ANNOTATED
INSTRUCTOR'S EDITION

Third Edition

Simon & Schuster
HANDBOOK
for WRITERS

Lynn Quitman Troyka
with Ann B. Dobie
and Emily R. Gordon

PRENTICE HALL
Englewood Cliffs, New Jersey 07632

For David,
who makes it all an adventure

Publisher: J. Philip Miller
Development Editor: Joyce Perkins
Production Editors: John Rousselle, Alison Gnerre, Keith Faivre
Acquisitions Editor: Alison Reeves
Art Director: Christine Wolf
Interior Design and Page Layout: Lorraine Mullaney
Cover Design: Ray Lundgren Graphics, Ltd.
Prepress Buyer: Herb Klein
Manufacturing Buyer: Bob Anderson
Production Assistance: Jenny Moss

© 1993, 1990, 1987 by Lynn Quitman Troyka

f t w
AFW3124

Printed in the United States of America

10   9   8   7   6   5   4   2   1

ISBN 0-13-813882-6

Prentice-Hall International (UK) Limited, *London*
Prentice-Hall of Australia Pty. Limited, *Sydney*
Prentice-Hall Canada Inc., *Toronto*
Prentice-Hall Hispanoamericana, S.A., *Mexico*
Prentice-Hall of India Private Limited, *New Delhi*
Prentice-Hall of Japan, Inc., *Tokyo*
Simon & Schuster Asia Pte. Ltd., *Singapore*
Editora Prentice-Hall do Brasil, Ltda., *Rio de Janeiro*

Contents

Brief Contents of Student Edition

Preface to the Annotated Instructor's Edition

This *Annotated Instructor's Edition (AIE)* of the *Simon & Schuster Handbook for Writers,* Third Edition, seeks to enhance instructors' enjoyment of the teaching of writing. The two major sections of the *AIE* correspond to my two major purposes in composing this volume.

One purpose of the *AIE* is to set forth the intellectual grounding of the *Simon & Schuster Handbook for Writers.* To achieve this, the volume's front section is the collection of five bibliographic essays that summarize current scholarship in rhetoric and composition. Commissioned exclusively for the *AIE,* the essays are intended as catalysts for study and discussion among faculty, including teaching assistants and part-time instructors. New for the Third Edition is an essay on teaching composition to speakers of other languages. Updated for the Third Edition are essays on the writing process, the history of rhetoric, writing across the curriculum, and testing. These essays help me meet the challenge that I set for myself with the *Handbook:* to demonstrate that effective teaching of composition relies upon theory and research outcomes translated into practice honed by experience.

The second purpose of the *AIE* is to give instructors multiple resources to draw upon while teaching. The *AIE* consists of an exact duplicate of the student edition of the *Handbook* along with a potpourri of teaching tips, background information on material in the text, quotations about writing, brief biographies of some of the writers quoted, alternate examples, and answers to the exercises. Accompanying the answers are Coverage listings, a feature begun in the Second Edition and expanded here, to reflect my goal of crafting exercises in which each major concept receives balanced attention. Coverage information can help teachers pinpoint student misunderstandings and design further instruction. Also, new for the Third Edition, I have added many annotated citations of timely, relevant journal articles and scholarly books.

I also intend this volume for growth. I cordially invite instructors to send proposed annotations (or comments or suggestions) for the next edition of the *AIE* to me c/o College English Editor, Prentice Hall, Englewood Cliffs, NJ 07632. Of course, any item published will carry the byline of its contributor.

For their invaluable help with the preparation of this *AIE,* I want to thank many key people. As she did for the Second Edition, Ann B. Dobie, University of Southwestern Louisiana, spearheaded my effort to compile useful, lively annotations for the *AIE,* Third Edition; her admirable expertise and wisdom are evident throughout. James C. MacDonald, University of Southwestern Louisiana, a newcomer to the project, contributed significantly to the annotations for a number of chapters. Emily R. Gordon, Hofstra University, as a result of her fine work with the *AIE,* First Edition, continues to enhance these pages. I am deeply grateful to the scholars who generously share their knowledge through the unusual forum of specially commissioned bibliographic essays for the beginning of this volume (listed here in the order their essays appear): Josephine Koster Tarvers, In*Scribe Communications, William F. Woods, Wichita State University; Barbara E. Walvoord, Loyola College in Baltimore; Emily R. Gordon, Hofstra University; and Joy Reid, University of Wyoming. At Prentice Hall, Joyce F. Perkins, Senior Development Editor, nurtured this project with a solid vision of its purpose and an unshakable determination to tame a truly overwhelming flood of variables. Others whose help was important include Phil Miller, Editor in Chief for Humanities; Mark Tobey, Editor, Humanities Supplements; Gina Sluss, Senior Marketing Manager for English; Tracy Augustine, former Senior Editor for English and current Director of Marketing for the Humanities and Social Sciences; and Helene Capparelli, Kara Hado, and Heidi W. Moore.

Lynn Quitman Troyka

The Composing Process: An Overview

Josephine Koster Tarvers

On the surface, rhetoricians used to suppose, the composing process looked easy to explain. All we had to do was to explain how ideas got into a writer's head, and from there onto paper. But more than three decades of research into the composing process have convinced us that this process is far more complex than we initially thought. In this essay, I discuss briefly some of the major theories about the composing process, to show you not only where these theories intersect but also where they differ, and conclude with suggestions about applying these theories to your teaching.

First of all, when we speak of the "composing process," we are amalgamating a number of processes, both psychological and physical, both for discovering ideas and actually committing them to writing. Research suggests that each person's writing process is different and that it changes with the writer's age, experience, level of knowledge about the subject, and

JOSEPHINE KOSTER TARVERS is president of In*Scribe Communications, a consulting firm that works with writers in the workplace. She has taught writing, grammar theory, history of the language, and other courses in language, gender, and medieval literature at Rutgers and the University of North Carolina at Chapel Hill. Her recent publications include Teaching Writing: Theories and Practices, *3rd edition (1991) and* Women and Men *(1992). She is currently at work on a book examining English women's literacy in the late Middle Ages.*

particular writing situation. It also depends on the environment a writer is working in, the culture that writer grew up in, and the people who give that writer feedback about a particular piece of writing. So when you see a book or article like this talk about "the writing process" or "the composing process," you must begin by remembering that it is radically compressing a complex group of actions and decisions.

Until the mid-1960s, few writing books or writing theorists even talked about a writing process, for writing was a *product* you generated, not a group of actions. But in that decade, for the first time rhetoricians began to talk about writing as an activity that had distinct stages (what we now call a stage-model theory). Most variations acknowledged some shared stages of the process: a period of gathering information and noting down ideas, one of "roughing out" those ideas, and one in which the information is reshaped and adjusted according to the writer's intentions and certain conventions of linguistic etiquette. We call these stages *planning* or *prewriting; drafting* or *writing;* and *revising* or *editing.* The stage-model theories, though, attempt to narrow, rather than broaden the focus of composing.

D. Gordon Rohman and Albert O. Wlecke are credited with the first exploration of the stage-model theory. In *Pre-Writing* [25], they argue that a pre-assimilation of ideas occurs in the mind before writing, and that writers must learn to "picture the process" in order to imitate it consciously. They suggest techniques such as keeping journals, writing meditations, and developing analogies as ways for students to discover their messages. They also insist on the separation from and primacy of prewriting over other stages of the composing process, and that the composing process is essentially linear, views that have been assailed by later theorists.

Another noted stage-model theorist is Peter Elbow. In *Writing Without Teachers* [8], he promotes the technique of *freewriting*, which encourages writers to record ideas quickly and continuously, without the premature editing for spelling, punctuation, and word choice that so often interrupts or destroys the writer's train of thought. One major criticism of systems like Elbow's, however, is that they privilege the initial stages of the writing process over the others. As a result, students enamored with prewriting may give scant attention to later stages, and produce less satisfactory results. Donald Murray attempts to counter this imbalance through use of a preliminary or "discovery" draft, where writers learn what other kinds of plans and explorations they might make before beginning the formal writing process. [22] But like Elbow, Murray emphasizes prewriting; revision in his scheme is the repetition of the prewriting stages of collecting, planning and developing as many times as is needed until the text is ready for editing.

As rhetoricians became more aware of the "holes" in stage-model theory, they turned more to psychology to learn how writers' minds may work. James Moffett, for instance, has based his work on the theories of Jean Piaget [2], who divided all childhood learning experiences into four stages, based on the behaviors children can learn in each stage (assimilation) and the changes they can make in those behaviors (adaptation). At each stage in Moffett's composing process [20], students are encouraged to return to the previous ones for help in planning and developing, so that their writing processes are not separate and linear but recursive, hierarchic, and spiraling, drawing on earlier knowledge to produce new kinds of writing for new audiences. In other words, they are encouraged to make *cognitive plans* [21].

The construction of cognitive plans is also central to the research in composing conducted by Linda Flower, John R. Hayes, and their many associates [14]. They base their conclusions on the study of "writing protocols," chronological descriptions of all the activities a writer uses in composing a text and transcripts of the writer narrating his or her decisions and choices in those activities. Flower and Hayes postulate a complex model of the composing process based on planning, translating, and reviewing texts. Planning involves probing one's own memory, organizing that information, and making an initial plan for producing a text. In translation, the writer puts sentences on paper, leading to a draft; in review the writer improves problem areas in the draft. This process is recursive: students might plan, generate, and revise one paragraph before moving on to another, or plan the whole essay, generate a draft, and revise globally, or use some combination of these processes. Composing is goal-directed, and students use different kinds of strategic knowledge in setting these goals and evaluating how effectively they have been realized. [11]

Flower and Hayes use their model to explain how writers solve the problems of moving from the planning to generating stages by juggling, discarding, or subdividing the constraints on their writing; by drawing on routines or familiar procedures (such as the five-paragraph theme); and by readjusting their goals and hypotheses. This latter stage, revision, has recently been investigated in more detail. More than a decade ago, Nancy Sommers [27,28] found that student writers frequently confuse revising with correcting, focusing only on "mistakes," whereas more experienced writers reconsider audience and purpose, paying attention to global issues. Sommers suggested that learning to distinguish between revising and editing in the composing process produces better student writing. Many scholars, following in Sommers's and Flower and Hayes's footsteps, have recently begun publishing their conclusions about *how* writers juggle the stages of composing, learning to move between the elements productively, to take advantage of their pauses, and to use heuristic planning strategies. [10, 24, 26]

The chief criticism of cognitive theories of the composing process is that they make writers too isolated; that is, such theories usually picture writers working alone, and ignore or downplay the social nature of writing and the writer's place in a community or communities of readers and writers. Such critics have developed a *social-constructionist* theory of the writing process, which argues that the writer, at whatever stage of a piece of writing, is working within the constraints and demands of the communities she or he belongs to. Thus, social constructionist views of the writing process are heavily influenced by the writer's purpose and audience. Richard Gebhardt [12] has suggested, in fact, that there are two large classes of composing processes, one in which the writer is relatively certain about audience, purpose, and the information these require, and one in which the writer discovers the relationship among these three elements. More recently, Maxine Hairston has proposed a three-category continuum [13] among these elements, calling the categories "message writing" needed to conduct well-understood business between writer and reader; "self-limiting writing" where the writer knows audience and purpose, and has the necessary information at hand; and "extended reflective writing," where the writer discovers information, purpose, and sometimes even the audience through the composing process.

Theorists like Kenneth Bruffee [4], Patricia Bizzell [3], and David Bartholmae [1] have expanded our knowledge of how communities influence writers; it is, in fact, safe to say that "social construction" and its paired term, "collaborative learning," are the watchwords for rhetorical theory in the early 1990s. Whether they will remain so is open to question, since evolving an understanding of the writing process is in itself an evolving process. Recently, even our notions of what defines a "community" have been called into question [19]; it's clear, then, that we still haven't pinned down the composing process, nor are we likely to in the near future.

Although no competing theories completely agree on descriptions of or labels for the composing process, most theorists agree in many respects about what is important in it:

■ The composing process contains several distinct stages. Each is important, and, depending on the kind of writing, the purpose, the writer's available fund of information, and the audience, each will require different amounts of attention for any particular writing task. No one stage is intrinsically "more important" than any other. As teachers, we must help our students gain experience in handling each stage, and overcome our instincts to emphasize the stage(s) most important to us.

■ Composing processes are recursive, not linear; only in the ideal world of textbooks do writers blithely choose an idea, make a neat outline, develop it, write about it, and make final cosmetic changes before presenting it to an audience. In reality, writers struggle, chew their pencils, cross out, go back, pause, reconsider, find other information, rack their brains, stare at the screen, juggle ideas, fling curses, and even start over from scratch in the process of composing a text. All of these may be positive actions in creating a text. We can help our students appreciate the recursive nature of writing by sharing our own drafts with them; when students see our corrections and stacks of paper, they are more likely to believe that such challenges face *all* writers, not just inexperienced ones.

■ Writing takes many forms, depending in each case on the writer's purpose and audience. Although writers may develop certain writing habits, their composing processes will vary with every writing occasion. We need to discuss with our students how those processes may change from professor to professor or boss to boss, or from routine memo to lab report to application letter to literary analysis.

■ Many techniques can stimulate the composing process; none are inherently "better" than others. Writers need to find the strategy or strategies which work best for them in each kind of writing situation they face. This means not only providing them with a repertoire of strategies to try, but also with the time to practice them.

■ Before writers actually begin *writing*, they need to find subjects and gather ideas and information to write about. The time this takes will be determined by the writer's purpose, audience, and existing fund of knowledge. By varying our assignments, we can help them learn to manipulate these variables.

■ The need to put ideas on paper "correctly" may inhibit writers. By drafting quickly and suspending editing until a text is nearly complete, many writers can compose more successful early drafts. Demonstrating techniques like freewriting and discovery drafts, for instance, can help students gain the courage to set aside the rules dinned in by previous teachers.

■ Many inexperienced writers do not distinguish between revising and editing. Revision allows writers to test drafts against their intentions and to add, delete, and rearrange what they have produced until it suits their purpose and audience. Working together as a class and then in small groups to revise pieces of student and professional writing will help students master true revising skills.

■ Editing is an act of social etiquette, in which writers decide how closely they wish their texts to conform to the audience's accepted conventions of language, and adjust their texts accordingly. Writers who choose to violate these conventions take their audience and purpose into account, and accept the consequences. Asking students to react to well- and poorly-edited copies of the same texts, and to answer questions such as "Which deserves the better grade? Which writer would you hire?" helps students see some of the real advantages of editing once a well-written document has been constructed.

Knowing what we do, then, about the composing process, how can we incorporate this knowledge into our teaching? We can encourage students to write frequently—and not always for grades—to make their own discoveries about the composing process. We can allow regular time in class for writing to help students develop the habit of writing. Students need to learn many different strategies to facilitate their composing. By introducing them to many planning and drafting strategies (not all at once!), we can help them become more productive writers. Questions of grammar, spelling, punctuation, and "where to start the next paragraph" often hinder students' attempts to produce texts; we can encourage them to postpone those worries and decisions until the editing stage, where they can be productively addressed. Students also need to learn to revise their papers to suit their purposes and audiences; by scheduling draft review sessions, encouraging peer editing, and holding conferences, we can direct students' attention away from "error-hunting" to more substantive questions.

Since students must also learn to write for audiences outside the classroom and in forms other than essay writing, we can provide them with practice by varying the design of our assignments. We can include other possibilities and other audiences, give students time in class not only to write, but to plan, discuss, reflect on, and generate ideas that prompt writing. We can work with our colleagues in other disciplines to provide writing across and throughout the curriculum, for many audiences and purposes. We can encourage students to practice these activities by collecting their notes and drafts along with the finished products. (Of course, the preliminary materials shouldn't be marked or graded, but we can examine them to help our students.)

And we shouldn't wait until *after* the student completes a document to offer our suggestions; rather, as Robert Zoellner has suggested [30], we need to intervene *during* the writing process, in a *talk–write* manner, so that students get maximum guidance. Zoellner uses a telling analogy: he says ski instructors don't tell novice skiers, "Ski down this slope, and I'll come back in about a week or so, look at the marks you made that still remain in the snow, and tell you what you should have done."[15] Rather, we need to be active coaches, helping writers through the process, giving them feedback, encouragement, and education. Above all, we can make our students more conscious of themselves as *writers*, people who have composing processes; teach them skills that let them work more effectively as writers; and help them realize that their texts are not merely products, but journeys—journeys of discovery, growth, and sometimes of liberation.

Annotated Bibliography of Suggested Readings

Below I list a number of works which deal, in part or totally, with the views of the writing process discussed above. This is by no means a complete bibliography, but will provide you with plenty of information and leads to follow. Abbreviations used are *CCC, College Composition and Communication; CE, College English;* NCTE, National Council of Teachers of English; *RTE, Research in the Teaching of English.*

1. Bartholmae, David. "Inventing the University." *When a Writer Can't Write: Research on Writer's Block and Other Writing Process Problems.* Ed. Mike Rose. NY: Guilford, 1986.

    Argues that students are often unaware of the conventions required by the academic community and must be familiarized with those if they are to succeed as writers.

2. Beard, Ruth M. *An Outline of Piaget's Developmental Psychology for Students and Teachers.* NY: NAL, 1969.

    Contains sections on the development of intelligence, on each of Piaget's four stages of cognitive growth, and on the implications of these theories for teachers.

3. Bizzell, Patricia. "Cognition, Convention, and Certainty: What We Need to Know about Writing." PRE/TEXT 3 (1983): 213–43.

    One of the first statements of the social-constructionist composing position, with a critique of other positions.

4. Bruffee, Kenneth. "Social Construction, Language, and the Authority of Knowledge." *CE* 48 (1986): 773–90.

    The theory and proposed practices underlying social construction.

5. Connors, Robert, and Cheryl Glenn. *The St. Martin's Guide to Teaching Writing.* 2nd ed. NY: St. Martin's, 1992.

    Overview to the profession, with an excellent chapter on the composing process and implications for your teaching.

6. Cooper, Charles R., and Lee Odell, eds. *Research on Composing: Points of Departure.* Urbana, IL: NCTE, 1978.

    Ten essays on the composing process by well-known specialists.

7. Elbow, Peter. *Writing With Power.* NY: Oxford UP, 1981.

    Emphasizes writing as a way of controlling one's world; discusses freewriting, revision, and peer editing, with many teaching suggestions.

8. ———. *Writing Without Teachers.* NY: Oxford UP, 1973.

    Encourages writers to break away from traditional practices (such as outlining) and to use other prewriting methods (especially freewriting) to discover new information.

9. Faigley, Lester, et al. *Assessing Writers' Knowledge and Processes of Composing.* Norwood, NJ: Ablex, 1985.

    Surveys the cognitive backgrounds of composing and the applications of this knowledge in pedagogy and theory.

10. ———, and Stephen Witte. "Analyzing Revision." *CE* 32 (1981): 400–14.

    There are two kinds of revision, surface (correcting minor flaws) and text-based (addressing larger concerns). The latter must be taught to students as an integral part of composing.

11. Flower, Linda. "The Construction of Purpose in Writing and Reading." *CE* 50 (1988): 528–50.

    A critique of earlier studies of writing, and of using protocols, and an elegant presentation of the Flower-Hayes theories.

12. Gebhardt, Richard C. "Initial Plans and Spontaneous Composition: Toward a Comprehensive Theory of the Writing Process." *CE* 44 (1982): 620–27.

    Identifies two relatively large groups of composing processes, one in which writers handle information they already possess, and another in which they discover the information they need.

13. Hairston, Maxine. "Different Products, Different Processes." *CCC* 37 (1986): 442–52.

Identifies and gives examples of the three kinds of composing, based on purpose, audience, and writer's information.

14. Hayes, John R., and Linda Flower. "Writing Research and the Writer." *American Psychologist* 41 (1986): 1106–13.

The fullest articulation of Flower and Hayes's theories to the date of publication, with full bibliography.

15. Heilker, Paul. "Public Products/Public Processes: Zoellner's Praxis and the Contemporary Composition Classroom." *Rhetoric Review* 10.2 (1992): 232–38.

Offers suggestions for incorporating talk–write pedagogy in the classroom.

16. Hume, Ann. "Research on the Composing Process." *Writing: Policies, Problems, and Possibilities.* Eds. Bruce Cronnell and Joan Michael. Los Alamitos, CA: Southwest Regional Laboratory of Educational Research and Development, 1982.

A comprehensive, detailed account of research on composing to about 1981.

17. Kantor, Kenneth. "Classroom Contexts and the Development of Writing Institutions: An Ethnographic Case Study." *RTE* 17 (1983): 72–94.

Case study of seven high-school students in a creative writing class, focusing on the revision stage of composing.

18. Lindemann, Erika. *A Rhetoric for Writing Teachers.* 2nd ed. NY: Oxford UP, 1987.

An overview of theories and research in the teaching of writing, with suggestions for classroom applications. A comprehensive and accessible summary for beginners and experts alike, with an extensive bibliography.

19. Lyon, Arabella. "Re-Presenting Communities: Teaching Turbulence." *Rhetoric Review* 10.2 (1992): 279–90.

Warns of the dangers in not exploring what we mean by "community" and "collaboration."

20. Moffett, James. *Teaching the Universe of Discourse.* Boston: Houghton, 1968.

A theory of discourse, drawing on students' cognitive development in producing increasingly more abstract texts. Emphasizes the relations between speaker and audience and speaker and subject.

21. ——— and Betty Jane Wagner. *Student-Centered Language Arts and Reading K–12.* 4th ed. Portsmouth, NH: Boynton-Cook/Heinemann, 1992.

A complete language arts text based on Moffett's discourse theory.

22. Murray, Donald M. *A Writer Teaches Writing.* 2nd ed. Boston: Houghton, 1985.

A book of advice for writers who are teachers, teachers who are writers, and nearly everyone else involved in composing. Sections on each of the stages of composing, with many teaching strategies and a full bibliography.

23. Odell, Lee, and Dixie Goswami, eds. *Writing in Nonacademic Settings.* NY: Guilford, 1985.

Fourteen essays on composing outside of the composition classroom.

24. Reither, James A. "Writing and Knowing: Toward Redefining the Writing Process." *CE* 47 (1985): 620–28.

Reminds us that the process (singular) is actually processes (plural), which are socially and culturally dependent.

25. Rohman, D. Gordon, and Albert O. Wlecke. *Pre-Writing: The Construction and Application of Models for Concept-Formation in Writing.* USOE Cooperative Research Project No. 2174. East Lansing: Michigan State University, 1964.

The writing process has three distinct stages: prewriting, writing, and revising. Prewriting has primacy; students can improve prewriting by keeping journals, writing meditations, and constructing analogies.

26. Scardamalia, Marlene, and Carl Bereiter. "Written Composition." *Handbook of Research on Teaching.* 3rd ed. Ed. Merlin C. Wittrock. NY: Macmillan, 1985.

A thorough survey of all areas of research on writing, including the composing process.

27. Sommers, Nancy. "Responding to Student Writing." *CCC* 33 (1982): 148–56.

> Students confuse revision with correction because teacher comments usually focus on errors in editing. When teachers comment on matters of revision, students learn to pay more attention to this stage of composing.

28. ———. "Revision Strategies of Student Writers and Experienced Adult Writers." *CCC* 31 (1980): 378–88.

> Suggests that major differences between students and experienced writers are the manner and amounts of their revisions; students make few revisions and focus on correctness, while adults are more willing to address global issues and to address the needs of their readers.

29. Warnock, John. "The Writing Process." *Research in Composition and Rhetoric.* Eds. Michael G. Moran and Ronald Lunsford. Westport, CT: Greenwood, 1984.

> A review of recent research and theory of composing.

30. Zoellner, Robert. "Talk–Write: A Behavioral Pedagogy for Composition." *CE* 30 (1969): 267–320.

> Monograph explaining and advocating this pedagogy, which has recently been "rediscovered" by the rhetorical community.

The History of Rhetoric: An Overview

William F. Woods

From its beginnings in Sicily around 450 B.C., rhetoric has been known as the art or "science" of persuasive discourse, the theory and practice of how to use available means of persuasion to affect the opinions of an audience. The earliest known treatise on rhetoric, by Corax of Syracuse, was a response to the citizens' need to speak well in litigations over land rights. A little more than a century later, Aristotle wrote his famous *Rhetoric* [item 15 in the Annotated Bibliography at the end of this essay] a work based on a systematic description of persuasive oratory as it was practiced in the law courts and the assembly of Athens. The key to Aristotle's approach to persuasion is *probability*. Logic can demonstrate a truth, but rhetoric can show that a position is worthy of belief— that it has a high probability of being true. Thus, while logical proofs are to be preferred in philosophical or scientific works, the persuasiveness of rhetoric is more effective in speaking or writing about practical affairs, and for a general audience.

WILLIAM F. WOODS is Associate Professor of English at Wichita State University, where he teaches medieval literature and the history of rhetoric. Some of his recent published articles are "The Reform Tradition in Nineteenth-Century Composition Teaching," Written Communication 2 (October 1985): 377–90; "The Cultural Tradition of Nineteenth-Century "Traditional Grammar Teaching," Rhetoric Society Quarterly 15 (nos. 1–2, 1985): 3–12; and "Emelye's Role in The Knight's Tale." Studies in Philology 88 (1991), 276–306.

Aristotle's *Rhetoric* assumes that there are three modes of appeal that can be used to reach an audience: the appeal to logic or reason (*logos*, in the Greek), the appeal to emotion (*pathos*), and the appeal to the moral or ethical sense (*ethos*). In themselves, these modes are only guidelines—ways of orienting the speaker to the task. However, each of the modes was also associated with certain kinds of discourse, as well as with the rhetorical devices proper to that sort of appeal. Perhaps the easiest way to give the flavor of Aristotle's rhetoric is to describe some of the devices he suggests for appealing to the mind, heart, and moral character of an audience.

As Aristotle saw it, the appeal to reason (*logos*) involved the use of certain basic concepts—fundamental, universally recognized formulas for thinking and expressing thought. Aristotle calls them the "common topics," because they are the commonplaces of thought. *Definition*, for example, is the classification of a subject, which in practice means identifying it by placing it in a class with other similar things (e.g., Man is an animal) and then further defining it by pointing out characteristics (*differentiae*) that distinguish it from the other things in that class (Man is a rational animal—"an animal that thinks"). The other topics that belong to the appeal to reason are as familiar and essential to us as definition. *Comparison* brings out the similarity, the difference, and the degree of difference between two subjects. *Relationship* refers to patterns such as cause and effect, antecedent and consequence, contraries, and contradictions. *Circumstance* refers to the process we go through in deciding whether something is or was possible or impossible, given the particular circumstances; here we are defining the subject in relation to its occasion, or context.

These common topics were not originated by Aristotle, of course. He merely gave them names, grouped them, and showed how they function in persuasive discourse. In the history of rhetoric since Aristotle, however, the topics have been one of the most useful and enduring parts of classical rhetorical theory. In the Middle Ages and the Renaissance they were adapted to theories of logical proof. In the nineteenth and twentieth centuries they have been used mainly as patterns for the development and organization of paragraphs and essays. All of these uses are valid, for the topics are simply a formalized reflection of the ways in which we think, and so they enter into every intellectual task. Indeed, we need to keep in mind that the topics are both fundamental and versatile, hard to pigeonhole. They are handy for organizing one's thoughts, for shaping a paragraph, for arranging an essay—but they can also lend incisive clarity to efforts to revise a piece of writing; they can be a productive guide to the solving of a problem; and they can help writers to think about a subject in ways that will extend the material, unfolding its implications. That is why Aristotle also identified the topics as aids to *invention,* or the *discovery* of arguments for or against a position.

The second kind of appeal Aristotle talks about (*pathos*) is the appeal to the emotions—to the heart. Aristotle recognized that the most powerful appeals are those that harness the primal human emotions, our tendencies to feel protectiveness, anger, envy, pride, fear, desire. Aristotle and the rhetoricians who came after him devoted considerable thought to what we would call "audience psychology"—the types of emotions, and the types of people who experience them—but they also tried to identify the kinds of subjects that would evoke such an emotional response. What are the types of description, they asked, that powerfully involve an audience by helping them to place themselves within an imagined experience? What are the phrases and the words associated with

deeply felt issues? And then there were the stylistic effects associated with emotional states. The periodic or suspended sentence, for instance, was thought to create tension and a feeling of building to climax. The "rhetorical" question had its place here, as did the use of exaggeration (hyperbole), metaphor, and various other figures of speech. The study of style has always been closely connected with the appeal to the emotions. That is why the Sophists, professional orators who flourished about the second century A.D., were both praised and condemned for their panegyrics (elaborate eulogies and other ceremonial speeches) which appealed to the emotions but were not always calculated to inspire careful thought.

The third mode of appeal (*ethos*) is best described as a perceived relationship between the character of the speaker or writer, and the social and ethical beliefs of the audience. It is an appeal to ethical values, perhaps, but it also has much to do with the ability of the audience to *identify* with the speaker, to accept him or her as someone who speaks for *them.* This appeal often derives as much from the personal qualities of a speaker or writer as it does from the overt content of the discourse. "Is this a person like us, who shares our values, and whose opinion can be trusted?" These are the sorts of questions addressed by the ethical appeal, which has a great deal to do with the *tone* of a piece of writing, and therefore with its syntax and choice of words. Tone also depends on the purpose of the discourse (to explain, persuade, entertain, etc.), and on the level of style adopted by the writer or speaker. Classical rhetoricians after Aristotle liked to identify three levels of style: (1) the high, or grand style (appropriate for epics and for the sublime, high-flown passages of persuasive oratory); (2) the middle ("pleasing," ornate) style associated with literary works and with ceremonial oratory; and (3) the low or plain style associated with the language of instruction and everyday affairs. More recently, linguists have tended to identify levels of style by their social function. For instance, Martin Joos [33] identifies five levels of usage: frozen (genteel), formal, consultative, casual, and intimate.

It is worth noting that Aristotle's three modes of appeal—*logos, pathos,* and *ethos*—reflect a basic way

WILLIAM F. WOODS

in which western culture has conceived or "pictured" the mind ever since the days of Plato. We say *mind, body,* and *spirit,*—or *reason, memory, imagination*—as if thought and substance were somehow united by a perceptive consciousness: our bond with the world outside us and the source of our state of being. Indeed, there is a basic "threeness" that runs through classical discussions of art and psychology like a magic thread. For example, beginning, middle, and end stood for the parts of a narrative or dramatic plot (Aristotle again). Invention, arrangement (organization), and style were the three essential phases of composition as classical rhetoricians described it. That is, writers first *discover* and gather together their materials, then they *arrange* them, and finally they *express* them in language that is appropriate to the aim, audience, and circumstances of the discourse. Memory and the techniques of delivery were also included as parts of rhetoric, but they were not directly involved in what we in our industrial age call the "process" of writing. The actual teaching of rhetoric in classical times again took the form of a sequential, three-stage program: *precept,* the learning of principles; *practice,* under the supervision of a grammar or rhetoric teacher; and *imitation* of the style and structure of various model passages.

As oratory gave way to written rhetoric in the seventeenth and eighteenth centuries (a recurrent trend in the history of rhetoric), it became easier to characterize discourse by its literary form rather than by its appeal to an audience. Whereas ancient oratory had been divided into deliberative (persuasive), epideictic (ceremonial), and judicial (courtroom) oratory, the rhetorical spectrum by the 1700s had broadened to admit formal letters (epistles), history, argument, narration, description, persuasion, and poetry. Since spoken and written discourse were both represented, it was now customary to describe them as the art of "rhetoric and *belles lettres*" (borrowing a term from French literary criticism, which was then enjoying a period of authority). The theory of rhetoric was also changing. Rhetoricians had followed the empiricist philosophers (e.g., Locke) in assuming that language and thought reflected sense impressions, especially those received through sight. They further assumed

that the forms of discourse must derive from the different patterns of language we use to record our perceptions, to form a "point of view," and to influence the opinions (views) of others. For example, we record our perceptions of things (thus, *descriptive* writing); we record our perceptions of events, or "things in action" (*narrative* writing); we interpret the pattern, or "logic" of relationships in the things and events perceived (*expository,* or explanatory writing); finally, we arrange our perceptions as proof, in support of our point of view (*argumentative* writing; "persuasion" generally meant spoken persuasive discourse). Authors of nineteenth-century textbooks on written rhetoric ("composition") found in these four terms, and in the kinds of writing they implied, a comprehensive schema for describing the teaching of writing.

These four "modes of discourse" [3] (which had little or nothing to do with Aristotle's three modes of appeal) were a typical feature of composition textbooks after 1850; they continued to shape teachers' approaches to English composition for at least the next hundred years. Rightly or wrongly, the four modes are now associated with the more conservative side of nineteenth-century composition teaching, which borrowed much from traditional methods of teaching English (and before that, Latin) grammar. There were other emphases, other theories at work in nineteenth-century composition teaching, but that period is remembered mainly for its drills, for the practice of having students memorize principles of grammar and style, for its increasing tendency to stress exposition (essay writing), and for giving first priority to the structuring of sentences, paragraphs, and essays. This was also a pedagogy associated with the rigorous methods and the sometimes endearing eccentricities of writing masters and textbooks writers like Alexander Bain, George Quackenbos, and A. S. (Adams Sherman) Hill.

But while the main thrust of nineteenth-century rhetoric and composition teaching was on style and structure, the *character* of the speaker or writer was beginning to receive a new emphasis. In a time when political, religious, and artistic individualism was much respected, the mental nature of the individual

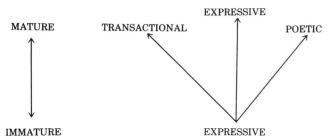

Figure 1

thinker, writer, and student became a serious subject of inquiry. The ultimate results of this spirit of romantic individualism, and the studies of child nature that accompanied it, can be seen today in the contemporary work of James Britton [29], a British educator specializing in research on student writing.

Britton's central insight was that written discourse can be described in terms of "function categories" (see Figure 1) which represent what the writer is doing, in each case, in the act of writing. Writing is no longer seen as reflecting three aspects of the mind; rather, writing is assumed to represent three basic types of observed language behavior (which may, of course, reflect three types of mental activity).

In Britton's first function category, the *transactional*, students are participating in a problem, discussion, or other event: they are getting things done with words. The language relates closely to the needs of the audience and to the features of the task at hand. Language here is seen as a means to an end. In the second category, the *expressive*, the students express their responses to an outside situation in language that relates closely to their own points of view or inner experiences of the situation. Here the language is less a way of getting things done than it is a way of putting feelings into an intelligible form; thus, expressive discourse probably serves the writer's needs more than it does the needs of the audience or the demands of the task at hand. In the third category, the *poetic*, the writer is a spectator to the problem or situation at hand and uses language that relates closely to the overall concept, or "global context," of what is being done, created, or argued. Here the writer is more a disinterested analyst than a participa-

tor in an interactive task or someone trying to verbalize an inner experience.

The striking difference between Britton's system and the classical rhetorics is the centrality of the expressive, or personal, aspect of writing. Britton assumes that child language *begins* as expressive discourse and diversifies as the child grows older; the transactional and poetic modes are gradually acquired, and the resources of the expressive mode are further developed. So while Aristotle's three modes of appeal were intended as ways of describing the impact of discourse on an audience, Britton's function categories are ways of identifying the kinds of discourse that emerge from three kinds of writing behavior. To put it another way, while Aristotle's modes are reader-oriented, Britton's categories are writer-oriented, since they describe discourse as the reflection of mental processes associated with certain adaptive social behaviors. Because of this emphasis on behavior, Britton's discussions are helpful to teachers trying to figure out "where students are coming from" in each of the various assignments that they write. Also, Britton's work may be a corrective influence on those who think of expressive discourse as a sloppy aberration from expository writing, or believe it should surface only in creative writing courses. Despite some real differences in theoretical orientation, however, Aristotle and Britton are not mutually exclusive. Teachers who have studied Aristotle's account of the appeals to the reason and the emotions will probably arrive at a better appreciation of Britton's transactional and poetic functions than those who come to Britton with no preparation in rhetoric.

In fact, even though social and historical conditions are vastly different now than they were in ancient Greece, Aristotle's *Rhetoric* continues to stand us in good stead, for the truth is that there have been no modern Aristotles, and no modern rhetoric has made the impact on rhetorical tradition that Aristotle and Cicero did. James Kinneavy [34] has come as close to that goal as anyone, perhaps, in his attempt to write a comprehensive modern theory of rhetoric, or "discourse," as he calls it, to allow for the enlarged role of writing in modern communication.

WILLIAM F. WOODS

Figure 2 (Adapted from Kinneavy)

Kinneavy's achievement is to distinguish the basic kinds of discourse and describe the forms and characteristics that are essential to each of them. He derives four kinds of discourse from a theory of communication which he expresses by the familiar "communication triangle" (see Figure 2). The three points of the triangle refer to (1) the *writer*, (2) the *audience*, and (3) the *subject* of discourse, while the body of the triangle refers to (4) the *signal*, which is, in this case, the written language that conveys the message.

Each of these four terms is the point of origin for one of the four *aims*, the purposes for which we produce discourse: (1) Discourse that derives from the point of view or "inner experience" of the writer is *expressive* (as in Britton's function theory). (2) Discourse that is oriented more toward the audience's concerns, ideas, and feelings is called *persuasive* (as in Aristotle's theory of rhetoric). (3) Discourse that is meant to represent accurately a subject of investigation is called *reference* discourse—this aim includes the nonpersuasive aspects of most academic and scientific writing, as well as what we call *expository* prose. (4) Discourse that is self-referential or mimetic in purpose and that is meant to be used or enjoyed for its own sake is called *literary* discourse or literature (similar to Britton's *poetic* function category but not synonymous with it).

Unlike Britton, Kinneavy is not concerned mainly with the development of students' discourse toward maturity. His emphasis is on the description of the kinds of writing and on their use, rather than on the way they evolve in childhood or the ways they have evolved in history. We can generalize by calling Kinneavy's work a comprehensive, painstaking description of the ways prose writing is used or understood in the twentieth century. In this sense his work is reminiscent of Aristotle's systematic, analytical description of persuasive oratory in fourth-century Athens. A basic understanding of Kinneavy's four aims lends a perspective on written communication; moreover, it gives us a way of thinking about the entire profession of teaching writing. For example, it makes sense of the differences between the kinds of writing we find in personal experience papers and term papers. It also helps in defining the intellectual tasks we expect students to carry out when they write a particular assignment; for instance, a term paper is predominantly a piece of reference discourse and requires the skills of observation, distinction, comparison, and so forth. In general, teachers who know the four aims, and the features associated with them, can shape their students' writing with more confidence because they will have a better sense of the goals of each assignment. And for those who wish to backtrack Kinneavy's research and pursue their own investigations in one direction or another, full bibliographies are appended to each chapter of his book [34].

At the far end of our history lies rhetoric's growing edge, the gradual assimilation of modern theory and contemporary research into the body of the discipline. Slowly, the ideas of major theorists like I.A. Richards [38], Kenneth Burke [30], Chaim Perelman [37], and Stephen Toulmin [39], are entering our shared assumptions about written rhetoric, and research findings have begun to shape our teaching methods [VI]. But the central concerns, and thus the distinguishing traits of today's rhetoric have more to do with our students: a varied lot, they reflect, in their challenging array of needs and abilities, the fragmentation that characterizes not only our own profession, but academia at large and the arenas of national and international politics.

Responding to social changes beginning with the immigration and urbanization early in the century, rhetoric teaching has recurrently transformed itself, deepening its resources and broadening its scope to provide effective instruction for non-traditional students. The crisis-related efforts that produced Sterling A. Leonard's *English Composition as a Social Prob-*

lem (1917), for example, or William Labov's *The Study of Non-Standard English* (1970), or Mina Shaughnessy's *Errors and Expectations* (1977), have enabled significant pedagogical advances, and they remind us that "fragmentation" can also mean growth. The recent emphasis on writing across the curriculum, with its implied sensitivity to differences in discourse and audience, is a broader, organizational response to this century-long groundswell of pluralism, and the idea of "discourse communities" is our response at the level of theory.

What is a discourse community? It is a useful phrase, a good metaphor, because it gives form to our ambivalent thoughts about rhetoric's fractured audience. If doctors (or sociologists, literary critics, street people) share a specialized body of knowledge, a common jargon, and a rhetoric that specifies the kinds of arguments acceptable within that group, then they belong to a community of shared discourse features. These communities are, in effect, political entities which tend to overflow social, economic and geographical boundaries. They are "city states of language," and as such Aristotle would have under-

stood them well, even though his rhetoric served a smaller, more unified world, and ours must speak to so many.

If there is a moral to be drawn from this lightning sketch of a few important works on rhetoric and composition, it is that a little knowledge is not a dangerous thing, but our only salvation. Not one of us has the time or dedication to absorb over two thousand years of rhetorical treatises, debates, and biases; even to desire such a thing is to miss the point badly. Our goal as teachers of writing is rather, by knowing something of the needs, ideas, and practices of former times, to understand more deeply and truly what we are engaged in doing and where we are tending. Neither Aristotle nor Kinneavy should be adopted as teachers' manuals. These two books, as well as the others that we have examined or that are listed in the bibliography, are parts of the history of our profession and should be sampled, experimented with, and pondered as we proceed with our own teaching, in our own times, in our own ways. To do so is to use history well; in so doing, we become rhetoricians—and enter history.

Annotated Bibliography of Suggested Readings

I. HISTORIES OF RHETORIC

1. Berlin, James. *Writing Instruction in Nineteenth-Century American Colleges.* Carbondale: Southern Illinois UP, 1984.

2. Bizzell, Patricia, and Bruce Herzberg, eds. *The Rhetorical Tradition: Readings from Classical Times to the Present.* Boston: St. Martin's, 1990.

> A superb anthology; the introductions and headnotes are in effect a substantial history of rhetoric.

3. Connors, Robert J. "The Rise and Fall of the Modes of Discourse." *CCC* 32 (1981): 444–55.

> A brief history of the growth and subsequent decline of the four "modes" of discourse (description, narration, exposition, and argumentation) in composition teaching.

4. Guthrie, Warren. "The Development of Rhetorical Theory in America, 1635–1850." *Speech Monographs* 13–16 (1946–49) and 18 (1951).

5. Halloran, Michael. "Rhetoric in the American College Curriculum: The Decline of Public Discourse." *Pre/Text* 3 (Fall 1982): 245–69.

6. Howell, Wilbur Samuel. *Eighteenth-Century British Logic and Rhetoric.* Princeton: Princeton UP, 1988.

7. ———. *Logic and Rhetoric in England, 1500–1700.* Princeton: Princeton UP, 1956.

> This classic study and its sequel catalog the changes rhetoric went through in response to the birth of empirical science and the resurgence of classical learning in the period between the early English Renaissance and the end of the seventeenth century.

WILLIAM F. WOODS

8. Kennedy, George A. *Classical Rhetoric and Its Christian and Secular Tradition from Ancient to Modern Times.* Berkeley: California UP, 1980.

>A reliable overview of rhetoric in its cultural tradition, but weaker in the periods following the Middle Ages. For those interested in Greek, Roman, or early Christian rhetoric, Kennedy's specialized works in those areas are standard sources.

9. Kimball, Bruce. *Orators and Philosophers: A History of the Idea of Liberal Education.* New York: Teacher's College, Columbia University, 1986.

>Examines the place of rhetoric in the development of the curriculum in England and America.

10. Murphy, James J. *Rhetoric in the Middle Ages.* Berkeley: California UP, 1974.

>The best survey of medieval rhetoric now available.

11. Reid, Ronald F. "The Boyleston Professorship of Rhetoric at Harvard." *QJS* 45 (1959): 239–57.

>Probably the best account of the nineteenth-century transition from spoken to written rhetoric.

12. Vickers, Brian. *Classical Rhetoric and English Poetry.* New York: St. Martin's, 1970.

13. ———. *In Defense of Rhetoric.* New York: Oxford UP, 1988.

>Excellent chapters on various periods in the history of rhetoric.

14. Woods, William F. "Nineteenth-Century Psychology and the Teaching of Writing." *CCC* 36 (1985): 20–41.

>Describes the three major theories of nineteenth-century psychology which parallel, and therefore illuminate, similar developments in the teaching of writing.

II. CLASSICAL AND MEDIEVAL THEORIES OF RHETORIC

15. Aristotle. *Rhetoric and Poetics.* Trans. Rhys Carpenter and Ingram Bywater. New York: Modern Library, 1984.

>This edition has the added benefit of a new preface by Edward P. J. Corbett, who edited the volume and contributed some useful bibliographies and notes to the text.

16. Augustine of Hippo. *De Doctrina Christiana,* trans. D. W. Robertson, Jr. Indianapolis: Bobbs-Merrill, 1958.

>Books I–III of this treatise are a guide to the reading and interpretation of the scriptures. Book IV (on preaching) is probably the most important statement of rhetorical theory in the Middle Ages.

17. Cicero. *De Oratore.* Trans. E. W. Sutton and H. Rackham. 2 vols. Loeb Classical Library. Cambridge, MA: Harvard UP, 1942.

>The comprehensive treatise that represents Cicero's mature rhetorical theory.

18. Corbett, Edward J. P. *Classical Rhetoric for the Modern Student.* 2nd ed. New York: Oxford UP, 1971.

>The best of the modern textbooks that make classical rhetorical theory and pedagogy available to teachers and students of English composition.

19. Quintilian. *Institutio Oratoria.* Trans. H. E. Butler. 4 vols. Loeb Classical Library. New York: Putnam's, 1921–22. See also J. J. Murphy's edition of Books 1, 2 and 10: *Quintilian on the Art of Speaking and Writing.* Carbondale: Southern Illinois UP, 1987.

>Quintilian was a teacher of rhetoric in Rome, under the Empire. His "Institute" of rhetoric is a thoroughgoing description of the art as it was practiced and taught during his times.

20. Anon. *Rhetorica Ad Herennium.* Trans. Harry Caplan. 2 vols. Loeb Classical Library. Cambridge, MA: Harvard UP, 1954.

>This relatively brief manual, and Cicero's early work *De Inventione (On Rhetorical Invention),* were the classical treatises which most influenced medieval rhetoric.

III. RENAISSANCE AND NEOCLASSICAL THEORIES OF RHETORIC

21. Erasmus, Desiderius. *On Copia of Words and Ideas (De Utraque Verborem ac Rerum Copia).* Trans. Donald B. King and H. David Rix. Milwaukee: Marquette UP, 1963.

>A much imitated treatise on the art of writing an "amplified," or richly developed style, which reflects a major emphasis in Renaissance rhetoric.

22. Fenelon. *Fenelon's Dialogues on Eloquence.* Trans. W. S. Howell. Princeton: Princeton UP, 1951.

"The greatest work on classical rhetoric written in French and the finest statement of the philosophical strand of the tradition since antiquity" (Kennedy).

23. Blair, Hugh. *Lectures on Rhetoric and Belles Lettres.* Ed. Harold F. Harding. 2 vols. 1783; Carbondale: Southern Illinois UP, 1965.

24. Campbell, George. *The Philosophy of Rhetoric.* Ed. Lloyd F. Bitzer. 1776; Carbondale: Southern Illinois UP, 1963.

25. Whately, Richard. *Elements of Rhetoric.* Ed. Douglas Ehninger. 1828; Carbondale: Southern Illinois UP, 1963.

Blair, Campbell, and Whately—sometimes called the "Scottish rhetoricians"—reflect the influence of empirical philosophy (e.g., Hume, Locke) on rhetorical theory; they also foreshadow the nineteenth-century shift in emphasis from spoken to written rhetoric (or "composition").

IV. NINETEENTH-CENTURY THEORIES OF RHETORIC

26. Adams, John Quincey. *Lectures on Rhetoric and Oratory, Delivered to the Classes of Senior and Junior Sophisters in Harvard University.* 2 vols. 1810; New York: Russell and Russell, 1962.

27. Channing, Edward T. *Lectures Read to the Seniors at Harvard College.* 1856; Carbondale: Southern Illinois UP, 1968.

28. DeQuincey, Thomas. *Essays on Rhetoric.* Ed. Frederick Burwick. Carbondale: Southern Illinois UP, 1967.

V. MODERN THEORIES OF DISCOURSE

29. Britton, James, et al. *The Development of Writing Abilities (11–18).* London: Macmillan Education, 1975.

Considered one of the best studies of how writing skills develop in young students. Britton offers a theory of composition based on extensive surveys of children's writing.

30. Burke, Kenneth. *A Grammar of Motives.* 1945; Berkeley: UP, 1969.

31. Gibson, Walker. *Tough, Sweet, and Stuffy: An Essay on Modern American Prose Styles.* Bloomington: Indiana UP, 1966.

A readable yet relatively sophisticated attempt to characterize prose styles by classifying their choice of words, syntax, and other features.

32. Hirsch, E. D., Jr. *The Philosophy of Composition.* Chicago: Chicago UP, 1977.

Known as a conservative approach to the theory of composition, Hirsch's book was nevertheless based on a careful study of discourse production, and it deserves a close reading.

33. Joos, Martin. *The Five Clocks.* Bloomington: Indiana UP, 1962.

A modern classification of the levels of style by reference to their use in a social context.

34. Kinneavy, James. *A Theory of Discourse.* 1971. New York: Norton, 1980.

Classifies the kinds of discourse according to purpose and describes the features associated with each of these purposes, or "aims." Grounded in the scholarship of linguistics, literature, communications, and philosophy, Kinneavy's is perhaps the reigning modern theory of discourse.

35. Moffett, James. *Teaching the Universe of Discourse.* Boston: Houghton, 1956.

Helpful in understanding the neo-progressive or student-centered attitudes toward teaching writing that dominated the Dartmouth Conference (1966) and later produced the "open classroom."

36. Ong, Walter J. "The Writer's Audience Is Always a Fiction." *PMLA* 90 (1975): 9–21.

In this milestone essay, Ong argues that writers project their own sense of an audience—an assumption that parallels current reader-response theory.

37. Perelman, Chaim and L. Olbrechts-Tyteca. *The New Rhetoric: A Treatise on Argumentation.* Notre Dame: University of Notre Dame Press, 1969.

38. Richards, I. A. *The Philosophy of Rhetoric.* New York: Oxford, 1936.

39. Toulmin, Stephen E. *The Uses of Argument.* Cambridge: Cambridge UP, 1958.

VI.   REFERENCE WORKS

40. Horner, Winifred, et al. *Historical Rhetoric: An Annotated Bibliography of Selected Sources in English.* Boston: Hall, 1980.

41. ———. *The Present State of Scholarship in Historical and Contemporary Rhetoric.* Columbia: University of Missouri Press, 1983.

42. Houlette, Forest. *Nineteenth-Century Rhetoric: An Enumerative Bibliography.* New York: Garland, 1989.

> Lists books and articles about rhetoric, composition, grammar, and the teaching of English which were published between 1800 and 1920.

43. Moran, Michael G. and Ronald F. Lunsford, eds. *Research in Composition and Rhetoric: A Bibliographical Sourcebook.* Westport, CT: Greenwood, 1984.

> A good supplement to Tate, *Teaching Composition.*

44. Mosenthal, Peter, et al., ed. *Research on Writing: Principles and Methods.* New York: Longman, 1983.

> Good discussions of empirical research and its basis in theory.

45. Tate, Gary, ed. *Teaching Composition: Twelve Bibliographical Essays.* Rev. and enlarged ed. Fort Worth: Texas Christian UP, 1987.

> Comprehensive overview of research in major areas related to rhetoric and composition.

Writing Across the Curriculum: An Overview

Barbara E. Walvoord

Halfway through a three-day workshop on writing across the curriculum that I was leading, a college chemistry instructor suddenly exclaimed, "This is really a workshop about thinking!" The "writing" in writing across the curriculum refers to the entire process of planning, gathering information, shaping, drafting, and revising.

BARBARA E. WALVOORD *is Professor of English and Director of Writing Across the Curriculum at the University of Cincinnati. She was co-founder and co-director of the Maryland Writing Project and the Baltimore Consortium for Writing Across the Curriculum. She was instrumental in founding and directing two institutional writing-across-the-curriculum programs—at Central College in Pella, Iowa, during the 1970s and at Loyola College in Maryland during the 1980s. She conducts workshops on writing across the curriculum for interdisciplinary faculty groups at colleges and community colleges. Her guide for teachers,* Helping Students Write Well, *now in its second edition, is published by the Modern Language Association. In addition, she has authored two textbooks as well as a number of articles on writing. Her latest book,* Thinking and Writing in College, *coauthored with Lucille McCarthy and others (Urbana: NCTE, 1991), reports the results of a seven-year study of students' thinking and writing processes in college classes in four disciplines.*

WHY USE WRITING IN THE DISCIPLINES?

Why and how should instructors in the disciplines integrate this "writing" into their courses? One explanation lies in theories about the close relationship between thought and language. We experience this bond when we find ourselves thinking and discovering *as* we write. Philosopher Susanne Langer proposes that sense data are translated into symbols, which themselves are our ideas [item 11 in the Annotated Bibliography at the end of this essay]. In order to think and learn, we manipulate symbols by talking to ourselves in what psychologist Lev Vygotsky calls "inner speech"—the mediator between thought and language [22, p. 149]. "Thought is born through words," he says [22, p. 153].

A body of research in psychology [summarized in Walvoord, 23, pp. 3–5] indicates that when people verbalize an idea, they can remember it longer,

BARBARA E. WALVOORD

understand it more thoroughly, and manipulate it in more sophisticated ways. Writing is one of the most effective modes for learning. "When I think back on my own student days, I realize I learned and retained more when I wrote" recalls Laurence Shute [19], an instructor at California Polytechnic Institute. "I'm going to give my students the same opportunity." He describes how, after a workshop on writing across the curriculum, he is "now rethinking every course I offer from the perspective of how to assign some kind of writing in each class." Because writing and thinking develop in complex ways across a student's years of schooling, every instructor needs to support that development.

Another reason for integrating writing across the disciplines is that a biologist and a literature teacher think, write, explore, use evidence, and pose questions in different ways. Walvoord and McCarthy [24] demonstrate how differently questions of evaluation and problem-solving are handled in classrooms in biology, history, psychology, and business. Faigley and Hansen [4] show how differently an English instructor and a sociology instructor may react to a student's writing in sociology. Bartholomae [1] and Bizzell [3] have described some characteristics of writing and thinking common to the academic community as a whole and have explored how different these modes are from students' customary ways of thinking and writing outside the academy.

Elaine Maimon [12] characterizes students as "strangers" to the academic conversation. She recalls her own experience as a "stranger" when she was a new faculty member at a small college, joining a group of her new colleagues at lunch the first day, and understanding little of their talk, filled as it was with references to people, events, and ongoing debates unknown to her. As she gradually became part of the conversation of those lunchtime tables, so we, as college instructors, seek to help our students become participants in the conversations by which our disciplines advance and transmit knowledge. A discipline, as Bazerman [2] has noted, is heavily dependent upon written conversation. Each instructor, by helping students develop their ability to use language within a discipline, can contribute to students' ability to join

the conversation of the discipline, and, more broadly, of educated people.

For further explication of the theories that undergird writing across the curriculum, see Fulwiler [5, 6] and Parker and Goodkin [16].

WHAT MIGHT FACULTY IN THE DISCIPLINES DO?

The following discussion of how faculty in the disciplines might implement writing across the curriculum relies on the example of a history instructor, John R. Breihan of Loyola College in Maryland, and a biology instructor, Virginia Johnson Anderson of Towson State University in Maryland. I have worked closely with both of them over the past nine years and have coauthored with them chapters in a book on how students write and think in the disciplines [24].

In any discipline, planning a college course that effectively integrates writing and thinking begins with clarification of course goals. For example, the biology instructor wanted her students to master a body of information and to be able to use the scientific method. The history instructor's goal was to help his students understand and write historical arguments.

The next step in course planning is to examine whether present practices are meeting the course goals. The biologist, who lectured to classes of more than 100 students, had been testing content by short-answer tests that often called for comparison/contrast, definition, or the explanation of a process. Tests sometimes showed her, too late, where students had not mastered lecture or laboratory material. Also, students were not skilled at handling comparison/contrast or shaping definitions and explanations in the ways that she wanted. She wondered whether, even in such a large class, there were ways to use writing to facilitate learning rather than just testing it.

The historian had been assigning essay tests, a term paper, and quizzes, but was very unhappy with the quality of student thinking and writing. He realized that he himself wrote arguments about material he knew well, he redrafted and revised many times, and he sought responses to drafts from colleagues. His essay tests, in contrast, were eliciting hasty, loosely connected "fact dumping" from students, and students' term papers were often thinly veiled paraphrases of library sources. Quizzes encouraged students to concentrate on the individual facts of their readings rather than on the arguments and lines of inquiry. At the end of the semester, he found himself writing, often in despair or frustration, red-ink comments on students' papers, telling them what they had done wrong and justifying the grades he was giving them. But his comments, he suspected, were neither carefully read nor fully used by his students. His traditional writing assignments, he concluded, neither were based on his own experience as a writer, nor were furthering his course goals as effectively as he wished.

To discover how they might better help students to learn, the biologist and the historian next took two steps: they examined their students and they explored what other teachers were doing. For example, the biologist recognized that students were passive (sometimes sound asleep) in lecture, and that in lab they went through the instructions cookbook style, sometimes without knowing the broader implications of what they were doing. The historian carefully examined his students' writing to identify specific competencies that his students needed for argument but did not always possess when they entered his class. He saw, for example, that they did not always know how to identify, in their reading, material that could be used as pros and cons for an argument, or how to categorize primary source material into factors such as social, economic, and religious, or how to defend a position on a debatable historical issue. As one of his history students said, "In high school we took the answers out of the book. I am not accustomed to writing arguments" [Walvoord and McCarthy, 24, p. 102].

The instructors also explored the options other teachers had used to integrate writing and learning in their courses. Such options are discussed, for example, in Fulwiler [5], Fulwiler and Young [7], Griffin [8], Stanford et al. [20], Thaiss [21], and Walvoord [23]. Other suggestions about using writing in disciplines

outside English appear in journals, conference presentations, and documents that can be accessed through the computerized data base ERIC, using the search terms listed as item 26 in the bibliography at the end of this essay. A review of the literature on teaching strategies shows that instructors are:

- Using a wide variety of types of writing rather than relying only on essay tests and term papers.
- Using not just formal polished writing, but also informal writing such as journals, dialogues, responses to readings, and exploratory essays to help their students apply, challenge, and muse about what they read and learn.
- Varying their responses to student writing according to the type of writing, the goal, and the instructor's available time. For example, the instructor will respond to journals differently than to a formal, polished research paper.
- Guiding the writing process: helping students to select topics, generate ideas, and plan, shape, and revise their writings, rather than merely giving the assignment and then collecting the finished product, with little attention to students' writing and thinking processes.

This last teaching approach is based on a body of literature that shows major differences between the writing processes of experienced writers and the processes of novice writers. The research is summarized in Hayes and Flower [9]. In brief, experienced writers appear to draw upon a broader base of knowledge, generate more comprehensive plans and goals for the writing task, and plan and revise with greater attention to the structure and purpose of the entire paper rather than merely to local issues.

Most writing-across-the-curriculum programs in colleges and universities across the country have begun with workshops for faculty to explore the theories and options we have just discussed. One description of such a workshop appears in Raimes [17]. Others, including descriptions of the larger programs of which workshops are a part, appear in McLeod [14] and Fulwiler and Young [7]. McLeod and Soven's 1992 collection [15] discusses many aspects

BARBARA E. WALVOORD

of starting and nurturing a WAC program. David Russell [18] places the movement in historical perspective. More can be located through ERIC, using the search terms listed as item 25 in the bibliography at the end of this essay.

Building on such a workshop and also on their careful observation of their students, the biologist and historian revised their courses to integrate writing more effectively than before, but not to bury themselves under an insupportable avalanche of student papers which they had to "correct." To do this, they used four strategies: (1) they substituted a more effective type of writing assignment for a less effective one, (2) they shifted their own time from a less effective activity to a more effective one, (3) they sometimes moved a former in-class activity into out-of-class time so as to make more time for in-class writing or writing-based activities, and (4) they varied their responses to student writing depending on its purpose.

For example, the historian abandoned the essay tests and the long, final term paper in favor of three short but carefully crafted historical essays. Now his students were able to shape and reshape their arguments in the same way that he and other historians did. To help them further, the historian shifted his time investment from the end of the writing process to the middle—that is, instead of spending most of his time writing extensive comments on finished writings where students, faced with an unchangeable grade, were not motivated to read and apply his suggestions, he shifted his time to respond to students' *drafts.* When the final papers came in, he made much shorter and more general comments, trying to give students the one or two broad pieces of advice they could carry with them into the next paper or the next course. On the basis of his comments to their drafts, students were often able to see where their arguments were weak and then to apply their new understanding immediately by revising their arguments. The instructor was gratified by the improvement in his students' ability to shape historical arguments, and now, eleven years later, he is still doing draft response, despite the time it takes, because he shifted his time to make his load manageable.

The historian also instituted a series of informal writings, done outside of class, all designed to help students master the skills necessary to the historical arguments. For example, for one writing, students were asked to discuss, in a paragraph, how the material from that day's reading could be used as evidence in an argument over whether Louis XIV was a "good" king. On another day, students had to list the "economic," "social," "political," and "religious" factors from a series of first-hand accounts of seventeenth-century riots. The instructor was teaching students to read for arguments, not just for disconnected facts or mere summary, and he was teaching them to categorize data as historians do. The results of these exercises began to show in the essays. Because these short writings fed into the essays and because their primary purpose was to help students with reading and thinking, the instructor did not mark the writings extensively for grammar and punctuation, nor did he even try to comment on every point of content and structure. Rather, he read the short writings very quickly and concentrated on making one or two suggestions. For each short writing that met a minimum standard, the student accumulated points toward the final course grade. Further discussion of this historian (John R. Breihan) and his methods appears in Walvoord [23], Walvoord and McCarthy [24], and in Mallonee and Breihan [13].

Other instructors may use informal writings in different ways. The historian arranged for all writing to be completed by students outside of class; however, the biologist used class time during her lectures for writing, because she felt it was better to help students become active learners than to "cover" more material they would not learn. She would stop the lecture and ask students to write for five minutes on questions such as "Summarize the most important ideas of last Friday's lecture" or "Compare the phylum we've covered today to the phylum we covered last time." To help her students understand the implications of their lab work, she asked them, before they began the lab, to write, for example, "Why are we using E $coli$ in the lab today?" Sometimes she asked students to share their writings with a peer in the next seat, or used them to encourage questions. Students kept all these short writings in their own folders, and at the end of the semester each student would choose three of his or her best short writings, polish them, and turn them in for a grade.

WHAT MIGHT ENGLISH FACULTY DO?

The role of the writing teacher in writing across the curriculum may encompass three areas: (1) articulation of the freshman composition course with other courses students take, (2) exemplification of strategies for integrating writing and learning, and (3) coordination of campus writing-across-the-curriculum activities.

Chapters 36–40 on "Writing Across the Curriculum" in the *Simon & Schuster Handbook for Writers,* Third Edition attempt to prepare composition students to understand the kinds of thinking and writing they will meet in other disciplines. In some schools, teachers of composition and teachers in the disciplines have agreed on basic terms or texts that will be required in the composition courses and used later by

other teachers as well. Some instructors ask students to analyze the characteristics of writing in various disciplines or professions.

Instructors who teach writing often also teach literature. The literature class can be a model for the effective integration of writing and learning.

On most campuses it is the writing instructors who initiate and coordinate writing-across-the-curriculum programs. However, instructors in other disciplines must quickly become spokespeople and leaders in the effort, and the writing instructors must coordinate rather than dominate the program.

The task of integrating writing and learning within courses across the disciplines, including composition, is complex and difficult. Some of our best attempts so far, however, have come when instructors in composition and other disciplines identify their goals, examine their students' needs and their own practices, and then institute teaching strategies that seem best calculated to help students learn to participate in the ongoing conversation of the discipline and of the academy.

Annotated Bibliography of Suggested Readings

1. Bartholomae, David. "Inventing the University." *When a Writer Can't Write: Studies in Writer's Block and Other Composing-Process Problems.* Ed. Mike Rose. New York: Guilford, 1985.

> Characterizes various levels of students' ability to "invent" the university—that is, to adopt the specialized language and persona of someone who is a member of the discipline's community.

2. Bazerman, Charles. "What Written Knowledge Does: Three Examples of Academic Discourse." *Philosophy of the Social Sciences* 11 (1981): 361–87.

> Points out that academic disciplines are primarily bound by their exchange of written communication, and analyzes the features of that writing.

3. Bizzell, Patricia L. "What Happens When Basic Writers Come to College?" *College Composition and Communication* 37 (1986): 294–301.

> "Basic writers" (i.e., those least well prepared for college) face a conflict of world view, which may force them to give up old world views.

4. Faigley, Lester, and Kristin Hansen. "Learning to Write in the Social Sciences." *College Composition and Communication* 36 (1985): 140–49.

> Explores the learning and writing process of students in college social science classes and shows the differing reactions of social science and English teachers to the same piece of student writing.

5. Fulwiler, Toby. *Teaching with Writing.* Portsmouth, NH: Boynton, 1987.

> A guide for teachers in all disciplines who want to integrate writing with learning. Includes theoretical

BARBARA E. WALVOORD

background on the interconnection of writing and learning, as well as practical suggestions for activities such as using journals or helping students revise.

6. ———. "Writing as an Act of Cognition." *Teaching Writing in All Disciplines.* Ed. C. Williams Griffin. San Francisco: Jossey, 1982.

Explains how students learn through writing, particularly relying on James Britton. Discusses implications for classroom teachers in all disciplines.

7. Fulwiler, Toby, and Art Young, eds. *Writing Across the Curriculum: Programs, Practices, and Problems.* Portsmouth, NH: Boynton, in press.

Describes a number of outstanding writing-across-the-curriculum programs across the country.

8. Griffin, C. Williams, ed. *Teaching Writing in All Disciplines.* San Francisco: Jossey, 1981.

A collection of essays about the practical and theoretical issues in writing across the curriculum.

9. Hayes, John R., and Linda S. Flower. "Writing Research and the Writer." *American Psychologist* 41 (1986): 1106–13.

Summarizes research on the organization of cognitive processes underlying the act of writing, specifically the processes of planning, sentence generating, and revising.

10. Kolln, Martha. "Closing the Books on Alchemy." *College Composition and Communication* 32 (1981): 139–51.

Explores the often misinterpreted research results on students' errors in punctuation and usage. Concludes that instruction in "grammar" should be integrated with writing experiences for students.

11. Langer, Susanne. *Philosophy in a New Key.* 3rd ed. Cambridge, MA: Harvard UP, 1957.

Describes human ability to perform "symbolic transformation" as the key to both scientific and humanistic problems.

12. Maimon, Elaine P. "Talking to Strangers." *College Composition and Communication* 30 (1979): 364–69.

Instructors are guides who help their students become part of the conversation of the academy. Explores implications of this concept for classroom teachers in all disciplines.

13. Mallonee, Barbara, and John R. Breihan. "Responding to Students' Drafts: Interdisciplinary Consensus." *College Composition and Communication* 36 (1985): 213–31.

Reports the team teaching experience of a history instructor and a writing instructor, exploring the points of difference with which they struggled and the areas of consensus they believe appropriate for teachers of writing and other disciplines.

14. McLeod, Susan, ed. *Strengthening Programs for Writing Across the Curriculum.* San Francisco: Jossey, 1988.

A collection of essays about supporting established writing-across-the-curriculum programs. Discusses issues such as developing programs beyond the initial workshops, finding continuing funding, assessing the program, and developing research projects.

15. McLeod, Susan, and Margot Soven, eds. *Writing Across the Curriculum: A Guide to Developing Programs.* Newbury Park, CA: Sage, in press.

16. Parker, Robert, and Vera Goodkin. *The Consequences of Writing: Enhancing Learning in the Disciplines.* Upper Montclair, NJ: Boynton, 1987.

Describes the origins of the writing-across-the-curriculum movement and its theoretical background. Shows how writing is used in five courses in different disciplines.

17. Raimes, Ann. "Writing and Learning Across the Curriculum: The Experience of a Faculty Seminar." *College English* 41 (1980): 797–801.

Describes a series of writing-across-the-curriculum seminars held during the academic year at Hunter College.

18. Russell, David. *Writing in the Academic Disciplines, 1870–1990: A Curricular History.* Carbondale, IL and Edwardsville, IL: Southern Illinois UP, 1991.

19. Shute, Laurence. "Getting Them to Write." Letter to the Editor. *New York Times* 5 Nov. 1988: 26.

A letter to the editor from a faculty member at California State Polytechnic University, urging teachers in the disciplines to integrate writing into their classrooms.

20. Stanford, Gene, and the Committee on Classroom Practices. *How to Handle the Paper Load.* Classroom Practices in Teaching English, 1979–1980. Urbana: National Council of Teachers of English, 1979.

Practical suggestions for teachers at all levels and in all disciplines, about how to use writing for learning.

21. Thaiss, Christopher, ed. *Writing to Learn: Essays and Reflections on Writing Across the Curriculum.* Dubuque: Kendall, 1983.

Essays about the writing-across-the-curriculum experiences and teaching strategies of faculty from a variety of disciplines at George Mason University.

22. Vygotsky, Lev S. *Thought and Language.* Cambridge, MA: MIT Press, 1962.

Shows how children and adults use language as a mediator between humans and the world of physical stimulation so that humans can react in terms of their own symbolic conception of reality.

23. Walvoord, Barbara E. Fassler. *Helping Students Write Well: A Guide for Teachers in All Disciplines.* 2nd ed. New York: MLA, 1986.

Guides college teachers in all disciplines through the process of planning a course that integrates writing and learning, guiding students' writing processes, and responding to student writers.

24. Walvoord, Barbara E., and Lucille McCarthy, with contributions by Virginia Johnson Anderson, John R. Breihan, Susan Miller Robison, and A. Kimbrough Sherman. *Thinking and Writing in College.* Urbana: National Council of Teachers of English, 1991.

The results of a seven-year naturalistic study of students' thinking and writing processes as they fulfilled their normal assignments in college classes in four disciplines.

25. *ERIC descriptors:* For articles on the content and structure of writing across-the-curriculum workshops: "Higher-Education," "Writing-Across-the-Curriculum," "Workshops," and inclusive dates.

26. *ERIC descriptors:* For articles on using writing in a particular discipline: "Higher-Education," "Writing Instruction," the name of the discipline, and inclusive dates.

Essay Testing: An Overview

Emily R. Gordon

The pressure on composition programs to "measure up" continues to increase. Our colleagues in colleges and universities complain about students' inability to write intelligibly, and even we composition instructors occasionally question the standards being applied in some writing classes. The pressure from the larger community is even more intense: parents, facing increasing tuition bills, demand that their children obtain salable skills; periodic tax revolts call into question the success of open admissions and compensatory programs, while demand increases in class size; personnel officers throughout industry complain that college graduates lack the writing skills needed for even entry-level positions. In response to all these pressures, more and more colleges have turned to uniform examinations to generate statistics that will support existing programs or argue for desired programs. These schools also increasingly are using such tests to determine student placement and to assess achievement against criteria for graduation.

Sometimes administrators see short-answer, objective tests as the most efficient way of making placement and graduation determinations. Yet, because essay tests are an important indicator of proficiency in composition, experts urge that essay tests be administered in place of, or in concert with, objective tests whenever possible.

This discussion first addresses the philosophical and pedagogical rationale for essay testing, then presents a plan for administering the examination, and finally explains the two most commonly used scoring procedures.

USES OF AN ESSAY TEST

Perhaps one of the most obvious characteristics of essay testing is that it is time-consuming. However,

EMILY R. GORDON is Adjunct Instructor of English at Hofstra University, where she teaches composition and business communication. She is co-author of the Simon & Schuster Workbook for Writers *(with Lynn Quitman Troyka) and author of the* Diagnostic and Competency Tests to Accompany the Simon & Schuster Handbook for Writers, *and she is a member of the editorial board of the* Journal of Basic Writing. *She holds an M.A. in English Literature from Queens College of the City University of New York and is currently pursuing a Ph.D. in Composition at New York University. She serves as a reader for the Educational Testing Service, for Queensborough Community College of the City University of New York, and for Hofstra University; she also acts as Chief Reader and consultant to private institutions implementing holistically scored essay tests.*

when essay testing is compared with objective testing, it becomes obvious that the time is well spent. Objective testing is simple to administer and grade and, when properly normed, it is highly predictive of students' composition skills. (For those who wish to complement essay tests with objective tests, Prentice Hall offers *Diagnostic and Competency Tests to Accompany the Simon & Schuster Handbook for Writers* [item 6 in the Annotated Bibliography at the end of this essay], a series of matching test forms useful for pre- and post-testing.)

Objective testing is only an indirect measure. It tests students' ability to manipulate the language of others rather than the ability to compose, a process that requires attention to multiple, overlapping concerns of audience, purpose, message, organization, grammar, diction, and mechanics.

Certainly, essay testing presents a few difficulties. Departmental consensus must be reached regarding the reason for testing, the skills to be evaluated, the test's wording, and scoring standards. Costly clerical and administrative support is essential to the reproduction of examinations, scheduling of testing and scoring facilities, notification of students, and recording and interpretation of scores.

Is this investment of time, energy, and resources worthwhile? The experts think so. According to Marie Jean Lederman [10], past University Dean for Academic Affairs of the City University of New York, essay tests serve as rites of passage to the world in which our students will eventually function: "drawing material together into a coherent written whole is vital to membership in a group of educated adults" (p. 45).

Essay testing also has other, more immediate, benefits. Preparing the prompt and scoring guidelines brings an English department together. Faculty share in the process of determining the purpose of the examination and deciding what constitutes acceptable and unacceptable writing for a particular situation. Participation in scoring contributes to a sense of unity among instructors and gives them a rare opportunity to share their responses and their underlying philosophy, a discussion that does not end with the last test paper.

Additional benefits of essay testing appear in the classroom. Where objective tests reign, institutions teach objective-test-taking. Conversely, where essay tests are given, instructors teach essay-test-taking strategies: brainstorming, outlining, thesis statements and topic sentences, relevant detail, supporting anecdotes and examples, editing, and proofreading. Finally, when students are required to take essay tests, they (and their parents and the community) realize that writing is important.

The benefits of giving essay tests may be summarized as follows:

- Instructors of English focus on the essay rather than on isolated grammatical errors.
- By sharing a uniform set of standards, instructors are less likely to use idiosyncratic standards in their own classrooms.
- More attention is placed on the teaching of writing as a process. Editing and proofreading skills are placed in perspective, as final steps rather than as ends in themselves.
- Faculty and administrators unite in the pursuit of a common goal.
- Assessment results can be used to revise curricula.
- Faculty in other disciplines see that writing is being stressed and so may be more willing to incorporate it into their own courses.
- Students take writing more seriously, realizing it can and will be evaluated.

ESSAY TEST TOPICS

Selecting a test topic (a prompt) depends upon two factors: the purpose of the examination and the amount of time available for testing. The two most commonly used time limits are 20 minutes and 50 minutes. Untimed essays also are a possibility, but the procedure is usually too cumbersome when large numbers of students are involved.

Purposes for testing can be divided into two broad categories: placement within a sequence of courses including exemption from a required course) and exit from a program (for example, a departmental final for Freshman Composition or a graduation requirement). An exit examination seeks to ascertain whether certain minimum standards have been met. In this situation, a 20-minute test can provide enough information for readers to distinguish competent from incompetent writing.

A placement examination, in contrast, is given to a much more heterogeneous population. Far subtler distinctions must be made. It is not uncommon for one examination to be used to place students in one of as many as seven courses within a sequence. When such fine distinctions are being made, a 50-minute test is a necessity.

Students need to be prepared for whatever time limit has been set, by being given practice essays in class. If this is not possible, letters sent to students notifying them that they will be writing an essay test should specify the time limit.

The Qualities of a Good Topic

What makes a good essay topic? The Educational Testing Service offers some solid advice in their pamphlet for new readers of the English Composition Test [2]:

> [A good essay topic] must be self-explanatory; it must be defined and limited. It must be a topic that every student . . . can be expected to have some information about. It must be a topic so stimulating that every candidate will have something to say immediately. It must be a topic that young and inexperienced candidates can write about intelligently. (1)

Research by Gordon Brossell has done much to clarify what makes an effective topic. Brossell [1] shows how an overly elaborate prompt inhibits composition. Teachers have known for years that students need prompts that guide their thinking, that one-word prompts ("excellence" or "freedom") elicit fuzzy essays. In an effort to stimulate thought, some test-makers go too far in the other direction and offer students elaborate scenarios. The results are startlingly poor, with many students doing little more than parroting the prompts. Brossell's work shows that

prompts of a few sentences work better than longer ones; students receive enough information to stimulate thought, but not so much as to intimidate them.

More recently, Brossell has joined with James Hoetker to make specific suggestions for generating useful topics [9]. In 1983 Hoetker and Brossell agreed to write a set of topics for Florida's College-Level Academic Skills Test (CLAST). Working with the underlying assumption that "wording and content of a topic may affect what and how well a student writes" (p. 328), they wrote short, simple topics, all having the same form. Their goal was to eliminate any factors that might misdirect students. To compensate for the varying intellectual backgrounds of students, Hoetker and Brossell engineered topics that let students write about the subjects they knew best. The resulting formula is modeled on the parts of the traditional definition: a category, a linking verb, a class specification, and differentiating criteria. The student is given the class specification and differentiating criteria. He or she then must supply an example of that category. By changing the class specification or the criteria, testers can produce similar topics.

> "A book/ that many students read/ that may affect them harmfully."
>
> "A book/ that many students read/ that may affect them beneficially."
>
> "A course/ that many students take/ that may affect them in important ways."

Topics such as these have produced positive results. Essays tend to have strong thesis statements rather than the rambling openings typical of essays written in response to earlier CLAST topics.

Despite the burgeoning interest in essay assessment over the last twenty years, the sharing of findings has been a haphazard affair. Leo Ruth and Sandra Murphy [11] have gone a long way toward correcting this situation. Drawing upon the work of ten leading practitioners ("'exemplars' of wise practice"), formal research in diverse areas (psychometrics, writing topics, and discourse theory), and their own experiences with the Bay Area Writing Project (1980–82), Ruth and Murphy suggest guidelines for designing topics for writing assessment. The scope of this review is impressive, and its tone is even-handed. The various studies are not always in agreement about the best way to reduce misinterpretation of text; test writers, students, and test readers do not all interpret directions and prompts in the same way, nor do student-writers and teacher-readers see the same essay in the same way. Ruth and Murphy point future research in the direction of reducing these "misfirings." Their book is presented not as the endpoint of research, but as a compilation of findings to date. They call emphatically for further exploration of the best way to create assessment situations in which writers can produce their best work.

Suggested Topics

You might want to create topics using the Hoetker/Brossell model above, or you may wish to use topics of the types illustrated below.

1. The following prompts guide students toward informative writing without imposing particular structures. Students are thus able to demonstrate their ability to organize an essay by choosing appropriate rhetorical strategies.

- Describe a visit to the dentist. Use specific details and anecdotes to convince the reader that your dental visits are as pleasant or unpleasant as you believe they are.
- What is your favorite color? Explain what this color represents that makes it special for you. Use specifics, such as details and anecdotes, to support your generalizations.
- Describe a formal social gathering that you have attended, such as a wedding or funeral. Compare the appearance and behavior of people on such an occasion with the way they usually look and behave.
- What career do you plan to pursue? Explain the reasons why you chose this field and tell what you hope to accomplish.
- Pick something you know how to do well, and teach someone how to do it. Be sure to include all the necessary steps and define any unusual terms.

2. Persuasive essays can be given focus if students are asked to agree or disagree with a brief statement. Often writers adapt this part of the prompt into a clear thesis statement. Background, such as that given here, stimulates thinking and suggests sources of evidence.

Follow each of the suggested prompts below with these directions: *Agree or disagree with this statement. Support your position with evidence based on your own experience, observation of others, and reading.*

- Overall, Americans feel the elderly are useless. We tear our older people away from their friends and send them off to live in nursing homes. Television and movies routinely portray the elderly as helpless, easily confused, and having little interest in life.
  In the United States, we have mistaken ideas about older people. [Insert above directions here.]
- Anyone who has ever tried to drive through the center of a large city must realize that something is wrong. Too many cars enter the central business districts, creating massive traffic jams that prevent emergency vehicles from passing, pollute the air, and waste gasoline.
  Private cars should be banned in the center of large cities. [Insert above directions here.]
- People have been arguing for years about whether boys and girls who return from school to an empty house are at a disadvantage. Some studies indicate that because these latchkey children do not have the supervision of an adult during the afternoon, they spend too much time alone watching television or getting into trouble. Other studies show, however, that latchkey children grow up to be responsible, self-confident adults.
  Children who return from school to a home without adult supervision suffer. [Insert above directions here.]
- In recent years, students from the United States have scored lower than students from Europe and Asia on tests of basic academic skills and reasoning ability. Seeking an explanation, some people have suggested that American schools

are too easy. They say students are not made to think through problems nor are they given enough homework to help them practice new skills.

American high schools are too easy. [Insert above directions here.]

- The world seems to get noisier every day. Garbage trucks and the people who pick up the trash make a terrible noise. The sound of machinery coming from construction sites can make it impossible to concentrate. Also some people play their stereos at top volume in the middle of the night.

Local governments should enact laws to control noise pollution. [Insert above directions here.]

3. Some prompts enable students to choose whether they wish to inform or persuade their readers. With these prompts, students must make their own decisions about purpose, audience, and organization.

Follow each of the suggested prompts below with these directions: *Relate this statement to your personal experiences and your observation of others. You may also want to draw on your reading in your response.*

- Worries can be very distracting.
- Every person is a mirror of his or her parents.
- The only thing permanent in life is change.
- The person who speaks in anger will probably regret it.
- Every right brings with it an equal obligation.

4. More experienced writers can be asked to respond to brief quotations. However, the literary cadence of even the shortest quotations makes such prompts challenging. Again, students need to make independent decisions about audience, purpose, and organization.

Follow each of the suggested prompts below with these directions: *Relate this statement to your personal experiences and your observation of others. You may also want to draw on your reading in your response.*

- We must make the best of those ills which cannot be avoided. —ALEXANDER HAMILTON
- In a dream you are never eighty. —ANNE SEXTON
- Common sense is the knack of seeing things as they are, and doing things as they ought to be done. —JOSH BILLINGS
- Understanding is a two-way street. —ELEANOR ROOSEVELT
- Difficulties strengthen the mind, as labor does the body. —SENECA

ADMINISTERING AN ESSAY TEST

Administration of an essay test may be seen as having five stages: organization, on-site preparation, proctoring, scoring, and reporting. The first three stages are discussed below; scoring procedures are discussed in the next section. Reporting methods depend upon the facilities available at each institution; however, students should receive prompt written notice of their test scores, along with an explanation of what further steps they should take.

Organizing an Essay Test

Before the actual test day, certain essential preparations must be made.

1. After the department or a committee has decided what skills are being tested, a suitable topic must be chosen and directions written.
2. The examination must be reproduced and stored in a secure area.
3. The day (or days) for administering the test must be chosen and announced.
4. Unless the test will be administered during regular classes, a test location must be selected.
5. Time for scoring must be scheduled, and a location must be reserved.
6. Supplies must be ordered: blue books, pencils, perhaps microphones.

7. If any students who will take the test are not currently in English classes, letters must be written and mailed to their homes, telling them of the nature, time, place, and *significance* of the examination.
8. Student aides must be hired to help with paperwork and distribution and collection of materials.

On-Site Preparation for an Essay Test

If the test is to be given in individual English classes, someone must see that each teacher receives sufficient question sheets, blue books, and pencils a day in advance. Scrap paper is not necessary, since question sheets or the back of the blue book may be used.

If the test is to be given outside regular classes, each proctor should pick up supplies an hour before the test is scheduled to begin. This will give the proctor time to prepare the test room and greet early arrivals.

Since posting the time distracts some students seriously, try to have a working clock in each room, if possible. If no clock is available, then posting the time at 10- or 15-minute intervals is essential.

Proctoring an Essay Test

Proctors should not spend all their time at the desk reading, but neither should they be constantly pacing. The recommended procedure is to stay in the front of the room making occasional supportive eye contact with students.

To ensure uniform administration of the examination, the test committee should prepare a script—or at least a detailed set of directions—for all proctors. In this way, students are guaranteed a fair policy on such matters as time limit and use of dictionaries, and no students will receive more guidance than others.

SCORING AN ESSAY TEST

The two most widely used procedures for assessing essay examinations are holistic and analytical scoring. Studies indicate that holistic scoring is more efficient and reliable than analytical, but both systems are discussed here so that departments may select the one most in keeping with their needs.

Holistic Scoring

The underlying assumptions of holistic scoring are well stated in the Educational Testing Service pamphlet on scoring the English Composition Test [2]:

> The basic assumptions of holistic scoring are that each of the factors involved in writing skill is related to all the others and that no one factor can be separated from the others. Readers must judge each essay as a whole; they must read each paper for the impression its totality makes. A misspelled word, a comma splice, a sentence fragment, a misplaced modifier should carry no great weight in scoring an otherwise well-written paper. The candidate is entitled to make some mistakes: he or she is writing hurriedly in a tense situation. (2)

Holistic scoring has several advantages. First, by considering each essay as a whole, readers are encouraged to focus on writing as a process leading to a unified product, rather than as a series of minimally connected errors. Second, training enables readers to discover their implicit priorities and the rationales behind them. Third, because readers see a wider range of writing skill than is found in any single course, their perspective is enlarged and therefore their ability to grade their own students fairly increases. Fourth, having two readers per paper reduces the chances of any idiosyncratic judgments and increases reliability in assessment.

Admittedly, holistic scoring also has a few disadvantages. First, scoring sessions take time, especially when training is properly conducted. Second, scoring sessions can be expensive. Release time or stipends need to be provided to participating faculty, and additional clerical help must be hired and trained. Someone at the institution must have extensive experience with holistic scoring in order to organize a reading and conduct training. If no such person is available, a consultant must be hired to act as chief reader and to train an on-campus successor. Finally, holistic scoring neither diagnoses specific weaknesses nor prescribes appropriate action.

However, despite these drawbacks, holistic scoring is preferred by most experts in the field. A brief

EMILY R. GORDON

overview of holistic scoring follows; anyone interested in a more thorough presentation is referred to Edward M. White's *Teaching and Assessing Writing* [13].

A great deal of work occurs behind the scenes before the reading begins. The chief reader, assistant chief reader(s), and table leaders read a large sampling of the essays. From these, they select papers representing various levels of skill, and they assign scores that, in their experienced judgment, reflect the quality of these essays *in relation to the other essays written in response to this particular prompt.* These essays, reflecting the entire range of scores, will be used to train the readers.

The scoring procedures are designed to promote uniform standards. The session begins with the chief reader presenting the topic to the readers and explaining the purpose behind that topic. He or she then discusses key aspects of evaluating the papers, such as the amount of emphasis to be placed on surface features and what constitutes an off-topic response.

The chief reader next explains the process of scoring: Two readers independently grade each essay, and their scores are either recorded in code or covered with removable tape, so that the second reader is not influenced by the first. After a paper has been read twice, clerks decode the scores. If the scores match or are within one point of each other, they are totaled to give the paper's final score. If scores are more than one point apart, a third, highly experienced, reader independently scores the essay, and the two most closely matching scores are added together.

Then the chief reader explains the scoring scale. The number of scores on a scale vary depending upon the purpose of the examination. Common scoring systems include a four-point scale (recommended for uncomplicated situations, such as exiting a course or program) and a six-point scale (useful for making the finer discriminations needed to place students within a course sequence). Sample four- and six-point scales are given in Appendices A and B. Studies indicate that even-numbered scales are preferable, because tired readers are likely to fall toward a neutral middle score, if one is available, rather than making the

sometimes difficult distinction between passing and failing essays. Whatever the number of scoring options on a scale, 1 represents the lowest score and the highest number represents the top score. The following discussion assumes a six-point scale.

Readers, initially working with the sample essays selected by the chief reader and his or her associates, are urged to decide on scores using a two-stage process. First, they must decide if an essay is above average (4 to 6) or below average (1 to 3). The second step is to decide if a passing paper is just above average (4), clearly above average (5), or well above average (6), and if a failing paper is just below average (3), clearly below average (2), or well below average (1).

Since no score exists to label a paper as exactly average, each reader must decide if such a piece is ever-so-slightly above or below average. In fact, one reader may give a score of 3 and another a 4. Some scoring systems treat this split grade as a pass; others treat it as a disagreement and refer the paper to a third reader. Each institution needs to agree on a policy for such scores.

During training, participants read and score up to twenty sample essays. Scores are tabulated, and in cases where readers disagree among themselves or with the scores given by the chief reader and his or her assistants, discussions are held to clarify criteria. Sample essays are read until readers have absorbed appropriate standards and are scoring consistently and accurately. Only then does actual reading of "live" essays begin.

To ensure that standards remain consistent, the reading is interrupted periodically for ongoing training. Even highly experienced readers need to participate in these sessions because they, as much as any beginner, tend to score more harshly when tired. As before, sample essays are read, scored, and discussed in an effort to maintain consensus. As a safeguard between training sessions, table leaders randomly select for review several of each reader's scored essays. If the two rate an essay differently, they discuss the reasons behind the scores. The table leader does not force a reader to change a score, but instead seeks to clarify how that score was determined and whether appropriate criteria are being applied.

The reading continues until all papers have been read twice (or three times, if necessary). Compilation of scores and reporting are left to clerical support personnel.

Analytical Scoring

The assumption behind analytical scoring is that the evaluation of discrete writing skills can be used to rate a whole piece of writing and simultaneously provide a prescription for further work.

Analytical scoring has a few advantages. First, the scoring of a limited number of preselected criteria makes reader training minimal. Second, students and teachers receive specific diagnoses; as a result, student objections to placement decisions are easily handled and teachers know immediately in what areas their students need work. Third, papers are read just once, reducing the clerical workload.

However, the disadvantages of analytical scoring are significant. First, measuring separate skills is incompatible with the philosophy that writing is a process leading to a single, complex product. Second, counting errors encourages readers (teachers who will carry the lesson of the reading back to their students) to focus on weaknesses rather than strengths. Finally, although each essay is read only once, that reading can take far longer than two readings done holistically.

If your department feels, nevertheless, that analytical scoring best suits its needs, two key decisions need to be made. First, decide what categories will be scored. Limit the number of characteristics to be rated, or readers will have to spend far too much time on each essay. Second, since points are awarded for high, middle, and low skill in each area, define what merits a high, middle, or low score. For some qualities, counting the number of errors will do. However, some important features of essay writing (among them, ideas, organization, and tone) do not easily lend themselves to quantification.

Anyone desiring more information about analytical scoring should see Paul B. Diederich's *Measur-*

ing Growth in English [4], which features an analytical scale and an explanation of the criteria for high, middle, and low scores in each of eight areas.

APPENDIX A

A Four-Point Scale

4   This essay is *among the best* written on the topic. It is organized around a clear thesis that is relevant to the prompt. The essay contains numerous appropriate details and examples in support of generalizations. Paragraphs follow a logical order and exhibit unity and coherence. Sentences are grammatically correct and demonstrate the writer's mastery of subordination and coordination. Diction is lively, showing the writer's understanding of levels of diction, denotation and connotation, and metaphor. Errors in punctuation, mechanics, and usage are rare.

3   This essay is a *slightly better–than–average response* to the prompt. A thesis clearly states the author's purpose, although some sentences may not relate to that purpose. The essay contains appropriate details and examples in support of generalizations. Paragraphs generally follow a logical order; they exhibit unity and coherence most of the time. Sentences are usually grammatically correct and reflect some grasp of subordination and coordination. Diction is adequate, but not especially lively. Some errors in punctuation, mechanics, and usage occur, but they do not seriously interfere with meaning.

2   This essay is a *somewhat below–average response* to the prompt. It may lack a thesis statement altogether; if one is present, little is done to provide support. The essay contains some details and examples, but they may not be relevant to the generalizations which they follow. Paragraphs may relate to the thesis, but they are usually underdeveloped, vague, or lacking in unity and coherence. Sentences may be ungrammatical, il-

logical, or unsophisticated; they show little under-standing of subordination or coordination. Diction is lackluster and sometimes inappropriate. Errors in punctuation, mechanics, and usage sometimes inter-fere with meaning.

1   This essay is a *well-below-average response* to the prompt. It may lack a thesis; if one is present, it is very weak. Details and examples are lacking or inappropriate. Most generalizations are com-pletely unsupported or supported with other, often redundant, generalizations. Paragraphs are undeveloped and incoherent, and they have little connection to any thesis or to one another. Sentences may be illogical or badly construct-ed; most consist of simple subject-verb-object combinations, with little or no use of subor-dination and coordination. Diction is immature and often non-idiomatic. Errors in punctuation, mechanics, and usage seriously interfere with meaning.

APPENDIX B

A Six-Point Scale

6   This essay is *among the very best* written on the topic. It contains a clear thesis and is well organ-ized throughout. Generalizations are supported with relevant details and explanations. Sentences demonstrate a mastery of basic grammar, as well as subordination, coordination, and parallel structure. Diction is highly appropriate. Punctua-tion, mechanics, and usage are almost always correct.

5   This essay is *clearly an upper-half response* to the topic. It contains a thesis and is generally well organized, including transitions between and within most paragraphs. Most generalizations are supported with appropriate details and examples. Sentence structure is generally correct, indicating some control of subordination, coordination, and parallel structure, although some errors may oc-cur in especially complicated sentences. Diction is appropriate. Punctuation, mechanics, and usage

are usually correct; whatever errors do occur are not particularly confusing to the reader.

4   This essay is a *slightly above-average response* to the topic. It contains a thesis and is fairly well organ-ized, although digressions or omissions may oc-cur. An attempt is made to support generaliza-tions with appropriate details and examples. While sentence structure is correct enough to be clear, it is often unsophisticated, with little use of subordination, coordination, or parallel structure. Diction is usually appropriate, but some slang and regionalisms may be present and vocabulary may be limited. Agreement, tense, and posses-sion are usually, although perhaps not always, correct. Punctuation shows an understanding of sentence boundaries, but other punctuation may sometimes be nonstandard. Spelling, including homonyms, is generally correct.

3   This essay is a *slightly below-average response* to the topic. Although the connection to the prompt is apparent, the thesis is either missing or vague. Most, but not all, paragraphs are underdeveloped and lacking in unity and coherence. Transitions within and between paragraphs are also missing. Sentence structure is monotonous and unsophis-ticated; few errors may occur because sentences are kept very simple, or there may be frequent errors in sentence punctuation. Diction is often inappropriately informal, and vocabulary is often inexact. Indirect and direct discourse are con-fused. Common words are sometimes mis-spelled.

2   This essay is *clearly a lower-half response* to the topic. Some attempt has been made to discuss the prompt, but ideas generally remain undeveloped. Supporting details and examples are rare; repeti-tion and irrelevancies are common. Paragraph development is minimal. Sentence structure is elementary and often unclear. Diction is highly informal, more appropriate to conversation than to academic writing. Sound-alike words are fre-quently confused, and vocabulary is juvenile. Errors in punctuation, mechanics, and usage are common.

1 This essay is *among the weakest* written on the topic. It has no thesis or pattern of organization, and its connection to the prompt may not be apparent. Errors in grammar, punctuation, mechanics, usage, and spelling are so frequent as to seriously distract the reader. This grade is also given to any essay that is too brief to judge.

Annotated Bibliography of Suggested Readings

1.   Brossell, Gordon. "Rhetorical Specification in Essay Examination Topics." *College English* 45 (1983): 165–73.

> Based upon experimental evidence, Brossell calls into question the assumed superiority of essay test prompts that provide detailed scenarios and that specify fictional speakers, purposes, and audiences. His findings suggest that the prompts most likely to elicit good impromptu responses are those that make only a brief statement about a subject before asking for a personal response.

2.   Conlan, Gertrude. *How the Essay in the College Board English Composition Test Is Scored: An Introduction to the Reading for Readers.* Princeton: Educational Testing Service, 1985.

> This pamphlet is given to new readers of the English Composition Test, the essay portion of the College Board's English Achievement Test. The discussion, outlining how holistic scoring procedures operate for this particular test, is noteworthy for its emphasis on the respect due student writers.

3.   Cooper, Charles R., and Lee Odell, eds. *Evaluating Writing: Describing, Measuring, Judging.* Urbana: National Council of Teachers of English, 1977.

> The editors present six essays, each discussing a different method of assessing writing. See especially "Holistic Evaluation of Writing" by Charles R. Cooper and "Primary Trait Scoring" by Richard Lloyd-Jones.

4.   Diederich, Paul B. *Measuring Growth in English.* Urbana: National Council of Teachers of English, 1974.

> Diederich suggests ways of improving the reliability of essay scoring and argues that a properly graded final essay examination (supported by a short-answer test) can accurately assess each student's writing ability.

5.   Fishman, Judith. "Do You Agree or Disagree: The Epistemology of the CUNY Writing Assessment Test." *WPA: Writing Program Administration* 8 (1984): 17–25.

> Fishman takes issue with the agree/disagree format of the much imitated Writing Assessment Test of the City University of New York, saying that it does not elicit each student's best writing. This critique is responded to by Greenberg [7] and by Troyka [12].

6.   Gordon, Emily R. *Diagnostic and Competency Tests to Accompany the Simon & Schuster Handbook for Writers.* 2nd ed. Englewood Cliffs, NJ: Prentice Hall, 1990.

> This testing package offers two matching forms of diagnostic tests for use on IBM and Apple II computers (Form CX and Form CY); two different matching forms of printed diagnostic tests (Form A and Form B); and two matching forms of printed competency tests (Form AA and Form BB), along with guidelines for administration and scoring.

7.   Greenberg, Karen L. "Writing Assessment Test Design: Response to Two *WPA* Essays." *WPA: Writing Program Administration* 9 (1985): 31–40.

> Greenberg responds to Fishman's charges (see item 5 above), noting that a competence test need not measure each student's best work, but must evoke thoughtful essays from members of a heterogeneous population while remaining valid and reliable.

8.   Greenberg, Karen L., Harvey S. Wiener, and Richard A. Donovan, eds. *Writing Assessment: Issues and Strategies.* New York: Longman, 1986.

Three leading founders of the National Testing Network in Writing have gathered essays by major figures in writing assessment. The volume presents an overview of the issues facing the testing community, and several of the essays indicate fruitful directions for additional work.

9.   Hoetker, James, and Gordon Brossell. "A Procedure for Writing Content-Fair Essay Examination Topics for Large-Scale Writing Assessment." *College Composition and Communication* 37 (1986): 328–35.

Based on their work for Florida's College-Level Academic Skills Test, Hoetker and Brossell suggest that essay prompts based on the structure of formal definition reduce the chances of student misinterpretation and help students focus on subjects about which they are knowledgeable.

10.   Lederman, Marie Jean. "Why Test?" *Journal of Basic Writing* 7 (1988): 38–46; rpt. Greenberg, Wiener, and Donovan [see item 8 above].

Lederman places testing in a historical perspective in order to demonstrate that testing is a rite of passage. Hence the values and essential skills of a society must be determined and acknowledged by those developing tests.

11.   Ruth, Leo, and Sandra Murphy. *Designing Writing Tasks for the Assessment of Writing.* Norwood: Ablex, 1988.

Ruth and Murphy analyze a large body of studies conducted on variables in writing-topic design and on the potential for misinterpretation of topics and directions among test writers, students, and readers.

12.   Troyka, Lynn Quitman. "The Phenomenon of Impact: The CUNY Writing Assessment Test." *WPA: Writing Program Administration* 8 (1984): 27–35.

Writing in response to Fishman's attack on the CUNY WAT (see item 5 above), Troyka recounts the successes of the examination and provides guidelines for the development of unbiased assessment topics.

13.   White, Edward M. *Teaching and Assessing Writing.* San Francisco: Jossey, 1986.

White draws together previously hard-to-find information as he makes a case for schools using essay tests to evaluate writing ability. He shows how such tests can be fair, reliable, and economical and how they foster a variety of changes beneficial to students and teachers.

Teaching Composition to Speakers of Other Languages: An Overview

Joy Reid

Even experienced teachers of composition whose students are native English speakers may experience discomfort and puzzlement when they find non-native speakers of English (ESL students)* in their classes. New or inexperienced composition teachers of native English speakers may face those same feelings as they first begin to teach; however, they usually have the advantage that, at the very least, *they* have been the kinds of students they are teaching. Past experience as native English-speaking students, if not as teachers, prepares them to understand both the expectations of their students and the clues—verbal and nonverbal—that native English speakers (NESs) offer in the classroom: heads nodding, note-taking, raised eyebrows, shifting in seats, interrup-

tions, and the like. When new teachers, experienced with NESs or not, encounter ESL students, however, they may have only limited knowledge about and experience with diverse cultures.† The expected protocols for question-asking, teacher–student exchanges, and group work that seem so "normal" in a class of NESs may be foreign to ESL students.

Initially, the experience of teaching composition to ESL students may parallel the "blind-random" setting on an exercise "step" machine: at this setting, the rhythm of the stepping slows and speeds up automatically and randomly, and so the stepper is "blind": he or she does not control when the rhythm will change or in what direction. Almost certainly the inexperienced teacher of ESL students encounters periods of "randomness," of surprising incidents, time frames and rhythms; furthermore, because of the cultural differences between the teacher and the students, and among the students themselves, the randomness is frequently not preceded by any clues—it occurs "blindly." The results: frustration and misperceptions for both teachers and students. This essay discusses several major areas in which the needs of ESL students differ from those of NESs; it provides informa-

JOY REID teaches in the English Department and coordinates the ESL support program at the University of Wyoming. She has published ESL composition textbooks as well as articles on discourse analysis, computers and composition, learning styles, the writing–reading connection, and the change process. Her newest book is Teaching ESL Writing *(Regents/Prentice-Hall, 1993).*

*To avoid confusion between native English speakers (NESs) and non-native speakers of English (NNSs), students for whom English is not a first language are called English as a Second Language (ESL) students in this essay, although of course English may be their third or fourth language.

†Richard Samovar and Larry Porter (1991) describe culture as the overall system of perceptions and beliefs, values and patterns of thought that direct and constrain a social group, from the way the group uses space to the meaning of widened eyes, and from the way members of the group approach relationships to the ways they view the world. Language—verbal, nonverbal, and written communication—is an integral part of culture.

JOY REID

tion from experienced ESL composition teachers concerning the identification of typical problems—and suggests solutions—in the NES/ESL composition class.

INTERNATIONAL VS. RESIDENT ESL STUDENTS

In much the same way that NESs differ in background knowledge, motivation, and perspective, it is important to realize that ESL students are not a homogeneous group. Aside from the clear diversity in language and cultural backgrounds, ESL students in U.S. colleges and universities can also be described in terms of the scenarios in which they acquired their second language. Specifically, most of the "international" (or "visa") students, those students who travel to the U.S. from their homelands to attend post-secondary institutions, differ from ESL students who have grown up in the U.S., who have graduated from U.S. high schools, and/or who may be U.S. residents/citizens.

Students who have studied English outside the U.S., English as a foreign language (EFL), and who have entered post-secondary institutions in the U.S. following several years of EFL study in their native countries, have, for the most part, acquired English *visually*; they have learned about the structures of the language, but their practice in producing English has been limited to the classroom. Furthermore, as Ilona Leki [item 13 in the Annotated Bibliography below] points out, not many educational systems appear to teach rhetorical patterns directly in the school setting; in most countries outside the U.S. there are virtually no courses in writing. Therefore, many international students have underdeveloped rhetorical skills. Moreover, because cultures evolve writing styles appropriate to their own histories and the needs of their societies, many international students have assumptions about the presentation of written ideas that are appropriate for their native discourse communities (that is, the expectations and needs of audiences in their native cultures). These assumptions may be inappropriate for U.S. academic discourse communities.

In contrast, U.S. residents (that is, ESL students who have lived and attended secondary schools in the U.S.) have acquired much of their English through their *ears*. Although they may have had ESL classes alongside their regular public school work, their English has been learned mainly through immersion in the language. In some cases, the same may be true in their first language: although they speak that language fluently, they may not read or write it fluently. As a result of this aural basis, their spoken language may be fluent and comprehensible, and their writing may appear fluent. However, because these students have limited knowledge of the structures of English, their writing may appear more or less phonetic with little demonstration of the structures (e.g., correct use of verb tenses, prepositions, word forms) of the language. This single difference between international and resident ESL students bears directly on the strengths and weaknesses these students bring to their writing classes, and significantly affects the ways teachers can approach writing processes with the ESL students in each group.

CROSS-CULTURAL AND INTERCULTURAL COMMUNICATION

At the same time composition teachers are struggling to accommodate ESL student needs, their ESL students may also be struggling to adjust their perceptions to a "foreign" classroom environment; that is, "blind-random" occurs on both sides of the desk. Even ESL students who have attended U.S. public schools and have lived in the U.S. most of their lives carry many of their first-culture values, needs, and expectations into their second-language classrooms. Collections of essays about cross-cultural issues, edited by Patricia Byrd [1] and Joyce Valdes [17], have shown that cultural differences between (and among) ESL students and their teachers may include differences across cultures of how students view teachers and in student attitudes toward teaching and learning. The degree of authority invested in and expected from the teacher, as well as the degree to which the teacher directs and dominates class activities, depends to a large extent on culture. For example, many Asian cultures, both in North America and in Asia, have a tradition of deference: questioning a person in authority—a parent, a teacher—is disrespectful, and passive learning is the key to success. In a U.S. college composition class, however, such behavior may be seen as inappropriately silent and non-participatory. In contrast, the strong cooperative values and high level of social responsibility of many Latin societies, in both North and South America, make the highly individualized and competitive values of many U.S. students seem unpleasantly aggressive. For the newly arrived international student, the adjustment may be even more jarring: a class in the U.S. must look like a structureless, anarchical situation for learning. In the U.S., composition students are expected to take an active part in the learning process, asking questions, challenging each other and their teachers, working (often loudly) in groups. Consequently, many ESL students must learn a variety of different assumptions about both learning and teaching. In fact, a truly multicultural class can result in substantial classroom imbalance in perspectives and even cross-cultural tensions as students and teachers struggle to find appropriate behaviors and interactions.

Contrastive Rhetoric

Robert Kaplan first defined contrastive rhetoric [9] when he sought to discover whether organizational patterns of written material vary from culture to culture. In his investigation of 600 student expository paragraphs, written in English by native speakers of many non-English language backgrounds, Kaplan used philosophical, psychological, anthropological, and linguistic insights to describe the differences between the essentially linear English paragraph, which does not tolerate digression or repetition, and paragraphs that he classified generally as Semitic, Oriental, Romance, and Russian. He represented the differences graphically; at the same time he cautioned that "much more detailed and more accurate descriptions are required before any meaningful contrastive system can be elaborated" (p. 12).

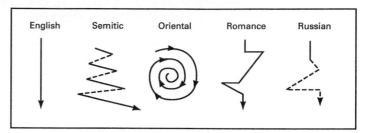

Kaplan's Contrastive Rhetoric Diagram

Since the appearance of Kaplan's article, the notion of contrastive rhetoric, along with the issues surrounding the transfer of rhetorical patterns in second language writing, has grown into an area of study. Research reported by proponents of this theory, published in collections edited by Kaplan [10] and by Ulla Connor and Robert Kaplan [4] demonstrate that the style in which each culture organizes and presents written material reflects the preferences of that particular culture. As a result, ESL writers often intuitively employ a rhetoric and sequence of thought that violate the expectations of the native reader; when they write for readers in another culture, they often have problems with the identifying audience expectations and communicating with different discourse communities.

Even *within* a language, there appear to be different rhetorical rules and conventions that govern different categories of texts. Leki [14] indicates that in U.S. academic classes, discipline-specific writing conventions differ in such diverse areas as length of sentences, choice of vocabulary, acceptability of using first person, extent of using passive voice, degree to which writers are permitted to interpret, and amount of metaphorical language accepted. According to William Grabe and Robert Kaplan [6], the ESL writer is also likely to have a different notion of what constitutes evidence, of the order in which evidence should best be presented, and of the amount of evidence needed in order to explain something to/or persuade the reader. Consequently, ESL students can face misunderstanding and even failure in their academic

JOY REID

written work because they are often unaware of the content expectations and of the rhetorical problems in their prose.

While such differences between ESL and NES writers may affect communication in a U.S. academic discourse community, they should not be stigmatized as deficiencies. As Alan Purves and his colleagues note, differences among rhetorical patterns do not represent differences in cognitive ability but rather differences in cognitive style [14]. After all, arrangement and presentation of ideas as well as style, can all be defined, practiced, and valued in many ways. However, ESL writers (like NESs) must acquire the appropriate background knowledge necessary to identify and fulfill the expectations of the U.S. academic audience; knowledge about appropriate language use, content, and genre can empower ESL students.

Recent articles on cognition and the theory of expertise indicate that the problems students encounter as a result of their contrastive rhetorics may be partially solved by strategy training. Such research, for example, suggests that novice NES writers who attempt to perform in areas of knowledge in which they have little or no specific background rely on general strategies, particularly a dependence on "what the teacher wants." These students need—and often demand—that the teacher be more and more specific about form, content, and language that the student can imitate. Then, as students begin to develop more specific writing strategies (as they become more experienced writers), they gain more knowledge of and practice in such specific writing strategies as reading and analyzing academic assignments, generating ideas, getting started, overcoming writer's block, revising, determining audiences, writing for a purpose, and so forth.

While many NES writers are inexperienced with the specific strategies used by experienced NESs in academic discourse communities, many ESL students are unaware even of the general strategies of English writing. And there is no reason to assume that ESL writers will acquire the conventions of English without assistance. For ESL students, then, the composition course is much more than a skills course; it is also a *content* course in which they need to learn about audience and purpose, levels of content specificity, and academic formats, perhaps for the first time. The students need to know that writing involves not only linguistic processes but social and cognitive processes as well: when it is appropriate to write, what is appropriate to write for an identified audience in a specific situation, and how to organize ideas appropriately for that audience and purpose. In addition, ESL students (and less experienced NES writers as well) need to learn repertoires of strategies to generate ideas, draft pieces of writing, and encounter feedback from peers and teachers. To assist their ESL students toward these goals, composition teachers may well need to be more didactic; certainly they must become cultural informants for their students, by *researching* U.S. academic writing assignments and the discourse communities that design, assign, and evaluate those assignments. They can gather that information, identify the rules of use of that discourse community, and provide opportunities for students to identify, understand, practice and fulfill the expectations of the U.S. academic discourse communities they will enter.

Schema Theory

Successful communication rests on background knowledge and experience that is shared by writers and readers; the prior knowledge of student writers necessarily influences what, and how, they write. Patricia Carrell's research [2] with ESL readers and writers defines this previously acquired background knowledge as *schema*. If we think of the brain as a computer, ideas and words are "input" into "files" (or databases), which are in turn modified by that new information; these files are analogous to our background knowledge structures called schemata. Carrell found it useful to distinguish three forms of schema: linguistic (language knowledge), content (topic knowledge), and formal schemata (knowledge of the rhetorical structures of different types of texts). First, because the effectiveness of written communication and reader interpretation depends on the successful interaction between writer and reader, language knowledge—linguistic schema—plays an integral part in ESL writing. Second, the background of the writer in the subject of the text—content schema—determines, in part, the comprehension. Finally, formal or rhetorical schema includes knowledge that Connor [3] describes as such structural text elements as the relationships among items of information, the subordination and coordination of this information, paragraph structures, and cohesion devices. Carrell's research indicated that when language *and* form *and* content are familiar and expected, writing is relatively easy, but when one or the other (or all) are unfamiliar, efficiency, effectiveness, and success for the writer can be problematic.

Since ESL writers organize and present material in ways that are different from NESs, Carrell indicates that, by providing necessary cultural information about the rhetorical organization of U.S. academic expository text and audience expectations of such text, teachers will help their ESL students' writing to be more effective. In other words, teachers must help their ESL writing students to acquire appropriate schemata. In order to do so, teachers need (a) to become informed about appropriate U.S. academic discourse patterns; (b) to inform their ESL writing students about discourse differences and audience expectations; and (c) to provide practice and experience with the new schema.

ACCURACY AND FLUENCY

Teachers of ESL writers will almost certainly face student essays with linguistic and rhetorical problems that are related to (a) the first languages of the students and/or (b) "developmental" problems that are the result of limitations in students' previous education. It is unfortunate that the language errors of ESL student writers rarely approximate those of NESs either in number or in kind, and that their visibility immediately triggers negative responses in readers. While an error that interferes with clear communication is unacceptable in both NES and ESL writing, an understanding of the logical bases for second language error in writing may mediate the visceral reaction that excludes other components of the student writing.

The question of error and the dichotomy between fluency and accuracy have existed in language teaching for decades: should the language teacher concentrate on one or the other? Traditionally, accuracy has been defined as the focus on discrete elements of the rules of language, while fluency has been defined as the focus on the communication of ideas without consideration of discrete language elements. This is probably a false dichotomy. A focus on fluency does not necessarily exclude consideration of the systematic properties of language; after all, it is not possible to communicate successfully without some knowledge and monitoring of the language of the message. Similarly, a focus on accuracy demands concentration on discrete points of language, but does not necessarily curb creativity and self-expression, ignore cognitive processes, or overlook personality traits of the learner.

At the basis of the accuracy–fluency controversy is the question of error. Once thought to be deviant behavior, error—in both first and second language acquisition—is now seen as a natural phenomenon. Of course, errors in written language can be due to inattention, memory lapse, or indifference. Moreover, in an in-class writing situation, NESs as well as ESL students will make hasty "performance errors." However, as Barbara Kroll [11] points out, ESL errors are generally neither random nor sporadic nor deviant; instead, they are systematic, regular, and rule-governed, the result of intelligence, not stupidity. Errors come from a conscious or unconscious attempt by students to use what they have learned.

ESL language errors are influenced by three factors: native language transfer, overgeneralization, and difficulty level. First, when second language students encounter a language form, they often infer rules from previous knowledge of their first language; they "transfer" that knowledge into a hypothesis about the second language. For that reason, students from the same language background may well make some of the same types of errors, though their hypotheses (and therefore the resulting language) may not be exactly the same. For example, native speakers of Spanish may use adjectives that have both gender and number and that follow, rather than precede, the verb (e.g., the flowers *reds*) because these rules apply in Spanish. Such first-language transfer occurs not only with grammatical structures but also with first-language writing skills and strategies as well; ESL writers often transfer both good and weak writing skills from their first language into English, and many ESL students who have not developed good strategies for writing in their first language will not have appropriate strategies to transfer to their second language.

Overgeneralization of rules is a somewhat different reason for error: ESL students may hypothesize, consciously or subconsciously, about a language form by extending the use of a rule they have learned in the second language. For instance, if the rule says that third-person singular verbs must take an "s" (i.e., "he runs"), ESL students may "overgeneralize" the rule to include second-person singular verbs (i.e., "you runs"). The hypothesis is incorrect, but it *is* a systematic application of a rule. In each of these cases, students who can identify or "monitor" for language errors can learn to reformulate new hypotheses and adopt new learning strategies to correct the errors.

Finally, if a language rule is particularly complex or difficult, students may make errors as they attempt to construct the language form, or they may avoid the form altogether. Level of difficulty is a complicated concept, for it is in part dependent on both first language differences and prior student experience. For example, while English is a subject–verb–object (SVO) language, Korean is a subject–object–verb (SOV) language, and word order is relatively free. A sentence in English, translated into Korean and then retranslated, word for word, into English, shows the differences:

English: Even though I told John not to take the Chemistry class, he took it.
Korean: Even though I John Chemistry class not to take told John it took.

In addition to word order, many Asian languages are "tonal": That is, they have few or no inflections (such as verb tense and plural markers). Chinese, for instance, is a language that has no verb tenses and no articles; learning the complex rules for verb tense is an enormous task, and implementing those rules expands the task geometrically. Many of the rules for article use in English are at best eccentric; correct use of articles for an ESL student whose native language does not have articles is extremely difficult. For instance, try formulating the rules needed for the following examples and consider the consequent decisions Asian ESL students must make:

She considered him (a) genius.
(X) (The) number seven is lucky.
(The) only girl at (the) party was Nanan.
(A/The) funny picture on (a/the) page

and

going to (a/the) church	vs.	going to (X) church
going to (a/the) store	vs.	going (X) (X) home
going on (a/the) journey	vs.	going to (X) work

For Arabic speakers, relative clauses are easier to use than auxiliary verbs in English because relative clauses in Arabic parallel use in English (though in Arabic, the relative clause requires the use of a personal pronoun, resulting in such structures as "The man who likes coffee *he* . . ."). In contrast, there are no auxiliary verbs in Arabic, so a structure like "She *taking* a class" is a common error. In short, ESL students are similar to other students of languages: native-like accuracy in non-native language writing is a life-long struggle, so both students and their teachers must expect language errors in student writing.

Error is an integral part of the learning process during a child's first language acquisition; however, quick intervention (say, by the mother of the young child) and direct or indirect correction, as well as continued exposure to correct language, allows the child to reformulate language hypotheses. Consider, however, the child raised in a relatively standard American English atmosphere who, as an adult, learns that she uses one English structure incorrectly: lay/lie. Having habituated that error for her first twenty-five years, she spends the next twenty-five "monitoring" for that error, thinking about the rules governing lay/lie before she uses those words, "unlearning," relearning, practicing, and, more often than not, avoiding that structure. Such habituated or "fossilized" behavior, whether a single grammatical structure or an inappropriate oral response, are for the person making the error easy to identify but difficult to monitor, and that behavior is nearly impossible to change permanently, at least in a short period of time. For the ESL student with not one but rather dozens of habituated language errors, writing flawless English prose is at best an overwhelming prospect.

In light of these facts, teachers should see most ESL errors as a normal, natural, and necessary part of the learning process. Teachers of ESL students who are interested in their students' errors may fruitfully investigate contrastive analysis studies that examine features of a native language (e.g., English) that contrast with features of another language (e.g., Spanish, Japanese) to determine what areas of second language learning are most likely to cause difficulty for their students. In such an investigation, teachers may well discover that the students themselves are the best sources of contrastive analysis information and, importantly, that asking students to analyze (and perhaps to log) their errors may prove beneficial to their learning processes. Another interesting area for examination is "error gravity" studies, in which researchers investigate the "irritation" or "acceptance" levels of NESs—usually university non-ESL faculty—to specific second language errors. That is, the studies focus on what second language errors interfere most with NES comprehension in order to help teachers and students prioritize language errors and edit more successfully. For example, Roberta Vann and her colleagues [18] investigated the responses of 164 faculty members to twelve typical ESL errors. They found that most respondents did not judge all errors as equally severe; incorrect word order (as in the direct translation of the Korean sentence above) was considered the most serious, and spelling errors the least severe.

Kroll [11] demonstrates that ESL writing proficiency can be broadly divided into *plus–syntax* and *minus–syntax*, *plus–rhetoric* and *minus–rhetoric*: "one paper can provide insightful commentary on a substantive topic while replete with problems in spelling and punctua-

tion [+rhetoric and −syntax]. Another paper can exhibit a wide range of sentence structures, flawless syntax, adherence to mechanics, yet lack development and support of its central thesis [−rhetoric and +syntax]" (p. 40). Still another paper may be hard to read because it contains both second language errors and a lack of coherence [−rhetoric and −syntax]. In terms of the two broad categories of ESL students described in this essay, typical international student writing will demonstrate limited coherence, and particularly a limited knowledge of academic forms and audience expectations [−rhetoric]. In contrast, typical resident student writing will often demonstrate [−syntax]; that is, the writing will be fluent but contain many language errors.

EVALUATION

Given the problems any second language learner can have with accuracy in writing, the problem of evaluation facing the composition teacher with ESL students is substantial. For the NES teacher, ESL language errors are even more visible (and so, perhaps, irritating) than common NES errors; looking beyond the errors to rhetorical and contextual successes or problems may therefore be difficult. "Lowering standards" or asking less of ESL student writing is not a viable solution, yet language errors must be seen in perspective: ESL students may have adequate knowledge of correct usage but find it difficult to produce accurate prose consistently. There is more, much more, to successful written communication than the use of articles. Therefore, as teachers develop criteria for evaluation by which the student writers will be judged, those criteria should be carefully developed, realistically grounded in the discourse communities the students will face outside the classroom, and explicitly articulated. The composition teacher might consider giving a separate grade for language, or even giving several grades for each paper in areas of focus for that paper: coherence, use of detail, audience awareness, etc. Such a grading scheme would allow students to identify more easily their writing strengths and weaknesses.

JOY REID

Liz Hamp-Lyons [8] notes that evaluation works best and is most fair to learners when it takes into account who the learner is, the situation in which the writer produces writing, and the overall context in which educational success is to be measured for the student writer. The objectives of correction, response, and evaluation are long-term improvement and cognitive change; sending students back into the writing process in order to work again (and again) with their writing is often more successful for the students than memorizing grammar rules. Moreover, students learn to do best what teachers can demonstrate. Researchers Ann Fathman and Elizabeth Whalley [5] found that teacher response/intervention during the writing process and teacher correction of error has impact when the feedback is clear. In other words, the response/correction must adequately describe the problem and then suggest methods of correction. Research has repeatedly shown that working with student errors in the context of their writing is more beneficial than studying discrete grammar points out of context. Teachers must also help ESL students monitor for error and to edit their almost-completed work for specific language problems.

Just as important, students must have the appropriate schema to be able to learn. Marking errors that students do not identify as errors is ineffectual; asking students to "organize" when they think they already have is at best confusing for the students. Instead, early intervention and explanation modes can assist students to identify and solve language problems before evaluation occurs. For example, teachers might begin by marking, but not correcting, language errors, then asking students to (a) distinguish between errors they immediately recognize (and can therefore monitor) and (b) those errors they do not recognize (and so need intervention and explanation). Identifying and then prioritizing language errors can make monitoring for error easier for ESL students. Next, careful planning of peer review and response groups can help ESL students to identify language problems and solutions; however, peer activities must allow ESL students to give as well as receive assistance. Conferencing, individually or in small groups, is another intervention technique that can prove useful for ESL students. Lynn Goldstein and Susan Conrad [7] discuss the problems and the benefits of conferencing with ESL students about specific language and rhetorical problems during the drafting process; they agree that successful conferencing can strengthen writing skills and develop the independent decision-making so vital in successful writing. In addition, the students must have the strategies to deal with peer and teacher feedback and to correct their errors, the time to digest and then to practice corrections. In short, feedback without follow-up (in the form of discussion, practice, graded revisions) will be less than effective. Finally, as Robin Scarcella and Rebecca Oxford point out [16], strategy training in the processes of composing, drafting, and editing will facilitate student learning; knowledge of resources other than the teacher (e.g., reference books and textbooks, peers, the campus writing center, peer editors) will enable students to seek help outside of class even after the class has ended.

CONCLUSION

Identifying and studying the differences in communication styles and strategies between cultures is worthwhile, even necessary, for both ESL students and their teachers. The more understanding that exists, the better prepared teachers will be to communicate effectively with their students; the more students understand about those differences, the more easily they will fulfill their own and other people's expectations. In an ESL class, the differences in cultural knowledge can be dramatic; students without appropriate linguistic, content, and/or formal schemata encounter difficulty communicating effectively. However, acquiring relevant cultural schemata can facilitate the learning process by enabling students to learn the social processes and the rhetorical conventions for written communication with academic discourse communities.

How teachers focus on ESL students in their classrooms depends, at least in part, on their goals for all students, on how and for whom they want to empower those students. If, as Robert Land and Catherine Whitley [12] suggest, the objective of a composition class is "to acquire enough facility with Standard Written English (SWE) to succeed in school and in the workplace" (284), an effective pedagogy would include teaching composition not only as a skills course but also as a content course. Grabe and Kaplan [6] have indicated that, for ESL students, the content of a composition course must include such areas as composing strategies, coherence systems and mechanisms, language features, rhetorical patterns, audience characteristics and expectations, and genre conventions.

Annotated Bibliography of Suggested Readings

1. Byrd, P., ed. *Teaching Across Cultures in the University ESL Program.* Washington, D.C.: NAFSA, 1986.

> An excellent collection of articles that provides background discussions of relevant issues in cross-cultural communication, useful descriptions of cultural programs developed at several institutions, and explanations of materials and methods developed by individual teachers for use in cross-cultural classrooms.

2. Carrell, P. L. "Text as Interaction: Some Implications of Text Analysis and Reading Research for ESL Composition." *Writing Across Languages: Analysis of L2 Text.* Eds. U. Connor and R. B. Kaplan. Reading, MA: Addison-Wesley, 1987. 47–56.

3. Connor, U. "Introduction." *Coherence in Writing.* Eds. Ulla Connor and Ann Johns. Alexandria, VA: TESOL, 1990. 1–5.

4. Connor, U., and R. Kaplan, eds. *Writing Across Languages: Analysis of L2 Text.* Reading, MA: Addison-Wesley, 1987.

> This collection of articles describes the concept of contrastive rhetoric, discusses empirical research in the contrastive rhetoric of many languages with English, and suggests applications of such research in the teaching of ESL writing. The book is an excellent sourcebook for information concerning contrastive rhetoric.

5. Fathman, A., and E. Whalley, "Teacher Response to Student Writing: Focus on Form vs. Content." *Second Language Writing: Research Insights for the Classroom.* Ed. Barbara Kroll. New York: Cambridge UP, 1990. 178–90.

6. Grabe, W., and R. Kaplan, "Writing in a Second Language: Contrastive Rhetoric." *Richness in Writing: Empowering ESL Students.* Eds. D. Johnson and D. Roen. New York: Longman, 1989. 263–83.

7. Goldstein, L. M., and S. M. Conrad, "Student Input and Negotiation of Meaning in ESL Writing Conferences." *TESOL Quarterly* 24(3) (1990): 441–60.

8. Hamp-Lyons, L. *Assessing ESL Writing in Academic Contexts.* Norwood, NJ: Ablex, 1992.

> This collection of articles written by the growing number of researchers in ESL testing focuses on the testing of ESL writing. It follows a clear, carefully written explanation of the issues in this research area; the assessment issues discussed range from validity questions concerning commercial writing tests to practical questions concerning classroom testing. Other issues discussed include cross-cultural assessment, academic literacy, criteria and scoring models, needs assessment, and models of feedback.

9. Kaplan, R. B. "Cultural Thought Patterns in Intercultural Education." *Language Learning* 16 (1966): 1–20.

10. Kaplan, Robert B., ed. *Annual Review of Applied Linguistics: 1982.* Rowley, MA: Newbury House Publishers, 1983.

> The third volume of the series is directed toward studies related to written text, more specifically to

contrastive rhetoric articles that study the rhetorical differences between English and such languages as German, Hindi, Korean, Mandarin, and Marathi. Kaplan introduces the collection and provides an integrative essay in conclusion.

11.　Kroll, Barbara, ed. *Second Language Writing: Research Insights for the Classroom.* New York: Cambridge UP, 1990.

This seminal collection of thirteen articles is addressed to teachers-in-training and to experienced teachers in the field of ESL teaching as well. It is divided into two sections: the first presents "the current state of thinking on what the teaching of writing to nonnative speakers entails" (p. 3); the second section presents a "variety of specific studies, each focused on a different aspect of writing and/or the writing classroom" (pp. 3–4).

12.　Land, R., and C. Whitley. "Evaluating Second Language Essays in Regular Composition Classes: Toward a Pluralistic Society." *Richness in Writing: Empowering ESL Students.* D. Johnson and D. Roen, eds. New York: Longman, 1989. 284–93.

13.　Leki, I. *Understanding ESL Writers: A Guide for Teachers.* New York: St. Martin's Press, 1992.

Written particularly for NES teachers of NES freshman English classes in which there are non-native speakers of English, the focus of this book is on immigrant students rather than international students: that is, students who may have had limited *study* of the English language, either in their native country or in the U.S., but whose oral (and listening) skills may be highly developed, the result of immersion in U.S. schools and culture. Their problems with reading and writing, and the problems faced by their teachers, are discussed in clear and cogent detail, with practical suggestions offered that are based on second language acquisition research and composition theory.

14.　Purves, Alan, ed. *Writing Across Languages and Cultures: Issues in Contrastive Rhetoric.* Newbury Park, CA: Sage Press, 1988.

The collection of research articles from scholars of several countries address the issue of cultural expec-

tations in the assessment of writing by non-native speakers of a language. How these writers deviate from the norms of the foreign culture in the kinds of material they choose, the style, and the organization of their prose is examined by the researchers.

15.　Samovar, L., and R. Porter, eds. *Intercultural Communication: A Reader,* 6th ed. Belmont, CA: Wadsworth, 1991.

This book contains interesting and informative articles by a large number of international educators in the field of cross-cultural communication. Each chapter examines current issues in the field, ranging from the sociocultural necessity of effective communication to cultural-specific essays, from the impact of Confucianism in East Asia to Arabic concepts of effective persuasion, to the cultural patterns of the Masai.

16.　Scarcella, R., and R. Oxford. *The Tapestry of Learning: The Individual in the Communicative Classroom.* Boston: Heinle and Heinle, 1992.

The authors present their approach to teaching, which is analogous to the weaving of many strands into a tapestry. The foundation of this approach defines the role of the teacher as information-gatherer, decision maker, motivator, facilitator of group dynamics, provider of language input, counselor and friend, provider of feedback, and promoter of a multicultural perspective. The book offers the theoretical bases for the approach and sequenced activities for the language classroom.

17.　Valdes, Joyce M., ed. *Culture Bound: Bridging the Cultural Gap in Language Teaching.* Cambridge: Cambridge UP, 1986.

This collection of articles brings together representative theoretical and practical material in the field of cross-cultural communication. Part I contains articles focusing on language, thought, and culture as they affect language learning. Part II presents cultural phases of particular groups and practical applications of intercultural communication theory.

18.　Vann, R., Meyer, D. E., and F. D. Lorenz. "Error Gravity: A Study of Faculty Opinion of ESL Errors." *TESOL Quarterly* 18(3) (1984): 427–40.

Third Edition

Simon & Schuster
HANDBOOK
for WRITERS

Lynn Quitman Troyka

PRENTICE HALL
Englewood Cliffs, New Jersey 07632

Library of Congress Cataloging-in-Publication Data

Troyka, Lynn Quitman
    Simon and Schuster handbook for writers / Lynn Quitman Troyka. —
3rd ed.
        p.   cm.
    Includes index.
    ISBN 0-13-813767-6
    1. English language—Rhetoric—Handbooks, manuals, etc.
    2. English language—Grammar—1950-   —Handbooks, manuals, etc.
    I. Title.   II. Title: Simon and Schuster handbook for writers.
    PE1408.T696   1993
    808'.042—dc20   92-27200
                                                                            CIP

> *For David,*
> *who makes it all an adventure*

Publisher: J. Philip Miller
Development Editor: Joyce Perkins
Production Editors: John Rousselle, Alison Gnerre, Keith Faivre
Acquisitions Editor: Alison Reeves
Art Director: Christine Wolf
Interior Design and Page Layout: Lorraine Mullaney
Cover Design: Ray Lundgren Graphics, Ltd.
Prepress Buyer: Herb Klein
Manufacturing Buyer: Bob Anderson
Production Assistance: Jenny Moss

Printed in the United States of America

10   9   8   7   6   5   4   2   1

ISBN 0-13-813767-6

Prentice-Hall International (UK) Limited, *London*
Prentice-Hall of Australia Pty. Limited, *Sydney*
Prentice-Hall Canada Inc., *Toronto*
Prentice-Hall Hispanoamericana, S.A., *Mexico*
Prentice-Hall of India Private Limited, *New Delhi*
Prentice-Hall of Japan, Inc., *Tokyo*
Simon & Schuster Asia Pte. Ltd., *Singapore*
Editora Prentice-Hall do Brasil, Ltda., *Rio de Janeiro*

Contents

9 Case of Nouns and Pronouns 225

10 Pronoun Reference 237

Preface

TO INSTRUCTORS

The Third Edition of the *Simon & Schuster Handbook for Writers* seeks to solidify and extend my commitment in earlier editions to demonstrate that students are empowered, not intimidated, by knowledge. I believe that information about writing processes and writing products can provide critical access to habits of mind that dramatically increase students' chances to fulfill their academic, business, and personal potentials. My vision, therefore, is that this *Handbook* serve both as a classroom text and as a comprehensive reference volume for college and the years afterwards. My goals are to provide uncomplicated yet complete explanations, a tone that conveys my enduring respect for students, and an accessible format.

In composing the Third Edition, I drew on many conversations held over the past few years—sometimes in person and sometimes on paper—with instructors and with students in dozens of colleges about what works best in a writer's handbook. I also relied, as before, on respected traditional and contemporary rhetorical theory, composition research, language studies, learning theory, and modern practices in the teaching of writing. This new edition retains the innovations that have always set this *Handbook* apart, is revised throughout to enhance clarity, and adds new features.

- The *Handbook* starts with six chapters about the whole essay, thereby giving students a context for studying writing.
- It sets the scene with a short first chapter about purposes and audiences for writing, thereby explaining the *why* of writing before turning to writing processes and writing products. **New for this edition,** writer's tone is discussed, tied to concepts of purpose and audience.
- It explains the writing process, emphasizing that steps in the process are rarely linear and always vary with the writer, the topic, and the writing situation.

■ It illustrates variations of writing purposes and processes with three complete student essays. Two have a persuasive purpose. **New for this edition,** the essay with an informative purpose has been replaced with a different example; it is shown evolving from planning and shaping through three complete drafts with student and instructor comments.

■ It devotes an extensive chapter to critical thinking as it affects reading, reasoning, and writing processes. **New for this edition,** the presentation of logical fallacies is refined.

■ It offers a separate chapter on writing argument, with the two student essays that have a persuasive purpose, each taking a different position on the same topic.

■ It covers all topics of grammar, style, language, punctuation, and mechanics, with explanations and examples to facilitate visual as well as verbal learning. The widely acclaimed additions to the Second Edition, Focus on Revising sections, once again apply concepts of revision to matters of grammar, language, and style. Occurring eleven times, each Focus on Revising invites students to reexamine their own writing and to work with two case studies of students revising.

■ **New for this edition,** the chapter on avoiding plagiarism and on using sources to quote, paraphrase, and summarize is reorganized to conform more closely to students' decision-making processes when conducting research.

■ **New for this edition,** coverage of research writing is expanded to five chapters. The dual processes of conducting research *and* writing about that research are integrated throughout. Two complete student research papers are now provided—one in MLA style and an entirely new paper in APA style—each accompanied by detailed explanations of the student's research and writing processes. The very popular Process Notes, introduced in the Second Edition with the MLA-style research paper, again narrate the student's decision-making and composing processes, thus demonstrating that critical thinking is central to research writing.

■ It contains a separate chapter on documenting sources, with a free-standing "mini-handbook" about using MLA style and APA style. Its pivotal section, with red tinted edges for instant identification, starts with a directory and then illustrates 42 examples in both MLA and APA styles.

■ It includes four chapters on writing across the curriculum. **New for this edition,** a chapter on writing about literature, which features three new complete student essays, one each on fiction, drama, and poetry. The last is a literary research paper that analyzes two works by Jamaican-born poet Claude McKay.

■ **New for this edition,** extensive attention to the concerns of students for whom English is a second language. Using a three-way integrated strategy, the material includes new ESL notes sprinkled throughout the text, new ESL sections at the end of selected existing chapters, and six new ESL chapters (in all-new Part 9) on aspects of language and grammar that require more detailed explanation.

In writing the *Simon & Schuster Handbook for Writers,* I strive to be inclusive of all people. Role stereotyping and sexist language are avoided; *man* is not used generically for the human race; male and female writers are represented equally in examples; and many ethnic groups are represented in the mix of student and professional writing examples. Also, in the Third Edition, I retain and add to the pool of pedagogic innovations in prior editions.

■ **New for this edition,** a guide on how to use this *Handbook* occupies the inside back cover. It walks students through five steps for locating information, and it visually displays location elements and content elements on each page of the *Handbook.*

■ Charts in tinted boxes present guidelines, checklists, grammar patterns, and summaries. **New for this edition,** the 184 charts are numbered for easier reference throughout the text. An alphabetized list of charts follows the index.

■ Clusters of examples have related content so that students can focus on concepts without being distracted by a new topic in each example.

■ Connected discourse in exercises replicates the processes of revising and editing as closely as possible. Almost half the exercises have been replaced for freshness of content. My goal is for students to practice skills and simultaneously enjoy the chance to acquire interesting information about a wide range of topics.

■ Content from across the curriculum is used for all examples, exercises, and case studies in the "Focus on Revising" sections.

■ A four-color design reinforces the conceptual framework of the material. Most important, blue is the color that signals revision in examples and in the background shade for "Focus on Revising" sections.

■ An ❖**ALERT** ❖ system helps students remember smaller matters in larger contexts. For example, a brief Punctuation Alert in an explanation of coordination puts into context a particular function of a comma. A brief Usage Alert in a discussion of restrictive and nonrestrictive elements puts into context choosing between *that* and *which*. This dual-entry system, which augments but does not replace full chapters on each separate topic, helps students handle the interplay of variables during writing.

■ A degree symbol (°) after a word or phrase signals that the term is defined in Glossary of Terms at the back of this *Handbook*. This features allows students to concentrate on the material at hand, with the assurance that they can easily locate a definition they might need. They no longer need feel frustrated by what might seem a pileup of unfamiliar words that are necessary for talking about some aspects of writing.

■ Response symbols incorporate the instantly popular Complimentary Symbols that I introduced in the Second Edition. Designed to facilitate praise of student writing, they now coexist with traditional correction symbols.

As a college student, I never encountered a handbook for writers. Questions about writing nagged at me, so I took to handbooks instantly when I discovered them in graduate school. I loved to browse through them, sometimes to locate specific information and sometimes simply to root around and make discoveries. Had I imagined then that I might some day set my hand to composing such a book, I would have either howled with laughter or frozen with panic. Now that I have completed the Third Edition of the *Simon & Schuster Handbook for Writers,* I am amazed that I ever began the First Edition. Which proves, it seems to me, that anyone can write, as long as she or he begins; that a *Handbook* can be an evolving text, as long as colleagues and students are graciously willing to join in the conversations that these pages seek to invite; and that students, empowered by knowledge, can write successfully.

TO STUDENTS

As I was writing the Third Edition of the *Simon & Schuster Handbook for Writers*, you, the students, were consistently on my mind. My goal is to provide you with useful, accessible information about writing processes and about written products so that you can write as effectively as possible. If I have succeeded, you will want to keep the *Handbook* as a reference source throughout your college years and afterwards.

Given the variety of information that this handbook includes, where might you begin? Rest assured, few people read it straight through from beginning to end. Instead, people browse. They get to know the *Handbook*'s contents by scanning the Overview of Contents on the inside front cover, or the more detailed Table of Contents, or the Index. When they spot a topic they want, they turn to the section that discusses it. To locate information as efficiently as possible, consult the guide to using your *Handbook* just inside the back cover.

Also, to further understand the rationale of the *Handbook*, you might want to read the Preface to Instructors on the previous pages. Let me call attention to two features discussed there: the 184 charts and my special use of the degree mark (°). I have designed the charts so that when you encounter new information, you can see it in a nutshell before turning to the more complete explanations and examples; or when you want to refresh your memory, you can find the essentials quickly. Also throughout the book, **when a degree mark (°) follows a term, it signals that you can find the definition of the word in the Glossary of Grammatical and Selected Composition Terms toward the back of the book.** I always define a term when used the first time, but often I must repeat it in other places. Whenever you encounter an unfamiliar term marked with the degree symbol, you will know that you can locate its meaning easily.

I hope this *Handbook* proves a trusted companion and friendly resource. Whether or not you use it as a class text, hold onto it throughout your college career and beyond so that you can look up whatever information you might need when you write. Keep it close at hand in your permanent library along with a dictionary and other reference books. As you use it, please feel welcome to write me with reactions, suggestions, and questions not answered in the *Handbook*. Here's the address: Lynn Quitman Troyka, c/o English Editor, Prentice Hall, Englewood Cliffs, NJ 07632. I promise to answer.

ACKNOWLEDGMENTS

Being able to turn for counsel and comfort to a community of students, teachers, personal friends, and family reaffirmed my conviction that writing is an intensely private yet social act for both writer and reader. To each person I name here goes my deep gratitude. Any shortcomings these pages reveal are mine, not theirs.

For both the Second and Third Editions of the *Handbook,* the participation and moral support of Ann B. Dobie, University of Southwestern Louisiana, has been indispensible: She coordinated my efforts to identify exemplary student writing, contributed to the pool of replaced exercises, and—most importantly—as senior contributing author of the *Annotated Instructor's Edition (AIE),* shared her admirable expertise and wisdom. Emily R. Gordon, Hofstra University and Queensborough Community College, again lent her keen intelligence as senior author of the *Workbook,* author of the testing package, and co-contributing author of the *AIE.* For advising me expertly about English as a second language (ESL), a subject I have rarely taught, I thank Dorothy V. Lindman, Brookhaven College, for her crucial, comprehensive suggestions throughout; Alice Maclin, DeKalb College, author of the *Simon & Schuster ESL Workbook for Writers,* for valuable guidance; and Warren Herendeen, Mercy College, for his sensitive insights, especially for the Preface for ESL Students that introduces Part Nine. Pat Morgan, Louisiana State University, played an essential role in preparing the pool of replaced exercises. Dawn Adamson Dobie was similarly important concerning student writing.

I am particularly delighted to thank the many students who contributed generously to the Third Edition, especially those whose writing is credited where it appears in this book. Also, Kristen Black, currently a college junior, was centrally influential with her incisive review of the previous edition (including interviews with other students), updates on electronic databases, and design advice. Aileen Morgan, currently a college sophomore, offered penetrating commentary on the Second Edition and multiple insights into writing research papers. Connie M. Didier, currently a graduate student, helped enormously with the new APA-style research paper. Kevin Dupre advised well on student writing. Lisa Lavery served as my excellent administrative assistant during the formative months of the Third Edition.

For their lively, comprehensive comments in Focus Groups, I thank Phyllis Brown, Santa Clara University; Joanne Ferreira, State University of New York at New Paltz and Fordham University; Paula Gillespie, Marquette University; Mary Multer Greene, Tidewater

Community College at Virginia Beach; Matilda Delgado Saenz, North Lake College; and Carolyn West, Daytona Beach Community College.

For serving in pivotal roles as advisors, log keepers, and/or ongoing consultant-reviewers, I am grateful for the scholarship and dedication to student writers of Duncan Carter, Portland State University; Jo Ellen Coopersmith, Utah Valley Community College; Thomas Copeland, Youngstown State University; Michael Goodman, Fairleigh Dickinson University, for business writing; Rebecca Innocent, Southern Methodist University, for writing with computers; James MacDonald, University of Southwestern Louisiana; Pamela T. Pittman, University of Central Oklahoma; Kirk Rasmussen, Utah Valley Community College; and Judith Stanford, Rivier College.

I benefited also from the reviews for the Third Edition by these astute reviewers: Nancy Westrich Baker, Southeast Missouri State University; Robert S. Caim, West Virginia University at Parkersburg; Joe R. Christopher, Tarleton State University; Jo Ellen Coopersmith, Utah Valley Community College; Lory Hawkes, DeVry Institute of Technology, Irving; Janet H. Hobbs, Wake Technical Community College; Frank Hubbard, Marquette University; Ursula Irwin, Mt. Hood Community College; Denise Jackson, Southeast Missouri State University; Myra Jones, Manatee Community College; Judith C. Kohl, Dutchess Community College; Eileen Schwartz, Purdue University at Calumet; Lisa Sebti, Central Texas College; John S. Shea, Loyola University at Chicago; Tony Silva, Purdue University; Bill M. Stiffler, Harford Community College; and Roseanna B. Whitlow, Southeast Missouri State University.

In writing the Third Edition, I drew frequently on extremely helpful reviews of my *Simon & Schuster Concise Handbook* (1992). I therefore also thank Norman Bosley, Ocean County College; John L. Hare, Montgomery College; Margo K. Jang, Northern Kentucky University; Susan J. Miller, Santa Fe Community College; Jon F. Patton, University of Toledo; Edward J. Reilly, St. Joseph's College; Peter Burton Ross, University of the District of Columbia; Jack Summers, Central Piedmont Community College; and Vivian A. Thomlinson, Cameron University.

Over the course of my writing the prior editions of the *Handbook*, the reviews of many colleagues helped me draft and revise. I renew my thanks to all of them.

At Prentice Hall/Simon & Schuster, many stellar people contributed to a team effort. The unseen but always present voice that graces each chapter of the *Handbook* belongs to Joyce F. Perkins, Senior Development Editor for English. Uncannily making miracles happen on an awesomely tight schedule, she is every author's ideal editor with her soaring intelligence, nurturing warmth, and gritty determination to be true to students and teachers. Phil Miller, Publisher for Humanities and Social Sciences, lent his special brand of optimism and outstanding judgment. Gina Sluss, Senior Marketing Manager for English, offered key counsel with her energizing commitment to excellence. Tracy Augustine, former Senior Editor for English and current Director of Marketing for Humanities and Social Sciences, contributed her superb vision and spirit. Christine Wolf, Art Director for Humanities, solved problems and offered a steady-flowing creativity. Others at Prentice Hall mattered much: Ed Stanford, President of the College Division; Will Ethridge, Vice President/Editorial and Marketing Director; Alison Reeves, Executive Editor for English; Stephen K. Deitmer, Managing Editor of College Book Editorial Development, for strengthening the Second Edition immeasurably; Carol Carter, Director of Marketing for Business and Economics; Bud Therien, Publisher for Art and Music; Jan Stephan, Managing Editor for Humanities Production; John Rousselle, Keith Faivre, and Alison Gnerre, Production Editors; and Kara M. Hado and Heidi W. Moore, Editorial Assistants.

Closer to home, friends and family surrounded me with the moral support and patience that help a writer thrive: Susan Bartlestone; Kristen and Dan Black; Rita and Hy Cohen; Ruth Davis; Elaine Gilden Dushoff, my cousin; Elliott Goldhush; Emily R. Gordon; Warren Herendeen; Edith Klausner, my sister; Jo Ann Lavery; Marilyn Miaz; Kate Morgan Jackson; Jerrold Nudelman; Claire Perlmutter; Belle and Sidney Quitman, my parents; Betty Renshaw; Magdalena Rogalskaja; Shirley and Don Stearns; Marilyn and Ernest Sternglass; Elsie Tischler; Muriel Wolfe; and Gideon Zwas. Above all, I am grateful to my husband, David Troyka, for his discerning reader's eye, his unflagging belief in my work, and for the joy of each new day with him.

LYNN QUITMAN TROYKA

SUPPLEMENTARY MATERIALS

As in other editions, the supplementary materials for the Third Edition of the *Simon & Schuster Handbook for Writers* assist teachers and students alike to use the text easily and to enhance the learning experience. The following list suggests the range of supplements available with the Third Edition but is not exhaustive.

Print Supplements for Instructors

- *Annotated Instructor's Edition, Third Edition,* by Lynn Quitman Troyka with Ann Dobie and Emily R. Gordon
- *Strategies for Teaching Writing* by Linda Julian
- *Teaching Writing Across the Curriculum* by Ann Gebhard
- *A Guide to the Simon & Schuster Handbook for Writers, Third Edition, and its Teaching and Learning Package*
- Answer Keys to the *Handbook, Workbook,* and *ESL Workbook*
- Diagnostic and Competency Tests
- Response Symbols Chart

Print Supplements for Students

- *Simon & Schuster Workbook for Writers, Third Edition* by Emily R. Gordon and Lynn Quitman Troyka
- *Simon & Schuster ESL Workbook for Writers* by Alice Maclin
- *Prentice Hall/New York Times Contemporary View Program: Writing*
- *Rough Drafts* by Kathleen Shine Cain
- *Model Research Papers for Writers*
- *Supplementary Essays for Writers*
- *The Research Organizer*
- *Webster's Dictionary* offers
- *Preparing for TASP* for Texas only
- *Preparing for CLASP* for Florida only

Audio-Visual Supplements

- ABC News/Prentice Hall Video Library: Composition
- *Using the Simon & Schuster Handbook for Writers, Third Edition: A Transparency Guide*
- Transparency Masters: Simon & Schuster Handbook for Writers, Third Edition
- Prentice Hall/Simon & Schuster Transparencies for Writers
- *Profiles of a Writer* Video Series
- Critical Thinking Audio Study Cassette

Software Supplements

- On-Line Handbook
- Bibliotec bibliography generator (MLA, APA, CBE)
- Blue Pencil Tutorial and Blue Pencil Authoring System
- Computerized Diagnostic and Competency Tests

For more information, contact your Prentice Hall representative or write the Marketing Manager for Humanities, Prentice Hall College Book Division, Englewood Cliffs, NJ 07632.

THE NEW YORK TIMES and **PRENTICE HALL** are sponsoring **A CONTEMPORARY VIEW,** a program designed to enhance student access to current information of relevance in the classroom. Through this program, the core subject matter provided in the text is supplemented by a collection of time-sensitive articles from one of the world's most distinguished newspapers, **THE NEW YORK TIMES.** These articles demonstrate the vital, ongoing connection between what is learned in the classroom and what is happening in the world around us.

To enjoy the wealth of information of **THE NEW YORK TIMES** daily, a reduced subscription rate is available in deliverable areas. For information, call toll-free: 1-800-631-1222.

PRENTICE HALL and **THE NEW YORK TIMES** are proud to co-sponsor **A CONTEMPORARY VIEW: Writing.** We hope it will make the reading of both textbooks and newspapers a more dynamic, involving process. In newspaper format, with a range of articles and opinion pieces on topics that interest today's students, **A CONTEMPORARY VIEW: Writing** not only demonstrates purposeful writing but can serve to initiate it as well.

 THE ABC NEWS/PRENTICE HALL VIDEO LIBRARY: COMPOSITION

Prentice Hall and ABC News have joined together to bring the most thoroughly integrated and comprehensive video libraries to the college market. These professional presentation packages offer both feature and documentary-style videos from a variety of ABC's award-winning news programs, including *World News Tonight, Nightline, 20/20, Primetime Live,* and others. Features in the **Composition** Video Library present current topics that can serve as springboards to discussion and writing.

CREDITS

We gratefully acknowledge permission to reprint from the following sources:

CLARA BENNETT. Excerpt from letter to the editor of *Newsday* by Clara Bennett, President of the Board of Trustees, Nassau County Library System. Reprinted with the kind permission of Clara Bennett.

THE NEW YORK TIMES

Excerpt from "Personal Computers" by Erik Sanberg Diment. Copyright © 1985 by The New York Times Company. Reprinted by permission.

Excerpt from "What Brand of Laughter Do You Use?" by Roger Rosenblatt in *The New York Times*, November 17, 1991. Copyright © 1991 by The New York Times Company. Reprinted by permission.

Excerpt from "Safe Lifting Techniques" by John Warde in *The New York Times*, March 11, 1990. Copyright © by The New York Times Company. Reprinted by permission.

Excerpt from "Older than Forks, Safer than Knives" by Dena Kleiman in *The New York Times*, January 17, 1990. Copyright © 1990 by The New York Times Company. Reprinted by permission.

Excerpt from "A Hoarder's Life: Filling the Cache—And Finding It" by Jane E. Brody in *The New York Times*, December 3, 1991. Copyright © 1991 by The New York Times Company. Reprinted by permission.

Excerpt from "Researchers Trace Empathy's Roots to Infancy" by Daniel Goleman in *The New York Times*, March 28, 1989. Copyright © 1989 by The New York Times Company. Reprinted by permission.

NEWSDAY.

Excerpt from "Fighting Racism with Inclusion" by Randolph H. Manning in *Newsday*, October 7, 1990. Copyright © 1990 by Newsday. Reprinted by permission.

Excerpt from "Depth of Field" by Susan Howard in *Newsday*, January 1, 1991. Copyright © 1991 by Newsday. Reprinted by permission.

Excerpt from "If Lightning Strikes" by Gerald Secor Couzens in *Newsday*, August 13, 1988. Copyright © 1988 by Newsday. Reprinted by permission.

Excerpt from "A Slice of History" by Lisa Pratt from *The Newsday Magazine*, April 29, 1990. Copyright © 1990 by Newsday. Reprinted by permission.

READER'S DIGEST. Excerpt from "That Astonishing Creature—Nature" by Jean Nathan in the *Reader's Digest*, January 1984. Copyright © 1984 by Reader's Digest Association and reprinted by permission.

OXFORD UNIVERSITY PRESS. Entry for *celebrate* excerpted from the *Oxford English Dictionary* (new edition 1989) by permission of Oxford University Press.

SIMON & SCHUSTER, INC. The entry for *celebrate* is from *Webster's New World Dictionary*, Third College Edition. © 1988 Simon & Schuster, Inc. Reprinted by permission of the publisher.

UNIVERSITY OF OKLAHOMA PRESS. Excerpt from "What Is Poverty?" by Jo Goodwin Parker in *America's Other Children* by George Henderson. Copyright © 1971. Published by the University of Oklahoma Press and reprinted with their permission.

H. W. WILSON COMPANY. Entry on "Communication, nonverbal" is excerpted from *Readers' Guide to Periodical Literature*, March 1979-February 1980. Copyright © 1980 The H. W. Wilson Company and reprinted with their permission.

About The Author

Lynn Quitman Troyka earned her Ph.D at New York University and has taught at the City University of New York (CUNY), including Queensborough Community College, the Center for Advanced Studies in Education at the Graduate School, and in the graduate program in Language and Literacy at City College. She is now Senior Research Associate in the Instructional Resource Center, CUNY.

Photograph © Jill Krementz

Former editor of the *Journal of Basic Writing*, Dr. Troyka has written articles for journals such as *College Composition and Communication, College English*, and *Writing Program Administration* and in books from Southern Illinois Press, Random House, and Boynton/Cook. She is an author in the area of composition/rhetoric for the *Encyclopedia of English Studies and Language Arts*, Scholastic, 1993.

Dr. Troyka is author the *Simon & Schuster Concise Handbook*, Prentice Hall, 1992; and *Structured Reading*, Third Edition, Prentice Hall, 1989. She is co-author (with Richard Lloyd-Jones, John Gerber, et al.) of *A Checklist and Guide for Reviewing Departments of English*, Associated Departments of English of the Modern Language Association, 1985; of *Steps in Composition*, Fifth Edition (with Jerrold Nudelman), Prentice Hall, 1990; and of the *Simon & Schuster Workbook for Writers*, Third Edition (with Emily R. Gordon), Prentice Hall, 1993.

Dr. Troyka has been a consultant to numerous federal and state agencies, including the National Endowment for the Humanities and Educational Testing Service. She has also been a consultant and/or guest lecturer at dozens of colleges and universities. She has also been a featured speaker at local, national, and international meetings. She is a past chair of the Conference on College Composition, of the College Section of the National Council of Teachers of English, and of the Writing Division of the Modern Language Association.

"All this information," says Dr. Troyka, "tells what I've done, not who I am. I am a teacher. It is my life's work, and I love it."

I Writing An Essay

When you write an essay, you engage in a process. The parts of that process vary with the writer and the demands of the subject. Part One explains all aspects of the act of writing, and of thinking and reading in relation to writing, so that you can evolve your personal style of composing and thereby become an effective writer.

BACKGROUND

In "Teaching for the University: Is 'Good Writing' Relative?" (*California English* 24 [May–June 1988]: 12), Lucinda Hillbrink calls for greater attention to audience on the part of freshman writers.

QUOTATION ABOUT WRITING

I shall live badly if I do not write, and I shall write badly if I do not live.

—Françoise Sagan

TEACHING TIP

To start a course in composition, you might ask students to think of personal experiences that support the four claims about writing that open this chapter. To get things started, you might talk about a few of your own experiences that support the claims. Do you recall a college paper you wrote? What do you remember about its contents and the experience of writing it? Have you found that writing about something makes you better able to teach it? Have you ever discovered what you wanted to say—or a connection among the ideas you already had in mind—as the words were formed "at the point of utterance"?

To encourage students to share their experiences, you might ask them first to jot down some notes and then participate in a discussion. If the group is large, you might divide it into small groups and give each group specific directions (written are more effective than oral) about what to discuss. The directions can have students discuss in turn each question listed in the paragraph above. You can appoint one person to serve as informal chair and another as secretary of the group. After a suitable amount of time, you might ask each group to report to the whole class.

1 Thinking about Purposes and Audiences

Why write? In this age of telephones and tape recorders, television and film, computers and communication satellites, why should you bother with writing? The answer has overlapping parts, starting with the inner life of a writer and moving outward.

Writing is a way of thinking and learning. Writing gives you unique opportunities to explore ideas and understand information. By writing, you come to know subjects well and make them your own. Even thirty years later, many people can recall details about the topics and content of essays they wrote in college, but far fewer people can recall specifics of a classroom lecture or a textbook chapter. Writing helps you learn and gain authority over knowledge. As you share what you learn, you also teach. When you write for a reader, you play the role of a teacher, someone who knows the material sufficiently well to organize and present it clearly.

Writing is a way of discovering. The act of writing allows you to make unexpected connections among ideas and language. As you write, thoughts emerge and interconnect in ways unavailable until the physical act of writing begins. An authority on writing, James Britton, describes discovery in writing as "shaping at the point of utterance." Similarly, a well-known writer, E. M. Forster, talked about discovery during writing by asking, "How can I know what I mean until I've seen what I said?" You can expect many surprises of insight that come only when you write and rewrite, each time trying to get closer to what you want to say.

Writing creates reading. Writing is a powerful means of communication. It creates a permanent, visible record of your ideas for others to read and ponder. Reading informs and shapes human thought. In an open society, everyone is free to write and thereby to create reading for other people. For that freedom to be exercised,

1b

however, the ability to write cannot be concentrated in a few people. All of us need access to the power of the written word.

Writing ability is needed by educated people. In college, you are expected to write many different types of assignments. Also, most jobs in today's technological society require writing skill for preparing documents ranging from letters to formal reports. Indeed, throughout your life, your writing will reveal your ability to think clearly and to use language effectively.

1a Understanding the elements of writing

Writing can be explained by its elements: *Writing is a way of communicating a message to a reader for a purpose.* Each word in this definition carries important meaning. **Communicating** in writing means sending a message that has a destination. The **message** of writing is its content, which you can present in a variety of ways. Traditionally, forms for writing are divided into *narration, description, exposition,* and *argumentation.* In this handbook, narration and description are two among many strategies for developing ideas, explained in section 4f. Exposition and argumentation are the major **purposes** for academic writing, explained in section 1b. The role of the **reader** of academic writing, often referred to as the audience, is explained in section 1c.

1b Understanding purposes for writing

Writing is often defined by its **purpose.** Writing purposes have to do with goals, sometimes referred to as *aims of writing* or *writing intentions.* Thinking about purposes for writing means thinking about the motivating forces that move people to write. As a student, you might assume that your only purpose for writing is to fulfill a class assignment. More is involved, however. As a writer in college, you are challenged to shape your writing purpose to suit the content of your material and the style of your writing. Major purposes for writing are shown in Chart 1.

The purposes of writing *to express yourself* and *to create a literary work* contribute importantly to human thought and culture. This handbook, however, concentrates on the two purposes most prominent and practical in your academic life: *to inform a reader* and *to persuade a reader.*

BACKGROUND

A Theory of Discourse by James L. Kinneavy explores the fundamental purposes for which people use language. Kinneavy explains the centrality of the concept of *purpose* in writing:

> Purpose in discourse is all important. The aim of a discourse determines everything else in the process of discourse. "What" is talked about, the oral or written medium which is chosen, the words and grammatical patterns used—all of these are largely determined by the purpose of the discourse (48).

Kinneavy is enthusiastic about the potential for composition as a field of scholarship:

> It is the thesis of this work that the field of composition—or discourse as it will presently be termed—is a rich and fertile discipline with a worthy past which should be consulted before being consigned to oblivion, an exciting present, and a future that seems as limitless as either linguistics or literature (2).

Kinneavy's theories, and those of similar bent that focus on purposes for writing, are widely accepted today among scholars and teachers. Other modern influential theorists who concentrate on writers' purposes include the highly respected James Britton, who classifies purposes as *poetic, expressive,* and *transactional.*

In "On Intention in Student Texts" (*Encountering Student Texts: Interpretive Issues in Reading Student Writing,* ed. Bruce Lawson, Susan Sterr Ryan, and W. Ross Winterowd [NCTE, 1989]), Sharon Crowley discusses problems that can result from expecting writers always to have a clear purpose in mind before writing. Writers often discover their purpose as they write, and their purpose may change from draft to draft.

PURPOSES FOR WRITING*   1

- to express yourself
- to inform a reader
- to persuade a reader
- to create a literary work

---

1   **Writing to inform a reader**

Informative writing seeks to give information and, frequently, to explain it. This writing is known also as **expository writing** because it expounds on, or sets forth, ideas and facts. *Informative writing focuses mainly on the subject being discussed.* Informative writing includes reports of observations, ideas, scientific data, facts, statistics. It can be found in textbooks, encyclopedias, technical and business reports, nonfiction, newspapers, and magazines.

When you write to inform, you are expected to offer information with a minimum of bias. You aim to educate, not persuade. Like all effective teachers, you need to present the information completely, clearly, and accurately. The material should be verifiable by additional reading, talking with others, or personal experience. For example, consider this passage that aims to inform the reader.

> In 1914 in what is now Addo Park in South Africa, a hunter by the name of Pretorius was asked to exterminate a herd of 140 elephants. He killed all but 20, and those survivors became so cunning at evading him that he was forced to abandon the hunt. The area became a preserve in 1930, and the elephants have been protected ever since. Nevertheless, elephants now four generations removed from those Pretorius hunted remain shy and strangely nocturnal. Young elephants evidently learn from the adults' trumpeting alarm calls to avoid humans.
>
> —CAROL GRANT GOULD, "Out of the Mouths of Beasts"

---

*Adapted from the ideas of James L. Kinneavy, a modern rhetorician, discussed in *A Theory of Discourse.* 1971; New York: Norton, 1980.

This passage is successful because it *communicates* (transmits) a *message* (about young elephants learning to avoid humans) to a *reader* (a person who might become or already is interested in the subject) for a *purpose* (to inform). In this passage, the writer's last sentence states the main idea. The other sentences offer support for the main idea.

CHECKLIST FOR INFORMATIVE WRITING   2

- Is its major focus the subject being discussed?
- Is its primary purpose to inform rather than persuade?
- Is its information complete and accurate?
- Can its information be verified?
- Is its information arranged for clarity?

---

2   Writing to persuade a reader

Persuasive writing seeks to convince the reader about a matter of opinion. This writing is sometimes called **argumentative** because it argues a position. (Because the techniques of written argument can be especially demanding on a writer, this handbook devotes all of Chapter 6 to them.)

Persuasive writing focuses mainly on the reader, whom the writer wants to influence. When you write to persuade, you deal with the debatable, that which has other sides to it. Persuasive writing seeks to change the reader's mind or at least to bring the reader's point of view closer to the writer's. Even the writer who feels sure that the reader's position on the subject will never change is expected to argue as convincingly as possible.

To be persuasive, you cannot merely state an opinion. Your reader expects you to offer convincing support for your point of view. Such support often relies upon information that explains and defends a point of view. Persuasive writing, therefore, often calls for informative writing (see 1b-1) to provide the evidence that lends strength to an argument. Examples of persuasive writing include editorials, letters to the editor, reviews, sermons, business or research proposals, opinion essays in magazines, and books that argue

BACKGROUND

Linda Flower assesses the role of purpose in *The Construction of Purpose in Writing and Reading* (Pittsburgh: Center for the Study of Writing, 1988), concluding that it is constructive, cognitive, and rhetorical. It deserves attention because it can provide meaning and coherence in a piece of writing.

BACKGROUND

Writing is sometimes classified according to four modes of discourse: *narration, description, exposition,* and *argumentation.* These modes describe the *what* of writing. They describe characteristics that written products seem to feature, although much overlap exists. A writer can narrate an incident in the service of arguing an opinion; a writer can describe a scene in the service of offering information.

This handbook starts with the *why* of writing. Thus it begins with *purposes* for writing. Purposes are familiar territory for instructors used to modes, because two of the modes are purposes: people write for the purpose of informing (expositing) and for the purpose of persuading (arguing). Purposes are based on the notion that people write for a reason; most college writing is done either to inform or to persuade. Research shows that few writers sit down and say to themselves, "I am going to write a comparison and contrast essay"; instead they say to themselves, "I want to give my readers some information" or "I want to convince my readers to change their minds." In the service of those purposes, writers compare and contrast, narrate, describe, draw analogy, and so forth.

Narration and description are discussed fully in Chapter 4, "Writing Paragraphs," along with many other writing strategies for idea development, including process, definition, comparison and contrast, cause-and-effect relationship, and analogy.

BACKGROUND

In "Purpose and Composition Theory: Issues in the Research" (*Journal of Advanced Composition* 9 [1989]: 97–111), Nancy Roundy Blyler discusses current theories about purpose in writing, pointing out that further investigation of definition, influences, writers' awareness, process, and pedagogy is called for. In "Purpose and Professional Writers" (*Technical Writing Teacher* 16 [Winter 1989]: 52–67), she looks at professional writers' concepts of purpose, concluding that for them it is based on situation, reader, and text.

QUOTATION ABOUT WRITING

Writing represents a unique mode of learning—not merely valuable, not merely special, but unique.

—Janet Emig

QUOTATION ABOUT WRITING

Whenever citizens are seen routinely as enemies of their own government, writers are routinely seen to be the most dangerous enemies.

—E. L. Doctorow

QUOTATION ABOUT WRITING

The desire to write grows with writing.

—Erasmus

BACKGROUND

The relationship of reader and writer is the subject of a study reported by Gesa Kirsch in "Authority in Reader–Writer Relationships" (*Reader* 19 [Spring 1989]: 56–67). Kirsch uses protocol study and theories of audience to examine how writers conceive of their readers during the composing process and how writers establish authority with them.

a point of view. For example, consider this passage that aims to persuade the reader.

> The search for some biological basis for math ability or disability is fraught with logical and experimental difficulties. Since not all math under-achievers are women, and not all women are mathematics-avoidant, poor performance in math is unlikely to be due to some genetic or hormonal difference between the sexes. Moreover, no amount of research so far has unearthed a "mathematical competency" in some tangible, measurable substance in the body. Since "masculinity" cannot be injected into women to test whether or not it improves their mathematics, the theories that attribute such ability to genes or hormones must depend for their proof on circumstantial evidence. So long as about 7 percent of the Ph.D.'s in mathematics are earned by women, we have to conclude either that these women have genes, hormones, and brain organization different from those of the rest of us, or that certain positive experiences in their lives have largely undone the negative fact that they are female, or both.
>
> —Sheila Tobias, *Overcoming Math Anxiety*

This passage is successful because it sends a *message* (about math ability and disability) to a *reader* (a person who might become or already is interested in the subject) for a *purpose* (to persuade a reader that math ability or disability is not related to gender). The writer's first sentence summarizes the point of view that she argues in the rest of the paragraph. The other sentences support the writer's assertion.

CHECKLIST FOR PERSUASIVE WRITING   3

- Is its major focus the reader?
- Is its primary purpose to convince rather than inform?
- Does it offer information or reasons to support its point of view?
- Is its point of view based on sound reasoning and logic?
- Are the points of its argument arranged for clarity?
- Does it evoke an intended reaction from the reader?

EXERCISE 1-1

For each paragraph, decide if the dominant purpose is *informative* or *persuasive*. Then, answer the questions in Chart 2 or Chart 3 in relation to the paragraph, and explain your answers.

A.   Trees are living archives, carrying within their structure a record not only of their age but also of precipitation and temperature for each year in which a ring was formed. The record might also include the marks of forest fires, early frosts and, incorporated into the wood itself, chemical elements the tree removed from its environment. Thus, if we only knew how to unlock its secrets, a tree could tell us a great deal about what was happening in its neighborhood from the time of its beginning. Trees can tell us what was happening before written records became available. They also have a great deal to tell us about our future. The records of past climate that they contain can help us to understand the natural forces that produce our weather, and this, in turn, can help us plan.

—JAMES S. TREFIL, ''Concentric Clues from Growth Rings Unlock the Past''

B.   We know very little about pain, and what we don't know makes it hurt all the more. Indeed, no form of illiteracy in the United States is so widespread or costly as ignorance about pain—what it is, what causes it, and how to deal with it without panic. Almost everyone can rattle off the names of at least a dozen drugs that can deaden pain from every conceivable cause—all the way from headaches to hemorrhoids. There is far less knowledge about the fact that about ninety percent of pain is self-limiting, that it is not always an indication of poor health, and that, most frequently, it is the result of tension, stress, idleness, boredom, frustration, suppressed rage, insufficient sleep, overeating, poorly balanced diet, smoking, excessive drinking, inadequate exercise, stale air, or any of the other abuses encountered by the human body in modern society.

—NORMAN COUSINS, *Anatomy of an Illness*

C.   Although Littleman, my eleven-year-old poodle, has never been separated from his thirteen-year-old mother, Simone, they are remarkably different. Simone weighs in at about ten pounds with very delicate, sophisticated features and coarse, curly hair. Slightly shorter, Littleman tops the scale at no more than seven pounds and is quite handsome with his teddy-bear features and soft wavy hair. Simone was the first dog in the family and is a pedigreed poodle. In many ways she is the picture of a thoroughbred, with her snobby attitude and nonchalant manners. On the other hand, Littleman came into the family a year later with four other puppies of pure breeding, but they were never registered. Unlike his mother, Littleman is very friendly, almost to the point of being pesty at times.

—LINDA NEAL, student

ANSWERS: EXERCISE 1-1

A. Dominant purpose is informative. It meets the criteria.

B. Dominant purpose is persuasive. It meets the criteria.

C. Dominant purpose is persuasive. It meets the criteria.

D. Dominant purpose is informative. It meets the criteria.

E. Dominant purpose is persuasive. It meets the criteria.

QUOTATION ABOUT WRITING

I started writing because of a terrible feeling of powerlessness: I felt I was drifting and obscure, and I rebelled against that. I didn't see what I could do to change my condition. I wanted to control rather than be controlled, to ordain rather than be ordained, and to relegate rather than be relegated.

—Anita Brookner

QUOTATION ABOUT WRITING

I can say now that one of the big reasons [for writing] was this: I instinctively recognized an opportunity to transcend some of my personal failings—things about myself I didn't particularly like and wanted to change but didn't know how.

—John Steinbeck

D.   During the past generation, the amount of time devoted to historical studies in American public schools has steadily decreased. About twenty-five years ago, most public high-school youths studied one year of world history and one of American history, but today, most study only one year of ours. In contrast, the state schools of many other Western nations require the subject to be studied almost every year. In France, for example, all students, not just the college-bound, follow a carefully sequenced program of history, civics and geography every year from the seventh grade through the twelfth grade.

—DIANE RAVITCH, ''Decline and Fall of Teaching History''

E.   For the past few years, our city has been in a downward slump, especially in terms of its recreational facilities and economy. Our parks and buildings have been the target of considerable vandalism. The lake, which has been sorrowfully neglected, could be improved with more trees, better roads, and additional security. Our unemployment is the highest in the state and our economy the worst. Both situations could be improved by attracting new industries to our city. Reclaiming our land by planting orange trees, onions, and melons would help the farm economy. Our city could be one of the best places to live if it would employ its available work force to effect these kinds of improvements.

—GERARDO ANTONIO GARZA, student

ANSWERS: EXERCISE 1-2

A. Answers will vary. Samples have to come from a single issue of a newspaper. Editorials, essays, letters to the editor, and reviews can serve as examples of writing with the dominant purpose of being persuasive. News reports can serve as examples of informative writing.

B. Answers will vary, as for above.

ANSWERS: EXERCISE 1-3

For each topic the student should write one paragraph (or more, according to how you have assigned the exercise) with an informative purpose and one paragraph with a persuasive purpose. The student should also be prepared to discuss (orally or in writing, according to your assignment) the differences in the two treatments of the same topic.

EXERCISE 1-2

A. In a single issue of a newspaper, find one informative article and one persuasive article. Consulting section 1b, explain why you identify them as you do. Next, for each article, go back to Chart 2 or Chart 3, whichever is appropriate for the purpose you have identified, and answer the questions. Explain each answer.

B. Repeat this process with a magazine.

EXERCISE 1-3

Consulting section 1b, assume that you have to write on each of these topics twice, once to inform and once to persuade your reader. Be prepared to discuss how your two treatments of each topic would differ.

1. diets
2. Canada
3. garbage
4. gym shoes
5. sense of humor
6. automobile insurance
7. forest fires
8. video cassette recorders (VCRs)
9. beach erosion
10. weight training

1c Understanding audiences for writing

Good writing is often judged by its ability to reach its intended **audience.** To be effective, informative and persuasive writing (see 1b) need to be geared to the fact that someone is "out there" to receive the communication. If you write without considering your reader, you risk communicating only with yourself.

As a writer for one or more readers, you need to consider who your audience is, especially concerning their background. For example, in writing meant to persuade people to vote for a particular candidate, if you imply disrespect for people who stay home and raise children, you risk losing votes of many homemakers and their spouses. Or, if you want to persuade lawmakers that homemakers should be allowed to draw from the Social Security system, you would need to address some of the lawmakers' practical concerns, such as the impact of your proposal on the federal budget.

Also, as you write, you need to think about what you can assume an audience already knows. For example, a sales report filled with technical language assumes that its readers know the specialized vocabulary. The general reading public would have trouble understanding such a report. But if the material were rewritten without technical terms, general readers could understand it.

If you know or can reasonably assume even a few of the characteristics listed in Chart 4, your chances of reaching your audience improve. The more explicit information that you have about your audience, the better you can think about how to reach it. Often, of course, you can only guess at the details. The chart can help you get started.

CHECKLIST OF BASIC AUDIENCE CHARACTERISTICS   4

WHO ARE THEY?

- age, gender
- ethnic backgrounds, political philosophies, religious beliefs
- roles, such as student, veteran, parent, wage earner, voter, other
- interests, hobbies

WHAT DO THEY KNOW?

- level of education
- amount of general or specialized knowledge about the topic
- preconceptions brought to the material

You might find that some students feel inhibited in their writing when they have to think about an audience for their writing. Studies show that some students misunderstand the concept of audience. They think it means that writers should act as if someone is constantly looking over their shoulders. Other students have trouble with the concept of audience because they think that they can never say something that would be unpopular with their audience. Some students might not want to admit these or other misunderstandings of the concept, so you might want to clear up the matter without asking anyone to give you their negative impressions. Once you start talking about the subject, you will often find that the students start chiming in to help you get at their concerns.

The concept of audience is meant to help writers get their message across. The concept is supposed to facilitate, not block. A writer is not expected to tell readers what they want to hear even if the writer disagrees with the readers. A writer is, however, expected to choose words the readers know and to use a tone suitable to the occasion. As writer Gary Provost says in "How to Make the Reader Like You," published in *Writer's Digest* in September 1986:

> You need some sense of your reader's knowledge. If you're writing a report for oceanographers, mention the *dorsal carapace* and the *chelipeds* if you must, but if you're writing a brochure for visitors to a public aquarium, please write *shell* and *claws.* Remember that any time, you don't have your entire vocabulary to work with. You have only that portion of your vocabulary that you share with the readers (37–38).

BACKGROUND

Robert Brooke and John Hendricks, in *Audience Expectations and Teacher Demands* (Carbondale, IL: Southern Illinois UP, 1989), discuss two of the problems that students face in learning to write for different audiences in a composition course. One problem is that students know that, whatever audience the paper is purportedly written for, the teacher will be the one who reads and evaluates the essay. Another problem is that writing to an audience means establishing a relationship with that audience and creating an identity within a community. Students, especially in their first year in college, are often uncertain about their identities, trying to establish themselves in new communities —in college classes, dormitories, fraternities, sororities, majors, and professions. Often students are not sure whether they even belong in these communities. Writing to audiences, especially unfamiliar ones, as they try to understand the expectations of the teacher who will grade their papers is difficult, Brooke and Hendricks write, and students need support. The authors suggest that students need to feel "secure in their classroom positions," to feel a strong sense of membership or community in the class, and to feel secure about their relationship to the teacher before they can tackle difficult problems of audience (67). Early class discussions, group work, and journal writing can bring out class expectations and insecurities, clarify the support students can expect from the teacher and each other, and give students an opportunity to explore their identities in the unfamiliar world of college.

QUOTATION ABOUT WRITING

[Writing is] the sense of being in contact with people who are part of a particular audience that really makes a difference to me.

—Sherley Anne Williams

1 Understanding the general reading public

The **general reading public** is composed of educated, experienced readers, people who frequently read newspapers, magazines, and books. These readers often have some general information about the subject you are dealing with, but they enjoy learning something new or seeing something from a different perspective. The general reading public expects material to be clear and to be free of advanced technical information.

2 Understanding your instructor as a reader

When you write for a class assignment, your audience will almost certainly be your **instructor.** Sometimes, especially when you are planning or revising your work, your instructor might want other students in your class to collaborate as an audience. In most cases, however, your final audience remains your instructor.

Your instructor is a member of the general reading public and also someone who recognizes that you are an apprentice. Your instructor knows that few students are experienced writers or complete experts on their subjects. Still, your instructor always expects your writing to reflect that you took time to learn the material thoroughly and to write about it well. In part, therefore, an instructor is a *judge,* someone to whom you must demonstrate that you are doing your best. Instructors are very experienced readers who can quickly recognize a minimal effort or a negative attitude (as when a paper carries a tone that suggests "Tell me what you want and I'll give it to you").

Think of your instructor as a representative reader, someone who is typical of the audience you want to reach. *Inexperienced writers sometimes wrongly assume that instructors will fill in mentally what is missing on the page.* Instructors expect what they read to include everything that the writer wants to say or imply. Do not leave out material. Even if you write immediately after your instructor has heard you give an oral report on the same subject, write as if no one is aware of what you know.

Your instructor is also an *academic,* a member of a group whose professional life centers on intellectual endeavors. You must, therefore, write within the constraints of academic writing. For example, if you are told to write on a topic of your choice, you definitely do not have total freedom to choose. Your topic must have some intrinsic intellectual interest. For example, an essay should not merely give directions on how to cut a wedding cake or use an eraser.

3 Understanding specialists as readers

Specialists are members of the general reading public who have expert knowledge on specific subjects. In writing for specialists, you are expected to know the specialty and also to realize that your readers have advanced expertise.

Specialized readers often share not only knowledge but also assumptions, interests, and beliefs. For example, they may be members of a club that concentrates on a hobby, such as amateur astronomy or orchid raising. They may have similar backgrounds, such as having immigrated from another country or having worked at a similar job. They may have similar views on matters related to religion and politics. When you write for readers who share specialized knowledge, you have to balance the necessity to be thorough with the demand not to go into too much detail about technical terms and special references.

1d Understanding the effect of tone

The **tone** of your writing is established by *what you say* and *how you say it*. Tone underlies much of written communication. This section gives a brief overview of tone, with references to longer discussions that you can consult elsewhere in this handbook.

The tone in your writing needs to be shaped to your purpose for writing (see 1b) and awareness of your audience (see 1c). Your tone reveals your attitude both toward the material about which you are writing and toward anyone you expect to read your writing. For example, if your tone implies that you feel superior to your readers, your material will be condescending and distasteful. Similarly, if your tone hints that you are uninformed or unsure, your readers will quickly lose confidence in what you are saying.

In your academic writing, you want to achieve a reasonable tone, both in the content of your material and in your choice of words. For example, readers might think a writer unreasonable who distorts information or tries to manipulate emotions unfairly by using slanted language (see 21a-4): for example, avoid biased words such as "the corrupt, deceitful politician" when "the politician being investigated for taking bribes" is more evenhanded. Also, a reader

BACKGROUND

Many teachers find that despite their best efforts to make students aware of the importance of audience for their writing, their essays continue to sound as if they were produced for a nameless, faceless reader. Bennett A. Rafoth, in a study of freshman college writers (*RTE* 23 [October 1989]: 273–290), found that they often tend to postpone concern for audience until they begin revising their work. In "Audience Awareness: Methods and Madness" (ERIC ED 276 007), R. J. Willey describes several strategies teachers can use to help students become more conscious of whom they are writing for.

QUOTATION ABOUT WRITING
Writing is making sense of life.
—Nadine Gordimer

QUOTATION ABOUT WRITING
I wrote my first novel because I wanted to read it.
—Toni Morrison

QUOTATION ABOUT WRITING
Writing is a dog's life, but the only life worth living.
—Gustave Flaubert

QUOTATION ABOUT WRITING
I write books to find out about things.
—Rebecca West

can infer from sexist language (see 21b) that a writer is insensitive to gender issues in word choice: for example, avoid "policeman" in favor of the less sexist "police officer." Similarly, pretentious language (see 21e-1) reflects negatively on a writer because it tries to obscure the obvious: for example, avoid overblown words such as "the occurrence that transpired" when you mean "the event that happened."

As important, when you move from writing privately for yourself to writing for an audience, the level of formality (see 21a-1) in your writing should reflect your goal. Although readers enjoy lively language, they can be jarred by an overly informal tone being injected into a serious discussion. Readers of academic writing expect to be treated respectfully. A medium level of formality is most effective. For example, in a newspaper report about the results of an election, you would not refer to the loser or winner as *guy* or *gal*, no matter how relaxed the candidate's demeanor. Likewise, in the middle of a serious critique, using *pretty* as a synonym for *very* or *fairly* would be out of place (as in "The weak script was helped by some pretty good acting").

EXERCISE 1-4

Each of these passages was written for a general reading audience. Consulting sections 1c and 1d, read each paragraph and decide (1) if its tone is appropriate for academic writing and (2) if the choice of words assumes knowledge that only a specialist would have.

A.   Pernicious anemia, a uniformly fatal disease, was spectacularly reversed by liver extract (much later found to be due to the presence of vitamin B_{12} in the extracts). Diabetes mellitus could be treated—at least to the extent of reducing the elevated blood sugar and correcting the acidosis that otherwise led to diabetic coma and death—by the insulin preparation isolated by Banting and Best. Pellagra, a common cause of death among the impoverished rural populations in the South, had become curable with Goldberger's discovery of the vitamin B complex and the subsequent identification of nicotinic acid. Diphtheria could be prevented by immunization against the toxin of diphtheria bacilli and, when it occurred, treated more or less effectively with diphtheria antitoxin.

—LEWIS THOMAS, "1933 Medicine"

B.   Forty-five minutes south of the capital city by train, in the small suburb of Myorenji, near Yokohama, 13-year-old Naoko Masuo returns from school, slips quietly into her family's two-story house and settles into her homework. She is wearing a plaid skirt and blue blazer, the uniform of the Shoe-ei Girls School, where she is a seventh-grader. ''I made it,'' her smile seems to say. For three years, when she was in fourth through sixth grades in public school, Naoko's schedule was high-pressure: she would rush home from school, study for a short time and then leave again to attend *juku,* or cram school, three hours a day three times a week. Her goal was to enter a good private school, and the exam would be tough.

—Carol Simons, ''Kyoiku Mamas''

C.   Without mucus, a slug would quickly be invaded by a host of microbial denizens and die. It would also be immobile, for slugs require mucus underfoot on which to crawl. Secreted from the pedal gland, located just beneath the head, the mucus flows down to the slug's single muscular foot. Like a miniature asphalt machine, the slug first lays its road and then, with wavelike motions of its foot, moves over it. As the mucus ''road'' dries, it becomes a silvery map of a slug's travels.

—Scott McCredie, ''They're Still Slimy, But Naked Snails
Are Finding New Friends''

D.   The consumer of electricity usually accepts the fact that power outages frequently occur during wind and thunderstorms. However, when outages occur during calm and dry weather, the consumer becomes upset and blames the power company. In reality, most non-weather-related outages occur either because of circumstances beyond the control of the power company or in order to insure the safety of its workers. Squirrels and other animals with the ability to reach the top of power poles cause outages by unknowingly completing a circuit between a hot wire and a ground wire, an act which can knock out power to many houses. Occasionally, rehabilitating old lines to decrease future outages forces the power company to kill the lines temporarily to insure safety. And, a power company that purchases its power from larger companies often loses power because of trouble on the other company's line.

—Burl Carraway, student

E.   My husband and I constantly marvel at the fact that our two sons, born of the same parents and only two years apart in age, are such completely opposite human beings. The most obvious differences became apparent at their births. Our first born, Mark, was big and bold—his intense, already wise eyes, broad shoulders, huge and heavy hands, and powerful, chunky legs gave us the impression that

ANSWERS: EXERCISE 1-4

A. (a) The tone is appropriate for academic writing.
   (b) The material assumes a specialized reader who would be familiar with words such as *diabetes mellitus, acidosis,* and *bacilli.*

B. (a) The tone is informal and may be inappropriate for academic writing in some courses.
   (b) The material does not assume a specialized reader.

C. (a) The tone is appropriate for academic writing.
   (b) The material assumes a specialized reader who would be familiar with words such as *microbial, mucus, pedal,* and *gland.*

D. (a) The tone is appropriate for academic writing.
   (b) The material assumes a small amount of specialized knowledge, though the gist of the message can be understood from the context. Specialized words include *outages, hot wire,* and *ground wire.*

E. (a) The tone is informal and may be inappropriate for academic writing in some courses.
   (b) The material does not assume a specialized reader.

QUOTATION ABOUT WRITING

Many people who want to be writers don't really want to be writers. They want to *have been* writers. They wish they had a book in print.

—James Michener

he could have walked out of the delivery room on his own. Our second son, Wayne, was delightfully different. Rather than have the football physique that Mark was born with, Wayne came into the world with a long, slim, wiry body more suited to running, jumping, and contorting. Wayne's eyes, rather than being intense like Mark's, were impish and innocent. When Mark was delivered, he cried only momentarily, then seemed to settle into a state of intense concentration, as if trying to absorb everything he could about the strange, new environment he found himself in. Conversely, Wayne screamed from the moment he first appeared until the nurse took him to the nursery. There was nothing helpless or pathetic about his cry either—he was damned angry!

—ROSEANNE LABONTE, student

2 Planning and Shaping

2a Understanding the writing process

Many people assume that a real writer can pick up a pen (or sit at a typewriter or word processor) and magically write a finished product, word by perfect word. Experienced writers know better. They know that **writing is a process,** a series of activities that start the moment they begin thinking about a subject and end when they complete a final draft. Experienced writers know, also, that good writing is rewriting. Their drafts are filled with additions, deletions, rearrangements, and rewordings.

For example, on the next page you can see how the paragraph you just read was reworked into final form. Notice that two sentences were dropped, two sentences were combined, one sentence was added, and various words were dropped, changed, or added. Such activities are typical of writing.

Writing is an ongoing process of considering alternatives and making choices. The better you understand the writing process, the better you will write and the more you can enjoy writing. For the sake of explanation, the parts of the writing process are discussed separately in this chapter. In real life, the steps overlap, looping back and forth as each piece of writing evolves.

Understanding writing as a multistage process allows you to work efficiently, concentrating on one activity at a time rather than trying to juggle all of the facets of a writing project simultaneously. An overview of the steps in the writing process is given in Chart 5. If you are a writer who likes to visualize a process, see the diagram on page 17. A straight line would not be adequate because it

TEACHING TIP

The facsimile of my writing and revising at the opening of this chapter is completely authentic (though the handwriting is not mine because I tend to scrawl illegibly). I have included this draft to show students that most teachers and professional writers *evolve* a text rather than produce it in one swoop. When I do this in my writing classes, the students never fail to be surprised that their instructor's first draft could be so rough. You might also call attention to the clumsy opening sentences that I deleted and to other revisions that I made in my first draft.

You might also bring in a few examples of your own drafts. A paragraph or two can suffice. And if you use a word processor, as I do, plan ahead and keep those sentences you love to delete with the press of a key. I have found that a few students sometimes think that my rough drafts are better than their final drafts, but I try to emphasize that such a reaction misses the point. After all, I am not as much of an apprentice writer as the students are. And I am trying to better my writing from a base of where I am, not from a base that I started at back in college.

QUOTATION ABOUT WRITING

The best time for planning . . . is when you're doing the dishes.

—Agatha Christie

BACKGROUND

Over the past decade a number of theories about the process of writing have emerged. In *Discourse: A Critique and Synthesis of Major Theories* (New York: MLA, 1989), Timothy W. Crusius provides a helpful analysis of those put forward by James Kinneavy, James Moffett, James Britton, and Frank D'Angelo. Crusius pulls their views together in an attempt to find a unified view of the concept.

Draft and Revision of Opening Paragraph in Chapter 2 by Lynn Troyka

AN OVERVIEW OF THE WRITING PROCESS

Planning calls for you to gather ideas and think about a focus.

Shaping calls for you to consider ways to organize your material.

Drafting calls for you to write your ideas in sentences and paragraphs.

Revising calls for you to evaluate your draft and, based on your decisions, rewrite it by adding, cutting, replacing, moving—and often totally recasting material.

Editing calls for you to check the technical correctness of your grammar, spelling, punctuation, and mechanics.

Proofreading calls for you to read your final copy for typing errors or handwriting legibility.

plan **2a**

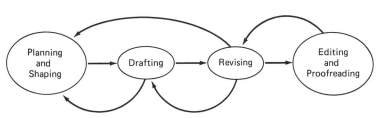

Visualizing the Writing Process

would exclude the recursive nature of writing. The arrows on the diagram imply movement. Planning is not over when drafting begins, drafting is not necessarily over merely because the major activity shifts to revision, and editing sometimes inspires writers to see the need for additional revising—and perhaps some new planning.

As you work with the writing process, rest assured that there is no *one* way to write. When you start, allow yourself to move through each stage of the writing process and see what is involved. Then as you gain experience, begin to observe what works best for you. Once you have a general sense of the pattern of *your* writing process, you can adapt the process to suit each new situation that you encounter as a writer.

Most writers struggle some of the time with ideas that are difficult to express, sentences that will not take shape, and words that are not precise. Do not be impatient with yourself, and do not get discouraged. Writing takes time. The more you write, the easier it will be, but remember that experienced writers know that writing never happens magically.

An aside about the words used to discuss writing: Instructors refer to written products in different ways. Often the words are used interchangeably, but sometimes they have specific meanings for specific instructors. Listen closely and ask if you are unsure of what you hear. For example, the words *essay*, *theme*, and *composition* usually—but not always—refer to writing that runs from about 500 to 1,000 words. This handbook uses *essay*. The words *report* and *project* usually mean writing that draws on outside sources. The word *paper* can mean anything from a few paragraphs to a long and detailed report of a complex research project. This handbook uses *paper* to refer to research writing.

BACKGROUND

Lester Faigley classifies composing process theories into three categories—expressive, cognitive, and social—in "Competing Theories of Process: A Critique and a Proposal" (*College English* [October 1986]: 527–542). Expressive or neoromantic views, associated with Donald Stewart, Ken Macrorie, and Peter Elbow, emphasize writing with integrity, spontaneity, and originality. Cognitive theories, associated with Linda Flower, Janice Lauer, and Barry Kroll, have drawn on research on cognitive development by Jean Piaget and others, as well as on cybernetic theory, and describe composing as a recursive problem-solving activity. Social views of composing processes, a diverse group of theories influenced by poststructuralism, ethnography, the sociology of science, and Marxism, hold that writing "can be understood only from the perspective of a society rather than a single individual" (535) and explain the composing processes of writers in terms of their relationship to a community or culture. James Berlin, Patricia Bizzell, and David Bartholomae are among those advocating social theories. "Each view of process," Faigley writes, "has provided teachers with ways of resisting static methods of teaching writing" (537).

BACKGROUND

Donald Graves was the first to use the term *rehearsing* to describe the activities that precede a completed draft. In *Balance the Basics: Let Them Write* (Ford Foundation Papers on Research About Learning, 1978), he discusses the stage of the writing process in which the writer (mentally and on paper) prepares to write, without yet knowing what that writing will be. Drawing conclusions from his observations of children writing, Graves points out the importance of experimenting with meaning, form, and voices, an attitude of play that is important in making meaning. It allows the writer to make unexpected relationships from surprising inner voices.

BACKGROUND

On several occasions (e.g., "Understanding Composing," *CCC* 31 [December 1980]: 363 –369), Sondra Perl has described the writing process as recursive, the several stages of planning, drafting, and revising occurring not in a straight, linear fashion, but doubling back on one another as the work takes shape. In the *New York University Education Quarterly* (1979), p. 18, she refers to the process as "retrospective structuring." "Composing," she writes, "does not occur in a straightforward, linear fashion. The process is one of accumulating discrete words or phrases down on the paper and then working from these bits to reflect upon, structure, and then further develop what one means to say." The reaching back and sensing forward have what she describes as "a clarifying effect," the written form serving, as it does, as a window on the intended meaning.

QUOTATION ABOUT WRITING

Had I known the answer to any of these questions, I would never have needed to write.

—Joan Didion

TEACHING TIP (see Chart 6)

The concept of a "writing situation" might be new to many students. It is an inclusive term for the combination of topic, purpose, audience, and special requirements such as word or time limits. Each of these four variables influences every decision a writer makes. You might want to ask your students to memorize that short list of key variables: TOPAS (with the two letters "to" for "top-ic") can be an easy memory device for students. These variables are especially important in narrowing a topic, as demonstrated by the inclusion of "writing situation" in the examples for narrowing a topic.

2b Adjusting for each writing situation

Writing begins with thinking about each **writing situation.** Your thinking involves answering the questions in Chart 6. Then you adjust your writing process (see 2a) to accommodate each particular writing situation.

ELEMENTS THAT INFLUENCE EACH WRITING SITUATION 6

- topic: what will you be writing about in this situation?
- purpose: what will be your writing purpose in this situation?
- audience: who will be your audience in this situation?
- special requirements: how much time were you given, and what length should the paper be?

Underlying all aspects of the writing situation is the **topic.** If you must choose your own topic or narrow an assigned topic, keep in mind the constraints of academic writing (see 2c). If the topic is assigned, you must not go "off the topic." Whatever the topic, *you* are the starting place for your writing. Draw upon yourself as a source. Whatever you have seen, heard, read, and even dreamed contributes to your fund of ideas and knowledge. Keep in mind the need to marshall specific support for the points you make about your topic.

The writing situation includes the **purpose** for your writing. For academic writing in college, the major **purposes** are *to inform* and *to persuade* (see 1b). Effective informative and persuasive writing succeed in part because they reflect a clear sense of purpose. Some writing assignments include or clearly imply a statement of purpose. For example, your purpose is informative if you are writing about the dangers of smoking. Conversely, your purpose is persuasive if you are writing an argument against smoking. When an assignment does not stipulate the writing purpose, one of your tasks is to choose either an informative or persuasive purpose based on the topic, what you want to say about it (often referred to as the *focus*), and how you develop what you want to say.

For college writing, your **audience** (see 1c) is often primarily, though not exclusively, your instructor. Your instructor is both a member of the general reading public and an academic. Some writing assignments name a specialized audience, which means your readers have more technical knowledge than does the general reading public. You have to write to their level. Sometimes an assignment stipulates that the writing will be read by other students in the class. In such situations, students serve as surrogate instructors, so you are expected to write with the same tone and level of information as you would for your instructor alone.

Special requirements influence every writing situation. These include the time allotted for the assignment, the expected length of the writing, and other practical constraints. If an assignment is due in one week, you have to expect that your instructor wants writing that shows more than one day's work. If the paper is due overnight, it has to be written more hastily, though never carelessly. If research is required, you have to build time for it into your schedule.

Your assignment is a major resource for you as you write. Refer to it often. Ideally, your instructor writes the assignment on the board or distributes it on paper. Some instructors, however, only announce an assignment, in which case you are expected to write it down. Try to record every word spoken, always ask questions if you need clarifications, and write down the answers you get or any given in response to other students' questions.

To give you examples of the writing process in progress, this chapter shows you the work of two actual students—Dawn Seaford and Daniel Casey—as they plan and shape their essays. Then in Chapter 3, Dawn Seaford's essay is discussed as it evolves through three drafts (shown in section 3f). Daniel Casey's essay is developed in Chapter 6, and its final draft appears in section 6h. Here is the written statement of the assignment that each student received.

Dawn Seaford was given this assignment: Write an essay of 700 to 800 words in which you explain how to face an extraordinary challenge—you choose what challenge. You can write with an informative purpose (see 1b-1) or a persuasive purpose (see 1b-2). Expect to write three drafts. Your first draft (in rough form, showing your comments to yourself and changes you made) and your second (cleanly typed) draft are due in one week. I will read your second draft as an "essay in progress" and will make comments to help you toward a third, final draft. That third, final draft (cleanly typed) is due one week after I hand back your second draft with my comments.

Daniel Casey was given this assignment: Write an essay of 500 to 700 words that argues about whether holidays have become too commercialized in the United States. Your final draft is due in one week. Bring your earlier drafts to class for possible discussion.

BACKGROUND

Writers, both amateurs and professionals, tend to devise rituals that help them begin and carry out a piece of writing. Some of them are elaborate, some of them relatively simple. They are identifiable by the fact that they are repeated actions that seem to be irrelevant to the task at hand but that are in some way helpful to the writer looking for ideas and ways to express them. Some are silly, such as using the same coffee mug each time one writes, or illogical, such as sweeping the front walk before getting started, but the fact is that they are effective in helping a writer make the transition from some other activity to that of composition.

Writers who are in the process of devising writing rituals can make their individual habits more productive by being aware of which steps are helpful and which are not. They can begin by asking themselves questions about where, when, and with what they write. Where do they get the most work done? Does it afford them access to materials they need? Is it free from interruptions? Does it make them comfortable but not too relaxed? Can they see well? Do they have room to spread out notes and books? What time of day or night do they usually do their writing? Are they alert and energetic at that time? Does it give them a block of time in which to work? Do they use a typewriter? A legal pad? A word processor? A spiral notebook? What objects, environments, or activities that are not directly connected with writing provide a sense of well-being during the process? The answers will vary from one writer to another, but for best results the process should remain fairly constant with the individual.

Rituals are habits that provide structure—reassurance that the writer has done a task this way once before. With each repetition they become more comfortable, making the writer feel more competent, more at home with the act of writing.

ANSWERS: EXERCISE 2-1

1. The purpose is to inform. Because the assignment is for a biology class, the audience will likely be the instructor and perhaps other students in the class; these people are specialists. The assumption about an audience of specialists is further confirmed by the time limit of twenty minutes, which means that the student has to pack in many technical terms and processes in a short period of time. The special requirements include the twenty-minute time limit and, implied by the wording of the assignment, in-class writing.

2. The purpose is to persuade. The audience is the general reading public (such as the course instructor and students in the class). The special requirements include a 500- to 700-word limit and a due date of one week.

3. A student receiving this assignment has many decisions to make. The purpose can be either informative or persuasive, depending on the student's focus on the topic. The audience can be the general reading public or specialists, according to the student's judgment; if the political science course is advanced, chances are that the instructor expects the writing to be addressed to specialists. The only stated special requirement is a length of 1,000 words. The student should ask the instructor when the assignment is due and if the assignment calls for research. The student might also want to set a purpose and audience and check them with the instructor before proceeding, if time permits.

4. The purpose is to persuade. The audience is readers of the college's student newspaper; they could be considered specialists in that they share the experience of attending the same college, but they are not specialists in technicalities concerning the functioning of college libraries. The special requirements include a 300-word limit, the need to draw on personal experience, and

➜

Seaford read her assignment with an eye toward analyzing the elements of her writing situation. The *topic* was how to face an extraordinary challenge, a subject that Seaford realized she would have to narrow considerably (for her process of narrowing the topic, see 2c-2). For a writing *purpose*, Seaford tentatively chose an informative purpose, knowing that as she got further into her planning, she might change her mind. She saw that her instructor was to be her *audience* and that the *special requirements* of length and time were given in the assignment.

Casey read his assignment to analyze his writing situation. He saw immediately that most elements were stated. The *topic* was commercialization of holidays in the United States, and the *purpose* persuasive because students were expected to adopt and argue a position about the topic. The *audience* was the instructor, though Casey realized that the class might hear or see earlier drafts once the final draft was finished. The *special requirements* of length and time were given in the assignment.

EXERCISE 2-1

Consulting section 2b, for each assignment listed below, answer these questions: (a) Is its purpose to inform or to persuade? (b) Is the audience the general reading public or specialists? (c) What special requirements of length and time are stated or implied?

1. *Biology:* You have twenty minutes to list and explain three ways that the circulatory system contributes to homeostasis in the human body.
2. *English:* Write a 500- to 700-word essay arguing for or against tougher academic requirements for student athletes. This assignment is due in one week.
3. *Political Science:* Write a 1,000-word essay about television's impact on elections.
4. *English:* Write a 300-word editorial for the student newspaper praising or criticizing the college's library. Draw on your personal experience. Also, interview at least one member of the library staff for his or her reaction to your point of view.
5. *Art:* Write a one-paragraph summary of the difference between a wide-angle lens and a telephoto lens.

2c **Choosing a topic for writing**

Choosing a topic calls for using good judgment and making sound decisions. Experienced writers know that the quality of their writing depends on how they handle a topic. Always think through a topic before you rush in and get too deeply involved to pull out within the time allotted.

Of course, some assignments leave no room for making choices about the topic. You may be given very specific instructions such as "Explain how oxygen is absorbed from the lungs," or you may be asked to describe the view from your classroom window. Your job with such assignments is to do precisely what is asked and not go off the topic.

1   Selecting a topic on your own

Some instructors ask students to choose their own topic. In such situations, do not assume that all subjects are suitable for informative or persuasive writing in college. Academic settings call for topics that can reflect your ability to think ideas through. For example, the old reliable essay about a summer vacation is probably not safe territory for a college essay if you have nothing extraordinary to report. Your essays need to dive into issues and concepts, and they should demonstrate that you can use specific, concrete details to support what you want to say. Conversely, the need for specifics should not tempt you to write very technical information when an audience is unfamiliar with the particular specialized vocabulary.

When you choose a topic on your own, you will have little success with topics that are so narrow that give you little to say. For example, you might reach a dead end if you tried to write a 500-word essay about what your cat looks like while sleeping, unless you are asked for a description of a common sight or observation report for a zoology course.

2   Narrowing an assigned topic

The real challenge in dealing with topics comes when you choose or are assigned a subject that is very broad. You have to *narrow the subject.* Narrowing means thinking of subdivisions of the subject, of different areas within the subject. Most very broad subjects can be broken down in hundreds of ways, but you need not think of all of them. When one seems possible, think it through before rushing in, however. Think whether the topic as narrowed can be developed well in writing. **What separates most good writing from bad is the writer's ability to move back and forth between general statements and specific details.**

Cont'd.
the need to interview a library staff member. The student should ask the instructor when the assignment is due.

5. The purpose is to inform. Because the assignment is only one paragraph and is for an art class, chances are high that the audience is the course instructor and perhaps other students in the class. As assumption of some specialized knowledge is appropriate (unless the instructor says to write the material for people totally unfamiliar with the topic). The special requirements include the one-paragraph limit and, perhaps implied by the wording of the assignment, in-class writing.

BACKGROUND

In his article "To Be Read" (*English Journal* 57 [May 1968]: 686–692; rpt. *Rhetoric and Composition: A Sourcebook for Teachers and Writers,* ed. Richard L. Graves [Portsmouth, NH Boynton/Cook, 1984]), Ken Macrorie discusses, among other issues, ways to help students arrive at a topic worth their effort. He begins by asking them for freewriting that strives to be honest (in contrast to phony), followed by discussion of strong passages that seem to speak the truth, a slowly developing focus on one subject, an effort to tighten the expression, and then an extension of the discussion to a full-length writing. By acting as editor instead of "grader" or "corrector," the teacher establishes a situation closer to that in which "real" writing takes place. Macrorie describes traditional "themes," papers assigned by teachers on topics that have no context, as papers that are "not meant to be *read*, but *corrected.*"

BACKGROUND

Much of what we know about the composing processes of students comes from the work of three researchers and their colleagues. James Britton in Britain's School Council Project *The Development of Writing Abilities, 11–18* (London: Macmillan Education, 1975) found that "writing is a deliberate act; one has to make up one's mind to do it." Once we decide to write, he points out, we begin the process by prewriting, which involves our trying to understand and solve a particular writing problem. Also fundamental to our current understanding of the writing process is the work of Janet Emig, reported in *The Composing Processes of Twelfth Graders* (NCTE Research Report No. 13 [Urbana: NVTE, 1971]). As the title suggests, she followed in detail the methods of high school seniors as they made their way through writing tasks. Finally, John R. Hayes and Linda S. Flower have provided a model for other researchers with their "thinking aloud" protocols, verbal descriptions of what writers report they think and do while they compose ("Identifying the Organization of Writing Processes" and "The Dynamics of Composing: Making Plans and Juggling Constraints," *Cognitive Processes in Writing*, ed. Lee W. Gregg and Erwin R. Steinberg [Hillsdale, N.J.: Lawrence Erlbaum Associates, 1980], pp. 3–50). Although the methods and terminology of these investigators vary, they arrive at fundamental agreement about the writing process.

QUOTATION ABOUT WRITING

Writing is just having a sheet of paper, a pen and not a shadow of an idea of what you're going to say.

—Françoise Sagan

For example, if the subject is marriage, you might decide to talk about what makes marriages successful. But you cannot depend merely on generalizations such as "In successful marriages husbands and wives learn to accept each other's faults." You need to explain why accepting faults is important, and you need to give concrete illustrations of what you are talking about.

As you narrow a broad subject to obtain a writing topic, keep in mind the writing situation (see 2b) of each assignment. Think about what you can handle well according to the conditions of each assignment.

SUBJECT	*Music*
WRITING SITUATION	freshman composition class
	informative purpose
	instructor as audience
	500 words, one week
POSSIBLE TOPICS	the moods music creates
	classical music of the Renaissance
	country western music as big business
SUBJECT	*Cities*
WRITING SITUATION	Sociology course
	Persuasive purpose
	Students and then instructor as audience
	500 to 700 words, one week
POSSIBLE TOPICS	comforts of city living
	discomforts of city living
	why city planning is important
SUBJECT	*Mythology*
WRITING SITUATION	Humanities course
	Informative purpose
	Instructor as audience, someone who is a specialist in mythology
	1,000 words, two weeks
POSSIBLE TOPICS	the purpose of myths
	comparison of Navaho and Roman myths explaining why seasons change

Dawn Seaford had to narrow the topic of her assignment (see page 19) because the words "an extraordinary challenge" were too vague and general. To stimulate her thinking, Seaford used some of the techniques for gathering ideas presented in the rest of this chapter. What helped her the most were using a journal (see her *plan* **2d**

work in 2e), freewriting (see her work in 2f), and mapping (see her work in 2i). As a result of using those techniques, Seaford decided to write about the extraordinary challenge of having to face a natural disaster. Her essay is discussed in Chapter 3 as it evolves through three drafts (shown in section 3f).

Daniel Casey did not have to narrow his topic because it was stated in his assignment (see page 19): the commercialization of holidays in the United States. He did, however, have to choose a position to argue on the topic. What helped him the most were brainstorming (see his work in 2g), asking the "journalist's questions" (see his work in 2h), and using a subject tree (see his work in 2-1). The development of Casey's essay is discussed in Chapter 6, and his final draft appears in section 6h.

EXERCISE 2-2

Consulting section 2c, for five of these general topics, think of three narrowed topics that would be suitable for a 500- to 700-word essay in a writing course. Assume that each essay is due in one week and that the audience is the general reading public, as represented by the course's instructor. List your three narrowed topics and explain briefly why each is suitable for the writing situation. Then think of one topic that interests you and is not on this list, and repeat the exercise with that topic.

1. computers
2. movies
3. political campaigns
4. Halloween
5. literature
6. popular music
7. self-respect
8. driver training
9. imagination
10. slang

2d   Gathering ideas for writing

Techniques for gathering ideas, sometimes called *prewriting strategies* or *invention techniques,* can help you discover how much you know about a topic. You need this information before you decide to write on a topic. Sections 2e through 2k describe various ways, listed in Chart 7, to gather ideas for writing.

Students sometimes worry that they have nothing to write about. Often, however, students know far more than they give themselves credit for. The challenge is to uncover what is there but seems not to be. As you use these various techniques for gathering ideas, find out which work best for *you.* Use only those that you find helpful for *your* style of thinking. Your goal is to discover ideas and to narrow your focus to a topic (see 2c) suitable for a given writing situation (see 2b).

TEACHING TIP

Students may be surprised to learn that all writers find the blank sheet of paper (or empty computer screen) a source of anxiety. The experienced writer knows that the most effective way to move past that feeling is to write *something,* regardless of its value. Once the clean surface has words on it, other words follow more easily. Unrelated ideas, notes, questions, examples—all help to relieve the writer's discomfort with getting started. A good habit to cultivate is to jot down responses and reactions to writing tasks as soon as they are given.

ANSWERS: EXERCISE 2-2

Answers will vary, but each topic should have an explanation of why it would be suitable for the writing situation described in the exercise.

BACKGROUND

Lev Vygotsky's theories about inner speech have attracted increased interest over the past few years. One analyst, James Thomas Zebroski, finds that Vygotsky's ideas support writing as process ("Vygotsky's Ideas Gaining Favor among Compositionists," *Composition Chronicle* 2 [March 1989]: 4–5).

QUOTATION ABOUT WRITING

I am a camera with its shutter open, quite passive, recording, not thinking.

—Christopher Isherwood

QUOTATION ABOUT WRITING

I have tried simply to write the best I can; sometimes I have good luck and write better than I can.

—Ernest Hemingway

TEACHING TIP: JOURNALS

Students often have trouble thinking of journal topics. Frequently the result is journals that read like parodies of diaries, shopping lists, descriptions of meals or clothes, transcripts of routine conversations. You can avoid this problem if you give students suggested topics. In addition to offering students something to write about, such topics act as models for the creation of original topics. You might distribute this list in groups of five or ten so that they can last for most of a semester.

1. How do you feel about having to keep a journal? How do you feel about writing? Explain.

2. Why are you in college? If there is something else you would rather be doing, what is it? Why are you in school instead?

3. What is your definition of success? Do your friends tend to share your definition or to have a different one? Discuss.

4. Do you think information about sex should be taught at home, in school, or both? Why?

5. How does your religion affect your daily life? Have you ever had to defend or explain your religious beliefs to someone? Do you think you were effective? Why or why not?

6. Do you plan to marry someday? Why? What do you expect married life to be like? (If you are married, were your expectations fulfilled? Why or why not?)

7. What do you want as a career? How are you preparing for it? How did you choose this career? Have you ever had to defend or explain your choice to parents or friends? Do you think you were effective? Why or why not?

8. Is the United States really a melting pot? Should immigrant children be educated in English or in their native languages? Should there be non-English radio and television stations in the United States? For each question, why or why not?

9. If you could give advice to your friend(s), what would you say?

➜

WAYS TO GATHER IDEAS FOR WRITING	7

- Keeping an idea book (see 2e)
- Writing in a journal (see 2e)
- Freewriting (see 2f)
- Brainstorming (see 2g)
- Using the journalist's questions (see 2h)
- Mapping (see 2i)
- Reading for writing (see 2j)
- Incubating (see 2k)

No one technique of generating ideas always works for all writers in all situations. Experiment. If one method does not provide enough useful material, try an alternative. Also, even if one strategy produces some good material, try another to see what additional possibilities turn up.

2e   Keeping an idea book and writing in a journal

Your ease with writing will grow as you develop the habits of mind that typify writers. Professional writers are always on the lookout for ideas to write about and for details to develop their ideas. They listen, watch, talk with people, and generally keep their minds open. For this reason, many writers always carry an **idea book**—a pocketsize notebook—to jot down ideas that spring to mind. Good ideas can melt away like snowflakes. If you keep an idea book handy throughout your college years, you will find that your powers of observation become increasingly strong.

Many writers, both amateur and professional, write in a **journal.** Keeping a journal gives you the chance to have a "conversation on paper" with yourself. Fifteen minutes a day can be enough—before going to bed, between classes, on a bus. *You* are your audience, so the content and tone can be as personal and informal as you wish.

Unlike a diary, a journal is not merely for listing what you did that day. In a journal you put down your thoughts. You can draw on your reading, your observations, your dreams. You can respond to quotations, react to movies or plays, or think through your opinions, beliefs, and tastes. Writing is a way of discovering, of allowing thoughts to emerge as the physical act of writing moves along.

Keeping a journal can help you in three ways. First, writing every day gives you the habit of productivity. The more you write, the more you get used to the feeling of words pouring out of you onto paper, the easier it will become for you to write in all situations. Second, a journal instills the habit of close observation and thinking. Third, a journal serves as an excellent source of ideas when you need to write in response to an assignment.

Here is an excerpt of a journal entry by Dawn Seaford made about 6 months before she got the assignment to write an essay about facing a challenge (see page 19). Seaford lives in Wichita, Kansas, an area of the United States where clusters of severe tornadoes are not unusual. When reading through her journal for ideas for her essay, Seaford realized that having to face a natural disaster can be an extraordinary challenge.

> April 27, 1991: Yesterday was terrifying. Really strong tornadoes crashed through Wichita in the early evening. My family always drills on what to do when tornado warnings come, but that doesn't stop the terror I feel. Luckily, none of those tornadoes hit our neighborhood, but the alert lasted for hours. McConnell Air Force Base just east of us got hit hard. Many buildings, including the hospital and dozens of on-base houses, were flattened. The trailer park in Andover was destroyed by huge twisters that hurled mobile homes around like toys and killed many people. Tornadoes are called "natural disasters," but they don't seem natural to me!

An Excerpt from Dawn Seaford's Journal

2f Using freewriting

Freewriting is writing nonstop. It means writing down whatever comes into your mind without stopping to worry about whether the ideas are good or the spelling is correct. When you freewrite, you do nothing to interrupt the flow. Let your mind make all kinds of associations. Do not censor any thoughts or flashes of insight. Do not

Cont'd.

10. Where do you go when you feel like being alone? Why?

11. Where do you go when you feel sociable? Why?

12. Does anything make you depressed? What? What do you do when you feel this way? What advice can you give others who feel this way?

13. What is your favorite place? What makes it so special?

14. What do you think your life will be like in the year 2000? What will your family life be like? What work will you be doing? Where will you be living? How will technology have influenced your life?

15. Who is your favorite relative? Why?

16. If you could change one thing about your personality, what would it be? Why?

17. If you could change one aspect of the way you look, what would it be? Why?

18. In what ways is college *not* what you expected? In what ways *is* it what you expected?

19. If you could be given a talent you do not already have, what would it be?

20. What is the most expensive thing you ever bought? Why did you buy it? How did you get the money? Was it worth the money?

21. How would you feel if you were told that you had to cook a healthy dinner for six people, including yourself? Who would you go to for advice or help? What would you serve? How successful do you think the dinner would be?

22. Who are some of the most important people in your life? Why? How do you let these people know how much they mean to you?

23. If you could travel anywhere on this planet, where would you like to go? Why? Where would you least like to go? Why?

24. If you could live in any earlier time period, what period would you choose? Why?

➜

Cont'd.

25. What is your favorite kind of movie? Why? What are its characteristics? What is the best movie of that kind that you have ever seen?

26. How does the weather affect your mood?

27. Do you enjoy playing a sport? Why or why not? What sport do you enjoy the most? Why?

28. If you were fated to be a public figure, what would you want to be: politician, rock star, movie star, environmental activist, news reporter? Why? What would your life be like? How would you treat people less famous than you?

29. If you were to be reincarnated as an animal that reflected your behavior in this life, what would you be? Why? If you could choose what animal to be, what would you be? Why?

30. What teacher has had a great deal of influence on you? Describe the teacher and his or her effect on you.

QUOTATION ABOUT WRITING

Looking back, I imagine I was always writing. Twaddle it was too. But better far write twaddle or anything, anything, than nothing at all.

—Katherine Mansfield

BACKGROUND

In "Toward a Phenomenology of Freewriting" (*Journal of Basic Writing* 8 [Fall 1989]: 42–71), Peter Elbow discusses why freewriting is fundamental to his work. He explains that it helps him as a writer and as a teacher because it allows him to move "more easily and fully" into writing and thinking.

go back and review. Do not cross out. Some days your freewriting might seem mindless, but other days it can reveal interesting ideas to you.

Freewriting helps get you used to the "feel" of pen moving across paper or of fingers in constant motion on the keyboard of a typewriter or computer. Freewriting works best if you set a goal, such as writing for fifteen minutes or until you have filled one or two pages. Keep going until you reach that goal, even if you must repeat a word over and over until a new word comes to mind.

If you use a word processor, you can avoid the temptation to stop and criticize your writing by doing "invisible writing." Dim the monitor screen so you cannot see your writing. The computer's memory will still be recording your ideas, but you will not be able to see them until you brighten the screen again. The same effect is possible for writing by hand if you use a worn-out ballpoint pen and a piece of carbon paper between two sheets of paper.

Focused freewriting means starting with a set topic. You may focus your freewriting in any way you like—perhaps with a phrase from your journal or a quotation you like. Use the focus as a starting point for writing down as many of your thoughts as you can until you meet the time or page limit you have set as a goal. Again, do not censor what you say. Keep moving forward.

As with journals, freewriting can be a source for ideas and details to write about. Dawn Seaford's home in Wichita, Kansas, is located in a part of the United States where clusters of severe tornadoes are not unusual. Here is a brief excerpt from her focused freewriting when she was thinking about facing the challenge of natural disasters.

> OK, so I live in "tornado alley." Tornadoes, twisters funnel-shaped monsters. We're always prepared for them. Drill, drill—at home, at school, my parents at work. For me, the big thing is my head. Fear. Being mentally prepared, and that's not just knowing the practical stuff. No more thoughts—tornadoes tornadoes tornadoes even if I <u>could</u> move away from here, I'd probably run into some other natural disaster like a hurricane, or a volcano eruption, or an earthquake.

An Excerpt from Dawn Seaford's Freewriting

EXERCISE 2-3

Consulting section 2f, freewrite for five minutes on one of these topics. Then think of one topic that interests you and is not on this list, and freewrite on that topic.

1. worrying
2. procrastinating
3. a dream vacation
4. taking tests
5. playing a sport
6. comedians on television
7. libraries
8. chocolate
9. falling in love
10. world peace

2g Using brainstorming

Brainstorming means making a list of all random ideas that come to mind associated with a topic. The ideas can be listed as words, phrases, or even random sentences. Let your mind range freely, generating quantities of ideas before eliminating some.

You can brainstorm in one concentrated session or over several days, depending on how much time is available for the assignment. In courses that permit collaborative work, brainstorming in groups can work especially well because one person's ideas bounce off the next person's, and collectively more ideas get listed.

Brainstorming is done in two steps. First, you make a list. Then you go back and try to find patterns in the list and ways to group the ideas into categories. Set aside any items that do not fit into groups. If an area interests you but its list is thin, brainstorm on that area alone. If you run out of ideas, ask yourself questions to stimulate your thinking. You might try exploratory questions about the topic, such as: What is it? What is it the same as? How is it different? Why or how does it happen? How is it done? What caused it or results from it? What does it look, smell, sound, feel, or taste like?

Daniel Casey's essay, discussed in Chapter 6, develops an argument concerning the benefits of the commercialization of holidays. For Casey's final draft, see section 6h. Realizing that his position was surely open to a great deal of debate, Casey used the technique of brainstorming to help himself think through his opinion. On the next page is an excerpt from the ideas as they came to Casey at random. The items followed by an asterisk (*) are those Casey chose for his fourth paragraph—about the spirit of the holidays—of his essay, shown in section 6h.

TEACHING TIP

In *Writing with Power* (New York: Oxford UP, 1981), Peter Elbow suggests that keeping a freewriting diary can help an aspiring writer. Writing for only ten minutes a day can provide "a brief mind sample" of that day. He also discusses a variance of freewriting called looping, which allows the reader a degree of control over the material that the mind produces. Looping involves a series of freewritings about a subject. After writing nonstop for several minutes for the first loop, the writer composes a "center of gravity sentence" that summarizes the main idea in the first loop as precisely as possible. The freewriting of the second loop responds to the center of gravity sentence. For each new loop, the writer should compose a new center of gravity sentence, each loop further refining and elaborating on the main idea. You may want to ask students to try looping as an in-class prewriting activity for a paper, to help choose a topic or to discover a tentative thesis statement.

QUOTATION ABOUT WRITING

Writing is no trouble: you just jot down ideas as they occur to you. The jotting is simplicity itself—it is the occurring which is difficult.

—Stephen Leacock

QUOTATION ABOUT WRITING

I need noise and interruptions and irritation: irritation and discomfort are a great starter. The loneliness of doing it any other way would kill me.

—Anita Brookner

QUOTATION ABOUT WRITING

All you need is a room without any particular interruptions.

—John Dos Passos

ANSWERS: EXERCISE 2-4

Class discussion will likely reveal disagreement about the main categories and the distribution of items. You can emphasize the role of the individual writer as decision maker. The list might be arranged in this way:

A. *Appeals of adverstisement:* Celebrities (as salespeople), self-esteem (appeal to), sex appeal, suitability for readership, status symbols, level of sophistication

B. *Use of color:* black and white vs. color, stimulates senses

C. *Language:* amount of writing, connotations of words, intentional misuse of English, witty language, facts, slogans

D. *Layout:* size of advertisement, placement of objects, product identification, grabs readers' attention, focal point, clarity of design

Note: Imagination and *creativity* do not fit because they are part of all these and thus too general.

ANSWERS: EXERCISE 2-5

Answers to this exercise will vary. The writer should be able to explain the principle that underlies each grouping.

EXCERPT FROM BRAINSTORMED LIST

people feel cheerful*
the economy is stimulated
people give to charities
strangers exchange friendly greetings*
everyone gives and gets gifts
children love visiting Santa (and the Easter Bunny)*
festive atmosphere in stores*
sending greeting cards helps friends stay in touch*
arouses positive sentimental feelings
stimulates good will

EXERCISE 2-4

Here is a brainstormed list for an assignment in marketing class on advertising strategies in magazines. Consulting section 2g, look over the list and group ideas. Some ideas may not fit into any group.

intentional misuse of English	black and white vs. color
status symbols	level of sophistication
suitability for leadership	imagination
grabs readers' attention	stimulates senses
product identification	witty language
placement of objects	facts
sex appeal	focal point
slogans	amount of writing
self-esteem of reader	clarity of design
celebrities	connotations of words
layout	suitability for audience
size of advertisement	creativity

EXERCISE 2-5

Consulting section 2g, brainstorm on a subject that interests you. First make a random list. Then group ideas within the list. If you cannot think of a subject, use one from Exercise 2-2 or Exercise 2-3.

2h   Using the journalist's questions

Journalist's questions ask *Who? What? When? Why? Where? How?* Asking these questions forces you to approach a topic from several different perspectives.

Daniel Casey used the journalist's questions to explore and expand his thinking about specific benefits of the commercialization of holidays in the United States. His answers to the questions helped him decide that he had enough details to write an effective essay (for his final draft, see section 6h).

WHO	Who specifically benefits from the commercial aspects of holidays?
WHAT	What specific benefits result from commercialization of holidays?
WHEN	When specifically do beneficial holidays fall?
WHY	Why specifically do some people object to the commercial aspects of holidays?
WHERE	Where specifically can evidence of benefits be seen or felt?
HOW	How do specific commercial aspects of holidays create benefits?

EXERCISE 2-6

Consulting section 2h, ask the journalist's questions about one of these subjects: day-care centers, watching soap operas, eating junk food, or shoplifting. Then think of one topic that interests you and is not on this list, and ask the journalist's questions about that topic.

2i Using mapping

Mapping, also called *clustering* or *webbing,* is much like brainstorming (see 2g), but it is more visual and less linear. Many writers find that mapping frees them to think more creatively by associating ideas more easily.

To map, start with your topic circled in the middle of a sheet of unlined paper. Next, draw a line radiating out from the center and label it with the name of a major subdivision of your topic. Circle it and from that circle radiate out to more specific subdivisions. When you finish with one major subdivision of your subject, go back to the center and start again with another major division. As you go along, add anything that occurs to you for any section of the map. Continue the process until you run out of ideas. The technique of mapping, by the way, also can be used the same way as using a subject tree (see 2l-1): to lay out the logical relationships of ideas to each other. But as did Dawn Seaford, many writers seem to prefer to use mapping for

BACKGROUND

In "Invention Again; or How the Skeptic Got Into Hot Water" (*Journal of Teaching Writing* 4 [Fall 1985]: 184–192), Jeanne Simpson points out the importance of identifying "the kind of heuristic needed and the quality of the one chosen." She particularly values those methods that are "reusable and reliable." Her ideas are expanded in a book published a few years later called *The Elements of Invention* (New York: Macmillan, 1990).

ANSWERS: EXERCISE 2-6

Each student will come up with a different response, but each one should be encouraged to write as detailed an answer as possible. Here is a sample response for item 2, *watching soap operas:*

who?—housewives, college students of both sexes, an increasing number of males of all ages, unsupervised young children; *what?*—watching soap operas regularly; *where?*—everywhere from office lounges in companies to college dorm rooms and nursing homes; *how?*—some for whole afternoons, some for selective viewing of only one or two shows, some openly, some secretly; *why?*—to escape reality, perhaps, or possibly simply to relax regularly or to keep up with peers' interests

Since long before the invention of universities, not to mention university programs in creative writing, authors have acquired their authority in four main ways—first, by paying a certain sort of attention to the experience of life as well as merely undergoing it; second, by paying a certain sort of attention to the works of their great and less great predecessors in the medium of written language, as well as merely reading them; third, by practicing that medium themselves, usually a *lot* (Charles Newman, the writer and critic, declares that the first prerequisite for aspiring writers is sufficient motor control to keep their pens moving left to right, line after line, hour after hour, day after day, and I would add year after year, decade after decade); and fourth, by offering their apprentice work for discussion and criticism by one or several of their impassioned peers, or by some more experienced hand, or by both.

—John Barth

TEACHING TIP

I've had great success asking students to write at least one journal entry a week that responds to (*not* summarizes) something that they have read. Students should include a photocopy of the article or pages from the book they've read. On the first day of class I show them a photocopy and sample entry as a model.

ANSWERS: EXERCISE 2-7

Answers will vary, but they should look somewhat like the model above Exercise 2-7.

discovering ideas already known but not remembered. You use the techniques as they suit you best.

Here is an excerpt from mapping by Dawn Seaford that she used while searching for ideas to use in her essay about preparing to face natural disasters (for the three drafts of her essay, see section 3f). After Seaford finished mapping, she was satisfied that she had enough information to use in her essay.

Dawn Seaford's Mapping

EXERCISE 2-7

Think of a topic about which you have some information. Use mapping to chart what you know. Start with the topic in the middle of a blank page. Work out from there.

2j Using reading for writing

The process of reading as it relates to critical thinking as you write essays is discussed at length in Chapter 5. Also, ways of reading sources for use in your research writing are discussed at length in Chapters 31 through 35.

This section explains that _all_ you have ever read—that is, your general fund of **prior knowledge**—can enhance your thinking of ideas when you plan and shape essays. Be careful, however. Often, reading is not part of assignments given for college essays (in contrast to assignments for research papers, which always imply the expectation that students will read and draw upon outside sources). Unless an assignment for an essay specifically says that you can refer to outside sources, _ask your instructor before you use any._ Many instructors want students to use what they already know—their prior knowledge—at the time of the assignment.

How can you use your prior knowledge gained from reading to help you think of ideas to write about? Use the techniques explained in 2e through 2k. They are designed to help you remember—that is, "discover"—what you already know. You will likely surprise yourself, once you let your mind roam freely as you use whichever techniques help you the most. If you are like some students who tend to freeze when they first get a writing assignment, feeling "sure" that they know nothing about the topic, you have much company. To overcome such feelings, move rapidly beyond any negative thoughts by immediately starting to use one or more of the techniques; if one does not work for you, try some others.

Dawn Seaford, whose essay in three drafts appears in section 3f, realized while she was mapping (see 2i) that her prior knowledge went beyond her personal experience with tornadoes. She had read in newspapers and magazines about other natural disasters such as earthquakes and hurricanes. Her mapping also made her aware that the survival tactics she knew for facing a tornado could apply to surviving many different kinds of natural disasters.

Daniel Casey, whose essay appears in final draft in section 6h, realized that he was arguing for a position that many people, including his instructor, might strongly disagree with. Not until he asked the journalist's questions (see 2h) and answered them did he feel confident that he knew enough specific details to support his argument.

TEACHING TIP

In _The Elements of Invention_ (New York: Macmillan, 1990), Jeanne H. Simpson suggests six guidelines for students using any invention system:

1. Try to do all the steps in an invention system. If you don't, the world won't end, but you might miss a good opportunity to explore an idea.

2. Ignore redundancies. Most invention systems will have you repeating yourself a bit. It's all right to do that. In fact, you may get a better grip on a slippery idea the second time you write about it.

3. Write as much as you can in response to any step in a system. Don't worry about the beauty of your writing; the main thing is to get your ideas down on paper where you can see them and work with them.

4. Forget about grammar, punctuation, and spelling for now. . . . Just dump the ideas down however you can. You can clean them up later.

5. Keep going, even if you are drawing a blank. Make the pen, pencil, or cursor move no matter what. . . . Eventually, something will occur to you.

6. Reward yourself when you've finished a good workout with an invention system. Take a break, perhaps have a snack. A mental "cool-down" period is often as important as a physical one; use it to help you gain some perspective on what you have written so far (2–3).

"Doing invention the right way," Simpson writes, "just means doing it consistently and with commitment. The only wrong answer in invention is a blank page" (3).

When you allow your ideas to **incubate,** you give them time to grow and develop. Incubation works especially well when you need to solve a problem in your writing (for example, if material is too thin and needs expansion, if material covers too much and needs pruning, or if connections among your ideas are not clear for your reader). Time is a key element for successful incubation. Arrange your time to make sure that you will not be interrupted. You need time to think, to allow your mind to wander, and then to come back and focus on the writing. Sometimes incubating an idea overnight permits sleep to help you discover or clarify an idea.

One helpful strategy is to turn attention to something entirely different from your writing problem. Concentrate *very hard* on that entirely different matter so that your conscious mind is totally distracted from the writing problem. After a while, relax and guide your mind back to the writing problem you want to solve.

Another strategy is to allow your mind to relax and wander, without concentrating on anything special. Open your mind to random thoughts, but do not dwell on any one thought very long. After a while, guide your mind back to the writing problem you are trying to solve. When you come back to the writing problem, you might see solutions that did not occur to you before.

If incubation does not work at first, practice the technique to give your mind the chance to adjust to this approach. Then you can decide whether incubation is helpful to you.

2l   Shaping ideas by grouping and sequencing

Once you have gathered ideas on a topic as a result of any or all of the planning activities in this chapter (see 2e to 2k), you are ready to group and sequence your ideas. This allows you to see whether you need to narrow or refine your topic further. **Shaping** activities are related to the idea that writing is often called *composing,* the putting together of ideas to create a *composition,* one of the synonyms for *essay.* To shape the ideas that you have gathered, you need to group them (see 2l-1) and sequence them (see 2l-2).

As you shape and order ideas, keep in mind that the form of an essay is related to the classical notion of a story's having a beginning, a middle, and an end. An academic essay always has an introduction,

---

TEACHING TIP

Journal writing and freewriting are often unpopular with students at first, but on their end-of-the-semester evaluations of my classes, students consistently mention these activities as being among the most helpful in my course. Perhaps one of the reasons students resist at first is that they don't believe that journal writing and freewriting will not be corrected or graded. It is important, however, to respond to students' journals, although you should not feel obliged to read and respond to every entry of every journal. Responses should not be directive or critical but should create an informal dialogue with students that encourages them to discuss their ideas and experiences in greater depth and detail.

In "Evaluating Writing to Learn: Responding to Journals" (*Encountering Student Texts: Interpretive Issues in Reading Student Writing,* ed. Bruce Lawson, Susan Sterr Ryan, and W. Ross Winterowd [NCTE, 1989]), Richard Beach describes how his students viewed his responses to their journals. They appreciated his positive responses and the indirectness of his criticisms ("I missed more specific comments to some of the readings"). They found it helpful when Beach described the strategies that they used in their writing—"listing," "mapping," "contrasting," "citing evidence"—but not when he merely restated their ideas. Students particularly liked comments that disclosed something about Beach himself and his experiences connected to what they were writing ("This reminds me of . . . .") as well as questions that engaged them in dialogue or otherwise indicated Beach's interest in what they had to say. But questions such as "What are some other related experiences?" often implied that students had not fulfilled a teacher's expectations. Comments that linked their entries to their papers or to class discussions—"This is something to think about for paper II"—were especially valuable (188–190).

a body, and a conclusion. The length of each paragraph is in proportion to the overall length of the essay. Introductory and concluding paragraphs are generally shorter than body paragraphs, and no body paragraph should overpower the others by its length. (Types of paragraphs useful for academic writing are discussed in Chapter 4.)

1 Grouping ideas

When you group ideas, you make connections and find patterns. As you do this, put each batch of related ideas into its own group. As you create groups, use the concept of **levels of generality** to help you make decisions. One idea is more general than another if it falls into a larger, less specific category than the other.

For example, "cures for diseases" is more general than "cures for cancer." Also, "bank account" is more general than "checking account." In turn, "checking account" is more general than "business checking account" or "regular checking account." And those terms are more general than "account 221222 at the E-Z Come, E-Z Go Bank." Remember that generality is a relative term. Each idea exists in the context of a whole relationship of ideas. An idea may be general in relationship to one set of ideas, but specific in relation to another set.

To group ideas, review the material you accumulated while gathering ideas (see 2e through 2k). Then look for general ideas. Next, group less general ideas under them. If you find that your notes contain only general ideas, or only very specific details, return again to gathering techniques to supply what you need. One of the standard tools for ordering ideas is making a "subject tree." It resembles mapping (see 2i). It shows ideas and details in order from most general at the top to most specific at the bottom.

Daniel Casey used a subject tree while shaping his essay that takes the position that benefits result from the commercialization of holidays in the United States (for his final draft, see section 6h). He used the subject tree to lay out the ideas in his third paragraph according to their relative levels of generality. The technique of using a subject tree, by the way, also can be used the same way as mapping (see 2i): to discover ideas that a writer already knows. But as did Daniel Casey, many writers seem to prefer using a subject tree for checking the interrelationships of the ideas once they have been discovered during mapping. You use the techniques as they suit you best.

QUOTATION ABOUT WRITING

The actual process of writing . . . demands complete, noiseless privacy, without even music; a baby howling two blocks away will drive me nuts.

—William Styron

TEACHING TIP

Mapping is a relatively new concept. It is likely that many of your students—and perhaps even you—have not heard of it before now. Mapping can be a refreshing change of pace in place of or in addition to other more traditional idea-gathering techniques. Because mapping is highly visual, it holds a special appeal for some students. Those who hate to do anything formal (such as an outline or even a list) find the apparent anarchy of a map enticing. Students are often engaged by the bunch of balloons developing on the board. Because entire branches of a map can be omitted from an actual essay, dead ends and short roads are not "errors."

Some students take to mapping readily. Others, especially in the beginning, may prefer to have some guidance, at least in the selection of subtopics. For example, an assignment calling for a persuasive essay about air pollution might benefit from a map based on the senses. Ask students to write an example of air pollution in a circle in the center of the page. Then have them draw a line for each sense and circle the name of that sense (smell, taste, sight, hearing, touch). The students can then draw additional lines and circles for each branch of the map.

BACKGROUND

Jeanette Harris explores the subject of invention in "Rethinking Invention" (*Freshman English News* 17 [Fall 1988]: 13–16). She calls for teachers to encourage students to include introspection and exploration of subjects in their heuristics.

TEACHING TIP

To teach the journalist's questions effectively, you might ask students to bring in some newspaper articles that cover the *w*'s in the first paragraph or two. Consider, for example, this brief opening paragraph (a single sentence) from an article in the *New York Times* (April 16, 1989) about a tragic incident at an English soccer game.

> London, April 15—At least 93 people were killed and more than 180 others were injured today when soccer fans surged forward in severely overcrowded stands at a match in the northern English city of Sheffield, according to police and hospital officials.

Who: Ninety-three people attending a soccer match
What: Were killed
When: April 15, 1989
Why: The fans surged forward
Where: Sheffield, England

BACKGROUND

Maxine Hairston states in "Different Products, Different Processes: A Theory about Writing" (*College Composition and Communication* [December 1986]: 442–452) that experienced writers employ different composing processes for different types of writing. Experienced writers generally give little thought to composing "routine maintenance or message writing"—brief notes and memos, lists, thank-you letters, and other short, simple writing that keeps "organizations and personal relationships functioning" (443). In extended "self-limiting" writing such as summaries, most reports, and essay examinations, writers know most of what they want to say and accomplish before they begin. Writers work mainly on organization, style, stance, and tone as they draft and revise, often following "traditional formulas," but skilled writers usually are able to complete these writing tasks easily and quickly, unless the paper is for a partic-

➜

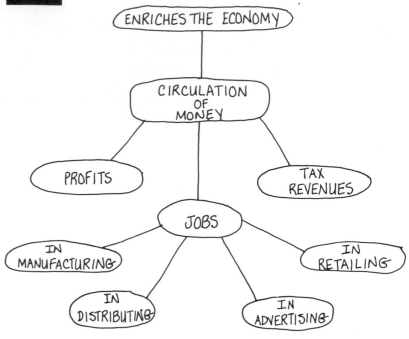

Grouping Ideas by Using a Subject Tree

2 Sequencing ideas

When you sequence ideas for writing, you decide what you want your readers to encounter first, second, and on until the last. When readers can follow your line of reasoning, they are more likely to understand the message that you want your material to deliver.

Within paragraphs, you can present ideas in any of the many ways explained in Chapter 4. Within an essay, the sequence in which you put those paragraphs reveals to your reader your evolving material. The three most common ways to sequence ideas within whole essays are listed in Chart 8.

COMMON WAYS TO SEQUENCE IDEAS WITHIN AN ESSAY   8

- ■ **Climactic order:** from least to most important
- ■ **Chronological order:** according to a time sequence
- ■ **Spatial order:** according to physical location

Climactic order, also called *emphatic order,* moves from least to most important. Ideas are arranged according to degree of impact on your reader or importance to your subject. The order builds to a climax—the most significant point. (Daniel Casey's essay shown in section 6h is an example of climactic order.) Climactic order also operates in essays that move from the simplest to most complex idea, or from the most familiar to least familiar idea.

Chronological order presents ideas according to a time sequence. Chronological order is frequently used in narrating a series of events. Chronological order is also useful when writing about a sequence of steps or actions. (The third, final draft of Dawn Seaford's essay shown in section 3f is an example of chronological order of actions to take.)

Spatial order presents ideas arranged according to their physical locations in relation to one another. This can include top to bottom, near to far, left to right. Spatial order is useful for such topics as describing a stage set or a street scene. Similarly, it would work well for moving from the East Coast to the West Coast or the opposite when comparing historic preservation programs in New York, Chicago, and San Francisco.

2m Shaping writing by drafting a thesis statement

A **thesis statement** is the central message of an essay. It is evidence that you have something definite to say about the topic. An effective thesis statement prepares your reader for the essence of what you discuss in an essay. As the writer, you want to compose a thesis statement with care so that it accurately reflects the content of your essay. If you find a mismatch between your thesis statement and the rest of your essay, revise to coordinate them better. The basic requirements for a thesis statement appear in Chart 9.

Some instructors ask for more than the basic requirements. For example, you might be required to put your thesis statement at the end of your introductory paragraph. (The drafts of the student essay in Chapter 3 provides a good example.) Also, many instructors require that the thesis statement be contained in one sentence. Other instructors permit two sentences if the material to be covered warrants such length. All requirements, basic and additional, are designed to help you think in structured patterns that communicate clearly with readers.

In most writing situations, all parts of a thesis statement might not accurately reflect what you say in the essay until you have written

Cont'd.
ularly important or difficult audience (444). "Extended reflective writing" is usually the most time-consuming and difficult but often the most satisfying to write. In these writings, writers make sense of their lives and their world and discover most of what they want to say only as they write. This kind of writing requires writers to "take risks because they are working at the edge of their abilities, operating in unfamiliar territory" (445). Writing courses, Hairston argues, should give students opportunities to practice self-limiting writing as well as reflective writing.

BACKGROUND

In "Writing as Process: How Writing Finds Its Own Meaning" (*Eight Approaches to Teaching Composition,* ed. Timothy Donovan and Ben McClelland [NCTE, 1980], pp. 3–20), Donald Murray discusses four forces that interact as the writer goes through the stages of rehearsing, drafting, and revising, moving in a recursive manner from exploration to clarification. They are the forces of collecting and connecting, writing and reading. Although writing may be ignited by any one of these forces in conjunction with any other, says Murray, once writing has begun, all of them begin to interact with each other. The writer is often unaware of this interaction, as innate curiosity leads naturally to the act of collecting information, which at some point calls for control and order that make the act of connecting necessary. Connections, in turn, make the writer see information in a new way, hence generating more collected data. The acts of writing and reading act in a similar fashion. The writer sets down what is heard mentally, then reads the product, checking it against what was heard, then rewrites it. Murray asserts that although each writing act is a complex, instantaneous interaction, the scale tips rapidly from one force to the other in response to the various needs of the writer dealing with rehearsing, drafting, or revising.

BACKGROUND

In his essay "Recent Developments in Rhetorical Invention" (*Teaching Composition: 12 Bibliographical Essays,* ed. Gary Tate [Fort Worth: Texas Christian UP, 1987], pp. 1–38), Richard Young classifies the theoretical bases for teaching invention into four main categories: classical invention, romantic invention, dramatism, and tagmemic invention. Classical invention refers to various systems based on the theories of ancient Greek and Roman rhetoricians such as Aristotle and Cicero. Romantic invention, associated with D. Gordon Rohman, tries to tap into the mysterious nonconscious and nonrational creative powers of the mind and often eschews formal methods of invention. Dramatistic invention is based on Kenneth Burke's pentad of agent, scene, act, agency, and purpose, first described in *A Grammar of Motives* (1945). Tagmemic invention is derived from Kenneth Pike's tagmemic linguistic theory, but it has its fullest realization in Richard Young, Alton Becker, and Kenneth Pike's *Rhetoric: Discovery and Change* (1950).

BASIC REQUIREMENTS FOR A THESIS STATEMENT   9

1. It states the essay's **subject**—the topic that you are discussing.
2. It reflects the essay's **purpose**—either to give your readers information or to persuade your readers to agree with you.
3. It includes a **focus**—your assertion that conveys your point of view.
4. It uses **specific language**—vague words are avoided.
5. It *may* briefly state the major subdivisions of the essay's topic.

---

one or more drafts. To start shaping your essay, however, you need a **preliminary thesis statement.** Often a preliminary thesis statement is too broad ("Natural disasters are dangerous") or too vague ("People should be prepared to face natural disasters"). Expect to revise a preliminary thesis statement as you write successive drafts of your essay, but an early version gives you direction in your writing. When you revise into a **final thesis statement,** make sure that it applies clearly to the content of your essay as it has evolved through its drafts.

Consider the final thesis statement in Dawn Seaford's essay on preparing for natural disasters. (For her three drafts, see section 3f.)

> Anyone who faces the possibility of a natural disaster can reduce its destructive, life-threatening power by being well-prepared ahead of time.

Seaford's thesis statement reveals that the *topic* is natural disasters, the *purpose* is to inform (see 1b-1), and the *focus* is the need to be well-prepared ahead of time in order to reduce a natural disaster's power. The thesis statement avoids vague language by using specific words such as "destructive, life-threatening power."

Here are more examples. These thesis statements are written for 500- to 700-word essays with an **informative purpose** (see section 1b-1). The ineffective versions resemble some types of preliminary thesis statements. The effective versions are final thesis statements written by students after they had gathered and grouped ideas. Note that the good versions contain the five Basic Requirements listed in Chart 9.

TOPIC	*classical music*
NO	Classical music combines many different sounds.
YES	Classical music can be played by groups of various sizes, ranging from chamber ensembles to full symphony orchestras.
TOPIC	*malpractice suits*
NO	There are many kinds of malpractice suits.
YES	Most people are familiar with malpractice suits against medical doctors, but an increasing number of suits are being filed against lawyers, teachers, and even parents.
TOPIC	*women artists*
NO	The paintings of women are getting more attention.
YES	During the past ten years the works of artists Mary Cassatt and Rosa Bonheur have finally gained widespread critical acclaim.

For a persuasive purpose, Daniel Casey wrote this thesis statement for his essay about the commercialization of holidays (see section 6h):

After all, commercial uses of holidays benefit the economy and lift people's spirits.

Casey's thesis statement reveals that the *topic* is commercialization of holidays, the *purpose* is to persuade, and the *focus* is the benefits of holidays' commercial uses.

Here are ineffective and effective thesis statements written for 500- to 700-word essays with a **persuasive purpose.** The ineffective versions resemble some types of preliminary thesis statements. The effective versions are final thesis statements written by students after they had gathered and grouped ideas. The material here on city living is built on one of the "possible topics" evolved in section 2c-2. Note that the good versions contain the first four Basic Requirements listed in Chart 9. Two of the good versions also include the fifth characteristic: the major subdivisions of the topic.

TOPIC	*discomforts of city living*
NO	The discomforts of living in a modern city are many.
YES	Rising crime rates, increasingly overcrowded conditions, and growing expenses make living comfortably in a modern city difficult.

TOPIC	*government loans for higher education*
NO	The federal government has inadequate loan programs for people seeking higher education.
YES	Congress should enact a law setting up an education loan account for each U.S. citizen for college or for retraining.
TOPIC	*deceptive advertising*
NO	Deceptive advertising can cause many problems for consumers.
YES	Deceptive advertising can cost consumers not only money but also their health.

The *No* examples of thesis statements shown above suffer from being too broad. They are so general that they offer no focus, and readers cannot predict the essay's thrust.

Another type of ineffective thesis statement results from an overly narrow focus. In such cases, the thesis statement is closer in scope to a topic sentence that begins a paragraph.

NO	The classical composer Béla Bartók was Hungarian.
YES	Although best-known today as a composer, Béla Bartók was also an important ethnomusicologist, who studied Hungarian folk music in his native country as well as at Columbia University in New York.
NO	Car thefts on Silver Avenue between First and Second Streets are intolerable.
YES	Neighbors have overcome language obstacles and differences in customs to combat increasing car thefts on Silver Avenue.

EXERCISE 2-8

Each of the following sets of sentences offers several versions of a thesis statement. Within each set, the thesis statements progress from weak to strong. The fourth thesis statement in each set is the best. Based on the Basic Requirements listed in Chart 9, identify the characteristics of the fourth thesis statement in each set. Then explain why the other choices in each set are weak. (The first set relates to the material in Exercise 2-4.)

A. 1. Advertising is complex.
   2. Magazine advertisements appeal to readers.
   3. Magazine advertisements must be creative.
   4. To appeal to readers, magazine advertisements must skillfully use language, color, and design.

ANSWERS: EXERCISE 2-8

A. The fourth thesis statement succeeds because it states a main idea (about magazine adverstisements' appeal to readers); it reflects a purpose (to persuade); it has a focus (that magazine advertisements must be skillfully done); and it briefly presents subdivisions (language, color, and design). The first and second thesis statements are too general, showing neither a purpose nor a focus. The third thesis statement shows a persuasive purpose but is still too general and has no focus ("must" is not explained).

B. The fourth thesis statement succeeds because it states a main idea (about playing tennis for fun and exercise); it reflects a purpose (to inform); it has a focus (what is required for playing tennis for fun and exercise); and it briefly presents subdivisions (agility, stamina, and strategy). The first statement is too general ("excellent" is a very broad term) and shows no purpose or focus. The second statement is also too vague ("fun" is a very broad term when used without a context) and shows no purpose or focus. The third statement reflects an informative purpose but lacks a focus ("various skills" is too vague).

C. The fourth statement succeeds because it states a main idea (characters in *Hamlet* seek revenge); it reflects a purpose (to inform); it has a focus (all three characters seek revenge); and it briefly states the major subdivisions (Hamlet, Fortinbras, and Laertes). The first statement is much too general, and though it suggests an informative intent, the statement lacks a focus. The second and third statements reflect an informative purpose but lack a focus ("must" and "want" are vague words here).

➔

B. 1. Tennis is excellent exercise.
2. Playing tennis is fun.
3. Tennis requires various skills.
4. Playing tennis for fun and exercise requires agility, stamina, and strategy.
C. 1. *Hamlet* is a play about revenge.
2. Hamlet must avenge his father's murder.
3. Some characters in *Hamlet* want revenge.
4. In *Hamlet*, Hamlet, Fortinbras, and Laertes all seek revenge.
D. 1. Maintaining friendships requires work.
2. To have good friends, a person must learn how to be a good friend.
3. To be a good friend, a person must value the meaning of friendship.
4. Unless a person is sensitive to others and communicates with them honestly, that person will not be able to build strong friendships.
E. 1. Many people are uninterested in politics.
2. Adults have become increasingly dissatisfied with the political process.
3. Fewer adults than ever vote in local elections.
4. Fewer college students participated in state primaries and voted in state elections this year than in either of the last two elections.

EXERCISE 2-9

Here are writing assignments, narrowed topics, and tentative thesis statements. Evaluate each thesis statement according to the Basic Requirements in Chart 9.

1. **Marketing assignment:** 700- to 800-word persuasive report on the college's cafeteria. *Audience:* the instructor and the cafeteria's manager. *Topic:* cafeteria conditions. *Thesis:* the college cafeteria could attract more students if it improved the quality of its food, its appearance, and the friendliness of its staff.
2. **Music assignment:** 300- to 500-word review of a performance. *Audience:* the instructor and other students in the class. *Topic:* the local symphony's final spring concert. *Thesis:* The ''Basically Beethoven'' program that ended the local symphony's spring season was pleasing.
3. **Chemistry assignment:** 800- to 1,000-word informative report about the ozone layer. *Audience:* the instructor and visiting students and

Cont'd.

D. The fourth statement succeeds because it states a main idea (strong friendships); it reflects a purpose (to persuade); it has a focus (what builds strong friendships); and it briefly states the major subdivisions (sensitivity and communication). The first statement uses vague language (''maintaining'' and ''work''), and it suggests neither a persuasive nor informative intent. The second statement reflects a persuasive purpose but depends on ''good'' used in a vague sense. The third statement reflects a persuasive purpose but ''value'' is too vague to provide a focus.

E. The fourth statement succeeds because it states a main idea (college students voting); it reflects a purpose (to inform); and it has a focus (how these students voted in state primaries and state elections this year compared with the last two years). The first statement relies on too much vague language (''many,'' ''people,'' ''uninterested'') and it lacks a purpose or focus. The second statement suggests an informative purpose, but it relies on vague language (''dissatisfied'' and ''political process'') and it lacks a focus. The third statement suggests an informative purpose but lacks a focus.

ANSWERS: EXERCISE 2-9

1. The thesis is good because it reflects the purpose (to persuade), states a main idea, and focuses specifically on logical subdivisions of the topic.

2. The thesis suggests that the concert review will do what such reviews should do: evaluate in an attempt to persuade a reader. The words ''was pleasing,'' however, are too vague; they need to be revised to be more specific. A brief indication of subdivisions might help the thesis communicate its message.

➡

ANSWERS: EXERCISE 2-9, *continued*

3. The thesis, though specific and focused, does not reflect a careful response to the assignment: the assignment requires an informative report, but this thesis reflects a persuasive purpose.

4. This thesis is good because it states a main idea, reflects a purpose (to inform), and includes a focus.

5. This thesis does not address the assignment adequately because it deals only with liberal arts majors (not all of the seniors) and reflects an informative rather than a persuasive purpose, as was required by the assignment.

QUOTATION ABOUT WRITING

My writing is a conscious letter to myself. It's a way for me to hold on to pieces as I grow and change and get on with my life.
—Joan Stein

TEACHING TIP

Several computer programs for invention are commercially available that incorporate Aristotle's topics; Kenneth Burke's pentad; Young, Becker, and Pike's tagmemic system; freewriting; problem-solving; and other pre-writing activities. Several of these programs are described in *The Computer in Composition Instruction: A Writer's Tool* (ed. William Wresch [NCTE, 1984]).

---

instructors attending a seminar at State College. *Topic:* recent research on the ozone layer. *Thesis:* The United States should increase efforts to slow the destruction of the ozone layer.

4. **Journalism assignment:** 200- to 300-word article about campus crime. *Audience:* the instructor, the student body, and the college administration. *Topic:* recent robberies. *Thesis:* During the fall term, campus robberies at State College equaled the number of robberies that took place in the prior five years combined.

5. **Business writing assignment:** 400- to 500-word persuasive report about the career-counseling services of State College. *Audience:* college seniors, career counselors, and the instructor. *Topic:* job placement for seniors. *Thesis:* State College's liberal arts graduates are hired mainly by business and industry.

2n Knowing how to outline

Many writers find outlining a useful planning strategy. If you are working from an outline and make changes in organization as you write, be sure to revise your outline at the end if you are expected to submit it as part of an assignment. An outline helps pull together the results of gathering and ordering ideas and preparing a thesis statement. It also provides a visual guide and checklist. Some writers always use outlines; others prefer not to. Writers who do like outlines use them at various points in the writing process: for example, before drafting, to arrange material; during drafting to keep track of evolving material; or while revising, to check the logic of an early draft's organization. Especially for academic writing, outlines can clearly reveal flaws: missing information, undesirable repetitions, digressions from the thesis. Some instructors require outlines because they want students to practice planning the arrangement and organization of a piece of writing.

An **informal outline** does not have to follow all the formal conventions of outlining. An informal outline is particularly useful for planning when the order within main ideas is still evolving or when topics imply their own arrangement, such as spatial arrangement for describing a room. An informal outline can also be considered a *working plan,* a layout of the major parts of the material intended for an essay. Here is part of an informal outline that served as a working plan for Dawn Seaford when she was writing her essay on preparing to face a natural disaster. (For Seaford's techniques of gathering ideas for writing, see 2e, 2f, and 2i; for the three drafts of her essay, see section 3f.) This excerpt includes the essay's thesis statement and the essay's fourth paragraph.

Thesis Statement: Anyone who faces the possibility of a natural disaster can reduce its destructive, life-threatening power by being well prepared ahead of time.

> *survival plans*
>> everyone gets an assignment
>> monitor the radio
>> emergency supplies
>> everyone accounted for
> what to do if separated
> conferences to review plans
> hold drills

Sample Informal Outline

A **formal outline** follows conventions concerning content and format. The conventions are designed to display material so that relationships among ideas are clear and so that the content is orderly. A formal outline can be a *topic outline* or a *sentence outline*. Each item in a topic outline is a word or phrase; each item in a sentence outline is a complete sentence. Formal outlines never mix the two.

Many writers who use formal outlines find that a sentence outline brings them closer to drafting than does a topic outline. For example, a topic outline carries less information with the item "Gathering information" than does a sentence outline with the corresponding item "Gathering information is the first step to being well-prepared."

When writing a formal outline, use the pattern shown in Chart 10. Also, as you outline, observe the following conventions:

1. **Numbers, letters, and indentations.** All parts of a formal outline are systematically indented and numbered or lettered. Capital roman numerals (I, II, III) signal major subdivisions of the topic. Indented capital letters (A, B) signal the next level of generality. Further indented arabic numbers (1, 2, 3) show the third level of generality. Indented lowercase letters (a, b) show the fourth level, if there is one. The principle here is that within each major subdivision, each succeeding level of the outline shows more specific detail than the one before it. If an outline entry is longer than one line, the second line is indented as far as the first word of the preceding line.

BACKGROUND

A demonstration of the effectiveness of using process pedagogy, as opposed to more traditional methods of instruction, is provided by Mary J. Meiser in "A Cognitive-Process Approach to College Composition: A Comparative Study of Unskilled Writers" (*Dissertation Abstracts International* 45 [January 1985]: 2018A). In this study she describes the progress made by two basic writing classes, one of them concentrating on grammar and specific writing strategies, the other on process instruction. The latter made more significant gains in all areas of evaluation.

TEACHING TIP

You may want to ask your students to test their thesis statements by exchanging them with one another. By asking the readers to answer questions about the thesis statements, the writers may discover weaknesses (and strengths) that were not apparent to them. Some questions they can ask are the following:

1. Is the main idea, the central point, clearly stated?

2. Is the purpose of the essay clear?

3. What is the purpose: to inform or persuade?

4. What is the focus of the essay?

5. Does the thesis statement identify the major subdivisions of the essay's topic?

6. Does it make the topic seem interesting?

7. Can this thesis be developed in the time available?

8. Can this thesis be developed in an essay of the length planned?

9. Is the thesis limited enough for development, but general enough to be worth the effort?

10. Is the thesis stated in specific terms? Does it avoid overly general, vague ones?

BACKGROUND

Defining themselves and assuming the roles of a college writer are often difficult challenges for students, according to David Bartholomae in "Inventing the University" (*Perspective on Literacy*, ed. Eugene R. Kintgen, Barry M. Kroll, and Mike Rose [Carbondale, IL: Southern Illinois UP, 1988]). Bartholomae believes that "all writers, in order to write, must imagine for themselves the privilege of being 'insiders'—that is, of being both inside an established and powerful discourse, and of being granted a special right to speak" (277). But students are seldom able to write as insiders or authorities, for they lack knowledge not only of the subject matter, but also of the vocabulary, audience, and genres of college writing. Students, then, "have to assume privilege without having any" (278). This problem is compounded by the fact that many high school and college assignments—exams, reports, and summaries—ask students to write "outside the working discourse of the academic community, where they are expected to admire and report on what we do, rather than inside that discourse, where they can do its work and participate in a common enterprise" (278).

TEACHING TIPS

Writers use outlines in a variety of ways. They turn to them, for example, at different stages of the composing process. Whereas some find it productive to move from mapping or freewriting directly into a listing of ideas in a particular order, using the outline to plan the drafting process, others use outlines to check the organization of a draft after it is written, testing to see if the paper has order and balance. Some writers find topic outlines helpful; some prefer a sentence outline. Each writer has to find the shaping strategies that prove to be most effective in his or her case.

PATTERN FOR FORMAL OUTLINE OF AN ESSAY   10

Thesis Statement:. . . . .

I. First main idea. . . . .

   A. First subdivision of the main idea. . . . .

      1. First reason or example. . . . .

      2. Second reason or example. . . . .

         a. First supporting detail. . . . .

         b. Second supporting detail. . . . .

   B. Second subdivision of the main idea. . . . .

II. Second main idea. . . . .

---

2. **More than one entry at each level.** At all points on an outline, there is no I without a II, no A without a B, and so on. Unless a category has at least two parts, it cannot be divided. If a category has only one subdivision, you need to either eliminate that subdivision or expand the material to at least two subdivisions.

NO   A. At home, an assignment for each person
           1. Monitoring the radio for updates
        B. If separated, where to meet after the crisis ends

YES   A. At home, responsibility for each person
        B. If separated, where to meet after the crisis ends

YES   A. At home, an assignment for each person
           1. Monitoring the radio for updates
           2. Taking charge of emergency supplies
        B. If separated, where to meet after the crisis ends

plan **2n**

3. **Levels of generality.** All subdivisions are at the same level of generality. A main idea cannot be paired with a supporting detail.

NO
A. At home, an assignment for each person
B. Monitoring the radio for updates
C. Taking charge of emergency supplies
D. If separated, where to meet after the crisis ends

YES
A. At home, an assignment for each person
B. If separated, where to meet after the crisis ends

4. **Overlap.** Headings do not overlap. What is covered in subdivision 1, for example, must be quite distinct from what is covered in subdivision 2.

NO
A. At home, an assignment for each person
   1. Monitoring the radio for updates
   2. Listening for radio reports on the crisis

YES
A. At home, an assignment for each person
   1. Monitoring the radio for updates
   2. Taking charge of emergency supplies

5. **Parallelism.** All entries within a level are parallel. For example, all might start with the *-ing* forms of verbs°*. (For more about parallelism in outlines, see 18h).

NO
A. Monitoring the radio for updates
B. Take charge of emergency supplies

YES
A. Monitoring the radio for updates
B. Taking charge of emergency supplies

YES
A. Monitor the radio for updates
B. Take charge of emergency supplies

6. **Capitalization and punctuation.** Except for proper nouns°, only the first word of each entry is capitalized. In a sentence outline, end each sentence with a period. Do not punctuate the ends of entries in a topic outline.

7. **Introductory and concluding paragraphs.** The content of the introductory and concluding paragraphs is not part of a formal outline. The thesis statement comes before (above) the roman numeral I entry.

---

*Throughout this book, a degree mark (°) indicates that you can find the definition of the word in the Glossary of Terms in this handbook.

TEACHING TIP

The notion of *focus* in a thesis statement might be new to some students. A useful analogy can be that the topic is the subject but the focus is the predicate. Without predication, sentences make no assertion. As Josephine Miles said in her important monograph "Working Out Ideas: Predication and Other Uses of Language": "Sentence making is predication, and to predicate is to assert an idea, selecting and treating facts from a point of view." Predication says something about, asserts something about, answers a question about, takes a position about the topic. It may, for example, define the topic, describe it, evaluate it, compare it to something, explain its purpose, or identify its causes. The topic of this section of *The S & S Handbook for Writers* is "a thesis statement." The predicate of the opening sentence of the section makes an assertion about "a thesis statement" by defining what one is—it "is the central message of an essay." A different predicate—for example, that a thesis statement "helps the writer focus the essay"—would change the focus, purpose, and direction of this section.

QUOTATION ABOUT WRITING

Prose is architecture, not interior decoration.
—Ernest Hemingway

ALTERNATE EXERCISE

Write thesis statements for persuasive papers on the following topics, making sure that they have the five characteristics of a good thesis statement listed in the Basic Requirements chart.
1. Topic: rock music
2. Topic: athletic scholarships
3. Topic: ethnic foods
4. Topic: a holiday ritual
5. Topic: mothers and daughters

TEACHING TIP

Students can practice making outlines by dealing with published essays. They will sometimes discover that an essay lacks a clearly defined order, or, on the other hand, they may find ideas in the work that they missed before dividing it into its major headings and subheadings. You should prepare students for this exercise by composing an outline of one or two short essays with the class, perhaps including one essay without a well-defined organization. You may find it helpful to use an overhead projector for displaying the essay or writing the outline. Students can then prepare a topic outline or a sentence outline on a different essay. You might ask them to compare their outlines to see if they each found the same emphases and order of development.

BACKGROUND

For those teachers who encounter difficulty in following the various invention theories proposed by Kenneth Burke and Ken Macrorie, as well as by Richard Young, Alton Becker, and Kenneth Pike, help is available in Peggy Parris's "Helping Snoopy through the Dark and Stormy Night: Heuristics for Creative Writing" (*Iowa English Bulletin* 33 [1984]: 26–30). She discusses how Burke's pentad, Young, Becker, and Pike's tagmemic matrix, and Macrorie's freewriting can be used to teach creative writing.

TEACHING TIP

If your students have trouble organizing an outline, you might suggest that they write each item on a 3 × 5 index card. The ability to move the cards around, make piles, and easily eliminate items often facilitates students' work.

BUILDING A FORMAL OUTLINE

11

1. Numbers, letters, and indentations signal groupings and levels of importance.
2. Each level has more than one entry.
3. All subdivisions are at the same level of generality.
4. Headings do not overlap.
5. Entries are grammatically parallel (see Chapter 18).
6. Only the first word of each entry is capitalized. (All proper nouns are also capitalized, of course.)
7. Periods end each sentence in a *sentence outline* but not the items in a *topic outline.*
8. The introductory and concluding paragraphs are omitted, but the thesis statement is usually given above the outline itself (see examples at end of this chapter).

Here is a topic outline of the final draft of Dawn Seaford's essay on natural disasters (shown in 3f). A sentence outline starts on the opposite page so that you can compare the two types of outlines.

TOPIC OUTLINE

Thesis Statement: Anyone who faces the possibility of a natural disaster can reduce its destructive, life-threatening power by being well prepared ahead of time.

I. Natural disasters occuring in the United States
  A. Earthquakes on the West Coast
  B. Tornadoes in the Southern and Midwestern states
  C. Hurricanes at the Gulf of Mexico and on the Atlantic Coast

II. Gathering information
  A. Learning which natural disaster
  B. Minimizing exposure
    1. The basement during a tornado
    2. Outside or inside during an earthquake
      a. Outside to a wide open area
      b. Inside under a strong desk or table
    3. In from the coast during a hurricane

C. Memorizing which radio and TV stations for information
D. Locating hospitals and public shelters
III. Developing and rehearsing survival plans
    A. At home, an assignment for each person
        1. Monitoring the radio for updates
        2. Taking charge of emergency supplies
        3. Accounting for everyone
    B. If separated, where to meet after the crisis ends
    C. For entire household, review conferences and drills
IV. Acquiring and storing survival supplies
    A. Fire extinguisher
    B. First aid kit and medicines
    C. Water and food
    D. Portable radio, light sources, and extra batteries
    E. Books, family games, and jigsaw puzzles

SENTENCE OUTLINE

Thesis Statement: Anyone who faces the possibility of a natural disaster can reduce its destructive, life-threatening power by being well prepared ahead of time.

I. Natural disasters occur in specific areas of the United States.
    A. Earthquakes hit the West Coast.
    B. Tornadoes sweep across the Southern and Midwestern states.
    C. Hurricanes strike at the Gulf of Mexico and on the Atlantic Coast
II. Gathering information is the first step to being well-prepared.
    A. People should learn what natural disaster might strike.
    B. People should minimize exposure to danger.
        1. During a tornado, a basement can be safe.
        2. During an earthquake, outside or inside can be safe.
            a. If outside, get to a wide open area.
            b. If inside, get under a strong desk or table.

BACKGROUND

In the chapter on "Shaping Discourse" in *A Rhetoric for Writing Teachers*, 2nd ed. (New York: Oxford UP, 1987, pp. 158–170), Erika Lindemann warns teachers and students against making inflexible writing plans that cause them to force ideas into a prescribed form. In particular, she points out that slavishly following an outline can limit a writer's options. It can, for example, prevent a writer from discovering the material's organic unity or from making choices that might improve the piece. Rigid adherence to an outline, says Lindemann, can create an inadequate and incomplete understanding of the paper, since an outline may offer little help in determining proportions or deciding on rhetorical strategies. In addition, it may also divert a writer from considering audience and purpose.

TEACHING TIP

John B. Lord describes an exercise that he has used to teach the outline and thesis statement in "The Taxonomy of Subject Matter: An Introduction to Outlining" (*Writing Exercises from Exercise Exchange*, ed. Littleton Long [NCTE, 1976]). To prepare a paper on a subject such as "The Causes of Automobile Accidents," the class brainstorms for ideas, and each idea is written on the board as it is suggested. When the class runs out of ideas, Lord asks the students to look for duplications and overlappings on the list. After that Lord guides the class into organizing the ideas into major divisions and then into subdivisions, creating an outline. The final step of the exercise is to compose a thesis statement for the outlined paper.

You may want to take Lord's exercise further and have the class write a draft of the paper together, perhaps dividing students into groups, with each group responsible for writing a section of the paper. The class can then hear and discuss each group's section and suggest revisions.

BACKGROUND

If you are interested in reading more about the writing process, in addition to the scholarship already mentioned in this chapter, you might like to look at "A Description of the Composing Processes of College Freshman Writers" by Sharon Pianko (*Research in the Teaching of English* 13 [February 1979]: 5–22). Also interesting is "The Composing Processes of Unskilled College Writers" by Sondra Perl (*Research in the Teaching of English* 13 [December 1979]: 317–336).

TEACHING TIP

Computers are increasingly helpful in organizing material and preparing outlines. Several software programs are commercially available for use in creating short outlines that can be expanded into more complex ones. They encourage experimentation with ideas and arrangements because they are flexible. Outlines can be quickly and easily expanded by the addition of subheadings or tightened by the removal of subheadings from the screen, though the writer can keep them available for possible inclusion.

3. During a hurricane, areas in from the coast can be safe.
C. People should memorize which radio and TV stations give reliable, complete information.
D. People should know the locations of hospitals and public shelters and how to get to them.

III. Developing and rehearsing survival plans comes next.
   A. At home, each person can have an assignment.
      1. One person monitors the radio for updates.
      2. Another person takes charge of emergency supplies.
      3. Another person checks that everyone is accounted for.
   B. If separated, everyone knows where to meet after the crisis ends.
   C. Entire household holds review conferences and drills.

IV. Then, acquiring and storing survival supplies is important.
   A. A fire extinguisher must be close at hand.
   B. A first aid kit and medicines must be up-to-date.
   C. Water and food supplies for a few days are essential.
   D. A portable radio and light sources, along with many extra batteries, are indispensible.
   E. Books, family games, and jigsaw puzzles can be helpful.

EXERCISE 2-10

Here is a sentence outline. Consulting section 2n, revise it into a topic outline. Then decide which form you would prefer as a guide to writing, and explain your decision.

Thesis Statement: Common noise pollution, although it causes many problems in our society, can be reduced.

I. Noise pollution comes from many sources.
   A. Noise pollution occurs in many large cities.
      1. Traffic rumbles and screeches.
      2. Construction work blasts.
      3. Airplanes roar overhead.
   B. Noise pollution occurs in the workplace.
      1. Machines in factories boom.

2. Machines used for outdoor construction thunder.
C. Noise pollution occurs during leisure-time activities.
   1. Stereo headphones blare directly into eardrums.
   2. Film soundtracks bombard the ears.
   3. Music in discos assaults the ears.
II. Noise pollution causes many problems.
   A. Excessive noise damages hearing.
   B. Excessive noise alters moods.
   C. Constant exposure to noise limits learning ability.
III. Reduction in noise pollution is possible.
   A. Pressure from community groups can support efforts to control excessive noise.
   B. Traffic regulations can help alleviate congestion and noise.
   C. Pressure from workers can force management to reduce noise.
   D. People can wear earplugs to avoid excessive noise.
   E. Reasonable sound levels for headphones, soundtracks, and discos can be required.

ANSWER: EXERCISE 2-10
Answer may vary from the following:
I. Sources of noise pollution
   A. Large cities
      1. Traffic
      2. Construction work
      3. Airplanes
   B. Workplace
      1. Factory machines
      2. Outdoor construction machines
   C. Leisure-time activities
      1. Stereo headphones
      2. Film soundtracks
      3. Disco music
II. Problems from noise pollution
   A. Damages hearing
   B. Alters moods
   C. Limits learning ability
III. How to reduce noise pollution
   A. Pressure from community groups
   B. Traffic regulations
   C. Pressure on management by workers
   D. Earplugs
   E. Reasonable sound levels

QUOTATION ABOUT WRITING
In any work that is truly creative, I believe, the writer cannot be omniscient in advance about the effects that he [or she] proposes to produce. The suspense of a novel is not only in the reader, but in the novelist, who is intensely curious about what will happen to the hero.

—Mary McCarthy

3 Drafting and Revising

In the writing process, drafting and revising follow from planning and shaping, discussed in Chapter 2. **Drafting** means getting ideas onto paper in sentences and paragraphs. In everyday conversation, people usually use the word *writing* when they talk about the activities involved in drafting. In discussing the writing process, however, the word *drafting* is more descriptive. It conveys the idea that the final product of the writing process is the result of a number of versions, each successively closer to what the writer intends and to what will communicate clearly to readers. **Revising** means taking a draft from its preliminary to its final version by evaluating, adding, cutting, moving material, editing, and proofreading.

3a Getting started

If ever you have trouble getting started when the time arrives for drafting (or any other part of the writing process), you are not alone. When experienced writers get stalled, they recognize what is happening and deal with it. If you run into a writing block, it may be the result of one of these common myths about writing.

MYTH	Writers are born, not made.
TRUTH	Everyone can write. Writers do not expect to ''get it right'' the first time. Being a good writer means being a patient rewriter.
MYTH	Writers have to be ''in the mood'' to write.
TRUTH	If writers always waited for ''the mood'' to descend, few would write at all. After all, news reporters and other professional writers often have to meet deadlines.
MYTH	Writers have to know how to spell every word and to recite the rules of grammar perfectly.

TRUTH	Writers do not let spelling and grammar block them. They write and then check themselves. A good speller is someone who does not ignore the quiet inner voice that urges checking a dictionary. Similarly, writers use a handbook to check grammar rules.
MYTH	Writers do not have to revise.
TRUTH	Writers expect to revise. Once words are on paper, writers can see what readers see. This "re-vision" helps writers revise so that their writing delivers its intended message.
MYTH	Writing can be done at the last minute.
TRUTH	Drafting and revising take time. Ideas do not leap onto paper in final, polished form.

Once you realize the truths behind myths about writing, you can try the time-proven ways that experienced writers get started when they are blocked. To make these suggestions work, suspend judgment; do not criticize yourself when trying to get underway. The time for evaluation comes during revision, but revising too soon can stall some writers. While the writing that results from these ideas is most certainly not a final draft, having something on paper to work with is a comfort—and can serve as a springboard to drafting.

1. **Avoid staring at a blank page.** Fill up the paper. Relax and allow your hand to move across the page or keyboard. Write words, scribble, or draw while you think about your topic. The movement of filling the paper while thinking can help stimulate your mind to turn to actual drafting.

2. **Use "focused freewriting"** (see 2f). Think about your topic, and write sentences about it nonstop for ten minutes or until you fill a few pages. Some of the sentences you write can help you begin actual drafting.

3. **Visualize yourself writing.** Many professional writers say that they write more easily if they first picture themselves doing it. Before you get up in the morning, when you are waiting for a bus, or as you are walking to classes, summon a full visual image of yourself writing. Imagine yourself in the place where you usually write, with the materials you need, busy at work.

4. **Picture an image or scene, or imagine a sound or taste, that relates to your topic.** For example, to report on a concert, recall the sound of your favorite part. Describe what you see or hear.

5. **Write about your topic in a letter to a friend.** This gives you a chance to relax and chat on paper to someone you like and feel comfortable with. The letter can lead to a less informal draft.

TEACHING TIP

Students may be skeptical of the value of picturing themselves working. Share with them these examples of successful people who use visualization: John Ueless, a champion pole-vaulter, used visualization before each meet. He would see himself winning by clearing the bar at a particular height. In his mind, he rehearsed every movement, as well as seeing the crowd and even smelling the grass when pole-vaulting out of doors.

Jack Nicklaus says that visualization gives him a "winning feeling": "This gives me a line to the cup just as clearly as if it's been tattooed on my brain. With that feeling, all I have to do is swing the club and let nature take its course."

You might want to give students time to visualize in class prior to writing. Tell them to close their eyes and sit comfortably. Tell them to imagine themselves reading a question and realizing they know how they want to respond. Tell them to imagine themselves making a list of notes, rearranging their material, or writing. At each stage, remind them to imagine themselves feeling confident and successful. Then have them write. Later, discuss how they felt when writing this time in contrast to their past experiences. This technique often does little for people at first, so try to give your students frequent opportunities to employ visualization techniques.

QUOTATION ABOUT WRITING

There is always a point in the writing of a piece when I sit in a room literally papered with false starts and cannot put one word after another and imagine that I have suffered a small stroke, leaving me apparently undamaged but actually aphasic.

—Joan Didion

BACKGROUND

In an article published in *U.S. News & World Report* (November 9, 1987, p. 106), Erica E. Goode cites tips for people who tend to procrastinate. They include the following helpful suggestions.

1. Break your work into small, clearly defined steps. Instead of vowing vaguely to "catch up on paperwork," resolve to spend one hour sorting out the papers on your desk.

2. Reward yourself for progress toward your goal. Ice cream is nice, as is a walk in the park.

3. The hardest step to take is the first, so pick something easy. A task that can be polished off in fifteen minutes is a good one for a starter.

4. Set a series of small but realistic deadlines rather than a final date.

5. Enlist support. Other people may be able to tell you if you're setting up expectations that are impossible to meet.

TEACHING TIP

Your students may find it helpful to keep a writing log. At the top of each piece of writing they can note where, when, and how they are working. The more detailed the notations, the more they will help students to draw conclusions about the manner in which their best writing takes place. After making a number of such notations, the students can write a paragraph evaluating the approaches used, trying to assess their effectiveness.

QUOTATION ABOUT WRITING

Let your literary compositions be kept from the public eye for nine years at least.

—Horace

6. Write your material as if you are someone else. Take your pick: you can be a friend writing to you, an instructor writing to you or a whole class, your parent writing to you, a person in history writing to you or to someone else. Once you take on a role, you might feel less inhibited about writing.

7. Switch your method of writing. If you usually typewrite or use a word processor, try writing by hand. If you usually use a pen, switch to a pencil. Whenever you write by hand, especially when you are having trouble getting started, try to treat yourself to good quality paper. The pleasure of writing on smooth, strong paper helps many experienced writers want to keep going.

8. Start in the middle. If you do not know what you want to write in your introductory paragraph, start with a body paragraph. Write from the center of your essay out, instead of from beginning to end.

As you use these springboards to drafting, seek out places and times of the day that encourage you to write. You might write best in a quiet corner of the library; at 4:30 a.m. at the kitchen table before anyone else is awake; or outside when people are walking by. Most experienced writers find that they concentrate best when they are alone, working without the risk of interruption. But occasionally background noise—in a crowded cafeteria, for example—might be comforting. Be sure, however, not to mislead yourself: you will not write well or efficiently while you are talking to other people, stopping now and then to jot down a sentence or two. Also, do not mistake delaying tactics for preparation: You do need pencil and paper (or their equivalent) to write, but you do not need fifteen perfectly sharpened pencils sitting in a neat row.

3b Knowing how to draft

Once you have your ideas planned and shaped for an essay, you are ready to **compose** them on paper. When you compose, you put together sentences and paragraphs into a unified whole. A *first draft* is a preliminary draft. Its purpose is to get your ideas onto paper, not to refine grammar and style (they come later, during revising). First drafts are not meant to be perfect; they are meant to give you something to revise. According to your personal preferences and each writing situation, you can use any of these ways (or your own ways) of writing a first draft.

1. **Put aside all your notes from planning and shaping.** Write a "discovery draft." As you write, be open to discovering ideas and making connections that spring to mind during the physical act of writing. When you finish a discovery draft, you can decide to use it either as a first draft or as part of your notes when you write a structured first draft.
2. **Keep your notes from planning and shaping in front of you and use them as you write.** Arrange your notes in a preliminary sequence, and write a structured first draft. Work through all of your material. Depending on the expected length of your essay, draft either the entire essay or blocks of one or two paragraphs at one time.
3. **Use a combination of approaches.** When you know the shape of your material, write according to that structure. When you feel "stuck" about what to say next, switch to writing as you would for a discovery draft.

The direction of drafting is forward: *keep pressing ahead.* If you are worried about the spelling of a word or a point in grammar, underline the material so that you can come back later and check it—and keep moving ahead. If you cannot think of a word that says precisely what you want, write an easy synonym and circle it so that you will remember to change it later—and move on. If you are worried about your sentence style or the order in which you present the supporting details within a paragraph, write *Style?* or *Order?* in the margin so that you can return to that spot later to revise—and press forward. If you feel that you are running dry, reread what you have written—but only to propel yourself to further writing, not to distract you into rewriting.

As you draft, use the essay's thesis statement as your springboard. A thesis statement has great organizing power. It expresses the central theme that controls and limits what the essay will cover (see 2m, including Chart 9).

As you use your thesis statement, remember that its role is to serve as a connecting thread that unifies the essay. **Unity** is important for communicating clearly to an audience. You achieve unity when all parts of the essay relate to the thesis statement and to each other. An essay is unified when it meets two criteria: (1) the thesis statement clearly ties into all topic sentences: see 4b; and (2) the support for each topic sentence—the paragraph development—contains examples, reasons, facts, and details directly related to the topic and, in turn, to the thesis statement: see 4c.

Equally important, your essay must be **coherent** to communicate clearly to an audience. An essay is coherent when it supplies guideposts that communicate the relations among ideas. Coherence

QUOTATION ABOUT WRITING

After making a start, children sometimes decide that it won't do and begin again. The strength of their conviction that a new start must be made, even though the teacher may have no complaints about what has been written, is sometimes remarkable. They are not easily persuaded to reconsider a decision to reject what they have done. Some seem to make a habit of rejecting their beginning, and rarely complete anything. These may be timid children for whom committing themselves to paper at all—"finding a tone to talk with" and "being oneself in talking"—imposes a severe strain.

—James Britton,
The Development of Writing Abilities

BACKGROUND

Janet Emig suggests that the reason many experienced writers prefer to write in longhand is that it gives them more time to think. The slower pace of handwriting, as opposed to the typewriter (or word processor), allows ideas to develop and surface ("Hand, Eye, Brain: Some 'Basics' in the Writing Process," *Research on Composing: Points of Departure*, ed. Charles Cooper and Lee Odell [Urbana: NCTE, 1978]; 61).

BACKGROUND

To gather examples of student writing for the *S & S Handbook*, Prentice Hall sponsored a project that enlisted the help of faculty across the United States. Dubbed the "Student Writing Project," this search resulted in my being able to draw on a bank of student essays (all in three drafts) and student paragraphs. The names of the participating faculty appear in the handbook's "Preface to the Instructor."

BACKGROUND

In "Revision Strategies of Student Writers and Experienced Writers" (*CCC* 31 [December 1980]; 46–49) Nancy Sommers makes distinctions between revising and editing. The former, she points out, encompasses the entire composition and often takes several times to complete; the latter, which has the purpose of polishing the text, deals with grammatical and usage problems. During the process of revision, the writer not only focuses on stylistic concerns, but also continues to mold the text to its purpose and audience. Sommers points out that student writers, in contrast to experienced writers, are more likely to edit than to revise. They approach revising primarily as a matter of rewording: eliminating repetition, finding synonyms, deleting words. Less frequently do they deal with rearrangement or addition of material. Experienced writers, on the other hand, continue to search for the shape of their discussion as they revise, making changes primarily in sentences, by addition and deletion. Sommers suggests the appropriate uses of revision in a question she raised a year earlier in "The Need for Theory in Composition Research" (*CCC* 30 [February 1979]; 48). She asks: "Instead of thinking of revision as an activity at the end of the process, what if we thought of revision as a process of making a work congruent with what a writer intends—a process that occurs throughout the writing of a work?"

QUOTATION ABOUT WRITING

To write is to write is to write is to write is to write is to write is to write.

—Gertrude Stein

QUOTATION ABOUT WRITING

I can't write five words but that I change seven.

—Dorothy Parker

is achieved through the use of transitional expressions, pronouns, repetition, and parallel structures. These techniques operate within paragraphs and to connect paragraphs (see 4d).

When you write, plan your practical arrangements. For example, try to work in a place where you are comfortable and will not be disturbed. If someone comes along and interrupts, you might lose a train of thought or an idea that has flashed into your mind. Also, keep enough paper at hand so that you use only one side of each sheet of paper. Later you will need to spread your full draft in front of you so that you can physically see how the parts relate to one another. As you write, leave large margins and plenty of room between lines so that you have space to enter changes later on.

To give you examples of the writing process used by college students, this chapter discusses the drafting and revising of two students—Dawn Seaford and Daniel Casey, each of whom wrote in response to the assignments shown on page 19. You can see three complete drafts of Seaford's essay in this chapter (section 3f). Also, you can see the final draft of Daniel Casey's essay in section 6h. For examples of Seaford's and Casey's uses of the techniques of planning and shaping before they began drafting, see sections 2b through 2n.

3c   Knowing how to revise

To **revise** you must evaluate. You assess your first (or subsequent) draft and decide where improvements are needed. Then you make the improvements and evaluate each on its own as well as in the context of the surrounding material. The revision process continues until you are satisfied that the essay is the best that you can make it in the time available. Keep in mind that academic writing, especially through the vehicle of revision, is an engaging intellectual endeavor that encourages students to stretch to the maximum.

To revise successfully you need first to *expect to revise*. Some people think that anyone who revises is not a good writer. Only the opposite is true. Writing is largely revising. Experienced writers know that the final draft of any writing project shows on paper only a fraction of the decisions made from draft to successive draft. Revision means "to see again," to look with fresh eyes. Good writers can truly *see* their drafts and rework them so that they evolve and improve.

To revise successfully you need also to distance yourself from each draft. You need to read your writing with objective eyes. A natural reaction of many writers is to want to hold onto their every word, especially if they had trouble getting started with a draft. If you ever have such feelings, resist them and work on distancing yourself from the material. Before revising, give yourself some time for that rosy glow of authorial pride to dim a bit. The classical writer Horace recommended waiting nine years. Given the hectic pace of modern life, you do not have that much time. But do try to wait a few hours before going back to look anew at your work.

If an objective perspective still eludes you, try reading your draft aloud; hearing the material can give you a fresh new sense of content and organization. Another useful method is to read the paragraphs in reverse order, starting with the conclusion; eventually, of course, you must read your essay from beginning to end, but to achieve distance you can temporarily depart from that sequence.

1 Knowing the steps and activities of revision

Once you understand the attitudes that underlie the revision process, you are ready to move into actual revising.

To revise, you work to improve your draft at all levels: whole essay, paragraph, sentence, and word. A revised draft usually looks quite different from its preceding draft. To revise effectively you likely need to engage in all the activities in Chart 12 and Chart 13.

As you engage in each activity, keep in mind the whole picture. Changes affect more than the place revised. Check that your separate changes operate well in the context of the whole essay or a particular paragraph. As with drafting (see 3b), getting distance from your material allows you the chance to be more objective.

Revising is usually separate from editing (see 3d). Editing involves concentrating on important surface features such as correct spelling and punctuation. During revising, you pay attention to the meaning that you want your material to deliver effectively.

2 Using the organizing power of your thesis statement and essay title during revision

As you revise, pay special attention to your essay's thesis statement and title. Both features can help you stay on the track. Also, they orient your reader to what to expect, which helps you communicate your message as clearly as possible.

If your **thesis statement** (see 2m, especially Chart 9) does not match what you say in your essay, you need to revise either the thesis statement or the essay—and sometimes both. A thesis statement, must present the topic of the essay, the writer's particular focus on that topic, and the writer's purpose for writing the essay. The first draft of a thesis statement is often merely an estimate of what will be covered in the essay. Early in the revision process, check the accuracy of your estimate. Then use the thesis statement's controlling power to bring it and your essay in line with each other.

12

STEPS FOR REVISING

1. Shift mentally from suspending judgment (during idea gathering and drafting) to making judgments.
2. Read your draft critically to evaluate it. Be guided by the questions on the Revision Checklist in this chapter or by material supplied by your instructor.
3. Decide whether to write an entirely new draft or to revise the one you have. Do not be overly harsh. While some early drafts serve best as "discovery drafts" rather than first drafts, many early drafts provide sufficient raw material for the revision process to get underway.
4. Be systematic. Do not evaluate at random. You need to pay attention to many different elements of a draft, from overall organization to choice of words. Some writers prefer to consider all elements concurrently, but most writers work better when they concentrate on different elements sequentially during separate rounds of revision.

13

MAJOR ACTIVITIES DURING REVISION

- **Add.** Insert needed words, sentences, and paragraphs. If your additions require new content, return to idea-gathering techniques (see 2d through 2k).
- **Cut.** Get rid of whatever goes off the topic or repeats what has already been said.
- **Replace.** As needed, substitute new words, sentences, and paragraphs for what you have cut.
- **Move material around.** Change the sequence of paragraphs if the material is not presented in logical order (see 2e-2). Move sentences within paragraphs or to other paragraphs if any paragraph arrangement seems illogical (see 4c).

TEACHING TIP

You might want to emphasize to your students that the change in attitude is fairly sharp when writers switch from generating prose to revising it. Making students aware of this fact often helps them understand and feel comfortable with the notion of writing as a process.

BACKGROUND

Diana Hacker and Betty Renshaw (*Writing with a Voice* [Boston: Little, Brown, 1985], p. 26) have compiled a list of reasons students are reluctant to revise their writing. They include the following:

1. I wait until the last minute, so there's no time to rewrite.

2. My first draft is the best I can do. I can't improve it.

3. I don't know whether my first draft is any good or not, so how can I improve it?

4. I don't know where to begin, and I wouldn't know when to stop.

5. Well, frankly, I'm lazy.

6. When I tinker with my sentences, they just turn out worse.

7. I don't really care about what I'm writing, so I just want to get it over with.

8. Rewriting is too messy. I like to work with clean-looking pages.

9. I'm such a bad writer I hate to read my own writing.

10. Rewriting is my instructor's responsibility.

11. Rewriting is painful. I can't stand the agony.

12. If I can't get it right the first time, I must be stupid.

QUOTATION ABOUT WRITING

I do a lot of revising. Certain chapters six or seven times. Occasionally you can hit it right the first time. More often, you don't.

—John Dos Passos

Each writer's experience with revising a thesis statement varies from essay to essay. Dawn Seaford wrote a number of versions of her thesis statement before she started drafting. After writing her first draft, Seaford checked the thesis statement and satisfied herself that it communicated what she wanted to say. But she decided to change parts of her essay to conform more closely to her thesis statement. (For an example of a thesis statement being revised for a research paper, from the first through the final draft, see 32p).

The **title** of an essay also plays an important organizing role during revision. An effective title can set you on your course and tell your reader what to expect. (Some writers like to start a first draft with a title at the top of the page to focus their thinking.) As they revise drafts, they revise the title as needed. An effective title might not come to mind until you have drafted, revised, and edited your essay, by which time your thinking about your topic has crystallized.

Titles can be *direct* or *indirect*. A *direct title* tells exactly what the essay will be about. A direct title contains key words under which the essay would be cataloged in a library or other database system. The title of Dawn Seaford's essay shown in 3f is direct: "Being Prepared for Natural Disasters." Similarly, the title of Daniel Casey's essay in section 6h is direct: "Commercialism at Holiday Time Benefits the Nation." Each title is specific and prepares the reader for the topic of the essay.

A *direct title* should not be too broad. An overly broad title implies that the writer has not thought through the essay's content. An unsatisfactory title for Seaford's essay would be "Natural Disasters." Conversely, a direct title should not be too narrow. Equally unsatisfactory would be a title that is overly long—for example, by listing the topics of most of the essay's body paragraphs: "Being Prepared with Knowledge, Preplanning, and Survival Supplies for Natural Disasters."

An *indirect title* is also acceptable in some situations, according to the writer's taste and instructor's requirements. An indirect title hints at the essay's topic. It presents a puzzle that can be solved by reading the essay. This approach can be intriguing for the reader, but the writer has to make sure that the title is not too obscure. For example, for Dawn Seaford's essay a satisfactory indirect title would be "Danger Defused," but an unsatisfactory, overly indirect title would be "The Test."

Whether direct or indirect, a title stands alone. For example, Dawn Seaford (whose essay's good title is "Being Prepared for Natural Disasters") would have been wrong had she written as her essay's first sentence: "Such preparation is very important" or "Everyone should do this." Chart 14 gives guidelines for titles.

3   Using revision checklists

Revision checklists can help you focus your attention as you evaluate your writing to revise it. Either use a checklist provided by

BACKGROUND

In "Disabling Fictions: Institutionalized Delimitations of Revision," Jeffrey G. Carroll describes revision as "layered and organic." He argues that it needs "less naming of parts and more dialogue between and among the forces that stimulate, affect, and require writing" (*Rhetoric Review* 8 [Fall 1989]: 62–72).

TEACHING TIP

To help students become aware of the importance of titles, you can ask them to experiment with devising alternative titles, both direct and indirect ones, for each other's essays or for short essays that they find in magazines. Before doing so, they should be able to state the thesis of the piece they intend to retitle. They can then explain their rationale for the new titles in a short informative paragraph.

QUOTATION ABOUT WRITING

A title is the writer's stamp of approval of her or his work.

—Sue V. Lape

QUOTATION ABOUT WRITING

You'll find a title and it'll have a certain excitement for you; it will evoke the book, it will push you along. Eventually, you will use it up and you will have to choose another title. When you find the one that doesn't get used up, that's the title you go with.

—E. L. Doctorow

PROCESS/PRODUCT DEBATE

Writers are judged in the outside world by their products, not their processes. Teaching students to view writing as process is extremely useful as an instructional technique and as a guide to what real writers do. But telling students that product does not matter is to mislead them about what they will face in other courses and in the workplace.

The call for balance has been made particularly well by one of the editors of the journal *Research in the Teaching of English* in the "Musings" column in May 1984, excerpted here.

> Yet that separation has been replaced by another that is likely to be equally unproductive. In the enthusiasm provoked by a focus on process, we have sometimes lost sight of the enterprise in which the process is engaged. Though our best philosophers have always warned us against false dualisms, our best research has often defined itself in reaction to the limitations of previous work. Thus the initial enthusiasm for the study of process was conditioned by a rejection of the earlier preoccupation with product. The research that has followed has been extraordinarily productive, extending both our theoretical understanding and our practical approaches. Yet one characteristic of any new idea is that, in the course of exploring its implications most fully, we learn not only its strengths but also its limitations. The strengths of the process studies of the last decade have been many, and the weaknesses minor relative to the insights we have gained. But as happens with most paradigms, we seem now to be approaching a point where the limitations as well as the advantages of process-oriented research are beginning to be clear.
>
> In particular, the separation of process and product is beginning to reemerge as the unnatural dualism that our past might

➔

GUIDELINES FOR ESSAY TITLES   14

- ■ Do not wait until the last minute to tack on a title. You might write a title before you start to draft or while you are revising, but always check as you review your essay, to make sure that the title clearly relates to the content of the evolving essay.
- ■ For a direct title, use key words relating to your topic, but do not reveal your entire essay.
- ■ For an indirect title, be sure that it hints accurately and that its meaning will be clear once a reader finishes your essay.
- ■ Do not use quotation marks or underlining with the title (*unless* your title includes another title; see section 30f).
- ■ Do not refer to your essay title with words like *it* or *this,* as if the title were part of the first sentence in the essay.

---

your instructor, or compile your own based on the revision checklists in Chart 15 and Chart 16. The checklists here are comprehensive and detailed; do not let them overwhelm you. Feel free to adapt them to your writing assignments as well as to your personal weaknesses and strengths. Also, the checklists here move from the **larger elements** of the whole essay and paragraphs to the **smaller elements** of sentences and words. This progression for the sake of self-evaluation works well for many writers. (To see how Dawn Seaford used these Revision Checklists, see section 3f.)

REVISION CHECKLIST: THE WHOLE ESSAY AND PARAGRAPHS   15

The answer to each question should be "yes." If it is not, you need to revise. The reference numbers in parentheses tell you what chapter or section of this handbook to consult.

1. Is your essay topic suitable and sufficiently narrow (2c)?
2. Does your thesis statement communicate your topic and focus (2m) and your purpose (1b)?
3. Does your essay reflect awareness of your audience (1c)?
4. Is your tone appropriate (1d)?
5. Is your essay logically organized (2l-2) and are your paragraphs logically arranged (4e)?
6. Have you cut material that goes off the topic?
7. Is your reasoning sound (5e–5g) and do you avoid logical fallacies (5h)?

➔

REVISION CHECKLIST: WHOLE ESSAY AND PARAGRAPHS (*cont'd.*)   15

8. Is your introduction related to the rest of your essay (4g)?
9. Does each body paragraph express its main idea in a topic sentence as needed (4c)? Are the main ideas clearly related to the thesis statement, and have you covered all that your thesis statement ''promises'' (2m)?
10. Are your body paragraphs sufficiently developed with concrete support for their main idea (4c)?
11. Have you used necessary transitions (4d-1, 4d-5)?
12. Do your paragraphs maintain coherence (4d)?
13. Does your conclusion provide a sense of completion (4g)?
14. Does your title reflect the content of the essay (3c-2)?

REVISION CHECKLIST: SENTENCES AND WORDS   16

The answer to each question should be ''yes.'' If it is not, you need to revise. The reference numbers in parentheses tell you what chapter or section of this handbook to consult.

1. Have you eliminated sentence fragments (13)?
2. Have you eliminated comma splices and fused sentences (14)?
3. Have you eliminated confusing shifts (15a)?
4. Have you eliminated misplaced and dangling modifiers (15b and 15c)?
5. Have you eliminated mixed and incomplete sentences (15d and 15e)?
6. Are your sentences concise (16)?
7. Do your sentences show clear relationships among ideas (17)?
8. Do you use parallelism to help your sentences deliver their meaning gracefully, and do you avoid faulty parallelism (18)?
9. Does your writing reflect variety and emphasis (19)?
10. Have you used exact words (20b)?
11. Is your usage correct (Usage Glossary)?
12. Do your words reflect an appropriate level of formality (21a-1)?
13. Do you avoid sexist language (21b); slang and colloquial language (21a-3), slanted language (21a-4), cliches, (21d) and artificial language (21e)?

Cont'd.

suggest it would inevitably become. Indeed, when reading, writing, or spoken language processes are separated from the ends they serve, we lose the essence of the process itself. Process does not consist of isolated behaviors that operate willy-nilly, but of purposeful activities that lead toward some end for the person who has chosen to engage in them.

Everyone seems to agree that process is good. So do we. The issue we raise is whether any process can ever be looked at alone. This comes from our belief that just as top-down and bottom-up approaches are interactive, so too do all processing behaviors need to be looked at interactively, as they interrelate with their outcomes. For us, process only has meaning as it works toward some end. Examination of *only* the means keeps us from understanding the most interesting complications of the human mind as it works in different ways toward different destinations.

—Judith A. Langer

TEACHING TIP

Students may find it helpful to know that the strengths and weaknesses in a piece of writing are often easier for the writer to recognize if a ''cooling off'' period intervenes between the time of writing and the time of revision. If there is an opportunity to put the piece away for a day or so, the writer returns to it not as the composer, but as a reader, thus finding it easier to spot confusing passages or awkward statements. Since students are not famous for working far ahead of schedule, they should be encouraged to provide at least a few hours to distance themselves from the writing before trying to revise it. On the other hand, if too much time elapses between the draft and the rereading, a writer is likely to lose the sense of purpose and meaning that accompanied the original effort.

4   Knowing how to use criticism

When criticism is constructive, you can learn a great deal about your writing through the eyes of others. Still, you have much company among writers if your initial reaction to criticism is defensive. Someone else's reactions to your writing can feel like an intrusion at first. Writing is a personal act, even when a writer is trying to communicate with a reader. The more you write, however, the more you will come to welcome constructive criticism.

The eyes of another person, someone who cares to help you improve, can give you an objective view of your material. Useful criticism helps you move your writing closer to what a reader needs to complete the act of communication. In working with comments, look at each one separately. First, make sure that you understand what the comment says. If you are unsure, ask. Next, be open-minded about the comment. If you resist every comment, you will miss many opportunities to improve. Finally, use the comments to revise according to what you think will improve your draft.

5   Knowing how to be a peer critic

Being a **peer critic** means using structured procedures to react to and make suggestions about another student's writing. Peer critiquing is an interactive communication process. It involves reading and thinking together, asking and explaining, talking and listening. As a student writer, be sure that your instructor wants you to use peer critiquing before you do so. There can be a fine line between giving opinions and doing others' work for them.

When you are a peer critic, you are part of a respected tradition of colleagues helping colleagues. Professional writers often seek to improve their rough drafts by asking other writers for comments. When you give comments as a student writer, know that you are not expected to be an expert. What you do offer can be quite valuable: opinions from the point of view of a writer who understands what his or her peer is going through. Try always to base your comments on an understanding of the writing process and of the features that characterize effective writing. The more concrete and specific your comments, the more helpful. The comment "this is good" might seem pleasant, but it says little. What makes the writing "good": ideas, patterns of organization, sentences, words?

When you receive comments from a peer critic, remain open-minded about what is said. Constructive criticism can help you read your writing in a fresh way that results in better revision. Encourage your peer to be honest. You, however, are the person who decides which comments to use, and which to ignore, when revising.

If your instructor distributes a list to guide peer discussion, follow it carefully. If you are expected to decide what to discuss with peers, you can use or adapt the revision checklists in this handbook section. Guidelines for being an effective peer critic are in Chart 17.

GUIDELINES FOR BEING AN EFFECTIVE PEER CRITIC   17

- Think of the writing as "work in progress."
- Think of yourself in the role of a coach, not a judge.
- After reading your peer's writing, give a brief summary of what you have read. This provides a check to determine that what you understand is what the writer intended.
- Be sure to compliment. Being specific, point out what you think is well done.
- Be sure to offer honest, constructive suggestions for improvement. Being specific, point out what you think needs revision.
- As you work through the material, invite the writer to ask questions and say how you might be most helpful.
- When possible, write down your comments to give to your peer (or provide for your peer to take notes while you comment).

3d   Knowing how to edit

When you **edit,** you are expected to check the technical correctness of your writing. You pay attention to surface features of your writing, such as grammar, spelling, and punctuation, and the correct use of capitals, numbers, italics, and abbreviations. Writers sometimes refer to editing as revising (see 3c). In this handbook, editing is discussed separately because editing focuses more on presentation than on meaning.

If you edit too soon in the writing process, you might distract yourself from checking to see if your material delivers its meaning effectively. You are ready to edit when you have a final draft that contains suitable content, organization, development, and sentence structure. Your job during editing is not to generate a new draft but to fine-tune the surface features of the draft you have. Once you have polished your work, you are ready to transcribe it into a final copy and proofread (see 3e) it.

Editing is crucial in writing. No matter how much attention you

Many of us have had the experience of reading what is supposedly a student's revision of an essay we have already read and responded to, only to find that most of our comments have been ignored; the revision turns out to be the original essay with a few spelling errors corrected. Sometimes students do not know how to respond fully to an instructor's comments.

One step in demystifying comments is to have the class collectively respond to the instructor's comments on Tara Foster's second draft. Ask the students to read the instructor's comments on Tara Foster's essay and decide what Foster might do in response to each one. You might lead a discussion of the options for fixing each problem. As you come to each comment, allow sufficient time for students to think about and draft revisions or to look up the needed information in their *S & S Handbook for Writers.* Invite students to offer their revisions at each comment, and keep students alert to the many good alternatives that can emerge in response to the instructor's questions. You might also point out that responses are more likely to be identical to the coded comments of the instructor because most of them call for corrections of grammar or punctuation.

An alternative to the class discussion comment-by-comment is to assign the entire revision as a home or class exercise. Then students can discuss their thought-through answers and compare their results.

As much as possible, try to use copies of the material or overhead transparencies for the discussion of alternate complete third drafts. Students often cannot follow the discussion if too much relies on memory of various similar versions.

have paid to planning, shaping, drafting, and revising, you must edit carefully. Slapdash editing will distract your readers and, in writing for assignments, lower your grade.

Editing takes patience. Inexperienced writers sometimes rush editing, especially if they have revised well and feel that they have prepared a good essay. When you edit, resist any impulse to hurry. Matters of grammar and punctuation take concentration—and frequently the time to check yourself by looking up rules and conventions in this handbook. As you edit, be systematic. Use a checklist supplied by your instructor or one that you compile from the editing checklist in Chart 18.

EDITING CHECKLIST   18

The answer to each question should be "yes." If it is not, you need to edit. The reference numbers in parentheses tell you what chapter of this handbook to consult.

1. Is your grammar correct (7 to 14)?
2. Is your spelling correct, and are your hyphens correct (22)?
3. Have you correctly used commas (24)?
4. Have you correctly used all other punctuation (25 through 29)?
5. Have you correctly used capital letters, italics, abbreviations, and numbers (30)?

3e Knowing how to proofread

When you **proofread,** you check a final version carefully before handing it in. To make sure that your work is an accurate and clean transcription of your final draft, proofread after you revise (see 3c) and edit (see 3d). If you try to proofread while you edit, one process might distract from the other.

Proofreading involves a careful, line-by-line reading of your writing. You may want to proofread with a ruler so that you can focus on one line at a time. Starting at the end also helps you avoid becoming distracted by the content of your paper. Another effective proofreading technique is to read your final draft aloud, to yourself or to a friend. This can help you hear and see errors that might have slipped past your notice.

In proofreading, look for letters or words inadvertently left out. If you handwrite your material, be legible. If you type, neatly correct any typing errors. If a page has numerous errors, retype the page. Do not expect your instructor to make allowances for crude typing; if you cannot type well, arrange to have your paper typed properly. No matter how hard you have worked on other parts of the writing process, if your final copy is inaccurate or messy, you will not reach your audience successfully. For guidelines for typing the final draft of your essays, see Appendix B.

3f Case study: A student writing an essay

This section is a case study of a student, Dawn Seaford, going through the process of writing an essay. As you examine her three drafts, refer back to her writing assignment on page 19. In addition, look at the discussion of how she shaped her ideas (see 2l-2) and wrote her thesis statement (see 2m). See 2n for sample outlines.

1 Writing and revising a first draft

Dawn Seaford wrote about how to face an extraordinary challenge. As a result of using planning techniques (see 2e, 2f, and 2i), she chose the topic of being prepared for natural disasters, and decided that her writing purpose would be *to inform* (see 1b-1). She then wrote the first draft, expecting to revise it later.

As Seaford revised her first draft, she worked systematically through the larger elements of the whole essay and paragraphs, and then she turned to her sentences and words. As she did this, she referred to the Revision Checklists in Chart 15 and Chart 16. Here is Seaford's first draft, along with her notes to herself about revisions she wanted to make when she wrote her second draft.

FIRST DRAFT, REVISED BY STUDENT

Being prepared for Natural Disasters

A disaster is called "natural" when nature, rather than people, ~~can be said to run~~ cause severe property damage and even death. ~~wild.~~ Some natural disasters can happen suddenly, and others can be forecast by weathermen. [when nature gets violent] What can people do to protect themselves? Anyone who faces a natural disaster can reduce its power by being well [I need more punch in my thesis statement] →

BACKGROUND

Many instructors are strongly attracted to the use of peer revision and editing groups, since they provide immediate feedback from an audience other than the teacher, plus the increased opportunity for one-on-one consultations between teacher and student. Some even build entire courses around the workshop model. A concise statement of how to use the classroom as a writing workshop appears in Chapter 12 of Erika Lindemann's *A Rhetoric for Writing Teachers*, 2nd ed. (New York: Oxford UP, 1987), pp. 184–186. Her suggestions include the following guidelines for teachers:

1. Use groups of no more than three students. Let students work with whomever they choose, as long as they do the work.

2. Assign specific work and define it concretely. Begin with brief tasks of 10 to 20 minutes, expanding the work period to a maximum of 30 or 35 minutes as students become comfortable working with each other.

3. Suggest specific questions, especially in the beginning, that writers and readers can ask each other. The session should begin with a writer's explanation of some strategy in the paper. Readers should begin by noting strengths of the writing. When readers or writers identify a problem, they should explain why it is a problem and suggest a solution.

4. Stay involved with what is going on, but avoid taking control. Initially make sure that each group is underway, then listen, from a distance, to each group, intervening only when one is not making progress. Refrain from giving "the answer" to groups that ask for help. Instead, pose questions that will help them discover a solution to their problems.

The result, according to Lindemann, is a classroom that realizes the primary objective of a writing course: "students and teachers writing and discussing each other's work."

BACKGROUND

In "Revision with a Computer: Seven Strategies" (*The English Record* 39 [1988]: 18–21), James Strickland outlines revision techniques that can be taught to writers who have used word processing to enter text into a text file. He suggests the following helpful strategies. (They can be used in conjunction with Appendix A in this handbook.)

1. Students create cumulative sentences through the addition of noun phrases, verb phrases, and absolutes, as suggested by Christensen's generative rhetoric, which adds right-branch modifiers to sentences, elaborates on the basic premise, explains a term, or completes a thought. Students can return at any point in the text to add information, which may generate more ideas. Strickland comments that word processing "encourages cumulative sentence revision because it moves the text over to make room for the new modifiers, and with 'word-wrap' and 'paragraph reformatting' features, it adjusts everything so that the text looks untouched."

2. To check the coherence of a text, students select the MVS, the "most valuable sentence" of each paragraph. Working with a renamed copy of their text file to protect the original, they delete all but the MVS from each paragraph, producing a compressed version of the writing. As Strickland points out, it is "a map of the forward motion of the essay, a top-level view of its structure."

3. Using the compressed text as an outline, the writer returns to the original text to create the "stairway of elaboration," sentences and paragraphs added to improve coherence. It is a process of expansion. Using the metaphor of the stairway to explain the process, Strickland says the writer is like a builder who can increase the number of stairs but can also elaborate on each step, making it wider and deeper. ➡

---

prepared ahead of time.

Most natural disasters are confined to specific geographic areas. The west coast *gets* damaging earthquakes, most southern and midwestern states *get* devastating tornadoes, and areas near the Gulf of Mexico and the Atlantic Ocean *get* violent hurricanes. These different natural disasters, and others as dangerous, teach people one common lesson––advance preparation ~~spells~~ *can mean* survival.

Newspapers and television news jump at the chance to tell stories of survival and to show pictures of storm damage. It's as if someone seems to enjoy frightening everyone with horror stories. (But that's nothing new!)

Knowledge is the first step to being well-prepared for a natural disaster. *Most of all,* ~~People~~ need to know exactly what natural disaster can strike *their area and* how they can minimize exposure to danger. The *safest place* during a tornado is the basement. The *safest place* during an earthquake is outside in wide open areas, or inside under strong desks or tables. The *safest place* during a hurricane is far enough from the coast that huge water surges are not a threat. ~~Being swept away and drowning in a water surge is horrible.~~

Learn where hospitals and public shelters are located and alternate routes *to them if some routes are blocked*. Memorize

(handwritten annotations: "get" 3 times FIX!; I've crowed too much into one sentence; I like this sentence; I'm off the topic here; I need more word variety; I'll combine these 2 ¶s into 1 ¶; I feel I'm rambling here.)

➡

which radio and TV stations can be relied upon to give complete weather forecasts and crisis warnings.

People need to be ready to ~~swing into action~~. *develop and rehearse plans for surviving a natural disaster.* During a crisis when everyone is at home~~x~~, *,* ~~E~~each person can have a specific assignment. For instance, one person can monitor the radio, another can take charge of emergency supplies, and someone else can check that everyone is accounted for~~.~~ *, including young children.* If household members are separated, a different plan is called for. The plan should include where to meet after the crisis ends. The possibility of reuniting is greater if each family member is familiar with the emergency plans that affect everyone else when away from home: at day care centers, schools, work, and other places. Of course, no plan (is good) unless review conferences and drills are held. *weak word*

When crisis plans are in place, each household should concentrate on collecting emergency supplies~~,~~ *for surviving a natural disaster.* Because fires fed by severed gas and electrical lines are not unusual. A large fire extinguisher ~~is needed~~. *should be close at hand.*

A fully stocked first aid kit and ample medicines must be up-to-date. Other items can include books, family games, and jigsaw puzzles to help people from (going nuts) waiting around. Sealed bottled water and nonperishable food

I think this is too informal

I'll move this to ¶ end—Most to least important →

Cont'd.

4. To teach the copy/move function of the software, which can rearrange and reorganize parts of a text, an instructor can ask students to move their concluding paragraph to the opening of the essay, and the introductory one to the end. Reading the rearranged work can lead to a new understanding of the purposes of beginnings and endings, specifically that writers' discoveries are often made at the end of a writing attempt, after they find what they wanted to say, and that readers usually need to know about that discovery at the beginning.

5. Stylistic revision can be carried out with the search-and-replace function of the software to find what Strickland calls "fuzzy" words—such as *very, really, quite, rather,* excessive *which* phrases, *th* words, and nominalizations. After they have been identified, the writer can decide if and how they are to be revised.

6. A spell checker helps students edit their orthography. By pointing out questionable spellings and offering alternative ones, the computer repeats, according to Strickland, the time-honored injunction to "look it up in the dictionary."

7. The final strategy is a computer conversation, which Strickland calls collaborative revision. Writers respond to each other's writing by way of on-line conversations: a new version of writers talking to each other about their work.

The value of revision with a computer, says Strickland, is that students see their work as a fluid text that can be easily added to, subtracted from, rearranged, and manipulated.

> ✓should be stored where they are secure yet
> ⟨to last a few days⟩
> instantly available for sudden evacuation. A
> *along with lots of batteries,*
> portable radio and light sources ⌃are
>
> indispensable.
>
> The forces of nature can be ~~sometimes~~
> ~~benign and sometimes~~ brutal. ~~The benign~~
> ~~aspects are easy to appreciate and enjoy.~~ Some
> *comma*
> people ~~might prefer to ignore that reality⦵~~ *splice;*
> *I fixed*
> ~~they~~ feel "sure" that no natural disaster could *it*
> *be* **violent enough to**
> ever ~~touch~~ them. The people who respect the
>   ⌃
> potential deadly power of nature and who
>
> prepare in advance to face it, however, are
>
> usually the ones who meet the disaster
>
> successfully.

2 Revising a second draft

After Dawn Seaford finished writing and entering notes to herself on her first draft (see 3f-1), she revised her work into a second draft and typed a clean copy to give to her instructor. As stated in the assignment (see page 19), Seaford's instructor considered the second draft an ''essay in progress,'' so that all comments by the instructor were aimed at helping Seaford write an effective third, final draft.

Here is Seaford's second draft with two types of comments from the instructor: *questions* to stimulate Seaford to clarify and expand on ideas in the draft as well as section *codes*—the number-letter combinations—for Seaford to consult in this handbook.

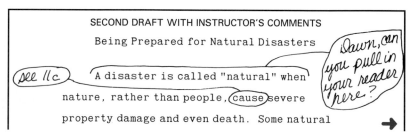

> SECOND DRAFT WITH INSTRUCTOR'S COMMENTS
>
> Being Prepared for Natural Disasters
>
> ⟨see 11c⟩ A disaster is called "natural" when
>
> nature, rather than people, ⟨cause⟩ severe
>
> property damage and even death. Some natural
>
> *Dawn, can you pull in your reader here?*

see 21b.

disasters can happen suddenly, and others can be forecast by (weathermen). What can people do to protect themselves when nature gets violent? Anyone who faces the possibility of a natural disaster can reduce its destructive, life-threatening power by being well prepared ahead of time.

good thesis statement

good narrowing of focus

see chart 140

In the United States, most natural disasters are confined to specific geographic areas. For example, the (w)est (c)oast can be hit by damaging earthquakes at any time. Most (s)outhern and (m)idwestern states can be hit by devastating tornadoes. Areas near the Gulf of Mexico and the Atlantic Ocean can be hit by violent hurricanes. These different natural disasters, and others as dangerous, teach people one common lesson—advance preparation can mean survival.

Do you want to repeat these?

Knowledge is the first step to being well-prepared to face a natural disaster. Most of all, people need to know exactly what natural disaster can strike their area and how they can minimize exposure to danger. The safest place during a tornado is the (basement). The most secure place during an (earthquake is outside in wide open areas or inside under strong desks or tables. The best place during a hurricane is far enough from the coast that huge water surges are not a threat. (Learn) which

Is Knowledge a step?

Can you help your reader more? See 4d-1

R what?

why?

15a

Cont'd.

reading their work—and real people ask questions when they are puzzled. Therefore, whenever possible, phrase your reactions as questions. Instead of writing *"unclear,"* ask "How does this relate to your thesis?" If you do not have time to write many questions, try to get at least one in per paper. Psychologically, people can't help but answer questions—at least in their own minds. So, to ask a question is to guarantee an answer. And with the answer in mind a student can revise.

Whenever time permits, a good description deserves more than "nice" scribbled in the margin; you might say "You really made me see the lake at sundown." If a student tells you about a cooking disaster, you might say "You had me laughing in sympathy. The same thing happened to me." Such comments validate students' experiences and also demonstrate compassionate reading.

In many cases, reaction comments are most useful in the final response to an essay. Many students turn to the end of their essays before reading marginal comments. After the grade, this is the part of our response that is most crucial to students. The final comment is our total impression, while the margins represent a kind of running commentary. To be useful, a closing comment needs to clarify our response, not duplicate the grade: a student whose grade has jumped from *D* to *B* knows his or her work is "better," so try to be specific.

A useful end comment consists of at least several sentences. A serviceable pattern consists of a personal response, a sentence about the content and organization of the piece (positive as well as negative observations—see the end comment to Foster), and, where pertinent, a few sentences about a recurring mechanical or grammatical issue (e.g., "Try to hear and pronounce the ends of words. You frequently omit *-s* and *-ed* endings, resulting in tense and number errors that can confuse a reader").

TEACHING TIP

Revising is a process just as composing is a process. Students may find it helpful to examine the steps they go through when revising, editing, and proofreading. Here are some questions they can use to look carefully at how they approach these final stages of writing a paper.

1. How did you make the mental shift from suspending judgment to making judgment?

2. Did you use the questions in the Revision Checklist in this chapter or material supplied by your instructor?

3. How did you decide whether to write an entirely new draft or to revise the one you had?

4. If you had readers other than the teacher, how did you use their suggestions? Did you use all of them? None of them?

5. Did you reconsider your original purpose and audience?

6. Did you need to make any changes in your introduction or conclusion because of other changes in your text?

7. Was your original title still appropriate?

8. Did you consider different elements of your writing during separate rounds of revision?

9. How much new material did you add? In how many places did you add new words, sentences, or paragraphs?

10. How much material did you delete? In how many places did you cut out words, sentences, or paragraphs?

11. How many changes in the sequence of paragraphs did you make?

12. Did you use a checklist, either the one in this chapter, your own, or one supplied by your instructor, to examine your writing for grammar, spelling, punctuation, or capitalization problems?

➡

radio and TV stations can be relied upon to give complete weather forecasts and crisis warnings. Also, teach yourself where hospitals and public shelters are located and alternate routes to them if routes are blocked.

[Can you make this more concise? See 16a-3]
15a

People need to develop and rehearse plans for surviving a natural disaster. During a crisis when everyone is at home, each person can have a specific assignment. For instance, one person can monitor the radio, another can take charge of emergency supplies, and someone else can check that everyone is accounted for, including young children. [If household members are separated, a different plan is called for. The plan should include where to meet after the crisis ends.] The possibility of reuniting is greater if each family member are familiar with the emergency plans that affect everyone else when away from home: at day care centers, schools, work, and other places. Of course, no plan can work well unless review conferences are scheduled and drills are held.

[What is the relation between this and prior ¶?]
[See 25d for another option]
[Can you combine these sentences?]
see 11g
[when? for whom?]

When crisis plans are in place, each household should concentrate on collecting emergency supplies for surviving a natural disaster. Because fires fed by severed gas and electrical lines are not unusual. A large fire extinguisher should be close at hand. A fully stocked first aid kit and ample reserves of medicines must be up-to-date. Sealed bottled

[sentence fragment see 13b]

➡

water and nonperishable food to last a few days
should be stored where they are secure yet *very good specific details*
instantly available for sudden evacuation. A
portable radio and light sources, along with
sp: see 22e
many extra batteries, are <u>indispensable</u>. Other
items include books, family games, and jigsaw
puzzles to help stranded people pass the time
and stay calm.

   The forces of nature can be brutal.
Still, some people feel "sure" that no natural
disaster could ever be violent enough to
conquer them. The people who respect the
potential deadly power of nature and who
prepare in advance to face it, however, are *Can a disaster be "met"?*
usually the ones who(meet the disaster)
successfully.

Your choice of the challenge of a natural disaster is an excellent response to the assignment. Also, your information is helpful and clear. I'm pleased with your self-revisions from your 1st draft. As you revise further, think about my questions, reactions, and suggestions. I'm looking forward to your final draft.

Cont'd.

13. Did you edit your paper in a single reading or look for possible errors in a series of readings?

14. Did you read your paper aloud to find errors? Did you start at the end? Did you read it line by line?

15. Did you reconsider the format of your paper?

TEACHING TIP

A personal editing checklist, a list of problems that recur from one piece of writing to the next, can help any writer spot potential trouble spots. You may want to suggest that students go through returned papers, listing each marked error and grouping those that are similar, such as spelling errors, subject-verb agreement errors, and comma splices. After becoming aware of the kinds of problems that are most likely to occur, the writer can devise ways of checking new manuscripts to make sure they are not present. For example, if the *s* is left off most third-person singular verbs, the writer should go through a new paper checking each such construction for agreement.

QUOTATION ABOUT WRITING

What makes me happy is rewriting. . . . It's like cleaning house, getting rid of all the junk, getting things in the right order, tightening things up.

—Ellen Goodman

3

Revising, editing, and proofreading a final draft

Seaford revised her essay in a third, final draft by working with the instructor's comments. Seaford started with the larger elements of the essay by thinking about the instructor's questions and suggestions. Next, Seaford used the codes—the number-letter combinations—that referred her to specific sections in this handbook concerning matters of word choice, style, grammar, and punctuation. She also referred to the Revision Checklists, Charts 15 and 16. Before typing a clean copy of her third, final draft, Seaford edited her writing by referring to the Editing Checklist in Chart 18. Here is the third, final draft of Seaford's essay. The labels in the margins are guideposts for you *only* in this handbook; do not use them on your final drafts.

THIRD, FINAL DRAFT BY STUDENT

title   Being Prepared for Natural Disasters

introduction: defining a term and asking a question   A natural disaster can strike almost anywhere at anytime. A disaster is called "natural" when nature, rather than people, is responsible for causing severe property damage and even death. Some natural disasters can happen suddenly, and others can be forecast by meteorologists. What can people do to protect themselves when nature gets violent? Anyone who faces the possibility of a natural disaster can

thesis statement   reduce its destructive, life-threatening power by being well prepared ahead of time.

background information on the topic   In the United States, most natural disasters are confined to specific geographic areas. For example, the West Coast can be hit by damaging earthquakes at any time. Most Southern and Midwestern states can be swept by devastating tornadoes, especially in the spring, summer, and early fall. The Gulf of Mexico and the Atlantic Ocean can experience violent hurricanes in late

➡️

BACKGROUND

In "The Apple in the Center" (*Writing Lab Newsletter* 9 [November 1984]: 9–10), Beatrice Jacobson assesses the impact of computers on the writing process, concluding that they make all of its stages easier and faster. She points out that computers make students want to write more. Students also gain a sense of professionalism when writing on computers.

In her study of student writers using computers, Wendy Colby Boserra found that students spent more time and energy revising and editing their work when using word processors, but that they did not significantly increase their prewriting ("Effects of Word Processors upon the Writing Processes of Basic Writers," *Dissertation Abstracts International* 48 [July 1987]: 34A).

QUOTATION ABOUT WRITING

When you say something, make sure you have said it. The chances of your having said it are only fair.

—E. B. White

summer and fall. These different natural
disasters, and others as dangerous, teach people
one common lesson——advance preparation can mean
survival.

support: first
action to take

      Gathering information is the first step to
being well–prepared to face a natural disaster.
Most of all, people need to know exactly what
natural disaster can strike their area, and how
they can minimize exposure to danger. For
example, the safest place during a tornado is the
basement of a sturdy building. The most secure
place during an earthquake is outside in wide open
areas, away from anything that might collapse
overhead, or inside under strong desks or tables
that can protect against falling ceilings or
walls. The best place during a hurricane is far
enough from the coast that huge water surges are
not a threat. Next, everyone should memorize
which radio and TV stations give reliable,
complete weather forecasts and crisis warnings.
Also, people need to learn where hospitals and
public shelters are located and alternate routes
to them if some streets are blocked.

support:
second action
to take

      Once people have information about the local
risk of a natural disaster, they need to develop
and rehearse plans for surviving it. During a
crisis when everyone is at home, each person can
have a specific assignment. For instance, one
person can monitor the radio for the latest
information and instructions; another can take
charge of emergency supplies; and someone else
can check that everyone is accounted for,
including young children. If household members
are separated, the plan should include where to
meet after the crisis ends. The possibility of
reuniting is greater if each family member is
familiar with the emergency plans that affect ➡

BACKGROUND
In "Proofreading: A Review of the Literature and Suggestions for Teaching Techniques" (*Maryland English Journal* 21 [Spring 1987]: 63–70), Elaine Ware argues for proofreading techniques that slow the reader down and limit the number of steps in the process.

QUOTATION ABOUT WRITING
You know when you think about writing a book, you think it is overwhelming. But, actually, you break it down into tiny little tasks any moron could do.
—Annie Dillard

QUOTATION ABOUT WRITING

I love spending an hour or two with a dictionary and a thesaurus looking for a more nearly perfect word. Or taking my pen and ruthlessly pruning all the unnecessary adjectives, or fooling around with the rhythm of a sentence or a paragraph by changing a verb into a participle or making any number of little changes that a magazine editor I work with calls "mouse milking."

—Marie Winn

everyone else when away from home: at day care centers, schools, work, and other places. Of course, no plan can work well unless review conferences are scheduled and drills are held frequently for the entire household.

support: third action to take

When crisis plans are in place, each household should concentrate on collecting emergency supplies for surviving a natural disaster. Because fires fed by severed gas and electrical lines are not unusual, a large fire extinguisher should be close at hand. A fully stocked first aid kit and ample reserves of medicines must be up-to-date. Sealed bottled water and nonperishable food to last a few days should be stored where they are secure yet still instantly available for sudden evacuation. A portable radio and light sources, along with many extra batteries, are indispensable. Less crucial but very helpful items include books, family games, and jigsaw puzzles to help stranded people pass the time and stay calm.

conclusion: call for awareness

The forces of nature sometimes can be brutal. Still, some people feel "sure" that no natural disaster could ever be violent enough to conquer them. The people who respect the potential deadly power of nature and who prepare in advance to face it, however, are usually the ones who meet the challenge successfully.

4 Writing Paragraphs

4a Understanding paragraphs

A **paragraph** is a group of sentences that work in concert to develop a unit of thought. Paragraphing permits you to subdivide material into manageable parts and, at the same time, to arrange those parts into a unified whole that effectively communicates its message.

Paragraphing is signaled by indentation. The first line is indented five spaces in a typewritten paper and one inch in a handwritten paper. (Business letters are sometimes typed in "block format," with paragraphs separated by a double space but no paragraph indentations. Generally block format is not appropriate for essays.)

The purpose of a paragraph helps to determine its structure. In college, the most common purposes for academic writing are to inform and to persuade (see 1b). Some paragraphs introduce, conclude, or provide transitions. Most paragraphs, however, are **topical paragraphs,** also called *developmental paragraphs* or *body paragraphs*. They consist of a statement of a main idea, and specific, logical support for that main idea. Consider paragraph 1, a topical paragraph that seeks to inform. (To help discussion and reference in this chapter, a red number appears at the left side of each sample paragraph.)

1   The cockroach lore that has been daunting us for years is mostly true. Roaches can live for twenty days without food, fourteen days without water; they can flatten their bodies and crawl through a crack thinner than a dime; they can eat huge doses of carcinogens and still die of old age. They can even survive "as

71

Cont'd.

portant the contents. In some cases, a reader can get the idea that the piece doesn't conclude so much as trail off. This is because newspaper articles are written on the assumption that they will *not* be read from beginning to end. Editors may cut off the last few inches of a story to make it fit on a page; readers may go only as far as the first paragraph.

These differences have several implications in the writing classroom. First, most newspaper articles and many magazine articles make poor models for paragraphing (unless you are teaching journalism). Be aware that composition textbooks often include some newspaper and magazine articles as model essays. Second, encouraging students to read a newspaper regularly may make them better informed and expose them to new vocabulary used in complete sentences, but such reading alone is not likely to help them form subconscious ideas about paragraph structure that can be usefully applied to academic writing. To learn to write essays, the student must—at least part of the time—read essays.

One way to show your students the difference between essay paragraphing and newspaper paragraphing is to give them copies of pieces dealing with the same experience: a newspaper account of a fire and an essay (such as an editorial) written in response to the event; a newspaper account of a trial and a magazine essay discussing the case. Ask students to list the differences. At minimum, they will mention differences in length, number of paragraphs, and the presence of personal opinion. They may also notice the lack of a thesis statement and of a conclusion in the newspaper article and the presence of both in the essay.

You might also ask students how satisfied they would be if they were given only the first paragraph of the newspaper article and of the essay. The article's introduction will probably be far more satisfying in terms of

➔

much radiation as an oak tree can," says William Bell, the University of Kansas entomologist whose cockroaches appeared in the movie *The Day After*. They'll eat almost anything—regular food, leather, glue, hair, paper, even the starch in book bindings. (The New York Public Library has quite a cockroach problem.) They sense the slightest breeze, and they can react and start running in .05 seconds; they can also remain motionless for days. And if all this isn't creepy enough, they can fly too.

—JANE GOLDMAN, "What's Bugging You"

Goldman states her main idea in the first sentence. She then gives concrete examples supporting her claim that there is much truth to the lore about cockroaches. This paragraph relates to the thesis° of the whole essay: "Roaches cannot be banished from the world, but they can be controlled in people's homes and apartments."

Consider this topical paragraph that seeks to persuade. It, too, consists of a main idea and support.

2   The public library is the best, most democratic, most economical mechanism ever devised to provide access to information and enlightenment on issues that range from the intensely personal to those that are global in nature. Individuals of all ages and from all walks of life, community groups, agencies, businesses, unions, and government institutions of every kind increasingly turn to the public library for assistance. It is the only library that is available to everyone in the community. Typically, it receives half of 1 percent of the government's budget yet serves 30 to 50 percent of the people. No other community service is more cost effective.

—CLARA BENNETT, President of the Board of Trustees,
Nassau County Library System

Bennett states her main idea in the first two sentences. The second sentence narrows the focus of the first and sets the stage for the supporting statements that follow.

Goldman's and Bennett's paragraphs demonstrate the three major characteristics of an effective paragraph. They are shown in Chart 19.

Understanding paragraph structure can help you at various points during your writing process. Before drafting (see 3b), you might decide to subdivide your material into paragraphs and to develop each in an effective way. If you prefer to plan less at first and instead write a "discovery" or a rough draft that gets all your ideas down on paper, you can later sort out your material and arrange it into manageable paragraphs. When revising (see 3c), you might find that a particular paragraph is weak because it does not clearly state its main idea or it does not develop that idea well. Also, you might

19
MAJOR CHARACTERISTICS OF AN EFFECTIVE PARAGRAPH

- ■ **Unity:** clear, logical relationship between the main idea of a paragraph and supporting evidence for that main idea (see 4b and 4c).
- ■ **Coherence:** smooth progression from one sentence to the next within a paragraph (see 4d).
- ■ **Development:** specific, concrete support for the main idea of the paragraph (see 4e and 4f).

notice that although each paragraph is well structured on its own, the paragraphs do not work together very well. This chapter offers you paragraphing options to consider as you plan, draft, and revise your writing.

4b Writing unified paragraphs

A paragraph is **unified** when all its sentences clarify or help support the main idea. Unity is lost if a paragraph goes off the topic by including sentences unrelated to the main idea. Here is a paragraph about databases, which lacks unity because two *deliberately added* sentences go off the topic.

> **NO**   We have all used physical databases since our grammar school days. Grammar school is known today as grade school or elementary school. Our class yearbooks, the telephone book, the shoebox full of receipts documenting our deductions for the IRS—these are all databases in one form or another, for a database is nothing more than an assemblage of information organized to allow the retrieval of that information in certain ways. Anyone who is well organized has a better chance of succeeding in college or in the business world.

In the preceding paragraph, the second and last sentences wander away from the topic of databases. As a result, unity is lost. A reader quickly loses patience with material that rambles and therefore fails to communicate a clear message. Paragraph 3 is the original version. It is unified because all its sentences, including the ones adding interesting details, relate to the subject of databases.

Cont'd.

information, less satisfying in terms of graceful presentation, background, pacing, and the like.

Another way to underscore the difference between the genres is to give students (or assign them to find) a meaty newspaper article—the kind that runs for two pages, usually about a scandal or a major crime. Have them rewrite the article as an essay. Before the students write, you might discuss with them the kinds of changes they anticipate making.

BACKGROUND

In *Errors and Expectations* (New York: Oxford UP, 1977), Mina Shaughnessy points out that just as novice writers must learn the structure of sentences and words by viewing them in unfamiliar, more abstract ways, they must similarly develop a new way of thinking if they are to learn paragraph and essay structure. She names two types of instruction that have merit: practice in "seeing" structure in a wide range of written materials, and practice in recognizing thought patterns that frequently appear in conventional writing tasks for college.

BACKGROUND

u·ni·ty (yoó nə tē) n. *pl* -ties (1) The state, property, or product of being united physically, socially, or morally; oneness; opposed to *division, plurality.*

—*Britannica World Language Dictionary,* Edition of Funk and Wagnalls Standard, p. 1373.

BACKGROUND

Many of the conventions followed by contemporary writers did not exist in the ancient world. For example, words were not divided from each other until sometime in the seventh century A.D., and word division was not systematically practiced until the eleventh. Some marks of punctuation, such as the question mark and the exclamation mark, evolved during the Middle Ages. Paragraphs had been indicated since pre-Christian days, first by short horizontal strokes or wedge-shaped signs. Later they were noted in Latin manuscripts by a new line. At the same time, it became the practice to indicate the beginning of a new paragraph with enlarged letters, sometimes extending the length of the page. Such elaborate figures became the ancestors of our capital letters. The paragraph as it is known today took shape late in the seventeenth century but was not systematically described until the nineteenth century, when Alexander Bain published his *English Composition and Rhetoric* (1866).

TEACHING TIP

To help students to make connections between what happens in the classroom and what goes on in their lives in other situations, you may want to encourage them to look for topic sentences in the newspapers and magazines they read. They may be surprised to discover that in materials published for a nonacademic setting, topic sentences occur at beginnings and endings of paragraphs, just as they do in textbook examples. In some cases they will probably find that paragraphs manage to make a unified statement without the presence of a stated topic sentence. The examples they find can provide a basis for class discussion.

YES   3

We have all used physical databases since our grammar school days. Our class yearbooks, the telephone book, the shoebox full of receipts documenting our deductions for the IRS—these are all databases in one form or another, for a database is nothing more than an assemblage of information in certain ways. A telephone book, for example, assuming that you have the right one for the right city, will enable you to find the telephone number for, say, Alan Smith. Coincidentally it will also give you his address, provided there is only one Alan Smith listed. Where there are several Alan Smiths, you would have to know the address, or at least part of it, to find the number of the particular Alan Smith you had in mind. Even without the address, however, you would still save considerable time by the telephone database. The book might list 50,000 names but only 12 Alan Smiths, so at the outset you could eliminate 49,988 telephone calls when trying to contact the elusive Mr. Smith.

—ERIK SANBERG-DIMENT, "Personal Computers"

The sentence that contains the main idea of a paragraph is called the **topic sentence.** It shapes and controls the content of the rest of the paragraph.

Some paragraphs use two sentences to present a main idea. In such cases, the topic sentence is followed by a **limiting** or **clarifying sentence,** which serves to narrow the paragraph's focus. In paragraph 3, the second sentence is its topic sentence, and the third sentence is its limiting sentence. The rest of the sentences support the main idea.

Professional essay writers do not always use topic sentences, because these writers have the skill to carry the reader along without explicit signposts. Student writers are often advised to use topic sentences so that their essays will be clearly organized and their paragraphs will not stray from the controlling power of each main idea.

Topic sentence at the beginning of a paragraph

Most informative and persuasive paragraphs place the topic sentence first so that a reader knows immediately what to expect.

To travel the streets of Los Angeles is to glimpse America's ethnic future. At the bustling playground at McDonald's in Koreatown, a

4   dozen shades of kids squirt down the slides and burrow through tunnels and race down the catwalks, not much minding that no two of them speak the same language. Parents of grade-school children say they rarely know the color of their youngsters' best friends until they meet them; it never seems to occur to the children to say, since they have not yet been taught to care.

             —NANCY GIBBS, "Shades of Difference"

Sometimes the main idea in the topic sentence starts a paragraph and is then restated at the end of the paragraph.

5   *Every dream is a portrait of the dreamer.* You may think of your dream as a mirror that reflects your inner character—the aspects of your personality of which you are not fully aware. Once we understand this, we can also see that every trait portrayed in our dreams has to exist in us, somewhere, regardless of whether we are aware of it or admit it. *Whatever characteristics the dream figures have, whatever behavior they engage in, is also true of the dreamer in some way.*

             —ROBERT A. JOHNSON, *Inner Work*

Topic sentence at the end of a paragraph

Some informative and persuasive paragraphs reveal the supporting details before the main idea. The topic sentence, therefore, comes at the end of a paragraph. This approach is particularly effective for building suspense and for dramatic effect. This arrangement forces readers to move through all the details before encountering the organizing effect of a main idea.

Paragraphs 6 and 7 end with a topic sentence. In paragraph 6, the main idea is fairly easy to predict as the specific suggestions accumulate. In paragraph 7, the main idea is less predictable, and it is thus more satisfying for some readers but more challenging for others.

6   Burnout is a potential problem for any hard working and persevering student. A preliminary step for preventing student burnout is for students to work in moderation. Students can concentrate on school every day, provided that they do not overtax themselves. One method students can use is to avoid concentrating on a single project for an extended period of time. For example, if students have to read two books for a midterm history test, they should do other assignments at intervals so that the two books will not get boring. Another means to moderate a workload is to regulate how many extracurricular projects to take on. *When a workload is manageable, a student's immunity to burnout is strengthened.*

             —BRADLEY HOWARD, student

BACKGROUND

The use of topic sentences by published writers has been the subject of a great deal of research and study over the past two decades. Richard Braddock's "The Frequency and Placement of Topic Sentence in Expository Prose" (*Research in the Teaching of English* [1974]: 287–302; rpt. *The Writing Teacher's Sourcebook,* ed. Gary Tate and Edward P. J. Corbett, 2nd ed. [New York: Oxford UP, 1988]) reports the surprising information that in the 25 essays he examined, he found topic sentences in paragraphs only 13 percent of the time. Admitting that it is difficult to know exactly what a topic sentence is, he also points out that "percentages vary greatly among individual writers." Several years later, in 1979, William Irmscher reported in *Teaching Expository Writing* (New York: Holt, Rinehart and Winston, p. 98) that his graduate students found topic sentences in 40 to 50 percent of the paragraphs they analyzed, a significantly higher percentage than Braddock discovered. The percentages have varied in other studies, but most have found that under half of the paragraphs in published writing begin with topic sentences.

Braddock, however, ends his study with the opinion that "often the writing in the 25 essays would have been clearer and more comfortable to read if the paragraphs had presented more explicit topic sentences" (301). Frank J. D'Angelo agrees in "The Topic Sentence Revisited" (*College Composition and Communication* [December 1986]: 431–441), arguing that recent research shows that people are able to read faster and remember and comprehend more material when a paragraph begins with a sentence that states the main idea and indicates the organization of the paragraph that follows. D'Angelo does not suggest that every paragraph begin with a topic sentence, but believes that writers improve the readability of their papers by beginning many of their paragraphs with topic sentences.

ALTERNATE EXAMPLE: TOPIC SENTENCE AT BEGINNING

A school that devotes itself totally and unequivocally to salable skills, especially in a time of high unemployment, sending young men and women into the world armed with only a narrow range of skills, is also sending lambs into the lion's den. If those people gain nothing more from their studies than supposedly salable skills, and can't make the sale because of changes in the job market, they have been cheated. But if those skills were more than salable, if study made them better citizens and made them happier to be human beings, they have not been cheated. They will find some kind of job soon enough. It might even turn out that those humanizing and liberating skills are salable. Flexibility, an ability to change and learn new things, is a valuable skill. People who have learned how to learn can learn outside of school. That is where most of us have learned to do what we do, not in school. Learning to learn is one of the highest liberal skills.

—Robert A. Goldwin, "Is It Enough to Roll with the Times?"

ANSWERS: EXERCISE 4-1

A. The topic sentence is the first sentence.

B. The topic sentence is the last sentence.

C. The topic sentence is the first sentence, and the second sentence is a limiting sentence.

D. The topic sentence is implied. The main idea is that peanuts, while nutritious, are also high in calories.

E. The topic sentence is the first sentence.

7 Most people do not lose ten dollars or one hundred dollars when they trade cars. They lose many hundreds or even a thousand. They buy used cars that will not provide them service through the first payment. They overbuy new cars and jeopardize their credit, only to find themselves "hung," unable even to sell their shiny new toys. *The car business is one of the last roundups in America, the great slaughterhouse of wheeling and dealing, where millions of people each year willingly submit to being taken.*

REMAR SUTTON, *Don't Get Taken Every Time*

Topic sentence implied

Some paragraphs make a unified statement without the use of a topic sentence. Writers must construct such paragraphs carefully so that a reader can easily discern the main idea.

8 The Romans were entertained by puppets, as were the rulers of the Ottoman Empire with their favorite shadow puppet, Karaghoiz, teller of a thousand tales. In the Middle Ages, puppets were cast as devil and angel in religious mystery and morality plays until cast out entirely by the church. For centuries, there has been a rich puppetry heritage in India that matches that country's multilayered culture. The grace of Bali is reflected in its stylized, ceremonial rod and shadow puppets. The Bunraku puppets of Japan, unequaled for technique anywhere in the world, require a puppet master and two assistants to create one dramatic character on stage.

—DAN CODY, "Puppet Poetry"

Cody uses many examples to communicate the main idea that puppets have been popular in many cultures over time. A reader does not expect to puzzle over material, so implied topic sentences must be very clear, even though they are silent.

EXERCISE 4-1

Consulting sections 4a and 4b, identify all topic sentences, limiting sentences, and topic sentences repeated at the ends of paragraphs. If there is no topic sentence, compose an implied one.

A. 9 A good college program should stress the development of high-level reading, writing, and mathematical skills and should provide you with a broad historical, social, and cultural perspective, no matter what subject you choose as your major. The program should teach you not only the most current knowledge in your field but also—just as important—prepare you to keep learning throughout your life. After all, you will probably change jobs, and possibly even careers, at least six times, and you'll have other responsibilities, too—perhaps as a spouse and as a parent and certainly as a member of a community whose bounds extend beyond the workplace.

—FRANK T. RHODES, "Let the Student Decide"

B.   The once majestic oak tree crashes to the ground amid the destructive flames, as its panic-stricken inhabitants attempt to flee the fiery tomb. Undergrowth that formerly flourished smolders in ashes. A family of deer darts furiously from one wall of flame to the other, 10 without an emergency exit. On the outskirts of the inferno, fire fighters try desperately to stop the destruction. Somewhere at the source of this chaos lies a former campsite containing the cause of this destruction—an untended campfire. This scene is one of many which illustrate how human apathy and carelessness destroy nature.

—ANNE BRYSON, student

C.   Rudeness is not a distinctive quality of our own time. People today would be shocked by how rudely our ancestors behaved. In the colonial period, a French traveler marveled that "Virginians do not use napkins, but they wear silk cravats, and instead of carrying white handkerchiefs they blow their noses either with their fingers or with a 11 silk handkerchief that also serves as a cravat, a napkin, and so on." In the 19th century, up to about the 1830s, even very distinguished people routinely put their knives in their mouths. And when people went to the theater, they would not just applaud politely—they would chant, jeer, and shout. So, the notion that there has been a downhill slide in manners ever since time began is just not so.

—"Horizons," *U.S. News & World Report*

D.   Peanuts contain no cholesterol and a lot of nutrition. A 3.5-12 ounce package of unsalted peanuts contains more than half of your daily protein requirement. But peanuts are far from a health food. That same 3.5-ounce package also contains 564 calories.

—LOUISE KLEIN, "Peanut Gallery"

E.   There are at least two important reasons for the surplus of women in urban areas. First, cities are the best places for women to find jobs. Men account for 79 percent of the nation's farmers, 85 percent of miners, and 95 percent of loggers. But the service economy is urban and dominated by women. The second reason is 13 the high death rate for young men in inner cities. The Bronx, for example, has only about 47 men for every 53 women in the target age group—the highest disparity of any county in New York State. Higher male mortality also explains the female skew in some rural counties, such as many of those that include Indian reservations.

—BRAD EDMONDSON AND BLAYNE CUTLER, "Where the Boys Are"

BACKGROUND

The theory that paragraph structures often resemble sentence structures was presented by Francis Christensen in "A Generative Rhetoric of the Paragraph" (*Notes Toward a New Rhetoric* [New York: Harper & Row, 1967]). He points out that the topic sentence is parallel to the base clause of a sentence, and the supporting sentences are parallel to the added sentence modifiers. Given such a structure, the paragraph, like the sentence, develops with *addition* that has *direction of modification* or *direction of movement*. When sentences are added to develop a topic, they are usually at a lower *level of generality*, and the more sentences the writer adds, the denser the *texture*. To use this structural analysis of the paragraph to generate paragraphs, Christensen proposes nine principles that can be applied and taught. Your students should not regard these principles as laws but as rules of thumb that can help them generate certain kinds of paragraphs but cannot be applied to all writing situations.

1. The paragraph may be defined as a sequence of sentences that are related by coordination and subordination.

2. The most general sentence of the sequence is often the topic sentence, the sentence on which the others depend.

3. The topic sentence is typically the first sentence of the sequence. Topics may be established explicitly or may be only suggested.

4. Simple sequences are of two sorts—coordinate and subordinate. In a coordinate sequence, repetition of structure—parallelism—is necessary; in a subordinate sequence, repetition must be avoided, each added sentence taking a different form.

➜

4c   ## Supporting the main idea of a paragraph

As a writer, when you know how to achieve effective **paragraph development,** your material is far more likely to deliver its message to your reader. Most successful topical paragraphs that seek to inform or persuade (see 1b) contain a generalization, which is communicated in the topic sentence of the paragraph (see 4b). But more is needed. In writing most topical paragraphs, you must be sure to *develop the paragraph.* Development is provided by specific, concrete details that support the generalization. Without development, a topical paragraph contains only the broad claim of the generalization. It goes around in circles because it merely repeats the generalization over and over. It therefore does little to inform or persuade the reader.

Here is a paragraph that is unsuccessful because it contains one generalization restated four times in different words. Compare it with paragraph 1, an example of a successful paragraph, early in this chapter.

> **NO**   The cockroach lore that has been daunting us for years is mostly true. Almost every tale we have heard about cockroaches is true. These tales have been disheartening people for generations. No one seems to believe that it is possible to control roaches.

This *No* paragraph is stalled. It goes nowhere. Such material does not hold the reader's interest because it neither informs nor persuades.

When you write a topical paragraph, remember that **what separates most good writing from bad is the writer's ability to move back and forth between generalizations and specific details.** A successful topical paragraph includes a generalization and specific, concrete supporting details.

Using detail is one of the keys to effective, successful development in topical paragraphs. Details bring generalizations to life by providing concrete, specific illustrations. "RENNS" is a memory device you can use to check whether you have included sufficient detail in a topical paragraph. Chart 20 explains RENNS. A well-supported paragraph usually has only a selection of RENNS, so do not expect your paragraphs to have all categories in the list. Also, RENNS does not mean that the supporting details must occur in the order of the letters in RENNS. To see RENNS in action, read the many sample paragraphs in this chapter with an eye for the details. Also, consider paragraphs 14, 15, and 16 especially.

USING "RENNS" TO CHECK FOR SPECIFIC, CONCRETE DETAILS 20

- ■ **R**easons
- ■ **E**xamples
- ■ **N**ames
- ■ **N**umbers
- ■ **S**enses (sight, sound, smell, taste, touch)

Here is a paragraph that has three of the five types of RENNS. Locate as many RENNS as you can before you read the analysis that follows the paragraph.

> U.S. shores are also being inundated by waves of plastic debris. On the sands of the Texas Gulf Coast one day last September, volunteers collected 307 tons of litter, two-thirds of which was plastic, including 31,733 bags, 30,295 bottles, and 15,631 six-pack yokes. Plastic trash is being found far out to sea. On a four-day trip from Maryland to Florida that ranged 100 miles offshore, John Hardy, an Oregon State University marine biologist, spotted "Styrofoam and other plastic on the surface, most of the whole cruise."

14

"THE DIRTY SEAS," *Time*, August 1, 1988

Paragraph 14 succeeds because it does more than merely repeat its topic sentence, which is its first sentence. It develops the topic sentence by offering concrete, specific illustrations to support the generalization that waves of plastic debris are inundating U.S. shores. It has Examples, including the kinds of litter found washed up on the beach and seen offshore. It has Names, such as Texas Gulf Coast; bags, bottles, six-pack yokes, which describe more specifically the general idea of 307 tons of litter; Maryland; Florida; John Hardy; Oregon State University; marine biologist; and Styrofoam. It has Numbers that describe the volume of litter collected (307 tons), the number of specific items (such as 31,733 bags and 30,295 plastic bottles), and the 100-mile distance from shore where John Hardy found floating plastic litter.

Here is a paragraph that has four of the five types of RENNS. Locate as many RENNS as you can before you read the analysis of RENNS that follows the paragraph.

> We live in a changed world from that of 1888, and we are a changed nation. Our founders knew an America with rising

Cont'd.

5. The two sorts of sequence combine to produce the commonest sort—the mixed sequence. The opportunity to generate the paragraph lies here with the addition of subordinate sentences to clarify and of coordinate sentences to emphasize or to enumerate.

6. Some paragraphs have no topic sentence; in these cases the topic can usually be inferred from the preceding paragraph, where it may be implied or placed.

7. Some paragraphs have sentences at the beginning or at the end that do not belong to the sequence. They furnish a transition either to the new paragraph (at the beginning) or from the current paragraph (at the end), or they may provide a conclusion or coda at the end.

8. Some paragraphing is illogical.

9. Punctuation should be by the paragraph, not by the sentence. Paragraph punctuation involves choosing whether to make compound sentences or not.

BACKGROUND

The article "Structure and Form in Non-Narrative Prose" (*Teaching Composition: 12 Bibliographical Essays*, ed. Gary Tate [Texas Christian UP, Fort Worth, TX 1987]) outlines three main approaches to the paragraph: as "in effect, an expanded sentence," as "a self-contained unit of writing," and as "a subdivision in a total discourse" (72). The first approach is most closely associated with Francis Christensen, the second with Alexander Bain, and the third with Paul Rodgers, Jr. Larson also notes a new conception of the paragraph proposed by Rochelle Smith in "Paragraphing for Coherence: Writing as Implied Dialogue" (*College English* [January 1984]: 8–21) in which each paragraph is seen as the next step in a dialogue of questions, responses, and confirmations between a writer and a reader.

ANSWERS: EXERCISE 4-2

A (paragraph 9). Reasons include learning current knowledge, keeping you learning through life, having a job, being a spouse, a parent, and a member of the community. Examples include job, spouse, parent, and member of the community. Number named is six.

B (paragraph 10). Names include oak, deer, fire fighters. Senses are invoked by sound of crashing oak, sight of flames, "fiery tomb," smoldering in ashes, deer family darting furiously, and the smell (implied) of burning trees.

C (paragraph 11). Examples include colonial Virginians using their cravats as handerkerchiefs and people putting their knives in their mouths. Names include the French traveler, distinguished people, people in the theater. Numbers include the dates 1830 and the 19th century. Senses include the noise—chants, jeers, and shouts—made by the audience in the theater.

D (paragraph 12). Reasons include the fact that a package of peanuts provides half the daily protein requirement. Names include peanuts, package, and protein. Numbers include the 3.5-ounce package, 564 calories.

E (paragraph 13). Reasons include cities are the best places for women to find jobs, and the death rate is higher for young men in cities. Example named is the Bronx. Names used are the Bronx, New York State. Numbers include 79 percent, 85 percent, 95 percent, and 47 men for every 53 women.

ANSWERS: EXERCISE 4-3

Obviously answers will vary considerably, but the main goal is to help students distinguish between generalities and good detail. Perhaps having each student share with the class what he or she considers the best detail in his or her paragraph would help make this point.

15 expectations, while we see a superpower riddled with self-doubt. Tropical rain forests were a mysterious challenge in 1888. The challenge in 1988 is saving them from disappearance. Automobiles had just been invented, and airplanes were unknown. Would our founders be impressed by rush-hour traffic, a brown cloud over Denver, or aerial gridlock at Chicago's O'Hare Airport? Could they have conceived of a Mexico City with 20 million people in an atmosphere so murky that the sun is obscured, so poisonous that school is sometimes delayed until late morning, when the air clears?

—GILBERT M. GROSVENOR, "Will We Mend Our Earth?"

Paragraph 15 succeeds because it does more than repeat its topic sentence, which is the first sentence. The paragraph develops its topic sentence with specific, concrete illustrations of the changed world that makes the United States a changed nation. It has Examples, including rain forests disappearing, automobiles and the rush-hour traffic they cause, airplanes and the aerial gridlock they cause, and air pollution that cars and planes cause. It has Names: America, Denver, Chicago's O'Hare Airport, and Mexico City. It has Numbers: the years 1888 and 1988, and 20 million people. And it elicits one of the five senses: the *sight* of a "brown cloud" over Denver and the *sight* of a murky atmosphere that obscures the sun.

Some well-developed paragraphs have a single extended example to support the topic sentence.

16 He was one of the greatest scientists the world has ever known, yet if I had to convey the essence of Albert Einstein in a single word, I would choose *simplicity*. Perhaps an anecdote will help. Once, caught in a downpour, he took off his hat and held it under his coat. Asked why, he explained, with admirable logic, that the rain would damage the hat, but his hair would be none the worse for its wetting. This knack of going instinctively to the heart of the matter was the secret of his major scientific discoveries—this and his extraordinary feeling for beauty.

—BANESH HOFFMAN, "My Friend, Albert Einstein"

EXERCISE 4-2

Reread the paragraphs in Exercise 4-1 and identify the RENNS (consult 4c) in each paragraph.

EXERCISE 4-3

Using your own words to complete the thought, fill in the blanks with a word or phrase that is specific. Then choose one of the five as a topic sentence and write a well-developed paragraph. Use as many RENNS (consult 4c) as you need to give the topic sentence concrete, specific support.

WRITING COHERENT PARAGRAPHS ¶ *coh* 4d

1. The place where I feel most comfortable is _____.
2. _____ can cause major problems for students.
3. Budgeting time is a skill I _____.
4. The greatest U.S. asset is _____.
5. Getting a good job depends largely on _____.

4d Writing coherent paragraphs

A paragraph is **coherent** when its sentences are related to each other, not only in content but also in grammatical structures and choice of words. To achieve coherence in your writing, write each sentence of a paragraph so that it flows sensibly from the one before. A coherent paragraph gives a reader a sense of continuity. Note in paragraphs 17 through 20 that each sentence continues from the previous sentence, by use of the techniques of coherence listed in Chart 21. As you draft and revise, monitor continuity in your paragraphs.

TECHNIQUES OF COHERENCE   21

- Use **transitional expressions** effectively (4d-1)
- Use **pronouns** effectively (4d-2)
- Use **deliberate repetition** effectively (4d-3)
- Use **parallel structures** effectively (4d-4)

---

1 Using transitional expressions

Transitional expressions are words and phrases that signal connections among ideas. By signalling how ideas relate to each other, you achieve coherence in your writing. Commonly used transitional expressions are listed in Chart 22. When you use them, be sure to vary your choices within each list to achieve variety in your writing. ❖ COMMA ALERT: Transitional expressions are usually set off with commas; see 24b-3. ❖ Here are some illustrations:

CONTINUITY BY ADDITION

Woodpeckers use their beaks to find food and to chisel out nests. **In addition,** they claim their territory and signal their desire to mate by drumming their beaks on trees.

BACKGROUND

The concept of the paragraph as a self-contained or organic unit of language first appeared in *English Composition and Rhetoric* (1866), a textbook by Alexander Bain, professor of rhetoric at the University of Aberdeen in Scotland. Bain defined the paragraph as "a collection of sentences with unity of purpose" and declared unity, coherence, and emphasis to be the characteristics of an effective paragraph, a proclamation that has had a vast influence on textbooks ever since. He gave students seven guidelines for achieving these effects:

1. Distribution into sentences: The paragraph is composed of individual sentences, each with its own unity, working together to form the whole.

2. Explicit reference: The connection of each sentence to the ones preceding it must be clear.

3. Parallel construction: Consecutive sentences that carry the same meaning or idea should be formed alike.

4. Indication of the theme: The first sentence should indicate the scope of the paragraph.

5. Unity: Unity derives from a sustained purpose and admits no digressions or irrelevancies.

6. Consecutive arrangement: Related topics should be placed close together.

7. Marking of subordination: The principal and subordinate statements should have their relative importance clearly indicated, just as such elements in a sentence do.

Later textbooks influenced by Bain, notably Fred Newton Scott and Joseph Villiers Denney's *Paragraph-Writing* (1891), treated the paragraph as an "essay in miniature" and encouraged a meristic or parts-to-whole approach to teaching the essay, first teaching students how to write sentences and paragraphs and then teaching them to put these parts together to build essays.

BACKGROUND

The concept of the paragraph as a subdivision of a paper is explained in "A Discourse-Centered Rhetoric of the Paragraph" by Paul C. Rodgers, Jr. (*College Composition and Communication* [February 1966]: 2–11). He argues against an organic conception of the paragraph, stating that writers decide on the length and shape of their paragraphs based on many considerations—emphasis, tone, appearance on the printed page. What a writer does in one paragraph will affect how he or she structures the preceding and following paragraphs. Rick Eden and Ruth Mitchell take a similar position in "Paragraphing for the Reader" (*College Composition and Communication* [December 1986]: 416–430). They argue that paragraphing is not part of the process of generating material for writing but part of the revising and editing process, when the writer "refines and shapes material already on the page" (417). With audience, purpose, appearance, and other considerations in mind, a writer shapes paragraphs to manipulate readers' expectations and attention to improve their comprehension and to emphasize some points over others. Rodgers, as well as Eden and Mitchell, argue against a meristic approach to teaching in favor of a holistic or whole-to-parts approach, in which students learn to write paragraphs in the context of writing entire essays.

CONTINUITY BY CONTRAST

Most birds communicate by singing. Woodpeckers, **however,** communicate by the duration and rhythm of the drumming of their beaks.

CONTINUITY BY RESULT

Woodpeckers communicate by drumming their beaks on dry branches or tree trunks. **As a result,** they can communicate across greater distances than songbirds can.

COMMON TRANSITIONAL EXPRESSIONS AND THE RELATIONSHIPS THEY SIGNAL 22

RELATIONSHIP	WORDS
ADDITION	also, in addition, too, moreover, and, besides, furthermore, equally important, then, finally,
EXAMPLE	for example, for instance, thus, as an illustration, namely, specifically,
CONTRAST	but, yet, however, on the other hand, nevertheless, nonetheless, conversely, in contrast, still, at the same time,
COMPARISON	similarly, likewise, in the same way,
CONCESSION	of course, to be sure, certainly, granted,
RESULT	therefore, thus, as a result, so, accordingly,
SUMMARY	hence, in short, in brief, in summary, in conclusion, finally,
TIME SEQUENCE	first, second, third, next, then, finally, afterwards, before, soon, later, meanwhile, subsequently, immediately, eventually, currently,
PLACE	in the front, in the foreground, in the back, in the background, at the side, adjacent, nearby, in the distance, here, there,

Consider how the transitional expressions (shown in boldface) help to make this paragraph coherent.

> **In addition to** causing viewers to lose touch with society, television has had negative effects on viewers' imagination. Before the days of television, people were entertained by exciting radio shows such as *Superman, Batman,* and "War of the Worlds." **Of course,** the listener was required to pay careful attention to the story if all details were to be comprehended. **Better yet,** while listening to the stories, listeners would form their own images of the actions taking place. When the broadcaster would give brief descriptions of the Martian space ships invading earth, **for example,** every member of the audience would imagine a different space ship. **In contrast,** television's version of "War of the Worlds" will not stir the imagination at all, **for** everyone can clearly see the actions taking place. All viewers see the same space ship with the same features. Each aspect is clearly defined, and **therefore,** no one will imagine anything different from what is seen. **Thus,** television cannot be considered an effective tool for stimulating the imagination.
>
> —TOM PARADIS, "A Child's Other World"

17

2 | Using pronouns

When you use pronouns that clearly refer to nouns or other pronouns (see Chapter 10), you help your reader follow the bridges you build from one sentence to the next. Consider how the pronouns, shown in boldface, help make the following paragraph coherent.

> The funniest people I know are often unaware of just how ticked off **they** are about things until **they** start to kid around about them. Nature did not build **these** people to sputter or preach; instead, in response to the world's irritations, **they** create little plays in their minds—parodies, cartoons, fantasies. When **they** see how funny **their** creations are, **they** also understand how really sore **they** were at **their** sources. **Their** anger is a revelation, one that works backward in the minds of an audience: the audience starts out laughing and winds up fuming.
>
> —ROGER ROSENBLATT, "What Brand of Laughter Do You Use?"

18

---

3 Using deliberate, selective repetition

You can achieve coherence by repeating key words in a paragraph. A key word is usually one related to the main idea in the topic sentence or to a major detail in one of the supporting sentences. Repeating a key word now and then helps your reader follow your material. This technique must be used sparingly, however, because you risk being monotonous. The shorter a paragraph, the less likely that repeated words will be effective.

Consider how the careful reuse of key words (shown in boldface) helps make this paragraph coherent.

19

> Anthropologist Elena Padilla, author of *Up from Puerto Rico*, describing Puerto Rican **life** in a poor and squalid district of New York, tells **how** much people know about each other—**who** is to be trusted and **who** not, **who** is defiant of the law and **who** upholds it, **who** is competent and well informed and **who** is inept and ignorant—and **how** these things are known from the **public life** of the sidewalk and its associated enterprises. These are matters of **public** character. But she also tells **how** select are those permitted to drop into the kitchen for a cup of coffee, **how** strong are the ties, and **how** limited the number of a person's genuine confidants, those **who** share in a person's **private life** and **private affairs. She** tells **how** it is not considered **dignified** for everyone to know one's **affairs.** Nor is it considered **dignified** to snoop on others beyond the face presented in **public.** It does violence to a person's **privacy** and rights. In this, the people she describes are essentially the same as the people of the mixed, Americanized city street on which I **live,** and essentially the same as the people **who live** in high-income apartments or fine town houses, too.
>
> —Jane Jacobs, *The Economy of Cities*

4 Using parallel structures

Parallel structures can help you achieve coherence in a paragraph. **Parallelism** is created when grammatically equivalent forms are used several times. The repeated tempos and sounds of parallel structures reinforce connections among ideas and create a dramatic effect. Be aware, however, that a thin line exists between effective parallelism (see Chapter 18) and lack of conciseness (see Chapter 16).

In paragraph 20, the authors use many parallel structures (shown in boldface) including a parallel series of words: *the sacred, the secular, the scientific.* They also use parallel phrases°: *sometimes smiled at, sometimes frowned upon.* They end the paragraph with a group of six parallel clauses°, starting with *banish danger with a gesture.*

20   Superstitions are **sometimes smiled at** and **sometimes frowned upon** as observances characteristic of the old-fashioned, the unenlightened, children, peasants, servants, immigrants, foreigners or backwoods people. Nevertheless, they give all of us ways of moving back and forth among the different worlds in which we live—**the sacred, the secular,** and **the scientific.** They allow us to keep a private world also, where, smiling a little, we can **banish danger with a gesture** and **summon luck with a rhyme, make the sun shine in spite of storm clouds, force the stranger to do our bidding, keep an enemy at bay,** and **straighten the paths of those we love.**

—Margaret Mead and Rhoda Metraux, "New Superstitions for Old"

5   Showing relationships among paragraphs

Paragraphs in an essay do not stand in isolation. You can use the techniques of coherence discussed in this chapter to communicate relationships among paragraphs in an essay. Transitional expressions, pronouns, deliberate repetition, and parallel structures can all help you link ideas from paragraph to paragraph throughout an essay.

One excellent way to connect paragraphs is to start a new paragraph with a reference to the previous paragraph. Passage 21 uses this technique. Also, the student essays and research papers throughout this handbook make the connections among paragraphs that help to maintain coherence in longer pieces of writing.

Passage 21 shows two full paragraphs and the start of a third paragraph from an essay on health-care costs in the journal *Science.* Repeated words connecting these paragraphs include *commission, commissioners, list,* and *Oregon.* The "It sounds great" sentence tightly links the first and second paragraphs: a reader does not know what "sounds great" without the information in the first paragraph about cost-benefit ratios. In a similar way, the opening sentence of the third paragraph, "While commission members dismiss the first draft's failure . . . ," creates another strong link to the second and first paragraphs. From these two paragraphs a reader can understand the reference to "first draft's failure."

I am not complaining that the brewing and baking were taken over by the men. If they can brew and bake as well as women or better, then by all means let them do it. But they cannot have it both ways. If they are going to adopt the very sound principle that the job should be done by the person who does it best, then that rule must be applied universally. If the women make better office-workers than men, then they must have the office work. If any individual woman is able to make a first-class lawyer, doctor, architect or engineer, then she must be allowed to try her hand at it. Once lay down the rule that the job comes first and you throw that job open to every individual, man or woman, fat or thin, tall or short, ugly or beautiful, who is able to do that job better than the rest of the world.

—Dorothy L. Sayers, "Are Women Human?"

EXTRA EXERCISE B

Rewrite the following paragraph using transitional words and phrases to make it more coherent. Combine and rearrange the sentences where necessary.

Americans are beginning to recognize the importance of regular exercise. Jogging gives the heart a good workout. It can damage the runner's ankles and calves. Jogging by itself does little to exercise the upper body. Some people prefer to walk. Bicycling is popular. In a pleasant setting it provides visual pleasures as well as a way to burn up calories. Some people ride a stationary bicycle at home. They can watch television while they rotate the pedals. Swimming involves the upper body as well as the legs. It allows a person to exert as much energy as possible without straining muscles. On a hot summer day swimming seems more like fun than exercise.

QUOTATION ABOUT WRITING

I don't know why I am so helplessly led to condensation in both my fiction and my essays. Some people find it hard to follow my meaning because I don't spell it out, not entirely. My writing is simple but I like to be sort of emphatic and let it go. I remember when I was writing exams in school I'd be the first one finished. All these people writing away. As I look back on it I think I didn't want to tell the teacher what he already knew, but to try to get at things from an angle—nothing very grand, just a little twist.

—Elizabeth Hardwick, *Writers at Work*

ANSWERS: EXERCISE 4-4

A (paragraph 22). *Pronouns:* her, she. *Deliberate repetition:* Kathy, arms, hands opened, closed. *Parallel structures:* Many parallel clauses, starting with "Her shoulders raised"; open hands reaching out and closed hands bringing back.

B (paragraph 23). *Pronouns:* we, this. *Deliberate repetition:* we. *Parallel structures:* Once set in motion, must remain in motion; we must.

➜

---

21 Oregon's commission thought it had the solution. And so did all the newspapers, magazines, and television stations that covered the commission's announcement last May. A means had been found, the stories went, to assign a cost-benefit rating to nearly 2,000 medical procedures. The basis of the list was a mathematical formula. All that had to be done was to feed piles of data into a computer, and the machine would respond with a list of procedures, carefully ordered according to their cost-benefit ratios.

It sounds great. But the list the computer actually spit out last May left the 11 commissioners reeling. Take thumb-sucking and acute headaches: treatments for these problems ranked higher than those for cystic fibrosis and AIDS. Immunizations for childhood diseases did not appear. Deeply embarrassed, the commissioners hastily withdrew the list, and three months later Oregon appears to be no closer to a second version. The current prognosis: a revised list is not expected until some time in the fall.

While commission members dismiss the first draft's failure as unimportant, it does indicate the complexity of the problem they face. [The paragraph continues, discussing specific details of the problem's complexity.]

—Virginia Morell, "Oregon Puts Bold Health Plan on Ice"

EXERCISE 4-4

Consulting section 4d, Identify the techniques of coherence—words of transition, pronouns, deliberate repetition, and parallel structures—in each paragraph.

A.   22 Kathy sat with her legs dangling over the edge of the side of the hood. The band of her earphones held back strands of straight copper hair which had come loose from two thick braids that hung down her back. She swayed with the music that only she could hear. Her shoulders raised, making circles in the warm air. Her arms reached out to her side; her opened hands reached for the air; her closed hands brought the air back to her. Her arms reached over her head; her opened hands reached for a cloud; her closed hands brought the cloud back to her. Her head moved from side to side; her eyes opened and closed to the tempo of the tunes. Kathy was motion.

—Claire Burke, student

B.   23 Newton's law may have wider application than just the physical world. In the social world, racism, once set into motion, will remain in motion unless acted upon by an outside force. The collective "we" must be the outside force. We must fight racism through education. We must make sure every school has the resources to do its job. We must present to our children a culturally diverse curriculum that reflects our pluralistic society. This can help students understand that prejudice is learned through contact with prejudiced people, rather than with the people toward whom the prejudice is directed.

Randolph H. Manning, "Fighting Racism with Inclusion"

C. Elephant shrews come into the world nose first, and "nose first" they go through the rest of their nervous lives. Ever alert for
24 danger, these tiny mammals depend on their noses as we do our eyes, mapping their twilight world primarily by scent. Their long, flexible noses twitch constantly, probing, sniffing, and exploring every detail of their brushy, dry habitat.

Susan Lumpkin, "The Elephant Shrew—By a Nose!"

D. The snow geese are first, rising off the ponds to breakfast in the sorghum fields up the river. Twenty thousand of them, perhaps more, great white birds with black wing tips rising out of the darkness into the rosy reflected light of dawn. They make a sweeping turn, a cloud of wings rising above the cottonwoods. But *cloud* is the wrong word.
25 They do not form a disorderly blackbird rabble but a kaleidoscope of goose formations, always shifting, but always orderly. The light catches them—white against the tan velvet of the hills. Then they are overhead, line after line, layer above layer of formations, and the sky is filled with the clamor of an infinity of geese.

Tony Hillerman, *Hillerman Country*

E. A full-grown brown bear can weigh more than 1,000 pounds, stand 12 feet tall on its hind legs and outrun a horse for short distances. Technically, brown bears are the same species as the grizzly bear—the one known as *Ursus arctos*. There are some differences, however. Brown bears occupy the coastal rim of southern
26 Alaska and parts of the Yukon and British Columbia. Grizzlies are found farther inland, for the most part; their range also includes much of western Canada and some of Montana, Idaho, and Wyoming. Brownies tend to be larger; grizzlies tend to have a more dish-shaped face and a more pronounced hump. The main difference, however, is that brown bears have access to migrating salmon and grizzlies don't.

—Boyd Norton, "It's a Good Thing McNeil's Big Bears Get Plenty to Eat"

EXERCISE 4-5

Reread the paragraphs in Exercise 4-1, and then, consulting section 4d, identify all techniques of coherence—words of transition, pronouns, deliberate repetition, and parallel structures.

Cont'd.

C (paragraph 24). *Pronouns:* they, their, we, our. *Deliberate repetition:* nose first. *Parallel structures:* come nose first, go first; probing, sniffing, exploring.

D (paragraph 25). *Pronouns:* them, they. *Transitional expressions:* first, but, then. *Deliberate repetition:* cloud, always, line, layer. *Parallel structures:* always shifting but always orderly, line after line, layer above layer.

E (paragraph 26). *Transitional expressions:* however, also. *Deliberate repetition:* brown bear, grizzlies. *Parallel structures:* Brownies tend to be, grizzlies tend to be.

ANSWERS: EXERCISE 4-5
Students are likely to find more examples than the answers given here.

A (paragraph 9). *Transitional expressions:* after all, too. *Pronoun:* you. *Parallel structure:* historical, social, cultural; as a parent, as a member of the community.

B (paragraph 10). *Deliberate repetition:* destructive, destruction, destroy. *Parallel structure:* crashes, smolders, darts, lies.

C (paragraph 11). *Pronouns:* our, they. *Transitional expressions:* and, so. *Deliberate repetition:* people.

D (paragraph 12). *Transitional expressions:* but, that same. *Deliberate repetition:* peanuts, contains.

E (paragraph 13). *Transitional expressions:* first, but, second, for example. *Deliberate repetition:* men, women.

ANSWERS: EXERCISE 4-6

Each paragraph will obviously differ in content, but this exercise should help students see that they need to support general statements with graphic details (developed through RENNS) that are smoothly linked by the techniques of coherence discussed in 4b: transitional expressions, pronouns, repetition, and parallelism.

BACKGROUND

In "A Tagmemic Approach to Paragraph Analysis" (*College Composition and Communication* [December 1965]: 237–242; rpt. *Rhetoric and Composition: A Sourcebook for Writing Teachers,* ed. Richard L. Graves [Portsmouth, NH Boynton/Cook, 1984]), A. L. Becker notes that paragraphs for exposition often follow two basic patterns: topic–restriction–illustration (TRI) and problem–solution (PS).

The TRI pattern has three "slots"—topic, restriction, and illustration. It begins with a topic sentence or proposition in the **T** slot. The **R** slot defines, restates, or explains the proposition at a lower level of generality. The **I** slot often provides one or more examples, an extended analogy, or a series of comparisons that describe or exemplify the topic at a still lower level of generality.

The problem–solution or PS pattern states a problem or effect in the opening **P** slot, sometimes in question form, and follows by stating the solution or cause in the **S** slot. If the explanation of the solution or cause is extended, it may follow the TRI pattern. Becker illustrates both the TRI and PS patterns with a paragraph from Frank Gibney's *Five Gentlemen of Japan:*

➡

EXERCISE 4-6

Consulting sections 4c and 4d, develop three of the following topic sentences into paragraphs that are unified with RENNS and techniques of coherence. After you finish, list the RENNS and the techniques of coherence you have built into each paragraph.

1. Newspaper comic strips reflect many current problems.
2. What constitutes garbage in the United States says a great deal about American culture.
3. Children are taught to compete at too early an age.
4. Learning to do laundry can be perilous to one's clothes.
5. College athletics is big business.

4e Arranging a paragraph

Arranging a paragraph means putting its sentences into an order logical for communicating the message of the paragraph clearly and effectively. This section shows you the most common choices for arrangements of topical paragraphs. Choices include sequencing according to time and to location; moving from general to specific, from specific to general, and from least to most important; and progressing from problem to solution.

As you write, you might prefer to postpone your final decisions about the arrangement of your paragraphs until after you have written a first draft. As you revise, you can experiment to see how your sentences can be arranged for greatest impact.

According to time

A paragraph arranged according to time is put into a *chronological sequence*. It tells what happened or what is happening during a period of time.

> Other visitors include schools of dolphin swimming with synchronized precision and the occasional humpback whale. Before 1950, these 14-meter marine mammals were a common sight in the waters of the Great Barrier Reef as they passed on their annual migration between Antarctic waters and the tropics, where their calves were born. Then in the 1950s whaling stations were set up on the New South Wales and Queensland coasts, and together with the long-established Antarctic hunts by the Soviet Union and America, whales were slaughtered in their thousands. By the time the whaling stations on the eastern Australian coast closed in the

27

early 1960s, it was estimated that only two hundred remained in these waters. Today, their numbers are slowly increasing, but sightings are still rare.

—ALLAN MOULT, "Volcanic Peaks, Tropical Rainforest, and Mangrove Swamps"

According to location

A paragraph arranged according to location is put into a *spatial sequence.* It describes the position of objects relative to one another, often from a central point of reference. The topic sentence usually establishes a location that serves as the orientation for all other places mentioned. The other sentences in the paragraph often use transitional expressions (see Chart 22) that indicate *place.*

28 The old store, lighted only by three fifty-watt bulbs, smelled of coal oil and baking bread. In the middle of the rectangular room, where the oak floor sagged a little, stood an iron stove. To the right was a wooden table with an unfinished game of checkers and a stool made from an apple-tree stump. On shelves around the walls sat earthen jugs with corncob stoppers, a few canned goods, and some of the two thousand old clocks and clockworks Thurmond Watts owned. Only one was ticking; the others he just looked at.

—WILLIAM LEAST HEAT MOON, *Blue Highways*

From general to specific

An arrangement of sentences from the general to the specific is the most common organization for a paragraph. Seen in many of the examples earlier in this chapter, a general-to-specific arrangement begins with a topic sentence (and perhaps is followed by a limiting or clarifying sentence) and ends with specific details.

29 Unwanted music is privacy's constant enemy. There is hardly an American restaurant, store, railroad station or bus terminal that doesn't gurgle with melody from morning to night, nor is it possible any longer to flee by boarding the train or bus itself, or even by taking a walk in the park. Transistor radios have changed all that. Men, women and children carry them everywhere, hugging them with the desperate attachment that a baby has for its blanket, fearful that they might have to generate an idea of their own or contemplate a blade of grass. Thoughtless themselves, they have no thought for the sufferers within earshot of their portentous news broadcasts and raucous jazz. It is hardly surprising that RCA announced a plan that would pipe canned music and pharmaceutical commercials to 25,000 doctors' offices in eighteen big cities— one place where a decent quietude might be expected. This raises a

Cont'd.

(P) How obsolete is Hearn's judgment? **(S1) (T)** On the surface the five gentlemen of Japan do not themselves seem to be throttled by this rigid society of their ancestors. **(R)** Their world is in fact far looser in its demands upon them than it once was. **(I)** Industrialization and the influence of the West have progressively softened the texture of the web. Defeat in war badly strained it. A military occupation, committed to producing a democratic Japan, pulled and tore at it. **(S2) (T)** But it has not disappeared. **(R)** It is still the invisible adhesive that seals the nation-hood of the Japanese. **(I)** Shimizu, Sanada, Yamazaki, Kisfi and Hirohito were all born within its bonds. Despite their individual work, surroundings and opinions, they have lived most of their lives as cogs geared into a group society. Literally as well as figuratively speaking, none of them has a lock on his house door.

ALTERNATE EXAMPLE: SPATIAL SEQUENCE

The wash [low land that is sometimes flooded, at other times nearly dry] looked perfectly dry in my headlights. I drove down, across, up the other side and on into the night. Glimpses of weird humps of pale rock on either side, like petrified elephants, dinosaurs, stone-age hobgoblins. Now and then something alive scurried across the road: kangaroo mice, a jackrabbit, an animal that looked like a cross between a raccoon and a squirrel—the ringtail cat. Farther on a pair of mule deer started from the brush and bounded obliquely through the beams of my lights, raising puffs of dust which the wind, moving faster than my pickup truck, caught and carried ahead of me out of sight into the dark. The road, narrow and rocky, twisted sharply left and right, dipped in and out of tight ravines, climbing by degrees toward a summit which I would see only in the light of the coming day.

—Edward Abbey, "The Most Beautiful Place on Earth"

whole new criterion for choosing a family physician. Better to have a second-rate healer content with the sounds of his stethoscope than an eminent specialist poking to the rhythms of Gershwin.

—WILLIAM ZINSSER, *The Haircurl Papers*

From specific to general

A less common arrangement moves from the specific to the general. Like paragraphs 6 and 7 earlier in this chapter, a paragraph with such an arrangement ends with a topic sentence and begins with the details that support the topic sentence.

30 Replacing the spark plugs probably ranks number one on the troubleshooting list of most home auto mechanics. Too often this effort produces little or no improvement, as the problem lies elsewhere. Within the ignition system the plug wires, distributor unit, coil, and ignition control unit play just as vital a role as the spark plugs. However, performance problems are by no means limited to the ignition system. The fuel system and emissions control system also help determine engine performance, and each of these systems contains several components which equal the spark plug in importance. The do-it-yourself mechanic who wants to provide basic care for a car should be able to do more than change the spark plugs.

—DANNY WITT, student

From least to most important

A sentence arrangement that moves from the least to the most important is known as *climactic order* because it saves the climax for the end. This arrangement can be effective in holding the reader's interest because the best part comes at the end. In informative and persuasive writing, this type of arrangement usually calls for the topic sentence at the beginning of the paragraph, although sometimes the topic sentence works well at the end. Here is a climactic paragraph that begins with a topic sentence.

31 But probably the most dumbfounding of nature's extraordinary creations is the horned toad of our Southwest. A herpetologist once invited me to observe one of these lizards right after it had molted. In a sand-filled glass cage I saw a large male. Beside him lay his old skin. The herpetologist began to annoy the beast with mock attacks, and the old man of the desert with his vulnerable new suit became frightened. Suddenly his eyeballs reddened. A final fast lunge from my friend at the beast and I froze in astonishment—a fine spray of blood shot from the lizard's eye, like fire from a dragon! The beast struck back with a weapon so shocking that it terrifies even the fiercest enemy.

—JEAN GEORGE, "That Astonishing Creature—Nature"

From problem to solution

An effective arrangement can be to present a problem and move quickly to a suggested solution. The topic sentence presents the problem and the next sentence—the limiting or clarifying sentence—presents the main idea of the solution. The rest of the sentences give the specifics of the solution.

> When I first met them, Sara and Michael were a two-career couple with a home of their own, and a large boat bought with a large loan. What interested them in a concept called voluntary simplicity was the birth of their daughter and a powerful desire to raise her themselves. Neither one of them, it turned out, was willing to restrict what they considered their "real life" into the brief time before work and the tired hours afterward. "A lot of people think that as they have children and things get more expensive, the only answer is to work harder in order to earn more money. It's not the only answer," insists Michael. The couple's decision was to trade two full-time careers for two half-time careers, and to curtail consumption. They decided to spend their money only on things that contributed to their major goal, the construction of a world where family and friendship, work and play, were all of a piece, a world, moreover, which did not make wasteful use of the earth's resources.

32

—LINDA WELTNER, "Stripping Down to Bare Happiness"

EXERCISE 4-7

For each paragraph, arrange the sentences into a logical sequence. Begin by locating the topic sentence and placing it at the beginning of the paragraph. As you work, consult sections 4b and 4c.

PARAGRAPH A

1. Handel, through his use of a major key and a dynamic and melismatic melody in the Hallelujah Chorus of his *Messiah,* gives us a sense of hopeful elation.

2. Although defined as "the art of arranging sounds with reference to rhythm, pitch and tone quality" by Funk and Wagnall, music is, in reality, much, much more.

ANSWERS: EXERCISE 4-7

Answers to this exercise may vary; alternate versions that can be defended are acceptable.

A. In the original paragraph, the sentences appeared in this order: 2, 5, 4, 6, 1, 3.

B. In the original paragraph, the sentences appeared in this order: 3, 7, 6, 1, 5, 2, 4.

C. In the original paragraph, the sentences appeared in this order: 5, 3, 1, 4, 2.

3. Chopin, on the other hand, through his use of the minor mode, bass register and slow tempo, conveys to us the feeling of sullen despair in the third movement of his Second Piano Sonata.

4. There is no doubt that we experience certain feelings when we fall under its hypnotic influence.

5. For example, music is surely the art of creating emotional responses through the skillful manipulation of sounds.

6. Examples of this power can be found among the works of any of the great composers.

—Kevin Kerwood, student

PARAGRAPH B

1. After a busy day, lens wearers often do not feel like taking time out to clean and disinfect their lenses, and many wearers skip the chore.

2. When buying a pair of glasses, a person deals with just the expense of the glasses themselves.

3. Although contact lenses make the wearer more attractive, glasses are easier and less expensive to care for.

4. However, in addition to the cost of the lenses themselves, contact lens wearers must shoulder the extra expense of cleaning supplies.

5. This inattention creates a danger of infection.

6. In contrast, contact lenses require daily cleaning and weekly enzyming that inconvenience lens wearers.

7. Glasses can be cleaned quickly with water and tissue at the wearer's convenience.

—Heather Martin, student

PARAGRAPH C

1. Indeed, there are moments today—amid outlaw litter, tax cheating, illicit noise and motorized anarchy—when it seems as though the scofflaw represents the wave of the future.

2. Already, Riesman says, the ethic of U.S. society is in danger of becoming this: ''You're a fool if you obey the rules.''

3. Yet it is painfully apparent that millions of Americans who would never think of themselves as lawbreakers, let alone criminals, are taking increasing liberties with the legal codes that are designed to protect and nourish their society.

4. Harvard sociologist David Riesman suspects that a majority of Americans have blithely taken to committing supposedly minor derelictions as a matter of course.

5. Law-and-order is the longest-running and probably the best-loved political issue in U.S. history.

—FRANK TIPPET, "A Red Light for Scofflaws"

EXERCISE 4-8

Consulting sections 4b and 4e, first identify all topic sentences. Then identify the arrangement or arrangements that organize the sentences in each paragraph. Choose from time, location, general to specific, specific to general, least to most important, and problem to solution.

A.   A combination of cries from exotic animals and laughter and gasps from children fills the air along with the aroma of popcorn and peanuts. A hungry lion bellows for dinner, his roar breaking through the confusing chatter of other animals. Birds of all kinds chirp endlessly at curious children. Monkeys swing from limb to limb performing gymnastics for gawking onlookers. A comedy routine by
33 orangutans employing old shoes and garments incites squeals of amusement. Reptiles sleep peacefully behind glass windows, yet they send shivers down the spines of those who remember the quick death many of these reptiles can induce. The sights and sounds and smells of the zoo inform and entertain children of all ages.

—DEBORAH HARRIS, student

B.   No one even agrees anymore on what "old" is. Not long ago, 30 was middle-aged and 60 was old. Now, more and more people are living into their 70s, 80s and beyond—and many of them are living
34 *well,* without any incapacitating mental or physical decline. Today, old age is defined not simply by chronological years, but by degree of health and well being.

—CAROL TAVRIS, "Old Age Is Not What It Used to Be"

C.   Surprisingly, the very first Chinese to set foot on United States soil were not adventurers or laborers in search of gold but students in search of knowledge. In 1847, a year before the glitter of that metallic substance caught the eye of John Marshall on the south bank of the American River, an American missionary, the Reverend S. R. Brown,
35 had brought with him three Chinese boys to the United States to study at the Monson Academy in Massachusetts. One of them was Yung Wing, who later graduated from Yale and who attained high office in the Chinese government. He was successful in persuading the Emperor to send other students to the United States for specialized

ANSWERS: EXERCISE 4-8

Students will likely see more than one arrangement in some of these paragraphs. *Note:* You might also ask students to analyze these paragraphs in light of what was previously discussed in this chapter: topic sentence, words in topic sentences that create focus and control (4a), development with RENNS (4c), and techniques of coherence (4d).

A (paragraph 33). Topic sentence last; specific to general

B (paragraph 34). Topic sentence last; problem to solution (and perhaps time)

C (paragraph 35). Topic sentence first; general to specific; (and perhaps least to most important)

D (paragraph 36). Topic sentence first; least to most important

E (paragraph 37). Topic sentence first and repeated last; time (and perhaps general to specific)

QUOTATION ABOUT WRITING

Within time and type, then, the individual writer makes his [or her] own unique combinations of choice. What it seems to me important for the young writer to know is what these choices are, how they have been made in the past, and how he [or she] may make them in the present. They are not infinitely various, for example, but limited and significant for certain tones and attitudes. . . .

—Josephine Miles "The Paragraph and Beyond," *CCC*, October 1963, pp. 146–154.

training and education, almost all of whom eventually rendered distinguished service to their country, then emerging from her self-isolation.

—BETTY LEE SUNG, *Mountain of Gold: The Story of the Chinese in America*

D.   Lately, bee researchers have been distracted by a new challenge from abroad. It is, of course, the so-called "killer bee" that was imported into Brazil from Africa in the mid-1950s and has been heading our way ever since. The Africanized bee looks like the Italian bee but is more defensive and more inclined to attack in force. It
36   consumes much of the honey that it produces, leaving relatively little for anyone who attempts to work with it. It travels fast, competes with local bees and, worse, mates with them. It has ruined the honey industry in Venezuela and now the big question is: Will the same thing happen here?

—JIM DOHERTY,
"The Hobby That Challenges You to Think Like a Bee"

E.   When children begin to play with other children and when they finally go to school, their names take on a public dimension. The child with a "funny" name is usually in for trouble, but most kids are proud of their names and want to write them on their books and pads and homework. There was a time when older children carved their names or initials on trees. Now that there are so many people and so few
37   trees, the spray can has taken over from the jackknife, but the impulse to put one's identifying mark where all the world can see it is as strong as ever. The popularity of commercially produced name-on objects of every kind, from teeshirts to miniature license plates, also attests to the importance youngsters (and a lot of grown-ups too) place on claiming and proclaiming their names.

—CASEY MILLER AND KATE SWIFT, "Women and Names"

ANSWERS: EXERCISE 4-9

Answers will vary according to how each student conceives of each subject. Comparisons of the methods of arrangement can reveal the multiplicity of available choices.

EXERCISE 4-9

Often more than one arrangement can be effective for discussing a subject. Think through the topics listed here and consider what arrangement (one or more) might be effective for discussing the subject. Consulting section 4e, choose from general to specific, specific to general, least to most important, problem to solution, location, and time. Be ready to explain your choices. As long as you can give a convincing rationale, you will be correct.

1. ways to make friends
2. automobile accidents
3. how to combine work and college
4. role of the U.S. Supreme Court

5. what parents of teenagers can learn from William Shakespeare's play *Romeo and Juliet*
6. the role of computers at home
7. traveling by bus
8. how to survive an earthquake
9. the problems with junk food
10. music favorites today

4f Knowing patterns for developing a paragraph

Patterns for **paragraph development** in informative and persuasive writing (see 1b) have evolved as writers have sought methods to express their ideas most effectively. When you know a variety of patterns for paragraph development, you have more choices when you are seeking ways to help your paragraphs deliver their meanings most effectively.

For the purpose of illustration, the patterns in this section are discussed separately. In essay writing, however, paragraph patterns often overlap. For example, narrative writing often contains descriptions; explanations of processes often include comparisons and contrasts; and so on. As you write paragraphs of various patterns, you will likely find that many patterns share characteristics. Your goal is to use paragraph patterns in the service of communicating meaning, not for their own sakes.

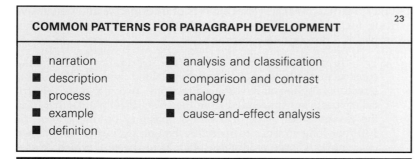

COMMON PATTERNS FOR PARAGRAPH DEVELOPMENT 23

- narration
- description
- process
- example
- definition
- analysis and classification
- comparison and contrast
- analogy
- cause-and-effect analysis

1 Using narration

Narrative writing tells about what is happening or what has happened. In informative and persuasive writing, narration is

BACKGROUND

Richard M. Coe, in *Process, Form, and Substance: A Rhetoric for Advanced Writers*, 2nd ed. (Englewood Cliffs, NJ: Prentice Hall, 1990), groups patterns of development into report and explanatory patterns and into analytic and progressive patterns. Description and narration are report patterns that depend on observation and "compose our perceptions" (261). Explanatory patterns (comparison/contrast, classification and division, definition, analogy, process analysis, causal explanation, and logical progression), on the other hand, are "abstracted" from description and narration to explain and make distinctions (301). Analytic patterns (description, comparison/contrast, classification and division, definition, and analogy) report and explain in static and spatial terms. Progressive patterns (narration, process, cause and effect, and logical progression), in contrast, are organized by time, and report and explain process and change.

usually written in chronological sequence. Narrative paragraphs that illustrate other aspects of informative and persuasive writing include paragraphs 16, 21, 31, and 54.

Here is another example of a narrative paragraph. Its main idea appears in the next-to-last sentence, when Gordon Parks explains what kind of "weapon" cameras have been for him.

38   Gordon Parks speculates that he might have spent his life as a waiter on the North Coast Limited train if he hadn't strolled into one particular movie house during a stopover in Chicago. It was shortly before World War II began, and on the screen was a hair-raising newsreel of Japanese planes attacking a gunboat. When it was over the cameraman came out on stage and the audience cheered. From that moment on Parks was determined to become a photographer. During his next stopover, in Seattle, he went into a pawnshop and purchased his first camera for $7.50. With that small sum, Parks later proclaimed, "I had bought what was to become my weapon against poverty and racism." Eleven years later, he became the first black photographer at Life Magazine.

—SUSAN HOWARD, "Depth of Field"

2   Using description

Descriptive writing appeals to a reader's senses—sight, sound, smell, taste, and touch. Descriptive writing permits you to share your sensual impressions of a person, a place, or an object. Descriptive paragraphs that illustrate other aspects of informative and persuasive writing include paragraphs 1, 14, 18, 19, and 28. Here is another example of a descriptive paragraph.

39   To a fugitive from the surface world, an underground construction site seems like a cave filled with unidentifiable structures angling off in various directions. Two rust-coated electrical conduits are suspended from the street-level planks that form the cavern's roof. A vertical slab of masonry on one side of the 150-foot-long corridor turns out to be one wall of an abandoned coal chute. A large pipe perpendicular to the rest, which crosses the corridor, is a sewerline connector. The place has a strange bluish light at the end open to the outside, where a large blue curtain has been hung to keep out the weather. A little swirl of dust and gas collects near the roof of the tunnel, and there is an occasional whiff of sewage. Ladders, tools, and plank walkways clutter the narrow workspace. At the point where the corridor

ends, a dozen pipes and conduits of varying sizes disappear into a solid 12-foot-high wall of New York dirt.

—DONALD DALE JACKSON,
"It Takes a 'Sixth Sense' to Operate Underneath the Streets of New York"

3 Using process

Process is a term used for writing that describes a sequence of actions by which something is done or made. Usually a process description is developed in chronological order. For an example, see paragraph 40. To be effective, process writing must include all steps. The amount of detail depends on whether you want to instruct the reader about how to do something or you want to offer a general overview of the process. Here is a process description written to give the reader a general picture. A process description that gives directions appears in paragraph 41.

> Making chocolate is not as simple as grinding a bag of beans. The machinery in a chocolate factory towers over you, rumbling and whirring. A huge cleaner first blows the beans away from their accompanying debris—sticks and stones, coins and even bullets can fall among cocoa beans being bagged. Then they go into another machine for roasting. Next comes separation in a winnower, shells sliding out one side, beans falling from the other. Grinding follows, resulting in chocolate liquor. Fermentation, roasting and "conching" all influence the flavor of chocolate. Chocolate is "conched"—rolled over and over against itself like pebbles in the sea—in enormous circular machines named conches for the shells they once resembled. Climbing a flight of steps to peer into this huge, slow-moving glacier, I was expecting something like molten mud but found myself forced to conclude it resembled nothing so much as chocolate.

40

—RUTH MEHRTENS GALVIN, "Sybaritic to Some, Sinful to Others"

Here is a process description that gives the reader specific, step-by-step instructions.

> Carrying loads of equal weight like paint cans and toolboxes is easier if you carry one in each hand. Keep your shoulders back and down so that the weight is balanced on each side of your body, not suspended in front. With this method, you will be able to lift heavier loads and also to walk and stand erect. Your back will not be strained by being pulled to one side.

41

—JOHN WARDE, "Safe Lifting Techniques"

BACKGROUND

In *A Conceptual Theory of Rhetoric* (Boston: Little, Brown, 1975) Frank D'Angelo points out that the act of thinking involves relating objects and events to each other and to one's own past experiences. In other words, by thinking, we organize perceptions into patterns that are ultimately expressed in paragraphs. The process inevitably causes the categories to which we assign paragraphs to overlap. D'Angelo explains:

> Description, for example, is related to definition. Describing something provides a means of analyzing and identifying it. Defining is a kind of abstract description. Definition, division into parts, and classification share fundamental relationships: to define is to limit or set boundaries to a thing by separating it from other things (division); to define is to put the thing to be defined into a class (classification); to classify is to divide into categories, so classification and division are related categories. Exemplification is related to definition (giving examples is one way of defining), to division in parts (examples are parts of wholes), and to classification (each example is a member of a group or class of persons and things) (p. 44).

4 Using example

A paragraph developed by example uses illustrations to provide evidence in support of the main idea. Examples are highly effective for developing topical paragraphs. They supply a reader with concrete, specific information. Many of the sample paragraphs in this chapter are developed with examples, among them paragraphs 1, 3, 5, 6, 14, and 29. Here is another paragraph with examples used to develop the topic sentence.

42   One major value of rain forests is biomedical. The plants and animals of rain forests are the source of many compounds used in today's medicines. A drug that helps treat Parkinson's disease is manufactured from a plant that grows only in South American rain forests. Some plants and insects found in rain forests contain rare chemicals that relieve certain mental disorders. Discoveries, however, have only begun. Scientists say that rain forests contain over a thousand plants that have great anticline potential. To destroy life forms in these forests is to deprive the human race of further medical advances.

—GARY LEE HOUSEMAN, student

5 Using definition

A paragraph of definition develops a topic by explaining the meaning of a word or a concept. A paragraph of definition is an *extended definition*—it is more extensive than a dictionary denotation (although the paragraph may include a dictionary definition). An effective paragraph of definition does not use abstractions to explain abstractions. Here is a paragraph that offers an extended definition of chemistry.

43   Chemistry is that branch of science which has the task of investigating the materials out of which the universe is made. It is not concerned with the forms into which they may be fashioned. Such objects as chairs, tables, vases, bottles, or wires are of no significance in chemistry; but such substances as glass, wool, iron, sulfur, and clay, as the materials out of which they are made, are what it studies. Chemistry is concerned not only with the composition of such substances, but also with their inner structure.

—JOHN ARREND TIMM, *General Chemistry*

6 Using analysis and classification

Analysis (sometimes called *division*) divides things up. Classification groups things together. A paragraph developed by analysis divides one subject into its component parts. Paragraphs of analysis written in this pattern usually start by identifying the one subject and continue by explaining that subject's distinct parts. For example, here is a paragraph that identifies a new type of zoo design and then analyzes changes in our world that have brought about that design.

44

> The current revolution in zoo design—the landscape revolution—is driven by three kinds of change that have occurred during this century. First are great leaps in animal ecology, veterinary medicine, landscape design, and exhibit technology, making possible unprecedented realism in zoo exhibits. Second, and perhaps most important, is the progressive disappearance of wilderness—the very subject of zoos—from the earth. Third is knowledge derived from market research and from environmental psychology, making possible a sophisticated focus on the zoo-goer.
>
> —Melissa Greene, "No Rms, Jungle Vu"

A paragraph developed by classification groups information according to some scheme. The separate groups must be *from the same class*—they must have some underlying characteristics in common. For example, different types of building violations can be classified into two large, general groups—inside violations and outside violations. Here is a paragraph that discusses many violations grouped in these two main categories.

45

> A public health student, Marian Glaser, did a detailed analysis of 180 cases of building code violation. Each case represented a single building, almost all of which were multiple-unit dwellings. In these 180 buildings, there were an incredible total of 1,244 different recorded violations—about seven per building. What did the violations consist of? First of all, over one-third of the violations were exterior defects: broken doors and stairways, holes in the walls, sagging roofs, broken chimneys, damaged porches, and so on. Another one-third were interior violations that could scarcely be attributed to the most ingeniously destructive rural southern migrant in America. There were, for example, a total of 160 instances of defective wiring or other electrical hazards, a very common cause of the excessive number of fires and needless tragic deaths in the slums. There were 125 instances of inadequate, defective, or inoperable plumbing or heating. There were 34 instances of serious infestation by rats and roaches.
>
> —William Ryan, "Blaming the Victim"

EXTRA EXERCISE C

Write a paragraph defining one of the terms listed below. You may find it helpful to begin by determining the class (genus) of the term and the characteristics that distinguish it from other members of the class. Means for developing paragraphs that have been discussed earlier in this chapter, such as examples and illustrations, can be used to develop the definition. In a paragraph of definition, synonyms, etymological information, and contrasting examples are also helpful.

1. chemistry
2. extrasensory perception
3. movies
4. weather
5. physical fitness

EXTRA EXERCISE D

The sentences in the following paragraph of definition have been jumbled. Indicate which is the topic sentence, then record the order of the remaining sentences by numbering them.

_____**1.** It is the sum total of substantive things called economic goods.

_____**2.** In other words, wealth is a stock, while income is a flow of economic goods.

_____**3.** The wealth of a nation is the stock of economic goods owned by its inhabitants as individuals or as members of the national group.

_____**4.** Most economists use the term "economic goods" to refer to those sources of satisfaction which are scarce enough to be able to command a price.

_____**5.** Wealth differs from income because it is the sum of the goods owned at a particular time as opposed to the goods consumed during a specific period.

ANSWERS: EXTRA EXERCISE D

The order of sentences in the paragraph of definition above should be 3, 1, 4, 5, 2.

7   **Using comparison and contrast**

Comparison deals with similarities, while contrast deals with differences. Paragraphs using comparison and contrast can be structured in two ways. A *point-by-point structure* allows you to move back and forth between the two items being compared. A *block structure* allows you to discuss one item completely before discussing the other.

PATTERNS FOR COMPARISON AND CONTRAST   24

POINT-BY-POINT STRUCTURE

Student body: college *A,* college *B*
Curriculum: college *A,* college *B*
Location: college *A,* college *B*

BLOCK STRUCTURE

College A: student body, curriculum, location
College B: student body, curriculum, location

Here is a paragraph structured point-by-point for comparison and contrast.

> In the business environment, tone is especially important. Business writing is not literary writing. Literary artists use unique styles to "express" themselves to a general audience. Business people write to particular persons in particular situations, not so much to express themselves as to accomplish particular purposes, "to get a job done." If a reader does not like a novelist's tone, nothing much can happen to the writer short of failing to sell some books. In the business situation, however, an offensive style may not only prevent a sale but may also turn away a customer, work against a promotion, or even cost you a job.
>
> —JOHN S. FIELDEN, "What Do You Mean, You Don't Like My Style!"

46

Here is a block-form comparison of games and business.

> Games are of limited duration, take place on or in fixed and finite sites and are governed by openly promulgated rules that are enforced on the spot by neutral professionals. Moreover, they are performed by relatively evenly matched teams that are counseled

47

and led through every move by seasoned hands. Scores are kept, and at the end of the game, a winner is declared. Business is usually a little different. In fact, if there is anyone out there who can say that the business is of limited duration, takes place on a fixed site, is governed by openly promulgated rules that are enforced on the spot by neutral professionals, competes only on relatively even terms, and performs in a way that can be measured in runs or points, then that person is either extraordinarily lucky or seriously deluded.

—WARREN BENNIS, "Time to Hang Up the Old Sports Clichés"

8 Using analogy

Analogy is a type of comparison. It compares objects or ideas from different classes—things not normally associated. For example, a fatal disease has certain points in common with war. Analogy is particularly effective when you want to explain the unfamiliar in terms of the familiar. Often a paragraph developed with analogy starts with a simile or metaphor (see 21c) to introduce the comparison. Here is a paragraph developed by analogy that starts with a simile and then explains the effect of casual speech by comparing it to casual dress.

48

> Casual dress, like casual speech, tends to be loose, relaxed and colorful. It often contains what might be called "slang words": blue jeans, sneakers, baseball caps, aprons, flowered cotton housedresses, and the like. These garments could not be worn on a formal occasion without causing disapproval, but in ordinary circumstances they pass without remark. "Vulgar words" in dress, on the other hand, give emphasis and get immediate attention in almost any circumstances, just as they do in speech. Only the skillful can employ them without some loss of face, and even then they must be used in the right way. A torn, unbuttoned shirt, or wildly uncombed hair can signify strong emotions: passion, grief, rage, despair. They are most effective if people already think of you as being neatly dressed, just as the curses of well-spoken persons count for more than those of the customarily foul-mouthed.

—ALISON LURIE, *The Language of Clothes*

9 Using cause-and-effect analysis

Cause-and-effect analysis involves examining outcomes and reasons for those outcomes. Causes lead to an event or an effect; and

QUOTATION ABOUT WRITING

Sometimes you get a line, a phrase, sometimes you're crying, or it's the curve of a chair that hurts you and you don't know why, or sometimes you just want to write a poem, and you don't know what it's about. I will fool around on the typewriter. It might take me ten pages of nothing, of terrible writing, and then I'll get a line, and I'll think, "That's what I mean!" What you're doing is hunting for what you mean, what you're trying to say. You don't know when you start.

—Anne Sexton

ALTERNATE EXAMPLE: ANALOGY

Consider the analogies developed by George Herbert in this short poem.

The Coming of Good Luck

So Good Luck came, and on my roof did
  light,
Like noiseless snow, or as the dew of
  night:
Not all at once, but gently, as the trees
Are, by the sun beams, tickled by degrees.

EXTRA EXERCISE E

To practice the principles of classification, arrange the following terms into three groups based on their similarities. Give each group a heading.

1. violin
2. helmet
3. bulb
4. conductor
5. perennial
6. referee
7. concerto
8. Joe Montana
9. blossom
10. baton
11. Mozart
12. quarterback
13. leaves and stems
14. spectators
15. nursery

ANSWERS: EXTRA EXERCISE E

Symphony Orchestra
violin
conductor
concerto
baton
Mozart
Football
helmet
referee
Joe Montana
quarterback
spectators
Flowers
bulb
perennial
blossom
leaves and stems
nursery

effects result from causes. Section 5f describes making reasonable connections between causes and effects. Here is a paragraph developed through a discussion of how television (the cause) becomes indispensable (the effect) to parents of young children.

49   Because television is so wonderfully available as child amuser and child defuser, capable of rendering a volatile three-year-old harmless at the flick of a switch, parents grow to depend upon it in the course of their daily lives. And as they continue to utilize television day after day, its importance in their children's lives increases. From a simple source of entertainment provided by parents when they need a break from child care, television gradually changes into a powerful and disruptive presence in family life. But despite their increasing resentment of television's intrusions into their family life, and despite their considerable guilt at not being able to control their children's viewing, parents do not take steps to extricate themselves from television's domination. They can no longer cope without it.

—Marie Winn, *The Plug-In Drug*

EXERCISE 4-10

Consulting section 4f, identify the pattern or patterns each paragraph illustrates. Choose from narration, description, process, example, definition, analysis, classification, comparison and contrast, analogy, and cause and effect.

A.   50   What was South Vietnam still seems like a different country from the North—more commercial, more casual, seemingly less wrapped up in political correctness. The main market in Hanoi had little to offer except local vegetables, a few plastic tools, and the incongruously colonial-looking green pith helmets that most northern men wear. (Hanoi's market also featured several tubs of live bullfrogs while we were there. Two market ladies chatted with each other while lopping the frogs' legs off with strokes of their cleavers.) In Saigon, there are rows of "shop-houses," the tan-colored buildings with red-tile roofs and open storefronts that are found throughout Southeast Asia, and stores selling paintings, lacquerware, and a few cheap imported calculators and digital watches. In Hanoi, there are virtually no private cars—the streets look the way China's must have looked fifteen or twenty years ago, dense with bicycle traffic but very quiet. In Saigon, there are lots of motorcycles and a few private cars, including original Mustangs and other veteran American models. Still, no place in Vietnam has anything like the bustle of a typical Southeast Asian trading center.

—James Fallows, "No Hard Feelings?"

B.

51   I retain only one confused impression from my earliest years: it is all red, and black, and warm. Our apartment was red: the upholstery was of red moquette, the Renaissance dining-room was red, the figured silk hangings over the stained-glass doors were red, and the velvet curtains in Papa's study were red too. The furniture in this awful sanctum was made of black pear wood; I used to creep into the knee-hole under the desk and envelop myself in its dusty glooms; it was dark and warm, and the red of the carpet rejoiced my eyes. That is how I seem to have passed the early days of infancy. Safely ensconced, I watched, I touched, I took stock of the world.

—SIMONE DE BEAUVOIR, *Memoirs of a Dutiful Daughter*

C.

52   In the case of wool, very hot water can actually cause some structural changes within the fiber, but the resulting shrinkage is minor. The fundamental cause of shrinkage in wool is felting, in which the fibers scrunch together in a tighter bunch, and the yarn, fabric, and garment follow suit. Wool fibers are curly and rough-surfaced, and when squished together under the lubricating influence of water, the fibers wind around each other, like two springs interlocking. Because of their rough surfaces, they stick together and cannot be pulled apart.

—JAMES GORMAN, "Gadgets"

D.

53   *Hard,* in terms of wood, really means *harder* to cut, but most hardwoods are also fine and even-grained. They are not apt to split, and they take polish well. For these reasons, they are generally better for small wood carving than the softwoods; most sculptors prefer to use hardwoods for large pieces, too. All the fruitwoods, like cherry, apple, pear, and orange, are hard, and so are oak, mahogany, walnut, birch, holly, and maple. Hardwoods range in color from the almost white of holly to the almost black of walnut. Oak and mahogany are the most open-grained, and therefore more apt to split. They are probably less good for small carvings than the other kinds.

—FLORENCE H. PETTIT, *How to Make Whirligigs and Whimmy Doodles*

E.

54   After our lunch, we drove to the Liverpool public library, where I was scheduled to read. By then, we were forty-five minutes late, and on arrival we saw five middle-aged white women heading away toward an old car across the street. When they recognized me, the women came over and apologized: They were really sorry, they said, but they had to leave or they'd get in trouble on the job. I looked at them. Every one of them was wearing an inexpensive, faded housedress and, over that, a cheap and shapeless cardigan sweater. I felt

ANSWERS: EXERCISE 4-10

Some paragraphs can be interpreted to illustrate more than one pattern. This is a basic list only. *Note:* Exercise 4-13 asks students to analyze these paragraphs for many other features.

A (paragraph 50). comparison and contrast—point by point, example

B (paragraph 51). description, narration, analysis, example

C (paragraph 52). cause and effect, definition, analogy

D (paragraph 53). analysis, definition, example

E (paragraph 54). narration

F (paragraph 55). analogy

G (paragraph 56). example, classification

honored by their open-mindedness in having wanted to come and listen to my poetry. I thought and I said that it was I who should apologize: I was late. It was I who felt, moreover, unprepared: What in my work, to date, deserves the open-minded attention of blue-collar white women terrified by the prospect of overstaying a union-guaranteed hour for lunch?

—JUNE JORDAN, ''Waiting for a Taxi''

F.   In many ways, chopsticks are the culinary equivalent of the stick shift. They enhance the act of eating and make it more participatory, tactile, not to mention fun. They give a certain ceremony to consumption and force the calorie-conscious diner to focus on the ritual of gustation, and therefore on the amount of food being shoveled into the mouth at any time.

55

—DENA KLEIMAN, ''Older than Forks, Safer than Knives''

G.   Lacking access to a year-round supermarket, the many species —from ants to wolves—that in the course of evolution have learned the advantages of hoarding must devote a lot of energy and ingenuity to protecting their stashes from marauders. Creatures like beavers and honeybees, for example, hoard food to get them through cold winters. Others, like desert rodents that face food scarcities throughout the year, must take advantage of the short-lived harvests that follow occasional rains. For animals like burying beetles that dine on mice hundreds of times their size, a habit of biting off more than they can chew at the moment forces them to store their leftovers. Still others, like the male MacGregor's bowerbird, stockpile goodies during mating season so they can concentrate on wooing females and defending their arena de l'amour.

56

—JANE BRODY, ''A Hoarder's Life: Filling the Cache—And Finding It''

ANSWERS: EXERCISE 4-11

Each student's paragraph will differ, but they all should have in common a clear use of RENNS and techniques of coherence.

EXERCISE 4-11

Consulting section 4f, write three of the following paragraphs.

1. A classification of drivers.
2. A personal definition of *political freedom*.
3. A narrative of your first experience as an authority figure.
4. A cause-and-effect analysis of the increase in crime in the United States.
5. An analogy about learning to use a college library.

4g   Writing introductory, transitional, and concluding paragraphs

Introductory, transitional, and concluding paragraphs are generally shorter than the topical paragraphs with which they appear.

Introductory paragraphs

In informative and persuasive writing, an introductory paragraph sets the stage and prepares a reader for what lies ahead. Introductions provide a bridge from the reader's mind to yours. In so doing, it needs to arouse the reader's interest in your subject. An introduction must clearly relate to the rest of your essay. If it points in one direction and your essay goes off in another, your reader will be confused, even annoyed, and will likely stop reading.

For college writing, many instructors require that an introductory paragraph include a statement of the thesis of the essay, so that the central idea of the essay is clearly available early on. Many instructors want students to demonstrate from the start that all parts of any essay are related. Professional writers do not necessarily include a thesis statement in their introductory paragraphs; with experience comes skill at maintaining a line of thought without overtly stating a central idea. Student writers, however, often need to practice explicitly and demonstrate openly external clues to essay organization. As you write successive drafts of an essay, expect to revise your introduction, in whole or part, so that it works well in concert with your other paragraphs.

When instructors require a thesis statement, they often want it to be in the last sentence or two of the introductory paragraph. Here is an example of an introductory paragraph with a thesis statement (shown in italics).

> 57   Most sprinters live in a narrow corridor of space and time. Life rushes at them quickly, and success and failure are measured by frustrating, tiny increments. Florence Griffith Joyner paints her running world in bold, colorful strokes. *For her, there's a lot of romance to running fast.*
>
> —CRAIG A. MASBACK, "Siren of Speed"

You can see additional examples of introductory paragraphs with a thesis statement in the last sentence in the student essays in sections 3f and 6h.

An introductory paragraph often includes one or more **introductory devices,** listed in Chart 25, that serve to stimulate a reader's interest in the subject of the essay. Usually the introductory device precedes the thesis statement.

BACKGROUND

"Write leads, not introductions," teacher and journalist Donald M. Murray advises in *Learning by Teaching* (Portsmouth, NH: Boynton/Cook, 1982, p. 109). "The introduction tells the reader what you intend to say. The lead draws the reader right into the subject. The introduction gets between the reader and the subject; the lead is the subject evolving." Murray points out that people reading a newspaper, magazine, or journal often decide whether to read an article after just five seconds of reading. "Clearly the writer must realize that he or she has ten lines or less in which to capture and hold the reader.

"The discipline of the lead, however, is not only a service to the reader, it is an opportunity for the writer. As the title helps the writer focus on the subject, so does the lead. The lead eliminates much of what might intrude upon the subject. It focuses, it establishes the dimensions of the piece. It often identifies the audience, and it sets the voice." Murray says that he frequently composes fifty leads or first paragraphs before continuing a draft.

SELECTED DEVICES FOR INTRODUCTORY PARAGRAPHS 25

- Provide relevant background information.
- Tell an interesting brief story or anecdote.
- Give a pertinent statistic or statistics.
- Ask a provocative question or questions.
- Use an appropriate quotation.
- Make a useful analogy.
- Define a term used throughout the essay.
- Identify the situation.

Here is an introduction that uses two anecdotes before its thesis statement (shown in italics).

> On seeing another child fall and hurt himself, Hope, just nine months old, stared, tears welling up in her eyes, and crawled to her mother to be comforted—as though she had been hurt, not her friend. When 15-month-old Michael saw his friend Paul crying, Michael fetched his own teddy bear and offered it to Paul; when that didn't stop Paul's tears, Michael brought Paul's security blanket from another room. *Such small acts of sympathy and caring, observed in scientific studies, are leading researchers to trace the roots of empathy—the ability to share another's emotions—to infancy, contradicting a longstanding assumption that infants and toddlers were incapable of these feelings.*
>
> —Daniel Goleman, "Researchers Trace Empathy's Roots to Infancy"

58

The key to the effectiveness of an introductory device is how well it relates to the essay's thesis and to the material in the topical paragraphs. An introductory device must be well integrated into the paragraph, not mechanically slotted in for its own sake. Note how smoothly the message of the quotation in the following introduction becomes a dramatic contrast that leads into the thesis statement (shown in italics).

> "Alone one is never lonely, says May Sarton in her essay "The Rewards of Living a Solitary Life." Most people, however, do not share Sarton's opinion: They are terrified of living alone. They are used to living with others—children with parents, roommates with roommates, friends with friends, husbands with wives. When the statistics catch up with them, therefore, they are rarely prepared. *Chances are high that most adult men and women will need to know how to live alone, briefly or longer, at some time in their lives.*
>
> —Tara Foster, student

59

In the following paragraph, the author uses a question and some dramatic description to arouse interest and to set the stage for his thesis statement (shown in italics).

60 What should you do? You are out riding your bike, playing golf, or in the middle of a long run when you look up and suddenly see a jagged streak of light shoot across the sky, followed by a deafening clap of thunder. *Unfortunately, most outdoor exercisers do not know whether to stay put or make a dash for shelter when a thunderstorm approaches, and sometimes the consequences are tragic.*

—GERALD SECOR COUZENS, "If Lightning Strikes"

In the following paragraph, statistics and numbers help the author lead into his thesis statement (shown in italics).

61 In a Milwaukee suburb, a teenage gang awarded points to members for vandalizing streetlights and lawns. A 16-year-old in Santa Clara County, California, took 12 classmates to look at the body of his ex-girlfriend. None of them told police. Later, the boy was charged with her murder. In Chicago's affluent North Shore suburbs, more than 40 teenagers have taken their own lives in the past two years. *These episodes point up what many social scientists regard as one of the most significant—and disturbing—trends of recent years: A new generation of American teenagers is deeply troubled, unable to cope with the pressures of growing up in what they perceive as a world that is hostile or indifferent to them.*

—STANLEY N. WELLBORN, *Troubled Teenagers*

As you write your introductory paragraphs, keep in mind the guidelines in Chart 26.

WHAT TO AVOID IN INTRODUCTORY PARAGRAPHS   26

- Do not be too obvious. Avoid bald statements such as "In this paper I will discuss violence on television" or "My assignment asks me to discuss Hamlet's inability to take action."
- Do not apologize. Avoid self-critical statements such as "I do not have much background in this subject," "Of course, other people are more expert in this subject than I am," or "I am not sure if I am right, but here is my opinion."
- Do not use overworn expressions such as "Haste makes waste," "A penny saved is a penny earned," "Love is what makes the world go around," and "War is hell."

Transitional paragraphs

A transitional paragraph usually consists of one or two sentences that help you move from a few pages on one subtopic to the next large group of paragraphs on a second subtopic. Transitional paragraphs are uncommon in short essays. In longer papers written for college, transitional paragraphs sometimes recapitulate the thesis° in the context of what was just discussed and what will follow.

Here is a two-sentence transitional paragraph written as a bridge between a lengthy discussion of people's gestures and the coming long discussion of people's eating habits.

62   Like gestures, eating habits are personality indicators, and even food preferences and attitudes toward food reveal the inner self. Food plays an important role in the lives of most people beyond its obvious one as a necessity.

—JEAN ROSENBAUM, M.D., *Is Your Volkswagon a Sex Symbol?*

Concluding paragraphs

A concluding paragraph serves to bring your discussion to an end that logically follows from your thesis° and its discussion. A conclusion that is merely tacked onto an essay does not give the reader a sense of completion. An ending that flows gracefully and sensibly from what has come before it reinforces the writer's ideas and enhances an essay. A concluding paragraph often includes one or more **concluding devices,** listed in Chart 27.

BACKGROUND

According to Aristotle's *Rhetoric,* the conclusion of an argument can have as many as four functions. It should create a favorable impression toward the speaker and an unfavorable impression toward the speaker's opponents. It should emphasize the points of the speaker while minimizing the points of the opposition. It should appeal strongly to the audience's emotions. And it should summarize the chief points of the argument.

SELECTED DEVICES FOR CONCLUDING PARAGRAPHS	27

■ Call for awareness, action, or similar type of resolution.
■ Look ahead to the future.
■ Summarize the main points of the essay, but avoid doing this in essays of only one or two pages.
■ Use the devices for introductory paragraphs (see Chart 25), but avoid using the same device in both the introduction and the conclusion of the essay.

Here is a concluding paragraph that summarizes an essay that discusses pizza, including the many versions of pizzalike foods enjoyed by various cultures throughout time.

63 For a food that is traced to Neolithic beginnings, like Mexico's tortillas, Armenia's lahmejoun, Scottish oatcakes, and even matzohs, pizza has remained fresh and vibrant. Whether it is galettes, the latest thin-crusted invasion from France with bacon and onion toppings, or a plain slice of a cheese pie, the varieties of pizza are clearly limited only by one's imagination.

—LISA PRATT, "A Slice of History"

The essay for which the following conclusion was written is a condemnation of racism as demonstrated by the existence of urban ghettos. This concluding paragraph reinforces the message of the essay by calling for awareness and, by extension, action.

64 It is a terrible, an inexorable, law that one cannot deny the humanity of another without diminishing one's own: in the face of one's victim, one sees oneself. Walk through Harlem and see what we, this nation, have become.

—JAMES BALDWIN, "Fifth Avenue, Uptown: A Letter from Harlem"

The following conclusion ends an essay that discusses the risks of genetic engineering. The author points to the future and calls for action.

65 I am not advocating that we stop the development of the new biology. I believe that we can achieve wonderful and important results with it. But we do need to ensure that its application is both peaceful and safe. We have to learn from the history of nuclear physics and organic chemistry. Indeed, I believe we have no real choice. We cannot afford to develop the new biological technologies without controlling them.

—SUSAN WRIGHT, "Genetic Engineering: The Risks"

As you write your concluding paragraphs, keep in mind the guidelines in Chart 28.

WHAT TO AVOID IN CONCLUDING PARAGRAPHS   28

- Do not go off the track. Avoid introducing an entirely new idea or adding a fact that belongs in the body of the essay.
- Do not reword your introduction. Check to see if the introduction and conclusion are interchangeable; if they are, revise.
- Do not announce what you have done. Avoid statements such as "In this paper I have discussed violence on television."

➡

BACKGROUND

"The perfect ending should take the reader slightly by surprise and yet seem exactly right," writes William Zinsser in *On Writing Well*, 4th ed. (Perennial Press, 1990). A good ending "is like the curtain line in a theatrical comedy. We are in the middle of a scene (we think) when suddenly one of the actors says something funny, or outrageous, or epigrammatic, and the lights go out. We are momentarily startled to find the scene over, and then delighted by the aptness of how it ended. What delights us, subconsciously, is the playwright's perfect control."

TEACHING TIP: EXERCISE 4-12 (pages 110-11)

One way to help students succeed with this exercise is to talk them through these imaginary essays before they think about the beginnings and endings. A class discussion about what details might support the topics of each paragraph will strengthen students' understanding of the importance of evidence. At the same time, it will give students a fuller concept of the essay on which to base their introductory and concluding paragraphs. When the students write the introductions and conclusions, alert them to the lists of useful devices and of "what to avoid," explained in section 4e.

ANSWERS: EXERCISE 4-13

1. **Topic sentences**
   A (paragraph 50). first sentence
   B (paragraph 51). first sentence
   C (paragraph 52). second sentence
   D (paragraph 53). first sentence
   E (paragraph 54). last sentence
   F (paragraph 55). first sentence
   G (paragraph 56). first sentence

2. **RENNS**
   A (paragraph 50). *Reasons:* Hanoi's main market has little to offer. Saigon has rows of "shop-houses." Hanoi has bicycles, while Saigon has motorcycles and a few private cars. *Examples:* The specific products in each market. *Names:* South Vietnam, Hanoi, Saigon, China, Mustangs. *Senses:* The sight of the frogs' legs being chopped off, the sight of dense bicycle traffic.

   B (paragraph 51). *Examples:* upholstery, Renaissance dining room, figured silk hangings over stained-glass doors, velvet curtains, black pear wood. *Names:* Renaissance dining room, Papa's study, black pear wood. *Senses:* sight of red and black, sight of "dusty glooms," darkness, watching, touching.

   C (paragraph 52). *Reasons:* felting causes wool to shrink, wool fibers stick together and cannot be pulled apart. *Names:* wool, fiber, yarn, fabric, garment. *Senses:* curly, rough surfaces

   D (paragraph 53). *Reasons:* not even grained, not apt to split, take polish well. *Examples:* fruitwoods, cherry, apple, pear, orange, oak, mahogany, walnut, birch, holly, maple. *Senses:* white of holly, almost black of walnut.

   E (paragraph 54). *Names:* Liverpool public library, middle-aged white women, old car, faded housedress, shapeless cardigan sweater. *Numbers:* forty-five, five.

➡️

WHAT TO AVOID IN CONCLUDING PARAGRAPHS (*continued*)

- Do not make absolute claims. Avoid statements such as "This proves that. . . ." Always qualify your message with expressions such as "This *seems* to prove. . . ."
- Avoid logical fallacies (see 5f). Concluding paragraphs are particularly vulnerable to errors in reasoning.
- Do not apologize. Avoid statements such as "I may not have thought of all the arguments, but what I do say is valid."

EXERCISE 4-12

Consulting section 4g, write an introduction and conclusion for each essay informally outlined below. To gain additional experience, write an alternate introductory and concluding paragraph for one of the essays.

A. Humor in current movies
   Thesis: Today's movies illustrate several types of humor.
   Topical paragraph 1: slapstick
   Topical paragraph 2: understatement and overstatement
   Topical paragraph 3: wit

B. Uses of computers
   Thesis: Many new applications for computers are emerging in the worlds of business, finance, and the arts.
   Topical paragraph 1: business
   Topical paragraph 2: finance
   Topical paragraph 3: the arts

C. Starting a new job
   Thesis: Starting a new job demands much concentration.
   Topical paragraph 1: learning or adapting skills
   Topical paragraph 2: fitting in with co-workers
   Topical paragraph 3: adjusting to the surroundings

D. Violence on television
   Thesis: Violence on television is harmful to children.
   Topical paragraph 1: cartoons
   Topical paragraph 2: series
   Topical paragraph 3: made-for-television movies

E. Adjusting to college

Thesis: Many challenges face students as they adjust to college.

Topical paragraph 1: financial

Topical paragraph 2: emotional

Topical paragraph 3: academic

EXERCISE 4-13

Reread the paragraphs in Exercise 4-10 and do the following.

1. Consulting section 4b, identify all topic sentences, limiting sentences, and implied topic sentences.
2. Consulting section 4c, identify all RENNS.
3. Consulting section 4d, identify all techniques of coherence.
4. Consulting section 4e, identify paragraph arrangements.

F (paragraph 55). *Reasons:* chopsticks are like the stick shift because they enhance and give ceremony to the act of eating, force the eater to focus on the act. *Names:* chopsticks, stick shift. *Senses:* tactile.

G (paragraph 56). *Reasons:* animals hoard because food is not available to them all year around. *Examples:* beavers, honeybees, desert rodents, burying beetles, etc. *Names:* ants, wolves, creatures, goodies, MacGregor's bowerbird, etc.

3. Techniques of coherence. In this order, if they appear: transitional expressions *(te)*, pronouns *(p)*, deliberate repetition *(dr)*, and parallel structures *(ps)*.

A (paragraph 50). *te:* still; *dr:* Hanoi, Saigon; *ps:* In Saigon there are/in Hanoi, there are.

B (paragraph 51). *p:* I; *dr:* red, black; *ps:* red, and black, and warm / I watched, I touched, I took stock.

C (paragraph 52). *te:* but; *p:* their, they.

D (paragraph 53). *te:* too, therefore; *p:* they, other kinds; *dr:* hardwoods, apt; *ps:* all verbs in simple present, they are.

E (paragraph 54). *te:* by then, moreover. *p:* our, I, we, they, them, their, it. *ps:* I thought and I said.

F (paragraph 55). *te:* not to mention, therefore. *p:* they, it. *dr::* they.

G (paragraph 56). *te:* for example, still, so. *p:* their, they. *dr::* others. *ps:* creatures / others / still others.

4. Paragraph arrangement

A (paragraph 50). general to specific

B (paragraph 51). least to most important

C (paragraph 52). general to specific

D (paragraph 53). general to specific

E (paragraph 54). time, least to most important

F (paragraph 55). general to specific

G (paragraph 56). general to specific

5 Reading and Thinking Critically

5a Understanding critical thinking

Thinking is not something you choose to do, any more than a fish "chooses" to live in water. To be human *is* to think. But while thinking may come naturally, awareness of *how* you think does not. Thinking about thinking is the key to thinking critically. When you think critically, you take control of your conscious thought processes. Without such control, you risk being controlled by the ideas of others. Indeed, critical thinking is at the heart of a liberal (from the Latin word for *free*) education.

The word **critical** here has a neutral meaning. It does not mean taking a negative view or finding fault, as when someone criticizes another person for doing something wrong. The essence of critical thinking is thinking beyond the obvious—beyond the flash of visual images on a television screen, the alluring promises of glossy advertisements, the evasive statements by some people in the news, the half-truths of some propaganda, the manipulations of slanted language and faulty reasoning.

Critical thinking is an attitude as much as an activity. If you face life with curiosity and a desire to dig beneath the surface, you are a critical thinker. If you do not believe everything you read or hear, you are a critical thinker. If you find pleasure in contemplating the puzzle of conflicting ideologies, theories, personalities, and facts, you are a critical thinker.

Activities of the mind and higher-order reasoning—the core of a college education—are processes of contemplation and deliberation. These processes take time. They contrast with the glorification of speed in today's culture: fast foods, instant mixes, self-developing film, short-spurt images in movies and videos. If you are among the people who assume that speed is a measure of intelligence, consider this true anecdote about Albert Einstein. The first time that Banesh Hoffman, a scientist, was expected to talk about his work to Albert Einstein, Hoffman was speechless and overawed. Einstein instantly put Hoffman at ease when he said: "Please go slowly. I don't understand things quickly."

Critical thinking in academic courses is rooted in the activities of analysis, synthesis, and critical assessment. These activities apply when you think about academic lectures and discussions, when you read your textbooks and other assignments, and when you conduct your daily life. They are summarized in Chart 29.

ACTIVITIES FOR CRITICAL READING AND THINKING 29

1. **Analysis:** break ideas into their component parts so that you can consider them separately.
2. **Synthesis:** make connections among different ideas or components of ideas, seeking relationships and interactions with which to tie them together.
3. **Critical assessment:** examine the quality of the ideas for soundness of reasoning and of logic.

5b Understanding the reading process

Reading, like writing, helps you to come to "know," to compose meaning. In college, reading assignments assume that you have the ability to read critically. A critical reader reads with a questioning mind, open to new ideas but careful to recognize when material is distorted because it is incomplete. A critical reader also recognizes when material is slanted to manipulate the reader improperly, or is based on incorrect information. If you understand **the reading process,** you can effectively meet the demands of critical reading.

Reading is not a passive activity. It involves more than looking at words. Reading is an active process—a dynamic, meaning-making encounter involving the interaction of the page, eye, and brain. When you read, your brain actively makes connections between what you know already and what is new to you. You comprehend and learn new material by associating it with material you already know.

BACKGROUND

Robert J. Tierney and P. David Pearson write that it is important to understand reading and writing "as essentially similar processes of meaning construction," active and recursive processes of composing ("Toward a Composing Model of Reading," *Language Arts* [1983]: 568–580; rpt. *Perspectives on Literacy,* ed. Eugene R. Kintgen, Barry M. Kroll, and Mike Rose [Carbondale, IL: Southern Illinois UP, 1988]). Like writers, readers plan by determining their purposes for reading a text, assessing what they know about the topic, focusing their goals and topics, and questioning themselves. Each reader's goals and knowledge influence how he or she reads and understands the text. Like writers, when they begin readers approach the text with particular goals and review what they know about a subject and then discover, revise, and delete goals and call up other knowledge as they read.

Like writers, readers draft, at first trying to discover a lead or hypothesis that will help them make sense of the rest of the text, refining and developing that lead as they read, making connections and filling in gaps in the text with their own inferences and knowledge, and trying to fit all the pieces of the text together into a coherent whole. Readers and writers also both engage in aligning. Readers take a stance (passive, critical, sympathetic, challenging) in relation to the author to better enable them to construct meaning from the text, just as writers take a stance toward their audiences.

Readers and writers both need to revise. Readers need to reflect on and evaluate the meanings they have constructed from the text, rereading the text and questioning and revising their interpretations. Finally, readers and writers need to monitor themselves as they compose, distancing themselves from the meaning they compose and examining their composing activities. Readers and writers should both be in dialogue with their "other self," to determine how well they are accomplishing their purposes.

Experts who have researched the reading process report that the key activity in reading is **making predictions.** As you read, your brain is always involved in guessing what is coming next. Once it discovers what comes next, it either confirms or revises its prediction and moves on. For example, if you encountered a chapter title "The Heartbeat," your predictions could be diverse, ranging from romance to how the heart pumps blood. As you read on, you would confirm or revise your prediction according to what you found—you would be in the realm of romance if you encountered a paragraph about lovers and roses, and you would be in the realm of biology if you encountered material that included diagrams of the physiology of the heart.

Predicting during reading happens at split-second speed without the reader's being aware of it. Without predictions, the brain would have to consider infinite possibilities for assimilating every new piece of information; with predictions, the brain can narrow its expectations to reasonable proportions.

Deciding on your **purpose for reading** before you begin to read can help your prediction process. Purposes for reading vary. Most reading in college is for the purpose of learning new information, appreciating literary works, or reviewing notes on classes or readings. These types of reading involve much *rereading;* one encounter with the material rarely suffices. Vladimir Nabokov, a respected novelist and lecturer on literature, observed: "Curiously enough, one cannot *read* a book: one can only *reread* it. A good reader, a major reader, an active and creative reader, is a rereader."

Your purpose in reading determines the speed at which you can expect to read. When you are hunting for a particular fact in an almanac, you can skim the material until you come to what you want. When you read about a subject that you know well, your brain is familiar with the material, so you can move somewhat rapidly through most of it, slowing down when you come to new material. When you are unfamiliar with the subject, your brain needs time to absorb the new material, so you have to slow down.

5c   Reading to learn from textbooks

To learn efficiently from a textbook, you can apply three universals that have parallels in the writing process, as explained in Chart 30. These universals help you use what you know about the reading process to study and think critically.

UNIVERSALS IN READING TO LEARN		30
SKIM	Like *planning* (see Chapter 2) in the writing process, **skimming** means getting ready to read.	
READ	Like *drafting* (see 3a-3b) in the writing process, **reading** means moving through the material, according to your purpose for reading.	
REINFORCE	Like *revising* (see 3c) and *editing* (3d) in the writing process, **reinforcing** means rereading, clarifying, fine tuning, and getting into final form.	

QUOTATION ABOUT READING

We always read for some purpose—unless some sad, bad, mad schoolteacher has got hold of us. There is no such thing as merely reading words; always through the words we are trafficking or trying to traffic with things—things gone by, present, to come or eternal.

—I. A. Richards, "How to Read a Page"

BACKGROUND

In a 1982 study of high school students (*Learning from Expository Text: The Interaction of Text Structure with Reader Characteristics,* National Institute of Education), Diane Schallert and Robert J. Tierney discovered that most students believe that the mark of a competent reader is the ability to read a text once quickly and remember much of what was read. As a result, students seldom saw a need to reread a text, to reflect on what they had read, or to question their interpretations and, in fact, often viewed these practices as inefficient. In order to learn critical reading practices, students need support and encouragement from teachers, just as they do to learn and use planning and revising strategies when they write.

Various structured systems for applying these universals have been suggested by experts in reading. Here is one widely endorsed system, popularly known as SQ3R.*

S = *Survey.* Surveying is part of *skimming.* You survey to get an overview of the material before you start reading closely. As you survey, your brain begins unconsciously to make predictions about the material.

If you are surveying a textbook, first quickly survey the entire text, and then as you read each chapter, survey it more slowly. If the material has headings, subheadings, words in italics or boldface, or visuals, use them as a road map during your surveying. If you are reading a book that has no headings, (1) read the title; (2) establish a general sense of the length of the material you need to read; (3) read the opening and closing paragraphs—unless you do not want to know the ending—and, if the material is long, glance over some intervening paragraphs.

Q = *Question.* Questioning is part of *skimming.* Asking questions stimulates your brain to prepare for learning. Experiments have shown that college students who actively use structured questioning before reading improve dramatically in comprehension and in recall over both short and long periods of time. Question in small chunks, in contrast to covering large amounts of material during surveying. If you are reading a textbook, it is best to question when you encounter

*Originated by Francis P. Robinson in 1946, the system has been adapted by many others since. The version here is adapted for college students.

each new subsection. Working in small chunks allows your brain to narrow its focus and to make more accurate predictions about what is coming next.

Ask questions deliberately and consciously. Base your questions on titles, key words, headings, and any other material that seems to be central. Here are some examples, based on section 5a.

TITLE	Thinking Critically
QUESTION	What is "thinking critically"?
KEY WORD	critically
QUESTION	What does "critically" mean here?
HEADING	Understanding the reading process
QUESTIONS	What is the reading process? What should I understand about it?

Answers during questioning do not necessarily have to be precise. The goal is to get your thinking started so that your brain will be alerted to focus on key matters as you read.

R = *Read.* Reading is the core activity in SQ3R. The speed at which you read depends on your purpose. Surveying and questioning before you start reading will allow you to get more meaning out of the written word. The full meaning will emerge on the literal level, the inferential level, and the evaluative level (these three levels are explained in 5d).

If you have trouble comprehending as your read, try the suggestions in Chart 31.

HOW TO HELP YOUR READING COMPREHENSION   31

- If you are reading about an unfamiliar subject, you need to associate new material to what you already know. In such a situation, take the time to build up your store of information by reading easier material in other sources on the subject; of course, you must return as quickly as possible to the more difficult material that you are required to read, but establishing a knowledge base will ease your way.

- Comprehension can elude you if your mind wanders, thus taking up some of your brain's activity with extraneous material. If this happens, be fiercely determined to concentrate and resist the appeal of other thoughts. Do whatever it takes. Arrange for silence or music, for being alone or in a crowded library's reading room, for studying at your best time of day (some people concentrate better in the morning, others in the evening). ➡

BACKGROUND

In *The Elements of Critical Reading* (New York: Macmillan, 1991, pp. 13–27), John Peters explains several useful elementary reading habits.

1. Examine organizational features. "When you first encounter a text of any kind, you should pause to examine its outward features. Depending on the kind of text, those may include cover, title page, table of contents, chapter or section divisions, glossary, notes, bibliography, and other accessories" (13). They will provide a useful first impression of the text.

2. Know when the text was written.

3. Determine apparent aims. "Spot reading" selected passages (also known as "prereading" and "x-raying") "allows you to inspect parts which can give you an idea of the text's aims and audience level" (15). Generally, begin with the preface or the opening paragraphs and, with nonfiction texts, then skip to the conclusion because it often summarizes the main points and purposes of the text. You should also drift a little back and forth through the center of the text, "eyeing those spots where expository writing often focuses its aims" (15–16), such as the first and last paragraphs of a section, the first sentence of each body paragraph, and any visual aids and illustrations. ➡

HOW TO HELP YOUR READING COMPREHENSION (*continued*)

- You cannot comprehend new material unless you have allotted sufficient time to work with it. College students are pulled in many different directions and have to discipline themselves to balance their class, study, social, and job (if any) schedules with the unavoidable, time-consuming demands of a reading and studying schedule. Nothing prevents learning so much as lack of time.

- If you are unfamilar with some of the key terms in your reading, you cannot get the full meaning of the material. Take the time to make a list of them and locate their meanings. Many textbooks have a list of key terms (often called a "glossary") at the end of each chapter or at the back of the book (as in this handbook). Any words are listed in a good dictionary (see 20a). As you read, keep your list next to your book so that you can consult it easily (alphabetical order helps in a list of over five words).

R = *Recite*. Reciting is part of *reinforcing*. Reciting calls for you to look away from the page and repeat the main points, aloud or to yourself. For best success, recite in chunks—subsections of textbook chapters, for example. Do not try to cover too much material at once. Knowing ahead of time that when you finish a section you will have to recite stimulates your concentration during reading. If you cannot recite the main points of the material, reread it and try again. If you still have trouble, survey and question again. Then reread.

R = *Review*. Reviewing is part of *reinforcing*. When you finish reading, survey again. This process refreshes your memory about the initial overview you got during surveying. It also gives you a larger framework into which to fit new material you have just learned. Be honest with yourself about what you cannot recall and need to reread. The next day, and again about a week later, repeat your review—always adding whatever new material you have learned since the previous review. As much as time permits, re-review at intervals during a course. The more reinforcement, the better.

Collaborative learning can help you reinforce what you learn from reading. Ask a friend or classmate who knows the material well to discuss it with you, even test you. Conversely, offer to teach the material to someone, and you will know quickly whether or not you have mastered it sufficiently to communicate it.

Writing can help you reinforce your learning. There is little that promotes authority over knowledge as does writing about it. Keep a learning log: draw a line down the center of your notebook page; on

Cont'd.

4. Adapt to the genre. "From nonfiction you should usually expect an orderly discussion such as you might hear at a lecture or business meeting. In general, your relation to nonfiction is that of a student, colleague, or general reader who wants information upon which to base opinions, decisions, or future activity related to the subject—but it's a good idea to be slightly skeptical, aware that a text may have misinformation or raise more questions than it answers" (16–17).

5. Listen to the language. Reading only for the message of the text, ignoring its emotions, tone, and rhythms, can cause a reader to miss much of what the text offers as well as much of the pleasure in reading.

6. Become aware of contrasts. "It is said that there are two sides to everything. As a reader you should become aware of the contrasts within a text. The inner structure is bound to reveal a play of opposites that close reading uncovers" (21).

7. Get to the heart of the matter. "For some readers, the heart of a text may be a passage or series of passages that seem to tie everything together and coordinate the flow of ideas throughout the entire work" (23). "The 'heart' can also be viewed as a sort of overall personality that characterizes the text. . . . But on the best occasions and as a result of our patient attentiveness, the heart of a text may reveal itself in the fullness of its meaning, both logical and emotional, and make us feel that we truly *know* what we've read" (25).

8. Sense what may be missing. "Of the many responses that reading can inspire, a few may be strong while plenty of others remain inactive. The intensity of your feelings is important, but so is the absence of those emotions which a text might have brought you but did not. . . . Knowing what a text means to you depends on your sense of what is present or missing in the relationship you've just concluded" (26).

one side take notes on the reading material, and on the other side list key words, ask questions, make connections among ideas, and have a "conversation on paper" with the material. Also, you can master difficult sections by writing paraphrases, the techniques of which are described in 31d.

EXERCISE 5-1

Consulting section 5c, (1) List the steps you usually go through when you read a textbook. (2) Next, apply SQ3R to reading a chapter in a textbook. (3) Observe your SQ3R reading process and list the steps you go through. (4) Compare the two lists—what you usually go through and what you did when you used the SQ3R system. Note how your lists are alike and how they are different. (5) Write a brief discussion that compares your two lists and that explains which steps in either or both lists helped you learn most successfully from your reading.

5d Reading critically

During the reading process, the full meaning of a literary passage or of an essay emerges on three levels: the **literal,** the **inferential,** and the **evaluative.** If you are like most readers, you stop reading at the literal level. Unless you move to the next two levels, however, your critical reading and thinking skills will suffer.

STEPS FOR READING CRITICALLY   32

1. **Read for literal meaning:** read "on" the lines to see what is stated.

2. **Read to make inferences:** read "between" the lines to see what is not stated but implied.

3. **Read to evaluate:** read "beyond" the lines to assess the soundness of the writer's reasoning, the accuracy of the writer's choice of words, and the fairness of the writer's treatment of the reader.

---

1 Reading for literal meaning

Reading for literal meaning, sometimes called *reading "on" the line,* calls for you to understand what is said. It does not include impressions or opinions about the material. Depending on the

5d

discipline in which you are reading, the literal level has to do with (1) the key facts, the central points in a line or argument, or the central details of plot and character; and (2) the minor details that lend texture to the picture. You need to understand the literal meaning of a passage, before you move beyond it to the next two levels crucial for critical thinking.

The more vocabulary you know, the more likely you are to understand the literal meaning of your reading. When you encounter unfamiliar words while reading, try to figure them out by using clues from the context of the material (for advice on using context clues, see 20c-2). If you cannot figure out a word's meaning, underline or highlight it to remind yourself to look it up after your first reading and before you begin your second.

When you encounter a complex writing style, take time to "unpack" the sentences. Try to break them down into shorter units or reword them into a simpler style. Do not assume that all writing is clear merely because it is in print. Authors write with a rich variety of styles, and not all are equally accessible on a first reading.

When you find a concept that you need to think through, take the time to come to know the new idea. Although no student has unlimited time for reading and thinking, rushing through material to "cover" it rather than understand it ends up costing more time in the long run.

2   **Reading to make inferences**

Reading to make inferences, sometimes called *reading "between" the lines,* means understanding what is implied but not stated. Often you have to infer information, or background, or the author's purpose. Consider this passage:

> How to tell the difference between modern art and junk puzzles many people although few are willing to admit it. The owner of an art gallery in Chicago had a prospective buyer for two sculptures made of discarded metal and put them outside his warehouse to clean them up. Unfortunately, some junk dealers, who apparently didn't recognize abstract expressionism when they saw it, hauled the two 300-pound pieces away.
>
> —ORA GYGI, "Things Are Seldom What They Seem"

The literal meaning is that many people cannot tell the difference between art and junk. Two abstract metal sculptures were carted away as junk when an art dealer left them outside a warehouse to clean them.

Now read the material inferentially. You can begin with the

QUOTATION ABOUT READING

Rereading books is an antisocial habit. If I keep it up, I'm not going to be invited out anymore. It's a pity, because rereading books has become a sort of addiction. If a book is really good, it deserves to be read again, and if it's great, it should be read at least three times.

It's not a question of paying homage to the book, but of doing it justice. In a first reading, you're distracted by pleasure, excitement, curiosity. The book may so seize you that you rush through it in a kind of delirium. In my own case, the more I like a book, the more slowly I read, and this has its distractions too. When you read slowly, as the speed-reading courses point out, you have time to free-associate to the material, and this blurs your recollection of it, confusing stimulus and response. Yet I wouldn't want to give up these associations, this spontaneous talking back to a book, because it's one of the things that makes reading so valuable. In mingling your ideas and feelings with the author's, you raise and complicate the level of your own imagining.

—Anatole Broyard, "About Books: Reading and Other Excesses"

unexplained statement "few are willing to admit" they do not know the difference between art and junk. Reading between the lines, you realize that people feel embarrassed *not* to know; they feel uneducated, or without good taste, or perhaps left out. With this inference in mind, you can move to the last two sentences, in which the author offers not only the literal irony (see 21c) of the art's being carted away as junk, but also the implied irony that the people who carted it away are not among those who might feel embarrassed. This implied irony suggests that the people either do not care if they know the difference between art and junk (after all, they assumed it was junk and went on their way) or they "apparently" (a good word for inference making) want to give the impression that they do not know the difference. Thus, it is the art dealer who ends up being embarrassed, for it is he who created the problem by leaving the sculptures outdoors unattended.

The process of inferring is a critical thinking skill that adds not only texture but also invaluable background to facilitate the interpretation of a passage. As you read to make inferences, consult Chart 33.

CHECKLIST FOR MAKING INFERENCES DURING READING   33

1. What is being said beyond the literal level?
2. What is implied rather than stated?
3. What words need to be read for their implied meanings (connotations) as well as for their stated meanings (denotations)? (For more about word meanings, see 20b-1.)
4. What information does the author expect me to have before I start to read the material?
5. What does the author seem to assume are my biases?
6. What information does the author expect me to have about his or her background, philosophy, and the like?
7. What do I need to be aware of concerning author bias?

---

3   Reading to evaluate

Evaluative reading, sometimes called *reading "beyond" the lines,* is essential for critical thinking. Once you know an author's literal meaning (see 5d-1), and once you have drawn as many inferences (see 5d-2) as possible from the material, you must evaluate.

Evaluative reading calls for many skills, including knowing

how to recognize faulty reasoning (5e–5g), logical fallacies (5h), slanted language (21a-4), and artificial language (21e). Evaluative reading also demands the ability to recognize the impact of an author's tone, to detect prejudice, and to differentiate fact from opinion, as summarized in Chart 34.

CHECKLIST FOR EVALUATIVE READING 34

1. Is the author's tone appropriate?
2. Is the author showing signs of prejudice?
3. What am I reading that is fact, and what is opinion?

Recognizing whether an author's tone is appropriate

Tone is communicated by all aspects of a piece of writing, from the writer's choice of words to the content of the message (see 1d). An author's tone should be appropriate to the author's purpose (see 1b) and audience (see 1c). For example, most academic writing should not use language that is either informal or overly stiff and formal (see 21a-1).

Most authors use a serious tone, but sometimes they use humor to get their point across; if you read such material exclusively for its literal meaning, you will miss the point. Here is a passage from an argument against the destruction of buildings that house small, friendly neighborhood stores and their replacement by large, impersonal buildings.

> Every time an old building is torn down in this country, and a new building goes up, the ground floor becomes a bank. The reason for this is that banks are the only ones who can afford the rent for the ground floor of the new buildings going up. . . . Most people don't think there is anything wrong with this, and they accept it as part of the American free-enterprise system. But there is a small group of people in this country who are fighting for Bank Birth Control.
>
> —ART BUCHWALD, "Birth Control for Banks"

Buchwald clearly respects his readers, for he expects that they will realize that (1) although he is talking only of banks, the banks stand for many aspects of urban renewal; (2) the first sentence is an exaggeration intended to elicit a smile—Buchwald is being slightly ridiculous to get across his point; and (3) the group "Bank Birth Control" does not exist—it is Buchwald's creation to advance his argument.

EXTRA EXERCISE A

Determine which of the following sentences state facts and which state opinions.

1. Nuclear fusion releases energy.

2. Nuclear fusion is a possible solution of our energy problems.

3. Solar energy has attracted a great deal of public attention over the past decade.

4. Many people hope that it will produce a clean, nonpolluting means of heating our homes and offices.

5. Oil and gas production in the United States has been falling for over a decade.

6. The petroleum industry is shrinking yearly.

7. In the interest of national security, the petroleum industry should be encouraged by government legislation.

8. The early pioneers generated energy from the wind on the frontier.

9. Such nonpolluting means of creating energy should replace those produced by fossil fuels immediately.

10. Because natural gas, methane, is a clean fuel, the government should encourage its use.

ANSWERS: EXTRA EXERCISE A

1. fact
2. opinion
3. fact
4. fact
5. fact
6. fact
7. opinion
8. fact
9. opinion
10. opinion

Most readers are wary of a highly emotional tone whose purpose is not to give information but to incite the reader.

NO   Urban renewal must be stopped! Urban redevelopment is ruining this country. Money-hungry capitalists are robbing treasures from law-abiding citizens! Corrupt politicians are murderers, caring nothing about people being thrown out of their homes into the streets.

Writers of such material do not respect their readers, for such writers assume that readers do not recognize screaming in print when they see it. Discerning readers instantly know the tone here is emotional and unreasonable. The exaggerations (robbing treasures, politicians as murderers) hint at the truth of some cases, but they are generalizations too extreme to be taken seriously.

On the other hand, if a writer's tone sounds reasonable and moderate, readers are more likely to pay attention.

YES   Urban renewal is revitalizing our cities, but it has caused some serious problems. While investors are trying to replace slums with decent housing, they must also remember that they are displacing people who do not want to leave their familiar neighborhoods. Surely a cooperative effort between government and the private sector can lead to creative solutions.

Detecting prejudice

Writers often express opinions, which readers should expect to be based on sound reasoning (see 5e-5h). **Prejudice** is revealed in negative opinions based on beliefs rather than on facts or evidence. Negative opinions might be expressed in positive language, but the underlying assumptions are negative. Prejudicial statements are like these: *Poor people like living in crowded conditions because they are used to the surroundings, Women are not aggressive enough to succeed in business, Men make good soldiers because they enjoy killing.* Often writers imply their prejudices rather than state them outright. Detecting underlying negative opinions that distort information is important for critical reading, because discerning readers must call into question any argument that rests upon a weak foundation. (See also Hasty Generalization in 5h.)

Differentiating fact from opinion

Facts are statements that can be verified. A person may use experiment, research, and/or observation to verify facts. Opinions are statements of personal beliefs that are open to debate. *Opinions* often contain information that cannot be verified, such as abstract ideas.

An author sometimes intentionally blurs the difference between fact and opinion, and a discerning reader must be able to tell the difference. Sometimes that difference is quite obvious.

A. A woman can never make a good mathematician.
B. Although fear of math is not purely a female phenomenon, girls tend to drop out of math sooner than boys, and adult women experience an aversion to math and math-related activity that is akin to anxiety.

Because of the word *never*, statement *A* is clearly an opinion. Statement *B* seems to be factual. Knowing who made these statements can sometimes help a reader distinguish between fact and opinion. Statement *A* is by a male Soviet mathematician living in Russia, as reported by David K. Shipler, a well-respected veteran reporter on Russian affairs for the *New York Times;* statement *B* is in a book called *Overcoming Math Anxiety* by Sheila Tobias, a university professor who has undertaken research studies to find out why many people dislike math. Thus, statement *B* can be confirmed to be fact.

One aid in differentiating between fact and opinion is to *think beyond the obvious.* For example, is "Strenuous exercise is good for your health" a fact? Although the statement has the ring of truth, it is not a fact. People with severe arthritis or heart trouble could be harmed by some forms of exercise. Also, what does "strenuous" mean—a dozen pushups, jogging, aerobics, or playing tennis?

A second aid in differentiating between fact and opinion is to *remember that facts sometimes masquerade as opinions, and opinions sometimes try to pass for facts.* Evaluative reading demands concentration and a willingness to deal with matters that are relative and sometimes ambiguous. For example, in an essay for or against capital punishment, you would likely evaluate the argument differently if you knew that the author is currently on death row, or a disinterested party with a philosophy to discuss.

At times, however, the stance of the author is less clear. Consider these statements:

C. The common wart usually occurs on the hands, especially on the backs of the fingers, but they may occur on any part of the skin. These dry, elevated lesions have numerous projections on the surface.
D. Warts are wonderful structures. They can appear overnight on any part of the skin, like mushrooms on a damp lawn, full grown and splendid in the complexity of their architecture.

QUOTATION ABOUT READING

My education was the liberty I had to read indiscriminately and all the time, with my eyes hanging out.

—Dylan Thomas

QUOTATION ABOUT WRITING

In any work that is truly creative, the writer cannot be omniscient in advance about the effects that he or she proposes to produce. The suspense . . . is not just in the reader, but in the writer, who is intensely curious about what will happen.

—Mary McCarthy

QUOTATION ABOUT READING

Books: The most effective weapon against intolerance and ignorance.

—Lyndon Baines Johnson

QUOTATION ABOUT READING

Whenever I feel uneasy about my writing, I think: What would be the response of the people in the book if they read the book? That's my way of staying on track. Those are the people for whom I write.

—Toni Morrison

Both statements are about warts. Judging only from the words—often all the evidence available—and without knowing who the authors are, we might say that *C* is fact and *D* is opinion.

Information about the authors can make your judgments more subtle and therefore more reliable. Statement *C* is from a respected medical encyclopedia; thus it can be confirmed as fact. Statement *D* is by Lewis Thomas, a distinguished physician, hospital administrator, researcher, and writer who won the National Book Award for his popular essays revealing the intricacies of biology to laypeople. Given this information and the comparatively benign nature of the material, the words in *D* move into the realm of fact—fact drawing on metaphor (see 21c) to illustrate its point. The author is trying to bring the facts to life by looking at them in a new way and explaining them inventively.

ANSWERS: EXERCISE 5-2

1. opinion
2. opinion
3. opinion
4. fact
5. fact (It's a dictionary definition.)
6. opinion
7. fact
8. fact
9. opinion
10. fact

ANSWERS: EXERCISE 5-3

Answers may vary somewhat, but here is a fairly complete list of possibilities:

A. Literal information

1. It is the first of February.
2. "Everyone" (see implied information, below) is talking about starlings.
3. Starlings came to this country on a passenger liner from Europe.
4. "This country" is the United States. (Central Park and New York are mentioned.)

➔

EXERCISE 5-2

Consulting section 5d, decide if each statement is a fact or an opinion. When the author and source are provided, explain how that information influences your judgment.

1. Jogging promotes good mental health.
2. Cotton clothing is more comfortable than polyester clothing.
3. "Every journey into the past is complicated by delusions, false memories, false namings of real events." (Adrienne Rich, poet, *Of Woman Born*)
4. Edmund Hillary performed two major feats: he not only led the first successful climb to the top of Mount Everest but also he led the first group to cross the Antarctic continent from sea to sea.
5. "History is the branch of knowledge that deals systematically with the past." (*Webster's New World Dictionary*, Third College Edition)
6. "Rock music encourages passions and provides models that have no relation to any life the young people who go to universities can possibly lead, or to the kinds of admiration encouraged by liberal studies." (Allan Bloom, a professor at the University of Chicago, *The Closing of the American Mind*)
7. The earth's temperature is gradually rising.
8. Slaves in ancient Egypt were often killed when they finished building a pyramid so that they could not reveal the entrances to thieves who would loot the tombs.
9. "You change laws by changing lawmakers." (Sissy Farenthold, political activist, interview reported in *The Bakersfield Californian*)

10. "But since it opened to the public in 1982, Elvis's place in suburban Whitehaven, a 30-minute drive from downtown Memphis, has attracted more than 3 million visitors. That figure makes it one of the top house attractions in the U.S. This year alone, some 640,000 people will visit Graceland, and in the process they will spend more than $10 million on tickets, food, and souvenirs." (J. D. Reed, "The Mansion Music Made," *Time*)

EXERCISE 5-3

Consulting section 5d, after you read this passage, (1) list all literal information, (2) list all implied information, and (3) list the opinions stated.

EXAMPLE   The study found many complaints against the lawyers were not investigated, seemingly out of a "desire to avoid difficult cases."

—Norman F. Dacey

Literal information: Few complaints against lawyers are investigated.
Implied information: The words "difficult cases" imply a coverup: lawyers, or others in power, hesitate to criticize lawyers for fear of being sued, or for fear of a public outcry if the truth about abuses and errors were revealed.
Opinions: None—all is factual because it refers to, and contains a quote from, a study.

A.   It is the first of February, and everyone is talking about starlings. Starlings came to this country on a passenger liner from Europe. One hundred of them were deliberately released in Central Park, and from those hundred descended all of our countless millions of starlings today. According to Edwin Way Teale, "Their coming was the result of one man's fancy. That man was Eugene Schieffelin, a wealthy New York drug manufacturer. His curious hobby was the introduction into America of all the birds mentioned in William Shakespeare." The birds adapted to their new country splendidly.

—Annie Dillard, *Terror at Tinker Creek*

B.   In recent years, the Soviet Union has been taking increasing interest in its Russian roots. As a result, Soviet archeologists and restorers are in the enviable position of having more government funds than they can spend. What they lack, they say, are experts to do the job. Only 2.5 percent of Novgorod has been explored; Yanin estimates that at least 20,000 more manuscripts are buried beneath the city. At the current rate of excavation, it will take a thousand years to exhaust the dig.

—Ruth Daniloff, "Letters from Medieval Russia"

Cont'd.

5. One hundred starlings were deliberately released in Central Park.
6. From these 100 are descended the countless millions of starlings today.
7. Edwin Way Teale said, "Their . . . Shakespeare."
8. Eugene Schieffelin was a wealthy New York drug manufacturer.
9. Schieffelin's hobby was introducing into America all the birds mentioned in Shakespeare.
10. The starlings adapted to their new country.

A. Implied information
1. "Everyone" is used for effect; the author does not mean each and every person.
2. By saying that the birds came "on a passenger liner" (rather than, for example, "in the cargo hold of a ship") the author begins to alert the reader to expect the unexpected (in this case, that someone wanted to introduce to America all the birds in Shakespeare).
3. Central Park is in New York City. (This is information the author assumes the reader has.)
4. "One man's fancy" are words that suggest that the man had somewhat unusual tastes.
5. The drugs that Schieffelin manufactured were legitimate, not illegal.
6. See item 2 in "Opinions" below.

A. Opinions
1. (In Teale's opinion) Schieffelin's hobby was somewhat strange ("curious").
2. (In Dillard's opinion) the starlings adapted too well ("splendidly"); here Dillard assumes that the reader knows that flocks of starlings can be a nuisance and even a danger (e.g., getting into airplane engines).

➜

5e

EXERCISE 5-3 ANSWERS, *cont'd.*

B. Literal information

1. In recent years, the Soviet Union has been taking increasing interest in its Russian roots.
2. Soviet archaeologists and restorers have more government funds than they can spend.
3. They say that they do not have enough experts to do the job.
4. Only 2.5 percent of Novgorod has been explored.
5. Yanin estimates that at least 20,000 more manuscripts are buried beneath the city. (See also "Opinions," item 3, below.)
6. At the current rate of excavation, it will take a thousand years to exhaust the dig. (See also "Opinions," item 4, below.)

B. Implied information

1. The Soviets had not taken an interest in their roots until recent years.
2. It is because of this recent interest that more government money has become available for archaeologists and restorers.
3. The Soviets cannot do the job without more experts.
4. Novgorod is worth exploring.

B. Opinions

1. It is enviable to have so much government money that it cannot be spent.
2. Although "they say" they lack experts, they might not.
3. Yanin's estimates are his opinion (based on his expertise).
4. "A thousand years" is an opinion (based on estimating the current rate).

C. Literal information

1. Gandhi envisaged a constitution and government for an independent India.

➡

C.   The kind of constitution and government Gandhi envisaged for an independent India was spelled out at the forty-fifth convention of the All-India Congress, which began at Karachi on March 27, 1931. It was a party political convention the like of which I had not seen before—nor seen since—with its ringing revolutionary proclamations acclaimed by some 350 leaders, men and women, just out of jail, squatting in the heat under a tent in a semicircle at Gandhi's feet, all of them, like Gandhi, spinning away like children playing with toys as they talked. They made up the so-called Subjects Committee, selected from the five thousand delegates to do the real work of the convention, though in reality, it was Gandhi alone who dominated the proceedings, writing most of the resolutions and moving their adoption with his customary eloquence and surprising firmness.

—William L. Shirer, *Gandhi: A Memoir*

5e ## Using evidence to think critically

The cornerstone of all reasoning is evidence. Readers expect writers to provide solid evidence for any assertion made or conclusion reached. Writers who successfully communicate their messages use evidence well to support their assertions or conclusions. Evidence consists of facts, statistical information, examples, and opinions of experts.

1 ### Using evidence effectively

Keep these guidelines in mind as you gather, evaluate, and use evidence.

GUIDELINES FOR USING EVIDENCE EFFECTIVELY   35

1. Use sufficient evidence.
2. Use representative evidence.
3. Use relevant evidence.
4. Use accurate evidence, whether from primary or secondary sources.
5. Qualify the claims you make based on the evidence.

---

1. **Evidence should be sufficient.** In general, the more evidence, the better. A survey that draws upon a hundred respondents is likely to be more reliable than a survey involving only ten. As a writer, you may convince your reader that violence is a serious problem in the high schools on the basis of two specific examples, but you will be more convincing if you can give five examples—or, better still, statistics for a school district, a city, or the nation.

2. **Evidence should be representative.** Readers expect as much objectivity and fairness as possible. People should not trust an assertion or conclusion if it is based on only some members of a group being discussed. An assertion or conclusion must be based on a truly *representative*, or typical, sample of the group. A political pollster would not get representative evidence by asking questions of the first 1,500 people to walk by a street corner in Austin, Texas, because no such group would truly represent the various regional, racial, political, and ethnic subgroups of the American electorate. Leading political and media pollsters, like those who do the Gallup polls and the Nielsen ratings, use sophisticated sampling techniques to try to ensure that their evidence is representative.

3. **Evidence should be relevant.** Evidence should relate directly to the assertion made. Determining relevance can demand subtle thinking. Suppose you read evidence that one hundred students who had watched television for more than two hours a day throughout their high school years earned significantly lower scores on the Scholastic Aptitude Test than one hundred students who had not. Would you conclude that students who watch less television perform better on achievement tests? Closer examination of the evidence might reveal other, more important differences between the two groups—differences in geographical region, family background, socioeconomic group, and perhaps quality of schools attended. Your evidence would be both ample and representative but your conclusion would not be *relevant to* the evidence.

4. **Evidence must be accurate.** Without accuracy, evidence is useless. Evidence must therefore come from reliable sources. For reliable evidence, you can refer to *primary sources* or *secondary sources* (see 5e-2). Equally important, once you have reliable evidence, you need to present it carefully so that you do not misrepresent or distort it when you communicate it to others.

5. **Evidence should be qualified.** Evidence rarely justifies claims that use words such as *all, certainly, always,* or *never.* Conclusions

Cont'd.

2. The constitution was spelled out at the forty-fifth convention of the All-India Congress.
3. The Congress began at Karachi on March 27, 1931.
4. The Congress was a political convention.
5. The Congress was attended by some 350 leaders.
6. The leaders were both men and women.
7. The leaders were just out of jail.
8. The leaders squatted in the heat under a tent in a semicircle at Gandhi's feet.
9. They all worked at spinning wheels.
10. They made up the so-called Subjects Committee, which was selected from the 5,000 delegates.
11. Gandhi wrote most of the resolutions and moved their adoption.

C. Implied information
1. India was not independent before March 27, 1931.
2. Even though the Congress had met 45 times, India was still not independent.
3. The Congress took more than one day—it only "began" on March 27, 1931.
4. Most of the leaders likely were revolutionaries who had been political prisoners—because all were "just out of jail."
5. The leaders were very dedicated—they were willing to squat in the heat under a tent.
6. The ruling government did not provide the basic amenities for a convention: room in a building, decent ventilation, chairs, tables, and so forth.
7. The leaders' sitting at Gandhi's feet implies how they respected him. ➜

EXERCISE 5-3 ANSWERS, *cont'd.*

8. Gandhi often worked at a spinning wheel as he spoke.

9. Everyone's spinning implies that they wanted to imitate Gandhi.

10. Five thousand people is too large a group to get policy matters decided.

11. Gandhi dominated the proceedings because everyone respected him so much.

C. Opinions

1. The author had not seen before—or since—a political convention like this one in achievement and tone.

2. The revolutionary proclamations were "ringing."

3. The leaders were spinning away like children playing with toys as they talked.

4. Gandhi dominated the proceedings.

5. Gandhi wrote and spoke with his customary eloquence and surprising firmness.

are more reasonable when qualified with words such as *some, many, a few, probably, possibly, perhaps, may, usually,* and *often.* Remember that today's "facts" may be revised as time passes, information changes, and knowledge grows.

---

2 | **Understanding primary and secondary sources as evidence**

Primary sources present first-hand evidence based on your own or someone else's original work or direct observation. First-hand evidence has the greatest impact on a reader. Consider this eyewitness account:

> Poverty is dirt. . . . Let me explain about housekeeping with no money. For breakfast I give my children grits with no oleo or cornbread without eggs and oleo. This does not use up many dishes. What dishes there are, I wash in cold water and with no soap. Even the cheapest soap has to be saved for the baby's diapers. Look at my hands, so cracked and red. Once I saved for two months to buy a jar of Vaseline for my hands and the baby's diaper rash. When I had saved enough, I went to buy it and the price had gone up two cents. The baby and I suffered on. I have to decide every day if I can bear to put my cracked sore hands into the cold water and strong soap. But you ask, why not hot water? Fuel costs money. If you have a wood fire it costs money. If you burn electricity, it costs money. Hot water is a luxury. I do not have luxuries. . . .
>
> —Jo Goodwin Parker, in *America's Other Children*

As a reader and as a writer, remember that not all eyewitness accounts are equally reliable. What is it about Parker's account that makes you trust what she says? She is specific. She is also authoritative. It is doubtful that anyone would have invented the story about being two cents short of the price of a jar of Vaseline. As a writer of personal observations, you need to be as specific as possible—to prove that you truly saw what you say you saw. Use language that appeals to all five senses: describe sights, sounds, and experiences that could have been seen, heard, or experienced only by someone who was there. Show your readers *your* cracked, red hands.

Primary sources can provide invaluable reports of observations. Few will ever see the surface of the moon or the top of Mt. Everest. People rely, therefore, upon the first-hand reports of the astronauts and mountain climbers who have been there. History depends heavily on letters, diaries, and journals—the reports of eyewitnesses.

Surveys, polls, and experiments are some of the means by which people extend their powers of observation beyond what can be "seen" in the everyday sense of the word. These surveys, polls, and experiments must be carefully controlled—through weighing, measuring, or quantifying information that would otherwise not be available. Jo Parker could look at her hands. Who can see, however, the attitude of the American public toward marriage, toward a presidential candidate, toward inflation? For evidence on these matters, polls or surveys are necessary, and they constitute primary evidence.

Secondary sources report, describe, comment on, or analyze the experiences or the work of others. As evidence, a secondary source is at least once removed from the original work, the direct observation, or the first-hand experience. Still, such evidence can have great value and enormous impact. Consider this second-hand, reported observation.

> The immediate causes of death from nuclear attack are the blast wave, which can flatten heavily reinforced buildings many kilometers away, the firestorm, the gamma rays and the neutrons, which effectively fry the insides of passersby. A school girl who survived the American nuclear attack on Hiroshima, the event that ended the Second World War, wrote this first-hand account:

> > Through a darkness like the bottom of hell, I could hear the voices of the other students calling for their mothers. And at the base of the bridge, inside a big cistern that had been dug out there, was a mother weeping, holding above her head a naked baby that was burned bright red all over its body. . . . But every single person who passed was wounded, all of them, and there was no one, there was no one to turn to for help. And the singed hair on the heads of the people was frizzled and whitish and covered with dust. They did not appear to be human, not creatures of this world.

> —CARL SAGAN, *Cosmos*

As with Parker's eyewitness account, the strength or value of a second-hand account hinges on the reliability of the reporter. That reliability is a function of how specific, accurate, and authoritative the observations are. Here the standard maxim "consider the source" becomes crucial. An expert's reputation must stem from some special experience (as the parents of many children could be "experts" on child reading) or training (as an accountant could be an expert on taxes). Because the author of the example paragraph, Carl Sagan, is a respected scientist, scholar, and writer, his report of the schoolgirl's eyewitness account is likely to be reliable, authoritative, worthwhile secondary evidence.

QUOTATION ABOUT READING

A reflection on having once read 800 pages of *War and Peace* in one day:

It took me a long time to forget the way I read that book. For a long time it seemed to me I had betrayed reading itself. Coming back to it now, I still find it disturbing. Something had been sacrificed in my quick dash through the book—another reading altogether. I had limited myself to the story at the expense of a deep, receptive, non-narrative reading of Tolstoy's writing itself. It was as though I had realized that day, once and for all, that a book consists of two layers: on top, the readable layer I had read that day on the train, and underneath, a layer that was inaccessible. You only sense its existence in a moment of distraction from the literal reading, the way you see childhood through a child. It would take forever to tell what you see, and it would be pointless.

—Marguerite Duras, "On Tolstoy, Racine, and Reading by the Light of the Book"

BACKGROUND

In *Illiterate America* (1985) Jonathan Kozol cites figures from a 1979 Ford Foundation study that places the number of illiterate Americans at about 60 million. Supporting those assertions are United Nations statistics that rank the United States forty-ninth in literacy among 158 U.N. countries.

QUOTATION ABOUT READING

The one thing I regret is that I will never have time to read all the books I want to read.

—Françoise Sagan

Although Carl Sagan referred to (and presumably quotes) an eyewitness account, the evidence becomes a secondary source because it is appearing in Sagan's work. It is secondary because while you can feel quite confident that Sagan is fully and fairly representing what the schoolgirl said, *you* cannot be sure of that unless you see her original account. If you were to use Sagan's version of her account as evidence, it would be third-hand evidence: one person (you) further removed from Sagan and the original source (the schoolgirl). Chart 36 gives guidelines for evaluating a secondary source.

CHECKLIST FOR EVALUATING A SECONDARY SOURCE   36

1. **Authoritative:** Is the source written by an expert or a person whom you can expect to write credibly on the subject?

2. **Reliable:** Does the material appear in a reputable publication— in a book published by an established publisher or a respected journal or magazine?

3. **Well known:** Do you find the source cited elsewhere as you read about the subject? (Doing so indicates fairly wide acceptance of the authority of the source.)

4. **Well supported:** Is the source *based on* primary evidence, such as someone else's first-hand experience or observation?

5. **Balanced tone:** Is the source's language relatively objective (therefore more reliable) or slanted (therefore likely not reliable)?

6. **Current:** Is the material current (therefore more reliable) or outdated (therefore likely not reliable)?

EXERCISE 5-4

Consulting Section 5e, decide the following: (a) Would each passage constitute primary or secondary evidence? (b) Is the evidence acceptable? Why or why not?

1. I went one morning to a place along the banks of the Madeira River where the railroad ran, alongside rapids impassable to river traffic, and I searched for any marks it may have left on the land. But there was nothing except a clearing where swarms of insects hovered over the dead black hen and other items spread out on a red cloth as an offering to the gods of macumba, or black magic. This strain of African origins in Brazil's ethnic character is strong in the Northwest Region.

—WILLIAM S. ELLIS, ''Brazil's Imperiled Rain Forest''

2.   In the fall of 1982, only 4.7 percent of first-year college students indicated an interest in elementary or secondary teaching as a career. In 1970 that percentage was more than 19 percent. And there are other equally disturbing statistical measures. More than a third of the nation's teachers have told pollsters that if they had to start their own careers over again, they would not select teaching. Thirteen out of every 100 teachers say they *certainly* would not become teachers again, and 30 more maintain they *probably* would not do so.

—MARY HATWOOD FUTRELL "Towards Excellence"

3.   Most climatologists believe that the world will eventually slip back into an ice age in 10,000 to 20,000 years. The Earth has been unusually cold for the last two to three million years, and we are just lucky to be living during one of the warm spells. But the concern of most weather watchers looking at the next century is with fire rather than ice. By burning fossil fuels and chopping down forests, humans have measurably increased the amount of carbon dioxide in the atmosphere. From somewhere around 300 parts per million at the turn of the century, this level has risen to 340 parts per million today. If the use of fossil fuels continues to increase, carbon dioxide could reach 600 parts per million during the next century.

—STEVE OLSON, "Computing Climate"

4.   Back in the days when large families were desired for their labor, at least children knew they were really needed. Today's child, overwhelmed with possessions and catered to endlessly by parents, is struggling with feelings of worthlessness. Even with labor-saving devices, big families are a lot of work. My children know they have to pitch in, and they know we appreciate their help. Maybe I don't have time to read to the three-year-old, but the eight-year-old does—to the benefit of them both.

—SARA L. SMITH, "Big Families Can Be Happy, Too"

5.   Marriages on the frontier were often made before a girl was half through her adolescent years, and some diaries record a casualness in the manner in which such decisions were reached. Mrs. John Kirkwood recounts.

The night before Christmas, John Kirkwood . . . the path finder, stayed at our house over night. I had met him before and when he heard the discussion about my brother Jasper's wedding, he suggested that he and I also get married. I was nearly fifteen years old and I thought it was high time that I got married so I consented.

—LILLIAN SCHLISSEL, *Women's Diaries of the Westward Journey*

131

ANSWERS: EXERCISE 5-4

1. *Primary evidence:* The author is describing his own experiences in a first-person narrative. It can be assumed to be reliable since a reliable journal, *National Geographic*, published the account.

2. *Impossible to determine from this excerpt.* Although this paragraph reports poll results, we do not know from it whether the author is citing a poll she conducted or reporting others' results. The paragraph describes the results of a poll. This information seems reliable because of the facts, although if Futrell later includes information about the design of the poll—the size, the representativeness of the sample, and other questions that might have influenced these answers—the argument will be even more reliable.

3. *Secondary evidence:* The assertions in this paragraph are carefully qualified and seem well substantiated by evidence. The material was published in a reliable science magazine.

4. *Primary evidence:* This is an eyewitness account. This argument is based on some assumptions that the reader might not share. For example, are all of today's children "struggling with feelings of worthlessness"? On the other hand, Smith is a suitable expert to discuss the effects of a large family on her children's needing to pitch in and help. Additional specific examples about Smith's family and testimony from people in other big families would strengthen this argument.

5. *Both secondary and primary evidence:* The opening paragraph presents secondary evidence, but the quoted material that follows this paragraph serves to make Schlissel's observations reliable. The second paragraph presents primary evidence—a first-hand account from a diary by Mrs. John Kirkwood.

You may want to ask your students to think about their own experiences, analyzing them for their causes and effects. You might ask your students to diagram these causes and effects and to write some of these diagrams on the board for discussion. The questions that follow can help to stimulate students' thinking.

1. How did you get your first job?
2. What did you learn from that job?
3. Whose advice is particularly important to you?
4. How do you reach a decision?
5. What difference do you expect college to make in your life?
6. Why do you have a particular way of doing something?
7. How do you make friends?
8. Who is the most important person in your life? Why?
9. When did you learn to drive a car?
10. What will you be doing in ten years?

5f Evaluating cause and effect to think critically

Cause and effect is a type of thinking that seeks to establish some relationship, or link, between two or more specific pieces of evidence. Regardless of whether you begin your thinking with a cause or an effect, you are working with this basic pattern:

BASIC PATTERN FOR CAUSE AND EFFECT

Cause A ⟶ produces ⟶ effect B

You may seek to understand the effects of a known cause (for example, studying two more hours each night):

More studying ⟶ produces ⟶ ?

Or you may attempt to determine the cause or causes of a known effect (for example, recurrent headaches):

? ⟶ produces ⟶ recurrent headaches

If you want to use reasoning based on a relationship of cause and effect, evaluate the connections carefully. As you evaluate cause-and-effect relationships, keep in mind the guidelines in Chart 37.

GUIDELINES FOR EVALUATING CAUSE-AND-EFFECT RELATIONSHIPS   37

- Establish a clear relationship between events.
- Determine whether the events can be repeated.
- Avoid oversimplifying: Look for multiple causes and/or effects.

1. **Is there a clear relationship?** When you read or write about causes and effects, carefully think through the reasoning. Causes and effects normally occur in chronological order: *first* a door slams, *then* a pie that is cooling on a shelf falls. But suppose you are walking down the sidewalk when, first, a car backfires, and then the person walking in front of you falls to the ground. Does this mean that the backfire is related to the fall? A cause-and-effect relationship must be linked by more than chronological sequence.

The fact that *B* happens after *A* does not prove that it was caused by *A*.

2. **Is there a pattern of repetition?** To establish the relationship of *A* to *B*, there must be proof that every time *A* was present, *B* occurred—or that *B* never occurred unless *A* was present. The need for a pattern of repetition explains why the Food and Drug Administration performs thousands of tests before declaring a new food or medicine safe for human consumption.

3. **Has oversimplification been avoided?** The basic pattern of cause and effect—single cause, single effect—rarely gives the full picture. Most complex social or political problems have **multiple causes,** not a single cause and a single effect.

It is oversimplifying to assume that high schools were the only cause of the nationwide decline in scores on the Scholastic Aptitude Test between 1964 and 1984. Not only would it be unfair to high schools, it would also be ignoring a variety of other possible important causes, such as television viewing habits, family life, level of textbooks, and so on. Similarly, one cause can produce **multiple effects:**

Some people are guilty of oversimplification of effects in how they present diets. A certain diet, for example, may bring about weight reduction and may lower salt intake, but the dieter may also suffer from the loss of valuable nutrients not included in the diet.

5g Understanding reasoning processes to think critically

To think critically you need to be able to understand reasoning processes. When you understand them you can recognize and

---

evaluate them in your reading and use them correctly in your writing. **Induction** and **deduction** are reasoning processes, natural thought patterns that people use every day to think through ideas and to make decisions. Inductive and deductive reasoning are summarized in Chart 38.

COMPARISON OF INDUCTIVE AND DEDUCTIVE REASONING		38
	INDUCTIVE REASONING	DEDUCTIVE REASONING
ARGUMENT BEGINS	with specific evidence	with a general claim
ARGUMENT CONCLUDES	with a general claim	with a specific statement
CONCLUSION IS	reliable or unreliable	true or false
REASONING IS USED	to discover something new	to apply what is known

1 **Recognizing and using inductive reasoning**

Induction is the process of arriving at general principles from particular facts or instances, as summarized in Chart 39. Suppose that you go to the Registry of Motor Vehicles to renew your driver's license, and you have to stand in line for two hours until you get the document. Then a few months later, when you return to the Registry for new license plates, a clerk gives you the wrong advice, and you have to stand in two different lines for three hours. Another time you go there in response to a letter asking for information, and you discover that you should have brought your car registration form, although the letter failed to mention that fact. You conclude that the Registry is inefficient and seems not to care about the convenience of its patrons. You have arrived at this conclusion by means of induction.

SUMMARY OF INDUCTIVE REASONING
39

1. **Inductive reasoning moves from the specific to the general.** It begins with the evidence of specific facts, observations, or experiences and moves to a general conclusion.

2. Inductive conclusions are considered *reliable* or *unreliable*, not true or false. An inductive conclusion indicates probability, the degree to which the conclusion is likely to be true. Frustrating though it may be for those who seek certainty, inductive thinking is, of necessity, based only on a sampling of the facts.

3. An inductive conclusion is held to be reliable or unreliable in relation to the quantity and quality of the evidence (see 5e) supporting it.

4. Induction leads to new "truths." Induction can support statements about the unknown on the basis of what is known.

---

2 | **Recognizing and using deductive reasoning**

Deduction is the process of reasoning from general claims to a specific instance. If several unproductive visits to the Registry of Motor Vehicles have convinced you that the Registry cares little about the convenience of its patrons (as the experiences described in 5g-1 suggest), you will not be happy the next time you must return. Your reasoning might go something like this:

The Registry wastes people's time.
I have to go to the Registry tomorrow.
Therefore, tomorrow my time will be wasted.

You reached the conclusion—"therefore, tomorrow my time will be wasted"—by means of deduction.

Deductive arguments have three parts: two **premises** and a **conclusion.** This three-part structure is known as a **syllogism.** The first premise of a deductive argument may be a fact or an assumption. The second premise may also be a fact or an assumption.

Whether or not an argument is **valid** has to do with the argument's form or structure. Here the word *valid* is not the general term people use in conversation to mean "acceptable" or "well

QUOTATION ABOUT READING

QUOTATION ABOUT READING

Do not dictate to your author; try to become him. Be his fellow-worker and accomplice. If you hang back, and reserve and criticize at first, you are preventing yourself from getting the fullest possible value from what you read. But if you open your mind as widely as possible, then signs and hints of almost imperceptible fineness, from the twist and turn of the first sentences, will bring you in the presence of a human being unlike any other. Steep yourself in this, acquaint yourself with this, and soon you will find that your author is giving you, or attempting to give you, something far more definite.

—Virginia Woolf, "How Should One Read a Book?"

QUOTATION ABOUT WRITING

The Latin roots of the word *induction* give us a clue as to how this method of arguing works: *in* = into + *ducere* = to lead— literally, "to lead into." After noting a series of similar phenomena, we draw some conclusion, we make some generalization about all phenomena of that kind. In other words, after observing a number of similar examples of something, we are "led into" a conclusion about all examples of that kind.

—Edward P. J. Corbett, *The Elements of Reasoning*

TEACHING TIP

Using analogy is a way to think inductively. An analogy compares two dissimilar objects, ideas, or experiences by focusing on what they have in common. For example, some people make an analogy between the role of a teacher and that of a coach. Like coaches, teachers train people in fundamentals through repetition and practice, recommend changes in technique, and try to inspire excellence. However, despite points of similarity, two dissimilar items remain dissimilar.

First, coaches work primarily with the body rather than the mind, developing physical rather than mental skills. Second, team coaches praise the team player while good teachers reward independence and originality. Thus the analogy between teachers and coaches breaks down at some point.

In the absence of other evidence, an analogy will not *prove* anything. Nevertheless, although an analogy can always be shown as flawed under close scrutiny, it can still help explain a point and thus help persuade an audience.

grounded." In the context of reading and writing logical arguments, the word *valid* has a very specific meaning. A deductive argument is *valid* when the conclusion logically follows from the premises. The following argument is valid.

VALID

PREMISE 1	When it snows, the streets get wet. [fact]
PREMISE 2	It is snowing. [fact]
CONCLUSION	Therefore, the streets are wet.

The following argument is invalid.

INVALID

PREMISE 1	When it snows, the streets get wet. [fact]
PREMISE 2	The streets are wet. [fact]
CONCLUSION	Therefore, it is snowing.

The invalid argument has acceptable premises because the premises are facts. The argument's conclusion, however, is wrong. It ignores other reasons for why the streets may be wet. The street could be wet from rain, from street-cleaning trucks that spray water, or from people using hoses to cool off the pavement or to wash their cars. Because the conclusion does not follow logically from the premises, the argument is invalid.

The following argument is also invalid. The conclusion does not flow from the premises (the car may not start for many reasons other than a dead battery).

INVALID

PREMISE 1	When the battery is dead, a car will not start. [fact]
PREMISE 2	My car will not start. [fact]
CONCLUSION	My battery is dead.

When a premise is an assumption, the premise must be able to be defended with evidence. The argument at the top of the opposite page is valid. Its conclusion flows logically from the premises. An argument's validity, however, is independent of its truth. Is premise 1 true? Different economists will offer different opinions. *Only if both premises are true is an argument true.* This argument may be true or false depending on whether the first premise is true or false. The writer must support the claim that is the first premise.

log **5g**

VALID (AND POSSIBLY TRUE)

PREMISE 1	When the unemployment rate rises, an economic recession occurs. [assumption: the writer must present evidence in support of this statement]
PREMISE 2	The unemployment rate has risen. [fact]
CONCLUSION	An economic recession will occur.

The following argument is valid. Its conclusion follows from its premises. Is the argument, however, true? Because the argument contains an assumption in its first premise, the argument can be true only if the premise is proved true. Such proof is not possible. Therefore, although the argument is valid, it is not true.

VALID (BUT NOT TRUE)

PREMISE 1	If you buy a Supermacho 357 sports car, you will achieve instant popularity. [assumption]
PREMISE 2	Kim just bought a Supermacho 357 sports car. [fact]
CONCLUSION	Kim will achieve instant popularity.

In any deductive argument, beware of premises that are implied but not stated—called **unstated assumptions.** Remember that an argument can be logically valid even though it is based on wrong assumptions. The response to such an argument is to attack the assumptions, not the conclusion. Often the assumptions are wrong. For example, suppose a corporation argued that it should not be required to install pollution control devices because the cost would cut into its profits. This argument rests on the unstated assumption that no corporation should do something that would lower its profits. That assumption is wrong, and so is the argument. But it can be shown to be wrong only when the assumptions are challenged. Similarly, if someone says that certain information has to be correct because it was printed in a newspaper, the person's deductive reasoning is flawed. Here the unstated assumption is that everything in a newspaper is correct—which is not true. Whenever there is an unstated assumption, supply it and then check to make sure it is true. Deductive reasoning is summarized in Chart 40.

ALTERNATE EXAMPLES

Invalid:

Some circular things are bubbles.
Some human heads are circular things.
Some human heads are bubbles.

Valid:

All mammals are animals.
All whales are mammals.
Therefore, all whales are animals.

SUMMARY OF DEDUCTIVE REASONING

40

1. **Deductive reasoning moves from the general to the specific.** The three-part structure that makes up a deductive argument includes two premises and a conclusion drawn from them.

2. A deductive argument is valid if the conclusion logically follows from the premises.

3. A deductive conclusion may be judged true or false. If both premises are true, the conclusion is true. If the argument contains an assumption, the writer must prove the truth of the assumption to establish the truth of the argument.

4. Deductive reasoning applies what the writer already knows. Though it does not yield anything new, it builds stronger arguments than does inductive reasoning because it offers the certainty of a conclusion's being true or false.

ANSWERS: EXERCISE 5-5

1. Invalid. The shirt's being expensive does not mean that it shares other characteristics of faddish clothing.

2. Valid. The conclusion follows logically from the premises.

3. Invalid. Some outstanding literary works have not received a Pulitzer Prize.

4. Invalid. All states do send representatives, but that does not mean that all representatives come from a state.

5. Valid. The argument is valid, although some people may not agree that all risks are frightening.

6. Valid. The conclusion flows logically from the premises.

7. Invalid. The premises do not contain the conclusion. It is impossible to know whether this magazine is part of "most."

8. Invalid. The qualifying word "usually" in the first premise leaves open the possibility that there are science fiction novels that are not violent.

9. Valid. The conclusion is contained in the premises.

10. Invalid. The first premise does not stipulate that all great college basketball teams come from the Midwest (and Georgetown is among universities not in the Midwest that produce great basketball teams).

EXERCISE 5-5

Consulting section 5g-2, ignore for the moment whether the premises seem to you to be true, but determine if each conclusion is *valid*. Explain your answer.

1. Faddish clothes are expensive.
   This shirt is expensive.
   This shirt must be part of a fad.

2. When a storm is threatening, small-craft warnings are issued.
   A storm is threatening.
   Small-craft warnings will be issued.

3. The Pulitzer Prize is awarded to outstanding literary works.
   The Great Gatsby never won a Pulitzer Prize.
   The Great Gatsby is not an outstanding literary work.

4. All states send representatives to the United States Congress.
   Puerto Rico sends a representative to the United States Congress.
   Puerto Rico is a state.

5. All risks are frightening.
   Changing to a new job is a risk.
   The change to a new job is frightening.

6. Before an occupancy permit can be issued, a new home must be inspected.
   Our new home has been issued an occupancy permit.
   Our new home has been inspected.

7. Most weekly news magazines give only superficial coverage of world affairs.
    This is a weekly news magazine.
    This will give only superficial coverage of world affairs.

8. Science fiction novels are usually violent.
    This is a science fiction novel.
    This novel is obviously violent.

9. All veterans are entitled to education benefits.
    Elaine is a veteran.
    Elaine is entitled to education benefits.

10. Midwestern universities produce great college basketball teams.
    Georgetown has a great college basketball team.
    Georgetown is a midwestern university.

5h Recognizing and avoiding logical fallacies

Logical fallacies are flaws in reasoning that lead to illogical statements. They tend to occur most often when ideas are being argued, although they can be found in all types of writing. Most logical fallacies masquerade as reasonable statements, but they are in fact attempts to manipulate readers by reaching their emotions instead of their intellects, their hearts rather than their heads. Most logical fallacies are known by labels; each indicates a way that thinking has gone wrong during the reasoning process.

Hasty generalization

A **hasty generalization** occurs when someone generalizes from inadequate evidence. If the statement "My hometown is the best place in the state to live" is supported with only two examples of why it is pleasant, the generalization is hasty. **Stereotyping** is a type of hasty generalization that occurs when someone makes prejudiced, sweeping claims about all of the members of a particular religious, ethnic, racial, or political group: "Everyone from country X is dishonest." **Sexism** occurs when someone discriminates against people on the basis of sex. (See 11q and 21b for advice on how to avoid sexist language, a form of sexism, in your writing.)

False analogy

A **false analogy** is a comparison in which the differences outweigh the similarities, or the similarities are irrelevant to the claim the analogy is intended to support. "Old Joe Smith would

TEACHING TIP

Many students enjoy finding and correcting logical fallacies in newspaper editorials and opinion columns, as well as in the work of their peers. You might distribute copies of works containing fallacies, as a spur to class discussion or for revision. A less adept class might benefit from a preliminary lesson based on a list of logical fallacies you can cull from assorted sources (newspapers, political literature, advertisements, student papers, etc.); tell the students all the passages are illogical and have them explain why, as a prelude to revision (oral or written, as time allows).

Your analytically minded students may be interested in additional logical fallacies:

A *question-begging phrase* (sometimes called *alleged certainty*) presents something as certain that is open to debate: "Everyone knows" and "It is obvious that" are typical phrases that beg the question. This statement is flawed: "It is common knowledge that jobs in Texas pay more than do jobs in Idaho"; this statement is logical: "A recent government survey revealed that, on the average, workers in the oil fields of Texas are paid more than are loggers in the timber ➡

139

industries of Idaho.'' *To correct:* Drop the phrase and substitute evidence that supports your claim.

A *complex question* (also known as a *loaded question*) contains one or more unproven assumptions: ''Are you still spending time with known drug addicts?'' Notice what happens when you try to answer such a question. If you say ''yes,'' you are guilty. If you say ''no,'' you are still guilty, because you are admitting that you used to spend time with drug addicts. *To correct:* Split the question into its parts (''Are you still spending time with those people?'' ''Are those people drug addicts?'') and deal with each separately.

Appeal to fear uses scare tactics instead of legitimate evidence. Such an argument implies danger: ''Anyone who stages a protest against the government is a communist, so we must outlaw all protests.''

Appeal to the people (also known as *ad populum*) draws on whatever the people hold dear—for example, country, religion, or family. This approach tries to sway people by using a favorable label instead of providing reasons: ''A vote for Joe Smith is a vote for the flag.''

Name-calling attaches an unpleasant label to something or someone. Consider how a label can stop people from thinking: ''Jane Jones was once an alcoholic, so she cannot possibly say anything of value about politics.''

Appeal to pity attempts to arouse sympathy: ''He embezzled $1,500 of company money, but after all, his wife recently died and his child needs surgery.''

The *genetic fallacy*, a special form of *hasty generalization*, predicts something about a person based on that person's origins: ''Joe Smith is from New York City, so he knows how to deal with street crime.'' Often this fallacy involves a person's religion, sex, race, or economic status.

never make a good President because an old dog cannot learn new tricks.'' Homespun analogies like this often seem to have an air of wisdom about them, but just as often they fall apart when examined closely. Learning the role of the President is hardly comparable to a dog's learning new tricks.

Circular argument

A **circular argument,** also called **begging the question** or **circular definition,** is an assertion merely restated in slightly different terms: ''Boxing is a dangerous sport because it is unsafe.'' Here, ''unsafe'' conveys the same idea as ''dangerous'' rather than adding something new. This ''begs the question'' because the conclusion is the same as the premise.

Irrelevant argument

An **irrelevant argument** is called **non sequitur** in Latin, which translates as ''it does not follow.'' This flaw occurs when a conclusion does not follow from the premises: ''Jane Jones is a forceful speaker, so she will make a good mayor.'' It does not follow that someone's ability to be a forceful speaker means that person would be a good mayor.

False cause

The fallacy of **false cause** is called **post hoc, ergo propter hoc** in Latin,—which means ''after this, therefore because of this.'' This fallacy results when someone assumes that because two events are related in time, the first one *causes* the second one. This cause-and-effect fallacy is very common. ''A new weather satellite was launched last week, and it has been raining ever since'' implies—illogically— that the rain (the second event) is a result of the satellite launch (the first event).

Self-contradiction

Self-contradiction occurs when two premises are used that cannot simultaneously be true: ''Only when nuclear weapons have finally destroyed us will we be convinced of the need to control them.'' This statement is self-contradictory in that no one would be around to be convinced if everyone had been destroyed.

Red herring

A **red herring,** sometimes referred to as **ignoring the question,** sidetracks an issue by bringing up a totally unrelated issue: ''Why worry about pandas becoming extinct when we should be concerned about the plight of the homeless?" Someone who introduces an irrelevant issue hopes to distract the audience as a red herring might distract bloodhounds from a scent.

Argument to the person

An **argument to the person,** also known as **ad hominem,** attacks a person's appearance, personal habits, or character instead of dealing with the merits of the individual's arguments, ideas, or opinions. "We could take her position in favor of jailing child abusers seriously if she were not so nasty to the children who live next door to her" is one type of ad hominem attack. It seems so reasonable to belittle suggestions about dealing with child abusers from someone who may (or may not) be nasty to the children next door. In truth, however, the suggestions, not the person who makes them, must be dealt with. The person who argues is *not* the argument.

Guilt by Association

Guilt by association is a kind of ad hominem attack implying that an individual's arguments, ideas, or opinions lack merit because of that person's activities, interests, or associates. The claim that because Jack belongs to the International Hill Climbers Association, which declared bankruptcy last month, he is unfit to be mayor uses guilt by association.

Bandwagon

Bandwagon, also known as **going along with the crowd** or **ad populum,** implies that something is right because everyone is doing it, that truth is determined by majority vote: "Smoking is not bad for people because millions of people smoke."

False or irrelevant authority

Using **false or irrelevant authority,** sometimes called **ad verecundiam,** means citing the opinion of an "expert" who has no claim to expertise about the subject at hand. This fallacy attempts to transfer prestige from one area to another. Many television commercials rely on this tactic—a famous tennis player praising a brand of motor oil or a popular movie star lauding a brand of cheese.

Card-stacking

Card-stacking, also known as **special pleading,** ignores evidence on the other side of a question. From all the available facts, the person arguing selects only those that will build the best (or worst)

QUOTATION ABOUT WRITING

Logic is in the eye of the logician.
—Gloria Steinem

QUOTATION ABOUT WRITING

I've always disliked words like *inspiration.* Writing is probably like a scientist thinking about some scientific problem, or an engineer about an engineering problem.
—Doris Lessing

possible case. Many television commercials use this strategy. When three slim, happy consumers rave about a new diet plan, they do not mention that (a) the plan does not work for everyone and that (b) other plans work better for some people. The makers of the commercial select evidence that helps their cause and ignore any that does not.

The either-or fallacy

The either-or fallacy, also known as **false dilemma,** offers only two alternatives when more exist. Such fallacies often touch on emotional issues and can therefore seem accurate at first. When people reflect, however, they quickly come to realize that more alternatives are available. Here is a typical example of an either-or fallacy: "Either go to college or forget about getting a job." This statement implies that a college education is a prerequisite for all jobs, which is not true.

Taking something out of context

Taking something out of context separates an idea or fact from the material surrounding it, thus distorting it for special purposes. Suppose a critic writes about a movie saying, "The plot was predictable and boring but the music was sparkling." Then an advertisement for the movie says, "Critic calls this movie 'sparkling.'" The critic's words have been taken out of context—and distorted.

Appeal to ignorance

Appeal to ignorance assumes that an argument is valid simply because it has not been shown to be false. Conversely, something is not false simply because it has not been shown to be true. Appeals to ignorance can be very persuasive because they prey on people's superstitions or lack of knowledge. Here is a typical example of such flawed reasoning: "Since no one has proven that depression does not cause cancer, we can assume that it does." The absence of opposing evidence proves nothing.

Ambiguity and equivocation

Ambiguity and **equivocation** describe expressions that are not clear because they have more than one meaning. An ambiguous expression may be taken either way by the reader. A statement such as "They were entertaining guests" is ambiguous. Were the guests amusing to be with or were people giving hospitality to guests? An equivocal expression, by contrast, is one used in two or more ways

---

EXTRA EXERCISE C

Each analogy here can be defended. Like all analogies, each can also be attacked. First, defend each one—give one or more arguments to show that the two parts of the analogy are similar and are relevant to the claim being made. Second, attack each one by pointing out how they are not similar. Finally, offer other types of evidence that would help make the claim ultimately more convincing.

1. Like warfare, the aim of football is to destroy.

2. Don't bother to take your books home over vacation. Vacation is like a "study date"—no studying ever takes place.

3. Taking care of a group of young children is like trying to string beads without a knot on the end of the string.

4. The atom is like a small solar system, with its own "sun" and its own satellites.

within a single argument. If someone argued that the President *played a role* in arms control negotiations and then, two sentences later, said that the President was *playing a role* when he called himself "the education President," the person would be equivocating.

SUMMARY OF LOGICAL FALLACIES   41

- **Hasty generalization:** generalizing from inadequate evidence. Stereotyping is hasty generalization using prejudiced claims about a group of people.
- **False analogy:** using a comparison in which the differences outweigh the similarities, or in which the similarities are irrelevant to the claim the analogy is intended to support
- **Circular argument:** asserting the same point merely in slightly different terms
- **Irrelevant argument:** reaching a conclusion that does not follow from the premises
- **False cause:** assuming that because two events are related in time, the first caused the second
- **Self-contradiction:** using two premises that cannot both be true
- **Red herring:** sidetracking the issue by raising a second, unrelated issue
- **Argument to the person:** attacking the person making the argument rather than the argument itself
- **Guilt by association:** attacking a person's ideas because of that person's interests or associates
- **Bandwagon:** implying that something is right or is permissible because "everyone" does it
- **False or irrelevant authority:** citing the opinion of a person who has no expertise about the subject
- **Card-stacking:** ignoring evidence on the other side of a question
- **The either-or fallacy:** offering only two alternatives when more exist
- **Taking something out of context:** distorting an idea or fact by separating it from the material surrounding it
- **Appeal to ignorance:** assuming that an argument is valid simply because there is no evidence on the other side of the issue
- **Ambiguity and equivocation:** using expressions that are not clear because they have more than one meaning

---

ANSWERS: EXTRA EXERCISE C

Answers will vary. Answers here are intended to be suggestive.

1. *Pro:* Both involve uniformed "teams" inflicting injury upon each other in pursuit of territorial gain. *Con:* Football is played according to rules, with clear time limits, for entertainment. *To revise:* Add statistics on actual injuries inflicted upon high school, college, and professional football players, as well as evidence of asocial attitudes (if any) developed by players.

2. *Pro:* In both cases, serious intentions readily give way to the pursuit of pleasure. *Con:* A study date ostensibly has a serious purpose whereas vacation, by definition, is unstructured free time. *To revise:* Add eyewitness accounts or reported observations about how time was spent on actual study dates, actual vacations.

3. *Pro:* Both are nearly impossible to control. The moment you get one "on the string," the others fall off. *Con:* Beads are much easier to control. *To revise:* Provide eyewitness accounts of babysitting experiences.

4. *Pro:* Both have large centers with smaller objects orbiting them. *Con:* The sun is chemically more complex than the nuclei of atoms; planets orbit the sun because of gravity rather than electrical charge. *To revise:* Other than listing additional similarities, the analogy cannot be made stronger—the properties of the solar system and of the atom are what they are.

ANSWERS: EXERCISE 5-6

1. *False authority.* A movie star is not an authority on the CIA.

2. *Red herring.* The social issue is introduced to divert attention from the real issue —whether or not money should have been spent to rescue the whales.

3. *Irrelevant argument,* or *non sequitur.* A person can be nervous about something and still be very good at it.

4. *Circular argument.* "Dishonest" is merely a slightly different term for "deceitful."

5. *Argument to the person,* or *ad hominem.* These people are being attacked for materialism, but they are perhaps excellent environmentalists, whose cars and shoes are irrelevant to their environmental stance.

6. *Appeal to ignorance.* Just because no evidence exists for one side of the argument does not mean that the other side of the argument is valid.

7. *False cause,* or *post hoc ergo propter hoc.* The sequence of events does not prove any connection between them.

8. *False analogy.* Analogies are dangerous in argument because they equate things that are not the same. Riding a bicycle is much different from learning to run a company, and although the skills for riding a bicycle remain the same, those of running a company may change with the economy and other pressures so that one could "fall" if he or she did not adopt those skills.

9. *Self-contradiction.* Medicare cannot be free if it is paid for.

10. *Either-or.* Reading good literature is not the only way to appreciate culture.

EXERCISE 5-6

Consulting section 5h, identify and explain the fallacy in each item. If the item does not contain a logical flaw, circle its number.

EXAMPLE   Seat belts are the only hope for reducing the death rate from automobile accidents. [This is an *either-or fallacy* because it assumes that nothing but seat belts can reduce the number of fatalities from car accidents.]

1. Joanna Hayes should write a book about the Central Intelligence Agency (CIA). She has starred in three films that show the inner workings of the CIA.

2. It is ridiculous to have spent thousands of dollars to rescue those two whales from being trapped in the Arctic ice. Why, look at all of the people trapped in jobs that they don't like.

3. Every time my roommate has a math test, she becomes extremely nervous. Clearly, she is not good at math.

4. Plagiarism is deceitful because it is dishonest.

5. The local political coalition to protect the environment would get my support and that of many other people if its leaders did not drive cars that get poor gasoline mileage.

6. UFO's must exist because no reputable studies have proven conclusively that they do not.

7. Water fluoridation affects the brain. Citywide, students' test scores began to drop five months after fluoridation began.

8. Learning to manage a corporation is exactly like learning to ride a bicycle: once you learn the skills, you never forget how, and you never fall.

9. Medicare is free; the government pays for it from taxes.

10. Reading good literature is the one way to appreciate culture.

6 Writing Argument

When writing **argument** for your college courses, you seek to convince a reader to agree with you concerning a topic open to debate. A written argument states and supports one position about the debatable topic. Support for that position depends on evidence, reasons, and examples chosen for their direct relation to the point being argued. One section of the written argument might present and attempt to refute other positions on the topic, but the central thrust of the essay is to argue for one point of view.

Taking and defending a position in a written argument is an engaging intellectual process, especially when it involves a topic of substance about which universal agreement is unlikely. The ability to think critically by analyzing, synthesizing, and assessing (see Chart 29 in section 5a) is challenged by the activity of examining all sides of a topic, choosing one side to defend, and marshaling convincing support for that one side.

If you are among the people who find any type of arguing distasteful, you are not alone. But rest assured that written argument differs drastically from everyday, informal arguing. Informal arguing sometimes originates in anger and might involve bursts of temper or unpleasant emotional confrontations. Written argument, in contrast, can always be a constructive activity. When you write an argument, you can disagree without being disagreeable. An effective written argument sets forth its position calmly, respectfully, and logically. Any passion that underlies a writer's position is evident not from angry words but from the force of a balanced, well-developed, clearly written discussion.

The ability to argue reasonably and effectively is an important skill that people need not only in college but throughout their lives—in family relationships, with friends, and in the business world. People engage in debates (perhaps more often in speaking than in writing) that call for an exchange of solidly supported views.

BACKGROUND

There is an increasing amount of scholarship on the significance of argumentation in the development of American society. For example, in "Early Twentieth-Century American Origins of Argumentation" (*Dissertation Abstracts* 49 [March 1989]: 2449A), Kathryn Jeanine Congalton examines early developments in argumentation and academic debate in this country. In "Who Reads John Locke? Words and Acts in the American Revolution" (*The American Scholar* [Autumn 1989]: 545–556), Oscar Handlin and Lillian Handlin examine the influence of Locke's writings on the American Revolution.

BACKGROUND

Although rhetoric, as defined by Aristotle, appears in the speeches and debates of the epics and plays of ancient Greece, its principles were not systematically formulated until the fifth century B.C. Corax of Syracuse, recognizing the need for a system by which citizens of Sicily could argue in the courts to recover property that they had lost during the reign of Thrasybulus, began to set down the principles of argumentation. Lacking documents to prove their claims, ordinary citizens had to argue their cases by relying on inferential reasoning and probability. Tisias, the student of Corax, extended the study of rhetoric from the courtroom and wrote speeches for other people to deliver. Others who quickly followed to develop the art of rhetoric, or persuasion, include Gorgias of Leotini (*fl.* 420 B.C.), known principally for his ornate style characterized by extensive use of figures of speech, and Isocrates (436–338 B.C.), one of the leading Athenian teachers of rhetoric and an author of influential books on rhetorical theory.

Once you become adept at the techniques of written argument, you can use them equally effectively for oral argument.

Much of the material in the earlier chapters of this handbook can help you compose a written argument. A list of useful sections is given in Chart 42. This chapter concentrates on the special demands of writing argument. The writing of two student essays is discussed in this chapter, and the final draft of each essay appears in section 6h.

MATERIAL FROM EARLIER CHAPTERS IN THIS HANDBOOK TO USE WHEN WRITING AN ARGUMENT 42

- Checklist for persuasive writing (1b-2)
- Audiences for writing (1c)
- Establishing a suitable tone (1d)
- Choosing a topic (2c)
- The writing process: planning and shaping (Chapter 2)
- The writing process: drafting and revising (Chapter 3)
- Writing paragraphs (Chapter 4)
- Reading and thinking critically (Chapter 5)
- Using evidence to think critically (5e)
- Analyzing cause and effect (5f)
- Using inductive and deductive reasoning (5g)
- Avoiding logical fallacies (5h)

The terms *persuasive writing* and *argumentative writing* often are used interchangeably. When a distinction is made between them, persuasive writing is the broader term. It includes advertisements, letters to editors, emotional pleas in speeches or writing, and formal written arguments. The focus of this chapter is formal written argument as usually assigned in college courses.

6a　Choosing a topic for a written argument

When you choose a topic for written argument, be sure that it is open to debate. Be careful not to confuse matters of information with matters of debate. Facts are matters of information, not debate. An essay becomes an argument when it takes a position concerning the fact or other piece of information.

FACT	Students at Deitmer College **are required** to take physical education.
POSITION OPEN TO DEBATE	Students at Deitmer College **should not be** required to take physical education.
OPPOSITE POSITION OPEN TO DEBATE	Students at Deitmer College **should be** required to take physical education.

A written argument could take one of these opposing positions and defend it. The essay could not argue for two or more sides, though it might mention other points of view and attempt to refute them.

When you are assigned a written argument, be sure to read and think through the assignment carefully. Instructors construct assignments for written argument in a number of ways. You might be given both the topic and the position to take on that topic. In such cases, you are expected to fulfill the assignment whether or not you agree personally with the given point of view. You are judged on your ability to marshal a defense of the assigned position and to reason logically about it. Another type of assignment is unstructured, requiring you to choose the debatable topic and the position to defend. In such cases, the topic that you choose should be **suitable for college writing** (see 2c-1). The topic should not be trivial (for example, the best way to chew gum). The topic should be **narrowed sufficiently** (see 2c-2) to fit the writing situation. You are judged on your ability to think of a debatable topic of substance, to narrow the topic so that your essay can include general statements and specific details, to choose a defensible position about that topic, and to present and support your position convincingly. If you cannot decide what position you agree with personally because all sides of a debatable topic have merit, do not get blocked. You need not make a lifetime commitment to your position. Rather, concentrate on the merits of one position, and present that position as effectively as possible.

The two sample essays at the end of this chapter were written in response to the assignment shown in the box below. This assignment states the topic but asks students to take a position about it.

Lindsey Black and Daniel Casey were given this assignment: Write an essay of 500 to 700 words that argues about whether holidays have become too commercialized in the United States. Your final draft is due in one week. Bring your earlier drafts to class for possible discussion.

EXTRA EXERCISE A

Which of the following topics are concerned with fact and which state a position open to debate?

1. The term *journalism* refers to the business of publishing a regularly recurring text.

2. Television news programs are more influential than they should be.

3. Journalists in the United States operate under the protection of the First Amendment to the Constitution.

4. Most reporters are biased in their descriptions of political figures.

5. The government should not let journalists have access to information dealing with national security.

6. Journalism involves both reporting the news and forming public opinion.

7. Reporters should verify a controversial story with two sources before running it.

8. Weekly newspapers are becoming increasingly popular in large cities.

9. Cartoons furnish one of the more entertaining features of newspapers.

10. Television commentators should not give their own opinions about political and social matters.

ANSWERS: EXTRA EXERCISE A

1. fact
2. opinion
3. fact
4. opinion
5. opinion
6. fact
7. opinion
8. fact
9. opinion
10. opinion

Chapter Two of this book, Planning and Shaping, lists four aspects of writing situations that affect the decisions that the writer makes. They are (1) the topic, (2) the purpose, (3) the audience that will read or hear it, and (4) the special requirements that influence every writing situation, such as deadlines and length. For explanations of each aspect, see Section 2b.

TEACHING TIP

Persuasive writing has much in common with argumentation. Both aim to lead the audience to agreement with the opinions of the writer. Persuasion additionally attempts to induce the reader to commit to a particular action. Advertising is probably the form of persuasive writing we encounter most often in the course of our daily lives. Because students enjoy looking at familiar advertisements in an analytical way, you may want to ask them to bring their favorites to class, or perhaps you will prefer to provide some. Helpful background information is available in several articles found in *Advertising Age*. For example, see the issue of April 18, 1988 for suggestions about the study of print advertising and its influence on what we read in popular magazines; the July 18, 1988 issue examines television commercials. The September 24, 1987 issue is also helpful for classes interested in analyzing contemporary advertising.

BACKGROUND

In an article entitled "Teenagers and Advertising," the *Quarterly Review of Doublespeak* (14 [April 1988]: 10) reports on the negative responses teenagers have to television commercials. The article suggests that teenage students need to study advertising so that they can deal with its persuasive techniques more capably.

Black and Casey analyzed the four aspects of the **writing situation** (see 2b) reflected in the assignment. The essay *topic* is stated (whether holidays have become too commercialized in the United States). The essay's *purpose* is persuasive, but students are free to choose the position to argue for (the student can choose to argue that the holidays have become too commercialized *or* that they have not become too commercialized). The *audience* for the essay is not specified and is therefore assumed to be the instructor and, perhaps, other members of the class. The *special requirements* include the essay's length (between 500 and 700 words) and the time for getting the essay into final draft (one week).

6b Developing an assertion and a thesis statement for written argument

An **assertion** is a statement that gives a position about a debatable topic and that can be supported by evidence, reasons, and examples (including facts, statistics, names, experiences, and experts). The thinking process that moves you from a topic to a defensible position calls, first, for you to make an assertion about the topic. The exact wording of the assertion often does not find its way into the essay, but the assertion serves as a focus for your thinking and your writing.

TOPIC	*The commercialization of holidays*
ASSERTION	Holidays have become too commercialized.
ASSERTION	Holidays have not become too commercialized.

Next, using your assertion as a base, you compose a **thesis statement** (see 2m) to use in the essay. It states the position that you present and support in the essay. The first thesis statement below comes from Lindsey Black's essay in section 6h; the second one comes from Daniel Casey's essay in 6h.

THESIS STATEMENT	The spirit of the holidays is being destroyed by commercialism.
THESIS STATEMENT	Commercial uses of holidays benefit the nation's economy and lift people's spirits.

Before you decide on an assertion—the position that you want to argue—you need to explore the topic. Do not rush into deciding on your assertion. Try to wait until you have as full a picture as possible. Consider all sides. Remember that **what mainly separates most good writing from bad is the writer's ability to move back**

and forth between general statements and specific details. Try to avoid a position that limits you to *only* general statements or to *only* specific details. In deciding on your assertion, use the memory device of RENNS (see 4c) to see whether you can marshall sufficient details to support your generalizations.

Even if you know immediately what assertion you want to argue for, do not stop there. The more you think through all sides of the topic, the broader will be the perspective that you bring to your writing. Also, as you think through your position and consider alternative points of view, be open to changing your mind and taking an opposite position. Before too long, however, do settle on a position; switching positions at the last minute lessens your chances of writing an effective essay.

To stimulate your thinking about the topic and your assertion about it, use the techniques for gathering ideas explained and illustrated in sections 2e through 2k. Jot down your thoughts as they develop. Do not lose the unique opportunity that the act of writing gives you to discover new ideas and fresh insights. Writers of effective arguments often list for themselves the various points that come to mind, using two columns to represent visually two contrasting points of view. (Head the columns with labels that emphasize contrast: for example, *agree* and *disagree* or *for* and *against*.) The lists can then supply ideas during drafting and revising.

Whenever possible, use outside resources for developing an assertion. These include talking with other people and conducting research. Getting points of view from other people helps you explore a debatable topic. As you talk with people, interview them rather than argue with them. Your goal is to come to know opposing points of view, so resist any temptation to "win" a verbal argument; people sometimes hesitate to offer their ideas fully and openly when their listener is hostile. If your assignment permits you to use the library, do so. Written argument can be particularly enhanced when your position is supported with facts and reference to experts. (For complete information about the process and techniques of research, consult Chapter 32.)

EXERCISE 6-1

Develop an assertion and a thesis statement for a written argument on each of the following topics. You may choose any defensible position.

EXAMPLE **Topic:** *Book censorship in high school*
Assertion: *Books should not be censored in high school.*
Thesis statement: *When books are taken off high school library shelves and are dropped from high school curricula, students are denied exposure to an open exchange of ideas.*

BACKGROUND
Many techniques for discovering means of developing a subject have been devised over the past decade. It is helpful to be reminded, however, that the ancient Greeks long ago devised a set of topics—*topoi*, meaning "places or regions"—that can be used to generate "arguments" to persuade an audience. They suggest material for the writer who does not have a ready opinion on a subject or an effective way to present it. They include the topics of definition (including genus and division), comparison (similarity, difference, and degree), relationship (cause and effect, antecedent and consequence, contraries, and contradictions), circumstance (the possible and impossible, past and future fact), and testimony (authority, testimonial, statistics, maxims, law, and examples). They remain the basis for many arguments of a general nature presented today. Particular kinds of argument were (and are) drawn from special topics devised to suit the type of discourse chosen by the writer. For example, the writer, or speaker, engaged in judicial discourse is concerned with justice and injustice, making it necessary to establish whether something happened (evidence), what it is (definition), and what kind of thing it is (cause and effect).

BACKGROUND
In a paper given at the Wyoming Conference on Freshman and Sophomore English in 1983, Mary C. Fenton explored four models for teaching argumentative discourse. Her synthesis of the models is explained in "Teaching Persuasion: A Positive Approach," found in ERIC ED 233 396.

ANSWERS: EXERCISE 6-1
Assertions and thesis statements will vary for this exercise.

6c

BACKGROUND

Available from ERIC is Karen Quinn and Ann Matsuhashi's article "Stalking Ideas: The Generation and Elaboration of Arguments," in which they report on specific college students who used reading to generate argumentative writing (ERIC ED 257 043).

EXTRA EXERCISE B

Practice devising assertions and thesis statements by working with some of the following topics.

1. Safety on interstate highways

2. The importance of knowing a second language

3. U.S. Savings Bonds as investments

4. The use of television with commercials in elementary school classrooms

5. Diminishing access to clean water

6. The future of motion pictures

7. Violence on television

8. The need for greater airport security

9. Computer literacy as a requirement for high school graduation

10. Sex education in public schools

BACKGROUND

Because of the increasing use of peer reader-response groups in writing classrooms, there is a growing interest in how they can be used to teach argumentative writing more effectively. In "Developing a Position Statement in the Collaborative Classroom" (*Exercise Exchange* 34 [Spring 1989]: 3–5), Peg Peoples suggests an answer. She describes a group activity that she has found to be helpful in getting students to see both sides of an issue.

1. television
2. prisons
3. drugs and athletics
4. diets for weight loss
5. grades

6c Structuring written argument

No one structure fits all written argument. For college courses, most written arguments include certain elements. Lindsay Black's essay in section 6h uses a structure based on the **classical pattern of argument** developed by the ancient Greeks and Romans and still highly respected today. Daniel Casey's essay in section 6h uses a modified form of that structure. Chart 43 will help you recognize the elements in a written argument.

ELEMENTS IN A WRITTEN ARGUMENT 43

1. **Introductory paragraph:** sets the context for the position that is argued in the essay. (For a discussion of introductory paragraphs, see 4g.)

2. **Thesis statement:** states the position being argued. In a short essay, the thesis statement often appears at the end of the introductory paragraph. (For a discussion of thesis statements, see 2m.)

3. **Background information:** gives the reader basic information needed for understanding the position being argued. This information can be part of the introductory paragraph (as in Daniel Casey's essay in section 6h) or can appear in its own paragraph (as in Lindsey Black's essay in section 6h).

4. **Reasons or evidence:** supports the position being argued. This material is the core of the essay. If the support consists of evidence, consult the discussion in 5e. Also, be sure that your reasoning is logical (see 5g). Each type of evidence or reason usually consists of a general statement backed up with specific details or examples. Depending on the length of the essay, one or two paragraphs are devoted to each reason or type of evidence.

➡

ELEMENTS IN A WRITTEN ARGUMENT *(continued)*

The best sequence for presenting the complete set of reasons and types of evidence depends on the impact you want to achieve. Moving from evidence most familiar to the reader to evidence least familiar helps the reader move from the known to the unknown. This order might catch the reader's interest early on. Moving from evidence least important to evidence most important might build the reader's suspense. (For more about various types of paragraph arrangement, see 4e.)

5. **Anticipation of likely objections and responses to them:** mentions positions opposed to the one being argued and rebuts them briefly. In classical argument, this "refutation" appears in its own paragraph, immediately before the concluding paragraph (as in Lindsey Black's essay). An alternative placement is immediately after the introductory paragraph, as a bridge to the rest of the essay; in such arrangements the essay's thesis statement falls either at the end of the introductory paragraph or at the end of the "refutation" paragraph (as in Daniel Casey's essay in section 6h). In still another arrangement, each paragraph that presents a type of evidence or reason (item 4 on this list) also mentions and responds to the opposing position.

6. **Concluding paragraph:** brings the essay to an end that flows logically and gracefully from the rest of the essay. It does not cut off the reader abruptly. (For a discussion of concluding paragraphs, see 4g.)

6d Considering the audience for written argument

The purpose of written argument is to convince a reader—the audience—about a matter of opinion. Key factors in considering audience are discussed in 1c. When you write argument, consider one additional factor about audience: the degree of agreement expected from the reader.

When a topic is emotionally charged, chances are high that any position being argued will elicit either strong agreement or strong disagreement. For example, topics such as abortion, capital punish-

BACKGROUND

Classical persuasion consisted of six parts that represented six basic functions. Although the writer or orator was granted some flexibility in how and in what order the parts were presented, they provided effective guidelines for presenting an argument. Often used today, the six parts of an argument, according to the classical precept, are:

1. *Exordium,* meaning "beginning a web." As an introduction, the purpose of the exordium is to attract the attention of the audience, indicate the subject, and favorably dispose the audience to what will follow.

2. *Narratio.* In this section, now usually referred to as "statement of fact," the issue is defined by stating pertinent facts about the subject. It is, therefore, basically expository.

3. *Partitio.* If the thesis has not yet been identified, it will be presented here, along with an indication of how the rest of the argument will be organized. The purpose of partition is to prepare the reader or listener for what will follow.

4. *Confirmatio.* Arguments to support the thesis, forming the bulk of the piece, are developed at this point. The question of the order of presentation of arguments is critical to the effectiveness of the confirmation.

5. *Refutatio.* Opposing arguments are considered and rendered ineffective in the refutation section. To ignore them is to risk letting them appear to be more attractive than one's own thesis. The refutation may be placed at various points in the piece, depending on where it will be most effective.

6. *Peroratio.* While the classical rhetoricians used a number of different terms to indicate the conclusion of a piece, it usually furnished a summary of proofs and refutations, a restatement of the major points, and a recreation of emotional and ethical appeals.

BACKGROUND

The ideal format of a Rogerian argument, according to Richard Coe (*Form and Substance,* John Wiley and Sons, 1981, pp. 342–343) follows this pattern:

Introduction. State the subject as a problem rather than as an issue to interest your audience in reading about something with which they disagree.

Fair statement of the opposing position. In this section the writer states the reader's position in a manner that seems fair and accurate to the reader.

Statement of contexts in which that position may be valid. Here the writer is trying to show readers that he or she understands their position by asserting that it is valid in some contexts.

Fair statement of the writer's position. The goal of this section is to get readers to understand the writer's position as fairly and thoroughly as the writer has understood theirs.

Statement of contexts in which the writer's position is valid. The writer tries to get readers to look at the problem from new perspectives and in new contexts.

Statement of how readers would benefit by adopting at least some elements of the writer's position. The writer appeals to readers' self-interest. In this section the writer's position turns from a threat to a promise.

ment, and gun control arouse very strong emotions in many people. Such topics are emotionally loaded because they touch on matters of personal beliefs, including religion and individual rights. A topic such as the commercialization of holidays (see the two essays in section 6h) is somewhat less emotionally loaded. Even less emotionally loaded, yet still open to debate, are topics such as whether everyone needs a college education or whether Computer X is better than Computer Y.

The degree to which a reader might be friendly or hostile can influence what strategies you use to try to convince that reader. For example, when you anticipate that many readers will not agree with you, consider using techniques of **Rogerian argument.** Rogerian argument has been adapted from the principles of communication developed by psychologist Carl Rogers. Communication, according to Rogers, is eased when people find common ground in their points of view. The common ground in a debate over capital punishment might be that both sides find crime to be a growing problem today. Once both sides agree about the problem, they might have more tolerance for the divergence of opinion concerning whether capital punishment is a deterrent to crime.

6e Defining terms in written argument

When you **define terms,** you explain what you mean by key words that you use. Words are key words when they are central to the message that you want to communicate. The meaning of some key words is readily evident. Key words open to interpretation, however, should be made specific enough to be clear.

NO	Commercialism at holiday time is **bad.**
YES	Commercialism at holiday time is **ruining the spirit of the holidays.**
YES	Commercialism at holiday time **tempts too many people to spend more money than they can afford.**

Some key words might vary with the context of a discussion and should be explained in an essay. Abstract words such as *love, freedom,* and *democracy* have to be explained because they have different meanings in different contexts. In his paper (see 6h), Daniel Casey uses *economy,* a word with many meanings, in the topic sentence of the third paragraph of his essay. He explains *economy* as the *ongoing circulation of money,* and he uses the rest of the paragraph to explain how that circulation operates. In this way, Casey makes clear that he is not referring to any of the other meanings of *economy:* the management of finances, the avoidance of waste, or the efficient use of resources.

Other key terms might be unfamiliar to the reader even though they are known words. For example, Casey opens his essay with the words *signs of commercialism.* Although each word by itself is familiar, the term is not. Casey therefore gives examples to illustrate the concept. In so doing, he creates an effective introduction to his essay by bringing the reader to a quick understanding of his topic.

Many students ask whether they should use actual dictionary definitions in an essay. Looking words up in a dictionary to understand precise meanings is a very important activity for writers. Quoting a dictionary definition, however, is not always wise. Dictionary definitions tend to be overused in student writing, and they are often seen as the "easy way out." Using an **extended definition** is usually a more effective approach, which is what Casey did for *economy* in the third paragraph of his essay. (For another example of extended definition, of *chemistry,* see paragraph 43 in 4f-5.) If you do use a dictionary definition in your writing, be sure to work it into your material gracefully. Do not simply tack it on abruptly to what you are saying. In general, do not rely on it for your opening sentence. Also, be aware that references to a dictionary must be complete. Do not simply refer to "Webster's," which is far too general. Each dictionary has its own name, such as *Webster's New World Dictionary.*

6f Reasoning effectively in written argument

When you reason effectively, you increase your chances of convincing your reader to agree with you. In many instances, of course, you cannot expect actually to change your reader's mind. The basis for a debatable position is often personal opinion or belief, neither of which can be expected to change as the result of one written argument. Nevertheless, you still have an important goal: to convince your reader that your point of view has merit. People often "agree to disagree," in the best spirit of intellectual exchange. Round-table discussions among various experts heard on National Public Radio (NPR) or television's Public Broadcast System (PBS) are conducted in such a spirit.

The opposite positions taken by Lindsey Black and Daniel Casey (see 6h) concerning commercialism at holiday time stem from their personal beliefs and perceptions of the world. Black feels that

EXTRA EXERCISE C
The following persuasive paragraph is not as effective as it could be because it uses undefined abstract words and words that vary in meaning with the context in which they appear. Rewrite the paragraph, improving its persuasiveness by defining key words that may be vague to the reader.

Some Americans react strongly to actions that show disrespect for our flag. They revere it as a symbol of the values for which the United States is known around the world. They are quick to rise up against those who would use their freedom to desecrate Old Glory, calling them traitors to the Constitution and all it upholds: our rights and our democratic form of government. Calling for a Constitutional amendment, they even want to restrict our freedoms by making it illegal to misuse the flag. Wouldn't such an amendment show disrespect for the freedom the flag represents?

A SAMPLE REWRITE FOR EXTRA EXERCISE C

Some Americans react strongly to acts that they construe to be insulting to our flag. Television news footage showing the flag being burned or torn apart makes them violently angry because they revere it as a symbol of the freedom and liberty for which this country is known around the world. They are quick to rise up against fellow citizens who use their freedom to desecrate Old Glory, calling them traitors to the Constitution and its guarantees of legislative representation and civil rights, such as the right of free speech. Calling for a Constitutional amendment, they even want to restrict citizens' freedoms by making it illegal to misuse the flag. But what constitutes misuse: wearing it? letting it fly outside on a rainy day? displaying it on a banquet table? A more important question is: Wouldn't such an amendment show disrespect for the freedom the flag represents?

ALTERNATE EXAMPLES

Logical Appeal

According to a recent publication of the Equal Employment Opportunity Commission, at the present rate of "progress" it will take forty-three years to end job discrimination—hardly a reasonable timetable.

If our goal is educational and economic equity and parity—and it is—then we need affirmative action to catch up. We are behind as a result of discrimination and denial of opportunity. There is one white attorney for every 680 whites, but only one black attorney for every 4,000 blacks; one white physician for every 659 whites, but only one black physician for every 5,000 blacks; and one white dentist for every 1,900 whites, but only one black dentist for every 8,400 blacks. Less than 1 percent of all engineers—or of all practicing chemists—is black. Cruel and uncompassionate injustice created gaps like these. We need creative justice and compassion to help us close them.

—Jesse Jackson, "Why Blacks Need Affirmative Action"

Emotional Appeal

A child's world is fresh and new and beautiful, full of wonder and excitement. It is our misfortune that for most of us that clear-eyed vision, that true instinct for what is beautiful and awe-inspiring, is dimmed and even lost before we reach adulthood. If I had influence with the good fairy who is supposed to preside over the christening of all children I should ask that her gift to each child in the world be a sense of wonder so indestructible that it would last throughout life, as an unfailing antidote against the boredom and disenchantments of later years, the sterile preoccupation with things that are artificial, the alienation from the sources of our strength.

I sincerely believe that . . . it is not half so important to *know* as to *feel*. If facts are the seeds that later produce knowledge and wisdom, then the emotions and the impres- ➤

commercialism is ruining the holidays. Casey recognizes the existence of commercialism, but he sees it as beneficial. The chance of either person convincing the other is slight. What can happen, however, is that each person can respect the quality of the other's argument.

An argument of good quality relies on three types of appeals to reason: the logical, the emotional, and the ethical. Chart 44 gives a summary of how to use the three appeals.

GUIDELINES FOR REASONING EFFECTIVELY IN WRITTEN ARGUMENT 44

- **Be logical:** use sound reasoning.
- **Enlist the emotions of the reader:** enlist the values and beliefs of the reader, usually by arousing "the better self" of the reader.
- **Establish credibility:** show that you as the writer can be relied upon as a knowledgeable person with good sense.

The most widely used appeal in written argument is the **logical appeal,** called *logos* by the ancient Greeks. Logical reasoning is sound reasoning. This type of reasoning is important in all thinking and writing. Chapter 5 of this handbook, therefore, is a close companion to this chapter. Logical reasoning calls for using evidence well, as explained in 5e. Logical reasoning also means analyzing cause and effect correctly, as explained in 5f. A sound argument uses patterns of inductive reasoning and deductive reasoning, as explained in 5g. A sound argument also clearly distinguishes between fact and opinion, as explained in 5d-3. Finally, sound reasoning means avoiding logical fallacies, as explained in 5h.

Written argument for college courses relies heavily on logic. Both Lindsey Black and Daniel Casey (see 6h) used logical reasoning throughout their essays. While the reader might not agree with the reasons or types of evidence presented, the reader can respect the logic of their arguments.

The **emotional appeal,** called *pathos* by the ancient Greeks, can be effective when used in conjunction with logical appeals. The word *emotional* has a specific meaning in this context. It means arousing and enlisting the emotions of the reader. Often it arouses the "better self" of the reader by eliciting sympathy, civic pride, and other feelings based on values and beliefs. Effective emotional appeals use description and examples to stir emotions, but they leave the actual stirring to the reader. Restraint is more effective than excessive sentimentality.

Both Casey and Black (see 6h) use emotional appeals in their essays, but always in conjunction with a logical presentation of material. Casey appeals to the emotions when in his fifth paragraph he mentions stores giving toys to children in hospitals. But he does not overdo it. He does not say that anyone who disagrees with him hates children and feels no pity for their suffering from dreadful illnesses that ravage their tiny bodies. If he had indulged in such excesses, the reader would resent being manipulated and therefore would probably reject his argument. Black appeals to the emotions when she writes in her second paragraph about the origins of the holiday spirit. With restraint, she mentions the meaning of each holiday. She does not attempt to tell the reader how to feel; she simply points out facts that support the logic of her argument and that might also stir the reader's pride in country and heritage.

The **ethical appeal,** called *ethos* by the ancient Greeks, means establishing the ethics and credibility of the writer. Credibility is gained if the writer uses correct facts, undistorted evidence, and accurate interpretations of events. Readers do not trust a writer who states opinions as fact or who makes a claim that cannot possibly be supported. The statement "A child who does not get gifts for Christmas suffers a trauma from which recovery is impossible" is an opinion as well as an exaggeration. It has no place in written argument.

Ethical appeals cannot take the place of logical appeals, but the two types of appeals work well together. One effective way to make an ethical appeal is to draw on personal experience. (Some college instructors do not want students to write in the first person, so ask your instructor before you use it.) If you use personal experience, always be sure that it relates directly to a generalization that you are supporting. Also, be aware that a personal experience can say as much about the writer as about the experience. For example, if Casey had been a volunteer at a hospital when gifts from a local business were distributed, the story of the experience not only would have supported his claim in his fifth paragraph, but also would have illustrated his good character.

6g Establishing a reasonable tone in written argument

To be reasonable, you have to be fair. By anticipating opposing positions and responding to them (see 6c), you have a particularly

Cont'd.

sions of the senses are the fertile soil in which the seeds must grow. The years of early childhood are the time to prepare the soil. Once the emotions have been aroused—a sense of the beautiful, the excitement of the new and the unknown, a feeling of sympathy, pity, admiration or love—then we wish for knowledge about the object of our emotional response.

Rachel Carson, *The Sense of Wonder*

Ethical Appeal
Our tragedy today is a general and universal physical fear so long sustained by now that we can even bear it. There are no longer problems of the spirit. There is only the question: When will I be blown up? Because of this, the young man or woman writing today has forgotten the problems of the human heart in conflict with itself which alone can make good writing because only this is worth writing about, worth the agony and the sweat.

He must learn them again. He must teach himself that the basest of all things is to be afraid; and, teaching himself that, forget it forever, leaving no room in his workshop for anything but the old verities and truths of the heart, the old universal truths lacking which any story is ephemeral and doomed —love and honor and pity and pride and compassion and sacrifice. Until he does so, he labors under a curse. He writes not of love but of lust, of defeats in which nobody loses anything of value, of victories without hope and, worst of all, without pity or compassion. His griefs grieve on no universal bones, leaving no scars. He writes not of the heart but of the glands.

—William Faulkner,
Nobel Prize Acceptance Speech

QUOTATION ABOUT WRITING
Mere knowledge of the truth will not give you the art of persuasion.

—Plato

QUOTATION ABOUT WRITING

Real communication occurs . . . when we listen with understanding. What does this mean? It means to see the expressed idea and attitude from the other person's point of view, to sense how it feels to him, to achieve his frame of reference in regard to the thing he is talking about.

—Carl Rogers

BACKGROUND

The theories of Carl Rogers have had important consequences for the teaching of argumentative writing. If Rogerian argument is of interest to you, you will want to read an article by Nathaniel Teich (*Journal of Advanced Composition* 7 [1987]: 52–61). In it he argues against the existence of Rogerian rhetoric. However, he goes on to suggest that Rogerian principles can supplement the teaching of policy arguments.

BACKGROUND

In "Using Toulmin's Model of Argumentation" (*Journal of Teaching Writing* 6 [Spring 1987]: 81–92) Joan Karback reviews the structure of warrants, grounds, and claims. She finds Toulmin's model to be an effective one because it is flexible, it has value as a heuristic, and it focuses on audience.

good chance to show that you are fair. When you alert your reader to other ways of thinking about the issue, you demonstrate that you have not ignored other positions. Doing this implies respect for the other side, which in turn makes the tone (see 1d) of the essay more reasonable.

To achieve a reasonable tone, choose your words carefully. Avoid words that exaggerate. Use figurative language, such as similes and metaphors (see 21c), to enhance your point rather than distort it. No matter how strongly you disagree with opposing arguments, never insult the other side. Name-calling is impolite, shows poor self-control, and demonstrates poor judgment. The more emotionally loaded a topic (for example, abortion, capital punishment, and gun control), the more might be the temptation to use angry words. Words such as *stupid* or *pigheaded,* however, say more about the writer than about the issue.

Artificial language (see 21e) also ruins a reasonable tone. The *Yes* example that follows is used by Daniel Casey as the first sentence in his essay in section 6h. Compare its impact with what would happen if Casey had used the *No* example.

NO   Emblems of commercial enterprise are ubiquitously visible as the populace prepares for the celebration of festivals and commemorations throughout the venerable United States of America.

YES   Signs of commercialism at holiday time are easy to see in the United States.

6h   Writing and revising a written argument

Lindsey Black chose the position that holidays have become too commercialized. Daniel Casey, on the other hand, chose the position that the commercialization of holidays has advantages. The final draft of each essay appears at the end of this chapter. The labels identify the structural elements of written argument discussed in 6c.

In an early draft of her essay, Black wrote an introduction that included the background information on the holidays, now in her second paragraph. When she revised, she moved the information to a separate paragraph because she saw that the introductory paragraph was too long and the thesis statement was being overshadowed. Also, she felt that a separate paragraph giving background information had the additional advantage of giving her the space to use an emotional appeal (see 6f). An early draft of Black's third paragraph consisted only of the topic sentence and the last three sentences of the final draft. When she revised, Black saw that she needed more examples to support the generalization in her topic sentence. She added the material about greeting cards and about time and stress.

Daniel Casey wrote a discovery draft (see 3b) to explore further the ideas that he evolved while planning his essay: for his brainstorming, see section 2g; for his use of the journalist's questions, see section 2h; for the sequencing of his ideas, see section 2l-2. As he wrote his draft, he discovered, for example, that he needed to define the term *signs of commercialism* by giving specific examples. He also found that he had two reasons he could develop in support of his thesis: an enriched economy and an enhanced spirit. He wanted a third reason, so he interviewed some friends who worked in a shopping mall, and they mentioned what some of the stores do for the community at holiday time. The second paragraph of Casey's essay was the next-to-last paragraph in an early draft. He moved it when he revised because he decided that it built an effective bridge to his thesis statement.

As both Black and Casey revised, they consulted the Revision Checklists in 3c to remind them of general principles of writing, and they looked over the checklist in Chart 45.

EXERCISE 6-2

Choose a topic below, and write an essay that argues for a debatable position about the topic. Apply all the principles you have learned in this chapter.

1. animal experimentation
2. nuclear power
3. value of the space program
4. celebrity endorsements
5. day-care centers
6. surrogate mothers
7. gun control
8. school prayer
9. optimism
10. highway speed limits

REVISION CHECKLIST FOR WRITTEN ARGUMENT   45

1. Does the thesis statement concern a debatable topic (see 6b)?
2. Is the material structured well for a written argument (see 6c)?
3. Do the reasons or evidence support the thesis statement? Are the generalizations supported by specific details? (See 6c.)
4. Are opposing positions mentioned and responded to (see 6c)?
5. Are terms defined (see 6e)?
6. Are the appeals to reason used correctly and well (see 6f)?
7. Is the tone reasonable (see 6g)?

TEACHING TIP

Most newspapers, including campus newspapers, carry numerous pieces of persuasive discourse in the letters to the editor, daily columns, and editorials. You may want to ask students to bring examples to class that can be analyzed in terms of assertions and thesis, as well as the order and means of development.

A different kind of experience, but an equally interesting one, can come from analysis of a longer, more sustained argument, such as Thoreau's essay "Civil Disobedience" or Martin Luther King, Jr.'s "Letter from Birmingham Jail."

EXTRA EXERCISE D

Analyze the following paragraphs to discover the dominant appeal of each.

1. We observe today not a victory of party but a celebration of freedom—symbolizing an end as well as a beginning—signifying renewal as well as change. For I have sworn before you and Almighty God the same solemn oath our forebears prescribed nearly a century and three quarters ago.

The world is very different now. For man holds in his mortal hands the power to abolish all forms of human poverty and all forms of human life. And yet the same revolutionary beliefs for which our forebears fought are still at issue around the globe—the belief that the rights of man come not from the generosity of the state but from the hand of God.

We dare not forget today that we are the heirs of that first revolution. Let the word go forth from this time and place, to friend and foe alike, that the torch has been passed to a new generation of Americans—born in this century, tempered by war, disciplined by a hard and bitter peace, proud of our ancient heritage—and unwilling to witness or permit the slow undoing of those human rights to which this nation has always been committed, and to which we are committed today at home and around the world.

—John F. Kennedy, "Inaugural Address"
➡

Lindsey Black
Professor Gregory
English 101
April 10, 19XX

Commercialism Is Ruining the Holidays

introduction: identification of the situation

Holidays should be special occasions that have religious, historical, and cultural significance. Increasingly, however, holidays in the United States are turning into little more than business opportunities. From coast to coast, the jingles and beeps of cash registers drown out the traditional sounds of holiday observance. The spirit of the holidays is being destroyed by commercialism.

thesis statement

background: origins and significance

The origins of the holiday spirit are varied in the United States. Thanksgiving reminds Americans to be grateful for their blessings, and the Fourth of July stimulates pride in the founding of the nation. Labor Day is a tribute to workers. Memorial Day honors soldiers who died in defense of the country, and Veterans Day honors all veterans of the armed forces. Christmas and Easter have great religious significance to Christians. Holidays used to be occasions for people to come together and celebrate their heritages. Today, however, the overriding message of the holidays is "spend money."

evidence: one type

The most visible evidence that commercialism now dominates holidays is the unfortunate emphasis on spending money in preparation for religious holidays. For example, buying and mailing Christmas cards has become standard practice for individuals, families, and industry. How many people can ignore the social and the business pressures to mail cards? The commitment of money and time for this activity is
➡

not small. The gift situation is equally stressful. Although exchanging gifts on Christmas or Hanukah was always part of the celebration, the thought behind the present used to be the point. Today, however, advertising--particularly on television--sets a high standard of expectations. Can home-baked cookies compare to a microwave oven? Can hand-drawn, handwritten cards be as impressive as elaborate greeting cards that play music?

evidence: another type

Other evidence that commercialism is ruining holidays is the emphasis on shopping for bargains rather than on activities related to cultural history. Huge sales held before holidays, and often on the holiday itself, are advertised heavily in newspapers, on television, and on radio. Veterans Day has become the day to buy fall and winter clothing at reduced prices, and Memorial Day means specially lowered prices on products for the coming summer. Parades and ceremonies on Labor Day honoring the workers of America get less attention than back-to-school sales. The image of the family gathering on Thanksgiving Day is being replaced with the image of the family shopping the day after Thanksgiving, when stores are more crowded than any other day except the day before Christmas.

major likely objections and responses to them

In spite of all this, not all people are troubled by the spirit of commercialism on holidays. Many people enjoy the festivity of exchanging cards and gifts. Some people feel that the chance to buy at sales helps them stay within their budgets and therefore enjoy life more. What these people do not realize is that the festive spirit of giving can quickly turn sour when large amounts of money are suddenly not available for necessities. Also, these people do not realize that holiday sales tend to lure shoppers into

Cont'd.

2. Harlem got its first private project, Riverton—which is now, naturally, a slum—about twelve years ago because at that time Negroes were not allowed to live in Stuyvesant Town. Harlem watched Riverton go up, therefore, in the most violent bitterness of spirit, and hated it long before the builders arrived. They began hating it at about the time people began moving out of their condemned houses to make room for this additional proof of how thoroughly the white world despised them. And they had scarcely moved in, naturally, before they began smashing windows, defacing walls, urinating in the elevators, and fornicating in the playgrounds. Liberals, both white and black, were appalled at the spectacle. I was appalled by the liberal innocence—or cynicism, which comes out in practice as much the same thing. Other people were delighted to be able to point to proof positive that nothing could be done to better the lot of the colored people. They were, and are, right in one respect: that nothing can be done as long as they are treated like colored people. The people in Harlem know they are living there because white people do not think they are good enough to live anywhere else. No amount of ''improvement'' can sweeten this fact. Whatever money is now being earmarked to improve this, or any other ghetto, might as well be burnt. A ghetto can be improved in one way only: out of existence.

—James Baldwin, ''Fifth Avenue Uptown: A Letter from Harlem'' ➡

ANALYSIS OF APPEALS
IN EXTRA EXERCISE D

1. In his Inaugural Address, John F. Kennedy makes extensive use of ethical appeal. By referring to the "solemn oath" he had just taken before God and the American people, he calls attention to his commitment to work for that which is good and right. When, in reference to the complexity of the modern world, he again invokes the name of God as the source of "the rights of man," he underscores the high moral calling of his office. In the final paragraph, he appeals to the ethical sense of the audience by exhorting citizens to join him in the struggle to make a better world. By using the pronoun *we*, he repledges himself to work with all Americans for the spread and preservation of those beliefs on which this country was founded.

2. James Baldwin's comments about Riverton seethe with anger, bitterness, and even hatred. The strong emotions that the reader hears and feels emanate not only from words such as "violent bitterness of spirit," "hated it," "hating it," and "despised them," but from the images of destruction that he provides: "smashing windows, defacing walls, urinating in the elevators, and fornicating in the playgrounds." Any positive term that Baldwin uses, such as "improvement," he puts in quotation marks, suggesting its unreality.

spending more money than they had planned, often for things that they did not think they needed until they saw them "on sale."

conclusion: call for awareness

Holiday celebrations in the United States today have more to do with the wallet than the spirit. Some people refuse to participate in the frenzy of a commercial interpretation of holidays, of course. But for too many people, holidays are becoming stressful rather than joyful, and upsetting rather than uplifting.

Daniel Casey
Professor Gregory
English 101
April 10, 19XX
Commercialism at Holiday Time Benefits the Nation

introduction: gives background

Signs of commercialism at holiday time are easy to see in the United States. Christmas decorations begin their call to consumers in October. Memorial Day and Labor Day remind shoppers to prepare for the seasonal change in clothing fashions. Halloween and Easter mean children can make toll calls to the Great Pumpkin or the Easter Bunny.

presentation and refutation of opposite view

Some people disapprove of these commercial uses of holidays in the United States. These people feel that the meaning of a holiday gets lost when television is blaring news of the latest holiday sale or expensive gift item. Many people also feel that the proliferation of gifts and greeting cards creates stressful pressure on budgets and ruins any pleasure derived from giving and receiving. No one, however, has to forget the meaning of a holiday simply because commerce is involved. In fact, commercialism can ➡

increase people's enjoyment of the holidays.

thesis statement

After all, commercial uses of holidays benefit the nation's economy and lift people's spirits.

reason: one effect

Commerce at holiday time in the United States enriches the economy. Prosperity in the United States is based on the ongoing circulation of money, which holidays encourage. When people spend money on gifts and holiday products, jobs are created. The jobs are in many sectors of the economy: manufacturing, distribution, advertising, and retailing. Jobs help people support their families. Profits help business and industry grow. Salaries and profits bring about tax revenues that support schools, police, hospitals, and other government services.

reason: second effect

In addition to economic benefits, commercial activity enhances the spirit of holidays. Most people feel more cheerful at holiday time. Everyone takes part in one big party. Advertising related to holidays, along with stores filled with holiday products, creates an atmosphere of festivity across the nation. Being able to say "Happy Thanksgiving" or "Merry Christmas" to strangers while shopping breaks down barriers and helps everyone feel part of one big family. The festivity on the streets, in malls, and in stores is infectious. Giving and getting gifts and greeting cards helps people stay in touch with each other and express their feelings. Children look forward all year to wearing a store—bought costume for Halloween, sitting on Santa's lap in a department store, and talking to the Easter Bunny at the local shopping mall.

reason: third effect

The holiday activities that help businesses prosper also inspire many businesses to improve everyone's quality of life. Many companies, for

➡

example, organize collections of clothing and preparation of hot meals for needy people at holiday time. Toy stores often give away toys for Christmas and Hanukah to children in hospitals and in caretaking homes. Macy's department store annually delights people of all ages with its Thanksgiving Day Parade in New York City. The entire nation is invited to enjoy the parade in person or on television. In small towns and large cities, many businesses sponsor fireworks, mounted and displayed safely by professionals, to celebrate the Fourth of July. Good will and good business go together to everyone's benefit at holiday time.

conclusion: summary of main points

The United States is a nation blessed with economic strength and resourceful people. While commercialism can detract from the true meaning of a holiday, it does not have to. People can discipline themselves to balance the spiritual with the commercial. Americans recognize that the advantages of a stimulated economy and a collective festive spirit are worth the effort of such self-discipline.

II Understanding Grammar

When you understand grammar, you have one tool to help you think about and discuss the ways that your sentences deliver their meaning to your readers. Part Two describes the elements of language and explains the standard rules for using those elements. As you use Chapters 7 through 12, remember that grammar is only a tool. Other parts of this handbook offer you additional perspectives on writing and the choices that writers can make.

7 Parts of Speech and Structures of the Sentence

When you recognize **parts of speech** and **structures of the sentence**, you have one way to describe how words are put together to create meaning.

PARTS OF SPEECH

Knowing **parts of speech** gives you a basic vocabulary for identifying words and understanding how language works. Sections 7a through 7i explain the **noun, pronoun, verb, adjective, adverb, preposition, conjunction,** and **interjection.** As you use this material, be aware that no part of speech exists in a vacuum. To identify a word's part of speech correctly, see how the word functions in the sentence you are analyzing. Often, the same word functions differently in different sentences.

We ate **fish.** [*Fish* is a noun. It names a thing.]
We **fish** on weekends. [*Fish* is a verb. It names an action.]

7a Recognizing nouns

A **noun** names a person, place, thing, or idea. For a list of types of nouns, see Chart 46. Nouns function as subjects°,* objects°, and complements°.

❖ ESL NOTE: Sometimes a suffix (a word ending) can help you identify the part of speech. Words with the following *suffixes* are usually nouns: *-ness, -ence, -ance, -ty,* and *-ment.* For more about suffixes, see 20c-1 and 22e. ❖

*Throughout this book, a degree mark (°) indicates that you can find the definition of the word in the Glossary of Terms in this handbook.

Articles often appear with nouns. These little words—*a, an, the*—are also called **limiting adjectives, noun markers,** or **noun determiners.** *A* and *an* "limit" a noun less than *the* does: *a plan, the plan.* When you choose between *a* and *an*, remember that *a* is the right word to use when the word following it starts with a consonant sound: *a carrot, a broken egg, a hip; an* is the right word to use when the word following it starts with a vowel sound: *an egg, an old carrot, an honor.*

NOUNS			46
PROPER	names specific people, places, or things (first letter is always capitalized)	**John Lennon, Paris, Buick**	
COMMON	names general groups, places, people, or things	**singer, automobile**	
CONCRETE	names things experienced through the senses: sight, hearing, taste, smell, and touch	**landscape, pizza, thunder**	
ABSTRACT	names things *not* knowable through the senses	**freedom, shyness**	
COLLECTIVE	names groups	**family, team**	
NONCOUNT OR MASS	names "uncountable" things	**water, time**	
COUNT	names countable items	**lake, minutes**	

❖ ESL NOTE: In English, the letters *h* and *u* can have either a vowel sound (*an* hour, *an* unlikely result) or a consonant sound (*a* house, *a* university). If you are not sure which article to use with an *h*- or *u*-word, check the pronunciation in the dictionary. For more information about when to use articles, see Chapter 42 ESL. ❖

WHERE TO FIND MORE INFORMATION RELATED TO NOUNS

BACKGROUND

The effectiveness of teaching grammar in composition courses has long been a controversial subject, with research studies on the subject dating to 1906. In 1963 Richard Braddock, Richard Lloyd-Jones, and Lowell Shoer declared: "In view of the widespread agreement of research studies based upon many types of students and teachers, the conclusion can be stated in strong and unqualified terms: the teaching of formal grammar has a negligible or, because it usually displaces some instruction and practice in composition, even a harmful effect on improvement in writing" (*Research in Written Composition*, NCTE, 37–38). Reviewing research studies since 1963, George Hillocks, Jr. likewise concluded: "If schools insist upon teaching the identification of parts of speech, the parsing or diagramming of sentences, or other concepts of traditional school grammar (as many still do), they cannot defend it as a means of improving the quality of writing" (*Research on Written Composition*, NCTE, 1986, 138).

Despite such negative assessments, most composition teachers, faced with student writing that fails to adhere to basic conventions of standard English grammar, recognize an obligation to deal with students' lack of understanding. As Mina Shaughnessy points out in *Errors and Expectations* (New York: Oxford UP, 1977, p. 128), one inevitably comes to the question of "how to help students reduce their errors to a level that is tolerable to their readers." In answer to that question, many continue to argue for teaching grammar as part of writing instruction, among them Janice Neubleib ("The Relation of Formal Grammar to Composition," *College Composition and Communication* 23 [1977]: 247–50), Patrick F. Basset ("Grammar—Can We Afford Not to Teach It?," *NASSP Bulletin* 64.10 [1980]: 55–63), and Mary Apes ("Tracing Errors to Their Sources: A Study of the Encoding Processes of Adult Basic Writers," *Journal of Basic Writing* 4 [Spring 1985]: 4–33).

7b Recognizing pronouns

A **pronoun** takes the place of a noun. The word (or words) a pronoun replaces is called its **antecedent.** Pronouns have three cases: subjective case, objective case, and possessive case. For a detailed discussion of pronoun case, see Chapter 9.

PRONOUNS 47

PERSONAL *I, you, they, her, its, ours,* and others	refers to people or things	**I** saw **her** take your book to **them.**
RELATIVE *who, which, that*	introduces certain noun clauses° and adjective clauses°	The book **that** I lost was valuable.
INTERROGATIVE *who, whose, what, which,* and others	introduces a question	**Who** called?
DEMONSTRATIVE *this, these, that, those*	points out the antecedent°	Is **this** a mistake?
REFLEXIVE; INTENSIVE *myself, themselves,* and other *-self* or *-selves* words	reflects back to the antecedent; intensifies the antecedent	They claim to support **themselves.** I **myself** doubt it.
RECIPROCAL *each other, one another*	refers to individual parts of a plural antecedent	We respect **each other.**
INDEFINITE *all, anyone, each,* and others	refers to nonspecific persons or things	**Everyone** is welcome here.

TEACHING TIP

According to Marcia Farr and Harvey Daniels in *Language Diversity and Writing Instruction* (NCTE, 1986, 45–46), recent research has identified "fifteen key factors associated with effective writing instruction":

1. Teachers who understand and appreciate the basic linguistic competence that students bring with them to school, and who therefore have positive expectations for students' achievements in writing.

2. Regular and substantial practice in writing, aimed at developing fluency.

3. The opportunity to write for real, personally significant purposes.

4. Experience in writing for a wide range of audiences, both inside and outside of school.

5. Rich and continuous reading experience, including both published literature of acknowledged merit and the work of peers and instructors.

6. Exposure to models of writing in process and writers at work, including both teachers and classmates.

7. Instruction in the processes of writing; that is, learning to work at a given writing task in appropriate phases, including prewriting, drafting, and revising.

8. Collaborative activities for students that provide ideas for writing and guidance for revising works in progress.

9. One-to-one writing conferences with the teacher.

10. Direct instruction in specific strategies and techniques for writing.

11. Reduced instruction in grammatical terminology and related drills, with increased use of sentence-combining activities.

12. Teaching of writing mechanics and grammar in the context of students' actual compositions, rather than in separate drills or exercises.

13. Moderate marking of surface structure errors, focusing on sets or patterns of related errors.

David is an accountant. [noun]
He is an accountant. [pronoun]
David gave **his** report to the finance committee. [The pronoun *his* replaces the antecedent *David*.]

WHERE TO FIND MORE INFORMATION RELATED TO PRONOUNS
Pronoun case	Chapter 9
Pronoun reference to antecedents	Chapter 10
Pronoun and antecedent agreement	11m-11p

EXERCISE 7-1

Consulting sections 7a and 7b, underline and label all nouns (N) and pronouns (P). Circle all articles.

EXAMPLE   Treadmills can be ⓐ way to fitness and rehabilitation.

1. Not only humans use them.
2. Scientists conduct experiments by placing lobsters on treadmills.
3. Scientists can study a lobster when it is fitted with a small mask.
4. The lobster may reach speeds up to a kilometer an hour.
5. Through the mask, researchers can monitor the heartbeat of the crustacean that they are studying.

7c Recognizing verbs

Main verbs express action, occurrence, or state of being. For a detailed discussion of verbs, see Chapter 8.

I **dance.** [action]
The audience **became** silent. [occurrence]
Your dancing **was** excellent. [state of being]

❖ ESL NOTE: If you are not sure whether a word is a verb, try putting the word into a different tense. If the sentence still makes sense, the word is a verb. (For an explanation of verb tense, see 8g.)

NO   He is a **changed** man. He is a **will change** man. [The sentence does not make sense when the verb *will change* is substituted, so *changed* is not functioning as a verb.]

YES   The store **changed** owners. The store **will change** owners. [Because the sentence still makes sense when the verb *will change* is substituted, *changed* is functioning as a verb.] ❖

Cont'd.
14. Flexible and cumulative evaluation of student writing that stresses revision and is sensitive to variations in subject, audience, and purpose.
15. Practicing and using writing as a tool of learning in all subjects in the curriculum, not just in English.

ANSWERS: EXERCISE 7-1
1. Not only humans[N] use them.[P]
2. Scientists[N] conduct experiments[N] by placing lobsters[N] on treadmills.[N]
3. Scientists[N] can study ⓐ lobster[N] when it[P] is fitted with ⓐ small mask.[N]
4. The lobster[N] may reach speeds[N] up to ⓐ kilometer[N] ⓐn hour.[N]
5. Through the mask,[N] researchers[N] can monitor the heartbeat[N] of the crustacean[N] that[P] they[P] are studying.

BACKGROUND
In late antiquity and the Middle Ages, grammar, rhetoric, and logic were organized into the *trivium*, the three language arts of education. The trivium and *quadrivium* (geometry, arithmetic, astronomy, and music) together formed the Seven Liberal Arts. Grammar meant the study of Latin until the eighteenth and nineteenth centuries, when English and other vernacular languages began to displace Latin as the language of education.

A HUMOROUS NOTE
Each year the number of children coming to the mall to see Santa Claus grew larger, so the store owners decided to hire additional Santas and station them around the mall. The most experienced Santa was in charge. He referred to the trainees as his "Subordinate Clauses."

BACKGROUND

Grammar is one of the oldest fields of study in Western education. Greek and Roman boys were enrolled in grammar schools to study language and literature in preparation for the study of rhetoric in their adolescence. The *praelectio* was the central exercise of these schools. After reading a model of good or bad writing, the teacher dissected it meticulously and systematically, one word and sometimes one syllable at a time. The *praelectio* identified parts of speech, inflections, gender, meter, figures of speech, and other grammatical and stylistic concerns in the model; provided background about the work; discussed its meaning; noted errors and ineffective passages; and praised eloquent passages. As students advanced, they analyzed the works themselves, answering the teacher's questions. Each student's composition was also subject to the same microanalysis.

TEACHING TIP

In the chapter on "Common Errors" in *Errors and Expectations* (New York: Oxford UP, 1977, pp. 90–159), Mina Shaughnessy recommends approaching the study of grammar inductively by encouraging students not only to have the right answers but to know why they do what they do. "Grammar," she states, "is more a way of thinking, a style of inquiry, than a way of being right." Students who have been introduced to key concepts in grammar have a frame within which to recognize, analyze, and address their own problems. They can develop their editorial skills by looking closely at their own work to mine those concepts. They can practice and improve them by carrying out appropriate exercises and drills.

Main verbs can act as **linking verbs,** as shown in Chart 48. Also, main verbs can combine with **auxiliary verbs** to form verb phrases, as shown in Chart 49.

48

LINKING VERBS

Linking verbs are main verbs that indicate a state of being or a condition. They link a subject° with a subject complement—a word (or words) that renames or describes the subject. Think of a linking verb as an equal sign between a subject and its complement.

- Linking verbs may be forms of the verb *to be* (*am, is , was, were;* see 8c for a complete list).

George Washington **was** president.

SUBJECT   LINKING VERB   COMPLEMENT = DESCRIBES SUBJECT

- Linking verbs may deal with the senses (*look, smell, taste, sound,* and *feel*).

George Washington **sounded** confident.

SUBJECT   LINKING VERB   COMPLEMENT = DESCRIBES SUBJECT

- Certain other verbs that convey a sense of existing or becoming—*appear, seem, become, get, grow, turn, remain, stay,* and *prove,* for example—can be linking verbs.

George Washington **grew** old.

SUBJECT   LINKING VERB   COMPLEMENT = DESCRIBES SUBJECT

- To test whether a verb other than a form of *to be* is functioning as a linking verb, substitute *was* for a singular subject or *were* for a plural subject. If the sentence makes sense, the original verb is functioning as a linking verb.

NO   George Washington **grew** a beard → George Washington **was** a beard. [*Grew* is not functioning as a linking verb.]

YES   George Washington **grew** old → George Washington **was** old. [*Grew* is functioning as a linking verb.]

WHERE TO FIND MORE INFORMATION RELATED TO VERBS

auxiliaries *be, do, have*   8e

forms of *be, do, have*   8e

AUXILIARY VERBS   49

Auxiliary verbs, also called **helping verbs,** are forms of *be, do, have, can, may, might, will,* and others. Auxiliary verbs combine with main verbs to make **verb phrases.**

- I **am shopping** for new shoes.
  - AUXILIARY VERB   MAIN VERB
  - VERB PHRASE

- Clothing prices **have soared** recently.
  - AUXILIARY VERB   MAIN VERB
  - VERB PHRASE

- Leather shoes **might cost** hundreds of dollars.
  - AUXILIARY VERB   MAIN VERB
  - VERB PHRASE

EXERCISE 7-2

Consulting section 7c, underline all verbs.

EXAMPLE   A famous holiday poem <u>was published</u> only because of a good-hearted thief.

1. Clement C. Moore wrote the poem for his three daughters.
2. Moore intended it as a private gift, not for publication.
3. He called the poem "An Account of a Visit from St. Nicholas."
4. Mysteriously and fortunately, the poem was mailed to a newspaper editor.
5. Today we know that poem as "The Night Before Christmas."

QUOTATION ABOUT WRITING
The Middle Ages envisioned the goddess of grammar, Grammatica, as an old woman. In one later incarnation, she is depicted as severe, with a scalpel and a large pair of pincers. Her right hand, which is by her side, grasps a bird by its neck, its mouth open as if in a gasp or a squawk. All this was emblematic, meant as a memory aid for the budding grammarian. But, Lord, how fitting the choices of emblem were—the living thing being strangled, beak open but silent, muted by the goddess Grammatica. And the scalpel, the pincers, are reminders to the teacher to be vigilant for error, to cut it out with the coldest tool.

—Mike Rose

ANSWERS: EXERCISE 7-2
1. Clement C. Moore <u>wrote</u> the poem for his three daughters.

2. Moore <u>intended</u> it as a private gift, not for publication.

3. He <u>called</u> the poem "An Account of a Visit from St. Nicholas."

4. Mysteriously and fortunately, the poem <u>was mailed</u> to a newspaper editor.

5. Today we <u>know</u> that poem as "The Night Before Christmas."

BACKGROUND

William Safire makes the point that understanding grammar helps us to perceive emphasis and meaning. For example, if at a wine tasting someone says, "They taste *good*," we know that the reference is to the wines, but if we hear "They taste *well*," we know that someone has made a comment about the tasters.

—William Safire,
"Going Gentle on My Mind"

TEACHING TIP

As students explore their own dialects, you might ask them how they might say the following in a conversation with a close friend.

1. They have a blind date for a party next weekend.

2. They need to spend extra time studying for the next history test because they did not do well on the last one.

3. They have been given a homework assignment in math, but they do not understand the directions.

4. They play basketball every day.

5. They admire each other's talent.

TEACHING TIP

To help students become aware of adverbs and how they function, you may want to provide a series of sentences that have blanks to be filled in with appropriate adverbs. For example:

The cat sat _____ under the kitchen table, _____ watching the mouse scampering _____ly, _____ly, almost _____ly.

7d Recognizing verbals

Verbals are verb parts functioning as nouns°, adjectives°, or adverbs°. For types of verbals, see Chart 50.

WHERE TO FIND MORE INFORMATION RELATED TO VERBALS

making verbs show accurate time sequences with verbals	8k
pronoun case with infinitives	9g
sentence fragments with verbals, not verbs	13a

VERBALS 50

INFINITIVE *to* + simple form° of verb	1. noun°: names an action, state, or condition	**To eat** now is inconvenient.
	2. adjective° or adverb°: describes or modifies	Still, we have far **to go.**
GERUND *-ing* form of verb	noun°: names an action, state, or condition	**Eating** in turnpike restaurants can be an adventure.
PAST PARTICIPLE *-ed* form of regular verb° or equivalent in irregular verb°	adjective°: describes or modifies	**Boiled, filtered** water is usually safe to drink.
PRESENT PARTICIPLE *-ing* form of verb	1. adjective°: describes or modifies	**Running** water may not be safe.
	2. noun°: see *Gerund,* above	

❖ ESL NOTE: For information about using gerunds and infinitives, see Chapter 45ESL. ❖

7e Recognizing adjectives

Adjectives modify—that is, they describe or limit—nouns°, pronouns°, and word groups that function as nouns. For a detailed discussion of adjectives, see Chapter 12.

I saw a **green** tree. [*Green* modifies the noun *tree.*]
It was **leafy.** [*Leafy* modifies the pronoun *it.*]
The flowering trees were **beautiful.** [*Beautiful* modifies the noun phrase *the flowering trees.*]

Descriptive adjectives, like *leafy* and *green,* can show levels of intensity: *green, greener, greenest; leafy, more leafy, most leafy.* **Proper adjectives** are formed from proper nouns: *American, Victorian.*

❖ ESL NOTE: These suffixes usually indicate that a word is an adjective: *-ful, -ish, -less,* and *-like.* For more information about suffixes, see 20c-1 and 22e. ❖

Some other words that are assumed to be quite different from adjectives nevertheless function to limit nouns; they are therefore classified as adjectives. They are known as **limiting adjectives.** Articles, one type of limiting adjective, are discussed in 7a and Chapter 42ESL; Chart 51 lists other types. Most of the words in the chart also function as pronouns. To identify each word's part of speech, see how it functions in a sentence.

That car belongs to Harold. [*that* = demonstrative adjective]
That is Harold's car. [*that* = demonstrative pronoun]

LIMITING ADJECTIVES	51
DEMONSTRATIVE *this, these, that, those*	**Those** students rent **that** house.
INDEFINITE *any, each, other, some,* and others	**Few** films today have complex plots.
INTERROGATIVE *what, which, whose*	**What** answer did you give?
NUMERICAL *one, first, two, second,* and others	The **fifth** question was tricky.
POSSESSIVE *my, your, their,* and others	**My** violin is older than **your** cello.
RELATIVE *what, which, whose, whatever,* and others	We don't know **which** road to take.

TEACHING TIP
To give students a sense of the range of uses for -*ing* words, you might hand out a list of -*ing* words and ask your students to use each word in three different sentences: in one as a noun, in another as an adjective, and in a third as part of a verb phrase. You can start with the chart of verbals and/or with Section 7m. Then you can collect the sentences and select 25 to 30 to reproduce and distribute. As an exercise or quiz, you can ask the students to identify each -*ing* word as a noun, an adjective, or part of a verb phrase. Often the author of a sentence is eager for others to get the identification correct and is therefore quite willing to explain the answer. You might use these -*ing* words or any others: (1) swimming, (2) painting, (3) flying, (4) reading, (5) cooking.

Here are some possible responses (the words appear first as nouns, then as adjectives, and finally as parts of verb phrases):
1. *Swimming* is fun. The *swimming* pool is crowded. She is *swimming* laps.
2. Oil *painting* requires an eye for detail. The *painting* equipment is in the shed. We will be *painting* the bedroom this weekend.
3. He likes *flying.* The *flying* squirrel leaped out of sight. Are you *flying* to Vancouver?
4. *Reading* is the basis of many other skills. The *reading* room at the library has comfortable chairs. What are you *reading*?
5. *Cooking* is a creative experience. The *cooking* class meets on Wednesday evenings. I am *cooking* something special for your birthday.

QUOTATION ABOUT WRITING
A *dependent clause* is like a dependent child: incapable of standing on its own but able to cause a lot of trouble.
—William Safire, "About Language"

BACKGROUND

The English language has many grammars, some of them based on opposing theories and spawning contrasting pedagogies. For example, prescriptive grammarians hold that some forms are inherently correct or incorrect, but descriptive grammarians argue that no form is any more correct than another. As concern grew during the latter part of the nineteenth century over the writing competence of college freshmen, prescriptivists called for increased efforts to improve the correctness of students' prose. Their concern was apparent not only in college curricula, but also in the popularity of magazines for the general public that promised the uncertain writer and speaker a guide to correctness. Christopher Gould describes one such publication ("Josephine Baker's *Correct English*," *Righting Words*, November/December 1988). Josephine Baker's *Correct English* was issued continuously between 1899 and 1950. The journal as well as her sixteen books (which went through 53 editions in 38 years) were published with the purpose of preserving the English language from the mistakes of careless speakers. The post–World War II shift of influence from the prescriptive to the descriptive grammarians is evident in the 1949 NCTE call for a "completely revised method of teaching the English langue." The two new fundamentals were to be "the ability to read intelligently" and "the ability to express ideas and thoughts to others clearly."

QUOTATION ABOUT WRITING

Like everything metaphysical the harmony between thought and reality is to be found in the grammar of the language.
—Wittgenstein, *Zettel*

WHERE TO FIND MORE INFORMATION RELATED TO ADJECTIVES

adjectives, not nouns, as modifiers	12f
bad and *badly*	12d
capitalizing proper adjectives	30e
commas with two or more adjectives	24c, 24d
comparatives and superlatives: *-er, more; -est, most*	12e
dangling modifiers	15c
double negatives	12c
determiners (expressions of quantity)	41bESL
good and *well*	12d
misplaced modifiers	15b
placement of adjectives	43bESL

7f Recognizing adverbs

An **adverb** modifies—that is, describes or limits—verbs°, adjectives°, other adverbs, and entire sentences. For a detailed discussion of adverbs, see Chapter 12.

Chefs plan meals **carefully.** [*Carefully* modifies the verb *plan.*]
Vegetables provide **very** important vitamins. [*Very* modifies the adjective *important.*]
Those potato chips are **too** highly salted. [*Too* modifies the adverb *highly.*]
Fortunately, people are learning that salt can be harmful. [*Fortunately* modifies the entire sentence.]

Many adverbs are easy to recognize because they are formed by adding *-ly* to adjectives: *sadly, loudly, normally.* Some adjectives, however, end in *-ly*: *brotherly, lovely.* Also, many adverbs do not end in *-ly: very, much, always, not, yesterday, so,* and *well* are a few that do not.

Descriptive adverbs can show levels of intensity, usually by adding *more* (or *less*) and *most* (or *least*): *more happily, least clearly.*

Conjunctive adverbs modify by creating logical connections in meaning. For a list of conjunctive adverbs, see Chart 52. Conjunctive adverbs can appear in the first position of a sentence, in the middle of a sentence, or in the last position of a sentence.

Therefore, we consider Isaac Newton an important scientist.
We consider Isaac Newton, **therefore,** an important scientist.
We consider Isaac Newton an important scientist, **therefore.**

Relative adverbs are words such as *where* and *when* used to introduce adjective clauses.° For a full explanation, see 7o-2.

CONJUNCTIVE ADVERBS AND THE RELATIONSHIPS THEY EXPRESS		52
RELATIONSHIP	**WORDS**	
ADDITION	*also, furthermore, moreover, besides,*	
CONTRAST	*however, still, nevertheless, conversely, nonetheless, instead, otherwise*	
COMPARISON	*similarly, likewise,*	
RESULT OR SUMMARY	*therefore, thus, consequently, accordingly, hence, then,*	
TIME	*next, then, meanwhile, finally, subsequently,*	
EMPHASIS	*indeed, certainly,*	

WHERE TO FIND MORE INFORMATION RELATED TO ADVERBS

adverbs as modifiers	7m-2, 12b
badly and *bad*	12d
comparatives and superlatives	12e
placement of adverbs	43cESL
punctuation with conjunctive adverbs	14e, 24f, 25c
splitting infinitives with adverbs	15b-3
well and *good*	12e

EXERCISE 7-3

Consulting 7d, 7e, and 7f, underline and label all adjectives (ADJ) and adverbs (ADV).

```
          ADJ        ADV                              ADJ
EXAMPLE   Working parents often need someone who will care for small

          children.
```

1. Concerned parents eagerly seek child-care that provides a stable environment where children are treated kindly.
2. Child-care has recently become a highly profitable industry.
3. Most working parents take their children to private or corporate day-care centers, rather than to an individual baby sitter.
4. Typically, children require care only during the business day.
5. However, hours in the early morning, late evening, or the weekend are also in demand.

7g Recognizing prepositions

Prepositions function with other words in **prepositional phrases.** A list of common prepositions appears in Chart 53. Prepositional phrases often set out relationships in time or space: *in April, under the orange umbrella.*

In the fall, we will hear a concert **by our favorite tenor.**
After the concert, he will fly **to Paris.**

Some words that function as prepositions also function as other parts of speech. To check whether a word is a preposition, see how it functions in its sentence.

The mountain climbers have not radioed in **since** yesterday. [preposition]
Since they have left the base camp, the mountain climbers can communicate with us only by radio. [subordinating conjunction: see 7h]
At first I was not worried, but I have **since** changed my mind. [adverb: see 7f]

WHERE TO FIND MORE INFORMATION RELATED TO PREPOSITIONS

gerunds after prepositions	45bESL
objects of prepositions	9b
repetition of prepositions, in parallel forms	18e
unintentional omission of prepositions	15e-3
using prepositions of time and place	44aESL
using prepositions with verbs (phrasal verbs)	44bESL

ANSWERS: EXERCISE 7-3

1. Concerned (adj); eagerly (adv); stable (adj); where (adv); kindly (adv)
2. recently (adv); highly (adv); profitable (adj)
3. Most (adj); working (adj); private (adj); corporate (adj); day-care (adj); rather (adv); than (adv); individual (adj); baby (adj)
4. Typically (adv); only (adv); business (adj)
5. early (adj); late (adj); also (adv)

A HUMOROUS NOTE

Misplaced prepositions and prepositional phrases can sometimes turn the serious into the comical, as Richard Lederer demonstrates in sentences he has collected from various publications.

- The patient was referred to a psychiatrist with a severe emotional problem.
- The judge sentenced the killer to die in the electric chair for the second time.
- Two cars were reported stolen by the Groveton police yesterday.
- Please take time to look over the brochure that is enclosed with your family.
- Berra had driven over with his wife, Carmen, from their home in a Mercedes for the softball game.

From Richard Lederer, *Anguished English* (*Wyrick and Company*, 1987)

TEACHING TIP

According to Forrest Burt, who teaches writing at Texas A & M, sentence-combining "in reverse" can improve the syntactical fluency of students. He suggests giving them sentences to break into "kernels." Take, for instance, this sentence:

Appearing before the dour, skeptical judge, Henry Winston, a carpenter who had not worked for over three months, said that he hijacked the bakery truck because he wanted to feed his family.

COMMON PREPOSITIONS		53
about	concerning	onto
above	despite	on top of
according to	down	out
across	during	out of
after	except	outside
against	except for	over
along	excepting	past
along with	for	regarding
among	from	round
apart from	in	since
around	in addition to	through
as	in back of	throughout
as for	in case of	till
at	in front of	to
because of	in place of	toward
before	inside	under
behind	in spite of	underneath
below	instead of	unlike
beneath	into	until
beside	like	up
between	near	upon
beyond	next	up to
but	of	with
by	off	within
by means of	on	without

7h Recognizing conjunctions

A **conjunction** connects words, phrases°, or clauses°. **Coordinating conjunctions** join two or more grammatically equivalent structures.

Here is the sentence broken into its kernels:

- Henry Winston appeared before the judge.
- The judge was dour and skeptical.
- Henry Winston said SOMETHING.
- Henry Winston was a carpenter.
- Henry Winston had not worked for over three months.
- Henry Winston hijacked the bakery truck.
- Henry Winston wanted SOMETHING.
- Henry Winston feeds his family.

Here are sentences that Burt suggests using:

1. They intended to buy groceries when they came home from work, but when they saw the heavy, cold rain falling, they decided to take a taxi, which was standing on the corner.

2. The consequences of pedantic, cryptic, sometimes deceptive language are funny, unless efficient communication is the purpose for which we resort to language.

BACKGROUND

In the eighteenth century Scottish rhetoricians such as Joseph Priestley (better known today for discovering oxygen) and George Campbell opposed the prescriptive grammars of the time. In his influential *The Philosophy of Rhetoric* (1776), Campbell wrote, ''It is not the business of grammar to give law to the fashions which regulate our speech. On the contrary, from its conformity to these, and from that alone, it derives all its authority and value.'' His statement ''Good usage is national and reputable and present'' became the guiding principle of grammarians for the next two centuries.

BACKGROUND

Most people think of the English they speak as being the standard version. People who use other forms, they assume, have dialects. The fact is that most of us speak a dialect, a language reflective of a particular region, class, or group of persons. The written version of the language that our society has generally agreed upon, called Edited American English (EAE), is used in most printed materials and in public utterances. EAE is discussed for students in Section 21a–2.

A HUMOROUS NOTE

Dangling participial phrases can produce some unintended meanings, such as these:

- Plunging 1,000 feet into the gorge, we saw Yosemite Falls.
- He rode his horse across Highway 12 and up and down the sidewalk in front of the saloon a good half hour before deputies arrived, shouting obscenities and being obnoxious.
- Locked in a vault for 50 years, the owner of the jewels has decided to sell them.

    Richard Lederer, *Anguished English*
    (Wyrick and Company, 1987)

QUOTATION ABOUT WRITING

Language, like the body, is so comfortable and familiar that we hardly notice its presence or complexity. Yet once examined closely, the accomplishment of any ordinary speaker is rather astonishing. He can produce and understand an indefinite number of new sentences—sentences he has never encountered previously.

    —Richard Ohmann,
    "Grammar and Meaning"

COORDINATING CONJUNCTIONS AND THE RELATIONSHIPS THEY EXPRESS

54

RELATIONSHIP	WORDS
ADDITION	*and*
CONTRAST	*but, yet*
RESULT OR EFFECT	*so*
REASON OR CAUSE	*for*
CHOICE	*or*
NEGATIVE CHOICE	*nor*

We hike **and** camp every summer. [*and* joins two words]

I love the outdoors, **but** my family does not. [*but* joins two sentences]

Correlative conjunctions also join equivalent grammatical structures. They function in pairs.

CORRELATIVE CONJUNCTIONS

55

both . . . and	not only . . . but (also)
either . . . or	whether . . . or
neither . . . nor	not . . . so much as

Both English **and** Spanish are spoken in many homes in the United States.

Anyone who knows two or more languages **not only** can understand multiple cultures **but also** can communicate with a wider range of people.

Subordinating conjunctions introduce dependent clauses°, structures that are grammatically less important than those in an independent clause° within the same sentence.

SUBORDINATING CONJUNCTIONS AND THE RELATIONSHIPS THEY EXPRESS		56
RELATIONSHIP	**WORDS**	
TIME	*after, before, once, since, until, when, whenever, while*	
REASON OR CAUSE	*as, because, since*	
RESULT OR EFFECT	*in order that, so, so that, that*	
CONDITION	*if, even if, provided that, unless*	
CONTRAST	*although, even though, though, whereas*	
LOCATION	*where, wherever*	
CHOICE	*rather than, than, whether*	

Many people were happy **after** they heard the news.
Because it snowed, school was canceled.

WHERE TO FIND MORE INFORMATION RELATED TO CONJUNCTIONS

agreement with correlative conjunctions	11d, 11n
commas with coordinating conjunctions	24a
punctuating dependent clauses that start with subordinating conjunctions	24b-1
semicolons with coordinating conjunctions	25b
using coordinating conjunctions for sentence coordination	17a-17d

7i Recognizing interjections

An **interjection** is a word or expression that conveys surprise or another strong emotion. Alone, an interjection is usually punctuated with an exclamation point. As part of a sentence, an interjection is set off with a comma (or commas). In academic writing, use interjections sparingly, if at all.

TEACHING TIP

To help students become aware of what conjunctions do, you might want to distribute the following passage from "Salvation" by Langston Hughes. Omit all conjunctions and ask students to supply them. When the passage is complete, ask students to discuss the function and the effect of each word they supplied. Then distribute the original, complete passage.

I was saved from sin *when* I was going on thirteen. *But* not really saved. It happened like this. There was a big revival at my Auntie Reed's church. Every night for weeks there had been much preaching, singing, praying *and* shouting, *and* some very hardened sinners had been brought to Christ, *and* the membership of the church had grown by leaps *and* bounds. Then just *before* the revival ended, they held a special meeting for children, "to bring the young lambs to the fold." My aunt spoke of it for days ahead. That night I was escorted to the front *and* placed on the mourners' bench with the other young sinners, who had not yet been brought to Jesus . . . Then I was left all alone on the mourners' bench. My aunt came *and* knelt at my knees *and* cried, *while* prayers *and* songs swirled all around me in the little church. The whole congregation prayed for me alone, in a mighty wail of moans *and* vices. *And* I kept waiting serenely for Jesus, waiting, waiting—*but* he didn't come. I wanted to see him, *but* nothing happened to me. Nothing! I wanted something to happen to me, *but* nothing happened.

QUOTATION ABOUT WRITING

In all speech, words and sense are as the body and the soul.

—Ben Jonson

Alas!
Hooray! I got the promotion.
Oh, they are late.

EXERCISE 7-4

Consulting sections 7a through 7i, identify the part of speech of each numbered and underlined word. Choose from noun, pronoun, verb, adjective, adverb, preposition, coordinating conjunction, correlative conjunction, and subordinating conjunction.

Some people[1] have had tantalizing[2] clues to the possibility of life after[3] death. Near-death experiences have been reported[4] by more than eight million people in[5] many cultures. Today, researchers are studying[6] these strange[7] experiences. Some people report that thinking[8] was extraordinarily[9] fast and clear. Others[10] describe intense[11] feelings of peace and[12] joy[13], accompanied by[14] brilliant light. Still others mention[15] enhanced[16] vision or[17] hearing. Furthermore[18], they seemed to be watching themselves[19] from a distance[20]. Researchers believe[21] that[22] these experiences are both[23] too numerous and[23] too[24] similar[25] to ignore.

STRUCTURES OF THE SENTENCE

When you know how sentences are formed, you have one tool for understanding the art of writing.

7j Defining the sentence

The sentence has several definitions, each of which views it from a different perspective. On its most mechanical level, a sentence starts with a capital letter and finishes with a period, question mark, or exclamation point. A sentence can be defined according to its purpose. Most sentences are **declarative;** they make a statement: *Sky diving is dangerous.* Some sentences are **interrogative;** they ask a question: *Is sky diving dangerous?* Some sentences are **imperative;** they give a command: *Be careful.* Some sentences are **exclamatory:** *How I love sky diving!* Grammatically, a sentence contains an independent clause (a group of words that can stand alone as an independent unit): *Sky diving is dangerous.* Sometimes a sentence is described as a "complete thought," but the concept of "complete" is too subjective to be reliable.

An infinite variety of sentences can be composed, but all sentences share a common foundation. Sections 7k through 7p present the basic structures of sentences.

7k   Recognizing subjects and predicates

A sentence consists of two basic parts: a **subject** and a **predicate.**

The **simple subject** is the word or group of words that acts, is described, or is acted upon.

> The **telephone** rang. [Simple subject, *telephone*, acts.]
>
> The **telephone** is red. [Simple subject, *telephone*, is described.]
>
> The **telephone** was being connected. [Simple subject, *telephone*, is acted upon.]

The **complete subject** is the simple subject and its modifiers (all the words that describe or limit it): *The red telephone rang.*

A **compound subject** consists of two or more nouns or pronouns and their modifiers: *The telephone and doorbell rang.*

The **predicate** is the part of the sentence that contains the verb. The predicate tells what the subject is doing or experiencing or what is being done to the subject.

> The telephone **rang.** [*Rang* tells us what the subject, *telephone*, did.]
>
> The telephone **is** red. [*Is* tells what the subject, *telephone*, experiences.]
>
> The telephone **was being connected.** [*Was being connected* tells what was being done to the subject, *telephone*.]

A **simple predicate** contains only the verb: *The lawyer listened.* A **complete predicate** contains the verb and its modifiers°: *The lawyer*

WORLD HISTORY

Sentence comes from the Latin *sententia*, a way of thinking, an opinion, a sentiment. In Latin, *sententia* also referred to a formally expressed opinion or a pithy saying, such as a maxim or aphorism, and *sentence* was used in this way by the fourteenth century. The more limited use of *sentence* to describe a grammatically complete passage began in the fifteenth century.

BACKGROUND

In "Grammar and Meaning," Richard Ohmann describes a simple study that demonstrated the vast creative possibilities of language. Twenty-five people were asked to describe a picture in a sentence, and the words from these sentences were fed into a computer, which was programmed to estimate how many accurate statements about the picture could be composed from those words. The computer's *conservative* estimate was 19.8 billion different sentences.

TEACHING TIP

In "Forward to the Basics: Getting Down to Grammar" (*College Composition and Communication* 35 [1984]: 362–367), Robert De-Beaugrande suggests a simple technique for students to use to identify subjects and predicates. Students are asked to make up a "who/what" question about a statement and then to compare the question and statement. *"The predicate of the statement is all the words you used again in the 'who/what' question,"* DeBeaugrande tells his students; *"the subject is the rest."*

> The Queen of Hearts made some tarts.
>
> *Who* made some tarts?
>
> (predicate = made some tarts)
>
> (subject = The Queen of Hearts)

TEACHING TIP

Erasmus, in his *De Copia,* demonstrated 150 ways of phrasing the Latin sentence *Tuae literae me magnopere delectarunt* (Your letter has delighted me very much). Given so many possibilities for stating a simple fact, how does a writer decide which is "better" or "best"? Some of the criteria for judgment include economy, grace, emphasis, rhythm, as well as appropriateness to subject, occasion, audience, and authorial voice.

To help students develop critical judgment about syntax, you may want to ask them to explore how many ways they can restate a single sentence, and then to evaluate which is the most effective. For example, how many ways can they state the following? Of the statements they compose, which is best?

1. Your suggestion has pleased me a great deal.

2. Photographs of our family bring back many pleasant memories.

3. When I look at my birth certificate, I often wonder what was going on when I was born.

listened carefully. A **compound predicate** contains two or more verbs: *The lawyer* **listened and waited.**

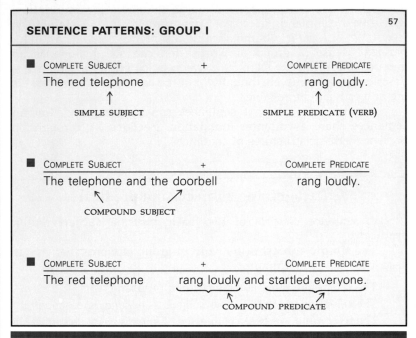

ANSWERS: EXERCISE 7-5

1. Family businesses / generate 60 percent of the U.S. gross national product.

2. Families / own or control more than three-quarters of American businesses.

3. These businesses / employ 40 million people.

4. Family firms / have grown more rapidly than non-family firms in recent years.

5. Some graduate programs in business administration / offer family-business studies.

EXERCISE 7-5

Consulting section 7k, use a slash to separate the complete subject from the complete predicate.

EXAMPLE   The standard image of a family business / is the simple mom-and-pop grocery store.

1. Family businesses generate 60 percent of the U.S. gross national product.

2. Families own or control more than three-quarters of American businesses.

3. These businesses employ 40 million people.

4. Family firms have grown more rapidly than non-family firms in recent years.

5. Some graduate programs in business administration offer family-business studies.

71   Recognizing direct and indirect objects

Direct objects and **indirect objects** occur in the predicate° of a sentence.

A **direct object** receives the action—it completes the meaning—of a transitive verb°. To find a direct object, make up a *whom?* or *what?* question about the verb.

An **indirect object** answers a *to whom? for whom? to what?* or *for what?* question about the verb. Chart 58 shows the relationships of direct and indirect objects in sentences.

SENTENCE PATTERNS: GROUP II   58

■ COMPLETE SUBJECT   +   COMPLETE PREDICATE

The caller   offered   money.

                          ↑   ↑

                         VERB   DIRECT OBJECT

■ COMPLETE SUBJECT   +   COMPLETE PREDICATE

The caller   offered the lawyer money.

                ↑   ↑   ↑

                VERB   INDIRECT   DIRECT

                        OBJECT   OBJECT

EXERCISE 7-6

Consulting section 7l, draw a single line under all direct objects and a double line under all indirect objects.

EXAMPLE: Car owners pay <u>mechanics</u> a high <u>price</u> for repairs.

1. New automotive technology has given cars sophisticated electronic systems to control their operations.
2. Mechanics today must own expensive tools and diagnostic equipment.
3. For example, expensive computers give mechanics vital information about cars' problems.
4. Competent mechanics take expensive refresher courses each year.
5. These expenses raise costs to customers.

ANSWERS: EXERCISE 7-6

1. New automotive technology has given cars sophisticated electronic <u>systems</u> to con̲t̲r̲o̲l̲ their <u>operations</u>.

2. <u>Mechanics</u> today must own expensive tools and diagnostic <u>equipment</u>.

3. For example, expensive computers give <u>mechanics</u> vital <u>information</u> about cars' problems.

4. Competent mechanics take expensive refresher <u>courses</u> each year.

5. These expenses raise <u>costs</u> to <u>customers</u>.

7m   Recognizing complements, modifiers, and appositives

1   Recognizing complements

A **complement** occurs in the predicate° of a sentence. It renames or describes a subject° or an object°.

A **subject complement** is a noun°, pronoun°, or adjective° that follows a linking verb (for an explanation of linking verbs, see 7c, especially Chart 48). Some systems of grammar use the term **predicate nominative** for a noun used as a subject complement and the term **predicate adjective** for an adjective used as a subject complement.

An **object complement** is a noun° or an adjective° that follows a direct object and either describes or renames it (for an explanation of direct objects, see 7l). Chart 59 shows the relationships of subject and object complements in sentences.

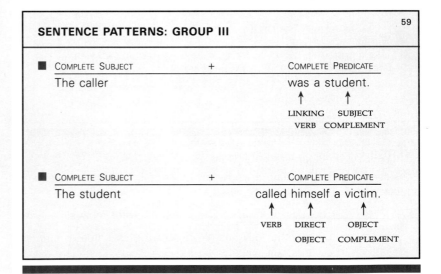

SENTENCE PATTERNS: GROUP III   59

■ COMPLETE SUBJECT   +   COMPLETE PREDICATE
The caller   was a student.
                                       ↑   ↑
                                   LINKING   SUBJECT
                                    VERB   COMPLEMENT

■ COMPLETE SUBJECT   +   COMPLETE PREDICATE
The student   called himself a victim.
                                      ↑   ↑   ↑
                                    VERB   DIRECT   OBJECT
                                            OBJECT COMPLEMENT

EXERCISE 7-7

Consulting section 7m-1, underline all complements and identify each as a subject complement or an object complement.

EXAMPLE   Most Americans rate their water supply <u>acceptable</u>. (object complement)

1. Industrial waste and pesticides can make water hazardous to drink, however.
2. The purity of river water is often suspect.
3. Water that looks, smells, or tastes peculiar should be tested for pollutants.
4. Even clean-looking water may be contaminated.
5. Home filter systems can make water safe.

2 Recognizing modifiers

Modifiers are adjectives° and adverbs°. They can appear in the subject or the predicate of a sentence.

The **large red** telephone rang. [adjectives *large* and *red* modifying the noun° *telephone*]

The lawyer answered **quickly.** [adverb *quickly* modifying the verb° *answered*]

The student was **extremely** upset. [adverb *extremely* modifying adjective *upset*]

Therefore, the lawyer spoke gently. [adverb *therefore* modifying the independent clause° *the lawyer spoke gently.*]

Chart 60 shows two common patterns for modifiers in sentences.

SENTENCE PATTERNS: GROUP IV — 60

COMPLETE SUBJECT + COMPLETE PREDICATE
The red telephone / rang.
↑ ADJECTIVE

COMPLETE SUBJECT + COMPLETE PREDICATE
The telephone / rang very loudly.
↓ ADVERBS

ANSWERS: EXERCISE 7-7
1. hazardous (object complement)
2. suspect (subject complement)
3. peculiar (subject complement)
4. contaminated (subject complement)
5. safe (object complement)

TEACHING TIP
You might help students expand short, choppy sentences by asking them to add modifiers that describe and tell *where, when,* and *how.* For example: Sigmund Freud was a doctor. Sigmund Freud was a Viennese doctor who influenced twentieth-century thinking about nervous diseases.

BACKGROUND
For an early, landmark work on expanding sentences by adding and directing modifiers, see Francis Christensen's "A Generative Rhetoric of the Sentence," in *Notes Toward a New Rhetoric,* 2nd ed., ed. Bonniejean Christensen (New York: Harper & Row, 1978, pp. 23–44). Christensen maintains that instructional time is most effectively spent in dealing with the cumulative sentence. This type of sentence presents the main clause first, then adds details that "move backward . . . to modify the statement of the main clause or more often to explicate or exemplify it, so that the sentence has a flowing and ebbing movement, advancing to a new position and then pausing to consolidate it, leaping and lingering as the popular ballad does." The additions are usually at a lower level of generality, going back over the main point in a more concrete and specific manner. Christensen argues that a writer generates ideas while composing multilevel sentences rich with details that expand the opening clause.

3 Recognizing appositives

An **appositive** is a word or group of words that renames the noun° or noun group preceding it. Most appositives are nonrestrictive, which means they are not necessary for identifying the noun being renamed. Chart 61 shows two patterns for appositives in sentences. ❖ PUNCTUATION ALERT: Use a comma or commas to separate a nonrestrictive appositive° from whatever it renames (see 24e-2). ❖

The victim's story, **a tale of broken promises,** was complicated. [*A tale of broken promises* renames the noun° *story.*]

The lawyer consulted an expert, **her law professor.** [*Her law professor* renames the noun° *expert.*]

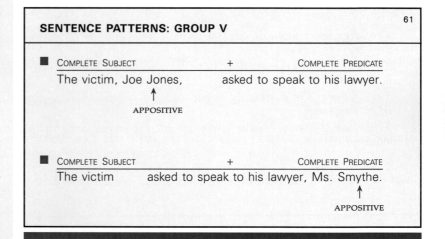

SENTENCE PATTERNS: GROUP V 61

COMPLETE SUBJECT	+	COMPLETE PREDICATE
The victim, Joe Jones,		asked to speak to his lawyer.

APPOSITIVE

COMPLETE SUBJECT	+	COMPLETE PREDICATE
The victim		asked to speak to his lawyer, Ms. Smythe.

APPOSITIVE

7n Recognizing phrases

A **phrase** is a group of related words that contains only a subject° or only a predicate°. A phrase cannot stand alone as an independent unit. Phrases function as parts of speech.

A **noun phrase** functions as a noun° in a sentence.

The **modern population census** dates back to the **seventeenth century.**

A **verb phrase** functions as a verb° in a sentence.

> Two military censuses **are mentioned** in the Bible.
> The Romans **had been conducting** censuses every five years to establish tax liabilities.

A **prepositional phrase,** which always starts with a preposition°, functions as an adjective° or an adverb°.

> After the collapse **of Rome,** the practice was discontinued **until modern times.**
> William the Conqueror conducted a census **of landowners in newly conquered England in 1086.** [three prepositional phrases in a row]

An **absolute phrase** usually contains a noun or pronoun and a participle°. It modifies the entire sentence to which it is attached.

> **Census-taking being the fashion,** Quebec and Nova Scotia took sixteen counts between 1665 and 1754.
> Eighteenth-century Sweden and Denmark had complete records of their populations, **each adult and child having been accounted for.**

A **verbal phrase** is a word group that contains a verbal. Verbals are infinitives°, present participles°, and past participles°. **Infinitive phrases** function as nouns° or modifiers°. (An infinitive is the simple form° of a verb, usually preceded by the word *to;* see 8b-2.) **Participial phrases** function as adjectives°. Participial phrases can be formed from a verb's present participle (its *-ing* form) and from its past participle (the *-ed* form of a regular verb or the irregular form; see 8d).

> In 1624, Virginia began **to count its citizens** in a census. [infinitive phrase = direct object]
> **Going from door to door,** census takers interview millions of people. [participial phrase = adjective modifying *census takers*]
> **Amazed by some people's answers,** the census takers always listen carefully. [participial phrase = adjective modifying *census takers*]

Gerund phrases function as nouns°. Telling the difference between a gerund phrase and a participial phrase using a present participle can be tricky because both use the *-ing* verb form. The key is to determine how the verbal phrase is functioning: a gerund phrase functions only as a noun°, and a participial phrase functions only as a modifier°.

TEACHING TIP

Combining sentences by using modifiers and appositives can not only reduce repetition but also create more graceful statements. Students are sometimes surprised by what they produce when they are asked to combine several choppy sentences into a single effective one. For example, the following separate sentences, repetitious and boring, can be turned into a single fluent one by combining them through the use of modifiers and appositives.

1. The president of the company resigned.
2. The president's name is Karen McCrae.
3. She resigned in protest against company policies.
4. She objected to the governing board's refusal to grant maternity leave to women employees.
5. She had been president of the company for seven years.
6. The company's name is General Services, Inc.

Here is one possible combination:

> Karen McCrae, the president of General Services, Inc., for seven years, resigned in protest against the governing board's refusal to grant maternity leave to women employees.

TEACHING TIP

Because students sometimes feel that phrases are peculiar constructions of grammar books, you might find it useful to reproduce and distribute copies of a newspaper article on a popular subject. Ask students to identify noun phrases, verb phrases, and prepositional phrases. Students will be amazed at how often phrases appear in "real" writing. Class discussion might next cover the functions of the noun phrases and prepositional phrases (subject, object, complement, adjective, adverb).

ANSWERS AND COVERAGE: EXERCISE 7-8

Answers will vary. Here is one set of possibilities.

1. Juliette Low lived in England for a time *and learned* [verb phrase] about Boy Scouting from its founder, Sir Robert Baden-Powell.

2. His sister Agnes Baden-Powell had started a similar organization, *called Girl Guides* [verbal (participial) phrase], for girls.

3. Low returned to Savannah in 1912 *to start the first U.S. Girl Scout troop there* [infinitive phrase].

4. *"Scout" being more suitable to the adventuresome U.S. spirit than "Guide"* [absolute phrase], Low called her organization "Girl Scouts."

5. *The girls' hiking, camping, riding horses, and climbing trees* [noun phrase using gerunds] were activities not considered suitable for young ladies.

6. *Refusing to let anyone tell her that girls were not capable of vigorous activities* [verbal (participial) phrase], Low recruited volunteers and raised money so that the girls could have challenging experiences.

7. *A fact unknown to most of her friends* [noun phrase] was that Low had become partially deaf as a young woman.

8. Low made her hearing loss an asset *by asking for help* [prepositional phrase] for the girls but never hearing a refusal [for parallelism with *asking*, the second independent clause has been changed to a gerund phrase].

9. Most people found it impossible to turn her away, *her persistence being a significant factor in the early success of Girl Scouting* [absolute phrase].

10. *With members in the United States, the Virgin Islands, Guam, and Puerto Rico* [prepositional phrase], today Girl Scouts of the U.S.A. serves girls in more than three hundred councils.

Including each person in the census was important. [gerund phrase = noun used as the subject]

Including each person in the census, Abby spent many hours on the crowded city block. [participial phrase = modifier used as adjective describing *Abby*]

EXERCISE 7-8

Consulting section 7n, combine each set of sentences into a single sentence, converting one sentence in each set into a phrase. Choose from among noun phrases, verb phrases, prepositional phrases, participial phrases, and gerund phrases. You can omit, add, or change words. Most sets can be combined in several equally correct ways, but be sure to check that your combined sentence makes sense.

EXAMPLE: Juliette Gordon Low is the founder of Girl Scouting in the United States. She was born in Savannah, Georgia in 1860.

Juliette Gordon Low, the founder of Girl Scouting in the United States, was born in Savannah, Georgia, in 1860. (noun phrase)

1. Juliette Low lived in England for a time. There she learned about Boy Scouting from its founder, Sir Robert Baden-Powell.

2. His sister Agnes Baden-Powell had started a similar organization for girls. It was called Girl Guides.

3. Low returned to Savannah in 1912. She started the first U.S. Girl Scout troop there.

4. "Scout" was more suitable to the adventuresome U.S. spirit than "Guide." Thus Low called her organization "Girl Scouts."

5. The girls hiked and camped and rode horses and climbed trees. These activities were not considered suitable for young ladies.

6. Low refused to let anyone tell her that girls were not capable of vigorous activities. She recruited volunteers and raised money so that the girls could have challenging experiences.

7. Low had become partially deaf as a young woman. This fact was unknown to most of her friends.

8. Low made her hearing loss an asset. She asked for help for the girls, but she never heard a refusal.

9. Most people found it impossible to turn her away. Her persistence was a significant factor in the early success of Girl Scouting.

10. Today, Girl Scouts of the U.S.A. serves girls in more than three hundred councils. It has members in the United States, the Virgin Islands, Guam, and Puerto Rico.

7o   Recognizing clauses

A **clause** is a group of words that contains a subject and a predicate. Clauses are divided into two categories: **independent clauses** (also known as *main clauses*) and **dependent clauses** (including **subordinate clauses** and **relative clauses**).

1   Recognizing independent clauses

An **independent clause** contains a subject° and a predicate°. It can stand alone as a sentence because it is an independent grammatical unit (see 7j). Chart 62 shows the basic pattern.

SENTENCE PATTERNS: GROUP VI		62
THE SENTENCE		
INDEPENDENT CLAUSE		
COMPLETE SUBJECT	+	COMPLETE PREDICATE
The telephone		rang.

2   Recognizing dependent clauses

A **dependent clause** contains a subject° and a predicate° but cannot stand alone as a sentence. A dependent clause must be joined to an independent clause (see 7o-1).

Some dependent clauses are **subordinate clauses.** They start with subordinating conjunctions. Each subordinating conjunction expresses a relationship between the meaning in the dependent clause and the meaning in the independent clause (see 7h).

Adverb clauses start with subordinating conjunctions and function as adverbs. Adverb clauses modify verbs°, adjectives°, other adverbs°, and entire independent clauses°. Adverb clauses usually answer some question about the independent clause: *how? why? when?* or *under what conditions?* ❖ PUNCTUATION ALERT: When an

TEACHING TIP

Imitation can be an effective means of expanding students' sentence-writing strategies. You can provide some samples, asking students to write a sentence on another topic, following the pattern of clauses and phrases in the model. Here are some varied possibilities for imitation, though you may want to choose your own.

- For three thousand years, poets have been enchanted and moved and perplexed by the power of their own imagination.

  —Jacob Bronowski, "The Reach of Imagination"

- The sea, which looks so near and so tempting, is often difficult to reach.

  —Henry Miller, "The Big Sur"

- Hearing the rising tide, I think how it is pressing also against other shores I know—rising on a southern beach where there is no fog, but a moon edging all the waves with silver and touching the wet sands with lambent sheen, and on a still more distant shore sending its streaming currents against the moonlit pinnacles and the dark caves of the coral rock.

  —Rachel Carson, "The Enduring Sea"

BACKGROUND

Marilyn Sternglass, in "Sentence-Combining and the Reading of Sentences" (*College Composition and Communication* 31 [1980], 325–328), maintains that sentence combining shows students how to cluster groups of words into phrases and clauses. This activity improves students' ability to recognize word groups as meaning-bearing units. She finds strong justification for including sentence-combining activities in writing classes, not only for their positive effect on writing skills, but also because they improve a student's ability to read sentences.

adverb clause comes before its independent clause, the clauses are usually separated by a comma (see 24b-1). ❖

> **If the bond issue passes,** the city will install sewers. [The adverb clause modifies the verb *install;* it explains "under what conditions."]
>
> They are drawing up plans as quickly **as they can.** [The adverb clause modifies the adverb *quickly;* it explains "how."]
>
> The homeowners feel happier **because they know the flooding will soon be better controlled.** [The adverb clause modifies the adjective *happier;* it explains "why."]

Adjective clauses (also called *relative clauses*) start with relative pronouns, the most common of which are *who, which,* and *that,* or relative adverbs such as *when, where,* or *why.* Adjective clauses modify nouns° and pronouns°.

> The car **that Jack bought** is practical. [The adjective clause describes the noun *car; that* refers to *car.*]
>
> The day **when I can buy my own car** is getting closer. [The adjective clause modifies the noun *day; when* refers to *day.*]

Chart 63 shows common sentence patterns for adverb and adjective clauses.

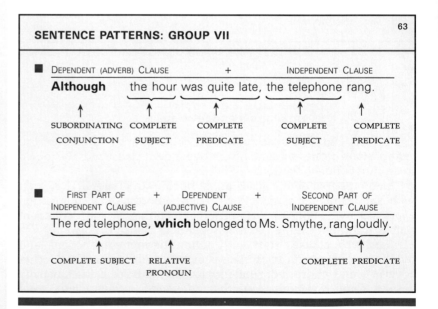

When you write adjective clauses, use *who, whom, whoever, whomever,* and *whose* when the antecedent° is a person or an animal with a name or a special talent.

> The Smythes, **who collect cars,** are wealthy.
>
> Their dog Bowser, **who is quite large,** is spoiled.

When you write adjective clauses, use *which* or *that* if the antecedent° is a thing or an animal. Either *which* or *that* begins restrictive° adjective clauses, and *which* begins nonrestrictive° ones. ❖ PUNC-TUATION ALERT: When an adjective clause is nonrestrictive, use commas to separate it from the independent clause°. (A restrictive clause is essential to limit meaning; a nonrestrictive clause is nonessential; see 24e.) ❖

> The car **that I want to buy** has a cassette player.
>
> The car **which I want to buy** has a cassette player. [The adjective clause is restrictive, and so either *that* or *which* may be used.]
>
> My current car, **which I bought used,** needs major repairs. [The adjective clause is nonrestrictive, so it begins with *which* and is set off with commas.]

Sometimes, *that* can be omitted from a sentence. For purposes of grammatical analysis, however, the omitted *that* is considered to be implied and therefore present.

> The car [that] **I buy** will have to get good mileage.

Often the word *that* makes a sentence easier to understand. Be sure to use *that* when it makes your writing clearer.

> Pat Smythe saw **that** Dale Smythe, along with her dog, was not in the car.

EXERCISE 7-9

Consulting section 7o-2, underline the dependent clauses. Write (ADJ) at the end of adjective clauses and (ADV) at the end of adverb clauses.

EXAMPLE   A coral reef, <u>which is composed of millions of living organisms</u> (ADJ), may take thousands of years to grow.

1. Although it appears to be a hard rock, almost like a boulder, a coral reef is actually very fragile.
2. Reefs are easily damaged by swimmers because even the slightest contact can weaken a section of reef and broken segments might take a hundred years to grow back.

To improve students' recognition of adjective and adverb clauses, as well as to increase their powers of concentration, you may want to read aloud the following passage from Katherine Anne Porter's "Memories of the Old South." Ask students to note every use of an adverb or adjective clause by listening for key words such as relative pronouns and subordinating conjunctions. After you read the passage, you may want to distribute and discuss it.

> In my grandmother's day, in Texas, everybody seemed to remember that man *who* had a way of showing up with a dozen grains of real coffee in his hand, *which* he exchanged for a month's supply of corn meal. My grandmother parched a mixture of sweet potato and dried corn *until* it was black, ground it up and boiled it, *because* her family couldn't get over its yearning for a dark hot drink in the mornings, but she would never allow them to call it coffee. It was known as That Brew. . . . The woman *who* made That Brew and the soldier *who* ate the bacon rind had been bride and groom in a Kentucky wedding somewhere around 1850. Only a few years ago a cousin of mine showed me a letter from a lady then rising ninety-five *who* remembered that wedding *as if* it had been only yesterday.

ANSWERS: EXERCISE 7-9

1. *Although it appears to be a hard rock, almost like a boulder* (ADV), a coral reef is actually very fragile.

2. Reefs are easily damaged by swimmers *because even the slightest contact can weaken a section of reef and broken segments might take a hundred years to grow back* (ADV).

➜

ANSWERS: EXERCISE 7-9, *continued*

3. Boats *that bring swimmers near the reef* (ADJ) also cause damage and pollution, spewing sewage and petroleum products *that make the water poisonous to the delicate reef system* (ADJ).

4. *When either too many nutrients or too many toxins are present in the water* (ADV), coral dies quickly.

5. Cool temperatures, destructive waves, and fast-growing algae are natural elements *that can fatally injure the reef system* (ADJ).

BACKGROUND

Professor Joe R. Christopher, Tarleton State University, responded to my invitation in the first edition of this text to send in material for the second edition. He writes:

> In addition to the simple, compound, complex, and compound-complex sentences usually listed in handbooks, there is one idiomatic pattern which is acceptable as an English sentence but which does not fit any of these patterns very comfortably; it may be considered a variation of the compound sentence, but the comparative forms it uses and the appearance of a comma without a conjunction make it an oddity.

Thus, this less common construction used to create balanced sentences joins independent clauses with a comma but without a conjunction. It yields an interdependent, comparative structure. Here are a few examples based on what Professor Christopher sent in:

- The higher he climbed, the thinner the air became.
- The closer the coyote approached, the more Louisa and Frank were mesmerized by its eyes.
- The more miles the trip [takes], the more exhausted you feel.

3. Boats that bring swimmers near the reef also cause damage and pollution, spewing sewage and petroleum products that make the water poisonous to the delicate reef system.

4. When either too many nutrients or too many toxins are present in the water, coral quickly dies.

5. Cool temperatures, destructive waves, and fast-growing algae are natural elements that can fatally injure the reef system.

Noun clauses begin with many of the same words as adjective clauses do: *that, who, which,* and their derivatives, as well as *when, where, whether, why,* or *how.* Noun clauses, however, do not modify°; they replace nouns°.

Promises are not always dependable. [noun]
What politicians promise is not always dependable. [noun clause]
The electorate often cannot figure out the **truth.** [noun]
The electorate often cannot know **what the truth is.** [noun clause]

Because they start with similar words, noun clauses and adjective clauses are sometimes confused with each other. A noun clause *is* a subject°, object°, or complement°. An adjective clause *modifies* a subject, object, or complement. The word starting an adjective clause has an antecedent° in the sentence. The word starting a noun clause does not.

Politicians understand **whom they must please.** [Noun clause is an object; *whom* does not need an antecedent here.]
Politicians **who make promises** sometimes fail to keep them. [Adjective clause modifying *politicians* is the antecedent of *who.*]

Elliptical clauses are grammatically incomplete for the deliberate purpose of concise prose (see Chapter 16). Elliptical clause gets its name from the word *ellipsis,* meaning "omission." An elliptical clause delivers its meaning only if the missing elements can be filled in from context. Sometimes an omission, although grammatically acceptable, interferes with the ability of a sentence to deliver its meaning. Commonly omitted in an elliptical clause are the relative pronouns *that, which,* or *whom* in adjective clauses, the subject° and verb° in adverb clauses°, and the second half of a comparison.

Engineering is one of the majors **[that] she considered.** [relative pronoun omitted]
After [he was granted] a retrial, he was released. [subject and verb omitted]
Broiled fish tastes better **than boiled fish [tastes].** [second half of the comparison omitted]

EXERCISE 7-10

Consulting section 7o, combine each of the following pairs of sentences using some of the subordinating conjunctions and relative pronouns from this list. Some pairs may be combined in a variety of ways. Create at least one elliptical clause. Subordinators may be used more than once, but try to use as many different ones as possible.

which	because	of which	since	if
while	as	how	that	although

EXAMPLE   Famine occurs. Insects or rodents destroy crops or stored food.

When insects or rodents destroy crops or stored food, famine occurs.

1. Destruction of crops has been a problem for ages. The human race has an equally long history of trying to eliminate pests.
2. The earliest pesticides were not very effective. The earliest pesticides included sulfur, lead, mercury, and arsenic.
3. We now realize something. These original pesticides are poisonous.
4. They accumulate in the soil. They can limit or stop plant growth.
5. Some pests develop immunity to the chemicals. The pests are never completely destroyed.
6. The surviving pests reproduce quickly, passing on resistant genes. A new generation of resistant pests takes the place of those killed.
7. New pesticides are manufactured organic chemicals. The most famous is DDT, dichlorodiphenyltrichloroethane.
8. No one thought about something. DDT would contaminate and threaten the entire planet.
9. Some birds have trouble forming eggs. DDT accumulates in them.
10. In 1971 a special committee began reviewing pollutants. DDT was one.

7p   **Recognizing sentence types**

Sentences can be **simple, compound, complex,** and **compound-complex.**

1   **Recognizing simple sentences**

A **simple sentence** is composed of a single independent clause° with no dependent clauses°.

191

ANSWERS: EXERCISE 7-10

Answers to this exercise will vary somewhat. Below is one set of possibilities. Note that the directions require students to write at least one elliptical clause.

1. While destruction of crops has been a problem for ages, the human race has an equally long history of trying to eliminate pests.

2. The earliest pesticides, which included sulfur, lead, mercury, and arsenic, were not very effective. (An elliptical alternative is: Not very effective, the earliest pesticides included sulfur, lead, mercury, and arsenic.)

3. We now realize that these original pesticides are poisonous. (An elliptical alternative is to drop *that*.)

4. If they accumulare in the soil, they can limit or stop plant growth.

5. Because some pests develop immunity to the chemicals, the pests are never completely destroyed.

6. Since the surving pests reproduce quickly, passing on resistant genes, a new generation of resistant pests takes the place of those killed.

7. New pesticides are manufactured organic chemicals of which the most famous is DDT, dichlorodiphenyltrichloroethane.

8. No one thought about how DDT would contaminate and threaten the entire planet. (An ellipical alternative to drop *about how*.)

9. Some birds have trouble forming eggs because DDT accumulates in them.

10. In 1971 a special committee began reviewing pollutants, of which DDT was one.

TEACHING TIP

The class discussion of compound sentences may be a good time to review compounding of all sorts. A series of examples to show compound subjects, objects, verbs, adjectives, adverbs, phrases, and clauses may help your students see the compound sentence as the final step in a logical progression.

John F. Kennedy and Richard M. Nixon were the candidates in the 1960 presidential election. [compound subject] Kennedy won the election because of his popularity in *the South and the East.* [compound object of preposition] Many people admired *his energy and his wholesomeness.* [compound object] He *made* respected cabinet appointments *and sponsored* far-sighted legislation. [compound verb] The first months of his administration were *smooth-running and successful.* [compound adjectives] However, the period *quickly and unexpectedly* came to an end. [compound adverbs] There were many successes: *establishment of the Alliance for Progress to aid Latin America, increased foreign aid to underdeveloped nations, the development of the Peace Corps, and reduced tariffs to encourage foreign trade.* [compound noun phrases] *Yet within a few months, an attempt by Cuban exiles to invade Cuba failed, Communist forces expanded their operations in Laos and Vietnam, and the East Germans built the Berlin Wall.* [compound independent clauses, which comprise a compound sentence]

This is probably also a good time to point out the difference between sentences such as these:

John F. Kennedy was President of the United States and a hero to many young people. [compound subject complement] John F. Kennedy was President of the United States, *and he was* a hero to many young people. [compound sentence]

Charlie Chaplin was born in London on April 16, 1889.
He was a mime and became famous for his character the Little Tramp.

2 Recognizing compound sentences

A **compound sentence** is composed of two or more independent clauses°. These clauses may be connected by a coordinating conjunction *(and, but, for, or, nor, yet,* or *so)* or by a semicolon. ❖ PUNCTUATION ALERT: Use a comma before a coordinating conjunction connecting two independent clauses; see 24a. ❖

His father died early, **and** his mother often had to spend time in mental hospitals.
Many people enjoy Chaplin films; **however,** some critics dislike his work.

3 Recognizing complex sentences

A **complex sentence** is composed of one independent clause° and one or more dependent clauses°. ❖ PUNCTUATION ALERT: When a dependent clause comes before its independent clause, the clauses are usually separated by a comma (see 24b-1). ❖

When times were bad, Chaplin lived in the streets. [dependent clause starting *when;* independent clause starting *Chaplin*]
When Chaplin was performing with a troupe which was touring the United States, he was hired by Mack Sennett, **who owned the Keystone Comedies.** [dependent clause starting *when;* dependent clause starting *which;* independent clause starting *he;* dependent clause starting *who*]

4 Recognizing compound-complex sentences

A **compound-complex sentence** joins a compound sentence (see 7p-2) and a complex sentence (see 7p-3). It contains two or more independent clauses° and one or more dependent clauses°.

Chaplin's comedies were immediately successful, **and** his salaries were huge **because of the enormous popularity of his tramp character, who was famous for his tiny mustache, baggy trou-**

sers, big shoes, and trick derby. [independent clause starting *Chaplin's;* independent clause starting *his salaries;* dependent clause starting *because;* dependent clause starting *who*]

Once studios could no longer afford him, Chaplin co-founded United Artists, **and** then he was able to produce and distribute his own films. [dependent clause starting *Once;* independent clause starting *Chaplin;* independent clause starting *then he was able*]

EXERCISE 7-11

Consulting section 7p, identify each sentence as simple, compound, complex, or compound-complex.

EXAMPLE   The restoration of Ellis Island was started in 1983 and completed in 1990. (simple)

1. Immigrants from many nations have come to the United States through New York City for hundreds of years.
2. The Federal government took control over immigration from New York State in 1891, and Ellis Island was designated as a federal immigration center in 1892.
3. Although it was built to accommodate half a million immigrants a year, Ellis Island saw the arrival of almost double that number in 1907.
4. On the average, 80 percent of the immigrants passed inspection each day, while 20 percent were detained to be checked for disease or the ability to support themselves, but only 2 percent of the Ellis Island immigrants were ever refused admission.
5. Because the two World Wars and more restrictive immigration laws dramatically reduced the number of immigrants to the United States, Ellis Island eventually became much quieter.
6. Concern about security risks during World War II led officials to confine illegal aliens in detention centers.
7. Ellis Island was designated a detention center for illegal aliens during World War II; it also served as a training center for the U.S. Coast Guard.
8. Immigration slowed to a trickle after World War II, and the aging facility was no longer needed.
9. Ellis Island, which was officially closed in 1954, was left with forty-two structures decaying under the effects of time, weather, and vandalism.
10. Ellis Island was targeted for restoration in the 1980s, and today the Ellis Island Immigration Museum honors all immigrants who entered the United States through any point.

ANSWERS: EXERCISE 7-11

1. simple
2. compound
3. complex
4. compound-complex
5. complex
6. simple
7. compound
8. compound
9. complex
10. compound-complex

8 Verbs

8a Understanding verbs

Verbs convey information about what is happening, what has happened, and what will happen. In English, a verb tells of an action, an occurrence, or a state of being.

Many people **overeat** on Thanksgiving. [action]
Mother's Day **fell** early this year. [occurrence]
Memorial Day **is** tomorrow. [state of being]

Verbs also convey information by various changes in their forms, as explained in Chart 64.

INFORMATION VERBS CONVEY	64
PERSON	who or what acts or experiences an action—the **first person** (the one speaking), the **second person** (the one being spoken to), or the **third person** (the person or thing being spoken about)
NUMBER	how many subjects act or experience an action—**one** (singular) or **more than one** (plural)
TENSE	when an action occurs—in the **past, present,** or **future** (see 8g–8k)
MOOD	what attitude is expressed toward the action—**indicative, imperative,** or **subjunctive** (see 8l–8m)
VOICE	whether the subject acts or is acted upon—the **active voice** or the **passive voice** (see 8n–8o)

VERB FORMS

8b Recognizing the forms of main verbs

A **main verb** names an action (*people **dance***), an occurrence (*Mother's Day **fell** early this year*), or a state of being (*Memorial Day **is** tomorrow*).

1 Identifying a main verb's three principal parts

Every main verb has three principal parts: a simple form, a form for past tense, and a form for past participle.

The **simple form** shows an action, an occurrence, or a state of being that is taking place in the present: *We **celebrate** Thanksgiving.* The simple form is also the basis for the future tense (see 8g).

The **past tense** indicates an action, an occurrence, or a state of being completed in the past: *We **enjoyed** Christmas.* If the past tense of a verb is **regular,** it is formed by adding *-ed* or *-d* to the simple form. If the past tense is **irregular,** the forms change in various ways (***go, went, gone***); for a list of irregular verbs, see Chart 65 in section 8d.

The **past participle** in regular verbs uses the same form as the past tense. In irregular verbs, the forms for the past tense and the past participle usually differ. Also, a past participle can combine with an auxiliary verb in a **verb phrase** (see 8e): *We **have observed** Passover for years.* Past participles combine with auxiliary verbs to form perfect tenses (see 8i) and passive-voice verbs (see 8n-8o). Used alone (without an auxiliary verb), a past participle functions as an adjective°: ***crumbled*** *cookies,* ***stolen*** *pies.*

2 Recognizing present participles and infinitives

Verbs also have a **present participle.** It is formed by adding *-ing* to the simple form: *eating, falling, learning.* Alone, a present participle can never function as a verb. To function as a verb, the present participle must combine with an auxiliary verb in a verb phrase (see 8e). Used alone, present participles function as adjectives° (*a **diving** board*) or nouns° (***Swimming*** *is good exercise*). When a present participle functions as a noun, it is called a **gerund.**

The **infinitive** is another verb form that functions as a noun or an adjective, but not as a verb. Infinitives use the simple form and usually, but not always, are preceded by *to.*

TEACHING TIP

Some students may feel overwhelmed by verb tenses—which they may perceive to be infinite in number—with the result that they refuse to face the fearsome verb and thus pick a form at random (or so it seems to us). It may be helpful to show them the basic distinction between tense and aspect.

Time can be divided into past, present, and future. *Tense* refers to the reflection of one of these times in a verb. Therefore, there are three basic tenses: past, present, future. *Aspect* says something about the way the action is experienced. The progressive aspect (*to be* + *ing*) shows an action still in progress and the perfect aspect (*has, have,* or *had* + past participle) shows a completed action or one being continued into the present from a specific point in the past. *Mood,* which describes conditions such as certainty, necessity, and possibility, is a separate issue, and so is *voice.* A verb can show all four qualities, but you might want to focus on the interplay of tense and aspect first.

It may be useful to go over a chart, such as the one below, with your students, discussing the possible uses of each tense.

TO LOVE

Time	Form	Tense
present	{ love	simple present
	{ am, is, are loving	present progressive
past	loved	simple past
	{ was, were loving	past progressive
	{ has, have loved	present perfect
	{ had loved	past (or pluperfect)
	{ has, have been loving	present perfect progressive
	{ had been loving	past (or pluperfect) progressive
future	{ will love	future
	{ will be loving	future progressive
	{ will have loved	future perfect
	{ will have been loving	future perfect progressive

195

TEACHING TIP

Leaving the *-s* off verbs is a common error, even among students who can quote the rule for its use. Many of these students speak or have studied second languages that have much more complex systems of verb endings. A discussion of the English *-s* in the context of other languages the students know may reduce the number of carelessly omitted *-s*'s. You can let students know, jokingly, that anyone who accurately writes and speaks French, Spanish, or Italian and still doesn't bother to keep track of "one little '*s*'" is too strange to be believed.

Here is a comparison of the verb *speak* (present tense) in four languages, with endings shown in boldface. When no pronouns are given, the pronoun is communicated by the verb's ending.

ENGLISH

Singular	*Plural*
I speak	we speak
you speak	you speak
he, she, it speak**s**	they speak

SPANISH

hablo	habl**amos**
habl**as**	habl**áis**
habl**a**	habl**an**

ITALIAN

parlo	parl**iamo**
parl**i**	parl**ate**
parl**a**	parl**ano**

FRENCH

je parl**e**	nous parl**ons**
tu parl**es**	vous parl**ez**
il, elle, on parl**e**	ils, elles parl**ent**

To own a bakery is my dream. [*to own* = infinitive functioning as noun subject°]

The owner wants you **to bake** cookies. [*to bake* = infinitive as noun object°]

We heard you **leave**. [*leave* = infinitive, without *to*, as noun object]

Participles or infinitives functioning as nouns or modifiers are called **verbals** (or *nonfinite verbs*). For more about verbals, see 7d.

❖ ESL NOTE: For information about using gerunds and infinitives as objects° after certain verbs, see Chapter 45ESL. ❖

8c   Using the *-s* form of verbs

The *-s* form of a verb occurs in the third-person singular in the present tense°. The *-s* ending is added to a verb's simple form: *smell, smells.*

The bread **smells** delicious.

The verbs *be* and *have* are irregular verbs. For the third-person singular, present tense, *be* uses **is** and *have* uses **has.**

The cheesecake **is** popular.

The eclair **has** chocolate on top.

Even if you tend to drop the *-s* or *-es* ending when you speak, do not forget to use it when you write. Proofread carefully for the correct use of the *-s* form. (For an explanation of the *-s* form of verbs in subject–verb agreement, see 11b.)

Also, although some dialects of spoken English use forms such as *he be* and *the bakery have* for third-person singular in the present tense, academic writing requires *he is* and *the bakery has*.

EXERCISE 8-1

Consulting sections 8b and 8c, rewrite each sentence, changing the subject to the word given in parentheses. Change the form of the italicized verb to match this new subject. Keep all sentences in the present tense.

EXAMPLE   Often in literature, a colorful figure *suggests* particular feelings or special characteristics. (colorful figures)

                 Often in literature, *colorful figures suggest* particular feelings or special characteristics.

1. A green figure *appears* in ancient folklore. (Green figures)

2. These characters *represent* nature, fertility, and growing things. (This character)

3. This fertility symbol *takes* part in dances and other celebrations of spring's return. (These fertility symbols)
4. In many cultures, any signs of spring *trigger* festivals that *emphasize* the color green. (any sign of spring) (a festival)
5. Today, a person who *has* a talent for gardening *is* said to have a green thumb, and green giants *adorn* one company's cans of vegetables. (people who) (a green giant)

8d   Using regular and irregular verbs

A **regular verb** forms its past tense and past participle by adding *-ed* or *-d* to the simple form. Most verbs in English are regular. Some English verbs are **irregular.** They form the past tense and past participle in various ways. For a list of the most common irregular verbs, see Chart 65.

SIMPLE FORM	PAST TENSE	PART PARTICIPLE
enter	enter**ed**	enter**ed**
smile	smil**ed**	smil**ed**
swim	**swam**	**swum**
drive	**drove**	**driven**

✤ SPELLING ALERT: For information about when to change a *y* to an *i* when adding the *-ed* ending, see 22e-1. For information about when to double a final consonant before the *-ed* ending, see 22e-1. ✤

Speakers sometimes skip over the *-ed* sound, hitting the sound lightly or not at all. Even if you are not used to hearing or pronouncing this sound, do not forget to add it when you write. Proofread carefully for *-ed* endings.

    NO   The cake was **suppose** to be tasty.

    YES   The cake was **supposed** to be tasty.

About two hundred verbs in English are **irregular.** Unfortunately, a verb's simple form does not provide a clue about whether the verb is irregular or regular. Irregular verbs do not consistently add *-ed* or *-d* to form the past tense and past participle. Some irregular verbs change an internal vowel to make past tense and past participle: *sing, sang, sung.* Some change an internal vowel and add an ending other than *-ed* or *-d; grow, grew, grown.* Some use the simple form throughout: *cost, cost, cost.*

Although you can always look up the principal parts of any verb, memorizing any you do not know is much more efficient in the long run. Consult Chart 65.

TEACHING TIP

Some of your students may speak a nonstandard English dialect. Black English is perhaps the most discussed of these, but nonblack rural and inner-city students and students (of any color) from former British colonies and U.S. protectorates may also speak nonstandard dialects.

Two-dialect students can pick up changes in vocabulary comparatively easily. Their verbs, however, might need to be monitored with care. You might consider reviewing the following chart with such students:

NONSTANDARD ENGLISH	STANDARD ENGLISH
Present Tense	
I	I
you ⎫	you ⎫
we ⎬ *loves*	we ⎬ *love*
they ⎭	they ⎭
he, she, it *love*	he, she, it *loves*
Past Tense	
I	I
you ⎫	you ⎫
we ⎬ *love*	we ⎬ *loved*
they ⎭	they ⎭
he, she, it *love*	he, she, it *loved*

EXTRA EXERCISE A

For practice identifying verbs and forming past-tense verbs, rewrite the following paragraph from Gretel Ehrlich's essay "Spring," changing the present-tense verbs to past tense. (Answers are in italics.)

Recuperation is *(was)* like spring: dormancy and vitality collide *(collided)*. In any year I'm *(I was)* like a bear, a partial hibernator. During January thaws I stick *(stuck)* my nose out and peruse *(perused)* the frozen desolation as if reading a book whose language I don't *(didn't)* know. In March I'm *(I was)* ramshackle, weak in the knees, giddy, dazzled by broken-backed clouds, the passing of Halley's comet, the on-and-off strobe of sun. Like a sheepherder I X *(Xed)* out each calendar day as if time were *(no change, subjunctive voice)* a forest through which I could clear-cut *(no change, subjunctive voice)* a way to the future. My physicist friend straightens *(straightened)* me out on this point too. The notion of "time passing," like a train through a landscape, is *(was)* an illusion, he says *(said)*. I hold *(held)* the Big Ben clock taken from a dead sheepherder's wagon and look *(looked)* at it. The clock measures *(measured)* intervals of time, not the speed of time, and the calendar is *(was)* a scaffolding we hang *(hung)* as if time were *(no change, subjunctive voice)* rushing water we could harness *(no change, subjunctive voice)*. Time-bound, I hinge *(hinged)* myself to a linear bias—cause and effect all laid out in a neat row—and in this we learn *(learned)* two things: blame and shame.

COMMON IRREGULAR VERBS

65

SIMPLE FORM	PAST TENSE	PAST PARTICIPLE
arise	arose	arisen
awake	awoke *or* awaked	awaked *or* awoken
be (is, am, are)	was, were	been
bear	bore	borne *or* born
beat	beat	beaten
become	became	become
begin	began	begun
bend	bent	bent
bet	bet	bet
bid (offer)	bid	bid
bid (command)	bade	bidden
bind	bound	bound
bite	bit	bitten *or* bit
blow	blew	blown
break	broke	broken
bring	brought	brought
build	built	built
burst	burst	burst
buy	bought	bought
cast	cast	cast
catch	caught	caught
choose	chose	chosen
cling	clung	clung
come	came	come
cost	cost	cost
creep	crept	crept
cut	cut	cut
deal	dealt	dealt
dig	dug	dug
dive	dived *or* dove	dived
do	did	done
draw	drew	drawn
drink	drank	drunk

➡

COMMON IRREGULAR VERBS *(continued)*

SIMPLE FORM	PAST TENSE	PAST PARTICIPLE
drive	drove	driven
eat	ate	eaten
fall	fell	fallen
feed	fed	fed
feel	felt	felt
fight	fought	fought
find	found	found
flee	fled	fled
fling	flung	flung
fly	flew	flown
forbid	forbade *or* forbad	forbidden
forget	forgot	forgotten *or* forgot
forgive	forgave	forgiven
forsake	forsook	forsaken
freeze	froze	frozen
get	got	got *or* gotten
give	gave	given
go	went	gone
grow	grew	grown
hang (suspend)*	hung	hung
have	had	had
hear	heard	heard
hide	hid	hidden
hit	hit	hit
hurt	hurt	hurt
keep	kept	kept
know	knew	known
lay	laid	laid
lead	led	led
leave	left	left
lend	lent	lent

*When it means to execute by hanging, *hang* is a regular verb: "In wartime, armies routinely **hanged** deserters."

➡

BACKGROUND

Old English, ancestor of our language as we know it today, used only two tenses, present and past. All other information, such as number, person, mood, and voice, was indicated by inflectional endings. All that remains of the personal endings is the *-es* or *-s* of the third person singular, which comes from the Middle English and Early Modern English *-eth* used by Chaucer, translators of the King James Bible, and Shakespeare. English verbs, like all their Germanic cognates, are distinguished by their division into weak and strong classes. In Old English the strong classes indicated tense by changing the medial vowels; the weak ones did so by their endings. After the Norman Invasion, when French and Latin became the languages of power (the court and the church), many strong English verbs became weak, adopting the *-ed* ending to indicate tense changes. New verbs admitted to the language were all placed in the weak category. Today the mixture of strong and weak forms makes it necessary for English speakers to memorize the principal parts of irregular verbs.

QUOTATION ABOUT WRITING

Grammar is the prism through which all writing is refracted.

—Patricia Robertson

WORD HISTORY

An *auxiliary verb* is also called a *helping verb*, and, not surprisingly, *auxiliary* comes from *auxiliarius*, a Latin word for *help*. Linking verbs were, until recently, often called *copulative verbs*. This usage dates back to the seventeenth century and comes from the Latin *copulativus*, meaning *connective*.

COMMON IRREGULAR VERBS *(continued)*

SIMPLE FORM	PAST TENSE	PAST PARTICIPLE
let	let	let
lie	lay	lain
light	lighted *or* lit	lighted *or* lit
lose	lost	lost
make	made	made
mean	meant	meant
pay	paid	paid
prove	proved	proved *or* proven
quit	quit	quit
read	read	read
rid	rid	rid
ride	rode	ridden
ring	rang	rung
rise	rose	risen
run	ran	run
say	said	said
see	saw	seen
seek	sought	sought
send	sent	sent
set	set	set
shake	shook	shaken
shine (glow)*	shone	shone
shoot	shot	shot
show	showed	shown *or* showed
shrink	shrank	shrunk
sing	sang	sung
sink	sank *or* sunk	sunk
sit	sat	sat
slay	slew	slain
sleep	slept	slept

*When it means to polish, *shine* is a regular verb: ''We **shined** our shoes.''

COMMON IRREGULAR VERBS *(continued)*

SIMPLE FORM	PAST TENSE	PAST PARTICIPLE
sling	slung	slung
speak	spoke	spoken
spend	spent	spent
spin	spun	spun
spring	sprang *or* sprung	sprung
stand	stood	stood
steal	stole	stolen
sting	stung	stung
stink	stank *or* stunk	stunk
stride	strode	stridden
strike	struck	struck
strive	strove	striven
swear	swore	sworn
sweep	swept	swept
swim	swam	swum
swing	swung	swung
take	took	taken
teach	taught	taught
tear	tore	torn
tell	told	told
think	thought	thought
throw	threw	thrown
understand	understood	understood
wake	woke *or* waked	waked *or* woken
wear	wore	worn
wring	wrung	wrung
write	wrote	written

EXERCISE 8-2

Consulting section 8d, in each blank write the correct past-tense form of the regular verb (simple form) in parentheses.

EXAMPLE: Rising annual temperatures over the last ten years (cause)
<u>**caused**</u> many scientists to predict climate changes.

ANSWERS: EXERCISE 8-2

1. contained
2. believed; occurred
3. feared; contributed
4. pointed; released; acted
5. absorbed; warmed

1. The 1980s (contain) _____ six of the warmest years ever recorded.
2. Some scientists (believe) _____ that rises and falls in annual temperatures (occur) _____ naturally over time.
3. Others (fear) _____ that human behavior (contribute) _____ to a warming climate.
4. They (point) _____ out that fossil fuels (release) _____ gases that (act) _____ like a layer of insulation around the earth.
5. This layer (absorb) _____ heat and (warm) _____ the earth's atmosphere.

ANSWERS: EXERCISE 8-3

1. wore, flew
2. knew, had
3. rose
4. found
5. sought, took
6. made
7. forbade
8. understood, began
9. sought, grew
10. led

EXERCISE 8-3

Consulting section 8d, in each blank write the correct past-tense form of the irregular verb (simple form) in parentheses. Use the list of irregular verbs in Chart 65.

EXAMPLE   The colorful butterflies (begin) **began** to arrive a few at a time in November.

1. As the month of November (wear) _____ on, millions of black, white, and orange flocks of monarch butterflies (fly) _____ through the sky.
2. Scientists (know) _____ that the monarch butterfly (have) _____ been migrating between Canada and Mexico for more than ten thousand years.
3. Zoologists visiting from the University of Florida (rise) _____ early to observe the migration of these butterflies.
4. In 1975, the scientists (find) _____ evidence suggesting that monarch butterflies might be threatened by the destruction of the Mexican forests for farmland.
5. A group concerned about the monarchs (seek) _____ help from the Mexican government, which in 1980 (take) _____ legal steps to protect the butterflies.
6. Laws were passed that (make) _____ it illegal to establish agricultural development in or around the monarch retreats.
7. The laws also (forbid) _____ logging, an industry essential to many local residents.
8. Conservation groups (understand) _____ the peasants' concerns and (begin) _____ looking for ways to help these people.
9. For example, scientists (seek) _____ ways to improve production of crops that (grow) _____ on existing farmland.
10. Also, residents of the area (lead) _____ tours of sightseers through the regions.

8e Using auxiliary verbs to form verb phrases

Auxiliary verbs, also called **helping verbs,** are forms of the verbs *be, do, have,* and others. They deserve special attention because they occur very frequently in English and their different forms vary more than usual. The forms are shown in Chart 66 and Chart 67. Auxiliary verbs combine with main verbs° to make **verb phrases.**

> The gym **is closing** early today. [*is* = auxiliary verb; *closing* = main verb; *is closing* = verb phrase]

❖ USAGE ALERT: Academic writing requires standard forms and uses of *be: He **is** (not **be**) walking to work.* ❖

THE FORMS OF THE VERB *BE*			66
SIMPLE FORM°	be	**-*s* FORM**	is
PAST TENSE°	was, were	**PRESENT PARTICIPLE**	being
PAST PARTICIPLE°	been		

PERSON°	**PRESENT TENSE°**	**PAST TENSE**
I	am	was
you (singular)	are	were
he, she, it	is	was
we	are	were
you (plural)	are	were
they	are	were

❖ ESL NOTE: When an auxiliary verb is used with a main verb, the auxiliary may change form to agree with a third-person singular subject (see 8c), but the main verb does not change.

NO	**Does** the library **closes** at 6:00?
YES	**Does** the library **close** at 6:00? ❖

The verb *be,* along with its various forms, is also a **linking verb.** It joins a subject° to its subject complement°. When *be* functions as a linking verb, it takes on the role of a **main verb°** rather than that of an auxiliary verb.

> The gym **is** a busy place. [*gym* = subject; *is* = linking verb; *busy place* = subject complement]

EXTRA EXERCISE B

Identify all modal auxiliaries in the following passage. (Answers are in italics.)

Most professionals in the field of medicine agree that the public *ought to* be better informed about recent developments in medical science. One of the tools that patients frequently experience but *may* know little about is the X-ray. Its discoverer, Professor Wilhelm Roentgen, thought he *might* have a powerful new means of examining the body when, in 1895, he saw the glimmer of a fluorescent screen. His discovery meant that medical professionals *could* peer into the innermost recesses of the body without surgery. For example, Dr. William B. Cannon realized that fluoroscopy *could* be used to examine the alimentary canal or digestive system. Today X-ray means that doctors *can* carry diagnostic methods to previously inaccessible areas of the human body by painless techniques. A list of all of the diagnostic uses of X-ray films *would* be too lengthy to include here, but it is safe to say that they *can* be used on all parts of the body. Of course, because improper use of X-rays *may* be harmful, technologists *should* have adequate training. They *must* complete a rigorous course of study before being allowed to operate X-ray machines.

QUOTATION ABOUT WRITING

True ease in writing comes from art, not chance,
As those move easiest who have learned to dance.
'Tis not enough no harshness gives offense,
The sound must seem an echo to the sense.

—Alexander Pope

A HUMOROUS NOTE

The English major was working for the summer as morning shift manager at a fast-food restaurant. One day her least reliable worker was missing again. She called over a friend of the boy and asked, "Where's Bill?"

"He decided to lay on the beach," replied the friend.

Not wishing to embarrass the worker but unable to overcome the urge to correct him the manager whispered, "Lie."

"All right," he said with a shrug, "Bill had to take his cat to the vet for an emergency appendectomy."

THE FORMS OF THE VERBS *DO* AND *HAVE*				67

SIMPLE FORM	do	**SIMPLE FORM**	have
PAST TENSE	did	**PAST TENSE**	had
PAST PARTICIPLE	done	**PAST PARTICIPLE**	had
***-s* FORM**	does	***-s* FORM**	has
PRESENT PARTICIPLE	doing	**PRESENT PARTICIPLE**	having

The verbs *can, could, may, might, must, shall, should, will,* and *would* are **modal auxiliary verbs.** Modal auxiliaries work in concert with the simple form° of main verbs to communicate a meaning of ability, permission, obligation, advisability, necessity, or possibility.

❖ ESL NOTE: For more about modal auxiliary verbs, see Chapter 46ESL. ❖

> Exercise **can lengthen** lives. [possibility]
> The exercise **must occur** regularly. [necessity, obligation]
> People **should protect** their bodies. [advisability]
> **May** I **exercise?** [permission]
> She **can jog** for five miles. [ability]

EXERCISE 8-4

Consulting section 8e, use auxiliary verbs from the list below to fill in the blanks. Use each auxiliary verb only once.

~~might~~   can   was   will   have   would

EXAMPLE   A shy person or one who is nervous about making conversation just __might__ find help at Ireland's Blarney Castle.

1. The block of limestone known as the Blarney Stone _____ set in a tower in 1446 at Blarney Castle.

2. According to legend, when the king of the castle saved an old woman from drowning, she promised the king that if he kissed the stone, he _____ be able to speak sweetly and convincingly.

3. Since then, Irish people claim that anyone who kisses the Blarney Stone _____ receive the gift of eloquence.

4. Today, a person who _____ speak witty words of flattery is said to have "the gift of blarney."

5. Tourists who _____ heard the legend travel to the castle near Cork, Ireland, hoping that the Blarney Stone will work its magic on their words.

ANSWERS: EXERCISE 8-4

Note: The following answers create the only possible set. Although both *can* and *will* would be correct in item 3, only *can* is correct in item 4. (Used in item 4, *will* creates a tense-sequence error.)

1. was
2. would
3. will
4. can
5. have

EXERCISE 8-5

Consulting section 8e, use each of the auxiliary verbs listed below to fill in the blanks. For some sentences, more than one correct answer is possible, but use each auxiliary verb only once.

must   should   will   can   ~~are~~   do

EXAMPLE   After years of being ignored by car dealers, women **are** finally being recognized as intelligent customers.

1. In the next few years, women _____ buy about half the cars sold in the United States.
2. To be effective, car salespeople _____ pay attention to the woman buyer.
3. The old ideas that women are interested only in style and color _____ change.
4. Salespeople now realize that women _____ understand technical information about a car's performance.
5. A salesperson _____ expect both men and women buyers to evaluate factors like dependability, value, safety, and comfort.

8f Using intransitive and transitive verbs

A verb is **intransitive** when the context does *not* require an object° to complete its meaning: *I sing loudly.* Most verbs are intransitive. A verb is **transitive** when the context requires an object to complete its meaning: *I need a guitar.* Some verbs are transitive only (for example, *need, have, like, owe, remember*). To compare how intransitive and transitive verbs operate, see Chart 68.

The verbs *lie* and *lay* are particularly confusing. *Lie* is intransitive (it does not need an object). *Lay* is transitive (it needs an object). Some of their forms, however, are similar. Get to know these forms, if you do not already, so that you can use them with ease.

	LIE	LAY
SIMPLE FORM	lie	lay
PAST TENSE	lay	laid
PAST PARTICIPLE	lain	laid
-s FORM	lies	lays
PRESENT PARTICIPLE	lying	laying

To *lie* means to recline, to place oneself down, or to remain; to *lay* means to place something down. Note from the examples that the

ANSWERS AND COVERAGE: EXERCISE 8-5

This exercise has many possible sets of answers. Only item 4 is invariable and only by default. Its answer must be *do* because *do* cannot be used in any other item. Here is one set of answers.

1. will [*should* is acceptable, suggesting speculation; *will* is more definite]

2. must [*should* is acceptable, suggesting possibility; *can* is acceptable but less appropriate than *must* or *should*]

3. should [*will* is acceptable, suggesting certainty; *should* is acceptable, suggesting possibility; although both *can* and *must* are grammatically acceptable, they suggest a fervent stance that is less appropriate in tone than the other choices]

4. do [only item where *do* is correct]

5. can [*should* is acceptable, suggesting possibility; although *must* is grammatically correct, its suggestions of either demand or resignation are inappropriate in tone; *will* is grammatically correct but the singular subject is logically inappropriate for a predictive general statement—compare *Salespeople will expect . . .*]

ALTERNATE EXAMPLES OF *LIE* AND *LAY*

You lie down, you lay down, and you've lain down; whenever you die, you'll be laid to rest.

—Mary Ellen Thornton

Here lies a man who was killed by lightning; He died when his prospects seemed to be brightening.

—Anonymous

Here lies the body of Ann Mann, Who lived to be an old woman And died an Old Mann.

—Anonymous

EXTRA EXERCISE C

Circle all transitive verbs and underline all intransitive verbs in the following paragraph.

1. Yellowstone National Park is the oldest and largest park in the national system.

2. It lies in the northwestern corner of Wyoming, slightly overlapping the boundaries of Montana on the north and Idaho on the west and south.

3. The planners originally designed the park to run 62 miles east–west and 54 miles north–south.

4. Yellowstone has several lofty plateaus, and the Continental Divide crosses it.

5. The Yellowstone River flows north into Yellowstone Lake, then through its canyon across Montana to join the Missouri.

6. The most famous sights in Yellowstone Park are the geysers.

7. The park has more than 3,000 springs, pools, and geysers.

8. Old Faithful is the most famous of the geysers, but in the same basin with it are a number of other impressive water jets.

9. Wildlife in the park, which includes bear, deer, elk, antelope, and mountain sheep, is protected.

10. The magnificent evergreen forests, severely damaged by fire in the summer of 1988, are beginning to sprout again.

ANSWERS: EXTRA EXERCISE C

1. is (intransitive)
2. lies (intransitive)
3. designed (transitive)
4. has (transitive); crosses (transitive)
5. flows (intransitive)
6. are (intransitive)
7. has (transitive)
8. is (intransitive); are (intransitive)
9. includes (transitive); is (intransitive)
10. are (intransitive)

COMPARISON OF INTRANSITIVE AND TRANSITIVE VERBS   68

INTRANSITIVE (OBJECT° NOT NEEDED)	TRANSITIVE (OBJECT NEEDED)
The cat **sees** in the dark. [*In the dark* is not a direct object°; it is a modifier°.]	The cat **sees** the dog [*dog* = direct object]
I can **hear** well. [*Well* is not a direct object; it is a modifier.]	I can **hear** you. [*you* = direct object]
We **teach** tomorrow. [*Tomorrow* is not a direct object; it is a modifier.]	We **teach** French. [*French* = direct object]

---

word *lay* is both the past tense of *lie* and the present-tense simple form of *lay*.

INTRANSITIVE

PRESENT TENSE	The hikers **lie** down to rest.
PAST TENSE	The hikers **lay** down to rest.

TRANSITIVE

PRESENT TENSE	The hikers **lay** their backpacks on a rock. [*Backpacks* is an object.]
PAST TENSE	The hikers **laid** their backpacks on a rock. [*Backpacks* is an object.]

EXERCISE 8-6

Consulting section 8f, in each blank write the correct word from each pair in parentheses.

EXAMPLE   Memory of last year's outdoor camping trip (lies, lays) <u>lies</u> heavy on my mind.

1. Planning on two days and a night in the woods, we left early and were soon (lying, laying) _____ our supplies in the shade of an old oak tree.

2. We were sure the supplies could safely (lay, lie) _____ in that spot all afternoon.

3. When the sun rose higher in the sky, the shade moved so that each bundle of food (lay, laid) _____ in the sun for hours.

4. As the spot where our gear was (laying, lying) _____ heated up, our food over-heated and spoiled.
5. While we (lay, laid) _____ hungry in our tent that night, we vowed not to go camping again.

VERB TENSE

8g Understanding verb tense

Verbs use **tense** to express time. They do this by changing form. English has six verb tenses, divided into simple and perfect groups. The three **simple tenses** divide time into present, past, and future. The **present tense** describes what is happening, what is true at the moment, and what is consistently true: *Rick **wants** to speak Spanish fluently.* The **past tense** tells of an action completed or a condition ended: *Rick **wanted** to improve rapidly.* The **future tense** indicates action yet to be taken or a condition not yet experienced: *Rick **will want** to progress even further next year.*

The three **perfect tenses** also divide time into present, past, and future. They show more complex time relationships than do the simple tenses, as explained in 8i.

The three simple tenses and the three perfect tenses also have **progressive forms**. These forms show an ongoing or a continuing dimension to whatever the verb describes, as explained in 8j. Chart 69 summarizes verb tenses and progressive forms.

✦ ESL NOTE: Chart 69 shows that most verb tenses are formed by combining one or more auxiliary verbs° with the simple form°, the present participle°, or the past participle° of a main verb°. Auxiliary verbs are important in the formation of most tenses, so be sure not to omit them.

| NO | I talking to you. |
| YES | I am talking to you. ✦ |

8h Using the simple present tense

The **simple present tense** uses the simple form of the verb (see 8b-1). It describes what is happening now, what occurs regularly,

---

ANSWERS AND COVERAGE: EXERCISE 8-6

1. laying [3rd person plural past progressive of *lay*]
2. lie [simple form of *lie* with modal auxiliary verb *could*]
3. lay [3rd person singular past tense of *lie*]
4. lying [3rd person singular past progressive of *lie*]
5. lay [3rd person plural past tense of *lie*]

EXTRA EXERCISE D

Identify the tenses of the verbs in the following sentences.

1. My neighbor walks to work every morning.
2. Thomas is studying for his chemistry examination.
3. I will take my lunch with me to the park.
4. The secretary has been typing the manuscript for days.
5. Her mother will be speaking with the supervisor in the morning.
6. Ms. Conrad had been planning to change jobs when her company was sold.
7. I closed my bank account yesterday.
8. We will have discussed the topic by the time you get to the meeting.
9. The program has generated a great deal of interest.
10. The babies in the nursery were crying when I went in.
11. The public will be seeing more of him in the next few years.
12. The children had taken a nap before they left for the beach.

➡

ANSWERS: EXTRA EXERCISE D

1. present
2. present progressive
3. future
4. present perfect progressive
5. future progressive
6. past perfect progressive; past
7. past
8. future perfect; present
9. present perfect
10. past progressive
11. future progressive
12. past perfect; past

EXTRA EXERCISE E

What meanings are expressed by use of the present tense in the following statements?

EXAMPLE

One yard is equal to thirty-six inches. (It is a fact, true in the past, present, and future.)

1. December 21 is the shortest day of the year.
2. My employer works every weekend.
3. We are going to my grandmother's house for Christmas.
4. She is to assume her duties as college president on the first of the month.
5. The rain is beating against the windows.
6. Hamlet postpones his revenge throughout the five acts of the play.
7. A stitch in time saves nine.
8. Passover comes in three weeks.
9. Shakespeare's plays entertain audiences of all ages and cultures.
10. College students learn that they must be serious about their studies.

➡

SUMMARY OF TENSES—INCLUDING PROGRESSIVE FORMS

69

SIMPLE TENSES

	REGULAR VERB	IRREGULAR VERB	PROGRESSIVE FORM
PRESENT	I talk	I eat	I am talking; I am eating
PAST	I talked	I ate	I was talking; I was eating
FUTURE	I will talk	I will eat	I will be talking; I will be eating

PERFECT TENSES

	REGULAR VERB	IRREGULAR VERB	PROGRESSIVE FORM
PRESENT PERFECT	I have talked	I have eaten	I have been talking; I have been eating
PAST PERFECT	I had talked	I had eaten	I had been talking; I had been eating
FUTURE PERFECT	I will have talked	I will have eaten	I will have been talking; I will have been eating

and what is a general truth. In addition, it describes a future event that has a fixed time.

> The students **study** hard. [happening now]
> Their class **meets** every day. [regularly occurring action]
> Mastering the material **takes** time. [general truth]
> The semester **ends** before the middle of December. [fixed-time future event]

❖ VERB ALERT FOR WRITING ABOUT LITERATURE: Use the present tense to describe or discuss action in a work of literature, no matter how old the work.

> In Shakespeare's play *Romeo and Juliet,* Juliet's father **wants** her to marry Paris, but Juliet **loves** Romeo. The play **depicts** the tragedy of ill-fated loved.

For describing or discussing action prior to or after the action you are describing or discussing, use the correct sequence of tenses as explained in 8k. ❖

8i Forming and using the perfect tenses correctly

The **perfect tenses** generally describe actions or occurrences completed, or to be completed, before a more recent point in time. They use the past participle (see 8b-1) together with auxiliary verbs° to form verb phrases°. For the present perfect, use *has* for third-person° singular subjects° and *have* for all other subjects, along with the past participle. For the past perfect, use *had* with the past participle. For the future perfect, use *will have* with the past participle.

PRESENT PERFECT	Our government **has offered** to help. [action completed but condition still in effect]
PRESENT PERFECT	The drought **has created** terrible hardship. [condition completed and still prevailing]
PRESENT PERFECT	We **have believed** always in freedom of speech. [condition true once and still true]
PAST PERFECT	The tornado barely **had passed** when the heavy rain started. [Both events occurred in the past; the earlier event, *the tornado passed*, was completed before the later event, *the rain started*, took place, so the earlier event uses *had*.]
FUTURE PERFECT	Egg production on the chicken farm **will have reached** 500 per day by next year. [The event will be complete before specified or predictable time.]

8j Forming and using progressive forms

Progressive forms show action or condition that is ongoing. They use the present participle (the *-ing* form) of the verb together with auxiliary verbs° to form verb phrases°.

For the present progressive, use the form of *be* that fits with the subject in person° and number°, plus the present participle: *I am thinking*, *you are thinking*, *she is thinking*. For the past progressive, use *was* or *were* to fit with the subject in person and number, plus the present participle: *I was thinking*, *you were thinking*, *she was thinking*. In all the other progressive tenses (future, present perfect, and future perfect), none of the auxiliary verbs change form to show person or number. Chart 69 shows progressive forms for all tenses.

ANSWERS: EXTRA EXERCISE E

1. stating a general truth
2. describing habitual action
3. describing a fixed-time future event
4. describing a fixed-time future event
5. describing what is happening now
6. discussing "timeless" events
7. stating a general truth
8. describing a fixed-time future event
9. describing a "timeless" activity
10. describing a regularly occurring action

EXTRA EXERCISE F

Identify each verb that takes the past tense or a perfect tense in the following paragraph. (Answers are in italics.)

Embroidery *has been* a popular form of needlework since earliest history. The earliest pieces of embroidery still extant *were produced* in Egypt during the sixteenth century B.C. Fragments of Greek origin from the fourth century B.C. *have been found* in the Crimea. The oldest known Chinese embroideries *were done* in chain stitch, but Turkish pieces from the same period (200 B.C.–220 A.D.) show several complex stitches as well as appliqué and patchwork. Clearly, ancient peoples all over the world *produced* elaborate embroidery of great richness and elaboration.

In the early medieval period in Europe the finest embroideries *must have been* those made at Constantinople. Some other pieces from that time *have been found* in the tomb of St. Cuthbert at Durham, England. One of the most famous works of the Middle Ages is the Bayeux tapestry, which *was produced* around the end of the eleventh century. Since the Renaissance, European embroidery *has been* of three main types: peas-

➜

EXTRA EXERCISE F, *continued*

ant embroidery (colorful and produced to be used), amateur embroidery (complicated but not useful), and professional embroidery (works of art).

Embroidery *had* always *been employed* for the decoration of garments, but from the sixteenth to the nineteenth century it *was used* far more extensively than it *has been* in the present century. Whereas it *had been used* to decorate ecclesiastical garments, with the Renaissance it *became* a means of ornamenting carpets, bookbindings, gloves, and shoes as well. Upholstered furniture is still sometimes embroidered, though not as often as it once *was*.

The first embroidery machine *was invented* in 1829. With its appearance, embroidered products that *had been* exclusively handmade *became* industrial products.

PRESENT PROGRESSIVE	The smog **is making** their eyes tear. [event taking place at the time]
PAST PROGRESSIVE	Stationery made from recycled paper **was selling** well last week. [event continuing from the past within stated limits]
FUTURE PROGRESSIVE	Because more people **are starting** to recycle, we **will be expecting** more buyers to shop for recyclable products. [future event that will continue for some time and that depends on another action]
PRESENT PERFECT PROGRESSIVE	Scientists **have been warning** us about air pollution for years. [event ongoing in the past that is likely to continue in the future]
PAST PERFECT PROGRESSIVE	Our neighborhood **had been recycling** many years before yours did. [ongoing condition in the past that has been ended by something stated]
FUTURE PERFECT PROGRESSIVE	In May, the college recycling center **will have been operating** for five years. [event ongoing until some specific future time]

ANSWERS AND COVERAGE: EXERCISE 8-7

1. reveals [present]; believe [present]

2. has been proven [present perfect]

3. conducted [past]

4. had caught [past perfect]

5. has [present]

6. wash [present]; reduce [present]

7. have discovered [present perfect]; does [present]; catch [present]

8. has lost [present perfect]

9. has been discovered [present perfect]

10. has been found [present perfect]; will have spent [future perfect]

EXERCISE 8-7

Consulting sections 8g through 8j, select the verb in parentheses that best suits the meaning. If there is more than one possible answer, be prepared to explain the differences in meaning between them.

EXAMPLE   Most people (caught, will catch) a cold sometime during the next year.

Most people *will catch* a cold sometime during the next year.

1. A recent poll (reveals, has been revealing) that 82 percent of people (believe, will be believing) kissing spreads colds.

2. Fortunately, this belief (proves, has been proven) false.

3. Doctors at a large New York medical center recently (conduct, conducted) research concerning the common cold.

4. They interviewed hundreds of people who (had been catching, had caught) a cold during the previous year.

5. The researchers concluded that cold viruses are most likely to be communicated when a person (has, will have had) hand contact with someone who is sick.

6. People who conscientiously (wash, are washing) their hands significantly (reduce, are reducing) the danger of catching a cold.

7. Through various tests and observations, doctors (discover, have discovered) that exposure to cold weather (does, did) not make a person (catch, have been catching) a cold.

8. During the past decade, the American economy (loses, has lost) more than five million dollars per year from lost wages and medical expenses due to the common cold.

9. Unfortunately, no cure (has been discovered, will have been discovered) for this persistent illness.

10. By the time a miracle drug (has been found, was being found), millions of Americans (are spending, will have spent) millions of dollars in trying to relieve their miseries.

8k Using accurate tense sequence

When you want your sentences to deliver messages about actions, occurrences, or states that occur over time, you must depend on verb tenses in sequences. These sequences often include more than one verb. Using **accurate tense sequences** correctly—that is, showing the time relationships correctly—is important for clear communication.

SUMMARY OF SEQUENCE OF TENSES 70

WHEN INDEPENDENT-CLAUSE° VERB IS IN THE SIMPLE PRESENT TENSE°, FOR THE DEPENDENT-CLAUSE° VERB:

■ Use the present tense to show same-time action.

  The director **says** that the movie **is** a tribute to Chaplin.

  I **avoid** shellfish because I **am** allergic to it.

■ Use the past tense° to show earlier action.

  I **am** sure that I **deposited** the check.

■ Use the present perfect tense° to show a period of time extending from some point in the past to the present.

  They **claim** that they **have visited** the planet Venus.

■ Use the future tense° for action to come.

  The book **is** open because I **will be reading** it later.

  ➡

EXTRA EXERCISE G

Supply the progressive form of an appropriate verb in the blanks in the following sentences. (Answers will vary.)

1. Don't bother me now; I am _____.

2. My brother is _____ to apply for a job in France.

3. The committee is _____ at 5 P.M.

4. The professor was _____ on the topic of the European Common Market.

5. The doctor was _____ in the hospital.

6. My dog was _____ in the yard.

7. I can't go swimming because I am _____.

8. The garden is _____ more beautifully every day.

9. Whose car is _____ in the driveway?

10. The telephone has been _____ all day.

EXTRA EXERCISE H

Circle the verbs in the following sentences, then name their tenses and explain what meaning is expressed by them.

1. Dolphins, porpoises, and whales belong to the order Cetacea, which are not fish, but mammals.

2. They give birth to their young, nourish them with milk, and have warm blood.

3. Once whales probably lived on the land and walked on four legs, but now they are completely aquatic.

4. Once they had left the land and moved to the water, their body structure changed radically.

5. Because they are land mammals that have become adapted to an aquatic existence, if water enters their lungs, they will die.

6. Consequently, when a whale is diving beneath the surface, it literally holds its breath by closing its nostrils.

7. Whales dive for different periods of time to various depths.

8. The humpback whale has been known to remain submerged for twenty minutes and the blue whale for fifty, though both could probably remain longer if necessary.

9. For years scientists have been researching the depths to which the various types of whale can dive.

10. The sperm whale has been known to dive to a depth of over 3,000 feet, subjecting it to a pressure of around 1,400 pounds per square inch.

➜

SUMMARY OF SEQUENCE OF TENSES *(continued)*

WHEN INDEPENDENT-CLAUSE VERB IS IN THE PAST TENSE, FOR THE DEPENDENT-CLAUSE VERB:

■ Use the past tense to show earlier action.

> I **ate** dinner before you **offered** to buy me pizza.

■ Use the past perfect tense° to show earlier action.

> The sprinter **knew** she **had broken** the record.

■ Use the present tense to state a general truth.

> Christopher Columbus discovered that the world **is** round.

WHEN INDEPENDENT-CLAUSE VERB IS IN THE PRESENT PERFECT OR PAST PERFECT TENSE, FOR THE DEPENDENT-CLAUSE VERB:

■ Use the past tense.

> The agar plate **has become** moldy since I **poured** it last week.

> Sugar prices **had** already **declined** when artificial sweeteners first **appeared.**

WHEN THE INDEPENDENT-CLAUSE VERB IS IN THE FUTURE TENSE, FOR THE DEPENDENT-CLAUSE VERB:

■ Use the present tense to show action happening at the same time.

> You **will be** rich if you **win** the prize.

■ Use the past tense to show earlier action.

> You **will** surely **win** the prize if you **remembered** to mail the entry form.

■ Use the present perfect tense to show future action earlier than the action of the independent-clause verb.

> The river **will flood** again next year unless we **have built** a better dam by then.

WHEN THE INDEPENDENT-CLAUSE VERB IS IN THE FUTURE PERFECT TENSE°, FOR THE DEPENDENT-CLAUSE VERB:

■ Use either the present tense or the present perfect tense.

> Dr. Chang **will have delivered** 5,000 babies by the time she **retires.**

> Dr. Chang **will have delivered** 5,000 babies by the time she **has retired.**

❖ **USAGE ALERT:** When an independent-clause verb is in the future tense, do not use a future tense in the dependent clause.

NO	The river **will flood** again next year unless we **will build** a better dam.
YES	The river **will flood** again next year unless we **build** a better dam. [Dependent-clause verb *build* is in the present tense.]
YES	The river **will flood** again next year unless we **have built** a better dam by then. [Dependent-clause verb *have built* is in the present perfect tense.] ❖

Tense sequences that include infinitives° or participles° must be correct. The **present infinitive** can name or describe an activity or occurrence coming either at the same time or after the time expressed in the main verb°.

> I **hope to buy** a used car. [*To buy* comes at a future time. *Hope* is the main verb, and its action is now.]
>
> I **hoped to buy** a used car. [*Hoped* is the main verb, and its action is over.]
>
> I **had hoped to buy** a used car. [Had hoped is the main verb, and its action is over.]

The **present participle** (a verb's *-ing* form) can describe action happening at the same time.

> **Driving** his new car, the man **smiled.** [The driving and the smiling happened at the same time.]

To describe an action that occurs before the action in the main verb, use the perfect infinitive (*to have eaten, to have worried*); the past participle°; or the present perfect participle (*having eaten, having worried*).

> Candida **is said to have written** fifty short stories in college. [The perfect infinitive *to have written* comes earlier in time than the saying.]
>
> **Pleased** with the short story, Candida **sent** it off to several magazines. [The past participle *pleased* comes earlier in time than the mailing.]
>
> **Having sold** one short story, Candida **invested** in a word processor. [The perfect participle *having sold* comes earlier in time than the investing.]

EXERCISE 8-8

Consulting section 8k, select the verb form in parentheses that best suits the sequence of tenses. Be ready to explain your choices.

ANSWERS: EXTRA EXERCISE H

1. belong (present tense, expresses a general truth); are (present tense, expresses a general truth)

2. give (present tense, expresses a general truth); nourish (present tense, expresses a general truth); have (present tense, expresses a general truth)

3. lived (past tense, expresses past event); walked (past tense, expresses past event); are (present tense, expresses current fact)

4. had left (past perfect tense, expresses an act completed in the past before another one took place); changed (past tense, expresses an act completed in the past)

5. are (present tense, expresses current truth); have become adapted (present perfect tense, act begun and completed in the past but continuing into the present); enters (present tense, expresses general truth); will die (future tense, expresses future action)

6. is diving (present progressive tense, expresses an action taking place at the moment); holds (present tense, expresses regularly occurring action)

7. dive (present tense, expresses habitual action)

8. has been known (present perfect tense, expresses action in the past which continues into the present); could remain (present tense with modal auxiliary, expresses possible action)

9. have been researching (present perfect progressive, expresses action ongoing in the past and likely to continue in the future); can dive (present tense with modal auxiliary, expresses possible action)

10. has been known (present perfect tense, expresses action in the past that continues into the present)

ANSWERS AND COVERAGE: EXERCISE 8-8

1. stretches [independent and dependent clauses both present]

2. came [ind. clause past perfect progressive, dep. clause past]

3. saw; had not been receiving [ind. clause past, dep. clause past perfect progressive]

4. established [ind. and dep. clauses both past]

5. had been providing [ind. clause past perfect progressive, dep. clause past]

6. learn; have been made [ind. clause present, dep. clause present perfect]

7. allowed; had been providing [ind. clause past, dep. clause past perfect progressive]

8. gave [ind. and dep. clauses both past]

9. has been criticized [ind. clause present perfect, dep. clause present]

10. plan [ind. clause present followed by infinitive, no dep. clause]

EXAMPLE Over seventy-five years ago, after Albert Schweitzer left Europe, he (traveled, had traveled) up the Ogooue River in Africa.

Over seventy-five years ago, after Albert Schweitzer left Europe, he *traveled* up the Ogooue River in Africa.

1. The Ogooue is a vast, brown waterway that (stretched, stretches) across the central African wilderness.

2. Schweitzer had been traveling for many days when he (had come, came) to a small village.

3. He (had been seeing, saw) that the natives (have not been receiving, had not been receiving) proper health care.

4. Even though Schweitzer anticipated difficulties, he (establishes, established) a jungle clinic.

5. When Schweitzer died at age ninety, he (was providing, had been providing) medical treatment to the native population for over fifty years.

6. Today visitors to the clinic (learned, learn) that many changes (had been made, have been made) over the years.

7. For example, a few years ago an electrical link with the nearest city (has allowed, allowed) the staff to shut down the noisy generators that (have been providing, had been providing) all the clinic's power.

8. Impressed by Schweitzer's work, European and American donors (gave, had given) money for five new buildings, which were completed in the late 1970s.

9. Although nearly everyone admires Schweitzer, he (has been criticized, had been criticized) for ignoring preventive medicine.

10. Doctors presently at the clinic (planned, plan) to address this issue by giving workshops on nutrition and hygiene.

EXERCISE 8-9

The verbs in each of the following sentences are in correct sequence. For each sentence, change the main verb as directed in the parentheses. Then, consulting section 8k, adjust dependent verbs, infinitives, or participles if necessary to maintain correct verb sequence. Some sentences may have several correct answers.

EXAMPLE If people exercise regularly, their physical fitness improves almost daily. (Change *exercise* to *would exercise*.)

If people *would exercise* regularly, their physical fitness *would improve* almost daily.

1. As research studies show, regular exercise boosts oxygen in the blood and increases physical endurance. (Change *show* to *showed.*)
2. Another effect of exercise was that it caused the body to produce substances linked to feelings of well-being. (Change *was* to *is.*)
3. People who exercise regularly for several months sometimes find that exercise makes them more creative because it helps them to think clearly and concentrate well. (Change *makes* to *can make.*)
4. After several months, exercisers also had a better sense of their own capabilities and exhibited signs of greater self-esteem. (Change *had* to *will have.*)
5. Because effective exercise required that a person make and observe a consistent routine, regular exercisers became efficient time managers. (Change *required* to *requires.*)

MOOD

81   Understanding mood

Mood refers to the ability of verbs to convey a writer's attitude toward a statement. The most common mood in English is the **indicative mood**. It is used for statements about real things, or highly likely ones, and for questions about fact.

> **INDICATIVE**   The door to the tutoring center opened.
> She seemed to be looking for someone.
> Do you want to see a tutor?

The **imperative mood** expresses commands and direct requests. When the subject is omitted in an imperative sentence—and it often is—the subject is implied to be either *you* or the indefinite pronoun *anybody, somebody,* or *everybody.* ♣ PUNCTUATION ALERT: A strong command is followed by an exclamation point; a mild command or a request is followed by a period (see 23a and 23e). ♣

> **IMPERATIVE**   Please shut the door.
> Watch out, that hinge is broken!

The **subjunctive mood** expresses conditions including wishes, recommendations, indirect requests, and speculations. The subjunctive mood is used less often in English than it once was.

> **SUBJUNCTIVE**   If **I were** you, I would ask for a tutor.

ANSWERS: EXERCISE 8-9

1. As research studies *showed,* regular exercise *boosted* oxygen in the blood and *increased* physical endurance.

2. Another effect of exercise *is* that it *causes* the body to produce substances linked to feelings of well-being.

3. People who exercise regularly for several months sometimes find that exercise *can make* them more creative because it *helps* [or *can help*] them to think clearly and concentrate well.

4. After several months, exercisers also *will have* a better sense of their own capabilities and *will exhibit* signs of greater self-esteem.

5. Because effective exercise *requires* that a person make and observe a consistent routine, regular exercisers *become* efficient time managers.

ALTERNATIVE EXAMPLES OF SUBJUNCTIVE MOOD

People find it interesting to speculate about how the future *could be* affected if a single aspect of our world *were* different today. For example, if the average yearly temperature *were* only a few degrees higher, the oceans *would* rise due to the melting of the polar icecaps. If serious worldwide droughts *were* to occur in several successive summers, the food supply *would* dwindle. Unless science *were* able to divert the swelling oceans or grow crops without the use of water, civilization as we know it *would be* radically changed. It is, consequently, important that mankind *recognize* the importance of environmental decisions. The world *should* not act as though the future *were* inevitably bad. If, in the early part of this century, the industrialized world *had considered* the effects of water and air pollution, our world *would be* a healthier one today.

EXTRA EXERCISE I

Select the verb in parentheses that best suits the meaning. If there is more than one possible answer, be prepared to explain the differences in meaning.

EXAMPLE

In the United States in 1964, only 64.4 percent of the eligible voters (turned, had turned, were turning, had been turning) out to vote. In the United States in 1964, only 64.4 percent of the eligible voters *turned* out to vote.

1. By the 1970 congressional elections, this figure (fell, had fallen, was falling, had been falling) to about 50 percent.

2. The figure (remained, has remained, will have remained) at about 50 percent through the mid-1980s.

3. These low turnouts (compare, are comparing, have been comparing) poorly to the voting records of many other countries.

4. The USSR (leads, has led, has been leading) the world, with an impressive 99.6 percent reported voter turnout.

5. Many other countries (had, have had, were having) voter turnouts of over 95 percent, including Czechoslovakia, East Germany, and Hungary.

6. Many other countries (require, are requiring, have been requiring) their citizens to vote.

7. Of the countries that require their citizens to vote, however, only the Netherlands (ranks, is ranking, has been ranking) in the top twenty countries, at 92.1 percent.

8. In Argentina, despite mandatory voting, fewer people (vote, have been voting, are voting) than in the United States.

9. Some authorities say that Americans cannot vote because they are at work, and these authorities (have suggested, had suggested, had been suggesting) that voting take place on Sundays.

➡

For the **present subjunctive,** use the simple form of the verb (see 8b-1) for all persons° and numbers°.

> The prosecutor asks that **she testify** [not *testifies*] again.
> It is important that **they be** [not *are*] allowed to testify.

For the **past subjunctive,** use the same form as the simple past tense: *I wish that I had* a car. The one exception is for the past subjunctive of *be:* use *were* for all persons and numbers.

> I wish that **I were** [not *was*] leaving on vacation today.
> They asked if **she were** [not *was*] leaving on vacation today.

1 Using the subjunctive in *if* clauses and some *unless* clauses for speculations or conditions contrary to fact

In dependent clauses introduced by *if* and sometimes by *unless,* use the subjunctive to describe speculations or conditions contrary to fact.

> If **it were** [not *was*] to rain, attendance at the race would be disappointing.

In an *unless* clause, the subjunctive signals that what the clause says is highly unlikely.

> Unless **rain were** [not *was*] to create floods, the race will be held this Sunday.

Be very aware that not every clause introduced by *if* requires the subjunctive. Use the subjunctive only when an *if* clause describes a speculation or condition contrary to fact.

INDICATIVE	If **she is** going to leave late, **I will** drive her to the race. [Her leaving late is highly likely.]
SUBJUNCTIVE	If **she were** going to leave late, **I would** drive her to the race. [Her leaving late is speculation.]

2 | Using the subjunctive for conjectures in dependent clauses introduced by *as if* or *as though*

Use the subjunctive to express conditions that are possible but cannot be confirmed.

The runner looked as if **he were** [not *was*] winded.

3 | Using the subjunctive for wishes, indirect requests, recommendations, and demands in dependent *that* clauses

Use the subjunctive for things that people wish for, ask for, or demand but that have not yet become reality.

I wish that this **race were** [not *was*] over.

It is important that the **doctor attend** [*not attends*] the race because the judges are demanding that **he examine** [not *examines*] the runners.

4 | Using the subjunctive with modal auxiliary verbs for speculations and conditions contrary to fact in dependent clauses

The modal auxiliary verbs *would, could,* and *should* are often used with the subjunctive. They convey the notion of speculations and conditions contrary to fact.

If the **runner were** [not *was*] faster, **I would** expect stiffer competition.

When an independent clause contains *would have,* be sure to use *had* in any dependent *if* clause.

NO	If I **would have** trained for the race, I **would have** won.
YES	If I **had** trained for the race, I **would have** won the race.

Sometimes the word *should* appears in the *if* clause to convey speculation.

Should the runners jump the starting gun, the **official would** [not *will*] restart the race.

Cont'd.

10. Other authorities (had been saying, have said, have been saying) that complicated residency laws are the problem.

11. In 1855, despite only 2,000 registered voters in Kansas, 6,000 ballots were cast in an election when people from neighboring Missouri (crossed, were crossing, had been crossing) the state line to vote for candidates in sympathy with Missouri's policies.

12. Episodes like this (led, have led, were leading, have been leading) to the enactment of strict residency laws for voters.

ANSWERS: EXTRA EXERCISE I

Other answers than these may be possible.
1. fell
2. remained
3. compare
4. leads
5. have had
6. require
7. ranks
8. vote
9. have suggested
10. have said
11. crossed
12. have led

TEACHING TIP

In *Teaching One-to-One: The Writing Conference* (NCTE, 1986), Muriel Harris suggests that teachers help students with tense shift problems by taking a passage and asking students to identify the tense of every sentence. After several sentences most students recognize problems in the tense sequence.

5	Using the subjunctive in certain standard expressions that appear in everyday language

If I **were** you . . .   Please let me **be.**
If only I **were** there . . .   **Be that as it may** . . .
Come what **may** . . .   Far **be** it from me . . .

EXERCISE 8-10

Consulting sections 8l and 8m, fill in the blanks with the appropriate subjunctive form of the verb in parentheses.

EXAMPLE   To improve a patient's general health, a doctor may ask that the person (diet) __diet__.

1. Suppose that George thought he (to be) _____ in good physical shape.
2. George's doctor, however, believed it important he (lose) _____ at least twenty pounds.
3. Medical experts urge that dieters (to be) _____ aware that the family may be uncooperative.
4. A jealous family member may even wish that the overweight person (gain) _____ weight.
5. For example, an insecure spouse may demand that the dieter (eat) _____ a food forbidden for that diet.

VOICE

8n   Understanding voice

Voice refers to verbs' ability to show whether a subject° acts or receives the action named by the verb. English has two voices: active and passive. In the **active voice,** the subject performs the action.

> Most clams live in salt water. [The subject *clams* does the acting; clams *live.*]
> They burrow into the sandy bottoms of shallow waters. [The subject *they* does the acting; they *burrow.*]

In the **passive voice,** the subject is acted upon, and the person or thing doing the acting often appears as the object° of the preposition *by.* Verbs in the passive voice add forms of *be* and *have,* as well as *will,* as auxiliaries to the past participle° of the main verb°.

ANSWERS AND COVERAGE: EXERCISE 8-10

1. were [subjunctive for conjecture, irregular verb *to be*]

2. lose [subjunctive for recommendation, regular verb]

3. be [subjunctive for recommendation, irregular verb *to be*]

4. gain [subjunctive for wish, regular verb in subjunctive form]

5. eat [subjunctive verb for demand, regular verb in subjunctive form]

ALTERNATE EXAMPLE: NECESSARY PASSIVE VOICE

In the days of Aristotle, air was believed to be one of four fundamental substances that could not be further subdivided into constituent components.

> —Frederick K. Lutgens and Edward J. Tarbuck, *The Atmosphere*

QUOTATION ABOUT WRITING

Grammar is a piano I play by ear. All I know about grammar is its power.

> —Joan Didion

Clams are considered a delicacy by many people. [The subject *clams* is acted upon by *people,* the object of the preposition *by*]

They are also admired by crabs and starfish. [The subject *they* are acted upon by *crabs and starfish,* the objects of the preposition *by.*]

Your decisions about audience (see 1b) and purpose (see 1c) for your writing should influence the voice that you choose for a sentence. Misusing voice usually creates problems of writing style rather than problems of incorrect grammar. To make your writing clear, use voice consistently in sentences on the same topic. For ways to identify and correct confusing shifts in voice, see 15a-2.

80 Writing in the active voice, not the passive voice, except to convey special types of emphasis

Because the active voice emphasizes the doer of an action, active constructions are more direct and dramatic. Active constructions also use fewer words than passive constructions (see 16a-2). Most sentences in the passive voice can easily be converted to the active voice.

PASSIVE   African tribal masks are often imitated by Western sculptors.

ACTIVE   Western sculptors often imitate African tribal masks.

The passive voice, however, does have some uses. If you learn what they are, you can use the passive to advantage.

1 Using the passive voice when the doer of the action is unknown or unimportant

When no one knows who or what did something, the passive voice is useful.

The lock **was broken** sometime after four o'clock. [Who broke the lock is unknown.]

When the doer of an action is unimportant, writers often use the passive voice.

In 1899, the year I was born, **a peace conference was held** at The Hague. [The doers of the action—holders of the conference—are unimportant to White's point.]

—E. B. WHITE, "Unity"

Identify the verbs in the following sentences, then decide if they are in the active or the passive voice.

1. Windsor Castle is an official residence of the monarchs of Great Britain.

2. In the year 1070 William the Conqueror built a fortress on the site it now occupies.

3. It was improved by succeeding rulers until the reign of Edward III (1327–1377).

4. Edward III demolished the old castle and built a new one.

5. Additions were made by later kings of England.

6. Sir Christopher Wren was asked by Charles II to design several important additions.

7. The state apartments are open to the public when the royal family is not in residence.

8. The state apartments include the grand staircase, state bedrooms, and reception rooms.

9. Many rulers were buried at Windsor Castle, including Henry VIII.

10. St. George's Chapel, one of the most beautiful parts of the castle, was built in the fifteenth century and redecorated throughout the following centuries.

ANSWERS: EXTRA EXERCISE J

1. is, active voice

2. built, active voice; occupies, active voice

3. was improved, passive voice

4. demolished, active voice; built, active voice

5. were made, passive voice

6. was asked, passive voice

7. are, active voice; is, active voice

8. include, active voice

9. were buried, passive voice

10. was built, passive voice; [was] redecorated, passive voice

TEACHING TIP

"To choose between the active and the passive," writes Joseph M. Williams, "we have to answer three questions: First, must our audience know who is performing the action? Second, are we maintaining a logically consistent string of subjects? And third, if the string of subjects is consistent, is it the right string of subjects?" (*Style: Ten Lessons in Clarity and Grace,* 3rd ed. [Chicago: Scott, Foresman, 1989], p. 24). Writers may choose the passive voice when they don't know the agent of the action, don't care, or want to keep that information confidential. Writers may also choose the voices of verbs "to create a sequence of sentences with subjects that the reader will feel are consistent, logically related," to avoid "constantly shifting from one unrelated subject to another" (p. 25).

2 Using the passive voice to focus attention on the action rather than on the doer of the action

The passive voice emphasizes the action, while the active voice focuses on the doer of the action. In a passage about important contributions to the history of science, you might want to emphasize a doer by using the active voice.

| ACTIVE | **Joseph Priestley discovered** oxygen in 1774. |

But in a passage summarizing what is known about oxygen, you may want to emphasize what was done.

| PASSIVE | **Oxygen was discovered** in 1774 by Joseph Priestley. |

| PASSIVE | The news that the dictator had fled **was received** before the order to storm the palace **could be given.** [Emphasis is on events, not on the doers of the action.] |

| ACTIVE | Before **the commander could give** the order to storm the palace, **he received** the news that the dictator had fled. [Emphasis is on the people rather than the actions.] |

3 Using active or passive voice in the social and natural sciences

Many writers in scientific disciplines (see Chapter 38) overuse the passive voice. Yet style manuals for scientific disciplines agree with the advice given in this section: Prefer the active voice. "Verbs are vigorous, direct communicators," point out the editors of the *Publication Manual of the American Psychological Association* (the APA). "Use the active rather than the passive voice."*

EXERCISE 8-11

Consulting sections 8n and 8o, determine first whether each of these sentences is in the active or the passive voice. Second, rewrite the sentence in the other voice. Then decide which voice best suits the meaning, and be ready to explain your choice.

*American Psychological Association, *Publication Manual of the American Psychological Association* (Washington: APA), 32.

EXAMPLE   Scientists were fooled by a horse and its owner about one hundred years ago. [passive voice]

Ah horse and its owner fooled scientists about one hundred years ago. [active voice]

1. Around the turn of the century, Berlin newspapers carried a story about a clever horse.

2. The horse was named Clever Hans by his owner.

3. Answers to math problems were given by taps from the horse's hoofs.

4. Many people suspected some kind of fraud.

5. Two zoologists and a horse trainer were called in to investigate by the people who doubted Hans's talents.

6. Even with Hans's master out of the horse's sight, Hans still provided perfect answers to every question.

7. A young psychologist still entertained doubts.

8. People who did not know the answers to the problems were used by the psychologist to ask Hans questions.

9. The math test was failed by Clever Hans.

10. Apparently Clever Hans had been reading small, subconscious human gestures that indicated the correct answers.

ANSWERS AND COVERAGE: EXERCISE 8-11

Rewrites may vary somewhat from the possibilities shown here. Coverage is five passive to active sentences; five active to passive sentences.

1. Active; rewrite in passive: Around the turn of the century, a story about a clever horse was carried by Berlin newspapers.

2. Passive; rewrite in active: The horse's owner named him Clever Hans.

3. Passive; rewrite in active: The horse gave answers to math problems by tapping his hoofs.

4. Active; rewrite in passive: Fraud was suspected by many people.

5. Passive; rewrite in active: People who doubted Hans's talents called in two zoologists and a horse trainer to investigate.

6. Active; rewrite in passive: Even with Hans's master out of the horse's sight, perfect answers to every question were still provided by Hans.

7. Active; rewrite in passive: Doubts were still entertained by a young psychologist.

8. Passive; rewrite in active: The psychologist used people who did not know the answers to the problems to ask Hans questions.

9. Passive; rewrite in active: Clever Hans failed the math test.

10. Active; rewrite in passive: Apparently small, subconscious human gestures that indicated the correct answers had been read by Clever Hans.

Focus on Revising

REVISING YOUR WRITING

If you have trouble with your verbs when you write, including unnecessary use of the passive voice, go back to your writing and locate the problems. Using this chapter as a resource, revise your writing to correct these kinds of problems: *-s* endings (see 8c); *-ed* endings (see 8d); auxiliary verbs (see 8e); transitive and intransitive verbs, including lie and lay (see 8f); tenses (see 8g–8j); tense sequences (see 8k); the subjunctive mood (see 8l–8m); active versus passive voice (see 8n–8o).

CASE STUDY: REVISING TO ELIMINATE VERB ERRORS

In these case studies, you can observe a student writer revising. Then, you have the chance to revise other student writing on your own.

Observation

A student wrote the following draft for a course called Popular Culture. The assignment called for choosing one year in which important contributions were made to popular culture in the United States and then writing about it. While this paragraph is well organized and offers good examples to support its topic, the draft's effectiveness is diminished by the presence of errors in verb forms and verb tense, and by the unnecessary use of the passive.

Read through the draft. The verb errors are highlighted and explained. Before you look at the student's revision, revise the material yourself. Then compare what you and the student did.

unneeded passive voice: 8n

A number of important contributions in the year 1925 likely will be agreed upon by anyone who has studied popular culture in the United States. The

-ed missing: 8d

Charleston, a dance most often associate with the 1920s, had become popular in 1925. Along

past perfect tense used; need simple past: 8i

present tense used; need simple past: 8h

with the new dance comes a new fashion trend. If a woman

COVERAGE: PARTICIPATION ESSAY, page 223–224

At election time, government leaders and the media always *encouraged* [8h: simple present needed] citizens to exercise one of their most basic rights: the right to

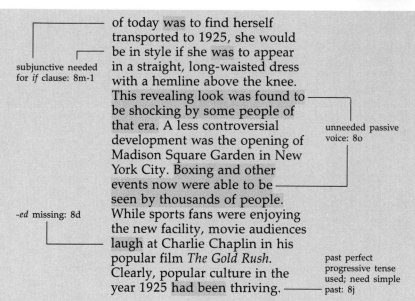

subjunctive needed for *if* clause: 8m-1

of today was to find herself transported to 1925, she would be in style if she was to appear in a straight, long-waisted dress with a hemline above the knee. This revealing look was found to be shocking by some people of that era. A less controversial development was the opening of Madison Square Garden in New York City. Boxing and other events now were able to be seen by thousands of people. While sports fans were enjoying the new facility, movie audiences laugh at Charlie Chaplin in his popular film *The Gold Rush.* Clearly, popular culture in the year 1925 had been thriving.

unneeded passive voice: 8o

-ed missing: 8d

past perfect progressive tense used; need simple past: 8j

Here is how the student revised the material to eliminate the verb errors. In revising from the unneeded passive voice to the active voice, the student had alternatives in word choice. Your revisions into the active voice might differ in wording from the student's.

Anyone who has studied popular culture in the United States likely will agree upon a number of important contributions in the year 1925. The Charleston, a dance most often associated with the 1920s, became popular in 1925. Along with the new dance came a new fashion trend. If a woman of today were to find herself transported to 1925, she would be in style if she were to appear in a straight, long-waisted dress with a hemline above the knee. Some people of that era found this revealing look shocking. A less controversial development was the opening of Madison Square Garden in New York City. Thousands of people could now see boxing and other events. While sports fans were enjoying this new facility, movie audiences laughed at Charlie Chaplin in his popular film *The Gold Rush.* Clearly, popular culture in the year 1925 was thriving.

Participation

A student wrote the following draft for a course called Introduction to Women's Studies. The assignment was to write a brief report ➡

COVERAGE PARTICIPATION
ESSAY, *continued*

vote. How many young women today realize that until the Nineteenth Amendment to the United States Constitution *was approve* [8d: -ed needed] in 1920, women in the United States were *deny* [8d: -[*i*]ed needed] the right to vote?

In the 1830s, almost a century before the Nineteenth Amendment was approved, *the battle for women's rights was being waged by Elizabeth Cady Stanton and other leading women.* [8o: unneeded passive voice] In 1848, the first women's rights convention *take* [8h: present tense used; need simple past of irregular verb] place in Seneca Falls, New York. Stanton *rises* [8f: present tense of intransitive verb used; simple past needed] to the occasion and produced what was *call* [8d: -ed needed] "A Declaraton of Sentiments." Its inspiration *lays* [8f: -*s* form of transitive verb used; past tense of intransitive verb needed] in the Declaration of Independence, but it revealed one shortcoming in Thomas Jefferson's language. Instead of the words "all men are created equal," Stanton's document *proclaim* [8d: -ed needed] that "all men and women are created equal."

Later, Stanton *was working* [8j: past progressive form used; simple present needed] to convince California Senator Aaron Sargeant to propose a constitutional amendment that would give women the vote. *It was introduced to the U.S. Congress by him in 1878.* [8o: unneeded passive voice] Forty years later the amendment was approved, but Stanton never *seen* [8d: past participle of irregular verb used; simple past needed] the victory because she died eighteen years before the amendment became law. Her legacy lives and should be remembered by all women when the time *come* [8c: simple present used; -*s* form needed] to vote.

ANSWER: PARTICIPATION ESSAY

This version revises the errors in verb forms and verb tense and the unnecessary use of the passive voice. Answers might vary slightly, especially in the revisions of the passives. Also, answers will vary if students have revised for content, organization, or style.

At election time, government leaders and the media always encourage citizens to exercise one of their most basic rights: the right to vote. How many young women today realize that until the Nineteenth Amendment to the United States Constitution was approved in 1920, women in the United States were denied the right to vote?

In the 1830s, almost a century before the Nineteenth Amendment was approved, Elizabeth Cady Stanton and other leading women waged the battle for women's rights. In 1848, the first women's rights convention took place in Seneca Falls, New York. Stanton rose to the occasion and produced what was called "A Declaration of Sentiments." Its inspiration lay in the Declaration of Independence, but it revealed one shortcoming in Thomas Jefferson's language. Instead of the words "all men are created equal," Stanton's document proclaimed that "all men and women are created equal."

Later, Stanton convinced California Senator Aaron Sargeant to propose a constitutional amendment that would give women the vote. He introduced it to the U.S. Congress in 1878. Forty years later the amendment was approved, but Stanton never saw the victory because she died eighteen years before the amendment became law. Her legacy lives and should be remembered by all women when the time comes to vote.

about a significant contribution to society in the United States. The material is concise and logical, but the draft's effectiveness is diminished by errors in verb forms and verb tense and by the unnecessary use of the passive voice.

Read through the draft. Then revise it to eliminate the errors. Also, make any additional revisions you think would improve the content, organization, and style of the material.

At election time, government leaders and the media always encouraged citizens to exercise one of their most basic rights: the right to vote. How many young women today realize that until the Nineteenth Amendment to the United States Constitution was approve in 1920, women in the United States were deny the right to vote?

In the 1830s, almost a century before the Nineteenth Amendment was approved, the battle for women's rights was being waged by Elizabeth Cady Stanton and other leading women. In 1848, the first women's rights convention take place in Seneca Falls, New York. Stanton rises to the occasion and produced what was call "A Declaration of Sentiments." Its inspiration lays in the Declaration of Independence, but it revealed one shortcoming in Thomas Jefferson's language. Instead of the words "all men are created equal," Stanton's document proclaim that "all men and women are created equal."

Later, Stanton was working to convince California Senator Aaron Sargeant to propose a constitutional amendment that would give women the vote. It was introduced to the U.S. Congress by him in 1878. Forty years later the amendment was approved, but Stanton never seen the victory because she died eighteen years before the amendment became law. Her legacy lives and should be remembered by all women when the time come to vote.

9 Case of Nouns and Pronouns

9a Understanding case

Case refers to the different forms that nouns° and pronouns° take to deliver information. Case communicates how the noun or pronoun relates to other words in a sentence.

Nouns "show" case only in the possessive, by the use of the apostrophe (see Chapter 27) or by an *of* construction. Pronouns have three cases: subjective case, objective case, and possessive case.

Personal pronouns, the most common type of pronouns, have a full range of cases that show changes in **person** (first, second, and third person) and **number** (singular and plural). For more about the concepts of person and number, see Chart 78 in section 11a.

CASES OF PERSONAL PRONOUNS   71

	SUBJECTIVE		OBJECTIVE		POSSESSIVE	
PERSON	SING.	PLUR.	SING.	PLUR.	SING.	PLUR.
FIRST	I	we	me	us	my/mine	our/ours
SECOND	you	you	you	you	your/yours	your/yours
THIRD	he she it	they	him her it	them	his her/hers its	their/theirs

A pronoun in the **subjective case** functions as a subject°.

We were going to get married. [*We* is the subject.]

John and **I** wanted an inexpensive band to play at our wedding. [*I* is part of the compound subject *John and I.*]

He and **I** found a one-person band we could afford. [*He* and *I* are compound subjects.]

A pronoun in the **objective case** functions as a direct object°, an indirect object°, or the object of a preposition°.

We saw **him** perform in a public park. [*Him* is the direct object.]

We showed **him** our budget. [*Him* is the indirect object.]

We understood each other and shook hands with **him.** [*Him* is the object of the preposition *with.*]

A pronoun in the **possessive case** indicates possession or ownership. For a discussion of the possessive case before gerunds, see 9h. ❖ PUNCTUATION ALERT: Do not use an apostrophe for a personal pronoun in the possessive case (see 27b). ❖

The **musician's** contract was in the mail the next day. [*Musician's,* a noun in the possessive case, indicates ownership.]

Our signatures quickly went on the contract. [*Our,* a pronoun in the possessive case, indicates possession.]

His was entered soon after. [*His,* a pronoun in the possessive case, indicates ownership and also implies the inclusion of the noun *signature.*]

The pronouns **who** and **whoever** also change form for case changes, as explained in 9e.

9b   Using the same cases for pronouns in compound constructions as in single constructions

A compound construction contains more than one subject° or object°.

He saw the eclipse of the sun. [single subject]

He and **I** saw the eclipse of the sun. [compound subject]

That eclipse astonished **us.** [single object]

That eclipse astonished **him** and **me.** [compound object]

A compound construction has no effect on the choice of pronoun case. A compound subject uses the subjective case, and a compound object uses the objective case. Sometimes, however, people make the mistake of switching cases for compounds. If you are ever unsure which case to use, try the "drop test."

Temporarily drop all of the compound elements *except* the pronoun in question, and then follow the steps in Chart 72.

TEST FOR COMPOUND SUBJECTS		72
EXAMPLE	**Janet and (me, I)** read that the moon has one-eightieth the mass of the earth.	
DROP	Janet and	
TEST	Which reads correctly: "**Me** read that the moon has one-eightieth the mass of the earth" or "**I** read that the moon has one-eightieth the mass of the earth"?	
ANSWER	**I**	

This "drop test" works also when both parts of the compound subject are pronouns: *She and I* [not *Her and me*] *read that the moon has one-eightieth the mass of the earth.* The same "drop test" works for compound objects, as shown in Chart 73.

TEST FOR COMPOUND OBJECTS		73
EXAMPLE	The instructor told **Janet and (I, me)** that the moon has one-fiftieth the volume of the earth.	
DROP	Janet and	
TEST	Which reads correctly: "The instructor told **I** that the moon has one-fiftieth the volume of the earth" or "The instructor told **me** that the moon has one-fiftieth the volume of the earth"?	
ANSWER	**me**	

BACKGROUND ON LANGUAGE

Joseph M. Williams explains in *Origins of the English Language* (New York: Free Press, 1975, 248–49) that changes in the second-person singular pronouns (subjective and objective cases) are rooted in the Roman Empire of the fourth century A.D. At that time there were two emperors, one in Rome and one in Constantinople. People speaking to either emperor were required to use the plural form of address. The practice of using the plural as a sign of respect slowly spread to France, where *tu* is the second-person singular pronoun and *vous* the plural. During the thirteenth century, in imitation of the *tu/vous* of the French nobles who occupied their country, the English began using *thee* (objective), *thou* (subjective), and *you* the same way. *You* became a mark of mutual respect in conversations among the elite and a sign of deference when a person spoke to a social superior. In contrast, *thee/thou* became a sign of intimacy among members of the same family or among those who believed in the same things.

TEACHING TIP

The "drop test" can be more effective if students are given both oral and written activities in which they are asked not only to select correct pronouns from prepared sentences but also to generate their own sentences using pronouns as parts of compounds.

This "drop test" works also when both parts of the compound object are pronouns: *The instructor told **her** and **me*** [not ***she** and **I***] *that the moon has one-fiftieth the volume of the earth.*

These principles apply to all sequences of pronouns (for example, the rules that govern *her and me* apply also to *me and her*). Also, when you write compound constructions that contain pronouns, do not commingle pronouns in the subjective case with pronouns in the objective case: for example, neither *him and I* (objective and subjective) nor *she and me* (subjective and objective).

When pronouns in a prepositional phrase° are compound, do not allow pronouns to slip into the wrong case. A prepositional phrase always has an object°, so any pronouns that follow words such as *to, with, from,* and *for* must be in the objective case.

NO	The instructor gave an assignment **to Sam and I.** [*To* is a preposition; *I* is in the subjective case and cannot follow a preposition.]
YES	The instructor gave an assignment **to Sam and me.** [*To* is a preposition; *me* is in the objective case, so it is correct.]
NO	The instructor spoke **with he and I.** [*With* is a preposition; both *he* and *I* are in the subjective case and cannot follow a preposition.]
NO	The instructor spoke **with him and I.** [*With* is a preposition; *him* is in the objective case, so it is correct. *I* is in the subjective case and cannot follow a preposition.]
YES	The instructor spoke **with him and me.** [*With* is a preposition; *him* and *me* are both in the objective case, so this construction is correct.]

Between is a preposition that frequently leads people to pronoun error. A pronoun after *between*, like those after other prepositions, must always be in the objective case.

NO	The instructor divided the work **between Sam and I.** [*Between* is a preposition; *I* is in the subjective case and cannot follow a preposition.]
YES	The instructor divided the work **between Sam and me.** [*Between* is a preposition; *me* is in the objective case, so it is correct.]

If you are in doubt when you use pronouns in prepositional phrases use the "drop test" for compound objects in Chart 73.

EXERCISE 9-1

Consulting section 9b, select the correct pronoun from each pair in parentheses and write it in the blank.

EXAMPLE   A friend who works with (I, me) __me__ decided to have her eyes examined.

Both ¹(her, she) _____ and her supervisor agreed that she should make an appointment to see an eye doctor. She asked ²(me, I) _____ to help her find a good opthalmologist. ³(We, Us) _____ two together searched through the telephone yellow pages. The name "Dr. John Bright" looked promising, so ⁴(she and me, her and me, she and I, her and I) _____ called ⁵(he, him) _____ . When the time for her appointment came, my friend had to leave work early, and she asked ⁶(we, us) _____ to answer her telephone. Another of our sales representatives and ⁷(I, me) _____ were able to cover all her calls. When my friend returned, she asked ⁸(him and me, him and I, he and I) _____ for her messages. Curious, ⁹(we, us) _____ asked how her doctor visit went. She laughed and said, "Between you and ¹⁰(I, me) _____ Dr. Bright needs to change his approach." Then she explained to ¹¹(us, we) _____ that the doctor had asked ¹²(her, she) _____ whether she had trouble threading needles or reading recipes. "No," she had told ¹³(he, him) _____ "but I do have difficulty reading the fine print in *The Wall Street Journal*."

Matching noun and pronoun cases

When *we* (subjective case) occurs with a noun, the noun must be functioning as a subject°; when *us* (objective case) occurs with a noun, the noun must be functioning as an object°. The "drop test" in 9b can be adapted here. Temporarily drop the noun following the pronoun and test which pronoun reads correctly.

EXAMPLE	**(We, Us)** tennis players practice hard.
TEST	**Us** practice hard. **We** practice hard.
ANSWER	**We** tennis players practice hard. [*Tennis players* is the subject, so the pronoun must be in the subjective case.]
EXAMPLE	Our coach tells **(we, us)** tennis players to practice hard.
TEST	Our coach tells **we** to practice hard. Our coach tells **us** to practice hard.
ANSWER	Our coach tells **us** tennis players to practice hard. [*Tennis players* is the object, so the pronoun must be in the objective case.]

ANSWERS AND COVERAGE:
EXERCISE 9-1

1. she [subj. case]
2. me [obj. case]
3. We [subj. case]
4. she and I [subj. case]
5. him [obj. case]
6. whoever [subj. case]
7. I [subj. case]
8. him and me [obj. case]
9. we [subj. case]
10. me [obj. case]
11. us [obj. case]
12. her [obj. case]
13. him [obj. case]

BACKGROUND

In *Talkin and Testifyin: The Language of Black America* (Boston: Houghton Mifflin, 1977; rpt. Wayne State UP, 1986), Geneva Smitherman-Donaldson writes that the cases of personal pronouns in Black English are not as differentiated as in Standard English:

> Thus, for example, with the third person plural pronoun, *they*, the same form serves for subject, possessive, and so-called reflexive as in *The expressway bought they house* and *They should do it theyselves*. In the case of the third person singular pronoun, *he*, we will hear both *He gone* and *Him cool*, and in the reflexive, *He did it all by hisself*. At an earlier stage in the development of Black English, forms like *he book* (for *his book*) and *she house* (for *her house*) were prominent, but these have gradually disappeared. (29)

EXTRA EXERCISE A

From the pronouns in parentheses, select the correct one and circle it.

1. My friend and (I, me) agreed long ago that we would someday take a romantic ocean cruise together.

2. (We, Us) and a few friends would sail the legendary seas and dock at exotic ports.

3. Together, (they, them) and (we, us) would shop in the mysterious bazaars of ancient cultures and eat the spicy foods of distant lands.

4. Unfortunately, an unexpected misfortune was visited on (she, her) and (I, me).

5. (She, her) and (I, me) both discovered that we had chicken pox on the day we were to leave.

6. Instead of visiting romantic places, the romantic places visited (she, her) and (I, me).

7. Our friend Tom gave (we, us) travel books with pictures of the many places we longed to see.

8. They were the same books someone had given (he, him) when he missed his trip to Mexico.

9. I guess (we, us) will have to give them to (whoever, whomever) can't make the next scheduled vacation trip.

ANSWERS TO EXTRA EXERCISE A

1. I
2. We
3. they, we
4. her, me
5. She, I
6. her, me
7. us
8. him
9. we, whoever

The same principles hold when pronouns occur in an **appositive**—a word or group of words that renames the noun or noun phrase° preceding it. The "drop test" in 9b can be adapted here. Temporarily drop the noun and test which pronoun reads correctly.

EXAMPLE	The winners, **(she, her)** and **(I, me),** advanced to the finals.
TEST	The winners, **her** and **me,** advanced to the finals. [*Her* and *me* rename the subject, *the winners,* so objective pronouns are incorrect.]
ANSWER	The winners, **she** and **I,** advanced to the finals.

9d Using the subjective case of pronouns after linking verbs

A **linking verb** connects a subject° to a word that renames it. Linking verbs indicate a state of being (*am, is, are, was, were,* etc.), relate to the senses (*look, smell, taste, sound, feel*), or indicate a condition (*appear, seem, become, grow, turn, remain,* and *prove*).

Because a pronoun coming after any linking verb renames the subject, the pronoun must be in the subjective case.

The contest winner was **I.** [*I* renames *the contest winner,* the subject, so the subjective case is required.]

The ones who will benefit are **they** and **I.** [*They* and *I* rename *the ones who will benefit,* the subject, so the subjective case is required.]

May I please speak to Guy? This is **he.** [*He* renames *this,* the subject, so the subjective case is required.]

Who is there? It is **I.** [*I* renames *it,* the subject, so the subjective case is required.]

In speech and informal writing, the objective case is sometimes substituted in the constructions shown in the last two examples above. In academic writing, always use the subjective case in such constructions.

EXERCISE 9-2

Consulting sections 9a through 9d, select the correct pronoun of each pair in parentheses and write it in the blank.

EXAMPLE   The two of you have suggested that (we, us) **we** roommates all have sausage and mushroom pizza for dinner tonight.

After much discussion, Kari and [1](I, me) _____ have reached a decision. We thought carefully about what you and Saroya have asked Kari and [2](I, me) _____ to do, because it is [3](we, us) _____ who have to live with [4](you and she, you and her) _____ for the rest of the semester. Because Kari hates mushrooms and I hate sausage, this proposal has no appeal whatsoever for either [5](she, her) _____ or [6](I, me) _____. We have now thought of a compromise that should satisfy you two as well as [7](we, us) _____. Tell Saroya that tonight's pizza eaters can certainly be you and [8](she, her)_____, but hamburgers are on the menu for Kari and [9](I, me)_____.

9e   Using *who*, *whoever*, *whom*, and *whomever*

The pronouns *who* and *whoever* are in the subjective case. The pronouns *whom* and *whomever* are in the objective case. They do not change form.

1   Using *who*, *whoever*, *whom*, and *whomever* in dependent clauses

CASES OF RELATIVE AND INTERROGATIVE PRONOUNS		74
SUBJECTIVE	**OBJECTIVE**	**POSSESSIVE**
who whoever	whom whomever	whose ---------

Pronouns such as *who, whoever, whom,* and *whomever* start many **dependent clauses°**. To determine what pronoun case is correct in a dependent clause, you need to find out whether the pronoun is functioning as a subject° or an object° in its own clause. Because informal spoken English tends to blur distinctions between *who* and *whom*, some writers cannot rely entirely on what sounds right.

To check your use of *who* and *whom*, adapt the "drop test" in 9b. Temporarily drop everything in the sentence up to the pronoun in question, and then make substitutions. Remember that *he, she, they, who,* and *whoever* are subjects, and *him, her, them, whom,* and *whomever* (the *-m* forms and *her*) are objects.

QUOTATION ABOUT WRITING

For my money we should get rid of "whom" (and "whomever" and "whomsoever") completely, irrevocably, immediately. Whom and the like are show-off words, painstakingly crafted to let you know you are in the company of a superior being. But more often than not they get in the way—of meaning, of style, of the natural flow of language . . .

Whom is unnatural in everyday speech.

For whom are you looking? Well, well, whom have we here? It's not what you know but whom you know. I forgot whom I was going to see. All these constructions are right, but that is about all they have going for them.

Real English doesn't take this guff. It laughs off a stiff, labored sentence like "For whom are you looking?" and says instead, "Who're you looking for?" There is no confusion here about who is who.

—John Allemang, "The Objectionable Pronoun," *The Toronto Globe and Mail*, June 30, 1990

TEST FOR *WHO*/*WHOM* IN SUBJECTIVE CASE	75
EXAMPLE	I wondered **(who, whom)** would vote.
DROP	I wondered
TEST	Try *he* and *him* (or *she* and *her*): "**He** would vote" or "**Him** would vote."
ANSWER	**He.** Therefore, because *he* is subjective, *who*, which is also the subjective, is correct: "I wondered **who** would vote."

The subjective case is called for even when expressions such as *I think* or *he says* come between the subject and verb. Ignore these expressions in determining the correct pronoun: *She is the candidate who [I think] will get my vote.* The same four-step "drop test" works for *whoever*:

> Voter registration drives attempt to enroll **whoever** is eligible to vote. ["**He** (not *him*) is eligible to vote" proves that the subjective case of **whoever** is needed.]

TEST FOR *WHO*/*WHOM* IN OBJECTIVE CASE	76
EXAMPLE	Volunteers go to senior citizen centers hoping to enroll people **(who, whom)** others have ignored.
DROP	Volunteers go to senior citizen centers hoping to enroll people.
TEST	Try *they* and *them* at the end of the sentence: "Others have ignored **they**" or "Others have ignored **them**."
ANSWER	**Them.** Therefore, because *them* is objective, *whom*, which is also objective, is correct: "Volunteers go to senior citizen centers hoping to enroll people **whom** others have ignored."

The same four-step "drop test" works for *whomever:*

> The senior citizens can vote for **whomever** they wish. ["The senior citizens can vote for **him** (not *he*)" proves that the objective case of **whomever** is needed.]

2 | Using *who* and *whom* in questions

At the beginning of questions, use *who* if the question is about the subject° and *whom* if the question is about the object°. To determine whether the case is subjective or objective, recast the question into a statement using *she* or *her* (or *he* or *him*).

> **Who** watched the space shuttle lift-off? ["*I* watched the space shuttle lift-off" uses the subjective pronoun *I. Who* is therefore correct.]
>
> Are those the people **who** are visiting from Kenya? ["*They* are visiting from Kenya" uses the subjective pronoun *they. Who* is therefore correct.]
>
> Ann admires **whom**? ["Ann admires *her*" uses the objective pronoun *her. Whom* is correct.]
>
> **Whom** does Ann admire? ["Ann admires *her*" uses the objective pronoun *her. Whom* is therefore correct.]
>
> To **whom** does Ann speak about becoming an astronaut? ["Ann speaks to *them* about becoming an astronaut" uses the objective pronoun *them. Whom* is therefore correct.]

EXERCISE 9-3

Consulting section 9e, select the correct pronoun of each pair in parentheses and write it in the blank.

EXAMPLE   Is there an age group of children (who, whom) __who__ do not tell lies?

If the word *liar* means ¹(whoever, whomever) _____ makes false statements with the intent to deceive, then even three- and four-year-olds fit the definition. Studies show that young children will lie to ²(whoever, whomever) _____ they think might be angered by the truth. Because young children may not define lying the way adults do, ³(whoever, whomever) _____ the child considers to have given false information may be considered a liar. For example, a parent ⁴(who, whom) _____ changes plans because of bad weather may be accused of lying by a young child. To the child ⁵(who, whom) _____ the change affects, the original statements were false and therefore the person ⁶(who, whom) _____ made them is a liar.

TEACHING TIP

If your students have trouble choosing the appropriate pronoun after *than* or *as*, you might try expanding elliptical comparisons with them to verify the best choice. Here are a few practice sentences.

1. You are taller than (I, me). [*I*]

2. Your parents are taller than (me, mine). [*mine*]

3. My brother is as short as (I, me). [*I*]

4. Your sisters are as smart as (me, mine). [*mine*]

EXTRA EXERCISE C

Circle the correct pronoun in each pair in parentheses.

1. Carl's resolution to study more is a result of (him, his) making poor grades last semester. [*his*]

2. The Dean almost required (he, him) to stay out a semester. [*him*]

3. His parents were angry about (him, his) partying too much. [*his*]

4. Not only as bright as his older brother, Carl was also as lazy as (he, him). [*he*]

5. He worked more diligently after his parents called (he, him) to see how he was doing. [*him*]

6. (Them, Their) calling was evidence that they cared about (he, him). [*Their, him*]

7. After that incident, (him, his) studying became more serious. [*his*]

EXTRA EXERCISE D

From each group of pronouns in parentheses, select the correct word.

9f **Using the pronoun case that reflects intended meaning after *than* or *as***

A sentence of comparison often can be clear even though some of the words following *than* or *as* are implied but not directly stated. For example, the word *are* does not have to be expressed at the end of this sentence: *My two-month-old Saint Bernard is larger **than** most full-grown dogs [are].*

When a pronoun follows *than* or *as*, the pronoun case carries essential information about what is being said. For example, these two sentences convey two very different messages, simply because of the choice between the words *me* and *I* after *than.*

1.   My sister loved that dog more **than me.**
2.   My sister loved that dog more **than I.**

Sentence 1 means "My sister loved that dog more *than she loved me.*" On the other hand, sentence 2 means "My sister loved that dog more *than I loved it.*" To make sure that any sentence of comparison delivers its message clearly, either include all words in the second half of a comparison or mentally fill in the words to check that you have chosen the correct pronoun case.

9g **Using the objective case when a pronoun is in an infinitive phrase**

An **infinitive** is the simple form° of a verb usually, but not always, following *to: to laugh, to dance.* Objective pronouns serve as both subjects° and objects° of infinitives.

> Our tennis coach expects **me to serve.** [The word *me* is the subject of the infinitive *to serve,* and so it is in the objective case.]
> Our tennis coach expects **him to beat me.** [The word *him* is the subject of the infinitive *to beat,* and *me* is the object of the infinitive; both are in the objective case.]

9h **Using the possessive case before gerunds**

A **gerund** is a verb's *-ing* form functioning as a noun°. (*Brisk walking is excellent exercise.*) When a noun or pronoun precedes a gerund, the possessive case is called for. (*Kim's brisk walking built up* *his stamina.* **His brisk walking** *built up his stamina.)* In contrast, a present participle—a form that also ends in *-ing*—functions as a modifier. It does not take the possessive case. (*Kim,* **walking briskly,** *caught up to me.*)

The possessive case, therefore, communicates important information. Consider these two sentences, which convey two different messages, entirely as a result of the possessive:

1. The detective noticed the **man staggering.**
2. The detective noticed the **man's staggering.**

Sentence 1 means that the detective noticed the man; sentence 2 means that the detective noticed the staggering. The same distinction applies to pronouns:

1. The detective noticed **him** staggering.
2. The detective noticed **his** staggering.

In conversation, such a distinction is often ignored, but readers of academic writing expect that information will be precise. Consider the difference in the following two examples:

| GERUND (AS SUBJECT) | The **governor's calling for a tax increase** surprised her supporters. |
| PARTICIPLE (AS MODIFIER) | The governor, **calling for a tax increase,** surprised her supporters. |

EXERCISE 9-4

Consulting sections 9f, 9g, and 9h, select the correct pronoun of each pair in parentheses and write it in the blank.

EXAMPLE   Thomas Edison had literally hundreds of bad ideas, but most people remember (him, his) __his__ creating inventions that were uniformly brilliant.

When evaluating creativity, the average person might say, "I know many people more talented than [1](I, me) _____; I do not think of [2](me, my) _____ being creative at all." What most people fail to realize is that [3](their, them) _____ being creative is a part of [4](their, them) _____ being human. Many people accept the myth that a creative person is far more gifted than [5](them, they) _____, but research shows that the ability of average human beings to adapt and survive in a changing world proves that [6](them, they) _____ are creative. Others believe the harmful myth that a creative person makes fewer mistakes than [7](them, they) _____, when, in fact, a creative

EXAMPLE

My softball teammates and (myself, me, I) are confident we will make the finals this year. [*I*]

1. I am so certain that I have already bought (me, myself) a new glove to celebrate. [*myself*]

2. Every practice session the coach tells the others and (me, myself) that we are getting better and better. [*me*]

3. The sponsor (himself, hisself), Big Al of Big Al's Used cars, even comes to games now. [*himself*]

4. The other women and (I, myself) are glad that our hard work has paid off. [*I*]

5. We had an exhibition game against our husbands, who tired (theirselves, themselves) out and lost by four runs. [*themselves*]

ANSWERS AND COVERAGE: EXERCISE 9-4

1. I [subjective case, 9f]
2. my [possessive case, 9h]
3. their [possessive case, 9h]
4. their [possessive case, 9h]
5. they [subjective case, 9f]
6. they [subjective case, 9a]
7. they [subjective case, 9f]
8. their [possessive case, 9h]
9. them [objective case, 9g]

person usually has more ideas, both good ones and bad ones, than other people. A creative person does not stop to rate ideas or to agonize over [8](their, them) _____ being accurate, but simply continues to generate [9](them, they) _____ .

9i Reserving *-self* forms of pronouns for reflexive or intensive use

A **reflexive pronoun** always uses the objective case, because this *-self* form is always the object of a verb°, a preposition°, or a verbal°. *The detective disguised **himself**. He relied on **himself** to solve the mystery.*

Intensive pronouns provide emphasis by making another word more intense in meaning: *The detective felt that his career **itself** was at stake.* In academic writing avoid nonstandard forms of reflexive and intensive pronouns: *hisself* is nonstandard for *himself; theirself, theirselves, themself,* and *themselfs* are nonstandard for *themselves.*

Do not use *-self* pronouns alone, without another noun° or pronoun° to refer to: *The detective and **I** (not *myself*) had a long talk. He wanted my partner and **me** (not *myself*) to help him.*

Focus on Revising

REVISING YOUR WRITING

If you make errors with the case of nouns and pronouns when you write, go back to your writing and locate the errors. Using this chapter as a resource, revise your writing to correct the problems.

CASE STUDY

The case study at the end of Chapter 10 offers you the chance to observe and participate in a revision that eliminates errors in pronoun case (this chapter) and pronoun reference (Chapter 10).

10 Pronoun Reference

A pronoun° always refers to a noun° or another pronoun, which is called the pronoun's **antecedent.** The term **pronoun reference** refers to this pronoun-antecedent relationship. For writing to communicate a clear message, each pronoun must relate directly to an antecedent.

Consider these sentences in which each pronoun has a clear referent.

> **Facts** do not cease to exist just because **they** are ignored.
>
> —ALDOUS HUXLEY

> I have found that the best way to give advice to **children** is to find out **what they want** and then advise **them** to do **it.**
>
> —HARRY S TRUMAN

> **I** knew a woman, lovely in **her** bones,
> When small birds sighed, **she** would sigh back at **them;**
>
> —THEODORE ROETHKE, "I Knew a Woman"

HOW TO CORRECT FAULTY PRONOUN REFERENCE 77

- Make a pronoun refer clearly to a single nearby antecedent (see 10a).
- Place pronouns close to their antecedents (see 10b).
- Make a pronoun refer to a definite antecedent (see 10c).
- Do not overuse *it* (see 10d), and reserve *you* only for direct address° (see 10e).
- Use *who, which,* and *that* correctly (see 10f).

10a Making a pronoun refer clearly to a single antecedent

When pronoun reference is unclear, the meaning gets muddled. Be sure that each pronoun that you use refers clearly to a single, nearby antecedent. If you find that you need the same pronoun to refer to more than one antecedent, revise the passage by replacing some pronouns with nouns° so that all the remaining pronouns clearly refer to a single antecedent.

NO In 1911, **Roald Amundsen** reached the South Pole just thirty-five days before **Robert F. Scott** arrived. **He** [who? Amundsen or Scott?] had told people that **he** was going to sail for the Arctic but then **he** turned south for the Antarctic. Then on the journey home, **he** [who? Amundsen or Scott?] and **his** party froze to death just a few miles from safety.

YES In 1911, **Roald Amundsen** discovered the South Pole just thirty-five days before **Robert F. Scott** arrived. **Amundsen** had told people that **he** was going to sail for the Arctic but then **he** turned south for the Antarctic. On the journey home, **Scott** and **his** party froze to death just a few miles from safety.

When you use more than one pronoun in a sentence, be sure that each has a clear antecedent.

> **Robert F. Scott** used **horses** for **his** trip to the Pole, but **they** perished quickly because **they** were not suited for travel over ice and snow.

Said and *told*, when used with pronouns that refer to more than one person, are particularly likely to create confusion for readers. Quotation marks and slight rewording can clarify meaning.

NO   Her mother told her she was going to visit Alaska.
YES Her mother told her, "You are going to visit Alaska."
YES Her mother told her, "I am going to visit Alaska."

10b Placing pronouns close to their antecedents for clarity

If too much material comes between a pronoun and its antecedent, even though they may be logically related, unclear pronoun reference results. Readers lose track of the meaning of a passage if they have to trace back too far to find the antecedent of a pronoun.

NO **Alfred Wegener,** a highly trained German meteorologist and professor of geophysics and meteorology at the University of Graz in Austria, was the first person to suggest that all the continents on earth were originally part of one large land mass. According to this theory, the supercontinent broke up long ago and the fragments drifted apart. **He** named this supercontinent Pangaea. [Although *he* can refer only to *Wegener,* too much material intervenes between the pronoun and its antecedent.]

YES **Alfred Wegener,** a highly trained German meteorologist and professor of geophysics and meteorology at the University of Graz in Austria, was the first person to suggest that all the continents on earth were originally part of one large land mass. According to his theory, the supercontinent broke up long ago and the fragments drifted apart. **Wegener** named this supercontinent Pangaea.

At the beginning of a new paragraph within an essay, many writers avoid using a pronoun to refer to a name in a prior paragraph. They prefer to repeat the name instead, particularly when the prior paragraph is long or when the subject matter is complex. Your repeating the name can help your reader follow more easily the message that you want your material to deliver.

EXERCISE 10-1

Consulting sections 10a, and 10b, revise so that each pronoun refers clearly to a nearby antecedent. Either replace pronouns with nouns or restructure the material to clarify pronoun reference.

EXAMPLE Georgia O'Keeffe's art has amazed and enlightened Americans for nearly three generations. O'Keeffe was born in 1887 and died in 1985, having lived ninety-eight years. She grew up on a farm near Sun Prairie, Wisconsin, the second of seven children. Her mother believed in the importance of her children's education. Realizing she had artistic talent, she took her to a nearby town for art lessons.

(Here is one acceptable revision for the last sentence: *Realizing that O'Keeffe had artistic talent, her mother took her to a nearby town for art lessons.*)

A HUMOROUS NOTE

Carelessly placed pronouns can result in some unintentionally funny statements, as Richard Lederer demonstrates in *Anguished English* (Wyrick and Company, 1987). Consider the difference between what the writers of the following sentences meant to say and what they really said.

1. Anti-nuclear protestors released live cockroaches inside the White House Friday, and these were arrested when they left and blocked a security gate.

2. My mother wants to have the dog's tail operated on again, and if it doesn't heal this time, she'll have to be put away.

3. About two years ago, a wart appeared on my left hand, which I wanted removed.

4. Guilt, vengeance, and bitterness can be emotionally destructive to you and your children. You must get rid of them.

ANSWERS: EXERCISE 10-1

Answers may vary somewhat. Some students may think that some of the pronouns replaced here with nouns are acceptable, but clarity is the issue—avoiding intervening information that distracts the reader, ambiguous references, and so on. Possible answers follow.

By the time Georgia O'Keeffe was twelve, she told a friend that she had made up her mind about her future. O'Keeffe was determined to become an artist. When she grew up, she attended art school in Chicago and then in New York City. Later, she spent two years as a commercial artist and then held a teaching job in Texas. The landscape of Texas impressed her deeply.

In 1916 O'Keeffe sent some charcoal drawings to a woman friend in New York. The friend took them to the renowned art dealer Alfred Stieglitz, who was astounded by O'Keeffe's talent. Stieglitz fell in love first with O'Keeffe's drawings, then with her letters, and finally with her. In 1924 Stieglitz and O'Keeffe were married, although she never wore a wedding ring or used the name "Mrs. Stieglitz."

Because O'Keeffe wanted to return to the landscapes of the Southwest, she began spending her summers alone at a ranch in New Mexico. She spent her winters in New York with her husband. In New Mexico, her work flourished. She was inspired by the spectacular cliffs, bleached animal bones, and constantly changing skies of that region of the United States. After Stieglitz died, O'Keeffe moved permanently to the area of Santa Fe, New Mexico.

By the time Georgia O'Keeffe was twelve, she told a friend that she had made up her mind about her future. She was determined to become an artist. When she grew up, she attended art school in Chicago and then in New York City. Later, she spent two years as a commercial artist and then held a teaching job in Texas. The landscape of Texas impressed her deeply.

In 1916 she sent some charcoal drawings to a woman friend in New York. She took them to the renowned art dealer Alfred Stieglitz, who was astounded by her talent. He fell in love first with her drawings, then with her letters, and finally with her. In 1924 he and she were married, although she never wore a wedding ring or used the name "Mrs. Stieglitz."

Because she wanted to return to the landscapes of the Southwest, she began spending her summers alone at a ranch in New Mexico. She spent her winters in New York with him. In New Mexico, her work flourished. She was inspired by the spectacular cliffs, bleached animal bones, and constantly changing skies of that region of the United States. After he died, she moved permanently to the area of Santa Fe, New Mexico.

10c Making a pronoun refer to a definite antecedent

1 Not using a pronoun to refer to a noun's possessive form

A noun's possessive form cannot be the antecedent° to a pronoun, unless the pronoun is also in the possessive case.

NO	The **geologist's** discovery brought **him** fame. [The pronoun *him* is not possessive and therefore cannot refer to the possessive *geologist's*.]
YES	The **geologist** became famous because of **his** discovery.
YES	The **geologist's** discovery was **his** alone.

2 Not using a pronoun to refer to an adjective

An adjective° cannot be an antecedent. A pronoun, therefore, cannot refer to an adjective.

NO	Avery likes to study **geological** records. **That** will be her major. [*That* cannot refer to the adjective *geological.*]
YES	Avery likes to study **geological** records. **Geology** will be her major.

3   Making *it, that, this,* and *which* refer to only one antecedent

When you use *it, that, this,* and *which,* check to see that the referent of these pronouns can be determined easily by your readers.

NO	Comets usually fly by the earth at 100,000 m.p.h., whereas asteroids sometimes collide with the earth. **This** interests scientists. [Does *this* refer to the speed of the comets, comets flying by the earth, or asteroids colliding with the earth?]
YES	Comets usually fly by the earth at 100,000 m.p.h., whereas asteroids sometimes collide with the earth. **This difference** interests scientists. [Adding a noun after *this* or *that* is an effective way to make your meaning clear.]
NO	A fireball, caused by the impact of either a comet or an asteroid, rose twelve miles somewhere above central Siberia in 1908, but **it** is still unknown. [Does *it* refer to the cause of the fireball or its size and location?]
YES	A fireball, caused by the impact of either a comet or an asteroid, rose twelve miles above central Siberia in 1908, but **the source of the explosion** is still unknown.
NO	I told my friends that I was going to major in geology, **which** annoyed my parents. [What does *which* refer to?]
YES	My parents were annoyed because I discussed my major with my friends.
YES	My parents were annoyed because I chose to major in geology.

4   Using *they* and *it* precisely

The expression *they say* cannot take the place of stating precisely who is doing the saying. Your reader is entitled to more than a *they* to provide authority for a statement.

BACKGROUND

Pronoun reference errors can have several causes. Sometimes the errors occur when students try to improve a sentence in revision without paying attention to how the changes affect the relationship between a pronoun and its referent. Sometimes, as Mina Shaughnessy writes in *Errors and Expectations* (New York: Oxford UP, 1977, p. 114), errors in pronoun reference and agreement are signs of problems a student has with perception, with keeping track of what he or she has written in previous sentences and clauses. Shaughnessy also points out that the impersonal conventions of much academic writing compared to other kinds of writing also make pronoun reference errors more likely. Analytical style often "pushes writers out of reportage (description and narration), where experience grounds their generalizations, into vaguer statements about a *person* or *they* or *one*, which are more difficult to control, or even care about."

TEACHING TIP

In *Teaching One-to-One: The Writing Conference* (NCTE, 1986), Muriel Harris describes several methods for helping students with pronoun reference problems in their papers. (1) Have students circle each pronoun and draw a line to the antecedent. (2) Ask the student to clarify the meaning of a pronoun that has a vague antecedent. (3) React as a reader to confusing pronouns by pointing out the different possible meanings that the pronoun could have. "After a few rounds of this," Harris writes, "most students eventually begin to anticipate reader problems with their pronouns" (132).

NO	**They** say that earthquakes are becoming more frequent.
YES	**Seismologists** say that earthquakes are becoming more frequent.

   In speech, common statements are *It said on the radio* or *In Washington they say*. Because such expressions are inexact and wordy, they should be avoided in academic writing: ***The newspaper reports*** [not *It said in the newspaper*] *that minor earthquakes occur almost daily in* California.

5	**Not using a pronoun in the first sentence of a work to refer to the work's title**

   When referring to a title, repeat or reword whatever part of the title you want to use.

TITLE	Geophysics as a Major

FIRST SENTENCE

NO	This subject unites the sciences of physics, biology, and ancient life.
YES	Geophysics unites the sciences of physics, biology, and ancient life.

10d Not overusing *it*

It has three different uses in English.

1. *It* is a personal pronoun: *Doug wants to visit the 18-inch Schmidt telescope, but **it** is on Mount Palomar.*
2. *It* is an expletive, a word that postpones the subject: ***It is*** *interesting to observe the stars.*
3. *It* is part of idiomatic expressions of weather, time, or distance: ***It is sunny. It is midnight. It*** *is not far to the hotel.*

All of these uses are acceptable, but combining them in the same sentence can create confusion.

NO	Because our car was overheating, **it** came as no surprise that **it** broke down just as **it** began to rain. [*It* is overused here even though all three uses—2, 1, and 3 above, respectively—are acceptable.]
YES	**It** came as no surprise that our overheating car broke down just as the rain began to fall.

See section 16a-1 for advice about revising wordy sentences that use expletive structures, and see section 11f for advice about using singular verbs with *it* expletives.

10e   Using *you* only for direct address

In academic writing, *you* is not a suitable substitute for specific words that refer to people, situations, and occurrences. Exact language is always preferable. Also, *you* used for other than direct address tends to lead to wordiness. This handbook uses *you* to address you directly as the reader; it never uses *you* to refer to people in general.

NO	Uprisings in prison often occur when **you allow** overcrowded conditions to continue. [Are you, the reader of this handbook, allowing the conditions to continue?]
YES	Uprisings in prison often occur when **the authorities allow** overcrowded conditions to occur.
NO	In many states, **you have your prisons** with few rehabilitation programs. [Do you, the reader, have few programs? Also, are the prisons yours?]
YES	In many states, **prisons have** few rehabilitation programs.
NO	In Russia **you** usually have to stand in long lines to buy groceries. [Are you, the reader, planning to do your grocery shopping in Russia?]
YES	**Russian consumers** usually have to stand in long lines to buy groceries.

EXERCISE 10-2

Consulting sections 10a to 10e, rewrite each sentence so that all pronoun references are clear. If you consider a passage correct as written, circle its number.

EXAMPLE   They say that slips of the tongue happen to everyone.

Psychologists say that slips of the tongue happen to everyone. (Revision avoids imprecise use of *they say*.)

1. It is interesting to note that it is thought that slips of the tongue might be the result of more than merely momentary mental lapses.
2. Sigmund Freud's theories include what he thought about the connection between slips of the tongue and unconscious thoughts.
3. Most psychologists agree, however, that a simple slip does not indicate that you are covering up deeply hidden secrets.

BACKGROUND

The usefulness of pronouns is clearly demonstrated by W. Nelson Francis and Henry Kucera in their *Frequency Analysis of English Usage* (Boston: Houghton, Mifflin, 1982). After analyzing a substantial body of publications in Edited American English, Francis and Kucera determined the frequency with which specific words are used. They report that when compared with other words, the following pronouns were ranked as follows in frequency of usage.

Word	Rank
he	10
it	12
his	15
I	20
they	30
you	33
she	37
we	41
him	42

ANSWERS: EXERCISE 10-2

Answers will vary somewhat. Here is one set of possibilities.

1. Interestingly, slips of the tongue might be the result of more than merely momentary mental lapses. (Revision eliminates overuse of *it*.)

2. Sigmund Freud developed theories about the connection between slips of the tongue and unconscious thoughts. (Revision eliminates the pronoun *be* referring to a noun in the possessive case.)

3. Most psychologists agree, however, that simple slips do not indicate that a person is covering up deeply hidden secrets. (Revision drops *you* because it was not used for direct address.)

ANSWERS: EXERCISE 10-2, *continued*

4. Research reports by psychologists and language experts say that ordinary slips of the tongue provide important clues about how the brain processes information. (Revision eliminates the imprecise *It says.*)

5. Correct

6. Information about slips can also be very interesting. (Revision eliminates having *it* refer to more than one antecedent.)

7. When people are suffering from anxiety, and when people have a great deal on their minds, they tend to make more slips because they are distracted. (Revision eliminates *this* referring to more than one antecedent.)

8. Correct

9. The first person to have written about slips of the tongue was the linguist Meringer, who published a book on the subject in 1895 and whose ideas helped Sigmund Freud develop a theory of the unconscious mind. (Revision clarifies who *he* refers to.)

10. People are less likely to make slips of the tongue if they do not make other kinds of slips, as forgetting people's names or bumping into things. (Revision replaces *you* not used for direct address.)

QUOTATION ABOUT WRITING

We are all apprentices in a craft where no one ever becomes a master.

—Ernest Hemingway

---

4. It says in research reports by psychologists and language experts that ordinary slips of the tongue provide important clues about how the brain processes information.

5. Understanding the slips and why they occur has scientific value.

6. It can also be very interesting.

7. When people are suffering from anxiety, and when people have a great deal on their minds, they tend to make more slips. This is the result of being distracted.

8. A slip can occur when a person uses a familiar expression of speech the meaning of which is wrong for the occasion.

9. The first person to have written about slips of the tongue was the linguist Meringer, who published a book on the subject in 1895. Sigmund Freud was helped by Meringer's ideas. He developed a theory of the unconscious mind.

10. You are less likely to make slips of the tongue if you do not make your other kinds of slips, such as forgetting people's names or bumping into things.

10f Using *who, which,* and *that* correctly

Who refers to people or to animals with names or special talents.

Theodore Roosevelt, who served from 1901 to 1909 as the twenty-sixth President of the United States, inspired the creation of the stuffed animal known as the "teddy bear."

Lassie, who was known for her intelligence and courage, was actually played by a series of male collie dogs.

Which and *that* refer to animals, things, and sometimes anonymous or collective groups of people. Some writers use *which* both for restrictive clauses (clauses that add essential information to a sentence) and for nonrestrictive clauses (clauses that could be omitted from a sentence without changing the essential meaning). Other writers reserve *which* for nonrestrictive clauses and *that* for restrictive clauses. You can follow either practice as long as you are consistent in each piece of writing. For help in distinguishing between restrictive and nonrestrictive clauses, see 24e.

The zoos **that most delight children** display newborn animals as well as animals that can be touched safely. [*That* introduces information essential for understanding which zoos are being referred to.]

Zoos, **which delight most children,** have been attracting fewer visitors each year. [*Which* introduces information that could be dropped from the sentence without changing the essential message.]

Who can be used for restrictive and nonrestrictive clauses alike.

♣ COMMA ALERT: Set off nonrestrictive clauses with commas. Do not set off restrictive clauses with commas (see 24e). ♣

EXERCISE 10-3

Consulting section 10f, fill in the blanks with *who, which,* or *that.*

EXAMPLE   Psychologists have found that most people **who** believe that the moon influences behavior actually believe that others, not they themselves, are affected by the moon.

1. Does the moon really affect human behavior? Ancient people believed the power _____ came from the moon was divine.

2. The word *lunatic,* _____ is derived from the Latin *luna,* suggests that people _____ are exposed to the moon become mad.

3. The moon, _____ has been credited by some researchers with influencing the stock market, is also thought by some experts to affect agricultural yields.

4. Some nurses _____ work in hospital delivery rooms claim it is the moon _____ stimulates labor pains to begin.

5. The moon may also affect certain groups of people, _____ include sleepwalkers and those_____suffer from migraine headaches.

ANSWERS AND COVERAGE: EXERCISE 10-3

Note: Reserving *that* for restrictive clauses and *which* for nonrestrictive clauses when the relative pronoun's referent is a thing (rather than a person) is a useful distinction. Because it is an often-ignored distinction, item 1 and the second part of item 4 show both *that* and *which* as acceptable. (Nonrestrictive relative clauses that have inanimate or nonhuman referents use *which.*)

1. that [restrictive reference to *power,* a thing; *which* is also acceptable]

2. which [nonrestrictive reference to *word lunatic,* a thing]

3. which [nonrestrictive reference to *moon,* a thing]

4. who [reference to *nurses,* people; restrictive]; that restrictive reference to *moon,* a thing; *which* is also acceptable]

5. which [nonrestrictive reference to *groups,* a thing]; who [restrictive reference to *those,* which refers to *people*]

Focus on Revising

REVISING YOUR WRITING

If you make errors in pronoun reference when you write, go back to your writing and locate the errors. Using this chapter as a resource, revise your writing to correct the problems.

CASE STUDY: REVISING TO CORRECT NOUN AND PRONOUN CASE AS WELL AS PRONOUN REFERENCE

In these case studies, you can observe a student writer revising. Then you have the chance to revise other student writing on your own.

Observation

A student wrote the following draft for a course called Twentieth-Century American History. The assignment was to write about an influential woman in American politics. This material is well organized as a narrative and offers good examples to support its topic, but the draft's effectiveness is diminished by errors in noun and pronoun case as well as in pronoun reference.

Read through the draft. The errors are highlighted and explained. Before you look at the student's revision, revise the material yourself. Then compare what you and the student did.

Few people who have grown up in the United States are unaware of Franklin Delano Roosevelt many accomplishments. Not everyone, however, knows much about one of his most valued aides and advisors: his wife Eleanor. In fact, it was her who was the strongest supporter in his decision to seek the governorship of New York as well as the presidency of the United States.

After he was stricken with polio in 1921, his legs were paralyzed. His mother, who

possessive case of noun needed: 9a

objective case used; need subjective case after linking verb: 9d

repeat noun at start of new paragraph: 10b

subjective case used; need objective case: 9e

Eleanor did not always agree with, urged Franklin to retire from politics. But Eleanor, with the approval of physicians and friends, urged him to continue with his career. Franklin listened to her, and he was elected governor of New York in 1928 and president of the United States in 1932.

should refer to a single antecedent: 10a

objective case used; calls for subjective case for correct comparison: 9f

repeat noun at start of new paragraph: 10b

As the new president's wife, she quickly showed that she cared as much about the nation as him. No sooner had her and her husband settled into the White House than she began touring the country and speaking to sharecroppers, slum dwellers, and unemployed workers. A first lady taking it upon herself to spread political messages created quite a stir across the nation. Even more unusual was her support of what were then unpopular causes, such as civil rights. This did not represent Franklin Roosevelt policy.

objective case used; need subjective case in the compound: 9a

subjective case used; need possessive case before gerund: 9h

this should refer to an antecedent of one word: 10c-3

Through lecture tours, radio broadcasts, newspaper columns, and press conferences for women reporters, she changed forever the world perception of the role of first lady of the United States.

possessive case of noun needed: opening Chapter 9

possessive case of noun needed: opening Chapter 9

antecedent too far away; repeat noun: 10b

Here is how the student revised the draft to correct errors in noun and pronoun case as well as in pronoun reference. In a few places, the student had alternatives for correcting the errors. Your revision, therefore, might not be exactly like this one, but it should deal with each error highlighted on the draft.

Few people who have grown up in the United States are unaware of Franklin Delano Roosevelt's many accomplishments.

COVERAGE: PARTICIPATION ESSAY, pages 248–249

Television programming mirrors the society that watches it. In the 1950's, *you saw* [10e: not a direct address] situation comedies with a traditional family with a father who was the breadwinner, a mother who enjoyed housekeeping, and children who were always adorable. Later, *they* [10c: pronoun should refer to a definite antecedent] replaced the traditional families seen on *Father Knows Best* and *Leave It to Beaver* with people which [10f: *who* needed] fit a broader definition of "family."

Reflecting an updated concept of family life in the 1970's, situation comedies like *All in the Family* portrayed nontraditional situations. A young couple lived with the *wife* [intro material for Chapter 9: possessive case needed for noun] parents. One spinoff from that series involved the father, his business, and him [9h: a gerund, so possessive case needed] raising a foster child alone. The long-running *Mary Tyler Moore Show* featured single women *whom* [9e: subjective case, *who* needed] were supporting themselves, raising children, and enjoying good friendships.

As working women have become the norm in society, situation comedies have changed to portray women who juggle home and career. Lead roles on situation comedies portray women as lawyers, architects, and factory workers. Some shows include unemployed husbands and husbands whose wives make more money than *them* [9f: after *than* subjective case needed for this meaning].

COVERAGE: PARTICIPATION ESSAY, *Continued*

In many ways today, however, *they* [10c: pronoun should refer to a definite antecedent] still differ from reality. In contrast to real life, most comedies show no child who is ever inconvenienced by parents or upset about *them* [9h: a gerund, so possessive case needed] working at demanding jobs. And parents are never too busy or too tired for the children. The kitchen is still primarily the domain of the woman, and it is *her* [9d: subjective case needed after a linking verb] *who* [9e: objective case, *whom* needed] the children usually turn to for personal advice.

As traditional patterns in family life are changing, so are the situations shown on television comedy series. It seems clear that it [10d: overuse of it] will not be long before *us* [9c: wrong case, *we* needed] viewers will see more comedies that come closer to reality.

ANSWER: PARTICIPATION ESSAY

This version revises the errors in noun and pronoun case and in pronoun reference. Answers might vary slightly. Also, answers will vary if students have revised for content, organization, or style.

Television programming mirrors the society that watches it. In the 1950's, situation comedies showed a traditional family with a father who was the breadwinner, a mother who enjoyed housekeeping, and children who were always adorable. Later, the writers of situation comedies replaced the traditional families seen on *Father Knows Best* and *Leave It to Beaver* with people who fit a broader definition of "family."

Reflecting an updated concept of family life in the 1970's, situation comedies

Not everyone, however, knows much about one of his most valued aides and advisors: his wife Eleanor. In fact, it was she who was the strongest supporter in his decision to seek the governorship of New York as well as the presidency of the United States.

After Franklin was stricken with polio in 1921, his legs were paralyzed. His mother, whom Eleanor did not always agree with, urged Franklin to retire from politics. But Eleanor, with the approval of physicians and friends, urged him to continue with his career. Franklin listened to his wife, and he was elected governor of New York in 1928 and president of the United States in 1932.

As the new president's wife, Eleanor Roosevelt quickly showed that she cared as much about the nation as he did. No sooner had she and her husband settled into the White House than she began touring the country and speaking to sharecroppers, slum dwellers, and unemployed workers. A first lady's taking it upon herself to spread political messages created quite a stir across the nation. Even more unusual was her support of what were then unpopular causes, such as civil rights. Eleanor's making public statements in support of such causes did not represent Franklin Roosevelt's policy.

Through lecture tours, radio broadcasts, newspaper columns, and press conferences for women reporters, Eleanor Roosevelt changed forever the world's perception of the role of first lady of the United States.

Participation

A student wrote the following draft for a sociology course called Faces of America. The assignment was to discuss the changing culture in the United States as reflected on television. The material is well organized and uses specific details, but the draft's effectiveness is diminished by errors in noun and pronoun case and in pronoun references.

Read through the draft. Then revise it to eliminate the errors. Also, make any additional revisions you think would improve the content, organization, and style of the material.

Television programming mirrors the society that watches it. In the 1950s, you saw situation comedies with a traditional family with a father who was the breadwinner, a mother who enjoyed housekeeping, and children who were always adorable. Later, they ➡

replaced the traditional families seen on <u>Father Knows Best</u> and <u>Leave It to Beaver</u> with people which fit a broader definition of "family."

Reflecting an updated concept of family life in the 1970s, situation comedies like <u>All in the Family</u> portrayed nontraditional situations. A young couple lived with the wife parents. One spinoff from that series involved the father, his business, and him raising a foster child alone. The long-running <u>Mary Tyler Moore Show</u> featured single women whom were supporting themselves, raising children, and enjoying good friendships.

As working women have become the norm in society, situation comedies have changed to portray women who juggle home and career. Lead roles on situation comedies portray women as lawyers, architects, and factory workers. Some shows include unemployed husbands and husbands whose wives make more money than them.

In many ways today, however, they still differ from reality. In contrast to real life, most comedies show no child who is ever inconvenienced by parents or upset about them working at demanding jobs. And parents are never too busy or too tired for the children. The kitchen is still primarily the domain of the woman, and it is her who the children usually turn to for personal advice.

As traditional patterns in family life are changing, so are the situations shown on television comedies series. It seems clear that it will not be long before us viewers will see more comedies that come closer to reality.

ANSWER: PARTICIPATION ESSAY, *Continued*

like *All in the Family* portrayed nontraditional situations. A young couple lived with the wife's parents. One spinoff from that series involved the father, his business, and his raising a foster child alone. The long-running *Mary Tyler Moore Show* featured single women who were supporting themselves, raising children, and enjoying good friendships.

As working women have become the norm in society, situation comedies have changed to portray women who juggle home and career. Lead roles on situation comedies portray women as lawyers, architects, and factory workers. Some shows include unemployed husbands and husbands whose wives make more money than they do.

In many ways today, however, situation comedies still differ from reality. In contrast to real life, most comedies show no child who is ever inconvenienced by parents or upset about their working at demanding jobs. And parents are never too busy or too tired for the children. The kitchen is still primarily the domain of the woman, and it is she to whom the children usually turn for personal advice.

As traditional patterns in family life are changing, so are the situations shown on television comedy series. It seems clear that before long we viewers will see more comedies that come closer to reality.

11 Agreement

The concept of *agreement* in human affairs implies the aligning or matching of ideas. Grammatical agreement also is based on matching. Rules governing agreement are not difficult, but their applications can seem tricky. Indeed, almost everyone has to consult a handbook once in a while to check one or another rule for agreement. This chapter discusses agreement between subjects and verbs (see 11a through 11l) and between pronouns and antecedents (see 11m through 11r).

SUBJECT–VERB AGREEMENT

11a Understanding subject–verb agreement

Subject–verb agreement means that subjects (see 7k) and verbs (see 7c and Chapter 8) in clauses (see 7o) must "match" in form. To agree grammatically, subjects and verbs must match in number (singular or plural) and in person (first, second, or third person). For an explanation of the major concepts in grammatical agreement, consult Chart 78.

The **firefly glows** with luminescent light. [*firefly* = singular subject in the third person; *glows* = singular verb in the third person]

Fireflies glow with luminescent light. [*fireflies* = plural subject in the third person; *glow* = plural verb in the third person]

This **insect is** nocturnal. [*insect* = singular subject in the third person; *is* = singular verb in the third person]

These **insects are** nocturnal. [*insects* = plural subject in the third person; *are* = plural verb in the third person] *agr* **11b**

	78

MAJOR CONCEPTS IN GRAMMATICAL AGREEMENT

- **Number,** as a concept in grammar, refers to *singular* and *plural.*
- The **first person** is the speaker or writer. *I* (singular) and *we* (plural) are the only subjects that occur in the first person.

SINGULAR   **I** see a field of fireflies.

PLURAL   **We** see a field of fireflies.

- The **second person** is the person spoken or written to. *You* (for both singular and plural) is the only subject that occurs in the second person.

SINGULAR   **You** see a shower of sparks.

PLURAL   **You** see a shower of sparks.

- The **third person** is the person or thing being spoken or written of. Most rules for subject–verb agreement involve the third person.

SINGULAR   The **scientist sees** a cloud of cosmic dust.

PLURAL   The **scientists see** a cloud of cosmic dust.

11b Using the final -*s* or -*es* either for plural subjects or for singular verbs

Subject–verb agreement often involves one letter: *s*. The basic pattern is shown in Chart 79. Be aware that the -*s* added to subjects and the -*s* added to verbs have very different functions.

Most **plural subjects** are formed by adding an -*s* or -*es*: *lip* becomes *lips*; *princess* becomes *princesses*. Exceptions include most pronouns (*they, it*) and a few nouns that for singular and plural either do not change (*deer, deer*) or change internally (*mouse, mice; child, children*); for information about spelling plural nouns, see 22c.

Singular verbs in the present tense of the third person are formed by adding -*s* or -*es* to the simple form of the verb: *laugh, laughs; kiss, kisses.* Even the exceptions—the verbs *be (is)* and *have (has)*—end in *s*.

EXTRA EXERCISE A

Fill in the blank with the correct present-tense form of the verb in parentheses.

EXAMPLE

Psychologists often (to use)_____projective tests to investigate clients' unconscious memories and drives. [*use*]

1. Psychologists sometimes (to present) _____ their clients with questions to which there are no correct answers.

2. The client then (to tell) _____ what he (to see) _____, thus showing the psychologist some of his inner self.

3. The popular *Rorschach Psychodiagnostic Inkblot Test* (to require) _____ the client to examine ten cards containing symmetrical inkblots and say what he (to think) _____ each means.

4. Next, the client (to point) _____ out where in the blot he (to find) _____ each image or idea.

5. Several scoring systems (to exist) _____ to help psychologists interpret clients' responses.

ANSWERS: EXTRA EXERCISE A

1. present
2. tells; sees
3. requires; thinks
4. points; finds
5. exist

ANSWERS: EXERCISE 11-1

Answers will vary. Each set of sentences must use the subject once as a singular and once as a plural, and the verbs must agree accordingly.

PATTERN FOR BASIC SUBJECT–VERB AGREEMENT	79

The **student works** long hours.
SINGULAR SUBJECT — SINGULAR VERB

The **students work** long hours.
PLURAL SUBJECT — PLURAL VERB

The **student laughs** at the idea that **students watch** too much television.

Most part-time **jobs involve** ten or twenty hours a week.

Studying requires all remaining time.

Here is a memory device to help you visualize how, in most cases, the *s* works in agreement. The *-s* (or *-es*) can take only one path at a time, going either to the top or to the bottom.

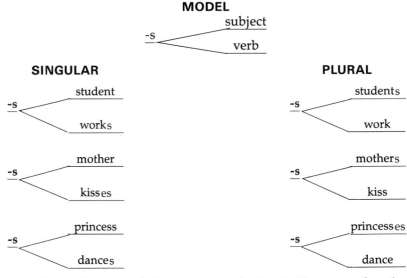

MODEL

-s → subject / verb

SINGULAR

-s → student / works
-s → mother / kisses
-s → princess / dances

PLURAL

-s → students / work
-s → mothers / kiss
-s → princesses / dance

The principle of the memory device holds, even for the exceptions discussed earlier in this section: *It* (singular pronoun) *is late; the **mice** (plural with internal change) are sleeping.*

❖ USAGE ALERT: Do not add *-s* to a main verb used with an auxiliary verb (a helping verb such as *be, do, can, might, must, would*; see 8e): *The coach **can walk** (not **can walks**) to campus.* ❖

EXERCISE 11-1

Consulting sections 11a and 11b, use the subject and verb in each set to write two complete sentences—one with the subject as a singular and one with the subject as a plural. Keep all verbs in the present tense.

1.	boat race	2.	flag fly	3.	critic applaud	4.	woman cheer
5.	chorus sing	6.	baby burp	7.	judge might decide	8.	winner kiss

11c Ignoring words between a subject and verb, for agreement

Words that separate the subject from the verb do not affect what the verb should agree with. The pattern is shown in Chart 80. Such intervening material often appears as a prepositional phrase°. Eliminate all prepositional phrases from consideration when you look for the subject of a clause.

NO   **Winners** of the state contest **goes** to the national finals.
[*Winners* is the subject. The verb must agree with it; *of the state contest* is a prepositional phrase.]

YES   **Winners** of the state contest **go** to the national finals.

PATTERN WHEN WORDS SEPARATE A SUBJECT AND VERB   80

The **student** *in my college class / in my college classes* **works** long hours.

SINGULAR SUBJECT   INTERVENING WORDS   SINGULAR VERB

The **students** *in my college class / in my college classes* **work** long hours.

PLURAL SUBJECT   INTERVENING WORDS   PLURAL VERB

Be especially careful with a construction that starts *one of the*. This construction takes a singular verb, to agree with the word *one*. Do not be distracted by a plural noun in the prepositional phrase.

EXTRA EXERCISE B

Fill in the blank with the correct present-tense form of the verb in parentheses.

EXAMPLE

In the eyes of many people, the Rorschach Inkblots (to be) _____ the psychologists' standard tool for getting at clients' hidden thoughts and feelings. [*are*]

1. Yet either the Holtzman Inkblot Technique or the Thematic Apperception Test (TAT) (to be) _____ given by psychologists who feel the Rorschach is unreliable.

2. Not only does the Holtzman series have more inkblots (45) than the Rorschach (10), but it also (to have) _____ a more standardized system of administration.

3. The TAT (to use) _____ a series of pictures showing people engaged in a wide range of activities.

4. Although the pictures show people in realistic situations, there (to be) _____ many possible acceptable answers.

5. It (to be) _____ the task of the person interpreting the picture to make up a story, deciding what has occurred and what the characters are thinking and feeling.

ANSWERS: EXTRA EXERCISE B

1. is
2. has
3. uses
4. are
5. is

EXTRA EXERCISE C

Rewrite the following passages making the following changes: For "children" substitute "a child." For "adults" substitute "an adult." For "unicorns" substitute "a unicorn." For "books" substitute "a book." For "a dragon" substitute "dragons." For "they" substitute "he," "she," or "it," considering the antecedent. Make sure that the verbs agree with the new subjects.

So I believe that we should trust our children. Normal children do not confuse reality and fantasy—they confuse them much less often than we adults do (as a great fantasist pointed out in a story called "The Emperor's New Clothes"). Children know perfectly well that unicorns aren't real, but they also know that books about unicorns, if they are good books, are true books. All too often, that's more than Mummy and Daddy know; for, in denying their childhood, the adults have denied half their knowledge, and are left with the sad, sterile little fact: "Unicorns aren't real." And that fact is one that never got anybody anywhere (except in the story "The Unicorn in the Garden," by another great fantasist, in which it is shown that a devotion to the unreality of unicorns may get you straight into the loony bin). It is by such statements as, "Once upon a time there was a dragon," or "In a hole in the ground there lived a hobbit"—it is by such beautiful non-facts that we fantastic human beings may arrive, in our peculiar fashion, at the truth.

—Ursula K. Le Guin, "Why Are Americans Afraid of Dragons?"

➡

NO	**One** of the problems **are** broken equipment.
YES	**One** of the problems **is** broken equipment.

Similarly, to locate the subject of a sentence, eliminate any phrases that start with *including, together with, along with, accompanied by, in addition to, except,* and *as well as.* Be sure that the verb agrees with the subject, not with the intervening material.

NO	**The moon,** as well as Venus, **are** visible in the night sky. [*The moon* is the subject. The verb must agree with it. Ignore *as well as Venus.*]
YES	**The moon,** as well as Venus, **is** visible in the night sky.
NO	**The Big Dipper,** along with many other constellations, **are** easy to learn to find. [*The Big Dipper* is the subject. The verb must agree with it. Ignore *along with many other constellations.*]
YES	**The Big Dipper,** along with many other constellations, **is** easy to learn to find.

11d Using verbs with subjects connected with *and*

When subjects are connected with *and*, they comprise a compound subject (see 7k) and require a plural verb. Chart 81 shows this pattern.

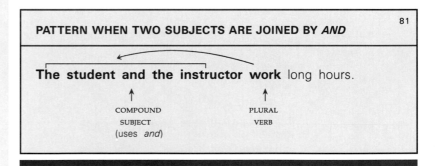

PATTERN WHEN TWO SUBJECTS ARE JOINED BY *AND*   81

The student and the instructor work long hours.

COMPOUND   PLURAL
SUBJECT   VERB
(uses *and*)

The Cascade Diner *and* the Wayside Diner *have* (not *has*) fried catfish today.

An exception occurs when *and* joins parts that combine to form a single thing or person.

My ***best friend and neighbor* makes** (not *make*) excellent chili. [The best friend is the same person as the neighbor. If two different people were involved, *makes* would become *make*.]

***Ham and cheese* is** (not *are*) a popular sandwich.

each, every

The words *each* and *every* remain singular even when they modify° a compound subject. Therefore, when *each* or *every* precedes a compound subject, the verb that follows it must be singular, not plural. (For information about verb agreement for *each* or *every* used alone, not as a modifier, see 11g.)

***Each* human hand and foot makes** (not *make*) a distinctive print.

To identify lawbreakers, ***every* police chief, sheriff, and federal marshal depends** (not *depend*) on such prints.

The same rule holds when the construction *one of the* follows *each* or *every*: ***Each* one of the robbers *is*** (not *are*) *now in prison.*

The only exception calls for a plural verb when *each* follows—rather than precedes—a compound subject: ***The Cascade Diner and the Wayside Diner each have*** (not *has*) *fried catfish today.*

❖ USAGE ALERT: Use either *each* or *every*, not both together, to single out something: ***Each*** (not *each and every*) *robber has been caught.* ❖

11e Making the verb agree with the subject closest to it

PATTERN WHEN SUBJECTS ARE JOINED BY *OR*

82

~~Either the instructor or~~
~~Either the instructors or~~ the **student knows** the answer.

↑ **SINGULAR SUBJECT** ↑ **SINGULAR VERB**

~~Either the instructor or~~
~~Either the instructors or~~ the **students know** the answer.

↑ **PLURAL SUBJECT** ↑ **PLURAL VERB**

So I believe that we should trust a child. A normal child does not confuse reality and fantasy—he or she confuses them much less often than an adult does (as a great fantasist pointed out in a story called "The Emperor's New Clothes"). A child knows perfectly well that a unicorn isn't real, but he or she also knows that a book about a unicorn, if it is a good book, is a true book. All too often, that's more than Mummy and Daddy know; for, in denying their childhood, an adult has denied half his or her knowledge, and is left with the sad, sterile little fact: "A unicorn isn't real." And that fact is one that never got anybody anywhere (except in the story "The Unicorn in the Garden," by another great fantasist, in which it is shown that a devotion to the unreality of unicorns may get you straight into the loony bin). It is by such statements as, "Once upon a time there were dragons," or "In a hole in the ground there lived a hobbit"—it is by such beautiful non-facts that we fantastic human beings may arrive, in our peculiar fashion, at the truth.

When subjects are joined with *or, nor, either . . . or, neither . . . nor,* or *not only . . . but (also),* make the verb agree with the subject closest to it. For subject–verb agreement, ignore everything before the final subject.

> ~~Not only the spider but also all other~~ **arachnids have** four pairs of legs.
>
> ~~Neither spiders nor~~ **flies tempt** my appetite.
>
> ~~Six clam fritters, four blue crabs, or one steamed~~ **lobster tempts** my appetite. [For less awkward wording, rearrange the items to place the plural subject next to the verb: *One steamed lobster, four blue crabs, or six clam fritters tempt my appetite.*]

11f Using verbs in inverted word order

In English, the subject of a sentence normally precedes its verb: *Astronomy is interesting.* Inverted word order means a change in the usual order. Most questions use inverted word order. Be sure to look *after* the verb, not before it, to check that the subject and verb agree.

> **Is astronomy** interesting?
>
> What **are** the **requirements** for the major?
>
> **Do John and Mary** study astronomy?

If you occasionally choose to write a sentence in inverted word order to convey emphasis (see 19f), be sure to locate the subject and then make the verb agree with it.

> Into deep space **shoot** probing **satellites.** [The plural verb *shoot* agrees with the inverted plural subject *satellites.*]
>
> On the television screen **appears** an **image** of Saturn. [The singular verb *appears* agrees with the inverted singular subject *image.*]

Expletive constructions use inverted word order. With the use of *there* or *it,* they postpone the subject. Check ahead in such sentences to identify the subject, and then make sure that the verb agrees with the subject. For advice on being concise by eliminating some expletives, see 16a-1.

> **There are** nine **planets** in our solar system. [The verb *are* agrees with the subject *planets.*]
>
> **There is** probably no **life** on eight of them. [The verb agrees with the subject *life.*]

It plus a singular form of the verb *be* can be an expletive construction as well: ***It is*** *astronomers who want new telescopes.*

EXERCISE 11-2

Consulting sections 11e and 11f, supply the correct present-tense form of the verb in parentheses.

EXAMPLE   Either sales and marketing or finance (to provide) **provides** the basic training for most top corporate executives.

1. To an outsider, the chief executive officer (CEO) of a company or conglomerate of companies (to seem) _____ to be an independent decision-maker.
2. Neither the economic climate nor a business's social responsibilities (to permit) _____ independence today, however.
3. There (to be) _____ many conflicting demands to reconcile from both stockholders and consumers.
4. Not only daily operations but also the public image of the corporation (to set) _____ the environment for a CEO.
5. It (to be) _____ up to the finance people to set the corporation's short-term goals.

11g Using verbs with indefinite pronouns

Indefinite pronouns are the type of pronouns (see 7b) that refer to usually unknown—thus the label "indefinite"—persons, things, quantities, or ideas. In context within a sentence, each indefinite pronoun takes on a very clear meaning. Most indefinite pronouns are singular and require a singular verb for agreement. A few indefinite pronouns can be singular or plural, depending on the meaning that a sentence intends to deliver. (For advice on avoiding sexist language° with indefinite pronouns, see 11q and 21b.)

COMMON INDEFINITE PRONOUNS 83

all*	each	many*	no one
another	either	more*	nothing
any	every	most*	one
anybody	everybody	neither	some*
anyone	everyone	nobody	somebody
anything	everything	none*	someone
			something

*can be singular or plural depending on context

TEACHING TIP
Controlled composition exercises are easy exercises to construct and are often useful for helping students with subject–verb agreement and other grammatical and stylistic concerns. A controlled composition exercise asks the student to copy a passage several sentences long—but to make one change in the passage that addresses an area in which the student needs to improve. For example, to work on subject–verb agreement, a student might rewrite a passage changing the verbs from past tense to present tense. For help with past-tense verb forms, a student might rewrite a different passage, converting the verbs from present tense to past tense. Although the exercise focuses the efforts of the student on one particular area, copying passages, like other imitation exercises, helps students develop syntactic fluency in other ways at the same time.

BACKGROUND ON LANGUAGE

Most of us spend a fair proportion of our time reminding students that indefinite pronouns (with the exception of *all, any, some,* and *none*) are always singular. Yet widespread informal usage does not adhere to this rule, and we hardly seem to make a dent in our students' habit of following *everyone, anybody,* and the like with *their.*

According to Martha Kolln of Pennsylvania State University, we shouldn't be too concerned about this usage. In ''Everyone's Right to Their Own Language'' (*College Composition and Communication* 37 [1986]: 100–102), she looks at the issue. Most handbooks treat this usage as, at best, informal, while some continue to label it an outright error. Yet, Kolln points out, studies of usage patterns indicate that *everybody* has been treated as a plural for over four hundred years and *everyone* for over two hundred, appearing this way in the works of Cardinal Newman, Shakespeare, and Swift. Despite this evidence (available since 1957), the rule stands—at least on the record.

Kolln argues for treating indefinite pronouns as we treat collective nouns. A collective noun such as *crowd* takes a singular verb but takes a plural pronoun when it clearly refers to more than one person. She gives as an example:

> At first *the crowd* was singing; then *they* began to laugh.

Kolln gives this example for indefinite pronouns:

> At first *everyone* in the room was singing; then *they* began to laugh.

In fact, a singular pronoun would be out of place in the second clause. She demonstrates that the same applies when the indefinite pronoun appears as the direct object or as the subject of a tag question.

Kolln ends by calling for the acceptance of the plural possessive pronoun (*their*) after collective indefinite pronouns:

➡

SINGULAR INDEFINITE PRONOUNS

Everything about that intersection **is** dangerous.

But whenever **anyone says** anything, **nothing is** done.

Everyone knows that **something** terrible **is** likely to happen.

The indefinite pronouns *each* and *every* demand a special measure of attention. They are always singular, no matter what intervening words come between one of them and its verb. (For advice on using *each* and *every* with subjects joined by *and,* see 11d.)

SINGULAR OR PLURAL INDEFINITE PRONOUNS

Each of us **has** (not *have*) to shovel snow; **each is** (not *are*) expected to help.

Every snowstorm of the past two years **has** (not *have*) been severe; **every has** (not *have*) caused massive traffic jams.

Some of our streams **are** polluted. [*Some* refers to the plural *streams,* so the plural verb *are* is correct.]

Some pollution **is** reversible, but **all** pollution **is** a threat to the balance of nature. [*Some* and *all* refer to the singular *pollution,* so the singular verb *is* is correct in both cases.]

All that environmentalists ask **is** to give nature a chance. [*All* has the meaning here of ''the entire thing'' or ''the only thing,'' so the singular verb *is* is correct.]

Winter has driven the birds south; **all are** gone. [*All* refers to *birds,* so the plural verb *are* is correct.]

❖ USAGE ALERT: Do not mix singular and plural when indefinite pronouns function as adjectives°, as in constructions such as *this kind, this type, these kinds,* and *these types. This* is singular, as are *kind* and *type; these* is plural, as are *kinds* and *types:* **This kind** *of weather* **makes** *me shiver.* **These kinds** *of sweaters* **keep** *me warm.* ❖

11h Using verbs in context for collective nouns

A **collective noun** names a group of people or things: *family, group, audience, class, number, committee, team,* and the like. When the group acts as one unit, use a singular verb. When the members of the group act individually, thus creating more than one action, use a plural verb.

The senior class nervously **awaits** final exams. [*Class* is acting as a single unit, so the verb is singular.]

The senior class were fitted for their graduation robes today. [Each member was fitted individually, but because there was more than one fitting the verb is plural.]

The couple in blue **is** engaged. [*Couple* refers to a single unit, so the verb is singular.]

The couple say their vows tomorrow. [Each of the two people will take a separate action, so because there is more than one action, the verb is plural.]

 11i   **Making a linking verb agree with the subject—not the subject complement**

Linking verbs indicate a state of being or a condition (see 7c). They connect the subject to its **complement**—a word that renames or describes the subject. You can think of a linking verb as an equal sign between a subject and its complement, called the **subject complement.**

The car **looks** new. [*The car = new; the car* is the subject, *looks* is the linking verb, and *new* is the subject complement.]

When you write a sentence that contains a subject complement, remember that the verb always agrees with the subject. For the purposes of agreement, ignore the subject complement.

NO	**The worst part** of owning a car **are** the bills. [The subject is *the worst part*, with which the verb *are* does not agree; the subject complement is *the bills*.]
YES	**The worst part** of owning a car **is** the bills. [The subject *the worst part* agrees with the verb *is*; the subject complement is *the bills*.]

When the wording of a sentence is revised so that the word or words that were the subject complement become the subject, the same rule applies: the verb always agrees with the subject. For the purposes of agreement, ignore the subject complement.

NO	**Bills is** the worst part of owning a car.
YES	**Bills are** the worst part of owning a car.

11j   **Using verbs that agree with the antecedents of *who, which,* and *that* as subjects**

The pronouns *who, which,* and *that* have the same form in singular and plural. Before deciding whether the verb should be singular or plural, find the pronoun's antecedents.

Cont'd.

These dicta that designate all indefinite pronouns as singular have no basis either in actual usage or in the rules of logic. Yet the current handbooks apply the same rule to all of the indefinite pronouns, whether they are collective or not, whether singular or not. (102)

Whether you agree or disagree with Kolln, the issue is certainly worth discussion.

BACKGROUND

Usage of masculine generic pronouns, "he or she," and the "singular *they*" (referring to a singular antecedent) has undergone considerable change in the last sixty years, according to Miriam Watkins Meyers in "Current Generic Pronoun Usage: An Empirical Study" (*American Speech* 65 [1990]: 228–237). A 1932 survey by Sterling A. Leonard reported that linguists "regarded *he or she* as established usage and singular *they* as established in some contexts." But a 1985 survey revealed that almost no American editors approved the singular *they* and only half preferred *he or she* to *he*. A 1982 study of college students found that 42 percent used *he*, 42 percent singular *they*, and only 7 percent *he or she*. Meyers's own study of writings by 392 adult college juniors and seniors, ranging from 22 to 64 in age, showed that "singular *they* is well established in the public writing of adult Americans" and that *he or she* is preferred increasingly to masculine generic pronouns. Women and younger adults are more likely to use alternatives to masculine generic pronouns than men and older adults.

ANSWERS AND COVERAGE: EXERCISE 11-3

1. works [11h, collective noun]

2. is [11i, verb agrees with subject, not subject complement]

3. encourage [11j, use of *that*]

4. say [11h, collective noun]; have [11j, use of *who*]

5. listens [11g, indefinite pronoun]; makes [11i, use of *who*]

The scientist will share the income from her new patent with the graduate **students who work** with her. [*Who* refers to *students,* so the plural verb *work* is used.]

George Jones is **the student who works** in the science lab. [*Who* refers to *student,* so the singular verb *works* is used.]

Be especially careful when you use *one of the* or *the only one of the* in a sentence before *who, which,* or *that.* If the pronoun refers to *one,* use a singular verb. If the pronoun refers to what comes after *one of the,* use a plural verb.

Tracy is one of the students **who talk** in class. [*Who* refers to *students,* so *talk* is plural.]

Jim is the only one of the students **who talks** in class. [*Who* refers to only *one,* so *talks* is singular.]

EXERCISE 11-3

Consulting sections 11g through 11j, supply the correct present-tense form of the verb in parentheses.

EXAMPLE   Everyone (to know) **knows** that a good laugh (to make) _____ most people feel better.

1. Now a group of humor consultants (to work) _____ to introduce laughter to American businesses.

2. They believe that the best introduction for a speech (to be) _____ jokes and humorous observations.

3. C. W. Metcalf has developed one of the programs that (to encourage) _____ people to laugh at their own problems.

4. A large number of personnel officers (to say) _____ they prefer to hire workers who (to have) _____ a sense of humor.

5. Sales representatives find that almost anyone (to listen) _____ more attentively to a person who (to make) _____ an amusing comment.

11k Using singular verbs with subjects that specify amounts and with singular subjects that are in plural form

Subjects that refer to sums of money, distance, or measurement are considered singular and take singular verbs.

Two hours is not enough time to finish that project.
Three hundred dollars is what we must pay.

Three-quarters of an inch is needed for a perfect fit.
Two miles is a short sprint for some serious joggers.

Many words that end in *-s* or *-ics* are singular in meaning and so need singular verbs, despite their plural appearance. These words include *news, ethics,* and *measles.* They also include *economics, mathematics, physics,* and *statistics* when these words refer to courses of study. Also, *the United States of America* is singular (see also 41c ESL).

The news gets better each day. [*News* is singular, so the singular verb *gets* is correct.

Statistics is required of science majors. [*Statistics* is a course of study, so the singular verb *is* is correct.]

Statistics show that a teacher shortage is coming. [*Statistics* refers to separate pieces of information, so the plural verb *show* is correct.]

Some nouns are singular in some contexts and plural in others. They include *politics* and *sports.* Such words agree with singular or plural verbs, depending on the meaning of the sentence.

Sports is a good way to build physical stamina.
Three **sports are** offered at the recreation center.

Some words require a plural verb even though they refer to one thing: *jeans, pants, scissors, clippers, tweezers, eyeglasses, thanks,* and *riches.* If, however, the word *pair* is used in conjunction with *jeans, pants, scissors, clippers, tweezers,* or *eyeglasses,* a singular verb is required to agree with *pair.*

My slacks need pressing.
My pair of slacks needs pressing.

Series and *means* have the same form in singular and plural, so the meaning determines whether the verb is singular or plural.

Six new television series are beginning this week.
A series of disasters is plaguing our production.

111 Using singular verbs for titles of written works, companies, and words as terms

Even when plural and compound nouns occur in a title, the title itself indicates one work or entity. Therefore, titles of written works are singular and require singular verbs.

Breathing Lessons by Anne Tyler **is** a prize-winning novel.

EXTRA EXERCISE D
In writing groups students can work together to edit the following sentences for subject–verb agreement.
1. When a couple move into a new apartment, they face many decisions.
2. One of the biggest choices have to do with how to decorate it.
3. Probably the most important decision of all are the color choices.
4. Green is one of the colors that looks good in any room.
5. Two hours are about all the time a person can spend looking at color samples without becoming confused.

ANSWERS: EXTRA EXERCISE D
1. When a couple *moves* into a new apartment, they face many decisions.
2. One of the biggest choices *has* to do with how to decorate it.
3. Probably the most important decision of all *is* the color choices.
4. Green is one of the colors that *look* good in any room.
5. Two hours *is* about all the time a person can spend looking at color samples without becoming confused.

If a word that is plural is referred to as a term, it requires a singular verb.

> *We* **implies** that I am included.
>
> During the Vietnam War, *protective reaction strikes* **was** a euphemism used by the U.S. government to mean *bombing*.

EXERCISE 11-4

Consulting sections 11k and 11l, supply the correct present-tense form of the verb in parentheses.

EXAMPLE   In the United States, most business cards (to show) <u>show</u> a person's name, address, and telephone number.

1. In some parts of the world, business cards (to make) _____ an important first impression.
2. One of the countries that almost (to require) _____ people to carry business cards is Japan.
3. In Japan, every businessperson, as well as most people in professions, (to need) _____ to carry a carefully designed card.
4. Everyone who (to use) _____ business cards must (to observe) _____ certain rules of etiquette and tradition.
5. The *Tokyo Times* (to publish) _____ articles on international business customs.
6. One of the most important parts of offering someone a business card (to be) _____ to exchange slight bows.
7. People also (to explain) _____ that a male visiting Japan should not (to use) _____ business cards with rounded corners, which (to be) _____ reserved for females.
8. Malaysian businesspeople, however, (to believe) _____ that anyone, male or female, (to be) _____ free to carry a round-cornered card.
9. The European community of countries (to be) _____ less strict in business card etiquette.
10. Throughout the world, the most important part of handling business cards (to be) _____ the customs of the country the person is visiting.

PRONOUN–ANTECEDENT AGREEMENT

11m
Understanding pronoun–antecedent agreement

Pronoun–antecedent agreement means that pronouns (such as *it, they, their;* see 7b) must "match" in form with their **antecedents,** the nouns°, noun phrases°, or other pronouns to which they refer. To

---

ANSWERS AND COVERAGE:
EXERCISE 11-4

1. make [11a, plural subject]

2. requires [11d, *one of the* construction]

3. needs [11d, use of *every* and intervening words between subject and verb]

4. uses [11g and 11j, indefinite pronoun and use of *who*]; observe [11b, modal auxiliary verb]

5. publishes [11l, title]

6. is [11d and 11i, *one of the* construction and agreement with subject, not subject complement]

7. explain [11a, plural subject]; use [11b, modal auxiliary verb]; is [use of *which*]

8. believe [11a, plural subject]; is [11g, indefinite pronoun]

9. is [11c, prepositional phrase intervening between subject and verb]

10. is [11i, agreement with subject, not subject complement]

QUOTATION ABOUT WRITING

I have rewritten—often several times—every word I have ever published. My pencils outlast their erasers.

—Vladimir Nabokov

agree grammatically, pronouns must match in number (singular or plural) and in person (first, second, or third person). Chart 84 shows these relationships. For explanations of the major concepts in grammatical agreement, consult Chart 78 in section 11a.

Agreement between pronouns and antecedents must be clear so that readers are not distracted by having to figure out the intended meaning of a sentence. (For related material on subjects and verbs, see 11a. Also, for advice about staying consistent in person and number, see 15a-1.)

> The **firefly** glows with luminescent light when **it** emerges from **its** nest at dusk. [The singular pronouns *it* and *its* match their singular antecedent *firefly*.]
>
> **Fireflies** glow with luminescent light when **they** emerge from **their** nests at dusk. [The plural pronouns *they* and *their* match their plural antecedent *fireflies*.]

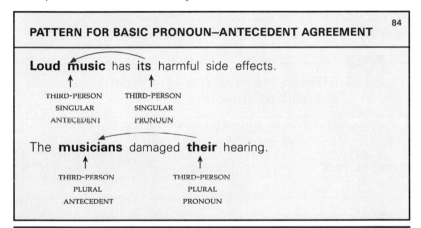

PATTERN FOR BASIC PRONOUN–ANTECEDENT AGREEMENT   84

Loud music has **its** harmful side effects.

THIRD-PERSON SINGULAR ANTECEDENT

THIRD-PERSON SINGULAR PRONOUN

The **musicians** damaged **their** hearing.

THIRD-PERSON PLURAL ANTECEDENT

THIRD-PERSON PLURAL PRONOUN

11n Using pronouns with antecedents connected with *and*

When two or more antecedents are connected with *and*, they require a plural pronoun, even if the separate antecedents are singular. (For related material on subjects and verbs, see 11d.)

> **The Cascade Diner *and* the Wayside Diner** closed for New Year's Eve to give **their** (not *its*) employees the night off.

An exception occurs when *and* joins singular nouns that combine to form a single thing or person.

263

EXTRA EXERCISE F

In writing groups students can work together to edit the inaccurate agreement of pronouns and antecedents in the following paragraph.

    Plaids have been a favorite fabric design for many centuries. It consists of bars of color crossing each other at right angles. Scotland is the home of the plaid, where they are called a tartan, or, in song, story, and legend, *plaidies*. The tartan, which distinguish the clan of their wearers, is ancient, but their origin is unknown. In its earliest forms they were pieces of cloth about two yards broad and four yards long, which was drawn round the waist in folds that was tightly buckled with a belt. The lower part came down to the knees, and the upper part fell over the left shoulder so that they left the right arm free. Early in the eighteenth century, the "belted plaid" disappeared. They were replaced by the kilt. The particular pattern of tartans which distinguish each clan must have been fixed before 1645, probably before 1600. Later, in 1746, trying to end the clan system, the British Parliament prohibited the Scots from wearing tartans. The action against it was taken following the Battle of Culloden where Prince Charles, Edward Stuart, grandson of James II, was defeated by the Duke of Cumberland. To be caught wearing them carried a penalty of six months' imprisonment. The kilt is worn today so that when the wearer is standing erect, their edges should reach the center of the kneecap. They should be made of a tartan associated with the name of the wearer. In the absence of a family claim to wear them, the Scots allow the wearing of the Royal Stuart tartan.

➡

My **best friend and neighbor** makes **his** (not *their*) excellent chili every Saturday. [The best friend is the same person as the neighbor. If two different people were involved, *his* would become *their*—and *makes* would become *make*.]

each, every

    The words *each* and *every* are singular. When *each* or *every* precedes antecedents joined by *and*, the pronoun must be singular. (For related material on subjects and verbs, see 11d. Also, for advice about pronoun agreement for *each* or *every* used alone, see 11p.)

    Each **human hand and foot** leaves **its** (not *their*) distinctive footprint.

The same rule holds when the construction *one of the* follows *each* or *every*: *Each one of the robbers left his* (not *their*) *fingerprints at the scene*.

    The only exception calls for a plural pronoun when *each* or *every* follows—rather than precedes—two antecedents joined by *and*: *The Cascade Diner and the Wayside Diner each closed for New Year's Eve to give their* (not *its*) *employees the night off*.

11o   Making the pronoun agree with the antecedent closest to it

    Antecedents joined by *or*, *nor*, or correlative conjunctions (such as *either . . . or*, *not only . . . but also*), often mix singular and plural; for a complete list, see Chart 55 in section 7h. For the purposes of agreement, ignore everything before the final antecedent. (For related material on subject–verb agreement, see 11e.)

PATTERN WHEN ANTECEDENTS ARE JOINED BY *OR*   85

~~Either the loudspeakers or~~ **the microphone** needs **its** electric cord repaired.

↑ SINGULAR ANTECEDENT   ↑ SINGULAR PRONOUN

~~Either the microphone or~~ **loudspeakers** need **their** electric cords repaired.

↑ PLURAL ANTECEDENT   ↑ PLURAL PRONOUN

Each night after the restaurant closes, either the resident mice or **the owner's cat** manages to get **itself** a good meal of leftovers.

Each night after the restaurant closes, either the owner's cat or **the resident mice** manage to get **themselves** a good meal of leftovers.

11p Using pronouns with antecedents that are indefinite pronouns

Indefinite pronouns are pronouns that refer to usually un-known—thus the label "indefinite"—persons, things, quantities, or ideas. In context within a sentence, each indefinite pronoun takes on a very clear meaning. Most indefinite pronouns are singular and require a singular antecedent for agreement. A few indefinite pro-nouns can be singular or plural, depending on the meaning a sen-tence intends to deliver. Chart 83 in section 11g lists common indefinite pronouns. (For related material on subjects and verbs, see 11g.)

SINGULAR INDEFINITE PRONOUNS

Everyone taking this course hopes to get **his or her** (not *their*) college degree within a year.

Anybody wanting to wear a cap and gown at graduation must have **his or her** (not *their*) measurements taken.

The indefinite pronouns *each* and *every* demand a special measure of attention. They are always singular, no matter what words follow. (For using *each* and *every* with antecedents joined by *and*, see 11n.)

Each of the students handed in **his or her** (not *their*) final term paper.
Each student **is** (not *are*) hoping for a passing grade.
Every student **needs** (not *need*) encouragement now and then.
Every student in my classes **is** (not *are*) studying hard.

SINGULAR OR PLURAL INDEFINITE PRONOUNS

All a student needs **is** encouragement from **his or her** parents. [*All* here means "the only thing"; the singular pronoun *all* is correct.]

The winter break has emptied the campus of students; **all** have left **their** dormitories for the comforts of home. [*All* refers to *students*, so the plural pronoun *their* is correct.]

None fear that **they** will fail. [The entire group does not expect to fail, so a plural noun is correct.]

None fears that **he or she** will fail. [No one individual expects to fail, so a singular pronoun is correct; note that *he or she* always functions as a singular pronoun (see Chart 86).]

ANSWERS: EXTRA EXERCISE F

Plaids have been favorite fabric *designs* for many centuries. *They* consist of bars of color crossing each other at right angles. Scotland is the home of the plaid, where *it* is called a tartan, or, in song, story, and legend, a *plaidie*. The tartan, *which distinguishes* the clan of *its wearer*, is ancient, but *its* origin is unknown. In its earliest form, *it* was *a piece* of cloth about two yards broad and four yards long, which was drawn round the waist in folds that *were* tightly buckled with a belt. The lower part came down to the knees, and the upper part fell over the left shoulder so that *it* left the right arm free. Early in the eighteenth century, the "belted plaid" disappeared. *It* was replaced by the kilt. The particular pattern of *tartan which distinguishes* each clan must have been fixed before 1645, probably before 1600. Later, in 1746, trying to end the clan system, the British Parliament prohibited the Scots from wearing *the tartan*. The action against it was taken following the Battle of Culloden where Prince Charles, Edward Stuart, grandson of James II, was defeated by the Duke of Cumberland. To be caught wearing *it* carried a penalty of six months' imprison-ment. The kilt is worn today so that when the wearer is standing erect, *its* edges should reach the center of the kneecap. *It* should be made of a tartan associated with the name of the wearer. In the absence of a family claim to wear *one*, the Scots allow the wearing of the Royal Stuart tartan.

EXTRA EXERCISE G

Rewrite this paragraph so that pronoun–antecedent agreement in person and number is maintained. It may also be necessary to change verbs or other words.

Buying stock involves many steps. Once a stockbroker receives an order, they call their firm's telephone clerk, who is located near the edge of the trading area. The telephone clerk summons his firm's floor broker by flashing their code number on a large electronic board posted in the trading area. Seeing their number, the floor broker goes to the telephone clerk and picks up the buy order. You then go to the small area set aside for trading in that company's stock. An employee of the Stock Exchange keeps track of all bids to buy and sell that particular stock. The floor broker makes an offer. If they are accepted by the selling broker, the stock is his. If you have bid too low, he must make another bid before someone else gets the stock. Then a reporter enters the deal into the Exchange computer, and they become part of the official record in seconds. After all this, the floor broker returns to the telephone clerk, who reports the deal to the original stockbroker, who bills the client.

11q Avoiding sexist pronoun use

In the past, grammatical convention specified using masculine pronouns to refer to indefinite pronouns: *"Everyone* open *his* book." Today, people are more conscious that the pronouns *he, his, him,* and *himself* exclude women, who comprise over half the population. Many experienced writers try to avoid using masculine pronouns to refer to the entire population. Chart 86 shows three ways to avoid using masculine pronouns when referring to males and females together. (For advice on how to avoid other types of sexist language, see 21b.)

WAYS TO AVOID USING ONLY THE MASCULINE PRONOUN TO REFER TO MALES AND FEMALES TOGETHER	86

Solution 1: Use a pair—but try to avoid a pair more than once in a sentence or in many sentences in a row. When you use a *he or she* construction, remember that it acts as a singular pronoun.

> **Everyone** hopes that **he or she** wins the scholarship.
>
> With the explosion of knowledge, no **doctor** can read outside **his or her** specialty.

Solution 2: Revise into the plural.

> **Many people** hope that **they** win the scholarship.
>
> With the explosion of knowledge, few **doctors** can read outside **their** specialties.

Solution 3: Recast the sentence.

> Everyone hopes to win the scholarship.
>
> With the explosion of knowledge, few doctors can read outside a small number of specialties.

11r With collective-noun antecedents, using singular or plural pronouns according to context

A **collective noun** names a group of people or things, such as *family, group, audience, class, number, committee,* and *team.* When the group acts as one unit, use a singular pronoun to refer to it. When the members of the group act individually, thus creating more than one action, use a plural pronoun.

The audience was cheering as **it** stood to applaud the performers. [The audience was acting as one unit, so the singular pronoun *it* is correct.]

The audience put on **their** coats and walked out. [Here the members of the audience were acting as individuals, so all the actions collect to become plural so that the plural pronoun *their,* is correct.]

The family is spending **its** vacation in Rockport, Maine. [All the family members went to one place together.]

The family are spending **their** vacations in Maine, Hawaii, and Rome. [Each family member went to a different place.]

EXERCISE 11-5

Consulting sections 11p through 11r, choose the proper pronoun to agree with its antecedent.

EXAMPLE   Many people wonder what gives rainbows (its, their) <u>their</u> colors.

1. A raindrop acts as a prism when sunlight enters (it, them) _____ .
2. For people to see a rainbow, (he, he or she, they) _____ must have their back to the sun and the raindrops in front of (them, him) _____ .
3. Rays of light come over the observer's head, and (they, it) _____ then enters into the raindrops.
4. A rainbow looks like an arch, but actually (they, it) _____ are part of a circle.
5. If two people are looking at a rainbow, each sees (their, his or her) _____ own version.
6. Because their angles of viewing are different, the observers each see a rainbow that is unique to (their, his or her) _____ eyes.
7. When people see one rainbow inside another, the outside rainbow has (its, their) _____ colors in reverse order.
8. A third and even a fourth rainbow may form, but (they, it) _____ is usually too faint to be seen.
9. A garden hose or lawn sprinklers can create (their, its) _____ own small rainbows.
10. To view a homemade rainbow, people must stand with (his or her, their) _____ back to the sun and the spray in front.

ANSWERS: EXERCISE 11-5

1. enters *it*
2. *they* must have . . . in front of *them*
3. *they* then *enter*
4. *it is* part
5. *his* or *her* own version
6. *their* eyes
7. *its* colors
8. *they* are usually
9. *their* own
10. with *their* back

REVISING YOUR WRITING

If you make errors in agreement when you write, go back to your writing and locate the errors. Using this chapter as a resource, revise your writing to correct the problems. Sections 11a through 11l discuss subject–verb agreement. Sections 11m through 11r discuss pronoun–antecedent agreement.

CASE STUDY: REVISING FOR AGREEMENT

In these case studies, you can observe a student writer revising. Then you have the chance to revise other student writing on your own.

Observation

A student wrote the following draft for a course in training as rehabilitation therapists. The assignment was to discuss the main idea of a film about handicapped athletes. The material offers a good summary of the film, but the draft's effectiveness is diminished by errors in subject–verb agreement and in pronoun–antecedent agreement.

Read through the draft. The errors are highlighted and explained. Before you look at the student's revision, revise the material yourself. Then compare what you and the student did.

> Last week students training as physical therapists saw a film about severely handicapped people participating actively in sports. The class know now that doing the impossible is becoming normal for many handicapped people.
> General fitness and eagerness to compete is among the reasons that a handicapped person might want to develop their skill in sports. All that is needed is a minimum of mobility and the will to train very hard. Either artificial

singular verb needed for this collective noun: 11h

verb should be plural for subjects joined by *and:* 11d

singular pronoun needed: 11m

the linking verb should agree with the subject: 11i

limbs—called *prostheses*—or a wheelchair allow many severely handicapped people to become athletes. Advances in design and material have led to better athletic equipment for the handicapped.

verb should agree with subject closer to it: 11e

Barriers are broken daily. Rafting, rock climbing, and basketball have found enthusiasts among the handicapped. Marathon racing, along with skiing and cycling, also have great appeal. Many have tried their skill at these sports. One competitive event for the handicapped was the eighth Paralympic Games, which was held in Seoul, South Korea, the site of the 1988 Olympics.

verb should agree with subject, not with words between subject and verb: 11c

plural verb needed to agree with this use of which: 11j

Every disabled athlete needs to train somewhat differently to accommodate their particular handicap. One of today's most versatile athletes compete in a triathlon event by wearing one kind of prosthesis for cycling, another for running, and none for swimming.

singular pronoun needed: 11p

singular verb needed to agree with one: 11c

Here is how the student revised the paragraph to correct the agreement errors. In a few places, the student had alternatives for the revision, so your revision might not match this one exactly. Your revision should, however, deal with each error highlighted on the draft.

Last week students training as physical therapists saw a film about severely handicapped people participating actively in sports. The class knows now that doing the impossible is becoming normal for many handicapped people.

General fitness and eagerness to compete are among the reasons that a handicapped person might want to develop his or her skill in sports. All that is needed are a minimum of mobility and the will to train very hard. Either artificial limbs—called *prostheses*—or a wheelchair allows many severely handicapped people to become athletes. Advances in design and material have led to better athletic equipment for the handicapped.

COVERAGE: PARTICIPATION ESSAY, page 270

Without kidney function, the body's ability to regulate fluids, blood pressure, red-cell production, protein levels, and blood chemistry *are* [11c: intervening words, singular verb needed] destroyed. If the kidneys no longer function, the standard prescription *are* [11i: linking verb, singular verb needed] dialysis treatments. Two or three times a week *are* [11k: amounts, singular verb needed] the norm for the treatments, which sometimes *continues* [11j: plural verb needed to agree with *treatments*] for months or even years. Dialysis, though, does not do everything that healthy kidneys *does* [11j: relative pronoun use here calls for plural verb].

Reregulating the amount of water in the blood and tissues *are* [11c: intervening words, singular verb needed] the best-known function of the kidney. Therefore, someone without functioning kidneys must be careful to keep *their* [11p: indefinite pronoun as antecedent, *his or her* needed] fluid intake within limits set by the doctor. Dialysis *help* [11a: singular subject calls for singular verb] to remove excess fluid. Reducing salt and controlling fluid intake also *helps* [11d: compound subject, plural verb needed]. Neither medical procedures nor diet *are* [11e: closest subject calls for singular verb] effective, however, without cooperation from the patient.

The whole family *are* [11h: collective noun calls for singular verb] affected, so it is important that the medical team *discuss* [11h: collective noun calls for singular verb] the functions of a healthy kidney with the patient and the family so that *he* [11n: compound antecedent calls for plural pronoun *they*] better understand the problems involved. Once the team makes *their* [11r: collective noun calls for singular pronoun *its*] treatment recommendations known, everyone can work together with greater patience and understanding.

ANSWER: PARTICIPATION ESSAY

This version revises the agreement errors. Answers will vary if students have revised for content, organization, or style.

Without kidney function, the body's ability to regulate fluids, blood pressure, red-cell production, protein levels, and blood chemistry is destroyed. If the kidneys no longer function, the standard prescription is dialysis treatments. Two or three times a week is the norm for the treatments, which sometimes continue for months or even years. Dialysis, though, does not do everything that healthy kidneys do.

Regulating the amount of water in the blood and tissues is the best-known function of the kidney. Therefore, someone without functioning kidneys must be careful to keep his or her fluid intake within limits set by the doctor. Dialysis helps to remove excess fluid. Reducing salt and controlling fluid intake also help. Neither medical procedures nor diet is effective, however, without cooperation from the patient.

The whole family is affected, so it is important that the medical team discusses the functions of a healthy kidney with the patient and the family so that they better understand the problems involved. Once the team makes its treatment recommendations known, everyone can work together with greater patience and understanding.

Barriers are broken daily. Rafting, rock climbing, and basketball have found enthusiasts among the handicapped. Marathon racing, along with skiing and cycling, also has great appeal. Many have tried their skill at these sports. One competitive event for the handicapped was the eighth Paralympic Games, which were held in Seoul, South Korea, the site of the 1988 Olympics.

Every disabled athlete needs to train somewhat differently to accommodate his or her particular handicap. One of today's most versatile athletes competes in a triathlon event by wearing one kind of prosthesis for cycling, another for running, and none for swimming.

Participation

A student wrote the following draft for a course called Introduction to Health Sciences. The assignment was to write about a function of the body. The material is concisely written and explains the material clearly, but the draft's effectiveness is diminished by pronoun–antecedent agreement errors and by subject–verb agreement errors.

Read through the draft. Then revise it to eliminate the errors. Also, make any additional revisions you think would improve the content, organization, and style of the material.

Without kidney function, the body's ability to regulate fluids, blood pressure, red-cell production, protein levels, and blood chemistry are destroyed. If the kidneys no longer function, the standard prescription are dialysis treatments. Two or three times a week are the norm for the treatments, which sometimes continues for months or even years. Dialysis, though, does not do everything that healthy kidneys does.

Regulating the amount of water in the blood and tissues are the best-known function of the kidney. Therefore, someone without functioning kidneys must be careful to keep their fluid intake within limits set by the doctor. Dialysis help to remove excess fluid. Reducing salt and controlling fluid intake also helps. Neither medical procedures nor diet are effective, however, without cooperation from the patient.

The whole family are affected, so it is important that the medical team discuss the functions of a healthy kidney with the patient and the family so that he better understand the problems involved. Once the team makes their treatment recommendations known, everyone can work together with greater patience and understanding.

12 Using Adjectives and Adverbs

12a Distinguishing between adjectives and adverbs

Both **adjectives** and **adverbs** are modifiers—words or groups of words that describe other words.

ADJECTIVE	The **brisk** *wind* blew. [Adjective *brisk* modifies noun *wind*.]
ADVERB	The wind *blew* **briskly.** [Adverb *briskly* modifies verb *blew*.]

The key to distinguishing between adjectives and adverbs is understanding that they modify different words or groups of words. As Chart 87 demonstrates, if you want to modify a noun° or pronoun°, use an adjective. If you want to modify a verb°, an adjective, or another adverb, use an adverb.

Inexperienced writers sometimes interchange adjectives and adverbs because of the *-ly* ending. Even though many adverbs do end in *-ly* (eat *swiftly*, eat *frequently*, eat *hungrily*), some do not (eat *fast*, eat *often*, eat *seldom*). To complicate matters further, some adjectives end in *-ly* (*lovely* flower, *friendly* dog). The *-ly* ending, therefore, is not a reliable way to identify adverbs.

EXERCISE 12-1

Consulting section 12a, first underline and label all adjectives (ADJ) and adverbs (ADV). Then go back and draw an arrow from each adjective and adverb to the word or words it modifies.

EXAMPLE   Do American teenagers frequently take jobs while attending high school?

ANSWERS: EXERCISE 12-1

1. Many American teenagers always worked very hard part-time jobs high school greater percentage teenage students ever before

271

ANSWERS: EXERCISE 12-1, *continued*

2. ADJ Reliable statistics

  ADV   ADJ ADV
almost one third of all

  ADJ   ADJ
ninth and tenth graders and

  ADV   ADJ
almost one half of

  ADJ   ADJ
all eleventh and twelfth graders

3.   ADV
Interestingly, they are

[whole clause] ⟶

    ADJ
working longer hours than the

  ADJ
high school students of

    ADJ   ADJ
twenty-five years ago

4. ADV   ADV
Not surprisingly, the number of

[whole clause] ⟶

         ADV
hours worked greatly influences

 ADJ
school performance.

5.   ADJ   ADV
important study conducted recently

 ADV   ADJ   ADJ
most eleventh and twelfth graders

  ADJ
weekly work schedule

  ADJ
twenty hours

 ADJ
their grades

12b   *ad*

1. Many American teenagers have always worked very hard at part-time jobs while going to high school, but a greater percentage of teenage students work today than ever before.

2. Reliable statistics reveal that almost one-third of all ninth and tenth graders and almost one-half of all eleventh and twelfth graders are employed.

3. Interestingly, they are working longer hours than the high school students of twenty-five years ago.

4. Not surprisingly, the number of hours worked greatly influences school performance.

5. An important study conducted recently at the University of California disclosed that most eleventh and twelfth graders can manage a weekly work schedule of twenty hours without damaging their grades.

SUMMARY OF DIFFERENCES BETWEEN ADJECTIVES AND ADVERBS   87

WHAT ADJECTIVES MODIFY	EXAMPLE
nouns°	The **busy** *lawyer* took a **quick** *look* at the members of the jury.
pronouns°	*She* felt **triumphant,** for *they* were **attentive.**

WHAT ADVERBS MODIFY	EXAMPLE
verbs°	The lawyer *spoke* **quickly** and **well.**
adverbs°	The lawyer spoke **very** *quickly.*
adjectives°	The lawyer was **extremely** *busy.*
independent clauses°	**Therefore,** *the lawyer rested.*

12b   Using adverbs—not adjectives—to modify verbs, adjectives, and other adverbs

Do not use adjectives as adverbs. Always use adverbs to modify verbs, adjectives, and other adverbs.

NO	The candidate inspired us **great**. [Adjective *great* cannot modify verb *inspired*.]
YES	The candidate inspired us **greatly**. [Adverb *greatly* can modify verb *inspired*.]
NO	The candidate felt **unusual** energetic. [Adjective *unusual* cannot modify adjective *energetic*.]
YES	The candidate felt **unusually energetic**. [Adverb *unusually* can modify adjective *energetic*.]
NO	The candidate spoke **exceptional forcefully**. [Adjective *exceptional* cannot modify adverb *forcefully*.]
YES	The candidate spoke **exceptionally forcefully**. [Adverb *exceptionally* modifies adverb *forcefully*.]

12c Not using double negatives

A **double negative** is a statement with two negative modifiers, the second of which repeats the message of the first. (This form, nonstandard today, was standard in the days of Chaucer and Shakespeare.) Negative modifiers include *no, never, not, none, nothing, hardly, scarcely,* and *barely.*

NO	The factory workers will **never** vote for **no** strike.
YES	The factory workers will **never** vote for **a** strike.

The words *not, no,* and *nothing* are particularly common in double negatives.

NO	The union members did **not** have **no** money in reserve.
YES	The union members did **not** have **any** money in reserve.
YES	The union members had **no** money in reserve.

If you use contractions, which many writers prefer to avoid in their academic writing, be especially careful not to use double negatives. When the word *not* is used in a contraction (such as *isn't, don't, didn't,* or *haven't*), the negative message carried by the contracted *not* applies to the entire statement. Do not let the *not* slip by your notice; do not add a second negative.

NO	He did**n't** hear **nothing**.
YES	He did**n't** hear **anything**.
NO	They have**n't** had **no** meeting.
YES	They have**n't** had **any** meeting.

LANGUAGE HISTORY

The rule banning double negatives in English is a relatively new one. Double, triple, and even quadruple negatives were acceptable in Old English and Middle English. They are also acceptable in many modern languages. In the eighteenth century, the first attempts were made to regularize English. It was then that the first English dictionaries and usage books were written. One of these was Robert Lowth's *Short Introduction to English Grammar*, in which he stated that "two Negatives in English destroy one another, or are equivalent to an affirmative." The new rich of the merchant class, eager to fit in by speaking and writing correctly, accepted Lowth's rule, and it became the standard despite the thousand-year history of acceptable double negatives in English.

BACKGROUND

In the chapter on vocabulary in *Errors and Expectations* (New York: Oxford UP, 1977), Mina Shaughnessy describes the use of modifiers by three groups of freshman writers. The few adverbs used by *basic* writers, she notes, usually come from the most overworked ones in the language, such as *too, very, quite,* and *hardly.* Similarly, basic writers modify their nouns and verbs with what she calls "the common adjectives": *a lot, many, good, easy, big, certain,* familiar words that slip into place without mental effort, thereby making it impossible for the writer to achieve the precision needed for complex consideration of the topic. *Intermediate* writers, moving closer to precise diction, use *-ly* adverbs and more specific adjectives. Although they are likely to use multiple adjectives, doing so does not usually increase the precision of the statement. *Advanced* freshman writers, working with more confidence, lean on adverbial conjunctions for paragraph cohesion—e.g., *furthermore, however, consequently*—and even include figurative language in an effort to be descriptive.

12d Using adjectives—not adverbs—as complements after linking verbs

Linking verbs indicate a state of being or a condition. They include *be (am, is, are, was, were)*; verbs related to the senses, including *look, smell, taste, sound,* and *feel*; and verbs such as *appear, seem, become, grow, turn, remain,* and *prove.* Linking verbs connect the subject° to a complement—a word that renames or describes the subject (see 7m-1). You can think of a linking verb as an equal sign between a subject and its complement.

The guests looked **happy.** [subject *guests* = adjective *happy*]

Problems can arise with verbs that function sometimes as linking verbs and sometimes as action verbs, depending on the structure of the sentence. As linking verbs, these verbs use adjectives in complements. As action verbs, these verbs use adverbs.

Zora **looks happy.** [*looks* = linking verb; *happy* = adjective]

Zora **looks happily** at the sunset. [*looks* = action verb; *happily* = adverb]

Bad—Badly

The words *bad* (adjective) and *badly* (adverb) are particularly prone to misuse with linking verbs such as *feel, grow, smell, sound, taste.* Only the adjective *bad* is correct when a verb is functioning as a linking verb. (When a verb functions as an action verb, *badly* is fine: Zora **played** the piano **badly.**)

FOR DESCRIBING A FEELING

NO	The student felt **badly.**
YES	The student felt **bad.**

FOR DESCRIBING A SMELL

NO	The food smelled **badly.**
YES	The food smelled **bad.**

Good—Well

Well functions both as an adverb and as an adjective. As a modifier°, *good* is always an adjective: *He wore his **good** suit. Well* is an adjective referring to good health, but it is an adverb in all other contexts.

You look **well** = You look to be in good health. [*well* = adjective]

You write **well** = You write skillfully. [*well* = adverb]

Except when *well* is an adjective referring to health, use *good* only as an adjective and *well* only as an adverb.

> **NO**   She sings **good.** [*sings* = action verb; adverb, not adjective, required; *good* is adjective]
>
> **YES**   She sings **well.** [*well* = adverb]

EXERCISE 12-2

Consulting sections 12b, 12c, and 12d, choose the correct uses of negatives and of adjectives and adverbs.

EXAMPLE   If Halloween and horror stories are a (good, well) **good** indicator, most people never want (nothing, anything) **anything** to do with bats.

1. Myths have labeled bats as (aggressively, aggressive) _____ and short-tempered, but biologists who (frequent, frequently) _____ handle bats call them (extreme, extremely) _____ shy and (gently, gentle) _____ .

2. These researchers who feel (bad, badly) _____ about the bats' terrifying reputation report that bats don't (never, ever) _____ act like the fearsome creatures in legends.

3. Bats (actual, actually) _____ (greedily, greedy) _____ eat insects by the millions, a fact that might make some people begin to feel (well, good) _____ about bats.

4. Varying (wide, widely) _____ in size and weight, some bats have a (terrifyingly, terrifying) _____ six-foot wingspan, while others weigh less than a penny.

5. Many people think bats come in nothing but neutral colors like mouse gray or brown, but some bats are (bright, brightly) _____ red or yellow.

12e   Using correct comparative and superlative forms of adjectives and adverbs

When comparisons are made, descriptive adjectives and adverbs often carry the message. Adjectives and adverbs, therefore, have forms that communicate relative degrees of intensity.

1   Using correct forms of comparison for regular adjectives and adverbs

Most adjectives and adverbs show degrees of intensity by adding *-er* and *-est* endings or by combining with the words *more,*

ANSWERS AND COVERAGE: EXERCISE 12-2

1. aggressive [12a, adj. modifies noun *bats*] frequently [12b, adv. modifies verb *handle*] extremely [adv. modifies adj. *shy*] gentle [12a, adj. modifies pronoun *them*]

2. bad [12d, adj. after linking verb *feel*] ever [12c, avoid double negative with *don't*]

3. actually, greedily [advs. modify verb *eat*] good [12d, adj. after linking verb *feel*]

4. widely [12b, adv. modifies adj. *varying*] terrifying [12a, adj. modifies noun *wingspan*]

5. bright [12d, adj. after linking verb *are*]

QUOTATION ABOUT LANGUAGE

Adjectives are used so freely these days that we feel almost naked, robbed, if we don't get at least a couple.

—Paul Stevens

WORD HISTORIES

Common irregular adjectives (and adverbs) can be confusing to students because the comparative and superlative forms seem unconnected to the positive form. The realization that these irregularities are only accidents of history rather than the product of difficult rules can make them less intimidating.

For example, *good* comes from the Old English *god*, related to the German *gut*, both of which come from the Indo-European word meaning *to be suitable*. *Better* and *best* come from Old English *betera* and *betst* respectively, based on the Indo-European word meaning *good*.

Another example is *worse* and *worst*, which come from their Old English synonyms: *wiersa* and *wyrsta*. However, *bad* does not come from *yfel*, the Old English word for *bad* or *evil*, but from Old English *baeddel*, meaning *hermaphrodite*. Perhaps your students would like to theorize about why this happened.

BACKGROUND

Adjectives can be made from nouns by adding different endings that sometimes color the meaning of the word. For example, an *-ish* ending can give a word a derogatory slant, as in *high-schoolish* or *childish*. On other occasions the *-ish* ending, and the *-y* ending, mean "similar to" or "becoming." For example, a *yellowish substance* or a *flowery paragraph* suggest a substance and paragraph that are not entirely yellow or flowered, but close. Materials often take an *-en* ending when they turn from nouns into adjectives (as in *wooden* and *silken*), and adjectives that suggest a Latin origin frequently end in *-al, -ar,* or *-ory* (as in *beneficial, oracular,* and *promissory*).

less, least (see Chart 88). A few adjectives and adverbs are irregular, as explained in 12e-2.

FORMS OF COMPARISON FOR REGULAR ADJECTIVES AND ADVERBS	88

FORM	FUNCTION
■ Positive	Used when nothing is being compared
■ Comparative	Used when two things are being compared, with *-er* ending or *more/less*
■ Superlative	Used when three or more things are being compared, with *-est* ending or *most/least*

POSITIVE	COMPARATIVE	SUPERLATIVE
green	greener	greenest
happy	happier	happiest
selfish	less selfish	least selfish
beautiful	more beautiful	most beautiful

Her tree is **green.**

Her tree is **greener** than his tree.

Her tree is the **greenest** tree on the block.

The choice of whether to use *-er, -est* or *more, most, less, least* depends largely on the number of syllables in the adjective or adverb.

- With **one-syllable words,** the *-er*, and *-est* endings are most common: *large, larger, largest* (adjective); *far, farther, farthest* (adverb).
- With **three-syllable words,** *more, most, less, least* are used.
- With **adverbs of two or more syllables,** *more, most, less, least* are used: *easily, more easily, most easily.*
- With **adjectives of two syllables,** practice varies: some take the *-er, -est* endings; others combine with *more* and *most.*

One general rule covers two-syllable adjectives ending in *-y:* use the *-er, -est* endings after changing the *-y* to *i: pretty, prettier, prettiest.* For other two-syllable adjectives, form comparatives and superlatives intuitively, based on what you have heard or read for a particular adjective.

Be careful not to use a **double comparative** or **double superlative**. The words *more, most, less, least* cannot be used if the *-er* or *-est* ending has been used.

He was **younger** [not *more younger*] than his brother.
Her music was the **snappiest** [not *more snappiest*] on the radio.
People danced **more easily** [not *more easier*] to her music.

2	**Using correct forms of comparison for irregular adjectives and adverbs**

A few comparative and superlative forms are irregular. They are listed in Chart 89. Memorize them so that they always spring easily to mind.

IRREGULAR COMPARATIVES AND SUPERLATIVES   89

POSITIVE [1]	COMPARATIVE [2]	SUPERLATIVE [3 +]
good (adjective)	better	best
well (adjective and adverb)	better	best
bad (adjective)	worse	worst
badly (adverb)	worse	worst
many	more	most
much	more	most
some	more	most
little	less	least

The Perkinses saw a **good** movie.
The Perkinses saw a **better** movie than the Smiths did.
The Perkinses saw **the best** movie that they had ever seen.

The Millers had **little** trouble finding jobs.
The Millers had **less** trouble finding jobs than the Smiths did.
The Millers had **the least** trouble finding jobs of everyone.

❖ USAGE ALERT: Do not use *less* and *fewer* interchangeably. Use *less* with noncountable items or values that form one whole. Use *fewer* with numbers or anything that can be counted: *They consumed* **fewer** *calories; the sugar substitute had* **less aftertaste.** ❖

EXTRA EXERCISE

Underline the adjectives and adverbs. If any adjective or adverb is in an incorrect form, write the correct form above it.

EXAMPLE

            more loudly
The music played   loud   in the disco than in the restaurant.

  1. The Joneses have the bigger tree on the block.

  2. Colorado has some of the most prettiest scenery in the country.

  3. Which of the sick twins has the highest fever?

  4. Juan is friendlier than his cousin.

  5. The more faster runner of the two received a ribbon.

  6. The red blouse is the most attractive in the store.

  7. Leontyne Price sings good.

  8. That is the worse coffee shop in town.

  9. Spain is near to Africa than most people realize.

10. Marc Chagall is the more famous modern artist from Russia.

ANSWERS: EXTRA EXERCISE

  1. biggest
  2. prettiest (drop *most*)
  3. higher
  4. Correct
  5. faster (drop *more*)
  6. Correct
  7. well
  8. worst
  9. nearer
10. most famous

ANSWERS: EXERCISE 12-3

Sentences called for in the second part of the instructions will vary. Here is the chart filled in.

POSITIVE	COMPARATIVE	SUPERLATIVE
big	bigger	biggest
hungry	hungrier	hungriest
hungry	more hungry	most hungry
quickly	more quickly	most quickly
important	more important	most important
thick	thicker	thickest
thirsty	more thirsty	most thirsty

BACKGROUND

"Jokes play across grammar," writes Josephine Miles in "The Humor of Composition" (*Composition and Literature: Bridging the Gap*, ed. Winifred Bryan Horner [Chicago: U of Chicago P, 1983]), and many jokes play on the "subtle tricks" of modifiers. In the following story, Miles observes, "a lot of superlative adjectives are shifted to one simple comparative":

> James Thurber and a friend attended the opening of a play that proved to be a bore from beginning to end. As they left the theater, the friend said, "That was the dullest, dreariest, and shoddiest play I ever saw."
> This off his chest, he continued, "And what did you think of it?"
> "Well," said the humorist, "I didn't think it was that good."

The punchline, Miles writes, depends on "Thurber's use of a predicate, a verb, and an intensive adverb instead of the negative adverb" (34). She does not, however, recommend analyzing jokes in class. That seems just as well.

EXERCISE 12-3

Consulting section 12e, do two things: First, complete this chart. Next, write sentences that set a context for each word in the completed chart.

EXAMPLE   *big:* Weighing 270 pounds and standing seven feet tall, he is big, even for a football player.

POSITIVE [1]	COMPARATIVE [2]	SUPERLATIVE [3+]
big		
		hungriest
	more hungry	
quickly		
important		
	thicker	
		most thirsty

12f Avoiding too many nouns as modifiers

Sometimes nouns—words that name a person, place, thing, or idea—function as modifiers° of other nouns: *truck driver, train track, security system.* These very familiar terms create no problems. However, when nouns pile up in a sequence of modifiers, the reader has difficulty figuring out which nouns are being modified and which nouns are doing the modifying. As you revise such sentences, you can use any of several routes to clarify your material.

SENTENCE REWRITTEN

NO   I asked my advisor to write **two college recommendation** letters for me.

YES   I asked my advisor to write **letters of recommendation** to **two colleges** for me.

ONE NOUN CHANGED TO POSSESSIVE CASE AND ANOTHER TO ADJECTIVE FORM

NO   Some students might take the **United States Navy examination** for **navy engineer training.**

YES   Some students might take the United States **Navy's** examination for **naval** engineer training.

NOUN CHANGED TO PREPOSITIONAL PHRASE

NO   Our **student advisor training program** has won awards for excellence.

YES   Our training program **for student advisors** has won awards for excellence. [Notice that this change requires the plural *advisors.*]

EXERCISE 12-4

Consulting all sections of this chapter, revise these sentences so that they are suitable for academic writing.

EXAMPLE   Animation is a little-understood, almost magical art that produces characters that are (remarkable, remarkably) **remarkably** human.

1. Not many people know that before computerization, animated characters were (most often, oftenest) _____ based on human beings, who had been asked to model for the animators.

2. The idea of using models worked (good, well) _____ because animators didn't (never, ever) _____ have to rely on their memories to draw lifelike movements of the human body.

3. Dopey in the 1937 film *Snow White and the Seven Dwarfs* was the (earliest, most early) _____ animated character to be based on a live model, a burlesque comedian named Eddie Collins.

4. A fact known to even (fewer, less) _____ people is that during the 1950s, animators used (elaborate, elaborately) _____ staged scenes complete with costumes and makeup and well-known stars.

5. In *Lady and the Tramp*, actress and singer Peggy Lee was the voice of Peg the Pekingese, and she also served (good, well) _____ as the model for one of the (sauciest, most sauciest) _____ walks in the history of animation.

ANSWERS AND COVERAGE:
EXERCISE 12-4

1. most often [12e, correct superlatives]

2. well [12b, adv. modifying verb *worked*] ever [12c, avoiding double negative]

3. earliest [12e, correct superlatives]

4. fewer [12e, correct comparatives] elaborately [12b, adv. modifying adjective *staged*]

5. well [12b, adv. modifying verb *served*] sauciest [12e, correct superlatives]

Writing
Correct
Sentences

 When you write correct sentences, you have a better chance of communicating clearly with your readers. Part Three offers you practical advice about how to avoid the most common sentence errors that interfere with the delivery of meaning. As you use Chapters 13 through 15, keep in mind that correct sentences give you a foundation on which you can build an effective, graceful, and memorable writing style.

13 Sentence Fragments

TEACHING TIP

Students sometimes create fragments as they attempt to write longer or more complicated sentences and experiment with their style. Without a range of syntactic structures available to them, students may try to vary the rhythm of their sentences, suggest pauses for emphasis, and establish sentence variety with the placement of periods. Fragments often appear because students begin using dependent clauses, participial phrases, elliptical constructions, and absolute phrases in their writing before they have enough knowledge and control of these structures. Students often benefit when they learn new sentence patterns as they learn to avoid fragments. Students who use periods to suggest a long pause may benefit from instruction on the dash (Chapter 29). Students creating fragments from dependent clauses, absolute phrases, and participial phrases may benefit from studying coordination and subordination (Chapter 17), parallelism (Chapter 18), and techniques for achieving sentence variety and emphasis (Chapter 19).

A sentence fragment occurs when a portion of a sentence is punctuated as a complete sentence. This chapter shows you how to distinguish between sentence fragments and complete sentences.

FRAGMENT	The telephone with redial capacity. [no verb°*]
REVISED	The telephone has redial capacity.
FRAGMENT	Rang loudly for ten minutes. [no subject°]
REVISED	The telephone rang loudly for ten minutes.
FRAGMENT	At midnight. [no verb° or subject°]
REVISED	The telephone rang at midnight.
FRAGMENT	**Because** the telephone rang loudly. [dependent clause° with subordinating conjunction°]
REVISED	Because the telephone rang loudly, the family was awakened in the middle of the night.
FRAGMENT	The telephone call **that** woke the family. [dependent clause° with relative pronoun°]
REVISED	The telephone call that woke the family was a wrong number.

Sentence fragments distract readers by intruding on the clarity of the message that you want your material to deliver.

NO	The lawyer was angry. When she returned from court. She found the key witness waiting in her office. [Was the lawyer angry when she returned from court or when she found the witness in her office?]

*Throughout this book, a degree mark (°) indicates that you can find the definition of the word in the Glossary of Terms in this handbook.

YES	The lawyer was angry when she returned from court. She found the key witness waiting in her office.
YES	The lawyer was angry. When she returned from court, she found the key witness waiting in her office.

When you check for sentence fragments, wait until the revising (see 3c) and editing (see 3d) stages of your writing process. While you are drafting (see 3b), if you suspect that you have written a sentence fragment, quickly underline or highlight the material without breaking your rhythm. Then you can check it later.

13a · Testing for sentence completeness

If you write sentence fragments frequently, you need a system to check that your sentences are complete. Here is a test you can use.

TEST FOR SENTENCE COMPLETENESS   90

1. **Is there a verb°?** If no, there is a sentence fragment.
2. **Is there a subject°?** If no, there is a sentence fragment.
3. **Do the subject and verb start with a subordinating word° and lack an independent clause° to complete the thought?** If yes, there is a sentence fragment.

QUESTION 1: Is there a verb?

If there is no verb, you are looking at a sentence fragment. Verbs convey information about what is happening, what has happened, or what will happen. In testing for sentence completeness, find a verb that can change form to communicate a change in time.

> Yesterday, the telephone **rang.**
> Now the telephone **rings.**

Verbals° do not function as verbs, so do not mistake a verbal for a verb. Verbals are gerunds° (-*ing* forms as nouns°), present participles° (-*ing* forms as modifiers°), past participles° (-*ed* or irregular past forms as modifiers), and infinitives° (*to* forms).

TEACHING TIP

To discuss fragments, you might ask students to bring in samples of public writing that contain fragments. Fruitful sources include advertisements, mail solicitations, and memos from companies where the students work. Collect, reproduce, and distribute a sampling of the passages. Ask students to identify all the fragments and to determine which, if any, are acceptable. Then have them revise the passages to eliminate the unacceptable fragments.

This lesson can be enlivened by the use of an overhead projector. Prepare transparencies of the original passages, and use a series of overlays to record and compare student revisions.

Students may ask why they must avoid unacceptable fragments when these errors can be found in published writing. You may want to discuss what impressions about the writers and their companies these errors create.

BACKGROUND

In a survey of 84 professionals representing 63 different occupations (Maxine Hairston, "Not All Errors Are Created Equal: Nonacademic Readers in the Profession Respond to Lapses in Usage," *College English* [1981]: 794–806), respondents ranked sentence fragments among the most serious of errors, below only "status markers" such as nonstandard verbs ("brung"), double negatives, and beginning a sentence with an objective pronoun.

QUOTATION ABOUT WRITING

Writing, I think, is an interestingly perverse occupation. It is quite sick in the sense of normal human enjoyment of life, because the writer is always *removed*, the way an actor never is.

—Edna O'Brien

FRAGMENT	Yesterday, the students registering for classes.
REVISED	Yesterday, the students **were** registering for classes.
FRAGMENT	Now the students registering for classes.
REVISED	Now the students **are** registering for classes.
FRAGMENT	Yesterday, told about an excellent teacher.
REVISED	Yesterday, I **was** told about an excellent teacher.
FRAGMENT	Now the students to register for classes.
REVISED	Now the students **want** to register for classes.

QUESTION 2: Is there a subject?

If there is no subject, you are looking at a sentence fragment. To find a subject, ask the verb "who?" or "what?"

FRAGMENT	Studied hard for class. [Who studied? unknown]
REVISED	The students studied hard for class. [Who studied? students]
FRAGMENT	Contained some difficult questions. [What contained? unknown]
REVISED	The test contained some difficult questions. [What contained? the test]

Every sentence must have its own subject. A sentence fragment without a subject often occurs when the missing subject is the same as the subject in the preceding sentence.

NO	The students formed a study group to prepare for the midterm exam. **Decided** to study together for the rest of the course.
YES	The students formed a study group to prepare for the midterm exam. **They decided** to study together for the rest of the course.
YES	The students formed a study group to prepare for the midterm exam, **and they decided** to study together for the rest of the course.

Imperative statements—commands and some requests—are an exception. They are not sentence fragments. Imperative statements imply the word "you" as the subject.

Run! = (You) run!
Study hard. = (You) study hard.
Please return my books. = (You) please return my books.

QUESTION 3: Do the subject and verb start with a subordinating word and lack an independent clause to complete the thought?

If the answer to Question 3 is "yes," you are looking at a sentence fragment. Subordinating words begin **dependent clauses.** A dependent clause cannot stand alone as an independent unit; it must be joined to an independent clause to be part of a complete sentence.

One type of subordinating word is a **subordinating conjunction.** A subordinating conjunction comes at the beginning of a dependent clause. Here are frequently used subordinating conjunctions. (For a more complete list that also tells the relationship each word expresses, see Chart 56 in section 7h.)

after	because	since	when
although	before	unless	whenever
as	if	until	where

FRAGMENT	**Because** she returned my books.
REVISED	**Because** she returned my books, I can study.
FRAGMENT	**When** I study.
REVISED	I have to concentrate **when** I study.

❖ PUNCTUATION ALERT: When a dependent clause starting with a subordinating conjunction, also called an adverb clause, comes before an independent clause, a comma usually separates the clauses (see 24b-1). ❖

Another type of subordinating word is a **relative pronoun.** The most common relative pronouns are *who, which,* and *that.*

FRAGMENT	The test **that** we studied for.
REVISED	The test **that** we studied for was cancelled.
FRAGMENT	The professor **who** taught the course.
REVISED	The professor **who** taught the course was ill.

Questions can begin with words such as *when, where, who,* and *which* without being sentence fragments: *When do you want to study? Where is the library? Who is your professor? Which class are you taking?*

ALTERNATE EXAMPLE

If your students have trouble recognizing dependent clauses as fragments, you may want to give them practice. Ask them to locate the fragments in the following mixture of complete and incomplete sentences. You might also ask them to combine the sentences so that each one is complete, being careful to separate with a comma each opening dependent clause from the independent one that follows.

Many elderly people have pets as companions. Because the elderly are often lonely. Nevertheless, pets make demands on their energy. For example, if a cat is sick, and when a dog must be bathed. Unless the owner has the strength and funds to care for the pet's needs. Then the pet is better off with a younger owner. Since the pet deserves a good home too. Before getting a cat or dog, people should be certain that they can provide adequate care.

TEACHING TIP

Dictating a passage like the one below for students to copy and punctuate can be a helpful exercise for students in identifying sentence boundaries. Students can compare their versions and discuss any differences.

We have a nine-acre lake on our ranch and a warm spring that feeds it all winter. By mid-March the lake ice begins to melt where the spring feeds in, and every year the same pair of mallards come ahead of the others and wait. Though there is very little open water they seem content. They glide back and forth through a thin estuary, brushing watercress with their elegant folded wings, then tip end-up to eat and, after, clamber onto the lip of ice that retreats, hardens forward, and retreats again.

—Gretel Ehrlich

TEACHING TIP

In *Grammar and the Teaching of Writing: Limits and Possibilities* (NCTE, 1991), Rei R. Noguchi proposes that students can identify declarative sentences and fragments if they attempt to transform the construction into tag questions and yes–no questions. For example, "Doing math problems isn't one of Billy's favorite activities" can be transformed into the tag question "Doing math problems isn't one of Billy's favorite activities, is it?" and the yes–no question "Isn't doing math problems one of Billy's favorite activities?" With fragments such as "Enjoyed the baseball game on Saturday" or "Whatever you could do to help my sister," students will find it impossible to create such questions unless they add words to the fragment, revealing that the construction was an incomplete sentence. You might ask students to try this method with Exercise 13-1.

ANSWERS: EXERCISE 13-1

Two pieces of information are given for each item: the reason for the sentence fragment and the number of the question in the "Test for Sentence Completeness" that explains what has caused each sentence fragment. (Exercise 13-3 asks students to correct the sentence fragments in this exercise.)

1. No verb; question 1
2. Starts with a subordinating word—without an independent clause to complete the thought; question 3
3. Complete sentence
4. No verb; question 1
5. No verb; question 1
6. No subject; question 2
7. Starts with a subordinating word but lacks an independent clause to complete the thought; question 3
8. No independent clause for clause beginning with *which*; question 3
9. Complete sentence
10. No subject; question 2

Chart 91 summarizes information on correcting a sentence fragment once you have identified its grammatical structure.

HOW TO CORRECT SENTENCE FRAGMENTS 91

REVISION STRATEGY

- If the sentence fragment is a dependent clause°, join it to an adjacent independent clause° (see 13b).
- If the sentence fragment is a dependent clause, revise it into an independent clause (see 13b).
- If the sentence fragment is a phrase°, join it to an adjacent independent clause (see 13c).
- If the sentence fragment is a phrase, revise it into an independent clause (see 13c).

EXERCISE 13-1

Using the Test for Sentence Completeness in Chart 90, check each word group. If a word group is a sentence fragment, explain what makes it incomplete. If a word group is a complete sentence, circle its number.

EXAMPLE   Urushiol the rash of poison ivy. [No verb; Question 1 in Chart 90.]

1. Urushiol from a crushed leaf or a broken stem of the poison ivy plant.
2. If ten people touch urushiol.
3. One person will have no reaction.
4. Nine people a rash.
5. One person sick enough for medical attention.
6. Penetrates the skin in minutes to cause an itchy rash.
7. Because urushiol can remain active for months on any object that touches it.
8. A mysterious rash, which has no apparent cause.
9. Although quickly washing in water can neutralize urushiol, soap can actually spread the rash.
10. Itches and oozes but is not contagious.

13b Revising dependent clauses punctuated as sentences

A **dependent clause** contains both a subject° and a verb° but also contains a subordinating word° (see 13a, Question 3). It cannot stand on its own as a sentence.

To correct a dependent clause punctuated as a sentence, you can either (1) join the dependent clause to an independent clause that comes directly before or after; if necessary, add words to the combined sentence so that it makes sense; or (2) drop the subordinating word; if necessary, add words to create an independent clause that makes sense.

FRAGMENT	Many people over twenty-five years of age are deciding to get college degrees. **Because they want the benefits of an advanced education.**
REVISED	Many people over twenty-five years of age are deciding to get college degrees because they want the benefits of an advanced education. [joined into one sentence]
REVISED	Many people over twenty-five years of age are deciding to get college degrees. They want the benefits of an advanced education. [subordinating conjunction dropped to create an independent clause]
FRAGMENT	College attracts many older students. **Who could not attend upon graduation from high school.**
REVISED	College attracts many older students who could not attend upon graduation from high school. [joined into one sentence]
REVISED	College attracts many older students. They could not attend upon graduation from high school. [relative pronoun dropped and *they* added to create an independent clause]

✚ USAGE ALERT: When trying to identify dependent clauses, be especially careful with words that indicate time—such as *after, before, since,* and *until*. In some sentences, they function as subordinating conjunctions, but in other sentences they function as adverbs° and prepositions°. Do not automatically assume when you see these words that you are looking at a dependent clause.

ALTERNATE EXAMPLE

In the paragraph that follows, words that indicate time sometimes function as subordinating conjunctions and sometimes as adverbs and prepositions. You might want to ask your students to locate those that act as subordinating conjunctions, indicated here by italics.

When Major Walter Slapton Wingfield invented lawn tennis in 1873, he merely combined several other racket games popular at the time. A century before, a "field tennis" club had been formed near London. *After* tennis came to the United States in 1878, it quickly spread throughout the country. Before Billie Jean King, however, professional tennis was mostly a male sport, and *until* it was broadcast on national television, many considered it to be an "elitist" one. Since then it has attracted spectator interest that rivals other major sports.

Before, the class was never full. Now it is overfilled. [These are two complete sentences. In the first sentence, *before* is an adverb° modifying the independent clause° *the class was never full.*]

Before this semester, the class was never full. [This is a complete sentence. *Before* is the preposition° in the prepositional phrase° *before this semester.*]

Before the professor arrived. [This is a dependent clause° punctuated as a sentence, so it is a sentence fragment. *Before* is a subordinating conjunction°.]

Before the professor arrived, the room was empty. [This is a complete sentence. The dependent clause precedes an independent clause.] ✣

EXERCISE 13-2

Consulting sections 13a and 13b, find and correct any sentence fragments. If a sentence is correct, circle its number.

EXAMPLE   Museums collect and exhibit artifacts. Which are human-made objects such as tools, weapons, and ornaments.

Museums collect and exhibit artifacts, which are human-made objects such as tools, weapons, and ornaments.

1. Artifacts offer glimpses of other cultures. Which include those of early inhabitants of the United States.

2. Although the archaeologists who obtain these artifacts are often funded by grants from the U.S. government.

3. Still, the Native American Indian descendants of those early peoples regard the archaeologists as thieves.

4. They are considered to be grave robbers. When the archaeologists take bones and burial artifacts.

5. Anthropologists and archaeologists who examine these Native American artifacts. They are able to reconstruct lifestyles and even human physical development.

6. At least eighteen states now have laws. That require or encourage the return of Native American remains to the tribes. Because Native Americans protested that the scientists were desecrating sacred ground.

7. Museums are being allowed to photograph and catalog the artifacts in their possession. After that, the artifacts must be returned to the tribes.

ANSWERS AND COVERAGE:
EXERCISE 13-2

Answers will vary. Here is one set of possible responses.

1. Artifacts offer glimpses of other cultures, which include those of early inhabitants of the United States. [dependent (relative) clause fragment attached to independent clause]

2. The archaeologists who obtain these artifacts are often funded by grants from the U.S. government. [subordinating conjunction dropped from dependent (adverb) clause]

3. Correct complete sentence

4. When the archaeologists take bones and burial artifacts, they are considered to be grave robbers. [dependent (adverb) clause fragment attached to independent clause]

5. Anthropologists and archaeologists who examine these Native American artifacts are able to reconstruct lifestyles and even human physical development. [subject and dependent (relative) clause fragment attached to independent clause]

6. Because Native Americans protested that the scientists were desecrating sacred ground, at least eighteen states now have laws that require or encourage the return of Native American remains to the tribes. [two dependent clauses (relative *that* clause and adverb *because* clause) added to independent clause]

7. Correct complete sentences

➡

8. Except for materials that were originally obtained with the permission of the tribes or those that the tribes agree can stay with researchers.

9. Even though the Smithsonian Institution, for example. It has already identified and returned over 300 skeletons to the tribes of origin. Museum officials plan to return even more artifacts to descendants.

10. Tribal councils are deciding whether all the artifacts will be reburied. Or whether some artifacts will remain available for further scientific study.

13c   Revising phrases punctuated as sentences

A **phrase** is a group of words that lacks a subject°, a verb°, or both. A phrase cannot stand on its own as a sentence. To revise a phrase punctuated as a sentence, you can either (1) rewrite it to become an independent clause°, or (2) join it to an independent clause that comes directly before or after.

A **verbal phrase** contains a verbal (an infinitive°, a past participle°, or a present participle°). It is not a sentence.

FRAGMENT	The mayor called a news conference last week. **To announce new programs for crime prevention and care for the homeless.** [verbal phrase containing infinitive *to announce*]
REVISED	The mayor called a news conference last week to announce new programs for crime prevention and care for the homeless. [joined into one sentence]
REVISED	The mayor called a news conference last week. She wanted to announce new programs for crime prevention and care for the homeless. [rewritten]
FRAGMENT	**Introduced by her assistant.** The mayor began with an opening statement. [verbal phrase containing past participle *introduced*]
REVISED	Introduced by her assistant, the mayor began with an opening statement. [joined into one sentence]
REVISED	The mayor **was** introduced by her assistant. She began with an opening statement. [rewritten]

Cont'd.

8. The exceptions are materials that were originally obtained with the permission of the tribes or those that the tribes agree can stay with researchers. [dependent (adverb) clause turned into independent clause]

9. Even though the Smithsonian Institution, for example, has already identified and returned over 300 skeletons to the tribes of origin, museum officials plan to return even more artifacts to descendants. [dependent (adverb) clause attached to independent clause; second independent clause attached for sense]

10. Tribal councils are deciding whether all the artifacts will be reburied or whether some [artifacts] will remain available for further scientific study. [dependent (adverb) clause attached to independent clause]

TEACHING TIP

To demonstrate how phrases can be turned into complete sentences, you might ask two students to read the following dialogue aloud in class, and then to improvise each comment as a sentence.

A: When are you coming?
B: In a minute.
A: Really?
B: Really.
A: Hurry up!
B: O.K. O.K. Just a second. How about Mother?
A: Who?
B: Mother.
A: Sure. Ready hours ago.

ANSWERS AND COVERAGE: EXERCISE 13-3

Answers will vary. Here is one set of possibilities.

1. Urushiol comes [verb supplied] from a crushed leaf or a broken stem of the poison ivy plant.

2. If ten people touch urushiol, one person will have no reaction [independent clause supplied].

3. Complete sentence

4. Nine people will have [verb supplied] a rash.

5. One person will be [verb supplied] sick enough for medical attention.

6. Urushiol [subject supplied] penetrates the skin in minutes to cause an itchy rash.

7. Urushiol can remain active for months on any object that touches it. [subordinating conjunction *Because* removed to make dependent (adverb) clause independent]

8. A mysterious rash, which has no apparent cause, appears [verb supplied].

9. Complete sentence

10. The rash [subject supplied] itches and oozes but is not contagious.

ANSWERS: EXERCISE 13-4

Answers will vary. Here is one possible revision.

An enterprising U.S. architect has constructed an aquarium in the Japanese city of Osaka to give visitors the experience of walking around the entire Pacific Ocean in only ninety minutes. What is this marvel? It is called "Ring of Fire" because the aquarium was designed to look like the Pacific coasts of Asia, the United States, and South America. The aquarium features a 1.4 million-gallon tank of sea water and also includes smaller tanks that represent the Pacific's richest coastal areas. In the water, brought to the aquarium from the Pacific Ocean by tanker, swim sea otters, penguins,

➔

FRAGMENT	**Hoping for strong public support.** She gave many examples of problems everywhere in the city. [verbal phrase containing present participle *hoping*]
REVISED	Hoping for strong public support, she gave many examples of problems everywhere in the city. [joined into one sentence]
REVISED	She was hoping for strong public support. She gave many examples of problems everywhere in the city. [rewritten]

A **prepositional phrase** starts with a preposition° (for a complete list, see Chart 53 in section 7g). It is not a sentence.

FRAGMENT	Cigarette smoke made the conference room seem airless. **During the long news conference.**
REVISED	Cigarette smoke made the conference room seem airless during the long news conference. [joined into one sentence]
REVISED	Cigarette smoke made the conference room seem airless. It was hard to breathe during the long news conference. [rewritten]

An **appositive** is one or more words that renames a noun°. It is not a sentence.

FRAGMENT	Most people respected the mayor. **A politician with fresh ideas and practical solutions.**
REVISED	Most people respected the mayor, a politician with fresh ideas and practical solutions. [joined into one sentence]
REVISED	Most people respected the mayor. She seemed to be a politician with fresh ideas and practical solutions. [rewritten]

A **compound predicate** contains two or more verbs°. To be part of a complete sentence, a predicate must have a subject. When the second half of a compound predicate is punctuated as a separate sentence, it is not a sentence.

FRAGMENT	The reporters asked the mayor many questions about the details of her program. **And then discussed her answers among themselves.**
REVISED	The reporters asked the mayor many questions about the details of her program and then discussed her answers among themselves. [joined into one sentence]

REVISED The reporters asked the mayor many questions about the details of her program. Then the reporters discussed her answers among themselves. [rewritten]

EXERCISE 13-3

Go back to Exercise 13-1 and revise any sentence fragments into complete sentences.

EXERCISE 13-4

Consulting sections 13a, 13b, and 13c, revise this paragraph to eliminate any sentence fragments. In some cases, you can combine word groups to create complete sentences; in other cases, you must supply missing elements to revise word groups. In your final version, check not only the individual sentences but also the clarity of the whole paragraph.

(1) An enterprising U.S. architect has constructed an aquarium. (2) In the Japanese city of Osaka. (3) To give visitors the experience of walking around the entire Pacific Ocean. (4) In only ninety minutes. (5) What is this marvel? (6) Called ''Ring of Fire.'' (7) Because the aquarium was designed to look like the Pacific coasts of Asia, the United States, and South America. (8) The aquarium features a 1.4 million-gallon tank of sea water. (9) And also includes smaller tanks. (10) Which represent the Pacific's richest coastal areas. (11) The water brought to the aquarium from the Pacific Ocean by tanker. (12) In it swim sea otters, penguins, and giant crabs. (13) Attracting attention is a giant whale shark, as well. (14) Visitors experiencing a sensation of floating in the sea, hopes Peter Chermayeff. (15) The designer of Osaka's incredible new aquarium.

13d Recognizing intentional fragments

Professional writers sometimes intentionally use fragments, sparingly, for emphasis and effect.

> The cars were jammed for 30 miles along the Karagatch road. Water buffalo and cattle were hauling carts through the mud. **No end and no beginning. Just carts loaded with everything they owned.** The old men and women, soaked through, walked along keeping the cattle moving.
>
> —ERNEST HEMINGWAY, *In Our Time*

The ability to judge the difference between an acceptable and unacceptable sentence fragment comes from much exposure to

Cont'd.

and giant crabs. Attracting attention is a giant whale shark, as well. Visitors will experience a sensation of floating in the sea, hopes Peter Chermayeff, the designer of Osaka's incredible new aquarium.

COVERAGE: EXERCISE 13-4

(1) complete sentence; (2) prepositional phrase; (3) infinitive phrase; (4) prepositional phrase; (5) complete sentence; (6) verbal phrase (past participle); (7) dependent clause with subordinating conjunction; (8) complete sentence; (9) compound predicate; (10) dependent clause with relative pronoun; (11) verbal phrase (past participle); (12) complete sentence; (13) complete sentence; (14) verbal phrase (present participle); (15) appositive

ANSWERS: EXERCISE 13-5, page 294

Answers will vary. Here is one set of possibilities.

Some of the most magnificent Easter eggs in the world were created by Peter Carl Fabergé, a master Russian goldsmith. In 1884, Czar Alexander III wanted a special Easter gift for his wife, the Czarina. Although Fabergé's first Imperial Easter egg appeared to be an ordinary hen's egg, the outer shell, made of gold, had been enameled to the off-white color of a hen's egg. It [*or* The shell] opened to reveal a yolk, also of gold, which contained a tiny chicken, elaborately crafted of several shades of gold. Hidden inside the chicken was a surprise, [*or* :] an intricate jewelled model of the imperial crown, which opened to reveal a tiny ruby egg. Because the Czar was so delighted, he commissioned Fabergé to create a new egg each Easter and gave the goldsmith one other instruction. The czar told Fabergé to include a surprise in each egg, which, of course, Fabergé wisely did.

reading the work of skilled writers. Many instructors, therefore, often do not accept sentence fragments in student writing until a student can demonstrate the consistent ability to write well-constructed complete sentences.

COVERAGE: EXERCISE 13-5

(1) phrase with no verb; (2) verbal phrase (past participle); (3) appositive; (4) verbal phrase (present participle); (5) dependent clause with subordinating conjunction; (6) verbal phrase (past participle); (7) verbal phrase (present participle); (8) complete sentence; (9) appositive; (10) dependent clause with relative pronoun; (11) dependent clause with subordinating conjunction; (12) complete sentence; (13) compound predicate; (14) appositive (infinitive phrase); (15) dependent clause with relative pronoun

EXERCISE 13-5

Consulting sections 13a, 13b, and 13c, revise this paragraph to eliminate any sentence fragments. In some cases, you can combine word groups to create complete sentences; in other cases, you must supply missing elements to revise word groups. In your final version, check not only the individual sentences but also the clarity of the whole paragraph.

(1) Some of the most magnificent Easter eggs in the world. (2) Created by Peter Carl Fabergé. (3) A master Russian goldsmith. (4) In 1884, Czar Alexander III, wanting a special Easter gift for his wife, the Czarina. (5) Although Fabergé's first Imperial Easter Egg appeared to be an ordinary hen's egg. (6) The outer shell made of gold that had been enameled to the off-white color of a hen's egg. (7) Opening to reveal a yolk, also of gold, which contained a tiny chicken, elaborately crafted of several shades of gold. (8) Hidden inside the chicken was a surprise. (9) An intricate jeweled model of the imperial crown. (10) Which opened to reveal a tiny ruby egg. (11) Because the Czar was so delighted. (12) He commissioned Fabergé to create a new egg each Easter. (13) And gave the goldsmith one other instruction. (14) To include a surprise in each egg. (15) Which, of course, Fabergé wisely did.

ANSWERS: EXERCISE 13-6

Answers will vary. Here is one set of possible answers.

Students looking for jobs need more than the "Help Wanted" section of a newspaper. One major tool is a carefully written résumé. A résumé should be written in a standard form (see Chapter 39) and proofread carefully to eliminate errors in spelling, punctuation, or grammar. For the content of the résumé students should analyze all types of experiences. A résumé can include not only paid jobs but also volunteer positions and extracurricular activities. Students have a better chance of getting a job if they have supervised other people, handled money, or taken on highly responsible tasks such as participating in political campaigns or chairing major committees at school. Many employers will consider student résumés, especially when the résumés include names of the students' supervisors.

EXERCISE 13-6

Consulting sections 13a, 13b, and 13c, revise this paragraph to eliminate any sentence fragments. In some cases, you can join word groups to create complete sentences; in other cases, you have to revise the word groups into complete sentences. In your final version, check not only the individual sentences but also the clarity of the whole paragraph.

(1) Students looking for jobs need more than the "Help Wanted" section of a newspaper. (2) One major tool, a carefully written résumé. (3) A résumé should be written in a standard form. (4) And proofread carefully to eliminate errors in spelling, punctuation, or grammar. (5) For the content of the résumé. (6) Students should analyze all types of experiences. (7) A résumé including not only paid jobs but also volunteer positions and extracurricular activities. (8) Students have a better chance of getting a job. (9) If they have supervised other people, handled money, or taken on highly responsible tasks. (10) Such as participating in political campaigns or chairing major committees at school. (11) Many employers will consider student résumés. (12) Especially when the résumés include names of the students' supervisors.

COVERAGE: EXERCISE 13-6

(1) complete sentence; (2) appositive; (3) complete sentence; (4) second half of compound predicate with no subject; (5) prepositional phrase; (6) complete sentence; (7) dependent (noun) clause; (8) complete sentence; (9) dependent clause with subordinating conjunction; (10) dependent (adverb) clause; (11) complete sentence; (12) dependent (adverb) clause

frag **13**

Focus on Revising

REVISING YOUR WRITING

If you write sentence fragments, go back to your writing and locate them. Then figure out why each is a sentence fragment by using the Test for Sentence Completeness in 13a. Next, revise each sentence fragment into a complete sentence, referring to 13a, 13b, and 13c.

CASE STUDIES: REVISING TO AVOID SENTENCE FRAGMENTS

In these case studies, you can observe a student writer revising. Then you have the chance to revise other student writing on your own.

Observation

A student wrote the following draft for a course called Introduction to the Novel. The assignment was to compose a paragraph about the childhood of a major novelist. This material is well organized as a narrative and tells an interesting story, but the draft's effectiveness is diminished by the presence of sentence fragments.

Read through the draft. The sentence fragments are highlighted. Before you look at the student's revision, revise the material yourself. Then compare what you and the student did.

dependent clause punctuated as a sentence: 13b

phrase—part of compound predicate—punctuated as a sentence: 13c

phrase—with past participle of verb—punctuated as a sentence: 13c

phrase—with -ing form of verb—punctuated as a sentence: 13c

The creative imagination of Victorian novelist Charlotte Brontë got an early start. When she was a child. Her father brought her brother, Branford, a set of wooden soldiers. Her father who was a clergyman and who wrote poetry and a novel as well as sermons. After he gave Branford the set. He told Charlotte and her sisters, Emily and Anne, each to pick one of the toy soldiers. And give it a name. Each sister then made up a history of her soldier. Soon creating tales of heroism. Inspired by the pleasure of telling stories. Charlotte, together with her brother, invented an

COVERAGE: PARTICIPATION ESSAY

In seventeenth-century England, from the death of Elizabeth I in 1603 to William of Orange's ascension to the throne in 1689 [13c: prepositional phrase punctuated as sentence]. The monarchy of England was the cause of unrest and uncertainty.

Queen Elizabeth I died single and childless in 1603. *Because she did not have a direct descendent* [13b: dependent clause punctuated as a sentence]. The throne passed to the Queen's cousin. *Who was crowned James I* [13b: dependent clauses punctuated as sentence]. Discord over the relative power of Parliament and the crown emerged under James I. *And erupted during the reign of James's son, Charles I* [13c; second half of compound predicate punctuated as sentence]. Incapable of resolving the conflicts, Charles I lost both the crown and his head to Oliver Cromwell's Puritan Revolution in 1649.

Holding fast to his anti-monarchy sentiments and refusing a crown [13c: participial phrase punctuated as sentence.] Oliver Cromwell did not establish a new line of English monarchs. Instead, he became Lord Protector of England. When Cromwell died, his son Richard lacked the charisma and political astuteness to hold on to power. As a result, the son of Charles I was recalled from France. *Where he had fled to live in safety.* [13b: dependent clause punctuated as sentence]. He was crowned Charles II in 1660. *And had very limited power, according to new laws passed by Parliament* [13c: second half of compound predicate punctuated as sentence]. Charles II sired no legitimate heirs, so the succession passed to his brother, James. *An apparently able man with one serious political handicap in seventeenth-century England* [13c: phrase punctuated as sentence]. He was Catholic, at a time when England feared that

293

COVERAGE: PARTICIPATION ESSAY, *cont'd.*

the Pope was plotting to reclaim England and rule it from Rome. *When the second wife of James baptized her newborn son Catholic* [13b: dependent clause punctuated as sentence]. Unease over James's rule escalated rapidly. *To ensure the safey of his wife and new son* [13c: phrase punctuated as sentence]. James sent them to France and followed soon after James's Protestant daughter Mary took the throne. *With her husband William of Orange* [13c: phrase puntuated as sentence]. A Dutchman who was a staunch supporter of Protestantism [13b: dependent clause punctuated as sentence]. Their union was so popular with the English that William continued to rule after Mary's death in 1694. Thus, the century that saw much upheaval and instability in England ended in relative calm.

ANSWER: PARTICIPATION ESSAY

This version is revised to correct the sentence fragments. Because of the many options available for corrections, answers will vary somewhat. Also, answers will vary if students have revised for content, organization, or style.

In seventeenth-century England, from the death of Elizabeth I in 1603 to William of Orange's ascension to the throne in 1689, the monarchy in England was the cause of unrest and uncertainty.

Queen Elizabeth I died single and childless in 1603. Because she did not have a direct descendent, the throne passed to the Queen's cousin who was crowned James I. Discord over the relative power of Parliament and the crown emerged under James I and erupted during the reign of James's son, Charles I. Incapable of resolving the conflicts, Charles I lost both the crown and his head to Oliver Cromwell's Puritan Revo- ➡

imaginary kingdom. With Angria as its name. Because she treasured her fantasies and wanted to remember them. Charlotte began to write them in notebooks. Wanting them to look like miniature editions of books. She printed in a tiny, almost microscopically small handwriting. Those notebooks stand as a reminder of how early in life Charlotte Brontë expressed her creativity.

dependent clause punctuated as a sentence: 13b

prepositional phrase punctuated as a sentence: 13c

phrase—using *-ing* form of verb— punctuated as a sentence: 13c

Here is how the student revised the paragraph to eliminate the sentence fragments. In many places, the student could correct the error in more than one way. Your revision, therefore, might not be exactly like this one, but it should not contain any sentence fragments.

The creative imagination of Victorian novelist Charlotte Brontë got an early start. When she was a child, her father brought her brother, Branford, a set of wooden soldiers. Her father was a clergyman who wrote poetry and a novel as well as sermons. After he gave Branford the set, he told Charlotte and her sisters, Emily and Anne, each to pick one of the toy soldiers and give it a name. Each sister then made up a history of her soldier, and each soon was creating tales of heroism. Inspired by the pleasure of telling stories, Charlotte, together with her brother, invented an imaginary kingdom with Angria as its name. Because she treasured her fantasies and wanted to remember them, Charlotte began to write them in notebooks. Wanting her notebooks to look like miniature editions of books, she printed in a tiny, almost microscopically small handwriting. Those notebooks stand as a reminder of how early in life Charlotte Brontë expressed her creativity.

Participation

A student wrote the following draft for a course called European History. The assignment was to discuss the political atmosphere of a European nation during the seventeenth century. This material is effectively organized for chronological presentation of information, and it uses specific details well. The draft's effectiveness, however, is diminished by the presence of sentence fragments. ➡

Read through the draft. Then revise it to eliminate the sentence fragments. Also, make any additional revisions that you think would improve the content, organization, and style of the material.

In seventeenth-century England, from the death of Elizabeth I in 1603 to William of Orange's ascension to the throne in 1689. The monarchy of England was the cause of unrest and uncertainty.

Queen Elizabeth I died single and childless in 1603. Because she did not have a direct descendant. The throne passed to the Queen's cousin. Who was crowned James I. Discord over the relative power of Parliament and the crown emerged under James I. And erupted during the reign of James's son, Charles I. Incapable of resolving the conflicts, Charles I lost both the throne and his head to Oliver Cromwell's Puritan Revolution in 1649.

Holding fast to his anti-monarchy sentiments and refusing a crown. Oliver Cromwell did not establish a new line of English monarchs. Instead, he became Lord Protector of England. When Cromwell died, his son Richard lacked the charisma and political astuteness to hold on to power. As a result, the son of Charles I was recalled from France. Where he had fled to live in safety. He was crowned Charles II in 1660. And had very limited power, according to new laws passed by Parliament. Charles II sired no legitimate heirs, so the succession passed to his brother, James. An apparently able man with one serious political handicap in seventeenth-century England. He was Catholic, at a time when the English feared that the Pope was plotting to reclaim England and rule it from Rome. When the second wife of James baptized her newborn son Catholic. Unease over James's rule escalated rapidly. To ensure the safety of his wife and new son. James sent them to France and followed soon after. James's Protestant daughter Mary took the throne. With her husband William of Orange. A Dutchman who was a staunch supporter of Protestantism. Their union was so popular with the English that William continued to rule after Mary's death in 1694. Thus, the century that saw much upheaval and instability in England ended in relative calm.

Cont'd.

lution in 1649.

Holding fast to his anti-monarchy sentiments and refusing a crown, Oliver Cromwell did not establish a new line of English monarchs. Instead, he became Lord Protector of England. When Cromwell died, his son Richard lacked the charisma and political astuteness to hold on to power. As a result, the son of Charles I was recalled from France, where he had fled to live in safety. He was crowned Charles II in 1660 and had very limited power, according to new laws passed by Parliament. Charles II sired no legitimate heirs, so the succession passed to his brother, James, an apparently able man with one serious political handicap in seventeenth-century England. He was Catholic, at a time when England feared that the Pope was plotting to reclaim England and rule it from Rome. When the second wife of James baptized her newborn son Catholic, unease over James's rule escalated rapidly. To ensure the safety of his wife and new son, James sent them to France and followed soon after. James's Protestant daughter Mary took the throne with her husband William of Orange, a Dutchman who was a staunch supporter of Protestantism. Their union was so popular with the English that William continued to rule after Mary's death in 1694. Thus, the century that saw much upheaval and instability in England ended in relative calm.

14 Comma Splices and Fused Sentences

A **comma splice** (or **comma fault**) is an error that occurs when a comma by itself joins independent clauses°. The only time that a comma is correct between two independent clauses is when the comma is followed by a coordinating conjunction (*and, but, for, or, nor, yet,* and *so*). The word *splice* means "to fasten ends together." The end of one independent clause and the beginning of another should not be fastened together with a comma alone.

COMMA SPLICE	The hurricane intensified, it turned toward land.

A **fused sentence** is an error that occurs when two independent clauses° are not joined by a comma with a coordinating conjunction (*and, but, for, or nor, yet,* and *so*) or by other punctuation. The word *fused* means "united as if by melting together." Two independent clauses cannot be united as if melted together. A fused sentence is also known as a *run-on sentence* or a *run-together sentence.*

FUSED SENTENCE	The hurricane intensified it turned toward land.

Comma splices and fused sentences are two versions of the same problem: incorrect joining of two independent clauses. A fused sentence, however, reveals less awareness of the need for a separation between the independent clauses.

Comma splices and fused sentences distract readers from understanding the meaning you want your material to deliver. If you tend to write comma splices and fused sentences, you might have trouble recognizing them, because they can seem to blend with surrounding sentences. Expect, therefore, to analyze your sentences individually. To do this, wait until you have finished drafting (see 3b) your material, so that the flow of your writing is not interrupted. If you suspect an error, quickly underline or highlight it and maintain the pace of your writing. You can check the sentences when you are revising (see 3c) and editing (see 3d).

Chart 92 shows you how to correct these errors and refers you to sections in this chapter for fuller explanations and illustrations.

HOW TO CORRECT COMMA SPLICES AND FUSED SENTENCES ^92

- Use a period (see 14b and 14e).

    The hurricane intensified. It turned toward land.

- Use a semicolon (see 14b and 14e).

    The hurricane intensified; it turned toward land.

- Use a semicolon and a conjunctive adverb° (see 14e).

    The hurricane intensified; then it turned toward land.

- Use a comma and a coordinating conjunction° (see 14c).

    The hurricane intensified, and it turned toward land.

- Revise one of two independent clauses° into a dependent clause° (see 14d).

    As the hurricane intensified, it turned toward land.

    The hurricane intensified as it turned toward land.

14a Recognizing comma splices and fused sentences

To recognize comma splices and fused sentences, you need to be able to recognize an independent clause. As was explained in 7j, an independent clause contains a subject° and predicate°. An independent clause can stand alone as a sentence because it is an independent grammatical unit.

SUBJECT	PREDICATE
Thomas Edison	was an American inventor.

If you tend to write comma splices, here is a useful technique for proofreading your work. Cover all the words on one side of the comma and see if the words remaining constitute an independent clause. If they do, cover that clause and uncover all the words on the

QUOTATION ABOUT WRITING

Word-carpentry is like any other kind of carpentry: you must join your sentences smoothly.

—Anatole France

BACKGROUND

In the second chapter of *Errors and Expectations*, entitled "Handwriting and Punctuation," (Oxford University Press: Oxford, UK 1977), Mina Shaughnessy observes that the urge to string sentences together reflects a need on the part of the writer for other ways of making links between sentences. Comma splices, for example, reflect a writer's effort to control a sentence, to simplify it by breaking it up into smaller segments by the use of a comma as a conjunction. She argues that punctuation should not be studied apart from other aspects of writing; instead, it should be integrated with work in composition, for "the process whereby writers *mark* sentences is related to the process whereby they *make* them." She suggests that punctuation skills will improve as novice writers study first to recognize and create simple subject and predicate phrases; second, to embed sentences in sentences (using *who, which, that, when,* and *if*); third, to embed appositional forms; and fourth, to embed *-ing* phrases.

297

TEACHING TIP

Students who write comma splices and/or fused sentences have a better chance of finding and correcting their errors if they can find a pattern in them. To help students detect patterns, set aside one class or conference session to have students review all the paragraphs and essays they have written for the course. First, if they have not already done so, they should correct all comma splices and fused sentences. Then they should tally the *types* of sentences involved, using for reference the chart Leading Causes of Comma Splices and Fused Sentences. Encourage students to create additional categories, if needed, for errors that do not fit the three basic patterns. Make yourself available to answer questions, and encourage students to ask advice of their peers. At the end of the exercise have students submit a review statement. Here is one student's response:

> Of the twelve comma splices and fused sentences I have written this semester, seven involved a second independent clause starting with a pronoun, four involved conjunctive adverbs, and one involved an explanation. I need to be careful, when I use a pronoun as the subject of an independent clause, to punctuate that clause as a sentence.

An explicit statement of results will force students to do the analysis, and the "I need to be careful . . ." sentence will force them to verbalize a plan of attack. Both steps work to overcome students' perceptions of punctuation errors as being random and uncontrollable.

You can then keep the statements on file (1) to help you determine who needs to work on a particular kind of comma splice or fused sentence, and (2) as a contract between you and each student acknowledging that he or she knows what to do—and will do it.

other side of the comma. If the second side of the comma is also an independent clause, you have written a comma splice. Also to help yourself avoid writing comma splices, become familiar with correct uses for commas, explained in Chapter 24.

Experienced writers sometimes use a comma to join very brief parallel° independent clauses, especially if a negative sentence is followed by a positive sentence: *Mosquitos do not bite, they stab.* Many instructors consider this form an error in student writing; you will never be wrong if you use a semicolon or period.

MAJOR CAUSES OF COMMA SPLICES AND FUSED SENTENCES   93

1. **Pronouns.** A comma splice or fused sentence often occurs when the second independent clause° starts with a pronoun°.

   NO   Thomas Edison was a productive inventor, **he** held over 1,300 U.S. and foreign patents.

   YES   Thomas Edison was a productive inventor. **He** held over 1,300 U.S. and foreign patents.

2. **Conjunctive adverbs and other transitional expressions.** A comma splice or fused sentence often occurs when the second independent clause starts with a conjunctive adverb (for a list, see Chart 52 in section 7f) or other transitional expression (for a list, see Chart 22 in section 4d-1). Remember that these words are *not* coordinating conjunctions *(and, but, or, nor, for, so,* and *yet),* so they cannot work in concert with a comma to join two independent clauses.

   NO   Thomas Edison was a brilliant scientist, **however,** his schooling was limited to only three months of his life.

   YES   Thomas Edison was a brilliant scientist. **However,** his schooling was limited to only three months of his life.

3. **Explanations or examples.** A comma splice or fused sentence often occurs when the second independent clause explains or gives an example of the information in the first independent clause.

   NO   Thomas Edison was the genius behind many inventions, among the best known are the phonograph and the incandescent lamp.

   YES   Thomas Edison was the genius behind many inventions. Among the best known are the phonograph and the incandescent lamp.

14b   Using a period or semicolon to correct comma splices and fused sentences

You can use a period or semicolon to correct comma splices and fused sentences. For the sake of sentence variety and emphasis, however, do not always choose punctuation to correct this type of error. (Other methods are discussed in 14c and 14d.) Strings of too many short sentences rarely establish relationships and levels of importance among ideas.

A **period** can separate the independent clauses° in a comma splice or fused sentence.

COMMA SPLICE	The Muir Woods National Monument is located in northern California, its dominant tree is the coast redwood.
FUSED SENTENCE	The Muir Woods National Monument is located in northern California its dominant tree is the coast redwood.
CORRECTED	The Muir Woods National Monument is located in northern California. Its dominant tree is the coast redwood.

A **semicolon** can separate the independent clauses° in a comma splice or fused sentence. Choose a semicolon only when the separate sentences are closely related in meaning. (See also 25a.)

COMMA SPLICE	The coast redwood is named "Sequoia" after a Cherokee Indian, he developed the first alphabet used by that tribe.
FUSED SENTENCE	The coast redwood is named "Sequoia" after a Cherokee Indian he developed the first alphabet used by that tribe.
CORRECTED	The coast redwood is named "Sequoia" after a Cherokee Indian; he developed the first alphabet used by that tribe.

14c   Using coordinating conjunctions to correct comma splices and fused sentences

When ideas in independent clauses° are closely related and grammatically equivalent, you can connect them with a coordinating conjunction (*and, but, or, nor, for, so,* and *yet*). If you are correcting a comma splice, insert a coordinating conjunction and retain the

---

QUOTATION ABOUT WRITING

I have grown fond of semicolons in recent years. The semicolon tells you that there is still some question about the preceding full sentence; something needs to be added; it reminds you sometimes of the Greek usage. It is almost always a greater pleasure to come across a semicolon than a period. The period tells you that that is that; if you didn't get all the meaning you wanted or expected, anyway you got all the writer intended to parcel out and now you have to move along. But with a semicolon there you get a pleasant little feeling of expectancy; there is more to come; to read on; it will get clearer.

—Lewis Thomas

BACKGROUND

Professional writers often intentionally separate two independent clauses with just a comma. The clauses in these comma splices never have internal commas and are normally short, balanced, and closely related in meaning. The teacher, of course, should decide whether to allow students to experiment with this form in their writing.

QUOTATION ABOUT WRITING

Wearing down seven number two pencils is a good day's work.

—Ernest Hemingway

TEACHING TIP

You might want to liven up a class by running a "revision contest." Divide the class into an even number of teams, each composed of four students. Tell the students that in preparation for the competition, everyone is to bring to class two paragraphs containing comma splices and fused sentences: (1) a published paragraph that the student has intentionally edited to have three such errors; and (2) an original paragraph written for the competition, containing three intentional comma splices or fused sentences. Ask each student to supply two copies of each paragraph: one for the contest and one filled in as an answer key.

On the day of the competition, pair up teams and have them exchange paragraphs. Collect the answer keys. Give the teams thirty minutes to revise the paragraphs they have received. When they finish, compare their revisions with the answer keys. Here is one way to score.

+5 points	for each correct revision
+2 points	for each minute by which a team beats the time limit
−5 points	for each incorrect revision, missed comma splice, or missed fused sentence
+5 points	added to the *finder's* team score for each unintentional error in end punctuation found in a contest paragraph (fragments, missing questions marks, etc.)
−10 points	deducted from the *writer's* team score for each unintentional error in end punctuation in a contest paragraph
+10 points	bonus for a perfect response

Team scores can be adjusted along a curve, if you wish, for group grades.

comma. If you are correcting a fused sentence, insert the coordinating conjunction along with a comma. ❖ PUNCTUATION ALERT: Use a comma before a coordinating conjunction that links independent clauses° (see 24a). ❖

❖ USAGE ALERT: When using a coordinating conjunction, be sure that it fits the meaning of the material. *And* signals addition, *but* and *yet* signal contrast, *for* and *so* signal cause, and *or* and *nor* signal alternatives. ❖

COMMA SPLICE	Redwood trees can grow to over 300 feet in height and up to 16 feet in diameter, their seeds are only a sixteenth of an inch long.
FUSED SENTENCE	Redwood trees can grow to over 300 feet in height and up to 16 feet in diameter their seeds are only a sixteenth of an inch long.
CORRECTED	Redwood trees can grow to over 300 feet in height and up to 16 feet in diameter, **but** their seeds are only a sixteenth of an inch long.
COMMA SPLICE	The foot-thick bark of the redwood tree is a barrier to destructive insects, the bitter chemicals and tannins in the bark further discourage insects and fungi.
FUSED SENTENCE	The foot-thick bark of the redwood tree is a barrier to destructive insects the bitter chemicals and tannins in the bark further discourage insects and fungi.
CORRECTED	The foot-thick bark of the redwood tree is a barrier to destructive insects, **and** the bitter chemicals and tannins in the bark further discourage insects and fungi.

EXERCISE 14-1

Consulting sections 14a, 14b, and 14c, revise any comma splices or fused sentences by using a period, a semicolon, or a coordinating conjunction and comma.

EXAMPLE   Huge numbers of people have become used to the speed of air travel, they do not like to take trains.

Huge numbers of people have become used to the speed of air travel. They do not like to take trains.

1. In the twenty-first century, a new type of transportation may be available, we may be riding superfast trains that connect major cities.

2. These trains, which are called maglevs, are moved along by magnets they provide a magnetic field that keeps the train just inches off the ground.

3. The French T.G.V. is the fastest rail train in use today it can travel 170 miles per hour, but an experimental maglev has traveled 260 miles per hour.

4. A group of transportation officials in Florida plans a train system connecting major cities, Tampa, Miami, and Orlando may soon be serviced by maglevs.

5. According to some experts, maglevs may someday replace railroad trains, they would use less energy and have fewer moving parts.

14d   Revising one of two independent clauses into a dependent clause to correct a comma splice or fused sentence

You can revise a comma splice or fused sentence by changing one of two independent clauses° into a dependent clause°. This method is suitable when one idea can logically be subordinated to the other.

One way to create a dependent clause is to insert a subordinating conjunction (such as *because* and *although*) in front of the subject and verb. (For a complete list of subordinating conjunctions, see Chart 56 in section 7h.) When using a subordinating conjunction, be sure that it fits the meaning of the material: for example, *as* and *because* signal reason, *although* signals contrast, *if* signals condition, and *when* signals time. ❖ PUNCTUATION ALERTS: (1) If you put a period after a dependent clause that is not attached to an independent clause, you will create the error called a *sentence fragment*; see Chapter 13. (2) Generally, use a comma after an introductory dependent clause that starts with a subordinating conjunction; see 24b-1. ❖

COMMA SPLICE	Gertrude Stein wanted to support struggling artists in the 1920s, she bought many paintings by Picasso and others.
FUSED SENTENCE	Gertrude Stein wanted to support struggling artists in the 1920s she bought many paintings by Picasso and others.
CORRECTED	**Because Gertrude Stein wanted to support struggling artists in the 1920s,** she bought many paintings by Picasso and others.

ANSWERS AND COVERAGE: EXERCISE 14-1, pages 300-301
The correction strategies will vary.
Here is one set of possibilities.

1. In the twenty-first century, a new type of transportation may be available. [14b, comma splice corrected by using a period] We may be riding superfast trains that connect major cities.

2. These trains, which are called maglevs, are moved along by magnets; [14b, fused sentence corrected by using a semicolon] they provide a magnetic field that keeps the train just inches off the ground.

3. The French T.G.V. is the fastest rail train in use today. [14b, fused sentence corrected by using a period] It can travel 170 miles per hour, but an experimental maglev has traveled 260 miles per hour.

4. A group of transportation officials in Florida plans a train system connecting major cities; [14b, comma splice corrected by using a semicolon] Tampa, Miami, and Orlando may soon be serviced by maglevs.

5. According to some experts, maglevs may someday replace railroad trains, and [14c, comma splice corrected by using a comma and a coordinating conjunction] they would use less energy and have fewer moving parts to service.

QUOTATION ABOUT WRITING

All morning I worked on the proof of one of my poems, and I took out a comma; in the afternoon I put it back.

        —Oscar Wilde

COMMA SPLICE	Gertrude Stein wrote many novels, short stories, essays, poems, plays, and one opera, she is better known for her art collection.
FUSED SENTENCE	Gertrude Stein wrote many novels, short stories, essays, poems, plays, and one opera she is better known for her art collection.
CORRECTED	Gertrude Stein wrote many novels, short stories, essays, poems, plays, and one opera **although she is better known for her art collection.**

Another way to create a dependent clause is to use a **relative pronoun** (*that, which, who*). This type of dependent clause is called an **adjective clause.** ❖ PUNCTUATION ALERT: To determine whether you need commas to set off an adjective clause, check whether it is restrictive° (essential), as explained in 24e. ❖

COMMA SPLICE	Gertrude Stein moved from America to Paris in 1902, she quickly became fascinated by impressionist painting.
FUSED SENTENCE	Gertrude Stein moved from America to Paris in 1902 she quickly became fascinated by impressionist painting.
CORRECTED	Gertrude Stein, **who moved from America to Paris in 1902,** quickly became fascinated by impressionist painting.

EXERCISE 14-2

Consulting sections 14a through 14d, revise any comma splices or fused sentences.

(1) Most sporting events have a positive effect on the economy. (2) They attract sports fans, they provide income for those who run the concessions, for example. (3) The longest sporting event in the world might be assumed to bring in correspondingly large profits, however, that is not the case. (4) The *Tour de France,* a cycling race that originated in 1903, covers over three thousand miles and lasts twenty-three days. (5) At least one-third of the workers in France take time off to watch the race they stay away from work for two-thirds of the time the race is in progress. (6) Because of the lost work hours, the total damage to the French economy is astronomical, it can add up to three-quarters of one percent of

ANSWERS: EXERCISE 14-2

(1) Most sporting events have a positive effect on the economy. (2) They attract sports fans, who provide income for those who run the concessions, for example. (3) The longest sporting event in the world might be assumed to bring in correspondingly large profits; however, that is not the case. (4) The *Tour de France,* a cycling race that originated in 1903, covers over three thousand miles and lasts twenty-three days. (5) At least one-third of the workers in France take time off to watch the race. They stay away from work for two-thirds of the time the race is in progress. (6) Because of the lost work hours, the total damage to the French economy is astronomical, adding up to three-quarters of one percent of the nation's gross national product. (7) That figure may not seem very large; nevertheless, it adds up to many millions of dollars annually. (8) Although French economists are very worried about the problem, they do not want the race discontinued because they also take time off to enjoy the festivities.

the nation's gross national product. (7) That figure may not seem very large, nevertheless, it adds up to many millions of dollars annually. (8) Although French economists are very worried about the problem, they do not want the race discontinued they also take time off to enjoy the festivities.

14e   Using a semicolon or a period before a conjunctive adverb or other transitional expression between two independent clauses

Conjunctive adverbs and other transitional expressions link ideas between sentences. Conjunctive adverbs and other transitional expressions that fall between sentences must be immediately preceded by a period or semicolon.

Conjunctive adverbs include such words as *however, therefore, also, next, then, thus, furthermore,* and *nevertheless,* (for a complete list, see Chart 52 in section 7f). Remember that these words are *not* coordinating conjunctions, which work in concert with commas to join independent clauses (see 14c). ❖ PUNCTUATION ALERT: A conjunctive adverb at the beginning of a sentence is usually followed by a comma (see 24b-3). ❖

COMMA SPLICE	Car theft has increased alarmingly in most major cities, **however,** one city has decided to fight back.
FUSED SENTENCE	Car theft has increased alarmingly in most major cities **however,** one city has decided to fight back.
CORRECTED	Car theft has increased alarmingly in most cities; **however,** one city has decided to fight back.
CORRECTED	Car theft has increased alarmingly in most major cities. **However,** one city has decided to fight back.

Transitional expressions include *for example, for instance, in addition, in fact, of course,* and *on the other hand* (see Chart 22 in section 4d-1 for a complete list). ❖ PUNCTUATION ALERT: A transitional expression at the beginning of a sentence is usually followed by a comma (see 24b-3). ❖

ANSWERS AND COVERAGE:
EXERCISE 14-3, pages 304-305

1. Sir Arthur Conan Doyle created the famous detective; however, [comma splice: conjunctive adverb] the stories are told through the voice of Sherlock Holmes's assistant, Dr. Watson.

2. Many people know Holmes through reading Doyle's stories; in addition, [fused sentence: transitional expression] the character of Sherlock Holmes has appeared on stage, screen, radio, and television.

3. Correct complete sentence

4. Learning the complex details of these stories is not easy; in fact, [fused sentence: transitional expression] many Holmes fans take great pride in being experts about the detective's life.

5. Much has been written about the character of Sherlock Holmes; indeed, [comma splice: conjunctive adverb] Sir Arthur Conan Doyle's detective has received considerable literary attention.

ANSWERS AND COVERAGE:
EXERCISE 14-4, pages 305-306

Answers will vary. Here is one set of possible revisions.

1. Some Cro-Magnon people were buried with many valuable possessions. We can assume, therefore, that Cro-Magnons had a society based on class distinctions. Also, they probably believed in an afterlife [two comma splices corrected with periods; 14b].

2. Correct complete sentence

3. A young boy and girl were buried together with many rings, ivory spears, and 8,000 ivory beads, which indicated their high rank [comma splice corrected with independent clause changed to dependent clause with relative pronoun *which*; 14d].

4. The living Cro-Magnons also wore jewelry; this practice indicates that they were not simply struggling to survive [comma splice corrected with a semicolon; 14b].

�![arrow]

COMMA SPLICE	In Boston stolen car reports are broadcast over the radio, **in fact,** a police officer "deputizes" about 500,000 listeners to be on the alert for stolen vehicles.
FUSED SENTENCE	In Boston stolen car reports are broadcast over the radio **in fact,** a police officer "deputizes" about 500,000 listeners to be on the alert for stolen vehicles.
CORRECTED	In Boston stolen car reports are broadcast over the radio; **in fact,** a police officer "deputizes" about 500,000 listeners to be on the alert for stolen vehicles.
CORRECTED	In Boston stolen car reports are broadcast over the radio. **In fact,** a police officer "deputizes" about 500,000 listeners to be on the alert for stolen vehicles.

A conjunctive adverb or other transitional expression can appear in more than one location within an independent clause°. In contrast, a coordinating conjunction *(and, but, or, nor, for, so, and yet)* can appear only between independent clauses that it joins.

Car theft has increased alarmingly in most major cities. **However,** one city has decided to fight back. [conjunctive adverb]

Car theft has increased alarmingly in most major cities. One city, **however,** has decided to fight back. [conjunctive adverb]

Car theft has increased alarmingly in most major cities. One city has decided, **however,** to fight back. [conjunctive adverb]

Car theft has increased alarmingly in most major cities. One city has decided to fight back, **however.** [conjunctive adverb]

Car theft has increased alarmingly in most major cities, **but** one city has decided to fight back. [coordinating conjunction]

EXERCISE 14-3

Consulting section 14e, revise any comma splices or fused sentences caused by a conjunctive adverb or other transitional expression. If an item is correct, circle its number.

EXAMPLE Sherlock Holmes is a most popular fictional detective in fact, his exploits have been translated into fifty-seven languages.

Sherlock Holmes is a most popular fictional detective. In fact, his exploits have been translated into fifty-seven languages.

1. Sir Arthur Conan Doyle created the famous detective however, the stories are told through the voice of Sherlock Holmes's assistant, Dr. Watson.
2. Many people know Holmes through reading Doyle's stories, in addition, the character of Sherlock Holmes has appeared on stage, screen, radio, and television.
3. The sixty original Holmes stories are important to Holmes's admirers consequently, they study these stories intently.
4. Learning the complex details of these stories is not easy in fact, many Holmes fans take great pride in being experts about the detective's life.
5. Much has been written about the character of Sherlock Holmes, indeed, Sir Arthur Conan Doyle's detective has received considerable literary attention.

EXERCISE 14-4

Consulting all sections in this chapter, revise all comma splices, using a different method of correction for each one. If an item is correct, circle its number.

EXAMPLE   Cro-Magnon people lived between 35,000 and 12,000 years ago, these ancient humans cared about status symbols.

Cro-Magnon people lived between 35,000 and 12,000 years ago. These ancient humans cared about status symbols.

1. Some Cro-Magnon people were buried with many valuable possessions, we can assume, therefore, that Cro-Magnons had a society based on class distinctions, also they probably believed in an afterlife.
2. In one 24,000-year-old grave that was found in Russia, for example, a man was buried in clothing decorated with over 3,000 ivory beads.
3. A young boy and girl were buried together with many rings, ivory spears, and 8,000 ivory beads, these possessions indicated their high rank.
4. The living Cro-Magnons also wore jewelry, this practice indicates that they were not simply struggling to survive.
5. People who were worried about mere subsistence would not have had the time and energy to spend hundreds of hours stringing beads, they would have had to devote every waking minute to securing food and shelter.

5. People who were worried about mere subsistence would not have had the time and energy to spend hundreds of hours stringing beads, for they would have had to devote every waking minute to securing food and shelter [fused sentence corrected with comma and coordinating conjunction; 14c].

ANSWERS: EXERCISE 14-5, page 306

Answers will vary. Here is one possible revision.

(1) During the nineteenth century, a number of fearless women traveled long distances from their homes. They visited places far more exotic than their native France or England. (2) Isabella Bird, for example, a British clergyman's daughter, began traveling and writing when she was in her forties; she often wrote by the light of a portable oil lamp and with a gun in her pocket. (3) In 1896, she celebrated her sixty-fourth birthday, and that same year she crossed northwest China hoping to reach Tibet. (4) While she was traveling, her guides collapsed with fever. Then her rice supply grew dangerously low. (5) Only when tribal warfare broke out, however, and the bridges were torn down did she turn around. (6) Like Isabella Bird, Flora Tristan, a native of France, proved her adventurous spirit when she sailed from France to Peru, a trip that inspired her to write a book. (7) The book was published in 1838; however, its title, *Peregrinations of a Pariah*, meaning "travels of an outcast," suggests that not everyone admired its courageous author.

COVERAGE: EXERCISE 14-5

(1) comma splice with pronoun; (2) comma splice with pronoun; (3) fused sentence with pronoun; comma splice with pronoun; (4) comma splice with conjunctive adverb; (5) correct; (6) comma splice with pronoun; (7) comma splice with conjunctive adverb

ANSWERS: EXERCISE 14-6

Answers will vary. Here is one possible revision.

(1) In the Nazca Desert of Peru, south of the capital city of Lima, the stony surface of the land is marked by enormous networks of strange lines that are believed to be over two thousand years old. (2) Some lines run perfectly straight for miles; in contrast, other lines form complex designs and figures of animals. (3) The scale of the designs is so huge, moreover, that from the ground no patterns are discernible. (4) From observation towers nearly fifty feet high the human eye can hardly notice the giant designs; however, they are startlingly clear from aircraft. (5) One theory proposes that the lines of Nazca marked airstrips for extraterrestrial spacecraft. Logically, though, that theory ignores too many of the designs in the pattern to be widely accepted. (6) Another theory suggests the figures are part of a huge astronomical calendar that might have been used to guide agricultural timetables. (7) Still another theory argues that the patterns were a part of traditional rituals; ceremonies involving hallucinogenic plants and rites reflecting cycles of regeneration might have incorporated the strange animal figures and patterns seen in the lines. (8) Anthropologists and archaeologists who study these strange networks of lines thus hope to solve the mystery of the origins of the lines of Nazca.

COVERAGE: EXERCISE 14-6

(1) comma splice with pronoun [14c, Cause 1]; (2) fused sentence with transitional expression [14e, Cause 2]; (3) correct complete sentence; (4) comma splice with conjunctive adverb [14c, Cause 1]; comma splice with transitional expression [14e, Cause 2]; (6) fused sentence with pronoun [14c, Cause 1]; (7) comma splice with examples in second clause [14b, Cause 3]; (8) comma splice with conjunctive adverb [14c, Cause 2]

EXERCISE 14-5

Consulting all sections in this chapter, revise any fused sentences, using as many different methods explained in this chapter as you can.

(1) During the nineteenth century, a number of fearless women traveled long distances from their homes they visited places far more exotic than their native France or England. (2) Isabella Bird, for example, a British clergyman's daughter, began traveling and writing when she was in her forties she often wrote by the light of a portable oil lamp and with a gun in her pocket. (3) In 1896, she celebrated her sixty-fourth birthday that same year she crossed northwest China she hoped to reach Tibet. (4) While she was traveling, her guides collapsed with fever then her rice supply grew dangerously low. (5) Only when tribal warfare broke out, however, and the bridges were torn down did she turn around. (6) Like Isabella Bird, Flora Tristan, a native of France, proved her adventurous spirit she sailed from France to Peru, a trip that inspired her to write a book. (7) The book was published in 1838 however, its title, *Peregrinations of a Pariah*, meaning "travels of an outcast," suggests that not everyone admired its courageous author.

EXERCISE 14-6

Consulting all sections in this chapter, revise all comma splices or fused sentences, using as many different methods of correction as you can. If a sentence is correct, circle its number. After you have corrected the comma splices and fused sentences, check not only the correctness of the individual sentences but also the clarity of the entire paragraph.

(1) In the Nazca Desert of Peru, south of the capital city of Lima, the stony surface of the land is marked by enormous networks of strange lines, they are believed to be over two thousand years old. (2) Some lines run perfectly straight for miles in contrast, other lines form complex designs and figures of animals. (3) The scale of the designs is so huge, moreover, that from the ground no patterns are discernible. (4) From observation towers nearly 50 feet high, the human eye can hardly notice the giant designs they are startlingly clear from aircraft. (5) One theory proposes that the lines of Nazca marked airstrips for extraterrestrial spacecraft, logically, though, that theory ignores too many of the designs in the pattern to be widely accepted. (6) Another theory suggests that the figures are part of a huge astronomical calendar it might have been used to guide agricultural timetables. (7) Still another theory argues that the patterns were part of traditional rituals, ceremonies involving hallucinogenic plants and rites reflecting cycles of regeneration might have incorporated the strange animal figures and patterns seen in the lines. (8) Scientists and archaeologists continue to study these strange networks of lines, thus, they hope to solve the mystery of the origins of the lines of Nazca.

Focus on Revising

REVISING YOUR WRITING

If you write comma splices or fused sentences, go back to your writing and locate them. Then figure out why each is an error by using Chart 93 in section 14a on Major Causes of Comma Splices and Fused Sentences. Next, using the explanations in 14b through 14e, revise your writing to eliminate the errors.

CASE STUDIES: REVISING TO AVOID COMMA SPLICES AND FUSED SENTENCES

In these case studies, you can observe a student writer revising. Then you have the chance to revise other student writing on your own.

Observation

A student wrote the following draft for a course called Introduction to Criminal Justice. The assignment was to discuss a current controversy in trial law. This material is well organized and presents its information clearly and fully. However, the draft's effectiveness is diminished by comma splices and fused sentences.

Read through the draft. The errors are highlighted and explained. Before you look at the student's revision, revise the material yourself. Then compare what you and the student did.

When fingerprinting was first introduced in the late nineteenth century, many judges hesitated to accept fingerprints as legal evidence. Recently, a similar controversy has arisen, it involves hypnosis. During this century, various state and federal courts have issued contradictory rulings on the admissibility of testimony obtained under hypnosis, however, in 1987 the United States Supreme Court ruled that such evidence is admissible. This

comma splice with pronoun *it:* 14a, Cause 1

comma splice with conjunctive adverb *however:* 14a, Cause 2 ruling is a major new development, but the public should not look to hypnosis as a miracle technique, because testimony obtained under hypnosis is no more reliable than that obtained when witnesses search their memories.

fused sentence with pronoun *it;* 14a, Cause 1

There is one major advantage of hypnosis it usually allows witnesses to recall incidents in far greater detail than they would otherwise. Hypnotized people will still recall what they think they saw or what they wished they had seen. In fact, it is possible for people to lie when hypnotized furthermore, a hypnotist can unintentionally lead witnesses to give certain responses.

fused sentence with conjunctive adverb *furthermore;* 14a, Cause 2

comma splice with explanation in second independent clause: 14a, Cause 3

One thing is certain, lively legal debates lie ahead. Hypnotists are not licensed professionals, they can be circus entertainers or serious practitioners. It would be up to a jury to decide on the competence of a hypnotist most people who sit on juries have no idea of what standards to apply.

comma splice with pronoun *they:* 14a, Cause 1

fused sentence with explanation in second independent clause: 14a, Cause 3

COVERAGE: PARTICIPATION ESSAY

(opposite page)

As consumers, when we buy clothes, we often make choices on the basis of the *fabric of an article of clothing, therefore,* [14a, Cause 2: comma splice with conjunctive adverb] fashion designers always pay attention to matters of composition and design in fabrics.

Fabric is composed of natural fibers, synthetic fibers, and blends of the two. Natural fibers include cotton, linen, and *wool, they* [14a, Cause 1: comma splice with pronoun] offer the advantages of durability and absorbency. Synthetic fibers include rayon, polyester, acrylic, or combinations of them and other synthetic *fibers they* [14a, Cause 1: fused sentence with pronoun] resist wrinkling and retain their color well. Fiber blends combine natural and synthetic fibers to create combinations such as cotton and polyester, which offer the advantages of each but have their own problems, such as retaining stains.

→

Here is how the student revised the paragraph to correct comma splices and fused sentences. In many places, the student could correct the errors in more than one way. Your revision, therefore, might not be exactly like this one, but it should deal with each error highlighted on the draft.

When fingerprinting was first introduced in the late nineteenth century, many judges hesitated to accept fingerprints →

as legal evidence. Recently, a similar controversy has arisen. It involves hypnosis. During this century, various state and federal courts have issued contradictory rulings on the admissibility of testimony obtained under hypnosis. However, in 1987 the United States Supreme Court ruled that such evidence is admissible. This ruling is a major new development, but the public should not look to hypnosis as a miracle technique, because testimony obtained under hypnosis is no more reliable than that obtained when witnesses search their memories.

There is one major advantage of hypnosis; it usually allows witnesses to recall incidents in far greater detail than they would otherwise. Hypnotized people will still recall what they think they saw or what they wished they had seen. In fact, it is possible for people to lie when hypnotized; furthermore, a hypnotist can unintentionally lead witnesses to give certain responses.

One thing is certain. Lively legal debates lie ahead. Hypnotists are not licensed professionals. They can be circus entertainers or serious practitioners. It would be up to a jury to decide on the competence of a hypnotist, but most people who sit on juries have no idea of what standards to apply.

Participation

A student wrote the following draft for a course called Introduction to Fashion Design. The assignment was to describe characteristics of fabric. This material is well organized and uses specific examples well, but the draft's effectiveness is diminished by comma splices and fused sentences.

Read through the draft. Then revise it to eliminate the comma splices and fused sentences. Also, make any additional revisions that you think would improve the content, organization, and style of the material.

As consumers, when we buy clothes, we often make choices on the basis of the fabric of an article of clothing, therefore, fashion designers always pay attention to matters of composition and design in fabrics.

Fabric is composed of natural fibers, synthetic fibers, and blends of the two. Natural fibers include cotton, linen, and wool, they offer the advantages of durability and absorbency. Synthetic fibers include rayon, polyester, acrylic, or combinations of them and other synthetic fibers they resist wrinkling and retain their ➔

Cont'd.

The design of fabric is affected by the way that the fabric is *produced, for example,* [14a, Cause 2: comma splice with transitional expression] a fabric can be produced on a loom to create woven fabrics such as crepe and *denim, conversely,* [14a, Cause 2: fused sentence with transitional expression] a fabric can be produced on a knitting machine to create fabrics such as jersey and velour. Once the basic fabric is being produced, special patterns can be woven or knit into it, *for instance,* [14a, Cause 2: comma splice with transitional expression] diagonal patterns can be woven into cotton fabrics for a geometric effect, and vertical patterns can be woven into a cable-stitched fabric for a thicker look and feel. Various finishes can further alter a fabric's *appearance stone* [14a, Cause 3: fused sentence with example] washing gives denim a worn look, and brushing gives flannel a softer look. Puckers or wrinkles can be set into a *fabric, these* [14a, Cause 1: comma splice with pronoun] features characterize fabrics such as seersucker and crinkle gauze.

These many options, and others, in fabrics permit fashion designers to satisfy the needs of many different types of *people, some* [14a, Cause 3: Fused sentence with example] consumers care more about being in style than building a long-lasting wardrobe, while others place high priority on ease of care or on comfortable fit.

ANSWER: PARTICIPATION ESSAY

This version revises the common splices and fused sentences. Answers might vary because of the options in correcting the errors. Also, answers will vary if a student revised the content, organization, or style.

ANSWER: PARTICIPATION ESSAY, *cont'd.*

As consumers, when we buy clothes, we often make choices on the basis of the fabric of an article of clothing. Therefore, fashion designers always pay attention to matters of composition and design in fabrics.

Fabric is composed of natural fibers, synthetic fibers, and blends of the two. Natural fibers include cotton, linen, and wool. They offer the advantages of durability and absorbency. Synthetic fibers include rayon, polyester, acrylic, or combinations of them and other synthetic fibers; they resist wrinkling and retain their color well. Fiber blends combine natural and synthetic fibers to create combinations such as cotton and polyester, which offer the advantages of each but have their own problems, such as retaining stains.

The design of fabric is affected by the way that the fabric is produced. For example, a fabric can be produced on a loom to create woven fabrics such as crepe and denim; conversely, a fabric can be produced on a knitting machine to create fabrics such as jersey and velour. Once the basic fabric is being produced, special patterns can be woven or knit into it. For instance, diagonal patterns can be woven into cotton fabrics for a geometric effect, and vertical patterns can be woven into a cable-stitched fabric for a thicker look and feel. Various finishes can further alter a fabric's appearance. Stone washing gives denim a worn look, and brushing gives flannel a softer look. Puckers or wrinkles can be set into a fabric; these features characterize fabrics such as seersucker and crinkle gauze.

These many options, and others, in fabrics permit fashion designers to satisfy the needs of many different types of people. Some consumers care more about being in style than building a long-lasting wardrobe, while others place a high priority on ease of care or on comfortable fit.

color well. Fiber blends combine natural and synthetic fibers to create combinations such as cotton and polyester, which offer the advantages of each but have their own problems, such as retaining stains.

The design of fabric is affected by the way that the fabric is produced, for example, a fabric can be produced on a loom to create woven fabrics such as crepe and denim, conversely, a fabric can be produced on a knitting machine to create fabrics such as jersey and velour. Once the basic fabric is being produced, special patterns can be woven or knit into it, for instance, diagonal patterns can be woven into cotton fabrics for a geometric effect, and vertical patterns can be woven into a cable-stiched fabric for a thicker look and feel. Various finishes can further alter a fabric's appearance stone washing, for example, gives denim a worn look, and brushing gives flannel a softer look. Puckers or wrinkles can be set into a fabric, these features characterize fabrics such as seersucker and crinkle gauze.

These many options, and others, in fabrics permit fashion designers to satisfy the needs of many different types of people, some consumers care more about being in style than building a long-lasting wardrobe, while others place a high priority on ease of care or on comfortable fit.

15 Sentences that Send Unclear Messages

A sentence can seem structurally correct at first glance, as if no grammatical principles of English had been violated, but can still have internal flaws that keep it from delivering a sensible message. To check for sentences that send the unclear messages listed in Chart 94, wait until you are revising (see 3c) and editing (see 3d). If you suspect a problem while you are drafting (see 3b), quickly underline or highlight the material and keep writing without breaking your rhythm. You can go back later and check yourself.

WAYS THAT SENTENCES SEND UNCLEAR MESSAGES   94

PROBLEM	SEE SECTION
■ Unnecessary shifts	
Person° and number°	15a-1
Subject° and voice°	15a-2
Tense° and mood°	15a-3
Direct discourse° and indirect discourse°	15a-4
■ Misplaced modifiers°	15b
■ Dangling modifiers°	15c
■ Mixed sentences	
Mixed constructions	15d-1
Faulty predication	15d-2
■ Incomplete sentences	15e
■ Missing pronoun subjects and expletives°	15ESL

QUOTATION ABOUT WRITING

In language clearness is everything.

—Confucius

QUOTATION ABOUT WRITING

It is not sufficient to know what one ought to say, but one must also know how to say it.

—Aristotle

QUOTATION ABOUT WRITING

Unless one is a genius, it is best to aim at being intelligible.

—Anthony Hope Hawkins

BACKGROUND

Clarity is one of the four virtues of style in classical rhetoric. The other three are correctness, appropriateness, and dignity or impressiveness. Theophrastus, a student of Aristotle, is credited with inventing the concept of the four virtues of style. The Stoics later added a fifth virtue—brevity.

QUOTATION ABOUT WRITING

Have something to say, and say it as clearly as you can. That is the only secret of style.
—Matthew Arnold

QUOTATION ABOUT WRITING

Writing is so difficult that I often feel that writers, having had their hell on earth, will escape all punishment hereafter.
—Jessamyn West

BACKGROUND

English emphasizes the number of every noun or pronoun in a sentence. In fact, it is impossible to talk or write about anything in English without signaling its number. English speakers take such information for granted, but the system is not universal. In Chinese, for example, the speaker decides if it is necessary to mention whether an item is singular or plural. Usually, number is considered irrelevant, and few sentences make any reference to it.

Many sentence flaws that send unclear messages can be hard to spot because of the way the human brain works. When writers know what they mean to say, they sometimes misread what is on the paper for what they intend. The brain unconsciously adjusts an error or fills in missing material. Readers, on the other hand, see only what is on the paper. For suggestions to help you see such flaws, see Chart 95.

NO Heated for 30 seconds, you get bubbles on the surface of the mixture. [This sentence says *you* are heated for 30 seconds.]

YES After the mixture is heated for 30 seconds, bubbles form on the surface.

NO After you boil the mixture for two minutes, it is cooled in a test tube. [This sentence shifts from *you* to *it* and from the active voice° to the passive voice.°]

YES After the mixture is boiled for two minutes, it is cooled in a test tube.

YES After boiling the mixture for two minutes, cool it in a test tube.

NO The chemical reaction taking place rapidly creates a salt. [Does *rapidly* refer to the place of the reaction or to the speed at which the salt is created?]

YES The chemical reaction takes place rapidly and creates a salt.

YES The chemical reaction rapidly creates a salt.

PROOFREADING TO FIND SENTENCE FLAWS · 95

- Finish your revision in enough time so you can put it aside and go back to it with fresh eyes that can spot flaws more easily.
- Work backwards, from your last sentence to your first, so that you can see each sentence as a separate unit free of a context that might lure you to overlook flaws.
- Ask an experienced reader to check your writing for sentence flaws. If you make an error discussed in this chapter, you likely make that error repeatedly. Once you become aware of it, you will have made a major step toward eliminating that type of error.
- Proofread an extra time exclusively for any error that you tend to make more than any other.

15a   Avoiding unnecessary shifts

Shift is a term for an abrupt, unneeded change of person°, number°, subject°, voice°, tense°, mood°, or kind of discourse (direct° or indirect°). Unnecessary shifts blur meaning. Readers expect to stay on the track that you as the writer start them on. If you switch tracks, your readers become confused.

1   Staying consistent in person and number

Person in English consists of the *first person (I, we)*, words that designate the speaker or writer; *second person (you)*, words that designate the one being spoken or written to; and *third person (he, she, it, they)*, words that designate the person or thing spoken or written about. All common nouns° are third-person words. (For more about person, see Chart 78 in section 11a.)

> **NO**   **They** enjoy feeling productive, but when a job is unsatisfying, **you** usually become depressed. [*They* shifts to *you*.]
>
> **YES**   **They** enjoy feeling productive, but when a job is unsatisfying, **they** usually become depressed.

Number refers to *singular* (one) or *plural* (more than one). Do not start to write in one number and then shift for no reason to the other number. Such shifting gives your sentences an unstable quality, and your message becomes fuzzy.

> **NO**   Because most **people** are living longer, an **employee** in the twenty-first century will retire later. [The plural *people* shifts to the singular *employee*.]
>
> **YES**   Because most **people** are living longer, **employees** in the twenty-first century will retire later.

A common cause of inconsistency in person and number is shifts to *you* (second person) from *I* (first person) or from a noun (third person) such as *person, the public,* or *people*. In academic writing, reserve *you* for sentences that address the reader directly; use the third person for general statements.

> **NO**   **I** enjoy reading forecasts of the future, but **you** wonder which will turn out to be correct. [*I*, which is first person, shifts to *you*, which is second person.]
>
> **YES**   **I** enjoy reading forecasts of the future, but **I** wonder which will turn out to be correct.

ALTERNATE EXAMPLE

To improve students' skills in recognizing person and number, you might ask them to read the following passage from Susan Allen Toth's "Cinematypes." Then ask students to work in groups to label the subject of each clause by person and number. (The subjects here appear in italics.)

> When *Pete and I* [third, first, plural] go to the movies, *we* [first, plural] take turns driving so *no one* [third, singular] owes anyone else anything. *We* [first, plural] leave the car far from the theater so *we* [first, plural] don't have to pay for a parking space. If *it's* [third, singular] raining or snowing, *Pete* [third, singular] offers to let me off at the door, but *I* [first, singular] can tell *he'll* [third, singular] feel better if *I* [first, singular] go with him while *he* [third, singular] finds a spot, so *we* [first, plural] share the walk too. Inside the theater *Pete* [third, singular] will hold my hand when *I* [first, singular] get scared if *I* [first, singular] ask him. *He* [third, singular] puts my hand firmly on his knee and covers it completely with his own hand. His *knee* [third, singular] never twitches. After a while, when the scary *part* [third, singular] is past, *he* [third, singular] loosens his hand slightly and *I* [first, singular] know *that* [third, singular] is a signal to take mine away. *He* [third, singular] sits companionably close, letting his *jacket* [third, singular] just touch my sweater, but *he* [third, singular] does not infringe. *He* [third, singular] thinks *I* [first, singular] ought to know *he* [third, singular] is there if *I* [first, singular] need him.

313

NO	By the year 2000, **Americans** will pay twice today's price for a car, and **you** will get twice the gas mileage. [*Americans,* which is third person, shifts to *you,* which is second person.]
YES	In 2000, **Americans** will pay twice today's price for a car, and **they** will get twice the gas mileage.

Another common cause of inconsistency in number is a shift from singular to plural in the third person. When a singular noun (for example, *employee*) or a singular third-person pronoun (for example, *someone*) is referred to with a pronoun, the pronoun should not be plural (for example, *they*). For a singular noun, use either *he* or *she* (or *he or she,* which acts as a singular pronoun). When you use words such as *employee* or *someone* in a general sense, without any specific "employee" or "someone" in mind, you might think that a "he" or "she" is not involved. Still, you have to choose a singular pronoun. Another choice is to change to the plural *employees,* in which case the plural pronoun *they* would be correct.

NO	When an **employee** is treated with respect, **they** usually feel highly motivated.
YES	When an **employee** is treated with respect, **he** or **she** usually feels highly motivated.
YES	When **employees** are treated with respect, **they** usually feel highly motivated.
YES	**Employees** who are treated with respect usually feel highly motivated.
YES	An **employee** who is treated with respect usually feels highly motivated.

Try to avoid sexist language when you use indefinite pronouns (such as *someone* or *everyone;* for a complete list, see 11g); see 11q and especially 21b for advice about nonsexist language.

❖ VERB ALERT: After you have revised person or number based on the advice here, check the verbs in the sentence to see whether any verb needs a change in number as well (see 8c). In the examples just shown, all Yes choices contain verb changes. ❖

EXERCISE 15-1

Consulting section 15a-1, eliminate shifts in person and number. Be alert to shifts between, as well as within, sentences.

(1) Hyperactivity in children is a problem that affects up to 6 percent of young boys and girls, although a boy is more likely to be affected than a girl. (2) Teachers can find teaching hyperactive children difficult, especially

---

ANSWERS: EXERCISE 15-1

Answers may vary somewhat because of the alternate ways to eliminate shifts in person and number.

(1) Hyperactivity in children is a problem that affects up to 6 percent of young boys and girls, although boys are more likely to be affected than girls. (2) Teachers can find teaching hyperactive children difficult, especially if the teachers do not know how to recognize the characteristics of such children. (3) In one study, teachers called as many as 30 percent of their students hyperactive. (4) In school, these children may daydream excessively, fidget a great deal, or talk. (5) They show other traits including tactlessly blurting out whatever is on their minds or racing around charging into people. (6) Hyperactive children are often impatient, cannot wait their turns, and are unable to follow directions. (7) New studies recently have been published. (8) They indicate that a key element in hyperactivity is a short attention span, possibly because these children eat too much sugar.

COVERAGE: EXERCISE 15-1

(1) 15a-1, shift in number, shift in number (2) 15a-1, shift in person, shift in number (3) no shift (4) no shift (5) 15a-1, shift in number (6) 15a-1, shift in number, shift in person (7) no shift (8) 15a-1, shift in number, shift in person.

if you do not know how to recognize the characteristics of such a child. (3) In one study, teachers called as many as 30 percent of their students hyperactive. (4) In school, these children may daydream excessively, fidget a great deal, or talk. (5) He shows other traits including tactlessly blurting out whatever is on their minds or racing around charging into people. (6) A hyperactive child is often impatient, cannot wait your turn, and are unable to follow directions. (7) New studies recently have been published. (8) It indicates that a key element in hyperactivity is a short attention span, possibly because we eat too much sugar.

---

2 **Staying consistent in subject and voice**

The **subject** of a sentence is the word or group of words that acts, is acted upon, or is described: *People* laugh, **people** *were entertained,* **people** *are nice.*

Some subject shifts are justified by the meaning of a passage: **People** *look forward to the future, but* **the future** *holds many secrets.*

Shifts in subjects are rarely justified when they are accompanied by a shift in **voice.** The voice of a sentence is either *active (People expect changes)* or *passive (Changes are expected).* (For information about active and passive voice, see 8n-8o.) Unnecessary shifts in subject and voice cause a sentence or longer stretch of writing to drift out of focus.

NO	Most **people expect** major improvements in the future, but some **hardships are also anticipated.** [The subject shifts from *people* to *hardships,* and the voice shifts from active to passive.]
YES	Most **people expect** major improvements in the future, but **they also anticipate** some hardships.
YES	Most people expect major improvements in the future but also anticipate some hardships.

---

3 **Staying consistent in tense and mood**

Tense refers to the ability of verbs to show time. Tense changes are required to describe time changes: *We will go to the movies after we finish dinner.* If tense shifts within or between sentences are illogical,

WORD HISTORY

According to the *Oxford English Dictionary* (OED), the word *voice* comes from the Latin word *vox,* meaning *voice* or *sound.* The earliest recorded statement in English using *voice* as a grammatical term is from 1382 by Wyclif: "A participle of a present tens, either preterit, or actif vois, eithir passif."

ALTERNATE EXAMPLE

To improve your students' skill in identifying subject and voice, you might ask them to work in groups to locate the subject and name the voice in each of the clauses in the following passage from Jack London's description of the San Francisco earthquake. (The subjects and verbs here appear in italics.)

The *earthquake* [subject] *shook* [active] down in San Francisco hundreds of thousands of dollars' worth of walls and chimneys. But the conflagration [subject] *that* [subject] *followed* [active] *burned* [active] up hundreds of millions of dollars' worth of property. *There* ["dummy" subject] *is* [active] no estimating within hundreds of millions the actual damage *that* [subject] *was wrought* [passive].

Not in history *has* a modern imperial city [subject] *been* so completely *destroyed* [passive]. *San Francisco* [subject] *is* [active] gone. *Nothing* [subject] *remains* [active] of it but memories and a fringe of dwelling houses on its outskirts. Its industrial *section* [subject] *is* [active] wiped out. Its social and residential *section* [subject] *is* [active] wiped out. The *factories* [subject] and *warehouses* [subject], the great *stores* [subject] and newspaper *buildings* [subject], the *hotels* [subject] and *palaces* [subject] of the nabobs, *all* [subject] *are* [active] *gone. There remains* [active] only the *fringe* [subject] of dwelling houses on the outskirts of *what* [subject] *was* [active] once San Francisco.

clarity suffers. (For information about correct sequences of tenses, see section 8k.)

NO	The campaign in the United States to clean up the movies **began** in the 1920s as civic and religious groups **try** to ban sex and violence from the screen. [The tense shifts from the past *began* to the present *try*.]
YES	The campaign in the United States to clean up the movies **began** in the 1920s as civic and religious groups **tried** to ban sex and violence from the screen.
NO	Producers and distributors **created** a film Production Code in the 1930s. At first, violating its guidelines **carried** no penalty. Eventually, however, films that **fail** to get the board's Seal of Approval **are not distributed** widely. [This shift occurs between sentences: the past tense *created* and *carried* shift to the present tense *fail* and *are not distributed*.]
YES	Producers and distributors **created** a film Production Code in the 1930s. At first, violating its guidelines **carried** no penalty. Eventually, however, films that **failed** to get the board's Seal of Approval **were not distributed** widely.

Mood refers to whether a sentence is a statement or question (*indicative mood*), a command or request (*imperative mood*), or a conditional or other-than-real statement (*subjunctive mood*). For information about mood, see section 8l. Shifts among moods blur the message of a passage.

NO	The Production Code included two guidelines about violence. **Do not show** the details of brutal killings, and **movies should not be** explicit about how to commit crimes. [The verbs shift from the imperative mood *do not show* to the indicative mood *movies should not be*.]
YES	The Production Code included two guidelines about violence. **Do not show** the details of brutal killings, and **do not be** explicit about how to commit crimes.
YES	The Production Code included two guidelines about violence. **Movies should not show** the details of brutal killings, and **should not be** explicit about how to commit crimes.

WORD HISTORY

According to the *Oxford English Dictionary* (OED), the term *mood* has been used since the sixteenth century to refer to verb forms that indicate commands or wishes. The earliest recorded use of the word in this way dates back to 1573, when a scholar named Golding asked a question that still concerns our students: "How shall men directly fynde the Coniugation, Nomber, Person, Tence, and Moode of Verbes togither in their Kynde?"

When we speak of the *mood* of a verb, we are not discussing its emotional state. *Mood* when it refers to a mental state is related to Latin *mos,* meaning *custom.* In contrast, *mood* used to discuss verbs is an alteration of *mode,* which comes from the Latin *modus,* meaning *measure, moderation,* or (most relevant here) *manner.* The earliest use of *mode* to refer to verbs dates back to 1520: "Sometyme of the infinytyve mode folowynge." Other early references make it clear that *mood/mode* was originally used for discussions of Greek and Latin rather than of English.

NO   The Code writers worried that if a crime were to be accurately depicted in a movie, it will encourage copycat crimes. [The sentence shifts from the subjunctive mood *if a crime were to be depicted* to the indicative mood *it will encourage.*]

YES   The Code writers worried that if a crime were to be accurately depicted in a movie, it would encourage copycat crimes.

<table>
<tr><td>4</td><td>Avoiding unmarked shifts between indirect and direct discourse within the same sentence</td></tr>
</table>

Indirect discourse reports speech or conversation and is not enclosed in quotation marks. **Direct discourse** repeats speech or conversation exactly and encloses the spoken words in quotation marks (see 24g). Sentences that merge indirect and direct discourse without quotation marks and other markers distort the message that you intend to deliver.

NO   A critic said that board members were acting as censors and **what you are doing is unconstitutional.** [The first clause is indirect discourse; the second clause shifts into unmarked direct discourse, garbling the message.]

YES   A critic said that board members were acting as censors and **that what they were doing was unconstitutional.** [This revision consistently uses indirect discourse.]

YES   A critic said that board members were acting as censors and added, **"What you are doing is unconstitutional."** [This revision uses indirect and direct discourse correctly, with quotation marks and other changes to distinguish reported words from spoken words.]

Changing a message from a direct-discourse version to an indirect-discourse version usually requires a change of verb tense and other grammatical changes. Simply removing the quotation marks is not enough.

NO   He asked **did we enjoy** the movie? [This version has the verb form needed for direct discourse, but the pronoun *we* is wrong and quotation punctuation is missing.]

YES   He asked **whether we enjoyed** the movie. [This version is entirely indirect discourse, and the verb has changed from *enjoy* to *enjoyed.*]

YES   He asked, **"Did you enjoy** the movie?" [This version is direct discourse. It repeats the original speech exactly, with correct quotation punctuation.]

ALTERNATE EXAMPLE

To improve your students' skill in identifying direct and indirect discourse, you might ask them to work in groups to identify the types of discourse found in the following passage from Russell Baker's "Country Living."

In the country, I am told, the trick is to let the weather roam free through the house. [indirect] "You're spoofing me, aren't you?" [direct] I asked the real-estate man. He wasn't.

In the country, he explained, you're supposed to wear long underwear all winter. [indirect] "It can get itchy if you don't have freezing wind coming between the logs," [direct] he said.

In the summer, you're expected to hang flypaper in the kitchen. "If your logs are chinked tightly they'll keep out the varmints that give your flypaper a businesslike appearance," [direct] he explained.

ANSWERS: EXERCISE 15-2

Answers will vary. Here is one set of possibilities.

1. Emmeline Pankhurst urged her two daughters to join the fight, but she asked whether they were prepared to commit civil disobedience.

2. Both Cristabel and Sylvia Pankhurst willingly adopted their mother's views and chained themselves to the gates of public buildings as they gave speeches urging that women be given the vote.

3. Some suffragists urged the Pankhursts to use "gentle persuasion," but most of their followers favored more radical action.

4. Suffragists once watched the Pankhursts climb into the rafters above the British Parliament and shout pro-vote slogans at important moments in the debate.

5. When British suffragists were arrested, they were often treated brutally, and they were noted for their brave persistence in spite of forced feedings aimed at breaking their hunger strikes.

COVERAGE: EXERCISE 15-2

(1) 15a-4, direct-indirect discourse shift (2) 15a-3, two tense shifts (3) 15a-2, subject and voice shift (4) 15a-1, shift in person (5) 15a-3, tense shift

ANSWERS: EXERCISE 15-3

(1) The robots of today can perform many more tasks than their earlier counterparts. (2) Twenty years ago, robots remained stationary and welded car bodies or lifted heavy steel bars. (3) Today's robots, on the other hand, perform work that includes cleaning offices, guarding hotel rooms, and inspecting automobiles. (4) At California's Memorial Medical Center of Long Beach, a doctor has performed brain surgery using a robot arm that allows her [or him] to drill into a person's skull and reach the brain ➡

EXERCISE 15-2

Consulting section 15a, revise these sentences to eliminate all incorrect shifts. (Some sentences can be revised several ways.)

EXAMPLE   British women began their fight for the right to vote later than their counterparts in the United States, but the British suffragist was far more militant.

British women began their fight for the right to vote later than their counterparts in the United States, *but the British suffragists were far more militant.*

1. Emmeline Pankhurst urged her two daughters to join the fight, but were they prepared to commit civil disobedience?

2. Both Cristabel and Sylvia Pankhurst willingly adopted their mother's views and chain themselves to the gates of public buildings as they give speeches urging that women be given the vote.

3. Some suffragists urged the Pankhursts to use "gentle persuasion," but more radical action was favored by most of their followers.

4. Suffragists once watched the Pankhursts climb into the rafters above the British Parliament, and you could hear them shout pro-vote slogans at important moments in the debate.

5. When British suffragists were arrested, they were often treated brutally, and they are noted for their brave persistence in spite of forced feedings aimed at breaking their hunger strikes.

EXERCISE 15-3

Consulting section 15a, revise this paragraph to eliminate incorrect shifts between, as well as within, sentences.

(1) The robots of today can perform many more tasks than its earlier counterpart. (2) Twenty years ago, a robot remained stationary and welded a car body or lifted heavy steel bars. (3) Today's robot, on the other hand, performs work that included cleaning offices, guarding a hotel room, and inspecting automobiles. (4) At California's Memorial Medical Center of Long Beach, a doctor has performed brain surgery using a robot arm that allows them to drill into a person's skull and reach your brain more accurately. (5) A robot recently joined the police force in Dallas, and a suspect was forced into surrendering by the robot. (6) When the robot broke a window, the suspect shouted "Help," and asked what is that? (7) Many people do not realize that service robots often prepare your fast food or sort the packages you brought to the post office. (8) In the near future, robots selling for about $20,000 will work without human assistance, and you will be able to buy a robot costing $50,000 that will do household chores.

15b Avoiding misplaced modifiers

A **modifier** is a word, phrase°, or clause° that describes other words, phrases, or clauses. A **misplaced modifier** is a describer that is positioned incorrectly in a sentence, thus distorting meaning. As you write and revise, always check to see that your modifiers are placed as close as possible to what they describe so that your reader will attach the meaning where you intend it to be.

1 Avoiding ambiguous placements

With **ambiguous placement,** a modifier is confusing to a reader because it can refer to two or more words in a sentence.

Limiting words (such as *only, not only, just, not just, almost hardly, nearly, even, exactly, merely, scarcely, simply*) can change meaning according to where they are placed. When you use such words, position them precisely. Consider how different placements of *only* change the meaning of this sentence: *Professional coaches say that high salaries motivate players.*

Only professional coaches say that high salaries motivate players. [No one else says this.]

Professional coaches **only** say that high salaries motivate players. [The coaches probably do not mean what they say.]

Professional coaches say **only** that high salaries motivate players. [The coaches say nothing else.]

Professional coaches say that **only** high salaries motivate players. [Nothing except high salaries motivates players.]

Professional coaches say that high salaries **only** motivate players. [High salaries do nothing other than motivate players.]

Professional coaches say that high salaries motivate **only** players. [No others on the team, such as coaches and managers, are motivated by high salaries.]

Squinting modifiers are ambiguous because they can describe both what precedes and what follows them. Since a modifier cannot do double duty, the reader must make a choice and may make the one that the writer did not intend. For clarity, revise the sentence, making sure that the modifier is positioned where its meaning is precise.

Cont'd.

more accurately. (5) A robot recently joined the police force in Dallas, and it forced a suspect into surrendering. (6) When the robot broke a window, the suspect shouted, "Help!" and asked, "What is that?" (7) Many people do not realize that service robots often prepare their fast food or sort the packages they bring to the post office. (8) In the near future, robots selling for about $20,000 will work without human assistance, and robots costing $50,000 will do household chores.

COVERAGE: EXERCISE 15-3

1. 15a-1, number
2. 15a-1, number between sentences 1 and 2; 15a-1, number within the sentence
3. 15a-1, number between sentences 1 and 3; 15a-3, tense; 15a-1, number within the sentence
4. 15a-1, number within the sentence; 15a-1, person
5. 15a-2, voice
6. 15a-4, indirect/direct discourse
7. 15a-1, person, 15a-3, tense
8. 15a-2, voice; 15a-1, number

TEACHING TIP

If your students feel that modifier placement is a slapdash business, you might ask them to look at some ludicrous sentences and have them try to draw what is written. Here are a few.

1. When people first saw whales, they were still wearing animal skins and had stone axes.
2. The man kissed the baby with a beard.
3. Walking down the street, the Eiffel Tower came into view.
4. The wildlife specialist said that most bears are dangerous on television.
5. Poison ivy is common in the forest which gives many people an itchy rash.

Working in groups, your students might enjoy experimenting with the following passage from Colin Fletcher's *The Winds of Mara* to see how movement of the italicized modifiers will change the meaning. The groups can compare their completed versions to see how many different readings have been created from the same original one simply by the change of location of modifiers.

> The lions continued their *slow and lazy* passage, directly toward us. Once a lioness stopped and turned her head to look *briefly* at the zebras, then walked on. A trio of cubs began to romp and tumble; an adult cuffed them into order. The gap between us narrowed. Soon we could see *magnificently self-assured* expressions on *golden* faces; then rib cages showing *faintly, sculpturally;* then muscles rippling beneath *powerful* haunches. Eventually it seemed as if we could see each hair adjusting to the animal's *slow and lazy* movements.

Pointing out that the rule against splitting an infinitive contradicts the principles of English grammar and the practice of our best writers, Cornelia and Bergen Evans demonstrate that meaning is sometimes distorted by adhering to it. They conclude that frequently the only way to avoid a split infinitive and still write good English is to avoid the infinitive. However, with the increasing use of the infinitive, in place of the *-ing* form or clause that was previously preferred, avoiding the infinitive may lead to wordy paraphrases that are not good English (*A Dictionary of Contemporary American Usage* [New York: Random House, 1957]).

NO	The football player being recruited **actively** believed each successive offer would be better. [What was active, the recruitment or the player's belief?]
YES	The football player being recruited believed **actively** that each successive offer would be better.
YES	The **actively** recruited football player believed each successive offer would be better.

2 Avoiding wrong placements

With **wrong placement,** modifying words are misplaced in a sentence, thus garbling the meaning.

NO	Most college athletic departments in the 1920s evolved from academic divisions, **especially those with large football programs.** [This sentence says that academic divisions, not athletic departments, had football programs.]
YES	Most college athletic departments in the 1920s, **especially those with large football programs,** evolved from academic divisions.

3 Avoiding awkward placements

Awkward placements are interruptions that seriously break the flow of a message and thereby distract your reader from understanding your material.

A **split infinitive** is one type of awkward placement. An **infinitive** is a verb form that starts with *to: to convince, to create.* When material comes between the *to* and its verb, it can interrupt meaning. This often happens when the intervening material could easily go before or after the infinitive.

NO	Orson Welles's radio drama "War of the Worlds" managed **to,** in October 1938, **convince** listeners that they were hearing an invasion by Martians.
YES	In October 1938, Orson Welles's radio drama "War of the Worlds" managed **to convince** listeners that they were hearing an invasion by Martians.

Often the intervening word that splits an infinitive is an adverb ending in *-ly.* Many such adverbs sound awkward unless they are placed either before or after the infinitive.

NO	People feared they would no longer be able **to happily live** in peace.
YES	People feared they would no longer be able **to live happily** in peace.

Nevertheless, sometimes an adverb seems awkward in any position except between *to* and the verb. Many readers, therefore, are not distracted by split infinitives like this one:

> Welles wanted **to realistically portray** a Martian invasion for the radio audience.

If you think your readers prefer that infinitives never be split, you can usually revise the sentence to avoid the split:

> Welles wanted his "Martian invasion" to sound realistic for the radio audience.

Interruptions of subjects and verbs by highly complex phrases or clauses disturb the smooth flow of a sentence.

NO	**The announcer,** because the script, which Welles himself wrote, called for perfect imitations of emergency announcements, **opened** with a warning that included a description of the "invasion."
YES	Because the script, which Welles himself wrote, called for perfect imitations of emergency announcements, **the announcer opened** with a warning that included a description of the "invasion."

When a **verb phrase** (a group of words that functions as a verb in a sentence: *was kissed, had been kissed*) is interrupted by words unrelated to the time sequence of the verb, the sentence lurches instead of flows. Your reader has to work too hard to understand the message that you want your sentence to deliver.

NO	Police switchboards **were,** not surprisingly, **jammed** with frantic phone calls.
YES	Not surprisingly, police switchboards **were jammed** with frantic phone calls.

When a verb and its object are interrupted by words that should modify both those elements, clarity often suffers.

NO	Many churches **held** for their frightened communities **"end of the world" prayer services.**
YES	Many churches **held "end of the world" prayer services** for their frightened communities.

TEACHING TIP

Students frequently become aware of problem sentences when they hear their papers read aloud. Particularly with long sentences, students sometimes compose chunk by chunk and fail to notice how the sections are connected. Reading aloud forces students to read the entire sentence, and hearing themselves stumble may signal a poorly constructed sentence. At home, students can read their papers into a tape recorder and then play back the tape to identify problem sentences. In class, student groups can listen for sentences that need revision as students read their papers aloud. Because some students make verbal corrections in their problem sentences when they read aloud without noticing a problem on the page, it is often useful to ask students to exchange their papers with another student and listen to that student read their paper aloud.

QUOTATION ABOUT WRITING

A good style should show no sign of effort. What is written should seem a happy accident.

—W. Somerset Maugham

TEACHING TIP

In *Revision: The Rhythm of Meaning* (Portsmouth, NH: Boynton/Cook, 1984), Marian M. Mohr suggests a sentence-revising exercise for small groups. Each student exchanges two problem sentences from his or her rough draft for two sentences by another student who has read the draft. Each student then suggests a couple of possible revisions for each sentence.

ANSWERS & COVERAGE: EXERCISE 15-4

Answers might vary somewhat. The final result must avoid all shifts.

1. If we look back in history, the origins of the automobile can be found in 1769 in France. [15b-3, interrupted verb phrase]

2. Because of his determination to travel without the assistance of animals, the Frenchman Nicholas Cugnot built the first self-propelled vehicle. [15b-3, separated subject and verb]

3. Only steam powered Cugnot's invention. [15b-1, squinting modifier]

4. The vehicle was run by a huge steam boiler that hung in front of its single front wheel. It was difficult to steer and hard to stop, and during a trial drive it knocked over a rock wall. [15b-3, separated subject and verb]

5. Beginning in 1860, the invention of various types of gas-combustion engines provided an alternative to clumsy steam power. [15b-2, wrong placement]

6. In Germany, two other inventors, Karl Benz and Gottlieb Daimler, were trying to invent a gas-driven vehicle. [15b-2, wrong placement]

7. They lived only sixty miles apart, but they did not know each other. [15b-1, ambiguous placement]

8. Benz is the man who finally produced the first car and was given credit for the invention of the automobile. [15b-1, ambiguous placement]

9. After the finishing touches had been added, the first car rolled out of a workshop in a small German town. [15b-3, interrupted verb phrase]

10. It rattled and banged down the street to announce loudly and dramatically a revolution in transportation. [15b-3, split infinitive]

ANSWERS: EXERCISE 15-5

1a. Frequently / , the microbiologist / used / old / methods / to explore / new / problems.

EXERCISE 15-4

Consulting section 15b, revise these sentences to correct any ambiguous, wrong, or awkward placements. If a sentence is correct, circle its number.

EXAMPLE   The invention of the first car took place in 1885, one of the greatest accomplishments in history.

The invention of the first car, *one of the greatest accomplishments in history,* took place in 1885.

1. The origins of the automobile can, if we look back in history, be found in 1769 in France.
2. The Frenchman Nicholas Cugnot, because of his determination to travel without the assistance of animals, built the first self-propelled vehicle.
3. Cugnot's invention only was powered by steam.
4. During a trial drive, the vehicle, which was run by a huge steam boiler that hung in front of its single front wheel and which was difficult to steer and hard to stop, knocked over a rock wall.
5. The invention, beginning in 1860, of various types of gas-combustion engines provided an alternative to clumsy steam power.
6. Two other inventors, Karl Benz and Gottlieb Daimler, were, in Germany, trying to invent a gas-driven vehicle.
7. Only they lived sixty miles apart, but they did not know each other.
8. Benz is finally the man who produced the first car and was given credit for the invention of the automobile.
9. The first car rolled, after the finishing touches had been added, out of a workshop in a small German town.
10. It rattled and banged down the street to loudly and dramatically announce a revolution in transportation.

EXERCISE 15-5

Consulting section 15b, combine each list of word groups to create all the possible logical sentences (each list offers more than one possibility). Insert commas as needed. Use a slash to indicate where each word or group of words ends. Explain differences in meaning, if any, among the alternatives you create.

EXAMPLE   college graduates
on the average
than do high school graduates
earn more money

A. On the average, / college graduates / earn more money / than do high school graduates. /

B. College graduates / earn more money, / on the average, / than do high school graduates. /

C. College graduates, / on the average, / earn more money / than do high school graduates. /

D. College graduates / earn more money / than do high school graduates, / on the average. /

1. the microbiologist
   frequently
   new
   to explore
   old
   used
   problems
   methods

2. to become
   engineering
   medicine
   the student
   a biomedical engineer
   studied
   successfully
   and

3. eagerly
   the computer specialists
   to solve problems
   worked
   artificial intelligence
   in
   only

4. know
   scientists
   that
   smoking
   lung
   not
   causes
   only
   cancer

5. air travel
   than travel by rail
   has become less expensive
   in many cases

15c Avoiding dangling modifiers

A **dangling modifier** describes or limits a word or words that are not stated in a sentence. Because a reader will "attach" the information in the dangling modifier to a noun or pronoun that *does* appear in the sentence, the writer's intended meaning is lost.

Dangling modifiers can be hard for a writer to spot. Aware of the intended meaning, the writer unconsciously supplies the missing material, but the reader usually sees only the error and realizes that the meaning is flawed.

Cont'd.

1b. The microbiologist / used / old / methods / to explore / new / problems / frequently.

1c. To explore / new / problems / , the microbiologist / used / old / methods / frequently.

1d. To explore / new / problems / frequently / , the microbiologist / used / old / methods.

2a. To become / a biomedical engineer / , the student / studied / engineering / and / medicine / successfully.

2b. The student / studied / engineering / and / medicine / successfully / to become / a biomedical engineer.

3a. Eagerly / , the computer specialists / worked / only / to solve problems / in / artificial intelligence.

3b. The computer specialists / worked / eagerly / only / in / artificial intelligence / to solve problems.

3c. Only / the computer specialists / worked / eagerly / in / artificial intelligence / to solve problems.

3d. The computer specialists / worked / eagerly / in / artificial intelligence / only / to solve problems.

4a. Not / only / scientists / know / that / smoking / causes / lung / cancer.

4b. Scientists / know / that / smoking / causes / not only lung cancer.

4c. Scientists / know / that / not / only / smoking / causes / lung / cancer.

5a. In many cases / , air travel / has become less expensive / than travel by rail.

5b. Air travel / has become less expensive / in many cases / than travel by rail.

5c. Air travel / has become less expensive / than travel by rail / , in many cases.

A HUMOROUS NOTE

Dangling modifiers can sometimes create statements that are unintentionally humorous. Consider the following examples collected and published by Richard Lederer in *Anguished English* (Wyrick and Company, 1988).

1. Locked in a vault for fifty years, the owner of the jewels has decided to sell them.

2. Do not sit in a chair without being fully assembled.

3. Washed from a layer of mudstone estimated to be more than three million years old, a young American paleoanthropologist has found several leg bones and a skull fragment.

TEACHING TIP

Students may realize that they have started a sentence with a dangling modifier when they move the modifier to follow the subject of the sentence. For example, "Shocked by her father's death, the family home became a refuge for Emily" becomes "The family home, shocked by her father's death, became a refuge for Emily" when the modifier follows the subject.

ANSWERS AND COVERAGE: EXERCISE 15-6

Answers may vary somewhat. Here is one set of possibilities.

1. To be successful, the student journalist must plan carefully. [dangling infinitive]

2. Being tense, an inexperienced journalist might begin on the wrong note. [dangling participle]

3. Until relaxed, the student journalist should mention only neutral topics. [unexpressed subject]

4. Correct

The first *No* example below says that the story's ending is doing the reading. The implied subject of the modifier is *we*, but nowhere is that subject stated—thus the modifier dangles. You can correct a dangling modifier by revising the sentence so that the intended subject is stated.

NO	**Reading Faulkner's short story "A Rose for Emily,"** the ending surprised us.
YES	**Having read Faulkner's short story "A Rose for Emily," we** were surprised by the ending.
YES	We read Faulkner's short story "A Rose for Emily" and were surprised by the ending.
NO	**When courting Emily, the townspeople** gossiped about her. [*The townspeople* were not courting Emily.]
YES	**When Emily was being courted by Homer Barron, the townspeople** gossiped about her.

Dangling modifiers are sometimes caused by unnecessary use of the passive voice (see 8n–8o).

NO	**To earn money, china-painting lessons** were offered by Emily to wealthy young women. [*China-painting lessons* cannot earn money.]
YES	**To earn money, Emily** offered china-painting lessons to wealthy young women.

EXERCISE 15-6

Consulting section 15c, identify and correct any dangling modifiers in these sentences. If a sentence is correct, circle its number.

EXAMPLE   Assigned to interview an unfriendly person, the experience can be instructive to a student journalist.

Assigned to interview an unfriendly person, *a student journalist can find the experience instructive.*

1. To be successful, careful plans must be made by the student journalist.

2. Being tense, the interview might begin on the wrong note for an inexperienced journalist.

3. Until relaxed, questions should mention only neutral topics.

4. After the journalist is more at ease, the person being interviewed might also relax.

mixed **15d**

5. With a list of questions, the interview process goes more smoothly for everyone involved.

6. Although easy to answer, mistakes are sometimes made on factual questions by a hostile interviewee.

7. By being analytic and evaluative, those mistakes can reveal a great deal to an experienced journalist.

8. Knowing how to pace an interview, the hard questions are more likely to be answered honestly after the interviewee has been caught off guard.

9. Until an interview is complete, the seasoned journalist always remains alert.

10. Essential information might be revealed when leaving.

15d Avoiding mixed sentences

A **mixed sentence** consists of parts that do not make sense together because the writer has lost track of the beginning of a sentence while writing the end. Careful proofreading, including reading aloud, can help a writer avoid this error.

1 Revising mixed constructions

A **mixed construction** starts out taking one grammatical form and then changes, derailing the meaning of the sentence.

NO	Because television's first transmissions in the 1920s included news programs quickly became popular with the public. [The opening dependent clause° starts off on one track, but the independent clause° goes off in another direction. What does the writer want to emphasize—the first transmissions or the popularity of news programs?]
YES	Television's first transmissions in the 1920s included news programs, which quickly became popular with the public. [The idea of the first transmissions is emphasized.]
YES	Because television's first transmissions in the 1920s included news programs, television quickly became popular with the public. [The idea of the popularity of the news programs is now emphasized.]

Cont'd.

5. With a list of questions, the interviewer can make the process go more smoothly for everyone involved. [unexpressed subject]

6. A hostile interviewee sometimes answers factual questions incorrectly, although they are easy to answer. [unnecessary passive voice]

7. By being analytic and evaluative, an experienced journalist can learn a great deal from those mistakes. [dangling participle]

8. Knowing how to pace an interview, a journalist will more likely get honest answers to hard questions after he or she has caught the interviewee off guard. [unexpressed subject]

9. Correct

10. Essential information might be revealed when the journalist is leaving. [unexpressed subject]

QUOTATION ABOUT WRITING
You write with ease to show your breeding,
But easy writing's curst hard reading.
—Richard Brinsley Sheridan

ALTERNATE EXAMPLES
What is inconsistent in the following mixed constructions? You might want to ask students to work in groups to revise these five sentences so that the parts make sense together.

1. Because you want to visit the great art museums of the world is why you should go to the Louvre in Paris.

2. Paris, the capital of France, one of the great museums of the world is located there.

3. Tourists from all over the world, the Louvre draws them.

4. The collection is composed of art works from many cultures is what distinguishes the Louvre.

BACKGROUND

In Chapter Three entitled "Syntax," of *Errors and Expectations* (New York: Oxford UP, 1977), Mina Shaughnessy presents an analysis of the causes of syntactic problems in the sentences produced by beginning students. She concludes that many such problems are linked to the manual process of writing, but others to the difficulty that nonwriters have learning the "dialect" of written formal English. Writing calls for specificity and coherence that are likely to seem "unnatural" because they are provided by other means in daily speech: gestures, tone of voice, tolerance for loose coordination, for example. In short, "the inexperienced writer is indeed not likely to have command of the language he needs to bring off the consolidations that are called for in writing." Another source of mismanaged syntax that has pedagogical implications is the beginning writer's lack of familiarity with how writers work. Unlike the speaker, the writer must have skills of encoding (handwriting, spelling, punctuation) and of experimenting with sentences (by additions, subtractions, substitutions, and inversions) to make meaning and statement fit as closely as possible. The third cause of syntactic problems, according to Shaughnessy, is the lack of confidence felt by novice writers in academic situations. She notes that self-doubt may be a memorable lesson they have learned in school. The solutions she suggests to help writers gain syntactic maturity are varied, including "direct intervention in the form of drills or grammatical explanations," pattern practice, and sentence-combining exercises. Shaughnessy attributes the greatest gains, however, to those times when the writer has to claim his or her meaning "within the constraints of a specific situation." It is "only as a writer," she asserts, "rather than as an exerciser" that a student can "develop the verbal responsiveness to his own thoughts and to the demands of his reader that produces genuinely mature syntax" (New York: Oxford UP, 1977).

NO   By doubling the time allotment for network news to thirty minutes increased the prestige of network news programs. [A prepositional phrase°, such as *by doubling,* cannot be the subject of a sentence.]

YES   Doubling the time allotment for network news to thirty minutes increased the prestige of network news programs. [Dropping the preposition *by* clears up the problem.]

YES   By doubling the time allotment for network news to thirty minutes, the network executives increased the prestige of network news programs. [Inserting a logical subject, *the network executives,* clears up the problem; an independent clause° is now preceded by a modifying prepositional phrase°.]

The phrase *the fact that* is sometimes the cause of a mixed sentence.

NO   The fact that quiz show scandals in the 1950s prompted the networks to produce even more news shows.

YES   The fact is that quiz show scandals in the 1950s prompted the networks to produce even more news shows. [The added *is* clarifies the meaning.]

YES   Quiz show scandals in the 1950s prompted the networks to produce even more news shows. [Dropping *the fact that* clarifies the meaning.]

2   Revising faulty predication

Faulty predication, sometimes called *illogical predication,* occurs when a subject and its predicate (see 7j) do not make sense together.

NO   The **purpose** of television **was invented** to entertain people.

YES   The **purpose** of television was to entertain people.

YES   **Television was invented** to entertain people.

One key cause of illogical predication is a breakdown in the connection between a subject and its complement. (A subject complement can be a noun°, a pronoun°, a noun clause° renaming a sentence subject, or an adjective° describing a sentence subject; see 7m-1.)

In the following *No* example, the subject complement *credible* could logically describe Walter Cronkite, but *Walter Cronkite* is not the

326

subject. The subject is *characteristic,* so the meaning calls for a subject complement that renames some characteristic of Walter Cronkite as a newscaster: thus, *credibility* instead of *credible.*

NO	As a newscaster, Walter Cronkite's outstanding **characteristic was credible.**
YES	As a newscaster, Walter Cronkite's outstanding **characteristic was credibility.** [The noun *credibility* renames *characteristic.*]
YES	As a newscaster, **Walter Cronkite was credible.** [The adjective *credible* describes the subject *Walter Cronkite.*]

Illogical predication is a problem in many constructions that include *is when* or *is where.* Avoid these phrases in academic writing.

NO	A disaster **is when** television news shows get some of their highest ratings.
YES	Television news shows get some of their highest ratings during a disaster.

Also, avoid *reason . . . is because* constructions. Use *reason . . . is that* instead. Remember that *because* means "for the reason that," so *reason . . . is because* literally means "reason . . . is for the reason that," which is repetitious.

NO	One **reason** television news captured national attention **is because** it covered the Vietnam War thoroughly.
YES	One **reason** television news captured national attention **is that** it covered the Vietnam War thoroughly.
YES	Television news captured national attention **because** it covered the Vietnam War thoroughly.

EXERCISE 15-7

Consulting section 15d, revise the mixed sentences below so that the beginning of each sentence fits logically with its end. If a sentence is correct, circle its number.

EXAMPLE   As a result of the increasing amount of sewage in the United States is a crisis in disposing of these wastes.

The increasing amount of sewage in the United States is creating a crisis in waste disposal.

1. The fact that millions of gallons of raw sewage are being dumped into the nation's waters are becoming unfit for use.

2. The reason that ecologists are extremely concerned is because waste disposal problems will get worse in the future.

Shaughnessy suggests that sentence problems often occur because students treat sentences as "a string of words" rather than as "a structure" (*Errors and Expectations*, p. 133). Faulty predication may occur when students begin a sentence with a well-conceived subject without looking ahead to the predicate that must follow. In "Getting Started" (*The Territory of Language: Linguistics, Stylistics, and the Teaching of Composition*, ed. Donald A. McQuade [Carbondale, IL: Southern Illinois UP, 1986]), Kenneth Bruffee suggests that students sometimes have a well-conceived predicate but do not know how to start the sentence to get to that predicate. Bruffee's explanation may be especially true when the predicate requires an abstract noun or a noun clause for a subject.

QUOTATION ABOUT WRITING

I only wish I could write with both hands, so as not to forget one thing while I am saying another.

—Teresa of Avila

ANSWERS AND COVERAGE:
EXERCISE 15-7

Answers will vary. Here is one set of possibilities.

1. Millions of gallons of raw sewage are being dumped into the nation's waters, which are becoming unfit for use. [15d-1, mixed construction with *the fact that*]

2. Ecologists are extremely concerned because waste disposal problems will get worse in the future. [15d-2, faulty predication with *reason is . . . because*]

➜

ANSWERS & COVERAGE: EXERCISE
15-7, *continued*

3. Multiple sewage spills in San Diego transformed a wildlife refuge into a public health hazard. [15d-1, mixed construction]

4. Also, hospital waste and other sewage created a fifty-mile-long slick that closed beaches in New Jersey and New York. [15d-2, faulty predication]

5. Correct

6. Sewage treatment plants were constructed that no longer are sufficient to handle today's volume of water. [15d-1, mixed construction]

7. One modern solution is the "greening" of sewage systems that occurs when trees are planted and then fertilized with sewage partially treated to retain soil nutrients. [15d-2, faulty predication with *is when*]

8. In Lubbock, Texas, recycled wastes keep a six-mile-long strip of community area green and lush. [15d-2, faulty predication with *is where*]

9. The source of pollution in some cities is the fact that storm runoffs from farmlands and urban streets are too huge and sudden to be handled without detention basins. [15d-1, mixed construction]

10. The problem is still enormous, because by the year 2005 the present 27 billion gallons of sewage a day will increase to 43 billion gallons, which means we have to take immediate, drastic action. [15d-1, 15d-2: mixed construction with *the fact that* and faulty predication with *reason . . . is because* and then mixed construction.]

3. Because of multiple sewage spills in San Diego transformed a wildlife refuge into a public health hazard.

4. Also, when hospital waste and other sewage created a fifty-mile-long slick closed beaches in New Jersey and New York.

5. This situation is similar to what happened in the nineteenth century, when sewage in overexpanded cities led to outbreaks of typhoid and cholera.

6. Back then sewage treatment plants were constructed no longer are sufficient to handle today's volume of waste.

7. One modern solution is "greening" of sewage systems is when trees are planted and then fertilized with sewage partially treated to retain soil nutrients.

8. In Lubbock, Texas, is where recycled wastes keep a six-mile-long strip of community area green and lush.

9. Because the source of pollution in some cities is storm runoffs from farmlands and urban streets are too huge and sudden to be handled without detention basins.

10. The fact is that the problem is still enormous, and the reason is because by the year 2005 the present 27 billion gallons of sewage a day will increase to 43 billion gallons means we have to take immediate, drastic action.

15e Avoiding incomplete sentences

An **incomplete sentence** is missing words, phrases, or clauses necessary for grammatical correctness or sensible meaning. Such omissions blur your meaning, and your reader has to work too hard to understand your message.

1 Using elliptical constructions carefully

An **elliptical construction** deliberately leaves out, rather than repeats, one or more words that appear elsewhere in the sentence. *I have my book and Joan's,* for example, is an acceptable way to express *I have my book and Joan's book.* An elliptical construction is correct only if the sentence contains the *exact* word or words omitted from the elliptical construction. Thus, *I have my book and Joan's* cannot be used to express *I have my book and Joan's books.*

328

NO   During the 1920s in Chicago, the cornetist Manuel Perez **was leading** one outstanding jazz group, Tommy and Jimmy Dorsey another. [The words *was leading* cannot take the place of *were leading,* which the subject *Tommy and Jimmy Dorsey* requires.]

YES   During the 1920s in Chicago, the cornetist Manuel Perez **was leading** one outstanding jazz group; Tommy and Jimmy Dorsey **were leading** another.

YES   During the 1920s in Chicago, the cornetist Manuel Perez **led** one outstanding jazz group, Tommy and Jimmy Dorsey another. [The verb *led* is correct both with *Manuel Perez* and with *Tommy and Jimmy Dorsey* and thus can be omitted after *Dorsey.*]

NO   The period of the big jazz dance bands **began** and **lasted through** World War II. [This sentence implies *through* after *began,* but *began* requires *in,* not *through.*]

YES   The period of the big jazz band **began in** and **lasted through** World War II.

2 | Making comparisons complete, unambiguous, and logical

In writing a comparison, be sure to include all words needed to make clear the relationship between the items or ideas being compared.

NO   Individuals with high concern for achievement make **better** business executives. [*Better* implies a comparison, but none is stated.]

YES   Individuals with high concern for achievement make **better** business executives **than** do people with little interest in personal accomplishments.

NO   Most personnel officers value high achievers more than risk takers. [Unclear: more than risk takers value high achievers, or more than personnel officers value risk takers?]

YES   Most personnel officers value high achievers more than they value risk takers.

YES   Most personnel officers value high achievers more than risk takers do.

NO   A risk taker's chance of success is very different. [Different from what?]

YES   A risk taker's chance of success is very different **from a high achiever's.**

BACKGROUND

Using "words which the hearer easily supplies" as a brief definition of *ellipsis,* Cornelia and Bergen Evans comment that speech, which is highly elliptical, would "scarcely be endurable otherwise." It is also "indispensable to the writer or speaker who wants to be brief and pithy, but it can easily cause confusion and obscurity and must be used with skill" (*A Dictionary of Contemporary American Usage* [New York: Random House, 1957]).

TEACHING TIP

Because conversation frequently includes incomplete comparisons, you might want to ask students to turn the following spoken dialogue into a paragraph written in the third person.

Speaker A: I'm so glad we came here. This restaurant is so much better.

Speaker B: You're right. A place that has fresh flowers on the tables is more appealing.

Speaker A: I always think linen napkins are nicer.

Speaker B: This place has a fine reputation for good service, but it's a shame that it's so much more expensive.

NO	Achievers value success **as much,** if not more than, a high salary. [Comparisons using *as . . . as* require the second *as.*]
YES	Achievers value success **as much as,** if not more than, a high salary.

In speech, sentences such as *That was such a difficult exam, You're so smart,* or *I'm too upset* are common. These constructions using *so, too,* and *such* as intensifiers imply that a completing thought has been omitted, and listeners can simply ask for more information if they need it. In academic writing, however, be sure to supply the completing information or take out the intensifier.

NO	Risk takers are often **such** innovative people.
YES	Risk takers are often **such** innovative people that some businesses seek them out as employees.
YES	Risk takers are often innovative people.

3 Proofreading carefully to catch inadvertently omitted articles, pronouns, conjunctions, and prepositions

Small words—articles°, pronouns°, conjunctions°, and prepositions°—needed to make sentences complete tend to drop out when a writer is rushing or is distracted. If you tend to omit small words, proofread your work an extra time exclusively to discover the missing words.

NO	On May 2, 1808, citizens Madrid rioted against French soldiers.
YES	On May 2, 1808, **the** citizens **of** Madrid rioted against French soldiers.
NO	On following day, captured rioters were taken into country and shot.
YES	On **the** following day, captured rioters were taken into **the** country and shot.
NO	The Spanish painter Francisco Goya recorded both the riot the execution in a pair of pictures painted 1814.
YES	The Spanish painter Francisco Goya recorded both the riot **and** the execution in a pair of pictures painted **in** 1814.

EXERCISE 15-8

Consulting section 15e, revise this paragraph to create correct elliptical constructions, to complete comparisons, and to insert any missing words.

(1) Engineering students use practical thinking to solve difficult problems as much as academic training. (2) One group students at the University California Berkeley received challenging assignment. (3) These students had to create a package that would allow an egg to be dropped as much, but not more than eighty feet onto cement without breaking. (4) This complex problem was considered and possible solutions analyzed by fourth-year chemical engineering student, Carla St. Laurent. (5) She gave so much thought to professor's challenge. (6) She created a mother hen made papier-maché that kept safe egg she dropped from fourth-floor window.

15
ESL

Supplying pronoun subjects and expletives

1

Supplying a missing pronoun as subject

Many languages omit a pronoun as a subject because the verb delivers the needed information. English, however, requires the use of the pronoun as a subject. Proofread carefully to be sure all needed pronouns appear in your sentences.

NO	Economics is an important subject in college; **is studied** all over the world. [A subject is not provided for the verb *is studied*.]
YES	Economics is an important subject in college; **it** is studied all over the world.
NO	In my family, **major** in economics or political science.
YES	In my family, **we** major in economics or political science.

2

Supplying missing expletives

Many languages do not use the structures that are called **expletives** in English. Expletives use *it* or *there* plus a form of the verb *be:* for example, *it is, there are, there were.* Often, an expletive adds unnecessary words to a sentence (see 16a-1), but in some sentences they are necessary to communicate a clear message. When you use an expletive, be sure to include both the verb and *it* or *there.*

Answers may vary somewhat. One set of possibilities is the following.

(1) Engineering students use innovative thinking to solve difficult problems as much as they use [15e-2, ambiguous comparison] theoretical knowledge. (2) One group of students at the University of California at Berkeley received a challenging assignment. [15e-3, small words omitted] (3) They had to create a package that would allow an egg to be dropped as much as, [15e-2, incomplete comparison] but not more than, eighty feet on to [15e-3, small word omitted] cement without breaking. (4) This complex problem was considered and possible solutions were [15e-1, incorrect elliptical] analyzed by fourth-year chemical engineering student Carla St. Laurent. (5) She gave so much thought to her professor's challenge that she came up with the winning solution. [15e-3, 15e-2: small word omitted, incomplete comparison] (6) She created a mother hen made of papier-maché that kept safe the egg dropped from a fourth-floor window. [15e-3, small words omitted]

ANSWERS: EXERCISE 15-ESL

1. In colleges and universities, where economists are common, they [15esl-1, missing pronoun subject] can teach and do research.

2. In government, there [15esl-2, missing expletive] are career opportunities as forecasters, statisticians, and even presidential advisors.

3. Harvard economist Jeffrey Sachs is an advisor to the new Russian government; he [15esl-1, missing pronoun subject] is advising on how to restructure the Russian economy.

4. Economists are applauded or ignored when the economy is strong; they [15esl-1, missing pronoun subject] are criticized when it [15esl-1, missing pronoun subject] is weak.

5. Businesses hire economics majors, too; there [15esl-2, missing expletive] is an up-to-date list of job opportunities for economists on file in the placement office.

NO	Many students at my school major in economics; **are** fifty economics majors in my graduating class.
YES	Many students at my school major in economics; **there are** fifty economics majors in my graduating class.

EXERCISE 15-ESL

Consulting section 15-ESL, find and correct any sentences where pronouns or expletives are missing.

EXAMPLE   Although most people think of economists in connection with the government, are many career possibilities for economics majors.

Although most people think of economists in connection with the government, *there are* many career possibilities for economics majors.

1. In colleges and universities where economists are common, can teach and do research.

2. In government, are career opportunities as forecasters, statisticians, and even presidential advisors.

3. Harvard economist Jeffrey Sachs is an advisor to the new Russian government; is advising on how to restructure the Russian economy.

4. Economists are applauded or ignored when the economy is strong; are criticized when is weak.

5. Businesses hire economics majors, too; is an up-to-date list of job opportunities for economists on file in the placement office.

Focus on Revising

REVISING YOUR WRITING

If you write sentences that send unclear messages, go back to your writing and locate the errors. Using this chapter as a resource, revise your writing to eliminate unnecessary shifts (15a), misplaced modifiers (15b), dangling modifiers (15c), mixed sentences (15d), and incomplete sentences (15e).

CASE STUDIES: REVISING TO CORRECT SENTENCES THAT SEND UNCLEAR MESSAGES

In these case studies, you can observe a student writer revising. Then you have the chance to revise other student writing on your own.

Observation

A student wrote the following draft for a course called Freshman Composition. The assignment was to compose a narrative of a personal experience with which other students in the class might sympathize. This narrative explains the experience clearly, uses specific examples well to illustrate the story, and draws on the writer's voice effectively. The draft's effectiveness is diminished, however, by the presence of sentences that send unclear messages by unnecessary shifts, misplaced modifiers, dangling modifiers, mixed sentences, and incomplete sentences.

Read through the draft. The unclear messages are highlighted and explained. Before you look at the student's revision, revise the material yourself. Then compare what you and the student did.

Moving to a different part of the United States was one of the most difficult experiences of my life. Looking forward to my senior year in high school, my father's company informed him that he had been transferred to Colorado Springs, and would we be ready to move in a month? I liked Boston much better than my father, so I was less than thrilled

dangling modifier: 15c

shift from direct to indirect discourse: 15a-4

ambiguous comparison: 15e-2

COVERAGE: PARTICIPATION ESSAY, pages 335-36

Most job hunters *enter business* [15e-3: missing word] world through a door labelled "Job Interviews." *Regardless of training and experience* [15c: dangling modifier], the interview is the occasion when an employer gets an impression of the candidate. What can a person do so that *you* [15a-1: shift in person] perform successfully at what is likely to be a fifteen-minute interview?

By understanding the objectives of the interview will help an applicant prepare [15d-1: mixed construction]. *An applicant who knows the company's needs is better equipped* [15e-2: incomplete comparison]. Most businesses with a position to fill interview with three basic questions in mind: Is this applicant qualified to do the job? Will this applicant perform if hired? Will *you* [15a-1: shift in person] fit into the work environment?

A job applicant can use a well-prepared résumé to present information about experience and training. At the interview, *applicants* [15a-1: shift in number] should be prepared to talk about courses taken, jobs held, and capabilities demonstrated. *Probing for specific details* [15c: dangling modifier], the applicant's abilities will be judged by the employer. *Job applicants will be judged by the employer. Job applicants should be aware that personal questions about marital status or plans to have children are illegal; however, such matters might be raised by some interviewers anyway* [15a-2: shift from passive to active voice]. *By preparing an answer like "Those areas of my life are personal," or "I make it a rule never to let my personal life interfere with business" will help an applicant's confidence* [15d-1: mixed construction].

A major concern of an interviewer is focused on whether the applicant would fit into the company [15d-2: faulty construction]. An applicant who plays *merely* ➔

incorrect elliptical construction: 15e-1

about having to leave. But after days of arguing and talking to my parents, I knew that the decision was final.

unnecessary shift in person and number: 15a-1

omitted word: 15e-3

When our family arrived in Colorado Springs, I was depressed. Our house was comfortable, about twice the size of our Boston apartment, but you had the feeling that it was in the middle of nowhere. Living in the outskirts of the city, I couldn't go anywhere without car. In Boston, all I have to do is hop on the "T" to go anywhere in the city.

unnecessary shift in tense: 15a-3

mixed construction: 15d-1

Also, by discovering that the expressions for some everyday things were different than in Boston was the place that I wanted to be. When I asked for a submarine, a thick sandwich on a long roll, the convenience store clerk said she didn't have kits for making model ships with a confused look. When buying something in Colorado, salespeople offered me what they called "a sack" instead of a bag. As far as I knew, a sack means that the quarterback has been tackled in football game.

misplaced modifier; wrong placement: 15b-2

dangling modifier: 15c

omitted word: 15e-3

misplaced modifier; ambiguous placement: 15b-1

Slowly, however, I began to realize that in Colorado even there are movies, fast-food restaurants, and shopping malls. Mostly, the people made the big difference for me. It didn't happily take long for me to get to know some students in my high school, and to, much to my surprise, find that most were eager to make me feel at home. By now, I can't imagine a better place to live than Colorado Springs.

misplaced modifier; awkward placement: 15b-3

Here is how the student revised the draft to correct the errors. In a few places, the student could correct the errors in more than one way. Your revision, therefore, might not be exactly like this one, but it should deal with each error highlighted on the draft.

Moving to a different part of the United States was one of the most difficult experiences of my life. At the time that I was looking forward to my senior year in high school, my father's company informed him that he had been transferred to Colorado Springs, and we would need to be ready to move in a month. I liked Boston much better than my father did, so I was less than thrilled about having to leave. But after days of arguing with and talking to my parents, I knew that the decision was final.

When our family arrived in Colorado Springs, I was depressed. Our house was comfortable, about twice the size of our Boston apartment, but I had the feeling that it was in the middle of nowhere. Living in the outskirts of the city, I couldn't go anywhere without a car. In Boston, all I had to do was hop on the "T" to go anywhere in the city.

Also, when I discovered that the expressions for some everyday things were different, Boston was the place that I wanted to be. When I asked for submarine, a thick sandwich on a long roll, the convenience store clerk looked confused and said she didn't have kits for making model ships. When I would buy something in Colorado, salespeople offered me "a sack" instead of a bag. As far as I knew, a sack means that the quarterback has been tackled in a football game.

Slowly, however, I began to realize that even in Colorado there are movies, fast-food restaurants, and shopping malls. Mostly, the people made the big difference for me. Happily, it didn't take long for me to get to know some students in my high school, and to find, much to my surprise, that most were eager to make me feel at home. By now, I can't imagine a better place to live than Colorado Springs.

Participation

A student working in the college peer counseling program for job hunters wrote the following draft for an article in the campus newspaper. This material shows a very good awareness of audience, and it contains well-organized, useful information. The draft's effectiveness is diminished, however, by the presence of sentences

Cont'd.

[15b-1: ambiguous placement of modifier] a role to impress an interviewer is making a mistake, particularly if *you* [15a-1: shift in person used in rest of essay] are offered a job that *you* [15a-1: shift in person used in rest of essay] are not suited for. *Present a natural image. Use the interview to find out how the company's work environment will fit your* [15a-1: shift in person used in rest of essay *personal style* [15a-3: shift in mood, with two imperative sentences].

ANSWER: PARTICIPATION ESSAY

This version is revised to eliminate errors that cause sentences to send unclear messages. Because options are available for handling corrections, answers will vary somewhat. Also, answers will vary if students have revised for content, organization, or style.

Most job hunters enter the business world through a door labelled "Job Interviews." Regardless of training and experience, the job candidate makes an impression on an employer during an interview. What can a person do so that he or she can perform successfully at what is likely to be a fifteen-minute interview?

Understanding the objectives of the interview will help an applicant prepare. An applicant who knows the company's needs is better equipped than someone who does not have such information. Most businesses with a position to fill interview with three basic questions in mind: Is this applicant qualified to do the job? Will this applicant perform if hired? Will this applicant fit into the work environment?

ANSWER: PARTICIPATION ESSAY, *continued*

A job applicant can use a well-prepared résumé to present information about experience and training. At the interview, an applicant should be prepared to talk about courses taken, jobs held, and capabilities demonstrated. Probing for specific details, the employer will judge the applicant's abilities. Job applicants should be aware that personal questions about marital status or plans to have children are illegal; however, some interviewers might raise such matters anyway. Preparing an answer like "Those areas of my life are personal" or "I make it a rule never to let my personal life interfere with business" will help an applicant's confidence.

A major concern of an interviewer is whether the applicant would fit into the company. An applicant who merely plays a role to impress an interviewer is making a mistake, particularly if the person is offered a job that he or she is not suited for. A wise job candidate presents a natural image and finds out whether the company's work environment fits his or her personal style.

that send unclear messages because of unnecessary shifts, misplaced modifiers, dangling modifiers, mixed sentences, and incomplete sentences.

Read through the draft. Then revise it to eliminate the errors. Also, make any additional revisions that you think would improve the content, organization, and style of the material.

Most job hunters enter business world through a door labeled "Job Interviews." Regardless of training and experience the interview is the occasion when an employer gets an impression of the candidate. What can a person do so that you perform successfully at what is likely to be a fifteen-minute interview?

By understanding the objectives of the interview will help an applicant prepare. An applicant who knows the company's needs is better equipped. Most businesses with a position to fill interview with three basic questions in mind: Is this applicant qualified to do the job? Will this applicant perform if hired? Will you fit into the work environment?

A job applicant can use a well-prepared résumé to present information about experience and training. At the interview, applicants should be prepared to talk about courses taken, jobs held, and capabilities demonstrated. Probing for specific details, the applicant's abilities will be judged by the employer. Job applicants should be aware that personal questions about marital status or plans to have children are illegal; however, such matters might be raised by some interviewers anyway. By preparing an answer like "Those areas of my life are personal," or "I make it a rule never to let my personal life interfere with business" will help an applicant's confidence.

A major concern of an interviewer is focused on whether the applicant would fit into the company. An applicant who plays merely a role to impress an interviewer is making a mistake, particularly if you are offered a job that you are not suited for. Present a natural image. Use the interview to find out how well the company's work environment will fit your personal style.

Writing Effective Sentences

When you write effective sentences, you move beyond correctness to writing characterized by style and grace. Part Four shows you various techniques of writing style that can enhance the delivery of your message. As you use Chapters 16 through 19, remember that writers can make choices to help form and content work in concert to create memorable prose.

16 Conciseness

Conciseness describes writing that is direct and to the point. Wordy writing is not concise. Wordiness irritates readers because it forces them to clear away excess words so that sentences can deliver their messages. Concise writing appeals to readers because it uses words economically.

HOW TO WRITE CONCISELY   96

- Eliminate wordy sentence structures (see 16a).
- Drop unneeded words (see 16b).
- Omit redundancies (see 16c).

16a Eliminating wordy sentence structures

Wordy sentence structures can make writing seem abstract and uninteresting. Whenever possible, revise to eliminate wordiness.

1 Revising unnecessary expletive constructions

An **expletive construction** consists of *it* or *there* along with a form of the verb *be* placed before the subject°* in a sentence. In some contexts, an expletive construction can create anticipation and provide emphasis, but usually expletive constructions are merely wordy. Removing the expletive and revising slightly eliminates wordy sentence structures.

*Throughout this book, a degree mark (°) indicates that you can find a definition of the word in the Glossary of Terms in this handbook.

338

NO	**It is** obvious that we missed class.
YES	Obviously, we missed class.
NO	**There was** a new teacher waiting for us.
YES	A new teacher was waiting for us.

❖ ESL NOTE: The *it* in an expletive construction is not a pronoun° referring to a specific antecedent°. The *it* is an "empty" word that fills the subject° position in a sentence but does not function as the actual subject. The actual subject appears after the expletive construction: *It was the **teacher** who answered the question.* (A more concise version is *The **teacher** answered the question.*)

The *there* in an expletive construction does not designate a place. The *there* indicates merely that something exists. Expletive constructions with *there* shift the sequence of the subject and verb° in a sentence, so that the actual subject appears after the expletive construction: ***There** are many **teachers** who can answer the question.* (A more concise version is *Many **teachers** can answer the question.*) ❖

2   Revising unnecessary passive constructions

In the **active voice,** the subject of a sentence *does* the action named by the verb°.

ACTIVE	**Professor Higgins teaches** public speaking. [*Professor Higgins* is the subject, and he does the action: he *teaches*.]

In the **passive voice,** the subject of a sentence *receives* the action named by the verb.

PASSIVE	**Public speaking is taught** by Professor Higgins. [*Public speaking* is the subject, which receives the action *taught*.]

The active voice adds liveliness as well as conciseness, so it is usually perferable. The simplest way to revise from the passive voice to the active voice is to make the doer of the action the subject of the sentence. (In a passive construction, the doer of an action is usually identified in a phrase starting with *by*.) When you want to switch from passive to active, turn the noun° or pronoun° in the *by* phrase into the sentence subject.

339

NO	Volunteer work **was done by the students** for extra credit in sociology. [The students are doers of the action, but they are not the subject of the sentence.]
YES	The **students did** volunteer work for extra credit in sociology.
NO	The new spending bill **was vetoed by the governor.** [The governor is the doer of the action, but he is not the subject of the sentence.]
YES	The **governor vetoed** the new spending bill.

Sometimes you can revise a sentence from passive voice to active voice by using a new verb. This method works especially well when you want to keep the same subject.

PASSIVE	**Britain was defeated** by the United States in the War of 1812.
ACTIVE	**Britain lost** the War of 1812 to the United States.
PASSIVE	Many **soldiers were stricken** with yellow fever.
ACTIVE	Many **soldiers caught** yellow fever.

Writers may sometimes have no choice but to use the passive voice, as when the doer of an action is unknown or when naming the doer would disrupt the focus of a sentence (see 8n–8o).

Writers sometimes, however, deliberately use the passive voice in sentence after sentence in the mistaken belief that it sounds "mature" or "academic."

NO	One very important quality developed by an individual during a first job is self-reliance. This strength was gained by me when I was allowed by my supervisor to set up and conduct my own survey project.
YES	During their first job, many individuals develop the very important quality of self-reliance. I gained this strength when my supervisor allowed me to set up and conduct my own survey project.
YES	During a first job, many people develop self-reliance, as I did when my supervisor let me set up and conduct my own survey project.

Be particularly alert for the passive voice that misleads readers because it hides information about who acts: *Cracks in the foundation of the structure had been found, but they were not considered serious.* Left out of the sentence is important information telling who found cracks and who decided that they were not serious.

3	**Combining sentences, reducing clauses to phrases, and reducing phrases to words**

As you revise your writing, check to see that it is not too wordy. When you need to be more concise, often you can combine sentences, reduce a clause° to a phrase°, or reduce a phrase to a single word.

Combining sentences

Look carefully at sets of sentences in your writing. You may be able to reduce the information in one sentence to a group of words that you can include in another sentence.

TWO SENTENCES

The *Titanic* was discovered seventy-three years after being sunk by an iceberg. The wreck was located in the Atlantic by a team of French and American scientists.

COMBINED SENTENCE

Seventy-three years after being sunk by an iceberg, the *Titanic* was located in the Atlantic by a team of French and American scientists.

TWO SENTENCES

The stern of the ship was missing and there was some external damage to the hull. Otherwise, the Titanic seemed to be in excellent condition.

COMBINED SENTENCE

Aside from its missing stern and external damage to its hull, the *Titanic* seemed to be in excellent condition.

For more advice about reducing sentence structures by combining sentences, see Chapter 17.

Reducing clauses

You can often reduce a clause° to a phrase°, sometimes simply by dropping the opening relative pronoun° and its verb°.

The *Titanic*, **which was a huge ocean liner,** sank in 1912.
The *Titanic,* **a huge ocean liner,** sank in 1912.

EXTRA EXERCISE

Rewrite each of the following groups of sentences as a single statement by reducing the information in one of them to a group of words that you can include in the other.

1. William Shakespeare had seven brothers and sisters. He was the third child.

2. He attended Stratford's free grammar school until he was about thirteen. Later he was apprenticed to a local tradesperson.

3. Anne Hathaway was eight years older than Shakespeare. He married her in 1582.

4. Their first child was born the next year. They named her Susanna.

5. In 1585 Anne bore twins. They were named Hamnet and Judith.

6. In 1597 Shakespeare moved from London back to Stratford. He bought a large house called New Place.

ANSWERS: EXTRA EXERCISE

Answers will vary, but here are some possibilities.

1. William Shakespeare was the third of eight children.

2. He attended Stratford's free grammar school until he was about thirteen, when he was apprenticed to a local tradesperson.

3. Shakespeare married Anne Hathaway, who was eight years his senior, in 1582.

4. Susanna, their first child, was born the next year.

5. In 1585 Anne bore the twins Hamnet and Judith.

6. In 1597 Shakespeare moved back from London to New Place, a large house in Stratford.

Truman Capote, known for a prose style marked by clarity and lucidity, never relented in his efforts to delete everything that marred the lean simplicity of his work. In *Music for Chameleons,* a book of essays published toward the end of his life, he included a description of an experience he had in a Moscow subway. To his surprise, he recognized a man who had lived in Capote's apartment building in New York ten years earlier. Blind, crippled, and dignified, Mr. Jones never left his apartment but received a steady stream of visitors and telephone calls. Suddenly he disappeared. Using the following excerpt from Capote's remembrance, you might ask students if they can find any words that can be deleted or phrases that can be reduced and revise the passage to be more concise.

—Ten years pass.

Now it is a zero-cold December afternoon, and I am in Moscow. I am riding in a subway car. There are only a few other passengers. One of them is a man sitting opposite me, a man wearing boots, a thick long coat and a Russian-style fur cap. He has bright eyes, blue as a peacock's.

After a doubtful instant, I simply stared, for even without the black glasses, there was no mistaking that lean distinctive face, those high cheekbones with the single scarlet star-shaped birthmark.

I was just about to cross the aisle and speak to him when the train pulled into a station, and Mr. Jones, on a pair of fine sturdy legs, stood up and strode out of the car. Swiftly, the train door closed behind him.

Revisions will vary, but here is one possibility:

Ten years later, on a zero-cold December afternoon, I am riding a Moscow subway. Among the few other passengers is a man sitting opposite me wearing boots, a thick long coat and a Russian-style fur cap. He has bright eyes, blue as a peacock's. ➡

Sometimes you can reduce a clause to a single word.

> The scientists held a memorial service for the passengers and crew members **who had died.**

> The scientists held a memorial service for the **dead** passengers and crew members.

You can create elliptical constructions° to reduce clauses. Be sure to omit only those words that are clearly implied (see 15e-1).

> **When they were confronted with disaster,** some passengers behaved heroically, **while others behaved selfishly.**

> **Confronted with disaster,** some passengers behaved heroically, **others selfishly.**

Keep your meaning clear when you reduce clauses. Making your writing concise should never get in the way of clarity.

Reducing phrases

Sometimes you can reduce phrases° to shorter phrases or to single words.

> Over fifteen hundred **travelers on that voyage** died in the shipwreck.

> Over fifteen hundred **passengers** died in the shipwreck.

> **Objects** found inside the ship **included unbroken** bottles of wine and expensive **undamaged** china.

> **Found undamaged** inside the ship were bottles of wine and expensive china.

4	Using strong verbs and avoiding nouns formed from verbs

Your writing will have more impact when you choose verbs° that are strong because they directly convey an action. *Be* and *have* are not strong verbs. Also, they tend to create wordy structures. When you revise weak verbs to strong ones, often you can reduce the number of words in your sentences.

WEAK VERB

The proposal before the city council **has to do with** locating the sewage treatment plant outside city limits.

STRONGER VERBS

The proposal before the city council **suggests** locating the sewage treatment plant outside city limits.

The proposal before the city council **argues against** locating the sewage treatment plant outside city limits.

WEAK VERBS

The board members **were of the opinion** that the revisions in the code **were not** changes they could accept.

STRONGER VERBS

The board members **said** that they **could not accept** the revisions in the code.

When you look for weak verbs to revise, look also for nominals (nouns derived from verbs, usually by added suffixes° such as *-ance*, *-ment*, or *-tion*). To achieve conciseness, turn a nominal back into a verb, thus reducing words and gaining impact.

NO	We **oversaw the establishment of** a student advisory committee.
YES	We **established** a student advisory committee.
NO	The building **had the appearance of** having been renovated.
YES	The building **appeared** to be renovated.

5   Using pronouns for conciseness

Pronouns°, which can replace nouns, can help you reduce wordiness. When changing nouns to pronouns, be sure that the antecedent of each pronoun is unambiguous (see 10a–10c) and that the agreement of pronouns and antecedents is correct (see 11m–11p).

NO	Queen Elizabeth II served as a driver and mechanic in World War II. **Elizabeth** joined the Auxiliary Territorial Service in 1944, while **the future queen** was still a princess. Although **Princess Elizabeth** did not know how to drive, she quickly learned how to strip and repair many kinds of engines.
YES	Queen Elizabeth II served as a driver and mechanic in World War II. **She** joined the Auxiliary Territorial Service in 1944, while **she** was still a princess. Although **she** did not know how to drive, she quickly learned how to strip and repair many kinds of engines.

Cont'd.

After a doubtful instant, I simply stared. I recognized, even without the black glasses, that lean distinctive face, those high cheekbones with the scarlet star birthmark.

I was about to cross the aisle and speak to him when the train pulled into a station, and Mr. Jones, on a pair of sturdy legs, stood and strode out of the car. Swiftly, the train door closed behind him.

TEACHING TIP

Joseph M. Williams (*Style: Ten Lessons in Clarity and Grace,* 3rd ed. [Glenview, IL: Scott, Foresman, 1989]) writes that "the first principle of clear writing" can be stated in two parts:

1. In the subjects of your sentences, name your cast of characters.

2. In the verbs of your sentences, name the crucial actions in which you involve those characters (9).

Richard Lanham states the same principle differently when he tells writers to ask "Who's kicking who?" and to put the "kicking" action into the main verb of the sentence.

Writers often state the crucial action with a noun instead of a verb—with "investigation" instead of "investigate," "discussion" instead of "discuss," or "agreement" instead of "agree." In such sentences the agent of the action often appears as the object of a preposition or is omitted entirely. Of course, writers sometimes need to name an action with a noun for proper emphasis.

EXERCISE 16-1

Consulting section 16a, combine each set of sentences to eliminate wordy constructions.

EXAMPLE   An event in the history of Scotland occurred in 1542 when Mary Stuart became queen of Scotland when she was only six days old. The death of James V, who was king of Scotland and also her father, followed Mary Stuart's birth.

Mary Stuart became queen of Scotland in 1542, when she was only six days old, after her father, King James V of Scotland, died.

1. Mary Stuart was too young to lift the crown. Mary Stuart could not hold the scepter. Mary Stuart was unable to repeat her solemn vows.
2. Her formal crowning, nevertheless, took place when she had reached the age of only nine months. The service was held in the chapel of Stirling Castle.
3. It is known that Mary was not the first monarch to ascend the throne as an infant. It was in 1422 in England that Henry VI, who was king of England, was crowned at the same age, which was nine months.
4. There was a decision made by her guardians when Mary was six years old, in 1548. The decision was to send the young queen to France, where she was supposed to prepare herself for marriage with Francis, who was the heir to the French throne.
5. Some famous and well-educated men and women were to be found living at the court of the French king. Mary was given the opportunity to observe and talk with these famous and well-educated people.
6. The young queen quickly learned the lessons that were taught to her. The reputation that she gained at court was for being witty and clever, and, in addition, she became known as being diplomatic.
7. When the time had arrived for Mary's marriage to take place, a French custom was broken by her. Her favorite color, which was white, was what she insisted on wearing. The royal seamstresses who sewed the gown warned her that in France white was not considered a color of good luck for a wedding.
8. What Mary was told by the seamstresses was that white was the traditional color of mourning for French queens who had lost a loved one. When Francis, who was Mary's young husband, died two years after the wedding, many people said the gown had been an omen that had predicted disaster.

➜

ANSWERS: EXERCISE 16-1

Answers will vary. Here is one set of possibilities.

1. Mary Stuart was too young to lift the crown, hold the scepter, or repeat her solemn vows.

2. She was formally crowned, nevertheless, in Stirling Castle chapel when she was only nine months old.

3. Mary was not the first infant monarch, for Henry VI was also only nine months old when he was crowned king of England in 1422.

4. In 1548, when Mary was six years old, her guardians decided to send her to France to prepare to marry Francis, the heir to the French throne.

5. Mary observed and talked with the famous and well-educated people who lived at the French king's court.

6. The young queen learned quickly and gained the reputation of being witty, clever, and diplomatic.

7. When Mary married, she broke a French custom by wearing white, her favorite color, even though the royal seamstresses warned her that white was bad luck for a wedding.

8. The seamstresses told Mary that white was the traditional color of mourning for French queens, so when Mary's young husband Francis died two years after the wedding, many people said the gown had been a disastrous omen.

9. It is known that in 1565 Mary married Lord Darnley, who was her cousin. The color of her gown for that wedding is not recorded by history.
10. Less than two years after the wedding, Lord Darnley was to fall victim to death. It was in 1567 that Lord Darnley died as a result of the fact that the house he was visiting was blown up because of political sabotage.

Cont'd.

9. In 1565, Mary married her cousin Lord Darnley, but history does not record the color of her wedding gown.

10. Lord Darnley died in 1567, less than two years after the wedding, when political saboteurs blew up the house he was visiting.

16b Eliminating unneeded words

To achieve conciseness, eliminate unneeded words that clutter sentences. Also, revise imprecise language so that six inexact words do not take the place of one precise word.

When a writer tries to write very formally or tries to reach an assigned word limit, **padding** usually results. Sentences loaded with **deadwood** contain empty words and phrases that increase the word count but lack meaning. If you find deadwood, clear it away.

PADDED	~~In fact,~~ the television station ~~which is situated in the local area~~ has won ~~a great~~ many awards ~~as a result of its having been involved in the~~ coverage of ~~all kinds of~~ controversial issues.
CONCISE	The local television station has won many awards for its coverage of controversial issues.
PADDED	The bookstore ~~entered the order for~~ the books ~~that the instructor has said will be utilized in~~ the course ~~sequence~~.
CONCISE	The bookstore ordered the books for the course.

Chart 97 lists typical empty words that are among the worst offenders. The chart also offers revised versions. Apply what is here to similar items not listed.

GUIDE FOR ELIMINATING EMPTY WORDS AND PHRASES   97

EMPTY WORD OR PHRASE	WORDY EXAMPLE	REVISION
as a matter of fact	*As a matter of fact,* statistics show that many marriages end in divorce.	Statistics show that many marriages end in divorce. ➡

TEACHING TIP

You might want to provide students with wordy phrases that commonly inflate and obscure English prose, asking them to find replacements that are more direct and effective. Here are some you can use, with suggested replacements; you can easily find others.

at this point in time	now
free up some space	make room
in the event that	if
my personal physician	my doctor
thunderstorm activity	thunderstorm
it is believed by many that	many believe
head up a committee	head a committee
experience some discomfort	hurt
in order to	to
making an effort to	trying to

QUOTATION ABOUT WRITING

Proper words in proper places, make the true definition of a style.

—Jonathan Swift

QUOTATION ABOUT WRITING

The language must be careful and must appear effortless. It must not sweat. It must suggest and be provocative at the same time.

—Toni Morrison

in a very real sense	In a very real sense, the drainage problems caused the house to collapse.	The drainage problems caused the house to collapse.
factor	The project's final cost was an essential factor to consider.	The project's final cost was essential to consider.
manner	The child touched the snake in a reluctant manner.	The child touched the snake reluctantly.
nature	His comment was of an offensive nature.	His comment was offensive.
type of	Gordon took a relaxing type of vacation.	Gordon took a relaxing vacation.
seems	It seems that the union called a strike over health benefits.	The union called a strike over health benefits.
tendency	The team had a tendency to lose home games.	The team often lost home games.
in the process of	We are in the process of reviewing the proposal.	We are reviewing the proposal.
exist	The crime rate that exists is unacceptable.	The crime rate is unacceptable.
in light of the fact that	In light of the fact that jobs are scarce, I am going back to school.	Because jobs are scarce, I am going back to school.

➡

for the purpose of	Work crews were dispatched *for the purpose of* fixing the potholes.	Work crews were dispatched to fix the potholes.
in the case of	*In the case of* the proposed water tax, residents were very angry.	Residents were very angry about the proposed water tax.
in the event that	*In the event that* you are late, I will leave.	If you are late, I will leave.
the point I am trying to make	*The point I am trying to make* is that news reporters should not invade people's privacy.	News reporters should not invade people's privacy.

EXERCISE 16-2

Consulting section 16b, eliminate unnecessary words or phrases. Be especially alert for empty words that add nothing to meaning.

EXAMPLE   In view of the fact that most people at some time or other in their lives face surgery, the effects of anesthesia are factors of great interest to the general public.

Because most people at some time face surgery, the effects of anesthesia are of great interest to the general public.

(1) It is a fact for many people that when they are anesthetized for surgery, that is to say so that they may have an operation performed, they feel no pain but still maintain some degree of consciousness. (2) Many fully anesthetized patients have a sense of being able to recognize sounds when they hear doctors and nurses alike talking in the operating room, the place where the surgery is performed. (3) In an experiment at the University of California at Davis Medical Center, eleven patients were given commands that were of a nonthreatening nature while they were under anesthesia. (4) It seems that while under anesthesia they were told to do a simple type of thing like pulling their ears during a postoperative interview.

QUOTATION ABOUT WRITING

Nothing you write, if you hope to be any good, will ever come out as you first hoped.

—Lillian Hellman

TEACHING TIP

Since empty words and phrases occur with some frequency in documents people receive every day, you might want to ask students to bring a memo from work, an advertising brochure from the mail, or a quotation from a newspaper that demonstrates useless verbal padding. (You may wish to bar documents written by teachers or administrators on campus.) The examples can be used for group discussion and revision, then presented to the class in their original as well as their revised form.

ANSWERS: EXERCISE 16-2

Answers will vary somewhat, but at the least students should revise the underlined words.

(1) It is a fact for many people that when they are anesthetized for surgery, that is to say so that they may have an operation performed, they feel no pain but still maintain some degree of consciousness. (2) Many fully anesthetized patients have a sense of being able to recognize sounds when they hear doctors and nurses alike talking in the operating room, the place where the surgery is performed. (3) In an experiment at the University of California at Davis Medical Center, eleven patients were given commands that were of a nonthreatening nature while they were under anesthesia. (4) It seems that while under anesthesia they were told to do a simple type of thing like pulling their ears during a post-operative ➡

Cont'd.

interview. (5) Patients who had been given the instruction had a tendency to pull on their ears six times more often than did patients who were given no orders. (6) It is interesting to note that it seems likely that the reason people can hear while they are anesthetized is because the highly specialized endings of the auditory nerve cells are hard for anesthetics to block. (7) Because of the fact that anesthesiologists are now aware of this phenomenon, many of them counsel surgeons to make positive, encouraging types of comments to patients under anesthesia. (8) As a matter of fact, some surgeons ask their patients to listen through earphones to music or to tapes with suggestions of a positive nature, which in a very real sense can speed and hasten recovery.

(5) Patients who had been given the instruction had a tendency to pull on their ears six times more often than did patients who were given no orders. (6) It is interesting to note that it seems likely that the reason people can hear while they are anesthetized is because the highly specialized endings of the auditory nerve cells are hard for anesthetics to block. (7) Because of the fact that anesthesiologists are now aware of this phenomenon, many of them counsel surgeons to make positive, encouraging types of comments to patients under anesthesia. (8) As a matter of fact, some surgeons ask their patients to listen through earphones to music or to tapes with suggestions of a positive nature, which in a very real sense can speed and hasten recovery.

16c   Revising redundancies

Planned repetition can create a powerful rhythmic effect (see 19g). The dull drone of unplanned repetition, however, can bore a reader and prevent the delivery of your message. Unplanned repetition, called **redundancy,** says the same thing more than once.

Certain redundant word pairs are very common. Avoid expressions like *each and every, null and void, forever and ever,* and *final and conclusive.* Other common redundancies are *perfectly clear, few* (or *many*) *in number, consensus of opinion,* and *reason is because.*

NO	Bringing the project to **final completion** three weeks early, the new manager earned our **respectful regard** when **the project was completed.**
YES	**Completing** the project three weeks early, the new manager earned our **respect.**
YES	The new manager earned our **respect** for **completing** the project three weeks early.
NO	**Astonished,** the architect **circled around** the building in **amazement.**
YES	**Astonished,** the architect **circled** the building.
YES	The architect **walked around** the building **in amazement.**

Notice how redundancies deaden a sentence's impact.

NO	The council members **proposed a discussion** of the amendment, but that **proposal for a discussion** was voted down after they had **discussed** it for a while.
YES	The council members' proposal to discuss the amendment was eventually voted down.

QUOTATION ABOUT WRITING

What is written without effort is in general read without pleasure.

—Samuel Johnson

QUOTATION ABOUT WRITING

Style consists in certain fashions, or certain eccentricities, or certain manners, of certain people, in certain situations, and possessed of a certain share of fashion or importance.

—Washington Irving

NO   The **consensus of opinion** among those of us who saw it is that the carton was **huge in size.**

YES   Most of us who saw the carton agree that it was huge.

❖ ESL NOTE: In all languages, words often carry an unspoken message—an *implied meaning*—that is assumed by native speakers of the language. Implied meaning can cause redundancy in writing. For example, *I sent a letter **by mail*** is redundant; in American English, *to send a letter* implies *by mail*. A good dictionary gives information about implied meaning of words (see the list of dictionaries in 20a). *Webster's New World Dictionary, Third College Edition,* for example, defines the verb *send* this way: "to dispatch, convey, or transmit (a letter, message, etc.) by mail, radio, etc." ❖

EXERCISE 16-3

Consulting section 16c, eliminate redundant words and phrases. Then revise the paragraph so that it is concise.

EXAMPLE   Many people will be surprised to learn that, amazingly enough, labor-saving household devices that are intended to save people from working hard as a matter of fact often do not accomplish their aim or goal.

Many people will be surprised to learn that labor-saving household devices often fail to accomplish their goal.

(1) Why would people pay good money and spend hard-earned dollars to buy labor-saving household appliances unless the devices really and truly lived up to their promise and saved work hours? (2) Think of the fact that time is saved in light of the fact that clothes are now washed in a washing machine instead of being washed on a washboard. (3) Today the vacuum cleaner now cleans floors in place of the broom doing all the sweeping and cleaning. (4) Instead of the manual egg beater people have the electric mixer. (5) Nevertheless, regardless of these inventions, homemakers in the United States spend about the same number of hours doing housework, laundry, and cleaning as people did in the year of 1910. (6) How could this situation and state of affairs come to be? (7) The reasons are because labor-saving household devices, in a very real sense, have not saved much labor nor have they lessened the time devoted to housework. (8) Surprisingly, it is amazing to note that people's wealth today is one essential factor to consider as a reason. (9) It seems that more people in this day and age compared with the year of 1910 can afford the expense of larger apartments or houses. (10) In addition, the level of cleanliness people expect of themselves has increased at about the same rate of speed as the advances in inventions.

ANSWERS: EXERCISE 16-3

Answers will vary somewhat, but at the least students should revise the underlined words and recast sentences as needed.

(1) Why would people pay good money and spend hard-earned dollars to buy labor-saving household appliances unless the devices really and truly lived up to their promise and saved work hours? (2) Think of the fact that time is saved in light of the fact that clothes are now washed in a washing machine instead of being washed on a washboard. (3) Today the vacuum cleaner now cleans floors in place of the broom doing all the sweeping and cleaning. (4) Instead of the manual egg beater, people have the electric mixer. (5) Nevertheless, regardless of these inventions, homemakers in the United States spend about the same number of hours doing housework, laundry, and cleaning as people did in the year of 1910. (6) How could this situation and state of affairs come to be? (7) The reasons are because labor-saving household devices, in a very real sense, have not saved much labor nor have they lessened the time devoted to housework. (8) Surprisingly, it is amazing to note that people's wealth today is one essential factor to consider as a reason. (9) It seems that more people in this day and age compared with the year of 1910 can afford the expense of larger apartments or houses. (10) In addition, the level of cleanliness people expect of themselves has increased at about the same rate of speed as the advances in inventions.

16 ESL Eliminating unneeded pronouns and adverbs

When a subject° or object° is separated from its verb°, avoid adding unneeded pronouns to go with the verb.

NO Winter storms that bring ice, sleet, and snow **they** can cause traffic problems. [*Winter storms* is the subject of the verb *can cause;* the pronoun *they* is unneeded.]

YES Winter storms that bring ice, sleet, and snow can cause traffic problems.

NO A car that has worn tires **it** is dangerous on wet or icy roads.

YES A car that has worn tires is dangerous on wet or icy roads.

Be especially careful not to add an unneeded pronoun after or within a relative clause (an adjective clause° starting with *that, which,* or *who*).

NO The car that I bought last month **it** was damaged in an accident.

YES The car that I bought last month was damaged in an accident.

NO The doors, which I had pinstriped **them** myself, were damaged in the accident.

YES The doors, which I had pinstriped myself, were damaged in the accident.

A related problem can occur when *where* or *when* is used as a relative adverb°, to introduce a relative (adjective) clause. Pronouns or adverbs can be unneeded additions in these sentences.

NO The curve **where** my car skidded **it** was icy. [The pronoun *it* is not needed.]

YES The curve where my car skidded was icy.

NO The curve **where** my car skidded **there** was icy. [The adverb *there* is unneeded.]

YES The curve where my car skidded was icy.

rep

16
ESL

EXERCISE 16-ESL

Consulting section 16-ESL, eliminate any unneeded pronouns or adverbs.

EXAMPLE   My car, which is much more convenient for me to use than the bus, it is a necessity.

My car, which is much more convenient for me to use than the bus, is a necessity.

1. A car-repair shop in my neighborhood it does good work.
2. I decided that was where I should go there for an estimate.
3. The mechanic who looked at the damage he asked how the accident had happened.
4. The tires, which had almost no tread left, they could not grip the icy pavement.
5. The car, which the mechanic said it needed new tires as well as new doors, it will be ready next week.

ANSWERS: EXERCISE 16ESL

1. A car-repair shop in my neighborhood [*it* deleted] does good work.

2. I decided that was where I should go [*there* deleted] for an estimate.

3. The mechanic who looked at the damage [*he* deleted] asked how the accident had happened.

4. The tires, which had almost no tread left, [*they* deleted] could not grip the icy pavement.

5. The car, which the mechanic said [*it* deleted] needed new tires as well as new doors, [*it* deleted] will be ready next week.

COVERAGE: PARTICIPATION ESSAY, page 372

College students seeking alternatives to dormitories, young adults moving out on their own, and newcomers to an area often rent apartments or houses. All of these potential renters should keep in mind that *renting or leasing* [16c: redundancy] involves a legal agreement between landlord and tenant. *It is recommended* [16a-1: expletive construction; also 16a-2: unnecessary passive] *that* anyone preparing to rent conduct *thorough and extensive* [16c: redundancy] *evaluations* [16a-4: noun from a verb] of the *entire situation* [16b: unneeded word] before making any decisions. *One major area to investigate is the evaluation of the type of landlord* [16b: unneeded words]. *It is also recommended* [16a-1: expletive construction; also 16a-2: unnecessary passive] *that* renters carefully examine the *condition and nature* [16c: redundancy] of the premises before any lease *is signed by them* [16a-2: unnecessary passive].

An initial step in the rent process is the investigation of the landlord [16b: unneeded words]. *Renters can determine the nature of* [16b: unneeded words] the landlord's management style by several strategies. A list of current and former tenants *of the facility* [16b: unneeded words] can *be requested* [16a-2: unnecessary passive] from the landlord. *Renters should not hesitate to contact a reasonable number of parties on the list. Renters should ask all of those with whom they come in contact whether the management of the property, in particular the landlord, is easy to contact if problems should arise and whether the landlord is willing to handle such problems without delay* [16a-3: combine sentences]. If anyone is *of the opinion* [16b: unneeded words] that the landlord has a poor reputation for handling problems properly, *it is better* [16a-1: expletive construction; also 16a-2: unnecessary passive] to find out before signing a lease or deposit check.

➡

Focus on Revising

REVISING YOUR WRITING

If you need to write more concisely, go back to your writing and locate wordy material. Using this chapter as a resource, revise your writing to eliminate wordiness in sentences (see 16a) and to avoid unneeded words (see 16b) and redundancy (see 16c).

CASE STUDY: REVISING FOR CONCISENESS

In these case studies, you can observe a student writer revising. Then you have the chance to revise other student writing on your own.

Observation

A student wrote the following draft for a course called Business Management. The assignment was to write a summary of a research study related to the course. This material summarizes the source material thoroughly, but the draft's effectiveness is diminished by a lack of conciseness.

Read through the draft. The wordy material is highlighted and explained. Before you look at the student's revision, revise the material yourself. Then compare what you and the student did.

Researchers in business management interviewed and talked to over two hundred people who have experienced important, major career defeats. The study was undertaken by the researchers for the purpose of discovering why some smart people fail at their careers while there are others who generally do not fail. The results show that in a very real sense many people lack the recognition that most careers involve getting along well with other people. It is often claimed by many employees who fail that

redundant: 16c

unneeded words: 16b

unnecessary expletive construction: 16a-1; and clause can be reduced to word: 16a-3

unnecessary passive construction: 16a-2

clause can be reduced to phrase: 16a-3

unneeded words: 16b

noun formed from verb: 16a-4

➡

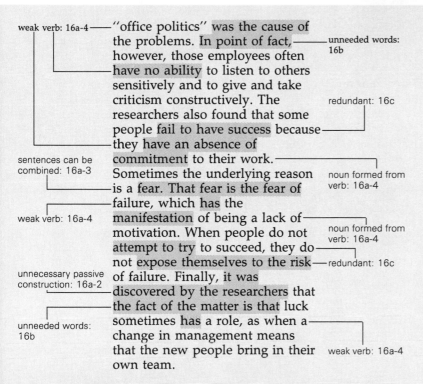

weak verb: 16a-4

"office politics" was the cause of the problems. In point of fact, however, those employees often have no ability to listen to others sensitively and to give and take criticism constructively. The researchers also found that some people fail to have success because they have an absence of commitment to their work. Sometimes the underlying reason is a fear. That fear is the fear of failure, which has the manifestation of being a lack of motivation. When people do not attempt to try to succeed, they do not expose themselves to the risk of failure. Finally, it was discovered by the researchers that the fact of the matter is that luck sometimes has a role, as when a change in management means that the new people bring in their own team.

unneeded words: 16b

redundant: 16c

sentences can be combined: 16a-3

noun formed from verb: 16a-4

weak verb: 16a-4

noun formed from verb: 16a-4

redundant: 16c

unnecessary passive construction: 16a-2

unneeded words: 16b

weak verb: 16a-4

Here is how the student revised the paragraph to achieve conciseness. In a few places, the student could correct the error in more than one way. Your revision, therefore, might not be exactly like this one, but it should eliminate the wordy material highlighted on the draft.

    Researchers in business management interviewed over two hundred people who have experienced major career defeats. The researchers wanted to discover why some smart people fail at their careers while others do not. The results show that many people do not recognize that most careers involve getting along well with other people. Many employees who fail claim that "office politics" caused the problem. However, those employees often do not listen to others sensitively and do not give and take criticism constructively. The researchers also found that some people fail because they are not committed to their work. Sometimes the underlying reason is a fear of failure, which manifests itself as a lack of motivation. When people do not try to succeed, they do

Cont'd.

    Also, *for the purpose of being* [16b: unneeded words] protected *in the event of* [16b: empty phrase] future disagreements, *it is recommended* [16a-1: expletive construction; also 16a-2: unnecessary passive] that renters inspect the premises carefully. If there is any *type of* [16b: empty words] damage in the apartment, the details should be *written down in a written inventory* [16c: redundancy] by the renters, and *it should be signed and dated by the renters and the landlord* [16a-2: unnecessary passive]. If any damages are to be repaired by the landlord, those promises should also be put in writing. *In the event that* [16b: empty words] any damage is present when renters leave the property, *it is* [16a-1: expletive construction] the renters who will probably be held legally liable for repairs since the landlord would be able to claim that the damage was done during the term of the renters' lease.

    In short, only after careful *consideration of the landlord and the premises should the renter even consider* [16c: redundancy *signing a lease or leaving a deposit or signing anything that might be legally binding* [16c: redundancy].

ANSWER: PARTICIPATION ESSAY

This version is revised for conciseness. Answers will vary but here is one possible revision. Also, answers will vary if students have revised content, organization, or style.

College students seeking alternatives to dormitories, young adults moving out on their own, and newcomers to an area often rent apartments or houses. All of these potential renters should keep in mind that renting involves a legal agreement between landlord and tenant. Anyone preparing to rent should thoroughly evaluate the situation before making any decisions. One factor to investigate is the landlord. Renters should also examine the condition of the premises carefully before they sign a lease.

First, renters should investigate the landlord. Renters can determine the landlord's management style by several strategies. They can ask the landlord for a list of current and former tenants. Renters should not hesitate to contact a reasonable number of parties on the list to ask them whether the landlord is easy to contact and prompt about handling problems. If anyone thinks that the landlord has a poor reputation, renters are better off knowing before they sign a lease or deposit check.

Also, to be protected against future disagreements, renters should inspect the premises carefully. If there is any damage in the apartment, the renters should make a written inventory, and they and the landlord should sign and date it. Also, renters should get in writing all promises of repairs. If any damage is present when renters leave the property, they will probably be held legally liable for repairs since the landlord would be able to claim that they caused the damage.

In short, only after carefully considering the situation should renters sign a lease or leave a deposit.

not risk failure. Finally, the researchers discovered that luck sometimes plays a role, as when a change in management means that the new people bring in their own team.

Participation

A student wrote the following draft for a journalism class called Feature Writing. The material is logically presented and informative, but the draft's effectiveness is diminished by wordy constructions, padding, and redundancies.

Read through the draft. Then revise it to eliminate the errors. Also, make any additional revisions you think would improve the content, organization, and style of the material.

College students seeking alternatives to dormitories, young adults moving out on their own, and newcomers to an area often rent apartments or houses. All of these potential renters should keep in mind that renting or leasing involves a legal agreement between landlord and tenant. It is recommended that anyone preparing to rent conduct careful and extensive evaluations of the entire situation before making any decisions. One major area to investigate is the evaluation of the type of landlord. It is also recommended that renters carefully examine the condition and nature of the premises before any lease is signed by them.

An initial step in the rent process is the investigation of the landlord. A list of current and former tenants of the facility can be requested from the landlord. Renters should not hesitate to contact a reasonable number of parties on the list. Renters should ask all of those with whom they come in contact whether the management of the property, in particular the landlord, is easy to contact if problems should arise and whether the landlord is willing to handle such problems without delay. If anyone is of the opinion that the landlord has a poor reputation for handling problems properly, it is better to find out before signing a lease or deposit check.

Also, for the purpose of being protected in the event of future disagreements, it is recommended that renters inspect the premises carefully. If there is any type of damage in the apartment, the details should be written down in a written inventory by the renters, and it should be signed and dated by the renters and the landlord. If any damages are to be repaired by the landlord, those promises should also be put in writing. In the event that any damage is present when renters leave the property, it is the renters who will probably be held legally liable for repairs since the landlord would be able to claim that the damage was done during the term of the renters' lease.

In short, only after careful consideration should the renter even consider signing a lease or leaving a deposit or signing anything that might be legally binding.

17 Coordination and Subordination

You can include **coordination** and **subordination** in your writing style to help you communicate relationships between two or more ideas. These techniques help your stylistic choices work in concert with the meaning that you want your sentences to deliver. While you are drafting (see 3b), concentrate on getting your ideas onto paper. Until you are a very experienced writer, expect to wait until you are revising (see 3c) to employ the full potential of coordination and subordination.

TWO IDEAS	The sky became dark gray.
	The air stilled ominously.
COORDINATED VERSION	The sky turned dark gray, and the air stilled ominously.
SUBORDINATED VERSION	As the sky turned dark gray, the air stilled ominously. [The *air* is the focus.]
SUBORDINATED VERSION	As the air stilled ominously, the sky turned dark gray. [The *sky* is the focus.]

COORDINATION

17a Understanding coordination

Coordination can produce harmony by bringing together related but separate elements to function smoothly in unison. Sections 17a through 17d explain coordination of independent clauses°. Coordinate sentences communicate balance in, or sequence of, the ideas that they contain. You can apply these same principles to the coordination of words, phrases°, and dependent clauses° (see also the explanation of parallelism, Chapter 18).

Patterns for coordinate sentences, also known as *compound sentences*, are shown in Chart 98. When you choose to coordinate sentences in your writing, keep these principles in mind:

- A coordinate sentence consists of two independent clauses that are grammatically equivalent.
- The coordinating of independent clauses must be justified by the meaning that you want your sentence to communicate.
- The independent clauses must be joined either by a coordinating conjunction (see Chart 98) or by a semicolon (see 25a and 25b).
- The coordinating conjunction must accurately express the relationship (see Chart 99) between the ideas in the independent clauses.
- If you are tempted to coordinate more than two independent clauses, do so with much care (see 17d-1 and 19b-2).

❖ CONJUNCTION ALERT: Do not confuse coordinating conjunctions with conjunctive adverbs (for example, *also, however, therefore;* for a complete list, see Chart 52 in section 7f). When conjunctive adverbs connect independent clauses, they function as explained in 7f and 14e. ❖

❖ PUNCTUATION ALERT: You will never be wrong if you use a comma before a coordinating conjunction that joins two independent clauses (see 24a).

The sky became dark gray, **and** the air stilled ominously.

The November morning had just begun, **but** it looked like dusk. ❖

PATTERNS FOR COORDINATE (COMPOUND) SENTENCES		98
Independent clause	**, and** **, but** **, for** **, nor** **, or** **, so** **, yet** **;**	independent clause

Here is an alternate example and a discussion of how it illustrates the contrast between coordination and subordination.

> When we toss a handful of good-luck rice at newlyweds, we're gracing them with one of the world's most important and versatile foods.
>
> —Jack Denton Scott, "Rice: A Food for All Reasons"

This sentence mentions (1) the idea of tossing rice at a wedding and (2) the fact that rice is an essential grain with many uses. Scott wants to stress the importance of rice as food because he puts that information in the independent clause. Rice as a ceremonial custom gives an ironic context to the main idea, but according to the way the sentence is written, it is a less important idea.

On the other hand, if Scott had been writing on marriage customs, he could have used subordination to provide a different emphasis:

> Although rice is one of the world's important and versatile foods, many Americans value it most as a good-luck symbol for newlyweds.

Here the independent clause stresses the connection of rice with weddings, and the food value of rice is mentioned as a less central point.

COORDINATING CONJUNCTIONS AND THE RELATIONSHIPS THEY EXPRESS		99
RELATIONSHIPS	**WORDS**	
addition	*and*	
contrast	*but, yet*	
result or effect	*so*	
reason or choice	*for*	
choice	*or*	
negative choice	*nor*	

17b Using coordinate sentences to show relationships

You can choose to use a string of short sentences for the impact that such style creates, as discussed in 19a. In most cases, however, a series of short sentences does not communicate well the relationships among the ideas. In such situations, coordination can help you avoid writing a series of short sentences that have unclear relationships.

UNCLEAR RELATIONSHIPS

We decided not to go to class. We planned to get the notes. Everyone else had the same plan. Most of us ended up failing the quiz.

CLEAR RELATIONSHIPS

We decided not to go to class, **but** we planned to get the notes. Everyone else had the same plan, **so** most of us ended up failing the quiz.

Overuse of coordination, however, can bore a reader with its unbroken rhythm (see 17d-2). For another technique to help you avoid an unwanted series of short sentences, see the discussion of subordination later in this chapter.

17c   Using coordinate sentences for effect

Coordinate sentences can help you communicate an unfolding of events.

> The first semester of my junior year at Princeton University is a disaster, **and** my grades show it. D's and F's predominate, **and** a note from the dean puts me on academic probation. Flunk one more course, **and** I'm out.
>
> —JOHN A. PHILLIPS AND DAVID MICHAELS, "Mushroom: The Story of an A-Bomb Kid"

F. Scott Fitzgerald, a U.S. writer of fiction and screenplays (1896–1940), often used coordination to achieve dramatic effect. In this passage, coordination underlines the contrasts that Fitzgerald draws:

> It was a hidden Broadway restaurant in the dead of night, **and** a brilliant and mysterious group of society people, diplomats, and members of the underworld were there. A few minutes ago the sparkling wine had been flowing, **and** a girl had been dancing gaily upon a table, **but** now the whole crowd were hushed and breathless.
>
> —F. SCOTT FITZGERALD, "The Freshest Boy"

17d   Avoiding the misuse of coordination

1   Avoiding illogically coordinated sentences

Coordination is illogical when ideas in the compounded independent clauses are not related. Your reader expects one part of a coordinate construction to lead logically to the other.

NO   Computers came into common use in the 1970s, and they sometimes make costly errors.

The statement in each independent clause is true, but the ideas are not related closely enough. The date computers became commonly used is unrelated to their making errors. The two ideas should not be coordinated. Here are ideas that do coordinate logically.

Cont'd.

King James Version

And it came to pass after these things, that God did tempt Abraham, and said unto him, Abraham: and he said, Behold, here I am. And he said, Take now thy son, thine only son Isaac, whom thou lovest, and get thee into the land of Moriah; and offer him there for a burnt offering upon one of the mountains which I will tell thee of. And Abraham rose up early in the morning, and saddled his ass, and took two of his young men with him, and Isaac his son, and clave the wood for the burnt offering, and rose up, and went unto the place of which God had told him. Then on the third day Abraham lifted up his eyes, and saw the place afar off. And Abraham said unto his young men, Abide ye here with the ass; and I and the lad will go yonder and worship, and come again to you. And Abraham took the wood for the burnt offering, and laid it upon Isaac his son; and he took the fire in his hand, and a knife; and they went both of them together.

Revised Standard Version

After these things God tested Abraham, and said to him, "Abraham!" And he said, "Here am I." He said, "Take your son, your only son Isaac, whom you love, and go to the land of Moriah, and offer him there as a burnt offering upon one of the mountains of which I shall tell you." So Abraham rose early in the morning, saddled his ass, and took two of his young men with him, and his son Isaac; and he cut the wood for the burnt offering, and arose and went to the place of which God had told him. On the third day Abraham lifted up his eyes, and saw the place afar off. Then Abraham said to his young men, "Stay here with the ass; I and the lad will go yonder and worship, and come again to you." And Abraham took the wood of the burnt offering, and laid it on Isaac his son; and he took in his hand the fire and the knife. So they went both of them together.

YES	Computers came into common use in the 1970s, and they are now indispensible for conducting business.
YES	Modern computer systems are often very complex, and they sometimes make costly errors.

2 | Avoiding the overuse of coordination

Overused coordination creates writing that reads as if it were whatever came into the writer's head. Readers become impatient with "babble" and quickly lose interest. When you are revising, be sure to check that your intended meaning justifies the use of coordination.

NO	Dinosaurs could have disappeared for many reasons, and one theory holds that the climate suddenly became cold, and another theory suggests that a sudden shower of meteors and asteroids hit the earth, so the impact created a huge dust cloud that caused a false winter. The winter lasted for years, and the dinosaurs died, for most of the vegetation they lived on died out.
YES	Dinosaurs could have disappeared for many reasons. One theory holds that the climate suddenly became cold, and another suggests that a sudden shower of meteors and asteroids hit the earth. The impact created a huge dust cloud that caused a false winter. The winter lasted for years, killing most of the vegetation that dinosaurs used for food.

In the revised version, the sentences deliver their meanings clearly.

Writers also overuse coordination if they fail to feature some ideas more prominently than others. Such writing tends to drone on monotonously.

NO	Laughter seems to help healing, so many doctors are prescribing humor for their patients, and some hospitals are doing the same. Comedians have donated their time to several California hospitals, and the nurses in one large hospital in Texas have been trained to tell each patient a joke a day.
YES	Laughter seems to help healing. Many doctors and hospitals are prescribing humor for their patients. Comedians have donated their time to several California hospitals, and the nurses in one large hospital in Texas have been asked to tell each patient a joke a day.

TEACHING TIP

In *Style: An Anti-Textbook* (New Haven: Yale UP, 1974), Richard Lanham attacks the pragmatic insistence "that words are for use, not enjoyment" and "that expression is a duty, not a pleasure" (10) to urge instructors to teach style as wordplay. "Prose written without joy," he warns, "can only be read in the same spirit" (10). Given the opportunity to play with new sentence patterns, students may surprise themselves with the ideas that they can express and the effects that they can create. Ask students to compose sentences following patterns such as "not only/ but also" and then to share their favorite sentences with the class.

ALTERNATE EXAMPLE: EXCESSIVE COORDINATION

Soap operas have earned a bad name, and they don't always deserve it. Some people may watch too many programs, or some people may take the plots too seriously, but that does not make the programs themselves unworthy. Years ago the soap opera viewer was regarded as unintelligent, but today studies show that many professionals take time each day to relax with their favorite continuing story. Some hospitals tell patients to watch soap operas to pass the time, or therapists sometimes urge their emotionally disturbed patients to watch certain programs. Later the patients discuss the characters' problems, and therapists encourage the patients to relate those problems to their own, and often the patients are helped by this process.

In the revised version, some ideas are kept separate and some are put into a coordinate sentence. (For another way to revise overused coordination, see the discussion of subordination, 17e through 17h.)

❖ ESL NOTE: If your instructor tells you that your sentences are too long and complex, practice limiting them. When you write your next paper, follow the advice of many ESL teachers: revise any sentence containing a combination of more than three independent and dependent clauses. ❖

EXERCISE 17-1

Consulting sections 17a through 17d, revise these sentences to eliminate illogical or overused coordination. If you think a sentence needs no revision, circle its number.

EXAMPLE   Anthropologists can tell the age of a skeleton by analyzing its structure and chemical makeup, and most people know this, but many do not know that skeletons can tell us much more.

Most people know that anthropologists can tell the age of a skeleton by analyzing its structure and chemical makeup, but many do not know that skeletons can tell us much more.

1. The life that a person leads often leaves marks on the bones, so anthropologists study stress marks on bones, and they often can figure out the life habits of a person, and they often can guess a person's occupation.
2. For example, the forearm bone is usually enlarged in baseball pitchers, and a similar enlargement appears in the skeletons of spear-throwing hunters from prehistoric times.
3. Also, women who always carry their babies on their backs have stress marks at the base of the spine, but a professional clarinet player usually has an irregular lower jaw.
4. Professor Kenneth A. R. Kennedy has compiled a list of over 140 skeletal marks that indicate occupation, and he teaches anthropology at Cornell University.
5. Professor Kennedy's work has great legal value, and it is also very practical, for it is another tool to help investigators identify accident and murder victims, and the information can provide clues about the identities of missing people, and it can help with identifying war casualties.

ANSWERS AND COVERAGE: EXERCISE 17-1
Answers will vary somewhat. Here is one set of possibilities.
1. The life that a person leads often leaves marks on the bones. Anthropologists who study stress markers on bones often can figure out the life habits and occupation of a person. [17d-2, overused]
2. Correct
3. Also, women who always carry their babies on their backs have stress marks at the base of the spine. In addition, a professional clarinet player usually has an irregular lower jaw. [17d-1, illogical]
4. Professor Kenneth A. R. Kennedy, who teaches at Cornell University, has compiled a list of over 140 skeletal markers that indicate occupation. [17d-1, illogical]
5. Professor Kennedy's work has great legal and practical value, for it is another tool to help investigators identify accident and murder victims, missing people, and war casualties. [17d-2, overused]

ANSWERS: EXERCISE 17-2

Answers will vary somewhat. Students have to choose ideas best given to effective compounding. They are to choose which ideas seem to have equal weight and could therefore be contained in compound sentences. Their final version should have no more than two compound sentences—all other sentences should be left as they are.

Many modern couples choose traditional weddings, and some do not. Some couples are very sentimental about how they met, so they decide to have unique marriage ceremonies. For example, a firefighter and his fiancée exchanged vows in a burning building. Two marathon runners got married while participating in a race. An adventurous couple said "I do" as they parachuted from an airplane. One modern wedding reportedly took place in a California hot tub. The guests and the Justice of the Peace got into the water with the bride and groom. Perhaps the next unusual wedding will be in outer space.

EXERCISE 17-2

Consulting sections 17a through 17d, revise this paragraph. Choose which ideas seem to have equal weight and could therefore be contained in compound sentences. Your final version should have no more than two compound sentences—all other sentences should be left as they are.

Many modern couples choose traditional weddings. Some do not. Some couples are very sentimental about how they met. They decide to have unique marriage ceremonies. For example, a firefighter and his fiancée exchanged vows in a burning building. Two marathon runners got married while participating in a race. An adventurous couple said "I do" as they parachuted from an airplane. One modern wedding reportedly took place in a California hot tub. The guests and the Justice of the Peace got into the water with the bride and groom. Perhaps the next unusual wedding will be in outer space.

SUBORDINATION

17e Understanding subordination

Subordination expresses the relative importance of ideas through their position in the sentence. Subordination makes a less important idea grammatically less prominent than a more important one. Sections 17e through 17h explain subordination of dependent and independent clauses: The more important idea appears in the independent clause—a group of words that can stand alone as a grammatical unit; the subordinated idea appears in the dependent clause—a group of words that cannot stand alone as a grammatical unit (see 7o-2). What information you choose to subordinate depends on the meaning that you want a sentence to deliver.

Major patterns of subordination with dependent clauses are shown in Chart 100. (For a discussion about commas in subordination patterns, see 24e.)

Two types of dependent clauses are adverb clauses and adjective clauses (see Chart 100). An **adverb clause** is a dependent clause that starts with a subordinating conjunction. Each subordinating conjunction has a specific meaning that expresses a relationship between the dependent clause and the independent clause, as shown in Chart 101.

An **adjective clause** is a dependent clause that can start with a relative pronoun (*who, which, that*), a relative adverb° (such as *where*), or a prepositional phrase° that includes a "relative" word (for example, has a preposition preceding the relative pronoun or relative adverb (for example, *to whom, above which*).

PATTERNS OF SUBORDINATION WITH DEPENDENT CLAUSES   100

SENTENCES WITH ADVERB CLAUSES

■ **Adverb clause,** independent clause.

> **After the sky grew dark,** the air stilled ominously.

■ Independent clause, **adverb clause.**

> Birds stopped singing, **as they do during an eclipse.**

■ Independent clause **adverb clause.**

> The shops closed **before the storm began.**

SENTENCES WITH ADJECTIVE CLAUSES

■ Independent clause **restrictive (essential)* adjective clause.**

> The weather forecasts warned of a storm **that might bring a thirty-inch snowfall.**

■ Independent clause, **nonrestrictive (nonessential)* adjective clause.**

> Spring is the season for tornados, **which rapidly whirl their destructive columns of air.**

■ Beginning of independent clause **restrictive (essential)* adjective clause** end of independent clause.

> Anyone **who lives through a tornado** recalls the experience.

■ Beginning of independent clause, **nonrestrictive (nonessential)* adjective clause,** end of independent clause.

> The sky, **which had been clear,** was turning gray.

*For an explanation of restrictive (essential) and nonrestrictive (nonessential) elements, see 24e.

QUOTATION ABOUT WRITING

Coordination is simply a way to show ideas that are equal in importance, but subordination indicates what's powerful and what isn't.

—Betty Jean Goodwin

QUOTATION ABOUT LANGUAGE

As I remained in the Third Form three times as long as anyone else, I had three times as much of it [sentence analysis]. I learned it thoroughly. Thus I got into my bones the essential structure of the ordinary British sentence—which is a noble thing.

—Winston Churchill

SUBORDINATING CONJUNCTIONS AND THE RELATIONSHIPS THEY EXPRESS	101	
RELATIONSHIPS	**WORDS**	
time	*after, before, once, since, until, when, whenever, while*	
reason or cause	*as, because, since*	
purpose or result	*in order that, so, so that, that*	
condition	*if, even if, provided that, unless*	
contrast	*although, even though, though, whereas*	
location	*where, wherever*	
choice	*rather than, whether*	

17f ### Choosing the subordinate conjunction appropriate to your meaning

Subordinating conjunctions express the relationship between major and minor ideas in sentences (see Chart 101). Consider the influence of the subordinating conjunction in each of the following sentences.

After you have handed it in, you cannot make any changes in your report. [time]

Because you have handed it in, you cannot make any changes in your report. [reason]

Unless you have handed it in, you cannot make any changes in your report. [condition]

Although you have handed it in, you can make changes in your report. [contrast]

I want to read your report **so that I can evaluate it.** [purpose]

Since you handed in your report, three more people have handed in theirs. [time]

Since I have seen the report, I can comment on it. [cause]

17g   Using subordination to show relationships

Subordination directs your reader's attention to the idea in the independent clause while at the same time using the idea in the dependent clause to provide context and support. Consider these examples (dependent clauses are in boldface).

As soon as I saw the elephant, I knew with perfect certainty that I ought not to shoot it.
> —GEORGE ORWELL, "Shooting an Elephant"

If they are very lucky, the passengers may catch a glimpse of dolphins playfully breaking water near the ship.
> —ELIZABETH GRAY, student

Subordination usually communicates relationships among ideas more effectively than does a group of separate sentences. (You may occasionally use a string of short sentences for impact; see 19a.)

UNCLEAR RELATIONSHIPS

In 1888, two cowboys had to fight a dangerous Colorado snowstorm. They were looking for cattle. They came to a canyon. They saw outlines of buildings through the snow. Survival then seemed certain.

CLEAR RELATIONSHIPS

In 1888, two cowboys had to fight a dangerous Colorado snowstorm **while they were looking for cattle. When they came to a canyon,** they saw outlines of buildings through the snow. Survival then seemed certain.

In the clear version, the first four short sentences have been combined into two complex sentences°. The last sentence is left short.

EXERCISE 17-3

Consulting sections 17e through 17g, combine each pair of sentences, using an adverb clause to subordinate one idea. Then revise each sentence so that the adverb clause becomes the independent clause. Refer to the list of subordinating conjunctions in Chart 100.

EXAMPLE   Shoes can be colorful, glamorous, or even witty. They are meant to protect the foot from some of the dangers of walking.

       a: *Although shoes can be colorful, glamorous, or even witty, they are meant to protect the foot from some of the dangers of walking.*

BACKGROUND

Sentence-combining exercises such as exercises 3, 4, 6, and 8 in this chapter, in which students are given two or more sentences and are asked to combine them into a single effective sentence to practice a specific sentence structure, were developed in the 1960s and 1970s by teachers applying principles of transformational grammar to writing instruction. Dozens of studies have found that while sentence combining has limitations, students who receive intensive instruction in sentence combining normally increase the complexity of their sentences and the overall quality of their writing (*Sentence Combining: A Rhetorical Perspective*, ed. Donald A. Daiker, Andrew Kerek, and Max Morenberg [Carbondale, IL: Southern Illinois UP, 1985]). Even brief use of sentence combining has been found to help improve the sentence complexity of some students. Several textbooks are devoted entirely to sentence combining, including *The Writer's Options* by Daiker, Kerek, and Morenberg, 2nd ed. (New York: Harper & Row, 1982) and *Sentence Combining: A Composing Book* by William Strong, 2nd ed. (New York: Random House, 1983).

ANSWERS: EXERCISE 17-3

Answers will vary. Here is one set of possibilities.

1a. Although sandals are worn primarily to protect the sole of the foot, they are also worn for comfort and style.

1b. Whereas they are also worn for comfort and style, sandals are worn primarily to protect the sole of the foot.

2a. After ornamentation was added to sandals worn by ancient peoples, footwear became a stylish article of clothing.

2b. When footwear became a stylish article of clothing, ornamentation was added to sandals worn by ancient people.

3a. Although sandalmakers were constrained by certain requirements in ancient Egyptian society, they had to cater to their clients' fashion whims.

3b. Because they had to cater to their clients' fashion whims, sandalmakers were constrained by certain requirements in ancient Egyptian society.

4a. For example, when the nobility demanded sandals with turned-up toes, peasants were expected to wear sandals with rounded or pointed toes.

4b. For example, whereas peasants were expected to wear sandals with rounded or pointed toes, the nobility demanded sandals with turned-up toes.

5a. As clothing had to be made from available materials, ancient Egyptian sandals were made of leather, woven palm leaves, or papyrus stalks.

5b. Clothing had to be made from available materials, so ancient Egyptian sandals were made of leather, woven palm leaves, or papyrus stalks.

b: *Although they are meant to protect the foot from some of the dangers of walking, shoes can be colorful, glamorous, or even witty.*

1. Sandals are worn primarily to protect the sole of the foot. They are also worn for comfort and style.
2. Ornamentation was added to sandals worn by ancient peoples. Footwear became a stylish article of clothing.
3. Sandalmakers were constrained by certain requirements in ancient Egyptian society. They had to cater to their clients' fashion whims.
4. For example, the nobility demanded sandals with turned-up toes. Peasants were expected to wear sandals with rounded or pointed toes.
5. Clothing had to be made from available materials. Ancient Egyptian sandals were made of leather, woven palm leaves, or papyrus stalks.

EXERCISE 17-4

Consulting sections 17e through 17g, combine each pair of sentences, using an adjective clause to make one idea subordinate to the other. Then revise each sentence so that the adjective clause becomes the independent clause. Use the relative pronoun given in parentheses.

EXAMPLE   The artist Pablo Picasso died in 1973 at the age of 92. He is best known for creating the Cubist style in art. (who)

a: *Pablo Picasso, who died in 1973 at the age of 92, is best known for creating the Cubist style in art.*

b: *Pablo Picasso, who is best known for creating the Cubist style in art, died in 1973 at the age of 92.*

1. Pablo Picasso had mastered all the traditional art techniques at a young age. He quickly became interested in experimenting with different styles. (who)
2. Picasso's style is characterized by designs that depart from strict reality. It is heavily influenced by the primitive art of Africa. (which)
3. Picasso created shapes. The shapes seemed to some people to be grotesque distortions of reality. (that)
4. An art critic enjoyed Picasso's use of geometric shapes to present multiple viewpoints of an object on one canvas. The art was nicknamed "Cubism" by the art critic. (who)
5. Experts agree that the entire body of Picasso's art is not solely in any one style. The entire body of Picasso's art is amazingly varied. (which)

17h   Avoiding the misuse of subordination

1   Avoiding illogical subordination

Subordination is illogical when the subordinating conjunction does not make clear the relationship between the independent and dependent clause (see Chart 101).

NO   Because Beethoven was deaf when he wrote his final symphonies, they are musical masterpieces.

The above sentence is illogical because it was not Beethoven's deafness that led to his writing symphonic masterpieces. Revising from *because* to *although* creates logical subordination.

YES   Although Beethoven was deaf when he wrote his final symphonies, they are musical masterpieces.

2   Avoiding the overuse of subordination

Overused subordination occurs when too many images or ideas crowd together, making your reader lose track of your intended message. If you have used more than two subordinating conjunctions or relative pronouns in a sentence, be skeptical about whether your meaning is clear.

NO   A new technique for eye surgery, which is supposed to correct nearsightedness, which previously could be corrected only by glasses, has been developed, although many doctors do not approve of it because it can create unstable eyesight.

YES   A new technique for eye surgery, which is supposed to correct nearsightedness, has been developed. Previously, nearsightedness could be corrected only by glasses. Because it can create unstable eyesight, many doctors do not approve of it, however.

In the revised version the first sentence has a relative clause, the second is a simple sentence°, and the third has a dependent clause starting with *Because*. Some words have been moved to new positions. The revision communicates its message more clearly because it

---

ANSWERS: EXERCISE 17-4

You might find that having students compare and discuss the differences in emphasis between the *a* and *b* answers to each item helps them clarify their understanding of the differences.

1a. Pablo Picasso, who had mastered all the traditional art techniques at a young age, quickly became interested in experimenting with different styles.

1b. Pablo Picasso, who quickly became interested in experimenting with different styles, had mastered all the traditional art techniques at a young age.

2a. Picasso's style, which is characterized by designs that depart from strict reality, is heavily influenced by the primitive art of Africa.

2b. Picasso's style, which is heavily influenced by the primitive art of Africa, is characterized by designs that depart from strict reality.

3a. Picasso created shapes that seemed to some people to be grotesque distortions of reality.

3b. The shapes that Picasso created seemed to some people to be grotesque distortions of reality.

4a. The art critic who enjoyed Picasso's use of geometric shapes to present multiple viewpoints of an object on one canvas nicknamed the art "Cubism."

4b. The art critic, who nicknamed the art "Cubism," enjoyed Picasso's use of geometric shapes to present multiple viewpoints of an object on one canvas.

5a. Experts agree that the entire body of Picasso's art, which is amazingly varied, is not solely in any one style.

5b. The entire body of Picasso's art, which experts agree is not solely in any one style, is amazingly varied.

ANSWERS: EXERCISE 17-5

Answers will vary considerably. Here is one possibility.

Although most parents continue to read their old favorites to their children, some experts question the value of traditional fairy tales. For instance, some experts think that fairy tales are too scary because they have characters like witches and dragons. These characters often frighten little children who are not yet mature enough to understand the difference between fantasy and reality. Other experts object to the theme of the "handsome prince and beautiful princess" which many fairy tales feature. The princess is always shown as weak, and the prince is always depicted as infallibly strong. Thus, children get a distorted impression of what they should expect of themselves and the opposite sex.

provides a variety of sentence structures (see 19a) while avoiding the clutter of overused subordination.

EXERCISE 17-5

Consulting section 17h, correct illogical or excessive subordination in this paragraph. As you revise, use not only some short sentences but also some correctly constructed adverb clauses. Also, apply the principles of coordination discussed in 17a through 17d, if you wish.

Although some experts question the value of traditional fairy tales, most parents continue to read old favorites to their children. For instance, some experts think that fairy tales are too scary because they have characters like witches and dragons which often frighten little children who are not yet mature enough to understand the difference between fantasy and reality, while other experts object to the theme of the "handsome prince and beautiful princess" which many fairy tales feature because the princess is always shown as weak while the prince is always depicted as infallibly strong so that children get a distorted impression about what they should expect of themselves and the opposite sex.

17i Achieving a balance between subordination and coordination

Coordination and subordination can sometimes be used in concert with each other.

When two Americans look searchingly into each other's eyes, emotions are heightened, **and** the relationship is tipped toward greater intimacy.

—FLORA DAVIS, "How to Read Body Language"

Varying sentence types can improve your ability to emphasize key points in your writing. Consider the following paragraph, which demonstrates a good balance in the use of coordination and subordination. It contains compound sentences (see 17a–17d), sentences that consist of dependent and independent clauses (see 17e–17h), and simple sentences°.

When I was growing up, I lived on a farm just across the field from my grandmother. My parents were busy trying to raise six children and to establish their struggling dairy farm. It was nice to have Grandma so close. **While my parents were providing the necessities of life,** my patient grandmother gave her time to her shy, young granddaughter. I always enjoyed going with Grandma and collecting the eggs that her chickens had just laid. Usually she knew which chickens would peck, **and** she was careful to let me gather the eggs from the less hostile ones.

—PATRICIA MAPES, student

Avoid using both a coordinate *and* a subordinate conjunction to express one relationship.

NO	**Although** the story was well-written, **but** it was too unbelievable.
YES	Although the story was well-written, it was too unbelievable.
YES	The story was well-written, but it was too unbelievable.

EXERCISE 17-6

Consulting all sections of this chapter, use subordination and coordination to combine these sets of short, choppy sentences.

EXAMPLE   New libraries are being built in record numbers in the United States. The number of people using public libraries is increasing too.

As the number of people using public libraries increases, record numbers of new libraries are being built in the United States.

1. Public libraries today are expanding their services. Librarians' roles are changing too.
2. Librarians are still expected to check books in and out. They are still expected to select books for the shelves. Now they also write grant proposals. They also campaign for bond issues.
3. Libraries are broadening the scope of their services. They still have one chief business. It is the circulation of books.
4. Libraries also circulate compact disks. They circulate videotapes. They circulate magazines. They offer literacy classes for adults. They have puppet shows for children. They have story hours for children, as well.
5. Technology is redefining the concept of a library. Many libraries today offer computerized databases. The databases can link one library with many other libraries. Each library no longer has to be only one physical location.

EXERCISE 17-7

Using topics you choose, imitate the style of three different examples shown in this chapter. Select from the quotations by Fitzgerald, Orwell, Gray, Davis, and Mapes.

ANSWERS: EXERCISE 17-6

Answers will vary. Here is one set of possibilities.

1. Because public libraries today are expanding their services, librarians' roles are changing.
2. Librarians, who are still expected to check books in and out and to select books for the shelves, now also write grant proposals and campaign for bond issues.
3. Although libraries are broadening the scope of their services, they still have one chief business, which is the circulation of books.
4. Libraries also circulate compact disks, videotapes, and magazines, and they offer literacy classes for adults as well as puppet shows and story hours for children.
5. Technology is redefining the concept of a library because many libraries today offer computerized databases that can link one library with many others so that each library no longer has to be only one physical place.

ANSWERS: EXERCISE 17-7

Students use a topic of their own to imitate the styles of three different examples shown in this chapter. Imitation has a proud tradition as a learning tool. The classic rhetoricians said that versatility in style came from (1) a study of principles, (2) practice in writing, and (3) imitation of the practice of others. For a modern interpretation of classical rhetoric, see Edward P. J. Corbett. *Classical Rhetoric for the Modern Student* (New York: Oxford UP, 1971), especially pp. 416 and 496–538.

ANSWERS: EXERCISE 17-8

Answers may vary. Here are two possibilities that students might enjoy comparing with their own.

1. Before the Anasazi Indians disappeared in the thirteenth century, they built cities in Colorado. They left behind an advanced culture, and archaeologists have been able to study them carefully. Because their beautiful buildings gleam in the afternoon sun, historians believe these structures may have started the legend of golden cities. Although in 1540 Francisco de Coronado tried to find the fabled cities of gold, he found no treasure.

2. The Anasazi Indians, who disappeared in the thirteenth century, built cities in Colorado. Because they left behind an advanced culture, archaeologists have been able to study them carefully. Historians believe their beautiful buildings that gleam in the afternoon sun may have started the legend of golden cities. In 1540 Francisco de Coronado tried to find the fabled cities of gold, but he found no treasure.

EXERCISE 17-8

Consulting all sections of this chapter, revise this passage by using coordination and subordination.

The Anasazi Indians built cities in Colorado. These Indians disappeared in the thirteenth century. They left behind an advanced culture. Archaeologists have been able to study them carefully. Their beautiful buildings gleam in the afternoon sun. Historians believe these structures may have started the legend of golden cities. In 1540 Francisco de Coronado tried to find the fabled cities of gold. He found no treasure.

Focus on Revising

REVISING YOUR WRITING

If you would like to use the techniques of coordination and subordination when you write, go back to your writing and locate sentences that you feel need improvement in style. Also, if you tend to misuse coordination and subordination, go back to your writing and locate the problems. Using this chapter as a resource, revise your writing: to use coordination effectively, see 17a through 17c; to correct coordination errors, see 17d; to use subordination effectively, see 17e through 17g; to correct subordination errors, see 17h; to balance coordination and subordination, see 17i.

CASE STUDIES

The case studies at the end of Chapter 19 offer you the chance to observe and participate in revisions of student writing that use coordination and subordination (this chapter), use parallelism (Chapter 18), and employ the techniques of variety and emphasis (Chapter 19).

18 Parallelism

This chapter advises you how to avoid **faulty parallelism** (18b through 18e) and how to use the grace and power of **parallelism** to strengthen your writing (18f and 18g). It also explains parallelism in outlines and lists (18h).

Many writers attend to parallelism when they revise (see 3c). If while you are drafting (see 3b) you think that your parallelism is faulty or that you can enhance your writing style by using parallelism, underline or highlight the material and keep your focus on getting ideas onto paper. When you revise, you can work on the places that you marked.

18a Understanding parallelism

Parallelism in writing, related to the concept of parallel lines in geometry, calls for the use of equivalent grammatical forms to express ideas of equal importance. An **equivalent grammatical form** is a word or group of words that matches—is parallel to—the structure of a corresponding word or group of words. See Chart 102.

Also, when you are expressing ideas of equal weight in your writing, parallel sentence structures can echo that fact and offer you a writing style that uses balance and rhythm to help deliver your meaning.

> **The deer** often come **to eat their grain, the wolves to destroy their sheep, the bears to kill their hogs, the foxes to catch their poultry.** [The message of the multiple, accumulating assaults is echoed by the parallel structures.]
>
> —J. HECTOR ST. JEAN DE CREVECOEUR,
> Letters from an American Farmer

WORD HISTORY

The *Oxford English Dictionary* (OED) has seven columns on *parallel* and related words. The OED reports the first use of *parallel* in 1549, in relation to geometry. *Parallelism* was used to describe biblical poetry in 1800, when Paley wrote of "correspondences between the Gospel of Mark and of Luke in sentences, words, and order of words."

TEACHING TIP

Classical rhetoric teaches that successful speaking or writing comes, in part, from the imitation of good examples. This imitation can take the form of copying passages verbatim or of imitating particular sentence patterns. Classical rhetoricians are not the only ones who have written about the benefits of imitation. Benjamin Franklin writes in his *Autobiography* (1771) of using essays in *The Spectator* as models for organization, sentence structure, and vocabulary. Malcolm X writes in his *Autobiography* of the benefits he gained from simply copying the dictionary in longhand. Winston Churchill and Somerset Maugham also write of the lessons they learned by imitating written models.

A possible first step in imitation is copying passages from favorite writers verbatim. This is not as brainless as it seems, for done properly it enables students to observe the details of an author's style. For this exercise to succeed, students should follow these guidelines adapted from Corbett, *Classical Rhetoric for the Modern Student* (New York: Oxford UP, 1990):

1. Students should read a piece through before beginning to copy it, in order to see the purpose and style of the whole. While working, they should read each sentence before beginning to write it. Once the passage has been completed, students should read their transcriptions in order again to "get a sense of the passage as a whole."

➡️

TEACHING TIP, Cont'd.

2. Students should copy for fifteen minutes per session. If they copy much longer, their minds will no longer focus on the work and the copying will become mechanical.

3. Students should copy by hand. Typing is too fast to allow students to see the qualities of a writer's style. Writing lets students work slowly enough to see the selection and placement of words, and the lengths and types of sentences.

4. Students should copy from a variety of authors. If they concentrate on one author to the exclusion of others, they may end up aping a single style rather than getting the feel of a variety of styles.

5. Students should copy patiently and with care. Too much speed can make the exercise meaningless. One way of controlling speed is to require that work be legible.

A second kind of imitation exercise uses sentences as patterns. The students duplicate the *kind, number,* and *order* of clauses and phrases in the model. The aim of this exercise is not to achieve a word-for-word correspondence with the model but rather to achieve an awareness of the variety of sentence structures of which the English language is capable (Corbett 495).

Parody can be an enjoyable imitation exercise for students. Writing a "restaurant review" of the cafeteria or a literary analysis of a comic book not only engages students in wordplay, but requires them to notice the stylistic and structural conventions of the model in order to make fun of them.

QUOTATION ABOUT WRITING

It doesn't matter how you write the first draft or even the second draft, but it makes all the difference in the world how you write the *final* draft.

—Elizabeth White

PARALLEL STRUCTURES   102

PARALLEL WORDS

Recommended exercise includes
running, swimming, and **cycling.** | The *-ing* words are parallel in structure and equal in importance.

PARALLEL PHRASES°

Exercise helps people **to maintain healthy bodies** and **to handle mental pressures.** | The phrases are parallel in structure and equal in importance.

PARALLEL CLAUSES°

Many people begin to exercise **because they want to look healthy, because they need to have stamina,** and **because they hope to live longer.** | The clauses starting with *because they* are parallel in structure and equal in importance.

18b Using words in parallel forms

To avoid faulty parallelism, be sure that words in parallel structures occur in the same grammatical form.

NO The strikers had tried **pleading, threats,** and **shouting.**

YES The strikers had tried **pleading, threatening,** and **shouting.**

YES The strikers had tried **pleas, threats,** and **shouts.**

Using words in parallel form can also serve to enhance the impact of the meaning that you want your material to deliver (see 18f and 18g).

18c Using phrases and clauses in parallel forms

To avoid faulty parallelism, be sure that phrases° and clauses° in parallel structures occur in the same grammatical form.

NO	The committee members **read the petition, discussed its major points,** and **the unanimous decision was to ignore it.**
YES	The committee members **read the petition, discussed its major points,** and **unanimously decided to ignore it.** [revised to parallel phrases]
NO	**The signers heard that their petition had not been granted, they became very upset,** and then **staged a protest demonstration.**
YES	**The signers heard that their petition had not been granted, they became very upset,** and then **they staged a protest demonstration.** [revised to parallel clauses]
YES	**The signers heard that their petition had not been granted, became very upset,** and then **staged a protest demonstration.** [revised to parallel phrases]

Using phrases and clauses in parallel form can also serve to enhance the impact of the meaning that you want your material to deliver (see 18f and 18g).

18d Using parallel structures with coordinating and correlative conjunctions and with *than* and *as*

1 Using parallel forms with coordinating conjunctions

The coordinating conjunctions are *and, but, or, nor, for, yet,* and *so* (for the relationship each expresses, see Chart 99 in section 17a). To avoid faulty parallelism, be sure that elements joined by coordinating conjunctions are parallel in grammatical form.

NO	**Love and being married** go together.
YES	**Love and marriage** go together.
YES	**Being in love** and **being married** go together.

BACKGROUND

In "Symmetrical Form and the Rhetoric of the Sentence" (*Essays on Classical Rhetoric and Modern Discourse,* ed. Robert J. Connors, Lisa S. Ede, and Andrea A. Lunsford [Carbondale, IL: Southern Illinois UP, 1984]), Richard Graves writes that parallel and balanced sentences are "part of the continuing human concern with the idea of symmetry, an idea which is rooted in our physiological being and touches many aspects of our collective lives" (171). The satisfaction that audiences have always taken from symmetry in language—as well as from symmetry in music, art, and architecture—is closely connected to the rhythms of the body, of walking, breathing, and the beating heart. Psychological studies suggest that symmetrical patterns are powerful aids for memory and comprehension. Even "the idea of justice carries with it the idea of balance and symmetry" (171).

TEACHING TIP

In *Style: Ten Lessons in Clarity and Grace,* 3rd ed. (Glenview, IL: Scott, Foresman, 1989), pp. 151–152, Joseph M. Williams suggests two simple ways to "enhance the rhythm and grace of coordination." First, a series of parallel clauses or phrases "will move more gracefully if each . . . is longer than the one before it." Second, writers can enhance parallel elements if they "consciously balance parts of phrases and clauses against one another.'

BACKGROUND

Martin Luther King, Jr. (1929–1968) was a powerful and eloquent speaker and writer for the civil rights movement in the United States. His works include *Stride Toward Freedom* (1958), *Strength to Love* (1963), *Why We Can't Wait* (1964), and *Where Do We Go from Here: Chaos or Community* (1967), as well as his famous "I Have a Dream" speech, which he delivered to a crowd of over 250,000 people in 1963 at a massive civil rights demonstration in Washington, D.C.

Among his best-known writings is his "Letter from Birmingham Jail," which he wrote from prison in 1963 in response to a published statement by eight Alabama clergymen who called his activities "unwise and untimely." In "The *Other* Beauty of Martin Luther King, Jr.'s 'Letter from Birmingham Jail'" (*College Composition and Communication* [February 1981]: 30–37), Mia Klein Anderson describes the musical, rhythmical effect of parallelism in King's powerful letter. King parallels clauses, nouns, verbs, adverbs, adjectives, and adjective/noun pairs, throughout the letter. Using antithesis and parallelism, he juxtaposes contrasting ideas with an engaging rhythm. King often combines parallelism with deliberate repetition of a word or group of words at the start of successive clauses, a rhetorical figure called *anaphora*. "Martin Luther King, Jr., knew that his effectiveness in reaching his wider audience would come both from what he said and from how he said it," Anderson writes. "The words can reach the mind, but the music and imagination can reach the heart and soul" (36).

QUOTATION ABOUT WRITING

Fine writing is generally the effect of spontaneous thoughts and a laboured style.
—William Shenstone

2 Using parallel forms with paired words (correlative conjunctions)

The correlative conjunctions are pairs of words that work in unison, such as *not only . . . but also, either . . . or,* and *both . . . and* (for more, see 7h). To avoid faulty parallelism, be sure that elements joined by correlative conjunctions are parallel in grammatical form. As you check your writing, pay particular attention to the correct placement of each half of the pair.

NO   Differing expectations for marriage **not only** can lead to disappointment **but also** to anger. [The words *can lead* apply to *disappointment* and to *anger*, so they belong before *not only*.]

YES   Differing expectations for marriage can lead **not only** to disappointment **but also** to anger.
                                              —Norman DuBois, student

3 Using parallel forms with *than* and *as*

To avoid faulty parallelism when you use *than* and *as* for comparisons, be sure that elements are parallel in grammatical form. Also, make sure that these comparisons are complete (see 15e-2).

NO   **Having a solid marriage** can be more satisfying **than** the **acquisition of wealth.**

YES   **Having a solid marriage** can be more satisfying **than** **acquiring wealth.**

YES   **A solid marriage** can be more satisfying **than wealth.**
                                              —Eunice Fernandez, student

18e Repeating function words in parallel elements

In a series of two or more parallel elements, be consistent in the second and subsequent elements about repeating or omitting function words. These include articles (*the, a, an*); the *to* of the infinitive° (for example, *to* love); prepositions (for example, *of, in, about*; for a complete list, see Chart 53 in section 7g). If you think that repeating such words clarifies your meaning or might help your reader catch the parallelism that you intend, use them.

NO   **To assign** unanswered letters their proper weight, **free us** from the expectations of others, **to give us** back to ourselves—here lies **the great, the singular** power of self-respect.

YES   **To assign** unanswered letters their proper weight, **to free us** from the expectations of others, **to give us** back to ourselves—here lies **the great, the singular** power of self-respect.

—JOAN DIDION, "On Self-Respect"

To avoid faulty parallelism when you use *who, which,* or *that* to start a series of clauses°, be sure to repeat or omit the words consistently in subsequent clauses.

I have in my own life a precious friend, a woman of 65 **who has** lived very hard, **who is** wise, **who listens** well, **who has** been where I am and can help me understand it; **and who represents** not only an ultimate ideal mother to me but also the person I'd like to be when I grow up.

—JUDITH VIORST, "Friends, Good Friends—and Such Good Friends"

We looked into the bus, **which was** painted blue with orange daisies, **had** picnic benches instead of seats, and **showed** yellow curtains billowing out its windows.

—KERRIE FALK, student

18f Using parallel, balanced structures for impact

Parallel structures characterized by balance serve to emphasize the meaning that sentences deliver. Balanced, parallel structures can be words, phrases, clauses, or sentences.

Deliberate, rhythmic repetition of parallel, balanced word forms and word groups reinforces the impact of a message. (For information about misused repetition, see 16c.) Consider the impact of this famous passage:

Go back to Mississippi, **go back to** Alabama, **go back to** South Carolina, **go back to** Georgia, **go back to** Louisiana, **go back to** the slums and ghettos of our northern cities, knowing that somehow this situation can and will be changed.

—MARTIN LUTHER KING, JR., "I Have a Dream"

If King had expressed the same idea with only minimal parallelism, his message would have been weaker. His structures reinforce the power of his message. An ordinary sentence would have been less effective: "Return to your homes in Mississippi, Alabama, South Carolina, Georgia, Louisiana, or the cities, and know that the situation will be changed."

A **balanced sentence** has two parallel structures, usually sentences, with contrasting content. A balanced sentence is a coordinate sentence (see 17a), characterized by opposition in the meaning of the two structures, sometimes with one cast in the negative: *Mosquitos do not bite, they stab.* Consider the impact of this sentence.

> By night, the litter and desperation disappeared as the city's glittering lights came on; by day, the filth and despair reappeared as the sun rose.
>
> —JENNIFER KIRK, student

Similarly, consider the impact of this famous sentence, which adds unusual word order (*ask not*, instead of *do not ask*) to its parallelism and balance.

> Ask not what your country can do for you, ask what you can do for your country.
>
> —JOHN F. KENNEDY

❖ COMMA ALERT: Authorities differ about using a comma or semicolon between the parts of a balanced sentence. In college, to prevent seeming to make the error of a comma splice (see Chapter 14), you are safer if you use a semicolon (or revise in other ways). ❖

18g Using parallel sentences in longer passages for impact

Parallel, balanced sentences in longer passages can create a dramatic unity through carefully controlled repetition of words and word forms. Consider this rich passage of repeated words, concepts, and rhythms.

> You ask me what is **poverty? Listen** to me. Here I am, dirty, **smelly,** and with no "proper" underwear on and with the **stench** of my rotting teeth near you. I will tell you. **Listen** to me. **Listen** without pity. I cannot use your pity. **Listen** with understanding. Put yourself in my dirty, worn-out, ill-fitting shoes, and hear me.
>
> **Poverty** is getting up every morning from a dirt- and illness-stained mattress. The sheets have long since been used for

diapers. **Poverty** is living in a **smell** that never leaves. **This is a smell** of urine, sour milk, and spoiling food sometimes joined with the strong **smell** of long-cooked onions. Onions are cheap. If you have **smelled** this **smell,** you did not know how it came. **It is the smell** of the out-door privy. **It is the smell** of young children who cannot walk the long dark way in the night. **It is the smell** of the mattresses where years of "accidents" have happened. **It is the smell** of the milk which has gone sour because the refrigerator long has not worked, and it costs money to get it fixed. **It is the smell** of rotting garbage. I could bury it, but where is the shovel? Shovels cost money.

—Jo Goodwin Parker, "What Is Poverty?"

EXERCISE 18-1

Reread the Jo Goodwin Parker passage above. Then, consulting sections 18a through 18e, discover all parallel elements in addition to those shown in boldface.

EXERCISE 18-2

Using topics you choose, imitate the writing style of three different passages shown in this chapter. Select from the quotations from De Crevecoeur, Didion, Viorst, King, Kennedy, or Parker.

EXERCISE 18-3

Consulting sections 18a through 18e, revise these sentences to eliminate errors in parallel structure.

EXAMPLE   Widely known as the sick-building syndrome, indoor air pollution causes office workers to suffer from burning eyes, from breathing that has become difficult, rashes that cause severe pain, and from throbbing headaches.

Widely known as the sick-building syndrome, indoor air pollution causes office workers to suffer *from burning eyes, difficult breathing, severely painful rashes, and throbbing headaches.*

1. In many new office buildings the windows are not only sealed shut but also the problem is that internal ventilation systems are inadequate and filthy.
2. Indoor pollutants include tobacco smoke, fumes from copy machines, carbonless paper releasing gas when used, cleaning chemicals, and even when rugs and draperies shed fibers.

ANSWERS: EXERCISE 18-1

Elements of parallelism in Parker's passage not shown in boldface are: *Repetitions:* you, me, I, dirty (dirt), pity, onions, mattress(es), urine (privy, "accidents"), long, it, shovels. *Paired words:* with / with. *Imperatives (mild commands):* Listen, Put, hear. *Contrasts:* pity and understanding, with / without. *Words in a series:* my dirty, worn-out, ill-fitting shoes; smell of urine, sour milk, and spoiling food.

ANSWERS: EXERCISE 18-2

Students use topics of their own to imitate the parallel style of three of the passages shown in this chapter: by Didion, Viorst, King, Kennedy, or Parker. Style imitation has a proud tradition as a learning tool. The classical rhetoricians said that versatility in style came from (1) a study of principles, (2) practice in writing, and (3) imitation of the practice of others. For a modern interpretation of classical rhetoric see Edward P. J. Corbett, *Classical Rhetoric for the Modern Student* (New York: Oxford UP, 1971), especially pp. 416 and 496–538.

ANSWERS AND COVERAGE: EXERCISE 18-3

Answers will vary. Here is one set of possibilities.

1. In many new office buildings today, *not only are the windows sealed shut but also the internal ventilation systems are inadequate and filthy* [18d-1, correlative conjunctions].

2. Indoor pollutants include tobacco smoke, *copy-machine fumes, carbonless-paper gases, cleaning chemicals, and even fibers* [18b, words] from rugs and draperies.

→

Cont'd.

3. Other pollutants come from outdoors when intake ducts for air into a ventilation system are located *over loading docks where trucks spew exhaust fumes or right next to streets and highways filled with truck and car traffic* [18c, clauses].

4. Environmental experts have studied sick buildings and made recommendations *that are easily implemented, that are not very costly, and that solve most of the problems of indoor pollution* [18e, repeating parallel function words].

5. Some of the simpler remedies range from frequently *cleaning air ducts and replacing air filters to rearranging office partitions* [18c, phrases] to allow air to flow more freely.

ANSWERS: EXERCISE 18-4

Answers may vary. Here is one set of possibilities.

1. The Tasaday had not developed even the most primitive forms of *agriculture, weaving, or pottery making.*

2. Animals and plants *provided their food,* leaves *provided their clothing,* **and** caves *provided their shelter.*

3. The Tasaday were unaware of **not only** *modern conveniences* **but also** *modern anxieties.*

4. The Philippine government decided *to protect* the tribe's Stone Age culture **and** *to ensure* the Tasaday's safety by declaring the forest a national preserve.

5. Throughout the ages, the Tasaday have never had a war, a fact **that** *amazes* anthropologists **and that** *inspires* peace-loving people everywhere.

QUOTATION ABOUT WRITING

Writers should be read—but neither seen nor heard.

—Daphne du Maurier

---

3. Other pollutants come from outdoors when intake ducts for air into a ventilation system are located over loading docks where trucks spew exhaust fumes, or streets and highways filled with truck and car traffic right next to air-intake ducts of buildings.

4. Environmental experts have studied sick buildings and made recommendations easily implemented and that are not costly, and they would be able to solve most problems that cause indoor air pollution.

5. Some of the simpler remedies range from frequently cleaning air ducts and air filters are often needing to be replaced, to rearranging of office partitions to allow air to flow more freely.

EXERCISE 18-4

Consulting sections 18a through 18e, combine the sentences in each numbered item, using techniques of parallelism.

EXAMPLE Philippine rain forests provide shelter for plants. They also protect animals. A Stone Age tribe called the Tasaday lives in a Philippine rain forest.

Philippine rain forests shelter plants, protect animals, and provide a home for a Stone Age tribe called the Tasaday.

1. The Tasaday had not developed even the most primitive forms of agriculture. They did not know how to weave. Making pottery was unknown to them.

2. Animals and plants provided their food. They used leaves as clothes. They lived in caves.

3. The Tasaday were unaware of modern conveniences. Also, they showed no evidence of modern anxieties either.

4. The Philippine government decided to protect the tribe's Stone Age culture. Also, the Tasaday's safety was ensured when the government declared the forest a national preserve.

5. Throughout the ages, the Tasaday have never had a war. This fact amazes anthropologists. The lack of war also inspires peace-loving people everywhere.

18h **Using parallelism in outlines and lists**

Items in formal outlines and lists must be parallel in grammar and structure. (For information about other issues of outline format and about how to develop an outline, see 2n.)

FORMAL OUTLINE NOT IN PARALLEL FORM
Reducing Traffic Fatalities

I.   Stricter laws
  A. Top speed should be 50 m.p.h. on highways.
  B. Higher fines
  C. Requiring jail sentences for repeat offenders.
II. The use of safety devices should be mandated by law.

FORMAL OUTLINE IN PARALLEL FORM
Reducing Traffic Fatalities

I.   **Passing** stricter speed laws
  A. **Making** 50 m.p.h. the top speed on highways
  B. **Raising** fines for speeding
  C. **Requiring** jail sentences for repeat offenders
II. **Mandating** by law the use of safety devices.

Although a nonparallel outline might serve as an informal, scratch outline for a writer's private purposes in the early stages of the writing process, only a parallel outline is acceptable as a final draft.

FORMAL LIST NOT IN PARALLEL FORM

Workaholics share these characteristics:

1. They are intense and driven.
2. Strong self-doubters.
3. Labor is preferred to leisure by workaholics.

FORMAL LIST IN PARALLEL FORM

Workaholics share these characteristics:

1. **They are** intense and driven.
2. **They have** strong self-doubts.
3. **They prefer** labor to leisure.

ALTERNATE EXAMPLES

Because parallelism gives statements a stately, dignified sound, it appears often in official declarations, as in the following.

1. . . . for the support of this declaration, with a firm reliance on the protection of Divine Protection, we mutually pledge to each other our Lives, our Fortunes, and our sacred Honor.

—The Declaration of Independence

2. It is rather for us to be here dedicated to the great task remaining before us—that from these honored dead we take increased devotion to that cause for which they gave the last full measure of devotion; that we here highly resolve that these dead shall not have died in vain; that this nation, under God, shall have a new birth of freedom; and that government of the people, by the people, for the people, shall not perish from the earth.

—Abraham Lincoln

3. We are saddened; we are stunned; we are perplexed.

—Earl Warren, on the death of John Kennedy

TEACHING TIP

To introduce students to creating parallel structures, you might want to begin with lists. For example, they can list the steps they go through when carrying out some ordinary task, such as changing a tire or baking cookies. Then students can incorporate those items in sentences that explain an activity. You might help get students started by offering sentences that need completion. Here are two examples:

Moving into one's first apartment can be expensive; you need to buy _____, _____, and _____. Settling into a new apartment can be tiring: hanging curtains, _____, _____, and _____.

ANSWERS: EXERCISE 18-5

I. Lack of information from some areas
   A. Politics
   B. Wars
   C. Cost
II. Computer problems
   A. Computer repairs not easily available in remote areas
   B. Garbled messages from unreliable computers
III. Unstable atmosphere
   A. Harsh weather
      1. South Pole
      2. North Pole
   B. Sudden shifts
   C. Lack of reliability over time

ANSWERS: EXERCISE 18-6

Answers will vary. See the answer to Exercise 18-2 for commentary on imitation as a learning device.

TEACHING TIP

Parallelism is easily found in advertising, public speeches, and promotional letters. You might ask students to bring to class examples that they see on television, or find in advertisements in magazines, newspapers, or their mail. You can then analyze the parallelism and discuss the effectiveness of the examples, including any instances of faulty parallelism (which appear in published material with surprising frequency).

EXERCISE 18-5

Consulting section 18h, revise this outline into parallel form.

Problems in Weather Forecasting

I. Information unavailable from some areas
   A. Politics leads some countries not to cooperate.
   B. If war breaks out, no one communicates about the weather.
   C. Cost
II. Computer problems
   A. Computer repairs not easily available in remote areas.
   B. Unreliable computers send garbled messages.
III. Unstable atmosphere
   A. The weather is harsh.
      1. South Pole
      2. The North Pole is extremely cold and windy.
   B. Conditions shift suddenly.
   C. There is a lack of reliability over time.

EXERCISE 18-6

Find the parallel elements in the following examples. Next, using your own topics, imitate the style of two of the examples.

1. Our earth is but a small star in a great universe. Yet of it we can make, if we choose, a plane unvexed by war, untroubled by hunger or fear, undivided by senseless distinctions of race, color, or theory.

   —STEPHEN VINCENT BENÉT

2. I think there are certain enduring ethical standards, enduring values that don't change with the times. My definition of the ethical public servant is one who acts in the public interest, who is truthful, credible, and honest, and who is able to turn from greed and selfhood to think in terms of others.

   —BARBARA JORDAN

3. I am lonely only when I am overtired, when I have worked too long without a break, when for the time being I feel empty and need filling up. And I am lonely sometimes when I come back home after a lecture trip, when I have seen a lot of people and talked a lot, and am full to the brim with experience that needs to be sorted out.

   —MAY SARTON, "The Rewards of a Solitary Life"

4. The more you live and the more you look, the more aware you are of a consistent pattern—as universal as the stars, as the tides, as breathing, as night and day—underlying everything.

—MARYA MANNES, "How Do You Know It's Good?"

5. Each afternoon around three-thirty, as some of the workers were about to go home to prepare their early dinners, Uncle Kwok slowly and deliberately ambled in through the Wong front door, dragging his feet heavily, and gripping in one hand the small black satchel from which he was never separated.

—JADE SNOW WONG, "Fifth Chinese Daughter"

Focus on Revising

REVISING YOUR WRITING

If you would like to use parallel structures correctly and effectively when you write, go back to your writing and locate sentences that need improvement in style. Using this chapter as a resource, revise your writing: to use parallel form with words, see 18b; to use parallel form with phrases and clauses, see 18c; to use parallel structures, see 18d; to use parallel form for long passages, see 18g; to use parallel form for formal outlines and lists, see 18h.

CASE STUDY

The case studies at the end of Chapter 19 offer you the chance to observe and participate in revisions of student writing that use parallelism (this chapter), that achieve a balance in coordination and subordination (Chapter 17), and that employ the techniques of variety and emphasis (Chapter 19).

19 Variety and Emphasis

19a Understanding variety and emphasis

Your writing style has **variety** when your sentence lengths and patterns vary. Your writing style is characterized by **emphasis** when your sentences are constructed to communicate the relative importance of their ideas.

Consider the following passage, which successfully employs key techniques of variety and emphasis. The authors vary their sentence length (see 19b), include a variety of structures (see 19c), and use different kinds of modifiers in various positions (see 19e).

> Henri Poincaré, a famous mathematician who lived in the nineteenth century, devised an exercise in imagination to help people understand the relativity of measures. Imagine that one night while you were asleep everything in the universe became a thousand times larger than before. Remember this would include electrons, planets, all living creatures, your own body, and all the rulers and other measuring devices in the world. When you awoke, could you tell that anything had changed? Is there any experiment you could make to prove that some change had occurred? According to Poincaré there is no such experiment.
>
> —JUDITH AND HERBERT KOHL, *The View from the Oak*

The techniques of variety and emphasis can move your writing beyond being correct to having style and grace. Rarely do variety and

---

HOW TO ACHIEVE VARIETY AND EMPHASIS   103

- Vary your sentence length to make your writing lively (see 19b).
- Use an occasional question, mild command, or exclamation (see 19c).
- Choose the subject of a sentence according to your intended meaning (see 19d).
- Add modifiers to basic sentences (see 19e).
- Invert standard word order (see 19f).
- Repeat important words or ideas (see 19g).

---

emphasis emerge during drafting (see 3b). Until you are a very experienced writer, you might not be able to apply the principles in this chapter until you are revising (see 3c).

19b   Varying sentence length

When you use a variety of sentence lengths, you communicate clear distinctions among ideas. Such a style can help your readers understand the focus of your material. Also, such a style avoids the unbroken rhythm of monotonous sentence length, which can lull your reader into inattention.

1   Revising strings of too many short sentences

Strings of too many short sentences rarely establish relationships and levels of importance among ideas. Readers cannot easily make distinctions between major and minor points. Such strings, unless deliberately planned in a longer piece of writing for occasional impact (see 19b-3), suggest that the writer has not thought through the material and decided what to emphasize. The style tends to read like that of young children.

Cont'd.

Evaluation	Professional	Student
A. Total number of words in the piece studied	____	____
B. Total number of sentences in the piece studied	____	____
C. Longest sentence (in no. of words)	____	____
D. Shortest sentence (in no. of words)	____	____
E. Average sentence (in no. of words)	____	____
F. Number of sentences that contain more than 10 words *over* the average sentence	____	____
G. Percentage of sentences that contain more than 10 words *over* the average sentence	____	____
H. Number of sentences that total 5 words or more *below* the average	____	____
I. Percentage of sentences that total 5 words or more below the average	____	____
J. Paragraph length longest paragraph (in no. of sentences)	____	____
shortest paragraph (in no. of sentences)	____	____
average paragraph (in no. of sentences)	____	____

You might want to try Corbett's analysis on a piece that you have written and share the results with the class.

NO	There is a legend. This legend is about a seventeenth-century Algonquin Indian. It says that he was inspired. He had an idea about popcorn. He transformed it into a gift. It was the first gift to a hostess in American history. He was invited to the Pilgrims' harvest meal. He brought along a bag of popcorn. This was a demonstration of good will. The occasion is honored to this day with Thanksgiving dinner.
YES	According to legend, in the seventeenth century an inspired Algonquin transformed popcorn into the first hostess gift in history. Invited to the Pilgrims' harvest meal, the Indian brought along a bag of popcorn as a demonstration of good will. The occasion is honored today with Thanksgiving dinner.

—PATRICIA LINDEN, "Popcorn"

In the revised version, the sentence structures permit key ideas to be featured. The two versions use almost the same short last sentence, but because the revised version leads up to it with longer sentences, the message in the last sentence is emphasized. In the revised version, ten sentences reduce to three and 74 words reduce to 47. (See also the explanation of conciseness, Chapter 16.)

2 | Revising a string of too many compound sentences

A **compound sentence** consists of two or more independent clauses° that are grammatically equivalent and that communicate balance or sequence in the ideas that they contain (see 17a). Too often, compound sentences are short sentences only strung together with *and* or *but,* without consideration of the relationships among the ideas.

NO	Science fiction writers are often thinkers, and they are often dreamers, so they let their imaginations wander. Jules Verne was such a writer, and he predicted space ships and atomic submarines, but most people did not believe airplanes were possible.
YES	Science fiction writers are often thinkers and dreamers who let their imaginations wander. Jules Verne was one such writer. He predicted space ships and atomic submarines before most people believed airplanes were possible.

In the revised version the relationships among the ideas are clear and key ideas are featured. In the last sentence a particularly obscure connection is clarified. For conciseness, one independent clause is reduced to a word, *dreamers*; another is reduced to a relative clause°, *who let their imaginations wander*; another starts a new sentence, *He predicted . . .*; and another is reduced to a subordinate clause°, *before most people . . . possible.*

3 **Revising for a suitable mix of sentence lengths**

To emphasize one idea among many others, you can express it in a sentence noticeably different in length or structure from the sentences surrounding it. Consider this passage, which carries its emphasis in one short sentence among longer ones:

> Today is one of those excellent January partly cloudies in which light chooses an unexpected landscape to trick out in gilt, and then shadow sweeps it away. **You know you are alive.** You take huge steps, trying to feel the planet's roundness arc between your feet. Kazantzakis says that when he was young he had a canary and a globe. When he freed the canary, it would perch on the globe and sing. All his life, wandering the earth, he felt as though he had a canary on top of his mind, singing.
>
> —ANNIE DILLARD, *Pilgrim at Tinker Creek*

A long sentence among shorter ones is equally effective.

> Mistakes are not believed to be part of the normal behavior of a good machine. **If things go wrong, it must be a personal, human error, the result of fingering, tampering, a button getting stuck, someone hitting the wrong key.** The computer, at its normal best, is infallible. I wonder whether this can be true.
>
> —LEWIS THOMAS, "To Err Is Human"

EXERCISE 19-1

Consulting sections 19a and 19b, revise these sets of sentences to vary the sentence lengths effectively.

1. Horror tales are not new. *Frankenstein* was written in the nineteenth century. It was written by Mary Shelley. She was the wife of the poet Percy Bysshe Shelly. *Frankenstein* tells the story of a scientist. He makes a monster. He makes it from a human corpse.

Cont'd.

equipment (a hatchet, a burlap sack) above our heads. [15] A mile more: of chastising horns, burs and briers that catch at our clothes; of rusty pine needles brilliant with gaudy fungus and molted feathers. [25] Here, there, a flash, a flutter, an ecstasy of shrilling remind us that not all the birds have flown south. [20] Always, the path unwinds through lemony sun pools and pitch vine tunnels. [12] Another creek to cross: a disturbed armada of speckled trout froths the water round us, and frogs the size of plates practice belly flops; beaver workmen are building a dam. [30] On the farther shore, Queenie shakes herself and trembles. [9] My friend shivers, too: not with cold but enthusiasm. [9] One of her hat's ragged roses sheds a petal as she lifts her head and inhales the pine-heavy air. [20] "We're almost there; can you smell it, Buddy?" she says, as though we were approaching an ocean. [17]

QUOTATION ABOUT WRITING

I think the single most important factor in any writing is its rhythm. A badly balanced sentence jars on me with something like physical pain!

—Helen Cresswell

ANSWERS: EXERCISE 19-1

In this exercise, the first item has too many short sentences, the second too many compounds, the third long and complicated sentences. Students will revise in various ways. Here is one set of possibilities:

1. Horror tales are not new. *Frankenstein* was written in the nineteenth century by Mary Shelley, the wife of the poet Percy Bysshe Shelley. *Frankenstein* tells the story of a scientist who makes a monster from a human corpse.

➡

Cont'd.

2. Another famous horror tale of the nineteenth century is "The Monkey's Paw," by W. W. Jacobs. It tells about an old English couple, parents of a teenage son, who get a monkey's paw. The paw has the power to grant three wishes. The father wishes for 200 pounds, but the money comes because their son is killed in an accident at work. The mother uses the second wish to bring her son back. Soon there is a knocking at their door. The mother rushes to unbolt it, but terrified of seeing a walking, rotting corpse, the father uses the last wish. The knocking stops.

3. After radios became common, horror programs broadcast their tales of terror into the living rooms of America. Many families, including children of all ages, grouped around the radio while they listened for the latest story of monsters and strange events. The many programs included *The Inner Sanctum*, which featured a creaking door, and *The Fat Man*, who had a madman's laugh. The scared, delighted audience came from different parts of the country, different occupations, and different economic and social groups.

BACKGROUND

Adding modifiers to basic sentences is the central feature of the "generative rhetoric" developed by Francis Christensen in *Notes Toward a New Rhetoric* (New York: Harper & Row, 1967) and *The Christensen Rhetoric Program* (New York: Harper & Row, 1968). The Christensen program teaches students various ways to expand a sentence by showing them model sentences, giving students a basic sentence and having them expand it following the pattern of the models, and then having students compose their own sentences according to that pattern. These exercises not only develop the style of students but also teach them ways of elaborating their ideas.

2. Another famous horror tale of the nineteenth century is "The Monkey's Paw," by W. W. Jacobs, and it tells about an old English couple with a teenage son, and they get a monkey's paw. It has the power to grant three wishes, so the father wishes for 200 pounds, but the money comes because their son is killed in an accident at work. The mother uses the second wish to bring her son back, and soon there is a knocking at their door, and the mother rushes to unbolt it, but the father is terrified of seeing a walking, rotting corpse, so he uses the last wish, and the knocking stops.

3. After radios became common, horror programs broadcast their tales of terror into the living rooms of America which were filled with families that included children of all ages who were grouped around the radio while they listened for the latest story of monsters and strange events. The many programs, which included *The Inner Sanctum*, which featured a creaking door, and *The Fat Man* who had a madman's laugh, scared and delighted the audience who came from different parts of the country, from different occupations, and from different economic and social groups.

19c Using an occasional question, mild command, or exclamation

To vary your sentence structure and to emphasize material, you can call on four basic sentence types. The most common English sentence is **declarative**. A declarative sentence makes a statement—it declares something. Declarative sentences offer an almost infinite variety of structures and patterns.

A sentence that asks a question is called **interrogative**. Occasional questions can help you involve your reader. A sentence that issues a mild or strong command is called **imperative**. Occasional mild commands are particularly helpful for gently urging your reader to think along with you. A sentence that makes an exclamation is called **exclamatory**. ✤ PUNCTUATION ALERT: A mild command ends with a period. A strong command or an exclamation ends with an exclamation mark. ✤

Consider the following paragraph, which uses the three basic sentence types found most frequently in academic writing: declarative, interrogative, and imperative.

Imagine what people ate during the winter as little as seventy-five years ago. They ate food that was local, long-lasting, and dull, like acorn squash, turnips, and cabbage. Walk into an American supermarket in February and the world lies before you:

grapes, melons, artichokes, fennel, lettuce, peppers, pistachios, dates, even strawberries, to say nothing of ice cream. Have you ever considered what a triumph of civilization it is to be able to buy a pound of chicken livers? If you lived on a farm and had to kill a chicken when you wanted to eat one, you wouldn't ever accumulate a pound of chicken livers.

— PHYLLIS ROSE, "Shopping and Other Spiritual Adventures in America Today"

EXERCISE 19-2

The paragraph below effectively varies sentence lengths and uses a question and a command. The result emphasizes the key points. Write an imitation of this paragraph, closely following all aspects except the topic. Choose your own topic.

EXAMPLE   If your topic were pets, your first sentence might be: *Why do most people buy expensive pure-bred dogs or cats when they want pets?*

Why do most people imagine hurricanes or bombs when they think of disasters? Consider the worst disaster in history. In 1347–1351, the black death killed over 75 million victims. A snow avalanche in Peru killed 25,000 in 1970, and a panic in an air raid shelter in Chungking, China, claimed 4,000 in 1941. Yet, the strangest disaster of all happened at the coronation of Czar Nicholas II when 5,000 were trampled to death in the stampede for free beer that was part of the celebration.

19d   Choosing the subject of a sentence according to your intended emphasis

The subject° of a sentence establishes the focus for that sentence. The subject you choose should correspond to the emphasis that you want to communicate to your reader.

Each of the following sentences, all of which are correct grammatically, contains the same information. Consider, however, how changes of the subject (and its verb°) influence meaning and impact.

> **Our study showed** that 25 percent of college students' time is spent eating or sleeping. [Focus is on the study.]
> **College students eat or sleep** 25 percent of the time, according to our study. [Focus is on the student.]

ANSWERS: EXERCISE 19-2

Answers may vary. Ask students to explain their choices. Here is one set of possibilities.

1. Easy Jet, a multi-race winner, was sold for 30 million dollars. That is more than the average combined yearly income of a town of 2,000 people!

2. What might the popularity of horse racing suggest about the American national character? We may be a nation of gamblers. On the other hand, we simply may want financial independence.

3. Tradition holds that no race horse can have a name that contains more than eighteen letters. Apostrophes, hyphens, and spaces count in the total! Longer names would take up too much room on written records.

4. Lotteries have become as popular as horse racing. Many states run lotteries to raise money for basic services earlier provided from taxes. Did you know that in many states school books are purchased with funds gambled on lottery tickets?

5. Some television commercials for lotteries show winners riding in limousines. Most lottery ticket holders lose, though. That tempting chance to win a million dollars has odds worse than a million to one!

Eating or sleeping occupies 25 percent of college students' time, according to our study. [Focus is on eating and sleeping.]
Twenty-five percent of college students' time **is spent** eating or sleeping, according to our study. [Focus is on the percentage of time.]

19e Adding modifiers to basic sentences for variety and emphasis

Adding modifiers° to basic sentences can provide you with a rich variety of sentence patterns.

1 Expanding basic sentences with modifiers

Sentences that consist only of a subject and verb usually seem very thin. You might use a very short sentence for its dramatic effect

---

WAYS TO EXPAND A BASIC SENTENCE   104

BASIC SENTENCE°	The river rose.
ADJECTIVE°	The **swollen** river rose.
ADVERB°	The river rose **dangerously.**
PREPOSITIONAL PHRASE°	**In April,** the river rose **above its banks.**
PARTICIPIAL PHRASES°	**Swollen by melting snow,** the river rose, **flooding the farmland.**
ABSOLUTE PHRASE°	**Trees swirling away in the current,** the river rose.
ADVERB CLAUSE°	**Because the snows had been heavy that winter,** the river rose.
ADJECTIVE CLAUSE°	The river, **which runs through vital farmland,** rose.

BACKGROUND

In *Classical Rhetoric for the Modern Student,* 3rd ed. (New York: Oxford UP, 1990), p. 422, Edward P. J. Corbett discusses how using different sentence openers can provide sentence variety. He lists several specific beginnings that are in common use:

A. Subject (e.g., *John* broke the window.)

B. Expletive (e.g., *It is plain that* . . .)

C. Coordinating conjunction (*and, but, or, nor, for, yet, so*)

D. Adverb word (e.g., *first, thus, moreover, nevertheless, namely*)

E. Conjunctive phrase (e.g., *on the other hand, as a consequence*)

F. Prepositional phrase (e.g., *after the game, in the morning*)

G. Verbal phrase (e.g., participial, gerundive, or infinitive: *To revise a sentence for emphasis,* you . . .)

H. Adjective phrase (e.g., *Tired but happy,* we . . .)

I. Absolute phrase (e.g., *The ship having arrived safely,* we . . .)

J. Adverb clause (e.g., *When the ship arrived safely,* we . . .)

K. Front-shift (e.g., inverted word order: *Gone was the wind. Happy were they to be alive.*)

in emphasizing an idea (see 19b-3). When you want to avoid a very short sentence, however, you can expand the basic sentence as illustrated in Chart 104. Your decision to expand a basic sentence will depend on the focus of each sentence and how it works in concert with its surrounding sentences.

EXERCISE 19-3

Consulting section 19e-1, expand each sentence by adding (a) an adjective, (b) an adverb, (c) a prepositional phrase, (d) a participial phrase, (e) an absolute phrase, (f) an adverb clause, and (g) an adjective clause.

1. We went to register for classes.
2. The lines were long.
3. The students seemed edgy.
4. The staff remained calm.
5. Both of us got the schedules we wanted.

| 2 | Positioning modifiers to create variety and emphasis |

Research on learning suggests that readers are more likely to retain the message that is at the very beginning or the very end of a sentence. Although you do not have unlimited choices about where to place modifiers, you do have some. Try to place them according to the emphasis that you want to achieve. At the same time, be sure to place your modifiers precisely within sentences so that you avoid the error of misplaced modifiers (see 15b).

A sentence that starts with a subject and verb and then provides additional information with modifiers that appear after the subject and verb is called a **cumulative sentence.** The cumulative sentence is the most common sentence structure in English; it is called "cumulative" because information accumulates. Sometimes the cumulative sentence is referred to as a **loose sentence** because it lacks the tightly planned structure of other sentence varieties. Such sentences, easy to read because they reflect how humans receive and pass on information, often do not provide impact, however.

In contrast, a **periodic sentence,** also called a *climactic sentence,* is highly emphatic. It builds up to the period, reserving the main idea for the end of the sentence. It draws the reader in as it builds to its climax. Periodic sentences can be very effective, but if they are overused they lose their punch.

ANSWERS: EXERCISE 19-3

Students are to expand each sentence by adding (a) an adjective, (b) an adverb, (c) a prepositional phrase, (d) a participial phrase, (e) an absolute phrase, (f) a subordinate clause, and (g) a relative clause. They can refer for guidance to the expansion techniques shown in Chart 104. The answers will vary considerably. Here is a possible set of answers for item 1:

a. We went to register for our college classes.

b. We went eagerly to register for classes.

c. We went to register for classes at the college.

d. Forced to wait until the storm passed, we went to register for classes, hoping we were not too late.

e. Clothing still unpacked in our dormitory, we went to register for classes.

f. As soon as we got to the college, we went to register for classes.

g. We, who had never attended college before, went to register for classes.

BACKGROUND

Periodic and cumulative sentences work by placing the weight of a sentence's message at one end. On the other hand, the balanced sentence, using the concept of parallel structure, presents two equally weighted pieces of meaning. Usually a punctuation mark and/or a coordinating conjunction acts as a centerpoint upon which the meaning balances, much like a see-saw on its base.

Freedom is the right to be wrong, not the right to do wrong.

—John Diefenbaker

ALTERNATE EXAMPLE

The following passage from a student paper employs different sentence types. You may want to discuss with students the effect of the mixture.

I froze when the voice said "Stop!" What did it want, I wondered, this voice that came from out of the shadows to my left? Although my knees were shaking. I hoped my voice would be steady. "What for?" I asked. "Because I said so, that's why. Don't go anywhere—yet." I didn't move, except that my eyes were almost popping out of my head trying to see the person with the voice. "Where's your car?" the voice asked. "Take me to it." "It's parked several blocks away," I objected. "Then go get it. Now!" "How do you know I'll come back?" I asked. "Because," the voice groaned, "I don't think you'd leave your best friend sitting in the street with a sprained ankle." "Well why didn't you say that in first place!" I shouted, then went to see if I could help Mike, the voice I thought I would know anywhere.

ALTERNATE EXAMPLES

1. The guests arrived. (Basic sentence)

2. The hungry guests arrived. (Adjective)

3. The hungry guests arrived late. (Adverb)

4. After the concert, the hungry guests arrived late in a thunderstorm. (Prepositional phrases)

5. Delayed by the weather, the hungry guests, running and laughing, arrived late. (Participles)

6. Shoes soaked from the rain, the hungry guests arrived. (Absolute phrase)

7. Because they were hungry, the guests hurried to the restaurant. (Adverb clause)

8. The guests, who were hungry, hurried to the restaurant. (Adjective clause)

PERIODIC   At midnight last night, on the road from Las Vegas to Death Valley Junction, **a car hit a shoulder and turned over.**

—JOAN DIDION, "On Morality"

CUMULATIVE   **A car hit a shoulder and turned over** at midnight last night on the road from Las Vegas to Death Valley Junction.

Another way to vary sentence structures is to start sentences with introductory words, phrases°, or clauses°. (For a discussion of commas with introductory material, see 24b.)

WORD   **Fortunately,** I taught myself to read before I had to face boring reading drills in school.

—ANDREW FURMAN, student

PHRASE   **Along with cereal boxes and ketchup labels,** comic books were the primers that taught me how to read.

—GLORIA STEINEM

CLAUSE   **Long before I wrote stories,** I listened for stories.

—EUDORA WELTY, *One Writer's Beginnings*

Often, modifiers may appear in several different positions within a sentence. Positioning modifiers offers you a chance to enhance your writing style with variety and emphasis. Here are sentences with the same modifiers in various positions. If you use this technique, be very careful to avoid placing modifiers in positions that create ambiguous meaning (see 15b-1).

Angrily the physician slammed down the chart, **sternly** speaking to the patient.

The physician slammed down the chart **angrily,** speaking **sternly** to the patient.

The physician **angrily** slammed down the chart, speaking to the patient **sternly.**

EXERCISE 19-4

Consulting section 19e, combine each set of sentences by changing one sentence to a clause, phrase, or word that will modify the other sentence.

EXAMPLE   According to a story about the Tower of Babel, all people once spoke the same language. The story appears in the Old Testament.

According to a story in the Old Testament about the Tower of Babel, all people once spoke the same language. [sentence changed to phrase]

1. The people of Babel tried to build a tower that would reach to heaven. They wanted to become famous.
2. God punished them for their arrogance. God made them all speak different languages.
3. Different languages create barriers between people. This is certainly true.
4. Some linguists have tried to develop universal languages. These linguists were ambitious.
5. The British linguist John Wilkins created an artificial language. This happened in 1668.
6. Wilkins wanted to promote universal communication. He made the rules of his invented language consistent and easy to learn.
7. The language had a written form that looked like Arabic. The form was difficult.
8. Another international language was created by L. L. Zamenhof, a Russian physician. This happened two hundred years later.
9. Zamenhof's language is based on European languages and is still used by some people today. It is called Esperanto.
10. The name of the language comes from a verb. The verb means *hope* in Spanish and French.

ANSWERS AND COVERAGE:
EXERCISE 19-4

Answers will vary. Here is one set of possibilities.

1. The people of Babel tried to build a tower that would reach to heaven because they wanted to become famous [clause].

2. God punished them for their arrogance by making them all speak different languages [phrase].

3. Different languages certainly [word] create barriers between people.

4. Some ambitious [word] linguists have tried to develop universal languages.

5. In 1668 [phrase], the British linguist John Wilkins created an artificial language.

6. Because Wilkins wanted to encourage universal communication [clause], he made the rules of his invented language consistent and easy to learn.

7. The language had a difficult [word] written form that looked like Arabic.

8. Two hundred years later [phrase], another international language was created by L. L. Zamenhof, a Russian physician.

9. Zamenhof's language, called Esperanto [phrase], is based on European languages and is still used by some people today.

10. The name of the language comes from a verb that means *hope* [clause] in Spanish and French.

19f   Inverting standard word order

Standard word order in the English sentence places the subject before the verb. Because this pattern is so common, it is set in people's minds, so any variation creates emphasis. Inverted word order places the verb before the subject. Used too often, inverted word order can be distracting; but used sparingly, it can be very effective.

STANDARD	**The mayor walked** in. **The governor walked** out.
INVERTED	In **walked the mayor.** Out **walked the governor.**
STANDARD	**The house** that shelters a friend **is happy.**
INVERTED	**Happy is the house** that shelters a friend.

—RALPH WALDO EMERSON

19g Repeating important words or ideas to achieve emphasis

You can repeat some words to help emphasize meaning, but choose the words carefully. Repeat only those words that contain a main idea or that use rhythm to focus attention on a main idea. Consider this passage, which uses deliberate repetition along with a variety of sentence lengths to deliver its meaning.

> Coal is **black** and it warms your house and cooks your food. The night is **black,** which has a moon, and a million stars, and is beautiful. Sleep is **black** which gives you rest, so you wake up **feeling good.** I am **black. I feel** very **good** this evening.

—LANGSTON HUGHES, "That Word *Black*"

Hughes repeats the word *black,* each time linking it to something related to joy and beauty. The rhythm that results from the deliberate repetition of *black* and *good* emphasizes Hughes's message and helps the reader remember it.

Be sure to use deliberate repetition sparingly, with central words, and only when your meaning justifies such a technique. Consider this passage, which is the result of limited vocabulary and a dull, unvaried style. Although few synonyms exist for the words *an insurance agent, car,* and *model,* some do. Also, the sentence structure has no variety.

NO	**An insurance agent** can be an excellent adviser when you want to buy a **car. An insurance agent** has records on most **cars. An insurance agent** knows which **models** tend to have most accidents. **An insurance agent** can tell you which **models** are the most expensive to repair if they are in a collision. **An insurance agent can** tell you which **models** are most likely to be stolen.
YES	If you are thinking of buying a new car, an insurance agent can be an excellent adviser. An insurance broker

---

ALTERNATE EXAMPLES

You might ask your students to explain the differences in emphasis in these sentences, which contain the same information presented in various ways.

1. Revelers wear bizarre costumes and dance in the streets on Mardi Gras, a day of carefree indulgence.

2. The bizarre costumes and dancing of revelers attract attention on Mardi Gras, a day of carefree indulgence.

3. Mardi Gras is a day of carefree indulgence marked by revelers' bizarre costumes and street dancing.

TEACHING TIP

Self-analysis of a writer's style can be an effective beginning to composing better sentences. You might encourage students to find out what kind of sentences they usually write (simple, compound, complex); the average length of the sentences and how often the sentences exceed or fall short of that length; and the rhetorical forms most often used (cumulative, periodic, balanced). This process can help students see how much variety (or lack of it) exists in their prose style. It will also reveal underused strategies of sentence composition. You may want to ask your students to gather such information about their sentences using a passage from one of their recent papers, and then to write a brief analysis that reviews the data and proposes specific changes that will enhance the passage's variety and emphasis. Computer style-checkers can greatly help a writer with this analysis.

has complete records on most automobiles. For example, he or she knows which models are accident prone. Did you know that some car designs suffer more damage than others in a collision? If you want to know which automobiles crumple more than others and which are least expensive to repair, ask an insurance agent. Similarly, some models are more likely to be stolen, so find out from the person who specializes in dealing with claims.

EXERCISE 19-5

Consulting all sections of this chapter, revise this paragraph to achieve emphasis through varied sentence length and deliberate repetition. You can reduce or increase the number of sentences, and you can drop words to reduce unneeded repetition. Each writer's revision will vary somewhat, but try to include at least one revision to a question or exclamation (19c) and one revision to an inverted word order (19f).

Pigeons adjust to many environments. Pigeons adjust to farm life. They adjust to city streets. In an urban setting they peck their livelihoods from garbage heaps, and they sometimes survive on crumbs tossed to them. They even thrive well in science labs. Recently, scientists wanted to find out something. The scientists wanted to know about the conceptual abilities of pigeons. The scientists were at the University of Iowa. The scientists worked with ordinary pigeons. The pigeons had been trapped on an Iowa farm. The pigeons were treated well by the scientists. The pigeons were given tests, and the tests required thinking ability. The pigeons had to assign pictures of objects to categories. The pigeons learn easily. The pigeons could tell apart photographs of different objects. The pictures were of separate items such as cats, flowers, people. The pictures even included manufactured items such as automobiles and furniture. Then a big surprise came. The scientists discovered that the pigeons did not learn by rote in that when photographs varied only slightly in different features or degrees of light, the pigeons could tell them apart. Humans can no longer doubt that pigeons are far smarter than they look.

EXERCISE 19-6

Consulting all sections of this chapter, use techniques of variety and emphasis to revise the following paragraph.

French educator Louis Braille was born in 1809. He became blind at three years of age. He was enrolled at the Institute for the Blind when he was ten. The Institute was in Paris. Braille devised a writing system for blind people consisting of raised dots on paper. Braille's accomplishment was of

ANSWERS: EXERCISE 19-5

Answers will vary. One possible revision is shown here. In this version, *pigeons* and *scientists* are deliberately repeated. Many short sentences are combined (in two places, three sentences are combined into one) into a variety of sentence types, and unneeded words are dropped in that process. The first compound sentence is revised to a simple sentence containing compound phrases. The second compound sentence is revised to contain a relative clause. Word order is inverted in one sentence, to which an exclamation point is added. One complex sentence is unpacked for greater clarity. The last sentence is revised into a question. Some sentences are not revised.

Pigeons adjust to many environments. Pigeons adjust to farm life, and they adjust to city streets where they peck their livelihoods from garbage heaps or from crumbs tossed to them. They even thrive well in science laboratories. Recently, scientists at the University of Iowa wanted to find out about the conceptual abilities of pigeons. The scientists worked with ordinary pigeons. The pigeons, trapped on an Iowa farm, were treated well by the scientists. The pigeons were given tests that required thinking ability. The pigeons had to assign pictures of objects to categories. The pigeons learned easily to tell apart photographs of different objects. The pictures were of separate items such as cats, flowers, people, and even manufactured items such as automobiles and furniture. Then came a big surprise! The scientists discovered that the pigeons did not learn by rote. When photographs varied only slightly in different features or degrees of light, the pigeons could tell them apart. Can humans doubt any longer that pigeons are far smarter than they look?

ANSWERS AND COVERAGE: EXERCISE 19-6

Answers will vary. This is a summary exercise, so it should reflect many of the techniques of variety and emphasis discussed in this chapter. Here is one answer; many others are possible.

Born in 1809 [19e-1, participial phrase to modify] French educator Louis Braille became blind at three years of age [19b-1, combined two short sentences], and he was enrolled at the Institute for the Blind [19b-3, compound sentence to vary sentence lengths] in Paris [19e-1, prepositional phrase to modify] when he was ten [19e-1, adverb clause to modify]. Braille devised for blind people a writing system that consisted of raised dots on paper [19e-1, adjective clause to modify]. At the time of this accomplishment of enormous benefit to humanity, Braille was only twenty [19e-2, periodic sentence]. Braille's system used 43 configurations of raised dots to represent individual letters of the alphabet, some combinations of letters, and some punctuation marks [19b-1, revised string of too many short sentences]. A modified version is still used today [19b-3, no change because effective short sentence among long sentences]. Did you know that Louis Braille was also a distinguished musician [19c, a question to vary sentence structures]? So talented was he [19f, inverted word order] that as an adult he played the violoncello and the organ to great acclaim throughout Paris [19e-1, prepositional phrases to modify]. Sadly, Braille died when only 43 years of age [no change].

ANSWERS: EXERCISE 19-7

Using their own topics, students imitate the variety and emphasis of two different passages shown in this chapter. They can choose from the Kohls, Dillard, Thomas, or Hughes. For a discussion of the technique of imitation, see the answer to Exercise 18-2.

enormous benefit to many people. At the time, he was only twenty years old. Braille's system used 43 configurations of raised dots. Some symbols represented individual letters of the alphabet. Other symbols stood for some combinations of letters. Still other symbols stood for some punctuation marks. A modified version is still used today. Few people know that Louis Braille was also a distinguished musician. He was so talented that as an adult he played the violoncello and the organ to great acclaim. He was known throughout Paris for his playing. Sadly, Braille died when only 43 years of age.

EXERCISE 19-7

Using topics you choose, imitate the variety and emphasis of two different passages shown in this chapter. Select from the quotations from the Kohls, Dillard, Thomas, or Hughes.

Focus on Revising

REVISING YOUR WRITING

If you would like to use variety and emphasis effectively when you write, go back to your writing and locate sentences that need improvement in style. Using this chapter as a resource, revise your writing: to vary sentence lengths effectively, see 19b; to use questions, mild commands, or exclamations effectively, see 19c; to choose sentence subjects for effective emphasis, see 19d; to add modifiers effectively, see 19e; to invert word order effectively, see 19f; to use repetition effectively, see 19g.

CASE STUDY: REVISING FOR EFFECTIVE USE OF SUBORDINATION, PARALLELISM, AND VARIETY AND EMPHASIS

In these case studies, you can observe a student writer revising. Then you have the chance to revise other student writing on your own.

Observation

A student wrote the following draft for her campus newspaper. The newspaper editor asked the student to compose a brief article about Soviet teenagers' interest in products made in the United States. The draft opens with an attention-getting reference and offers engaging information. The draft's effectiveness is diminished, however, by problems with subordination (Chapter 17), parallelism (Chapter 18), and variety and emphasis (this chapter).

Read through the draft. The sections that could be written more effectively are highlighted and explained. Before you look at the student's revisions, revise the material yourself. Then compare what you and the student did.

does not show relationships among ideas: 17g

In 1987, singer Billy Joel toured the former Soviet Union. He played to capacity crowds throughout the Soviet Union. A television special about the concert tour provided viewers in the United States with a startling picture of Soviet youth.

→

COVERAGE: PARTICIPATION ESSAY

Many people enjoy playing sports in high school and college. *Sports like football and basketball are team sports, and they can be fun to play, and they can keep players in excellent physical condition.* [17d-2: coordination overused] These sports have one major shortcoming, however. *They are hard to play after college. Finding enough people to make up two teams is usually difficult outside of school.* [17b: does not show relationship among ideas]

People plan to play sports over a lifetime. A wise choice is golf. This sport is not particularly popular in school. [17b: does not show relationship among ideas] Swinging a golf club promotes flexibility and agility. Also, golf players can maintain their physical conditioning if they *walk* the golf course briskly and *are carrying* [18b: not parallel form for words] their golf clubs. Golf courses often measure between three-and-a-half and five miles, which is a good distance for a workout. *Golfers begin to age. They can use a pull cart. The pull cart is for the bags. The pull cart helps prevent strain. The strain can be on muscles and joints. Then, golfers age further. The golfers have a new solution. They can use electric carts. Electric carts allow golfers to ride part or all of the course.* [19b: not a suitable mix of sentence lengths; and 17b: does not show relationship among ideas]

In addition to being physically demanding, golf offers a mental challenge. Most long-time, nonprofessional golfers know that they are playing against the golf course. They are not playing against someone who is *younger* and *has more strength.* [18b: not parallel form for words] In golf, the lower the score, the better. Professional golfers hope for scores in the high sixties or low seventies. My grandfather is a lifetime golf player. ➡

---

coordination overused: 17d-2

subordination illogical: 17h-1

parallel form needed: 18b and 18c

The concertgoers were wearing bluejeans, running shoes, and they had let their hair grow long and wore T-shirts. Simply put, they looked startlingly similar to American teenagers. The sight of a teenager in American-style clothing was nothing new in Russia, but most Americans did not realize this, for western products had been "hot items" over a decade in the Soviet Union, and popular items ranged from stereos to chewing gum.

Detente had started during the 1970s. This referred to the lessening of tension between the United States and the Soviet Union. Detente had led to a number of American businesses opening in Moscow. At the same time, the country had played host to hordes of American tourists and professionals. Soviet teenagers had seemed intrigued by whatever the visitors brought with them, although tourists had returned home with stories of Russian teenagers offering to buy the very jackets and shoes the Americans were wearing. Journalists had talked about and were publishing stories about a thriving black market in American cigarettes, records, and electronic gear.

Soviet teenagers had developed a big appetite for a wide range of U.S. styles and ➡

not a suitable mix of sentence lengths: 19b-3

parallel form needed: 18b and 18c

items. That appetite helped break
down barriers between the two
countries.

Here is how the student revised for effective use of subordination, parallelism, and variety and emphasis. In some places, the student could revise the material in more than one way. Your revision, therefore, might not be exactly like this one, but it should eliminate all the problems highlighted in the draft.

In 1987, singer Billy Joel toured the former Soviet Union and played to capacity crowds. A television special about the concert tour provided viewers in the United States with a startling picture of Soviet youth.

The concertgoers wore bluejeans, running shoes, long hair, and T-shirts. Simply put, they looked startlingly similar to American teenagers. Most Americans did not realize, however, that the sight of a teenager in American-style clothing was nothing new in Russia, for western products, from stereos to chewing gum, had been "hot items" for over a decade in the Soviet Union.

Detente, the lessening of tension between the United States and the Soviet Union that had started during the 1970s, led to a number of American businesses opening in Moscow. At the same time, the country had played host to hordes of American tourists and professionals. Soviet teenagers had seemed intrigued by whatever the visitors brought with them, and tourists returned home with stories of Russian teenagers offering to buy the very jackets and shoes the Americans were wearing. Journalists had talked about and published stories about a thriving black market in American cigarettes, records, and electronic gear.

Soviet teenagers had developed a big appetite for a wide range of U.S. styles and items. That appetite helped break down barriers between the two countries.

Participation

A student wrote the following draft for a course called Health and The Aging Process. The assignment was to write about sports that people can play all their lives. The material contains useful informa-

→

Cont'd.

Because he is 82, he still plays golf almost every day. [17h-1: illogical subordination] He says that his goal is to get a golf score that matches his age. Therefore, with each added year, he has a better chance to reach his goal. That is mental health!

ANSWER: PARTICIPATION ESSAY

This version revises the problems with coordination and subordination (Chapter 17), parallelism (Chapter 18), and variety and emphasis (this chapter). Answers will likely vary somewhat from this version because so many options are available. Also, answers will vary if students have revised for content, organization, or style.

Many people enjoy playing sports in high school and college. Team sports like football and basketball are fun to play and can keep players in excellent physical condition. These sports have one major shortcoming, however. They are hard to play after college, because finding enough people to make up two teams is usually difficult outside of school.

People who plan to play sports over a lifetime would be wise to choose golf, even though this sport is not particularly popular in school. Swinging a golf club promotes flexibility and agility. Also, golf players can maintain their physical conditioning if they walk the golf course briskly and carry their golf clubs. Golf courses often measure between three-and-a-half and five miles, which is a good distance for a workout. As golfers age, they can use a pull cart for the bags so that they do not strain their muscles and joints. Even later in life, golfers can use electric carts to ride the course.

ANSWER: PARTICIPATION ESSAY,
continued

In addition to being physically demanding, golf offers a mental challenge. Most long-time, nonprofessional golfers know that they are playing against the golf course. They are not playing against someone who is younger and stronger. In golf, the lower the score, the better. Professional golfers hope for scores in the high sixties or low seventies. My grandfather is a lifetime golf player. Although he is 82, he still plays golf almost every day. He says that his goal is to get a golf score that matches his age. Therefore, with each added year, he has a better chance to reach his goal. That is mental health!

tion logically presented, but the draft's effectiveness is diminished by problems with subordination (Chapter 17), parallelism (Chapter 18), and variety and emphasis (this chapter).

Read through the draft. Then revise it to eliminate the problems. Also, make any additional revisions you think would improve the content, organization, and style of the material.

Many people enjoy playing sports in high school and college. Sports like football and basketball are team sports, and they can be fun to play, and they can keep players in excellent physical condition. These sports have one major shortcoming, however. They are hard to play after college. Finding enough people to make up two teams is usually difficult outside of school.

People plan to play sports over a lifetime. A wise choice is golf. This sport is not particularly popular in school. Swinging a golf club promotes flexibility and agility. Also, golf players can maintain their physical conditioning if they walk the golf course briskly and are carrying their golf clubs. Golf courses often measure between three-and-a-half and five miles, which is a good distance for a workout. Golfers begin to age. They can use a pull cart. The pull cart is for the bags. The pull cart helps prevent strain. The strain can be on muscles and joints. Then, golfers age further. The golfers have a new solution. They can use electric carts. Electric carts allow golfers to ride part or all of the course.

In addition to being physically demanding, golf offers a mental challenge. Most long-time, nonprofessional golfers know that they are playing against the golf course. They are not playing against someone who is younger and has more strength. In golf, the lower the score, the better. Professional golfers hope for scores in the high sixties or low seventies. My grandfather is a lifetime golf player. Because he is 82, he still plays golf almost every day. He says that his goal is to get a golf score that matches his age. Therefore, with each added year, he has a better chance to reach his goal. That is mental health!

Using
Effective
Words

*When you use words effectively, you choose words that
communicate your message precisely. Part Five alerts you
to the meanings that reside in words and the effect that
words have on your readers. As you use Chapters 20 through 22,
keep in mind that words work in concert with effective sentence
structures and paragraphs to create good writing.*

The earliest dictionary, really a combination grammar and dictionary, was a tablet from Sumerian Nippur that attempted to enunciate the rules of language use. Not until the early seventeenth century was the first English dictionary produced by Henry Cockeram. The earliest attempt to list all the words in the English language was Nathaniel Bailey's *Universal Etymological English Dictionary* of 1721. Mulcaster had urged such a compilation as far back as 1582, but the only result was Robert Cawdrey's *Table Alphabeticall of Hard Words* (about 3,000 of them) published in 1604. Following Bailey's effort, dictionary makers dutifully tried to include all words, not just the difficult ones. Consequently, the seventeenth and eighteenth centuries saw the size of dictionaries grow substantially. Further innovations included Samuel Johnson's use of quotations to exemplify usage in his *Dictionary of the English Language* (1755) and Noah Webster's inclusion of quotations from the Founding Fathers in his *An American Dictionary of the English Language* (1828). Webster's nationalistic feelings were also evident in his insistence on American spellings. Contemporary dictionaries, such as *The American Heritage Dictionary of the English Language* and *Random House Dictionary*, include photographs, illustrations, and maps. Today's unabridged dictionaries include well over one million words, although the average adult is said to have a use-and-recognition vocabulary of between 30,000 and 60,000 words. A highly literate adult may know 100,000. Since it is estimated that only 20,000 to 30,000 words are in full use today, average adults can get along well, although they may not know nine out of ten words in the official language because these are terms from special fields with which they have no contact.

20 Understanding the Meaning of Words

American English, evolving over centuries into a rich language, reflects the many cultures that have merged in our melting-pot society. The earliest varieties of American English can be traced from sixteenth-century Elizabethan English—the language of Shakespeare. As the United States expanded, so did American English. Changes from Elizabethan forms occurred in vocabulary, spelling, and syntactic patterns. Distinctly American words originated colloquially—in spoken language—and words from all the cultures settling the United States became part of the language. Food names, for example, show how other languages and cultures loaned words to English. Africans brought the words *okra, gumbo,* and *goober* (peanut); Spanish and Latin American peoples contributed *tortilla, taco, burrito,* and *enchilada*. From German we got *hamburger, wiener,* and *pretzel;* Italian supplied *spaghetti, pasta, pizza,* and *antipasto;* and Yiddish is responsible for *gefilte fish, tsimmes,* and *bagel.* American English creates a truly international *smorgasbord,* a Scandinavian word meaning "a wide variety of appetizers and other tasty foods."

Etymology is the study of the origins and historical development of words, including changes in form and meaning. For example, *alphabet* originates from the names of the first two letters in Greek: *a = alpha, b = beta.* The meanings of some words change with time. For example, W. Nelson Francis points out in *The English Language,* the word *nice* "has been used at one time or another in its 700-year history to mean . . . foolish, wanton, strange, lazy, coy, modest, fastidious, refined, precise, subtle, slender, critical, attentive, minutely accurate, dainty, appetizing, agreeable."

To use American English well, you want to be aware of the kinds of information that dictionaries offer (20a), to know how to choose exact words (20b), and to use strategies that actively build your vocabulary (20c).

20a Using dictionaries

Good dictionaries show how language has been used and is currently being used. Each dictionary entry gives the meaning of the word and much additional important information. Many dictionaries also include essays on the history and use of language.

1 Understanding all parts of a dictionary entry

A dictionary entry usually includes items 1 through 11, and sometimes 12 and 13, discussed below. As you use the list, consult the entry shown here for *celebrate*, taken from *Webster's New World Dictionary*, Third College Edition.

Dictionary Entry for *Celebrate*

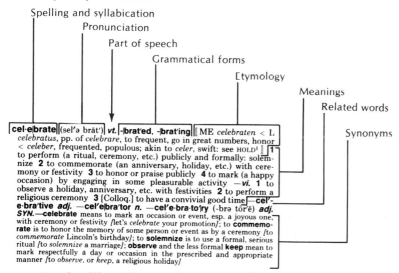

1. **Spelling.** If more than one spelling is shown, the first is the most commonly used, and the others are acceptable.

   Celebrate has only one spelling.

2. **Word Division.** Dots (or bars, in some dictionaries) separate the syllables of a word. Writers can hyphenate at syllables as long as the rules in section 22g are not violated. To help writers, *Webster's New World Dictionary*, Third College Edition, uses a hairline (a thin vertical line)

TEACHING TIP

Words dealing with cooking or food are often put to other uses. You can ask students to find the original meanings of the following words, then to write sentences in which they are used in situations that have nothing to do with food.

1. hodgepodge (a pot of beans, meat, and barley)
2. goulash (a Hungarian stew)
3. mishmash (an English stew dating back to the fifteenth century)
4. pastiche (a meat pie)
5. smorgasbord (a Swedish buffet)

TEACHING TIP

Students may find it interesting to discover that different dictionaries do not always provide the same information about specific words. To identify some differences (and even contradictions), you can ask students to bring to class their findings about the spelling, pronunciation, syllabification, etymology, and usage of the following words. Where differences appear, students can question and discuss the reasons for them.

1. gumbo
2. cab
3. broadcast
4. rhetoric
5. nachos

WORD DERIVATION

Georgia was named for King George II of England. *Virginia* was named for Elizabeth I, who was known as the Virgin Queen. Naming new territories after monarchs and their family members was a common practice among explorers who wanted to gain favor or give thanks for patronage.

to indicate any syllable that should not be used for hyphenating.

> *Cel·e|brate* has three syllables: *cel, e,* and *brate.* A hyphen is acceptable after *cel* but not after the second *e.*

3. **Pronunciation.** The symbols in parentheses show pronunciation. If more than one pronunciation is given, the first is the most common, and the others are acceptable. A guide to the pronunciation of the symbols appears in the front of most dictionaries, and some dictionaries provide a brief guide to the most common symbols at the bottom of pages.

> *Celebrate* is pronounced sel' ə brāt. The accent mark after the *l* means that the stressed syllable is *sel.* The unusual looking symbol /ə/, called a *schwa,* is pronounced "uh," as in *ago.* The line over the *a* indicates the long *a* sound, as in *ate.*

4. **Part of Speech Labels.** Abbreviations, explained in the front of the dictionary, indicate parts of speech. Many words can function as more than one part of speech.

> *Celebrate* is a transitive verb°* (**vt.**), for which four definitions are given; also, it is an intransitive verb° (**vi.**), for which three definitions are given.

5. **Grammatical Forms.** This information tells of variations in grammar: for a verb°, its principal parts and form variations; for a noun°, its plural when the spelling demands other than the addition of *s* only; for an adjective° or adverb°, its comparative form° and superlative form°.

> The principal parts of the verb *celebrate* are *celebrated* and *celebrating.*

6. **Etymology.** This information traces the way that the word has evolved through other languages over the years to become the word and meaning in current use.

> *Celebrate* comes from a Middle English (ME) word that is derived from the Latin (L). The meaning evolved from the idea of "going in great numbers, honoring," a meaning reflected by the first definition in the entry.

---

*Throughout this book, a degree mark (°) indicates that you can find the definition of the word in the Glossary of Terms in this handbook.

7. **Definitions.** If a word has more than one meaning, the definitions are numbered in most dictionaries from the oldest to the newest meaning. A few dictionaries start with the most common use.

> The oldest meaning of *celebrate* is given first, and its most recent use is given last (item 4 in the **vt.** list and item 3 in the **vi.** list).

8. **Usage Labels.** If the use of a word is special, a usage label explains how the word should be used. Chart 105 explains the most common usage labels in dictionaries.

> The most recent meaning of *celebrate* as an intransitive verb (**vi.**) is *colloquial*. Therefore, such use is informal (and probably should be avoided in academic writing).

9. **Field Labels.** When a word applies to a specialized area of study, such as chemistry or law, an abbreviation alerts a reader to the specialized meaning. For example, along with its everyday meanings, the word *center* has specialized meanings in these fields: sports, mechanics, the military, and politics.

10. **Related Words.** Words based on the defined word appear, with their part of speech, at the end of the definitions.

> Words related to *celebrate* are *celebrative* (adjective), *celebrator* (noun), and *celebratory* (adjective).

11. **Synonyms and Antonyms,** if any. Synonyms are words that are close in meaning. They are listed with their subtle differences explained. Also, for each word in the list of synonyms, a cross-reference appears at that word's entry so that the reader can tell where to find the complete list. For example, at the entry *commemorate*, this information appears: *SYN.* CELEBRATE. It means that synonyms for *commemorate* can be found at the entry for *celebrate*. Antonyms are words that are opposite in meaning to the word defined. Any antonyms are listed after any synonyms.

> *Celebrate* and four of its synonyms are listed and explained; it has no antonyms.

12. **Idioms,** if any. When the defined word is an idiom, either in itself or when combined with other words, it has a meaning that differs from its usual meaning. For example, in *Webster's New World Dictionary*, the entry for *ceiling* lists

---

TEACHING TIP

Many commonly used English words come directly from classical mythology. Maxwell Nurnberg and Morris Rosenblum suggest that students will enjoy finding the stories that have given us such words as *aegis, chimerical, cornucopia, protean, stentorian, stygian,* and *titanic*. They will add words to their vocabularies at the same time (*All About Words: An Adult Approach to Vocabulary Building* [New York: The New American Library, 1966]).

WORD DERIVATION

Nevada is a shortening of the Spanish *Sierra Nevada* ("snowy range"), a mountain range in eastern California.

WORD DERIVATION

New Mexico is a literal translation of the Spanish *Nuevo Méjico*. *Méjico* is the Spanish rendering of *Mexitli*, the name of an Aztec war god.

WORD DERIVATION

The state of *Pennsylvania* is named after a man and the local geography. *Sylvania* means "wooded land" in Latin. The *Penn* part is less clear. Some say that the *Penn* is William Penn, the colonist to whom King Charles II of England gave the land. Others say that under orders from King Charles, Penn named the land after his own late father, an English admiral. In either case, the admiral had died before the king could repay a debt of 16,000 pounds. The king gave the land to William Penn in settlement of the debt—and to keep the religious activist out of England.

BACKGROUND

In "English Language Teaching Dictionaries: Past, Present, and Future" (*English Today* 4 [April 1988]: 10–14), Della Summers reviews the development of English dictionaries for foreign students. She goes on to compare the coverage provided by three monolingual English language teaching dictionaries.

EXTRA EXERCISE A

Find the answers to the following questions in the dictionary you commonly use. Name the sections consulted for any answers you are unable to find.

1. When was the University of the South (in Tennessee) founded?

2. What is the population of Midland, Texas?

3. What was George Eliot's real name?

4. Who took the Elgin marbles to England?

5. When did Mary Cassatt live?

6. What is the highest peak in the Elk Mountains?

7. Where is the Bonneville Dam?

8. What large city is near Evanston?

9. What is the meaning of the abbreviation *e.g.*?

10. Where does a cockney live?

11. What is the zip code for Auburn University?

12. What is the mathematical symbol for infinity?

13. To what genus does the mandrill belong?

14. What is the size (in square miles) of Manitoba?

15. What is the etymology of *helicopter*?

WORD DERIVATION

Kentucky comes from the Iroquoian words for "level land."

and defines the idiom *hit the ceiling.* If an idiom is considered slang or colloquial, a usage label (see item 8 above and section 20a-2) alerts the reader.

13. **Examples.** Some definitions provide an example sentence that illustrates the defined word in use.

2 Understanding usage labels

Usage refers to the customary manner of using particular words or phrases. As a writer, you can refer to the **usage labels** in a dictionary to help you decide when a word is appropriate for use. For example, a word labelled *slang* usually is not suitable for academic writing, unless you are writing about the word itself. A word labelled *poetic* is likely to be found only in poetry, not in prose.

The concept of usage also applies to the customary manner of using certain words (for example, *among* versus *between*). For a list and explanation of such words, see the Usage Glossary toward the back of this handbook.

USAGE LABELS

105

LABEL	DEFINITION	EXAMPLE
COLLOQUIAL	Characteristic of conversation and informal writing	**pa** [father] **ma** [mother]
SLANG	Not considered part of standard language, but sometimes used in informal conversation	**whirlybird** [helicopter]
OBSOLETE	No longer used; occurred in earlier writing	**betimes** [promptly, quickly]
POETIC	Found in poetry or poetic prose	**o'er** [for *over*]
DIALECT	Used only in some geographical areas	**poke** [Southern: a bag or sack]

EXERCISE 20-1

Use a dictionary with entries that include a list of synonyms and some labels, as in the entry for *celebrate* on page 401. Then, assume that your audience is a student unfamiliar with such entries, and write an explanation of each part. Consult sections 20a-1 and 20a-2.

3 | Using unabridged dictionaries

Unabridged means "not shortened." Of the various kinds of dictionaries, unabridged dictionaries have the most in-depth, accurate, complete, and scholarly entries. They give many examples of current uses and changes in meanings of the word over time. They include infrequently used words that abridged dictionaries (see 20a-4) often omit.

The most comprehensive, authoritative unabridged dictionary of English is the *Oxford English Dictionary (OED)*. The *OED*, second edition, has twenty volumes defining more than 616,500 words and terms. The *OED* traces the history of each word and gives updated quotations to illustrate changes in meaning and spelling. The second edition of the *OED* consists of three parts: (1) the first edition of the *OED*, largely unchanged; (2) the contents of the four supplements that accompanied the first edition; and (3) approximately 5,000 words or terms new in the second edition.

Its comprehensive historical information and examples about English words make the *OED* a specialized dictionary (20a-5) as well as an unabridged dictionary. The following entry for *celebrate* is taken from the *OED*, second edition. It is only a small excerpt, but it serves to illustrate the kinds of information that you can get from the *OED*. Compare this material and format with the entry for *celebrate* on page 419 taken from *Webster's New World Dictionary*, Third College Edition. In addition to the usual dictionary features (see 20a-1), the *OED* offers a complete history of the word (*celebrate*'s first recorded use was in 1656). Note the historical examples of *celebrate* following its third meaning.

For most college students *Webster's Third New International Dictionary of the English Language* provides any needed information. This highly respected, one-volume work has more than 470,000 entries and is especially strong in new scientific and technical terms. It uses quotations to show various meanings, and its definitions are given in order of their appearance in the language.

Random House Dictionary of the English Language, second edition, is another one-volume work. It has more than 315,000 entries. Although it is the least detailed of the three unabridged dictionaries

ANSWERS: EXERCISE 20-1
Answers will vary.

WORD DERIVATION
Rhode Island's etymology is a mystery. There are two theories. According to one, Italian explorer Giovanni da Verrazano saw a resemblance between the island on which the city of Newport is now located and the Greek island of Rhodes. According to the second, Dutch explorers named the area *Roode Eylandt* ("red island") because of its red clay soil.

EXTRA EXERCISE B
List two synonyms for each of the following words. On the basis of information that you can find about them in a dictionary, explain the differences between the pairs of synonyms.

1. indulge   6. frugal
2. egotism   7. red
3. lazy   8. good
4. fame   9. govern
5. friendly   10. industry

TEACHING TIP
You may want to ask students to work in groups to research the origins of a slang expression, a commonly used phrase, or a regional expression of their own choice. The results can take the form of an oral report to the rest of the class.

WORD DERIVATION
Florida was named by explorer Ponce de Leon. The name is Spanish for "abounding in flowers."

BACKGROUND

In 1989 Oxford University published a second edition of the *Oxford English Dictionary*, commonly known as the *OED*. The idea for the first edition came from a paper delivered in 1857 to Britain's Philological Society by Richard Trench, Dean of Westminster; it was entitled "On Some Deficiencies in Our English Dictionaries." His concerns led the Society to make plans for compiling a completely new dictionary that would include "every word occurring in the literature of the language." In 1859 Herbert Coleridge, a grandson of the poet, became editor of the new work, expecting to publish it in two years. After his untimely death, he was succeeded by Frederick J. Furnivall, who agreed to devote four or five years to producing the first part of the dictionary. Overburdened by work, Furnivall in 1876 turned over his duties to James Murray, who agreed to produce a dictionary of between 6,000 and 7,000 pages within ten years. Beginning with one and three-quarters tons of materials collected by Furnivall, he made a public appeal for a thousand readers of English to assist with finding quotations for unusual as well as ordinary words. Working twelve to fifteen hours a day, with the help of his eleven children, Murray had, by 1894, completed sections A, B, C, and D, whereupon the work was first called *The Oxford English Dictionary*. Murray died in 1915 with a sixth of the work unfinished. The completed dictionary emerged in 1928 after 70 years of work by a series of devoted researchers. Since that time four supplements to the original work have been published.

The new edition combines the original *OED* and the supplements, which add 5,000 new words as well as revised, corrected, and updated information. Revision will continue, and new supplements will appear as time goes on. Meanwhile, the first edition is now available in a CD-ROM (Compact Disk —Read Only Memory) version that presents not only the full text of the *OED*, but also eight indexes.

Sample OED Entry

celebrate ('sɛlɪbreɪt), *v.* [f. prec., or on analogy of vbs. so formed. See -ATE³.]

(**1656** BLOUNT *Glossogr.*, *Celebrate*, to frequent, to solemnize with an Assembly of men, to make famous, also to keep a festival day or other time with great solemnity.)

3. To observe with solemn rites (a day, festival, season); to honour with religious ceremonies, festivities, or other observances (an event, occasion). Also *absol.* (see quot. 1937).

    1560 BIBLE (Genev.) *Lev.* xxiii. 32 From euen to euen shall ye celebrate [WYCL. halowe, COVERD. kepe] your Sabbath. **1591** SHAKS. *1 Hen. VI.* I. vi. 14 Feast and banquet in the open streets, To celebrate the ioy that God hath giuen vs. **1672** DRYDEN *Conq. Granada* I. i, With Pomp and Sports my Love I celebrate. **1697** —— *Virg. Georg.* I. 466 Celebrate the mighty Mother's Day. **1737** L. CLARKE *Hist. Bible* IX. (1840) I. 376 The Feast of Tabernacles being then celebrating. **1841** LANE *Arab. Nts.* I. 71 The Minor Festival ..is celebrated with more rejoicing than the other. **1929** *Randolph Enterprise* (Elkins, W. Va.) 26 Sept. 3/2 [He] came over..Sunday night to celebrate a little. **1937** PARTRIDGE *Dict. Slang* 136/1 *Celebrate*, v.i., to drink in honour of an event or a person; hence, to drink joyously. **1963** J. T. STORY *Something for Nothing* i. 40 It's Treasure's wedding day. Somebody's got to celebrate.

mentioned here, it is unique in including an atlas with color maps and appendixes that list reference books.

4   Using abridged dictionaries

Abridged means "shortened." Abridged dictionaries contain the most commonly used words. They are convenient in size and economical to buy, and they serve as practical reference books for writers and readers. Many good abridged dictionaries are referred to as "college" editions because they serve the needs of most college students.

Webster's New World Dictionary of American English, Third College Edition, has more than 170,000 entries and gives detailed etymologies. Names of people, places, abbreviations, and foreign expressions appear in the main body of the work (rather than in appendixes). Definitions appear in chronological order of their acceptance into the language. *Webster's New World Dictionary* has a contemporary American emphasis. It uses a star symbol (☆) for Americanisms— words that first became part of the language in the United States. It gives the origins of American place names (cities, states, rivers, and so on). It supplies usage labels for many words and gives synonyms, often in lists that explain distinctions among closely related words.

An appendix covers punctuation, italics, numbers, capitalization, abbreviations, and source documentation. Its introductory material includes essays on the English language and etymology. *Webster's New World Compact School and Office Dictionary* is based on *Webster's New World Dictionary*, Third College Edition. More complete than a "pocket" dictionary, it has 56,000 entries.

The American Heritage Dictionary of the English Language has more than 200,000 entries and 3,000 photographs, illustrations, and maps. This dictionary lists the most common meaning of a word first, departing from the traditional practice of listing the oldest meaning first. *The American Heritage Dictionary* has thorough guidance on usage and extensive notes on synonyms. It lists biographical and geographical names in a separate section. Its introductory material contains essays on language, culture, and usage, as well as sections on grammar, spelling, and pronunciation.

Random House College Dictionary, revised edition, has more than 173,000 entries. It gives the most common definition of a word first and has full synonymies. It includes recent technical words and is generously illustrated. Its introductory section presents essays on usage, dialects, and functional varieties of English; its appendixes include a style manual.

✤ ESL NOTE: A useful dictionary for students who speak English as a second language is the *Dictionary of Contemporary English* published by Longman. Some useful dictionaries of idioms are listed in Chart 106. ✤

5	**Using specialized dictionaries of English**

A specialized dictionary focuses on a single area, such as slang, word origins, synonyms, antonyms, usage, or almost any other aspect of language. Most college libraries include all or some of the volumes listed in Chart 106.

SPECIALIZED DICTIONARIES	106
SYNONYMS	*New Roget's Thesaurus of the English Language in Dictionary Form* ➡

BACKGROUND

Good news arrived in December 1985 for linguists, folklorists, and run-of-the-mill browsers. After an incubation period of almost one hundred years, volume one (A–C) of the *Dictionary of American Regional English (DARE)* arrived. Upon completion, *DARE* will contain over 60,000 regional words and expressions.

The roots of *DARE* go back to 1889 and the founding of the American Dialect Society. The society's purpose was to sponsor and record data for an American dialect dictionary. It had its own journal, which continues today as *The Publication of the American Dialect Society*. Compilation of a master file of entries for the dictionary began in 1917, and the society participated along the way in several other, smaller dialect dictionaries (the incomplete *Linguistic Atlas of the United States and Canada* and the *American Dialect Dictionary* [1944]).

In 1963 the society appointed Frederic G. Cassidy (editor of *The Dictionary of Jamaican English*) the *DARE* editor. He and his staff had at their disposal a hundred years of accumulated scholarship: the files of the American Dialect Society, linguistic and folklore journals, regional publications, diaries and other materials in library archives, records of folk speech, historical dictionaries, and linguistic atlases.

Astonishingly, Cassidy chose to go beyond the written word, and the *DARE* benefits from five years of original fieldwork aimed at finding out how people speak in their daily lives. Eighty-two trained fieldworkers, most of them graduate students in linguistics or the history of English, went across the United States conducting personal interviews.

The 2,777 informants represented 1,002 communities across the United States. The informants were chosen to create a balance of male and female, city and country, black and white, North and South. However, in order to preserve vanishing words, about two-thirds of the informants were 60 years ➡

SPECIALIZED DICTIONARIES (*continued*)

SLANG	*Dictionary of Slang and Unconventional English,* ed. Eric Partridge
	Dictionary of American Slang, ed. Harold Wentworth and Stuart Berg Flexner [out of print, but available in many libraries]
	The Thesaurus of Slang, by Esther Lewin and Albert E. Lewin.
ETYMOLOGIES	*Dictionary of Word and Phrase Origins,* ed. William Morris and Mary Morris
	Origins: A Short Etymological Dictionary of Modern English, ed. Eric Partridge [out of print, but available in many libraries]
USAGE	*Modern American Usage,* ed. Jacques Barzun
REGIONALISMS	*Dictionary of American Regional English,* ed. Frederic Cassidy
IDIOMS	*A Dictionary of American Idioms,* by Adam Makkai
	Dictionary of English Idioms, published by Longman Inc.
	NTC's Dictionary of American Idioms, by Richard A. Spears

20b Choosing exact words

The English language offers a wealth of words to choose among as a writer. **Diction,** the term for choice of words, affects the clarity and impact of the message that you want your sentences to deliver. As a writer, you want to use words that exactly fit the particular context of each piece of writing.

1 Understanding denotation and connotation

When you look up a word in the dictionary to find out what it means, you are looking for its **denotation.** For example, the denotation of the word *semester* is "a period of time of about eighteen weeks that makes up part of a school or college year."

Readers expect words to be used according to their established meanings for their established functions. Exactness is essential. When you use a thesaurus or dictionary of synonyms, be aware that subtle shades of meaning create distinctions among words that have the same general definition. These small differences in meaning allow you to be very precise in choosing just the right word, but they also oblige you to make sure that you know what precise meanings your words convey. For instance, describing a person famous for praiseworthy achievements in public life as *notorious* would be wrong. Although *notorious* means "well-known" and "publicly discussed"—which famous people are likely to be—*notorious* also carries the meaning "unfavorably known or talked about." George Washington is *famous*, not *notorious*. Al Capone, on the other hand, is *notorious*.

Here is another example. **Obdurate** means "not easily moved to pity or sympathy," and its synonyms include "inflexible, obstinate, stubborn, hardened." The synonym *hardened* for *obdurate*, however, might prompt someone unfamiliar with *obdurate* to use the word incorrectly.

NO   Footprints showed in the *obdurate* concrete.

Here are two correct uses of *obdurate:*

YES   The supervisor remained *obdurate* in refusing to accept excuses.

YES   My roommates, *obdurate* people who are unwilling to compromise, want to get rid of my pet boa constrictor.

Here is a final example of the importance of explicit meaning. Suppose a writer who is describing a mine shaft has used the word *deep* several times. Searching for a synonym, the writer consults a thesaurus and finds, among other alternatives for *deep*, the word *profound*. The writer then states: "Shaft 4, outside Woodville, is the most profound in the state." *Profound* means "deep" in reference to thoughts or ideas; it cannot be used in reference to a mine shaft.

Connotation refers to ideas implied, but not directly indicated, by a word. Connotations convey associations as emotional overtones beyond the direct, explicit definition of a word. For example, the word *home* usually evokes more emotion than does its denotation "a dwelling place" or its synonym *house*. *Home* may have very pleasant connotations of warmth, security, the love of family. Or *home* may

Cont'd.

old or older. Each questionnaire contained 1,847 questions. One questionnaire was filled in for each community. In some cases, one informant answered all the questions; in others, the questions were divided among a number of informants. The fieldworkers also brought back 1,843 tape recordings of conversations: a total of two million oral responses and 900 hours of tape recordings.

EXTRA EXERCISE D

Be prepared to discuss differences in the connotations of the following pairs of words.

1. passive—shy
2. giggle—snicker
3. buddy—cohort
4. brave—foolhardy
5. wise—intelligent
6. economical—miserly
7. aggressive—assertive
8. cook—chef
9. hairdresser—beautician
10. violinist—fiddler

TEACHING TIP

To underscore the importance of subtle shades of meaning and connotation, you might ask your students how they would react to each of the statements below. Once their egos are involved, students will quickly see that not all synonyms are created equal.

You are wrong.

You are incorrect.

What you say is false.

You are inaccurate.

You are imprecise.

You are evil.

You are improper.

You are unethical.

You are unrighteous.

You are bad.

You are willfully misleading.

BACKGROUND

Over time words change their meanings in several different ways. In *The Story of Our Language* (New York: Doubleday, 1962), Henry Alexander points out that a word may undergo a widening, in which it expands its range of meaning and is applied to new situations; a narrowing, by which it comes to refer to only a portion of the ideas or objects it originally covered; a lowering of meaning, wherein it takes on pejorative aspects; and a raising of meaning, by which it loses its unpleasant associations and acquires more positive ones. For example, *meat* has undergone a narrowing of meaning; it originally referred to all kinds of food, but now denotes what was earlier called flesh. The word *hussy*, with its contemporary uncomplimentary meaning, has experienced a lowering; it originally denoted a housewife.

TEACHING TIP

Following Henry Alexander's discussion of four ways in which words change their meaning over time, students can be asked to discover what types of change have occurred with the following words. Their findings will make an interesting report to the class.

1. chagrin
2. picture (n.)
3. miscreant
4. place
5. cafeteria
6. wanton
7. nice
8. stench
9. fond
10. wife

have unpleasant connotations of an institution for elderly or sick people. As a student writer, be aware of the potential of connotation to help your words deliver their meaning. Connotations are never completely fixed, for they can vary with different contexts for a word. Still, people can communicate effectively because most words have relatively stable connotations and denotations in most contexts.

Being sensitive to the differences between the denotation and connotation of a word is essential for critical thinking. Critical thinkers must first consider material at its literal level (see 5d-1). Doing so calls for dealing with the denotation of words. Next, critical thinkers must move to the inferential level (see 5d-2)—to what is implied although not explicitly stated. Connotations of words often carry the inferential message, as illustrated in Chart 107.

COMPARING DENOTATION AND CONNOTATION		107
SAMPLE WORD	**DENOTATION**	**CONNOTATION**
ADDITIVE	an added substance	in food, a preservative, but perhaps also harmful to health
CHEAP	inexpensive	of products, low quality; of people, stingy
NUCLEAR REACTOR MELTDOWN	unintentional meltdown of fuel rods in nuclear reactor	release of dangerous radiation; possibility of imminent death or eventual cancer; poisoning of food chain

EXERCISE 20-2

Drawing on section 20b-1, separate the words in each set into one of three groups: *Neutral* if you think the word has no connotations; *Positive* if you think it has good connotations; *Negative* if you think it has bad connotations. If you think a word fits in more than one group, put it under each heading that applies, and be ready to explain your choices. If you are unsure of a word, consult your dictionary.

EXAMPLE   alibi, excuse, pretext, reason, explanation

> *Neutral:* reason; *Positive:* explanation; *Negative:* alibi, pretext, excuse

1. fat, fleshy, stout, portly, rotund, chubby, plump, obese, corpulent, heavy, paunchy, overweight, rolypoly, large-sized
2. thin, lean, lanky, skinny, gaunt, scrawny, rawboned, slender, slim, slight, skin and bones
3. teacher, lecturer, instructor, professor, pedant, pedagogue, mentor, scholar, educator
4. politician, lawmaker, senator, representative, leader, demagogue, rabble-rouser
5. loyal, dedicated, devoted, determined, stubborn, firm, unyielding

2 | Using specific and concrete language to bring life to general and abstract language

Specific words identify individual items in a group (*Oldsmobile, Honda, Ford*). **General** words relate to an overall group (*car*). **Concrete** words identify persons and things that can be perceived by the senses—seen, heard, tasted, felt, smelled (the *black padded vinyl dashboard* of my car). **Abstract** words denote qualities, concepts, relationships, acts, conditions, ideas (*transportation*).

As a writer, you want to choose words suitable for your writing purpose (see 1b) and your audience (see 1c). Usually, specific and concrete words bring life to general and abstract words. Whenever you choose general and abstract words, be sure to supply enough specific, concrete details and examples to illustrate effectively your generalizations and abstractions. Consider how sentences with general words come to life when they are revised with words that refer to specifics.

GENERAL	My car has a great deal of power, and it is very quick.
SPECIFIC	My Trans Am with 220 horsepower can go from zero to fifty in six seconds.
GENERAL	The car gets good gas mileage.
SPECIFIC	The Dodge Lancer gets about 35 mpg on the highway and 30 mpg in the city.

ANSWERS: EXERCISE 20-2

The response to this exercise is likely to elicit much debate, given that shades of connotative meaning are often fairly personal. The list below is the result of a poll of the students in a half dozen classes; some votes were very close.

1. *Positive:* portly; *Neutral:* rotund, large-sized, overweight; *Negative:* fat, fleshy, stout, chubby, plump, obese, corpulent, heavy, paunchy, roly-poly

2. *Positive:* lean, lanky, slender, slim; *Neutral:* thin, slight; *Negative:* skinny, gaunt, scrawny, rawboned, skin and bones

3. *Positive:* mentor, scholar, educator; *Neutral:* teacher, lecturer, instructor, professor; *Negative:* pedant, pedagogue

4. *Positive:* senator, representative, leader; *Neutral:* politician, lawmaker; *Negative:* demagogue, rabble-rouser

5. *Positive:* loyal, dedicated, devoted, determined; *Neutral:* firm; *Negative:* stubborn, unyielding

WORD DERIVATION

Louisiana comes from *La Louisianne.* The French, who had controlled the Mississippi Valley before selling the area to the United States in 1803, had named the area after their king, Louis XIV.

EXTRA EXERCISE E

Working in groups and without a dictionary, compile a list of as many words as you can think of that begin with the following prefixes. How does the prefix affect the meaning of each of the words on your list? The group with the longest list can be declared the winner.

1. mono
2. retro
3. contra
4. sub
5. pre
6. auto
7. super
8. un
9. re
10. poly

EXTRA EXERCISE F

Using the following prefixes, devise new words, being prepared to explain their meaning.

1. inter
2. ante
3. anti
4. post
5. uni

ANSWERS: EXERCISE 20-3

Because of the many possibilities for rewording posed by this exercise, the answers are likely to vary widely. Students may enjoy comparing the different choices they have made. The important principle for revision is that the new versions should have a high degree of specificity and concreteness. Here is one set of possibilities.

The used 1988 Buick was exactly what we were looking for. It was a maroon two-door model with a vinyl top, and it was priced at several hundred dollars less than we were expecting to pay. The seats were covered in black fabric that looked brand new. It had a tape player, air conditioning, and automatic transmission. We were especially pleased that it could get 28 miles per gallon on the highway. The dealer said we could drive it off the lot that very day. The only problem was that he would not take our 1956 Chevrolet with the cracked windshield and bent right fender as a trade-in.

20c Increasing your vocabulary

The benefits of increasing your vocabulary are many. The more words you know, the more easily and the faster you can read. A large, rich vocabulary also helps you understand ideas and communicate them clearly and effectively in your writing. Use the techniques described in Chart 108.

TECHNIQUES FOR BUILDING YOUR VOCABULARY　108

TO FIND WORDS

■ Use a highlighter pen to mark all unfamiliar words in textbooks and other reading material. Then define the words in the margin so you can study the meaning in context. Use context clues (see 20c-2) to figure out definitions, or look up the words in a dictionary. Write each word and its definitions on an index card or in a notebook.

■ Listen carefully to learn how speakers use the language. Jot down new words to look up later. Write each word and its definitions on an index card or in a notebook.

TO STUDY WORDS

■ Select some words that you intend to study each week. Put the date next to the word so that you can keep track of your goals. Whenever you look up a word in your dictionary, put a small checkmark next to it. When you accumulate three checkmarks next to a word, it is time to learn that word.

■ Set aside time each day to study your selected words. Carry your cards or notebook to study in spare moments each day.

■ Use mnemonics (see 22b-2) to help you memorize words. Set a goal of learning eight to ten new words a week. *Use the words in your writing and, when possible, in conversation.*

■ Go back to words from previous weeks, whenever possible. List any words you have not learned well. Study them again, and *use* them.

TEACHING TIP

Knowledge of prefixes and suffixes can help students figure out the meanings of many words. If this skill is coupled with the ability to recognize root words, however, many students' power to decipher new words can increase dramatically. Fundamentally, a root word is a base to which prefixes and suffixes can be added. For example, *-graph* (from the Greek *-graphos,* "to write") refers to something that writes or records, as in *telegraph* or *graphite;* or to something written, as in *paragraph* or the *graphic arts; graphology* is the study of handwriting.

Here are a few of the most common Greek and Latin roots, their meanings, and a sample word built from each root.

LATIN

aequs	equal (equivalent)
amare, amatum	to love (amiable)
dicere, dictum	to say, to speak (diction)
manus	hand (manuscript)
omnis	all (omnipotent)
portare, portatum	to carry (porter)
scribere, scriptum	to write (scribble)
sentire, sensum	to feel (sense)
spirare, spiratum	to breathe (inspiration)
verbum	word (verb)

GREEK

bios	life (biology)
chronos	time (chronology)
gamos	marriage (bigamy)
geo-	earth (geology)
krates (-crat)	member of a group (democrat)
metron	to measure (thermometer)
pathos	suffering, feeling (sympathy)
phobos	fear (agoraphobia)
photos	light (photograph)
podos	foot (tripod)

1 **Knowing prefixes and suffixes**

Prefixes are syllables in front of a **root** word that modify its meaning. *Ante–* (before) placed before the root *bellum* (war) gives *antebellum,* which means "before the war." In American English, *antebellum* refers to the time before the Civil War.

Suffixes are syllables added to the end of a root word that modify its meaning. For example, *excite* is formed by adding the prefix *ex–* (out) to the past participle of *cierce* (to summon). It has various forms when suffixes are added: *excited, exciting, excitedly, excitement.* The part of speech of a word is often signaled by the suffix.

Knowing common prefixes and suffixes listed in Charts 109 and 110, is an excellent way to learn to decode unfamiliar words and increase your vocabulary.

PREFIXES		109
PREFIX	**MEANING**	**EXAMPLE**
ante-	before	*antebellum*
anti-	against	*antiballistic*
auto-	self	*autobiography*
contra-	against	*contradict*
dis-	not	*disagree*
extra-	more	*extraordinary*
hyper-	more	*hyperactive*
il-	not	*illegal*
im-	not	*immoral*
in-	not	*inadequate*
inter-	between	*interpersonal*
intra-	inside	*intravenous*
ir-	not	*irresponsible*
mal-	poor	*malnutrition*
mis-	not	*misunderstood*
mono-	one	*monopoly*
non-	not	*noninvolvement*
poly-	many	*polygamy* →

20c

PREFIXES (*continued*)		
post-	after	*postscript*
pre-	before	*prehistoric*
re-	back	*return*
retro-	back	*retroactive*
semi-	half	*semicircle*
sub-	under	*submissive*
super	more	*supernatural*
trans-	across	*transportation*
ultra-	more	*ultraconservative*
un-	not	*unhappy*
uni-	one	*uniform*

SUFFIXES   110

NOUNS		
SUFFIX	**MEANING**	**EXAMPLE**
-dom	state of	*freedom*
-hood	state of	*childhood*
-ness	state of	*kindness*
-ship	state of	*friendship*
-tion	act of	*integration*
-tude	state of	*solitude*

VERBS		
SUFFIX	**MEANING**	**EXAMPLE**
-ate	to make	*integrate*
-ify	to make	*unify*
-ize	to make	*computerize*

ADJECTIVES		
SUFFIX	**MEANING**	**EXAMPLE**
-able	able to be	*comfortable*
-ate	full of	*fortunate* ➡

EXTRA EXERCISE G

Working in groups and without a dictionary, compile a list of as many words as you can think of that end with the suffixes in the accompanying chart. What does the suffix tell you about the meaning of each word?

BACKGROUND

The growing public awareness of sexism in the English language has resulted in the appearance of numerous books and articles that examine the problem from a variety of viewpoints: those of the sociologist, the psychologist, and the anthropologist, as well as those of the linguist, the writer, and the historian. One of the most perceptive and comprehensive of these books is *Sexism and Language* by Nilsen, Bosmajian, Gershuny, and Stanley (NCTE, 1977). It addresses such matters as sexism in English vocabulary, in literature, in dictionaries, and in children's books. It concludes with the NCTE Guidelines for Nonsexist Use of Language.

BACKGROUND

In an interesting examination of the objectivity of dictionaries, Sidney Landau argues that many American dictionaries present misleading definitions of the word *abortion* ("A Matter of Life and Death," *English Today* 4 [October 1988]: 43–46).

20c

UNDERSTANDING THE MEANING OF WORDS

SUFFIXES (*continued*)

-ible	able to be	*compatible*
-ful	full of	*tactful*
-less	without	*penniless*
-ous	full of	*pompous*
-y	full of	*gloomy*

ANSWERS AND COVERAGE: EXERCISE 20-4

1. illogical [il-]
2. hypersensitive [hyper-]
3. antifreeze [anti-]
4. preexisting [pre-]
5. reconsider [re-]
6. unirail [uni-] *and* monorail [mono-]
7. improper [im-]
8. semicircular [semi-]
9. monotone [mono-]
10. maladjustment [mal-]

ANSWERS AND COVERAGE: EXERCISE 20-5

1. happiness [-ness; noun]
2. flirtation [-tion; noun]
3. roomy [-y; adjective]
4. agreeable [-able; adjective]
5. beautify [-ify; verb]
6. realize [-ize; verb]
7. ceremonious [-ious; adjective]
8. moveable [-able; adjective]
9. worthy [-y; adjective]
10. careless [-less; adjective]

EXERCISE 20-4

Consulting section 20c-1, add a prefix to each italicized word to match the definition given. Use a dictionary if necessary.

EXAMPLE   not *happy* = *unhappy*

1. not *logical*
2. excessively *sensitive*
3. against the *freeze*
4. *existing* before
5. *consider* again
6. one *rail*
7. not *proper*
8. half *circular*
9. one *tone*
10. poor *adjustment*

EXERCISE 20-5

Consulting section 20c-1, add a suffix to each italicized word to match the definition given. Notice that you will be changing the form of the word to match the exact definition. Consult a dictionary to verify spelling.

EXAMPLE   state of being *lazy* = laziness

1. state of being *happy*
2. act of *flirting*
3. full of *room*
4. able to *agree*
5. to make *beautiful*
6. to make *real*
7. full of *ceremony*
8. able to be *moved*
9. full of *worth*
10. without *care*

2   Using context clues to figure out word meanings

The familiar words that surround an unknown word can give you hints about the meaning of the new word. Such **context clues** include four main types.

416

1. **Restatement context clue.** You can figure out an unknown word when a word you know repeats the meaning: *He jumped into the* fray *and enjoyed every minute of the fight. Fray* means "fight." Sometimes a restatement is set off by punctuation. For example, parentheses contain a definition in this sentence: *Fatty deposits on artery walls combine with calcium compounds to cause* arteriosclerosis *(hardening of the arteries).* Sometimes a technical term is set off by punctuation after the definition of a term is given. For example, dashes set off a term after it is defined in this sentence: *The upper left part of the heart—the left* atrium—*receives blood returning from circulation.*

2. **Contrast context clue.** You can figure out an unknown word when an opposite or contrast is presented: *We feared that the new prime minister would be a* menace *to society, but she turned out to be a great peacemaker. Menace* means "threat"; the contrast that explains *menace* is *but she turned out to be a great peacemaker.* As you read, watch for words that express contrast (such as *but, however, nevertheless;* for a complete list see Chart 22 in 4d-1).

3. **Example context clue.** You can figure out an unfamiliar word when an example or illustration relating to the word is given: *They were* conscientious *workers, making sure that everything was done correctly and precisely.* A dictionary defines *conscientious* as "motivated by a desire to do what is right." The words "done correctly and precisely" are close to that meaning.

4. **General sense context clue.** You can use an entire passage to get a general sense of difficult words. For example, in *Nearly forty million Americans are overweight; obesity has become an epidemic,* chances are good that *epidemic* refers to something happening to many people. Sometimes a "general sense context clue" will not make clear a word's exact denotation. For example, you might guess that *epidemic* indicates a widespread threat, but you might miss the connection of the word *epidemic* with the concept of disease. Interpreting the meaning of a word from the general sense carries the risk of allowing subtle variations that distinguish one word from another to slip by. You might want, therefore, to check the exact definition in a dictionary.

Donald Hayes, in "Speaking and Writing:
Distinct Patterns of Word Choice" (*Journal of
Memory and Language* 27 [October 1988]:
572–585), examines patterns of diction at
various skills levels.

QUOTATION ABOUT WRITING

Appropriate words are like appropriate
clothes. Satin and silk don't work at a barbe-
cue, and denim looks strange at the annual
arts ball.

—Jane F. Bonin

TEACHING TIP

Because language varies from one geographic area to another, students who have
lived in several different parts of the country
often know expressions that are used in one
region but not in another. Other members of
a class may find it interesting to hear some
of those regionalisms, afterwards compiling
a list of words and phrases peculiar to their
own area.

BACKGROUND

What constitutes "correct" usage is not as
easy to define as it might seem. In a study of
what university teachers accept as correct,
Herb Smith discovered wide variation. He
reports his findings in "The Fallacy of 'Correct' Usage: An Empirical Study" (*English
Quarterly* 17 [Spring 1984]: 102–108).

21 Understanding the Effect of Words

As words communicate meaning (see Chapter 20), they have an
effect on the people reading or hearing them. As a writer, you want
to choose words carefully. Sometimes the choices available to you
are clearly either right or wrong, but often the choices are subtle. The
guidelines in Chart 111 can help you make good choices.

GUIDELINES FOR EFFECTIVE USE OF LANGUAGE   111

- Use proper level of formality (*see* 21a-1).
- Use edited American English (*see* 21a-2).
- Avoid slang or inappropriate colloquial words or regional words
  (*see* 21a-3).
- Avoid slanted language (*see* 21a-4).
- Avoid sexist language (*see* 21b).
- Use figurative language appropriately (*see* 21c).
- Avoid clichés (*see* 21d).
- Avoid artificial language (*see* 21e).

21a Using appropriate language

As a writer, you need to pay special attention to **tone** (see 1d)
and **diction** (see 20b). You want the words that you use to communicate your meaning as clearly and effectively as possible. Equally
important, your choice of words should work in concert with the

effectiveness of your sentence style (see Chapters 16–19) to create your individual style of writing.

1   Using appropriate levels of formality

Informal and highly formal levels of writing differ clearly in **tone.** They use different vocabulary and sentence structures. Tone in writing indicates the attitude of the writer toward the subject and toward the audience. Tone may be highly formal, informal, or somewhere in between.

Different tones are appropriate for different audiences (see 1c), different subjects, and different purposes (see 1b). An informal tone occurs in casual conversation or letters to friends. A highly formal tone, in contrast, occurs in sermons and proclamations.

Informal language, which creates an informal tone, may include slang, colloquialisms, and regionalisms (see 21a-3). In addition, informal writing often includes sentence fragments (see Chapter 13), contractions, and other forms that approximate casual speech. **Medium** language level uses general English: not too casual, not too scholarly. Unlike informal language, medium-level language is acceptable for academic writing. This level uses standard vocabulary (for example, *learn* instead of *wise up*), conventional sentence structure, and few or no contractions. A **highly formal** language level uses a multisyllabic Latinate vocabulary (*edify* instead of *learn*) and often stylistic flourishes such as extended or complex figures of speech. Academic writing, along with most writing for general audiences, should range from medium to somewhat formal levels of language.

INFORMAL	Ya know stars? They're a gas!
MEDIUM	Gas clouds slowly changed into stars.
FORMAL	The condensations of gas spun their slow gravitational pirouettes, slowly transmogrifying gas cloud into star.

—CARL SAGAN, "Starfolk: A Fable"

The informal example would be appropriate in a letter to a close friend or in a journal. The writer's attitude toward the subject is playful and humorous; the word choice and sentence structure assume great familiarity between writer and audience. The medium example would be appropriate in most academic and professional situations. The writer's attitude toward the subject is serious and straightforward. The formal example is addressed to an audience

---

After analyzing the sentences that follow, decide if they are in formal, medium, or informal language. Which words are particularly effective in establishing the level of usage in the sentence?

1. Weather forecasting is a pretty good field to be in.

2. My old man watches the TV weather news every morning.

3. It takes a lot of work to put a forecast together.

4. The Weather Bureau collects data from reporting stations that, after analysis, are reported to the public as forecasts, weather maps, and storm warnings.

5. The Bureau conducts research on a variety of topics from solar radiation and the ozone layer to snowfall patterns.

6. My father just wants to know if it's going to rain.

7. I can't get into all that stuff either.

8. You gotta admit that the Bureau has done plenty of good things.

9. In 1942 Dr. F. W. Reichelderfer was the recipient of a prestigious award for his pioneering work in advancing the practice of meteorology as applied to aeronautics.

ANSWERS: EXTRA EXERCISE A

1. Informal: pretty good, field, be in

2. Informal: old man

3. Informal: a lot of

4. Formal: collects data

5. Medium: familiar words, but no slang, throughout

6. Medium: just wants to know, it's, going to

7. Informal: get into, all that stuff

8. Informal: gotta admit, plenty, good things

9. Formal: recipient, prestigious award, practice of meteorology, applied to aeronautics

BACKGROUND

The subject of Standard English has been the focus of intense interest over the past decade. Numerous journal articles have approached the topic from a variety of viewpoints. Two recent treatments have been published by James Sledd and Samuel H. Stein. In "Product in Process: From Ambiguities of Standard English to Issues That Divide Us" (*College English* 50 [February 1988]: 168–176), Sledd argues that Standard English is a means of maintaining cultural domination over minorities. He examines the issue in terms of classroom instruction. Stein explores the effects of language that divides groups of people in an article entitled "The Language of Inequality" (*ETC: A Review of General Semantics* 45 [Spring 1988]: 52–56). He urges speakers and writers to refer to individuals as individuals.

EXTRA EXERCISE B

Rewrite the following advertisements so that they conform to edited American English.

1. Arizona. You don't have to rough it to love it. Because today's Arizona is more than cactus and high-country wilderness. It's world-class resorts. Fine dining. Year-round championship golf. It's all the natural beauty you've imagined, and more luxuries than you'd ever dream. Shopping. Exploring. Endless sunny blue skies . . . and all the history and spirit of the American West.

> Arizona, The Grand Canyon State
> *The New Yorker*, December 16, 1991

2. There are places in the heart where the hubris of civilization is stripped away. Summer cabins. Bungalows on the beach. A hidden lake touched by the first breath of autumn. Places with an unpretentious quality that we intuitively recognize as genuine and right. Such are the characteristics of our

➡

with considerable interest in and knowledge of scientific phenomena, such as readers of a science journal.

2 Using edited American English for academic writing

The language standards that you are expected to use in academic writing are those of **edited American English:** the accepted written language of a book like this handbook or a magazine like *U.S. News & World Report* or *National Geographic.* Such language conforms to widely established rules of grammar, sentence structure, punctuation, and spelling. Because advertising language and other language intended to reach and sway a large audience often ignore conventional usage, readers often encounter written English that varies from the standard. Do not let these published departures from edited American English influence you into believing they are acceptable in academic writing.

Edited English is not a fancy dialect for the elite. It is a practical form of the language that educated people use. As a student writer, you might find that early drafts of your essays contain language that departs from edited American English. When you use edited American English in your academic writing, you will not risk distracting your readers from the message you want to communicate. Do not, however, revise your words too early in the writing process (see Chapter 3), or you will risk being distracted from getting your ideas onto paper.

3 Avoiding slang and colloquial or regional language for most academic writing

Slang consists of coined words and new meanings attached to established terms. Slang words and phrases usually pass out of use quickly, although occasionally they become accepted into standard usage. **Colloquial** language is characteristic of casual conversation and informal writing: *The student flunked chemistry* instead of *the student failed chemistry.*

Slang words are used only in very informal situations. Sometimes slang terms are inventions: *beatnik* from the 1950s became *hippie* in the 1960s. In the 1980s, *yuppie* was popular. Sometimes slang terms are redefinitions of existing words. For example, *awesome* has been used informally for "excellent" or "wonderful," as has *wired* for "nervous." Slang varies according to time and place. For example, slang in New York City in the early 1990s has included *be sword* for "relax, be cool" and *say what?* for "excuse me?" These expressions might not communicate the same meanings to teenagers in California in the 1990s or to teenagers anywhere by the year 2000. At no time, however, does slang communicate accurate meanings in academic or business writing.

Regional language (also called *dialectal* language) is specific to some geographic areas. A *dragonfly* is a *snake feeder* in parts of Delaware, a *darning needle* in parts of Michigan, and a *snake doctor* or *ear sewer* in parts of the southern United States. Dialects are different from slang because dialectical differences reflect geographical regions and socioeconomic status. Using a dialect when writing for the general reading public tends to shut some people out of the communication. Except when dialect is the topic of the writing, academic writing rarely accommodates dialect well.

Although slang, colloquial words, and regional language are neither substandard nor illiterate, they are usually not appropriate for academic writing. Replacing them in your college writing allows you to communicate clearly with the large number of people who speak and write in medium or somewhat formal levels of language (see 21a-1).

---

4   **Avoiding slanted language**

To communicate clearly, you will want to choose words that convince your audience of your fairness as a writer. When you are writing about a subject on which you hold strong opinions, it is easy to slip into biased or emotionally loaded language. Such **slanted language** usually does not convince a careful reader to agree with your point. Instead, it makes the reader wary or hostile. For example, suppose you are arguing against the practice of scientific experimentation on animals. If you use language such as "laboratory Frankensteins" who "routinely and viciously maim helpless kittens and puppies," you are using slanted language. You want to use words that make your side of an issue the more convincing one. Once you start using slanted, biased language, readers feel manipulated rather than reasoned with.

21b   **Avoiding sexist language**

Sexist language assigns roles or characteristics to people on the basis of gender. Most women *and* men today feel that sexist

---

Cont'd.

outdoor clothing and gear. Created with an enduring sense of style and tradition. And imbued with the spirit of a place you once knew, and want to find again.

Eddie Bauer
The New Yorker, September 2, 1991

Quite simply, Hartmann is dedicated to building the best case. With the best leathers. The best tweed. The best vinyl. And the best locks. Hartmann. No one builds a better a case.

Hartmann Luggage
The New Yorker, May 29, 1989

Getting to gate 87 in two minutes isn't always easy. Anyone who travels on business knows how hard it can be. Which is why we've made getting AT&T so easy. Even at public phones that aren't automatically connected to AT&T. If you're calling long distance and you don't hear "AT&T" after the bong, simply hang up.

AT&T
The New Yorker, December 30, 1991

TEACHING TIP

Discussions about slanted language make students more aware of biased writing. A logical follow-up assignment is to ask them to be alert to loaded diction in news articles and television broadcasts. Examples are particularly abundant during an election year. The words and phrases students collect can be the basis of another lesson, this one specific and close to home.

language unfairly discriminates against both sexes. Sexist language inaccurately assumes all nurses and homemakers are female (and therefore refers to them as "she") and all physicians and wage earners are male (and therefore refers to them as "he"). One of the most widespread occurrences of sexist language is the use of the pronoun *he* to refer to someone of unidentified sex. Although tradition holds that *he* is correct in such situations, using only masculine pronouns to represent the human species excludes women and thereby distorts reality.

If you want to avoid sexist language in your writing, follow the guidelines in Chart 112. Also, you can avoid sexism by avoiding demeaning, outdated stereotypes, such as *women are bad drivers* or *men are bad cooks*. Do not describe a woman by her looks, clothes, or age (unless you do the same for men). Do not use the first name of one spouse when you use a title (such as *Mr., Dr.,* or *Mrs.*) and the last name for the other spouse: *Phil Miller* [not *Mr. Miller*] *and his wife, Jeannette, always travel on separate planes* or *Jeannette and Phil Miller live in Idaho.*

HOW TO AVOID SEXIST LANGUAGE   112

- Avoid using only the masculine pronoun to refer to males and females together. Use a pair of pronouns.

  NO   A doctor has little time to read outside **his** specialty.

  YES   A doctor has little time to read outside **his or her** specialty.

The "he or she" construction acts as a singular pronoun, and it therefore calls for a singular verb when it serves as the subject of a sentence. Try to avoid using the "he or she" construction, especially more than once in a sentence or in consecutive sentences. Revising into the plural may be a better solution.

  NO   A successful doctor knows that **he** has to work long hours.

  YES   Successful doctors know that **they** have to work long hours.

You may also recast a sentence to omit the gender-specific pronoun.

  NO   Everyone hopes that **he** will win the scholarship.

  YES   Everyone hopes to win the scholarship.

HOW TO AVOID SEXIST LANGUAGE (*continued*)

■ Avoid the use of *man* when men and women are clearly intended in the meaning.

NO   **Man** is a social animal.

YES **People** are social animals.

NO   A **man's** best friend is a dog.

YES A **person's** best friend is a dog.

■ Avoid stereotyping jobs and roles by gender when men and women are included.

NO	YES
chairman	chair, chairperson
policeman	police officer
businessman	businessperson, business executive
statesman	diplomat, prime minister, statesperson

NO   teacher . . . **she**; principal . . . **he**

YES teachers . . . **they**; principals . . . **they**

■ Avoid expressions that exclude either sex.

NO	YES
mankind	humanity
the common man	the average person
man-sized sandwich	huge sandwich
old wives' tale	superstition

■ Avoid using demeaning and patronizing labels.

NO	YES
lady lawyer	lawyer
male nurse	nurse
gal Friday	assistant
career girl	professional woman
coed	student

NO   My **girl** will send it.

YES My **secretary** will send it.

Heidi Moore will send it.

TEACHING TIP

In addition to the techniques given in Chart 112, How to Avoid Sexist Language, here are a few additional tactics.

1. When appropriate, use the first person or the second person.

No A person should always keep an eye on his luggage in airports.

Yes I should always keep my eye on my luggage in airports.

Yes We should always keep an eye on our luggage in airports.

Yes Keep an eye on your luggage in airports.

2. Repeat a noun or use a synonym in place of the troublesome pronoun.

No A preoccupied traveler is an easy target for thieves, who can pick his pocket in a second.

Yes A preoccupied traveler is an easy target for thieves, who pick a traveler's pocket in a second.

Yes A preoccupied traveler is an easy target for thieves, who can pick a tourist's pocket in a second.

3. Use *who*.

No A traveler has little to worry about, if he stays alert.

Yes A traveler who stays alert has little to worry about.

ANSWERS: EXERCISE 21-1

Answers will vary. Here are some possible nonsexist versions.

1. An individual's sense of space and distance is variable.

2. People establish their own "personal space" by what they can do, not what they can see, in a given area.

3. A parent is usually seen standing very close to his or her children. [*or* Parents are usually . . . to their children.]

4. Politicians, too, usually stand close to talk with one or two constituents but many feet away from large groups of people to whom they are talking.

5. The sizes of people's "bubbles" of personal space vary with their culture or ethnicity.

6. Germans will go to great lengths to preserve their "private sphere" at home and at work.

7. English businesspeople, however, are used to a common work space at the office.

8. For that reason, they are willing to exist close to their co-workers.

9. Some U.S. business executives use other people in the office to help protect their personal bubbles.

10. They have assistants [*or secretaries* or *receptionists*] announce all visitors and screen all phone calls.

BACKGROUND

In "A Sheepish Tongue" (*English Today* 4 [April 1988]: 24–25), Vernon Noble looks at the occupation of sheep-rearing to assess its contribution to the English language. He discusses metaphors, sayings, and colloquialisms that the field has provided for general usage.

EXERCISE 21-1

Consulting section 21b, revise the following sentences by changing sexist language to nonsexist language.

1. Man's sense of space and distance is variable.

2. Everyone establishes his own "personal space" by what he can do, not what he can see, in a given area.

3. A mother is usually seen standing very close to her children.

4. A lady politician, too, usually stands close to talk with one or two of her constituents but many feet away from large groups of people to whom she is talking.

5. The size of a person's "bubble" of personal space varies with his culture or ethnicity.

6. A German will go to great lengths to preserve his "private sphere" at home and at work.

7. An Englishman, however, is used to a common work space at the office.

8. For that reason, he is willing to exist close to his fellow workers.

9. Some U.S. businessmen use the ladies who work in the office to help protect their personal bubbles.

10. They have the office girls announce all visitors and screen all phone calls.

21c   Using figurative language

Figures of speech use words for more than their literal meanings, yet they are not merely decorative. **Figurative language** enhances meaning. It makes comparisons and connections that draw on one idea or image to explain another.

TYPES OF FIGURATIVE LANGUAGE   113

■ **Analogy:** a comparison of similar traits between dissimilar things (The length of an analogy can range from one sentence to a paragraph—see 4f-8—to an entire essay.)

A cheetah sprinting across the dry plains after its prey, the base runner dashed for home plate.

→

TYPES OF FIGURATIVE LANGUAGE (*continued*)

- **Irony:** the use of words to suggest the opposite of their usual sense

  > Told that the car repair would cost $2,000 and take at least two weeks, she said, "Oh, that would be wonderful!"

- **Metaphor:** a comparison between otherwise dissimilar things without using the word *like* or *as* (Be alert to avoid the error of a mixed metaphor, explained in the text.)

  > The rush-hour traffic bled out of all the city's major arteries.

- **Overstatement** (also called *hyperbole*): deliberate exaggeration for emphasis

  > Andrew Marvell says praising his love's eyes and forehead would take 100 years.

- **Personification:** the assignment of a human trait to a nonhuman thing

  > The book begged to be read.

- **Simile:** a direct comparison between otherwise dissimilar things, using the word *like* or *as*

  > Langston Hughes says that a deferred dream dries up like a raisin in the sun.

- **Understatement:** deliberate restraint for emphasis

  > It gets a little warm when the temperature reaches 105 degrees.

A mixed metaphor combines images that do not work well together. Consider this sentence, for example: *Milking the migrant workers for all they were worth, the supervisors barked orders at them.* Here the initial image is of taking milk from a cow, but the final image has supervisors barking, an action suggesting dogs. Avoid confusing your reader by combining two or more images that do not blend well.

EXERCISE 21-2

Consulting section 21c, identify each figure of speech. Also, revise any mixed metaphors.

1. The challenger, another Goliath, fell with the first blow.
2. They were captured by the glow of the moon, dragging them deeper and deeper into the sea.

WORD DERIVATIONS

Metaphor comes from *metapherein* (Greek for "to transfer"), a combination of *pherein* ("to carry") and *meta* ("over"). A metaphor carries over the meaning. The first recorded use of the word in English was by Henry VIII in 1533: "And rather than men would note a lye when they know what is meant, they will sooner by allegory or metaphor draw the word to the truth."

Simile comes from *similis* (Latin for "like"). Similes always contain *like* or *as*, making the comparison explicit. *Simile* was first used in 1393 in William Langland's "Piers Plowman."

TEACHING TIP

Sports have been a fertile field for metaphor in America. You might remind your students of these common metaphors. What does each mean within its sport? What does each mean in a general context? You might also ask students if they can add to the lists or start lists for other sports or interests. Many metaphors listed here are discussed in Tim Considine's "Starting from Scratch" (*New York Times*, June 8, 1985).

Soccer	*Football*
kick off	huddle
get the ball rolling	chalk talk
Baseball	a flag on the play
right off the bat	all-American
off base	*Boxing*
touch base with	answer the bell
go to bat for	a low blow
out of left field	below the belt
drop the ball	on the ropes

ANSWERS AND COVERAGE: EXERCISE 21-2

1. metaphor

2. mixed metaphor

➡

ANSWERS AND COVERAGE: EXERCISE 21-2, *continued*

3. personification
4. understatement
5. simile
6. analogy
7. overstatement
8. metaphor
9. simile
10. irony

3. The ocean screamed its fury.
4. Triple bypass heart surgery is no tea party.
5. The champion was like a cobra ready to strike.
6. The individual bees worked together in the hive, the separate parts of a single, purposeful animal.
7. The world ended when his parents divorced.
8. The inventor's ideas took root and grew, seeds becoming flowers.
9. At night, the lights along the bridge's suspension cables looked like a giant diamond necklace mounted on black velvet in a celestial jewelry showcase.
10. Changing a flat tire is exactly how I love to spend my time.

21d   Avoiding clichés

A **cliché** is an overused, worn-out expression that has lost its capacity to communicate effectively. Some comparisons, once clever, have grown trite: *dead as a doornail, gentle as a lamb, straight as an arrow.* If you have heard words over and over again, so has your reader. If you cannot think of a way to rephrase a cliché, delete the phrase entirely.

Clichés are not created simply by being repeated or by becoming overly familiar. English is full of word groups that are frequently used yet are not clichés (for example, *up and down* and *in and out*). Common patterns are not clichés and need not be avoided.

ANSWERS: EXERCISE 21-3

Answers to this exercise will vary. Here is one set of possibilities.

1. If you want a sale, you have to take control of the situation.

2. You can't be indirect when it comes to getting a sale.

3. Being aggressive means getting the attention of prospective buyers with an impressive sales presentation.

4. To make customers happy, give them a good product and good service.

5. Eventually customers realize that you are there to help them.

EXERCISE 21-3

Consulting section 21d, revise these clichés. Use the idea in each cliché for a sentence of your own in plain English.

1. If you want a sale, you have to take the bull by the horns.
2. You can't beat around the bush when it comes to getting a sale.
3. Being aggressive means knocking the socks off prospective buyers with an impressive sales pitch.
4. To make customers as happy as a lark, give them a good product and good service.
5. Slowly but surely, customers realize that you are there to help them.

21e   Avoiding artificial language

Sometimes student writers think that ornate words and complicated sentence structures make writing impressive. Experienced writers, however, work hard to communicate as clearly and directly as they can. As a student writer, avoid long, fancy words to explain a point. Try to make what you write as accessible as possible to your readers. Extremely complex ideas or subject areas may require complex terms or phrases to explain them, but in general the simpler the language, the more likely it will be understood.

1   Avoiding pretentious language

Pretentious language is too showy, calling undue attention to itself with complex sentences and polysyllabic words. Academic writing does not call for big words used for their own sake. Overblown words are likely to obscure your message.

> As I alighted from my vehicle, my clothing was besmirched with filth. [*Translation:* My coat got dirty as I got out of my car.]

> I hate it when he tries ostentatiously to flaunt his accoutrements recently acquired in the haberdashery shop. [*Translation:* I hate it when he tries to show off his new clothes.]

2   Avoiding unnecessary jargon

Jargon is specialized vocabulary of a particular group. It consists of words that an outsider might not understand. As you write, consider your purpose (see 1b) and audience (see 1c) to decide whether a word is jargon in the context of your material. For example, a football fan easily understands a sportswriter's use of words such as *punt, sacked,* and *safety,* but they are jargon to people not familiar with football. Specialized language evolves in every field: professions, academic disciplines (see Chapters 36–38), business, and even hobbies. Avoid using jargon unnecessarily. When you must use jargon for a general audience, be sure to explain the specialized meanings.

BACKGROUND

Jargon and euphemisms are not forms of language often recommended by teachers. However, Stephen Fry and David Shults have taken unusual positions in their articles on these kinds of expressions. Fry argues that jargon is sometimes preferable to plain language because people today lack a common understanding of many words ("Who Knows?: Purchasing Comprehension with Linguistic Currency," *ETC: A Review of General Semantics* 45 [Fall 1988]: 256–257). In "Soothespeak" Shults defends the use of some euphemisms (*Quarterly Review of Doublespeak* 15 [October 1988]: 11–12).

TEACHING TIP

Walker Gibson examines the meaning of the term *doublespeak* by searching out its origins, then expanding its definition ("On Defining Doublespeak," *Quarterly Review of Doublespeak* 14 [April 1988]: 8–9).

Students who are interested in finding examples of doublespeak should refer to *Quarterly Review of Doublespeak,* published by the National Council of Teachers of English. The journal publishes articles that report doublespeak in business, education, government, law, medicine, and the military. See, for example, Michael Johanel's "Edspeak 1988," an examination of doublespeak in education which was published in *QRD* in January 1988, or "Campaign '88 Doublespeak," which appeared in April of the same year. In addition, *QRD* makes annual awards for the most notable instances of doublespeak that have appeared in a given year.

This example shows acceptable specialized language. It is from a college textbook that assumes students know or can decipher the meaning of *eutrophicates, terrestrial,* and *eutrophic.*

ACCEPTABLE SPECIALIZED LANGUAGE

As the lake eutrophicates, it gradually fills until the entire lake will be converted into a terrestrial community. Eutrophic changes (or eutrophication) is the nutritional enrichment of the water, promoting the growth of aquatic plants.

—DAVIS AND SOLOMON, *The World of Biology*

3 Avoiding euphemisms

Euphemisms attempt to avoid the harsh reality of truth by using more pleasant-sounding, "tactful" words. The word *euphemism* comes from the Greek meaning "words of good omen" (*eu-,* "good" + *pheme,* "voice").

Euphemisms are, of course, sometimes necessary for tact in social situations (using *passed away* instead of *died* when offering condolences, for example). In other situations, euphemisms drain meaning from truthful writing. Unnecessary euphemisms might describe socially unacceptable behavior (for example, *Johnny has a wonderfully vivid imagination* instead of *Johnny lies*). Unnecessary euphemisms might try to hide unpleasant facts (*She is between assignments* instead of *She lost her job*).

4 Avoiding "doublespeak"

Doublespeak is artificial, evasive language. It aims to distort and deceive. For example, many automobile dealerships today have renamed "used cars" as "pre-owned cars" or "previously distinguished cars." A major corporation has described its notice that laid off 5,000 workers as a "career alternative enhancement package." The Pentagon has used "collateral damage" for unintended killing of innocent civilians.

To use doublespeak is to try to hide the truth, a highly unethical practice that seeks to control people's thoughts. So severe has the doublespeak problem become in our society that the National Council of Teachers of English yearly announces a Doublespeak Award to the "best" example of language that purposely misleads. A recent nominee for the award went to a foreign government for calling hostages "foreign guests" whose guards are "hosts." An award went to a U.S. Representative for saying the Congress "did not raise taxes," it "sought new revenues." Such misuses of language have devastating social and political consequences in a free society. As a writer, always avoid using doublespeak; use language truthfully.

5   Avoiding bureaucratic language

Bureaucratic language is stuffy and overblown.

You can include a page that also contains an Include instruction. The page including the Include instruction is included when you paginate the document but the included text referred to in its Include instruction is not included.

The irony in this example is that the writer seems to be trying to communicate very precisely. Bureaucratic language (or *bureaucratese*, the coined word to describe the style) is marked by unnecessary complexity. Always avoid such meaningless writing.

EXERCISE 21-4

Consulting section 21e, revise these examples of pretentious language, jargon, euphemism, "doublespeak," and bureaucratic language.

1. The memorandum previously circulated should be ignored and replaced by the memorandum sent before the previous one. The memorandum presently being held by the reader should be attached to the previous one.
2. At a commercial postal delivery service, the "least-best" drivers are the ones who have poor driving and/or delivery records.
3. She came within the venue of the law enforcement establishment.
4. It is with grave misgivings that I undertake this endeavor to instruct myself in the intricacies of computer programming.
5. They are awaiting a little bundle of joy from heaven.
6. The administrative assistant typed an epistle for his superior.
7. Her occupation is domestic engineering.
8. Our airline is experiencing "scheduling irregularities"; they are not called "delays."
9. The cat passed away and now reposes in the Slumber Pet Cemetery.
10. For fire safety, all homes must have a "combustion enunciator" to warn people of smoke.

Cont'd.

health is viewed as an evolving process which occurs throughout the life span of enfamilied selves in interrelationship with the ecosystem. Family health is perceived as expansion of consciousness of enfamilied selves."

■ When several women's groups protested the Pakistani law that accords the legal testimony of women half the weight of the testimony of men, Qazi Hussain Ahmed, leader of the Islamic Party, said, "These laws do not affect women adversely. Our system wants to protect women from unnecessary worry and save them the trouble of appearing in court."

        —*New York Times,* June 14, 1988, p. A1

ANSWERS AND COVERAGE: EXERCISE 21-4

1. The first memorandum you received should replace the one that followed it. Please attach this notice to the cancelled version [bureaucratic].

2. At a commercial postal delivery service, some employees have poor driving and/or delivery records [doublespeak].

3. She was arrested [jargon].

4. I am worried about teaching myself to become a computer programmer [pretentious].

5. They are expecting a baby [euphemism].

6. The administrative assistant typed a letter for his boss [pretentious].

7. She is a housewife [euphemism].

8. Our airline is experiencing delays [doublespeak].

9. When their cat died, they buried it at Slumber Haven Pet Cemetery [euphemism].

10. For fire safety, all homes must have a smoke alarm [bureaucratic].

Focus on Revising

REVISING YOUR WRITING

If you need to write using more effective words, go back to your writing and locate the ineffective words. Using this chapter as a resource, revise your writing to communicate effectively through using appropriate language (21a), avoiding sexist language (21b), correctly using figurative language (21c), and eliminating clichés (21d) and artificial language (21e).

CASE STUDY: REVISING FOR EFFECTIVE LANGUAGE

In these case studies, you can observe a student writer revising. Then you have the chance to revise other student writing on your own.

Observation

A student wrote the following draft for a course called American Government. The assignment was to present a situation in which legislation designed to protect the rights of one group necessarily infringes on the rights of another. The material focuses on the essential features of the controversy, but the draft's effectiveness is diminished by errors in the use of language.

Read through the draft. The errors are highlighted and explained. Before you look at the student's revision, revise the material yourself. Then compare what you and the student did.

slang: 21a-3

In 1961, Great Britain's Royal College of Physicians issued a report that served as a major downer for the tobacco industry worldwide. The report said that medical researchers had found that smoking was directly related to health problems. The Report of the U.S. Surgeon General confirmed those findings nine years later, and the U.S. Congress bureaucratic language: 21e-5

mixed metaphor: 21c

overly informal: 21a-1

sexist language: 21b

slanted language: 21a-4

pretentious language: 21e-1

inappropriate colloquial language: 21a-3

cliché: 21d

slang: 21a-3

slang: 21a-3

embarked on a policy of disallowing cigarette advertising on television. Then, in the late 1980s, a whole lot was widely known about the bad effects of smoking on smokers and nonsmokers alike. Advocates of a smoke-free environment began to get their feet wet and rushed into battle. "Clean air" ordinances, "smoke-free" work zones, and smoking bans on some airplane flights resulted.

These regulations have upset a vocal minority of smokers, who say that bans constitute "unfair discrimination." Sometimes actions speak louder than words. Before fines were legislated by the federal government, stewardesses and stewards on one airline found themselves physically grappling with selfish, unreasonable passengers who acted like pigs by insisting on lighting up during a nonsmoking flight. Before nonsmoking regulations went into effect at most restaurants across the nation, some dining establishments experienced an exodus of patrons to restaurants in nearby communities that had no smoking prohibitions. The days of being able to grab a smoke at any place and time seem to be over or smokers. Still, exchanging gripes is likely to continue between smokers and nonsmokers.

COVERAGE: PARTICIPATION ESSAY

The average person needs to sleep seven and a half to eight hours every twenty-four hours. What happens to a person when he loses *his* [21b: sexist language] needed *shut eye* [21a-3: slang]?

When a person does not sleep one night *his* [21b: sexist language] divergent thinking suffers. Divergent thinking calls for originality and flexibility. Convergent thinking, on the other hand, is possible. *Notwithstanding the deprivation of a sole night's lapse into a sleep modality* [21e-1: pretentious language], a person can perform routine, familiar tasks. Even those tasks, however, become almost impossible to do when a person loses *forty winks* [21a-3: colloquial] for two nights.

This information comes as a result of a study at Loughborough University in England. The researchers used a group of twenty-four healthy students. First, all the students took an *array of assessments that measure the duration of time it usually takes people to perform certain tasks of cognitive activity* [21e-1: pretentious language]. The tests had no right answers. Instead, the tests called for originality and the ability to elaborate on thoughts. Students had to be *quick on the uptake* [21d: cliche] to respond to the questions. One question required the students to think of as many uses as possible for a cardboard box. Another question asked students to imagine the consequences if

➡

COVERAGE: PARTICIPATION ESSAY, *continued*

clouds had strings attached to them that hung down to earth.

After the tests, the students were divided into two subgroups that were evenly matched on their scores on the thinking tests. One subgroup slept as usual. The other subgroup stayed up all night, fighting off any *somnolent* [21a: overly formal] feelings. The next day, all the students were retested. During the second night, the subgroup that had slept was once again allowed to sleep. The other subgroup again stayed up all night, even though the members felt *dead as dogs* [21d: cliché] All the students retook the tests the next day. On the average, the students who had spent two nights without sleep did far worse than did the students in the other subgroup. After one night, divergent thinking suffered; after two nights, convergent thinking *went into a nose dive* [21d: cliché].

This research has important implications for students. *Hitting the books* [21a-3: slang] all night before a test is *really a pretty* [21a-1: overly informal] bad mistake. Abilities to analyze information or answer an essay question are severely reduced after the loss of one night's sleep.

ANSWER: PARTICIPATION ESSAY

This version revises the errors in language use, though answers will likely vary somewhat from those shown here. Also, answers will vary if students have revised content, organization, or style.

The average person needs to sleep seven and a half to eight hours every twenty-four hours. What happens to a person who loses needed sleep?

When a person does not sleep one night, divergent thinking suffers. Divergent thinking calls for originality and flexibility. Convergent thinking, on the

Here is how the student revised the paragraph to correct errors in language use. In a few places, the student had alternatives for correcting the errors. Your revision, therefore, might not be exactly like this one, but it should deal with each error highlighted on the draft.

In 1961, Great Britain's Royal College of Physicians issued a report that hurt the tobacco industry worldwide. The report said that medical researchers had found that smoking was directly related to health problems. The Report of the U.S. Surgeon General confirmed those findings nine years later, and the U.S. Congress passed a law prohibiting cigarette advertising on television. Then, in the late 1980s, much was widely known about the bad effects of smoking on smokers and nonsmokers alike. Advocates of a smoke-free environment began to work actively for their cause. "Clean-air" ordinances, "smoke-free" work zones, and smoking bans on some airplane flights resulted.

These regulations have upset a vocal minority of smokers, who say that bans constitute "unfair discrimination." Sometimes the smokers have taken action. Before fines were legislated by the federal government, flight attendants on one airline found themselves physically grappling with passengers who insisted on smoking during a nonsmoking flight. Before nonsmoking regulations went into effect at most restaurants across the nation, some dining establishments lost customers to restaurants in nearby communities that had no smoking prohibitions. The days of being able to smoke at any place and time seem to be over for smokers. Still, friction is likely to continue between smokers and nonsmokers.

Participation

A student wrote the following draft for a course called Introduction to Psychology. The assignment was to explain the effects of sleep on thinking processes. The material is well organized and uses specific details, but the draft's effectiveness is diminished by errors in use of language.

Read through the draft. Then revise it to eliminate the errors. Also, make any additional revisions you think would improve the content, organization, and style of the material.

The average person needs to sleep seven and a half to eight hours every twenty-four hours. What happens to a person when he loses his needed shut-eye?

When a person does not sleep one night, his divergent thinking suffers. Divergent thinking calls for originality and flexibility. Convergent thinking, on the other hand, is possible. Notwithstanding the deprivation of a sole night's lapse into a sleep modality, a person can perform routine, familiar tasks. Even those tasks, however, become almost impossible to do when a person loses forty winks for two nights.

This information comes as a result of a study at Loughborough University in England. The researchers used a group of twenty-four healthy students. First, all the students took an array of assessments that measure the duration of time it usually takes people to perform certain tasks of cognitive activity. The tests had no right answers. Instead, the tests called for originality and the ability to elaborate on thoughts. Students had to be quick on the uptake to respond to the questions. One question required the students to think of as many uses as possible for a cardboard box. Another question asked students to imagine the consequences if clouds had strings attached to them that hung down to earth.

After the tests, the students were divided into two subgroups that were evenly matched on their scores on the thinking tests. One subgroup slept as usual. The other subgroup stayed up all night, fighting off any somnolent feelings. The next day, all the students were retested. During the second night, the subgroup that had slept was once again allowed to sleep. The other subgroup again stayed up all night, even though the members felt dead as dogs. All the students retook the tests the next day. On the average, the students who had spent two nights without sleep did far worse than did the students in the other subgroup. After one night, divergent thinking suffered; after two nights, convergent thinking went into a nose dive.

This research has important implications for students. Hitting the books all night before a test is really a pretty bad mistake. Abilities to analyze information or answer an essay question are severely reduced after the loss of one night's sleep.

Cont'd.

other hand, is possible. In spite of losing one night's sleep, a person can perform routine, familiar tasks. Even those tasks, however, become almost impossible to do when a person loses needed sleep for two nights.

This information comes as a result of a study at Loughborough University in England. The researchers used a group of twenty-four healthy students. First, all the students took a set of tests that measure how long certain thinking tasks usually take. The tests had no right answers. Instead, the tests called for originality and the ability to elaborate on thoughts. Students had to be clever and quick to respond to the questions. One question required the students think of as many uses as possible for a cardboard box. Another question asked students to imagine the consequences if clouds had strings attached to them that hung down to earth.

After the tests, the students were divided into two subgroups that were evenly matched on their scores on the thinking tests. One subgroup slept as usual. The other subgroup stayed up all night, fighting off any drowsy feelings. The next day, all the students were retested. During the second night, the subgroup that had slept was once again allowed to sleep. The other subgroup again stayed up all night, even though the members were exhausted. All the students retook the tests the next day. On the average, the students who had spent two nights without sleep did far worse than did the students in the other subgroup. After one night, divergent thinking suffered; after two nights, convergent thinking declined sharply.

This research has important implications for students. Studying all night before a test is surely a bad mistake. Abilities to analyze information or answer an essay question are severely reduced after the loss of one night's sleep.

22 Spelling and Hyphenation

You might be surprised to know this about good spellers: They do not always remember how to spell every word they write, but they are very skilled at sensing when they should check the spelling of a word. Try, therefore, not to ignore your quiet inner voice that doubts a spelling; listen to it and look up the word. At the same time, do not allow spelling doubts to interrupt the flow of your writing during drafting (see 3b). Underline or circle words you want to check, and go back to them when you are editing (see 3d) your writing.

How do you look up a word in the dictionary if you do not know how to spell it? If you know the first few letters, find the general area for the word and browse for it. If you do not know how a word begins, try to find it listed in a thesaurus under an easy-to-spell synonym°. When you are writing on a computer, you can usually use a program that checks spelling. Be careful, though, to proofread for spelling errors that result when you substitute another correctly spelled word for the word that you intend (for example, *whole* if you mean *hole*).

As you spell, be aware that the various origins and ways English-speaking people pronounce words make it almost impossible to rely solely on pronunciation to spell a word. What you *can* rely on is using a system of proofreading and using spelling rules.

22a Eliminating careless spelling errors

Many spelling errors are the result of illegible handwriting, slips of the pen, or typographical mistakes. Catching "typos" requires especially careful proofreading, using the techniques in Chart 114. (To handwrite corrections of typos, follow the guidance in Appendix B, section B3.)

<table>
<tr><td>114</td></tr>
</table>

TECHNIQUES FOR PROOFREADING FOR SPELLING

1. Slow down your reading speed so that you can concentrate on individual letters of words rather than on the meaning of the words.
2. Stay within your "visual span," the number of letters you can identify with a single glance (for most people, about six letters).
3. Put a ruler or large index card under each line as you proofread, to focus your concentration and vision.
4. Read each paragraph *backwards,* from the last sentence to the first. This method helps to prevent your being distracted by the meaning of the material.

22b Spelling homonyms and commonly confused words

Homonyms are words that sound exactly like others (*its, it's; morning, mourning*). There are also many words that sound so much alike that they are often confused with each other. A comprehensive list appears here (also, the most common sets are included in the Usage Glossary at the back of this handbook).

One source of confusion not covered by this list is "swallowed" pronunciation. For example, if a speaker fails to pronounce the letter *-d* at the end of words ("swallows" it), a writer may put down *use to, suppose to,* or *prejudice* when *used to, supposed to,* or *prejudiced* is required.

Another source of confusion is expressions that are always written as two words, not one: for example, *all right,* [not *alright*] and *a lot* [not *alot*].

The best way to remember how to distinguish between homonyms and between other commonly confused words is to use memory devices (mnemonics). For example, if you have trouble with the homonyms *stationary* and *stationery,* try this: *Stationary* means standing (*a* is in both) still while *stationery* is written (*e* is in both) on.

A HUMOROUS NOTE
In *Anguished English* (Wyrick and Company, 1988), Richard Lederer reprints some misspellings that convey unintended, and comical, meanings. Here are a few of those he has collected.

1. They gave William IV a lovely funeral. It took six men to carry the beer.
2. On Thanksgiving morning we could smell the foul cooking.
3. I am in the mists of choosing colleges.
4. During peek season the beach is covered with hundreds of bikini-clad beauties.
5. In Pittsburgh they manufacture iron and steal.

WORDS OFTEN MISSPELLED
Here is a collection of commonly misspelled words. To help you locate the words your students have difficulty with, the lists are organized in these categories: Word Endings (Suffixes), Double Consonants, Unstressed Syllables, Silent Letters and Blended Sounds, *ei/ie,* and Other Commonly Misspelled Words. It's a good idea to assign words for study in groups of 25 at a time.

Double Consonants

accommodate	committee	missile
accompanied	controlled	occasion
accomplish	different	occurred
accordion	disappear	parallel
accustomed	disappoint	processes
address	disapprove	quizzes
annihilate	efficient	satellite
appoint	equipped	stepped
appreciate	fulfill	succeed
appropriate	happened	suppose
arrest	harass	surround
bulletin	interrupt	tyranny
commercial	mirror	villain

BACKGROUND

Teachers looking for help in improving the spelling of basic writers should see Chopeta Lyons' article in the *Journal of Basic Writing* (*JBW* 4 [Fall 1985]: 80–83). She explains how such students can be taught to identify, analyze, and correct their errors.

WORDS OFTEN MISSPELLED

Word Endings (Suffixes)

acceptable	characteristic
accessible	Christianity
accidentally	commitment
accuracy	competent
acreage	competition
actually	completely
admission	confident
affectionately	consistent
aggression	continuous
announcement	convenient
apparent	coolly
appearance	criticism
approximately	criticize
arguing	cruelty
argument	curiosity
assassination	decision
attendance	definitely
barbarous	description
basically	desirable
beautiful	desperate
beginning	despicable
beneficial	
biggest	disastrous
bureaucracy	discussion
business	dormitory
	easily
calculator	elaborately
carrying	entirely
changeable	environment
changing	equipment

➡

HOMONYMS AND COMMONLY CONFUSED WORDS

accept	to receive
except	with the exclusion of
advice	recommendation
advise	to recommend
affect	to produce an influence on (*verb*°); an emotional response (*noun*°)
effect	result (*noun*); to bring about or cause (*verb*)
aisle	space between rows
isle	island
allude	to make indirect reference to
elude	to avoid
allusion	indirect reference
illusion	false idea, misleading appearance
already	by this time
all ready	fully prepared
altar	sacred platform or place
alter	to change
altogether	thoroughly
all together	everyone or everything in one place
are	plural form of *to be*
hour	sixty minutes
our	plural form of *my*
ascent	the act of rising or climbing
assent	consent
assistance	help
assistants	helpers
bare	nude, unadorned
bear	to carry; an animal
board	piece of wood
bored	uninterested
breath	air taken in
breathe	to take in air
brake	device for stopping
break	destroy, make into pieces
buy	to purchase
by	next to, through the agency of
capital	major city
capitol	government building
choose	to pick
chose	past tense of *to choose*
cite	to point out
sight	vision
site	a place

clothes	garments
cloths	pieces of fabric
coarse	rough
course	path; series of lectures
complement	something that completes
compliment	praise, flattery
conscience	sense of morality
conscious	awake, aware
council	governing body
counsel	advice
dairy	place associated with milk production
diary	personal journal
descent	downward movement
dissent	disagreement
dessert	final, sweet course in a meal
desert	to abandon; dry, sandy area
device	a plan; an implement
devise	to create
die	to lose life (*dying*); one of a pair of dice
dye	to change the color of something (*dyeing*)
dominant	commanding, controlling
dominate	to control
elicit	to draw out
illicit	illegal
eminent	prominent
immanent	living within; inherent
imminent	about to happen
envelop	to surround
envelope	container for a letter or other papers
fair	light-skinned; just, honest
fare	money for transportation; food
formally	conventionally, with ceremony
formerly	previously
forth	forward
fourth	number four
gorilla	animal in ape family
guerrilla	soldier specializing in unconventional, surprise attacks
hear	to sense sound by ear
here	in this place
hole	opening
whole	complete; an entire thing
human	relating to the species *homo sapiens*
humane	compassionate

Cont'd.

especially	insurance
evidently	intelligent
existence	interference
experiment	irrelevant
explanation	irresistible
extremely	irritated
finally	likelihood
financially	listening
generally	
government	liveliest
governor	livelihood
guidance	lying
happily	magnificent
hindrance	maintenance
hoping	manageable
humorous	management
hungry	marriage
	meanness
hurriedly	mischievous
hypocrisy	mysterious
ideally	narrative
idiosyncrasy	naturally
ignorant	necessary
illogical	noticeable
imaginary	noticing
immediately	nuisance
immensely	numerous
incalculable	occasionally
incidentally	occurrence
incredible	occurring
independent	official
indispensable	omission
individually	omitting
influential	opponent
innocuous	

➡

QUOTATION ABOUT WRITING
Bad spellers of the world, untie!

—Graffito

WORDS OFTEN MISSPELLED

Word Endings (Suffixes), *continued*

opportunity	questionnaire
opposite	rarity
oppression	reality
optimism	realize
ordinarily	really
originally	recession
particularly	recommend
peaceable	referring
peculiar	regulate
performance	rehearsal
permanence	religious
permissible	remembrance
politician	repetition
possession	representative
practicality	resemblance
predominant	ridiculous
preparation	scarcity
prevalent	scenery
prisoner	secretary
probably	senseless
professor	shining
prominent	shrubbery
pronunciation	significant
publicly	simply
pursuing	sincerely

BACKGROUND

In "English Spelling and Pidgin" (*English Today* [July 1988]: 29–35), Valerie Yule discusses how spelling systems are developed for English pidgins. She analyzes the factors that determine how closely pidgin spelling correlates with English spelling.

insure	buy or give insurance
ensure	guarantee, protect
its	possessive form of *it*
it's	contraction for it is
know	to comprehend
no	negative
later	after a time
latter	second one of two things
lead	heavy metal substance; to guide
led	past tense of *to lead*
lightning	storm-related electricity
lightening	making lighter
loose	unbound, not tightly fastened
lose	to misplace
maybe	perhaps
may be	might be
meat	animal flesh
meet	to encounter
miner	a person who works in a mine
minor	under age
moral	distinguishing right from wrong; the lesson of a fable, story, or event
morale	attitude or outlook, usually of a group
of	preposition indicating origin
off	away from
passed	past tense of *to pass*
past	at a previous time
patience	forbearance
patients	people under medical care
peace	absence of fighting
piece	part of a whole; musical arrangement
personal	intimate
personnel	employees
plain	simple, unadorned
plane	to shave wood; aircraft
precede	to come before
proceed	to continue
presence	being at hand; attendance at a place or in something
presents	gifts
principal	foremost (*adjective*°); school head (*noun*°)
principle	moral conviction, basic truth

quiet	silent, calm
quite	very
rain	water drops falling to earth; to fall like rain
reign	to rule
rein	strap to guide or control an animal (*noun*); to guide or control (*verb*)
raise	to lift up
raze	to tear down
respectfully	with respect
respectively	in that order
right	correct; opposite of *left*
rite	ritual
write	to put words on paper
road	path
rode	past tense of *to ride*
scene	place of an action; segment of a play
seen	viewed
sense	perception, understanding
since	measurement of past time; because
stationary	standing still
stationery	writing paper
than	in comparison with; besides
then	at that time; next; therefore
their	possessive form of *they*
there	in that place
they're	contraction for *they are*
through	finished; into and out of
threw	past tense of *to throw*
thorough	complete
to	toward
too	also; indicates degree (*too much*)
two	number following one
waist	midsection of the body
waste	discarded material; to squander, to fail to use up
weak	not strong
week	seven days
weather	climatic condition
whether	if
where	in which place
were	past tense of *to be*
which	one of a group
witch	female sorcerer

TEACHING TIP

A sophisticated relative of the spelling test is the dictation exercise. Passages can be created to test student ability to spell, punctuate, or capitalize. Here is a sample dictation passage aimed at testing whether students can distinguish among homonyms and commonly confused words. The context gives students clues to which word is intended (much as the sentences normally given as part of a spelling test do); at the same time, the paragraph format is more interesting than random illustrative sentences. (Homonyms and commonly confused words are in italics.)

The institution of marriage has received *its* share of public attention over the past few years. Rising divorce rates, *seen* as a symptom of a troubled society, have *led* people to question why some marriages *break* up and others succeed. One reason may be that the *effect* of courtship is to cause the bride and groom to *lose sight* of reality. Researchers *cite* evidence that some couples are *too* unrealistic. They *proceed* to the *altar* carrying romantic *illusions* about themselves, each other, and marriage itself. Having grown accustomed to *compliments* and *presents,* they find themselves walking down the *aisle* expecting a lifetime of romantic bliss to follow. The groom may assume that his bride is an *angel,* and she may *choose* to think of him as a *knight* on a white horse. They may fail to realize that one expects to *dominate* rather than *complement* the other, or that he lacks *patience* and she is not as *quiet* as she seems. *They're* reluctant to look at the *whole* situation until *later,* when they *are* called on to *accept* the serious responsibilities of marriage. The best *advice,* of *course,* is for husbands and wives to live by *principles* that *lead* them to treat each other *respectfully,* *lightening* each other's troubles and acknowledging each other's *rights.*

English orthography satisfies all the requirements of the canons of reputability under the law of conspicuous waste. It is archaic, cumbrous, and ineffective; its acquisition consumes much time and effort; failure to acquire it is easy of detection.

—Thorstein Veblen,
Theory of the Leisure Class

ANSWERS: EXERCISE 22-1

1. Council	**14.** used to
2. than	**15.** their
3. council	**16.** accept
4. cites	**17.** assistance
5. to	**18.** patience
6. are	**19.** personal
7. their	**20.** morale
8. too	**21.** raise
9. weak	**22.** principle
10. may be	**23.** already
11. passed	**24.** know
12. no	**25.** respective
13. Formerly	

TEACHING TIP

Much of the recent research on spelling improvements stresses the importance of using as many of the senses as possible during word study. You may want to suggest to students that they try to improve their visual memory by writing a word in the air, using a finger to make the troublesome letters especially large. Ask them to try to ➡

whose	possessive form of *who*
who's	contraction for who is
your	possessive form of *you*
you're	contraction for *you are*
yore	long past

EXERCISE 22-1

Consulting section 22b, select the appropriate homonym from each group in parentheses.

According to the (Council, Counsel) on Aging, the U.S. population over 85 is growing faster (than, then) any other segment of society. The (council, counsel) (cites, sites) statistics indicating that elderly people who have access (to, too, two) good health care (are, our) likely to outlive (their, there, they're) parents. If elderly parents grow (to, too, two) (weak, week) to care for themselves, responsibility for them (maybe, may be) (passed, past) to children (know, no) longer young themselves. (Formally, Formerly) (use to, used to) (their, there) parents making independent decisions, adult children must now learn to (accept, except) that parents may need (assistance, assistants) with some decisions. Aging parents must be treated with courtesy and handled with (patience, patients). Frequent (personal, personnel) visits help to keep parents' (moral, morale) high or to (raise, raze) low spirits. In (principal, principle), adult children (all ready, already) (know, no) how to behave with aging parents; they must sometimes be prepared to reverse their (respectful, respective) roles.

22c Spelling plurals

Plurals in English are formed in different ways. The rules are relatively easy to learn because they are consistent.

Most **plurals** are formed by adding *-s: leg, legs; shoe, shoes.* If the word ends in *-s, -sh, -x,* or *-z,* the plural is formed by adding *-es* to the singular: *dish, dishes; tax, taxes.*

When a noun ends in a "soft" *-ch* (the sound in *beach*), add *-es*: *beach, beaches*. When a word ends in a "hard" *-ch* (a *k* sound), add *-s* only: *stomach, stomachs*.

Plurals of words ending in -o are formed by adding *-s* if the *-o* is preceded by a vowel (*radio, radios; cameo, cameos*) and *-es* if the *-o* is preceded by a consonant (*potato, potatoes; veto, vetoes*). A few words ending in *-o* preceded by a consonant can take either *-s* or *-es*. The choice is yours, but always be consistent in each piece of writing: *cargo, cargoes, cargos; volcano, volcanoes, volcanos; tornado, tornadoes, tornados; zero, zeroes, zeros*.

Plurals of words ending in -f or -fe are formed sometimes by adding *-s* (*belief, beliefs*) and sometimes by changing the *-f* or *-fe* to *-ves* (*life, lives; leaf, leaves*). When a word ends in *-ff* or *-ffe*, simply add *-s*: *staff, staffs; giraffe, giraffes*.

Plurals of compound words are formed by adding *-s* or *-es* at the end of the whole compound word (*checkbook, checkbooks; player-coach, player-coaches*). When, however, the first word in a compound of separate or hyphenated words is the major word, add the *-s* or *-es* to the first word (*mile per hour, miles per hour; sister-in-law, sisters-in-law*). For information about using hyphens in compound words, see 22g-3.

Plurals formed by internal changes do not use the added *-s* or *-es* (*child, children; foot, feet; man, men; mouse, mice*). These plurals sound so different that they do not usually cause spelling problems, except for *woman* and *women*. Remember that these words add *wo-* to *man* and *men*.

Plurals of foreign words are formed according to the rules of each language. Latin words ending in *-um* usually form their plurals by changing the *-um* to *-a* (*curriculum, curricula; datum, data; medium, media; stratum, strata*). For Latin words ending in *-us*, the plural is *-i* (*alumnus, alumni; syllabus, syllabi*). Greek words with *-on* singular forms often change to *-a* in the plural (*criterion, criteria; phenomenon, phenomena*).

Plurals that retain their singular form are spelled the same for both singular and plural. Usually they are the names of animals or grains (*deer, elk, fish, quail, rice, wheat*).

Cont'd.
imagine a word as if it were on an outdoor movie screen. Then they can try to write the word mentally in "longhand." The auditory sense can be invoked by making exaggerated pronunciations. That is, the speaker emphasizes the problem portion of a word when saying it. For example, the person who habitually leaves off the final *-d* of *used* should practice pronouncing the word as "you said." The kinesthetic and tactile senses are combined when a writer records a problem word on paper using a different kind of medium to write the difficult spots, changing from a ball-point pen, for instance, to a crayon. This technique can include a visual element if the student puts the problem letters in red or some other bright color.

WORDS OFTEN MISSPELLED
Word Endings (Suffixes) (*continued*)

skiing	tragedy
strenuous	tremendous
stubbornness	truce
studying	unanimous
suburban	unconscious
succession	undoubtedly
sufficient	usage
summary	
superintendent	using
supersede	usually
suppress	valuable
surely	various
susceptible	vegetable
suspicious	vengeance
swimming	violence
technical	visible
temporary	writing
tendency	written

ANSWERS: EXERCISE 22-2

1. heroes	**8.** selves
2. brothers-in-law	**9.** bacteria
3. marches	**10.** staffs
4. stresses	**11.** tomatoes
5. sheep	**12.** shelves
6. teeth	**13.** wives
7. children	**14.** data
	15. loaves

COVERAGE: EXERCISE 22-2

(1) consonant before the final *-o;* (2) major word is the first word; (3) word ends in *-ch;* (4) word ends in *-s;* (5) name of animal; (6) internal change; (7) internal change; (8) word ends in *-f;* (9) foreign word; (10) word ends in *-ff;* (11) word ends in *-o* preceded by a consonant; (12) word ends in *-f;* (13) word ends in *-fe;* (14) foreign word; (15) word ends in *-f.*

WORDS OFTEN MISSPELLED

Unstressed Syllables (including syllables frequently not pronounced)

adolescent	apology
alcohol	article
amateur	aspirin
analysis	average
angel	bargain

➜

EXERCISE 22-2

Consulting section 22c, form the plurals of these words.

1.	hero	6.	tooth	11.	tomato
2.	brother-in-law	7.	child	12.	shelf
3.	march	8.	self	13.	wife
4.	stress	9.	bacterium	14.	datum
5.	sheep	10.	staff	15.	loaf

22d Spelling words with prefixes

Prefixes are syllables placed in front of words, either changing or adding to the word's meaning. For example, the prefixes *un*– and *in*– turn a word into its opposite (**un***cooperative*, **in***admissible*); *re*– adds the meaning "again" to a word (**re***create*, **re***incarnation*); and *pre*– adds the meaning "before" to a word (**pre***cook*, **pre***destination*). A prefix does not alter the spelling of the word to which it is added: for example, *un + reliable = unreliable; re + locate = relocate.* Some prefixes, however, do require hyphens (see 22g-2). For a complete list of prefixes, see 20c-1.

22e Spelling words with suffixes

A **suffix** is a word ending added to the basic (root) form of a word. A suffix cannot stand alone as a word. Suffixes can change a present-tense verb to past tense (*talk, talked*), an adjective to an adverb (*quick, quickly*), a verb to a noun (*govern, government*), or a noun to an adjective (*courage, courageous*). Often spelling is affected when a suffix is added to a word. Even though they have many exceptions, rules and other guidelines about suffixes can help you.

1 Using spelling rules for suffixes

Three spelling rules can help you add suffixes to words correctly. Whenever you are unsure, check your dictionary.

When to change a final *y* to *i*

Check the letter before the final *y* in the word. If it is a consonant, change the *y* to *i*, unless the suffix begins with an *i* (for example, *-ing*). If the letter before the *y* is a vowel, keep the final *y*. These rules do not apply to irregular verbs (see Chart 65 in 8d); spell these according to the principal parts of irregular verbs (for example, *buy, bought; fly, flew; pay, paid*).

fry, fried, frying   emplo**y**, emplo**yed**, emplo**ying**

When to drop a final *e*

Drop the final *e* when the suffix begins with a vowel (for example, *-ing*). Do not, however, drop the *e* if doing so would cause confusion; for example, the final *e* is needed to avoid confusing *dyeing* and *dying* (in *dying* the *y* to *i* rule also operates). Do not drop the final *e* when the suffix begins with a consonant (for example, *-ment: excitement, requirement*). Major exceptions are *argument, judgment,* and *truly*.

require, requir**ing**, requir**ement**   **like, liking, likely**
guid**e**, guid**ing**, guid**ance**

When to double a final letter

Check the final letter of a word. If it is a consonant, double it when adding a suffix—but only if it passes all three of these tests: (1) the last two letters of a word are a vowel followed by a consonant; (2) the word has one syllable or is accented on the last syllable; (3) the suffix begins with a vowel.

drop, dr**opped**   forg**et**, forg**etful**, forg**ettable**
beg**in**, beg**inning**   happ**en**, happ**ened**

---

2 **Using other guidelines for suffixes**

The *-d* and *-ed* suffixes change many verbs in the present tense into the past tense or into past-participle° forms: *change, changed; work, worked.* Do not rely on how words sound in conversa-

---

Cont'd.

boundary	imitate
cafeteria	integrate
calendar	interest
category	introduce
cemetery	laboratory
census	liable
certain	luxury
challenge	magazine
channel	manual
children	mathematics
chocolate	medicine
chosen	miniature
coarsely	particle
concentrate	perhaps
controversial	persuade
curious	physical
decorate	pigeon
delicate	pitiful
despair	pleasant
destroy	poison
develop	practical
disease	prepare
dispel	privilege
divide	propaganda
divine	pumpkin
ecstasy	purpose
embarrass	pursue
enemy	pursuit
escape	quandary
everything	rebel
exercise	recognize
family	regular
favorite	remember
grammar	reproduce
heroes	resources
holiday	restaurant
hundred	sacrifice
imagine	

➡

WORDS OFTEN MISSPELLED

Unstressed Syllables (including syllables frequently not pronounced), *continued*

saxophone	sponsor	tobacco
sentence	statistics	together
separate	strategy	tomorrow
several	surprise	typical
sheriff	temperature	vitamins
similar	therefore	Wednesday
sophomore	thorough	woman
specimen		women

WORDS OFTEN MISSPELLED

ei/ie

achievement	conscientious	relief
apiece	eighth	relieve
atheist	foreign	review
belief	forfeit	seize
believed	height	view
ceiling	leisure	weird
chief	lenient	
conceited	niece	
conceive	receive	

TEACHING TIP

Carol Chomsky suggests an exercise that can be used to clarify the spellings of words with silent consonants. She points out that it is helpful to associate each one with a root word in a different form that does not silence the letter. For instance, the *g* in *sign* is easily heard in *signature*; the silent *c* in *muscle* is apparent in *muscular*. Groups of words that have consonant alternation become easier to spell after the exchange is noted and discussed—as in *coincidental* and *coincidence*, *pirate* and *piracy*, in which the *t* and *c* are alternated ("Reading, Writing, and Phonology," *Harvard Educational Review* 40 [1970]: 287–309).

tion to guide your spelling. The *-d* sound at the end of verbs is not always clearly pronounced (for example, although you may hear "suppose to," write *supposed to*).

The -*ally* and -*ly* suffixes turn words into adverbs. The suffix -*ally* is added to words ending in -*ic* (*logic* + *ally* = *logically*). The suffix -*ly* is added to adjectives not ending in -*ic* (*quick* + *ly* = *quickly*).

There are no consistent rules for the use of **the -*able* and -*ible* suffixes.** More words end in -*able* (*advisable, comfortable*); some common words end in -*ible* (*audible, forcible*). The best rule is, "When in doubt, look it up."

There are also no consistent rules for the use of **the -*nce* and -*nt* suffixes.** Some words end in -*ance* (*compliance, defiance*). Usually, if a noun° ends in -*ance*, the adjective° form ends in -*ant* (*defiance, defiant*), and if a noun ends in -*ence*, the adjective form ends in -*ent* (*confidence, confident; convenience, convenient*).

The -*cede*, -*ceed*, and -*sede* suffixes have very dependable rules. Only one word ends in -*sede*: *supersede*. Three words end in -*ceed*: *exceed, proceed*, and *succeed*. All other words whose endings sound like these suffixes end in -*cede*: *concede, intercede, precede*.

22f Using the *ie, ei* rule

The old rhyme for *ie* and *ei* is usually true: "*i* before *e*, except after *c*, or when sounded like *ay*, as in *neighbor* and *weigh*."

I BEFORE *E*
believe, field, grief
EXCEPT AFTER *C*
ceiling, conceit
EXCEPT WHEN SOUNDS LIKE *AY*
neighbor, weigh, eight, vein

Some major exceptions are worth memorizing.

IE	conscience, financier, science, species
EI	either, neither, leisure, seize, counterfeit, foreign, forfeit, sleight, weird

EXERCISE 22-3

Consulting sections 22e and 22f, follow the directions for each group of words.

A. Add *-able* or *-ible:* 1. contempt; 2. resist; 3. believe; 4. reverse; 5. dispense.

B. Add *-ant* or *-ent:* 1. relev____; 2. promin____; 3. vari____; 4. resist____; 5. conveni____.

C. Drop the final *e* as needed: 1. manage + ing; 2. manage + ment; 3. complete + ly; 4. complete + ion; 5. create + ing.

D. Change the final *y* to *i* as needed: 1. study + ing; 2. study + ed; 3. supply + ed; 4. merry + ment; 5. vary + ous.

E. Double the final consonant as needed: 1. write + ing; 2. begin + ing; 3. stop + ed; 4. occur + ed; 5. question + ing.

F. Insert *ie* or *ei* correctly: 1. rel____f; 2. conc____ve; 3. n____ce; 4. dec____ve; 5. fr____ght.

22g Using hyphens correctly

1 Hyphenating at the end of a line

Unless the last word on a line would use up most of the right margin of your paper, do not divide it. If you must divide a word, try not to divide the last word on the first line of a paper, the last word in a paragraph, or the last word on a page. When you have to

CHECKLIST FOR HYPHENATING WORDS 115

- **Never divide single syllable or very short words.**

  NO we-alth, en-vy   YES wealth, envy

- **Never leave or carry over only one or two letters.**

  NO a-live, he-licopt-er   YES alive, heli-cop-ter

- **Always divide words only between syllables.**

  NO proc-ess   YES pro-cess

- **Always follow rules for double consonants.**

  NO ful-lness, omitt-ing   YES full-ness, omit-ting

ANSWERS: EXERCISE 22-3

A. 1. contemptible
2. resistible
3. believable
4. reversible
5. dispensable
B. 1. relevant
2. prominent
3. variant
4. resistant
5. convenient
C. 1. managing
2. management
3. completely
4. completion
5. creating
D. 1. studying
2. studied
3. supplied
4. merriment
5. various
E. 1. writing
2. beginning
3. stopped
4. occurred
5. questioning
F. 1. relief
2. conceive
3. niece
4. deceive
5. freight

COVERAGE: EXERCISE 22-3

A. (1), (2), and (4) are *-ible;* (3) and (5) are *-able.*

B. (1), (3), and (4) are *-ant;* (2) and (5) are *-ent.*

C. (1), (4), and (5) drop the final *e;* (2) and (3) retain it.

D. (1) retains the final *y;* (2), (3), (4), and (5) drop it and change to *i.*

E. (1) and (5) do not double the final consonant; (2), (3), and (4) double it.

F. (1) and (3) are *i* before *e;* (2), (4), and (5) are *e* before *i.*

WORDS OFTEN MISSPELLED
Silent Letters and Blended Sounds

acquainted	muscle
acquire	pamphlet
condemn	psychology
contradict	quantity
courteous	receipt
crowd	reminisce
dealt	rhythm
descend	safety
distinct	sandwich
empty	schedule
fascinate	sergeant
February	shoulder
foresee	source
foretell	souvenir
gauge	straight
group	strength
gruesome	stretch
guaranteed	strict
guard	technique
initiative	themselves
instead	though
knowledge	thought
length	through
library	trouble
meant	twelfth
mortgage	vacuum

BACKGROUND

Some grammarians point out that context usually clarifies whether a writer means *research* or *re-search*, *re-creation* or *recreation*, and other words beginning with the *re-* prefix. Carl Kane, writing in *The Cedar Rapids Gazette* (August 20, 1986), contends that hyphens should not be neglected. "Anything that might even temporarily mislead a reader should be eliminated. Throw in a hyphen. It can't hurt."

hyphenate, break the word only at a syllable, using the checklist in Chart 115. If you are unsure of how to divide a word into syllables, consult a dictionary (see 20a).

2 | Using hyphens with prefixes

If the last letter of a prefix is the same as the first letter of the base word, or if adding a prefix results in three vowels in a row, you may use a hyphen after the prefix: *anti-intellectual, re-ionize*. Some words are commonly spelled without this hyphen: for example, *cooperation, preeminent,* and *reexamine.*

If a word has a prefix followed by three or more letters, divide it after the prefix rather than between other syllables. Some prefixes are always separated from the base word with a hyphen, whether or not they are divided at the end of a line. (For information about spelling words with prefixes, see 22d. For a list of prefixes, see 20c-1.)

CHECKLIST FOR USING HYPHENS TO ATTACH PREFIXES   116

- **Always use hyphens when using the prefixes *all-, ex-, quasi-,* and *self-.***

  all-inclusive   self-reliant
- **Always use a hyphen when the base word is a proper name or a number.**

  pro-American   post-1950
- **Always use a hyphen when the base word is a compound.**

  anti-gun control   ex-president-elect
- **Always use a hyphen when confusion in meaning or pronunciation can occur.**

  re-dress ("dress again")   redress ("set right")
- **Always use hyphens when two prefixes are used with one base word.**

  pre- and post-war eras   two- or four-year colleges

---

3   Hyphenating compound words

A **compound word** consists of two or more words used together to form one word. Types of compound words are explained in Chart 117. To hyphenate compound words, use the guidelines in this section. (For information about spelling plurals of compound words, see 22c.)

TYPES OF COMPOUND WORDS   117

- **An open compound is spelled as two or more separate words without using any hyphens.**
  cedar shingles   night shift
- **A closed compound is spelled as one word without using any hyphens.**
  handbook   toothache
- **A hyphenated compound is spelled as two or more words joined with hyphens.**
  tractor-trailer   brother-in-law

As you write compound words, be aware that choosing between open and closed forms of words (such as *in to* or *into* and *may be* or *maybe*) calls for close attention to the meaning of the sentence: *She spoke **into** the microphone; she walked **in to** make the announcement.*

In general, when compound words are new or are coined for a specific purpose, they are spelled as open compounds. Many of those that become more widely used go through a stage of being spelled as hyphenated compounds. If they last in the language, they often come to be spelled as closed compounds. For example, *mini van* came into the language in the early 1980s. By the middle of the decade, *minivan* was the accepted spelling.

Also, when a compound acts as a modifier° before a noun°, it is usually hyphenated: ***well-dressed** teacher,* ***twenty-page** report.* That same modifier usually is not hyphenated when it comes after the noun, however: *the teacher was **well dressed;** the report was **twenty pages.*** Some familiar terms are unambiguous and easy to understand

---

WORDS OFTEN MISSPELLED
Other Commonly Misspelled Words

absence	material
across	mere
always	minutes
among	morning
ancestry	nevertheless
anxiety	nineteen
anywhere	ninety
authentic	ninth
awkward	nuclear
bachelor	omit
benefited	opinion
birthday	paid
compel	parole
consensus	pastime
cylinder	penetrate
defer	pertain
disagree	phase
disturb	prairie
exceed	pretty
expense	prevail
familiar	restaurant
forty	science
forward	speak
furniture	speech
grandeur	temperature
hesitate	until
hypocrite	vicious
intercede	wherever
laid	whether
license	wholly

QUOTATION ABOUT WRITING
Hooray for the hyphen! Or, rather, Hoo-ray!
—George Plimpton

447

and so do not require hyphens: for example, *genetic engineering laboratory, health insurance policy, junior high school, state sales tax.*

When the first word in a compound is an *-ly* adverb, when the first word is a comparative° or superlative°, or when the compound is a foreign phrase, the hyphen is omitted: **happily married** *couple,* **better fitting** *dress,* **least expected** *results,* **ex post facto law.**

When a compound is formed by two components of a combined unit of measure, the hyphen is used: *light-years, kilowatt-hour.*

Although most compound titles are not hyphenated (*state senator, vice principal, editor in chief*), many are. Hyphenated titles usually are nation names, actual double titles, or three-word titles: *Italian-American, broker-analyst, ambassador-at-large, father-in-law.*

4 | **Using hyphens with spelled-out numbers**

When you write spelled-out numbers, use hyphens according to the checklist in Chart 118.

CHECKLIST FOR USING HYPHENS IN SPELLED-OUT NUMBERS [118]

■ **Always use a hyphen between two-word numbers from twenty-one through ninety-nine.**

   thirty-five (35)   two hundred thirty-five (235)
   five hundred fifty thousand (550,000)

■ **Always use a hyphen between the numerator and denominator of two-word fractions.**

   one-half (1/2)   two-fifths (2/5)   seven-tenths (7/10)

Figures are usually easier for a reader to understand than spelled-out numbers (see 30l). If you need more than two words to spell out a fraction, use figures. If you cannot use figures for a special reason (for example, when a fraction starts a sentence that you cannot rearrange), use hyphens between the words of the numerator's number and the words of the denominator's number, but do not use hyphens between the numerator and the denominator: *two one-hundredths* (2/100); *thirty-three ten-thousandths* (33/10,000).

For numbers and words combined to form one idea or modifier°, use a hyphen between the number and the word: *50-minute class, 3-to-1 odds, 10-kilometer race.* If the word in the modifier is possessive°, omit the hyphen: *8 hours' pay, one week's work.* If you choose to spell out the numbers, hyphenate the same way: *fifty-minute class, three-to-one odds.*

EXERCISE 22-4

Consulting section 22g, in the blanks write the correct form of the word in parentheses according to the way it is used in the sentence.

1. The tiger is (all powerful)_____in the cat family.
2. (Comparison contrast)_____studies of tigers and lions show that the tiger is the (more agile)_____and powerful.
3. The tiger's body is a (boldly striped)_____yellow, with a white (under body)_____.
4. The tiger's maximum length is about (eleven feet)_____, about (one quarter)_____of which is accounted for by its tail, and its maximum weight is up to (five hundred)_____pounds.
5. The Bengal tiger, the largest of the family, is aggressive and (self confident)_____.
6. In India, where the Bengal is called a (village destroyer)_____, it has a reputation for going (in to)_____villages to hunt for food.
7. Entire villages have been temporarily abandoned by (terror stricken)_____people who have seen a Bengal tiger nearby
8. Villagers seek to protect their homes by destroying tigers with traps, (spring loaded)_____guns, and (poisoned arrows)_____.
9. Bengal tigers are also called (cattle killers)_____, although they attack domestic animals only when wild ones cannot be found.
10. Many people who do not live near a zoo get to see tigers only in (animal shows)_____, although (pro animal)_____activists try to prevent tigers' being used this way.

EXERCISE 22-5

Each paragraph contains eleven misspelled words. Circle the words, correct them, and match them to a section in this chapter. If the error does not fall under any particular section, describe the cause of the error in your own words.

1.   It seems that all we hear about now adays is the computer revolution. There are computers in librarys, schools, offices, and even in homes. Freinds of mine who once feared anything remotely associated with electronics now loudly sing the praises of word-processing, as if the typewriter were a product of the Stone Age. Last week I grew so weary of listenning to them that I decided to see for

ANSWERS: EXERCISE 22-4

1. all-powerful
2. Comparison-contrast; more agile
3. boldly striped; underbody
4. eleven feet; one-quarter; five hundred
5. self-confident
6. village destroyer; into
7. terror-stricken
8. spring-loaded; poisoned arrows
9. cattle killers
10. animal shows; pro-animal

COVERAGE: EXERCISE 22-4

1. *all-* prefixes hyphenated
2. hyphenated compound; open
3. *-ly* adverb as first word of compound; *under* prefixes spelled closed
4. not a double digit; fraction; not a double digit
5. *self-* prefixes hyphenated
6. open compound; closed compound
7. hyphenated compound
8. hyphenated compound; open compound
9. open compound
10. open compound; *pro-* prefix hyphenated before a vowel

ANSWERS: EXERCISE 22-5
1.

Incorrect	Correct	Rule Pattern
1. now adays	nowadays	22c-3
2. librarys	libraries	22d-1
3. freinds	friends	22d-2
4. listenning	listening	22d-1
5. assalted	assaulted	22c-4
6. occassional	occasional	22c-4
7. offerred	offered	22d-1
8. assistants	assistance	22c-1

➡

ANSWERS: EXERCISE 22-5, *continued*

	Incorrect	Correct	Rule Pattern
9.	tryed	tried	22d-1
10.	haveing	having	22d-1
11.	of	off	22c-1

2.

	Incorrect	Correct	Rule Pattern
1.	disobediance	disobedience	22d-1
2.	themselfs	themselves	22d-4
3.	they're	their	22c-1
4.	goverment	government	22c-4
5.	were	where	22c-1
6.	succeses	successes	22d-1
7.	beleived	believed	22d-2
8.	eliminateing	eliminating	22d-1
9.	testamony	testimony	22c-4
10.	non-violent	nonviolent	22e-2
11.	resistence	resistance	22d-1

myself exactly what these wonders of technology could do. As I cautiously approached my college's Writing Center, my ears were assalted by the click-click-click of keyboards, and an occassional screech from a printer. One of the tutors offered me her assistants in learning to use the machine. Within a mere twenty-five minutes I was typing happily, thinking all the while that I should have tryed this much sooner. Just as I began the conclusion of my English paper, the entire building was plunged into silent darkness. I was dismayed at the thought of haveing to wait until the following day to see the printout. Then the tutor told me the bad news: I had lost the entire essay when the electricity went of. My draft no longer existed. With poise and grace, I felt my way to the exit.

2.   Among the most effective voices for nonviolent resistance and civil disobediance in the twentieth century have been Mohandas Gandhi and Martin Luther King, Jr. Both were educated, middle-class men who found themselfs the objects of discrimination because of they're race. Gandhi first encountered racism when he visited South Africa around the turn of the century. After forcing the government to modify parts of the racial code in that country, he returned to his homeland, India, where he began a long quest to rid it of British rule. His succeses as well as his failures influenced a young minister from Georgia, Martin Luther King, Jr., who fiercely opposed segregation in the United States. King embraced Gandhi's warning that oppressed people must resist the temptation to answer violence with violence. They both beleived that once the oppressed resort to violence they become no better than their oppressors. King's success in eliminateing legally sanctioned segregation in the South, like Gandhi's success in freeing India from the British, is testamony to the effectiveness of non-violent resistence. It is ironic that these two apostles of peace died in the same way: victims of assassins' bullets.

VI

Using Punctuation and Mechanics

When you use punctuation and mechanics according to currently accepted practice, you avoid errors that interfere with the delivery of the meaning that you want to communicate. Part Six presents and explains the rules and conventions that readers have come to expect. As you use Chapters 23 through 30, remember that punctuation and mechanics are tools that help you deliver your message clearly to your readers.

Punctuation: what is it, after all, but another way of cutting up time, creating or negating relationships, telling words when to take a rest, when to get on with their relentless stories, when to catch their breath?

—Karen Elizabeth Gordon

BACKGROUND

In "What Good Is Punctuation?" (Center for the Study of Writing Occasional Paper, no. 2 [Berkeley: CSW, 1987]), Wallace Chafe reviews the functions of punctuation. In addition, he makes suggestions for teaching punctuation in the context of writing.

BACKGROUND

In 1988 Patricia Cordeiro published a study of the understanding first- and third-graders have of the use of the period. She found qualitative differences in the errors made by the two groups ("Children's Punctuation: An Analysis of Errors in Period Placement," *Research in the Teaching of English* 22 [February 1988]: 62–74).

23 The Period, Question Mark, and Exclamation Point

The period, question mark, and exclamation point are called **end punctuation** because they occur at the end of sentences.

I love you. Do you love me? I love you!

THE PERIOD

23a Using a period at the end of a statement, a mild command, or an indirect question

Unless a sentence asks a direct question (23c) or issues a strong command or emphatic declaration (23e), it ends with a period.

STATEMENT	A journey of a thousand leagues begins with a single step.
	—Lao-Tsu
MILD COMMAND	Put a gram of boldness into everything you do.
	—Baltasar Gracian
INDIRECT QUESTION	I asked if they wanted to climb Mt. Everest. [A direct question would end with a question mark: *I asked, ''Do you want to climb Mt. Everest?''*]

23b Using periods with most abbreviations

Most **abbreviations** call for periods, but some do not. Typical abbreviations with periods include *Mt., St., Dr., Mr., Ms., Mrs., Ph.D.,*

M.D., and *R.N.* In general, the word *professor* is spelled out, not abbreviated. Also, *a.m.* and *p.m.* are appropriate with exact times (such as *2:15 p.m.*) but should not be used instead of the word *morning, evening,* or *night.* Abbreviations without periods include the names of some organizations and government agencies (such as *CBS* and *NASA*). For more information about abbreviations, see 30h and 30i.

> Ms. Yuan, who works at NASA, lectured to Dr. Garcia's physics class at 9:30 a.m.

❖ PUNCTUATION ALERT: When the period of an abbreviation falls at the end of a sentence, the period serves also to end the sentence. ❖

THE QUESTION MARK

23c Using a question mark after a direct question

A **direct question** asks a question and ends with a question mark. In contrast, an **indirect question** reports a question and ends with a period (see 23a).

> How many attempts have been made to climb Mt. Everest? [An indirect question would be: *The tourists wanted to know how many attempts had been made to climb Mt. Everest.*]

❖ PUNCTUATION ALERT: Do not combine a question mark with a comma, a period, or an exclamation point. ❖

> **NO** She asked, "How are you?."
> **YES** She asked, "How are you?"

Questions in a series are each followed by a question mark, whether or not each question is a complete sentence. ❖ CAPITALIZATION ALERT: When questions in a series are not complete sentences, you can choose whether or not to capitalize the first letter, as long as you are consistent in each piece of writing.

> After the fierce storm had passed, the mountain climbers debated what to do next. Turn back? Move on? Rest for a while? ❖

When a request is phrased as a question, it does not always require a question mark, especially when the request is phrased as a question to achieve a polite tone: *Would you please send me a copy.*

QUOTATION ABOUT WRITING

GREEKANDLATINMANUSCRIPTSWERE USUALLYWRITTENWITHNOSPACEBE-TWEENWORDSUNTIL AROUND THE NINTH CENTURY AD ALTHOUGH·ROMAN·INSCRIPTIONS·LIKE·THE·FA-MOUS·TRAJAN·COLUMN·SOMETIMES·SEPARATED·WORDS·WITH·A·CEN-TERED·DOT·EVEN AFTER SPACING BECAME COMMON IT REMAINED HAPHAZARD FOREXAMPLE OFTEN A PREPOSITION WAS LINKEDTO ANOTHER WORD

A CENTERED DOT DIVIDED WORDS WHICH FELL AT THE END OF A LINE IN EARLY GREEK AND LATIN MANU-SCRIPTS AND THE MORE VISUALLY DISTINCT HYPHEN WAS INTRODUCED IN THE ELEVENTH CENTURY MEDIEVAL SCRIBES OFTEN PUT MARKS AT THE END OF SHORT LINES TO MAKE A SOLID TEXT

Period Styles: A History of Punctuation
Exhibition Catalog, The Herb Lubalin
Study Center of Design and Typography,
The Cooper Union for the Advancement
of Science and Art, p. 1

QUOTATION ABOUT WRITING

Punctuation is a group of supplementary visual cues which organize letters on a two-dimensional surface. Some kinds of punctuation merely format a text, without affecting its basic meaning: for example, abbreviations, hyphenated line breaks, word spacing, and the left-to-right direction of reading. Other forms affect the meaning of a text, like the comma, colon, period, and question mark, which stand in place of spoken pauses and intonations.

"Telegrammar: From Writing to Speech,"
Catalog, *Period Styles: A History of
Punctuation,* The Cooper Union

23d Using a question mark in parentheses

When a date or number is **unknown or doubtful** even after your very best research, you can use *(?)*.

Mary Astell, an English author who wrote pamphlets on women's rights, was born in 1666 *(?)* and died in 1731.

The word *about* is often a graceful substitute for *(?)*: *Mary Astell was born about 1666.*

Do not use *(?)* to communicate that you are unsure of information: *It might rain* [not *will rain (?)*] *today.* Also, your choice of words, not *(?)*, should communicate irony or sarcasm.

NO	Having the flu is a delightful (?) experience.
YES	Having the flu is as pleasant as almost drowning.

THE EXCLAMATION POINT

23e Using an exclamation point for a strong command or an emphatic declaration

An **exclamation point** can end a strong command or an emphatic declaration. A strong command gives a very firm order: *Look out behind you!* An emphatic declaration makes a shocking or surprising statement: *There's been an accident!* ♣ PUNCTUATION ALERT: Do not combine an exclamation point with a comma, a period, or a question mark. ♣

NO	"There's been an accident**!,**" cried my mother.
YES	"There's been an accident!" cried my mother.

23f Avoiding the overuse of exclamation points

In academic writing, your words, rather than exclamation points, should communicate the strength of your message. Reserve exclamation points for occasional emphatic dialogue. Use them only very rarely for a short emphatic declaration within a longer passage.

When we were in Nepal, we tried each day to see Mt. Everest. But each day we failed to see it. Clouds defeated us! The summit never emerged from a heavy overcast.

If you use exclamation points too often in academic writing, your reader will think that your judgment of urgency is exaggerated.

NO Mountain climbing can be dangerous! You must learn correct procedures! You must have the proper equipment. Take rope! Wear spiked boots! Carry special picks designed for mountaineering.

YES Mountain climbing can be dangerous. Without knowing correct procedures, climbers quickly can turn an outing into a disaster. Required mountaineering gear includes rope, spiked boots, and special picks.

Your choice of words, not (!), should communicate amazement or sarcasm.

NO At 29,141 feet (!), Mt. Everest is the world's highest mountain. I heard that Chris (!) wants to climb it.

YES At a majestically staggering 29,141 feet, Mt. Everest is the world's highest mountain. Surely, Chris lacks the stamina to climb it.

EXERCISE 23-1

Consulting sections 23a–23f, insert any needed periods, question marks, and exclamation points. Also delete any unneeded ones.

EXAMPLE The paintings of the great El Greco are associated with Spain, but he was actually born in 1541 on the island of Crete!

The paintings of the great El Greco are associated with Spain, but he was actually born in 1541 on the island of Crete.

1. After studying art in Crete, El Greco moved to Venice, Italy, before 1567 (?), apparently to study with the famous Venetian artist Titian.
2. Scholars wonder if Titian was referring to El Greco when Titian mentioned ''a talented young pupil'' in a letter to King Philip II?
3. El Greco later moved to Rome with a letter of introduction (dated Nov 19, 1590) to a rich, influential art patron, Cardinal Alessandro Farnese.
4. Cardinal Farnese introduced El Greco to the outstanding (!) people of the city.
5. By 1572, El Greco had moved to the city of Toledo in Spain, where he spent the rest of his life!

BACKGROUND

Bergen and Cornelia Evans in *A Dictionary of Contemporary American Usage* define an exclamation as a spontaneous expression of strong emotion, shown in speech by pitch and in writing by the exclamation point. Advising that exclamation points should be reserved for true exclamations ''and not wasted on sentences where commas would serve as well,'' they list several forms in which exclamations commonly appear. They may take the form of a sentence that begins with *how, what,* or *why,* in which the subject precedes the verb, as in *What a surprise this is!* They may appear as a declarative sentence, as in *The tree blew down!* They are often incomplete expressions, sometimes having a verb but no subject, as in *Bless your heart!*

ANSWERS AND COVERAGE: EXERCISE 23-1

1. After studying art in Crete, El Greco moved to Venice, Italy, probably before 1567 [23d, question mark deleted and *probably* added], apparently to study with the famous Venetian artist Titian.
2. Scholars wonder if Titian was referring to El Greco when Titian mentioned ''a talented young pupil'' in a letter to King Philip II. [23a, question mark deleted and replaced with period]
3. El Greco later moved to Rome with a letter of introduction (dated Nov. [period added] 19, 1590) to a rich, influential art patron, Cardinal Alessandro Farnese.
4. Cardinal Farnese introduced El Greco to the outstanding [23e, exclamation point deleted] people of the city.
5. By 1572, El Greco had moved to the city of Toledo in Spain, where he spent rest of his life. [23e, exclamation point deleted and replaced with period]

➡

Cont'd.

6. Toledo was a rich, cultured, and intellectual city where El Greco worked as a sculptor, painter, and architect. [23a, period added]

7. Toward the end of his life, El Greco suffered from a mysterious [23d, question mark deleted] illness that reduced his capacity for work. [23a, period added]

8. "Was El Greco's eyesight affected by the illness? [23c, question mark added]" is a question that has been asked for centuries. [23a, question mark deleted and replaced with period]

9. Visual problems might explain the elongated bodies in El Greco's portraits. [23a, question mark deleted and replaced with period]

10. From time to time, physicians write articles diagnosing [23d, question mark deleted] El Greco's illness based on this artist's paintings! [23e, acceptable exclamation point]

ANSWERS: EXERCISE 23-2

During World War II, U.S. soldiers' mail was censored. Specially trained people read the mail. Many people wanted to know why this was necessary. The censors had to make sure that no military information was disclosed. Return addresses often read "Somewhere in the Pacific Area" to keep strategic positions secret. Have you ever heard the story about the soldier who could not write his sweetheart for many months but finally had time? He wrote her a long letter explaining the delay and telling her that he loved her very much. All the woman received, however, was a tiny slip of paper that read: "Your boyfriend is fine. He loves you. He also talks too much! Sincerely, The Censor."

6. Toledo was a rich, cultured, and intellectual city where El Greco worked as a sculptor, painter, and architect

7. Toward the end of his life, El Greco suffered from a mysterious (?) illness that reduced his capacity for work

8. "Was El Greco's eyesight affected by the illness" is a question that has been asked for centuries?

9. Visual problems might explain the elongated bodies in El Greco's portraits?

10. From time to time, physicians write articles diagnosing (?) El Greco's illness based on this artist's paintings!

EXERCISE 23-2

Insert needed periods, question marks, and exclamation points.

During World War II, US soldiers' mail was censored Specially trained people read the mail Many people wanted to know why this was necessary The censors had to make sure that no military information was disclosed Return addresses often read "Somewhere in the Pacific Area" to keep strategic positions secret Have you ever heard the story about the soldier who could not write his sweetheart for many months but finally had time He wrote her a long letter explaining the delay and telling her that he loved her very much All the woman received, however, was a tiny slip of paper that read: "Your boyfriend is fine He loves you He also talks too much Sincerely, The Censor."

24 The Comma

The comma is the most frequently used mark of punctuation, occurring twice as often as all other marks of punctuation combined. Rules for the comma are many: the comma *must* be used in certain places, it *must not* be used in other places, and it is *optional* in still other places. To help you sort through the various rules and uses of the comma, consult Chart 119.

USES OF THE COMMA	119
■ Comma before coordinating conjunction°* linking independent clauses°	Section 24a
■ Comma after an introductory clause°, phrase°, or word	Section 24b
■ Commas to separate items in a series	Section 24c
■ Commas to separate coordinate adjectives°	Section 24d
■ Commas to set off nonrestrictive° (nonessential) elements	Section 24e
■ Commas to set off parenthetical and transitional expressions°, contrasts, words of direct address°, and tag sentences°	Section 24f
■ Commas with quoted words	Section 24g
■ Commas in names, dates, addresses, and numbers	Section 24h
■ Commas to clarify meaning	Section 24i
■ Commas misused or overused	Section 24j

*Throughout this book, a degree mark (°) indicates that you can find the definition of the word in the Glossary of Terms in this handbook.

The role of the comma is to group and separate sentence parts, helping to create clarity for readers. Consider the clarity of the following paragraph, which contains all needed punctuation except commas.

> **NO**   Among publishers typographical errors known as "typos" are an embarrassing fact of life. In spite of careful editing reviews and multiple readings few books are perfect upon publication. Soon after a book reaches the marketplace reports of errors embarrassments to authors and editors alike start to come in. Everyone laughed therefore although no one thought it was funny when an English textbook was published with this line: "Proofread your writing carefullly."

Here is the same paragraph with commas included.

> **YES**   Among publishers, typographical errors, known as "typos," are an embarrassing fact of life. In spite of careful editing, reviews, and multiple readings, few books are perfect upon publication. Soon after a book reaches the marketplace, reports of errors, embarrassments to authors and editors alike, start to come in. Everyone laughed, therefore, although no one thought it was funny, when an English textbook was published with this line: "Proofread your writing carefullly."

In the Yes paragraph, the meaning is clear. Each comma in it is used for a specific reason according to a comma rule.

Avoid two practices that can get writers into trouble with commas: (1) As you are writing, do not insert a comma just because you happen to pause to think before moving on. (2) As you reread your writing, do not insert commas according to your personal habits of pausing. Although a comma alerts a reader to a slight pause (except in dates and other conventional material), pausing is not a reliable guide for writers, because people's breathing rhythms, accents, and thinking spans vary greatly.

24a   **Using a comma before a coordinating conjunction that links independent clauses**

When **coordinating conjunctions** (*and, but, or, nor, for, so,* and *yet*) link independent clauses°, they create **compound sentences°**. Use a comma before the coordinating conjunction.

EXTRA EXERCISE A

Insert commas before coordinating conjunctions that separate independent clauses.

1. England, Scotland and Wales are located on the same island.

2. Wales is located on the western peninsula of the island and England and Scotland occupy the rest of it.

3. It is bounded on the east by the North Sea and on the south by the English Channel.

4. The Teutonic invaders of the fifth century had to struggle with native Britons for possession of the island for the Romans had virtually abandoned the island by that time.

5. Britain is the proper name of the whole island but England is the political name of the part conquered by the Angles.

6. Neither the Jutes nor the Saxons moved north for they chose to settle in what is today Kent or they moved on to Sussex, Wessex, and Essex.

7. The Scots were actually the people of Ireland yet a small colony they established in the northern part of the island eventually gave it its name.

8. The Norman Conquest of Britain was begun under William the Conqueror and was continued by his sons.

9. With few exceptions all the existing shires of England had been established at the time of the Norman Conquest but the boundaries were not always exactly the same as they are now.

10. Since the eleventh century the map of Britain has remained little changed yet the reins of power have shifted many times.

→

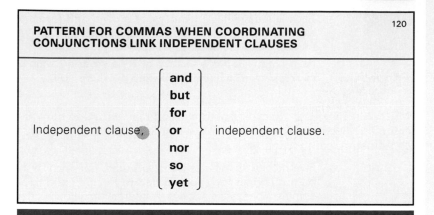

**PATTERN FOR COMMAS WHEN COORDINATING
CONJUNCTIONS LINK INDEPENDENT CLAUSES**

120

Independent clause, { and / but / for / or / nor / so / yet } independent clause.

The sky was dark gray, **and** the air stilled ominously.
The November morning had just begun, **but** it looked like dusk.
Shopkeepers closed their stores early, **for** they wanted to get home.
Soon high winds would start, **or** thick snow would begin silently.
Farmers had no time to continue harvesting, **nor** could they round up their animals in distant fields.
The firehouse whistle blew four times, **so** everyone knew a blizzard was closing in.
People on the road tried to reach safety, **yet** a few unlucky ones were stranded.

When the two independent clauses in a compound sentence are very short, some authorities omit the comma before the coordinating conjunction. However, you will never be wrong, and you avoid the risk of error, if you always use a comma in your college writing.

✤ COMMA CAUTION: Do not put a comma *after* a coordinating conjunction that links independent clauses.

NO	The sky was dark gray **and,** the air stilled ominously.
YES	The sky was dark gray, **and** the air stilled ominously. ✤

✤ COMMA CAUTION: Do not use a comma when a coordinating conjunction links *two* words, phrases°, or dependent clauses° only. Use commas for a series of three or more items (see 24c).

NO	Learning a new language demands **time, and patience.** [Two words linked by *and* use no comma.]
YES	Learning a new language demands **time and patience.**

BACKGROUND
The placement of a comma can have consequences that are highly important. Consider the following examples:
1. A comma once saved a man's life. Czar Alexander III had signed a death warrant reading: "Pardon impossible, to be sent to Siberia." Being sent to Siberia inevitably led to death. However, Czarina Maria Fyodorovna saved the man by altering the message to read: "Pardon, impossible to be sent to Siberia."
2. Elizabeth Langmore (Letters, *Time*, July 4, 1988) points out how very different it is to ask, "Have you seen the elephant eating Tom?" and "Have you seen the elephant eating, Tom?"
3. In the same publication, Grover Reynolds points out the difference between "Woman without her man has no reason for living," and "Woman: without her, man has no reason for living."
4. In another letter to *Time*, Leslie Bryant asks readers to decipher "That that is is that that is not is not is that it it is." With commas and periods, it reads "That that is, is. That that is not, is not. Is that it? It is."

ANSWERS: EXERCISE 24-1

Answers may vary slightly, especially for item 6. Here is one set of possibilities.

1. John Sutter and James Marshall searched for gold in the United States, and they found it in California in 1848.

➡

NO	Each language has **a beauty of its own, and forms of expression** which are duplicated nowhere else. [Two phrases linked by *and* use no comma.]
YES	Each language has **a beauty of its own and forms of expression** which are duplicated nowhere else.

—MARGARET MEAD, "UNISPEAK" ✤

✤ COMMA CAUTION: To avoid creating a comma splice°, do not use a comma to separate independent clauses unless they are linked by a coordinating conjunction (see 14c).

NO	Five inches of snow fell in two hours, one inch of ice built up when the snow turned to freezing rain. [The comma alone is insufficient. A coordinating conjunction must follow when the comma is used here.]
YES	Five inches of snow fell in two hours, **and** one inch of ice built up when the snow turned to freezing rain. [The coordinating conjunction *and* links the two independent clauses.]
YES	Five inches of snow fell in two hours. One inch of ice built up when the snow turned to freezing rain. [Independent clauses can become two separate sentences.] ✤

When independent clauses containing other commas are linked by a coordinating conjunction, you can choose to use a semicolon before the coordinating conjunction (see 25b). Base your decision on what would help your reader understand the material most easily.

Because temperatures remained low all winter, the snow could not melt until spring; **and** some people wondered when they would see grass again.

EXERCISE 24-1

Consulting section 24a, combine each pair of sentences using the coordinating conjunction shown in parentheses. When necessary, rearrange words. Insert commas before coordinating conjunctions that separate independent clauses.

EXAMPLE   Gold is a very rare metal. It was the first metal to be discovered. (yet)

Gold is a very rare metal, yet it was the first metal to be discovered.

1. John Sutter and James Marshall searched for gold in the United States. They found it in California in 1848. (and)

2. They tried to keep their discovery a secret. They did not want other people to find out about the riches. (for)
3. The news took half a year to reach the Atlantic coast. Then the word spread fast. (but)
4. President James Polk announced the discovery of gold in December 1848. The California gold rush began in 1849. (and)
5. Prospectors, adventurers, and business people rushed to the gold fields. Only a few of these people found enough gold to become rich. (yet)
6. The people who swarmed to California truly believed they could amass fortunes in gold. They would not have traveled the long trails to the Far West. (or)
7. As it turned out, John Sutter and James Marshall did not discover a significant amount of gold. They did not ever become rich. (nor)
8. Large numbers of people went to California looking for gold. They stayed even after the gold rush ended. (but)
9. Gold is highly malleable. A single ounce can be beaten into a thin film that would cover a hundred square feet. (so)
10. Medieval alchemists tried but failed to make gold out of cheaper metals. In the process of searching, they discovered strong acids that are extremely useful to modern industry. (yet)

24b Using a comma after an introductory clause, phrase, or word

Use a comma to signal the end of an introductory element and the beginning of an independent clause°.

PATTERN FOR COMMAS WITH INTRODUCTORY CLAUSES, PHRASES, AND WORDS 121

■ Introductory clause,
■ Introductory phrase, ⟶ independent clause.
■ Introductory word,

Cont'd.

2. They tried to keep their discovery a secret, for they did not want other people to find out about the riches.
3. The news took half a year to reach the Atlantic coast, but then the word spread fast.
4. President James Polk announced the discovery of gold in December 1848, and the California gold rush began in 1849.
5. Prospectors, adventurers, and business people rushed to the gold fields, yet only a few of these people found enough gold to become rich.
6. The people who swarmed to California truly believed they could amass fortunes in gold, or they would not have traveled the long trails to the Far West.
7. As it turned out, John Sutter and James Marshall did not discover a significant amount of gold, nor did they ever become rich.
8. Large numbers of people went to California looking for gold, but they stayed even after the gold rush ended.
9. Gold is highly malleable, so a single ounce can be beaten into a thin film that would cover a hundred square feet.
10. Medieval alchemists tried but failed to make gold out of cheaper metals, yet in the process of searching, they discovered strong acids that are extremely useful to modern industry.

COVERAGE: EXERCISE 24-1

1 and 4 use *and*; 3, 7, and 8, use *but*; 2 uses *for*; 6 uses *or*; 7 uses *nor*; 5 and 10 use *yet*; 9 uses *so*.

Some authorities omit the comma when an introductory element is very short and the sentence is clear without a comma. However, you will never be wrong if you use a comma after an introductory clause, phrase, or word in your college writing.

1 Using a comma after an introductory adverb clause

An adverb clause is a dependent clause (see 7o-2). It cannot stand alone as an independent unit because it starts with a subordinating conjunction (for example, *although, because, if;* for a complete list, see 7h). When an adverb clause precedes an independent clause, separate the clauses with a comma.

> **When it comes to eating,** you can sometimes help yourself more by helping yourself less.
>
> —RICHARD ARMOUR

2 Using a comma after an introductory phrase

A **phrase** is a group of words that cannot stand alone as an independent unit. It lacks a subject°, a predicate°, or both. Use a comma to set off a phrase that introduces an independent clause. (Types of phrases are explained in 7n.)

> **Between 1544 and 1689,** sugar refineries appeared in London and New York. [prepositional phrase°]
>
> **Obtained mainly from sugar cane and sugar beets,** sugar is also developed from the sap of maple trees. [past participle° phrase]
>
> **Beginning in infancy,** we develop lifelong tastes for sweet and salty foods. [participial phrase°]
>
> **To satisfy a craving for ice cream,** timid people sometimes brave midnight streets. [infinitive phrase°]
>
> **Eating being enjoyable,** we tend to eat more than we need for fuel. [absolute phrase°]

3 Using a comma after introductory words

Transitional expressions and **conjunctive adverbs** carry messages of a relationship between ideas in sentences and paragraphs.

Transitional expressions include *for example* and *in addition* (for a complete list, see Chart 22 in section 4d-1). Conjunctive adverbs include *therefore* and *however* (for a complete list, see Chart 52 in section 7f). When these introductory words appear at the beginning of a sentence, most writers follow them with a comma.

For example, fructose is fruit sugar that is metabolized as a blood sugar.

Interjections are introductory words that convey surprise or other emotions. Use a comma after an interjection at the beginning of a sentence: *Oh, we did not realize that you are allergic to cats. Yes, your sneezing worries me.*

❖ PUNCTUATION ALERT: Use a comma before and a comma after a transitional expression, conjunctive adverb, or interjection that falls within a sentence. Use a comma before such words that fall at the end of a sentence. ❖

EXERCISE 24-2

Consulting section 24b, insert commas where needed after introductory words, phrases, and clauses. If a sentence is correct, circle its number.

EXAMPLE   Although everyone values a car for transportation few people realize that a car can help them survive danger.

Although everyone values a car for transportation, few people realize that a car can help them survive danger.

(1) To protect your life in certain life-threatening circumstances you can use many resources from your car. (2) Surprisingly it contains many items that can help you survive. (3) For example a car's horn or its lights at night can alert rescuers as far as a mile away. (4) However these strategies will eventually deplete the car's battery. (5) A reservoir of oil is available under the hood. (6) Burned in a hubcap a quart will spew a miniature cloud visible for miles. (7) While some people know that any hose in the car can be used as a siphon to get at gasoline few realize that windshield washer tubing can be used for a life-saving tourniquet. (8) When you need a fire that will not go out for three to four hours you can burn a tire. (9) In most situations your car can serve as a bunkhouse. (10) Yes survival experts know that giving people this information saves lives.

TEACHING TIP

Group work in the writing classroom has become an increasingly popular teaching strategy in the last few years. Called by a variety of names (Reading-Response Groups, Peer Response Groups, Writing-in-Progress, for example), in all its forms the technique emphasizes sharing writing so that an audience besides the teacher can offer suggestions for improvement. Such groups can focus on any stage of the writing process, including editing. An article that discusses their use in classes for basic writers, "Ideas in Practice: Why Come to Class? Productive Class Time in a Developmental Writing Course" was published by Debra Gomez (*Journal of Developmental Education* 8 [1985]: 20–21). A more comprehensive view of why and how to organize writing groups for a writing class is offered by Anne Ruggles Gere in her book *Writing Groups* (Carbondale, IL: Southern Illinois UP, 1987).

ANSWERS: EXERCISE 24-2

1. circumstances, you
2. Surprisingly, it
3. For example, a
4. However, these
5. Correct
6. Burned in a hubcap, a
7. gasoline, few
8. hours, you
9. situations, your
10. Yes, survival

ANSWERS AND COVERAGE: EXERCISE 24-3

Answers may vary, but the following versions are possibilities.

1. When people bring fresh fruit back into the United States, they do not realize the dangers involved. [adverb clause]

2. For example, a person might bring back a mango or papaya to give as a gift. [introductory words—transitional expression]

3. Although fresh fruit carried into the United States may seem perfectly harmless, it may carry insects harmful to North American crops and livestock. [adverb clause]

4. To prevent the entry of illegal foods, the United States government passed a law forbidding people to carry certain fruits and vegetables through customs. [infinitive phrase]

5. Unfortunately, one traveler into the United States ignored the law in 1980 and smuggled some oranges that carried Mediterranean fruit flies. [introductory words—conjunctive adverb]

6. Because that one traveler was very selfish, many of California's orange groves were severely harmed. [adverb clause]

7. To wipe out the fruit flies, the government had to spend more than $100 million dollars. [infinitive phrase]

8. Recently, a new weapon has been developed to detect food smugglers. [introductory word—transitional expression]

9. Dressed in bright green jackets, beagles mingle with incoming travelers at five big-city airports in the United States. [participial phrase]

10. When the dogs sniff out food in bags or bundles, their human handlers alert customs officials to inspect the traveler's luggage. [adverb clause]

EXERCISE 24-3

Consulting section 24b, combine each set of sentences into one sentence that starts according to the directions in parentheses. You can add, delete, and rearrange words as needed. Be sure to use commas after introductory elements in the combined sentences.

EXAMPLE   Most travelers entering the United States are law-abiding people. They may be carrying illegal items. (clause beginning *although*)

Although most travelers entering the United States are law-abiding people, they may be carrying illegal items.

1. People bring fresh fruit back into the United States. They do not realize the dangers involved. (clause beginning *when*)

2. A person returning from the tropics might bring back a mango or papaya. The person might want to give the fruit as a gift. (begin with *for example*)

3. Fresh fruit carried into the United States may seem perfectly harmless. It may carry insects harmful to North American crops and livestock. (clause beginning *although*)

4. The United States government needed to prevent the entry of illegal foods. A law was passed forbidding people to carry certain fruits and vegetables through customs. (phrase beginning *to prevent*)

5. One traveler into the United States ignored the law in 1980. One traveler smuggled some oranges that carried Mediterranean fruit flies. (begin with *unfortunately*)

6. That one traveler was very selfish. Many of California's orange groves were severely harmed. (clause beginning *because*)

7. The government had to wipe out the fruit flies. This action cost more than $100 million dollars. (phrase beginning *to wipe out*)

8. A new weapon has been developed to detect food smugglers. This weapon has been developed recently. (begin with *recently*).

9. Beagles dressed in bright green jackets mingle with incoming travelers. The beagles work at five big-city airports in the United States. (phrase beginning *dressed*)

10. The dogs sniff out food in bags or bundles. Their human handlers alert customs officials to inspect the traveler's luggage. (clause beginning *when*)

24c Using commas to separate items in a series

A **series** is a group of three or more elements—words, phrases°, or clauses°—that match in grammatical form as well as in importance in the same sentence.

PATTERN FOR COMMAS IN A SERIES	122
■ word, word, and word	
■ word, word, word	
■ phrase, phrase, and phrase	
■ phrase, phrase, phrase	
■ clause, clause, and clause	
■ clause, clause, clause	

Marriage requires **sexual, financial, and emotional** discipline.

—Anne Roiphe, "Why Marriages Fail"

Culture is a way of **thinking, feeling, believing.**

—Clyde Kluckhohn, *Mirror for Man*

My love of flying goes back to those early days **of roller skates, of swings, of bicycles.**

—Teresa Wiggins, student

The big world of action is both dangerous and mysterious; you'll never really understand it. **Stay out of it, sit still, don't try.**

—Elizabeth Janeway, "Soaps, Cynicism, and Mind Control"

We have been taught **that children develop by ages and stages, that the steps are pretty much the same for everybody, and that to grow out of the limited behavior of childhood,** we must climb them all.

—Gail Sheehy, *Passages*

Some authorities omit the comma before the coordinating conjunction between the last two items of a series. This handbook does not recommend omitting this comma, for its absence can distort meaning and confuse a reader. If you never omit the comma in your academic writing, you will never be wrong.

When the items in a series contain commas or other punctuation, separate them with semicolons instead of commas (see 25d). This practice ensures that your sentence will deliver the meaning you intend.

> If it's a bakery, they have to sell cake; if it's a photography shop, they have to develop film; **and** if it's a dry-goods store, they have to sell warm underwear.
>
> —ART BUCHWALD, "Birth Control for Banks"

Numbered or lettered lists within a sentence are items in a series. Use commas (or semicolons if the items are long) to separate them when there are three or more items.

> To file your insurance claim, please enclose (1) a letter requesting payment, (2) a police report about the robbery, and (3) proof of purchase of the items you say are missing.

❖ COMMA CAUTION: Do not use a comma before the first item or after the last item in a series unless a different rule makes it necessary.

NO	Many artists, writers, and composers, have indulged in daydreaming and reverie.
YES	Many artists, writers, and composers have indulged in daydreaming and reverie.
NO	Such dreamers include, Miró, Debussy, Dostoevsky, and Dickinson.
YES	Such dreamers include Miró, Debussy, Dostoevsky, and Dickinson.
YES	Such dreamers include, of course, Miró, Debussy, Dostoevsky, and Dickinson. [The comma after *of course* is necessary to set off the phrase from the rest of the sentence.] ❖

EXERCISE 24-4

Consulting section 24c, insert commas to separate items in a series. If a sentence needs no commas, circle its number.

EXAMPLE   Recent studies show that people who watch television for more than a few straight hours are likely first to feel relaxed then to grow passive and eventually to develop self-contempt.

Recent studies show that people who watch television for more than a few straight hours are likely first to feel relaxed, then to grow passive, and eventually to develop self-contempt.

1. Viewers in the United States Canada West Germany and Italy ages 10 through 82 participated in a carefully designed study.

2. Participants agreed that for one week they would carry beepers listen for a signal about seven times a day and immediately fill in a form about their current mood and mental activity.

3. The participants were told to watch whatever amount of television they normally did and to do nothing special during the week of the study.

4. When viewing stretched on for hours, the viewers' responses showed that they lost their ability to concentrate that they felt increasingly unhappy and lonely and that they experienced guilt and anxiety.

5. A less expected problem was that after seeing so many beautiful competent captivating people on television the viewers felt inadequate and unable to compete.

24d Using a comma to separate coordinate adjectives

Coordinate adjectives are two or more adjectives° that equally modify a noun°. Separate coordinate adjectives with commas (unless the coordinate adjectives are joined by a coordinating conjunction such as *and* or *but*).

PATTERN FOR COMMAS WITH COORDINATE ADJECTIVES   123

coordinate adjective, coordinate adjective noun

COORDINATE ADJECTIVES

The **huge, restless** crowd waited for the concert to begin. [Both *huge* and *restless* modify *crowd*.]

The audience cheered happily when the **pulsating, rhythmic** music filled the stadium. [Both *pulsating* and *rhythmic* modify *music*.]

NONCOORDINATE ADJECTIVES

The concert featured **several new** bands. [*New* modifies *bands*; *several* modifies *new bands*.]

Each had a **distinctive musical** style. [*Musical* modifies *style*; *distinctive* modifies *musical style*.]

QUOTATION ABOUT WRITING

A world that has only periods is a world without inflections. It is a world without shade. It has a music without sharps and flats. It is a martial music. It has a jackboot rhythm. Words cannot bend and curve. A comma, by comparison, catches the gentle drift of the mind in thought, turning in on itself and back on itself, reversing, redoubling and returning along the course of its own sweet river music; while the semicolon brings clauses and thoughts together with all the silent discretion of a hostess arranging guests around her dinner table.

—Pico Iyer, "In Praise of the Humble Comma"

If you are not sure whether adjectives need a comma between them, use the "Tests for Coordinate Adjectives" in Chart 124. ❖ COMMA CAUTIONS: (1) Do not put a comma after a final coordinate adjective and the noun it modifies. (2) Do not put a comma between adjectives that are not coordinate. ❖

TESTS FOR COORDINATE ADJECTIVES   124

If either test given here works, the adjectives are coordinate and need a comma between them.

■ Can the order of the adjectives be reversed without changing the meaning or creating nonsense? If yes, use a comma.

NO   The concert featured **new several** bands. (Only *several new* makes sense.)

YES   The **huge, restless** (or *restless, huge*) crowd waited for the concert to begin.

NO   Each had a **musical distinctive** style. (Only *distinctive musical* makes sense.)

YES   The audience cheered happily as the **rhythmic, pulsating** (or *pulsating, rhythmic*) music filled the stadium.

■ Can the word *and* be inserted between the adjectives? If yes, use a comma.

NO   The concert featured **new and several** bands.

YES   The **large and restless** crowd waited.

ANSWERS: EXERCISE 24-5

1. correct

2. sophisticated, intricate system

3. bright, curious young chimp; cheerful, alert student; remarkable, unending desire

4. correct

5. exasperating, stubborn student; sharp, startling pinch

EXERCISE 24-5

Consulting section 24d, insert commas to separate coordinate adjectives. If a sentence needs no commas, circle its number.

EXAMPLE   A lively bright chimpanzee named Kanzi can communicate with humans.

A lively, bright chimpanzee named Kanzi can communicate with humans.

1. Kanzi communicates using a keyboard filled with complex geometric symbols.
2. Kanzi was not taught how to use the sophisticated intricate system.
3. The bright curious young chimp quickly and efficiently learned on his own by watching his mother being taught.
4. Kanzi has the most advanced linguistic abilities of any animal on

record, and he is a cheerful alert student with a remarkable unending desire to learn.

5. Kanzi sometimes can be an exasperating stubborn student who teases his teachers by doing exactly the opposite of what is asked, and he is not above giving his infant half-sister a sharp startling pinch if she is getting too much attention.

24e Using commas to set off nonrestrictive (nonessential) elements; not setting off restrictive (essential) elements

Perhaps the most difficult comma decisions are those related to **restrictive (essential)** elements and **nonrestrictive (nonessential)** elements. The comma usage rules themselves are easy. The difficult part comes in understanding what *restrictive, essential, nonrestrictive,* and *nonessential* mean. Before trying to master the rules, use Chart 125 to become familiar with the meaning of these terms. Then apply the definitions as you closely reread your writing and analyze what you want your reader to understand from your sentences.

DEFINITIONS OF "RESTRICTIVE" AND "NONRESTRICTIVE" 125

■ A **restrictive element** contains information **essential** for the reader to understand fully the meaning of the word or words that it modifies. It limits ("restricts") what it modifies.

> Some states retest drivers **over age 65** to check their driving competency.

The prepositional phrase° *over age 65* limits the word *drivers* so that a reader understands which drivers are being retested (not all drivers, only those over age 65). Therefore, *over age 65* is restrictive.

■ A **nonrestrictive element** is **not essential** for a reader to understand fully the word or words that it modifies. It describes but does not limit (does not "restrict") what it modifies.

> My parents, **who both are over age 65,** took a defensive driving course last year.

The relative clause° *who both are over age 65* describes *my parents,* but it is not essential to a reader's understanding which parents took a defensive driving course last year. Therefore, *who both are over age 65* is nonrestrictive.

Here are additional examples of restrictive and nonrestrictive elements.

RESTRICTIVE ELEMENTS

Some people **in my neighborhood** enjoy jogging. [The reader needs the information *in my neighborhood* to know which people enjoy jogging. The information is essential, so commas are not used.]

Some people **who are in excellent physical condition** enjoy jogging. [The reader needs the information *who are in excellent physical condition* to know which people enjoy jogging. The information is essential, so commas are not used.]

NONRESTRICTIVE ELEMENTS

An energetic person, Ed Stanford enjoys jogging. [Without knowing that Ed Stanford is energetic, the reader can understand that Ed Stanford enjoys jogging. The information is not essential, so commas are used.]

Ed Stanford, **who is in excellent physical condition,** enjoys jogging. [Without knowing that Ed Stanford is in excellent physical condition, the reader can understand the information that Ed Stanford enjoys jogging. The information is not essential, so commas are used.]

Ed Stanford enjoys jogging, **which is also my favorite pastime.** [Without knowing about my favorite pastime, the reader can understand the information that Ed Stanford enjoys jogging. The information is not essential, so commas are used.]

Once you understand the terms *restrictive, essential, nonrestrictive,* and *nonessential,* use Chart 126 to get to know the patterns for commas with nonrestrictive (nonessential) elements.

PATTERN FOR COMMAS WITH NONRESTRICTIVE ELEMENTS 126

- **Nonrestrictive element,** independent clause.
- Beginning of independent clause, **nonrestrictive element,** end of independent clause.
- Independent clause, **nonrestrictive element.**

❖ COMMA CAUTION: Remember, a restrictive element is essential. Do not set it off with commas (or any other punctuation) from the rest of the sentence. ❖

1 | Using commas to set off nonrestrictive (nonessential) clauses and phrases

Adjective clauses usually begin with relative pronouns or relative adverbs, such as *who, whom, that, which,* and *where.* Set nonrestrictive (nonessential) adjective clauses off with commas.

NONRESTRICTIVE CLAUSES

Farming, **which is a major source of food production,** may not always be dependent on the weather. [*Farming* in this sentence is not meant to be restricted by *which is a major source of food production,* so the information is not essential and commas are used.]

Organic farmers, **who use only natural substances to produce food,** disapprove of the widespread use of chemicals in commercial agriculture. [*Organic farmers* in this sentence is not meant to be restricted by *who use only natural substances to produce food,* so the information is not essential and commas are used.]

RESTRICTIVE CLAUSES

Much food **that is canned or frozen** is grown by the same large companies **that process it for consumption.** [The first restrictive clause limits the general word *food* to only food that is canned or frozen; the second one restricts the large companies to only those that process the food for consumption. The information in both cases is essential, and so commas are not used.]

❖ USAGE ALERT: In adjective clauses, use the relative pronoun *who* to refer to people. To refer to animals or things, some writers use the relative pronoun *which* both for restrictive and for nonrestrictive clauses. Other writers reserve *which* for nonrestrictive clauses and use *that* for restrictive clauses. You can follow either practice as long as you are consistent in each piece of writing. ❖

A **phrase** is a group of related words without a subject, a predicate, or both. Set nonrestrictive (nonessential) phrases off with commas.

NONRESTRICTIVE PHRASES

Farmers, **wanting the best possible yields,** use many techniques to enhance their crops' growth. [*Farmers* in this sentence is not meant to be limited by the phrase *wanting the best possible yields,* so the information is not essential and commas are used.]

RESTRICTIVE PHRASES

Farmers **retaining complete control over their land** are very hard to find these days. [*Farmers* in this sentence is meant to be narrowed to only those retaining complete control over their land, so the information is essential and commas are not used.]

471

2 Using commas to set off nonrestrictive appositives

An **appositive** is a word or group of words that renames the noun or noun group preceding it. A **nonrestrictive appositive** is not essential for the identification of what it is renaming; it is set off by commas.

NONRESTRICTIVE APPOSITIVE

The agricultural scientist, **a new breed of farmer,** controls the farming environment. [The appositive *a new breed of farmer* is not essential in identifying who controls the farming equipment, so the nonrestrictive appositive is set off with commas.]

Most appositives are nonrestrictive (nonessential). Once the name of something is given, words renaming it are not usually necessary to specify or limit it even more. In some cases, however, appositives are restrictive (essential) and are not set off with commas.

RESTRICTIVE APPOSITIVE

The agricultural scientist **Wendy Singh** has helped develop a new fertilization technique. [The appositive *Wendy Singh* is essential in identifying exactly which agricultural scientist has developed the new fertilization technique, so the restrictive appositive is not set off with commas.]

EXERCISE 24-6

Consulting section 24e and using your knowledge of restrictive and nonrestrictive clauses and phrases, insert commas as needed. If a sentence is correct, circle its number.

EXAMPLE   Elena Piscopia who began to study Aristotle at the age of seven took the examination for her doctoral degree.

Elena Piscopia, who began to study Aristotle at the age of seven, took the examination for her doctoral degree.

1. Elena Piscopia a resident of Venice was the first woman to receive a doctoral degree.
2. Many university officials reflecting the beliefs of their time opposed Elena's goal of higher education.
3. The doctoral examination of a woman a unique phenomenon in 1678 drew crowds of curious spectators.
4. Elena Piscopia who had prepared carefully for her questioners completed the examination easily.

ANSWERS AND COVERAGE:
EXERCISE 24-6

1. Elena Piscopia, a resident of Venice, was the first woman to receive a doctoral degree. [nonrestrictive appositive]

2. Many university officials, reflecting the beliefs of their time, opposed Elena's goal of higher education. [nonrestrictive participial phrase]

3. The doctoral examination of a woman, a unique phenomenon in 1678, drew crowds of curious spectators. [nonrestrictive appositive]

4. Elena Piscopia, who had prepared carefully for her questioners, completed the examination easily. [nonrestrictive relative clause]

→

5. Her replies which were given entirely in Latin amazed her examiners with their clarity and brilliance.

6. Elena Piscopia's father who was an exceptionally enlightened man for his time supported and encouraged his daughter's education.

7. Other women who lived in the 1600s were not so lucky.

8. Christine de Pisane widowed at 25 turned to writing to support herself and her three children.

9. She found herself unprepared and taught herself a complete course of study that included Latin, history, philosophy, and literature.

10. She later wrote *The City of Ladies* a book about women leading creative lives.

24f Using commas to set off transitional and parenthetical expressions, contrasts, words of direct address, and tag sentences

Words, phrases°, or clauses° that interrupt a sentence but do not change its essential meaning should be set off, usually with commas. (Dashes or parentheses can also set material off; see sections 29a and 29b.)

Conjunctive adverbs such as *however* and *therefore* (for a complete list, see Chart 52 in section 7f) and **transitional expressions** such as *for example* and *in addition* (for a complete list, see Chart 22 in section 4d-1) can express connections within sentences. When they do, set them off with commas.

> The American Midwest, **therefore,** is considered the world's breadbasket.
>
> California and Florida are important food producers, **for example.**

✤ COMMA CAUTION: Use a semicolon or a period—not a comma—before the conjunctive adverb or a transitional expression that falls between independent clauses. If you use a comma, you will create the error known as a comma splice (see Chapter 14). ✤

Parenthetical expressions are "asides," additions to sentences that the writer thinks of as extra. Set them off with commas.

> American farmers, **according to U.S. government figures,** export more wheat than they sell at home.
>
> A major drought, **sad to say,** reduces wheat crops drastically.

Cont'd.

5. Her replies, which were given entirely in Latin, amazed her examiners with their clarity and brilliance. [nonrestrictive relative clause]

6. Elena Piscopia's father, who was an exceptionally enlightened man for his time, supported and encouraged his daughter's education. [nonrestrictive relative clause]

7. None. [restrictive relative clause]

8. Christine de Pisane, widowed at twenty-five, turned to writing to support herself and her three children. [nonrestrictive participial phrase]

9. She found herself unprepared and taught herself a complete course of study, which included Latin, history, philosophy, and literature. [nonrestrictive relative clause]

10. She later wrote *The City of Ladies,* a book about women leading creative lives.

BACKGROUND

Erika Lindemann, in *A Rhetoric for Writing Teachers,* 2nd ed. (Oxford UP, 1987, p. 135) discusses how sentence combining can improve comma usage in student writing.

> Students who have learned to be careful about commas understandably "write around" the problem. Sentence-combining exercises not only illustrate how punctuation organizes sentence elements for a reader but also how to solve punctuation problems which for years have limited a student's range of syntactic options. Furthermore, the exercises sometimes expose misunderstood punctuation rules discussed in previous English classes . . . [and] grammatical labels [that] sometimes create punctuation problems. Sentence combining allows teachers to dispense with terminology altogether or, if they wish, to name constructions *after* students have practiced them.

Expressions of contrast describe something by stating what it is not. Set them off with commas.

Feeding the world's population is a serious problem, **but not an intractable one.**

We must work against world hunger continuously, **not just when emergencies develop.**

Words of **direct address** indicate the person or group spoken to. Set them off by commas.

Join me, **brothers and sisters,** to end hunger.

Your contribution to the Relief Fund, **Steve,** will help us greatly.

Tag sentences consist of a verb°, a pronoun°, and often the word *not*, generally contracted. Set off tag sentences with commas. If the tag sentence is a question, end it with a question mark.

Worldwide response to the Ethiopian famine was impressive, **wasn't it?**

Response to the next crisis will be as generous, **I hope.**

EXERCISE 24-7

Consulting section 24f, add necessary commas to set off transitional, parenthetical, and contrasting elements, words of direct address, and tag sentences.

EXAMPLE   Many well-known authors according to historical records have spent time in jail.

Many well-known authors, according to historical records, have spent time in jail.

1. Many well-known authors have been jailed for political reasons or for libel not for crimes against life or property.
2. Voltaire sad to say was jailed in 1717 for writing poems against the regent.
3. The British poet Richard Lovelace was jailed because of his political actions too.
4. O. Henry however served time for embezzling funds from the First National Bank in Austin, Texas.
5. It is ironic that many famous authors wrote important works of literature while they were jailed isn't it?

QUOTATION ABOUT WRITING

Unlike the period, question mark, exclamation, colon, dash, and parentheses, the comma has no clear special quality. . . . It is not a terminal marking like the period, a specialized coordinating mark like the semicolon, or an anticipatory mark like the colon. Even the dash, which comes nearest the comma in variety of uses, has a characteristic quality, and all the points except the dash have a much more limited number of uses. The comma may be used alone or in pairs; it may stand between coordinate expressions or may separate expressions of different grammatical rank; it may set off a group for emphasis or clearness even when the grammatical relation is close.

—George Summey, Jr.,
American Punctuation

ANSWERS AND COVERAGE: EXERCISE 24-7

Answers may vary slightly. Here is one set of possibilities.

1. Many well-known authors have been jailed for political reasons or for libel, not for crimes against life or property. [expression of contrast]

2. Voltaire, sad to say [parenthetical expression], was jailed in 1717 for writing poems against the regent.

3. The British poet Richard Lovelace was jailed because of his political actions, too. [transitional word]

4. O. Henry, however, [transitional word] served time for embezzling funds from the First National Bank in Austin, Texas.

5. It is ironic that many famous authors wrote important works of literature while they were jailed, isn't it? [tag sentence]

24g Using commas to set off quoted words from explanatory words

Use a comma to set off quoted words from short explanations in the same sentence. This rule holds whether the explanatory words come before, between, or after the quoted words.

PATTERNS FOR COMMAS WITH QUOTED WORDS   127

- Explanatory words, "Quoted words."
- "Quoted words," explanatory words.
- "Quoted words begin," explanatory words, "quoted words continue."

Speaking of ideal love, the poet William Blake wrote, "Love seeketh not itself to please."

"My love is a fever," said William Shakespeare about love's passion.

"I love no love," proclaimed poet Mary Coleridge, "but thee."

This use of commas is especially important in communicating conversations or other direct discourse. Explanatory words like *she said, they replied,* and *he answered* are called **speaker tags,** and they are always set off from immediately following words of direct discourse in the ways shown in the pattern chart.

Because explanatory words such as *that* or *as* create a different kind of grammatical setting (such as a noun clause° or a subject complement°) for the quoted words, do not separate the explanatory words from the quoted words with a comma. (For capitalization in quotations, see 30c.)

Shakespeare also wrote that "Love's not Time's fool."

The duke describes the duchess as being "too soon made glad."

Shaw's quip "Love is a gross exaggeration of the difference between one person and everybody else" delights me.

Sometimes words a person has spoken or written are conveyed through indirect discourse. The writer does not use direct quotation but instead paraphrases material. Do not use a comma after *that* in indirect discourse.

BACKGROUND

Here is the complete poem by William Blake quoted in 24g.

The Clod and the Pebble

"Love seeketh not itself to please,
Nor for itself hath any care,
But for another gives its ease,
And builds a Heaven in Hell's despair."

So sung a little Clod of Clay
Trodden with the cattle's feet,
But a Pebble of the brook
Warbled out these metres meet:

"Love seeketh only self to please,
To bind another to its delight,
Joys in another's loss of ease,
And builds a Hell in Heaven's despite."

BACKGROUND

Here is the complete poem by Mary Coleridge quoted in 24g.

My True Love Hath My heart and I Have His

None ever was in love with me but grief.
    She wooed me from the day that I was born;
She stole my playthings first, the jealous thief,
    And left me there forlorn.

The birds that in my garden would have sung,
    She scared away with her unending moan;
She slew my lovers too when I was young,
    And left me there alone.

Grief, I have cursed thee often—now at last
    To hate thy name I am no longer free;
Caught in thy bony arms and prisoned fast,
    I love no love but thee.

Shakespeare also wrote that people should be true to themselves.

✣ COMMA CAUTION: **When quoted words end with a question mark or an exclamation point, keep that punctuation even if explanatory words follow.**

QUOTED WORDS *"O Romeo! Romeo!"*

NO   "O Romeo! Romeo**!,"** called Juliet as she stood at her window.

NO   "O Romeo! Rome**o,"** called Juliet as she stood at her window.

YES "O Romeo! Romeo!" called Juliet as she stood at her window.

QUOTED WORDS *"Wherefore art thou Romeo?"*

NO   "Wherefore art thou Romeo**?,"** continued Juliet as she yearned for her new-found love.

NO   "Wherefore art thou Rome**o,"** continued Juliet as she yearned for her new-found love.

YES "Wherefore art thou Romeo?" continued Juliet as she yearned for her new-found love. ✣

EXERCISE 24-8

Consulting section 24g, punctuate the following dialogue correctly. If a sentence is correct, circle its number.

EXAMPLE   "Was anyone with the injured boy?," asked the admissions clerk.

"Was anyone with the injured boy?" asked the admissions clerk.

1. "His father" replied the ambulance driver "but he's unconscious."

2. "This boy looks like he needs surgery, but he is the son of the surgeon now on duty" said the clerk.

3. She explained in an agitated voice "Surgeons do not operate on their own family members."

4. "How can he be the surgeon's son when his father is still in the ambulance?" asked the driver.

5. With a disgusted look, the clerk told the driver "The surgeon is the boy's mother."

ANSWERS: EXERCISE 24-8

1. "His father," replied the ambulance driver, "but he's unconscious."

2. "This boy looks like he needs surgery, but he is the son of the surgeon now on duty," said the clerk.

3. She explained in an agitated voice, "Surgeons do not operate on their own family members."

4. Correct

5. With a disgusted look, the clerk told the driver, "The surgeon is the boy's mother."

COVERAGE: EXERCISE 24-8

1. explanatory words in the middle of a quotation

2. explanatory words at the end of a quotation

3. explanatory words at the beginning of a quotation

4. Correct (no comma should follow the question mark)

5. explanatory words at the beginning of a quotation.

24h Using commas in dates, names, addresses, and numbers according to accepted practice

When you write dates, names, and numbers, be sure to use commas according to accepted practice.

RULES FOR COMMAS WITH DATES   128

- Use a comma between the date and the year: **July 20,** 1969.
- Use a comma between the day and the date: **Sunday,** July 20, 1969.
- Within a sentence, use a comma on both sides of the year in a full date.

  > Everyone wanted to be near a television set on **July 20, 1969,** to watch Armstrong emerge from the lunar landing module.

- Do not use a comma in a date that contains the month with only a day or the month with only a year. Also, do not use a comma in a date that contains only the season and year.

  > The major news story during **July 1969** was the moon landing; news coverage was especially heavy on **July 21.**

- An inverted date takes no commas: **20 July 1969.**

  > People stayed near their television sets on **20 July 1969** to watch the moon landing.

RULES FOR COMMAS WITH NAMES, PLACES, AND ADDRESSES   129

- When an abbreviated title (Jr., M.D., Ph.D.) comes after a person's name, use a comma between the name and the title—**Rosa Gonzales,** M.D.—and also after the title if it is followed by the rest of the sentence:

  > The jury listened closely to the expert testimony of **Rosa Gonzales,** M.D. last week.

- When you invert a person's name, use a comma to separate the last name from the first: **Troyka,** David.   ➡

BACKGROUND

One of the most disputed topics in the teaching of composition concerns the effectiveness of formal grammar instruction in improving student writing. Opinions, many of them supported by research and experience, range from those that insist on the necessity for writers to understand the rules of grammar to those that would replace all such instruction with writing experience. Typical of the dialogue to be found in professional journals is a series of articles published in *College English* in 1985. Patrick Hartwell began the discussion by claiming that because teaching grammar does not improve student writing, teachers should look for more effective means of instruction ("Grammar, Grammars, and the Teaching of English" 47 [February 1985]: 105–127). The article was rebutted by Martha Kolln in "Comment on 'Grammar, Grammars, and the Teaching of Grammar' 47 (February 1985) and a Response," also published in *College English* 47 [December 1985]: 874–879). Additional comments from four theorists appeared, along with a final commentary from Hartwell, in the same journal, in October 1985 (641–650).

Another article dealing with the controversy is "John S. Mayher's "Grammar and Consciousness" (*Connecticut English Journal* 15 [Spring 1984]: 29–30), in which Mayher reports research to support his argument against teaching grammar to improve writing. Also, in "Three Reasons Why We Shouldn't Teach Grammar and One Why We Should (Sort Of)" (*Connecticut English Journal* 18 [Spring 1985]: 1–4), Robert C. Small argues that because grammar instruction is abstract, time-consuming, and ineffective, it should not be included in composition classes, but he suggests that it has a more appropriate place in linguistics courses.

QUOTATION ABOUT WRITING

The commas are the most useful and usable of all the stops. It is highly important to put them in place as you go along. If you try to come back after doing a paragraph and stick them in the various spots that tempt you you will discover that they tend to swarm like minnows into all sorts of crevices whose existence you hadn't realized and before you know it the whole long sentence becomes immobilized and lashed up squirming in commas. Better to use them sparingly, and with affection, precisely when the need for each one arises, nicely, by itself.

—Lewis Thomas

RULES FOR COMMAS WITH NAMES, PLACES, AND ADDRESSES (*continued*)

■ Use a comma to separate the names of a city and state: **Philadelphia, Pennsylvania.** If the city and state fall within a sentence, use a comma after the state as well, unless the state name ends the sentence and thus is followed by a period, question mark, or exclamation point.

The Liberty Bell has been on display in **Philadelphia, Pennsylvania,** for many years.

■ When you write a complete address as part of a sentence, use a comma to separate all the items, with the exception of the zip code. The zip code follows the state after a double space but no comma. Also, do not follow the zip code with a comma.

I wrote to **Mr. U. Lern, 10-01 Rule Road, Englewood Cliffs, New Jersey 07632** for the instruction manual.

RULES FOR COMMAS WITH LETTERS

130

■ For the opening of an informal letter, use a comma:

Dear Betty,

The opening of a business or formal letter takes a colon (:).

■ For the close of a letter, use a comma:

Sincerely yours,   **Best regards,**
Love,   **Very truly yours,**

RULES FOR COMMAS WITH NUMBERS

131

■ Counting from the right, put a comma after every three digits in numbers over four digits: **72,867   156,567,066**

■ A comma is optional for most four-digit numbers. Use a consistent style within a given piece of writing.

$1776	**$1,776**
1776 miles	**1,776 miles**
1776 potatoes	**1,776 potatoes**

➜

RULES FOR COMMAS WITH NUMBERS (*continued*)

- Do not use a comma for a four-digit year: **1990** (a year of five digits or more gets a comma: **25,000 B.C.**); in an address of four digits or more: **12161 Dean Drive;** or in a page number of four digits or more: **see page 1338**
- Use a comma to separate related measurements written as words: **five feet, four inches**
- Use a comma to separate a scene from an act in a play: **Act II, scene iv**
- Use a comma to separate a reference to a page from a reference to a line: **page 10, line 6**

EXERCISE 24-9

Consulting section 24h, insert commas where they are needed. If a sentence is correct, circle its number.

EXAMPLE   Perhaps Eden Texas offers people an earthly paradise.

Perhaps Eden, Texas, offers people an earthly paradise.

1. Eden Texas lies 165 miles north of San Antonio Texas and has a population of 1400.
2. A researcher reported in the summer of 1983 that there are 16 Edens listed in the zip code book.
3. Eden Prairie Minnesota must be an attractive spot, for its population soared between January 1 1970 and January 1 1980 from 6938 to 16263.
4. The citizens of Edenton North Carolina publish a brochure saying their town is the "South's Prettiest Town."
5. The brochure reports that the town is 135 miles from Raleigh North Carolina and has a population of 5264.

24i   Using commas to clarify meaning

Sometimes you will need to use a comma to clarify the meaning of a sentence, even though no other rule calls for one.

ANSWERS: EXERCISE 24-9

1. Eden, Texas, lies 165 miles north of San Antonio, Texas, and has a population of 1,400 **[or 1400]**.
2. Correct
3. Eden Prairie, Minnesota, must be an attractive spot, for its population soared between January 1, 1970, and January 1, 1980, from 6,938 **[or 6938]** to 16, 263.
4. The citizens of Edenton, North Carolina, publish a brochure saying their town is the "South's Prettiest Town."
5. The brochure reports that the town is 135 miles from Raleigh, North Carolina, and has a population of 5,264 **[or 5264]**.

COVERAGE: EXERCISE 24-9

1. comma after city and state; commas with numbers
2. correct
3. comma after city and state; commas with dates; comma with numbers
4. comma after city and state
5. comma after city and state; comma with numbers

24j ,

NO	Of the gymnastic team's twenty five were injured.
YES	Of the gymnastic team's twenty, five were injured.
NO	Those who can practice many hours a day.
YES	Those who can, practice many hours a day.
NO	George dressed and performed for the sellout crowd.
YES	George dressed, and performed for the sellout crowd.

ANSWERS: EXERCISE 24-10

1. Using specially prepared tape, recorders communicate hidden messages to listeners.

2. Some people who want to, learn supposedly without effort by listening to the tape.

3. Correct

4. Of the twenty, nine reported pilferage had decreased by about 37 percent.

5. Correct

EXERCISE 24-10

Consulting section 24i, insert commas to prevent misreading. If a sentence is correct, circle its number.

EXAMPLE   Though controversial subliminal learning appeals to many people.

Though controversial, subliminal learning appeals to many people.

1. Using specially prepared tape recorders communicate hidden messages to listeners.

2. Some people who want to learn supposedly without effort by listening to the tape.

3. To prevent shoplifting twenty major department stores started using subliminal tapes.

4. Of the twenty nine reported pilferage had decreased by about 37 percent.

5. Many people worry that governments or businesses might use subliminal learning to control people against their will.

BACKGROUND

In an article entitled "Pain and Suffering: Apostrophes and Academic Life" (*Journal of Basic Writing* 7 [Fall 1988]: 91–98), Irvin Hashimoto argues for tolerance on the part of teachers towards students' punctuation errors. He describes what happens when writers "wade into the wonderful sea of arbitrary punctuation."

24j Avoiding misuse of the comma

Using commas correctly helps you deliver your meaning to your reader. As a writer, you frequently have to make decisions about whether a comma is needed. If as you are drafting (see 3b) you are in doubt about a comma, insert and circle it clearly so that you can go back to it later when you are revising (see 3c) and think through whether it is correct. Throughout this chapter, most sections that discuss a correct use of the comma include a COMMA CAUTION to alert you to a related misuse of the comma. This section summarizes the most frequent misuses of the comma.

1 Avoiding misuse of a comma with coordinating conjunctions

Section 24a discusses the correct use of commas with sentences joined by coordinating conjunctions°. Do not put a comma *after* a coordinating conjunction that joins two independent clauses° unless another rule makes it necessary. Also, do not use commas to separate two items joined with a coordinating conjunction.

NO	The sky was dark gray **and,** it looked like dusk.
YES	The sky was dark gray, **and** it looked like dusk.
NO	**The moon, and the stars** were shining last night.
YES	**The moon and the stars** were shining last night.

2 Avoiding misuse of a comma with subordinating conjunctions and prepositions

Do not put a comma *after* a subordinating conjunction° or a preposition° unless another rule makes it necessary.

NO	**Although, the storm brought high winds,** it did no damage.
YES	**Although the storm brought high winds,** it did no damage.
NO	The storm did no damage **although, it brought high winds.**
YES	The storm did no damage **although it brought high winds.**
NO	People expected worse **between, the high winds and the heavy downpour.**
YES	People expected worse **between the high winds and the heavy downpour.**

3 Avoiding misuse of commas to separate items

Section 24c discusses the correct use of commas with items in a series. Do not use a comma *before* the first or *after* the last item in a series, unless another rule makes it necessary.

BACKGROUND

The power of the comma was demonstrated at the 1984 Republican National Convention. An item proposed for the party platform read "The Convention opposes any form of tax increase which would hurt the economy." Someone called for the addition of a comma, so that the item would read, "The Convention opposes any form of tax increase, which would hurt the economy."

That comma was a reflection of the conservative economic position of its proposer. In the first version of the sentence, *which* begins a restrictive clause. The author of the proposal was talking only of harmful tax increases and implying that nonharmful increases would be acceptable. In the second version, *which* begins a nonrestrictive clause. This author saw all tax increases as the same—harmful.

BACKGROUND

From a study of 100 basic writers, Carole McAllister and Richard Louth concluded that the use of a word processor raises the quality of students' revisions (ERIC ED 281 232).

NO	The gymnasium was decorated with, **red, white, and blue** ribbons for the Fourth of July.
NO	The gymnasium was decorated with **red, white, and blue,** ribbons for the Fourth of July.
YES	The gymnasium was decorated with **red, white, and blue** ribbons for the Fourth of July.

Section 24d discusses the correct use of commas with coordinate adjectives°. Do not put a comma after the final coordinate adjective and the noun it modifies. Also, do not use a comma between noncoordinate adjectives.

NO	The **huge, restless,** crowd waited.
YES	The **huge, restless** crowd waited.
NO	The concert featured **several, new** bands.
YES	The concert featured **several new** bands.

4 Avoiding misuse of commas with restrictive elements

Section 24e discusses the correct use of commas with restrictive (essential) elements° and nonrestrictive (nonessential) elements°. Do not use a comma to set off a restrictive (essential) element from the rest of a sentence.

| NO | Vegetables, **stir-fried in a wok,** are uniquely crisp and flavorful. [The information about being stir-fried in a wok is essential, so it is not set off with commas.] |
| YES | Vegetables **stir-fried in a wok** are uniquely crisp and flavorful. |

5 Avoiding misuse of commas with quotations

Section 24g discusses the correct use of commas with quoted material. Do not use a comma to set off indirect discourse° (often signalled by *that* or *as*).

NO	Jon **said that, he likes stir-fried vegetables.**
YES	Jon **said that he likes stir-fried vegetables.**
YES	Jon **said, "I like stir-fried vegetables."**

EXTRA EXERCISE B

Circle unnecessary commas and add needed commas where restrictive and nonrestrictive phrases, clauses, and appositives appear in the following sentences.

1. Elizabeth II, who is queen of the United Kingdom, was born in London in 1926.

2. She is the elder daughter of King George VI and Queen Consort Elizabeth, who is now known as the Queen Mother.

3. Her education, administered at home by private tutors, covered a wide variety of subjects.

4. She was married at Westminster Abbey to Philip Mountbatten, who was formerly Prince Philip of Greece.

5. He was created duke of Edinburgh, with all the rights and privileges of the title, on the eve of the marriage.

6. Prince Charles Elizabeth's first child was born on November 14, 1948.

7. Princess Anne the second child was born on August 15, 1950.

8. Elizabeth's father George VI died in 1952.

9. She was crowned, Queen of England, in Westminster Abbey a historic site on June 2, 1953.

10. Prince Charles, now heir apparent, thus became, the Duke of Cornwall.

➜

| 6 | Avoiding use of a comma to separate a subject from its verb, a verb from its object, a verb from its complement, and a preposition from its object |

NO   **Orville and Wilbur Wright, made** their first success-ful airplane flights on December 17, 1903. [As a rule, do not let a comma separate a subject from its verb.]

YES   **Orville and Wilbur Wright made** their first successful airplane flights on December 17, 1903.

NO   These inventors enthusiastically **tackled, the prob-lems** of powered flight and aerodynamics. [As a rule, do not let a comma separate a verb from its object°.]

YES   These inventors enthusiastically **tackled the problems** of powered flight and aerodynamics.

NO   Flying has **become, both** an important industry and a popular hobby. [As a rule, do not let a comma separate a verb from its complement°.]

YES   Flying has **become both** an important industry and a popular hobby.

NO   Airplane hobbyists visit Kitty Hawk's flight **museum from, all over the world.** [As a rule, do not let a comma separate a preposition° from its object.]

YES   Airplane hobbyists visit Kitty Hawk's flight museum **from all over the world.**

Because the comma occurs so frequently, advice against over-using it sometimes clashes with a rule requiring it. In such cases, follow the rule that calls for the comma.

The town of Kitty Hawk, North Carolina, attracts thousands of tourists each year. [Although the comma after *North Carolina* separates the subject and verb, it is required because the state is set off from the city and from the rest of the sentence; see 24h.]

EXERCISE 24-11

Some deliberately misused commas have been added in these sentences. Consulting 24j and the other sections in this chapter that are referred to in 24j, delete unneeded commas. If a sentence is correct, circle its number.

EXAMPLE   Airplanes started as little more than motorized, double-winged, gliders, and have advanced to supersonic transporta-tion in less than a century.

Airplanes started as little more than motorized, double-winged gliders and have advanced to supersonic transportation in less than a century.

1. Correct
2. She is the elder daughter of King George VI and Queen Consort Elizabeth, who is now known as the Queen Mother.
3. Her education, administered at home by private tutors, covered a wide variety of subjects.
4. She was married at Westminster Abbey to Philip Mountbatten, who was formerly Prince Philip of Greece.
5. Correct
6. Prince Charles, Elizabeth's first child, was born on November 14, 1948.
7. Princess Anne, the second child, was born on August 15, 1950.
8. Elizabeth's father, George VI, died in 1952.
9. She was crowned Queen of England in Westminster Abbey, a historic site, on June 2, 1953.
10. Prince Charles, now heir apparent, thus became the Duke of Cornwall.

ANSWERS AND COVERAGE: EXERCISE 24-11

1. Wilbur [omit: coordinating conjunction joining two nouns] and Orville Wright proved that people could fly in 1903.   ➔

Cont'd.

2. U.S. engineers were building [omit: do not separate verb from object] rocket planes for research as early as 1943.

3. The planes were built to withstand the intense air pressure [omit: clause is restrictive] that is present at Mach 1.

4. Mach 1 [omit: don't separate subject and verb] is defined as the speed of sound, [keep: opens nonrestrictive clause] which is approximately 738 miles per hour [omit: restrictive phrase] at sea level.

5. Finally, [optional keep: one-word transition] the Bell X-1, [keep: open nonrestrictive appositive] the product of many engineering challenges, [keep: close nonrestrictive appositive] was perfected.

6. Air Force Captain [omit: restrictive appositive] Charles E. Yeager [omit: restrictive appositive] reached Mach 1 and broke the sound barrier [omit: restrictive prepositional phrase] in a Bell X-1 rocket plane in 1947.

7. This [omit: do not separate subject and verb] was the first supersonic flight [omit: restrictive phrase] in history.

8. At first, [optional omit: the introductory phrase is short] all supersonic jets were military, [keep: coordinating conjunction joining two independent clauses] but Russia initiated commercial supersonic transport (SST) [omit: contextually restrictive] in 1968.

9. England and France, [keep: open parenthetical] you may remember, [keep: close parenthetical] cooperated with each other to build an SST, [keep: open appositive] the Concorde.

10. Landings of the Concorde SST at American airports [omit: do not separate subject and verb] has been a topic [omit: do not separate verb from object] of much debate, [keep: coordinating conjunction joining two independent clauses] for many people worry [omit: restrictive clause] that such planes might inflict long-term damage on areas around the airports.

1. Wilbur, and Orville Wright proved in 1903 that people could fly.

2. U.S. engineers were building, rocket planes for research as early as 1943.

3. The planes were built to withstand the intense air pressure, that is present at Mach 1.

4. Mach 1, is defined as the speed of sound, which is approximately 738 miles per hour, at sea level.

5. Finally, the Bell X-1, the product of many engineering challenges, was perfected.

6. Air Force Captain, Charles E. Yeager, reached Mach 1 and broke the sound barrier, in a Bell X-1 rocket plane in 1947.

7. This, was the first supersonic flight, in history.

8. At first, all supersonic jets were military, but Russia initiated commercial supersonic transport (SST), in 1968.

9. England and France, you may remember, cooperated with each other to build an SST, the Concorde.

10. Landings of the Concorde SST at American airports, have been a topic, of much debate, for many people worry, that such planes might inflict long-term damage on areas around the airports.

REVISING YOUR WRITING

If you make comma errors when you write, go back to your writing and locate the errors. Using this chapter as a resource, revise your writing to correct the errors. Use Chart 119 at the beginning of this chapter to help you locate each use of the comma.

CASE STUDY: REVISING FOR CORRECT USE OF COMMAS

In these case studies, you can observe a student writer revising. Then you have the chance to revise other student writing on your own.

Observation

A student wrote the following draft for a course called Introduction to Sociology. The assignment was to write about a person who organizes group efforts to improve society. This material is well organized and includes excellent specific details, but the draft's effectiveness is diminished by the presence of comma errors.

Read through the draft. The errors are highlighted and explained. Before you look at the student's revision, revise the material yourself. Then compare what you and the student did.

commas missing to set off nonrestrictive phrase: 24e-1

comma missing after introductory word: 24b-3

comma missing after introductory phrase: 24b-2

commas missing to set off nonrestrictive phrase: 24e-1

comma missing between coordinate adjectives: 24d

comma missing in a number of five digits: 24h

Millard Fuller, executive director of Habitat for Humanity, believes that all people have a right to decent housing. Habitat for Humanity an organization that depends on volunteer labor and donations of money and materials builds modest sturdy homes that are sold at cost to low-income families. Previously these families had rented substandard housing without plumbing or heat. The full cost of each Habitat home is approximately $28000. To buy a home each family has to make a

COVERAGE: PARTICIPATION ESSAY

Consumers often feel that choosing a new car is a *difficult time-consuming* [24d: commas for coordinate adjectives] matter. Most automobile customers tend to concentrate on *the price, the special features the look and the reputation* [24c: commas in a series] of the car. Truly *experienced informed* [24d: commas for coordinate adjectives] car buyers *however* [24f: commas for transitional word in middle of a sentence] carefully investigate the car manufacturer's grievance procedures.

A common mistake that consumers make is to assume that the *helpful friendly* [24d: commas for coordinate adjectives] car salesperson will help resolve problems with the automobile after it is purchased. In fact [24b: comma after introductory words] the salesperson's job is essentially finished once the car is *sold so a consumer* [24a: comma before coordinating conjunction that joins two independent clauses] with a complaint will usually *hear "You'll* [24g: comma before quoted words] have to talk to the service department."

If a car salesperson offers little or no help [24b: comma after introductory clause] a consumer may feel cheated by the indifference. One reaction *one felt by many people who end up with a lemon of a car* [24e: commas for nonrestrictive appositive] is to write an angry letter to the chief executive officer of the automobile manufacturer. *Before writing* [24b: comma after introductory phrase; also 24i: comma needed for clarity] the consumer should realize that complaints to the manufacturer are referred back to the dealership. *After all* [24b: comma after introductory words; also 24i: comma needed for clarity] dealerships and manufacturers are not owned and managed by the same people.

In some cases [24b: comma after introductory words] consumers may benefit from legal advice. States have varying ➡

small down payment and support a mortgage. The monthly mortgage payment is usually about $150⎸an amount less than [comma missing to set off nonrestrictive appositive: 24e-2] the monthly rent that the family had been paying for their indecent housing. Nevertheless⎸Habitat for Humanity is not a charitable organization. The families offered the homes must be able to take on the financial responsibility [commas missing between items in a series: 24c] involved⎸participate in the labor of building their house⎸and donate time to help build other houses. When Fuller asks people to [comma missing before quoted words: 24g] help⎸he says⎸"It's not your blue blood⎸your pedigree⎸or your [commas missing between items in a series: 24c] college degree. It's what you do with your life that counts." One famous volunteer recruited to take on a yearly assignment is Jimmy Carter⎸former President of the United States. The concept of Habitat for Humanity is catching on⎸for the number of new Habitat U.S. affiliates increased from 11 to 171 between 1980 and 1986. This seems like an excellent way to fight poverty housing⎸doesn't it? [comma missing to set off tag sentence: 24f]

[comma missing after introductory word: 24b-3]

[commas missing between items in a series: 24c]

[comma missing after introductory clause: 24b-1]

[comma missing to set off nonrestrictive appositive: 24e-2]

[comma missing between independent clauses joined by *for*: 24a]

Here is how the student revised to correct the comma errors. Compare it with your revision. Make sure that your revision has eliminated each of the errors highlighted in the draft.

Millard Fuller, executive director of Habitat for Humanity, believes that all people have a right to decent housing. Habitat for Humanity, an organization that depends on volunteer labor and donations of money and materials, builds modest, sturdy homes that are sold at cost to low-income families. Previously, these families had rented substandard housing without plumbing or heat. The full cost of each Habitat home is approximately $28,000. To buy a home, each family has to make a small down payment and support a mortgage. The monthly mortgage payment is ➡

usually about $150, an amount less than the monthly rent that the family had been paying for their indecent housing. Nevertheless, Habitat for Humanity is not a charitable organization. The families offered the homes must be able to take on the financial responsibility involved, participate in the labor of building their house, and donate time to help build other houses.

When Fuller asks people to help, he says, "It's not your blue blood, your pedigree, or your college degree. It's what you do with your life that counts." One famous volunteer recruited to take on a yearly assignment is Jimmy Carter, former President of the United States. The concept of Habitat for Humanity is catching on, for the number of new Habitat U.S. affiliates increased from 11 to 171 between 1980 and 1986. This seems like an excellent way to fight poverty housing, doesn't it?

Participation

A student wrote the following draft for a course called Introduction to Political Science. The assignment was to discuss an example of the power of consumers. The material is clear and logically presented, but the draft's effectiveness is diminished by comma errors.

Read through the draft. Then revise it to eliminate the errors. Also, make any additional revisions you think would improve the content, organization, and style of the material.

Consumers often feel that choosing a new car is a difficult time-consuming matter. Most automobile customers tend to concentrate on the price, the special features the look and the reputation of the car. Truly experienced informed car buyers however carefully investigate the car manufacturer's grievance procedures.

A common mistake that consumers make is to assume that the helpful friendly car salesperson will help resolve problems with the automobile after it is purchased. In fact the salesperson's job is essentially finished once the car is sold so a consumer with a complaint will usually hear "You'll have to talk to the service department."

If a car salesperson offers little or no help a consumer may feel cheated by the indifference. One reaction often felt by many people who end up with a lemon of a car is to write an angry letter to the chief executive officer of the automobile company.

Cont'd.
"lemon laws" to help consumers who purchase defective cars. In some states *for example* [24f: commas for transitional word in middle of a sentence] the existence of a problem, *that is unresolved*, [24e: drop commas with restrictive element] after six repair attempts by the dealership's service department can require a dealer to substitute a new vehicle. Chrysler Motors has the Customer Arbitration Board (CAB), which consists of a consumer advocate, a member of the general public, and an *independent, technical expert* [24d: drop comma with noncoordinate adjectives]. Any solution that the CAB proposes is binding on the dealer and Chrysler Motors.

It is comforting to know that a consumer, *who buys a lemon of a car,* [24e: drop commas with restrictive clause] is not always *helpless isn't it?* [24h: comma for tag question] Sometimes a lemon can be made into lemonade, right?

ANSWER: PARTICIPATION ESSAY
This version revises the comma errors. Answers will vary if students have revised content, organization, or style.

Consumers often feel that choosing a new car is a difficult, time-consuming matter. Most automobile customers tend to concentrate on the price, the special features, the look, and the reputation of the car. Truly experienced, informed car buyers, however, carefully investigate the car manufacturer's grievance procedures.

A common mistake that consumers make is to assume that the helpful, friendly car salesperson will help resolve problems with the automobile after it is purchased. In fact, the salesperson's job is essentially finished once the car is sold, so a consumer with a complaint will usually hear, "You'll have to talk to the service department."

If a car salesperson offers little or no

ANSWER: PARTICIPATION ESSAY, *continued*

help, a consumer may feel cheated by the indifference. One reaction, one felt by many people who end up with a lemon of a car, is to write an angry letter to the chief executive officer of the automobile manufacturer. Before writing, the consumer should realize that complaints to the manufacturer are referred back to the dealership. After all, dealerships and manufacturers are not owned and managed by the same people.

In some cases, consumers may benefit from legal advice. States have varying "lemon laws" to help consumers who purchase defective cars. In some states, for example, the existence of a problem that is unresolved after six repair attempts by the dealership's service department can require a dealership to substitute a new vehicle. Chrysler Motors has the Customer Arbitration Board (CAB), which consists of a consumer advocate, a member of the general public, and an independent technical expert. Any solution that the CAB proposes is binding on the dealer and Chrysler Motors.

It is comforting to know that a consumer who buys a lemon of a car is not always helpless, isn't it? Sometimes a lemon can be made into lemonade, right?

Before writing the consumer should realize that complaints to the manufacturers are referred back to the dealership. After all dealerships and manufacturers are not owned and managed by the same people.

In some cases consumers may benefit from legal advice. States have varying "lemon laws" to help consumers who purchase defective cars. In some states for example the existence of a problem, that is unresolved, after six repair attempts by the dealership's service department can require a dealer to substitute a new vehicle. Chrysler Motors has the Customer Arbitration Board (CAB), which consists of a consumer advocate, a member of the general public, and an independent, technical expert. Any solution that the CAB proposes is binding on the dealer and Chrysler Motors.

It is comforting to know that a consumer, who buys a lemon of a car, is not always helpless isn't it? Sometimes a lemon can be made into lemonade, right?

25 The Semicolon

25a Using a semicolon between closely related independent clauses

When independent clauses° are clearly related in meaning, you can separate them with a semicolon instead of a period. The choice is yours in relation to the meaning you want your material to deliver. A period signals complete separation between independent clauses; a semicolon tells readers that the separation is softer.

SEMICOLON PATTERN I   132

Independent clause; independent clause.

This is my husband's second marriage; it's the first for me.

—RUTH SIDEL, "Marion Deluca"

Our Constitution is in actual operation; everything appears to promise that it will last; but in this world nothing is certain but death and taxes.

—BENJAMIN FRANKLIN

❖ COMMA CAUTION: Do not use only a comma between independent clauses, or you will create the error called a comma splice (see Chapter 14). ❖

Punctuation contributes to art as well as to correctness, to style as well as to styling. Make it work for you, not just to develop prose that is "clear enough"—not just to prevent confusion—but to help you express yourself, or your characters express themselves. Don't lean on it; don't shy away from it; just *use* it—and in doing so, let it help you convey nuances too subtle for words alone to convey; let it help you evoke effects so delicate that talk would shatter them. And remember that if you frequently use more marks than usual—or fewer than usual—you will call attention to your craft, with the results possibly seeming artful rather than artistic, posturing rather than expressive. Nor do I for a moment suggest that punctuation can, or should, be charged with sole responsibility for effectiveness: descriptive detail, diction, sentence length, sentence rhythm, paragraph structure, timing—these and other elements of style can and must share the load.

—Robert M. Pierson, "Punctuation as Art"

ALTERNATE EXAMPLES

1. Each year people from all over the world visit the Tower of London; for centuries, it served as a prison for famous persons who were deemed to be enemies of the crown.

2. The Tower is located in the Borough of Stepney; it covers about eighteen acres.

3. The central portion, called the White Tower, was begun in 1078; it was modernized by Christopher Wren.

4. The Beauchamp Tower has 91 inscriptions of prisoners in it; the Bloody Tower served as the prison of Sir Walter Raleigh, who wrote an incomplete *History of the World* during his stay there in 1614.

5. The place of execution within the walls was Tower Green; there Anne Boleyn was beheaded in 1536.

25b Using a semicolon before a coordinating conjunction joining independent clauses containing commas

When independent clauses° are linked by a coordinating conjunction (*and, but, or, nor, for, yet, so*), a comma should separate them (see 24a), but there is one exception. When one of the independent clauses contains a comma, you can use a semicolon before the coordinating conjunction. Choose according to what would be easier for your reader.

SEMICOLON PATTERN II   133

- Independent clause, one that contains a comma, coordinating conjunction independent clause.
- Independent clause; coordinating conjunction independent clause, one that contains a comma.
- Independent clause, one that contains commas; coordinating conjunction independent clause, one that contains a comma.

When the peacock has presented his back, the spectator will usually begin to walk around him to get a front view; but the peacock will continue to turn so that no front view is possible.

—FLANNERY O'CONNOR, "The King of the Birds"

For anything worth having, one must pay the price; and the price is always work, patience, love, self-sacrifice.

—JOHN BURROUGHS

25c Using a semicolon when conjunctive adverbs or other transitional expressions connect independent clauses

You can use a semicolon between two independent clauses when the second clause begins with a conjunctive adverb (*therefore, however;* for a complete list, see Chart 52 in 7f) or other transitional expression (*in fact, as a result;* for a complete list, see Chart 22 in 4d-1). Your other option is to use a period, creating two sentences.

SEMICOLON PATTERN III 134
■ Independent clause; conjunctive adverb, independent clause. ■ Independent clause; transitional expression, independent clause.

The average annual rainfall in Death Valley is about two inches; **nevertheless,** hundreds of plant and animal species survive and even thrive there.

Patient photographers have spent years recording desert life cycles; **as a result,** all of us have watched barren sands flower after a spring storm.

❖ COMMA ALERTS: (1) Do not use *only* a comma between independent clauses connected by a conjunctive adverb or other words of transition, or you will create the error called a comma splice; see Chapter 14. (2) Usually use a comma *after* a conjunctive adverb or a transitional expression that begins an independent clause, although some writers omit the comma after short words, such as *then, next, soon.* ❖

25d Using a semicolon between long or comma-containing items in a series

When a sentence contains a series of phrases° or clauses° that are long or that contain commas, use a semicolon, not a comma, to separate the items. This practice enables your reader to read without having to stop to figure out where one item in the series ends and the next begins. (For information on using commas in a series, see 24c.)

SEMICOLON PATTERN IV 135
Independent clause containing a series of items, any of which contain a comma; another item in the series; another item in the series.

1. Black varieties of the leopard are common in humid parts of India; however, they are rare in Africa.
2. Leopards prey on monkeys, birds, and reptiles; consequently, they must hunt both in trees and on the ground.
3. A leopard begins its meal by tearing at the forequarters of its prey; in contrast, the tiger starts with the hindquarters of its victim.
4. One Indian leopard was alleged to have killed 200 human beings in two years before it was shot; similarly, a leopard in Ceylon used to lie in wait for passers-by on a main road.
5. The leopard's roar of belligerence is different from its mating call; nevertheless, both sound fierce to the human ear.

BACKGROUND
During the rise of printing, punctuation was to a large degree left up to the judgment of the compositor because vernacular languages, such as English, had not devised any strict conventions to follow. Because handwritten copy was often hard to read, and authors were not always sure of how to punctuate their texts, little effort was made to reproduce manuscripts with fidelity. The result was a free interpretation on the part of the printer.

ALTERNATE EXAMPLES

1. A newborn baby exhibits what we interpret to be fear at a sudden, loud, unexpected noise; the removal of parental, mechanical, or other physical support; and the appearance of strange, unexpected, unknown objects mixed with familiar ones.

2. A baby shows rage when its free, uninhibited movement is constrained; when its regular, nourishing feeding pattern is interrupted; or when its expected, traditional, physical comfort is disturbed.

3. Most practical jokes, such as unexpected, loud, exploding fireworks; collapsing, unstable seats; and mysterious, deceptive, disappearing objects are an exploitation of these situations.

4. Laughter can be explained in terms of feelings of malice or envy; awareness of contrast, incongruity, or ugliness; relief from this experience; or in terms of its more positive result, a feeling of sudden glory; a surge of vital feeling; or a sense of freedom.

ANSWERS AND COVERAGE: EXERCISE 25-1

1. . . . Conrad Gesner in 1559; he saw them . . . [25a, closely related independent clauses] person famous for growing exotic plants.

2. . . . a favorite flower; in fact, the tulip's name . . . [25c, transitional expression connecting independent clauses] comes from a Turkish word for *turban*.

3. . . . throughout Dutch society; it became a . . . [25a, closely related independent clauses] mark of good taste to have a garden full of them.

➜

Functioning as assistant chefs, the students chopped onions, green peppers, and parsley; sliced chicken and duck meat into strips; started a broth simmering; and filled a large, low, copper pan with oil before the head chef stepped to the stove.

25e Avoiding the misuse of the semicolon

1 Not using a semicolon after an introductory phrase or between a dependent clause and an independent clause

NO   Once opened; the computer lab will be well used.

YES Once opened, the computer lab will be well used.

NO   Although the new computers had arrived at the college; the computer lab was still being built.

YES Although the new computers had arrived at the college, the computer lab was still being built.

2 Using a colon, not a semicolon, to introduce a list

NO   The newscast featured three major stories; the latest pictures of Uranus, a speech by the president, and a series of brush fires in Nevada.

YES The newscast featured three major stories: the latest pictures of Uranus, a speech by the president, and a series of brush fires in Nevada.

EXERCISE 25-1

Consulting sections 25a–25e, insert semicolons where they are needed, and change any incorrectly used semicolons to correct punctuation. If a sentence is correct, circle its number.

EXAMPLE   In the seventeenth century, the citizens of Holland became victims of tulip madness, this mania became so intense that regular businesses were neglected while people bought and sold tulips.

In the seventeenth century, the citizens of Holland became victims of tulip madness; this mania became so intense that regular businesses were neglected while people bought and sold tulips.

1. Tulips were first noted in Holland by Conrad Gesner in 1559, he saw them in the garden of Counsellor Herwart, a person famous for growing exotic plants.

2. Herwart had gotten the onionlike bulbs from a friend traveling in Turkey, where tulips were a favorite flower, in fact, the tulip's name comes from a Turkish word for *turban*.

3. Growing tulips quickly became popular throughout Dutch society, it became a mark of good taste to have a garden full of them.

4. Soon, merchants and shopkeepers were competing to find the rarest specimens, consequently, prices for these prized bulbs soared.

5. As tulip bulb prices reached preposterous heights, Dutch businesses of all kinds began to suffer because money needed for other goods was tied up in tulip purchases.

6. In 1635, a person might invest 100,000 florins to buy forty bulbs, but four tons of beer cost 32 florins, twelve sheep 120 florins, a thousand pounds of cheese 100 florins, and a silver cup 60 florins.

7. In Amsterdam, a very rare tulip was exchanged for the following items; 4,600 florins, an expensive, gilded carriage, and two gray horses, complete with harnesses, bridles, and bells.

8. Brokers began to trade tulips on the stock exchanges, therefore, Dutch nobles, farmers, merchants, servants, and street-sweepers alike found themselves growing richer as prices rose.

9. One merchant discovered that a rare bulb was missing after a messenger had made a delivery, an hour later he found the messenger finishing lunch, which included the ''onion'' he had taken from the merchant's office.

10. Although Holland's tulip madness has calmed down considerably today; growing tulips is an important industry in that country.

EXERCISE 25-2

Combine each set of sentences into one sentence containing two independent clauses. Use a semicolon between the two clauses. You may add, omit, revise, and rearrange words. Try to use all the patterns in this chapter. More than one revision may be correct, so be ready to explain the reasoning behind your decisions.

EXAMPLE   Roller coasters have been around for a long time. Today's roller coasters barely resemble their ancestors. Today's roller coasters are scientifically designed.

Roller coasters have been around for a long time; however, today's scientifically designed roller coasters barely resemble their ancestors.

Cont'd.

4. . . . the rarest specimens; consequently, prices . . . [25c, conjunctive adverb connecting independent clauses]

5. Correct

6. . . . to buy forty bulbs; but four tons . . . [25b, coordinating conjunction joining independent clauses]

7. . . . following items: [25e-2, list introduced by colon, not semicolon] 4,600 florins; an expensive, gilded carriage; and two gray horses, complete with harnesses, bridles, and bells [25d, between comma-containing items in a series].

8. . . . on the stock exchanges; therefore, [25c, conjunctive adverb joining independent clauses] Dutch nobles, farmers, merchants, servants, [note that commas should be used between the items in the series here] and street-sweepers alike found themselves growing richer as prices rose.

9. made . . . a delivery; an hour later he found the messenger finishing lunch, which included the "onion" he had taken from the merchant's office [25a, closely related independent clauses containing one or more commas]

10. Although Holland's tulip madness has calmed down considerably today, growing tulips . . . [25e-1, use a comma, not a semicolon, to separate a dependent clause from an independent clause]

ANSWERS: EXERCISE 25-2

1. The first roller coaster in the United States, installed in the late nineteenth century, was part of an amusement park in the Coney Island section of New York City: it was named the "Switchback Gravity Pleasure Railway."

2. The first roller coaster was extremely primitive; it was built of wood, had only two inclines, and reached a downhill speed of a mere six miles per hour.

→

ANSWERS: EXERCISE 25-2, *continued*

3. Riders got on at the top of the first incline and climbed out when the train reached the bottom; then the riders walked up the hill to the top of the second incline and climbed in for the ride to the bottom.

4. Soon a chain drive for roller coasters was developed to power the train on the uphill parts; therefore, higher inclines could be built to give riders a greater thrill.

5. Major breakthroughs in roller-coaster design occurred in the 1970s, when roller coaster designers drew on advanced knowledge from physics, mathematics, and human physiology; and the designers used computer simulations to check their work.

6. Extraordinarily sophisticated scientific applications to roller coasters began to appear in the 1980s; in fact, some high school physics teachers were so impressed that they began to use examples of modern roller-coaster design to illustrate principles in physics.

7. A 360-degree circle cannot be used for a roller coaster loop because speed reduction at the top of a 360-degree circle could pull riders from their seats; in contrast, the tear-shaped clothoid loop has been found to permit roller-coaster riders to speed along safely upside down at 70 miles per hour.

8. The Shock Wave, opened in the late 1980s at an Illinois amusement park, has a height of 17 stories; a short downhill run of 70 miles per hour; rapidly reversing directions, patterned after a twisted pretzel; and a sequence of corkscrew spirals.

9. A recent visitor to New York's Coney Island amusement park reported that the 61-year-old wooden Cyclone was half-empty; and the new Double Loop, designed with the latest advances in roller-coaster engineering, drew huge crowds.

10. Many roller-coaster enthusiasts drive long distances to try out a new roller coaster; however, many other people are repelled by the thought of riding a roller coaster.

1. The first roller coaster in the United States was installed in the late nineteenth century. It was installed as part of an amusement park. The park was in the Coney Island section of New York City. It was named the "Switchback Gravity Pleasure Railway."

2. The first roller coaster was extremely primitive. It was built of wood. It had only two inclines. It reached a downhill speed of a mere six miles per hour.

3. Riders got on at the top of the first incline. Riders climbed out when the train reached the bottom. Then the riders walked up the hill to the top of the second incline. Once again they climbed in for the ride to the bottom.

4. Soon a chain drive for roller coasters was developed. The chain drive powered the train on the uphill parts. Higher inclines could be built. The higher inclines gave riders a greater thrill.

5. Major breakthroughs in roller-coaster design occurred in the 1970s. Roller coaster designers drew on advanced knowledge from physics, mathematics, and human physiology. The designers used computer simulations to check their work.

6. Extraordinarily sophisticated scientific applications to roller coasters began to appear in the 1980s. Some high school physics teachers were very impressed. The teachers began to use examples of modern roller-coaster design to illustrate principles in physics.

7. A 360-degree circle cannot be used for a roller coaster loop. Speed reduction at the top of a 360-degree circle could pull riders from their seats. The clothoid loop has been found to permit roller-coaster riders to speed along safely upside down at 70 miles per hour. A clothoid loop is tear shaped.

8. The Shock Wave opened in the late 1980s. It opened at an Illinois amusement park. It has a height of 17 stories. It has a short downhill run of 70 miles per hour. It has rapidly reversing directions, patterned after a twisted pretzel. It has a sequence of corkscrew spirals.

9. A recent visitor to New York's Coney Island amusement park gave a report. The report was that the 61-year-old wooden Cyclone was half-empty. The new Double Loop drew huge crowds. The Double Loop was designed with the latest advances in roller-coaster engineering.

10. Many people are roller-coaster enthusiasts. They drive long distances to try out a new roller coaster. Many other people are repelled by the thought of riding a roller coaster.

EXERCISE 25-3

Consulting sections 25a–25e, insert semicolons where they are needed. If a sentence is correct, circle its number.

EXAMPLE On April 20, 1960, the capital of Brazil was Rio de Janeiro, on April 21 of that year Brasilia became the new capital.

On April 20, 1960, the capital of Brazil was Rio de Janeiro; on April 21 of that year Brasilia became the new capital.

1. As early as colonial days, Brazilian officials had expressed a desire to move the capital inland they hoped that this move would encourage development.
2. When the Brazilian constitution was written in 1891, one clause stated that Rio de Janeiro should no longer be the capital.
3. In 1956 Juscelino Kubitschek was elected president of Brazil, one of his campaign promises was that a new capital would be built.
4. Kubitschek kept his promise, indeed, construction of the new capital began within a year.
5. Lucio Costa planned the layout of the streets, and Oscar Niemeyer designed the buildings.
6. When viewed from above, the city looks a little like a jet, with the suburban areas making up the wings and the government areas the fuselage.
7. The city officially became the capital in 1960, however, many governmental agencies remained in Rio de Janeiro for some time.
8. Many Brazilians argue that the capital should be returned to Rio de Janeiro, nevertheless, it appears that Brasilia will remain the seat of government.
9. The cost of the city was far too great to abandon it now, moreover, it has improved life in the interior regions.
10. Brasilia has helped the economy of the region, it has drawn people to the country's interior, expecially Planalto, it continues to serve the country well as the center of government.

EXERCISE 25-4

Consulting sections 25a–25e, combine each set of sentences into one sentence containing two independent clauses. Use a semicolon between the two clauses. You may omit, add, revise, or rearrange words. More than one answer may be correct.

ANSWERS: EXERCISE 25-3

1. As early as colonial days, Brazilian officials had expressed a desire to move the capital inland; they hoped that this would encourage development. [25a, between comma-containing independent clauses]

2. Correct

3. In 1956 Juscelino Kubitschek was elected president of Brazil; one of his campaign promises was that a new capital would be built. [25a, between closely related independent clauses]

4. Kubitschek kept his promise; indeed, construction of the new capital began within a year. [25c, between independent clauses joined by a transitional expression]

5. Lucio Costa planned the city; Oscar Niemeyer designed the buildings. [25a, between closely related independent clauses]

6. Correct

7. The city officially became the capital in 1960; however, many governmental agencies remained in Rio de Janeiro for some time. [25c, between independent clauses joined by a conjunctive adverb]

8. Many Brazilians argue that the capital should be returned to Rio de Janeiro; nevertheless, it appears that Brasilia will remain the seat of government. [25c, conjunctive adverb]

9. The cost of building the city was far too great to abandon it now; moreover, it has improved life in interior regions. [25c, conjunctive adverb]

10. Brasilia has helped the economy of the region; it has drawn people to the country's interior, especially Planalto; it continues to serve the country well as the center of government. [25a, a series of closely related independent clauses]

ANSWERS AND COVERAGE: EXERCISE 25-4

Answers will vary. Here is one set of possibilities.

1. Some postcards offer colorful views of exotic places or reproduce famous paintings; others feature portraits of famous persons. [25a, closely related independent clauses]

2. On postcard racks today you can find a wide variety of selections; you may find a classic scene from a Bogart film or a giant cactus with sunglasses. [25a, closely related independents]

3. Postcards have been popular for a long time; however, there was a so-called "Golden Age of Postcards" that lasted from the turn of the century to the Great Depression. [25c, independents joined by a conjunctive adverb]

4. Some rare postcards are extremely valuable; for example, a signed original by the artist Alphonse Mucha recently sold for $3,000. [25c, independents joined by a transitional expression]

5. The first postcard was designed in 1869 by Emmanuel Hermenn; four years later, the U.S. government began issuing especially designed "postal cards" with an illustration on one side and a space for an address and stamp on the other. [25a, comma-containing independents]

EXAMPLE   Postcards are more than a means of communication. They are miniature works of art. Some of them can be quite valuable.

Postcards are more than a means of communication; they are miniature works of art, some of them quite valuable.

1. Some postcards offer colorful views of exotic places. Some cards reproduce famous paintings. Others feature portraits of famous persons.

2. On postcard racks today you can find a wide variety of selections. You may find a classic scene from a Bogart film. On the other hand, you may see a giant cactus with sunglasses.

3. Postcards have been popular for a long time. However, there was a so-called "Golden Age of Postcards." That lasted from the turn of the century to the Great Depression.

4. Some rare postcards are extremely valuable. A signed original by the artist Alphonse Mucha is a good example. One of these cards recently sold for $3,000.

5. The first postcard was designed in 1869. It was designed by Emmanuel Hermenn. Four years later the U.S. government began issuing specially designed "postal cards." These cards had an illustration on one side and a space for an address and stamp on the other.

26 The Colon

26a Using a colon after an independent clause to introduce a list, an appositive, or a quotation

You can use a colon to introduce statements that summarize, restate, or explain what is said in an independent clause°.

COLON PATTERN I   136

- Independent clause: list.
- Independent clause: appositive.
- Independent clause: "Quoted words."

A colon can introduce a list only when the words before the colon are an independent clause. After phrases such as *the following* or *as follows,* a colon is usually required. A colon is not called for with the words *such as* or *including* (see 26d).

LISTED ITEMS

If you really want to lose weight, you need give up only three things: breakfast, lunch, and dinner.

The students' demands included the following: an expanded menu in the cafeteria, improved janitorial services, and more up-to-date textbooks.

BACKGROUND

A *colon* (in Greek *kōlon*) was originally a person's or an animal's limb. As such it came to be used to refer to a portion of a strophe in choral dancing, then to a division in prosody, and later to a principal clause in a sentence. Finally it became the sign marking the breathing space at the end of a clause.

Historically the colon as a mark of punctuation was preceded by the semicolon, but in English it had more use than the semicolon until the nineteenth century, when it was employed almost solely as a mark of anticipation. It began to regain prestige with the publication of Fowler's *A Dictionary of Modern English Usage* in 1926 and has experienced increased usage since that time.

QUOTATION ABOUT WRITING

The colon is usually a mark of addition or expectation, with emphasis on a following explanation, list, table, or quotation. With formal words (*as follows* or the like) it raps for attention; with easy wording it is little more formal than the somewhat lighter semicolon. It is not a series or balancing point like the semicolon; it seems to say "Watch carefully what comes next."

—George Summey, *American Punctuation*

497

QUOTATION ABOUT WRITING

Remember that colons—perhaps the mark we exploit least—generally mean that what is to come will explain what has just gone by. They imply identity, whereas semicolons imply "separate but equal" status. "I have just learned three facts: that St. Paul is the capital of Minnesota; that Helena is the capital of Montana; and that Lincoln is the capital of Nebraska." Everything after the colon adds up to "three facts"—whereas the three statements of fact, though they have much in common, are not identical (there are three, not one). Colons can also save words and create special effects. Compare:

- I admire her poetry. Its imagery is magnificent.
- I admire her poetry for its magnificent imagery.
- I admire her poetry: its imagery is magnificent.

All three versions are "correct." The first is emphatic and probably clear—or clear enough: *Probably* your reader will realize that the second sentence explains the first. The second version is clearer, and it flows along smoothly. The third is clearer than the first and just as clear as the second, and it gives us a unique kind of silence—not just a break (the period did *that*) but mild suspense. Your job is to decide which way of punctuating best expresses what *you* want to express.

—Robert M. Pierson, "Punctuation as Art"

QUOTATION ABOUT WRITING

An unnecessary mark is worse than useless. It is an interruption.

—George Summey, *American Punctuation*

A colon can introduce an appositive—a word or words that rename a noun° or pronoun°—but only if the introductory words are an independent clause.

APPOSITIVE

The Metropolitan Museum in New York City now owns the best-known works of Louis Tiffany's studio: those wonderful stained-glass windows. [*Stained-glass windows* renames *best-known works.*]

A colon can introduce a quotation, but only if the introductory words are an independent clause°. Use a comma, not a colon, if the introductory words are not an independent clause (see 24b).

QUOTATION

The little boy in *E.T.* did say something neat: "How do you explain school to a higher intelligence?"

—GEORGE F. WILL, "Well, *I* Don't Love You, E.T."

❖ QUOTATION ALERT: When a quotation is more than four lines, it must be *displayed* on lines indented ten spaces (see 28a). ❖

26b Using a colon between two independent clauses

When the first independent clause° explains or summarizes the second independent clause, a colon can separate them.

COLON PATTERN II 137
Independent clause: Independent clause.

❖ CAPITALIZATION ALERT: You can use a capital letter or a lower-case letter for the first word of an independent clause that follows a colon. Whichever you choose, be consistent in each piece of writing. This handbook uses a capital letter.

We will never forget the first time we made dinner at home together: He got stomach poisoning and for four days was too sick to go to work.

—LISA BALADENDRUM, student ❖

26c Using a colon to separate standard material

TITLE AND SUBTITLE

A Brief History of Time: From the Big Bang to Black Holes

HOURS, MINUTES, AND SECONDS

The plane took off at 7:15 p.m.
The track star passed the halfway point at 1:23:02.

In the military services, hours and minutes are written without colons (and always use four digits):

The staff meeting originally scheduled for Tuesday at 0930 will be held Tuesday at 1430 instead.

CHAPTERS AND VERSES OF THE BIBLE

Psalms 23:1–3   Luke 3:13

MEMO FORM

To: Dean Kristen Olivero
From: Professor Daniel Black
Re: Student Work-Study Program

SALUTATION OF FORMAL OR BUSINESS LETTER

Dear Ms. Morgan:

For the use of colons in documenting sources, see 33c–33d.

26d Avoiding misuse of the colon

A complete independent clause *must* precede a colon, except with standard material (see 26c). When you have not written an independent clause, do not use a colon.

NO	The cook bought: eggs, milk, cheese, and bread.
YES	The cook bought eggs, milk, cheese, and bread.

The words *such as, including, like,* and *consists of* can be tricky: Do not let them lure you into using a colon incorrectly (see 26a).

ALTERNATE EXAMPLES

1. To introduce quotations, summaries, lists:

   a. Alice Roosevelt Longworth's colorful reputation is exemplified by this remark: "I have a simple philosophy. Fill what's empty. Empty what's full. And scratch where it itches."

   b. Greek mythology comprises the description of the gods and the various stories told about them: it is a series of narratives depicting their personalities, functions, and relationships.

   c. Zeus, the supreme god of the Greeks, served in a number of capacities: as weather god, sender of rain and lightning, and ruler over the other gods.

2. To separate material:

   a. Eric Partridge is the author of *You Have a Point There: A Guide to Punctuation and Its Allies* as well as *Usage and Abusage: A Guide to Good English.*

   b. I will cite the work in the bibliography as follows:
   O'Connor, Flannery. "The Life You Save May Be Your Own." *The Realm of Fiction: Seventy-Four Stories.* Ed. James B. Hall and Elizabeth Hall. 3rd ed. New York: McGraw, 1977. 479–88.

   c. To: Professor Dorothy Bankston
   From: Professor Sylvia Iskander
   Re: Selection of textbooks

TEACHING TIP

Of all the elements of writing, punctuation is probably the most rule-bound. It makes more demands on a writer to be acquainted with the conventions governing its use. Edgar Schuster takes up the issue of writing rules in "Let's Get Off the Mythmobile" (*English Journal* 74 [October 1985]: 40–43), in which he refutes five commonly accepted requirements of grammar by citing examples from the work of several established authors who deviated from them.

ALTERNATE EXERCISE

You may want to ask your students to re-write the following sentences, omitting the colons. The students will probably have to divide each into several sentences.

1. The institution of marriage is generally divided by sociologists into four main types: monogamy, polygyny, polyandry, and group marriage.

2. An early reference to group marriage was made by Julius Caesar concerning the early Britons: "Ten and even twelve have wives common to them, and particularly brothers among brothers, and parents among their children."

3. Monogamy, the marriage of one man with one woman, is the most widely approved form in contemporary society: it is the basis of the modern family.

4. Polygyny is practiced by some religious sects: it is acceptable, for example, in some Arab countries.

5. Most American women do not generally favor such an arrangement: they have no desire to be one of several wives.

QUOTATION ABOUT WRITING

For what is Punctuation, and what its aim? It is the art of dividing a literary composition into sentences, and parts of sentences, by means of points, for the purpose of exhibiting the various combinations, connections, and dependencies of words. And what is this process but a means of facilitating that analysis and combination which must be made, consciously or unconsciously, before we can penetrate to the very core of an author's thoughts, and appropriate them as food for the life and growth of our own minds?

—John Wilson, *A Treatise on English Punctuation*, 32nd ed., 1899

NO	The health board discussed a number of problems, **such as:** poor water quality, an aging sewage treatment system, and the lack of an alternate water supply.
YES	The health board discussed a number of problems, **such as** poor water quality, an aging sewage treatment system, and the lack of an alternate water supply.
YES	The health board discussed a number of problems: poor water quality, an aging sewage treatment system, and the lack of an alternate water supply.

Do not use a colon to separate a phrase° or dependent clause° from an independent clause.

NO	Day after day: the drought dragged on.
YES	Day after day, the drought dragged on.
NO	After the drought ended: the farmers celebrated.
YES	After the drought ended, the farmers celebrated.

EXERCISE 26-1

Consulting sections 26a–26d, insert colons where they are needed and delete unnecessary ones. If a sentence is correct, circle its number.

EXAMPLE   Most runners ignore how slim their chances are of winning the New York Marathon, about 1 in 26,000.

Most runners ignore how slim their chances are of winning the New York Marathon: about 1 in 26,000.

1. Chefs in the most fashionable restaurants in large cities report a new dessert craze; chocolate cake with a melting chocolate center.

2. The chefs describe two principal types of cake: (1) those with a solid chocolate layer that melts in the oven and (2) those that are underbaked so the center stays semiliquid.

3. Although ingredients for the two versions of the cake vary, three are common in recipes for both, chocolate, sugar, and butter.

4. Unfortunately: lots of calories are common to both.

5. A book used in many business courses today is *Business Ethics; Concepts and Cases.*

6. Its author describes the primary aim of the book in these words "To introduce the reader to the ethical concepts that are relevant to resolving moral issues in business."

7. Among artists married to artists, two couples illustrate some interesting dynamics of fame, Lee Krasner and Jackson Pollack, both respected today, although Pollack is far more famous; and Georgia O'Keeffe and photographer Alfred Stieglitz, with O'Keeffe more famous than Stieglitz, at least in the last years of the twentieth century.

8. Insurance companies classify adventurous people such as: astronauts, drivers of hydroplanes, and auto race drivers, as bad risks.

9. Calling: "Max, Max," Belinda ran through the forest.

10. Cadets;
This year's graduation ceremony begins at 1400 hours, but tell your parents 200 p.m., so that no one will be confused.

11. On April 8, 1974, Babe Ruth's home run record was finally broken. Henry Aaron became the new home run king.

12. In the past century, vaccines have been developed for five diseases, diphtheria, measles, polio, typhoid fever, and whooping cough.

13. To;   All Employees
From;   Management
Re;   Vacation Schedules

14. In *Silent Spring,* the environmentalist Rachel Carson wrote these words about pollution, "The chemical barrage has been hurled against the fabric of life."

15. The city's budget crisis carries a message, How long can government continue to spend beyond its means?

ANSWERS AND COVERAGE: EXERCISE 26-1

1. craze: chocolate cake [26a, appositive]
2. Correct
3. both: chocolate [26a, list]
4. Unfortunately, lots [26d, not an independent clause]
5. *Ethics: Concepts* [26c, separate standard material]
6. words: "To [26a, quotation]
7. fame: Lee [26a, list]
8. such as astronauts [26a, not an independent clause]
9. Calling, "Max [26a, not an independent clause]
10. Cadets: [26c, formal salutation]
11. broken: Henry [26b, between two independent]
12. diseases: diphtheria [26a, list]
13. To: All; From: Management; Re: Vacation [26c, memo form]
14. pollution: "The [26a, quotation]
15. message: How [26b, between two independent clauses]

QUOTATION ABOUT WRITING
When we are very young, we tend to regard the ability to use a colon much as a budding pianist regards the ability to play with crossed hands: many of us, when we are older, regard it as a proof of literary skill, maturity, even of sophistication: and many, whether young, not so young, or old, employ it gauchely, haphazardly, or at best inconsistently.

—Eric Partridge, *You Have a Point There*

27 The Apostrophe

BACKGROUND

The English apostrophe was adopted from French, which had taken it from Latin *apostrophus*. It had, not surprisingly, come to Latin from Greek, in which it referred to elision or omission.

The apostrophe plays three major roles: it helps to form the possessive of nouns and some pronouns; it stands for one or more omitted letters; and it helps to form the plurals of letters and numerals. It does *not* help form plurals of nouns or the possessive case of personal pronouns.

27a Using an apostrophe to form the possessive case of nouns and indefinite pronouns

The **possessive case** serves to communicate ownership or close relationship.

| OWNERSHIP | The writer's pen |
| CLOSE RELATIONSHIP | The novel's plot |

Possession in nouns and certain indefinite pronouns can be communicated by phrases beginning with *of, (comments of the instructor, comments of Professor Montana)* or by an apostrophe in combination with an *-s (instructor's comments).*

1 Adding -'s to show possession when nouns and indefinite pronouns do not end in s

The **dean's** duties included working closely with the resident assistants. [*dean* = singular noun° not ending in *s*]

In one more year I will receive my **bachelor's** degree. [*bachelor* = singular noun not ending in *s*]

QUOTATION ABOUT WRITING

A well-educated American almost always tries, at least, to adhere as a rule to (his conception of) the national standard [of punctuation]; a well-educated Englishman is more likely, I think, to regard the practice he prefers, however idiosyncratic, as one that ought to be standard or at least permissible, whether the dons or the printers like it or not. In short, an American is likely to punctuate unconventionally only because he doesn't know any better; a Briton, at least the typical British writer, because he is jolly well sure he does.

—John W. Clark, *American Practice*

They care about their **children's** futures. [*children* = plural noun not ending in *s*]

An **indefinite pronoun** refers to nonspecific persons or things (for example, *any, few, someone, no one*; see 7b and 11g).

The accident was really **no one's** fault. [*no one* = indefinite pronoun not ending in *s*]

2	Adding -'*s* to show possession when singular nouns end in *s*

Most academic writers today use -'*s* to show possession when singular nouns end in *s*, although some writers prefer to use only the apostrophe. Be consistent in each piece of writing. This handbook uses -'*s*.

That **business's** system for handling complaints is inefficient.
Chris's ordeal ended.
Lee **Jones's** insurance is expensive.

When adding -'*s* could lead to tongue-twisting pronunciation, practice varies. All writers use the apostrophe. Some writers do not add the *s*; others do, for consistency with other practices.

Charles Dickens's story "A Christmas Carol" is a classic tale.

3	Using only an apostrophe to show possession when a plural noun ends in *s*

The **boys'** statements were recorded.
The newspapers have publicized several **medicines'** severe side effects recently.
Three **months'** maternity leave is in the **workers'** contract.

4	Adding -'*s* to the last word in singular compound words and phrases

His **mother-in-law's** corporation just bought out a competitor.
The **tennis player's** strategy was brilliant.
They wanted to hear **somebody else's** interpretation of the rule.

ALTERNATE EXERCISE

The questions that follow this brief paragraph are designed to point out how much information about the situation has been provided by the apostrophes. You may want to use the questions in a class discussion of apostrophe usage.

The jury's deliberations were over. Charles's lawsuit had at last come to an end. The defendants' lawyers seemed calm as they waited, but the prosecuting attorney's hands twitched with nervousness. Charles's and Robert's businesses would be either ruined or saved by the verdict of the court. Charles and his family's holdings would be seriously affected. The judge's face was impassive as he addressed the jury about its verdict. The jury foreman's voice trembled as he began to speak.

1. Does the writer think of the jury as a single body or as individuals?

2. Is there one defendant, or are there several?

3. Is there one prosecuting attorney, or are there several?

4. Do Charles and Robert own businesses together or separately?

5. Does Charles share in his family's holdings?

6. Why is there no apostrophe in *its verdict*?

7. Why do the words *jury's* (first sentence), *judge's* (next to last sentence), and *foreman's* (last sentence) end in '*s*?

ANSWERS: ALTERNATE EXERCISE

(1) a single body; (2) several; (3) one; (4) separately; (5) yes; (6) the personal pronoun is possessive without an apostrophe; (7) each word is a singular noun that does not end in -*s*

TEACHING TIP

Some instructors despair of ever having students remember the differences between certain common contractions and their homonyms (*their, they're; its, it's*). You might find it helpful to let students know how experienced writers recognize the differences. Many writers pronounce the two-word form of each possibility. If the two-word form makes no sense in that context, then the other word (usually a possessive pronoun) is needed. If the two-word form makes sense, experienced writers ask themselves if the informal contraction is appropriate. Of course, experienced writers do this in a microsecond, but some of our students need to do it slowly, consciously, and methodically.

I need to know if *their/they're* home. [I need to know if *they are* home.]

I need to know if *their/they're* gas meter is working. [I need to know if *they are* gas meter is working = nonsense; therefore, *their* is correct]

---

5 Adding -'s to only the last noun in joint or group possession

Olga and Joanne's books are valuable. [Olga and Joanne own the books together.]

Anne Smith and Glen Smith's article on solar heating interests me. [Anne Smith and Glen Smith wrote the article together.]

6 Adding -'s to each noun in individual possession

Olga's and Joanne's books are valuable. [Olga and Joanne each own some of the valuable books, but they do not own the books together.]

After the fire, **the doctor's and the lawyer's** offices had to be rebuilt. [The doctor and the lawyer had separate offices.]

❖ APOSTROPHE CAUTION: Do not use an apostrophe to indicate the plural form of a noun, unless you want to indicate possession or close relationship as explained in 27a-1 and 27a-3. ❖

27b Not using an apostrophe with the possessive forms of personal pronouns

Some pronouns have specific possessive forms, which do not include an apostrophe. Contrast them with contractions, discussed in 27c.

PRONOUN	POSSESSIVE FORM(S)
he	his
she	her, hers
it	its
we	our, ours
you	your, yours
they	their, theirs
who	whose

Be especially alert to *it's* and *its*, as well as *who's* and *whose*, which are frequently confused. (*It's* stands for *it is*; *its* is a personal pronoun showing possession. *Who's* stands for *who is*; *whose* is a personal pronoun showing possession.)

NO	The government has to balance **it's** budget.
YES	The government has to balance **its** budget.
NO	The professor **who's** class was canceled is at a meeting of bird watchers.
YES	The professor **whose** class was canceled is at a meeting of bird watchers.

❖ APOSTROPHE CAUTION: The following forms are nonstandard, so do not use them: *its', his', hers', her's, yours', your's, theirs', their's, whos',* and *our's.* ❖

27c Using an apostrophe to stand for omitted letters, numbers, or words in contractions

Contractions are words from which one or more letters have been intentionally omitted and in which apostrophes are inserted to signal the omission. Contractions are common in speaking and in informal writing, but many readers dislike them in academic writing. A major exception is *o'clock* (which stands for *of the clock*). To choose between a contraction and the full phrase, consider your audience and the level of formality you want. Chart 138 lists common contractions.

SOME COMMON CONTRACTIONS	138
aren't = are not	*she's* = she is, she has
can't = cannot	*there's* = there is
didn't = did not	*they're* = they are
don't = do not	*wasn't* = was not
he's = he is, he has	*we're* = we are
it's = it is	*weren't* = were not
I'd = I would, I had	*we've* = we have
I'm = I am	*who's* = who is
isn't = is not	*won't* = will not
let's = let us	*you're* = you are

Contractions can help to show informal speech or dialect, especially in dramatic or fiction writing.

You may want to see if students can locate all the unnecessary and misplaced apostrophes in the following paragraph.

(1) A good cook stay's busy doing many tasks that make cooking possible. (2) The oven's interior has to be cleaned, the pots' and pans' scrubbed, and the knives sharpened. (3) Once the kitchen is tidy, the grocery list's have to be made and menu's planned. (4) Then comes the shopping so that the pantry's shelves will be full. (5) When the chopping and stirring actually begin, most cook's pleasure begins. (6) The aromas' that come from the kitchen are a sign that someone is having a good time.

(1) stay's (present-tense verb); (2) oven's is correct; pots', pans' (nonpossessive nouns ending in -s); (3) list's (nonpossessive plural noun); menu's (nonpossessive plural noun); (4) pantry's is correct; (5) cook's (possessive plural noun); (6) aromas' (nonpossessive plural noun)

Scout yonder's been **readin'** ever since she was born, and she **ain't** even started school yet. You look right puny for **goin'** on seven.

—HARPER LEE, *To Kill a Mockingbird*

Apostrophes also indicate the omission of the first two numerals in years. Avoid this contraction in academic writing.

The class of '50 is having a reunion this year.

They moved from Vermont to Florida after the blizzard of '78.

27d Using an apostrophe to form plurals of letters, numerals, symbols, and words when used as terms

Billie always has trouble printing *W's.*

The address includes six *6's.*

The *for's* in the paper were all misspelled as *four's.*

When the keys jammed, a series of *&'s* showed on the computer screen.

✤ UNDERLINING ALERT: Always underline letters used as letters and words used as words in typewritten or handwritten material. In printed material, such words are set in italic type. If you use a computer and printer that can produce italics, you can use italics instead of underlining.

```
Many first-graders had trouble writing 8's and pro-
nouncing eight's phonetically.
```

Many first-graders had trouble writing *8*'s and pronouncing *eight*'s phonetically. ✤

For the plural form of years, two styles are acceptable: with an apostrophe (1980's) or without (1980s). Whichever form you prefer, use it consistently. This handbook uses the form without the apostrophe.

27e Avoiding misuse of the apostrophe

Do not overuse apostrophes by inserting them where they do not belong. Chart 139 lists the major causes for apostrophe errors. If you tend to make apostrophe errors, use Chart 139 to diagnose the causes of your problem; then stay conscious of them as you edit (see 3d) your writing.

LEADING CAUSES OF APOSTROPHE ERRORS

139

1. Do not use an apostrophe with the present-tense verb form.

   NO Cholesterol **plays'** an important role in how long we live.

   YES Cholesterol **plays** an important role in how long we live.

2. Do not add an apostrophe at the end of a nonpossessive noun ending in *s*.

   NO Medical **studies'** reveal that cholesterol is the primary cause of coronary heart disease.

   YES Medical **studies** reveal that cholesterol is the primary cause of coronary heart disease.

3. Use an apostrophe after the *s* in the possessive plural of a noun.

   NO The medical community is seeking more information from **doctor's** investigations into heart disease.

   YES The medical community is seeking more information from **doctors'** investigations into heart disease.

4. Do not use an apostrophe to form a nonpossessive plural.

   NO **Team's** of doctors are trying to predict who might be most harmed by cholesterol.

   YES **Teams** of doctors are trying to predict who might be most harmed by cholesterol.

QUOTATION ABOUT WRITING

Mechanics are a necessary part of the writing process. Without them the most profound statements would be misunderstood, but with them, sentences take on clarity. Mechanics tell us when new sentences begin, when they end, and when we should pause in our reading. Mechanics signal us when different ideas will be presented. They indicate when the words of another have been used and when people and places have been named. In short, they make an essay a finished product ready to be displayed in public.

—Andrew Hirt, *Comprehension and Composition*

EXERCISE 27-1

Consulting sections 27a and 27e, rewrite these sentences to insert -'s or an apostrophe alone to make the words in parentheses show possession. Delete the parentheses.

EXAMPLE Born in 1732, Franz-Josef Haydn, one of (Austria) most notable musicians, sang in (St. Stephan) Choir until, at age 16, his voice changed.

Born in 1732, Franz-Josef Haydn, one of Austria's most notable musicians, sang in St. Stephan's choir until, at age 16, his voice changed.

1. (Haydn) music has delighted (music lovers) ears for more than two centuries.

ANSWERS: EXERCISE 27-1

1. Haydn's; music lovers'
2. composer's; children's
3. Haydn's; today's
4. musicians'
5. musicians'; women's; men's; concertgoers'; Brahms's; Beethoven's; Ives's; Strauss's
6. players'
7. singer-composer's
8. Esterhazy's; life's
9. patron's; London's
10. music-maker's; homeland's

ANSWERS: EXERCISE 27-2

1. Athletic competition is encouraged in accordance with the participants' age and ability.

2. These athletes' training takes place in schools and other institutions.

3. Participants' handicaps do not prevent them from competing in sports from basketball to gymnastics and ice skating to wheelchair exercise.

4. The program's sponsor is the Joseph P. Kennedy, Jr., Foundation, which first sponsored the event in 1968.

5. The foundation's true beneficiary is American society, for a democracy's aim is equal opportunity and participation for all its members.

COVERAGE: EXERCISE 27-2

(1) plural possessive noun; (2) plural possessive noun; (3) plural possessive noun; (4) singular possessive noun; (5) singular possessive noun; singular possessive noun

ANSWERS: EXERCISE 27-3

(1) One of Albert Einstein's biographers tells about the famous physicist's encounter with a little girl in his neighborhood. (2) The little girl stared at Einstein's soaking wet feet and said, "Mr. Einstein, you've come out without your boots again!" (3) Einstein laughed and, pulling up his trousers, replied, "Yes, and I've forgotten my socks, too." (4) Most people aren't as forgetful as Einstein, but sometimes our memories let all of us down. (5) We may not be able to remember if our first job started in '81 or '82; we may forget whether our employer's husband spells his name with two *t*'s or with one. (6) No one is absolutely sure how memory works. (7) Dr. Barbara Jones's study of memory suggests that personality styles affect memory. (8) People with rigid personalities whose livelihoods depend on facts tend to have good memories. (9) Mr. Harry Lorayne's and Dr.

➜

2. The (composer) symphonies are still performed frequently, with the "Surprise Symphony" a favorite at (children) concerts.

3. Apart from recognizing (Haydn) music, however, (today) concertgoers would find little else familiar at an eighteenth-century (orchestra) performance.

4. Eighteenth-century (musicians) powdered wigs, satin breeches, and white stockings, colorful and elegant, were meant to be noticed.

5. Contemporary orchestral (musicians) black garb, usually (women) dresses and (men) tuxedos, is meant to keep (concertgoers) attention focused on (Brahms), (Beethoven), (Ives), or (Strauss) music, not on the people playing it.

6. Also, eighteenth-century (players) musical instruments differed from modern ones, in both appearance and sound.

7. In fact, 163 of the Austrian (singer-composer) compositions were written for the *baryton,* a now-obsolete instrument similar to a viola or cello.

8. In 1760, Prince Paul (Esterhazy) offer to hire Haydn as court musician freed him to pursue his (life) main purpose: composing.

9. After his (patron) death, Haydn left Austria to visit (London) musical world.

10. Although he died in 1809, this brilliant (music-maker) special legacy to Austria lives on because Haydn wrote his (homeland) national anthem.

EXERCISE 27-2

Consulting sections 27a, 27b, and 27e, rewrite these sentences so that each contains a possessive noun.

EXAMPLE   The Special Olympics is an international program promoting the physical fitness of mentally retarded children and adults.

> *The Special Olympics is an international program promoting mentally retarded children's and adults' physical fitness.*

1. Athletic competition is encouraged in accordance with the age and ability of the participants.

2. The training of these mentally retarded athletes takes place in schools and other institutions.

3. Handicaps of the participants do not prevent them from competing in sports from basketball to gymnastics and ice skating to wheelchair exercise.

4. The sponsor of the program is the Joseph P. Kennedy, Jr. Foundation, which first sponsored the event in 1968.

5. The true beneficiary of the foundation is American society, for the aim of a democracy is equal opportunity and participation for all its members.

EXERCISE 27-3

Consulting all sections in this chapter, correct any errors in the use of apostrophes in the paragraph below.

(1) One of Albert Einsteins biographers tells about the famous physicists encounter with a little girl in his' neighborhood. (2) The little girl stared at Einstein's soaking wet feet and said, ''Mr. Einstein, youve come out without you'r boots again!'' (3) Einstein laughed and, pulling up his trousers, replied, ''Yes, and Ive forgotten my socks, too.'' (4) Most people arent as forgetful as Einstein, but sometimes our memories' let all of us down. (5) We may not be able to remember if our first job started in '81 or 82; we may forget whether our employers' husband spells his name with two *t*s or with one. (6) No one is absolutely sure how memory works. (7) Dr. Barbara Jones study of memory suggests that personality style's affect memory. (8) People with rigid personalities who's livelihoods depend on facts tend to have good memories. (9) Mr. Harry Lorayne and Dr. Laird Cermak's studies of memory each provide a different approach to improving that useful faculty (10) Mr. Lorayne suggest's relating what you want to remember to something verbal or visual. (11) For instance, if you want to remember that your sister's-in-law's name is Rose, you would picture her wearing a rose corsage. (12) Dr. Cermaks suggestions include consideration of physiological factors. (13) He notes that doctors' are currently developing drugs that will prevent older people from losing the memories that are rightfully their's.

EXERCISE 27-4

Consulting all sections of this chapter, correct any errors in the use of apostrophes in the paragraph below.

(1) Every summer Twinsburg, Ohio, comes to life when over one thousand pair's of twins gather for the towns annual festival. (2) The conversation at the gathering usually involves twin's stories about tricking people by exchanging identities, about knowing each others thoughts, and about sharing secret's. (3) The stories' are entertaining, but many psychologists' find them informative as well. (4) Many studies' have involved identical twins' who were separated at birth. (5) Identical twins come from a single fertilized egg that split's soon after conception, resulting in two fetuses' with identical genes. (6) Although identical twins may look like carbon copies of each other, theyre like snowflakes: no pair is exactly alike.

Cont'd.

Laird Cermak's studies of memory each provide a different approach to improving that useful faculty. (10) Mr. Lorayne suggests relating what you want to remember to something verbal or visual. (11) For instance, if you want to remember that your sister-in-law's name is Rose, you would picture her wearing a rose corsage. (12) Dr. Cermak's suggestions include consideration of physiological factors. (13) He notes that doctors are currently developing drugs that will prevent older people from losing the memories that are rightfully theirs.

ANSWERS: EXERCISE 27-4

(1) Every summer Twinsburg, Ohio, comes to life when over one thousand pairs of twins gather for the town's annual festival. (2) The conversation at the gathering usually involves twins' stories about tricking people by exchanging identities, about knowing each other's thoughts, and about sharing secrets. (3) The stories are entertaining, but many psychologists find them informative as well. (4) Many studies have involved identical twins who were separated at birth. (5) Identical twins come from a single fertilized egg that splits soon after conception, resulting in two fetuses with identical genes. (6) Although identical twins may look like carbon copies of each other, they're like snowflakes: no pair is exactly alike.

28 Quotation Marks

Most commonly, quotation marks enclose **direct quotations**—spoken or written words from an outside source (see 28a). Quotation marks also set off some titles (see 28b), and they can call attention to words used in special senses (see 28c).

Always use quotation marks in pairs, and be especially careful not to omit the second (closing) quotation mark. **Double quotation marks** (" ") are standard. **Single quotation marks** (' ') are used only for quotation marks within quotation marks. In print, opening and closing quotation marks look slightly different from each other, but they look identical on a typewriter or computer printer. Examples of both print and typewritten quotation marks are in this chapter.

For information about the functions in quotations of brackets, see 29c; of the ellipsis, see 29d; of the slash, see 29e. For information about commas with quoted words, see 24g; about capital letters with quotations, see 30c.

28a Using quotation marks to enclose direct quotations of not more than four lines

Direct quotations are exact words from a print or nonprint source. When you use a quotation, always check carefully that you have recorded it precisely as it appeared in the original (see also 31c-1).

1 Using double quotation marks to enclose short quotations

A quotation is considered "short" if it can be typed or handwritten to occupy no more than four lines on a page. Short quotations are enclosed in double quotation marks. Longer quotations are not enclosed in quotation marks—they are **displayed**. In MLA style (see 33b-1; for APA style see 33b-2), a displayed quotation starts on a new line, with all typewritten lines indented ten spaces. (In the examples shown in this chapter, MLA parenthetical documentation is used; see 33b-1.)

SHORT QUOTATIONS

```
Hall explains the practicality of close conversational
distances: "If you are interested in something, your pupils
dilate; if I say something you don't like, they tend to
contract" (47).
```

```
Personal space "moves with us, expanding and contracting
according to the situation in which we find ourselves"
(Fisher, Bell, and Baum 149).
```

LONG QUOTATION (MORE THAN FOUR LINES)

```
Robert Sommer, an environmental psychologist, uses literary
and personal analogies to describe personal space:
```

```
        Like the porcupines in Schopenhauer's fable, people
        like to be close enough to obtain warmth and
        comradeship but far enough away to avoid pricking
        one another. Personal space . . . has been likened to
        a snail shell, a soap bubble, an aura, and "breathing
        room." (26)
```

✤ PUNCTUATION ALERT: In MLA documentation style (explained in 33b-1), the period goes *after* the parenthetical reference for a short quotation (not displayed); the period goes *before* the parenthetical reference for a displayed quotation. ✤

For more about displayed quotations, see Appendix B.

2	**Using single quotation marks for quotations within quotations**

When you quote four lines or less and the original words already contain quotation marks, use double quotation marks at the start and end of the directly quoted words. Then, substitute single quotation marks ('   ') wherever there are double quotation marks in the original source.

TEACHING TIP

You might point out to your students that typewriter face is used in 28a-1 so that writers can see how such material should look on their typed papers. All material is double spaced. A short quotation is "run in" with the writer's prose; a long quotation is displayed. For additional examples in typewriter face, you might direct your students' attention to the student research paper in Chapter 34. In particular, you might point out that paragraphs are indented five spaces and displayed quotations are indented ten spaces for all lines.

TEACHING TIP

As the study summarized in the margins of Chapter 31 points out, many students think that they are not plagiarizing as long as they use quotation marks to indicate material taken from sources. These students do not realize that they must also document the source. Now that MLA recommends a system of parenthetical references, the direction to "use footnotes" no longer can help college instructors deal easily with documentation. You might find it useful, therefore, to take some time to explain the word *documentation*, which, in contrast to *footnotes*, is not widely known to students inexperienced in writing research papers. You might also explain that the placement of the parenthetical reference depends on the length of the quotation. If the quotation is "run in," the parenthetical reference comes before the period; if the quotation is displayed, the parenthetical reference comes after the period.

When punctuation was first employed, it was in the role of the handmaid of prose; later the handmaid was transformed by the pedants into a harsh-faced chaperone, pervertedly ingenious in the contriving of stiff regulations and starched rules of decorum; now, happily, she is content to act as an auxiliary to the writer and as a guide to the reader.

—Harold Herd, *Everybody's Guide to Punctuation*, 1925

TEACHING TIP
You may want to divide the class into groups of three or four, asking two members of each group to assume the role of a particular person or type of person. Giving one of them an opening statement that is likely to generate a dialogue, you can ask the two to engage in a conversation with each other. When they have finished, the group can write what they heard, first as direct discourse, then as indirect discourse. The first writing can take the form of a short play, and the second a short story.

TEACHING TIP
One pleasant way to review the use of quotation marks is to have students "translate" passages of indirect discourse found in short stories into dialogues. Alternatively, students can be given a short scene from a play they enjoy and asked first to rewrite it as if it were a chapter in a short story. They can set the scene and present the dialogue as conversation, following the conventions of the short story rather than those of the play. Then they can rewrite the scene using indirect discourse in all the conversations.

ORIGINAL SOURCE

Personal space . . . has been likened to a snail shell, a soap bubble, an aura, and "breathing room."

—ROBERT SOMMER, *Personal Space: The Behavioral Bases of Design*, page 26

SINGLE QUOTATION MARKS WITHIN DOUBLE QUOTATION MARKS

Robert Sommer, an environmental psychologist, compares personal space to "a snail shell, a soap bubble, an aura, and 'breathing room'" (26).

If quotation marks are needed within a quotation of more than four lines, display it (see 28a-1), and be sure to use any quotation marks that appear within the original source.

3 | Using quotation marks correctly for short quotations of poetry and for direct discourse

A quotation of poetry is "short" if it is no more than three lines of the poem. As with short prose quotations, use double quotation marks to enclose the material. If you quote more than one line of poetry, use a slash with one space on each side to show the line divisions (see 29e).

As W. H. Auden wittily defined personal space, "some thirty inches from my nose / The frontier of my person goes. . . ."

For more about displayed quotations of poetry, see Appendix B. ❖ CAPITALIZATION ALERT: When you quote lines of poetry, follow the capitalization of your source. ❖

Quotation marks are also used to enclose speakers' words in **direct discourse°**. Whether you are reporting the exact words of a real speaker or making up dialogue in, for example, a short story, quotation marks let your readers know which words belong to the speaker and which words do not. Use double quotation marks at the beginning and end of a speaker's words, and start a new paragraph each time the speaker changes.

"I don't know how you can see to drive," she said.

"Maybe you should put on your glasses."

"Putting on my glasses would help you to see?"

"Not me; you," Macon said. "You're focused on the windshield instead of the road."

—ANNE TYLER, *The Accidental Tourist*

If one speaker's words require two or more paragraphs, use double quotation marks at the start of each paragraph *but* double quotation marks at the end of the last quoted paragraph *only*.

Indirect discourse reports what a speaker said. In contrast, direct discourse presents a speaker's exact words. Note that the difference between direct and indirect discourse is not only a matter of punctuation; usually the verb tenses differ. Do not enclose indirect discourse in quotation marks.

DIRECT DISCOURSE

The mayor said, "I intend to veto that bill."

INDIRECT DISCOURSE

The mayor said that he intended to veto that bill.

For advice on revising incorrect shifts between direct and indirect discourse, see 15a-4.

EXERCISE 28-1

Consulting section 28a, correct the use of double and single quotation marks. If a sentence is correct, circle its number.

EXAMPLE   According to J. F. Perkins, "O. Henry "solves" most of his short story plots with surprise endings.

According to J. F. Perkins, "O. Henry 'solves' most of his short story plots with surprise endings."

1. Canfield and Lebson write, No one understands the sleeping habits of these sharks.

2. In the last two lines of the poem, Dickinson creates a powerful contrast: Parting is all we know of heaven, / And all we need of hell.

3. "One can put up with "Service with a Smile" if the smile is genuine and not mere compulsory toothbaring," wrote Cornelia Otis Skinner. She did not, on the other hand, advocate 'Service with a Snarl.'

4. "Promises," said Hannah Arendt, are the uniquely human way of ordering the future.

5. According to Henry James, "Nothing . . . will ever take the place of the good old fashion of "liking" a work of art or not liking it."

6. Pauline Kael, the movie critic, notes that "certain artists can, at moments in their lives, reach out and unify the audience" and in so doing give people the opportunity for "a shared response.

7. Don't let anyone convince you that you can't fulfill your ambitions, warned the speaker, or you surely won't.

8. Why have women passion, intellect, moral activity—these three—

ANSWERS: EXERCISE 28-1

1. Canfield and Lebson write, "No one understands the sleeping habits of these sharks."

2. In the last two lines of the poem, Dickinson creates a powerful contrast: "Parting is all we know of heaven. And all we need of hell."

3. "One can put up with 'Service with a Smile' if the smile is genuine and not mere compulsory toothbaring." wrote Cornelia Otis Skinner. She did not, on the other hand, advocate "Service with a Snarl."

4. "Promises," said Hannah Arendt, "are the uniquely human way of ordering the future."

5. According to Henry James, "Nothing . . . will ever take the place of the good old fashion of 'liking' a work of art or not liking it."

6. Pauline Kael, the movie critic, notes that "certain artists can, at moments in their lives, reach out and unify the audience" and in so doing give people the opportunity for "a shared response."

7. "Don't let anyone convince you that you can't fulfill your ambitions," warned the speaker, "or you surely won't."

8. "Why have women passion, intellect, moral activity—these three—and a place in society where no one of the three can be exercised?" asked Florence Nightingale in the 1850s.

9. "In seven cases," the report continued, "outlets with the lowest prices had the highest percentages of defective merchandise."

10. Leslie Hanscom reports about the latest volume of the *Oxford English Dictionary.* "Most of the new words are originating in the USA."

➜

and a place in society where no one of the three can be exercised? asked Florence Nightingale in the 1850s.

9. "In seven cases, the report continued, outlets with the lowest prices had the highest percentages of defective merchandise.

10. Leslie Hanscom reports about the latest volume of the *Oxford English Dictionary,* Most of the new words are originating in the United States.

EXERCISE 28-2

Consulting section 28a, decide whether each sentence is direct or indirect discourse. Then rewrite each sentence in the other form.

EXAMPLE   In 1928 an elderly woman contacted a London auctioneer and asked, "Would you be interested in selling this manuscript?" (Direct discourse)

In 1928 an elderly woman contacted a London auctioneer and asked if he would be interested in selling a manuscript.

1. The auctioneer said that his company did sell manuscripts, but only original ones by famous authors.
2. "This manuscript is original," the woman replied.
3. "The author inscribed it with these words—'A Christmas gift to a dear child'—and I was that child," she continued.
4. Astonished, the auctioneer said, "Is this manuscript what I think it is?"
5. The woman acknowledged that it was the original Lewis Carroll manuscript of *Alice in Wonderland.*

28b Using quotation marks to enclose certain titles

When you refer to certain types of works by their titles, enclose the titles in quotation marks. Use quotation marks around the titles of short published works, like poems, short stories, essays, articles from periodicals, pamphlets, and brochures. Also use them around song titles and individual episodes of television or radio series.

Discuss the rhyme scheme of Andrew Marvell's "Delight in Disorder." [poem]

Have you read "Young Goodman Brown"? [short story]

One of the best sources I have found is "The Myth of Political Consultants." [magazine article]

"Shooting an Elephant" describes George Orwell's experience in Burma. [essay]

COVERAGE: EXERCISE 28-1

(1) direct discourse; (2) short poetry quotation; (3) quotation within a quotation; short quotation; (4) direct discourse following an interruption; (5) quoted word within a quotation; (6) closing quotation marks needed; (7) interrupted direct discourse; (8) direct discourse; (9) interrupted short quotation; closing quotation marks needed; (10) short quotation

ANSWERS: EXERCISE 28-2

Answers may vary in the rewritten sentences. Here is one set of possibilities.

1. *Indirect discourse.* The auctioneer said, "My company does sell manuscripts, but only original ones by famous authors."

2. *Direct discourse.* The woman replied that the manuscript was original.

3. *Direct discourse.* She said that the author inscribed it with the words "A Christmas gift to a dear child" and that she was that child.

4. *Direct discourse.* Astonished, the auctioneer asked if the manuscript was what he thought it was.

5. *Indirect discourse.* The woman said, "Yes, it is the original Lewis Carroll manuscript of *Alice in Wonderland.*"

Underlining is used for titles of many other types of works, such as books and plays. A few titles are neither underlined nor enclosed in quotation marks. (For useful lists showing how to present titles, see 30e and 30f). ❖ UNDERLINING ALERT: Underlining in typed or handwritten papers signals words that would appear in **italic type** if the paper were to be typeset. (Printed books, magazines, newspapers, and similar documents are "typeset.") If you use a computer and can produce italic type, you may choose either underlining or italics. Be consistent in each piece of writing. ❖

Do not put the title of your own paper in quotation marks when you place it on a title page or at the top of a page (see 28d).

EXERCISE 28-3

Consulting section 28b, correct any quotation mark errors. If a sentence is correct, circle its number.

1. Almost everyone who has had to make a difficult choice in life can relate to Robert Frost's poem The Road Not Taken.
2. On a *Twilight Zone* episode called Healer, the main character steals a magic artifact.
3. In her essay titled ''In Search of Our Mothers' Gardens, Alice Walker says that she found her own garden because she was guided by a ''heritage of a love of beauty and a respect for strength.''
4. Unable to get enough peace and quiet to write songs, such as his famous Over There and You're a Grand Old Flag, George M. Cohan would sometimes hire a Pullman car drawing room on a train going far enough away to allow him to finish his work.
5. A snake gives Sherlock Holmes the clue he needs to solve a puzzling murder in the mystery story The Speckled Band.

28c   **Using quotation marks for words used in special senses or for special purposes**

Writers sometimes enclose in quotation marks words or phrases meant ironically or in some other nonliteral way.

The proposed tax "reform" is actually a tax increase.
The "wonderful companion for children" snarled menacingly.

Writers sometimes put technical terms in quotation marks and define them the first time they are used. No quotation marks are used once such terms have been introduced and defined.

QUOTATION ABOUT WRITING

Manuscript: Something submitted in haste and returned at leisure.

—Oliver Herford

ANSWERS AND COVERAGE: EXERCISE 28-3

1. Almost everyone who has had to make a difficult choice in life can relate to Robert Frost's poem "The Road Not Taken" [title of poem].

2. On a *Twilight Zone* episode called "Healer," the main character steals a magic artifact [television episode].

3. In her essay titled "In Search of Our Mothers' Gardens," Alice Walker says that she found her own garden because she was guided by a "heritage of a love of beauty and a respect for strength" [essay title; closing quotation marks needed].

4. Unable to get enough peace and quiet to write songs, such as his famous "Over There" and "You're a Grand Old Flag," George M. Cohan would sometimes hire a Pullman car drawing room on a train going far enough away to allow him to finish his work [song titles].

5. A snake gives Sherlock Holmes the clue he needs to solve a puzzling murder in the mystery story "The Speckled Band" [short story title].

"Plagiarism"—the unacknowledged use of another person's words or ideas—can result in expulsion. Plagiarism is a serious offense.

The translation of a word or phrase can be enclosed in quotation marks. (Also underline any words or phrases that require translation.)

My grandfather usually ended arguments with *de gustibus non disputandum est* ("there is no disputing about tastes").

Words being referred to as words can be either enclosed in quotation marks or underlined. Follow consistent practice throughout a paper.

NO	Many people confuse "affect" and *effect*.
YES	Many people confuse "affect" and "effect."
YES	Many people confuse *affect* and *effect*.

28d Avoiding the misuse of quotation marks

Writers sometimes enclose in quotation marks words they are uncomfortable about using, such as slang in formal writing or a cliché. Do not use quotation marks around language you sense is inappropriate to your audience or your purpose. Take the time to find accurate, appropriate, and fresh words instead.

NO	They "eat like birds" in public, but they "stuff their faces" in private.
YES	They eat very little in public, but they consume enormous amounts of food in private.

Do not enclose a word in quotation marks merely to call attention to it.

NO	"Plagiarism" can result in expulsion.
YES	Plagiarism can result in expulsion.

When you refer to published or performed works by title, you will often need quotation marks (28b) or underlining (30f) to set the title off. When you put the title of *your* paper at the top of a page or on a title page, however, do not enclose it in quotation marks or underline it.

NO	"The Elderly in Nursing Homes: A Case Study"
YES	The Elderly in Nursing Homes: A Case Study

The only exception is if the title of *your* paper refers to another title or a word that requires setting off in quotation marks.

NO	Character Development in Shirley Jackson's Story The Lottery
YES	Character Development in Shirley Jackson's Story "The Lottery"

Do not put a nickname in quotation marks unless you are giving a nickname with a full name. When a person's nickname is widely known and used, you do not have to give both the nickname and the full name. For example, use *Senator Ted Kennedy* or *Senator Edward Kennedy*, whichever is appropriate to your audience and purpose. You do not have to write *Senator Edward "Ted" Kennedy*.

EXERCISE 28-4

Consulting section 28d, correct any incorrect use of quotation marks. If a sentence is correct, circle its number.

EXAMPLE   Many people confuse the spellings of "there," *their*, and *they're*.

Many people confuse the spellings of "there," "their," and "they're."

1. "Accept" and *except* sound enough alike to confuse many listeners.
2. "Mickey" Mantle, "Yogi" Berra, and Whitey Ford helped make the Yankees champions in the 1950s.
3. Although the district attorney thought it would be an "open and shut case," she found out that "life is full of surprises."
4. An "antigen" is any substance from outside the body that activates the body's immune system. Today scientists are focusing intensive research on "antigens."
5. *Valross,* whale-horse, is the Norwegian word from which we get *walrus*.

28e Following accepted practices for other punctuation with quotation marks

1 Placing commas and periods inside closing quotation marks

Because the class enjoyed F. Scott Fitzgerald's "The Freshest Boy," they were looking forward to his longer works.

ANSWERS: EXERCISE 28-4
1. "Accept" and "except" sound enough alike to confuse many listeners. [or *Accept* and *except* sound enough alike to confuse many listeners.]
2. Mickey Mantle, Yogi Berra, and Whitey Ford helped make the Yankees champions in the 1950s.
3. Correct
4. An "antigen" is any substance from outside the body that activates the body's immune system. Today scientists are focusing intensive research on antigens.
5. *Valross,* "whale-horse," is the Norwegian word from which we get *walrus*.

COVERAGE: EXERCISE 28-4
(1) consistent treatment needed; (2) nicknames; (3) correct; (4) second use of a technical term; (5) translation of a term

ALTERNATE EXAMPLES

1. Virginia Woolf was a member of the "Bloomsbury group," the name taken from the district of London in which she and her sister lived after the death of their father.

2. She was the author of many short stories, essays, and sketches, such as "The Mark on the Wall."

3. She was an early user of "stream of consciousness": an attempt to capture the truth of human experience by depicting aspects of an individual's personality.

4. Have you read her long essay called "A Room of One's Own"?

Ms. Rogers said, "Don't stand so close to me."
Edward T. Hall coined the word "proxemics."

For information about commas before quotations, see 24g.

2 Placing colons and semicolons outside closing quotation marks

We have to know "how close is close": we do not want to offend.
Some experts claim that the job market now offers "opportunities that never existed before"; others disagree.

3 Placing question marks, exclamation points, and dashes inside or outside closing quotation marks, according to the context

If a question mark, exclamation point, or dash belongs with the words enclosed in quotation marks, put that punctuation mark *inside* the closing quotation mark.

"Did I Hear You Call My Name?" was the winning song.
"I've won the lottery!" he shouted.
"Who's there? Why don't you ans—"

If a question mark, exclamation point, or dash belongs with words that are *not* included in quotation marks, put the punctuation *outside* the closing quotation mark.

Have you read Nikki Giovanni's poem "Knoxville, Tennessee"?
If only I could write a story like Erskine Caldwell's "The Rumor"!
Weak excuses—a classic is "I have to visit my grandparents"—change little from year to year.

ANSWERS: EXERCISE 28-5

1. One of the most famous passages in Shakespeare is Hamlet's soliloquy, which begins with the question "To be, or not to be?"

2. "Take this script," Rudyard Kipling said to the nurse who had cared for his first-born child, "and someday if you are in need of money you may be able to sell it at a handsome price."

➜

EXERCISE 28-5

Consulting section 28e, correct any errors in quotation marks and other punctuation with quotation marks. If a sentence is correct, circle its number.

1. One of the most famous passages in Shakespeare's plays is Hamlet's soliloquy, which begins with the question ''To be, or not to be''?

2. ''Take this script'', Rudyard Kipling said to the nurse who had cared for his first-born child'', and someday if you are in need of money you may be able to sell it at a handsome price.''

3. Ernest Hemingway claimed this was the source of his famous phrase ''a lost generation:'' in conversation with ''Papa'' Hemingway, a garage owner used the words to describe the young mechanics he employed.

4. After lulling the reader with a description of a beautiful dream palace in his poem Kubla Khan, Coleridge changes the mood abruptly: And 'mid this tumult Kubla heard from far / Ancestral voices prophesying war.

5. The words that Emma Lazarus wrote, ''Give me your tired, your poor, your huddled masses yearning to breathe free'', open the inscription on the Statue of Liberty.

Cont'd.

3. Ernest Hemingway claimed this was the source of his famous phrase "a lost generation": in conversation with Papa Hemingway, a garage owner used the words to describe the young mechanics he employed.

4. After lulling the reader with a description of a beautiful dream palace in his poem "Kubla Khan," Coleridge changes the mood abruptly: "And 'mid this tumult Kubla heard from far / Ancestral voices prophesying war."

5. The words of Emma Lazarus, "Give me your tired, your poor, your huddled masses yearning to breathe free," open the inscription on the Statue of Liberty.

COVERAGE: EXERCISE 28-5

(1) quotation is a question; (2) commas always placed inside closing quotation marks; (3) colon always placed outside closing quotation marks; (4) title of poem; quotation from poem; (5) commas always placed inside closing quotation marks

29 Other Marks of Punctuation

This chapter explains the uses of the dash (see 29a), parentheses (see 29b), brackets (see 29c), ellipsis (see 29d), and slash (see 29e).

THE DASH

29a Using the dash

The dash, or a pair of dashes, lets you interrupt a sentence's structure to add information. Such interruptions can fall in the middle or at the end of a sentence. Use dashes sparingly—if you do use them—so that their impact is not diluted by overexposure.

In typed papers, make a dash by hitting the hyphen key twice (--). Do not put a space before, between, or after the hyphens. In print, the dash is an unbroken line that is approximately the length of two hyphens joined together (—). In handwritten papers, make a dash slightly longer than a hyphen, using one unbroken line (–).

1 Using a dash or dashes to emphasize an example, a definition, an appositive, or a contrast

EXAMPLE

The care-takers—those who are helpers, nurturers, teachers, mothers—are still systematically devalued.

—ELLEN GOODMAN, "Just Woman's Work?"

DEFINITION

Although the emphasis at the school was mainly language— speaking, reading, writing—the lessons always began with an exercise in politeness.

—ELIZABETH WONG, *Fifth Chinese Daughter*

APPOSITIVE°

Two of the strongest animals in the jungle are vegetarians—the elephant and the gorilla.

—DICK GREGORY, *The Shadow that Scares Me*

CONTRAST

Tampering with time brought most of the house tumbling down, and it was this that made Einstein's work so important—and controversial.

—BANESH HOFFMANN, *"My Friend, Albert Einstein"*

Always place the words that you set off in dashes next to or near the words they explain. Otherwise, the interruption will confuse your reader.

NO   The current argument **is—one that parents, faculty, students, and coaches all debate fiercely—whether** athletes should have to meet minimum academic standards to play their sports.

YES   The current **argument—one that parents, faculty, students, and coaches all debate fiercely—is whether** athletes should have to meet minimum academic standards to play their sports.

---

2 | **Using a dash or dashes to emphasize an "aside"**

"Asides" are writers' comments within the structure of a sentence or a paragraph. In writing meant to seem objective, asides help writers convey their personal views. Consider your purpose (see 1b) and audience (see 1c) when deciding whether to insert an aside.

Television showed us the war. It showed us the war in a way that was—if you chose to watch television, at least—unavoidable.

—NORA EPHRON, *Scribble Scrabble*

✦ PUNCTUATION ALERTS: (1) If the words within a pair of dashes would take a question mark or an exclamation point if they were a separate sentence, use that punctuation before the second dash: *A first date—do you remember?—stays in the memory forever.* (2) Do not use commas, semicolons, or periods next to dashes. When such a possibility comes up, revise the sentence to avoid it. (3) Do not enclose dashes in quotation marks except when the words require them: *Many of George Orwell's essays—"A Hanging," for example—draw*

ALTERNATE EXAMPLES: DASH

Appositive
  Elizabeth Barrett Browning—the wife of Robert Browning—was probably a more popular poet than her husband in the nineteenth century.

Example
  Many students—elementary school, high school, and college students—find themselves taking required courses that they would not choose for themselves.

Definition
  A meaningful relationship—one that is satisfying to those involved and promises to last—is sought by most single people.

  Futuristic novels with a bleak vision of the prospects for the free individual characteristically portray a society in which history— knowledge of the past—has been systematically eliminated.

—Diane Ravitch, *"Decline and Fall of Teaching History"*

Dinner at the Huntercombe's possessed only two dramatic features—the wine was a farce and the food a tragedy.

—Anthony Powell

QUOTATION ABOUT WRITING

It [the dash] is a comfortable punctuation mark since even the most rigorous critic can seldom claim that any particular example of it is a misuse. Its overuse is its greatest danger, and the writer who can't resist dashes may be suspected of uncoordinated thinking.

—Cornelia and Bergen Evans

521

ANSWERS AND COVERAGE: EXERCISE 29-1

1. The adult blue, or lycaenid, butterfly is tiny—about big enough to cover a 20 cent stamp [explanation]

2. This personality—so runs the erroneous belief—will be revealed in all its splendor if the individual just forgets about courtesy . . .[aside].

3. We decide about our health habits—whether we exercise, what we eat, whether we smoke or drink [appositive].

4. Two large plots of land have been appropriated for lucrative wildlife parks—Masai Mara in Western Masailand and, in the east, Amboseli National Park, at the foot of snow-capped Mt. Kilimanjaro. [appositive]

5. Different as they were—in background, in personality, in underlying aspiration—these two great soldiers had much in common [explanation].

ALTERNATE EXAMPLES: DASH

Contrast
It's not right or wrong—it's just fattening.

An Aside
If you choose to vote for that candidate—and I don't care whether you do or not—then you have put yourself in the conservative camp.

Broken-Off Speech
"It's not that I don't love you, Tom, it's just that—"

on his experiences as a civil servant. *"Shooting an Elephant"—another Orwell essay—appears in many anthologies.* ♣

EXERCISE 29-1

Consulting section 29a, supply dashes in the following sentences.

EXAMPLE   In the Middle Ages nearly everyone believed as Aristotle had that the intellect was located in the heart.

In the Middle Ages nearly everyone believed—as Aristotle had—that the intellect was located in the heart.

1. The adult blue, or lycaenid, butterfly is tiny about big enough to cover a 20 cent stamp.

—MATTHEW DOUGLAS, ''The Butterfly Connection''

2. This personality so runs the erroneous belief will be revealed in all its splendor if the individual just forgets about courtesy. . . .

—MARGARET HALSEY, ''What's Wrong with 'Me, Me, Me'?''

3. We decide about our health habits whether we exercise, what we eat, whether we smoke or drink.

—JOAN BORYSENKO, *Minding the Body, Mending the Mind*

4. Two large plots of land have been appropriated for lucrative wildlife parks Masai Mara in Western Masailand and, in the east, Amboseli National Park, at the foot of snow-capped Mt. Kilimanjaro.

—KATHLEEN HUNT, ''Subduing the Lion Killers''

5. Different as they were in background, in personality, in underlying aspiration these two great soldiers had much in common.

—BRUCE CATTON, ''Grant and Lee: A Study in Contrasts''

PARENTHESES

29b   Using parentheses

Parentheses allow writers to interrupt a sentence's structure to add information of many kinds. Parentheses are like dashes in this function of setting off extra or interrupting words. Unlike dashes, which tend to make interruptions stand out, parentheses tend to deemphasize what they enclose.

Use parentheses sparingly, because their overuse can be very distracting for readers.

1   Using parentheses to enclose interrupting words

EXPLANATION

After they've finished with the pantry, the medicine cabinet, and the attic, they will throw out the red geranium (too many leaves), sell the dog (too many fleas), and send the children off to boarding school (too many scuffmarks on the hardwood floors).

—SUZANNE BRITT, "Neat People vs. Sloppy People"

In *division* (also known as *partition*) a subject commonly thought of as a single unit is reduced to its separate parts.

—DAVID SKWIRE, *Writing with a Thesis*

EXAMPLE

Though other cities (Dresden, for instance) had been utterly destroyed in World War II, never before had a single weapon been responsible for such destruction.

—LAURENCE BEHRENS AND LEONARD J. ROSEN, *Writing and Reading Across the Curriculum*

ASIDE

The older girls (non-graduates, of course) were assigned the task of making refreshments for the night's festivities.

—MAYA ANGELOU, *I Know Why the Caged Bird Sings*

The sheer decibel level of the noise around us is not enough to make us cranky, irritable, or aggressive. (It can, however, affect our mental and physical health, which is another matter.)

—CAROL TAVRIS, *Anger: The Misunderstood Emotion*

2   Using parentheses for certain numbers and letters of listed items

When you number listed items within a sentence, enclose the numbers (or letters) in parentheses. ✤ PUNCTUATION ALERTS: (1) Use a colon before a list only if the list is preceded by an independent clause; see 26b. (2) You can use commas or semicolons to separate items in a list that falls within a sentence, as long as you are consistent within a piece of writing. When any item itself contains punctuation, use a semicolon to separate the items so that your material is easily read. ✤

ALTERNATE EXAMPLES: PARENTHESES

Explanations
Most Americans try to be honest about filing their income tax returns (no matter how much it hurts to pay).

Examples
Many modern zoos (such as the Santa Barbara Zoo) try to present the animals so that young children can easily see them.

Asides
House plants are subject to bug infestations (at least mine are) which require special treatment if the attack is to be repelled.

ALTERNATE EXAMPLES: PARENTHESES

Numbers and letters
There are five basic ingredients in a good gumbo: (1) a roux, (2) chopped vegetables, (3) water, (4) seafood or chicken, and (5) seasonings.

Numerical repetition
A freshman is required to take twelve (12) hours of course work to be in regular status.

Expression of doubt
We have $900 (?) in the bank.

QUOTATION ABOUT WRITING

Though parentheses seem to say "here it is if you wish it; it's only an aside," such an aside may be intended for special notice—like many a remark that begins with the disarming *by the way* or *incidentally*.

—George Summey, *American Punctuation*

EXAMPLES OF PARENTHESES WITH OTHER PUNCTUATION

When eating at a formal restaurant (such as Chez Marcelle), a man is expected to wear a coat and tie.

Although the rain kept falling (and the river rising!), we decided to wait for the rescue boat instead of striking out on our own.

Casablanca has become a favorite film of many people too young to have seen it when it was originally released (or to have seen Bogart and Bergman in their other films).

BACKGROUND

Literally *parenthesis* indicates "an insertion beside" the basic meaning of the sentence because etymologically the Greek from which it comes (by way of Medieval Latin) is composed of *para,* beside, *en,* meaning in, and *thesis,* a placing, from *tithenai,* to place or put. Hence a parenthesis is a placing beside the principal meaning.

Four items are on the agenda for tonight's meeting: (1) current membership figures, (2) current treasury figures, (3) the budget for renovations, and (4) the campaign for soliciting additional public contributions.

In legal and some business writing, you can use parentheses to enclose a numeral that repeats a spelled-out number.

The monthly rent is three hundred fifty dollars ($350).
Your order of fifteen (15) gross was shipped today.

3 | Using other punctuation with parentheses

Do not put a **comma** before an opening parenthesis even if what comes before the parenthetical material requires a comma.

NO Although clearly different from my favorite film, (*The Wizard of Oz*) *Gone with the Wind* is an important film worth studying.

YES Although clearly different from my favorite film (*The Wizard of Oz*), *Gone with the Wind* is an important film worth studying.

You can use a **question mark** or an **exclamation point** with parenthetical words that occur within the structure of a sentence.

Looking for clues (what did we expect to find?) wasted four days.

A complete sentence enclosed in parentheses sometimes stands alone and sometimes falls within the structure of another sentence. Those that stand alone start with a capital and end with a period. Those that fall within the structure of another sentence do not start with a capital and do not end with a period.

NO Looking for his car keys (he had left them at my sister's house.) wasted an entire hour.

YES Looking for his car keys wasted an entire hour. (He had left them at my sister's house.)

YES Looking for his car keys (he had left them at my sister's house) wasted an entire hour.

Place quotation marks to enclose words that require them, but do not use quotation marks around parentheses that come before or after those words.

NO	Alberta Hunter **"(Down Hearted Blues)"** is better known for her jazz singing than for her poetry.
YES	Alberta Hunter **("Down Hearted Blues")** is better known for her jazz singing than for her poetry.

EXERCISE 29-2

Consulting section 29b, supply needed or useful parentheses.

EXAMPLE   We know that many imaginative people, artists and writers, for example, become so involved in their work that they forget to eat.

We know that many imaginative people (*artists and writers, for example)* become so involved in their work that they forget to eat.

1. Ann Landers and Dear Abby they are actually twin sisters are the most famous advice columnists in the country.
2. Nowadays you can order almost anything clothing, toys, greeting cards, and even meat through mail-order catalogs.
3. Some actors refuse to accept their Oscars, both George C. Scott and Marlon Brando, for example, refused their Best Actor awards even though the Academy Award is considered Hollywood's highest honor.
4. To be a President of the United States, a person must be 1 at least thirty-five years old and 2 a native-born American citizen.
5. Between 1970 and 1978, the price of gold on the free market went from under thirty-five dollars $35 to over two hundred forty dollars $240 an ounce.

BRACKETS

29c   Using brackets

1   Using brackets to enclose words you insert into quotations

When you work quoted words into your own sentences (see 31c), you may have to change the form of a word or two to make the quoted words fit into the structure of your sentence. Enclose any changes you make in square brackets. (The examples with brackets in this section use MLA style° of parenthetical references; see 33b-1.)

ALTERNATE EXAMPLES: BRACKETS

Insertion of words
Describing the end of grief, Marjorie Waters wrote, "[it] was a homecoming, a returning to myself made sweeter by the long separation."

—Marjorie Waters, "Coming Home"

To be reasonably comfortable for even short walks outdoors [in Moscow during the winter] it is necessary to wear coats of natural fur.

—Leona P. Schecter, "Moscow"

We hold these truths to be self-evident, that all men are created equal, that they are endowed by their Creator with certain unalienable [sic] Rights, that among these are Life, Liberty and the pursuit of Happiness.

—The Declaration of Independence

Brief parenthetical material inside parentheses
"The Declaration of Independence" (subtitled "The Unanimous Declaration of the Thirteen United States of America" [and published by Congress in 1776] is an eloquent assertion of human rights.

QUOTATION ABOUT WRITING

Surely the unnecessary profusion of straight lines, particularly on a printed page, is offensive to good taste, is an index of the *dasher's* profound ignorance of the art of punctuation, and, so far from helping to bring out the sense of an author, is better adapted for turning into nonsense some of his finest passages.

—John Wilson, *A Treatise on English Punctuation*, 32nd ed., 1871

ORIGINAL SOURCE

Surprisingly, this trend is almost reversed in Italy, where males interact closer and display significantly more contact than do male/female dyads and female couples.

—ROBERT SHUTER, "A Field Study of Nonverbal Communication in Germany, Italy, and the United States," page 305

QUOTATION WITH BRACKETS

Although German and American men stand farthest apart and touch each other the least, Shuter reported "this trend [to be] almost reversed in Italy" (305).

Enclose your words in brackets if you need to add explanations and clarifications to quoted material.

ORIGINAL SOURCE

This sort of information seems trivial, but it does affect international understanding. Imagine, for example, a business conference between an American and an Arab.

—CHARLES G. MORRIS, *Psychology: An Introduction*, page 516

QUOTATION WITH BRACKETS

"This sort of information [about personal space] seems trivial, but it does affect international understanding" (Morris 516).

Now and then you may find that an author or a typesetter has made a mistake in something you want to quote—a wrong date, a misspelled word, an error of fact. You cannot change another writer's words, but you want your readers to know that you did not make the error. To show that you see the error, insert the Latin word *sic* in brackets, right after the error. Meaning "so" or "thus," *sic* in brackets says to a reader, "It is thus in the original."

The construction supervisor points out one unintended consequence of doubling the amount of floor space: "With that much extra room per person, the tennants [*sic*] would sublet."

2 | **Using brackets to enclose very brief parenthetical material inside parentheses**

From that point on, Thomas Parker simply disappears. (His death [c. 1441] is unrecorded officially, but a gravestone marker is mentioned in a 1640 parish report.)

The abbreviation "c." means "about" when placed next to numerals that refer to time (see Chart 142 in section 30j).

THE ELLIPSIS

29d Using the ellipsis

An **ellipsis** is a set of three spaced dots (use the period key when typing). Its most important function is to show that you have left out some of the original writer's words in material you are quoting. When an ellipsis takes the place of one or more sentences, use four dots to show the period and then the ellipsis.

ORIGINAL SOURCE

Personal space is not necessarily spherical in shape, nor does it extend equally in all directions. (People are able to tolerate closer presence of a stranger at their sides than directly in front.) It has been likened to a snail shell, a soap bubble, an aura, and "breathing room."

—ROBERT SOMMER, *Personal Space: The Behavioral Bases of Design,* page 26

QUOTATION WITH WORDS IN A SENTENCE OMITTED

Sommer says, "It has been likened to . . . 'breathing room.' "

QUOTATION WITH SENTENCE OMITTED

Sommer uses similes to define its dimensions: "Personal space is not necessarily spherical in shape. . . . It has been likened to a snail shell, a soap bubble, an aura, and 'breathing room' " (26).

If an omission occurs at the beginning of your quoted words, you do not need to use an ellipsis to show the omission. Also you do not need to use an ellipsis at the end as long as you end with a complete sentence. (Otherwise, almost everything you quote would require an ellipsis.)

If you stop quoting before the end of the sentence in the original and your own sentence continues, use an ellipsis to show that the quoted sentence continues.

Personal space "has been likened to a snail shell, a soap bubble . . ." (Sommer 26), but the shape varies among cultures.

When a quotation comes at the end of your sentence but the quoted words are *not* the end of a sentence in the original source, you must use an ellipsis. If the quotation is not followed by parenthetical documentation, use (1) a sentence period after the last quoted word, (2) three spaced dots for the ellipsis, and then (3) closing quotation marks.

ELLIPSIS AT END OF SENTENCE WITHOUT PARENTHETICAL DOCUMENTATION°

Still, on that same page, Sommer says people have described personal space as "a snail shell, a soap bubble, an aura. . . ."

But if the quotation is followed by parenthetical documentation, use (1) three spaced dots for the ellipsis, (2) closing quotation marks, (3) the parenthetical reference, and then (4) the sentence period.

ELLIPSIS AT END OF SENTENCE WITH PARENTHETICAL DOCUMENTATION°

Sommer says people have described personal space as "a snail shell, a soap bubble, an aura . . ." (26).

When you delete words immediately after an internal punctuation mark in the quotation, omit that mark from your sentence unless it serves some purpose, and then add the three spaced dots for the ellipsis.

Sommer says that it has been likened to a snail shell . . . and "breathing room" (26).

THE SLASH

29e Using the slash

The **slash** is a diagonal line also known as a *virgule* or *solidus*.

1 Using the slash to separate quoted lines of poetry

If you quote more than three lines of a poem in writing, set the poetry off with space and indentations as you would a prose quotation of more than four lines (see 28a and Appendix B). For three lines or less, use a sentence format and enclose the poetry lines in quotation marks, with a slash to divide one line from the next. Leave a space on each side of the slash.

Consider the beginning of Anne Sexton's poem "Words": "Be careful of words, / even the miraculous ones."

Capitalize and punctuate each line as it is in the original, with this exception: End your sentence with a period if the quoted line of poetry does not have other end punctuation. If your quotation ends before the end of the line, use an ellipsis (see 29d).

2 | Using the slash for numerical fractions in typed manuscripts

If you have to type numerical fractions, use the slash to separate numerator and denominator and a hyphen to tie a whole number to its fraction: *1/16, 1-2/3, 2/5, 3-7/8* (For advice on using spelled-out and numerical forms of numbers, see 30l.)

3 | Using the slash for *and/or*

Try not to use word combinations like *and/or* for writing in the humanities. In academic disciplines where use of such combinations is acceptable, separate the words with a slash. Leave no space before or after the slash. In the humanities, listing both alternatives in normal sentence structure is usually better than separating choices with a slash.

NO	The best quality of reproduction comes from 35mm slides/direct-positive films.
YES	The best quality of reproduction comes from 35mm slides or direct-positive films.

EXERCISE 29-3

Consulting all sections in this chapter, supply needed dashes, parentheses, brackets, ellipses, and slashes. If a sentence is correct as written, circle its number. In some sentences you can choose between dashes and parentheses; when you make your choice, be ready to explain it.

EXAMPLE   Every year in the United States, four times the amount of money spent on baby food is spent on pet food $1.5 billion.

Every year in the United States, four times the amount of money spent on baby food is spent on pet food ($1.5 billion).

1. Albert Einstein's last words they were spoken in his native German will never be known because his attending nurse spoke only English.

2. During one five-week span in 1841, three different men served as President of the United States: 1 Martin Van Buren finished his term on March 3; 2 William Henry Harrison Van Buren's successor was inaugurated on March 4; and 3 John Tyler assumed the Presidency when Harrison died on April 6 after only thirty-two days in office.

ANSWERS: EXERCISE 29-3

Answers may vary slightly. Here are some possibilities.

1. Albert Einstein's last words—they were spoken in his native German—will never be known because his attending nurse spoke only English. [parentheses also acceptable]

2. During one five-week span in 1841, three different men served as President of the United States: (1) Martin Van Buren finished his term on March 3; (2) William Henry Harrison—Van Buren's successor—was inaugurated on March 4; and (3) John Tyler assumed the Presidency when Harrison died on April 6 after only thirty-two days in office.

3. Gold is so malleable that a single ounce can be beaten out into a thin film (less than 1/282,000th of an inch) that would cover 100 square feet. [dashes also acceptable]

4. Correct

5. The American portrait artist Charles Willson Peale made George Washington an innovative set of dentures—elks' teeth set in lead.

6. Henri Matisse's painting *Le Bateau* once hung in New York's Museum of Modern Art for forty-seven days (not to mention being viewed by about 116,000 people) before someone noticed that it was hung upside down. [dashes also acceptable]

7. When Thomas Edison learned that one of the batteries his company manufactured was defective, he offered a refund to all buyers—a pledge made good by $1 million from his own pocket.

8. In 1816 a strange chain of events (beginning with a volcanic eruption in the Dutch East Indies [now Indonesia]) caused New England to experience snow in June and killing frosts through July and August.

➡

ANSWERS: EXERCISE 29-3, *continued*

9. Although the identity of the famous Jack the Ripper was never proven, when the convicted murderer Dr. Thomas Cream was hanged his last words were the unfinished sentence, "I am Jack the—" [the . . ." also acceptable]

10. Maxine Kumin—the winner of the 1973 Pulitzer Prize for Poetry—wrote these memorable lines about calves as they are being born: "They come forth with all four legs folded in / like a dime-store card table." [parentheses also acceptable]

COVERAGE: EXERCISE 29-3

(1) dashes or parentheses for interruptive explanation; (2) parentheses for numbers of listed items, dash for explanatory material; (3) parentheses or dashes for definition; (4) correct; (5) dash for appositive; (6) parentheses or dashes for an aside; (7) dash for appositive; (8) brackets within parentheses for explanation within explanation; (9) dash for broken-off speech; (10) dashes or parentheses for appositive

---

ANSWERS: EXERCISE 29-4

Answers will vary greatly. When checking them, note whether the directions were followed.

1. only three lines of the sonnet, with slash marks between the first and second and between the second and third lines—quoted in a sentence.

2. parentheses to enclose the numbers 1–4 that label the list within a sentence

3. ellipsis to indicate an omission from a quotation, with the meaning of the whole still clear

4. dashes to set off a definition in a sentence

5. parentheses to enclose a brief example in a sentence

3. Gold is so malleable that a single ounce can be beaten out into a thin film less than 1 282,000th of an inch that would cover 100 square feet.

4. To get at every ounce of gold, miners have dug as deep as 2-1/2 miles.

5. The American portrait artist Charles Wilson Peale made George Washington an innovative set of dentures elks' teeth set in lead.

6. Henri Matisse's painting *Le Bateau* once hung in New York's Museum of Modern Art for forty-seven days not to mention being viewed by about 116,000 people before someone noticed that it was hung upside down.

7. When Thomas Edison learned that one of the batteries his company manufactured was defective, he offered a refund to all buyers a pledge made good by $1 million from his own pocket.

8. In 1816 a strange chain of events (beginning with a volcanic eruption in the Dutch East Indies (now Indonesia) caused New England to experience snow in June and killing frosts through July and August.

9. Although the identity of the famous Jack the Ripper was never proven, when the convicted murderer Dr. Thomas Cream was hanged his last words were the unfinished sentence, "I am Jack the."

10. Maxine Kumin the winner of the 1973 Pulitzer Prize for Poetry wrote these memorable lines about calves as they are being born: "They come forth with all four legs folded in / like a dime-store card table."

EXERCISE 29-4

Follow the directions for each item. Consulting sections 29a, 29b, 29d, and 29e, use dashes, parentheses, ellipses, and slashes as needed.

EXAMPLE Write a sentence using dashes that exclaims about love.

I am in love—again!

1. Write a sentence that quotes only three lines of Sonnet XLIII by Elizabeth Barrett Browning:
   How do I love thee? Let me count the ways.
   I love thee to the depth and breadth and height
   My soul can reach, when feeling out of sight
   For the ends of Being and ideal Grace.
   I love thee to the level of every day's
   Most quiet need, by sun and candlelight.
   I love thee freely, as men strive for Right;

I love thee purely, as they turn from Praise.
I love thee with the passion put to use
In my old griefs, and with my childhood's faith.
I love thee with a love I seemed to lose
With my lost saints, — I love thee with the breath,
Smiles, tears, of all my life! — and, if God choose,
I shall but love thee better after death.

2. Write a sentence that includes a list of four numbered items.

3. Quote a few sentences from a source. Choose one from which you can omit a few words without losing meaning. Correctly indicate the omission. At the end, give the source of the quotation.

4. Write a sentence in which you use dashes to set off a definition.

5. Write a sentence in which you use parentheses to enclose a brief example.

30 Capitals, Italics, Abbreviations, and Numbers

CAPITALS

30a Capitalizing the first word of a sentence

30a Capitalizing the first word of a sentence

Always capitalize the first letter of the first word in a sentence: *Records show that four inches of snow fell last year.* Practice varies for using a capital letter to start each question in a series of questions. Whichever practice you choose, be consistent throughout a piece of writing. Of course, if the questions are complete sentences, start each with a capital letter.

YES	What facial feature would most people change if they could? Their eyes? Their ears? Their mouth?
YES	What facial feature would most people change if they could? their eyes? their ears? their mouth?

Practice varies for using a capital letter for a complete sentence following a colon (see 26b). Whichever practice you choose, be consistent throughout a piece of writing. This handbook uses a capital letter after the colon.

A complete sentence enclosed in parentheses sometimes stands alone and sometimes falls within the structure of another sentence. Those that stand alone start with a capital letter and end with a period. Those that fall within the structure of another sentence do not start with a capital letter and do not end with a period.

> I did not know till years later that they called it the Cuban Missile Crisis. But I remember Castro. (We called him Castor Oil and were awed by his beard.) We might not have worried so much (what would the Communists want with our small New Hampshire town?) except that we lived 10 miles from an air base.
>
> —JOYCE MAYNARD, "An 18-Year-Old Looks Back on Life"

30b Capitalizing listed items correctly

In a **run-in list,** the items are worked into the structure of a sentence or a paragraph rather than arranged with each item on a new line. When the items in a run-in list are complete sentences, capitalize the first letter of each item.

> We found three reasons for the delay: (1) Bad weather held up delivery of raw materials. (2) Poor scheduling created confusion and slowdowns. (3) Lack of proper machine maintenance caused an equipment failure.

When the items in a run-in list are not complete sentences, begin each with a lower-case letter.

> The reasons for the delay were (1) bad weather, (2) poor scheduling, and (3) equipment failure.

In a **displayed list,** the items are set up vertically, one below the other. If the items are sentences, capitalize the first letter. If the items are not sentences, you may start each with a capital letter or a lower-case letter. Whichever you choose, be consistent in each piece of writing. ❖ PARALLELISM ALERT: Make list items parallel in structure; for example, if one item is a sentence, use sentences for all the items (see 18h). ❖

In a **formal outline,** each item must start with a capital letter (see 2n).

30c Capitalizing the first letter of an introduced quotation

If you have made quoted words part of the structure of your own sentence, do not capitalize the first quoted word.

> Mrs. Enriquez says that when students visit a country whose language they are trying to learn, they "absorb a good accent with the food."

If the words in your sentence serve only to introduce quoted words or if you are directly quoting speech, capitalize the first letter of the quoted words if it is capitalized in the original.

> Mrs. Enriquez says, "Students should always visit a country when they want to learn its language. They'll absorb a good accent with the food."

Do not capitalize the continuation of a one-sentence quotation within your sentence, and do not capitalize a partial quotation.

"Of course," she added, "the accent lasts longer than the food." Smiling, she encouraged me to "travel—and eat—to learn to speak Spanish."

30d Capitalizing I and O

Always capitalize the pronoun° *I*, no matter where it falls in a sentence or in a group of words or when it stands alone: *I love you, even though I do not want to marry you.* Always capitalize the interjection° *O: You are, O my fair love, a burning fever.* Do not capitalize the interjection *oh* unless it starts a sentence or is capitalized in material that you are quoting.

30e Capitalizing nouns and adjectives according to standard practice

Capitalize **proper nouns** (nouns° that name specific people, places, and things): *Mexico, Rome.* Also capitalize **proper adjectives** (adjectives° formed from proper nouns): *a Mexican entrepreneur, the Roman street.* Do not capitalize articles *(the, a, an)* accompanying proper nouns or proper adjectives.

A proper noun or adjective sometimes takes on a "common" meaning, losing its very specific "proper" associations. When this happens, the word loses its capital letter as well: *french fries, pasteurize.*

Many common nouns are capitalized when names or titles are added to them. For example, *lake* is not ordinarily capitalized, but when a specific name is added, it is: *Lake Mead.*

In your reading, expect sometimes to see capitalized words that this book says not to capitalize. How writers capitalize can sometimes depend on audience and purpose. For example, a corporation's written communications usually use *the Board of Directors* and *the Company*, not *the board of directors* and *the company*. Similarly, the administrators of your school might write *the Faculty* and *the College* or *the University*, words you would not capitalize in a paper. In specific contexts, adapt to the situation.

Chart 140 is a Capitalization Guide. Apply what you find in it to similar items not listed. Also, for information about using capital letters in addresses on envelopes, see 39a.

CAPITALIZATION GUIDE

140

	CAPITALS	LOWER-CASE LETTERS
NAMES	Mother Teresa (*also,* in place of their names: Mother, Dad)	my mother (*relationship*)
	Doc Holliday	the doctor (*role*)
TITLES	President Truman the President (*now in office*)	a president
	Democrat (*a party member*)	democrat (*a believer in democracy*)
	Representative Barbara Boxer	the congressional representative
	Senator Robert Dole	the senator
	Queen Elizabeth II	the queen
GROUPS OF HUMANITY	Caucasian (*race*)	white (*also* White)
	Negro (race)	black (*also* Black)
	Native American	
	Jew, Catholic	
ORGANIZATIONS	Congress	congressional
	the Ohio State Supreme Court	the state supreme court
	the Republican Party	the party
	Wang Corporation	the company
PLACES	Los Angeles	the city
	the South (*a region*)	turn south (*a direction*)
	Main Street	the street
	Atlantic Ocean [also the Atlantic]	the ocean
	the Black Hills	the hills
BUILDINGS	the Capitol (in Washington, D.C.)	the state capitol
	Ace High School	the high school
	China West Cafe	the restaurant
	Highland Hospital	the hospital ➡

ALTERNATE EXERCISE

Emily Dickinson and E. E. Cummings, both American poets, used and did not use capitalization in unusual ways. What is the effect of their highly individualistic use (and lack of use) of capital letters in the following poems?

Much Madness is divinest Sense—
To a discerning Eye—
Much Sense—the Starkest Madness—
'Tis the Majority
In this, as All, prevail—
Assent—and you are sane—
Demur—you're straightway dangerous—
And handled with a Chain—

          —Emily Dickinson, 1890

"next to of course god america i
love you land of the pilgrims' and so forth
  oh
say can you see by the dawn's early my
country 'tis of centuries come and go
and are no more what of it we should
  worry
in every language even deafanddumb
thy sons acclaim your glorious name by
  gorry
by jingo by gee by gosh by gum
why talk of beauty what could be more
  beaut-
iful than these heroic happy dead
who rushed like lions to the roaring
  slaugh-
ter
they did not stop to think they died
  instead
then shall the voice of liberty be mute?"

He spoke. And drank rapidly a glass of
  water

          —e.e. cummings, 1925

535

ALTERNATE EXERCISE

To point out the importance of capitalization, you might want to give your students a paragraph that has been typed with only lowercase letters. Then ask them to sort out the sentences and meaning, placing capital letters where they are needed. Here is a paragraph you can use:

> drugs are one of the techniques of western therapy of which we are most proud. however, drugs are used by healers in other cultures as well. rauwulfia root, for example, which was introduced into western psychiatry in the 1950s as resperine, a major tranquilizer, has been used in india for centuries as a tranquilizer and has also been in wide use in west africa for many years. another example is shock therapy. when electric shock therapy was introduced by cerletti in the 1930s, he was not aware that it had been used in some cultures for up to 4,000 years. the technique of applying electrical eels to the head of a patient is referred to in the writings of aristotle, pliny, and plutarch. what kind of results do therapists in other cultures—witch doctors—achieve? a canadian psychiatrist, dr. raymond prince, spent 17 months studying 46 nigerian witch doctors and judged that the therapeutic results were about equal to those obtained in north american clinics and hospitals.
>
> —Edwin Fuller Torrey, *The Mind Game*

ANSWERS TO ALTERNATE EXERCISE

The words capitalized in the original paragraph, grouped by sentences, are: Drugs, Western; However; Rauwulfia, Western, India, West Africa; Another; When, Cerletti; The, Aristotle, Pliny, Plutarch; What; A, Canadian, Dr. Raymond Prince, Nigerian, North American.

CAPITALIZATION GUIDE (*continued*)

	CAPITALS	LOWER-CASE LETTERS
SCIENTIFIC TERMS	Earth (*the planet*)	the earth (*where we live*)
	the Milky Way	the galaxy
		the moon, the sun
	Streptococcus aureus	a streptococcal infection
	Gresham's law	the theory of relativity
LANGUAGES, NATIONALITIES	Spanish	
	Chinese	
SCHOOL COURSES	Chemistry 342	a chemistry course
	my English class	
NAMES OF THINGS	the *Boston Globe*	the newspaper
	Time	the magazine
	Purdue University	the university
	Heinz Ketchup	ketchup
	the Dodge Colt	
TIMES AND SEASONS	Friday	spring, summer, fall,
	August	autumn, winter
HISTORICAL PERIODS	World War II	the war
	the Great Depression (*in the 1930s*)	the depression (*any economic depression*)
	the Reformation	an era, an age
		the eighteenth century
		fifth-century manuscripts
		the civil rights movement
RELIGIOUS TERMS	God	a god, a goddess
	Buddhism	a religion
	the Torah	
	the Koran	
	the Bible	
LETTER PARTS	Dear Ms. Tauber:	
	Sincerely,	
	Yours truly,	

CAPITALIZATION GUIDE (*continued*)

	CAPITALS	LOWER-CASE LETTERS
TITLES OF PUBLISHED AND RELEASED MATERIAL	"The Lottery" *A History of the United States to 1877* *Jazz on Ice*	[Capitalize the first letter of the first word and all other words except articles°, short prepositions°, and short conjunctions°]
COMPOUND WORDS	African-American post-Victorian Mexican-American Indo-European	
ACRONYMS° AND INITIALISMS	NATO FBI AFL-CIO UCLA NAACP IBM	
SOFTWARE	Microsoft Word DOS WordPerfect	[Capitalize software titles as shown in the program documentation. Do not underline these titles or enclose them in quotation marks.]

✤ ESL NOTE: When the subject of your paragraph or essay is a proper noun°, capitalize that word or words. ✤

EXERCISE 30-1

Consulting sections 30a through 30e, add capital letters as needed.

1. President Abraham Lincoln's secretary, whose name was Kennedy, and President John F. Kennedy's secretary, whose name was Lincoln, advised these ill-fated presidents not to go out just before their assassinations.

2. The first child of european parents to be born in north america was Snorro, whose mother was the widow of Leif Erickson's brother.

3. The ancient egyptians, the first to embalm their dead citizens, also embalmed their dead crocodiles.

ANSWERS: EXERCISE 30-1, *Cont'd.*

4. In 1659 *Massachusetts* outlawed *Christmas* and fined anyone celebrating the Holiday five Shillings.

5. Mark Twain, the author of *"The Celebrated Jumping Frog of Calaveras County,"* once refused to invest in a friend's invention, calling it a "Wildcat speculation." The invention was the telephone!

6. An artificial hand invented in 1551 by a *Frenchman* (his name was Ambroise Tare) had Fingers that moved by cogs and levers, thus enabling a handless member of the Cavalry to grasp the reins of his horse.

7. "Take care, *O* traitor," roared the hero, "Or your Villainy will do you in!"

8. Researchers at the *Institute* for *Policy Studies* of *Harvard University* discovered that the following jobs are considered most boring by those who hold them: (1) Assembly line worker, (2) elevator operator, (3) pool typist, (4) Bank Guard, (5) Housewife.

9. What is the most common item in a family medicine chest? Is it Aspirin? *Adhesive* bandages? *A* thermometer? *An* antibacterial agent? [lower case for *adhesive, a,* and *an* also acceptable]

10. "I don't care what you do, my dear," the Actress *Mrs.* Patrick Campbell is supposed to have said, "as long as you don't do it in the Street and frighten the horses!"

11. The letter announcing that the company was closing its doors and everyone was losing their jobs ended with the words *"Have* a happy day."

12. The book that has sold the most copies of any book throughout the world is the *Bible.*

13. I registered for *Biology* 101 and *History* 121, but the courses I wanted in psychology and in art were filled by the time I got to registration.

14. The *Capitol* building is located in the nation's capital.

15. The sun does not shine for 186 days at the *North Pole.*

4. In 1659 massachusetts outlawed christmas and fined anyone celebrating the holiday five shillings.

5. Mark Twain, the author of "the celebrated jumping frog of calaveras county," once refused to invest in a friend's invention, calling it a "wildcat speculation." The invention was the telephone!

6. An artificial hand invented in 1551 by a frenchman (his name was Ambroise Tare) had fingers that moved by cogs and levers, thus enabling a handless member of the cavalry to grasp the reins of his horse.

7. "Take care, o traitor," roared the hero, "Or your villainy will do you in!"

8. Researchers at the institute for policy studies of harvard university discovered that the following jobs are considered most boring by those who hold them: (1) assembly line worker, (2) elevator operator, (3) pool typist, (4) bank guard, (5) housewife.

9. What is the most common item in a family medicine chest? Is it aspirin? adhesive bandages? a thermometer? an antibacterial agent?

10. "I don't care what you do, my dear," the actress mrs. Patrick Campbell is supposed to have said, "as long as you don't do it in the street and frighten the horses!"

11. The letter announcing that the company was closing its doors and all employees were losing their jobs ended with the words "have a happy day."

12. The book that has sold the most copies of any book throughout the world is the bible.

13. I registered for biology 101 and history 121, but the courses I wanted in psychology and in art were filled by the time I got to registration.

14. The capitol building is located in the nation's capital.

15. The sun does not shine for 186 days at the north pole.

ITALICS (UNDERLINING)

In printed material, **roman type** is the standard; type that slants to the right is called **italic.** Words in italics indicate material that is underlined when typewritten or written by hand.

HANDWRITTEN   *Catch 22*

TYPED   Catch 22

TYPESET   *Catch 22*

30f Using standard practice for underlining titles and other words, letters, or numbers

Chart 141 provides a guide for making decisions about whether to underline. Apply what you find in it to similar items not listed.

GUIDE TO UNDERLINING   141

TITLES

UNDERLINE	DO NOT UNDERLINE
The Bell Jar [a novel]	your own paper's title
Death of a Salesman [a play]	
Collected Works of O. Henry [a book]	"The Last Leaf" [one story in the book]
Simon & Schuster Handbook for Writers [a book]	"Writing Paragraphs" [one chapter in the book]
Contexts for Composition [a collection of essays]	"Science and Ethics" [one essay in the collection]
The Iliad [a long poem]	"Nothing Gold Can Stay" [a short poem]
The African Queen [a film]	
Scientific American [a magazine]	"The Molecules of Life" [an article in a magazine]
The Barber of Seville [title of an opera]	Concerto in B-flat Minor
Symphonie Fantastique [title of a long musical work]	[identification of a musical work by form, number, and key. Use neither quotation marks *nor* underlining.]
Twilight Zone [a television series]	"Terror at 30,000 Feet" [an episode of a television series]
The Best of Bob Dylan [a record album or a tape]	"Mr. Tambourine Man" [a song or a single selection on an album or a tape]
	Lotus 1-2-3 [software program names are neither underlined nor enclosed in quotation marks]

the Los Angeles Times [a newspaper. Note: Even if *The* is part of the title printed on a newspaper, do not use a capital letter and do not underline it in your writing. In documentation°, omit the word *The*.] ➜

ALTERNATE EXAMPLES

Can your students cite the rules governing the following uses of capital letters?

1. The Koran is the sacred book of the Moslems.

2. A generation ago all high school students read Charles Dickens' novel *A Tale of Two Cities*.

3. The price of an airline ticket will increase on Monday, April 16.

4. My sister had her baby at Women's and Children's Hospital.

5. Spanish is now the primary language of many people in the Southwest.

6. Next semester I want to take Humanities 101.

7. The job with General Motors will give me the opportunity to travel.

8. John Steinbeck's novel *The Grapes of Wrath* tells the story of the Joad family coping with the problems of the Great Depression.

9. Earthbound people have always wondered about the possibility of life on Mars or Venus.

10. A history class cannot cover all aspects of the Renaissance.

11. The letter announcing that the company was closing its doors and everyone was losing their jobs ended with the words "Have a happy day."

12. The book that has sold the most copies of any book throughout the world is the *Bible*.

13. I registered for Biology 101 and History 121, but the courses I wanted in psychology and in art were filled by the time I got to registration.

14. The Capitol building is located in the nation's capital.

15. The sun does not shine for 186 days at the North Pole.

TEACHING TIP

To draw students' attention to standard (and perhaps nonstandard) capitalization practice, you may want to ask them to bring to class examples from advertising and newspapers that demonstrate the use of capital letters for a variety of purposes. The examples can be the basis for discussing reasons for using capital letters and the effectiveness with which they are used.

BACKGROUND

In the eighteenth century there was a movement to reduce the frequency with which capital letters were used. Nevertheless, the final text of the Declaration of Independence is liberally sprinkled throughout with capital letters. As evidence of how conventions regarding capitalization have changed, consider the following passage; you might rewrite it as a contemporary document.

> We hold these truths to be self-evident, that all men are created equal, that they are endowed by their Creator with certain unalienable Rights, that among these are Life, Liberty and the pursuit of Happiness. That to secure these rights, Governments are instituted among Men, deriving their just powers from the consent of the governed. That whenever any Form of Government becomes destructive of these ends, it is the Right of the People to alter or to abolish it and to institute new Government . . . as to them shall seem most likely to affect their Safety and Happiness.

ANSWERS: EXERCISE 30-2

1. The first rule in an old book about rules of etiquette reads, "Do not eat in mittens."

2. When he originated the role of Fonzie in the television series *Happy Days*, Henry Winkler earned about $750 per episode.

➡

GUIDE TO UNDERLINING (*continued*)

OTHER WORDS

the Intrepid [a ship; don't underline preceding initials like U.S.S. or H.M.S.]

aircraft carrier [a general class of ship]

Voyager 2 [names of specific aircraft, spacecraft, and satellites]

Boeing 747 [general names shared by classes of aircraft, spacecraft, and satellites]

summa cum laude [term in a language other than English]

burrito, chutzpah [widely used and commonly understood words from languages other than English]

What does our imply? [a word referred to as such]

the abcs; confusing 3s and 8s [letters and numbers referred to as themselves]

30g Underlining sparingly for special emphasis

Professional writers sometimes use italics to clarify a meaning or stress a point.

> Many people we *think* are powerful turn out on closer examination to be merely frightened and anxious.
>
> —MICHAEL KORDA, *Power!*

In your academic writing, rely on choice of words and sentence structures to convey emphasis.

EXERCISE 30-2

Consulting section 30f, eliminate unneeded underlining and quotation marks, and add needed underlining. Correct capitalization as necessary.

1. The first rule in an old book about Rules of Etiquette reads, "Do not eat in mittens."

2. When he originated the role of Fonzie in the television series "Happy Days," Henry Winkler earned about $750 per episode.

3. The Monitor and the Merrimac were the first iron-hulled ships to engage in battle.

4. Iowa's name comes from the Indian word <u>ayuhwa</u>, which means "sleepy ones."

5. The New York Times does not carry comic strips.

6. Judy Garland was the second-lowest-paid star in the film classic The Wizard of Oz; only the dog who portrayed <u>Toto</u> was paid less.

7. For distinguished accomplishments of people over age 70, we can look to Verdi, who wrote the song "Ave Maria" at age 85, and Tennyson, who wrote the short poem "Crossing the Bar" at age 80.

8. Handwriting experts say personality traits affect the way an individual dots an i and crosses a t.

9. The <u>Italian</u> word <u>ciao</u> is both a greeting and a farewell.

10. A sense of danger develops slowly in Shirley Jackson's short story <u>The Lottery</u>.

ABBREVIATIONS

30h Using abbreviations with time and symbols

Some abbreviations are standard in all writing circumstances. In some situations, you may choose whether to abbreviate or spell out a word. When choosing, consider your purpose for writing (see 1b) and your audience (see 1c). Then be consistent in each piece of writing. ❖ PUNCTUATION ALERT: Most abbreviations call for periods: *Mr., R.N., a.m.* Some do not, including names of organizations, government agencies, and postal service abbreviations (see 39a): *IBM, FBI, AZ.* When the period of an abbreviation falls at the end of a sentence, the period serves also to end the sentence. ❖

TIME

The abbreviations a.m. (A.M.) and p.m. (P.M.) can be used only with exact times, such as *7:15 A.M., 7:15 a.m.; 3:47 P.M., 3:47 p.m.* You can use capital or lower case letters, but be consistent in each piece of writing. ❖ USAGE ALERT: Use *a.m.* and *p.m.* only with numbers indicating time. Do not use them instead of the words *morning, evening,* and *night.* ❖

In abbreviations for years, A.D. precedes the year: *A.D. 977.* Conversely, B.C. (or B.C.E.) follows the year: *12 B.C.* (or 12 B.C.E.).

Cont'd.

3. The *Monitor* and the *Merrimac* were the first iron-hulled ships to engage in battle.

4. Iowa's name comes from the Indian word *ayuhwa,* which means "sleepy ones."

5. The *New York Times* does not carry comic strips.

6. Judy Garland was the second lowest paid star in the film classic *The Wizard of Oz;* only the dog who portrayed Toto was paid less.

7. For distinguished accomplishments of people over age 70, we can look to Verdi, who wrote the song "Ave Maria" at age 85, and Tennyson, who wrote the short poem "Crossing the Bar" at age 80.

8. Handwriting experts say personality traits affect the way an individual dots an *i* and crosses a *t.*

9. The Italian word *ciao* is both a greeting and a farewell.

10. A sense of danger develops slowly in Shirley Jackson's short story "The Lottery."

COVERAGE: EXERCISE 30-2

(1) underlining not needed because title is not cited; (2) omit underlining with proper name: underline title of television show; (3) underline names of ships; (4) omit underlining with proper name; (5) underline title of a newspaper (does not include *the*); (6) underline movie title, underlining not needed for proper name; (7) do not underline title of short literary or musical works; (8) underline letters used as themselves; (9) omit underlining with proper name; underline foreign word; (1) use quotation marks for titles of short works

QUOTATION ABOUT WRITING

The most famous abbreviation of antiquity, perhaps of all time, was SPQR—Senatus Populusque Romanus—the great insigne of Rome.

—Cornelia and Bergen Evans

The letters B.C. follow a date, while the letters A.D. precede a date. William Safire, essayist on language for the *New York Times,* reports in his column of June 22, 1986 that a plaque left on the moon by the first Americans to land there reads: "July 1969, A.D." He further reports that at the time he was a speechwriter at the White House and he approved the wording. He writes:

> In a century or so, I hope some descendant of mine will take a sharp stylus on some weekend rocket to the moon and, while awaiting a transfer rocket to Mars, will draw a little circle around the *A.D.* and put an arrow placing it in front of the word *July.* This will show that human beings in the early days of space were grammatically fallible; that mankind (since changed to *humankind,* but you can leave it the old way on the plaque, Junior) is forever editing, and that a little precision is a dangerous thing.

ALTERNATE EXERCISE

What is the difference in meaning suggested by the following changes in the italicized words?

1. **a.** *Six* different bodies compose the United Nations.
   b. Six different bodies compose the *United Nations.*
2. **a.** All members of the U.N. can send *five* representatives to the General Assembly.
   b. All members of the U.N. can send five representatives to the *General Assembly.*
3. **a.** The *primary* responsibility of the Security Council is to maintain international peace and security.
   b. The primary responsibility of the Security Council is to maintain *international* peace and security.

SYMBOLS

Symbols are seldom used in the body of papers written for courses in the humanities, but they are used in charts or similar format. Also, symbols can be appropriate in the sciences.

In the humanities, spell out *percent* and *cent* rather than using the symbols % and ¢. You can use a dollar sign with specific dollar amounts: *$23 billion, $7.85.* Let common sense and your readers' needs guide you.

30i Using abbreviations with titles, names and terms, and addresses

TITLES

Use either a title of address before a name: *Dr. Daniel Gooden* or an academic degree after a name: *Daniel Gooden, Ph.D.* Do not use both. Because *Jr., Sr., II, III,* and the like are considered part of the name, they can be used with both titles of address and academic degree abbreviations: *Dr. Martin Luther King, Jr.; Arthur Wax, Sr., M.D.* (The title *Professor* is usually not abbreviated.) ❖ COMMA ALERT: When you use an academic degree or *Jr.* or *Sr.,* insert a comma before it, and after it if it falls before the end of a sentence: *Martin Luther King, Jr., was a superb orator.* ❖

NAMES AND TERMS

If you use a long name or term frequently in a paper, you may abbreviate it using these guidelines: The first time, give the full term, with the abbreviation in parentheses immediately after the spelled-out form. After that, you can use the abbreviation alone.

Spain voted to continue as a member of the **North Atlantic Treaty Organization (NATO),** to the surprise of other **NATO** members.

You can abbreviate *U.S.* as a modifier (*the U.S. ski team*), but spell out *United States* when you use it as a noun.

NO	The **U.S.** has many different climates.
YES	The **United States** has many different climates.

ADDRESSES

If you include a full address—street, city, and state—in the body of a paper, you can use the state abbreviation (for a list, see Chart 144) for the state name. Spell out any other combination of a city and a state or a state by itself. ❖ COMMA ALERT: Use a comma before *and* after the state. ❖

NO	The Center for Disease Control in **Atlanta, GA,** sometimes quarantines livestock.
YES	The Center for Disease Control in **Atlanta, Georgia,** sometimes quarantines livestock.
YES	The Center for Disease Control in **Georgia** sometimes quarantines livestock.

30j Using abbreviations in documentation according to standard practice

Documentation means giving the source of any material that you quote (see 31c), paraphrase (see 31d), or summarize (see 31e). Styles of documentation are discussed in Chapter 33. Chart 142 gives scholarly abbreviations that you might find in the sources that you consult, as well as those that you need for documentation in your writing. Indexes and other reference books list the abbreviations that they use, along with their spelled-out forms, usually at the beginning or end of the volume.

COMMON SCHOLARLY ABBREVIATIONS 142

anon.	anonymous	i.e.	that is
b.	born	ms., mss.	manuscript, manuscripts
c. *or* ©	copyright	n.b.	note carefully
c. *or* ca.	about (with dates)	n.d.	no date (of publication, for a book)
cf.	compare		
col., cols.	column, columns	p., pp.	page, pages
d.	died	pref.	preface
ed.; eds.	edited by; editors	rept.	report, reported by
e.g.	for example	sec., secs.	section, sections
esp.	especially	v. *or* vs.	versus (legal case)
et al.	and others	vol., vols.	volume, volumes
f., ff.	and the following page, pages		

ALTERNATE EXAMPLES

Can your students cite the rule governing the following italicized words?

1. *Hamlet* is still one of the world's most frequently produced plays.

2. Several magazines, such as *Life* and *The Saturday Evening Post,* have significantly changed their format in recent years.

3. Some people prefer to keep up with current events by watching *CBS Evening News* instead of reading *USA Today.*

4. The reruns of *Star Trek* continue to attract viewers.

5. The *Challenger* disaster will be long remembered.

6. Children should know their *abc's* before starting first grade.

7. The literary works of the *fin de siècle* were shocking to many readers.

8. English has borrowed many words from other languages, such as *chauffeur, taco,* and *moccasin.*

9. *The Red Badge of Courage* is a modern epic.

10. The *Titanic* was thought to be invulnerable.

BACKGROUND

During the administration of President Franklin D. Roosevelt, a number of new government agencies became known by their initials. The Tennessee Valley Authority, for example, was called the TVA, and the National Industrial Recovery Act was the NIRA. World War II strengthened the policy of using initials without periods, and since that time it has been common practice to use an abbreviation without periods in place of some proper names, such as the UN (United Nations), USC (University of Southern California), the NYPD (New York Police Department), and DDT (dichlorodiphenyl-trichloroethane).

MONTH ABBREVIATIONS USED IN MLA STYLE° DOCUMENTATION   143

Jan.	January	May	(none)	Sept.	September
Feb.	February	June	(none)	Oct.	October
Mar.	March	Jl.	July	Nov.	November
Apr.	April	Aug., Ag.	August	Dec.	December

POSTAL ABBREVIATIONS   144

AL	Alabama		MT	Montana
AK	Alaska		NB	Nebraska
AZ	Arizona		NV	Nevada
AR	Arkansas		NH	New Hampshire
CA	California		NJ	New Jersey
CO	Colorado		NM	New Mexico
CT	Connecticut		NY	New York
DE	Delaware		NC	North Carolina
DC	District of Columbia		ND	North Dakota
FL	Florida		OH	Ohio
GA	Georgia		OK	Oklahoma
HI	Hawaii		OR	Oregon
ID	Idaho		PA	Pennsylvania
IL	Illinois		RI	Rhode Island
IN	Indiana		SC	South Carolina
IA	Iowa		SD	South Dakota
KS	Kansas		TN	Tennessee
KY	Kentucky		TX	Texas
LA	Louisiana		UT	Utah
ME	Maine		VT	Vermont
MD	Maryland		VA	Virginia
MA	Massachusetts		WA	Washington (state)
MI	Michigan		WV	West Virginia
MN	Minnesota		WI	Wisconsin
MS	Mississippi		WY	Wyoming
MO	Missouri			

30k Using *etc.*

The abbreviation *etc.* is from Latin *et cetera,* which means "and the rest." Do not use *etc.* in writing in the humanities. Acceptable substitutes are *and the like, and so on,* and *and so forth.*

EXERCISE 30-3

Consulting sections 30h, 30i, and 30j, revise this material so that abbreviations are used correctly.

1. In 1665, Harvard U. graduated its first N. American Indian, Caleb Cheeshateaumuck.
2. The first swim across the Eng. Channel took twenty-one hrs., forty-five mins.
3. According to most drs., the best places in the U.S. for allergy sufferers to live in are the deserts of AZ.
4. When Sandra Day O'Connor was appt. to the Supreme Ct. by Pres. R. Reagan in 1981, she became the 1st woman Supreme Ct. justice in Amer. history.
5. Many coll. students today are required to take courses in lit., soc. sci., and lang.
6. The energy crisis of 1973 prompted enforcement of a natl. speed limit of 55 mph.
7. It seems ironic that the paintings of Vincent van Gogh, who died penniless, now sell for millions of $.
8. The route of the Boston Marathon, run every Apr., covers twenty-six mi. between Hopkinton, MA, and Boston, MA.
9. At fifty mins. before the liftoff, the Sat. launch was postponed.
10. The UN bldg. in NYC has been a popular tourist attraction for yrs.

NUMBERS

30l Using spelled-out numbers

Depending on how often numbers occur in a paper and what they refer to, you will sometimes express the numbers in words and sometimes in figures. The guidelines here, like those in the *MLA Handbook for Writers of Research Papers,* Third Edition, are suitable for

TEACHING TIP
You might want to refer your students to section 23b for a discussion of the use of periods with abbreviations.

ANSWERS: EXERCISE 30-3

1. In 1665, Harvard University graduated its first North American Indian, Caleb Cheeshateaumuck.
2. The first swim across the English Channel took twenty-one hours, forty-five minutes.
3. According to most doctors, the best places in the United States for allergy sufferers to live in are the deserts of Arizona.
4. When Sandra Day O'Connor was appointed to the Supreme Court by President Ronald Reagan in 1981, she became the first woman Supreme Court justice in American history.
5. Many college students today are required to take courses in literature, social science, and language.
6. The energy crisis of 1973 prompted enforcement of a national speed limit of 55 mph.
7. It seems ironic that the paintings of Vincent van Gogh, who died penniless, now sell for millions of dollars.
8. The route of the Boston Marathon, run every April, covers twenty-six miles between Hopkinton, Massachusetts, and Boston, Massachusetts.
9. At fifty minutes before the scheduled liftoff, the Saturday launch was postponed.
10. The United Nations building in New York City has been a popular tourist attraction for years.

BACKGROUND

Conventions regarding written numbers differ from place to place and from one institution to another. Where Americans use a decimal point to separate numbers, for example, Europeans use a comma; in Britain an earlier practice called for a raised dot in that position. The traveler should also be aware that dates are cited in a different way in some other countries. The American who invites a British friend to a spring picnic on 6/1/93, the first day of June, will cause some confusion, because the invited person will assume the event is to take place in the snow, planned as it seems to be for January 6. The American military follows the European practice, even in letters, using as a heading, for instance, 2 July 1992 instead of July 2, 1992.

ALTERNATE EXERCISE

You may want to organize your class into competing teams, giving each in turn a postal abbreviation to which a member is to respond by naming a city in that state. For example, an acceptable answer for a player who is given the abbreviation MN would be Minneapolis. When a player cannot answer, the abbreviation is given to a player on the other team.

TEACHING TIP

Some writers mix suffixes with numerals: *1st, 33rd.* Traditional practice calls for the spelled-out word (the *first* robin), except for days, when only the numeral without a suffix should be used (November 1). When you clarify this issue for students, you might also want to point out that this is among the few cases in English in which formal spoken practice differs from formal written practice. That is, a person can say in a formal talk: "The crisis occurred on November 21st." In written form, however, the formal convention is November 21.

writing in the humanities. For the guidelines other disciplines follow, consult their style manuals (for a list, see 33g).

If conveying numerical exactness to your readers is not a prime purpose in your paper, and if you mention numbers only a few times, spell out numbers that can be expressed in one or two words: *Iceland's population increases by more than* **one** *percent a year, but that gain translates into fewer than* **three thousand** *individuals.*

❖ HYPHENATION ALERT: Use a hyphen between spelled-out two-word numbers from *twenty-one* through *ninety-nine.* (see 22g-4). ❖

If you use numbers fairly frequently in a paper, spell out numbers from *one* to *nine,* and use figures for numbers *10* and above. In the humanities, never start a sentence with a figure; spell out the number. In practice, you can usually revise a sentence so that the number does not come first.

Three hundred seventy-five dollars per credit is the tuition rate for nonresidents.
The tuition rate for nonresidents is $375 per credit.

If you are using specific numbers often in a paper (temperatures in a paper about climate, for example, or percentages, or any specific measurements of time, distance, or other quantities) use figures. If you are using an occasional approximation, spell out the numbers: *about five inches of snow.*

Do not mix spelled-out numbers and figures in a paper when they both refer to the same thing.

NO In four days, our volunteers increased from five to eight to 17 to 233.

YES In four days, our volunteers increased from 5 to 8 to 17 to 233. [All the numbers referring to volunteers are given in figures, but *four* is still spelled out because it refers to a different quantity—days.]

30m Using numbers according to standard practice

Standard practice requires figures for numbers in the cases covered in Chart 145.

GUIDE FOR USING SPECIFIC NUMBERS 145

DATES	August 6, 1941; 1732–1845; 34 B.C. to A.D. 230
ADDRESSES	10 Downing Street 237 North 8th Street Export Falls, MN 92025
TIMES	8:09 A.M.; 6:00 P.M.; six o'clock, *not* 6 o'clock; four in the afternoon (or 4 P.M.), *not* four P.M.
DECIMALS AND FRACTIONS	5:55; 98.6; 3.1416; 7/8; 12-1/4 three quarters, *not* 3 quarters; one-half
CHAPTERS AND PAGES	Chapter 27, page 245
SCORES AND STATISTICS	a 6–0 score; a 5 to 3 ratio; 29 percent
IDENTIFICATION NUMBERS	94.4 on the FM dial; call 1-212-555-XXXX
MEASUREMENTS	2 feet; 67.8 miles per hour; 1.5 gallons; 2 level teaspoons; 3 liters; 8-1/2″ × 11″ paper, *or* 8-1/2 × 11-inch paper
ACT, SCENE, AND LINE NUMBERS	act II, scene 2, lines 75–79
TEMPERATURES	43° F; 4° C
MONEY	$1.2 billion; $3.41; 25 cents *or* 25¢

EXERCISE 30-4

Consulting sections 30l and 30m, revise this material so that the numbers are in correct form, either spelled out or in figures.

1. The film *Quo Vadis* used thirty thousand extras and 63 lions.
2. The best time to use insecticides is four p.m. because that is when insects are most susceptible.
3. People in the United States spend six hundred million dollars a year on hot dogs.
4. 4/5 of everything alive on this earth is in the sea.

TEACHING TIP

William Safire, essayist on language for the *New York Times,* pointed out in his column of April 23, 1986, that practice varies greatly on how to write *noon* or *midnight* when the number 12 is involved. Some people use 12:00 A.M. for midnight while others use 12:00 P.M. The same is true for noon. Safire suggests using *12 noon* and *12 midnight* for greater clarity.

TEACHING TIP

Some students may need a review of Roman numerals. The major ones are: I = 1; V = 5; X = 10; L = 50; C = 100; D = 500; M = 1,000.

In academic writing, Roman numerals have few uses. They designate the major divisions in outlines; sometimes they are used in lists. They are used as parts of names and titles: *Peter Brown III, Queen Elizabeth II, Rocky IV.* You might remind students that Roman numerals are not interchangeable with arabic (regular) numerals in addresses, dates, or measurements.

ANSWERS: EXERCISE 30-4

1. The film *Quo Vadis* used 30,000 extras and 63 lions. [*or* thirty thousand extras and sixty-three lions.]
2. The best time to use insecticides is 4:00 p.m. because that is when insects are most susceptible.
3. People in the United States spend $600 million a year on hot dogs. [Also correct are the spelled-out form. $600,000,000 and 600,000,000 dollars, but $600 million is most appropriate for academic writing.]
4. Four-fifths of everything alive on this earth is in the sea.
5. The earliest baseball game on record was played in 1846 on June 19 [*or* 19th] for a final score of 23 to 1 in four innings. →

ANSWERS: EXERCISE 30-4, *Cont'd.*

6. Aaron Montgomery Ward started the first mail order company in the United States in 1872 at 825 North Clark Street in Chicago.

7. The record for a human's broad jump is about 28 feet, one-quarter inch, and the record for a frog's broad jump is 13 feet, 5 inches.

8. Two hundred fifty words per minute is the reading speed of the typical reader. [*or:* The typical reader reads 250 words per minute.]

9. The yearly income of the average family in the United States in 1915 was $687. [Spelled-out form for money is also correct.]

10. Three out of four people who wear contact lenses are between 12 and 23 years of age.

11. Vine Deloria counts 315 Native American "tribes" in the United States today.

12. It will be about thirty degrees warmer in April.

13. Her date of birth may have been 27 B.C.E.

14. One teaspoon of baking soda will neutralize the acid in the $1\frac{1}{2}$ cups of lemon juice.

15. They were born at 3:17 a.m. in 1900.

COVERAGE: EXERCISE 30-4

(1) numbers over 10 expressed in words and figures; (2) time; (3) money; (4) fraction; (5) date, words and figures mixed in statistics; (6) address; (7) statistics expressed with mixed figures and words; (8) sentence opened with figures; (9) date and money; (10) sentence opened with figures; (11) number over 10 expressed in words (12) number over 10 expressed in words; (13) year expressed in words; (14) sentence opened with figures; measurement expressed in words; (15) time and date expressed in words

5. The earliest baseball game on record was played in 1846 on June nineteenth for a final score of 23 to one in 4 innings.

6. Aaron Montgomery Ward started the first mail order company in the United States in 1872 at eight hundred twenty-five North Clark Street in Chicago.

7. The record for a human's broad jump is about twenty-eight feet, one-quarter inch, and the record for a frog's broad jump is 13 feet, 5 inches.

8. 250 words per minute is the reading speed of the typical reader.

9. The yearly income of the average family in the United States in nineteen fifteen was six hundred and eighty-seven dollars.

10. 3 out of 4 people who wear contact lenses are between 12 and 23 years of age.

11. Vine Deloria counts three hundred fifteen Native American "tribes" in the United States today.

12. It will be about 30 degrees warmer in April.

13. Her date of birth may have been twenty-seven B.C.E.

14. 1 teaspoon of baking soda will neutralize the acid in the one and one-half cups of lemon juice.

15. They were born at three seventeen a.m. in nineteen hundred.

30

Focus on Revising

REVISING YOUR WRITING

If you make errors in using capitals, italics, abbreviations, or numbers, go back to your writing and locate the errors. Using this chapter as a resource, revise your writing to correct the problems.

CASE STUDY: REVISING FOR CORRECT CAPITALS, ITALICS, ABBREVIATIONS, AND NUMBERS

In these case studies, you can observe a student writer revising. Then you have the chance to revise other student writing on your own.

Observation

A student wrote the following draft for a course called The United States in the Twentieth Century. The assignment was to discuss an important political moment that occurred between 1945 and the present. This material is well organized and includes many specific details, but the draft's effectiveness is diminished by the presence of errors in capitalization, italics (underlining), abbreviations, and numbers.

Read through the draft. The errors are highlighted and explained. Before you look at the student's revision, revise the material yourself. Then compare what you and the student did.

capital needed for
nationality: 30e

Many american people have forgotten some interesting details of the historic march on Washington, D.C., that took place in 1963. More than 200,000 people, black and white, linked

quotation marks, not italics, needed for song title: 30f

arms and chanted the song We Shall Overcome. Crowds listened peacefully to the sounds of Folksingers Joan Baez and Peter, Paul and Mary. Radio and television audiences felt the passion and power in the words of

lower case needed: 30e

➡

period needed for abbreviation: 30i

Dr Martin Luther King, Jr., who delivered the speech that rang with the now-famous phrase "I have a dream."

Historians marvel at the coalition that came together to sponsor the march. Labor leaders,

lower case needed: 30e

Church leaders, representatives of both pacifist and more militant civil rights organizations all joined together with a common goal—to make the country aware of the need for jobs and freedom for all people in the United States. Although initially opposed to the

capital needed for title: 30e

march, president John F. Kennedy finally endorsed it and met with its leaders early in the day. he later watched the rally on television.

capital needed for first word in sentence: 30a

Even more amazing was the orderliness of the demonstration. In anticipation of possible trouble,

numerals needed: 30l

almost six thousand police had been called out, and the armed services had 4,000 people standing by. The worst problem

lower case needed: 30e

that the Police had to deal with was traffic control. Even the

italics (underlining) not needed: 30g

sanitation department had little to do. After the march was over, the demonstrators cleaned up virtually all of the litter from the bag

lower case needed: 30e

lunches most of them had brought. The city and Nation had never seen anything like this march.

Here is how the student revised the essay to correct errors in capitalization, italics (underlining), abbreviations, and numbers.

Many American people have forgotten some interesting details of the historic march on Washington, D.C., that took place

COVERAGE: PARTICIPATION ESSAY

Benjamin Franklin played a leading role in the drive for *american* [capital needed for nationality: 30e] independence from the rule of England. He also helped improve the quality of daily life in many others ways.

in 1963. More than 200,000 people, black and white, linked arms and chanted the song "We Shall Overcome." Crowds listened peacefully to the sounds of folksingers Joan Baez and Peter, Paul and Mary. Radio and television audiences felt the passion and power in the words of Dr. Martin Luther King, Jr., who delivered the speech that rang with the now-famous phrase "I have a dream."

Historians marvel at the coalition that came together to sponsor the march. Labor leaders, church leaders, representatives of both pacifist and more militant civil rights organizations all joined together with a common goal—to make the country aware of the need for jobs and freedom for all people in the United States. Although initially opposed to the march, President John F. Kennedy finally endorsed it and met with its leaders early in the day. He later watched the rally on television.

Even more amazing was the orderliness of the demonstration. In anticipation of possible trouble, almost 6,000 police had been called out, and the armed services had 4,000 people standing by. The worst problem that the police had to deal with was traffic control. Even the sanitation department had little to do. After the march was over, the demonstrators cleaned up virtually all of the litter from the bag lunches most of them had brought. The city and nation had never seen anything like this march.

Participation

A student wrote the following draft for a course called Introduction to United States History. The assignment was to write about a leading figure around the time of the Revolutionary War. This material is well organized and uses specific examples well, but the draft's effectiveness is diminished by errors in capitalization, italics (underlining), abbreviations, and numbers.

Read through the draft. Then revise it to eliminate the errors. Also, make any additional revisions that you think would improve the content, organization, and style of the material.

Benjamin Franklin played a leading role in the drive for american independence from the rule of England. He also helped improve the quality of daily life in many other ways.

Franklin's devotion to social improvement showed itself in his efforts to improve the quality of daily life in Philadelphia, ➔

Cont'd.
writing the Constitution of the *U.S.* [United States needs to be spelled out as a noun: 30i].

Benjamin Franklin's legacy to our nation is his wisdom, energy, and rare and varied talents.

ANSWER: PARTICIPATION ESSAY

Benjamin Franklin played a leading role in the drive for American independence from the rule of England. He also helped improve the quality of daily life in many other ways.

Franklin's devotion to social improvement showed itself in his efforts to improve the quality of daily life in Philadelphia, where he worked as a printer. He proposed a city-paid police force and helped start up a volunteer fire department. He successfully campaigned for a library, and his writing about education led to the founding of the University of Pennsylvania. His first important contribution to politics was in organizing a militia to guard Philadelphia against raids threatened by French and Spanish ships.

Franklin gained prestige for his work with electricity. His flying a kite in a thunderstorm to learn more about lightning is a familiar image from colonial days. Beyond science, Franklin gained fame as a politician. He served in London as spokesperson for the American colonies. When negotiations with England fell apart, he returned to the colonies, where he helped write the Declaration of Independence. When war between the colonies and England broke out, he traveled to France as an ambassador to secure military and economic aid for the colonies. Franklin persuaded France to send 12,000 soldiers and 32,000 to Gen. George Washington. Franklin helped frame the treaty that finally gave the American colonies their independence, and he had a hand in writing the Constitution of the United States.

Benjamin Franklin's legacy to our nation is his wisdom, energy, and rare and varied talents.

where he worked as a printer. He proposed a city-paid Police force and helped start up a volunteer fire department. He successfully campaigned for a library, and his writing about education led to the founding of the university of Pennsylvania. His first important contribution to politics was in organizing a militia to guard Philadelphia against raids threatened by French and Spanish ships.

Franklin gained prestige for his work with electricity. His flying a kite in a thunderstorm to learn more about lightning is a familiar image from colonial days. Beyond science, Franklin gained fame as a politician. he served in London as spokesperson for the American colonies. When negotiations with England fell apart, he returned to the colonies, where he helped write the Declaration of Independence. When war between the colonies and England broke out, he traveled to France as an Ambassador to secure military and economic aid for the colonies. Franklin persuaded France to send twelve thousand soldiers and 32,000 sailors to Gen George Washington. Franklin helped frame the treaty that finally gave the American colonies their independence, and he had a hand in writing the Constitution of the U.S.

Benjamin Franklin's legacy to our nation is his wisdom, energy, and rare and varied talents.

PART

VII Writing Research

When you write research, you engage in two processes: doing research and writing a research paper. Part Seven explains how to find and write from sources, how to conduct research and write a paper based on your findings, and how to document your sources completely and accurately. As you use Chapters 31 through 35, be aware that writing research fosters habits of mind to draw upon in college and throughout your life.

All of us, unfortunately, have to deal with plagiarism from time to time. Techniques for plagiarism-proofing assignments are plentiful: requiring the submission in the student's own hand of working bibliographies, note cards, outlines, and rough drafts; assigning unusual topics and changing them every semester; replacing the semester-long research project with several shorter ones to prevent students from having time to contact research paper mills; limiting research to the use of a particular casebook. All of these work to some degree, but at the price of turning us into thought-police, ever on the alert for the student who might find a way around our system. We take on extra stress and extra paperwork—students continue to think of us as fussy creatures who demand they follow rituals peculiar to English classes. If we are not to continue to waste our energies tracking down plagiarized passages in the library stacks, we need to take steps to counter the mixed signals about plagiarism that our students have received over the years—and continue to receive.

Doris R. Dant, in "Plagiarism in High School: A Survey" (*English Journal* [Feb. 1986]: 81–84), makes several points about how students are taught to write reports in high school and the impact of this on plagiarism in college. In a survey of fourteen freshman composition classes at Brigham Young University (1984), she found that 17 percent of the students reported being advised by their high school teachers to copy "the information word for word from other sources." Dant also found that there was a correlation between the number of teachers who taught when to document sources and the students' avoidance of plagiarism. Students who reported that all their teachers explained how to credit sources were far more likely to understand the concept of plagiarism and to avoid copying reports ➡

31 Avoiding Plagiarism and Using Sources for Quoting, Paraphrasing, and Summarizing

The core of every college writing project is its content. For many writing assignments, the source of that content is expected to be your own. For many other assignments, you are expected to explain and support your ideas by drawing on outside sources, such as books, articles, films, and interviews (see Chapter 32).

Whenever you work with outside sources, you are expected to avoid plagiarism (see 31a) and to credit your sources by using documentation°* (see 31b). Quoting (see 31c), paraphrasing (see 31d), and summarizing (see 31e) are the techniques to use to incorporate information from sources. Guidelines for using outside sources in your writing are given in Chart 146.

GUIDELINES FOR USING OUTSIDE SOURCES IN YOUR WRITING 146

1. Avoid plagiarism by always attributing ideas and words that are not yours to their source.
2. Document sources accurately and completely.
3. Know how and when to use these techniques:
   - **Quotation:** the exact words of a source set off in quotation marks (see 31c)
   - **Paraphrase:** a detailed restatement of someone else's statement expressed in your own words and your own sentence structure (see 31d)
   - **Summary:** a condensed statement of the main points of someone else's passage expressed in your own words and sentence structure (see 31e)

---

*Throughout this book, a degree mark (°) indicates that you can find the definition of the word in the Glossary of Terms in this handbook.

31a Avoiding plagiarism

To **plagiarize** is to present another person's words or ideas as if they were your own. Plagiarism is like stealing. The word *plagiarize* comes from the Latin word for kidnapper and literary thief. Plagiarism is a serious offense that can be grounds for failure of a course or expulsion from a college. Plagiarism can be intentional, as when you submit as your own work a paper you did not write. Plagiarism is also intentional when you deliberately incorporate the work of other people in your writing without using documentation° to mention your source. Plagiarism can also be unintentional—but no less serious an offense—if you are unaware of what must be acknowledged and how to go about documenting. All college students are expected to know what plagiarism is and how to avoid it.

What should you document? Everything that you get from an outside source. You are required to document any material that you quote (see 31c), paraphrase (see 31d), or summarize (see 31e). Writing the words of others in your own words does not release you from the obligation to document.

To prevent plagiarism in your writing, take careful notes as you conduct research using outside sources. Here are practices that help researchers avoid plagiarism.

1. **Record complete documentation information.** Become entirely familiar with the documentation style you intend to use in your paper (see 31b). Make a master list of the documentation facts required for each source, and write down all the facts on a bibliography card (see 33a).

2. **Record documentation information as you go along.** Never forget to write down complete documentation facts. As you take notes, use clear handwriting. *When you write a research paper, your chances of unintentional plagiarism increase sharply if you have to recreate your research process. Do not expect to be able to relocate your sources or to reconstruct what came from the source and what was your own thinking.*

3. **Use a consistent note-taking system.** Always use different colors of ink or a code system to keep three things separate: (1) material paraphrased or summarized from a source; (2) quotations from a source; and (3) your own thoughts triggered by what you are reading. For quotations, always write clear, perhaps oversize, quotation marks that you will be certain to see later.

Cont'd.

than their peers who received such instruction from just a few of their teachers.

Only 47 percent of the students questioned understood, when they were seniors in high school, how to write an unplagiarized report. Among the untrained students, some felt that putting ideas into their own words and providing a bibliography (no parenthetical references or footnotes) was sufficient. Others felt that copying was fine provided that they supplied either footnotes, parenthetical references, or a bibliography (no quotation marks). Almost 6 percent had no idea what "plagiarism" meant. Not surprisingly, over 60 percent of the students in these groups reported having copied high school reports.

Some students, however, consciously plagiarize to receive higher grades, and it may be necessary to devote class time to a discussion of the ethics of plagiarism. In a 1985 survey of 150 freshmen at Indiana University ("How College Freshmen View Plagiarism," *Written Communication* [April 1988]: 203–221), Barry M. Kroll found that most students regarded plagiarism as a violation of one's responsibility to do one's own work, as a failure to give authors just credit for their work, or as theft of someone's ideas. Few students, however, identified deliberate plagiarism as lying, fraud, or a betrayal of trust—issues, Kroll believes, that students should be asked to consider in a class discussion.

EXTRA EXERCISE A

Which of the following statements should be documented and which need not be documented?

1. The Declaration of Independence was issued in 1776.

➜

What do you *not* have to document? When you write a paper that draws on outside sources, you are not expected to document common knowledge (if there is any on your topic) or your own thinking, as explained here.

Common knowledge

You do not have to document **common knowledge.** Common knowledge is information that most educated people know, although they might need to remind themselves of certain facts by looking up information in a reference book. For example, every educated person knows that the U.S. space program included moon landings. Some people might have to look in a reference book to remind themselves that Neil Armstrong, the first man to set foot on the moon, landed on July 20, 1969. That fact is common knowledge and does not have to be documented. You move into *the realm of research and the need to document* as soon as you get into less commonly known details about the moon landing: the duration of the stay on the moon, the size and capabilities of the spaceship, what the astronauts ate during their journey, and similar details. If you feel that you are walking a thin line between knowledge held in common and knowledge learned from research, be safe and document. Sometimes, of course, a research paper does not happen to contain common knowledge. For example, Amy Brown, whose research paper appears in Chapter 34, had no common knowledge about her topic of personal space. (In fact, Brown deliberately chose to write about a subject new to her.) Brown's research paper, therefore, consists of documented material from sources and her own thinking about the subject (see below).

Your own thinking

You do not have to document **your own thinking.** As you conduct your research, you learn new material by building on what you already know. You are expected to think about that new material, formulate a thesis statement° about it, and organize the information to write a research paper about it.

Be particularly careful about plagiarism slipping into a thesis statement. It is plagiarism to put a source's main idea into your words and pass that off as your thesis. Similarly, it is plagiarism to combine the main ideas of several sources, put them into your own words, and pass that off as your thesis. Your thesis statement must reflect your own thinking.

Here are illustrations of a student's own thinking, drawn from the research paper by Amy Brown in Chapter 34:

- the thesis statement (see paragraph 1)
- most organizing sentences (see, for example, the opening sentences of many paragraphs after paragraph 2; also see comment G)
- comments (see, for example, the sentence in paragraph 1 after the parenthetical reference; also the sentence in paragraph 13 after the paraphrase of Morris and parenthetical reference)
- transitional sentences (for example, the sentence in paragraph 13 after the summary of information from Davis and Skupien and parenthetical reference)
- the conclusion (see paragraph 14)

31b Understanding the concept of documentation

Documentation means acknowledging your sources by giving full and accurate information about the author, title, date of publication, and related facts. Whenever you quote (see 31c), paraphrase (see 31d), or summarize (see 31e), you must document your source according to correct documentation style°.

Documentation styles vary among the academic disciplines. In courses for which you write using outside sources, ask your instructor what documentation style you are expected to use. Chapter 33 explains and illustrates two major documentation styles: Modern Language Association (MLA) style and American Psychological Association (APA) style. Section 33g lists where to find documentation styles in other academic disciplines, and section 38g shows examples of documentation of sources in one style recommended by the Council of Biology Editors (CBE).

31c Using quotations effectively

Quotations are the exact words of a source set off in quotation marks (see 28a). Whereas paraphrase (see 31d) and summary (see 31e) distance your reader one step from your source, quotations give your reader the chance to encounter directly the words of your source. Guidelines for using quotations are in Chart 147.

Two conflicting demands confront you when you use quotations in your writing. Along with the effect and support of quota-

Cont'd.

2. The sediments on the ocean floor are the accumulation of silt carried by rivers to the sea, volcanic dust, coastal sands, and discarded shells of living creatures.

3. Levi Strauss, the inventor of blue jeans, came to the United States from Germany in 1848.

4. Coca-Cola is a popular soft drink all around the world.

5. According to Germaine Greer, the reason few women artists have achieved greatness is that they have historically internalized their oppression, thereby draining the energy required for creative work.

6. The United States is a substantially less secure society today than it was forty years ago.

7. The Olympic Games are held every four years.

8. The initials GNP stand for the term *gross national product.*

9. As a society we should read poetry because it makes us live more fully and live more deeply.

10. Henry David Thoreau lived at Walden Pond for two years.

ANSWERS: EXTRA EXERCISE A

1. No. Common knowledge.
2. Yes. Not common knowledge.
3. Yes. Not common knowledge.
4. No. Common knowledge.
5. Yes. Opinion of someone besides the writer.
6. No, if opinion of the writer. Yes, if opinion of someone besides the writer.
7. No. Common knowledge.
8. No. Common knowledge.
9. No, if opinion of the writer. Yes, if opinion of someone besides the writer.
10. No. Common knowledge.

BACKGROUND

Only in the last century has the paraphrase been taught mainly for research. For 2,000 years the paraphrase was an important exercise for developing style and teaching structure. In his *Institutio Oratoria* (A.D. 95), Roman educator Quintilian described a curriculum in which young boys began paraphrasing simple stories such as Aesop's fables and, as they grew older, were required to paraphrase longer and more complex texts by great writers. Quintilian believed that paraphrasing also improved students' appreciation for great writing and their ability to critique their own work.

QUOTATION ABOUT WRITING

You could compile the worst book in the world entirely out of selected passages from the best writers in the world.

—G. K. Chesterton

TEACHING TIP

In the belief that most students who plagiarize from their sources do so because they don't know how to avoid the problem, Kathleen Mouton has devised a technique that can be demonstrated in class to help students avoid taking notes that are too close to the words of the source. She suggests that instructors ask students to read a short, informative passage of material, then put it away and make notes from memory. Students can check afterwards to make sure that facts (such as dates and names) are correct. With larger amounts of material, students can stop frequently to make their notes, still being careful not to look at the source while recording the note.

tions, you also want your writing to be coherent and readable. You might seem to gain authority by quoting experts on your topic, but if you use too many quotations, you lose coherence as well as control of your own paper. In general, if more than a quarter of your paper consists of quotations, you have written what some people call a "scotch tape special." Having too many quotations gives readers— including instructors—the impression that you have not developed your own thinking and you are letting other people do your talking. Use quotations sparingly, therefore. When you draw on support from an authority, rely mostly on paraphrase (see 31d) and summary (see 31e).

GUIDELINES FOR USING QUOTATIONS

1. Use quotations from authorities in your subject to *support* what you say, not for your thesis statement° or main points.
2. Select quotations that fit your message.
3. Choose a quotation only if
   a. its language is particularly appropriate or distinctive;
   b. its idea is particularly hard to paraphrase accurately;
   c. the authority of the source is especially important to support your material;
   d. the source's words are open to more than one interpretation, so your reader needs to see the original.
4. Do not use quotations in more than a quarter of your paper; rely mostly on paraphrase and summary.
5. Quote accurately.
6. Integrate quotations smoothly into your prose (see 31c-4), paying special attention to the verbs that help you to do so effectively (see 31f).
7. Document your source. Set off quotations with quotation marks to **avoid plagiarism°** (see 31b).

---

1 Quoting accurately

When you use quotations, be very careful not to misquote a source. Always check your quotations against the originals—and then recheck. Mistakes are extremely easy to make when you are copying from a source into your notes or from your notes into your paper. If you photocopy material, mark off on the copy the exact place that caught your attention; otherwise, you might forget your impressions and have to spend time trying to reconstruct your thought processes.

If you have to add a word or two to a quotation so that it fits in with your prose, put those words in brackets (see 29c). Make sure that your additions do not distort the meaning of the quotation. The quotation below is taken from original material shown in section 31d-2. The bracketed material replaces the word *he* in the original quote. The meaning of *he* was clear in context, but in excerpted material a reader would not know to whom *he* referred. The bracketed information supplies words to clarify the material.

"If you hail from western Europe, you will find that [the person you are talking to] is at roughly fingertip distance from you" (Morris 131).*

If you delete a portion of a quotation, indicate the omission with an ellipsis (see 29d). When using ellipses, make sure that the remaining words accurately reflect the source's meaning. Also, make sure that your omission does not create an awkward sentence structure. Here is an example of effective use of an ellipsis:

ORIGINAL

Like the porcupines in Schopenhauer's fable, people like to be close enough to obtain warmth and comradeship but far enough away to avoid pricking one another. Personal space is not necessarily spherical in shape, nor does it extend equally in all directions. (People are able to tolerate closer presence of a stranger at their sides than directly in front of them.) It has been likened to a snail shell, a soap bubble, an aura, a "breathing room" (Sommer 26).

WITH ELLIPSIS

Like the porcupines in Schopenhauer's fable, people like to be close enough to obtain warmth and comradeship but far enough away to avoid pricking one another. Personal space . . . has been likened to a snail shell, a soap bubble, an aura, a "breathing room" (Sommer 26).

| 2 | Selecting quotations that are from accepted authorities and that fit your meaning |

Quotations enhance your message only when you use authorities who bring credibility to your discussion. You must be able to

---

*Parenthetical references are in MLA style (see Chapter 33).

EXTRA EXERCISE B

Working in small groups or in pairs, students can learn good techniques of paraphrasing by trying to find acceptable synonyms for key words in a passage. The italicized words and phrases in the following excerpts can be used for the exercise.

(1) It is clear that between what a man calls (a) *me* and what he simply calls (b) *mine,* the line is difficult to draw. We (c) *feel and act* about certain things that are ours very much as we (c) *feel and act* about ourselves. . . . In its widest possible sense, a man's Self is the sum total of all that he can call his, not only his (d) *body* and his (e) *psychic powers,* but his (f) *clothes* and his (g) *house,* his (h) *wife and his children,* his (i) *ancestors* and his (j) *friends,* his (k) *reputation* and his (l) *works,* his (m) *land and horses and yacht and bank account.* If they (n) *wax and prosper,* he feels triumphant, if they (o) *dwindle and die away,* he feels (p) *cast down*—not necessarily in the same degree for each thing, but in much the same way for all.

—William James, *Principles of Psychology*

(2) Subject to (a) *infinite variables* of winds and currents, of (b) *supply and demand,* of crops and markets, trade has a way of (c)

➔

justify every quotation that you decide to use. If you are unsure whether to quote, then either paraphrase (see 31d) or summarize (see 31e) the material. For example, Amy Brown, author of the student research paper in Chapter 34 about personal space, quoted from Edward T. Hall because he is an accepted authority on her topic. (See Chart 155 in 32g).

Similarly, choose words to quote that fit your context. If you force a quotation to fit your material, most readers will quickly discern the manipulation. Also, never hunt for a quotation simply because you want to include a particular authority's words.

3 Keeping long quotations to a minimum

When you use a quotation, your purpose is to supply evidence or support your assertion, not to reconstruct someone else's argument. If you need to present a complicated argument in detail and thus quote long passages, make absolutely *sure* every word in the quotation counts. Edit out irrelevant parts (using an ellipsis to indicate deleted material; see 31c-1).

If you must quote a long passage, you must be ready to defend your decision to use it by explaining the quotation's significance. Otherwise, your readers will likely skip over the long quotation— and your instructor will assume that you did not want to take the time to paraphrase (see 31d) or summarize (see 31e) the material. ❖ FORMAT ALERT: For instructions on how to arrange the format of a quotation on a page, see Appendix B. ❖

4 Integrating quotations smoothly into your prose

When you use quotations, you *must* integrate them smoothly into your sentences. Do not end up with choppy, incoherent sentences in which quoted portions do not mesh with the grammar, style, or logic of your prose. Consider these examples based on the original material in section 31c-1.

NO	Sommer says personal space for people "like the porcupines in Schopenhauer's fable, people like to be close enough to obtain warmth and comradeship but far enough away to avoid pricking one another" (26). [problem with grammar]
YES	Sommer says concerning personal space that "like the porcupines in Schopenhauer's fable, people like to be close enough to obtain warmth and comradeship but far enough away to avoid pricking one another" (26).

Perhaps the biggest complaint instructors have about student research papers is that some students simply stick in quotations without any rationale for their inclusion. When words are placed between quotation marks, they take on special significance concerning message as well as language. Without context-setting information, the reader cannot know how the writer connects the quotation with its surroundings. Check your writing carefully for quotations that are disembodied (some instructors call them "ghost quotations") and revise so that more than quotation marks differentiate between a quotation and your prose. Be aware that a quotation seldom should begin a paragraph; rely on your own topic sentence° to begin. Then use the quotation if it supports or extends what you have said.

To avoid disembodied quotations in your paper, you might mention the author's name as you introduce a quotation. Also give the title of the source that you are quoting, provided that doing so does not awkwardly interrupt the flow of language. Moreover, if the source is a noteworthy figure, you can give additional authority to your message by referring to his or her credentials as part of this introductory tag. Consider the treatments that follow this quotation, from the student research paper in Chapter 34.

SOURCE

Hall, Edward T. *The Hidden Dimension*. New York: Doubleday, 1966: 171.*

ORIGINAL MATERIAL

Therefore, people from different cultures, when interpreting each other's behavior, often misinterpret the relationship, the activity, or the emotions.

AUTHOR'S NAME

Edward T. Hall claims that "people from different cultures, when interpreting each other's behavior, often misinterpret the relationship, the activity, or the emotions" (171).*

AUTHOR'S NAME AND SOURCE TITLE

Edward T. Hall claims in *The Hidden Dimension* that "people from different cultures, when interpreting each other's behavior, often misinterpret the relationship, the activity, or the emotions" (171).

AUTHOR'S NAME, CREDENTIALS, AND SOURCE TITLE

Edward T. Hall, an anthropologist who has studied personal space, claims in *The Hidden Dimension* that "people from different cultures, when interpreting each other's behavior, often misinterpret the relationship, the activity, or the emotions" (171).

*Source information and parenthetical references are in MLA style (see Chapter 33).

Cont'd.

carving its own paths not always obedient to (d) *the mercantilist faith.* The faith (e) *was embodied* in Britain's Navigation Act, enacted under Oliver Cromwell in 1651 in the interests of the (f) *rising middle class* and the industrial towns and major trading ports— the so-called Cinque Ports, so long (g) *influential* in British history. Aimed specifically at the Dutch to protect British trade against its (h) *most dangerous rival,* the Act raised (i) *a wall of customs duties,* and permitted (j) *transshipment of goods* only in British (k) *bottoms* calling at British ports. The natural result had been (l) *maritime war* with Holland and (m) *bitter resentment* of customs duties in the Colonies, feeding the (n) *spirit of rebellion* which led to the American war. For Britain, the expense of fighting the Dutch and trying to (o) *suppress the American revolt* was more costly than anything that could be gained by the trade laws, causing (p) *higher taxes* at home and their natural consequence, a rise in (q) *domestic disaffection.* That was not the least of Britain's (r) *afflictions* in her (s) *embattled time.*

—Barbara W. Tuchman, *The First Salute*

ANSWERS: EXTRA EXERCISE B

Answers will vary, but here are possible responses.

(1) (a) my self, (b) my people and my things, (c) respond to and behave, (d) physical substance, (e) spiritual capacities, (f) dress, (g) home, (h) family, (i) lineage, (j) favored companions, (k) general character estimation by others, (l) accomplishments, (m) possessions, (n) increase and thrive, (o) decrease and disappear, (p) undone.

(2) (a) unlimited possibilities, (b) resources and desires, (c) going its own way, (d) commercial assumptions, (e) was contained, (f) growing bourgeois class, (g) a force, (h) greatest enemy, (i) tarriff barriers, (j) transfer of merchandise, (k) ships, (l) naval battles, (m) animosity, (n) defiant temper, (o) put down the American revolution, (p) greater levies, (q) discontent among the people, (r) ills, (s) period of struggle.

Occasionally quotations speak for themselves, but at times they do not. Usually the words you are quoting are part of a larger piece, and you know the connection that the quotation has to the original material. Without the original material, your reader may puzzle over why you included the quotation or may need to have the quoted material fully identified. A brief introductory remark gives your reader the needed information.

AUTHOR'S NAME AND INTRODUCTORY ANALYSIS

Edward T. Hall believes that people from different societies perceive personal space in varying ways, claiming that "people from different cultures, when interpreting each other's behavior, often misinterpret the relationship, the activity, or the emotions" (171).

In adding your own words to fit a quotation into your writing, you may interrupt the quotation.

"Therefore," claims Edward T. Hall, "people from different cultures, when interpreting each other's behavior, often misinterpret the relationship, the activity, or the emotions" (171).

EXERCISE 31-1

Read the original material. Then evaluate the passages that show unacceptable uses of quotations. Point out problems, and write a revision of each. End your quotations with this MLA parenthetical reference: (Siwolop 111).

ORIGINAL MATERIAL

This is from "Helping Computer Chips to Keep Their Cool" by Sana Siwolop in *Business Week,* January 25, 1988.

Engineers could improve the efficiency of engines, chemical reactors, furnaces, and other equipment if only they could supply them with electronic sensors. But computer chips can't take the heat. Most microchips develop amnesia long before the temperature climbs to the boiling point of water. But that may change. Researchers at North Carolina State University in Raleigh have successfully made microelectronic transistors that operate at temperatures of up to 1,200 F. The key: using silicon carbide, a material familiar to most people as the grit on sandpaper, instead of the crystalline silicon usually used for computer chips.

ANSWERS: EXERCISE 31-1

A. *Analysis:* The quotation does not relate clearly to the sentence it follows. A transitional introduction to the quotation is needed. *Acceptable* (answers will vary): Many problems are caused when sensitive equipment overheats. Until now, researchers have failed to develop sensors that would warn of such overheating mainly because nearly all "microchips develop amnesia long before the temperature climbs to the boiling point of water" (Siwolop 111).

B. *Analysis:* The quotation omits several words but does not provide an ellipsis to indicate where material has been deleted. *Acceptable* (answers will vary): Many researchers believe that they would be able to "improve the efficiency of engines . . . if only they could supply them with electronic sensors" (Siwolop 111).

C. *Analysis:* The sentence is grammatically incorrect. The quotation does not fit with the rest of the sentence. Words need to be added so that the information flows smoothly. *Acceptable* (answers will vary): Several new developments have taken place at North Carolina State University in Raleigh where researchers "have successfully made microelectronic transistors that operate at temperatures of up to 1,200 F" (Siwolop 111).

D. *Analysis:* The tense of the verb in the quotation shifts from the tense of the verb in the previous sentence. Brackets can be used to change the tense of the verb in the

→

UNACCEPTABLE USES OF QUOTATIONS

A. Many problems are caused when sensitive equipment overheats. "Most microchips develop amnesia long before the temperature climbs to the boiling point of water" (Siwolop 111).

B. Many researchers believe that they would be able to "improve the efficiency of engines and other equipment if only they could supply them with electronic sensors" (Siwolop 111).

C. Several new developments have taken place at North Carolina State University in Raleigh "have successfully made microelectronic transistors that operate at temperatures of up to 1,200 F" (Siwolop 111).

D. In the past, there have been serious problems with sensors designed to detect heat. Until recently, "computer chips can't take the heat" (Siwolop 111), but now that problem may be solved.

E. One of the problems in designing a heat sensor is that many "microchips develop amnesia before the temperature climbs up to the boiling point of water" (Siwolop 111).

EXERCISE 31-2

A. For a paper describing how and why twins make important contributions to scientific research, write a three- to four-sentence passage that includes your own words and a quotation from this material. After the quoted words, use this parenthetical reference: (Begley 84).

For over a century twins have been used to study how genes make people what they are. Because they share precisely the same genes but live in different surroundings under different influences, identical twins reared apart are helping science sort out which qualities of body and mind are shaped by our genes, and which by upbringing. Researchers needn't worry about running out of subjects: according to the Twins Foundation, there are approximately 4.5 million twin individuals in the United States alone, and about 70,000 more are born each year.

—Sharon Begley, "Twins"

B. For a paper arguing that it is difficult, if not impossible, to assure honesty in large-scale testing, quote from the Robbins material in Exercise 31-6. Be sure to include at least one numerical statistic in your quotation.

C. Write a three- to four-sentence passage that includes your own words and a quotation from a source you are using for a paper assigned in one of your courses. If you have no such assignment, choose any material suitable for a college-level paper. Your instructor might request a photocopy of the material from which you are quoting.

Cont'd.

quotation so that it agrees grammatically with the previous verb. *Acceptable* (answers will vary): In the past, there have been serious problems with sensors designed to detect heat. Until recently, "computer chips [couldn't] take the heat" (Siwolop 111) but now that problem may be solved.

E. *Analysis:* The quotation is inaccurate; the word "long" is omitted while "up" is added. *Acceptable* (answers may vary): One of the problems in designing a heat sensor is that many "microchips develop amnesia long before the temperature climbs to the boiling point of water" (Siwolop 111).

ANSWERS: EXERCISE 31-2

A. Answers will vary; here is one possibility:

Because genetic research is becoming increasingly important, scientists are seeking twins who are willing to participate in experiments either for pay or as volunteers. The Twins Foundation is confident that researchers will find the subjects they need because "there are approximately 4.5 million twin individuals in the United States alone, and about 70,000 more are born each year," (Begley 84).

B. Answers will vary; here is one possibility:

It is becoming increasingly difficult to assure that large-scale testing will be taken honestly. For example, in New York State students stole copies of the Regents exam, and because of their actions "1,200 principals received instructions from the State Education Commissioner to look for *unusual scoring patterns* that would show that students had the answers beforehand" (Robbins 12).

C. Answers will vary.

EXTRA EXERCISE C

Following the guidelines for writing a summary, summarize one of the following paragraphs.

1. The Elizabethan Age takes its name from the queen who reigned over England and Ireland from 1558 to 1603. She was an intelligent and gifted ruler, managing for decades to escape political disasters at home and abroad. Always an insightful judge of character, she achieved her success in large part because of her tendency to make use of the shrewdest people around her. However, her clear awareness of what she wanted and why she wanted it sometimes led her to go her own way, using a variety of means to reach the ends she desired. She was on occasion devious, even false, but she managed to outwit her opposition time after time. As a result, it was a glorious time in the history of Britain, for under her rule the nation rose from a relatively weak position among the nations of Europe to the highest rank. England's power and success grew rapidly in the sixteenth century, leaving it, at the death of Elizabeth I, a leader in navigation and exploration, in literary productivity—particularly in the drama—and in colonization of the New World.

2. When she died in 1986, Georgia O'Keeffe the person generated almost as much interest among the public as Georgia O'Keeffe the artist. Sometimes she was thought of as the wife and often-photographed model of Alfred Stieglitz, but more often she was pictured as a romantic recluse who, when she grew older, moved increasingly away from the world of art critics and historians and closer to the rugged but exotic New Mexico countryside and culture. In the long run, however, it will be for her art that she will be best remembered. Some viewers admire her abstractions, others her figurative works. Even those who disagree about the relative quality of her paintings agree that her art is memorable, clear, and strong. She painted with a distinctive, powerful, ➡

31d Paraphrasing accurately

When you **paraphrase,** you precisely restate in your own words a passage written (or spoken) by another person. The word *paraphrase* combines the Greek word for *tell* with the Greek prefix *para-*, meaning "alongside." Thus, *paraphrase* describes a parallel text, one that goes alongside an original writing. Your paraphrases offer an account of what various authorities have to say, not in their words but in yours. Guidelines for writing a paraphrase are in Chart 148. The ideas of authorities can give substance and credibility to your message and can offer support for your material. Equally important, the process of writing a paraphrase helps you untangle difficult passages and come to understand them. Paraphrasing forces you to read closely and to extract precise meaning from complex passages.

GUIDELINES FOR WRITING A PARAPHRASE 148
1. Say what the source says, but no more.
2. Reproduce the source's emphases.
3. Use your own words, phrasing, and sentence structure to restate the message. If certain synonyms are awkward, quote the material—but resort to quotation very sparingly.
4. Read over your sentences to make sure that they do not distort the source's meaning.
5. Expect your material to be as long as, and possibly longer than, the original.
6. Use verbs effectively to integrate paraphrases into your prose (see 31f).
7. **Avoid plagiarism°** (see 31a).
8. As you take notes, record all documentation facts about your source so that you can prevent plagiarism.

1 Restating material completely using your own words

When you paraphrase, restate the material—and no more. Do not skip points. Do not guess at meaning. Do not insert your own opinions or interpretations. If the source's words trigger your own thinking, do not lose your thought or assume you will recall it later. *Write down your thought, but make sure it is physically separate from your paraphrase:* in the margin, in a different color ink, or circled.

As you paraphrase, use your own words; otherwise you will be quoting. Use synonyms wherever you can, and use your own sentence structures. When you finish, read over your paraphrase to check that it makes sense and does not distort the meaning.

In paraphrasing, the farther you get from the original phrasing, the more likely you are to sound like yourself. Do not be surprised to find that when you change language and sentence structure you might also have to change punctuation, verb tense°, and voice°.

Sometimes, synonyms or substitute phrases are not advisable. Consider how each synonym fits into the flow of your sentence. For example, for a basic concept such as *people,* the phrase *homo sapiens* might make the material seem strained. Also, do not rename terms that the author identifies as coined; quote them. For example, in paragraph 2 of the student research paper in Chapter 34, Amy Brown does not use a synonym for Edward Hall's word "proxemics," because Hall originated it.

2 Avoiding plagiarism when you paraphrase

You must **avoid plagiarism** (see 31a) when you paraphrase. Even though a paraphrase is not a direct quotation, you *must* use documentation° to credit your source. Also, you *must* reword your source material, not merely change a few words. Compare these passages, based on a source used in the student research paper in Chapter 34:

SOURCE

Morris, Desmond. *Manwatching.* New York: Abrams, 1977: 131.*

ORIGINAL

Unfortunately, different countries have different ideas about exactly how close is close. It is easy enough to test your own "space reaction": when you are talking to someone in the street or in any open space, reach out with your arm and see where the nearest point on his body comes. If you hail from western Europe, you will find that he is at roughly fingertip distance from you. In other words, as you reach out, your fingertips will just about make contact with his shoulder. If you come from eastern Europe, you

---

*Source information throughout this chapter is in MLA style (see Chapter 33).

Cont'd.

personal vision, one that continues to speak strongly to viewers today. Her red poppies, purple hills, and bleached skulls fix themselves in the mind's eye not to be easily erased.

3. To the non-Scot, the tartan is perhaps the most picturesque and original costume in Europe. To a Scot, it is a costume of national distinction. Even without considering the causes for the veneration paid to it by the Highlanders, its merits are several. For one, it bears extraordinarily well the inclemency of weather. It also is economical, light, and unencumbering to the wearer, making it comfortable to wear in a variety of situations. In addition, the plaid of the tartan designates the clan, or family, of the wearer. In the mid-eighteenth century it came to be such a powerful symbol of Scottish culture that it was banned by the English in a law that was not repealed until 1782.

ANSWERS: EXTRA EXERCISE C

Here are possible summaries.

1. An "insightful judge of character," a clever and sometimes deceitful politician, and an independent and purposeful ruler, Elizabeth I, queen of England from 1558 to 1603, continually triumphed over her enemies and weathered political crises to help make England into one of the most powerful countries of Europe.

2. Although people occasionally identify Georgia O'Keeffe as photographer Alfred Stieglitz's model and wife or as a hermit artist from New Mexico, people will recall her finally for her paintings. Whatever their opinions of her art, all find it original, personal, forceful, and unforgettable.

3. The tartan is not only an important emblem of the Scottish people, but also an inexpensive, comfortable, and durable piece of clothing that Scots may wear for most occasions. Each plaid represents a different clan.

EXTRA EXERCISE D

Practice working quotations smoothly into your own writing by devising introductions to the following statements.

1. "Boys and girls grow up in different worlds, but we think we're in the same one, so we judge each other's behavior by the standards of our own."

—Deborah Tannen, *You Just Don't Understand: Men and Women in Conversation*

2. "Science does not aim at establishing immutable truths and eternal dogmas: its aim is to approach the truth by successive approximations, without claiming that at any stage final and complete accuracy has been achieved."

Bertrand Russell, *The ABC of Relativity*

3. "Femininity, in essence, is a romantic sentiment, a nostalgic tradition of imposed limitations."

—Susan Brownmiller, "Femininity"

4. "In books I've read since I was young I've searched for heroines who could serve as ideals, as models, as possibilities."

—Judith Viorst, "How Books Helped Shape My Life"

5. "Every gift we give carries with it our idea of what a present is. Perhaps it expresses our personality; perhaps, on the contrary, it is what we believe the recipient really wants, a choice based on careful listening for the slightest hint of what he longs for or needs or should have, even though he may not realize it."

—Margaret Mead and Rhoda Metraux, "The Gift of Autonomy"

will find you are standing at "wrist distance." If you come from the Mediterranean region, you will find that you are much closer to your companion, at little more than "elbow distance."

UNACCEPTABLE PARAPHRASE (UNDERSCORED WORDS ARE PLAGIARIZED)

Regrettably, different nations think differently about <u>exactly how close is close</u>. Test yourself: <u>when you are talking to someone in the street or in any open space</u>, stretch your arm out to measure how close that person is to you. If you are from western Europe, you will find that <u>your fingertips will just about make contact with the person's shoulder</u>. If you are from eastern Europe, <u>your wrist will reach the person's shoulder</u>. If you are from <u>the Mediterranean region, you will find that you are much closer to your companion</u>, when your elbow will reach that person's shoulder (Morris 131).*

ACCEPTABLE PARAPHRASE

People from different nations think that "close" means different things. You can easily see what your reaction is to how close to you people stand by reaching out the length of your arm to measure how close someone is as the two of you talk. When people from western Europe stand on the street and talk together, the space between them is the distance it would take one person's fingertips to reach to the other person's shoulder. People from eastern Europe converse at a wrist-to-shoulder distance. People from the Mediterranean, however, prefer an elbow-to-shoulder distance (Morris 131).*

The first attempt to paraphrase is not acceptable. All that the writer has done is simply change a few words. What remains is plagiarized because the passage keeps most of the original's language, has the same sentence structure, and uses no quotation marks. The documentation is correct, but it does not make up for the unacceptable paraphrasing.

The second paraphrase is acceptable. It captures the essence of the original in the student's own words.

EXERCISE 31-3

Read the original material and then the paraphrase that is unacceptable because it plagiarizes. Point out each example of plagiarism. Then write your own paraphrase. End it with this parenthetical reference: (Jacobs 141).*

*Parenthetical references are in MLA style (see Chapter 33).

ORIGINAL MATERIAL

This paragraph is from *The Death and Life of Great American Cities* by Jane Jacobs, published by Random House in 1961, page 141.

A good street neighborhood achieves a marvel of balance between its people's determination to have essential privacy and their simultaneous wish for differing degrees of contact, enjoyment, or help from the people around. This balance is largely made up of small, sensibly managed details, practiced and accepted so casually that they normally seem taken for granted.

UNACCEPTABLE PARAPHRASE (PLAGIARIZES)

A good neighborhood maintains an impressive balance between the people being determined to have privacy and wishing for varying degrees of contact, pleasure, or assistance from others nearby. People manage this with small details that are normally taken for granted (Jacobs 141).°

EXERCISE 31-4

A. For a paper on economic conditions in Third World countries, paraphrase this paragraph. End your paraphrase with this parenthetical reference: (Ehrenreich and Fuentes 87).*

For many Third World women, electronics is a prestige occupation, at least compared to other kinds of factory work. They are unlikely to know that in the United States the National Institute on Occupational Safety and Health (NIOSH) has placed electronics on its select list of high health-risk industries using the greatest number of toxic substances. If electronics assembly work is risky here, it is doubly so in countries where there is no equivalent of NIOSH to even issue warnings. In many plants toxic chemicals and solvents sit in open containers, filling the work area with fumes that can literally knock you out.

—Barbara Ehrenreich and Annette Fuentes, "Life on the Global Assembly Line"

B. Write a paraphrase of a paragraph of at least 150 words from one of the sources you are using for a paper assigned in one of your courses. If you have no such assignment, choose any material suitable for a college-level paper. Your instructor may request that you submit a photocopy of the original material to accompany your paraphrase.

*Parenthetical references are in MLA style (see Chapter 33).

Analysis: This paraphrase is unacceptable because it uses many words and phrases from the original. Also, the first sentence uses the same sentence structures. *Acceptable paraphrase* (answers will vary considerably): When people want to create a sense of neighborhood where they live, they need to balance their interest in privacy with their desire for knowing their neighbors. Practically without being conscious of it, people manage the details of their lives to achieve the balance they need (Jacobs 141).

A. Answers will vary; here is one acceptable paraphrase:

Women who live in underdeveloped or emerging countries frequently regard working with electronics as giving them higher status than other assembly line work. Most of these women are unaware that the electronics occupation may pose significant threats to their physical well-being. They have no way of knowing that NIOSH (National Institute on Occupational Safety and Health) has identified electronics plants in the United States as employing the largest amount of poison materials that may have a negative effect on workers' health in any industry. Certainly the dangers here in the United States are twice as threatening when they exist in Third World nations, which have no organization like NIOSH to act as watchdogs. In underdeveloped countries, the air in factories is often polluted with toxic vapors that arise from poisonous materials that are stored in uncovered vessels. The gas created by these chemicals and other substances is strong enough to make a worker lose consciousness (Ehrenreich and Fuentes 87).

31e

QUOTATION ABOUT WRITING

Quotations are the wisdom of the wise and the experience of ages.

—Isaac D'Israeli

QUOTATION ABOUT WRITING

Nothing is said that has not been said before.

—Terence

QUOTATION ABOUT WRITING

Be sure you go to the author to get at his meaning, not to find yours.

—John Ruskin

QUOTATION ABOUT WRITING

Originality consists in thinking for yourself, and not in thinking unlike other people.

—J. Fitzjames Stephen

QUOTATION ABOUT WRITING

Stay at home in your mind. Don't recite other people's opinions. I hate quotations. Tell me what you know.

—Ralph Waldo Emerson

QUOTATION ABOUT WRITING

I quote others only the better to express myself.

—Montaigne

31e Summarizing accurately

A **summary** reviews the main points of a passage and gets at the gist of what an author or speaker says. A summary condenses the essentials of someone else's thought into a few general statements. Guidelines for writing a summary are in Chart 149.

Summaries and paraphrases (see 31d) differ in one primary way. A paraphrase restates the original material completely; a summary is much shorter and provides only the main point of the original source.

149

GUIDELINES FOR WRITING A SUMMARY

1. Identify the main points and condense them without losing the essence of the material.
2. Use your own words to condense the message.
3. Keep your summary short.
4. Use verbs effectively to integrate summaries into your prose (see 31f).
5. **Avoid plagiarism°.**
6. As you take notes, record all documentation facts about your source so that you can prevent plagiarism.

Here is a summary based on the original material shown in section 31d-2. Compare it with the acceptable paraphrase in that section.

SUMMARY

Expected amounts of space between people when they are talking differs among cultures: in general, people from western Europe prefer fingertip to shoulder distance, from eastern Europe wrist to shoulder, and from the Mediterranean elbow to shoulder (Morris 131).*

Summarizing forces you to read closely and to comprehend clearly. Writing summaries can help you learn material, because the

---

*Parenthetical references are in MLA style (see Chapter 33).

31e

process helps lock information into your memory. Summarizing is probably the most frequently used technique for taking notes and for incorporating sources into papers.

1 | Isolating the main points and condensing without losing meaning

A summary captures the entire sense of a passage in very little space, so you must read through all the content before you write. Then isolate the main points by asking these questions: What is the subject? What is the central message on the subject? A summary excludes more than it includes, so you must make substantial deletions.

As you summarize, you trace a line of thought. Doing this involves deleting less central ideas and sometimes transposing certain points into an order more suited to summary. A summary should reduce the original by at least half. In summarizing a longer original—about ten pages or more—you may find it helpful to first divide the original into subsections and summarize each. Then group your subsection summaries and use them as the basis for further condensing the material into a final summary.

Condensing information into a table is another option you can use to summarize, particularly when you are summarizing numerical data. For an example, see paragraph 5 of the student research paper in Chapter 34: Table 1 summarizes ten pages of a source.

As you summarize, you may be tempted to interpret something the author says or make a judgment about the value of the argument. Your own opinions do not belong in a summary, but jot down your ideas immediately, so that you can use them later. *Be sure to place your ideas in your notes so that they are physically separate from your summary:* in the margin, in a different color ink, or circled.

Until you are experienced at writing summaries, you will likely have to revise them more than once. Always make sure that a summary accurately reflects the source and its emphases.

2 | Avoiding plagiarizing when you summarize

You must **avoid plagiarism°** (see 31a) when you summarize. Even though a summary is not a direct quotation, you *must* use documentation° to credit your source. Also, you *must* use your own words. Compare these passages, based on a source used in the student research paper in Chapter 34.

TEACHING TIP

Many activities in other courses require students to write about readings and employ paraphrasing and summarizing. Students are often asked to synthesize, analyze, respond to, and critique readings in exams and papers. They may compose book reviews, interpret literature, analyze arguments, and relate textbook material to experiments in lab reports. Paraphrasing and summarizing are also effective study techniques that can be applied to any reading assignment. They are particularly helpful to students trying to identify the main points of a piece of writing and relate them to each other. Students often disagree in identifying the main points of a text. For that reason, they often find it informative to compare their paraphrases and summaries, discussing why they made certain choices.

QUOTATION ABOUT WRITING

Why can't somebody give us a list of things that everybody thinks and nobody says, and another list of things that everybody says and nobody thinks.

—Dr. Oliver Wendell Holmes

QUOTATION ABOUT WRITING

One has to secrete a jelly in which to slip quotations down people's throats and one always secretes too much jelly.

—Virginia Woolf

TEACHING TIP

To give your students practice in note taking before they are assigned research paper topics, you might distribute copies of a newspaper or magazine article on a popular subject and ask your students to take notes in support of a particular thesis.

Once they (and you) are sure of their skills, the students can move on to more complex issues with confidence, but at first keeping to popular subjects will help interest students.

Encourage students to paraphrase, summarize, and quote as they feel necessary, and to take as many (or as few) notes as they feel would be useful in supporting a thesis. Then collect their notes and distribute copies of all or some sets of notes. As a class (or in groups), discuss the notes one set at a time.

1. Do all the notes support the thesis?
2. Are paraphrases accurate?
3. Are summaries accurate?
4. Are quotations appropriate and accurate?
5. Are quoted words within paraphrases and summaries placed in quotation marks?
6. Would any material be better presented in a different kind of note?

SOURCE

Hall, Edward T. *The Hidden Dimension.* New York: Doubleday, 1966: 109.*

ORIGINAL

The general failure to grasp the significance of the many elements that contribute to man's sense of space may be due to two mistaken notions: (1) that for every effect there is a single and identifiable cause; and (2) that man's boundary begins and ends with his skin. If we can rid ourselves of the need for a single explanation, and if we can think of man as surrounded by a series of expanding and contracting fields which provide information of many kinds, we shall begin to see him in an entirely different light. We can then begin to learn about human behavior, including personality types. . . . Concepts such as these are not always easy to grasp, because most of the distance-sensing process occurs outside the awareness. We sense other people as close or distant, but we cannot always put our finger on what it is that enables us to characterize them as such. So many different things are happening at once it is difficult to sort out the sources of information on which we base our reactions.

UNACCEPTABLE SUMMARY (UNDERSCORED WORDS ARE PLAGIARIZED)

Concepts such as identifying causes and determining boundaries are not always easy to grasp (Hall 109).*

ACCEPTABLE SUMMARY

Human beings make the mistake of thinking that an event has a "single and identifiable cause" and that people are limited by the boundaries of their bodies. Most people are unaware that they have a sense of interpersonal space, which contributes to their reactions to other people (Hall 109).*

The unacceptable summary does not isolate the main point, and it plagiarizes. The writer used almost all the language in the source.

The second summary is acceptable because it not only isolates the main idea but also recasts it in the student's words. One phrase—"single and identifiable cause"—is borrowed, but it is set off in quotation marks. No one would charge this student with plagiarism.

*Source information and parenthetical references are in MLA style (see Chapter 33).

EXERCISE 31-5

Read the original material and then the summary that is unacceptable because it plagiarizes. Point out each example of plagiarism. Then write your own summary. End it with this parenthetical reference: (Friedman 69).*

ORIGINAL MATERIAL

This is from *Overcoming the Fear of Success* by Martha Friedman, published by Seaview Books in 1980, page 69.

The manner in which we respond to negative criticism is a clue to the level of our self-esteem, which in turn is a good index to the degree of our fear of success. If we harbor a feeling of inadequacy, as many of us do, about something, no matter how slight, negative criticism can wipe us out. Many of us carry too many internalized low-esteem messages from the past, negative things our parents or siblings or teachers or schoolday peers said to us.

UNACCEPTABLE SUMMARY

Many people harbor feelings of low self-esteem as a result of internalized negative messages from the past, and if people respond badly to negative criticism, no matter how slight, it indicates a low level of self-esteem, which is also an excellent index of their fear of success (Friedman 69).*

EXERCISE 31-6

A. For a paper explaining the problems of large-scale competency testing, summarize this material. End your summary with this parenthetical reference: (Robbins 12).*

More and more states are requiring students to pass competency tests in order to receive their high school diplomas. And many educators fear that an increase in the use of state exams will lead to a corresponding rise in cheating. They cite the case of students in New York State who faced criminal misdemeanor charges for possessing and selling advance copies of state Regents examinations. Approximately 600,000 students take the Regents exams. And it proved impossible to determine how many of them had seen the stolen tests. As a result, 1,200 principals received instructions from the State Education Commissioner to look for *unusual*

*Parenthetical references are in MLA style (see Chapter 33).

ANSWERS: EXERCISE 31-5

Analysis: This summary is unacceptable because it uses many words and phrases from the original. *Acceptable summary* (answers will vary considerably): When people respond badly to negative criticism, they are revealing poor self-esteem that usually results from childhood experience and that also indicates that they are afraid of success (Freidman 69).

ANSWERS: EXERCISE 31-6

A. Answers will vary, but here is one possible summary:

A cloud hangs over testing programs because of an increase in cheating, as when students in New York State sold the state Regents examination in advance. This led to warnings that educators should watch for student scores that appear in unusual patterns (Robbins 12).

B. Answers will vary, but here is one possible summary:

Many women in underdeveloped countries regard electronics as a desirable career, but they are usually unaware that this industry has been identified by experts in the United States as posing serious threats to the health of workers (Ehrenreich and Fuentes 87).

C. Answers will vary.

scoring patterns that would show that students had the answers beforehand. This put a cloud over the test program.

—Stacia Robbins, ''Honesty: Is It Going Out of Style?''

B. Write a summary of your paraphrase of the Ehrenreich and Fuentes material in Exercise 31-4. End it with the parenthetical reference given.

C. Write a summary of one or two paragraphs that total about 200 words. Take it from a source you are using for a paper assigned in one of your courses, or select material suitable for a college-level paper. Your instructor may request that you submit a photocopy of the original material to accompany your summary.

31f Using verbs effectively to integrate source material into your prose

Many verbs can help you work paraphrases, summaries, and quotations into your writing smoothly. They are listed in Chart 150. Make sure to use these verbs without any strain of style. To see many of these verbs used, read the student research paper in Chapter 34. Note especially comment X, which goes with paragraph 10. As you use this list of verbs, be aware that some have rather specific meanings, while others are general enough to use in most situations. Choose them according to the meaning that you want your sentences to deliver.

VERBS USEFUL FOR PARAPHRASE, SUMMARY, AND QUOTATION   150

analyze	complain	find	offer	show
argue	concede	illustrate	point out	speculate
ask	conclude	insist	report	suggest
assert	consider	maintain	reveal	suppose
claim	describe	note	say	think
comment	explain	observe	see	write

32 The Processes of Research Writing

32a Understanding research writing

Research writing involves two processes: conducting research and writing a paper based upon it. The processes of researching and writing are interwoven throughout a research project. The **writing process** for a research paper is much like the writing process for all academic papers (see Chapters 1-3). The **research process** adds a new dimension throughout your writing process. In planning, you choose a suitable topic, refine it into a research question, use a search strategy to find and evaluate sources, and take notes (all these activities are explained in this chapter). In drafting and revising, you integrate sources into your research paper by quoting, paraphrasing, and summarizing (see Chapter 31).

Research writing seeks to answer questions. Few research assignments are stated as questions, but all assignments imply the need to search for answers. Seeing research as a quest for answers makes clear that you cannot know whether you have located useful material unless you know what you are looking for. Research questions, whether stated or implied, and the processes needed to answer them vary widely. You might be asked to explain information: "How does penicillin destroy bacteria?" You might be asked to argue one side of an issue: "Is Congress more important than the Supreme Court in setting social policy?"

To attempt to find answers, you must track down information from varied sources. *Attempt* is an important word in relation to research. Some research questions lead to a final, definitive answer, but some do not. In the preceding paragraph, the question about penicillin leads to a definitive answer (the antibiotic destroys the cell

All too often, the Research Paper looms over Freshman Composition like a thundercloud. It requires much time, students resent "doing" it, and the results are dismal. James Strickland ("The Research Sequence: What To Do Before the Term Paper," *College Composition and Communication* [May 1986]: 233–236) offers a useful semester plan that incorporates the research project into the ongoing concerns of Freshman Composition.

The sequence begins with an opinion paper in the form of a letter to the editor. No research is required, and Strickland encourages students to submit the letters to local papers (achieving a publication rate of almost 50 percent and a concomitant increase in students' self-esteem).

Strickland next splits the class into groups of readers whose jobs are to go over one another's letters and indicate what points need support to be more convincing. Wanting to close the holes in their arguments, students are now ready to learn the research skills they need.

As periodicals are the most likely source for the information students need, Strickland begins with the use of periodical indexes. Students must locate and read several articles bearing on their subjects to see if their "original position was accurate and/or reasonable." Students at this stage learn to decipher periodical indexes, to make bibliography notecards, and to paraphrase and take notes.

Based on their research, students now write "documented essays" on the subjects of their original letters to the editor. They are asked to imagine that, on the basis of their letters, they have been asked to write 750-word essays for the Sunday newspaper's magazine section. These two- to three-page essays provide an opportunity to revise the thrust of the original letters, and to use quotation and paraphrase in support of a thesis. Several parenthetical references or endnotes and a bibliography are standard.

→

walls of some bacteria); the question about social policy, on the other hand, leads not to a definitive answer but rather invites an informed opinion based on information gathered from research.

Research can be an engrossing, creative activity. By gathering information, analyzing its separate components, and composing a synthesis of it, you can come to know your subject deeply. As you write, you can make fresh connections and gain unexpected insights. Equally important, you can sample the pleasures of being a self-reliant learner, someone with the self-discipline and intellectual resources to locate and learn information independently.

If you are among those who feel overwhelmed by the prospect of research writing, you are not alone. Many researchers, whether inexperienced or experienced, share such feelings. When you break research writing into the series of steps described in this chapter, however, the project becomes far less intimidating.

32b Scheduling for research writing

Research writing takes time. Once you are aware of what is involved, you can plan ahead and budget your time intelligently. As soon as your instructor gives a research-paper assignment, work out a schedule for finishing each step. You might need one day for a number of steps and two weeks for another.

The more you do research-paper projects, the more skilled you will become at scheduling the work and handling it efficiently. The schedule in Chart 151 lists typical research steps (the parentheses give the section in which each step is discussed). No two research-paper projects are alike, so adapt the schedule to your needs. Also, you might find that all steps might not proceed in a straight line, but rather loop back and forth. Be flexible, but always keep an eye on the calendar.

32c Using a research log

A **research log** is like a diary. It becomes a record of your research process, especially your evolving thoughts about your work. Start a research log as soon as you get your assignment. Begin by entering the schedule (see 32b) you intend to follow. Use a separate notebook for the log, one that you can carry to the library and any other places where you conduct research.

SAMPLE SCHEDULE FOR A RESEARCH PAPER PROJECT 151

Assignment received (date)_____   **FINISH BY**

1. Keep a research log (see 32c). _____
2. Choose a suitable topic (see 32d). _____
3. Decide on purpose and audience (see 32e). _____
4. Gather needed equipment (see 32f). _____
5. Know how to evaluate sources (see 32g). _____
6. Determine documentation style (see 32j). _____
7. Use a search strategy (see 32h), take notes (see 32i), and make bibliographic cards (see 33a). *Use whichever steps fit your situation.* _____
8. Draft a preliminary thesis statement (see 32p). _____
9. Decide whether to interview experts (see 32h-1). _____
10. Decide whether to send for information (see 32h-2). _____
11. Use reference books (see 32k and 32l). _____
12. Use indexes to periodicals and read periodicals (see 32m). _____
13. Use the book catalog and read books (see 32n). _____
14. Use computerized databases (see 32o). _____
15. Compile a working list of sources to consult (see 33a). _____
16. Draft and revise a final thesis statement (see 32p). _____
17. Outline as required (see 32q). _____
18. Draft paper (see 32r). _____
19. Use parenthetical references (see 33b). _____
20. Revise paper (see 32r). _____
21. Compile a final Works Cited list (see 33c and 33d). _____

Assignment due (date)_____

Although much of your research log will never find its way into your research paper itself, its entries become invaluable aids as you progress from choosing a topic to gathering material to organizing information and finally to writing the paper. As a student expected to concentrate simultaneously on various courses, you can use a

Cont'd.

The next step is a "researched paper," using more thorough research and fuller documentation. This time students are asked to imagine that they have been invited to expand their Sunday newsmagazine piece into a full-size article (14–24 pages) for a major national magazine. Each student serves as "editor" to another student, in addition to writing his or her own article. The editor's job is to point out places in the essay where additional evidence is needed or where logic is unclear or faulty. The students explore a variety of heuristics as they seek to fill developmental gaps and correct logical flaws.

Overall, Strickland feels, the sequence has resulted in superior papers, exhibiting better documentation skills than papers written by students before he used this sequence. Student attitude has also changed in a positive way: students are more willing to go to the library, are more confident in their ability to do research, and complain less about assignments.

TEACHING TIP

A research log can become the basis for an "I-Search paper" describing the search conducted for the research paper. According to Ken Macrorie (*The I-Search Paper* [Portsmouth, NH: Boynton/Cook, 1988]), an I-Search paper tells the story of what the writer went through to learn something that he or she needed to know. Writing an I-Search paper encourages writers to reflect about the process of conducting their research, allows writers to describe the satisfactions and frustrations of their research, and, when well written, can tell an entertaining, suspenseful tale. Many I-Search papers follow a four-part outline:

1. What I Knew (and didn't know about my topic when I started out).

2. Why I'm Writing This Paper. . . .

3. The Search (story of the hunt).

4. What I Learned (or didn't learn . . .) (64).

BACKGROUND

The research paper originated when American universities adopted the research ideal and began developing a curriculum to educate students for careers in specialized disciplines. According to David R. Russell (*Writing in the Academic Disciplines, 1870–1990* [Carbondale, IL: Southern Illinois UP 1991]), young college instructors who had studied in research-oriented German universities began occasionally to assign a "scholarly thesis" in U.S. colleges around 1870. Ten years later many colleges began to require seniors to write a "graduating thesis" of 1,000 to 3,000 words, and by the 1890s these were frequently required in the new seminar courses for advanced students. At first instructors required little formal documentation in a thesis, but by the turn of the century, the typical thesis paper provided a bibliography, extensive footnotes, and charts and diagrams. Faculty regarded students as "apprentices" in a profession, and the thesis was an opportunity for students to develop the investigative skills needed to become experts in their fields, and to learn to address readers in their professions. The research paper soon moved into lower-level courses, and by 1931 high school students often were required to write a term paper in their junior or senior year.

Research paper instruction began to be offered in freshman composition courses in the 1920s. By the early 1980s, according to James E. Ford and Dennis R. Perry ("Research Paper Instruction in the Undergraduate Writing Program," *College English* [December 1982]: 825–831), 84 percent of freshman writing programs and 40 percent of advanced composition programs were teaching the research paper, and the research paper was a requirement in 78 percent of the freshman programs and 42 percent of the advanced programs.

research log to enhance your efficiency. A well-kept log traces your line of reasoning as your project evolves, tells where you ended each work session, and suggests what your next steps should be. Such a record means much less wasted time retracing a research path or reconstructing your thinking. Also, a research log plays the role of a journal (see 2e) in which you can "think on paper" by exploring ideas, analyzing information, and discovering insights that the physical act of writing makes possible. Like other examples in this chapter, the two excerpts from a research log shown here are by the student whose research paper about personal space appears in Chapter 34.

> Nov. 1: The assigned subject is communication. Must narrow! I've always wondered about "unspoken" communication, like the messages of body language or the idea of being comfortable when I have "my own space." My psychology textbook has the term "nonverbal communication." Check what it means.

> Nov. 15: Found Sommer's book, made a biblio. card, and photocopied p. 26. Excellent source. He is an environmental psychologist. Tone is calm, seems unbiased. I see I was overlapping two concepts: territory and personal space. Territory refers to places we carve out as our own — a chair in a classroom, a room in a house. Personal space is the "bubble" of space we carry around with us. We don't like intrusions in our bubbles.

Excerpts from Amy Brown's Research Log

Choosing and narrowing a topic for research writing

Instructors assign topics for research papers in a variety of ways. Some assign the specific topic. Others assign a general subject area and require you to narrow it to a topic that can be researched within the constraints of time and length imposed by the assignment. Still other instructors expect you to choose a topic on your own.

What if you have free choice of a research topic, but you develop what might be called "research topic block" because the task seems overwhelming? First, stay calm so that you can think clearly. Next, force yourself to get started. One way is to use the "BLB" system, explained in Chart 152, which has been worked out by students who have experience dealing with topic block.

152

OVERCOMING RESEARCH TOPIC BLOCK USING "BLB"

Use this system by taking one step at a time, without focusing on the entire project right away. Think positively and assure yourself that you *can* find a topic in the allotted time.

1. B-BROWSE for a subject where ideas can be found.

    ■ The **vertical file** (sometimes called the *pamphlet file*) in your college library contains materials too short or informal to be listed in a library's catalog. It can contain pamphlets and reports from medical groups (such as the Red Cross or the National AIDS Hotline); environmental groups (such as the World Wildlife Fund); socially conscious groups (such as Mothers Against Drunk Driving or the Council on Aging); and others. It might also contain informative booklets and reports published by the U.S. Government, the United Nations, and other governmental groups (some libraries store them separately, so check with a librarian).

    ■ **Textbooks** of yours or your friends—or even ones on reserve at the library or shelved in the college bookstore (if browsing is allowed). ➡

TEACHING TIP
Saying something original based on several sources is an imposing challenge for most students. Many instead treat the research paper as a knowledge-telling exercise in which they restate what they have read. The research paper becomes a string of quotations, paraphrases, and summaries that drown out the student's voice, lack purpose and focus, and often invite plagiarism. According to Margaret Kantz ("Helping Students Use Textual Sources Persuasively," *College English* [January 1990]: 74–91), "Writing an original persuasive argument based on sources requires students to apply material to a problem or to use it to answer a question, rather than simply to repeat it or evaluate it" (78). But students "have learned to see texts statically, as descriptions of truths, instead of as arguments" (79). This view encourages students simply to collect facts into a research paper in the belief that the facts will settle any disagreements and reveal the truth. Kantz recommends that teachers encourage students to regard the research paper and its sources "as existing to solve problems" (84). Students should try to understand what the author of a source was trying to accomplish and what audience was being addressed. They should treat facts as claims that could be challenged or interpreted differently. And they should write their research paper in order to solve a problem or answer a question for a particular audience.

BACKGROUND

As we struggle to teach the Research Paper, we may sometimes wonder if we are struggling alone. According to James E. Ford and Dennis R. Perry ("Research Paper Instruction in the Undergraduate Writing Program," *College English,* Dec. 1982, 825–31), we are definitely not alone.

Research paper instruction is currently being offered in 84.09% of freshman composition programs and in 40.03% of advanced composition programs. In general this high level of occurrence is fairly uniform in all types and sizes of institutions and in all regions of the country. There is, however, a slight tendency for research paper instruction to decrease as the size of the school increases (down to 71.06% in the large schools). Also, occurence is highest in the Rocky Mountain region (91.66%) and . . . lowest on the Pacific coast (72.40%). Instruction in the research paper is required in 78.11% of freshman composition programs offering it and 42.35% of advanced writing programs where it is offered. Although 4.16% of the schools not offering instruction in the research paper at the basic level indicated their reason for omitting it as "faculty think it unnecessary," the most common reason given for not offering it came under the "other" category, checked by 12.12%. About half of these (that is, about 6% of the total respondents) said the course was already too full to allow time for such instruction.

. . . No institution surveyed had eliminated a research paper requirement during the past five years and only two now have plans to do away with it. (827)

➡

OVERCOMING RESEARCH TOPIC BLOCK USING "BLB" *(continued)*

- The stacks at a library (if they are "open stacks") or perhaps the library's catalog (see 32n) or indexes to periodicals (see 32m).
- An encyclopedia article on a subject that interests you, as well as other encyclopedia articles cross-referenced there.

2. **L-L**OOK OVER all the items that interest you, focusing especially on major headings (often in bolder type than the rest of the material) and the first few pages. Try to get an idea of a subject's major subdivisions so that you avoid a topic that is too broad.

3. **B-B**RAINSTORM as soon as you think that an idea might have potential. Use the techniques for gathering ideas explained in sections 2d through 2k: freewrite, make lists, draw clusters of ideas, or whatever else helps you scan ideas in what you have found or what comes to mind. Also, carry pen and paper at all times so that you can jot down thoughts if a topic or related ideas suddenly occur to you.

Before deciding on a topic, check it using the guidelines for choosing a topic in Chart 153.

What if you have been assigned a general subject area for your research, but you are not sure how to narrow the subject into a topic appropriate for a research paper? Use the guidelines for choosing a topic for a research paper in Chart 153.

Communication was the general topic assigned to Amy Brown, the student whose research paper appears in Chapter 34. Her instructor required a paper of 1800 to 2000 words to be written in five weeks based on about twelve sources. To get started, Brown borrowed two textbooks from a friend, one an introduction to psychology and the other an introduction to business communications. Browsing through the textbooks helped Brown make her first major choice. She decided to focus on *nonverbal communication.* To further narrow her focus, Brown read a book that a psychology professor recommended during an interview. She then began to concentrate on *personal space*, a topic that particularly caught her interest. She was fascinated to learn that cultures have unspoken standards for the accepted distances between people who are conversing and interacting. Brown also liked the topic of personal

---

GUIDELINES FOR CHOOSING A TOPIC FOR A RESEARCH PAPER [153]

1. **Expect to think through various topics before making your final choice.** Avoid rushing; give yourself time to think. Keep your mind open to flashes of insight and to alternative ideas. Conversely, avoid allowing indecision to block you.

2. **Be practical.** Plan to do the work within the established time limit and paper length. Be sure that sufficient resources on your topic are available and accessible at your college and/or community library for a productive search strategy (see 32h).

3. **Choose a topic worth researching.** Avoid trivial topics. They prevent you from doing what student researchers are expected to do: investigate related ideas, think about them critically, and synthesize complex, perhaps conflicting, concepts.

4. **Try to select a topic that interests you.** Know that your topic will be a companion for a while, sometimes most of a semester. Select a topic that arouses your interest and allows you to sample the pleasure of satisfying your intellectual curiosity.

5. **Narrow the topic sufficiently.** Avoid topics that are too broad, such as *communication* or even *nonverbal communication*. Conversely, avoid topics that are too narrow to allow a suitable mix of generalizations and specific details.

6. **Confer briefly with a professor in your field of interest.** Ask for advice in narrowing your topic. Also, ask for the names of the major books and authorities on your topic.

---

space because her college had many sources to which she could refer. As she began to read closely on the topic, Brown evolved her research question: "How do standards for personal space differ among cultures?" The flow chart on page 580 illustrates Brown's process of narrowing the topic. Although this chart makes each decision seem to flow smoothly from the one before, the process in action is rarely neat and tidy. The process looks clear-cut only after all the thinking, debating, and choosing ends. Do not be surprised if you back out of dead ends and make some sharp turns as you define your choices and find a suitable path to a research question. To clarify your thinking, try charting your decision process as you go along.

Cont'd.
Ford and Perry also say:

> Not surprisingly, research paper instruction is offered more in freshman programs (50.56%) during the second semester of the freshman year, but it also is included in a significant number of courses offered during the first semester (41.57%). It is a feature in both semesters at 15.17% of the institutions. Such instruction on the advanced level most often comes during the sophomore year (63.83%), but it is common also during the junior year (46.81%). . . . Whenever it is offered, research paper instruction constitutes, on the average, a very considerable 34.66% of one basic course and 36.71% of an advanced course. (828)

TEACHING TIP

Students usually write more effective research papers if they formulate a tentative thesis after they have read and taken notes on a wide selection of sources but well before they begin drafting the paper, according to Sandra Stotsky ("On Developing Independent Critical Thinking: What We Can Learn from Studies of the Research Process," *Written Communication* [April 1991]: 193–212). "Finding a focus, or controlling idea," Stotsky suggests, "may well depend on how much information is gathered in an initial search process and how students organize and evaluate their initial notes. Categorizing, organizing, recategorizing, and reorganizing may be the most significant generative activities in the search process" (207).

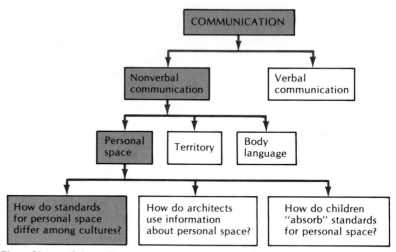

Flow Chart of Amy Brown's Narrowing Process

32e **Determining the purpose and audience for your research paper**

To fulfill the **purpose** for your research papers, you are expected to analyze, synthesize, and critically assess (see 5a, especially Chart 29) material that you gather during your research process. The question that guides your research process (see 32a) can help you determine your paper's purpose. If your question asks for facts, information and/or explanation, your purpose is to inform. For example, the question "How do standards for personal space differ among cultures?" requires an answer that calls for informative writing (see 1b-1).

On the other hand, if the question raised by a topic asks for an informed opinion *based* on information and other evidence, your purpose is to persuade (see 1b-2). For example, the question "Why should people be aware of intercultural differences in standards for personal space?" calls for persuasive writing. You may find that your paper's purpose shifts during the research process, as Amy Brown's purpose changed (see 34a). Remain open-minded as you work. By

32g

the time you are writing your paper, however, be sure to have defined your purpose.

The **audience** for your college writing is primarily, but perhaps not exclusively, your instructor (see 1c). When you think of writing for your instructor, remember that he or she plays two roles: a surrogate for the general reading public or a specialized reader and a person responsible for judging how well you have understood your material and the forms for presenting it. Sometimes the audience for a research paper includes other people—students in your class or perhaps specialists on your topic. Consider your reader's expertise on your topic, therefore, when you make decisions about content, specific details in explanations, and word choice.

32f Gathering equipment needed for research

Before starting your research, you need the proper equipment at hand to facilitate your work. Experienced researchers use equipment that helps them work efficiently. Gather the materials listed in Chart 154. Keep them separate from your regular books and materials so that you can locate them easily.

Color coding helps researchers in establishing categories for information. For example, you might use one color of index cards or colored clips for notes and another for bibliographic information. You might use one color ink for quotations (see 31c), another for paraphrases (see 31d) and summaries (see 31e), and a third for your own comments on a source.

32g Being ready to evaluate sources

As you conduct research, you are expected to locate **sources.** A source can be a book, article, videotape, or any other form of communication. Sources are rarely equally valuable. Before you start to gather information from sources, learn the criteria for evaluating them given in Chart 155. Then read with a critical eye.

As you evaluate sources, be aware of the difference between primary and secondary sources. **Primary sources** include original works of an author—novels, poems, short stories, autobiographies, diaries, first-hand reports of observations and of research, and so on. When you use primary sources, no one comes between you and your direct exposure to the author's own words. Also, you can conduct

TEACHING TIP

Students might feel overwhelmed if they had to do a research paper on, say, the role of the media in shaping public attitudes toward the Vietnam war or the impact of wheat sales to Russia on the American farmer. The problem has more to do with students' fears than the actual complexity of such assignments. Students' confidence can be built as research skills are developed if "accessible" topics are assigned—especially for preliminary exercises in library skills and note taking. Here are a few possibilities:

1. Write a biography of someone you would like to know more about: a sports figure, a cartoonist, a movie director, a state legislator, a deposed dictator.

2. Write an essay recommending a particular type or model of some fairly expensive consumer item that you are interested in buying yourself, such as a car, a VCR, or a microwave oven.

3. Write an essay recommending and explaining an eating regimen that can help someone lose weight, train for a sport, or control a health problem (e.g., diabetes or high blood pressure).

4. Imagine you are a travel agent who has been asked to plan a tour of Asia or Africa. Money is no object. You have been told to arrange stops in all countries with which the United States has friendly relations. Advise your clients of (1) entry requirements such as a visa and limitations on what they may bring into each country; (2) health precautions that they ought to take, including inoculations; and (3) local laws or customs that they must not violate, such as the non-use of alcohol or drugs.

5. If you have not chosen a career or major, write an essay exploring the pros and cons of a particular career or major that you are considering. If you have chosen your field, write an essay exploring a particular job in that field or arguing a position about an ethical or political problem in the field.

BASIC EQUIPMENT FOR CONDUCTING RESEARCH
154

1. A copy of your assignment.
2. A separate notebook to use for a research log (see 32c).
3. Pens or pencils (of several different colors) for taking notes. Pencil tends to blur when notes are shuffled and handled often.
4. Index cards for notes (see 32i) and for bibliographic information (see 33a). Use one index card per source to record bibliographic data, and a separate index card for each idea you take down in notes. Index cards give you the flexibility to move information around; pages in a notebook do not.
5. Whatever coins you need for the library's copying machines. (See 32i about photocopying.)
6. Paper clips, a small stapler, or rubber bands to help you organize index cards and other papers.
7. A book bag if you intend to check out books from the library. Librarians joke about researchers with wheelbarrows. You might need a backpack.

---

primary research such as a scientific experiment, a survey, or an interview. The data from such research becomes a primary source.

Secondary sources report, describe, comment on, or analyze someone else's work. The information comes to you second-hand, influenced by the intermediary between you and the primary source. Secondary sources explain events, analyze information, and draw conclusions. Consulting secondary sources gives you the opportunity to read closely (and listen closely, if you interview authorities) and thereby work to understand what scholars and other experts know about your subject.

32h Using a search strategy for conducting research

Inexperienced researchers can easily feel overwhelmed by a seemingly limitless choice of sources. Inexperience can tempt the student into mistaking activity for productivity. Going to the library

---

155

CRITERIA FOR EVALUATING SOURCES FOR RESEARCH

1. **Authoritative:** Check encyclopedias, textbooks, articles in academic journals, and bibliographies, and ask experts. If a particular name or a specific work is mentioned often, that source is probably recognized as an authoritative one on your topic. Also, to see whether the author of a source has a background that makes him or her an authority, consult one of the biographical references listed in 32k.

2. **Reliable:** Material published in academic journals (see 32m-2), by university presses, or by presses that specialize in scholarly books is considered reliable. Material published in newspapers, general readership magazines, and by large commercial publishers usually can be considered reliable, though cross-checking is advisable when possible.

3. **Well known:** Check several different sources. If the same information appears, the material is probably reliable.

4. **Well supported:** Check that each source supports assertions or information with sufficient evidence (see 5e). If the material expresses the source's point of view but offers little to back up that position, turn to another source.

5. **Balanced tone:** Read a source critically (see 5d through 5h). If the tone is unbiased and if the reasoning is logical, consider the source to be balanced.

6. **Current:** Check that the information is up-to-date. Sometimes long-accepted information is replaced or modified by new research. Check indexes to journals or computerized databases to see if anything newer has come along.

---

to spend days at the catalog to find everything even remotely related to a topic can be exhausting and fruitless when writing a college research paper.

Researchers can interview experts, send for information by mail, and—most of all—use the resources of a library efficiently. To be a productive researcher, use a **search strategy** to work systematically. A search strategy is an organized procedure that leads step-by-step from general to specific sources. No two research processes are exactly alike, so expect to adapt the search strategy explained in this section through section 32o to your needs. A search strategy is rarely as tidy as it seems to be when described in a textbook.

TEACHING TIP

In *Form and Substance* (New York: John Wiley, 1981) Richard Coe suggests that in establishing a broad overview of a subject, some sources are more helpful than others. He suggests using review articles that summarize major books and articles on a topic, a general textbook that includes the topic, a good encyclopedia, and the *Book Review Digest*. He points out that at this stage of the research process, it is not important to take notes. The writer should simply read quickly and broadly, getting a general background and watching for critical problems or researchable questions.

BACKGROUND

Before it was burnt down in the third century A.D., the famous library at Alexandria, Egypt contained as many as 700,000 scrolls. Under the Ptolemies (third century B.C. on) the library became a depository for copies of all important texts. Books were edited into a standard format, and systems of punctuation and accents were introduced. Textual scholarship, revisions of books to incorporate new knowledge, and the writing of new books went on constantly. Most of the books have been lost. Only those works which were widely copied and distributed have managed to survive. For example, evidence indicates that Aeschylus, Sophocles, Euripides, and Aristophanes wrote about 330 plays in total; only 43 remain.

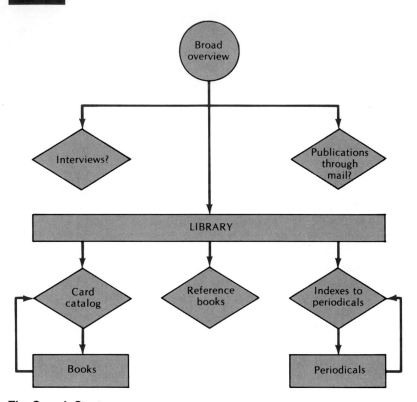

The Search Strategy

1 **Deciding whether to interview experts**

An expert can often offer valuable information, points of view concerning your topic, or advice. The faculty at your college or nearby colleges have special expertise about many topics. Corporations and professional organizations can often suggest experts in many fields; a customer service department or public relations office is a good place to begin. Public officials are sometimes available for interviews. Many federal and state government offices have employees who specialize in providing information to the public. If your topic relates to an event that your family or friends experienced, they qualify as experts.

If you want to interview other people, start early. It takes time to set up appointments and fit your research needs into other people's schedules. You may not always be granted the interviews you seek, but many people remember their own experiences doing academic research and try to help.

Prepare questions that use time efficiently. Know why you are interviewing the person and what you want to know. Ask questions that elicit information, not merely a "yes" or "no" answer. Be constructive; avoid language that shows bias or a hostile attitude. Experienced interviewers take notes or use a tape recorder so that they do not have to rely on their memories. (Always ask permission of the person you are interviewing.) Some people routinely refuse to allow their comments to be taped, so be ready with a note-taking system as a backup. For example, you might put each question on an index card with space left for your notes during the interview.

Evaluate carefully any information or opinion that you get from interviewing experts, using section 32g for guidance. Experts may have a slanted point of view in line with vested interests. Also, always follow up an interview, no matter how short, with a brief note of thanks. Aside from its being polite, this courtesy helps pave the way for the next student who might ask for an interview.

For details about creating and using questionnaires to gather research data, see 38a.

2 Deciding whether to send for information

Publications or other kinds of information about your topic may be available by mail. A month or more can go by before an inquiry is processed, so send early and leave time in your schedule to use the material. To be safe, never depend entirely on mail-order sources for your research. The material might not arrive in time or might turn out to be unsuitable. Also, remember that an effective research paper usually draws on a variety of sources, including those found in a library.

When you write to businesses, target your request carefully to get the material you need. If you are unsure of what is available, call the company and talk with someone in its public relations office, customer service department, or the equivalent. Large libraries sometimes have corporate reports and specialized technical reports on file, so check with a reference librarian *before* you order through the mail. Always evaluate corporate materials carefully for bias and promotion of special interests. To be useful, a corporate publication must go well beyond the kinds of information usually written for consumers.

BACKGROUND

During the Middle Ages, the libraries of Western Europe were affiliated with religious houses and cathedrals. The few private libraries belonged to bishops. The clergy were the only people who could read, and even if the level of literacy was sometimes low, the church maintained the tradition of schools and libraries. These religious libraries were quite small by twentieth-century standards. The largest (at Canterbury and Bury St. Edmunds) had 2,000 volumes each, but libraries of only a few hundred volumes were the rule. The libraries contained theological and biblical works, law books, classical texts, medical and historical works. Contemporary histories, written in monasteries, remain the best records of what happened during the period. In the thirteenth and fourteenth centuries, the rise of the new universities, the rediscovery of Aristotle (from Arabic), and the position of the friars as university teachers undermined the dominance of the monastic libraries. Although the university libraries were not open to undergraduates, the Franciscan friars opened their own libraries (some still survive in England), and they printed small, portable books which contrasted with the bulky illuminated manuscripts of the monasteries. The monastic libraries of England were destroyed in 1536–1540 (during Henry VIII's reign) and their books dispersed. In 1550, university libraries, schools, and churches were purged. Many treasures saved during the 1,000 years of the Dark Ages were lost.

Medieval libraries apparently were noisier than libraries today. Silent reading was not a common practice until the Renaissance. Until then, most people mumbled as they read. Carrels (small private enclosures) were invented so that readers would not disturb other people in the library with their noise.

United States government publications are available in an almost astounding variety. You can get information on population figures, weather patterns, agriculture, national parks, and much more. Large libraries often have many government documents on file, so ask a reference librarian before you send for the material. To find out what publications are available and how to order them, consult one of the directories listed below, found in the reference section of a large library. Many of these publications are now available on either computer databases or CD-ROM (a computer storage device using compact disk technology). Using a computer will eliminate the time that would be spent mailing materials and can provide you with more recently updated information. Find out from a reference librarian if the publications that you need are accessible by computer.

■ The *Monthly Catalog of United States Government Publications* is an up-to-date listing of all offerings. Items are cataloged according to subject.

■ *American Statistics Index (ASI)* is published in two volumes: the *Index*, which catalogues all statistical documents produced by government departments; the *Abstracts*, which gives concise summaries of the contents of the documents.

■ The *Congressional Information Service (CIS)*, indexes all papers produced by U.S. congressional panels and committees. These documents include the texts of hearings (for example, testimony about the plight of the homeless) and reports (for example, a comparative study of temporary shelters for the homeless).

3 Using all the resources of the library

Using the library as a resource takes time. Rodney Phillips, the director of special collections for the humanities and social sciences of the New York Public Library, is extremely familiar with the time needed to prepare a good undergraduate research paper. Division staff receives an average of 2,000 inquiries per day, and many of them are from students like you who want to know how to find information for their papers. To do a decent job, Mr. Phillips says, you will want to gather and look over at least 25 different items. Some you will need to skim, and some you will need to read slowly. You will need to take notes on many. "Plan to spend at least 15 hours in the library," Mr. Phillips says. "You will sometimes be frustrated to find that others have been there before you and taken books you want. Then you'll have to look further, just as they probably did. You will find that titles you thought were promising will not give you what you were after. Other sources might pay off enormously." Mr. Phillips says the typical undergraduate, new to research writing, expects to obtain a paper from one book and two or three other sources. These students, he states flatly, are not budgeting anywhere near the time that they need to do a good job.

Librarians are information experts. They are highly skilled at searching for and finding information. Reference librarians seek to help people learn how to use library resources well. Although the research task remains yours, asking for help from a librarian is normal and reasonable. Professor Mary Cope, who was chief of materials processing of the library at the City College of the City University of New York, says she holds "reference interviews" with students "to determine what they want to learn. We direct them, then, to the resources and tell them to return if they need more guidance." Professor Cope thinks that the best assistance she offers is to point out different aspects of subjects covered in reference sources. By doing so, she helps students narrow their topics.

Many colleges and large public libraries prepare written guides to their resources. Find out if your library has such a guide. With or without a guide, get to know your library well. Wander around and browse. Libraries differ from each other in physical layout and in the breadth and depth of resources.

---

4 **Compiling a list of headings or key words**

Researchers use headings and key words to look up information. **Headings** are subject categories in books and periodicals. **Key words** (sometimes called *descriptors* or *identifiers*) identify subject categories in periodicals and computerized databases. Knowing how to locate headings and key words is central to the research process. The people who prepare reference books, library catalog information, and indexes to periodicals do not have the resources to maintain an infinite number of headings, so they group information into categories and arrange efficient retrieval systems.

The Library of Congress cataloging system is one widespread system for organizing a library's materials. The categories into which this system groups materials are laid out in the *Library of Congress Subject Headings*. This invaluable multivolume resource, usually available also in computerized form, is described fully in 32n.

BACKGROUND

Benjamin Franklin organized the Library Company of Philadelphia in 1731. It was the first American subscription library. Its original purpose was to provide ready access to books for members of the Junto Club, a public service group to which Franklin belonged. Franklin himself said that he spent time at the library almost daily, learning foreign languages or reading for general knowledge.

Until the founding of the Library Company of Philadelphia in 1731, there were few public libraries in the American colonies. The earliest one was the library of Harvard College, founded in 1638 with around 400 volumes bequeathed by John Harvard. Libraries were established at Yale and at William and Mary around 1700. In the Southern colonies the Reverend Thomas Bray (1656–1730), working by appointment of the Bishop of London as commissary of the Anglican Church, established parochial libraries. In 1876 a report on *Public Libraries in the United States* stated: "So far as is known, there were, in 1776, twenty-nine public libraries in the thirteen American colonies, and they numbered altogether 45,623 volumes; in the year 1800 the number of libraries had increased to forty-nine, and the number of volumes to about 80,000." The Library of Congress, which contains over 72 million pieces of material (among them 16.5 million books and 31 million manuscripts), was begun by Congress in 1800 with a budget of $5,000. Today it costs over $150 million per year to operate.

As you conduct your search for sources, you have to locate the headings and key words that lead you to books and articles on your topic. For example, the topic *nuclear energy* is identified with various headings or key words: *energy, nuclear; atomic energy; energy, atomic; nuclear power; power, nuclear;* and so on. You have to "break the code" to figure out what words identify the category you are seeking in each source. As you conduct your research, keep an ongoing list in your research log of headings and key words that relate to your topic. Then when you approach a new source, your search process will be more efficient.

32i   Being ready to take useful notes

Your research process includes taking notes as you consult sources and recording your ideas as you move through the process. Taking good notes is the key to using sources well in your research paper. Together with your research log (see 32c) and bibliography cards (see 33a), your notes give you a complete record of your research and the information you found.

Notetaking is a decision-making process. The first decision concerns whether a source related to your topic is worth taking notes on. To decide, evaluate it according to the criteria in Chart 155 in 32g. If it seems to be a good source, take notes. If it does not, record its title and location in your research log along with a message to yourself about why you rejected it. What seems useless one day might have potential if you revise the focus of your paper or slightly reshape your topic.

The second decision concerns what to put into your notes. Knowing how to select material for notes comes with experience. Dive in and get that experience. Use critical reading skills (see 5d) to sort major information from minor information as it relates to your topic. Do not get bogged down in unimportant details. At the same time, do not overlook important material. Try for a reasonable balance.

When you begin taking notes, if you have only a general sense of your topic, read and take notes widely. Stay alert for ways to narrow your topic. Use your research log to keep track of your thoughts because ideas tend to pop in and out of mind during a selection process. Topic narrowing takes time and patience (for advice, see 32d). Taking notes, with a general focus, can help you "discover" ideas that come to mind once the physical act of writing words on paper begins. Do not get discouraged; all researchers cast about at first. Once you have narrowed your topic, take notes focused within the boundaries of your choice.

EXTRA EXERCISE A

To practice methods of preventing unconscious plagiarism, paraphrase or summarize the following paragraphs.

(1) Jane Austen, an English novelist, was born in 1775 the daughter of the Reverend George Austen, rector of Steventon and Deane, and Cassandra Leigh Austen. She was the youngest of seven children. Her childhood at Steventon was quiet, domestic, and moderately studious. Much of her spare time was spent in writing, mostly for her own amusement. In 1801 the family moved to Bath. After the death of her father in 1805, she settled in Chawton, where she remained until shortly before her death.

(2) Jane Austen began writing stories at an early age, and by the time she was twenty-two had completed one of her best known novels, *Pride and Prejudice.* Other works for which she is remembered include *Sense and Sensibility* and *Northanger Abbey*, which was published by her family after her death. The novels were not especially popular in Jane Austen's lifetime, but today are regarded as
➔

The third decision in the notetaking process concerns the form of your notes. **You must use procedures that prevent plagiarism.** This matter is so important that Chapter 31 is devoted to avoiding plagiarism and to the skills of quoting, paraphrasing, and summarizing. To plagiarize is to steal someone else's words and pass them off as your own. To avoid the risk of plagiarism, take notes in such a way that you will always be able to tell from your notes what is yours and what belongs to a source. You might want to use one color ink for *your* thoughts and another color ink for words that you take from sources in the form of quotations, paraphrases, or summaries.

To take notes, use index cards. Cards, in contrast to pages in a notebook, provide flexibility for organizing material to use in writing your paper. Never put notes from more than one source on the same index card. If your notes on a source require more than one index card, number the cards sequentially. (For example, if you use the labels "1 of 2" for the first card on a source and "2 of 2" for the second card on the same source, you can work efficiently.) If you take notes on more than one idea or topic from a particular source, start a new card for each new area of information. Head each index card with identifying information that clearly relates to one of your bibliographic cards (see 33a). Include the source's title and the number of the page or pages from which you are taking notes. Also, clearly identify the *type* of note on the card: quotation, paraphrase, or summary. A note card written by Amy Brown, the student whose paper is in Chapter 34, is shown below.

Hall, *Hidden*, p.109
Awareness of personal space
Summary: Most people are unaware that interpersonal distances exist and contribute to peoples' reactions to one another.

Note Card Summarizing a Source

589

Cont'd.
among the best novels in the English language. Although her people are neither intellectual nor heroic, and her plots are not elaborate, her skill at storytelling and drawing characters continues to please her readers.

(3) On the map, Mexico resembles a great funnel, or rather, a cornucopia, with its widest part towards the north and its smallest end twisting to the south and east, meeting there the sudden expansion of the Maya area. There are few regions in the world with such a diverse geography as we find within this area—Mexico is not one, but many countries. All the climatic extremes of our globe are found, from arctic cold near the summits of the highest volcanoes to the Turkish-bath atmosphere of the coastal jungle. Merely to pass from one valley to another is to enter a markedly different ecological zone.
—Michael D. Coe, *Mexico*, p. 12

(4) In 1773 we know that [Francisco] Goya was in Madrid, where he married Josefa Bayeau, the sister of the painter who had introduced him into Madrid society. His first important chance was a commission for a series of cartoons for tapestries, which Mengs (possibly advised by Bayeu, who had acquired a certain reputation and had become part of a group of young academic painters, which included his brothers) commissioned for the Royal Tapestry Factory at Santa Barbara. It was an important opportunity because it meant that Goya was admitted to court circles; in addition this kind of work allowed him great freedom in his choice of subject matter and of technique. Perhaps most important of all, the sketchy nature of the cartoon medium spared Goya the necessity of "finishing" his work. His style was slow to mature; until now he had displayed a dextrous hand but had shown no signs of genius.
—Margherita Abbaruzzese, *Goya*, p. 5

32j

ANSWERS: EXTRA EXERCISE A

Summaries and paraphrases will vary; here are sample answers to passages (1) and (2).

(1) Born in 1775, Jane Austen lived in Steventon until 1801, when her family relocated to Bath. She moved to Chawton in 1805 when her father died and lived there for almost the rest of her life. Her childhood was uneventful. She helped with the housework, studied, and often spent her free time writing.

(2) Jane Austen started writing fiction as a child and finished her first novel, *Pride and Prejudice*, when she was twenty-two. Although none of her novels, including *Sense and Sensibility* and *Northanger Abbey*, attracted much attention while she was alive, critics today consider Austen one of the greatest writers in English fiction because of her ability to make fascinating stories and characters out of simple plots and people.

(3) Mexico's geography is among the most heterogenous in the world. Widest at the northern border, narrowing and curving like a funnel toward the south, Mexico has a climate that ranges from the bitter cold at the peaks of its volcanoes to jungle heat and humidity along the coasts.

(4) The art and career of Goya benefitted from his contact with the upper class of Madrid. Thanks to Mengs and perhaps his brother-in-law Bayeau, Goya was hired by the Royal Tapestry Factory at Santa Barbara to design cartoons for tapestries. As a result, Goya not only came to know members of Spanish aristocracy; he also found more opportunity to select subject matter for his art and experiment with his craft and more time to develop as an artist. Goya did not develop his style quickly. By this time, his technique was accomplished, but his art lacked brilliance and depth.

Sommer, p. 26

The best way to learn the location of invisible boundaries is to keep walking until somebody complains. Personal space refers to an area with invisible boundaries surrounding a person's body into which intruders may not come. Like the porcupines in Schopenhauer's fable, people like to be close enough to obtain warmth and comradeship but far enough away to avoid pricking one another. Personal space ~~is not necessarily spherical in shape, nor does it extend equally in all directions. (People are able to tolerate closer presence of a stranger at their sides than directly in front.)~~ It has been likened to a snail shell, a soap bubble, an aura, and "breathing room." There are major differences between cultures in the distances that people maintain—Englishmen keep further apart than Frenchmen or South Americans. Reports

[handwritten annotations: "I'll paraphrase this" and "I'll quote this with ellipses"]

Photocopy of Source, with Annotations

Photocopying can save you time if you want a word-for-word record of a source. Photocopying, however, can be a seductive trap for researchers. It is a waste of time and money to photocopy everything you come across. Write your paraphrases and summaries as you go along. When you do photocopy, always mark the paper with (1) identifying information and (2) notations about what you consider important and why. Do not merely pile up stacks of photocopies without any record of your thought processes. A photocopy Amy Brown made and annotated is shown above.

32j Determining your documentation style

The term **documentation style** refers to a system for providing information about each source you have used in a research paper. Documentation styles vary among the disciplines. The **Modern Language Association** (MLA) has developed the style often used in the humanities (see 33b-1, 33c-1, and 33d). The **American Psychological Association** has developed the style often used in the social sciences (see 33b-2, 33c-2, and 33d).

Before you start consulting sources, know what documentation style you need to use. If your assignment does not specify a documentation style, ask your instructor which to use. As you take notes on each source, keep a record of that information so that you can document your sources correctly and fully.

32k

32k Using general reference books

General reference books usually contain summaries of vast amounts of information. They can provide a useful broad view, but as you conduct your research, you will likely want to use specialized reference books as well (see 32l). The *Guide to Reference Books* is a valuable resource. It covers reference works in all fields, describing general ones first, and then specialized ones. This book, or another like it, is worth getting to know well.

Most widely used reference works are available in computerized CD-ROM versions, and many libraries give students access to computer-based dictionaries, thesauruses, encyclopedias, bibliographies, and even atlases. Almanacs and statistical works on computer are kept more up-to-date than their printed counterparts and can often present information in several different ways. More specialized reference works, however, are usually not available in this form.

Encyclopedias

Articles in general encyclopedias such as *Collier's Encyclopedia* and *Encyclopedia Brittanica* summarize information about a wide variety of subjects. The articles can be useful for a broad overview but not as major sources for college-level research. They are written by specialists for nonspecialist readers. Many articles end with a brief bibliography of major works on the subject. Because encyclopedias take a long time to write and publish, some kinds of information in them quickly become outdated. Look for up-to-date editions and annual supplements.

To locate the information you want, start with the Index volume. If you cannot find what you are looking for, try alternate headings or key words (see 32h-4). General encyclopedias are not the place to look for reports on recent events or current research.

One-volume general encyclopedias cover subjects very briefly. You may want to consult one, such as *The New Columbia Encyclopedia* or the *Random House Encyclopedia,* to see whether a general subject area interests you enough for further research. A one-volume encyclopedia may also be useful when something comes up in your research that you need not explore fully but do need to understand in a general way. Also, specialized encyclopedias exist in many fields (see 32l).

BACKGROUND

Some very famous people have been librarians. A few of them may even have helped students with term papers.

- German diplomat and philosopher-mathematician Gottfried von Leibniz (1646–1716) served two terms as a librarian.

- British philosopher, economist, and historian David Hume (1711–1776) spent five years as a librarian at the Library of the Faculty of the Advocates at Edinburgh while writing his *History of England.*

- The infamous Casanova (1725–1798) served as a private librarian to royalty for thirteen years at the end of his life.

- Pope Pius XI (1857–1939) spent nineteen years at the Ambrosian Library in Milan, and he was then appointed chief librarian. In 1911, he began reorganization and updating of the Vatican Library, and in 1915 was named prefect of the Vatican Library. He went on to become pope in 1922.

- Archibald MacLeish (1892–1982), poet, playwright, Assistant Secretary of State, and three-time Pulitzer Prize winner, served as Librarian of Congress under Franklin D. Roosevelt.

- Mao Tse-Tung (1893–1976) at one time was assistant to the chief librarian of the University of Peking.

- J. Edgar Hoover (1895–1964) was a messenger and cataloguer in the Library of Congress as a young man.

Almanacs, Yearbooks, Fact Books

Almanacs—books such as *The World Almanac and Book of Facts*—briefly present a year's events and data in government, politics, sports, economics, demographics, and many other categories. *Facts on File* covers world events in a weekly digest and in an annual one-volume *Yearbook.*

Congressional Record and *Statistical Abstract* contain a wealth of data about the United States. *Demographic Yearbook* and *United Nations Statistical Yearbook* carry worldwide data. Other specialized yearbooks and handbooks are named in 32l.

Atlases

Atlases contain maps—and remember that seas and skies and even other planets have been mapped. These comprehensive books contain many kinds of geographic information: topography, climates, populations, migrations, natural resources, crops, and so on.

Dictionaries

Dictionaries define words and terms. The dictionaries described in section 20a define words in the English language and give various other information about these words. Also, specialized dictionaries exist in many academic disciplines to define words and phrases specific to a field (see 32l).

Biographical Reference Works

Biographical reference books give brief factual information about many famous people. They are good places to find dates and brief listings of major events or accomplishments in noted people's lives. (Do not confuse these works with full-length biographies or bestseller accounts about noted people.) Various *Who's Who* series cover noteworthy people, male or female, living or dead. *Current Biography: Who's News and Why* is published monthly, with six-month and annual cumulative editions. *Dictionary of American Biography* and *Webster's Biographical Dictionary* are very widely available.

Specialized biographical reference books focus on artists, musicians, important people of various historical periods or nationalities, and so on (see 32l).

Bibliographies

Bibliographies list books. *Books in Print* lists all books that are available through their publishers and sometimes other sources in the United States. This multivolume work classifies its entries by author name, title, and general subject headings, but it does not describe a book's content.

The *Book Review Digest* excerpts book reviews that have appeared in major newspapers and magazines. These excerpts of critics' opinions can help you evaluate a source (see 32g). This digest is published every year. The reviews appear in the volume that corresponds either to the year a book was published or to the one immediately following. The *Book Review Index* and *Current Review Citations* list where reviews have appeared but do not carry the actual reviews.

Consulting specialized bibliographies—ones that list many books on a particular subject—can be very helpful in your research process (see 32l). Annotated or critical bibliographies describe and evaluate the works that they list and are therefore especially useful.

321 Using specialized reference books

As you work your way into a research topic and use general reference books (see 32k), you will need increasingly specific information. Here are selected titles, grouped by general academic disciplines. This list can only hint at the wide variety available at many libraries.

BUSINESS AND ECONOMICS

A Dictionary of Economics
Encyclopedia of Advertising
Encyclopedia of Banking and Finance
Handbook of Modern Marketing

FINE ARTS

Crowells' Handbook of World Opera
International Cyclopedia of Music and Musicians
Oxford Companion to Art

HISTORY

Dictionary of American Biography
Encyclopedia of American History
An Encyclopedia of World History
New Cambridge Modern History

BACKGROUND

The Guinness Book of Records was founded as a result of the curiosity of Sir Hugh Beaver, the managing director of Arthur Guinness, Son and Co., Ltd. One day in 1954, Sir Hugh went bird hunting. He shot at some plovers—and missed. He started wondering if plovers were the fastest game birds, and he tried to satisfy his curiosity in the encyclopedia. Neither it nor any other reference work had the answer.

As a result, Sir Hugh decided that people needed a book that would accurately list record sizes, speeds, and durations. His plan was to have a copy of the book in every pub that sold Guinness stout, as an aid in settling bets. He set about finding someone to author such a book, and one of his executives recommended the McWhirter brothers. Trivia history was made.

Norris and Ross McWhirter, identical twin sons of a newspaper writer, had grown up around newspapers, magazines, and reference books. Their childhood hobby had been to collect information of the very type Sir Hugh was seeking. They had frequently found contradictions in their sources, and so as adults they had founded a company to verify these statistics and to "supply facts and figures to newspapers, yearbooks, encyclopedias, and advertisers."

Four months after Sir Hugh had interviewed them, the McWhirters published the first book in the series. The 198-page betseller became England's number one nonfiction best-seller in only four months. Immediately, readers began submitting their own fantastic facts. The McWhirters collected and checked these submissions, and soon an updated volume was on the way. Norris and Ross McWhirter acted as coeditors until 1975.

BACKGROUND

Libraries are as old as recorded history. In fact, they were the repository of the records of past civilizations. In what was ancient Mesopotamia, for example, temples and princely houses have been excavated that held thousands of clay tablets inscribed with epic poems, liturgic and magic texts, and commercial records. The palace of Ashurbanipal, who reigned from 668–633 B.C. in Nineveh, has provided tablets bearing stamps of ownership, catchwords, and sometimes source and place indications, thereby testifying to the existence of a well-developed cataloging system. In Egypt every temple had its library and school. Although the Egyptian collections were made on papyrus (and thus have been found mostly in graves and tombs rather than in temples), the content was similar. Much has been lost, but records often remain. In the temple at Edfu, for instance, a full catalogue of all the hieratical works the library contained was incised on the walls, bearing witness to what was once there.

LITERATURE

Cassell's Encyclopedia of World Literature
Dictionary of Literary Biography
A Dictionary of Literary Terms
MLA International Bibliography of Books and Articles on the Modern Languages and Literature
The Oxford Companion to American Literature
The Oxford Companion to English Literature

PHILOSOPHY AND RELIGION

Dictionary of the Bible
Eastern Definitions: A Short Encyclopedia of Religions of the Orient
Encyclopedia of Philosophy

POLITICAL SCIENCE

Foreign Affairs Bibliography
Political Handbook and Atlas of the World
Political Science Bibliographies

SCIENCE AND TECHNOLOGY

Encyclopedia of Chemistry
Encyclopedia of Computer Science and Technology
Encyclopedia of Physics
The Encyclopedia of the Biological Sciences
The Larousse Encyclopedia of Animal Life
The McGraw-Hill Encyclopedia of Science and Technology

SOCIAL SCIENCES

Dictionary of Anthropology
Dictionary of Education
Encyclopedia of Psychology
International Encyclopedia of the Social Sciences

FILM, TELEVISION, THEATER

International Encyclopedia of Film
International Television Almanac
The Oxford Companion to the Theatre

32m Using periodicals

Periodicals are magazines and journals published at set periods during a year. The key to using periodicals is to locate **indexes to periodicals.** These indexes list articles written between the dates listed on the cover on each edition. Many indexes are kept up-to-date with supplements between editions. Some but not all indexes include abstracts, which are brief summaries of each article.

Classification systems vary among indexes, so take time to learn how to decipher the codes and abbreviations in the index that you need. Most indexes include a guide for readers in the front or back of each volume and supplement, and the guide is usually also in a computerized database, if available. As you learn to use an index, update your list of headings and key words (see 32h-4) for future reference.

Indexes are packaged in a variety of ways. Some indexes are in yearly bound volumes and interim paperback updates. Depending on the systems at your library, some indexes may be on microfilm or microfiche. These may have to be accessed through computer terminals. Before you start using periodicals, get to know the systems at your library.

1 Using general indexes to periodicals

General indexes list articles in magazines and newspapers. Headings and key words on the same subject vary among indexes, so think of every possible way to look up the information you seek. Large libraries have many general indexes, among them these two major ones.

■ The *New York Times Index* catalogs all articles that have been printed in this encyclopedic newspaper since 1851. Supplements are published every two weeks in paperbound volumes. The supplements are organized into volumes (bound, in computerized databases, or on microfilm) periodically.

■ The *Readers' Guide to Periodical Literature* is the most widely used index to over 100 magazines and journals for general (rather than specialized) readers. Paperback supplements are published every two weeks. These supplements are organized into volumes (bound, in computerized databases, or on microfilm) periodically. This index does not include scholarly journals, so its uses are often very limited for college-level research. It can be useful, for

BACKGROUND

The first general index of magazine articles was *Poole's Index of Periodical Literature,* which lists articles from the years 1802 through 1906 and is still a valuable reference tool. The idea for *Poole's Index* originated in the 1840s when a college student from Yale, William Frederick Poole, noticed that the many periodicals in the Yale library were going unused because people could not find the articles they wanted except by going through the journals one by one. Poole decided to scan the periodicals himself, compile a list of articles, and organize the list under subject headings. At first he wrote out a single copy which he shared with others, but the demand for the list was so great that Poole published it in 1848. For many years Poole updated and expanded the index himself, until 1876, when he asked the American Library Association to sponsor the index and assign fifty librarians from across the United States to the project. Receiving no pay, each librarian went through a list of assigned magazines to record and classify the articles and then sent this information to Poole for the next volume of the index.

BACKGROUND

Under the strong influence of the Renaissance, Italy became the center of book collecting in the Western world. Florence was one of the major trading cities, because of the support of the princes, who served as patrons to scholars who searched for lost treasures of Greek and Latin literature. The scholars' efforts were in large measure responsible for transmitting classical learning to a new age through the works they found, translated, recopied, and sold. Among the princes of that time, Cosimo de Medici (1389–1464) is especially notable for building the Medici Library, the first public library in Europe to have been opened since the Romans. The Medicis invested $15 million from 1434 to 1469, collecting and commissioning copies of manuscripts. The collection acquired under their patronage, especially that of Cosimo and his successor, Lorenzo the Magnificent (1449–1492), are now housed in the Laurentian and National libraries of Florence.

getting a broad overview and for thinking of ways to narrow a subject. An entry from *Readers' Guide* showing listings for Communication, the subject of Amy Brown's research paper assignment, appears below.

COMMUNICATION, Nonverbal ——————————— Subject heading
Does your body *parle francais?* French body —————— Title of article
  language; teaching methods of L. Wylie pors ——— Author
  Time 113:107+ My 14 '79 ———————————— Periodical title
Watching your every move: what you reveal
  about yourself without saying a word. J.
  Marks. Teen 23:36+ Jl '79 ——————————— Vol. 23, p. 36+, July 1979
When tensions talk—listen! Subtle motion tells
  a story. E. Hamilton por Sci Digest 85:30-2+ ——— Has portrait
  Ap '79
Women smile less for success; study of job
  success by Wendy McKenna and Florence
  Denmark. M. B. Parlee. Psychol Today 12:16
  Mr '79
    See also
Eye—Movements ———————————————— Related subject
Gesture   headings
Sign language
Touch

Annotated Excerpt from *Readers' Guide to Periodical Literature*

2   Using specialized indexes to periodicals

Specialized indexes are much more helpful for most college-level research than are general indexes (see 32m-1). Specialized indexes help a researcher become a specialist in a particular topic. These indexes list articles published in academic and professional periodicals. Many specialized indexes carry an abstract (a summary) of each listed article.

Depending on their resources, libraries stock many or few specialized indexes in book form and in paperback supplements. Some libraries make available a computerized database that includes many different, specialized indexes. Commonly available specialized indexes include:

> *America: History and Life*
> *Applied Science and Technology Index*
> *Art Index*

Biological Abstracts

Biological and Agricultural Index

Business Periodicals Index

Education Index

Essay and General Literature Index

General Science Index

Humanities Index

*MLA International Bibliography of Books and Articles in the Modern
    Languages and Literatures*

Music Index

Psychological Abstracts

Social Science Index

Few libraries, by the way, subscribe to all the periodicals that are listed in these specialized indexes. Most libraries list the periodicals they carry. If possible, obtain a copy of this list before you use a specialized index so that you do not waste time seeking periodicals your library does not have. (You can check with a librarian to find out about the possibility of interlibrary loans of periodicals from other libraries, if time permits in your research schedule.)

Here is an entry from the *Humanities Index* that Amy Brown used in her research for the paper in Chapter 34. The abbreviations have the same meaning as those in the excerpt from the *Readers' Guide to Periodical Literature* on the opposite page.

> Nonverbal communication
>> *See also*
>> Expression
>> Gesture
> Background to kinesics. R. L. Birdwhistell. *Etc* 40:352-61
>> Fall '83
> Mediated interpersonal communication: toward a new
>> typology. R. Cathcart and G. Gumpert. *Q J Speech*
>> 69:267-77 Ag '83

Excerpt from *Humanities Index*

32n Using a library's book catalog

A **book catalog** is a list of all books in a library. Years ago, all libraries used a **card catalog** for their record of holdings. In recent years, many libraries have transferred their cards onto a **microfiche catalog** or store their catalog on computer.

BACKGROUND

One of the most famous libraries of antiquity was the one at Alexandria, founded by Ptolemy I (c. 323–285 B.C.) and greatly augmented by his son Ptolemy II Philadelphus (c. 285–247 B.C.) and his grandson Ptolemy III Euergetes (c. 247–221 B.C.). Manuscripts were imported from all parts of Greece and Asia, resulting in holdings that are estimated to have been as high as 700,000 papyrus rolls during the time of Caesar. Because of its riches, leading scholars of the Hellenistic world were drawn to it, resulting in a flurry of scholarly activity. Books were edited into a standard format, and systems of punctuation and accents were introduced. Textual scholarship, revisions of books to incorporate new knowledge, and the writing of new books went on constantly. Most of the books have been lost. Only those works which were widely copied and distributed have managed to survive. As the political importance of Alexandria waned, the library suffered from neglect. Finally, in 270 A.D., much of it was razed to the ground, and a good part of the rest was destroyed by fire a little over a century later.

BACKGROUND

Abdul Kassem Ismael (938–995), Grand Vizier of Persia, had a library of 117,000 volumes. When he traveled, he took his books along—all of them. He had 400 camels trained to walk in order; the books they carried remained in strict alphabetical sequence. His camel drivers doubled as librarians.

BACKGROUND

Swiss naturalist Konrad von Gesner (1516–1565) wrote the *Universal Library*, a summary of *all* books known in Hebrew, Greek, and Latin.

Often only part of the catalog is computerized, so check to see which items are included in your library's on-line catalog before you search. You may have to use the card catalog to locate materials that the library acquired before a certain date (usually whenever the computer system was installed).

An on-line catalog typically can perform two different functions: a *browse search,* which displays alphabetical lists of consecutive entries much like a conventional card catalog and a *key word search* (also called an *express search*), which looks for any entries containing the key words (see 32h-4). Choosing key words carefully is important when doing a computer search because words that are too general produce large, unwieldy lists of sources, many of which will be irrelevant. Conversely, words that are too specific may find too few citations or none at all. Ask a reference librarian for help in choosing key words; the *Library of Congress Subject Headings* is also a useful resource.

Many libraries are connected to other libraries' catalogs through a computer network that gives you access to the holdings of libraries other than your own. The largest such network is the OCLC (On-line Computer Library Center) system, which links thousands of libraries across the country. Many smaller networks connect libraries in a given state or region. If you feel you need materials not in your own library, accessing a network can tell you where they may be found, but make sure you have exhausted the resources of your own library before looking elsewhere. Once identified, materials from other libraries usually can be requested by a librarian through an interlibrary loan.

Whether the catalog is on cards, microfiche or computer, the same information is offered. Catalog information is organized alphabetically in three categories: authors' names, book titles, and subjects. In some libraries, authors and titles are in one file, subjects in another. In other libraries, the three types of information are filed together.

Each card in the card catalog or on microfiche contains much useful information. The **call number** is most important. Be sure to copy it down *exactly* as it appears, with all numbers, letters, and decimal points. The call number tells where the book is located in the stacks. If you are working in a library with open stacks (one where you can go into the book collection yourself), the call number leads you to the area in the library where all books on the same subject can be found. Being there can help you search for sources, even though some books might have been checked out and other books might be at the reserve desk. The call number is also crucial in a library with closed stacks. In this case, to get a book, you must fill in a call slip, hand it in at the call desk, and wait for the book to arrive. Be aware that if you have filled in the wrong number or an incomplete number, your wait will be in vain.

Libraries classify books according to one of two systems. You can tell what system a particular library uses from the call numbers on the catalog cards. Cards in the **Library of Congress system** have call numbers that start with a letter. Each letter indicates a major classification of information: *A* stands for general works, *B* for philosophy, *C* and *D* for history, and so on. Cards in the **Dewey Decimal system** have call numbers that start with numbers. Each number indicates a major classification of information: 0-99 signals general works, 100-199 philosophy, 200-299 religion, and so on. Find out what system your library uses, and ask for a complete list of the classifications.

BACKGROUND

Melvil Dewey (1851–1931) is famous for devising the Dewey Decimal System of book classification (1876). He was also a founder and editor of the *Library Journal* and of the American Library Association. In 1883, he became librarian at Columbia University, New York City, and founded its school of library economy, the first program to train and certify librarians. Dewey and the school moved to Albany, New York, where it became the State Library school. Dewey served as director of the New York State library (1899–1906), secretary of the University of the State of New York (1899–1900), and state Director of Libraries (1904–1906). He remade the state library into one of the most efficient in the country, and he set up traveling libraries and picture collections. His innovations were widely copied throughout the United States and abroad.

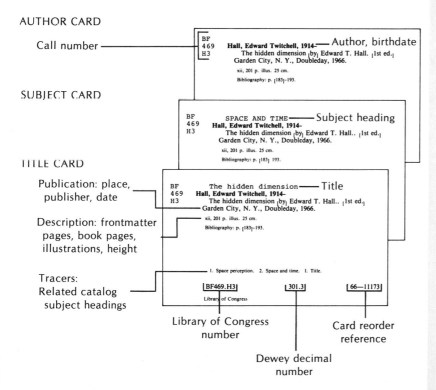

Library of Congress Catalog Cards

TEACHING TIP

Donnelyn Curtis and Stephen A. Bernhardt ("Keywords, Titles, Abstracts, and Online Searches: Implications for Technical Writing," *Technical Writing Teacher* [1991]: 142–161) write that a student who knows the title of one helpful book or article for his or her research paper can employ a popular "backdoor approach" (151) that librarians often use with difficult subjects. The database entry for that title will provide the student with subject headings that should be fruitful key terms for the search. Curtis and Bernhardt also recommend that students consult a thesaurus for alternative terms.

Tracers are another important feature of cards in the card catalog. Tracers are words, numbered and in fine print below a book's publication data, that give other headings used to classify information related to the subject of the card. Tracers are valuable hints for other topics to look up in the subject file of the card catalog when you want to find more about a subject. As you find tracers, be sure to add them to your list of headings and key words (see 32h-4).

At libraries that use the Library of Congress cataloging systems, the multi-volume *Library of Congress Subject Headings (LCSH)* is an indispensable guide. Available in the reference or reserve section of a library, it is a catalog of the subject headings (not title or author) used in the card catalog. This valuable resource helps you in three ways. First, you can look up your subject without having to go through the catalog. Second, if the term you are using is not in the catalog, it might be in the *LCSH* with a cross reference to the term used in the catalog. The expense and time is enormous to change subject headings in a catalog, so terms are not always up-to-date.

For example, until recently, sources related to "World War I" were filed in the catalog under "The European War." People who consulted the *LCSH* easily found out that the old term for "World War I" was still in effect, and they could continue with their research. Third, at each subject heading, you can find a list of tracers—related headings that can lead you to additional sources. As a bonus, the *LCSH* also lists related terms (marked by *x*) that are *not* used to classify information in the system; knowing these terms will help you avoid unproductive searching. All these terms can suggest alternate key words (see 32h-4) that you can use when searching through other sources. Amy Brown, whose research paper appears in Chapter 34, found the LCSH excerpts shown on the opposite page when she looked up "nonverbal communication" as well as "personal space."

32o **Using computerized databases**

A **computerized database** is a bibliographic computer file of articles, reports, and—less often—books. Each item in a computerized database provides information about title, author, and publisher. If the database catalogs articles from scholarly journals, the entry might also provide an *abstract* (a summary) of the material. Once you locate an entry that seems promising for your research, you must then track down the source itself. Some databases, however, such as ERIC and NEWSBANK, have the full texts of cited articles on microfiche. With such a system, each citation contains an abstract as

Excerpts from Library of Congress Subject Headings

well as a catalog number (for example, ERIC ED 139 580) which allows you to look up the microfiche—ask a librarian where this is stored—that contains the entire article.

Key words, as for on-line catalogs (see section 32l), are equally important when searching computerized databases, some of which contain as many as 100 million references. You must, therefore, choose which databases will be most helpful before you can begin to search. The DIALOG Information System, one of the largest databases, is a compilation of over 200 smaller databases likely in the humanities, the social sciences, business, science and technology, medicine, economics, and current events. Restrict your search to one database at a time. A reference librarian usually can help you choose the databases best suited to your research, but first you must be able to provide a specific, not vague, description of your research.

Computerized databases may be "on-line" (accessed through a telephone line and modem, such as DIALOG) or on CD-ROM (accessed in the library without having to connect to a distant computer). CD-ROM is thus cheaper and easier to use—generally an inexperienced user may follow simple on-screen instructions to search for entries. In contrast, on-line systems often must be used by trained librarians. On-line databases require the library to pay a fee for the time used and the number of entries requested. This fee is sometimes passed on to you, the user. Find out how much the charge

BACKGROUND

According to Curtis and Bernhardt, computers and the information explosion are changing the nature of indexing. Books and articles increasingly are indexed by title and keywords instead of by subject. Subject indexing requires readers to scan and classify each item for the index and is a slower, more expensive process than indexing by title and keywords, which can be done by computers. The process of having readers scan and classify makes it difficult and more expensive for indexes to adjust to the present rapid increase in journals and the development of new subject areas. Curtis and Bernhardt argue that the new emphasis on titles and keywords in indexes and computer searches means that writing teachers and students need to give more attention to composing titles.

32o

(1) Silver Platter 2.01   (2) PsycLIT Disc 2 (1/83 9/91)
    TI   DOCUMENT TITLE:Culture and the Self:Implications for cognition,
    emotion, and motivation.
    AU   AUTHOR(S): Marcus,Hazel R., Kitayamo, Shinobu
    IN   INSTITUTIONAL AFFILIATION OF FIRST AUTHOR: U Michigan, Research Ctr
    for Group Dynamics, Ann Arbor, US
(3) JN   JOURNAL NAME: PSYCHOLOGICAL REVIEW, 1991 Apr
    Vol 88(2) 224 253
(4) CC   CODEN:PORVAX
(5) IS   ISSN:0033295X
    LA   LANGUAGE:English
    PY   PUBLICATION YEAR : 1991
(6) AB   ABSTRACT: People in different cultures have strikingly different
    construals of the self,of others,and of the interdependence of the 2.
    These construals can influence, and in many cases determine,the very
    nature of the individual experience,including cognition,emotion,and
    motivation. Many Asian cultures have distinct conceptions of
    individuality that insist on the fundamental relatedness of individuals
    to each other. The emphasis is on attending to others,fitting in,and
    harmonious interdependence with them. American culture neither assumes
    nor values such overt connectedness among individuals. In contrast,
    individuals seek to maintain that independence from others by attending
    to the self and by discovering and expressing their unique inner
    attributes. As proposed herein, these construals are even more powerful
    than previously imagined. Theories of the self from both psychology and
    anthropology are integrated to define in detail the difference between a
    construal of the self as independent and a construal of the self as
    interdependent. Each of these divergent construals should have a set of
    specific consequences for cognition,emotion,and motivation;these
    consequences are proposed and relevant empirical literature is reviewed.
    (PsycLIT Database Copyright 1991 American Psychological Assn,all rights
    reserved)
(7) KP   KEY PHRASE:cultural construals of self and others; individual
    experience and cognition and emotion and motivation
(8) DE   DESCRIPTORS:CROSS CULTURAL DIFFERENCES; SELF PERCEPTION; SOCIAL
    PERCEPTION;COGNITION;EMOTIONAL STATES;LIFE EXPERIENCES; MOTIVATION
(9) CC   CLASSIFICATION CODE(S): 2830
(10) PO   POPULATION: Human
(11) UD   UPDATE CODE: 9109
(12) AN   PSYC ABS.VOL.AND ABS.NO.:78 23878
(13) JC   JOURNAL CODE: 1838

A CD—ROM Database Entry

is and whether the service is free for students—or you may be charged as much as a dollar or more per entry. Narrowing your search with apt key words is important to avoid your or your college's having to pay for a list of useless sources.

Recently, many databases previously available only on-line have been transferred to CD-ROM. The most popular databases on the DIALOG system, (such as the business, psychology, and scientific databases) are now available in this format, and many libraries are beginning to utilize CD-ROM rather than on-line databases. However, CD-ROM databases tend to be smaller and are updated less frequently than their on-line counterparts.

32o

(1)   The brand name of the CD ROM system. Another common name is DIALOG OnDisc.

(2)   The name of the database. The dates in parentheses list the earliest and latest dates covered on the disk.

(3)   The journal name, date, and volume, and inclusive page numbers for the full text of the article.

(4)   Numerical codes for the journal in which the article appears.

(5)   The journal's standard identification number.

(6)   The abstract of the article. An abstract provides just enough information to let a researcher decide whether to read the article itself. As a responsible researcher, you should always read an article yourself, quoting from it or paraphrasing or summarizing it in your own words, rather than quoting an abstract of the article.

(7)   The key phrases that very briefly sum up what the article is about and that can be very useful for scanning through large numbers of database entries for useful material.

(8)   The descriptors, or subject words under which the entry is listed, like subject cards in a card catalog. The underlined descriptors *cross-cultural differences* and *self-perception* are the words that were entered to start the search that found this entry.

(9)   A code for the subject of the article.

(10)   The group to which the article applies. This article is about humans in general. Other articles may be about more specific groups, such as Americans, dysfunctional families, paranoid schizophrenics, etc.

(11)   A code for when this article was added to the database.

(12)   The volume and abstract number where this entry can be found in the print version of *Psychological Abstracts*.

(13)   Numerical codes for the journal in which the article appears.

A Key for the CD–ROM Database Entry

Amy Brown, the student who wrote the research paper in Chapter 34, used a CD-ROM database to search for sources. After consulting a librarian and determining which specific databases were available at her college library, she decided to use the PsycLIT database (a computerized version of *Psychological Abstracts*, which includes about a dozen major journals related to psychology). With the help of a librarian, Brown chose key words such as *cross cultural differences, social perception,* and *labor force.* She combined these words with others to come up with a list of citations that she could manage to look up in a reasonable amount of time. One of those she found is shown on page 000; its numbered parts are explained above.

QUOTATION ABOUT WRITING

The computer is down. I hope it's something serious.

—Stanton Delaplane

32p

32p Drafting a thesis statement for a research paper

Drafting a **thesis statement** for a research paper is the beginning of the transition between the research process and the writing process. A thesis statement in a research paper is like the thesis statement in any essay: it tells the central theme (see 2m, especially Chart 9). Any paper must fulfill the promise of its thesis statement. Because readers expect unified material, the theme of the thesis must be sustained throughout a research paper.

Most researchers draft a **preliminary thesis statement** before or during their research process. They expect that they will revise the thesis somewhat after their research, because they know that the sources they will consult will enlarge their knowledge of a subject. Other researchers draft a thesis statement after the research process.

No matter when you draft your thesis statement, expect to write many alternatives. Your goal is to draft the thesis carefully so that it delivers the message you intend. In writing a **revised thesis statement,** take charge of your material. Reread your research log (see 32c). Reread your notes (see 32i). Look for categories of information. Rearrange your note cards into logical groupings. Begin to impose a structure on your material. As you draft a thesis statement, remember that one of your major responsibilities in a research paper is to support the thesis. Be sure that the material you gathered during the research process offers effective support. If it does not, revise your thesis statement, or conduct further research, or both.

Amy Brown, whose research paper appears in Chapter 34, drafted two different preliminary thesis statements before she composed one that worked well with her material.

FIRST PRELIMINARY VERSION	Standards for personal space vary among cultures.
NEXT PRELIMINARY VERSION	These different norms can lead to intercultural misunderstandings when people from different countries come together unaware of how their expectations concerning interpersonal distances can affect their reactions to each other.
FINAL VERSION	Everyone has expectations concerning the use of personal space, but accepted distances for that space are determined by each person's culture.

Brown knew that the first version of her thesis statement was too broad. Still, she used it as she wrote the first draft of her paper

QUOTATION ABOUT RESEARCH

A research paper is not a list of findings; it is the coherent communication of a meaningful pattern of information.

—Richard M. Coe, *Form and Substance*

because she knew she would revise it once she saw how the material from her research would come together in her paper. Brown wrote the second version of her thesis statement in the middle of her revising process, after she had written a few drafts of her paper. She knew that her second version was wordy and complicated. She composed her final thesis statement after she put her drafts aside for a few days and got some distance from her material.

As you revise your thesis statement, go back to the research question that guided your research process (see 32a). Your thesis statement should be one answer to the question. Here are examples of subjects narrowed to topics, focused into research questions, and then cast as thesis statements.

SUBJECT	*Rain Forests*
TOPIC	The importance of rain forests
RESEARCH QUESTION	What is the importance of rain forests?
THESIS STATEMENT (informative)	Rain forests provide the human race with many irreplaceable resources.
THESIS STATEMENT (persuasive)	Rain forests must be preserved because they offer the human race many irreplaceable resources.
SUBJECT	*Nonverbal Communication*
TOPIC	Personal space
RESEARCH QUESTION	How do standards for personal space differ among cultures?
THESIS STATEMENT (informative)	Everyone has expectations concerning the use of personal space, but accepted distances for that space are determined by each person's culture.
THESIS STATEMENT (persuasive)	To prevent intercultural misunderstandings, people must be aware of cultural differences in standards for personal space.
SUBJECT	*Smoking*
TOPIC	Curing nicotine addiction
RESEARCH QUESTION	Are new approaches being used to cure nicotine addiction?
THESIS STATEMENT (informative)	Some approaches to curing nicotine addiction are themselves addictive.
THESIS STATEMENT (persuasive)	Because some methods of curing addiction are themselves addictive, doctors should prescribe them with caution.

32r

TEACHING TIP

Composing a formal outline of an article read by the entire class can be either a small-group activity or a whole-class activity. It will not only provide practice for students in following formal outline form, but it will also help them, through discussion, to improve their ability to distinguish between major ideas, subordinate ideas, and supporting details. The instructor, however, needs to use care in selecting the article. Many professionally written pieces do not fall easily into outline form.

QUOTATION ABOUT RESEARCH

Research is the ability to investigate systematically and truly all that comes under your observation in life.

—Marcus Aurelius

QUOTATION ABOUT RESEARCH

. . . You should always collect more material than you will eventually use. Every article is strong in proportion to the surplus of details from which you can choose the few that will serve you best—if you don't go on gathering facts forever. At some point you must decide to stop researching and start writing.

—William Zinsser, *On Writing Well*

QUOTATION ABOUT RESEARCH

The process of doing research is not dissimilar from the process of writing anything else. It starts with a question, a problem, a topic which the writer examines, probes, and analyzes. The difference is that the writer is not alone in this game. When doing research, the writer participates with others who have also been taken with the subject.

—Ann Sullivan

32q Outlining a research paper

Some instructors require an outline of a research paper. To begin organizing your material for an outline, you might write an **informal outline.** Group the subcategories in your material until you are ready to write a formal outline.

A **formal outline** should be in the form discussed in section 2n. Head it with the paper's thesis statement. You can use a **topic outline** (a format that requires words or phrases for each item) or a **sentence outline** (a format that requires full sentences for each item). Do not mix the two types. For a sentence outline of the student's research paper in Chapter 34, see the early pages of 34b.

32r Drafting and revising a research paper

Drafting and revising a research paper have much in common with the writing processes for writing any type of paper (see Chapters 2 and 3). But more is demanded. You must demonstrate that you have followed the research steps in this chapter. You must demonstrate an understanding of the information you have located, and you must organize for effective presentation. Additionally, you must integrate sources into your writing without plagiarizing (see 31a) by properly using the techniques of quotation (see 31c), paraphrase (see 31d), and summary (see 31e). Also, you must use parenthetical references (see 33b) to document your sources. So many special demands take extra time for drafting, thinking, redrafting, and rethinking.

Expect to write a number of drafts of your research paper. Successive drafts help you gain authority over the information that you have learned from your research. The **first draft** is your initial attempt to structure your notes into a unified whole. It is also a chance to discover new insights and fresh connections. Only the act of writing makes such discovery possible. A first draft is a rough draft. It is a prelude to later work at revising and polishing. Chart 156 suggests some alternative ways to write the first draft of a research paper.

A **second and subsequent drafts** are the results of reading your first draft critically and revising it. If at all possible, get some distance from your material by taking a break of a few days (or a few hours, if you are pressed for time). Then, reread your first draft and

32r

SUGGESTIONS FOR DRAFTING A RESEARCH PAPER 156

- Some researchers work with their notes in front of them. They use the organized piles made for drafting a thesis statement (see 32p) and for outlining (see 32q). They spread out each pile and work according to the categories of information that have emerged from their material. They proceed from one pile to the next. They expect this process to take time, but they are assured of a first draft that includes much of the results of their research.

- Some researchers gather all their information and then set it aside to write a **partial first draft,** a quickly written first pass at getting the material under control. Writing this way helps researchers get a broad view of the material. The second step is to go back and write a **complete first draft** with research notes at hand. The researchers go over their partial draft slowly to correct information, add material left out, and—most important—insert parenthetical references (see 33b).

- Some researchers write their first draft quickly to get words down on paper when they feel ''stuck'' about what to say next. When they have a clear idea of how to proceed, they slow down and use their notes. These researchers draw on their experiences with gathering ideas (see 2d through 2k), shaping ideas (see 2l), getting started (see 3a), and drafting (see 3b).

TEACHING TIP

Since the processes of drafting and revising vary from one writer to another, students may gain insight into their own processes by interviewing one another about how they approach these stages of writing a research paper. They can base their interviews on the following questions.

1. Do you organize your note cards in piles?
2. Do you work with your notes in front of you?
3. Do you write the first draft without referring to your note cards?
4. Is your first draft a complete draft?
5. When do you insert parenthetical references?
6. Is your first draft composed slowly and carefully? Or quickly and sketchily?
7. Do you proceed immediately to a second draft, or do you let some time elapse between drafting and revising?
8. Do you show your work to other people for responses and suggestions?

think how it can be improved. You also might ask friends or classmates to read it and react.

Some researchers photocopy their first drafts and cut up the paper to move paragraphs and sentences around. If a new order suggests itself, the researchers tape the paper together in its new form. Researchers who have access to a computer will find this process considerably easier (see Appendix A).

As you work, pay attention to any uneasy feelings you have that hint at the need to rethink or rework your material. Experienced writers expect to revise; they know that writing is really rewriting. Research papers are among the most demanding composing assignments, and most writers have to revise their drafts more than a few times. As you revise, consult the Revision Checklists in 3c to remind yourself of general principles of writing. Also, consult the special revision checklist in Chart 157 for a research paper.

QUOTATION ABOUT RESEARCH

Research means to give each and every element its final value by grouping it in the unity of an organized whole.
—Pierre T. DeChardin

QUOTATION ABOUT RESEARCH

One of the skills of research is knowing when you have enough information; in considering too many side issues or too many perspectives, you may lose the main thread of your subject.
—Charles Bazerman, *The Informed Writer*

TEACHING TIP
Using the Revision Checklists in 3c and their own previously written and marked papers, students can devise individualized checklists for themselves to serve as reminders of their own problem areas. If, for example, they consistently leave the -s off third-person singular verbs, they should make that instance an item to be checked during the editing stage. Compiling such a checklist not only provides students with an efficient means of self-editing, it also makes them more conscious of where they need to exercise the greatest concern about mechanics.

QUOTATION ABOUT WRITING

Language exists only when it is listened to as well as spoken. The hearer is an indispensable partner.

—John Dewey

REVISION CHECKLIST FOR A RESEARCH PAPER   157

If the answer to any question in the list is "no," revise your draft.

1. Does the introductory paragraph lead effectively into the material (see 4g)?
2. Are you fulfilling the promise of the thesis statement (see 32p)?
3. Do the ideas follow from one another?
4. Do you stay on the topic?
5. Are important questions answered?
6. Do you avoid bogging down the paper with irrelevent or insignificant information?
7. Do you avoid leaving gaps in information?
8. Have you integrated source material without plagiarizing (see 31a)?
9. Have you used quotations, paraphrases, and summaries well (see Chapter 31)?
10. Have you used parenthetical references (see 33b) correctly, and has each tied in with a source listed in the Works Cited (or References) list at the end of the paper (see 33c and 33d)?
11. Have you used correct documentation forms (see 33b through 33d)?
12. Does the concluding paragraph end the material effectively (see 4g)?

The **final draft** shows that you have revised well. It shows also that you have edited (see 3d) and proofread (see 3e) for correct grammar, spelling, and punctuation. No amount of careful research and good writing can make up for a sloppy manuscript. Strive to make the paper easy to read. If any page is messy with corrections, retype it. If your instructor accepts handwritten papers, use ruled white paper that has *not* been torn out of a spiral notebook. (If at all possible, however, type your work because it will present itself better.) Use black or blue ink and write very legibly.

For a case study of a student writing an MLA-style research paper, including a narrative of the writing process in action, and a sample student research paper, see Chapter 34.

33 Documenting Sources for Research Writing

When you write a research paper, you always have to **document** your sources. To prepare to document, you want to create a working bibliography on cards (see 33a), so that you can keep careful track of all the sources on which you take notes. In your research paper itself, you are expected to document by giving information about your sources in two separate but equally important ways.

DOCUMENTATION REQUIREMENTS IN EVERY RESEARCH PAPER

1. Within the body of the paper, use **parenthetical references** (see 33b). Some courses might require endnotes or footnotes instead of parenthetical references (see 33f).
2. At the end of the paper, provide a **list of sources** (see 33c and 33d).

Two different documentation styles are featured in this chapter. The most frequently used style in the humanities was developed by the Modern Language Association (MLA). Another style used in some humanities and most social sciences was developed by the American Psychological Association (APA). MLA style and APA style for parenthetical references are given in 33b. MLA style and APA style for listing sources are given in 33c and 33d. Content notes are explained in 33e.

Never mix documentation styles. Use *only* MLA style, *only* APA style, or *only* a different style required by your instructor.

If you are expected to use a note system (footnotes or endnotes) of documentation, consult 33f. If you need to document in other than MLA style or APA style, consult 33g.

BACKGROUND

The term *bibliography* is derived from two Greek roots. The first is *biblia*, the plural form of the word meaning book or papyrus, so named after the Phoenician city *Byblos* (now Jubayl) from which papyrus was exported. *Biblia* has been responsible for many words in the English language dealing with books. For example, a *biblioclast* is a destroyer of books, and *bibliognost* refers to one who is knowledgeable about books. A *bibliolater* is a lover of books. A *bibliopegist* is a bookbinder.

The second Greek root is *graphos*, meaning *to write*. At one time *bibliography* meant *the writing of books*, but in the seventeenth century the term came to mean *writing about books*. At the same time, *bibliography* began to receive wide usage in Latin and began to replace such words as *catalogus* and *bibliotheca* in the titles of bibliographies, the making of which became increasingly important as bibliographers struggled to devise some type of organization for keeping track of the flood of publications that resulted from the invention of printing. Nevertheless, the term *bibliography* was not included in Samuel Johnson's dictionary of 1755 and was not found in the *Encyclopaedia Britannica* until its third edition in 1797. According to the *Oxford English Dictionary*, not until the early nineteenth century was the word *bibliography* first used to refer to "the systematic description and history of books, their authorship, printing, publication, editions, etc." or to a book about such matters.

33a Creating a working bibliography

To create a working bibliography, write out a bibliographic card for every source on which you take notes. (*Bibliography* literally means "description of books.") Include on each card all the bibliographic information you need to fulfill the requirements of the documentation style you are using. Also, for each card on a library source, write the call number in the upper left-hand corner, being careful to copy it exactly. (Depending on how recent they are and how the library stores them, magazines and journals may not have call numbers.) If you conduct research at more than one library, also note on the card the library where you found each source. You will then be able to relocate the source. When the time comes to compile a final list of sources for your research paper, you can easily arrange your bibliographic cards in alphabetical order. The bibliographic card here is for the research paper in Chapter 34.

HM
285
H3

Hall, Edward T. *The Hidden Dimension.* New York: Doubleday, 1969.

As you organize and write your paper, you may find that you have not drawn on certain sources at all, even though you took notes on them. In both MLA and APA documentation styles, list only the sources you mention in your paper. In MLA style, the list is called Works Cited; in APA style, the list is called References.

33b Documenting sources with parenthetical references

As you draft and revise your research paper, be sure to use **parenthetical references.** The purpose of parenthetical references is to lead your readers to the sources for your quotations (see 31c), paraphrases (see 31d), and summaries (see 31e). In the past, you may have used footnotes or endnotes to document your sources, but current practice in some of the humanities and most of the social sciences calls for parenthetical references. When you need to use footnotes or endnotes for documentation, refer to section 33f.

Make parenthetical references brief and accurate. To decide what to include in a reference, you need to consider what information about the source already appears in the sentence or immediate context. For illustrations and explanations of parenthetical references, consult section 33b-1 for MLA documentation style and section 33b-2 for APA documentation style. Chart 158 summarizes the functions of parenthetical references.

FUNCTIONS OF PARENTHETICAL REFERENCES WITHIN A PAPER 158

- They signal places in your paper where you have paraphrased, summarized, or quoted material from another source.
- They say exactly where that material is located in the source.
- They give information enabling a reader to find the source in the list of sources that appears at the end of your paper. (The list is called Works Cited in MLA documentation style and References in APA documentation style.)

---

1 Understanding the MLA system of parenthetical references

Quoted, paraphrased, or summarized material requires a parenthetical reference in MLA style to direct a reader to the full citation list called Works Cited, at the end of a paper. Parenthetical references contain the same information about a source whether you choose to quote it, paraphrase it, or summarize it.

In the first example on the next page, the author's name and the page number appear in parentheses. The author's name, which a reader needs in order to find an entry for the Works Cited list, is presented in parentheses because it does not appear elsewhere in the sentence. No punctuation separates the author's name from the page number. In the second example, the author's name is mentioned in the sentence, so only the page number appears in parentheses. In the third example, the author's name and the title of the work appear in the sentence, so only the page number is given in parentheses.

EXTRA EXERCISE A

Devise parenthetical references for the following quotation, paraphrase, and summary. The source is provided at the end of each selection.

1. "If indeed we note in his [Thomas Carlyle's] writings those passages in which the words and rhythms are most resonant, and the accent falls with the strongest emphasis, we shall find they are the expression of the cosmic wonder and terror which formed the darkly flaming background of all his thoughts." (Logan Pearsall Smith, "Thomas Carlyle: The Rembrandt of English Prose," *Reperusals and Re-Collections*, Harcourt, Brace and Company, Inc., 1936, p. 115.)

2. Ethologists study the traits that distinguish a group—a group of people or a group of animals. They try to discover how the group usually acts by observing its members in their natural surroundings, and to understand their behavior by testing it, when possible, in the laboratory. (Sally Carrighar, "Ethology," from *Wild Heritage*, Houghton Mifflin Company, 1965, pp. 174–175.)

3. May Sarton, who now lives in Maine, is the author of over forty books of poetry, fiction, journals, and memoirs. Since her first book of poetry appeared in 1937, and her first novel the year following, she has been known to the reading public as one who explores the solitary life and different forms of female creativity. She has been an influential figure in the Women's Movement. (Karen Saum, "May Sarton, *Writers at Work*, ed. George Plimpton, Viking Penguin Inc., p. 71.)

ANSWERS: EXTRA EXERCISE A

1. (Smith 115).
2. (Carrighar 174–75).
3. (Saum 71).

BACKGROUND

Nicolás Antonio (1617–1684) is credited with the creation of modern bibliography and the shaping of literary history into a scholarly discipline. His *Bibliotheca Hispana* is an index in Latin of Old World and New World Spanish writers after 1500. It also contains a history of earlier Spanish literature.

TEACHING TIP

Students often wonder why they need to be scrupulous in their documentation of information, sometimes thinking of the process as just another pointless but difficult exercise devised by the teacher. It may help them to understand the demands of documentation if you point out to them the reasons behind it. You will probably think of additional reasons, but here are some that you might find useful.

1. Using someone else's ideas or words is like using anything else that belongs to another person: The borrower has an ethical obligation to the owner not to claim the article as his or her own. Thus, the writer must acknowledge that the ideas or words of someone else belong to another person. In the case of long quotations—e.g., the reprinting of an entire work or a substantial portion of it—the writer must request and receive permission from the original author or publisher to use it.

2. Other researchers of the same subject may be intrigued by a reference to a particular work or author, causing them to look for the original so that they can read the entire piece. Citation of complete publication information will greatly simplify finding the original work or even the original passage.

➡

PARAPHRASE

People from the Mediterranean prefer an elbow-to-shoulder distance (Morris 131).

Desmond Morris notes that people from the Mediterranean prefer an elbow-to-shoulder distance (131).

In Manwatching: A Field Guide to Human Behavior, Desmond Morris notes that people from the Mediterranean prefer an elbow-to-shoulder distance (131).

When you quote fewer than four handwritten or typewritten lines, integrate the quoted material into your sentence.

SHORT QUOTATIONS

Personal space "moves with us, expanding and contracting according to the situation in which we find ourselves" (Fisher, Bell, and Baum 149).

Hall explains the practicality of close conversational distance, observing that "if you are interested in something, your pupils dilate; if I say something you don't like, they tend to contract" (47), which explains why in some cultures people speak to each other at close range.

When you quote more than four handwritten or typewritten lines, set off the quoted material from your own writing by indenting it ten spaces from the left margin. Do not put quotation marks around an indented quotation (also called a "displayed quotation").

LONG QUOTATION

Robert Sommer, an environmental psychologist, uses literary and personal analogies to describe personal space:

> Like the porcupines in Schopenhauer's fable, people like to be close enough to obtain warmth and comradeship but far enough away to avoid pricking one another. Personal space . . . has been likened to a snail shell, a soap bubble, an aura, and "breathing room." (26)

The reference is in parentheses at the end of the quotation and *after* the final period. Because the author's name is in the sentence that introduces the quotation, only the page number is given in the parenthetical reference.

Additional examples of parenthetical references in MLA style follow. To avoid lengthy parenthetical references, get in the habit of putting reference information into your sentence. Whether you put documentation information in a parenthetical reference or a sentence, remember that your reader must be able to find an entry in the Works Cited list for each reference to a source in your paper. If you have further questions about parenthetical references using MLA documentation style, consult the *MLA Handbook for Writers of Research Papers* (see 33g).

Work by one author—MLA

The examples Morris, Hall, and Sommer on the opposite page illustrate parenthetical references to a work by one author.

Work by two or more authors—MLA

If you use a source written by more than one author, you have the option of providing the names and page number in the parenthetical reference—(Leghorn and Parker 115)—or providing the names in the sentence itself, followed by just the page number in parentheses. If a book is by two or three authors, you must give all the names. If a book is by more than three authors, you can use the first author's name plus *et al.* either in the parenthetical reference—(Moore et al. 275)—or in the sentence. ❖ PUNCTUATION ALERT: For *et al.*, which is Latin for "and elsewhere" or "and others," be sure not to put punctuation after *et* and to put a period after *al.*, which is an abbreviation that requires a period wherever it appears in your sentence. ❖

One author with two or more works—MLA

If you use two sources by the same author, when you refer to either of the sources, supply the author's last name, an abbreviated title of the work, and the relevant page numbers—(Morris, Manwatching 95). Notice that a comma separates the author and underlined title, but no punctuation separates the title and page number. To shorten the parenthetical reference, use the author's name and the title of the work in your sentence and give only the page number in parentheses.

Cont'd.

3. Documentation protects the researcher from any charges of plagiarism. When all sources are acknowledged, there can be no doubt about what the researcher has gleaned from others and what is original.

4. References to sources inform the reader that the researcher has been thorough. The study which does not indicate that standard work in the field has been considered will be taken less seriously than the one that shows that the researcher is aware of what has already been written about the topic.

5. Particularly in science, the test of research findings is the replication of experiments by other researchers. They can repeat such work only if the steps of the process have been clearly documented, with careful reference to the work of others in the field.

TEACHING TIP

Because dealing with methods of documentation is tedious stuff for many students, working in groups can alleviate some of the frustration that they feel. Initially a class can work as a whole, with one or two people recording choices on the chalkboard. Later, small groups can work on documentation exercises in parenthetical documentation, footnoting, or preparation of lists of Works Cited or References.

QUOTATION ABOUT WRITING

l'écrivain original n'est pas celui qui n'imite personne, mais celui que personne ne peut imiter.

An original writer is not one who imitates no one, but one whom no one can imitate.

—François-René de Chateaubriand

BACKGROUND

Copyright is the term used to refer to a group of exclusive rights given for limited times to the authors or owners of original literary, dramatic, artistic, or musical writings. It includes the exclusive right to copy an author's work and to prevent others from doing so without permission. It also allows the owner to translate a work, to dramatize or arrange it, and to change it into other versions.

To be granted a copyright, a work must be original, but merit and aesthetic quality are of no importance. The law specifies several classes of works that can receive copyright protection. They include books, periodicals, musical compositions, dramatic works, motion pictures, works prepared for oral delivery, maps and other scientific or technical works, photographs, works of art, works of the graphic arts, and commercial prints and labels.

TEACHING TIP

Asking students to make up a title and citation for their imaginary autobiography, published this year by Prentice Hall, may inject a little fun into learning to cite a book.

Two or more authors with the same last name—MLA

If you use sources that include works by different authors with the same last name, you must supply the author's first and last names—(Charles G. Morris 516). Notice that no comma separates the author from the page numbers. To shorten the parenthetical reference, you can include the author's complete name in your sentence and give only the page numbers in parentheses.

Corporate author—MLA

If you use a source in which the "author" is the name of a corporation, an agency, or a group, a parenthetical reference can use the corporate author's name and relevant page number—(Boston Women's Health Collective 11). When possible, incorporate long names into your sentence to avoid a long parenthetical reference. The parentheses would then contain only the page number.

Work cited by title—MLA

If you use a source with no author given, substitute the title or abbreviated title for the author's name in the parenthetical reference —(Chicago 305)—or in the text itself. Notice that the title is underlined. If you use a shortened version of the title, be sure it starts with the word by which you alphabetize the source in your Works Cited list.

Multivolume work—MLA

Suppose you have used both volumes of a work by John Herman Randall, Jr. To cite a reference from one volume, indicate the volume number as well as the page number in the parenthetical reference—(Randall 1:64). Notice that a colon and a space separate the volume number and the page number. If the entry in the Works Cited list refers only to one volume of a multivolume work, give only the page number in the parenthetical citation—(Ernest 130). If you include the author's name in your sentence, supply only the page number, or the volume and page number, in the parenthetical reference.

Literary work—MLA

If you use an edition of a classic novel, play, or poem, give more information than a page reference. (Readers might be using other editions.) For prose works, in addition to a page number to your edition, give additional information about parts, sections, or chapters—(3; pt. 1, ch. 1). Notice that a semicolon separates the page number from other information. Use standard abbreviations, such as *pt.* (part), *sec.* (section), and *ch.* (chapter). For classic verse, plays, and poems, the MLA recommends that you omit page references altogether and cite divisions (canto, book, part, act, or scene and line), using periods to separate the various numbers—(King Lear 4.1.5–6). This means act 4, scene 1, lines 5–6 of Shakespeare's *King Lear*. Some instructors prefer roman numerals for citing acts and scenes—(King Lear IV.i).

One-page work—MLA

If you use a work that is only one page long, such as a short newspaper or magazine article, you can omit the page number in the parenthetical reference—("Hospitals"), though you must include it in the Works Cited list. The title is in quotation marks, not underlined, because it is a short work. If you include the work's author and title in your sentence, no parenthetical reference is needed.

Reference to more than one source—MLA

If more than one source has contributed to an idea or opinion in your paper, acknowledge multiple sources by putting all necessary information for each source in the parenthetical reference. Separate the sources with a semicolon—(Morris, Intimate 193; Mead 33).

Article in a book—MLA

If you use an article that appears in an edited book, give the name of the author of the article, not the editor of the book. If you were quoting from Ernesto Galarza's "The Roots of Migration," which appears in a book edited by Luis Valdez and Stan Steiner, you would use the following citation form: (Galarza 127).

An indirect source—MLA

If you are citing an author who has been quoted by another author, indicate both names: (Cather qtd. in McClave). This form tells the reader that you are citing the words of Willa Cather, that you found them in McClave's work, and that the Works Cited entry is the standard form for McClave's publication.

BACKGROUND

Until the middle of the fifteenth century, the only books available to Europeans were handwritten manuscripts, which were costly and often inaccurate. The development of printing made books available to the common people for the first time.

The major breakthrough in the history of printing was the invention of movable type, the making of a stamp for each letter on a separate base so that the letters could be assembled to form a page. Although this system was already known in China and Korea (where it was little used because of the large number of Chinese characters and the lack of suitable ink), its discovery in Europe was made independently. Credit for the European development is given to Johann Gutenberg (c. 1400–1468). Although his "Gutenberg Bible," printed in 1455, was not his first printed work, it is his most famous one.

Today it is often remarked that the world is going through another printing revolution. With the availability of copying machines, memory typewriters, word processing computer programs, and a variety of desktop printers, methods of producing printed material have undergone another major shift. Whereas only a few years ago having a document printed meant handing it over to a professional printer, today it is likely to be produced on equipment readily available in most offices and many homes.

BACKGROUND

As commonly used, the term *bibliography* sometimes refers to a science, sometimes to an art, and sometimes to the product of the art. As a science, it is an organized body of knowledge dealing with all aspects of books, both as physical objects and as the expression of ideas. Bibliography as an art consists of the techniques for finding, organizing, and presenting information about books. The bibliography that is produced by that art is a systematic listing of books that share common characteristics.

The objectives of bibliography may be analytical or systematic. Analytic bibliography tries to discover information about authorship, publication, and derivation of a text. Systematic bibliography, on the other hand, produces systematic lists of books. The result is many different kinds of bibliographies. For example, bibliographies may be critical (critically appraising the books they list), current or retrospective, comprehensive or selective, annotated or not, enumerative (presenting an inventory) or subject oriented (presenting content). In all their varied forms, they provide the modern researcher with invaluable assistance in finding out where to look to learn what is already known about a subject.

2 | Understanding the APA system of parenthetical references

Paraphrased, summarized, and quoted material requires documentation in the APA style of documentation. APA parenthetical references direct a reader to the full citation, listed on a separate page called References at the end of a paper.

In the APA system, integrate any quotation shorter than forty words into your own prose. (Section 31c-4 discusses how to work quotations smoothly into your own writing.) When you use a quotation longer than forty words, introduce it with your own words, and then set off the quotation from your words by starting it on a new line and indenting all lines of the quotation five spaces from the left margin. The parenthetical citation follows two spaces after the closing punctuation of the quotation. See the set-off quotation on page 686 in Chapter 35.

When you quote material, always include the page number with *p.* for one page or *pp.* for more than one page. Give the page number immediately after the end of the quotation, even in mid-sentence. If you do not mention the name of the author or the year in your sentence, include all three pieces of information in the parenthetical reference—(Morris, 1977, p. 131). Use a comma after the author and after the year. If your sentence includes the author's name, give the year of publication immediately after the name, even if the page number falls at a different place in the sentence—Morris (1977) found "elbow-to-shoulder distance" (p. 131) is preferred. If your sentence includes the author's name and the date of publication, then give only the page—(p. 131).

For paraphrased or summarized material, APA style allows the writer to decide whether or not to give a page number, depending on whether the reader is likely to want to know the specific location of information. Also, because a summary or paraphrase may use data from various places within a source, page numbers may be irrelevant. As a student writer, you might be required to give the page number so that your instructor can verify your information. Check with your instructor to find out the requirements in any class that calls for APA documentation style.

If you refer to a work more than once in a paper, give the author and date the first time that you mention the work, and then give only the author in subsequent mentions. There is one exception: If you are citing two or more works by the same author, each citation must include the date so that a reader knows which work is being cited—(Jones, 1989), (Jones, 1992).

Additional examples of parenthetical references in APA style follow. Whether you put documentation information in a parenthetical reference or a sentence, remember that your reader must be able to find an entry in the References list for each source cited in your paper. If you have further questions about parenthetical references using APA style, consult the *Publication Manual of the American Psychological Association* (see 33g).

Work by one author—APA

The examples of Morris on page 616 illustrate parenthetical references to a work by one author.

Work by two or more authors—APA

If you are citing a source by two authors, always use both last names. If the authors' last names do not appear in your prose, the parenthetical reference includes them and the year—`Worchel & Cooper, 1983`. Note that APA style permits the use of the ampersand—`&`—to stand for the word *and* in parenthetical citations. If you mention the authors in your own prose, however, use *and*—`Worchel and Cooper (1983) counted 2,123 occurrences`.

If a work has more than two authors but fewer than six, use all the authors' last names in the first reference but use only the last name of the first author followed by *et al.* for subsequent references. In the actual reference, do not underline any item—`(Peat et al., 1987)`.

If a work has six or more authors, use only the last name of the first author and *et al.* for the first citation and all other citations of the work.

Author(s) with two or more works in the same year—APA

If you use more than one source written in the *same year* by the same author(s), alphabetize the works by their titles for the References list, and assign letters (*a, b,* etc.) to them. Then, use the letters next to the year for works in the References list—`(1989a), (1989b)`. Use these formats in the parenthetical references—`(Jones, 1989a)`, and elsewhere, `(Jones, 1989b)`; for one citation of both references—`(Jones, 1989a, 1989b)`.

Two or more authors with the same last name—APA

If you use sources that include works by different authors with the same last name, use first- and middle-name initials in all text citations—`(A. J. Jones, 1992)`.

BACKGROUND

The Bibliographical Society of America was organized at the American Library Association's St. Louis Conference in 1904. It succeeded the Bibliographical Society of Chicago, which had been in existence for the preceding five years. The object of the society is "to promote bibliographical research and to issue bibliographical publications." Its membership is made up of professors, librarians, instructors, rare book dealers, collectors, and other bibliophiles. It is responsible for many publications dealing with published American writing.

EXTRA EXERCISE B

Using the following information, compile a Works Cited list following MLA style.

1. *Abraham Lincoln: The Man Behind the Myths,* by Stephen B. Oates. Harper & Row, Publishers, New York, Cambridge, Philadelphia, San Francisco, London, Mexico City, Sao Paulo, and Sydney, 1984.

2. Barbara W. Tuchman. *Practicing History.* Alfred A. Knopf, Inc. Copyright 1936, 1959, 1966, 1974, 1981. Introduction copyright 1981. New York.

3. *Time's Arrow, Time's Cycle: Myth and Metaphor in the Discovery of Geological Time.* Stephen Jay Gould. Harvard University Press, Cambridge, Massachusetts. 1987.

4. T. C. Smout. *A Century of the Scottish People, 1830–1950.* New Haven and London. 1986, Yale University Press.

5. Thomas J. Peters and Robert H. Waterman, Jr. *In Search of Excellence.* Harper & Row, Publishers, New York, 1982.

6. *The Man Who Mistook His Wife for a Hat, and Other Clinical Tales.* Oliver Sacks. New York. Summit Books. "The Autist Artist." No year of publication listed. Pages 204 through 223.

7. *The Rise and Fall of the House of Medici.* 1974. Penguin Books. New York. Christopher Hibbert.

8. *Capote: A Biography.* 1988. Simon & Schuster. New York. Gerald Clarke.

➡️

Corporate author—APA

If you use a source in which the "author" is the name of a corporation, an agency, or a group, a parenthetical reference gives that name as the author. In such citations, usually you should spell out the full name—(Boston Women's Health Collective, 1992). However, if the full name is long but it has a familiar abbreviated form, you can use the abbreviation after the first citation. In the first citation, give the full name and, in brackets, the abbreviation—(National Aeronautics and Space Administration [NASA], 1994). In subsequent citations, use the abbreviation—(NASA, 1994).

Work cited by title—APA

If you use a source that gives no author, substitute the title or the first two or three words of the title and the year—(Chicago Manual, 1982). The title is underlined because the source is a book. An article title appears in quotation marks—("The Research Organizer," 1991).

Reference to more than one source—APA

If more than one source has contributed to an idea or opinion in your paper, cite the sources alphabetically in a single reference and separate them with a semicolon—(Morris, 1977; Worchel & Cooper, 1983).

33c Documenting sources with a list of sources

In both MLA documentation style and APA documentation style, you must present a final list of sources. Use *only* MLA style or *only* APA style. Never mix them.

In MLA style, the list is called Words Cited. In APA style, the list is called References. Whichever style you follow, the list contains all sources referred to in your paper. Include only the sources from which you quote, paraphrase, or summarize. Do not include sources that you consulted but do not refer to in the paper. Begin the list on a new page that is numbered sequentially with the rest of your paper. Arrange entries alphabetically by author name. If the author's name is unknown, the entry is alphabetized by the first significant word of the title (not by *A, An,* or *The*).

For citing books, you may find most of the information you need on the title page or the copyright page (the reverse of the title page). For citing articles, the information you need usually appears on the cover, title page, or contents page of the magazine or journal, or sometimes on the first page of the article.

MLA documentation style for Works Cited is illustrated and explained in section 33c-1. APA documentation style for References is illustrated and explained in section 33c-2. Then on the red-bordered pages of 33d is a directory of forms, followed by an example of each form in MLA style and in APA style.

Computer software is available that will prepare a list of sources in MLA, APA, and several other documentation styles. As long as you enter data accurately, such software can be a great convenience.

The major differences between MLA style and APA style are summarized in Chart 159.

DOCUMENTATION FORMS FOR LIST OF SOURCES IN MLA STYLE AND APA STYLE   159

■ **TITLE OF LIST OF SOURCES**

    MLA Works Cited

    APA References

■ **FORMAT**

    MLA indents the second and subsequent lines five spaces.

    APA indents the second and subsequent lines three spaces.

■ **AUTHOR'S NAME**

    MLA includes first name and any middle initials.

    APA uses initials only for first name and includes middle initials.

■ **ORDER OF AUTHORS' NAMES FOR MORE THAN ONE AUTHOR**

    MLA reverses the order (last name, first name) only for the first name and uses regular order (first name, last name) for all subsequent names.

    APA reverses the order (last name, initials) for all names.

    ➡

DOCUMENTATION FORMS FOR LIST OF SOURCES IN MLA STYLE AND APA STYLE *(continued)*

■ **THE WORD *and* FOR LISTING MORE THAN ONE AUTHOR**

> **MLA** uses the word *and*.
>
> **APA** uses the ampersand (&).

■ **YEAR OF PUBLICATION**

> **MLA** gives the year toward the end of the citation.
>
> **APA** gives the year in parentheses followed by a period immediately after the author name.

■ **CAPITALIZATION IN TITLES**

> **MLA** capitalizes all major words in titles.
>
> **APA** *For books:* Capitalize only the first word, a word after a colon, and proper nouns in titles. *For names of journals and proceedings of meetings:* Capitalize the first word and all major words.

■ **QUOTATION MARKS FOR NAMES OF SHORTER WORKS**

> **MLA** uses quotation marks for the names of shorter works.
>
> **APA** omits quotation marks for the names of shorter works.

■ **CITING A SELECTION IN A LARGER WORK**

> **MLA** gives the name of the selection followed by a period. Then it gives the name of the larger work followed by a period.
>
> **APA** does the same but uses the word *In* to introduce the name of the larger work and names the editors, using normal order for the names, before the title of the larger work. ➡

DOCUMENTATION FORMS FOR LIST OF SOURCES IN MLA STYLE AND APA STYLE *(continued)*

■ **PUBLISHER**

> **MLA** uses short forms as long as they are clear: Prentice for *Prentice Hall.* Also, MLA uses UP for *University Press.*
>
> **APA** uses the complete name, but it drops words such as *Inc., Publishers,* and *Co.*

■ **PUBLICATION MONTH ABBREVIATIONS**

> **MLA** abbreviates all months except *May, June,* and *July* by using the first three letters followed by a period: *Dec., Feb.*
>
> **APA** does not abbreviate months.

■ **INCLUSIVE PAGE NUMBERS**

Inclusive page numbers give the starting page number and the ending page number of a cited work, such as one article in a journal or one chapter in a book. Using inclusive page numbers signals that the cited work is on those pages and all pages in between. If that is not the case, use the style shown below for discontinuous pages.

> **MLA** uses the full second number through 99. Then it uses only the last two digits, unless confusion would result: 103–04 is clear, but the full numbers are needed for 567–602.
>
> **APA** uses complete numbers.

■ **DISCONTINUOUS PAGES**

> **MLA** uses the starting page number followed by a plus sign (+): 32+.
>
> **APA** lists all pages, with discontinuous numbers set off by commas: 32, 44–45, 47–49, 50.

1 | Using MLA documentation style: the Works Cited list

Citing books—MLA

Citations for books have three main parts: author, title, and publication information (place of publication, publisher, and date of publication). Each part is followed by a period and two spaces. If the citation uses more than one line, use the regular margin for the first line and indent all other lines five spaces from the left margin.

AUTHOR	TITLE	PUBLISHING INFORMATION
Didion, Joan.	Salvador.	New York: Simon, 1983.

Many sources need additional items of information included in the citation. Indent all lines after the first line five spaces.

Chester, Laura, and Sharon Barba, eds. Rising Tides:
    Twentieth Century American Women Poets. Intro.
    Anaïs Nin. New York: Simon, 1973.

In the title, capitalize all major words. If several cities are listed for the place of publication, give only the first. If a foreign city might be unfamiliar to a reader, add an abbreviation of the Canadian province or country. You can shorten the publisher's name as long as the shortened version is easily identifiable. (*Prentice Hall* can be *Prentice*; *Oxford University Press* can be *Oxford UP*; *Simon & Schuster* can be *Simon*.) See 33d for a directory of forms followed by an example of each form in MLA style.

Citing articles—MLA

Citations for articles in periodicals (such as journals, magazines, and newspapers) contain three major parts: author, title of article, and publication information. The publication information usually includes the periodical title, volume number, year of publication, and inclusive page numbers (first through last).

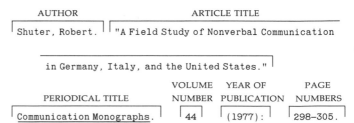

AUTHOR	ARTICLE TITLE		
Shuter, Robert.	"A Field Study of Nonverbal Communication		
	in Germany, Italy, and the United States."		

PERIODICAL TITLE	VOLUME NUMBER	YEAR OF PUBLICATION	PAGE NUMBERS
Communication Monographs.	44	(1977):	298–305.

When a month is part of a date of publication, spell out *May, June,* and *July,* but abbreviate all other months (use the first three letters followed by a period). Additional information may be required, depending on the source. Indent all lines after the first line five spaces. In the citation for an article, each part is followed by a period and two spaces. Within each part, use one space between each word and after punctuation. In the title, capitalize all major words.

❖ NUMBER ALERT: In citing inclusive page numbers, give the second number in full for numbers through 99 (for example, 23–24). For numbers 100 and above, give only the last two digits unless doing this would create confusion (for example, if you write 103–04, your reader can assume that you mean 103–104; however, 567–02 is not clear and should be written 567–602). ❖

See 33d for a directory of forms followed by an example of each form in MLA style. If you have further questions about citations using MLA style, consult the *MLA Handbook for Writers of Research Papers* (see 33g).

2	Using APA documentation style: the References list

Citing books—APA

Citations for books have four main parts: author, date, title, and publication information. After the first line, indent all lines three spaces.

AUTHOR	DATE	TITLE
Didion, J.	(1977).	A book of common prayer.

PUBLISHING INFORMATION

New York: Simon & Schuster.

Give the author's last name first and then the initial of the first and, if any, middle name. In the title, capitalize the first word, any proper nouns°, and the first word after a colon. If several cities are listed for place of publication, give only the first. If the city might be unfamiliar to a reader, add an abbreviation of the state (use U.S. Postal Service abbreviations), province, or country. Use the full publisher's name, but you may omit terms such as *Publishers, Co.,* and *Inc.* Give the latest copyright date for the edition you are using.

Citing articles—APA

Citations for articles in periodicals (such as journals, magazines, and newspapers) contain four major parts: author, date, title of article, and publication information. If a citation uses more than one line, use the regular margin for the first line and then indent the other lines 3 spaces from the left margin. For articles, the publication information usually includes the periodical title, volume number, and inclusive page numbers (first through last). For articles from newspapers or magazines, use *p.* or *pp.* before the page numbers. For articles in journals, use the page numbers only, without *p.* or *pp.* Spell out (do not abbreviate) a month used in a publication date.

AUTHOR	DATE	ARTICLE TITLE
Shuter, R.	(1977).	A field study of nonverbal communication

in Germany, Italy, and the United States.

PERIODICAL TITLE	VOLUME NUMBER	PAGE NUMBERS
Communication Monographs,	44,	298–305.

In the citation for an article, each of the parts (bracketed in the example above) ends with a period and two spaces. Within each part, use one space between words and after punctuation. Capitalize the title of the *article* according to the guidelines for a book title in APA style (see 33c-1). Capitalize the title of the *publication* that contains the article according to standard practice, as explained in Chart 140. ❖ NUMBER ALERT: Use complete inclusive page numbers (for example, 103–104, 344–347, 2334–2367). ❖

If you have further questions about citations using APA style, consult the *Publication Manual of the American Psychological Association* (see 33g).

33d Using MLA forms or APA forms for list of sources

The following directory is a numbered list corresponding to the forms shown in the examples that follow. The MLA style and the APA style appear together for each item so that you can compare them easily. Use *only* MLA style or *only* APA style. Never mix them.

MLA style permits underlining of a title of two or more words with either an unbroken or a broken line. (Some widely used word-processing programs underline with a broken line only.) APA style requires an unbroken line. Whatever your choice, be consistent in each piece of writing. This handbook uses an unbroken line for MLA style.

Not every possible documentation model is given. You may

find that you have to combine features of more than one model to document a particular source. You will also find more information in the *MLA Handbook* and APA *Publication Manual* (see 33g).

DIRECTORY

1. Book by one author
2. Book by two or three authors
3. Book by more than three authors
4. Two or more books by same author(s)
5. Book by group or corporate author
6. Book with no author named
7. Book with an author and an editor
8. Translation
9. Work in several volumes or parts
10. One selection from an anthology or an edited book
11. Two selections from one anthology or an edited book
12. Signed article in a reference book
13. Unsigned article in a reference book
14. Edition
15. Anthology or edited book
16. Introduction, preface, foreword, or afterword
17. Unpublished dissertations or essays
18. Reprint of an older book
19. Books in a series
20. Books with a title within a title
21. Government publication
22. Published proceedings of a conference
23. Article from a daily newspaper
24. Editorial, letter to the editor, review
25. Unsigned article from a daily newspaper
26. Article from a weekly or biweekly magazine or newspaper
27. Article in a monthly or bimonthly periodical
28. Unsigned article from a weekly or monthly periodical
29. Article from a collection of reprinted articles
30. Article in a journal with continuous pagination
31. Article in a journal that pages each issue separately
32. Interview
33. Published and unpublished letters
34. Lectures, speeches, and addresses

35. Films and videotapes
36. Recordings
37. Live performance
38. Works of art or musical compositions
39. Radio and television programs
40. Computer software
41. Information services: ERIC and NewsBank
42. Maps and charts

1. BOOK BY ONE AUTHOR

MLA   Welty, Eudora. One Writer's Beginnings. Cambridge: Harvard
             UP, 1984.

APA   Welty, E. (1984). One writer's beginnings. Cambridge:
             Harvard University Press.

2. BOOK BY TWO OR THREE AUTHORS

MLA   Leghorn, Lisa, and Katherine Parker. Woman's Worth. Boston:
             Routledge, 1981.

MLA   Kelly, Alfred H., Winfred A. Harbison, and Herman Belz. The
             American Constitution: Its Origins and Development. New
             York: Norton, 1983.

Give only the first author's name in reversed order; give other authors' names in normal order. Use commas to separate authors' names, including a comma before the *and* preceding the last name in the series. Give the names in the order in which they appear on the title page of the book.

APA   Leghorn, L., & Parker, K. (1981). Woman's worth. Boston:
             Routledge & Kegan Paul.

APA   Kelly, A. H., Harbison, W. A., & Belz. H. (1983). The American
             constitution: Its origins and development. New York:
             Norton.

Give each author's name in reversed order. Use initials for first and middle names. Use commas to separate authors' names, including a comma before the ampersand (the symbol &) with more than two authors. Give the names in the order in which they appear on the title page of the book. Note that the second word, *American,* is capitalized only because it is a proper adjective; *Its* is capitalized only because it is the first word of a subtitle that follows a colon.

3. BOOK BY MORE THAN THREE AUTHORS

MLA   Moore, Mark H., et al. Dangerous Offenders: The Elusive Target
of Justice. Cambridge: Harvard UP, 1984.

Give only the first author's name, in reversed order; *et al.* ("and others") indicates that three or more authors wrote the work.

APA   Moore, M. H., Estrich, S., McGillis, D., & Spelman, W. (1984).
Dangerous offenders: The elusive target of justice.
Cambridge: Harvard University Press.

Give last names and initials, in reversed order, for all authors, no matter how many.

4. TWO OR MORE BOOKS BY SAME AUTHOR(S)

MLA   Morris, Desmond. Manwatching: A Field Guide to Human
Behavior. New York: Abrams, 1977.

---, ed. Primate Ethology. London: Wiedenfeld, 1967.

When citing two or more books by the same author(s), give the name(s) in the first entry only. In the second and subsequent entries, use three hyphens and a periods to stand for exactly the same name(s). If the person served as editor or translator, put a comma and the appropriate abbreviation (*ed.* or *trans.*) following the three hyphens. Alphabetize the works listed according to book title, regardless of such labels as *ed.* or *trans.*, and regardless of the chronological order in which they were published.

APA   Morris, D., Ed. (1967). Primate ethology. London:
Wiedenfeld.

APA   Morris, D. (1977). Manwatching: A field guide to human
behavior. New York: Henry N. Abrams.

5. BOOK BY GROUP OR CORPORATE AUTHOR

MLA   The Boston Women's Health Collective. Our Bodies, Ourselves.
New York: Simon, 1986.

MLA   American Psychological Association. Publication Manual of the
American Psychological Association. 3rd ed. Washington:
APA, 1984.

Cite the full name of the corporate author first. Use the abbreviation *APA* for the publisher if readers are likely to recognize it. Otherwise, use the abbreviation *Amer. Psychol. Assn.* Do not abbreviate the author name.

APA The Boston Women's Health Collective. (1986). <u>Our bodies,</u>
<u>ourselves</u>. New York: Simon & Schuster.

APA American Psychological Association. (1984). <u>Publication</u>
<u>manual of the American Psychological Association</u> (3rd ed.).
Washington, DC: Author.

Cite the full name of the corporate author first. If the author is also
the publisher, use the word *Author* as the name of the publisher.

6. BOOK WITH NO AUTHOR NAMED

MLA <u>The Chicago Manual of Style</u>. 13th ed. Chicago: U of Chicago P,
1982.

If there is no author's name on the title page, begin the citation with
the title. Alphabetize the entry according to the first significant word
of the title (not *A, An,* or *The*).

APA <u>The Chicago manual of style</u> (13th ed.). (1982). Chicago:
University of Chicago Press.

If there is no author's name on the title page, begin the citation with
the title. Alphabetize the entry according to the first significant word
of the title (not *A, An,* or *The*).

7. BOOK WITH AN AUTHOR AND AN EDITOR

MLA Brontë, Emily. <u>Wuthering Heights</u>. Ed. David Daiches. London:
Penguin, 1985.

MLA Daiches, David, ed. <u>Wuthering Heights</u>. By Emily Brontë.
London: Penguin, 1985.

If what you refer to in your paper is the work of the book's author,
begin the citation with the author's name. If you refer instead to the
work of the editor, begin the citation with the editor's name.

APA Brontë, E. (1985). <u>Wuthering Heights</u> (D. Daiches, Ed.).
London: Penguin.

8. TRANSLATION

MLA Freire, Paulo. <u>Pedagogy of the Oppressed</u>. Trans. Myra Bergman
Ramos. New York: Seabury, 1970.

APA Freire, P. (1970). <u>Pedagogy of the oppressed</u> (M. B. Ramos,
Trans.). New York: Seabury Press.

9. WORK IN SEVERAL VOLUMES OR PARTS

MLA   Jones, Ernest. The Last Phase. New York: Basic, 1957. Vol. 3 of The Life and Work of Sigmund Freud. 3 vols.

MLA   Randall, John Herman, Jr. The Career of Philosophy. 2 vols. New York: Columbia UP, 1962.

If you are citing only one volume of a multivolume work, place this information after the publication date. You may end the entry giving the total number of volumes. MLA recommends using arabic numerals, even if the source uses roman numerals (*Vol. 6* for *Vol. VI*).

If you have drawn from two or more volumes of a multivolume work, give the total number of volumes.

APA   Randall, J. H., Jr. (1962). The career of philosophy (Vols. 1–2). New York: Columbia University Press.

10. ONE SELECTION FROM AN ANTHOLOGY OR AN EDITED BOOK

MLA   Galarza, Ernest. "The Roots of Migration." Aztlan: An Anthology of Mexican American Literature. Ed. Luis Valdez and Stan Steiner. New York: Knopf, 1972. 127–132.

Give the author and title of the selection first. Place titles of essays, short stories, or short poems in quotation marks. Underline the title of a book or a play. Then give the full title of the anthology. Next comes the editor information. Start with *Ed.*, which stands for "Edited by," whether there is one or more editors. Then give the name(s) of the editor(s), with the first name before the last. End the citation with the inclusive page numbers (first through last) of the selection; do not use the abbreviation *p.* or *pp.*

APA   Galarza, E. (1972). The roots of migration. In L. Valdez & S. Steiner (Eds.), Aztlan: An anthology of Mexican American literature (pp. 127–132). New York: Alfred A. Knopf.

The word *In* introduces the larger work from which the selection is taken.

11. TWO SELECTIONS FROM ONE ANTHOLOGY OR AN EDITED BOOK

MLA   Gilbert, Sandra M., and Susan Gubar. The Norton Anthology of Literature by Women. New York: Norton, 1985.

MLA   Kingston, Maxine Hong. "No Name Woman." Gilbert and Gubar 2337–47.

If you cite more than one selection from the same anthology, list the anthology as a separate entry with all the publication information. Also list each selection from the anthology by author and title of the selection, but give only the names of the editor(s) of the anthology and the page number(s) of the selection.

APA   Gilbert, S., & Gubar, S. (Eds.). (1985). <u>The Norton anthology of literature by women</u>. New York: W. W. Norton.

APA   Kingston, M. H. (1985). No name woman. In S. Gilbert & S. Gubar (Eds.), <u>The Norton anthology of literature by women</u>. New York: W. W. Norton.

You must provide full reference information for each selection from an anthology (or collection) you cite. Use *In* to show the larger work from which the selection is taken.

12. SIGNED ARTICLE IN A REFERENCE BOOK

MLA   Holt, Robert R. "Freud, Sigmund." <u>International Encyclopedia of the Social Sciences</u>. Ed. David L. Sills. 18 vols. New York: Macmillan, 1968.

If articles are alphabetically arranged in the work, omit the volume and page numbers. If the reference book is frequently revised, give only the edition and year of publication.

APA   Holt, R. R. Freud, Sigmund. In D. L. Sills (Ed.), <u>International encyclopedia of the social sciences</u> (pp. 1–11). New York: Macmillan.

The word *In* introduces the larger work from which the selection is taken.

13. UNSIGNED ARTICLE IN A REFERENCE BOOK

MLA   "Ireland." <u>Encyclopaedia Britannica</u>. 1974 ed.

APA   Ireland. (1974). In <u>Encyclopaedia Britannica</u>.

14. EDITION

MLA   Mandell, Maurice I. <u>Advertising</u>. 4th ed. Englewood Cliffs: Prentice, 1984.

When a book is not the first edition, the edition number appears on the title page. Place this information between the title and the publication information. Give the latest copyright date for the edition you are using.

APA   Mandell, M. I. (1984). Advertising (4th ed.). Englewood
         Cliffs, NJ: Prentice Hall.

15. ANTHOLOGY OR EDITED BOOK

MLA   Valdez, Luis, and Stan Steiner, eds. Aztlan: An Anthology of
         Mexican American Literature. New York: Knopf, 1972.

APA   Valdez, L., & Steiner, S. (Eds.). (1972). Aztlan: An anthology
         of Mexican American literature. New York: Alfred A. Knopf.

16. INTRODUCTION, PREFACE, FOREWORD, OR AFTERWORD

MLA   Boaz, Frank. Introduction. Patterns of Culture. By Ruth
         Benedict. 1934. Boston: Houghton, 1959.

If you are citing an introduction, preface, foreword, or afterword,
give its author's name first and then the name of the part cited.
Capitalize the first letter of the part cited, but neither underline it nor
put it in quotation marks. If the writer of the introduction, preface,
foreword, or afterword is different from the author of the book, give
the word *By* and the author's full name after the title. After the
publication information, give the inclusive page numbers (first
through last) of the part you are citing. Give page numbers from a
preface or an introduction in roman numerals, just as they appear in
the work.

APA   Boaz, F. (1959). Introduction. In Patterns of culture by
         R. Benedict. Boston: Houghton Mifflin. (Original work
         published 1934)

17. UNPUBLISHED DISSERTATIONS OR ESSAYS

MLA   Geissinger, Shirley Burry. "Openness versus Secrecy in
         Adoptive Parenthood." Diss. U. of North Carolina at
         Greensboro, 1984.

To cite an unpublished dissertation or essay (your own or another
person's), state the author's name first, then the title in quotation
marks (not underlined), then a descriptive label (such as *Diss.* or
Unpublished essay), then the degree-granting institution (for dissertations), and finally the date.

APA   Geissinger, S. B. (1984). Openness versus secrecy in adoptive
         parenthood. Unpublished dissertation, University of North
         Carolina at Greensboro.

18. REPRINT OF AN OLDER BOOK

MLA   Hurston, Zora Neale. Their Eyes Were Watching God. 1937.

Urbana: U of Illinois Press, 1978.

A republished book may be the paperback version of a book originally published as a hardbound, or it may be the reissue of a book. Republishing information can be found on the copyright page. Give the date of the original version before the publication information for the version you are citing.

APA   Hurston, Z. N. (1978). Their eyes were watching God. Urbana,

IL: University of Illinois Press. (Original work published

in 1937)

19. BOOK IN A SERIES

MLA   McClave, Heather. Women Writers of the Short Story. Twentieth

Century Views Series. Englewood Cliffs: Prentice, 1980.

APA   McClave, H. (1980). Women writers of the short story.

Englewood Cliffs, NJ: Prentice Hall.

20. BOOK WITH A TITLE WITHIN A TITLE

MLA   Lumiansky, Robert M., and Herschel Baker, eds. Critical

Approaches to Six Major English Works: Beowulf Through

Paradise Lost. Philadelphia: U of Pennsylvania P, 1968.

When a book title includes the title of another work that is usually underlined (such as a novel, play, or long poem), do *not* underline the incorporated title. If the incorporated title is usually enclosed in quotation marks (such as a short story or short poem), keep the quotation marks and underline the complete title of the book.

APA   Lumiansky, R. M., & Baker, H. (Eds.). (1968). Critical

approaches to six major English works: Beowulf through

Paradise Lost. Philadelphia: University of Pennsylvania

Press.

21. GOVERNMENT PUBLICATION

MLA   United States. Cong. House. Committee on the Judiciary.

Immigration and Nationality with Amendments and Notes on

Related Laws. 7th ed. Washington: GPO, 1980.

If a government publication has no stated author, use the government, governmental body, and/or government agency as the author, with periods and two spaces separating the parts. The U.S. government publishes books, reports, pamphlets, and other material. As a general rule, unless a specific person is named as author, consider the government (country, state, or other locality) to be the author. The government agency is named next. In the United States, the Government Printing Office (GPO) publishes most federal publications.

APA   United States Congresional House Committee on the Judiciary.

(1980). Immigration and nationality with amendments and

notes on related laws (7th ed.). Washington, DC: U.S.

Government Printing Office.

APA uses the complete name of a government agency as author when no specific person is named.

22. PUBLISHED PROCEEDINGS OF A CONFERENCE

MLA   Harris, Diana, and Laurie Nelson-Heern, eds. Proceedings of

NECC 1981: National Educational Computing Conference.

17-19 June 1981. Iowa City: Weeg Computing Center, U of

Iowa, 1981.

APA   Harris, D., & Nelson-Heern, L. (Eds.). (1981). Proceedings of

NECC 1981: National Education Computing Conference. Iowa

City: Weeg Computing Center, University of Iowa.

23. ARTICLE FROM A DAILY NEWSPAPER

MLA   Dullea, Georgia. "Literary Folk Look for Solid Comfort." New

York Times 16 Apr. 1986: C14.

Cite the title of the newspaper exactly as it appears on the masthead, ommitting any introductory *A* or *The*. If the city of publication is not in the title of the periodical, add it in square brackets after the title, not underlined: for example, Patriot Ledger [Quincy, MA]. Give the day, month, and year of the issue. Be sure to give the section letter as well as the page number, if appropriate: C14. If an article does not run on consecutive pages (if, for example, it starts on 23 and continues on 42), give the first page number and add a plus sign (23+).

APA   Dullea, G. (1986, April 16). Literary folk look for solid

comfort. New York Times, p. C14.

24. EDITORIAL, LETTER TO THE EDITOR, REVIEW

MLA   "Facing Space, After the Cold War." Editorial. <u>New York Times</u> 1 May 1989: A16.

MLA   Childress, Glenda Teal. Letter. <u>Newsweek</u> 9 June 1986: 10.

MLA   Linebaugh, Peter. "In the Flight Path of Perry Anderson." Rev. of <u>In the Tracks of Historical Materialism</u>, by Perry Anderson. <u>History Workshop</u> 21 (1986): 141–46.

APA   Facing space, after the cold war. (1989, May 1). [Editorial.] <u>New York Times</u>, p. A16.

APA   Childress, G. T. (1986, June 9). Letter to the editor. <u>Newsweek</u>, p. 10.

APA   Linebaugh, P. (1986). In the flight path of Perry Anderson [Review of <u>In the tracks of historical materialism</u>]. <u>History Workshop</u>, <u>21</u>, 141–146.

25. UNSIGNED ARTICLE FROM A DAILY NEWSPAPER

MLA   "Hospitals, Competing for Scarce Patients, Turn to Advertising." <u>New York Times</u> 20 Apr. 1986: 47.

Alphabetize in Works Cited by first word of title.

APA   Hospitals, competing for scarce patients, turn to advertising. (1986, April 20). <u>New York Times</u>, p. 47.

Alphabetize in References by first word of title.

26. ARTICLE FROM A WEEKLY OR BIWEEKLY MAGAZINE OR NEWSPAPER

MLA   Toufexis, Anastasia. "Dining with Invisible Danger." <u>Time</u> 27 Mar. 1989: 28.

If a periodical is published every week or every two weeks, give the complete date. First cite the day, then the month (abbreviated if necessary), and finally the year. Drop any introductory *A, An,* or *The* from the title of a periodical.

APA   Toufexis, A. (1989, March 27). Dining with invisible danger. <u>Time</u>, p. 28.

27. ARTICLE IN A MONTHLY OR BIMONTHLY PERIODICAL

MLA   Roosevelt, Anna. "Lost Civilizations of the Lower Amazon."
Natural History Feb. 1989: 74-83.

If a periodical is published monthly or every two months, give the month(s) and year.

APA   Roosevelt, A. (1989, February). Lost civilizations of the
lower Amazon. Natural History, pp. 74-83.

28. UNSIGNED ARTICLE FROM A WEEKLY OR MONTHLY PERIODICAL

MLA   "A Salute to Everyday Heroes." Time 10 July 1989: 46+.

APA   A salute to everyday heroes. (1989, July 10). Time, pp. 46-51,
54-56, 58-60, 63-64, 66.

29. ARTICLE FROM A COLLECTION OF REPRINTED ARTICLES

MLA   Curver, Philip C. "Lighting in the 21st Century." Futurist
Jan./Feb 1989:29-34. Rpt. in Energy Ed. Eleanor
Goldstein. Vol. 4. Boca Raton: Social Issues Resources
Series, 1990. Art. 84.

APA   Curver, P. C. (1990). Lighting in the 21st century. In Social
issues resources series. Energy (Vol. 4, Article 84). Boca
Raton: Social Issues Resources.

30. ARTICLE IN A JOURNAL WITH CONTINUOUS PAGINATION

MLA   Cochran, D. D., W. Daniel Hale, and Christine P. Hissam.
"Personal Space Requirements in Indoor versus Outdoor
Locations." Journal of Psychology 117 (1984): 132-33.

If a journal pages its issues continuously through an annual volume, give only the volume number before the year. (*National Geographic* is such a journal. If the first issue of a volume ends on page 224, for example, the second issue starts on page 225.) Notice that all numbers, even the volume, are arabic numerals.

APA   Cochran, D. D., Hale, W. D., & Hissam, C. P. (1984). Personal
space requirements in indoor versus outdoor locations.
Journal of Psychology, 117, 132-133.

The volume number is underlined.

31. ARTICLE IN A JOURNAL THAT PAGES EACH ISSUE SEPARATELY

MLA   Hashimoto, Irvin. "Pain and Suffering: Apostrophes and
Academic Life." Journal of Basic Writing 7.2 (1988):
91–98.

Some journals page each issue of an annual volume separately. (Each issue begins with page 1.) To cite articles from such journals, give both the volume number and the issue number (7.2 because 7 is the volume and 2 is the issue).

APA   Hashimoto, I. (1988). Pain and suffering: Apostrophes and
academic life. Journal of Basic Writing, 7(2), 91–98.

The volume number is underlined, and the issue number appears immediately after it, within parentheses.

32. INTERVIEW

MLA   Friedman, Randi. Telephone interview. 30 June 1992.

If you are citing a face-to-face interview, use Personal interview.

In APA style, a personal interview is considered personal correspondence and is not included in the References list. Cite the interview parenthetically in the text: Randi Friedman (personal communication, June 30, 1992).

Personal communications do not provide recoverable data, and so in the APA system, do not include personal communications in the References list. Personal communications can be cited only in the text of a paper: (R. Friedman, personal communication, June 30, 1992).

33. PUBLISHED AND UNPUBLISHED LETTERS

MLA   Lapidus, Jackie. Letter to her mother. 12 Nov. 1975. Between
Ourselves: Letters Between Mothers & Daughters. Ed.
Karen Payne. Boston: Houghton, 1983. 323–26.

MLA   Brown, Theodore. Letter to the author. 13 June 1988.

APA   Lapidus, J. (1983). Letter to her mother. In K. Payne (Ed.),
Between ourselves: Letters between mothers & daughters (pp.
323–326). Boston: Houghton Mifflin.

In the APA system, unpublished letters are considered personal communication and so do not appear in the References list. Personal communications are cited only in the text of a paper, as shown in item 32, Interview, above.

636

34. LECTURES, SPEECHES, AND ADDRESSES

MLA Kennedy, John Fitzgerald. Address. Greater Houston
Ministerial Association. Houston, Sept. 12, 1960.

APA Kennedy, J. F. (1960, September 12). Address. Speech
presented to the Greater Houston Ministerial Association,
Houston.

35. FILMS AND VIDEOTAPES

MLA Erendira. Writ. Gabriel Garcia Marquez. Dir. Ruy Guerra. With
Irene Pappas. Miramax, 1984.

APA Marquez, G. G. (Writer), & Guerra, R. (Director). (1984).
Erendira [Film]. New York: Miramax.

36. RECORDINGS

MLA Smetana, Bedřich. My Country. Cond. Karel Anserl. Czech
Philharmonic Orch. Vanguard, SV–9/10, 1975.

MLA Turner, Tina. "Show Some Respect." Private Dancer. Capitol,
ST–12330, 1983.

Begin the citation of a recording with either the composer, conductor,
or performer, depending on whom or what you are emphasizing in
your paper. Then give the information shown in the examples.

APA Smetana, B. (Composer). (1975). My country. Anserl
(Conductor). Czech Philharmonic Orch. (Recording No.
Sv–9/10). London: Vanguard Records.

APA Turner, T. (Performer). (1983). Show some respect. On Private
dancer [Album]. (Recording ST–12330). New York: Capitol
Records.

The word *On* is used to show where the selection came from.

37. LIVE PERFORMANCE

MLA The Real Thing. By Tom Stoppard. Dir. Mike Nichols. With
Jeremy Irons and Glenn Close. Plymouth Theatre, New York.
3 June 1984.

Begin with the title or a particular individual (for example, writer,
conductor, or director) if that is the emphasis in your paper.

APA Stoppard, T. (Author), Nichols, M. (Director), Irons, J.
(Performer), & Close G. (Performer). (1984, June 3). The
Real Thing [Live performance]. New York: Plymouth Theatre.

38. WORKS OF ART OR MUSICAL COMPOSITIONS

MLA   Cassatt, Mary. La Toilette. Art Institute of Chicago,
    Chicago.

MLA   Handel, George Frideric, Water Music.

Underline an opera, a ballet, or named instrumental music. Do not underline or put in quotation marks a composition identified only by form, number, and key.

APA   Cassatt, M. La toilette [Art work]. Chicago: Art Institute of
    Chicago.

APA   Handel, G. F. Water music [Musical composition].

39. RADIO AND TELEVISION PROGRAMS

MLA   The Little Sister. Writ. and dir. Jan Egleson. With Tracy
    Pollan and John Savage. Prod. Rebecca Eaton. American
    Playhouse. PBS. WGBH, Boston. 7 April 1986.

To cite radio or television programs, include all information shown in the example: the title of the program (underlined); the network; the local station and its city; and the date of the broadcast. For a series also supply the title of the specific episode (in quotation marks) before the title of the program and the title of the series (neither underlined nor in quotation marks).

APA   Egleson, J. (Writer and Director), Pollan T. (Performer),
    Savage, J. (Performer), & Eaton, R. (Producer). (1986,
    April 7). The little sister [Television program]. Boston:
    WGBH, PBS American Playhouse.

40. COMPUTER SOFTWARE

MLA   Microsoft Word. Vers. 5.0. Computer software. Microsoft,
    1989. MS—DOS 2.0 or higher or OS/2 1.0 512K, disk.

To cite computer software, give the writer of the program (if known), the title (underlined), a descriptive label, the distributor, and the year of publication. Add any other important information, such as the computer on which the program can be used, number of kilobytes or units of memory, the operating system, and the form of the program (cartridge, disk, or CD).

APA   Microsoft word. Vers. 5.0 [Computer software]. (1989).
    Microsoft. MS—DOS 2.0 or higher or OS/2 1.0. 512K, disk.

41. INFORMATION SERVICES: ERIC AND NEWSBANK

MLA   Breland, Hunter. Assessing Writing Skill. ERIC ED 286 920.

If the material in ERIC (Educational Resources Information Center) or any other information service was previously published, give the publishing information before the ERIC number.

MLA   Wenzell, Ron. "Businesses Prepare for a More Diverse Work
        Force." NewsBank, 1990. EMP 27:D12.

NewsBank provides microfiche copies of periodical articles on subjects such as politics, culture, finance, the environment, employment, and business. EMP refers to *Employment*, the subject group under which the Wenzell article is found.

APA   Breland, H. Assessing writing skill. (ERIC Document
        Reproduction Service No. ED 286 920).

If the material in ERIC (Educational Resources Information Center) or any other information service was previously published, give the publishing information before the ERIC number.

APA   Wenzell, R. (1990). Businesses prepare for a more diverse work
        force. (NewsBank Document Reproduction Service No. EMP
        27:D12).

42. MAPS AND CHARTS

MLA   The Caribbean & South America. Map. Falls Church: AAA, 1982.

APA   The Caribbean and South America [Map]. (1982). Falls Church,
        VA: American Automobile Association.

33e Using content endnotes or footnotes in MLA style

When you want to add observations to your paper that do not fit into your text, use endnotes or footnotes. In the MLA system, the page is headed *Notes* (in the APA system, the page is headed *Footnotes*). Charts 160 and 161 summarize formatting.

In MLA style, footnotes or endnotes serve two specific purposes. You can use them for commentary that does not fit into your paper but is still worth relating.

EXTRA EXERCISE D

Using the Directory for MLA and APA forms, give the number of the correct documentation models for the following works.

A. "Kids as Capital." Written by Jonathan Rauch. Published in *The Atlantic* in August 1989, pp. 56–61.

B. *The Nine Nations of North America.* Written by Joel Garreau. Published in Boston by Houghton Mifflin Company in 1981.

C. "Joe's Place." Written by Babette Fraser. Collected in *Her Work: Stories by Texas Women.* Edited by Lou Halsell Rodenberger. Published by Shearer Publishing in Bryan, Texas, in 1982.

D. "Looking for Luck in Bangkok." Poem written by Maxine Kumin. Published in *The New Yorker,* June 12, 1989, p. 42.

E. "Rhetorical Implications of School Discourse for Writing Placement." Written by Kathryn R. Fitzgerald. Published in *Journal of Basic Writing.* Spring 1988, Volume 7, No. 1, pp. 61–72.

F. "The Whitney Interprets Museums' Dreams." Written by Roberta Smith. Published in *The New York Times* on July 23, 1989, pp. 31 and 33.

G. *Her Work: Stories by Texas Women.* Edited and with an Introduction by Lou Halsell Rodenberger. Published by Shearer Publishing in Bryan, Texas, in 1982.

H. "The Priciest Pyre." No author given. Published in *Time,* July 31, 1989, p. 30.

I. *The Floating Opera.* Written by John Barth. Published in New York by Appleton-Century-Crofts in 1956.

J. *Literary San Francisco: A Pictorial History from Its Beginnings to the Present Day.* Written by Lawrence Ferlinghetti and Nancy J. Peters. Published by City Lights Books and Harper & Row, Publishers in San Francisco in 1980.

GUIDELINES FOR NOTE NUMBERS IN A PAPER

160

1. Put the number as near as possible to whatever you are referring to: at the end of a quotation, either direct or indirect, but after any punctuation that goes with whatever you are quoting.
2. Raise the number a little above the line of words; leave no extra space before the number.
3. Leave one space after the number except at the end of a sentence. Leave two spaces after the number before starting a new sentence.

EXAMPLE

We cannot know exactly why the Greeks included the myth of Icarus in their mythology or why Ovid wrote the myth down and included it in the Metamorphoses.[1] However, the

---

TEXT OF PAPER

Eudora Welty's literary biography, One Writer's Beginnings, shows us how both the inner world of self and the outer world of family and place form a writer's imagination.[1]

ENDNOTE WITH COMMENTARY

[1] Welty, who values her privacy, has resisted investigation of her life. However, at the age of 74, she chose to present her own autobiographical reflections in a series of lectures at Harvard University.

Also, you can use content notes for extensive lists of bibliographic information supporting points that you make. Otherwise, such information interrupts the flow of your paper.

TEXT OF PAPER

Barbara Randolph believes that enthusiasm is contagious (65).[2] Many psychologists have found that panic, fear, and rage spread more quickly in crowds than positive emotions do, however.

ENDNOTE WITH ADDITIONAL SOURCES

[2] Others agree with Randolph. See Thurman 21, 84, 155; Kelley 421–25; and Brookes 65–76.

33f Documenting sources with endnotes or footnotes in MLA style

You can put documentation information in notes either at the bottom of pages (footnotes) or on a separate page or pages following the end of your paper (endnotes). The content is the same, whether you use footnotes or endnotes. Unless your instructor requires footnotes, use endnotes because they are easier to manage when you are typing a paper (see Chart 161). For an example of a page of endnotes, see page 10 of the student research paper in Chapter 34.

GUIDELINES FOR FORMATTING ENDNOTES IN MLA STYLE 161

1. Center the word *Notes* two inches from the top of a separate page at the end of the paper. Do not put *Notes* in quotation marks or underline it.
2. Skip four lines before starting the note.
3. Indent the first line of each note five character spaces. Start other lines at the left margin.
4. Raise each note number a little above the words. Do not put a period after the number.
5. Leave one space between the note number and the first word.
6. Double space within *and* between endnotes.

EXAMPLE

Notes

[1] Publius Ovidius Naso. "Icarus and Daedalus," in Metamorphoses (Amsterdam: Wetstein and Smith, 1932), I, 257–260.

   [2] Pieter Brueghel, Landscape with the Fall of Icarus. Musée des Beaux Arts, Brussels, Belgium.

When a research paper refers to only one or two primary sources, some instructors permit students to use simplified documentation. A single note tells where quotations come from. If you do not give the full text of the primary source in the paper's appendix, give full publication information as in the following example:

TEACHING TIP

Using the information provided in Extra Exercise D, you can ask your students to provide a Works Cited or References list, following the models for the MLA or APA style provided in the text. Here is the MLA version:

Works Cited

Barth, John. *The Floating Opera*. New York: Appleton-Century-Crofts, 1956.

Ferlinghetti, Lawrence, and Nancy J. Peters. *Literary San Francisco: A Pictorial History from Its Beginnings to the Present Day*. San Francisco: City Lights Books and Harper & Row, 1980.

Fitzgerald, Kathryn R. "Rhetorical Implications of School Discourse for Writing Placement." *Journal of Basic Writing* 7.1 (Spring 1988): 61–72.

Fraser, Babette. "Joe's Place." *Her Work: Stories by Texas Women*. Ed. Lou Halsell Rodenberger. Bryan, TX: Shearer, 1982.

Garreau, Joel. *The Nine Nations of North America*. Boston: Houghton Mifflin, 1981.

Kumin, Maxine. "Looking for Luck in Bangkok." *New Yorker* 12 June 1989: 42.

"The Priciest Pyre." *Time* 31 July 1989: 30.

Rauch, Jonathan. "Kids as Capital." *Atlantic* Aug. 1989: 56–61.

Rodenberger, Lou Halsell, ed. *Her Work: Stories by Texas Women*. Bryan, TX: Shearer, 1982.

Smith, Roberta. "The Whitney Interprets Museums' Dreams." *New York Times* 23 July 1989: 31+.

Note forms for second and subsequent references in MLA style

After the first note for a source, shorten all further references to that source. If you cite only one work by an author, the author's last name and the page reference are enough:

⁸ Kelley, 731.

If you are citing more than one work by the same author, also include a shortened form of the title.

⁹ Eliot, <u>Mill</u>, 107.

¹⁰ Eliot, <u>Marner</u>, 24.

List of sources when note is used in MLA style

When you use MLA note style, you have two options for listing your sources at the end of a paper. You can list all sources consulted, not only the sources referred to or quoted from. If you do this, call the list Bibliography. Alternatively, you can list only the sources referred to or quoted from. If you do this, call the list Works Cited. Whatever your choice, MLA style calls for the format for Works Cited (see 33c- and 33d).

33g Using each discipline's documentation style

You can find MLA and APA documentation forms in section 33d for most of the sources that you use in academic papers. For an unusual source, consult the MLA or APA style manuals listed here.

The documentation styles of the various fields within the natural and technological sciences vary slightly from one another. Like MLA and APA, many other fields have manuals that explain the documentation style common to their professional journals. Many of these manuals are listed in this section. If you are writing in a field that does not have a style manual, refer to a journal in the field and imitate its documentation style.

In each course, ask your instructor what documentation style is required. If the choice is yours, use the style of your major field so that you can practice it, or follow the style of the subject of your course.

BIOLOGY

Council of Biology Editors Style Manual Committee. *CBE Style Manual.* 5th ed. Bethesda, MD: Council of Biology, 1983.

TEACHING TIP

Although the MLA style and the APA style are the most widely used systems of documentation, there are other style manuals in general use. They include *The Chicago Manual of Style,* 13th ed. (Chicago UP, 1982), and *Manual of Foreign Languages: For the Use of Librarians, Bibliographers, Research Workers, Editors, Translators, and Printers,* 4th ed. (George F. von Ostermann, Central, 1952). Since some disciplines have their own recommended style sheets, your students may find it helpful to know where to find the forms used in their various fields of study. For a list of such manuals, see the end of this chapter. For guidelines on Council of Biology Editors (CBE) style, see pages 724-25 in this book.

BACKGROUND

Additional professional style manuals include the following:

Geology: Suggestions to Authors of the Reports of the United States Geological Survey, 6th ed., Government Printing Office, 1978.

Law: A Uniform System of Citation, 14th ed., Harvard Law Review Association, 1986.

Medicine: International Steering Committee of Medical Editors, "Uniform Requirements for Manuscripts Submitted to Biomedical Journals," *Annals of Internal Medicine* 90 (Jan. 1979): 95–99.

Petroleum Geology: Bulletin of the American Association of Petroleum Geologists, AAPG, Tulsa, OK.

BIOMEDICINE

International Steering Committee of Medical Editors. "Uniform Requirements for Manuscripts Submitted to Biomedical Journals." *Annals of Internal Medicine* 90 (Jan. 1979): 95–99.

CHEMISTRY

American Chemical Society. *Handbook for Authors of Papers in American Chemical Society Publications.* Washington, DC: American Chemical Society, 1978.

ENGLISH, LANGUAGES, AND OTHER HUMANITIES

Modern Language Association. *MLA Handbook for Writers of Research Papers.* 3rd ed. New York: MLA, 1988.

LAW

Harvard Law Review. *A Uniform System of Citation.* 13th ed. Cambridge: Harvard Law Review Association, 1981.

MATHEMATICS

American Mathematical Society. *A Manual for Authors of Mathematical Papers.* 8th ed. Providence, RI: American Mathematical Society, 1984.

PHYSICS

American Institute of Physics. *Style Manual for Guidance in Preparation of Papers.* 3rd ed. New York: American Institute of Physics, 1978.

SOCIAL SCIENCES

American Psychological Association. *Publication Manual of the American Psychological Association.* 3rd ed. Washington: American Psychological Association. 1983.

34 Case Study: A Student Writing an MLA Research Paper

This chapter presents a case study of a student, Amy Brown, going through the processes of conducting research and writing a paper based on her findings. Section 34a narrates the processes. Section 34b shows Brown's final draft of her paper, along with commentary that draws attention to the paper's key elements. The commentary includes Process Notes that explain many of Brown's decisions during her writing process.

Amy Brown was given this assignment for a research paper:

Write a research paper on the general subject of "communication." The paper should run 1,800 to 2,000 words and should be based on a variety of sources. The final paper is due in five weeks. Interim deadlines for parts of the work will be announced. To complete this assignment, you need to engage in two interrelated processes: conducting research and writing a paper based on the research. Consult the *Simon & Schuster Handbook for Writers, Third Edition,* especially Chapter 32.

As you conduct your research, expect to establish a work schedule (32b), narrow the subject to a suitable topic (32d), determine your purpose and audience (32e), use a search strategy (32h), and keep a research log (32c) and take useful notes (32i). As you take notes, make sure that you record your information so that you can document your sources (Chapter 33) and avoid plagiarism (31a). As you write your paper based on your research, expect to engage in the writing process (32p through 32r, as well as all chapters in Part One).

34a Observing the processes of researching and writing a MLA-style research paper

Amy Brown faced many challenges as she worked on her assignment. Some decisions did not come easily, especially in the early stages of her research process. Brown expected the process to lead to a few puzzles and frustrations, and she resolved to remain patient with herself and the project.

Narrowing the subject of communication to a more **suitable topic** proved the most difficult challenge. Because the idea of unspoken messages among people interested her, Brown decided to concentrate on *nonverbal communication*. She used the term to start her research by compiling a list of **headings and key words** (32h) that she found in periodical indexes (32m) and her college library's catalog (32n). She located many words: *eye movements, gesture, sign language, body language, touch, expression, space perception, space and time,* and *territory.* Such a varied list confirmed what Brown had suspected: that nonverbal communication was too broad a subject for her paper. She thought she might write about expressions on people's faces when they use public transportation, but she realized that such a topic was too narrow because the library had almost no resources on it. At this point, Brown was getting discouraged and was tempted to switch to an entirely different aspect of communication, but she did not want to give up too soon. Brown wrote about her feelings and her current thinking in her **research log.** Doing this helped her think on paper and discover ideas. Her log also gave her a record of her thought processes in case something came up later that tied into her earlier thinking.

Deciding that more information would help her think of a suitable topic, Brown browsed through a psychology textbook and interviewed a psychology professor. One book that the professor recommended was especially interesting to Brown: *The Hidden Dimension,* by Edward T. Hall, which talks about personal space as a major factor in nonverbal communication. Personal space concerns the amount of physical distance people expect to maintain between themselves and other people during social interaction. When Brown read Hall, she recalled an experience she had had when a cousin had come for a weekend and had stayed three weeks while looking for a job. Brown's family lives in a small apartment, and although Brown likes her cousin, she felt that she had lost her "space" and she became cranky with her cousin. Brown knew that the crowding she had felt was not directly related to Hall's concept of personal space, but the idea of space as a part of communication intrigued her.

Hall calls the study of personal space *proxemics*. Brown assumed it was a key word and went to the library to look for books and articles. She drew several blanks. Nowhere could she find the term *proxemics*—not in the *Readers' Guide to Periodical Literature*, in any encyclopedia, or in the library's catalog. She then looked up the word in a dictionary, and the closest she could get was the word *proximity*. She looked up *proximity* and found nothing. She began to suspect that Hall had coined *proxemics*. Brown felt she was running out of time, and she considered switching to a different topic. But then she had a breakthrough. She tried a specialized index (see 32m-2), and the *Social Science Index* listed *proxemics* with the cross-reference "See personal space." She found numerous articles exploring aspects of personal space. Brown had "broken the code" and was very pleased. In her research log she wrote about her discovery, including all the information that she might need to find it again easily when it was time to take notes.

The key term *personal space* produced an important title in the library's catalog: *Personal Space,* by Robert Sommer. She also looked under *body language,* a term she had seen in the titles of a few articles listed in the *Social Science Index*. She found the book *Body Language,* by Julius Fast. At the back of Fast's book was a bibliography of key references. In it Hall's book and Sommer's book were listed, a fact that helped her confirm that Hall and Sommer were **authoritative, reliable sources,** two of the criteria used to evaluate sources (see 5e and 32g). Brown now knew that the books and articles she had found offered her a sufficient number of sources for her research.

Next, Brown was ready to formulate a **research question,** which would further narrow her topic. Brown was most interested in Hall's discussion of differing standards for personal space in different cultures. Brown brainstormed research questions. "What is personal space?" was too broad and lacked focus. "How do standards for personal space differ between North Americans and Arabs?" was too narrow for the resources in her college library. Then Brown settled on "How do standards for personal space differ among cultures?" (For a flow chart that shows Brown's narrowing process, see 32d.)

Now Brown was ready to think about her purpose and audience (see 1b, 1c, and 32e). For an audience, she chose a **general reader**—rather than a specialized reader—because she wanted to assume that the audience would know little about the topic of personal space. Deciding on a purpose proved more complicated. Brown started by wanting to write with a persuasive purpose, but she soon switched to an informative purpose. At first, she wanted to argue that people from different countries have serious trouble with cross-cultural communication unless they are aware of varying expectations concerning personal space. While reading and taking notes to answer her research question, however, Brown realized that she could not explain basic cross-cultural concepts *and* argue a position within the time and length limits of the assignment. She settled on an informative purpose.

Brown's research process now shifted to finding additional sources and taking notes. Earlier Brown had used a search strategy (32h) to help her think of a suitable topic. Now she used the search strategy again, this time to take notes on the sources she had found before and to find additional sources that would permit her to give a full picture in her paper.

Brown now had a working bibliography. Using MLA documentation style (see 33b-1, 33c-1, and 33d), she had made bibliography cards (see 33a) on three key books, fifteen articles, and two textbooks. It was time to read closely and take notes. Brown carefully headed each index card with the author of the source. Making sure to avoid plagiarism, she paraphrased, summarized, and copied quotations according to the techniques described in Chapter 31 of this handbook. Whenever she used an author's exact words, Brown wrote oversized quotation marks so that she would be sure to see them and thereby avoid plagiarism when using her notes.

While taking notes, Brown realized that some of the articles she had found were not as useful as she had thought. She rejected a few sources that were duplications of what she already had. Later, as she was writing her paper, she dropped a few sources that were related to personal space but not to her paper (for example, the duration of eye contact in different cultures). Her final version uses fourteen references.

In organizing her paper, Brown looked through her notes and saw that they fell into two piles: standards for personal space in North America and standards in other countries. She tried to outline the material and quickly realized that she would need to start with a definition of personal space. Going back through her cards, she created a third pile for definitions.

Composing her thesis statement was next. Brown wanted her thesis statement to be the last sentence of her introductory paragraph. She drafted a preliminary thesis statement to use as she wrote the first full draft of her paper. Later she revised the thesis statement (for a description of the evolution of her final thesis statement, see 32p). Here is an early draft of Brown's introductory paragraph; the last sentence contains the preliminary thesis statement.

> People know unconsciously what close is when
> they stand near other people during conversations.
> This relates to the concept of personal space—the
> amount of physical distance people expect during
> social interaction. Standards for personal space
> vary among cultures.

Brown knew that this early draft was flawed. It lacked interest, the word "this" was a vague pronoun reference, and the thesis statement did not give a full picture of the paper. She showed her draft to three friends and asked them to react. One friend, a major in psychology, had a newspaper clipping in his files that Brown thought would be a good source to draw on for introducing her essay. For Brown's final draft, see page 1 of her paper in 34b.

In writing her paper, Brown composed three drafts. In addition to rewriting her opening paragraph, Brown made other improvements as she revised. Her first draft lacked clear signals to readers about the material's organization. In her second draft, Brown used topic sentences to start many of her paragraphs, to help readers follow the sequence of presentation that she used. Brown felt that first draft relied too much on quotations. In her second draft, Brown used paraphrase (see 31d) and summary (see 31e). She also used quotations (see 31c), but only when an author's language carried some special significance (see, for example, Brown's third and fourth paragraphs) or helped establish the credibility of the information. In her third draft, Brown polished her word choice, corrected her grammar and spelling, and reworked her conclusion. Brown decided that the conclusion should be a "call to action" (see 4g), urging people to become sensitive to the concept of personal space and thereby avoid intercultural misunderstandings. Brown's first draft of a concluding paragraph was only one sentence long, so she knew it needed work.

Brown's final draft appears in 34b. Each page of the paper is accompanied by commentary that explains elements of the paper and that includes Process Notes that narrate Brown's thinking and writing processes.

QUOTATION ABOUT WRITING

A title page is like a tray of hors d'oeuvres; it suggests what is to come.

—Susie R. Rambo

BACKGROUND

A direct title tells exactly what the essay will be about. An indirect title hints at the essay's topic. In either case, it stands alone, not as part of the body of the essay. (See 3c-2.)

34b Analyzing an MLA-style research paper

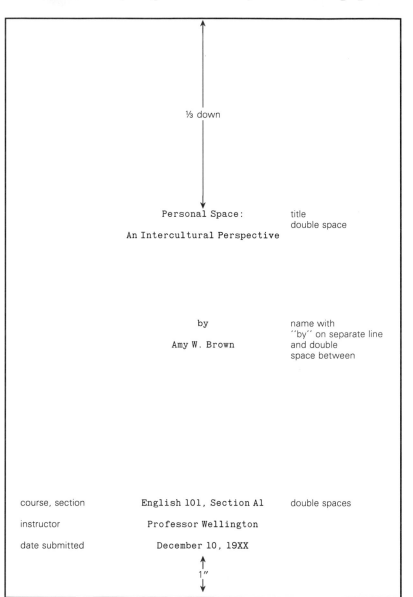

⅓ down

Personal Space: title
      double space
An Intercultural Perspective

by   name with
      "by" on separate line
Amy W. Brown   and double
      space between

course, section   English 101, Section A1   double spaces

instructor   Professor Wellington

date submitted   December 10, 19XX

1″

Cover page. If your instructor requires a cover page, use the format and types of information shown on the opposite page. Then on page 1 of your paper, repeat only the paper's title. A cover page is needed when an outline is included with the paper, as is the case with Amy Brown's paper. The outline appears on the next two pages.

First page. If your instructor does not require a cover page, follow the style shown below for heading your first page (MLA format). If you do use a cover page, use the format on the first page of Amy Brown's paper, page 654.

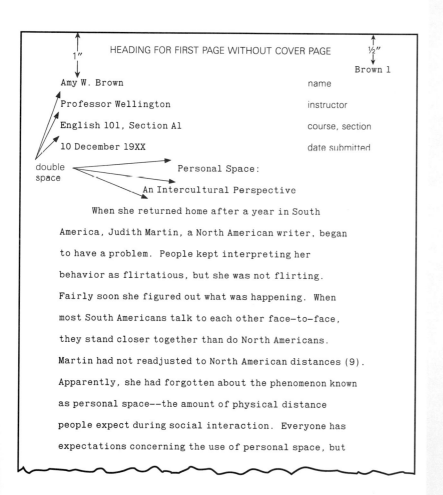

HEADING FOR FIRST PAGE WITHOUT COVER PAGE

1"

½"

Brown 1

Amy W. Brown — name

Professor Wellington — instructor

English 101, Section A1 — course, section

10 December 19XX — date submitted

double space

Personal Space:

An Intercultural Perspective

When she returned home after a year in South America, Judith Martin, a North American writer, began to have a problem. People kept interpreting her behavior as flirtatious, but she was not flirting. Fairly soon she figured out what was happening. When most South Americans talk to each other face-to-face, they stand closer together than do North Americans. Martin had not readjusted to North American distances (9). Apparently, she had forgotten about the phenomenon known as personal space--the amount of physical distance people expect during social interaction. Everyone has expectations concerning the use of personal space, but

1″

½″

Brown i

Outline

<u>Thesis</u> <u>statement</u>: Everyone has expectations concerning the use of personal space, but accepted distances for that space are determined by each person's culture.

I. Observations about personal space began about twenty years ago.

   A. Most people are unaware that interpersonal distances exist.

   B. Personal space depends on invisible boundaries.

   C. Personal space moves with people as they interact.

   D. People do not like anyone to trespass on their personal space.

II. Research reveals North Americans' expectations for personal space.

   A. Hall indentifies four zones for personal space.

   B. Subcultures help determine expectations for personal space.

   C. Age affects how people use personal space.

   D. Gender influences people's use of personal space.

III. Research reveals standards for personal space in countries other than the United States.

   A. Conversational distances vary in different cultures.

Brown ii

1. Western Europeans use fingertip-to-shoulder
   distance.

2. Eastern Europeans use wrist-to-shoulder
   distance.

3. Mediterraneans use elbow-to-shoulder
   distance.

B. Amounts of touching vary in different cultures.

C. Arabs prefer close interpersonal distances.

D. Japanese do not prefer close interpersonal
   distances.

Outline. Brown's instructor required a formal outline in the final draft of each student's research paper. To format her outline, Brown referred to sections 2n and 32q in this handbook. She numbered the pages with lower-case roman numerals to indicate that the outline comes before page 1 of the actual paper. She placed the name/page information in the upper right corner, and centered the word "Outline," using a capital letter to start it. She underlined the words "thesis statement" and placed them at the left margin. The thesis statement matches the last sentence of the first paragraph of her paper.

Brown used a **sentence outline,** not a topic outline (see 2n). To reflect the organization of her paper, she divided the material in the outline into three major parts, numbered I, II, and III. Each item in the three major parts she numbered A, B, etc. Part III. *A* needed more detail, so the added items are numbered 1, 2, and 3. The items in the outline are in parallel form: Each starts with a subject followed by a verb in the present tense°.

BACKGROUND

A formal outline (see 2n) follows conventions concerning content and format that ensure that relationships among ideas are clear and that the content is orderly. If it is a topic outline, each item in it is only a word or a phrase. If it is a sentence outline, each item is a complete sentence.

1   **A**

B

Personal Space:

An Intercultural Perspective

1   When she returned home after a year in South
America, Judith Martin, a North American writer, began
to have a problem. People kept interpreting her
behavior as flirtatious, but she was not flirting.
Fairly soon she figured out what was happening. When
most South Americans talk to each other face-to-face,
they stand closer together than do North Americans.
Martin had not readjusted to North American distances (9).
Apparently, she had forgotten about the phenomenon known
as personal space--the amount of physical distance
people expect during social interaction. Everyone has
expectations concerning the use of personal space, but
accepted distances for that space are determined by each
person's culture.   **C**

D

2   Observations about personal space began about
twenty years ago. Anthropologist Edward T. Hall was a
pioneer in the field. He became very interested in how
interpersonal distances affected communication between
people. In his aptly titled book <u>The Hidden Dimension</u>,
Hall coined the word "proxemics" to describe people's
use of space as a means of communication (1). As Hall's
book title indicates, most people are unaware that
interpersonal distances exist and contribute to people's
reactions to one another (109).   **E**

F

COMMENTARY

General Note: Amy Brown uses MLA Style° for the format of this paper. She also uses MLA style for parenthetical references (see 33b-1) and Works Cited (see 33c-1 and 33d).

A. **Page number.** Because Brown used a cover page, she used only the number 1 in the upper right-hand corner a half inch from the top. On the rest of the pages, she used the page number preceded by her last name.

B. **Title.** Brown's title prepares readers for her paper by giving the paper's major term (personal space) and the focus of her paper's discussion (more than one culture). ❖ PROCESS NOTE: In an earlier draft, Brown's title was "Proxemics: An Intercultural Perspective on the Need for Space." She rejected it because "space" was too general and "proxemics" was too technical. She then tried "Being Close: An Intercultural Perspective," but she revised the first half to avoid multiple meanings. ❖

C. **Introductory device.** Brown uses an anecdote. (For introductory devices, see 4g.) She wanted it to serve four functions: to make the abstract concept of personal space concrete and familiar; to tie into the paper's title; to lead into the thesis statement; and to capture readers' interest. ❖ PROCESS NOTE: For an early draft of Brown's introductory paragraph, see 34a. ❖

D. **Thesis statement.** The last sentence of Brown's introductory paragraph is her thesis statement. Emerging from the paper's title and opening anecdote, the thesis prepares readers for what to expect. ❖ PROCESS NOTE: To see the evolution of Brown's thesis statement, see 32k. ❖

E. **Evaluation of source.** Brown establishes Hall as an expert by identifying him as an anthropologist and as a pioneer on the subject of personal space. ❖ PROCESS NOTE: To see how Brown was able to confirm that Hall was an authoritative, reliable source, read 34a. ❖

F. **Parenthetical reference to author and book named in the text.** Brown uses two sources by Edward T. Hall. To keep them separate, she mentions Hall's name and the title of the work here. Her two parenthetical references include only the page numbers. The references are inserted before the periods that end the sentences. Brown uses quotation marks for the coined word "proxemics." (The other work by Hall is cited in paragraph 11.)

Brown 2

3   Personal space depends on invisible boundaries.   **G**
Those boundaries move with people as they interact.
Personal space gets larger or smaller depending on the   **H**
circumstances of the social interaction at any moment
(Fisher, Bell, and Baum 149). Robert Sommer, an   **I**
environmental psychologist, uses literary and visual
analogies to describe personal space:

> Like the porcupines in Schopenhauer's fable,   **J**
> people like to be close enough to obtain warmth
> and comradeship but far enough away to avoid
> pricking one another. Personal space . . . has
> been likened to a snail shell, a soap bubble,
> an aura, a "breathing room." (26)

4   People do not like anyone to trespass on their
personal space. As Worchel and Cooper explain, invasions
of personal space elicit negative reactions that range
from mild discomfort to retaliation to walking out on the
situation (539-40). The poet W. H. Auden threatens a
uniquely negative reaction to intrusions in his space.   **K**

> Some thirty inches from my nose
> The frontier of my person goes
> And all the untilled air between
> Is private pagus or demesne
> Stranger, unless with bedrooms eyes
> I beckon you to fraternize
> Beware of rudely crossing it
> I have no gun but I can spit.
>
>   (qtd. in Worchel and Cooper 539)   **L**

BACKGROUND

An ellipsis is a set of three spaced dots used to show that some of the original writer's words have been left out of a quotation. If an omission occurs at the beginning of a quotation, an ellipsis is not needed to show the omission. Also, an ellipsis is not necessary at the end of a quotation as long as it ends in a complete sentence. (See 29d.)

TEACHING TIP

Students sometimes think they are the only readers who skip over long quotations. You may want to assure them that they are not alone. The implication for students as writers, of course, is that when they feel they must include a lengthy quotation, in order to present a complicated idea in detail, for example, it is helpful to prepare the reader by explaining its importance. To make it as brief as possible, all irrelevant material should be deleted so that every word counts.

COMMENTARY

G. **Topic sentence.** Brown uses a topic sentence (see 4a) to start many of her paragraphs. ❖ PROCESS NOTE: Brown did not want to plagiarize. She thought carefully about what she could say in her paper without citing a source. Because she had read a great deal and had categorized her notes into logical units, she decided that her topic sentences—which she usually put at the beginning of her paragraphs—were her own and did not need citations. ❖

H. **Paraphase of original source.** ❖ PROCESS NOTE: In an earlier draft, Brown quoted the material and worked it into her prose. In her final draft, she uses a paraphase because she does not want too many quotations. ❖

I. **Parenthetical reference to author not named in the text.** The author and page of the source are added in parentheses.

J. **A long quotation.** A quotation of more than four typewritten lines is set off from the rest of the text. Brown introduces it with a colon because she has written a complete sentence (compare with paragraph 13). She indents the material 10 spaces and does not paragraph indent the first line. In the fourth line, Brown uses a three-dot ellipsis where she omitted words (the full original source is shown in 32i). The parenthetical page reference is placed after the punctuation that ends the quotation. The words "breathing room" are in quotation marks because they appear this way in the original source.

K. **Use of an unexpected source.** ❖ PROCESS NOTE: Brown realized that W. H. Auden is not a likely expert on personal space. She uses his poem nonetheless because she discovered it reprinted in a discussion of personal space by social psychologists, so she felt its content had credibility for her paper. She also decided that it would suit her audience well, given that the paper was for her freshman English class. ❖

L. **Parenthetical reference for an indirect source.** Brown did not find the poem in its original source (see comment K above). She relied on the indirect source. In her parenthetical reference, she used *qtd. in*, the abbreviation for "quoted in," to make it clear that the quoted words are Auden's and that they are to be found on page 539 of Worchel and Cooper's book. The Works Cited entry is for Worchel and Cooper's book.

Brown 3

5   Research provides information about the distances that North Americans prefer when interacting. The pioneering work was done by Hall. He observed the behavior of a group of middle–class adults in business and professions in the northeastern United States. He saw four zones of personal space; they are summarized and explained in Table 1.

M

Table 1

Hall's "Distance Zones"[a]

N

	Intimate	Personal	Social	Public
Close	0 to 6″	$1\frac{1}{2}'$ to $2\frac{1}{2}'$	4′ to 7′	12′ to 25′
Far	6″ to $1\frac{1}{2}'$	$2\frac{1}{2}'$ to 4′	7′ to 12′	25′ +

Source: Discussion in Hall, Hidden 110–20; also Henley 32–33; Fisher, Bell, and Baum 153.

O

[a] Selected illustrations of each zone are: Close Intimate: lovers, children with parents; Far Intimate: strangers in crowds; Close Personal: husband and wife talking on the street; Far Personal: friends talking on the street; Close Social: boss and subordinate at a meeting; Far Social: receptionist and people in a waiting room; Close Public: teacher and students in a classroom; Far Public: actors or public speakers with audiences.

P

COMMENTARY

M. **Word choice.** ✤ PROCESS NOTE: Before doing research for her paper, Brown had assumed that "American" meant someone from the United States. She discovered, however, that people from South America consider themselves Americans. Brown therefore uses "North American" to refer to people in the United States. ✤

N. **Table.** A table is an excellent way to summarize complex information that involves numbers and/or repeated categories. In MLA style°, a table should be placed as close as possible to the paragraph in which it is first mentioned. If a table cannot fit in the space remaining on the page, it can be placed on the next page after the end of the first paragraph on that page. Some instructors permit students to put tables on a separate page, called Appendix, at the end of the paper, but before "Notes" (if any) and "Works Cited." Brown uses the format described in the *MLA Handbook for Writers of Research Papers:* table number and title at the left margin, a lettered—not numbered—footnote, and source information immediately below the data, before the footnote. In MLA style, footnotes in tables are signaled with lower-case letters, and endnotes or footnotes are signaled by numbers (see paragraphs 11 and 13). ✤ PROCESS NOTE: In an early draft, Brown wrote sentences to present the information now in this table. She did not think of using a table until she showed her early draft to a friend who said that the material was hard to follow and boring. She then tried to condense the material, and as she was writing she thought a table would be a concise, clear, more lively way to present numerical information. ✤

O. **Source identification.** Because Brown uses two works by Hall, she includes a shortened title *(Hidden)* here so that readers will know which Hall work she is referring to. She uses semicolons to separate each item in a series of multiple references. The other Hall work is cited in paragraph 11.

P. **Choice of examples.** ✤ PROCESS NOTE: In writing the footnote to the table, Brown had many choices of illustrations for each zone. She chose the ones that seemed to her to be effective examples. ✤

Brown 4

6   Researchers working with Hall's data found that accepted interpersonal distances in the United States also depend on other factors. For example, subcultures help determine expectations concerning personal space. Fisher, Bell, and Baum report that groups of Hispanic-Americans generally interact more closely within their subculture than Anglo-Americans do within theirs. They further explain that "in general subcultural groups tend to interact at closer distances with members of their own subculture than with nonmembers" (158).

Q

R

7   Age also affects how people use personal space. Worchel and Cooper report that North American children seem unaware of boundaries for personal space until the age of four or five. As the children get older they become more aware of standards for personal space. By the time they reach puberty, they have completely adpated to their culture's standards for interpersonal distances (535-37).

R

S

8   Gender also influences people's use of personal space. For example, North American males' most negative reaction is reserved for anyone who enters their personal space directly in front of them. Females, on the other hand, feel most negative about approaches from the side. Also, females have smaller interpersonal distances than do males, although pairs of the same sex communicate across larger spaces than do pairs of males

T

COMMENTARY

Q. **Quotation within sentence.** Brown fits a quotation into her prose, using quotation marks to avoid plagiarism. ❖ PROCESS NOTE: Brown used a quotation because she felt that the material comparing one subgroup with another might be sensitive. She wanted her readers to have particular confidence in her presentation of the information. This is Brown's third quotation in her paper; the other two (paragraphs 3 and 4) are long quotations, which are displayed. This is a short run-in quotation, which Brown felt covered the material well and offered a change of pace in ways to integrate quotations. ❖

R. **Placement of parenthetical references.** Parenthetical references go immediately after a quotation or after a block of information from a source, as long as the material is not interrupted by the writer's own thinking.

S. **Word choice.** Brown uses *gender*, not *sex* here. ❖ PROCESS NOTE: In an early draft, Brown used "sex," not "gender." As she was reading journal articles, she saw that *gender* is used in discussions of comparisons between men and women. The psychology professor she had interviewed also used *gender*. She also checked Charles G. Morris's *Psychology: An Introduction*, a source she cites later in this paper. When she looked up *sex* in the index to that book, she found "Sex differences. See Gender differences." She decided to use *gender*, in her topic sentence and later in paragraph 8. ❖

T. **Paraphrase of an original source.** Brown uses a paraphase here. ❖ PROCESS NOTE: As Brown paraphrased her source, she resequenced it slightly to fit the logic of her paper. This practice is permitted only if the rearrangement does not distort the meaning of the original. Here is the original, from Worchel and Cooper, page 535 (the ellipsis indicates intervening material): "One of the most consistent findings in the personal space literature is that females have smaller personal spaces than males. . . . Further, smaller personal-space zones are found between male–female pairs than between same-sex pairs. . . . Males responded most negatively to frontal invasions of their space, whereas females reacted most negatively to invasions from the side." ❖

Brown 5

U

and females (Worchel and Cooper 535). The gender factor shifts, however, in high-density situations such as crowded subways or elevators in the United States. As Maines observes, when people have some choice about where they stand or sit in crowded settings, they gravitate to people of the same sex (100).

9   Expectations concerning personal space exist in all cultures, but such expectations vary greatly from culture to culture (Fast 29). Research reveals standards for personal space in countries other than the United States. For example, conversational distances vary between people from different countries, according to Desmond Morris, a British zoologist. He notes that when people from Western Europe stand on the street and talk, the space between them is the distance it would take one person's fingertip to reach the other's shoulder. People from Eastern Europe converse at a wrist-to-shoulder distance. People from the Mediterranean, however, prefer elbow-to-shoulder distance (131).

V

10   Permitted amounts of touching also illustrate intercultural differences in standards for personal space. Touching while conversing differs in Germany, Italy, and the United States, reports Robert Shuter, a communications specialist. His research shows that Germans and North Americans behave alike in that males stand farther apart and touch less when talking than do male-female pairs or female pairs. The opposite is

W

COMMENTARY

U. **Use of sources.** ✤ PROCESS NOTE: Brown wondered whether she needed a parenthetical reference three times (after the second, third, and fourth sentences in paragraph 8). Her instructor explained that the parenthetical reference is required only once, as long as the information does not spill over to another paragraph and the material is not interrupted by information from another source or by a comment of the writer. ✤

V. **Summary of original source.** Brown uses a summary to condense a source. ✤ PROCESS NOTE: Brown liked the informal tone of Morris's material, but she did not quote it so that she could avoid using too many quotations. ✤ Here is the original (which uses British, not American, rules for quotation marks).

> Unfortunately, different countries have different ideas about exactly how close is close. It is easy enough to test your own 'space reaction': when you are talking to someone in the street or in any open space, reach out with your arm and see where the nearest point on his body comes. If you hail from western Europe, you will find that he is at roughly fingertip distance from you. In other words, as you reach out, your fingertips will just about make contact with his shoulder. If you come from eastern Europe you will find you are standing at 'wrist distance'. If you come from the Mediterranean region you will find that you are much closer to your companion, at little more than 'elbow distance'.

W. **Transferring information from note to paper.** In paragraph 10, Brown uses the summary from her note card.

> Shuter, p. 305
> *Intercultural differences*
> Summary:
> Germans and N. Americans behave alike in that males stand farther apart and touch less while talking than do male-female pairs. The opposite is true in Italy, where males interact more closely and touch more during conversations than do male-female pairs or female pairs. Thus, Italian males expect to use personal space as females do in Germany and the United States.

Brown 6

true in Italy, where males interact more closely and touch more during conversations than do male—female pairs of female pairs. Shuter concludes that Italian males expect to use personal space as females do in Germany and the United States (305). In another experiment, adults were asked to put dolls in position for what was called "comfortable interaction." People from Italy and Greece placed the dolls closer together than did people from Sweden, Scotland, or the United States. Also, in doctors' waiting rooms, Australians were less likely to start conversations with strangers than were Indonesians (Worchel and Cooper 536).

11 Arabs prefer close interpersonal distances. Polhemus explains that Arab students move close together more often, confront each other directly, and touch each other more frequently when talking than do American students (21). In an interview called "Learning the Arabs' Silent Language," Hall notes that Arabs know the practicality of close conversational distances: "If you are interested in something, your pupils dilate; if I say something you don't like, they tend to contract" (47).[1] Hall explains that conversational distances of two feet——preferred by many Arabs——permit people to see each other's pupils better than does the typical North American distance of five feet (48).

X

Y

Z

COMMENTARY

X. **Word choice.** ❖ PROCESS NOTE: In an early draft, Brown used the word *explains* in most places where she presented information from a source. When she revised, Brown wanted to vary her word choice. She looked at Chart 150 in section 31f to get ideas for different words. In her final draft Brown uses forms of these words: *explain, note, report, conclude,* and *observe.* ❖

Y. **Quotation from an interview.** Brown quotes what Hall said at an interview. She can be sure of the exact wording because the interview is reported in a respected magazine. In general, professional writers check the wording of a quotation before they use it in print. When material is even slightly controversial, professional writers usually also reconfirm all paraphrases and summaries with the source. Some of the most highly respected publications have a staff whose sole job is to verify information and reconfirm quoted material. Some instructors require students to follow these practices. Also, some instructors prefer that material from an interview be paraphased or summarized, unless a student has tape-recorded an interview. ❖ PROCESS NOTE: While reading her sources, Brown repeatedly was impressed with the language of Edward T. Hall. She kept feeling that her paraphrases and summaries could not possibly do justice to Hall. But she resisted the temptation to quote him extensively. She was aware that a student research paper, in one sense, is an exercise in which a student is expected to demonstrate the ability to paraphrase and summarize well. She quoted Hall here and in paragraph 13 because he is a major reference for her paper and Brown felt that this material helped establish the credibility of her information. ❖

Z. **Comment in an endnote.** Brown uses an endnote to comment on her information. The number for the endnote is raised slightly above the line after the period ending the sentence. The endnote appears on Brown's page 9. ❖ PROCESS NOTE: Brown uses notes for information that she considers particularly interesting but that does not fit neatly into the logic of her paragraphs. Endnotes are placed at the end of a paper, on a separate sheet of paper labeled "Notes." ❖

Brown 7

12   Japanese do not prefer close interpersonal distances. Because the island of Japan is quite small for its population of about 120 million, public places are often very crowded. To cope, the people remain formal and aloof even when in very close proximity to one another (Fast 38).

13   People can easily be misunderstood if they are insensitive to how people from another culture use personal space. Clearly, what is considered obnoxious in one culture might be considered polite in another (Fisher, Bell, and Baum 167). As Hall says, virtually everything people are and do

> is associated with the experience of
> space. . . . Therefore, people from different
> cultures, when interpreting each other's
> behavior, often misinterpret the relationship,
> the activity, or the emotions. This leads to
> alienation in encounters or distorted
> communications. (Hidden 171)

In the next few years, more studies will be undertaken to uncover information about cultural differences in matters such as personal space (Davis and Skupien, xix). The information will be important. International understanding cannot thrive unless people recognize and accept such disparities. Charles G. Morris, a professor of psychology, explains that this information is important because without it people from different countries might misunderstand each other. He

AA

BB

CC

COMMENTARY

AA. **Concluding device.** In paragraphs 13 and 14, Brown concludes her paper with a call for action (for concluding devices, see 4g). ✤ PROCESS NOTE: In early drafts, Brown's concluding paragraph was quite long. In her final draft, Brown divided it into two paragraphs and added a relevant quotation. ✤ (See also Comment DD.)

BB. **Combined quotation from two paragraphs in original sources.** Brown combines into one quotation material from two paragraphs in Hall. She needs no punctuation to lead into the quotation (compare with colon used before next quotation) because her lead-in is an incomplete sentence. She uses a four-dot ellipsis to show that the quotation is taken from two paragraphs. Here is the original source (Hall, *Hidden* 171):

> This book emphasizes that virtually everything that man is and does is associated with the experience of space. Man's sense of space is a synthesis of many sensory inputs: visual, auditory, kinesthetic, olfactory, and thermal. Not only does each of these constitute a complex system—as, for example, the dozen different ways of experiencing depth visually—but each is molded and patterned by culture. Hence, there is no alternative to accepting the fact that people reared in different cultures live in different sensory worlds.
>
> We learn from the study of culture that the patterning of perceptual worlds is a function not only of culture but of *relationship, activity,* and *emotion.* Therefore, people from different cultures, when interpreting each other's behavior, often misinterpret the relationship, the activity, or the emotions. This leads to alienation in encounters or distorted communications.

CC. **Paraphrase of original source and using same last names.** ✤ PROCESS NOTE: In an early draft, Brown used a displayed quotation from Morris. When she revised, she decided to paraphrase so that she would not have too many quotations in her paper. Brown also had to accommodate two alike names: Desmond Morris, and Charles G. Morris. She differentiated by identifying the profession of each (Desmond Morris is identified in paragraph 9) and by using first and last names for each. ✤

Brown 8

imagines what might happen at a business meeting between North Americans and Arabs. The North American is most comfortable at a business conference when interpersonal distances are about three or four feet. In contrast, the Arab prefers less distance.[2] If the American backs away from the Arab, the American is considered cold and the Arab is considered pushy (Morris 516). All that is really going on is that each person is behaving according to cultural customs.

14   As international travel and commerce increase,   **DD** intercultural contact is becoming commonplace. Soon, perhaps, cultural variations in expectations for personal space will be as familiar to everyone as are cultural variations in food and dress. Until then, people need to make a special effort to learn one another's expectations concerning personal space. Once people are sensitive to such matters, they can stop themselves from taking the wrong step: either away from or toward a person from another culture.

COMMENTARY

DD. **Revising a concluding paragraph.** ❖ PROCESS NOTE: Brown rewrote her paragraph 14 almost as many times as she did her introductory paragraph. She wanted to get some punch into the ending. After many revisions, she wrote a last sentence that delivered the impact she was searching for. She also consulted Chart 28 in section 4g to remind herself what to avoid in conclusions. This helped her decide to get rid of the phrase "sort of discussed in this paper." The idea of using steps as a metaphor came to her nearly at the last minute, and she quickly worked it into her final draft. Here is a very early draft of paragraph 14. ❖

> Contact between cultures is happening more frequently. After all, international travel and commerce increase daily. It is urgent, therefore, that everyone knows that there are lots of variations among cultures in personal space. That means there are more differences than those in food and dress. Researchers' observations of the sort discussed in this paper help people understand more about the wide variety of expectations concerning proper amounts of interpersonal closeness and distance.

TEACHING TIP

So that students realize that not all research papers include endnotes, you may want to point out to them that endnotes are a convenient way to include information that makes an interesting addition to the discussion but is not essential to it. They may provide more detail than the average reader is interested in learning, or they may explain background information that enhances the subject but does not bear directly on it.

1″

½″
Brown 9

Notes   **EE**

[1] This might explain why some Arab leaders wear sunglasses indoors.

[2] Both Charles G. Morris and Edward T. Hall agree   **FF**
that North Americans prefer larger conversational distances than do Arabs. They do not, however, seem to agree on the precise distances. Morris says the distance is three to four feet. Hall says five feet. These differences do not detract, however, from the central point concerning the contrasts in cultural preferences.

COMMENTARY

EE. **Endnotes.** On a separate numbered page headed "Notes," Brown provides commentary that does not fit into the text of her paper. Notes in MLA style comment upon, explain, or clarify material written in the text. Each note starts with a number raised a half line and indented five spaces, paragraph style. Double spacing is used within and between all notes. The format of the page is the same as for other pages: the name/page line is one-half inch from the top edge of the page, in the right-hand corner. The word *Notes*, with the first letter capitalized, is centered one inch from the top edge of the paper.

FF. **Comments in endnotes.** ❖ PROCESS NOTE: Brown used notes to include this material. She felt that it was interesting information, but it did not fit into the paper itself. In her first note, Brown draws on her knowledge of newspaper photographs of some Arab leaders. Brown uses the second note to present a discrepancy in the information she found during her research process. She wanted to be sure not to gloss over this information, but she could not fit it into the body of her paper. ❖ In endnote 2, Brown uses the full names of the two people she mentions because she wants to differentiate between the two sources that have Morris as a last name. She uses the full name of Charles G. Morris, and to maintain parallelism°, she uses Hall's first name and middle initial.

TEACHING TIP

Even when a writer is very experienced in using a particular documentation system, it is helpful to have a handbook nearby for ready reference. For novice writers it is even more important not to work entirely from memory when it comes to making a Works Cited (MLA style) or References (APA style) list. Unusual citations will always appear, making it necessary to find a rarely used form, and because each period, comma, and space is stipulated, even common citations need scrupulous checking.

You may want to suggest to students that when they think they have finished their lists, they should make a final comparison of their forms with those found in this handbook (section 33d) to discover discrepancies that might otherwise be missed. Having students exchange lists and serve as editors for each other often helps to focus the minutiae of documentation more clearly. In these ways students can be sure that they are adhering precisely to the mandates of the selected system of documentation.

Brown 10

Works Cited

Davis, Martha, and Janet Skupien, eds. Body Movement **GG**
and Nonverbal Communication: An Annotated
Bibliography 1971–1981. Bloomington: Indiana UP,
1982.

Fast, Julius. Body Language. New York: Evans, 1970. **HH**

Fisher, Jeffrey D., Paul A. Bell, and Andrew Baum. **II**
Environmental Psychology. 2nd ed. New York: Holt,
1984.

Hall, Edward T. The Hidden Dimension. New York:
Doubleday, 1966.

---. Interview. "Learning the Arabs' Silent Language." **JJ**
With Kenneth Friedman. Psychology Today Aug. 1979: **KK**
44–54.

Henley, Nancy M. Body Politics: Power, Sex, and
Nonverbal Communication. Englewood Cliffs:
Prentice, 1977.

Maines, David R. "Tactile Relationship in the Subway as **LL**
Affected by Racial, Sexual, and Crowded Seating
Situations." Environmental Psychology and
Nonverbal Behavior 2 (1977): 100–108.

Martin, Judith. "Here's Looking at You." Newsday 27 **MM**
Jan. 1981, sec. 2: 9+.

Morris, Charles G. Psychology: An Introduction. 4th **NN**
ed. Chapter 16. Englewood Cliffs: Prentice, 1982.

Morris, Desmond. Manwatching: A Field Guide to Human
Behavior. New York: Abrams, 1977.

COMMENTARY

General Format.   A bibliography, called "Works Cited," is used in MLA documentation style (see 33c-1 and 33d). Entries must be in alphabetical order. Alphabetize by each author's last name, and if no author's name is given, alphabetize by the title. Indent five spaces after the first line of each entry. Punctuate and space between words and lines as shown. Double spacing is used within and between entries. Two spaces occur after each period in an entry.

GG.   **Entry for edited book.**   Inverted order for name of first editor (last name, first name), but regular order for second name. *University Press* abbreviated *UP.*

HH.   **Entry for book by a single author.**

II.   **Entry for book by three authors.**   Inverted order (last name, first name) for name of first author, but regular order for others. *Second edition* abbreviated to *2nd ed.* Publisher abbreviated from *Holt, Rinehart and Winston* to *Holt. (Note:* In a work with three or fewer authors, all names are listed; in a work by four authors or more, the first author is named and then *et al.* is used.)

JJ.   **Second work by same author.**   Three hypens and a period stand for the repetition of the preceding author's name. (*Note:* In such instances, works by the same author are listed alphabetically by title, not chronologically according to date of publication.)

KK.   **Entry for an interview published in a magazine.**   Entry listed by person interviewed, not by the person doing the interviewing. The page numbers are not preceded by *pp.*

LL.   **Entry for an article in a journal with continuous pagination.**   Article title in quotation marks. Journal title underlined. Then volume number, year (in parentheses), and page numbers without *pp.*

MM.   **Entry for an article in a daily newspaper.**   Title of article in quotation marks. Name of newspaper, *Newsday,* underlined. Date of newspaper in this order: day, month (abbreviation permitted), year. Then newspaper section and page numbers without *pp.* The + symbol is used *only* for newspaper articles when material continues on another page.

NN.   Publisher abbreviated from *Prentice Hall* to *Prentice.*

Brown 11

Polhemus, Ted. "Social Bodies." The Body as a Medium
    of Expression. Ed. Jonathan Benthall and Ted
    Polhemus. New York: Dutton, 1975. 13–35.

Shuter, Robert. "A Field Study of Nonverbal
    Communication in Germany, Italy, and the United
    States." Communication Monographs 44 (1977): 298–
    305.

Sommer, Robert. Personal Space: The Behavioral Bases of
    Design. Englewood Cliffs: Prentice, 1969.

Worchel, Stephen, and Joel Cooper. Understanding Social
    Psychology. 3rd ed. Homewood, IL: Dorsey, 1983.

OO

PP

COMMENTARY

OO. **Entry for article in a book.** Author of article heads the entry. Editors of book, with names in regular order, follow book title. Title of article in quotation marks. Title of book underlined. Page numbers—without *pp.*—after city of publication and publisher.

PP. **Entry for book by two authors.** Inverted order (last name, first name) for name of first author, but regular order for second name. Place of publication includes city *and* two-letter postal abbreviation for state because many readers might not know that Homewood is in Illinois.

You might want to explain that formats are of major importance in many disciplines other than English composition. The formats constitute "genres" that readers expect. The formats ease communication because readers know where to look for specific information: background, data, conclusions.

35 Case Study: A Student Writing an APA Research Paper

This chapter presents a student research paper written in the documentation style° of the American Psychological Association (APA). Section 35a discusses the researching (see Chapter 32), planning (see Chapter 2), drafting (see 3b and 32r), and revising (see 3c and 32r) processes of the student, Carlos Velez. Section 35b gives an abstract of the paper. Section 35c shows the final draft of the paper.

> *Carlos Velez was given this assignment for a research paper in a course called Introduction to Psychology:*
>
> Write a research paper of 1,800–2,000 words about an unconscious process in humans. For guidance, refer to the *Simon & Schuster Handbook for Writers, Third Edition,* Chapters 31 through 33. Use the documentation style of the American Psychological Association (APA) explained in Chapter 33. Your topic and working bibliography are due in two weeks. An early draft of your paper is due two weeks later (try to get it close to what you hope will be your last draft, so that comments from me and your peers can concretely help you write an excellent final draft). Your final draft is due one week after the early draft is returned to you with comments.

35a Observing the processes of researching and writing an APA-style research paper

After Carlos Velez read his assignment, he started **planning** by listing various unconscious processes in humans so that he could pick one most interesting to him. Referring to his class notes and the textbook from his psychology course, he found these topics: sleep, dreams, insomnia, biological clocks, daydreams, hypnosis, and meditation. He favored biological clocks because of his experiences with jet lag whenever he traveled between his home in California (in the Pacific Time Zone) and his grandparents' home in Puerto Rico (in the Eastern Time Zone).

Velez then checked to see whether the library at his college had enough sources useful for research on biological clocks. He was pleased to find books, journal articles, magazine and newspaper articles, and even a videotape of a Public Broadcasting System program on the subject. So that he could compile a working bibliography (see 33a) and, at the same time, try to find an approach to the topic suitable for a paper of 1,800–2,000 words, Velez began to read and take notes (see 32i). He saw entire books about biological clocks, so he realized that he would need to narrow the topic (see 32d) sufficiently to shape a thesis statement° (see 32p and 2m). The narrowing process worried him because he had been told in other college courses that his topics for research papers were too broad. He was determined this time to avoid that same problem.

The working bibliography that Velez submitted consisted of twenty-two sources, though he had read and rejected about six others as inadequate (he knew that this represented real progress for him). He did not intend to use them all in his paper, but he wanted them available as he wrote his early drafts. Not surprisingly, his instructor urged him to reduce the list by half once drafting began; otherwise Velez would risk writing too little about too much. He redoubled his efforts to read even more critically to evaluate his sources (see 32g) and weed out material. He got his list down to nineteen sources, took detailed notes (see 32i) on each, and began to group his material into emerging subtopics.

To start **drafting** his paper, Velez spread his note cards around him for easy reference, but he felt somewhat overwhelmed by the amount of information at hand, and he wrote only a few sentences. To break through, he decided to write a "discovery draft" (see 3b) to see what he had absorbed from his reading and note-taking. That very rough draft became his vehicle for many things, including creating an effective thesis statement°, inserting source information according to APA documentation style, and checking the logical arrangement of his material.

Revising for Velez started with his thesis statement°, a process that helped him further narrow his focus. He started with "Biological clocks are fascinating," which expressed his feelings but said nothing of substance. His next version served well as he revised his discovery

QUOTATION ABOUT WRITING

Writing represents a unique mode of learning—not merely valuable, not merely special, but unique. . . . Writing serves learning uniquely because writing as process-and-product possesses a cluster of attributes that correspond uniquely to certain powerful learning strategies.

—Janet Emig, "Writing as a Mode of Learning"

QUOTATION ABOUT WRITING

Writing is thinking on paper. Anyone who thinks clearly should be able to write clearly —about any subject at all.

—William Zinsser, *Writing to Learn*

draft into a true first draft: "Biological clocks, our unconscious time keepers, affect our lives in many ways including compatibility in marriage, family life, jet travel, work schedules, illnesses, medical treatments, and the space program." That version proved to Velez that he was covering too much for an 1,800-2,000–word research paper, and he wanted to drop material. He decided first to inform his readers about the phenomenon of biological clocks and then to discuss the effects of those clocks on people's alertness in the morning and later in the day, on travelers on jet airplanes, and on workers' performance. For his final draft, Velez used this more focused thesis statement: "Biological clocks, which are a significant feature of human design, greatly affect personal and professional lifestyles."

Using APA documentation style made Velez attend very closely to the details of correct parenthetical references (see 33b-2) within his paper and a correct list of References (see 33c-2 and 33d) at the end. Because he had used MLA documentation style° in other courses, he made sure not to confuse the two styles. For example, he saw that APA-style parenthetical references require a page number for a quotation but not for a paraphrase or summary (whereas MLA style requires a page number for all three). For the References list at the end of his paper, he found Chart 159 in section 33c especially helpful.

As Velez checked the logical arrangement of his material, he realized that because he had dropped some aspects of biological clocks when he finally narrowed his topic sufficiently, he needed a little more depth about those aspects that he was retaining. A few hours back in the library gave him what he needed. Having to retrace his steps had a dramatic impact on Velez: Now he saw the difference between researching a topic too broadly (and therefore gathering too many sources for the assignment) and researching a few aspects of a topic in depth by focusing on selected sources. His final draft, which appears in 35c, draws on twelve sources, a number that is down drastically from the twenty-two with which he started.

Preparing an abstract of an APA-style research paper

Although Carlos Velez was not required to include an **abstract** (a brief summary of a paper) with his research paper in psychology, abstracts are often required in courses that call for APA-style documentation of sources. Here is an abstract of the paper Velez wrote:

Circadian rhythms, which greatly affect human lives, often suffer disruptions in technological societies, resulting in such disorders as jet lag syndrome and seasonal affective disorder (SAD). With growing scientific awareness both of natural circadian cycles and the effects of disturbances of these cycles, individuals are learning how to control some negative effects.

35c ## Considering the final draft of an APA-style research paper

Biological Clocks

1

Biological Clocks:
The Body's Internal Timepieces

Carlos Velez

Biological Clocks
2

Biological Clocks:

The Body's Internal Timepieces

Life in modern, technological societies is built around timepieces. People set clocks on radios, microwave ovens, VCRs, and electric coffee makers. Students respond to bells that start and end the school day as well as dividing it into blocks of time. Almost everyone relies on clocks to manage time well. While carefully managing the minutes and hours each day, individuals are often encouraged or forced by current styles of family and work life to violate another kind of time: their body's time. Biological clocks, which are also known as circadian cycles, are a significant feature of human design that greatly affect personal and professional lifestyles.

The term "circadian," which is Latin for "about a day," describes the rhythms of people's internal biological clocks. Circadian cycles are in tune with external time cycles such as the 24-hour period of the earth's daily rotation as signaled by the rising and setting of the sun. Usually, humans set their biological clocks by seeing these cycles of daylight and darkness. Carefully designed studies conducted in caves or similar environments that let researchers control light and darkness have shown that most people create cycles slightly over 24 hours when they are not exposed to natural cycles of day and night (Allis & Haederle, 1989; Enright, 1980). Human perception of the external day-night cycle affects the production and release of a brain hormone, melatonin, which is important in initiating and regulating the sleep-wake cycle, as Alfred Lewy and other scientists at the National Institute of Health in Bethesda, Maryland, have found (Winfree, 1987).

Biological Clocks

3

An individual's lifestyle reflects that person's own circadian cycle. Scientists group people as "larks" or "owls" based on whether individuals are more efficient in the morning or at night. The idea behind the labels is that "in nature certain animals are diurnal, active during the light period; others are nocturnal, active at night. The "morning lark" and "night owl" connotations typically are used to categorize the human extremes" ("Are You," 1989, p. 11).

"Larks" who must stay up late at night and "owls" who must awaken early in the morning experience mild versions of the disturbances, called "jet lag," that time-zone travelers often encounter. Jet lag, which is characterized by fatigue and irregular sleep patterns, results from disruption of circadian rhythms, a common problem among those who travel great distances by jet airplane to different time zones:

> Jet lag syndrome is the inability of the internal body rhythm to rapidly resynchronize after sudden shifts in the timing. For a variety of reasons, the system attempts to maintain stability and resist temporal change. Consequently, complete adjustment can often be delayed for several days--sometimes for a week--after arrival at one's destination. (Bonner, 1991, p. 72)

Interestingly, research shows that the number of flying hours is not the cause of jet lag. Rather, "the number, rate, and direction of time-zone changes are the critical factors in determining the extent and degree of jet lag symptoms," according to Richard Coleman (1986, p. 67) in Wide Awake at 3 a.m.: By Choice or by Chance? Eastbound travelers find it harder than

Biological Clocks

4

westbound travelers to adjust, because traveling east forces people to go to bed before their biological clocks are ready for them to do so (Coleman).

Another group that suffers greatly from biological clock disruptions consists of people whose livelihoods depend on erratic schedules. This situation affects 20- to 30-million U.S. workers whose work schedules differ from the usual morning starting time and afternoon or early evening ending time (Weiss, 1989). Charles Czeisler, director of the Center for Circadian and Sleep Disorders at Brigham and Woman's Hospital in Boston, reports that 27 percent of the U.S. workforce does shift work (Binkley, 1990). Shift work can mean, for example, working from 7:00 a.m. to 3:00 p.m. for six weeks, from 3:00 p.m. to 11:00 p.m. for six weeks, and from 11:00 p.m. to 7:00 a.m. for six weeks. Many shift workers endure stomach and intestinal-tract disorders, and, on average, they have a three times higher risk of heart disease than non-shift workers (Bingham, 1989). In a 1989 report to the American Association for the Advancement of Science, Czeisler states that "police officers, [medical] interns, and many others who work nights perform poorly and are involved in more on-the-job accidents than their daytime counterparts" (Binkley, p. 26).

Other researchers confirm that safety is at risk during late-shift hours (Chollar, 1989). In a study of 28 medical interns observed during late night shifts over a one-year period, 25 percent admitted to falling asleep while talking on the phone, and 34 percent had at least one accident or near-accident during that period (Weiss, 1989). Investigations into the Challenger Shuttle explosion and the nuclear-reactor disasters at

Biological Clocks

5

Three-Mile Island and Chernobyl reveal critical errors made by people undergoing the combined stresses of lack of sleep and unusual work schedules (Toufexis, 1989).

One especially negative effect of an upset biological clock is a syndrome increasingly recognized as a medical problem: the disorder known as Seasonal Affective Disorder (SAD). Table 1 lists some of the major symptoms of SAD.

Table 1

Common Symptoms of Seasonal Affective Disorder

Sadness	Later waking
Anxiety	Increased sleep time
Decreased physical activity	Interrupted, unfreshing sleep
Irritability	Daytime drowsiness
Increased appetite	Decreased sexual drive
Craving for carbohydrates	Menstrual problems
Weight gain	Work problems
Earlier onset of sleep	Interpersonal problems

Note. From The Clockwork Sparrow (p. 204) by S. Binkley, 1990, Englewood Cliffs, NJ: Prentice Hall. Copyright 1990 by Prentice Hall, Inc.

SAD appears to be related to the short daylight (photoperiod) of winter in the temperate zones of the northern and southern hemispheres. The phenomenon of SAD not only illustrates the important role of circadian rhythms, but also it dramatically proves that an understanding of circadian principles can help scientists to improve the lives of people who experience disruptions of their biological clocks. Binkley claims that exposure to bright light for

Biological Clocks

6

periods of up to two hours a day during the short photoperiod days of winter reduces SAD-related "depression in 87 percent of patients . . . within a few days; relapses followed" (pp. 203-204) when light treatment ended.

Exposure to long periods of bright light is not, however, an appropriate solution for people whose safety is at risk because of continual assaults on their circadian cycles by shift schedules at work. Establishing work schedules more sensitive to biological clocks could reduce certain safety hazards. A group of police officers in Philadelphia were studied while on modified shift schedules (Locitzer, 1989; Toufexis, 1989). These officers changed between day shifts and night shifts less frequently than they had on former shift schedules; they rotated forward rather than backward in time; and they worked four rather than six consecutive days. Officers reported 40 percent fewer patrol-car accidents and decreased use of drugs or alcohol to get to sleep. Overall, the police officers preferred the modified shift schedules. Charles Czeisler, who conducted the study, summarizes the importance of these results: "When schedules are introduced that take into account the properties of the human circadian system, subjective estimates of work schedule satisfaction and health improve, personnel turnover decreases, and worker productivity increases" (Locitzer, 1989).

Scientists like Charles Czeisler are beginning to help individuals live harmoniously with their biological clocks. Growing awareness of the effects of such situations as shift work and travel across time zones is one significant step toward control. The use

Biological Clocks

7

of light to manipulate the body's sense of time is another. As more people become aware of how circadian rhythms affect lifestyles, the day might soon come when we can fully control our biological clocks instead of their controlling us.

Biological Clocks

8

References

Allis. T., & Haederle, M. (1989, June 12). Ace in the
      hole: Stefania Follini never caved in. People,
      p. 52.

Are you a day or night person? (1989, March). USA Today
      Magazine, p. 11.

Bingham, R. (Writer & Director). (1989). The time of
      our lives [Television production]. KCET
      Commercial Television of Southern California,
      PBS.

Binkley, S. (1990). The clockwork sparrow. Englewood
      Cliffs, NJ: Prentice Hall.

Bonner, P. (1991, July). Travel rhythms. Sky Magazine,
      pp. 72–73, 76–77.

Chollar, S., (1989, November). Safe solutions for
      night work. Psychology Today, p. 26.

Coleman, R. (1986). Wide awake at 3:00 a.m.: By choice
      or by chance? New York: W. H. Freeman.

Enright, J. T. (1980). The timing of sleep and
      wakefulness. Berlin: Springer–Verlag.

Locitzer, K. (1989, July/August). Are you out of sync
      with each other? Psychology Today, p. 66.

Toufexis, A. (1989, June 5). The times of your life.
      Time, pp. 66–67.

Weiss, R. (1989, January 21). Safety gets short shrift
      on long night shift. Science News, p. 37.

Winfree, A. (1987). The timing of biological clocks.
      New York: W. H. Freeman.

PART

VIII Writing Across the Curriculum

When you write for the different disciplines that you encounter during your college years, you become familiar with the perspectives and assumptions that underlie each discipline. Part Eight compares and contrasts the various disciplines so that you can respond effectively to the major types of writing assignments in each discipline. As you use Chapters 36 through 40, be aware that the information in this handbook serves as a resource for your entire college career and beyond.

BACKGROUND
Because only a few of the many helpful articles and books on writing across the curriculum have been mentioned in this chapter, you should know that bibliographies such as Robert M. McIlvaine and Joan C. Condravy's *Writing Across the Curriculum: An Annotated Bibliography* (ERIC/RCS [June 1983]: ERIC ED 234 421) are available. Other, more specialized bibliographies like Chris Madigan's "Writing Across the Curriculum Resources in Science and Mathematics: A Selected, Annotated Bibliography" (*Journal of College Science Teaching* 16 [February 1987]: 250–253) are also helpful.

BACKGROUND
In an article entitled "Defining Writing Across the Curriculum" (*WPA: Writing Program Administration* 11 [Fall 1987]: 19–24), Susan McLeod outlines two philosophical bases for WAC programs: cognitive and rhetorical. The first, associated with Janet Emig and James Britton, assumes that writing is a mode of thinking and learning. It emphasizes the use of journals and other ungraded writing assignments to assist learning. The latter, developed by Ken Bruffee, Elaine Maimon, and others, emphasizes the contextual and social constraints of writing. Because the discourse community is considered important to learning the conventions expected in a finished product, classes are likely to employ collaborative learning strategies and writing-response groups.

36 Comparing the Different Disciplines

36a Recognizing similarities and differences among the disciplines

The humanities, the social sciences, and the natural sciences each have their own perspectives on the world and their own philosophies about academic thought and research. To understand some of the differences among the disciplines, consider these three quite different paragraphs about a mountain.

HUMANITIES

The mountain stands above all that surrounds it. Giant timbers—part of a collage of evergreen and deciduous trees—conceal the expansive mountain's slope, where cattle once grazed. At the base of the mountain, a cool stream flows over rocks of all sizes, colors, and shapes. Next to the outer bank of the stream stands a shingled farmhouse, desolate, yet suggesting its active past. Unfortunately, the peaceful scene is interrupted by billboards and chairlifts, landmarks of a modern, fast-paced life.

SOCIAL SCIENCES

Among the favorite pastimes of American city dwellers is the "return to nature." Many outdoor enthusiasts hope to enjoy a scenic trip to the mountains, only to be disappointed. They know they have arrived at the mountain that they have traveled hundreds of miles to see because huge billboards are directing them to its base. As they look up the mountain, dozens of people are riding over the treetops in a chairlift, littering the slope with paper cups and food wrappers. At the base of the mountain stands the inevitable refreshment stand, found at virtually all American tourist attractions. Land developers consider such commercialization a way to preserve and utilize natural resources, but environmentalists are appalled.

NATURAL SCIENCES

The mountain is approximately 5,600 feet in height. The underlying rock is igneous, of volcanic origin, composed primarily of granites and feldspars. Three distinct biological communities are present on the mountain. The community at the top of the mountain is alpine in nature, dominated by very short grasses and forbs. At middle altitudes, a typical northern boreal coniferous forest community is present, and at the base and lower altitudes, deciduous forest is the dominant community. This community has, however, been highly affected by agricultural development along the river at its base and by recreational development.

These examples illustrate that each discipline has its writing traditions and preferences. The paragraph written for the humanities describes the mountain from the individual perspective of the writer—a perspective both personal and yet representative of a general human response. The paragraph written for the social sciences focuses on the behavior of people as a group. The paragraph written for the natural sciences reports observations of natural phenomena.

As you study and write in each of the academic disciplines, you become familiar with alternative ways of thinking. As you come to know the habits of mind that characterize each discipline, you develop specialized vocabularies that allow you to participate in the conversations of each discipline. As your perspectives are broadened, you gain lifelong access to the pleasures of informed insight— among the major benefits of a college education.

No matter what differences exist among the academic disciplines, all subject areas interconnect and overlap. Chart 162 lists similarities and differences.

SIMILARITIES AND DIFFERENCES IN WRITING ACROSS THE DISCIPLINES 162

SIMILARITIES

1. Consider your purpose, audience, and tone. — Chapters 1–2
2. Use the writing process to plan, shape, draft, revise, edit, and proofread. — Chapters 2–3
3. Develop a thesis. — Chapters 2–3

QUOTATION ABOUT WRITING

In schools where the lessons taught in English classes are not repeated and emphasized in the student's other classes, the knowledge and skills learned in those lessons tend to atrophy. We believe language skills deserve more conscious attention from teachers in all academic disciplines, and that teachers who recognize the role played by these "elementary" skills can help students increase their learning ability, improve their communication skills, and enhance their cognitive and emotional growth.

—Toby Fulwiler and Art Young, *Language Connections*

QUOTATION ABOUT WRITING

Problem solving is common ground for all the disciplines and fundamental to all human activities. . . . The discovery function of writing in the content areas, particularly in the scientific and technological fields, can help students become aware of the processes they use to solve problems.

—Carol Berkenkotter, "Writing and Problem Solving"

BACKGROUND

Many writing-across-the-curriculum programs offer support for instructors interested in developing new teaching techniques that involve writing. Such support often takes the form of workshops led either by a resident faculty member or by an outside consultant. At the workshops, instructors from varied disciplines discuss writing-to-learn strategies, evaluation methods, journal keeping, and related matters. One successful format is an off-campus "retreat" where instructors spend several days working on such issues. Many schools also have a director of writing who serves as a resource person for faculty members looking for help in introducing writing into their assignments and classroom activities.

BACKGROUND

Commenting that "there's almost no subject that can't be made accessible in good English," William Zinsser (*Writing to Learn* [New York: Harper & Row, 1988]) defines jargon as "the lingo of people in specialized fields who have infected each other with their private terminology and don't think there's any other way to say what they mean" (p. 66). He divides jargon into two main forms: buzzwords and special occupational terms. The first group is, for Zinsser, particularly objectionable because it is composed of words that "make the insider feel important when he uses them but that don't really mean anything" (p. 67). The second category consists of terms that some field has found it necessary to invent, terms that serve a particular need when professional people talk together. One proof of their value is that nonprofessionals quickly adopt them if they become important. The problem, according to Zinsser, arises when "jargon becomes a crutch—when its users become so dependent on their private terminology that they claim they can't express themselves in any other way" (p. 68).

BACKGROUND

To those teachers in other disciplines who fear that using writing to teach their course will be a waste of time or that they will not be able to evaluate students' work, Ruth Couch provides answers and suggestions for making writing-to-learn strategies work ("Dealing with Objections to Writing Across the Curriculum," *Teaching English in the Two-Year College* 16 [October 1989]: 193–196).

BACKGROUND

In *Programs That Work: Models and Methods for Writing Across the Curriculum* (Portsmouth, NH: Boynton/Cook, 1989), Toby Fulwiler and Art Young examine fourteen successful college and university WAC programs.

SIMILARITIES AND DIFFERENCES IN WRITING ACROSS THE DISCIPLINES *(continued)*

4.	Arrange and organize your ideas.	Chapter 2
5.	Use supporting evidence.	Chapters 2–4
6.	Develop paragraphs thoroughly.	Chapter 4
7.	Read and think critically, and use correct reasoning and logic.	Chapter 5
8.	Argue well.	Chapter 6
9.	Write effective sentences.	Chapters 16–19
10.	Choose words well.	Chapters 20–21
11.	Use correct grammar.	Chapters 7–15
12.	Spell correctly.	Chapter 22
13.	Use correct punctuation and mechanics.	Chapters 23–30

DIFFERENCES

1. Conduct research and select sources according to each discipline (see 36a-1).
2. Select a style of documentation appropriate to each discipline.
3. Follow manuscript format requirements, if any, in each discipline (see 36a-3).
4. Use specialized language, when needed, in each discipline (see 36a-4).

For example, in a humanities class you might read *Lives of a Cell*, by Lewis Thomas, a collection of essays about science and nature written by a noted physician and prize-winning author. As you consider the art of the writer, you will also be thinking deeply about biology and other sciences.

The four differences listed in Chart 162 are discussed in detail here.

1 **Conducting research and selecting sources according to each discipline**

Primary sources offer you first-hand exposure to information. No one comes between you and the exciting experience of discovering and confronting material on your own. Research methods differ among the disciplines when primary sources are used. In the humanities, existing documents are primary sources; the task of the researcher is to analyze and interpret these primary sources. Typical primary-source material for research could be a poem by Dylan Thomas, the floor plans of Egyptian pyramids, or early drafts of music manuscripts. In the social and natural sciences, primary research entails the design and undertaking of experiments involving direct observation. The task of the researcher in the social and natural sciences is to conduct the experiments or to read the first-hand reports of experiments and studies written by people who conducted them.

Secondary sources—articles and books about a primary source—are also important in all disciplines. In the humanities, you can learn much from the examples of others who have analyzed and interpreted primary sources. In the social and natural sciences, secondary sources can usefully synthesize findings in many areas and draw parallels that offer new insights.

2 | Selecting a style of documentation appropriate to each discipline

Writers use **documentation** to give credit to the sources they have used. A writer who does not credit a source is guilty of **plagiarizing**—a serious academic offense (see 31a). Styles of documentation differ among the disciplines.

In the humanities, many fields use the documentation style of the Modern Language Association (MLA). MLA documentation style is explained and illustrated in 33b through 33f. The student research paper in Chapter 34 and the student literary analysis in Chapter 37 use MLA documentation style. In the social sciences, most fields use the documentation style of the American Psychological Association (APA). APA documentation style is explained and illustrated in 33b through 33d. The student research paper in Chapter 35 uses APA documentation style. In the natural sciences, documentation styles vary, as is explained in 33g and 38g.

3 | Following manuscript format requirements, if any, in each discipline

As a reflection of the differences among academic disciplines, different formats are sometimes expected for presentation of material. These special formats have evolved to communicate a writer's purpose, to emphasize content by eliminating distracting variations in format, and to make the reader's work easier. Writing in the

TEACHING TIP

In 1984, the Modern Language Association (MLA) changed its recommended documentation style from a note system to a parenthetical system. Often, therefore, the MLA parenthetical system is called "new MLA" or "1984 MLA." You might want to point out to your students that the change in documentation style has implications for writing style. With the MLA note system, readers often had to get all source information in the note; with the parenthetical system, readers do not expect to have to divert their eyes (and attention) to learn about the source. The new preference is for writers to include as much information as gracefully as possible in the text, with the balance left for parentheses. The MLA style is explained in Chapter 33.

TEACHING TIP

Because the differences in documentation styles are easier to see from actual papers than to understand from a description, you may want to bring examples of research papers that use different documentation systems to class. The papers will make students aware that there is no single right way to cite sources; there is, instead, a way that is appropriate for a particular writing task and audience. The demonstration has the added benefit of showing students in various disciplines what is expected of them in their fields of study. If papers are not available for such use, you may want to show how a single note would be treated in the pre-1984 MLA style, the newer MLA style, and the APA style.

QUOTATION ABOUT WRITING

[Writing] conventions can vary greatly with different tasks and different disciplines, although many fields share similar ones. . . . Stylistically, the paper must "sound right." If you appear knowledgeable, believable, you will gain the confidence of your reader.

—Diane Bennett Durkin,
Writing in the Disciplines

TEACHING TIP

College students need to make connections, to see relationships among the ideas and data they meet in their various courses if they are to develop their skills in critical thinking. This chapter is designed, therefore, as a resource for students who want to apply what they have learned in composition classes to their writing in other courses. The material in this chapter is offered to help students see that what they learn in "writing class" is related to what they need to do as they write throughout their college careers and beyond.

You might want to point out that this chapter offers two important resources: (1) explanations and examples of various types of writing about literature, social sciences, and natural and technological sciences; and (2) presentation of documentation styles other than the MLA parenthetical system—which is presented and discussed in detail in Chapter 33.

QUOTATION ABOUT WRITING

The main assumption behind Writing Across the Curriculum seems to embody a resurrected sense of the responsibility of entire faculties and administrative bodies for the literary competence of the graduate. . . . Literacy is the concern of all faculty members since it is the cornerstone of education. Another assumption is that some rhetorical principles—careful description, explanation and proof, problems of definition and classification, and consideration of style and audience—transcend departments. Everyone can teach writing in a way. All faculty members can learn some general writing-teaching skills.

—James Kinneavy, interview, December 1984

humanities is less often subject to set formats, although writing is expected to be well organized and logically presented. Writing in the social and natural sciences often calls for set formats for specific types of writing.

4 Using specialized language, when needed, in each discipline

Specialized language is often referred to as **jargon.** Jargon is useful when it helps people who are specialists communicate easily with each other in a kind of "verbal shorthand." When specialized material is communicated to the general reading public, however, any jargon has to be defined so that everyone can understand the message. Jargon is not useful when it is unnecessarily obscure and overblown (see 21e-2).

All disciplines use specialized language to some extent. The specialized terms in the social and natural sciences are generally more technical and less accessible to nonspecialists than are those in the humanities. The more important that exactness is to a discipline, the more likely that many words will have specialized meanings. For example, consider the word *niche.* It has two generally known meanings: "a place particularly suitable to the person or thing in it," and "a hollowed space in a wall for a statue or vase." *Niche* in the natural sciences, however, has a very specialized meaning: "the set of environmental conditions—climate, food sources, water supply, enemies—that permit an organism or species to survive."

❖ USAGE ALERT: Many writers in scientific disciplines make a habit of writing in the passive voice. Yet style manuals for scientific writing agree with the advice you will find in 8o: Use the active voice except for purposes best fulfilled by the passive.* ❖

36b Using collaborative writing in various disciplines

If you are told to engage in **collaborative writing,** you will be expected to work with others in your class on a project. A collaborative writing group consists of two or more people, according to the instructor's directions. (Be aware that in many classes your instructor might prefer that you work alone on projects. To avoid any risk of charges of cheating or plagiarism, get permission from your instruc-

*You may want to look at section 2.06 in the *Publication Manual of the American Psychological Association,* Third Edition (36) and in the *CBE Style Manual,* Fifth Edition (38).

tor if you want to work collaboratively on your own with other students.)

Many professions require people to serve on committees, to reach general agreement, and to write reports of their deliberations and recommendations. Many businesses and academic fields require people to work together on reports or papers that draw upon the different skills and information each person in the group can contribute. Some college courses incorporate the experience of writing collaboratively. For example, in a marketing course, each of several groups might be expected to develop a new product, conduct research for marketing the product, and write a paper explaining 0their plan. Similarly, in a science course, a collaborative project might consist of jointly conducting an experiment, assessing its results, and writing a report.

Collaborative writing gives you the advantage of being able to share your knowledge and hear what others know. "Two heads are better than one" often proves true. Still, working with others on writing projects demands patience and graciousness. You have to work along with the pace of the group, listen carefully as you consider closely what others are saying, and contribute your part to the endeavor. Here are guidelines to help you function productively when writing collaboratively. Use them in conjunction with Guidelines for Being an Effective Peer Critic, given in Chart 17 in section 3c-5.

GUIDELINES FOR COLLABORATIVE WRITING   163

GETTING UNDERWAY

1. Get to know each other's names. If you exchange phone numbers, you can be in touch outside of class.

2. Participate in the group process. During discussions help to set a tone that encourages everyone to participate, including people who do not like to interrupt, who want time to think before they talk, or who are shy. If you are not used to contributing in a group setting, try to take a more active role.

3. Facilitate the collaboration. As a group, assign work to be done between meetings. Distribute the responsibilities as fairly as possible. Also, decide whether to choose one discussion leader or to rotate leadership.

PLANNING THE WRITING

4. After discussing the project, brainstorm (see 2g) or use other techniques to think of ideas (see 2d through 2j). ➜

QUOTATION ABOUT WRITING

But liberal learning does not permit us to hold on to any single answer for too long. As soon as you find one answer, you discover that that answer leads to other questions. Liberal learning can be unsettling. People like certainty, the right answer, the only way. Because of this desire for certainty and security, people can find themselves living with answers that other people have imposed upon them. In a free society, people learn to cultivate inquiring minds. They see that in broad areas of life there are no single right answers, that knowledge has a peculiar way of generating more questions, and that the world is more ambiguous than it appears. Liberal learning frees the mind to experience a sense of wonder at this ambiguous and fascinating world. F. Scott Fitzgerald writes, ''The test of a first-rate intelligence is the ability to hold two opposed ideas in the mind at the same time, and still retain the ability to function.'' A liberally educated person learns to use this first-rate intelligence to function—even to prevail—in the midst of ambiguity.

> —Elaine P. Maimon, et al.,
> *Writing in the Arts and Sciences*

TEACHING TIP

You might ask students to write contrastive paragraphs in the humanities, social sciences, and sciences using one of these topics:

a river	the *Titanic*
an automobile	an insect
a sport	an illness

GUIDELINES FOR COLLABORATIVE WRITING (*continued*)

5. As a group, choose the ideas that seem best. Incubate (see 2k), if time permits, and discuss the choices again.

6. As a group, divide the project into parts and distribute assignments as fairly as possible.

7. As you work on your part of the project, take notes so that you can be ready to report to the group.

8. As a group, sketch an overview (if you choose to outline, see 2n) of the paper to get a preliminary idea of how best to use the material contributed by individuals.

DRAFTING THE WRITING

9. Draft a first paragraph or two. This material sets the direction for the rest of the paper. Each member of the group can draft a version, but agree on one draft for these paragraphs before getting too far into the rest of the draft. Your group might rewrite once the whole paper has been drafted, but a preliminary beginning helps to focus everyone.

10. Work on the rest of the paper. Decide whether each member of the group should write a complete draft or a different part of the whole. Use photocopies to share work.

REVISING THE WRITING

11. Read over the drafts. Check that everything useful has been incorporated into the draft.

12. Use the Revision Checklists in section 3c-3 to decide on revisions. Work as a group, or assign sections to subgroups. Use photocopies to share work.

13. Agree on a final version. Assign someone to prepare it in final form and make photocopies.

EDITING THE WRITING

14. As a group, review photocopies of the final version. Do not leave the last stages to a subgroup. Draw on everyone's knowledge of grammar, spelling, and punctuation. And use everyone's eyes to proofread.

15. Use the Editing Checklist in section 3d to make sure that the final version has no errors. If necessary, retype. No matter how well the group has worked collaboratively, or how well the group has written the paper, a sloppy final version reflects negatively on the entire group.

37 Writing About Literature

Literature, which includes **fiction** (novels and stories), **drama** (plays and scripts), and **poetry** (poems and lyrics), has developed from age-old human impulses to discover and communicate meaning by telling stories, reenacting events, and singing or chanting. Reading and then writing about literature can deliver a related satisfaction: You have the chance to think about meaning and to tell others what you have found.

37a Understanding methods of inquiry into literature

All questions about literature require you to read a work closely. Some questions then ask you to deal with the material on a literal level (see 5d-1). You might be asked to explain the meaning of a passage in a novel, or to find out what historical events were going on when the work was written or what other scholars have said about some element of the work.

Other questions call for inferential reasoning (see 5d-2) and evaluative thinking (see 5d-3). You might be asked to discuss the effect of sound or rhythm or rhyme in a poem, or to compare characters in two plays by a particular playwright. Unlike inquiry in many other disciplines, you might also be asked to describe your response or reaction to a work of literature after a close, careful reading.

In each case, your answers must be thorough, well-reasoned, well-supported with evidence, and informed by knowledge of the work.

BACKGROUND

In "Composition and Literature: The Continuing Conversation" (*College English* 51 [October 1989]: 617–622), Ann Ruggles Gere reviews four books that discuss "new ways to teach." The focus is on making connections between reading and writing instruction.

QUOTATION ABOUT WRITING

A research paper is a report that an individual presents to others about the conclusions he or she has reached after investigating a subject and carefully assessing the information he or she has gathered.

—Susan M. Hubbuch, *Writing Research Papers Across the Curriculum*

QUOTATION ABOUT WRITING

Writing is the yeast of the learning process, not merely the frosting.

—Barbara E. Fassler Walvoord

BACKGROUND

Douglas Hesse takes up the question of how to teach students to think and write about literature by describing some nontraditional methods in "Some Alternatives to Plot, Theme, and Setting: Social Construction and Critical Thinking" (*Illinois English Bulletin* 76 [Winter 1989]: 12–22).

QUOTATION ABOUT WRITING

You can write about *anything*, and if you write well enough, even the reader with no intrinsic interest in the subject will become involved.

—Tracy Kidder

BACKGROUND

The relatively new school of literary theory known as Reader Response Criticism came about as a challenge to the Formalists, who had held sway in classrooms and journals for several decades. The Reader Response theorists, such as David Bleich, Norman Holland, Wolfgang Iser, Stanley Fish, and Jonathan Culler, rejected the affective fallacy of the New Critics, and asked whether it is the reader or the text that determines interpretation. Although the Reader Response critics vary widely in their theoretical assumptions, critical strategies, and pedagogical practices, they all conclude that understanding and evaluation are based on subjective opinion. There is no such thing as an unbiased, objective reading of a text.

A number of useful articles and books that address the various theories of Reader Response have recently been published. In addition to such primary sources as Iser's *The Implied Reader* (Baltimore: Johns Hopkins UP, 1974) and Fish's *Is There a Text in This Class?* (Cambridge: Harvard UP, 1980), there are helpful explanations in Steven Lynn's "A Passage into Critical Theory" (*College English* 52 [March 1990]: 258–269) and in Reed Way Dasenbrock's "Do We Write the Text We Read?" (*College English* 53 [January 1991]: 7–17). Charles Moran and Elizabeth Penfield have collected a number of readable essays on contemporary critical theory and assessed their use for teachers in *Conversations* (Urbana: NCTE, 1990).

37b Understanding purposes and practices in writing about literature

The general purposes of writing about literature are to inform and to persuade (see 1b). **Informative writing** includes explaining what a passage means or what constitutes a particular work's key elements. **Persuasive writing** includes arguing the merits of an evaluation or an interpretation. Reaction papers (see 37d-1) often combine informative and persuasive purposes. All writing about literature calls for you to analyze, synthesize, and assess critically (see Chart 29 in section 5a).

1 Using first and third person appropriately

Instructors usually have students use the first person° (*I, we, our*) to write about their points of view or personal evaluations, and the third person° (*he, she, it, they*) for other assignments. Be sure to inquire about and adapt to your instructor's requirements. In research papers, the first person is usually acceptable only when you present your personal experience, your own conclusions, or your personal views contrasted with those of the sources that you have consulted and documented°.

2 Using verbs in the present tense and the past tense correctly when writing about literature

When you describe or discuss a literary work or any of its elements, use the present tense°: *George Henderson **takes** control of the action and **tells** the other characters when to speak and when not to.* The present tense is also correct for discussing what the author has done in a specific work: *Because Susan Glaspell [the author] **excludes** Minnie and John Wright from the stage as speaking characters, she **forces** us to learn about them through the words of others.*

If you are discussing events that take place before the action of a literary work begins, a past-tense° verb is correct: *The characters **have gathered** [before the action starts] at the Wright farmhouse when the play begins.* Also use past tenses, as appropriate, to discuss historical events or biographical information: *Susan Glaspell **was** a social activist who **was** strongly **influenced** by the chaotic events of the early twentieth century.*

3 Using your own ideas and using secondary sources

Some assignments call only for your own ideas about the subject of your essay. Other assignments ask you to support your analysis with **secondary sources.** Secondary sources include books and articles in which an expert discusses material related to your topic. You can locate secondary sources by using the research process discussed in Chapter 32.

Whenever you use secondary sources, **avoid plagiarism** (see 31a). So that no reader thinks that the ideas of another person are yours, always document your sources (see 31b and Chapter 33). Also, to work material from secondary sources skillfully and gracefully into your writing, use the techniques of quotation (see 31c), paraphrase (see 31d), and summary (see 31e).

37c Using documentation style for writing about literature

If you use secondary sources° when you write about literature, you are required to credit your sources by using documentation°. Many college instructors require their students to use the documentation style of the Modern Language Association (MLA), an organization of scholars and teachers of language and literature.

The MLA updated its documentation style in 1984. A few instructors still prefer the style endorsed before 1984, which calls for footnotes or endnotes in the body of a paper and a Bibliography at the end (see 33f). Most instructors expect the newer MLA documentation style, which uses parenthetical references (see 33b-1) in the body of a paper and a Works Cited list (see 33c-1 and 33d) at the end of a paper. For an example, see the student research paper in Chapter 34, which uses MLA documentation style.

Some college instructors require their students to use the documentation style of the American Psychological Association (APA). This style calls for parenthetical references (see 33b-2) in the body of a paper and a References list (see 33c-2 and 33d) at the end of a paper. For an example, see the student research paper in Chapter 35, which uses APA documentation style.

QUOTATION ABOUT WRITING

Writing in the humanities involves an act of judgment or interpretation based on values. Humanists are especially concerned with skillful judgment—understanding and valuing ideas and creations. They encourage unique insight into past thought and action, asking of readers a similar interpretive skill —the ability to see new significance, impose a new structure, redefine meaning, or unveil assumptions. While interpretations may often conflict, making us question their reliability or validity, the goal is not reliability. Rather, the goal is to model reality in a way that helps us understand and appreciate it.

—Diane B. Durkin

BACKGROUND

In *Writing Themes About Literature*, 7th ed. (Prentice Hall, 1991), Edgar V. Roberts considers the objection that too much literary analysis "spoils" appreciation of a work. Pointing out that the purpose is not to "cut up literature like a frog and leave it in pieces," he explains that literary analysis should make it possible to see more in a work, to find greater appreciation of its literary excellence. To that end, he suggests four broad areas that literary analysis explores: (1) meaning, (2) structure, (3) style, and (4) background and influences.

TEACHING TIP

Some students find it helpful to keep a double entry journal as they read a long work such as a novel or play. In a notebook they draw a vertical line down the middle of the page. On one side they record significant events or passages from the reading material. On the other side they make personal comments about that portion of the text. The journal can serve as a seedbed for extended student writing, as a study guide, or simply as a record of initial responses to a work that may call for repeated readings.

37d Writing different types of papers about literature

Before you write a paper in which you refer or react to a literary work, be sure to read the work closely. To read well, use your understanding of the reading process (see 5b) and critical reading skills (see 5d).

1 Writing reaction papers

In a paper in which you react to a work of literature, you might ask and try to answer a central question that the work made you think about, criticize a point of view in the work, or present a problem that you see in the work. For example, if you are asked to respond to a play, you might write about why you did or did not enjoy reading the play, how the play does or does not relate to your personal experience or to your view of life, what the play made you think about and try to puzzle through. You can focus on the entire play or on a particular scene, character, or set of lines.

2 Writing book reports

A book report informs readers about the content of a book—by summarizing its plot and its theme and by discussing (1) the significance and purpose of the book, (2) how the book presents its content, and (3) who might be most interested in the book. When you discuss the significance of the book, try to relate it to your field of study. For example, if the book is a classic in children's literature, your focus for a literature class would differ somewhat from your focus for a course in psychology or education.

3 Writing interpretations

An interpretation discusses either what the author means by the work or what the work means personally to the reader. When you are writing an interpretation paper, always consider the questions in Chart 164.

37d

QUESTIONS FOR AN INTERPRETATION PAPER 164

1. What is the theme of the work?
2. How are particular parts of the work related to the theme?
3. If patterns exist in various elements of the work, what do they mean?
4. What message does the author convey through the use of major aspects of the work, listed in Chart 165.
5. Why does the work end as it does?

QUOTATION ABOUT LITERATURE

Great writers leave us not just their works, but a way of looking at things.

—Elizabeth Janeway

QUOTATION ABOUT LITERATURE

A classic is something that everybody wants to have read and nobody wants to read.

—Mark Twain

---

4 Writing analyses

Analysis is the examination of the relationship of a whole to its parts. In a **literary analysis,** you are expected to discuss your well-reasoned ideas about a work of fiction, poetry, or drama. To get to know the work well and to gather ideas for your analysis, read the work thoroughly, again and again. Watch for patterns in the aspects of literary analysis listed in Chart 165. Write notes as you go along so that you have a record of two important resources for your writing: the patterns you find in the material, and your reactions to the patterns and to the whole work.

MAJOR ASPECTS OF LITERARY WORKS TO ANALYZE 165

PLOT	The events and their sequence
THEME	Central idea or message
STRUCTURE	Organization and relationship of parts to each other and to the whole
CHARACTERIZATION	Traits, thoughts, and actions of the people in the plot
SETTING	Time and place of the action ➡

BACKGROUND
Diane P. Thompson suggests engaging
adult students in analysis by first asking
them to write lies, rewrite published stories,
and even create poems. After engaging in
their own creative experiences, they can
more readily take up literary analysis (*Teaching
English in the Two-Year College* 16 [February 1989]: 37–39).

QUOTATION ABOUT LITERATURE
Great literature is simply language charged
with meaning to the utmost possible degree.
—Ezra Pound

MAJOR ASPECTS OF LITERARY WORKS TO ANALYZE (*continued*)	
POINT OF VIEW	Perspective or position from which the material is presented—sometimes by a narrator or a main character
STYLE	How words and sentence structures present the material
IMAGERY	The pictures created by the words (similes, metaphors, figurative language)
TONE	The attitude of the author toward the subject of the work—and sometimes toward the reader—expressed through the choice of words and through the imagery
FIGURES OF SPEECH	Includes metaphor ° and simile ° (for a complete list and definitions, see the Chart 113 in 21c)
SYMBOLISM	The meaning beneath the surface of the words and images
RHYTHM AND RHYME	Beat, meter, repetition of sounds, etc.

37e Three case studies of students writing about literature

This section includes three student essays of literary analysis.
Two do not use secondary sources° (see 37e-1 and 37e-2) and one
does use them (see 37e-3). All three essays use MLA documentation
style (see Chapter 33 and 37c).

1 Student essay interpreting a plot element in a short story

The following essay interprets a plot element in Edgar Allan
Poe's story "The Tell-Tale Heart."

Born in 1809, Edgar Allan Poe was an important American journalist, poet, and fiction writer. In his short, dramatic life, Poe gambled, drank, lived in terrible poverty, saw his young wife die of tuberculosis, and died himself under mysterious circumstances at age 40. He also created the detective novel and wrote brilliant, often bizarre short stories that still stimulate the reader's imagination.

When Valerie Cuneo read Poe's "The Tell-Tale Heart," first published in 1843, she was fascinated by one of the plot elements: the sound of a beating heart that compels the narrator of the story to commit a murder and then to confess it to the police. In the following paper, Cuneo discusses her interpretation of the source of the heartbeat.

QUOTATION ABOUT LITERATURE

The cultivation of literary pursuits forms the basis of all sciences, and in their perfection consist the reputation and prosperity of kingdoms.

—Marques de Pombal,
Portuguese statesman

QUOTATION ABOUT LITERATURE

All good books are alike in that they are truer than if they had really happened.

—Ernest Hemingway

The Sound of a Murderous Heart

In Edgar Allan Poe's short story "The Tell—Tale Heart," several interpretations are possible as to the source of the beating heart that causes the narrator—murderer to reveal himself to the police. The noise could simply be a product of the narrator's obviously deranged mind. Or perhaps the murder victim's spirit lingers, heart beating, to exact revenge upon the narrator. Although each of these interpretations is possible, most of the evidence in the story suggests that the inescapable beating heart that haunts the narrator is his own.

The interpretation that the heartbeat stems from some kind of auditory hallucination is flawed. The narrator clearly is insane—his killing a kind old man because of an "Evil Eye" demonstrates this—and his psychotic behavior is more than sufficient cause for readers to question his truthfulness. Even so, nowhere else in the story does the narrator imagine things that do not exist. Nor is it likely that he would intentionally attempt to mislead us since the

➡

701

narrative is a confessional monologue through which he tries to explain and justify his actions. He himself describes his "disease" as a heightening of his senses, not of his imagination. Moreover, his highly detailed account of the events surrounding the murder seems to support this claim. Near the end of the story, he refutes the notion that he is inventing the sound in his mind when he says, "I found that the noise was not within my ears" (792). Although the narrator's reliability is questionable, there seems to be no reason to doubt this particular observation.

Interpreting the heartbeat as the victim's ghostly retaliation against the narrator also presents difficulties. Perhaps most important, when the narrator first hears the heart, the old man is still alive. The structure of the story also argues against the retaliation interpretation. Poe uses the first-person point of view to give readers immediate access to the narrator's strange thought processes, a choice that suggests the story is a form of psychological study. If "The Tell-Tale Heart" were truly a ghost story, it would probably be told in the third person, and it would more fully develop the character of the old man and explore his relationship with the narrator. If the heartbeat that torments the narrator is his own, however, these inconsistencies are avoided.

The strongest evidence that the tell-tale heart is really the narrator's is the timing of the heartbeat. Although it is the driving force behind the entire story, the narrator hears the beating heart only twice. In both of these instances, he is under immense physical and psychological stress—times when his own heart would be pounding. The narrator first hears the heartbeat with the shock of realizing that he has accidentally awakened his intended victim:

➡

> Meantime the hellish tattoo of the heart increased. It grew quicker and quicker, and louder every instant. The old man's terror must have been extreme! It grew louder, I say, louder every moment!—do you mark me well? I have told you that I am nervous: so I am. And now at the dead hour of the night, amid the dreadful silence of that old house, so strange a noise as this excited me to uncontrollable terror. (791)

As the narrator's anxiety increases, so does the volume and frequency of the sound, an event easily explained if the heartbeat is his own. Also, the sound of the heart persists even after the old man is dead, fading slowly into the background, as would the murderer's own heartbeat after his short, violent struggle with the old man. This reasoning can also explain why the narrator did not hear the heart on any of the seven previous nights when he looked into the old man's bedchamber. Because the old man slept and the "Evil Eye" was closed, no action was necessary (according to the narrator-murderer's twisted logic), and therefore he did not experience the rush of adrenaline that set his heart pounding on the fatal eighth visit.

The heart also follows a predictable pattern at the end of the story when the police officers come to investigate a neighbor's report of the dying old man's scream. In this encounter the narrator's initial calm slowly gives way to irritation and fear. As he becomes increasingly agitated, he begins to hear the heart again. The narrator clearly identifies it as the same sound he heard previously, as shown by the almost word-for-word repetition of the language he uses to describe it, calling it "a low, dull, quick sound—much such a sound as a watch makes when enveloped in cotton" [Poe's italics] (792). As the narrator-murderer focuses his attention on the sound, which ultimately ➡

overrides all else, his panic escalates until,
ironically, he is betrayed by the very senses that he
boasted about at the start of the story.

Work Cited

Poe, Edgar Allan. "The Tell—Tale Heart." American
Literature: A Prentice Hall Anthology. Vol. 1.
Ed. Emory Elliott, Linda K. Kerber, A. Walton
Litz, and Terence Martin. Englewood Cliffs:
Prentice, 1991. 789–792.

---

2 Student essay analyzing the characters in a drama

The following essay analyzes actions and interactions of the male and female characters in *Trifles,* a one-act play written by Susan Glaspell. Glaspell (1882–1948) was a feminist and social activist who wrote many plays for the Provincetown Players, a theater company she cofounded in Cape Cod, Massachusetts. She wrote *Trifles* in 1916, four years before women were allowed to vote in the United States. In 1917, Glaspell rewrote *Trifles* as the short story "A Jury of Her Peers." In both versions of the work, two married couples and the county attorney gather at a farmhouse where a taciturn farmer has been murdered, apparently by his wife. The five characters try to discover a motive for the murder. In doing so, they reveal much about gender roles in marriage and in the larger society.

After reading *Trifles,* Peter Wong said to his instructor, "No male today could get away with saying some of the things the men in that play say." The instructor encouraged Wong to analyze that reaction.

Gender Loyalties: A Theme in Trifles

Susan Glaspell's play Trifles is a study of
character even though the two characters most

➡

central to the drama never appear on stage. By excluding Minnie and John Wright from the stage as speaking characters, Glaspell forces us to learn about them through the observations and recollections of the group visiting the farmhouse where the murders of Minnie Wright's canary and of John Wright took place. By indirectly rounding out her main characters, Glaspell invites us to view them not merely as individuals but also as representatives in a conflict between the sexes. This conflict grows throughout the play as characters' emotions and sympathies become increasingly polarized and oriented in favor of their own gender. From this perspective, each of the male characters can be seen to stand for the larger political, legal, and domestic power structures that drive Minnie Wright to kill her husband.

George Henderson's speaking the first line of the play is no accident. Although his power stems from his position as county attorney, Henderson represents the political, more than the legal, sphere. With a job similar to a district attorney's today, he is quite powerful even though he is the youngest person present. He takes control of the action, telling the other characters when to speak and when not to and directing the men in their search for evidence that will establish a motive for the murder. As the person in charge of the investigation, George Henderson orders the other characters about. Mrs. Peters acknowledges his skill at oratory when she predicts that Minnie Wright will be convicted in the wake of his "sarcastic" cross-examination (speech 63).

Glaspell reveals much of the conflict in the play through the heated (but civil) exchanges between George Henderson and Mrs. Hale. His behavior (according to the stage directions, that of a gallant young politician) does not mask his belittling of Minnie Wright and of women in general:

➡

COUNTY ATTORNEY. I guess before we're through she may have something more serious than preserves to worry about.

HALE. Well, women are used to worrying over trifles. [The two women move a little closer together.]

COUNTY ATTORNEY. [With the gallantry of a young politician.] And yet, for all their worries, what would we do without the ladies? [The women do not unbend. He goes to the sink, takes a dipperful of water from the pail and pouring it into a basin, washes his hands. Starts to wipe them on the roller-towel, turns it for a cleaner place.] Dirty towels! [Kicks his foot against the pans under the sink.] Not much of a housekeeper, would you say, ladies?

(speeches 29–31)

As this excerpt shows, George Henderson seems to hold that a woman's place is in the kitchen, even when she is locked up miles away in the county jail. He shows so much emotion at the discovery of dirty towels in the kitchen that it is almost as if he has found a real piece of evidence that he can use to convict Minnie Wright, instead of an irrelevant strip of cloth. It is apparent that his own sense of self-importance and prejudicial views of women are distracting him from his real business at the farmhouse.

Sheriff Henry Peters, as his title suggests, represents the legal power structure. Like the county attorney, Henry Peters is also quick to dismiss the "trifles" that his wife and Mrs. Hale spend their time discussing while the men conduct a physical search of the premises. His response to the attorney's asking whether he is absolutely certain that the downstairs contains no relevant clues to the motive for the murder is a curt "Nothing here but kitchen things" (speech

25). Ironically, the women are able to reconstruct the entire murder, including the motive, by beginning their inquiries with these same "kitchen things." Sheriff Peters and the other men all completely miss the unfinished quilt, the bird cage, and the dead bird's body. When the sheriff overhears the women talking about the quilt, his instinctive reaction is to ridicule them, saying, "They wonder if she was going to quilt it or just knot it!" (speech 73). Of course, the fact that Minnie Wright was going to knot the quilt is probably the single most important piece of evidence that the group could uncover, since John Wright was strangled with what we deduce is a quilting knot. Although he understands the law, the sheriff seems to know very little about people, and this prevents him from ever cracking this case. His blindness is made clear when he chuckles his assent to the county attorney's observation that Mrs. Peters is literally "married to the law" (speech 145) and therefore beyond suspicion of trying to hinder the case against Minnie Wright. This assumption is completely wrong, for Mrs. Peters joins Mrs. Hale in suppressing the evidence and lying to the men.

Rounding out the male characters is Lewis Hale, a husband and farmer who represents the domestic sphere. Although Lewis Hale may not be an ideal individual, he provides a strong foil for John Wright's character. We might expect Lewis Hale, as Mrs. Hale's spouse, to be a good (or at least a tolerable) person, and, on the whole, he is. Although he too misses the significance of the "trifles" in the kitchen and mocks the activities of his wife and Mrs. Peters, he seems less eager than the other men to punish Minnie Wright—possibly because he knew John Wright better than they did. Lewis Hale is clearly reluctant to provide evidence against Minnie Wright when he speaks of her behavior after he discovers the body:

➡️

> HALE. She moved from that chair to this one
> over here [Pointing to a small chair in the
> corner.] and just sat there with her hands
> held together and looking down. I got a
> feeling that I ought to make some
> conversation, so I said I had come in to see
> if John wanted to put in a telephone, and at
> that she started to laugh, and then she
> stopped and looked at me--scared. [The
> county attorney, who has had his notebook
> out, makes a note.] I dunno, maybe it wasn't
> scared. I wouldn't like to say it
> was . . . (speech 23)

Lewis Hale is the only man who tries to bring up
the incompatibility of the Wrights' marriage, citing
John Wright's dislike for conversation and adding, "I
didn't know if what his wife wanted made much
difference to John--" (speech 9), but George Henderson
cuts him off before he can pursue this any further.
Lewis Hale is a personable and talkative man--not at
all like John Wright, whom Mrs. Hale likens to "a raw
wind that gets to the bone" (speech 103). Lewis Hale is
a social being who wants to communicate with the people
around him, as his desire for a telephone party line
indicates. The Hales' functional marriage shows that
gender differences need not be insurmountable, but it
also serves to highlight the truly devastating effect
that a completely incompatible union can have on two
people's lives. Mrs. Hale reminds us that even a
marriage that "works" can be dehumanizing:

> MRS. HALE. I might have known she needed
> help! I know how things can be--for women. I
> tell you it's queer, Mrs. Peters. We live
> close together and we live far apart. We all
> go through the same things--it's all just a
> different kind of the same thing. (speech
> 136)

→

The great irony of the drama is that the women are able to accomplish what the men cannot: They establish the motive for the murder. They find evidence suggesting that John Wright viciously killed his wife's canary—her sole companion through long days of work around the house. More important, they recognize the damaging nature of a marriage based upon the unequal status of the participants. Mrs. Hale and Mrs. Peters decide not to help the case against Minnie Wright, not because her husband killed a bird, but because he isolated her, made her life miserable for years, and cruelly destroyed her one source of comfort. Without hope of help from the various misogynistic, paternalistic, and uncomprehending political, legal, and domestic power structures surrounding her, Minnie Wright took the law into her own hands. As the characters of George Henderson, Henry Peters, and Lewis Hale demonstrate, she clearly could not expect understanding from the men of her community.

Work Cited

Glaspell, Susan. Trifles. Literature: An Introduction to Reading and Writing. 3rd ed. Edgar V. Roberts and Henry E. Jacobs. Englewood Cliffs: Prentice, 1992. 1018–1028.

3 | **Student research paper analyzing two poems**

The following essay is a literary analysis that uses secondary sources°.

Born in 1889 on the Caribbean island of Jamaica, Claude McKay moved to the United States in 1910 and became a highly respected African-American poet.

Paule Cheek chose to write about Claude McKay's nontraditional use of a very traditional poetic form, the sonnet. A sonnet has fourteen rhyming lines and develops one idea. In secondary sources Cheek found information about McKay's life that she felt gave her further insights into both the structure and the meaning of McKay's sonnets "The White City" and "In Bondage." Cheek used MLA documentation style (see Chapter 33 and 37c) in her paper.

Words in Bondage:

Claude McKay's Use of the Sonnet Form in Two Poems

The sonnet has remained one of the central poetic forms of Western tradition for centuries. This fourteen—line form is easy to learn but difficult to master. With its fixed rhyme schemes, number of lines, and meter, the sonnet form forces writers to be doubly creative while working within it. Many poets over the years have modified or varied the sonnet form, playing upon its conventions to keep it vibrant and original. One such writer was Jamaican—born Claude McKay (1889–1948).

The Jamaica of McKay's childhood was very different from turn—of—the—century America. Slavery had ended there in the 1830s, and McKay was able to grow up "in a society whose population was overwhelmingly black and largely free of the overt white oppression which constricted the lives of black Americans in the United States during this same period" (Cooper, The Passion of Claude McKay 5–6). This background could not have prepared McKay for what he encountered when he moved to America in his twenties. Lynchings, still common at that time, were on the rise, and during the Red Scare of 1919 there were dozens of racially motivated riots in major cities throughout the country. Thousands of homes were destroyed in these riots, and several African—Americans were tortured and burned at the stake (Cooper, Claude McKay: Rebel Sojourner in the Harlem Renaissance 97). McKay responded to these atrocities by raising an outraged

➡

cry of protest in his poems. In two of his sonnets from this period, "The White City" and "In Bondage," we can see McKay's mastery of the form, and his skillful use of irony in the call for social change.

McKay's choice of the sonnet form as the vehicle for his protest poetry at first seems strange. Since his message was a radical one, we might expect that the form of his poetry would be revolutionary. Instead, McKay gives us sonnets—a poetic form that dates back to the early sixteenth century and that was originally intended to be used exclusively for love poems. Critic James R. Giles notes that this choice

> . . . is not really surprising, since McKay's Jamaican education and reading had been based firmly upon the major British poets. From the point quite early in his life when he began to think of himself as a poet, his models were such major English writers as William Shakespeare, John Milton, William Wordsworth. He thus was committed from the beginning to the poetry which he had initially been taught to admire. (44)

McKay published both "The White City" and "In Bondage" in 1922, and they are similar in many ways. Like most sonnets, each has fourteen lines and is in iambic pentameter. The diction is extremely elevated. For example, this quatrain from "In Bondage" is almost Elizabethan in its word choice and order:

> For life is greater than the thousand wars
> Men wage for it in their insatiate lust,
> And will remain like the eternal stars,
> When all that shines to—day is drift and
> dust. (11. 8—12)

If this level of diction is reminiscent of Shakespeare, it is no accident. Both poems employ the English sonnet rhyme scheme (a b a b c d c d e f e f g g) and division into three quatrains and a closing →

couplet. McKay introduces a touch of his own, however. Although the English sonnet form calls for the "thematic turn" to fall at the closing couplet, McKay defies convention. He incorporates two turns into each sonnet, instead of one. This allows him to use the first "mini-turn" to further develop the initial theme set forth in the first eight lines while dramatically bringing the poem to a conclusion with a forcefully ironic turn in the closing couplet. Specifically, in "The White City," McKay uses the additional turn to interrupt his description of his "Passion" with a vision of "a mighty city through the mist" (line 9). In "In Bondage" he uses the additional turn to justify his desire to escape the violent existence that society has imposed upon his people.

McKay also demonstrates his poetic ability through his choice of words within his customized sonnets. Consider the opening of "In Bondage":

> I would be wandering in distant fields
> Where man, and bird, and beast, lives leisurely,
> And the old earth is kind, and ever yields
> Her goodly gifts to all her children free;
> Where life is fairer, lighter, less demanding,
> And boys and girls have time and space for play
> Before they come to years of understanding--
> Somewhere I would be singing, far away. (11. 1-8)

The conditional power of "would" in the first line, coupled with the alliterative "wandering," subtly charms us into a relaxed, almost dreamlike state, in which the poet can lead us gently through the rest of the poem. The commas in the second line force us to check our progress to a "leisurely" crawl, mirroring the people and animals that the line describes. By the time we reach the eighth line, we are probably ready to join the poet in this land of "somewhere . . . far away."

Then, this optimistic bubble is violently burst by the
closing couplet:

> But I am bound with you in your mean graves,
> O black men, simple slaves of ruthless slaves.
> (ll. 13–14)

In "The White City," McKay again surprises us.
This time, he does so by turning the traditional love
sonnet upside down; instead of depicting a life made
unendurable through an overpowering love, McKay shows
us a life made bearable through a sustaining hate:

> I will not toy with it nor bend an inch.
> Deep in the secret chambers of my heart
> I muse my life-long hate, and without flinch
> I bear it nobly as I live my part.
> My being would be a skeleton, a shell,
> If this dark Passion that fills my every mood,
> And makes my heaven in the white world's hell,
> Did not forever feed me vital blood.   (ll. 1–8)

If it were not for the presence of "life-long hate" in
line three, this opening would easily pass as part of a
conventional love sonnet. The emotion comes from "deep
in the secret chambers" of the speaker's heart (line 2),
it allows him to transcend "the white world's hell"
(line 7), and it is a defining "Passion." Once again,
however, McKay uses the couplet to defy our
expectations by making it plain that he has used the
form of the love sonnet only for ironic effect:
The tides, the wharves, the dens I contemplate,
Are sweet like wanton loves because I hate. (ll. 13–14)

McKay's impressive poetic ability made him a
master of the sonnet form. His language could at times
rival even Shakespeare's, and his creativity allowed
him to adapt the sonnet to his own ends. His ironic
genius is revealed in his use of one of Western
society's most elevated poetic forms in order to
critique that same society. McKay once described

➡

himself as "a man who was bitter because he loved, who
was both right and wrong because he hated the things
that destroyed love, who tried to give back to others a
little of what he had got from them . . ." (Barksdale and
Kinnamon, 491). As these two sonnets show, McKay gave
back very much indeed.

Works Cited

Barksdale, Richard, and Kenneth Kinnamon, eds. Black
     Writers of America: A Comprehensive Anthology.
     New York: Macmillan, 1972.

Cooper, Wayne F. Claude McKay: Rebel Sojourner in the
     Harlem Renaissance. Baton Rouge: Louisiana
     State UP, 1987.

———, ed. The Passion of Claude McKay. New York:
     Schocken Books, 1973.

Giles, James R. Claude McKay. Boston: Twayne, 1976.

McKay, Claude. "In Bondage." Literature: An
     Introduction to Reading and Writing. 3rd ed.
     Edgar V. Roberts and Henry E. Jacobs. Englewood
     Cliffs: Prentice, 1992. 740.

———, "The White City." Literature: An Introduction to
     Reading and Writing. 3rd ed. Edgar V. Roberts and
     Henry E. Jacobs. Englewood Cliffs: Prentice,
     1992. 937–38.

38 Writing in the Social Sciences and Natural Sciences

38a Understanding methods of inquiry in the social sciences

Disciplines in the **social sciences** include subject areas such as economics, education, geography, political science, psychology, and sociology. At some colleges, history is included in the social sciences; at others it is included in the humanities. The social sciences focus on the behavior of people as individuals and in groups.

Observation is a common method for inquiry in the social sciences. To make observations, take along whatever tools or equipment you might need: writing or sketching materials, and perhaps recording or photographic equipment. As you make observations, take very accurate and complete notes. If you use abbreviations to speed your note-taking, make sure you will later understand them when you need to write up your observations. In a report of your observations, tell what tools or equipment you used, because your method might have influenced what you saw (for example, your taking photographs may make people act differently than usual).

Interviewing is another common technique that social scientists use. Interviews are useful for gathering people's opinions and impressions of events. If you interview, remember that interviews are not always a completely reliable way to gather factual information, because people's memories are not precise. If your only source for facts is interviews, try to interview as many people as possible so that you can cross-check the information. Before you interview anyone, practice with whatever note-taking tools you might need, so that they do not intrude on the interview process (see also 32h-1).

QUOTATION ABOUT HISTORIANS

The first quality [of a historian] is to be true and impartial; the next is to be interesting.
—David Hume

QUOTATION ABOUT HISTORIANS

A historian is a prophet in reverse.
—Friedrich von Schlegel

QUOTATION ABOUT ECONOMISTS

If all economists were laid end to end, they would not reach a conclusion.
—George Bernard Shaw

QUOTATION ABOUT ECONOMISTS

I learned more about economics from one South Dakota dust storm than I did in all my years in college.
—Hubert Humphrey

QUOTATION ABOUT POLITICAL SCIENCE

Politics is not an exact science.
—Prince Otto von Bismarck

QUOTATION ABOUT POLITICAL SCIENCE

Politics is the science of how who gets what, when and why.
—Sidney Hillman

QUOTATION ABOUT PSYCHOLOGY

Gossip: sociologists on a mean and petty scale.
—Woodrow Wilson

Questionnaires can be useful for gathering information in the social sciences. When you administer a questionnaire, be sure that you ask a sufficient number of people to respond, so that you do not reach conclusions based on too small a sample of responses. To write questions for a questionnaire, use the guidelines in Chart 166.

GUIDELINES FOR WRITING QUESTIONS FOR A QUESTIONNAIRE ¹⁶⁶

166

1. First, define what you want to find out, and then write questions that will elicit the information you seek.
2. Phrase questions so that they are easy to understand.
3. Use appropriate language (see 21a), and avoid artificial language (see 21e).
4. Be aware that how you phrase your questions will determine whether the answers that you get truly reflect what people are thinking. Make sure that your choice of words does not imply what *you* want to hear.
5. Avoid questions that invite one-word answers about complex matters that call for a range of responses.
6. Test a draft of the questionnaire on a small group of people before you use it. If any question is misinterpreted or hard to understand, revise and retest it.

38b Understanding writing purposes and practices in the social sciences

Social scientists write to inform readers by presenting and explaining information (see 1b-1), or to persuade readers by arguing a point of view (see 1b-2).

Analysis (see 4f-6 and 5a) helps social scientists write about problems and their solutions. For example, an economist writing about a major automobile company in financial trouble might first break the situation into parts, analyzing employee salaries and benefits, the selling price of cars, and the costs of doing business. Next, the economist might show how these parts relate to the financial status of the whole company. Then the economist might speculate about how specific changes would help solve the company's financial problems.

Social scientists are particularly careful to **define their terms** when they write, especially when they discuss complex social issues. For example, if you are writing a paper on substance abuse in the medical profession, you first have to define what you mean by the terms *substance abuse* and *medical profession*. By *substance* do you mean alcohol and drugs or only drugs? How are you quantifying *abuse*? When you refer to the medical profession, are you including nurses and lab technicians or only doctors? Without defining these terms, you can confuse your readers or lead them to wrong conclusions.

Social scientists often use **analogy** (see 4f-8) to make unfamiliar ideas clear. When an unfamiliar idea is compared to one that is more familiar, the unfamiliar idea becomes easier to understand. For example, sociologists may talk of the "culture shock" that some people feel when they enter a new society. The sociologists might compare this "shock" to the reaction that someone living today might have if suddenly moved hundreds of years into the future or the past.

In college courses in the social sciences, some instructors ask students to write their personal reactions to information or experiences, in which case the first person (*I, we, our*) is acceptable. In most writing for the social sciences, however, writers use the third person (*he, she, it, one, they*). Also, because the emphasis is on people or groups being observed rather than on the person doing the observing, some social scientists use the passive voice° (see 8n–8o) rather than the active voice°. The *Publication Manual of the American Psychological Association,* the most commonly used style manual in the social sciences (see 38c), however, recommends the active voice whenever possible.

38c

Using documentation style in the social sciences

If you use secondary sources° when you write about the social sciences, you are required to credit these sources by using documentation°. The most commonly used documentation style° in the social sciences is that of the American Psychological Association (APA). The APA documentation style uses parenthetical references (see 33b-2) in the body of a paper and a References list (see 33c-2 and 33d) at the end of a paper.

For an example of a student research paper that uses APA documentation style, see Chapter 35.

BACKGROUND

In addition to case studies and research papers, students in social science classes are sometimes asked to write analyses of standard texts in a field of study and reports of personal investigation into a specific question. They may find it helpful to know that a textual analysis begins with clear identification of the articles to be reviewed by citation of titles, authors, and publication data. It should include an introduction to the topic under examination, a review of the major views of the subject, and an evaluation of the sources surveyed. The thesis of the paper should indicate that the student has formulated certain concepts about the subject and is able to support them with arguments. It should end with a list of references. The research report on an investigated question should state the purpose of the research, name the processes by which it was carried out, specify what equipment was used, explain the results, and conclude with generalizations about the subject. It should also include citation of any outside sources that were used. In the case of original research, the report should include a survey of related theories in the field, as well as an explanation of the importance of the study and the significance of the findings.

BACKGROUND

One of the objections often heard to implementing writing-to-learn techniques in non-English classes is that the large number of students in those courses make it impossible for student writing to be adequately read or evaluated. In "Writing to Learn in Large Lecture Classes," (*Journal of College Science Teaching* 19 [December 1989]: 158–163), Toby Fulwiler and Michael Strauss offer solutions to the problem by explaining such methods as keeping chemistry logs, visualizing informal thought, and holding laboratory workshops on writing.

38d Writing different types of papers in the social sciences

Two major types of papers in the social sciences are case studies and research papers.

1 Writing case studies in the social sciences

A **case study** is an intensive study of one group or individual. It is usually presented in a relatively fixed format, but the specific parts and order of case study formats vary. Most case studies contain the following components: (1) basic identifying information about the individual or group; (2) a history of the individual or group; (3) observations of the individual's or group's behavior; and (4) conclusions and perhaps recommendations as a result of the observations.

In writing a case study, describe situations; do not interpret them. Be sure to differentiate between fact and opinion (see 5d-3). For example, you may observe nursing-home patients lying in bed on their sides facing the door. Describe exactly what you see; do not interpret this observation as, say, patients watching for visitors. Perhaps medicines are injected in the right hip, and patients are more comfortable lying on their left side, thus facing the door.

2 Writing research papers in the social sciences

You may be assigned a **research paper** in the social sciences for which you must consult secondary sources°. (See 32l on using specialized reference books and 32m-2 on using specialized indexes.) These sources are usually articles and books that report, summarize, and otherwise discuss the findings of other people's research. For an example of a student research paper written for an introductory psychology course, see Chapter 35.

38e Understanding methods of inquiry in the sciences

Disciplines in the **natural sciences** include astronomy, biology, chemistry, geology, and physics. The sciences focus on natural phenomena. The purpose of scientific inquiry is discovery. Scientists formulate and test hypotheses in order to explain cause and effect (see 5f) systematically and objectively.

The **scientific method,** commonly used in the sciences to make discoveries, is a procedure for gathering information related to a specific hypothesis. The scientific method is the cornerstone of all inquiry in the sciences. Guidelines for using the scientific method are shown in Chart 167.

GUIDELINES FOR USING THE SCIENTIFIC METHOD 167

1. Formulate a tentative explanation—known as a **hypothesis**—for a scientific phenomenon. Be as specific as possible.
2. Read and summarize previously published information related to your hypothesis.
3. Plan and outline a method of investigation to uncover the information needed to test your hypothesis.
4. Experiment, exactly following the investigative procedures you have outlined.
5. Observe closely the results of the experiment, and write notes carefully.
6. Analyze the results. If they prove the hypothesis to be false, rework the investigation and begin again. If the results prove the hypothesis to be true, say so.
7. Write a report of your research. At the end, you might suggest additional hypotheses that might be investigated.

38f Understanding writing purposes and practices in the natural sciences

Scientists usually write to inform their audiences about factual information.

Exactness is extremely important in scientific writing. Readers expect precise descriptions of procedures and findings, free of personal biases. Scientists expect to be able to *replicate*—repeat step-by-step—the experiment or other process and get the same outcome as the writer.

Completeness is also essential in scientific writing. Without complete information, the reader might come to wrong conclusions.

BACKGROUND

Some social scientists divide research papers into two categories: the qualitative and the quantitative. Qualitative research, as the name implies, investigates human values, patterns, or other characteristics that cannot be described numerically. It usually includes the personal involvement of the researcher with the subject being studied through interviews, observation, and, in some cases, participation. Throughout the study, the researcher is looking for meaning and patterns, moving progressively towards formulation of a hypothesis, and ultimately, a theory. A major problem for students who attempt to do qualitative research is time. Because the researcher must suit his or her schedule to the availability of the subject, sometimes the semester (or quarter) is not long enough to compile sufficient data to formulate significant conclusions. Also, the student may on occasion find it impossible to be present when important events occur. The quantitative research paper, on the other hand, follows a more structured (and predictable) process. Dealing with subjects that can be tested and expressed numerically, it is appropriate for comparing situations or examining frequency of occurrence. In many cases the researcher begins with a hypothesis, designs a means of testing it, then goes on to prove or disprove it. It requires some skill and knowledge on the part of the researcher in the use of graphs, statistics, and other techniques of quantitative expression.

BACKGROUND

In an article published in *College Teaching* ("Integrating Writing in Developmental Mathematics," 37 [Fall 1989]: 140–142), Aparna B. Ganguli reports that when writing assignments are combined with mathematical instruction, weak students achieve higher math scores than their counterparts who receive more conventional instruction.

QUOTATION ABOUT WRITING

The universe is full of magical things, patiently waiting for our wits to grow sharper.

—Eden Phillpotts

QUOTATION ABOUT SCIENCE

I seem to have been only a boy playing on the seashore, and diverting myself in now and then finding a smoother pebble or a prettier shell than ordinary, whilst the great ocean of truth lay all undiscovered before me.

—Sir Isaac Newton

QUOTATION ABOUT SCIENCE

Creativity in science could be described as the act of putting two and two together to make five.

—Arthur Koestler

QUOTATION ABOUT WRITING IN THE NATURAL SCIENCES

With the rise of experimental methods in the eighteenth century, science has developed increasingly sophisticated methods of data collection, observation, and verification. Using carefully controlled laboratory environments, natural scientists must observe reactions, detail materials and procedures, and repeat experiments—all of which call for written records. They must immediately record observations, make entries for all reactions, and specify all facets of a procedure. The concern for methods suggests how pivotal to scientific training is the laboratory notebook and the laboratory report.

Diane Bennett Durkin,
Writing in the Disciplines

For example, a researcher may investigate how different types of soil affect plant growth. The researcher should report not only the analysis of each soil type, but also the amount of daylight each plant receives, the moisture content of the soil, the amount and type of fertilizer used, and all other related facts. Having all this information may lead the researcher to unexpected insights. For instance, plant growth may be less dependent on soil type than on a combination of soil type, fertilizer, and watering. This observation could be made only if the researcher had carefully noted all the facts.

The sciences generally focus on the experiment rather than the experimenter and on objective observation rather than subjective interpretation. Unless you are writing a personal-reaction paper, generally avoid using the first person (*I, we, our*) in writing science papers.

Use of the passive voice is common in scientific and technical writing. *The Council of Biology Editors Style Manual*, fifth edition, gives the same advice about voice that you will find in this handbook: Use the active voice except for the special purposes best fulfilled by the passive voice (see 8n and 8o).

When writing for the sciences, often you are expected to follow fixed formats, which are designed to summarize a project and present its results efficiently. In your report, organize the information to achieve clarity and precision. Writers in the sciences sometimes use charts, graphs, tables, diagrams, and other illustrations to present material. In fact, illustrations can sometimes explain complex material more clearly than words can.

38g Using documentation style in the natural sciences

If you use secondary sources° when you write about the sciences, you are required to credit your sources by using documentation°. Documentation styles° in the various sciences differ somewhat. Ask your instructor which style you should use. If your instructor has no preference, consult 33g for a list of available style manuals in the sciences, and try to locate the manual you need. If you cannot locate the manual, or if the science you are writing in does not have a style manual, find a journal that publishes research in that science and imitate its documentation style.

The Council of Biology Editors (CBE) publishes a style manual that gives advice specific to several scientific fields, including plant sciences, microbiology, animal sciences, chemistry and biochem-

38g

istry, and geography and geology. The *CBE Manual,* fifth edition, also gives general advice about documentation, mentioning several systems. One is the *Harvard System,* a "name-and-year" system very similar to the MLA and APA systems covered in this handbook (see Chapters 33, 34, and 35).

For style of a list of sources, the *CBE Manual* recommends following either a professional journal in the specific field or the *American National Standard for Bibliographic References,* a 1977 publication of the American National Standards Institute. Here are some examples of formats for common types of sources based on *American National Standard* guidelines. (The sources named match those in section 33d, for your ease of comparison.)

BOOK BY ONE AUTHOR

Welty, E. One writer's beginnings. Cambridge: Harvard University Press; 1984.

BOOK WITH MORE THAN ONE AUTHOR AND WITH A SUBTITLE

Kelly, A.H.; Harbison, W.A.; Belz, H. The American Constitution: its origins and development. New York: W.W. Norton & Co.; 1983.

TWO OR MORE BOOKS BY THE SAME AUTHOR(S)

Morris, D. Primate ethology. London: Wiedenfeld; 1967.

Morris, D. Manwatching: a field guide to human behavior. New York: Henry N. Abrams; 1977.

JOURNAL ARTICLE, ONE AUTHOR

Shuter, R. A field study of nonverbal communication in Germany, Italy, and the United States. Comm. Monogr. 44:298–305; 1977.

JOURNAL ARTICLE, MORE THAN ONE AUTHOR

Cochran, D.D.; Hale, W.D.; Hissam, C.P. Personal space requirements in indoor versus outdoor locations. J. Psych. 117:132–133; 1984.

UNSIGNED NEWSPAPER ARTICLE

Hospitals, competing for scarce patients, turn to advertising. The New York Times. 1986 Apr. 20; 47.

FILM

Erendira [Motion picture]. Miramax, 1984.

TEACHING TIP

Many scientists are also writers who have achieved popularity with the general reading public because of their ability to write clearly, interestingly, sometimes movingly about their fields of study. As reading has long been one of the ways people learn to write or to improve their writing styles, you may want to recommend to your students that they read some of the outstanding writers in their fields in an effort to discover new ways of communicating knowledge and opinions about their subject. For example, important essayists in the biological and botanical sciences include Charles Darwin, Loren Eiseley, Jane Goodall, Hans Zinsser, Arthur Hasler, Rachel Carson, and Carl Sagan. Physics and mathematics are the subjects of the work of George Harter, Pamela McCorduck, Christopher Evans, Charles Townes, and others. John McPhee writes compellingly about earth sciences, Lewis Thomas about medicine, and Fred Hoyle about astronomy. Journals that carry well-written articles about science include *Scientific American, Science, Astronomy, Physics Today, Nature, Genetics,* and *Sky and Telescope.*

BACKGROUND

Science and composition instructors interested in learning more about how to implement writing in the science classroom can turn to John S. Dickey's article "On Science Education" (*Journal of College Science Teaching* 19 [December 1989]: 132–133), in which he describes various writing activities and the use of video texts.

38h   Writing different types of papers in the natural sciences

Two major types of papers in the sciences are reports and reviews.

1   Writing science reports

Science reports tell about observations and experiments. Such reports may also be called "laboratory reports" when they describe laboratory experiments. Formal reports include the eight sections (including the title) described in Chart 168. Less formal reports, which are sometimes assigned in introductory college courses, might not include an abstract or a review of the literature. Ask your instructor which sections to include in your report.

PARTS OF THE SCIENCE REPORT   168

1. **Title.** This is a precise description of what your report is about.
2. **Abstract.** This is a short overview of the report.
3. **Introduction.** This section states the purpose behind your research and presents the hypothesis. Any needed background information and a review of the literature appear here.
4. **Methods and material.** This section describes the equipment, material, and procedures used.
5. **Results.** This section provides the information obtained from your efforts. Charts, graphs, and photographs help present the data.
6. **Discussion.** This section represents your interpretation and evaluation of the results. Did your efforts support your hypothesis? If not, can you suggest why not? Use concrete evidence in discussing your results.
7. **Conclusion.** This section lists conclusions about the hypothesis and the outcomes of your efforts, with particular attention to any theoretical implications that can be drawn from your work. Be specific in suggesting further research.
8. **References cited.** This list presents references cited in the review of the literature, if any. Its format conforms to the requirements of the documentation style in the particular science (see 33g and 38g).

SAMPLE SCIENCE REPORT (Excerpts)

An Experiment to Predict Vestigial Wings
in an F_2 Drosophila Population

INTRODUCTION

The purpose of this experiment was to observe
second filial generation (F_2) wing structures in
Drosophila. The hypothesis was that abnormalities in
vestigial wing structures would follow predicted
genetic patterns.

METHODS AND MATERIALS

On February 7, four Drosophila (P_1) were observed.
Observation was made possible by etherizing the
parents (after separating them from their larvae),
placing them on a white card, and observing them under a
dissecting microscope. The observations were recorded
on a chart.

On February 14, the larvae taken from the parents
on February 7 had developed to adults (F_1), and they
were observed using the same methods as on February 7.
The observations were recorded on the chart.

On February 19, the second filial generation (F_2)
was supposed to be observed. This was impossible
because they did not hatch. The record chart had to be
discontinued.

RESULTS

No observations of F_2 were possible. For the F_1
population, according to the prediction, no members
should have had vestigial wings. According to the
observations, however, some members of F_1 did have
vestigial wings.

[DISCUSSION SECTION OMITTED]

QUOTATION ABOUT SCIENCE

The most incomprehensible thing about the
world is that it is comprehensible.

—Albert Einstein

QUOTATION ABOUT WRITING

The ability to translate data and scientific
terms into clear, readable, interesting prose
is the most important criterion for judging
the success of an essay in a science course.

—Linda Simon

BACKGROUND

Over the past decade many teachers in
different disciplines have experimented
with ways to work together to improve
student writing and learning. In "A Freshman Writing Course in Parallel with a Science Course" (*College Composition and Communication* 36 [May 1985]: 160–165), A. M.
Wilkinson describes the joint efforts of instructors in biology and composition to design a freshman course for students concurrently enrolled in the two departments.
They hoped to give students practice in
writing clear, factual, scientific prose, expose them to some rhetorical forms characteristic of scientific writing, and give them
opportunities to rewrite. The results were
that students were more highly motivated.
They had to recall and review material that
they had already covered as they prepared
to write about it. In "Writing Across the
Curriculum: The Mentor Project" (*Teaching
English in the Two-Year College* 16 [May 1989]:
99–103), Diane Martin Jordan and Michael
Moorhead report on another program that
pairs English teachers with faculty from
other departments. Barbara Y. Stewart describes Swarthmore's writing-intensive laboratory courses in biology, which are taught
by biology and composition teachers, in
"Merging Scientific Writing with the Investigative Laboratory" (*Journal of College Science Teaching* 19 [November 1989]: 94–95).

BACKGROUND

James B. Livingston describes seven methods for improving student learning and writing in science courses in "Reading into the Subject of Science: Strategies for a More Literate Class" (*Science Teacher* 56 [February 1989]: 49–50). He covers lab journals, written reports, research papers, and other kinds of writing.

BACKGROUND

Steve Trombulak and Sallie Sheldon report in "The Real Value of Writing to Learning Biology" (*Journal of College Science Teaching* 18 [May 1989]: 384–388), that writing not only improves students' performance, but also increases their appreciation of science.

BACKGROUND

In "Implementing Writing Across the Curriculum: Strategies in the Biological Sciences" (*Dissertation Abstracts International* 50 [August 1989]: 339A), Joanna Theresa Ambron reports on the use of various heuristic devices and writing-to-learn strategies in biology courses. She discusses journal writing, freewriting, microthemes, and clustering.

QUOTATION ABOUT SCIENCE

I am actually not at all a man of science, not an observer, not an experimenter, not a thinker. I am by temperament nothing but a conquistador—an adventurer.

—Sigmund Freud

CONCLUSIONS

Two explanations are possible to explain vestigial wings in the F_1 population. Perhaps members from F_2 were present from the F_1 generation. This is doubtful since the incubation period is 10 days, and the time between observations was only 8 days. A second possible explanation is that the genotype of the male P_1 was not WW (indicating that both genes were for normal wings) but rather heterozygous (Ww). If this were true the following would be the first filial products in a 1:1 ratio:

$$P_1 \quad Ww \times ww$$
$$F_1 \quad Ww \; ww$$

Thus, the possiblity for vestigial wings would exist. The problem remains, however, that the ratio was not 1:1 2:1 (i.e., 24 normal to 12 abnormal). One explanation could be that the total number was not large enough to extract an average.

The hypothesis concerning predicted genetic patterns in F_2 could not be confirmed because the F_2 generation did not hatch. This experiment should be repeated to get F_2 data. A larger F_1 sample should be used to see if the F_1 findings reported here are repeated.

---

2 Writing science reviews

A **science review** is a paper discussing published information on a scientific topic or issue. The purpose of the review is to gather together for readers the current knowledge about the topic or issue.

Sometimes the purpose of a science review is to suggest a new interpretation of the old material. Any reinterpretation is based on a synthesis of old information with new, more complete information. In such reviews, the writer must marshal evidence to persuade readers that the new interpretation is valid.

If you are required to write a science review, (1) choose a very limited scientific issue currently being researched; (2) use information that is current—the more recently published the articles, books, and journals you consult, the better; (3) accurately summarize and paraphrase material—as explained in 31e and 31d; (4) document your sources (see 33g). If your review is more than two or three pages, you might want to use headings to help your reader understand the organization and idea progression of your paper. See 32l on using specialized reference books and 32m-2 on using specialized indexes.

QUOTATION ABOUT WRITING

It is difficult to overemphasize the importance of writing in the professional life of a scientist. The amount of time my colleagues and I spend writing is out of all proportion to the fraction of our training devoted to developing writing skills. "Publish or perish" is a cliché, but it carries the unmistakable implication that experimental work and elegant theories have no peer value until they have been put in manuscript form. I was shocked to find that the time and effort of writing was often equal to that of the research work being described. . . . The tasks of writing fall heavily on industrial scientists as well.

—C. G. Enke, "Scientific Writing:
One Scientist's Perspective"

QUOTATION ABOUT SCIENTIFIC WRITING

Bad scientific writing involves more than stylistic inelegance; it is often the outward and visible form of an inward confusion of thought.

—Peter F. Woodford, "Sounder Thinking
through Clearer Writing"

39 Business Writing

Business writing requires of you what other kinds of writing call for: understanding your audience and your purpose. This chapter explains how to write business letters (see 39a), job application letters (see 39b), and résumés (see 39c). As you write for business, use the guidelines listed in Chart 169.

GUIDELINES FOR BUSINESS WRITING 169

- Consider your audience's needs and expectations.
- Show that you understand the purpose for a business communication and the context in which it takes place.
- Put essential information first.
- Make your points clearly and directly.
- Use conventional formats.

39a Writing and formatting a business letter

Business letters are written to give information, to build good will, or to establish a foundation for discussions or transactions. Experts in business and government agree that the letters likely to get results are short, simple, direct, and human. Here is good, basic advice: (1) call the person by name; (2) tell what your letter is about in the first paragraph; (3) be honest; (4) be clear and specific; (5) use accurate English; (6) be positive and natural; (7) edit ruthlessly.

For business letters, use the guidelines in Chart 170 and the format on page 728. To avoid sexist language in the salutation of your

39a

letter, use the guidelines in Chart 171. For a business envelope, see page 732.

GUIDELINES FOR BUSINESS LETTERS

170

LETTERHEAD	If printed stationery is not available, type the company name and address centered at top of white paper, 8½ × 11″.
DATE	Put the date at the left margin under the letterhead, when typing in block form as shown in the example. When using paragraph indentations, type the date so that it ends at the right margin.
INSIDE ADDRESS	Direct your letter to a specific person. Be accurate in spelling the name and the address. If unsure of your information, telephone and ask questions of a secretary or other assistant.
SUBJECT LINE	Place at the left margin. In a few, concise words state the letter's subject.
SALUTATION	Use a first name only if you personally know the person. Otherwise, use *Mr.* or *Ms.* or whatever title is applicable with the person's last name. Avoid sexist language.
CLOSING	*Sincerely* or *Sincerely yours* are generally appropriate, unless you know the person very well and wish to use *Cordially.* Leave about four lines for your signature.
NAME LINES	Type your full name and title below your signature. The title can be on the same or the next line as your name.
SECOND PAGE	Head a second page with three items of information: the name of the person or company to which your letter is addressed, the number *2* or *page 2,* and the date. Place the information on three lines at the top left margin or on one line spaced across the top of the page.

TEACHING TIP

Some students expect business writing to involve rules about margins, indentations, and abbreviations. While such concerns do matter, they should take only a small part of your time. Format can be taught in just a few lessons; the emphasis in business writing is on audience, tone, and organization.

Audience. Business writers need to be acutely aware of their audiences. Since business correspondence is aimed at a particular individual or a limited group of individuals rather than the general audience essays are aimed at, in certain aspects business writing differs markedly from essay writing. The most obvious difference is that the use of *you* and *I/we* is preferable to the third person often used in essays.

Tone. The tone of business correspondence needs to be adjusted to suit the actual relationship between author and audience. It is perfectly conceivable that a businessperson might write a very formal memo to the staff of one department about lax security and a minute later write a relatively friendly memo to another department congratulating it for exceeding production goals. The key word in deciding on the appropriate tone is *relationship.* Your students can judge the nature of the relationship by asking themselves a few questions as they prepare to write: Who is the person I am writing to? How long and under what circumstances have we known one another? What do I want him or her to do? No matter what the relationship, correspondence should be written in standard, clear, and honest English. See Chapter 21 for discussions of levels of formality and artificial language.

Organization. The organization of a business document will vary with its purpose. To help students become familiar with the conventional forms of business letters, résumés, and memos, some examples are provided in this chapter.

39a

TEACHING TIP

Some people are fascinated by those initials and abbreviations they see in letters, at the left margin a few lines below the signature. Few of our students have any need to use these on a regular basis, but in case you are asked about these symbols, here's a quick review.

AS/kw The writer's initials followed by the typist's initials (known as reference initials). Practice varies in the use of capital and lowercase letters. Sometimes a colon is used: *AS:kw.*

Enclosures: Typed below the reference initials, a numeric notation alerts the opener of the mail to the presence of additional material: brochures, résumés, photographs. A multi-page enclosure counts as one. Sometimes the notation is written out as "Enc.: résumé and letter of reference."

cc: Ken Lane Typed below the reference initials, the abbreviation *cc* indicates that a carbon copy has been sent. Carbon paper is passé, but the abbreviation lingers. The notation is followed by a name or initials.

P.S. A postscript may be added after everything else to highlight a point made within the letter or to add a brief personal message. Do not use a postscript to add important information that you forgot to include in the letter; rewrite the letter. Strings of postscripts (P.P.S., etc.) are definitely not suitable for business writing.

BUSINESS LETTER FORMAT

letterhead
AlphaOmega Industries, Inc.
123456 Motor Parkway
Fresh Hills, CA 55555

date
December 28, 19XX

inside address
Ron R. London, Sales Director
Seasonal Products Corp.
5000 Seasonal Place
Wiscasset, ME 00012

subject line
Subject: Spring Promotional Effort

salutation
Dear Ron:

message
Since we talked last week, I have completed plans for the Spring promotion of the products that we market jointly. AlphaOmega and Seasonal Products should begin a direct mailing of the enclosed brochure on January 28.

I have secured several mailing lists that contain the names of people who have a positive economic profile for our products. The profile and the outline of the lists are attached.

Do you have additional approaches for the promotion? I would like to meet with you on January 6 to discuss them and to work out the details of the project.

Please call me and let me know if a meeting next week at your office accommodates your schedule.

closing
Sincerely,

Alan Stone

name, title
Alan Stone, Director of Special Promotions

WRITER'S/ typist's initials
AS/kw

copies
cc: Yolanda Lane, Vice President, Marketing

enclosures
Enc.: Brochure: Mailing Lists;
Customer Profile

39b

GUIDELINES FOR WRITING A NONSEXIST SALUTATION   171

You may want to send a business letter when you do not have a specific person to whom it should be addressed. Use the following steps to prepare a salutation.

1. Telephone the company to which you are sending the letter. State your reason for sending the letter, and ask for the name of the person who should receive it.

2. Use a first name only if you know the person. Otherwise, use *Mr.* or *Ms.* or an applicable title. Avoid a sexist title such as *Dear Sir.*

3. If you cannot find out the name of the person who should read your letter, use a generic title.

   NO   Dear Sir: [obviously sexist]

   Dear Madam/Sir or Dear Sir/Madam: [few women want to be addressed as ''Madam'']

   YES   Dear Personnel Officer:

   Dear IBM Sales Manager:

In addressing an envelope, remember that the best-written letter means nothing if it does not reach its destination. In the illustration on page 732, you will see the U.S. Postal Service guidelines for addressing envelopes so that they can be processed by machine. (Envelopes that must be sorted by hand add three days or more to mail-delivery time.)

39b Writing and formatting a job application letter

Chart 172 gives guidelines for a job application letter. A sample job application letter appears on page 731.

GUIDELINES FOR JOB APPLICATION LETTERS   172

| **YOUR ADDRESS** | Type your address in block style as you would on an envelope. Use as your address (with a ➡ |

TEACHING TIP: SALUTATIONS

The salutation is the first thing a reader sees, so it must be suitable if the letter is to be taken seriously. In most situations the salutation presents no problem, but sometimes the writer has to make a difficult decision. Here are some guidelines:

1. When the recipient's name is known: *Dear Mr._____; Dear Ms._____; Dear Mrs._____; Dear Miss_____.*

2. When the writer normally calls the recipient by his or her first name and when the letter is relatively informal: *Dear Heidi; Dear Elliot.*

3. When the letter is going to a position within an organization and the writer has not been able to get an individual's name: *Manager, Customer Service Department; Dear Manager.*

4. When the writer does not know the sex of the recipient: *Dear Mr. or Ms. Gery; Dear Director; Dear Mr. or Ms. Director.*

5. When the recipient is a group: *Dear Members of_____; Dear Committee Members.*

6. When there will be many anonymous recipients: *Dear Homeowners; Dear Student; Dear Customer.*

TEACHING TIP

Few letters are as difficult for students to write as those they send in hopes of getting a job interview. The following suggestions can be adapted to any job-seeking situation.

Before writing a letter of application, the student should already have prepared a stock résumé, one that can be used for any job in the student's area of interest. A properly written résumé will be good for six months to a year or more. As it lists the basics of a career to date, it should not have to be redone for each job sought.

In the cover letter, students should tell a prospective employer what they can bring to the job, why they feel they are qualified—not why they want the job. This is the place to expand upon the information listed in the résumé. Do not, however, summarize or repeat large parts of the résumé.

In paragraph 1, students should tell how they found out about the job (ad, friend with the company). In paragraphs 2 to 4, students should pick three skills or personal qualities that they know are needed for the job. These may include, but are not limited to, using office machines, driving a delivery truck, preparing a payroll, speaking a second language, being available for night shifts or out-of-town travel.

In the next paragraph, students should discuss their specific qualifications. They can draw upon work experience, education, volunteer work, family responsibilities, and hobbies. In the final paragraph, students should thank the reader for taking the time to consider the application. They should also express a wish for an interview at the employer's convenience and include a phone number and address.

GUIDELINES FOR JOB APPLICATION LETTERS (*continued*)

zip code) a place where you can be reached **by letter.**

DATE	Put the date below your address. Make sure that you mail the letter on either the same day or the next day; a delayed mailing can imply lack of planning.
INSIDE ADDRESS	Direct your letter to a specific person. Telephone the company to find out the name of the person to whom you are writing. Be accurate. A misspelled name can offend the receiver. A wrong address usually results in a lost letter.
SALUTATION	Be accurate. No one likes to see his or her name misspelled. In replying to an ad that gives only a post-office box number, omit the salutation and start your opening paragraph directly below the inside address. To avoid sexist language, use Chart 171.
INTRODUCTORY PARAGRAPH	State your purpose for writing and your source of information about the job.
BODY PARAGRAPH(S)	Interest the reader in the skills and talents you offer by mentioning whatever experience you have *that relates to the specific job*. Mention your enclosed résumé, but do *not* summarize it.
CLOSING PARAGRAPH	Suggest an interview, stating that you will call to make arrangements.
CLOSING	*Sincerely* or *Sincerely yours* are generally appropriate.
NAME LINES	Type your full name below your signature. Leave about four lines for your signature.
NOTATION	If you are enclosing any material with your letter, type *Enc.:* and briefly list the items.

JOB APPLICATION LETTER

422 Broward
University of Texas at Arlington
Arlington, Texas 75016
May 15, 19XX

Rae Clemens, Director of Human Resources
Taleno, Ward Marketing, Inc.
1471 Summit Boulevard
Houston, Texas 78211

Dear Ms. Clemens:

I am answering the advertisement for a marketing
trainee that Taleno, Ward placed in today's Houston
Chronicle.

Marketing has been one of the emphases of my course work
here at the University of Texas, Arlington, as you will
see on my enclosed résumé. This past year, I gained
some practical experience as well, when I developed
marketing techniques that helped to turn my typing
service into a busy and profitable small business.

Successfully marketing the typing service (with
flyers, advertisements in college publications, and
even a two-for-one promotion) makes me a very
enthusiastic novice. I can think of no better way to
become a professional than working for Taleno, Ward.

I will be here at the Arlington campus through August 1.
You can reach me by phone at 555-1976. Unless I hear
from you before, I'll call on May 25 about setting up an
interview.

Sincerely yours,

Lee Franco

Lee Franco

Enc.: Résumé

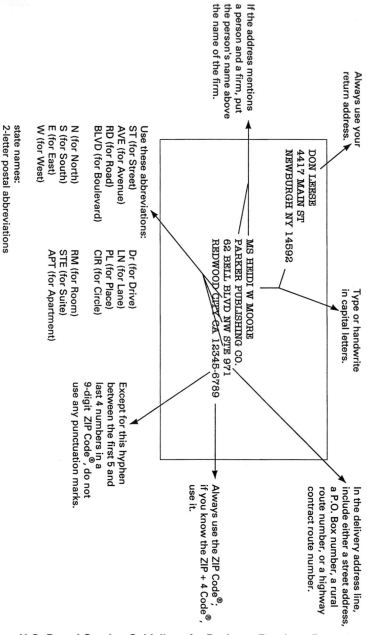

Always use your return address.

Type or handwrite in capital letters.

If the address mentions a person and a firm, put the person's name above the name of the firm.

Use these abbreviations:
ST (for Street)
AVE (for Avenue)
RD (for Road)
BLVD (for Boulevard)

N (for North)
S (for South)
E (for East)
W (for West)

Dr (for Drive)
LN (for Lane)
PL (for Place)
CIR (for Circle)

RM (for Room)
STE (for Suite)
APT (for Apartment)

state names:
2-letter postal abbreviations

DON LEESE
4417 MAIN ST
NEWBURGH NY 14592

MS HEIDI W MOORE
PARKER PUBLISHING CO.
62 BELL BLVD NW STE 971
REDWOOD CITY CA 12345-6789

In the delivery address line, include either a street address, a P.O. Box number, a rural route number, or a highway contract route number.

Always use the ZIP Code®, if you know the ZIP + 4 Code®, use it.

Except for this hyphen between the first 5 and last 4 numbers in a 9-digit ZIP Code®, do not use any punctuation marks.

U.S. Postal Service Guidelines for Business Envelope Format

39c Writing and formatting a résumé

A **résumé** is an easy-to-read, factual document that presents your qualifications for employment. All résumés cover certain standard items: name, address, phone number; education; past experience; skills and talents; publications, awards, honors, membership in professional organizations; list of references or a statement that they are "available upon request."

A résumé gives you an opportunity to present a positive picture of yourself to a prospective employer. Employers understand that college students may have limited experience in the business world. Think of headings that allow you to emphasize your strengths. For example, if you have never done paid work, do not use *Business Experience.* You can use *Work Experience* if you have done volunteer or other unpaid work. If the experience you offer an employer is that you have run school or social events, you might use *Organizational Experience.* If your greatest strength is your academic record, put your educational achievements first.

You may choose to arrange your résumé in emphatic order with the most important information first and the least important last. Or you may choose to arrange information in chronological (time) order, a sequence that is good for showing a steady work history or solid progress in a particular field. Lee Franco's résumé, which was sent with the job application letter on page 731, is on page 734. It uses emphatic order. Stephen Schmit's résumé, on page 735, uses chronological order.

When you are applying for a specific job, modify your basic résumé to emphasize your qualifications for that job. Lee Franco added the *Marketing Trainee* heading and the statement about relevant experience for becoming a marketing trainee to her basic résumé and positioned the *Marketing Experience* section first. These modifications help to send a message that Franco's qualifications for the marketing trainee position are better than other applicants'. If you keep your résumé on computer, you can easily tailor it to specific job opportunities.

Your résumé usually has to fulfill only one purpose: It has to convince the person who first looks at it to put it into the "Call for an interview" pile rather than into the wastebasket. To do that best, a résumé should be eye-catching and informative, and it should make its readers think, "We should talk to this person, who sounds likely to be an asset to our business."

TEACHING TIP
Most job applicants are aware of the importance of writing a good letter of application and of providing an attractive résumé. Many people, however, neglect to follow up these initial moves by writing thank-you letters for job interviews and follow-up letters to a potential employer who fails to respond.

You might want to remind students of other types of letters that can help them secure the job of their choice. They can also be asked to practice those additional forms.

BACKGROUND
Margaret Ann Smith examined students' sense of audience in a beginning management class. She also studied how their perceptions of writing changed and developed (*Dissertation Abstracts International* 50 [August 1989]: 330A).

BACKGROUND
Robert Morris College has been a leader in developing writing across the curriculum in higher education, particularly in business curricula. Donna J. Lund reports on the work being done there in "A Structural Approach to Integrating Write to Learn in All Disciplines" (ERIC ED 304 698).

EMPHATIC RÉSUMÉ

Lee Franco   MARKETING TRAINEE
422 Broward
University of Texas at Arlington
Arlington, Texas 75016
713–555–1976

The experience I acquired marketing my typing
service provided me with a good practical background
for a position as a marketing trainee.

MARKETING EXPERIENCE (program for campus typing
service)
    Evaluated typing–service capabilities; analyzed
    market for service; drew up and implemented
    marketing plan; produced 2–color flyer, designed
    print ads and wrote copy, developed and ran
    special promotion. August 19XX to February 19XX

BUSINESS EXPERIENCE
    Type–Right Typing Service: Ran campus typing
    service for two years. Duties included word
    processing (Wordstar, Displaywrite, SuperCalc),
    proofreading, billing and other financial
    record–keeping, and customer contact. August
    19XX to present.

    Archer & Archer Advertising: Worked as general
    assistant in the copy department under direct
    supervision of John Allen, Director. Duties
    included proofreading, filing, direct client
    contact. June 19XX to August 19XX.

ADDITIONAL EXPERIENCE
    Coordinated student–employment service at
    Hawthorne High School, Baton Rouge, Louisiana.
    Duties included contacting students to fill jobs
    with local employers, arranging interviews, and
    writing follow–up reports on placements.

EDUCATION
    University of Texas, Arlington
    B.A. May 19XX, Psychology, Marketing

EXTRACURRICULAR
    Marketing Club, Computer Graphics Society

References available upon request.

CHRONOLOGICAL RÉSUMÉ

Stephen L. Schmit
5230 St. Stephens Street
Boston, Massachusetts 02188

(617)555-8165

CAREER QUALIFICATIONS Technical writer trained in preparation of manuals, catalogues, and instructional materials. Experienced in writing computer documentation containing syntax formats.

WORK EXPERIENCE Northeastern University, Boston, MA, Reading and Writing Specialist, English Language Center, March-July 19XX, January-March 19XX.

Created individual lesson plans for each student assigned to the Reading and Writing Laboratory and developed materials for use in Laboratory programs. Ran the Laboratory for approximately 100 students 20 hours a week. Kept all records of students' work and prepared written and oral reports on student progress and laboratory operations.

Tutor of Foreign Students, September 19XX-present. Integrated foreign students into a large urban school and community and was a positive role model educationally and socially.

W. M. Mercer, Inc., Boston, MA, September-December 19XX.
Data processing and general office duties. Created and implemented a CRT search system for office personnel.

SPECIAL SKILLS BASIC programming; PASCAL, Edition, and graphics courses to be completed June 19XX.

EDUCATION Northeastern University, Boston, MA, Bachelor of Arts, June 19XX.

Concentration: English with minors in Economics and Technical Communications.

Activities: Selected to serve on the Residence Judicial Board, a faculty-staff-student group that adjudicates residence-hall disputes; Northeastern News reporter; Northeastern Yearbook staff.

40 Writing Under Pressure

When you write under the pressure of time constraints, you are expected to write as completely and clearly as possible. The demands of writing under pressure can sometimes seem overwhelming, but if you break the challenge into small, sequential steps and then focus on each step in turn, you can succeed. If you tend to freeze under pressure, force yourself to take some slow, deep breaths and use a relaxation technique such as counting backwards from ten. When you turn to the task, remember to break the whole into parts so that the process is easier to work through.

Writing answers for essay tests is one of the most important writing tasks that you face in college. Common in the social sciences and humanities, essay tests are becoming increasingly common in the natural sciences as well. Essay tests give you the chance to synthesize and apply your knowledge, thereby helping your instructor determine what you have learned. Essay tests demand that you recall information and also put assorted pieces of that information into contexts that lead to generalizations you can support.

40a Understanding cue words and key words

Most essay questions contain what is sometimes called a **cue word,** a word of direction that tells what the content of your answer is expected to emphasize. Knowing the major cue words and their meanings can increase your ability to plan efficiently and to write effectively. Be guided by the list of cue words and sample essay-test questions in Chart 173.

Each essay question also has one or more **key words** that tell you the information, topics, and ideas you are to write about. For example, in the question "Criticize the architectural function of the modern football stadium," the cue word is "criticize," and the key words are "architectural function" and "football stadium." To answer the question successfully, you must define "architectural function," then describe the typical modern football stadium (mentioning major variations when important), and then discuss how well the typical modern football stadium fits your definition of "architectural function."

CUE WORDS FOUND IN QUESTIONS FOR ESSAY TESTS

173

- **Analyze** means to separate something into parts and then discuss the parts and their meanings.

    Analyze Socrates's discussion of "good life" and "good death."

- **Clarify** means to make clear, often by giving a definition of a key term and by using examples to illustrate it.

    Clarify T. S. Eliot's idea of tradition.

- **Classify** means to arrange into groups on the basis of shared characteristics.

    Classify the different types of antipredator adaptations.

- **Compare and contrast** means to show similarities and differences.

    Compare and contrast the reproductive cycles of a moss and a flowering plant.

- **Criticize** means to give your opinion concerning the good points and bad points of something.

    Criticize the architectural function of the modern football stadium.

- **Define** means to give the definition of something and thereby to separate it from similar things.

    Define the term "yellow press."

- **Describe** means to explain features to make clear an object, procedure, or event.

    Describe the chain of events that constitutes the movement of a sensory impulse along a nerve fiber.

➡

TEACHING TIP
Some essay questions ask students to respond to a quotation. Here are some suggestions you can give your students to help them formulate their answers.

The quotation may come from a familiar source, such as the text for the course, or from an unfamiliar source. Whether the student is working with a familiar or unfamiliar source, the following guidelines can be helpful:

1. Read the quotation carefully.

2. Paraphrase the quotation on scratch paper to be as sure as possible of its meaning.

3. Ask the professor to explain any words that are unfamiliar, if that is permitted.

4. Determine what you are supposed to do with the quotation. Argue against it? Support it? Compare it with another idea in your course readings or lectures?

5. If you use language from the quotation in your answer, use quotation marks. Follow the guidelines for using quotations in section 31e.

TEACHING TIP

Many students feel anxious about writing under time limits, as in an exam, for instance. In addition to following the strategies for writing essay tests, they may find it helpful to have the following suggestions to follow.

1. Allow yourself enough time to arrive at least ten minutes before the exam is scheduled to begin so that you can easily find a chair and desk.

2. Bring all the materials you will need to write comfortably, including extra paper for jotting notes, extra pens, and any books that you are permitted to use for reference.

3. While you are waiting for the exam to begin, clear your mind by thinking about something other than the material you have studied. Mentally reviewing details at the last minute is likely to make you panic. Some people bring a pleasure book to read while they wait for the exam to be distributed.

BACKGROUND

Diane Durkin (*Writing in the Disciplines* [New York: Random House, 1987]) warns that students often go wrong in writing papers or answers to essay questions on tests because they spend too little time analyzing the task they are given. She suggests several steps that can help students understand assignments more clearly and thoroughly. She advises them to do the following:

1. Find the key verb in the assignment. Does it ask you to analyze? explain? define? summarize? If the verb is vague—e.g., *consider*—you must substitute another verb that is indicated by the question as a whole.

2. Determine the subject of the writing task. What is the topic?

3. Rewrite the assignment in a form that tells you precisely what you are to do.

CUE WORDS FOUND IN QUESTIONS FOR ESSAY TESTS *(continued)*

■ **Discuss** means to consider as many elements as possible concerning an issue or event.

> Discuss the effects of television viewing on modern attitudes toward violence.

■ **Evaluate** means to give your opinion about the value of something.

> Evaluate Margaret Mead's contribution to the field of anthropology.

■ **Explain** means to make clear or intelligible something that needs to be understood or interpreted.

> Explain how the amount of carbon dioxide in the blood regulates rates of heartbeat and breathing.

■ **Illustrate** means to give examples of something.

> Illustrate the use of symbolism in Richard Wright's novel *Native Son.*

■ **Interpret** means to explain the meaning of something.

> Give your interpretation of Maxine Kumin's poem ''Beans.''

■ **Justify** means to show or prove that something is valid or correct.

> Justify the existence of labor unions in today's economy.

■ **Prove** means to present evidence that cannot be refuted logically or with other evidence.

> Prove that smoking is a major cause of lung cancer.

■ **Relate** means to show the connections between two or more things.

> Relate increases in specific crimes in 1932–33 to the prevailing economic conditions.

■ **Review** means to reexamine, summarize, or reprise something.

> Review the structural arrangements in proteins to explain the meaning of the term *polypeptide.*

→

CUE WORDS FOUND IN QUESTIONS FOR ESSAY TESTS (*continued*)

■ **Show** means to point out or demonstrate something.

> Show what effects pesticides have on the production of wheat.

■ **Summarize** means to repeat briefly the major points of something.

> Summarize the major benefits of compulsory education.

■ **Support** means to argue in favor of something.

> Support the position that destruction of rain forests is endangering the planet.

40b Writing effective responses to essay-test questions

An effective response to an essay-test question is complete and logically organized. Here are two answers to the question, "Classify the different types of antipredator adaptations." The first one is successful; the second is not. The sentences are numbered for your reference, and they are explained on page 740.

ANSWER 1

(1) Although many antipredator adaptations have evolved in the animal kingdom, they all can be classified into four major categories according to the prey's response to the predator. (2) The first category is hiding techniques. (3) These techniques include cryptic coloration and behavior in which the prey assumes characteristics of an inanimate object or part of a plant. (4) The second category is early enemy detection. (5) The prey responds to alarm signals from like prey or other kinds of prey before the enemy can get too close. (6) Evasion of the pursuing predator is the third category. (7) Prey that move erratically or in a compact group are displaying this technique. (8) The fourth category is active repulsion of the predator. (9) The prey kills, injures, or sickens the predator, establishing that it represents danger to the predator.

TEACHING TIP

Here are two responses to an essay question in a course on criminal justice. It includes a quotation. The first answer is successful; the second is not. The sentences are numbered for your reference.

Essay Question: In his book *The Hidden Dimension*, Edward T. Hall says that "people from different cultures, when interpreting each other's behavior, often misinterpret the relationship, the activity, or the emotions. This leads to alienation or distorted communications" (171). Explain how Hall's observations might be important to a law enforcement professional. Use an example from lectures and reading in this course.

Answer 1
Successful Response

(1) Edward T. Hall believes that individuals whose cultural backgrounds differ may have trouble understanding each other. (2) This semester we learned that in some cultures it is considered rude to look another person in the eye when responding to an accusation or reprimand. (3) In the United States, on the other hand, many people believe that an individual who does not make eye contact is lying or feeling guilty. (4) Law enforcement professionals who are aware of Hall's findings may be less apt to make incorrect assumptions about the guilt or innocence of a person from a different culture. (5) Avoiding "alienation or distorted communications" (Hall 171) may prevent cases of false arrest and will almost certainly make for better relationships between members of the community and law enforcement professionals.

→

Continued from page 743

Answer 1 is successful because:

(1) Sentence 1 demonstrates that the student understands Hall's point.

(2) Sentences 2 and 3 provide what the question asks: an example from the course readings and lectures.

(3) Sentences 4 and 5 address the purpose of the question: to relate the quotation from Hall's book to the law enforcement profession.

(4) Sentence 5 contains a direct quotation from Hall that is appropriately used and correctly punctuated.

Answer 2
Unsuccessful Response

(1) Edward T. Hall thinks we might encounter alienation. (2) Why should law enforcement professionals have to worry about whether or not someone else can understand their culture? (3) There are too many other issues that are more important, like stopping drug traffic and preventing gang wars. (4) I am against Hall's idea and what he says about alienation and in encounters or distorted communication.

Answer 2 is unsuccessful because:

(1) Sentence 1 shows that the student does not understand what Hall is saying. The student uses words from the quotation but distorts their meaning.

(2) Sentences 2, 3, and 4 give the student's opinion, but do not address the purpose of the question: to apply the quotation to the law enforcement profession.

(3) No sentence in this answer gives an example from the course readings or lectures, although the question asks for one.

(4) Sentence 4 uses a direct quotation from Hall, but the quotation does not fit grammatically or logically with the rest of the sentence, nor is it properly punctuated.

ANSWER 2

(1) Antipredator adaptations are the development of the capabilities to reduce the risk of attack from a predator without too much change in the life-supporting activities of the prey. (2) There are many different types of antipredator adaptations. (3) One type is camouflage, hiding from the predator by cryptic coloration or imitation of plant parts. (4) An example of this type of antipredator adaptation is the praying mantis. (5) A second type is the defense used by monarch butterflies, a chemical protection that makes some birds ill after eating the butterfly. (6) This protection may injure the bird by causing it to vomit, and it can educate the bird against eating other butterflies. (7) Detection and evasion are also antipredator adaptations.

Here is an explanation of what happens, sentence by sentence, in the two answers on page 739 and at the top of this page.

	ANSWER 1	ANSWER 2
Sentence 1	Sets up classification system and gives number of categories based on key word	Defines key word
Sentence 2	Names first category	Throwaway sentence—accomplishes nothing
Sentence 3	Defines first category	Names and defines first category
Sentence 4	Names second category	Gives an example for first category
Sentence 5	Defines second category	Gives an example for second (unnamed) category
Sentence 6	Names third category	Continues to explain example
Sentence 7	Defines third category	Names two categories
Sentence 8	Names fourth category	
Sentence 9	Defines fourth category	

Answer 1 sets about immediately answering the question by introducing a classification system as called for by the cue word, *classify*. Answer 2, on the other hand, defines the key word, a waste of time on a test that will be read by an audience of specialists. Answer 1 is tightly organized, easy to follow, and to-the-point, whereas answer 2 rambles, never manages to name the four categories, and says more around the subject than on it.

40c Using strategies when writing under pressure

If you use specific strategies when writing under pressure, you can be more comfortable and your writing will likely be more effective. As you use the strategies listed in Chart 174, remember that your purpose in answering questions is to show what you know in a clear, direct, and well-organized way.

The more you use the strategies in the chart and adapt them to your personal needs, the better you will use them to your advantage. Try to practice them, making up questions that might be on your test and timing yourself as you write the answers. Doing this offers you another benefit: if you study by anticipating possible questions and writing out the answers, you will be very well prepared if one or two of them show up on the test.

STRATEGIES FOR WRITING ESSAY TESTS   174

1. Do not start writing immediately.

2. If the test has two or more questions, read them all at the start. Determine whether you are supposed to answer all the questions. Doing this gives you a sense of how to budget your time either by dividing it equally or by allotting more for some questions. If you have a choice, select questions about which you know the most and can write about most completely in the time limit.

3. Analyze each question that you answer by underlining the cue words and key words (see 40a) to determine exactly what the question asks.

4. Use the writing process as much as possible within the constraints of the time limit. Try to allot time to plan and revise. For a one-hour test of one question, take about 10 minutes to jot down preliminary ideas about content and organization, and save 10 minutes to reread, revise, and edit your answer. If you suddenly are pressed for time—but try to avoid this—consider

➡

TEACHING TIP

Some students have a harder time than others writing under a time limit. For those who have serious difficulty in pacing themselves, and thus suffer greater anxiety about the process, a few suggestions may help. Making an outline at the outset, or at least jotting down the major points to be covered, can save the student time by charting the direction of the answer. Leaving a few minutes at the end for quick editing will produce more polished copy. Some students leave blank space at the beginning of an answer so that an accurate introduction can be inserted after the answer is written. The student who has problems working efficiently under a time limit can improve his or her performance with practice. Before an examination, such a student should compose several questions an instructor is likely to ask, then, with a timer running, practice writing answers to them. A familiar process is always less threatening than an unfamiliar one.

BACKGROUND

The first use of the word *essay* to refer to a literary form was made by Montaigne in 1580 for his informal written reflections about himself and humankind in general. Resigning from a judicial post in 1570, he devoted himself to writing his *Essays*, an edition of Books I and II appearing in 1580 and the final emended edition of Books I, II and III in 1595. Close to the same time (1597) in England, Francis Bacon's *Essays* were written as "counsels for the successful conduct of life and the management of men." Since the seventeenth century, essayists in England and America have found an omnivorous audience for their work. The names of Addison, Steele, Lamb, Hazlitt, and Chesterton in England, Mencken, E. B. White, Lincoln Steffens and others in this country have proved as memorable as their counterparts in poetry, fiction and drama.

TEACHING TIP

Any instructor with more than a few weeks of classroom experience knows that making good essay questions for an examination is not a simple matter. Considerations regarding adequate coverage of material, clarity of instructions, and availability of time must play a part in what is asked and how it is asked as well. As a way to understand the students' task, and how one can reasonably expect it to be carried out, an instructor can always write the answers to the questions he or she poses. The results are often gratifying, but sometimes they reveal gaps in what is being tested, ambiguous directions, or unreasonable length. The teacher who recognizes these shortcomings before giving a test is more likely to have students who perform well than the teacher who finds out afterwards from the students themselves that there was not enough time to finish or that they were not sure what they were being asked to do.

STRATEGIES FOR WRITING ESSAY TESTS (continued)

skipping a question that you cannot answer well or a question that counts less toward your total score. If you feel blocked, try free writing (see 2f) to get your hand and your thoughts moving.

5. Support any generalizations with specifics (see 4c about using the formula RENNS for being specific).

6. Beware of ''going off the topic.'' Respond to the cue words and key words (see 40a) in the question, and do not try to reshape the question to conform to what you might prefer to write about. Remember, your reader expects a clear line of presentation and reasoning that answers the given question.

EXERCISE 40-1

Look back at an essay that you have written under time pressure. Read it over and decide whether you would change the content of your answer or the strategies you used as you were writing under pressure. List these specific strategies, and, if you think they were useful, add them to Chart 174.

IX Writing When English Is a Second Language

When English is your second language, you face the special challenge of needing to learn characteristics of English that native-born writers take for granted. Part Nine begins with a special ESL Preface to set the context for your using the rest of Part Nine, which explains the features of English that tend to give nonnative writers the most trouble. As you use Chapters 41 through 46, remember that learning to write English involves much more than studying separate features. As for writers in any language, the more time you spend actually writing, the faster you can become a fluent writer.

Often, students for whom English is a second language ask instructors to suggest ways to increase fluency in the writing of English. Given their varied backgrounds (culture, age, gender, and facility with language—both the first language and English), not all ESL students respond equally well to the same suggestion, so this idea has to be tailored accordingly.

Here is a variation on keeping a journal that can help ESL students think and express themselves somewhat more freely than they might be used to, at least compared with expectations in U.S. colleges. This variation starts where many ESL students are most comfortable: writing down facts and other types of information.

I suggest that students buy a thick notebook to keep a daily ESL journal. On the left side of each page, they should write a few sentences of information to help them easily recall the day's events. On the right side, they should write any kind of creative thought about those events: perhaps a story they recall, an interesting word to discuss, a mood to describe, or even a poem or dialogue. If they see a movie or read a book or a newspaper or magazine article, they should write down on the left side the title, the actors' or characters' names, and a factual summary of the material. On the right side, they should give their comments about what they liked or didn't. They might even try to write part of a movie script or a novel or a memory, just to practice and enjoy writing.

An added bonus is that students who keep an ESL journal are likely to find that they have done some work for many assignments even before the assignments have been given. Their journals can provide them with many subjects and examples to use when they are asked to write. Also, their practice with ideas in writing can make it easier for them to talk in class about their ideas.

Preface for ESL Students

Do you sometimes worry when you write in English? If you ever do worry about your English writing, let me assure you that you have much in common with me and with many U.S. college students. But as an ESL writer, you face a special challenge because you must attend to every word, every phrase, every sentence, and every paragraph in a way that native speakers of English do not.

You may be reassured to know that any errors you make as an ESL writer indicate that you are progressing through necessary stages of second-language development. Eventually, when you have passed through all the stages that all language learners must, you should be a proficient writer of English.

Unfortunately, there are no shortcuts. As with progress in speaking, listening, and reading comprehension in a new language, passing through the various stages of language development takes time. Some students have more available time than others, and some students have a home or study environment that enables faster learning of a new language. However, no matter how fast a language skill is learned, all the stages of language development must be experienced. Just as most adults make mistakes when they learn to play a new sport, few people write fluently and without error when they compose a first draft of a piece of writing. In fact, only rarely have even the most noted and experienced writers ever written something perfectly the first time.

What can you do to progress as quickly as possible from one writing stage to another? You might start by trying to remember what the typical school writing is like in your first language. Try to recall how ideas are presented in writing in your native language, especially when information has to be explained and when a matter of opinion has to be argued.

In recalling the typical style of school writing in your native language, compare it with what you are learning about writing style in American English. For example, most college writing in the United States has a very direct, straightforward basic structure. In a typical essay or research paper, the reader expects to find a **thesis statement**°,* which clearly states the overall message of the piece of writing, by the end of the first or second paragraph. Usually, each paragraph that follows relates directly to the thesis statement and starts with a sentence, called a **topic sentence**°, that tells the point of the paragraph. The rest of each paragraph usually supports the point by using reasons, examples, and other specific details. The final paragraph brings the essay or research paper to a reasonable, logical conclusion.

This handbook contains many examples of writing by U.S. college students. For essays, see sections 3f, 6h, and 37e. For research papers, see Chapters 34 and 35 and section 37e. Also, this handbook explains paragraph structures typically expected in U.S. college writing: see Chapter 4. By the way, these typical, basic structures do not apply to novels, plays, poems, or articles in most newspapers and magazines published in the United States.

Writing structures typical of your native language probably differ from those in this country. Always honor your culture's writing traditions and structures, for they reflect the richness of your heritage. At the same time, try to adapt to and practice the characteristic college writing style in the United States. Later, when you are writing fluently, your college instructors likely will encourage you to practice other American English writing styles that are less common and that allow greater liberty in organization and expression.

Over the past twenty years, many interesting observations have been made about the very real variations in school writing styles among people of different cultures and language groups. Research about these contrasts is ongoing, so scholars hesitate to generalize about them. Even so, interesting differences seem to exist. For example, many Spanish-speaking students feel that U.S. school writing lacks the sort of traditional introductory background observations that Spanish-language writing usually includes, yet U.S. composition teachers will often mark such introductory material as wordy or not sufficiently relevant to the central point of an essay or research paper. Traditional French school essays usually begin with a series of points that are discussed in the body of the essay and then repeated in reverse order in the conclusion. Japanese school writing customarily begins with references to nature. In some African nations, a ceremonial, formal opening is expected to start school

*Throughout this book, a degree mark (°) indicates that you can find the definition of the word in the Glossary of Terms in this handbook.

TEACHING TIP

Some ESL students ask instructors for advice about how to increase their spoken fluency in English (which, of course, transfers to their writing to some extent). Here are two tips based on experiences that ring true to some ESL students (depending on their backgrounds (culture, age, gender, available time, and facility with language—both first and English).

A story my husband tells is instructive about how to learn a second language. Years back, he was stationed near a small village in France with the U.S. Army. Having studied a little French in school, he gained much fluency when he visited the village's central square on his days off and chatted informally with young children who had come with their parents to play. He listened to and got to practice simple French conversation. The results were so good that he eventually served for a time as a French language teacher ("survival French") in the military service.

Also, a friend of mine who teaches ESL tells a parallel story. Some of his adult second-language students work in nursing homes. These students improve their English quite quickly because their elderly patients are often eager for conversation, and they tend to speak with and prefer to listen to slower speech.

TEACHING TIP

You might want to suggest that ESL students try to watch the news on TV, then listen to the same news on the radio, and then read about some of the same events in the newspaper. The repetitions, along with the variations in medium and language, can be instructive and reinforcing.

When learning a new language, teachers and classes help, but if students try to write a few sentences in English and then the next day read a newspaper, they might see a word or sentence similar to the one they tried to write the day before. It jumps at them from the page. They see written what they had been trying to say, and the next time that they try to write the same thing, they can do it.

TEACHING TIP

You might want to show some of your ESL writers a few of the published letters of Bartolomeo Vanzetti, the Italian immigrant to the United States who was sentenced to death in the 1920s for murders that he and many supporters insisted he did not commit. Vanzetti wrote from prison, in imperfect English that sometimes seems halfway between English and Italian. Even so, his letters are full of human passion and of love of humanity and nature. Frankly, I have read some writers in English who write more "correctly" than Vanzetti, but rarely have I encountered anything as beautiful as his letters.

writing as an expression of respect for the reader. As a person, I greatly enjoy discovering the rich variations in the writing traditions of the many cultures of the world. As a teacher, however, my responsibility is to explain the expectations in the United States.

The ESL chapters following this special ESL preface are designed to help you focus on the most obvious and frequent errors that many ESL writers make. I hope that Chapters 41 through 46, as well as the rest of this handbook, can be of great use to you.

LYNN QUITMAN TROYKA

41 ESL Singulars and Plurals

BACKGROUND

To set a context for Part IX, the *Annotated Instructor's Edition* of this handbook includes the specially commissioned bibliographic essay "Teaching Composition to Speakers of Other Languages: An Overview" by Joy Reid, University of Wyoming, who has written extensively about ESL. This essay represents the theoretical and practical stance toward students and the teaching that underlie the ESL material in this handbook.

HOW TO USE CHAPTER 41 ESL EFFECTIVELY

1. Use this chapter together with these handbook sections.
   - 7a nouns°
   - 8c *s* forms of verbs°
   - 11a-11l subject-verb agreement°
   - 12f nouns as modifiers°
2. Remember that throughout this handbook, **a degree mark (°)** after a word indicates that you can find the definition of the word in the Glossary of Terms toward the back of the book.
3. Also, use any **cross-references** (usually given in parentheses) to find full explanations of key concepts.

This chapter can help you choose between using singulars° (one) and plurals° (more than one). Section 41a discusses the concept of count nouns° and noncount nouns°. Section 41b discusses determiners° and nouns. Section 41c discusses three instances when the choice between singular and plural can be particularly confusing. Section 41d discusses some nouns with irregular plural forms.

41a Understanding the concept of count and noncount nouns

Count nouns name items that can be counted: *radio, street, idea, fingernail.* Count nouns can be singular° or plural° (*radios, streets*).

UNCOUNTABLE ITEMS   175

- **Groups of Similar Items Making Up "Wholes":** *clothing, equipment, furniture, luggage, mail, money, traffic,* and others
- **Abstractions:** *equality, fun, ignorance, health, knowledge, laziness, peace, pride, respect,* and others
- **Liquids:** *blood, coffee, gasoline, water,* and others
- **Gases:** *air, helium, oxygen, smog, smoke, steam,* and others
- **Materials:** *aluminum, cloth, cotton, tar, wood,* and others
- **Food:** *beef, bread, butter, macaroni, meat, pork,* and others
- **Particles or Grains:** *dirt, dust, hair, rice, salt, sugar, wheat,* and others
- **Sports, Games, Activities:** *chess, reading, sailing, soccer,* and others
- **Languages:** *Arabic, Chinese, Japanese, Spanish,* and others
- **Fields of Study:** *biology, computer science, history, literature, math,* and others (see llk for special problems with words ending in *-ics,* like *mathematics*)
- **Events in Nature:** *electricity, heat, moonlight, sunshine, thunder,* and others

---

Noncount nouns name things that are thought of as a whole and not separated into individual parts: *rice, knowledge, traffic.* (Noncount nouns are used in the singular form only.) Chart 175 lists eleven categories of uncountable items, and it gives examples of noncount nouns in each category.

If you want to check whether a noun is count or noncount, look it up in a dictionary such as the *Longman Dictionary of Contemporary English* or the *Oxford Advanced Learner's Dictionary.* These two dictionaries use the terms *countable* and *uncountable.* Noncount nouns are indicated by the letter *U.* Nouns without a *U* are always count.

Some nouns, including some listed in Chart 175, can be countable or uncountable. Most such nouns name things that can be meant individually or as "wholes" made up of individual parts depending on the meaning you want to deliver in each sentence°.

COUNT	You have a **hair** on your sleeve. [In this sentence, *hair* is meant as an individual, countable item.]
NONCOUNT	Kioko has black **hair**. [In this sentence, *hair* is meant as a whole.]
COUNT	The rains were late last year. [In this sentence, *rains* is meant as individual, countable occurrences of rain.]
NONCOUNT	The **rain** is soaking the garden. [In this sentence, particles of *rain* are meant as a whole.]

When you are editing your writing (see section 3d), be sure that you have not added a plural -*s* to any noncount nouns, for they are always singular in form. ❖ VERB ALERT: Be sure to use a singular verb with any noncount noun that functions as a subject° in your sentences. ❖

41b Using singular and plural nouns with determiners

Determiners, also called *expressions of quantity*, are a group of words that traditionally are called adjectives° but that are used to tell "how much" or "how many" about nouns. Additional names for determiners include *limiting adjectives°*, *noun markers*, and *articles°*. (For information about articles—the words *a*, *an*, and *the*—which occur in English more often than any other determiners, see Chapter 42 ESL.)

Choosing the correct determiner with a noun depends first on whether the noun is count° or noncount° (see 41a). For count nouns, you must also decide whether the noun is singular or plural. Chart 176 lists many determiners and singular count nouns, noncount nouns, and plural (count) nouns that they can accompany.
❖ USAGE ALERT: The phrases *a few* and *a little* convey the meaning "some": *I have **a few** rare books* means "I have *some* rare books." *They are worth **a little** money* means "They are worth *some* money."

Without the word *a*, *few* and *little* convey the meaning "almost none" or "not enough": *I have **few** [or very few] books* means "I have almost no books." *They are worth **little** money* means "They are worth *almost no* money." ❖

TEACHING TIP

Many ESL students are used to a style of pedagogy different from what they encounter in the United States. For example, U.S. colleges tend to be more test-oriented than those in other countries. Students may be surprised to find out that their placement or course grade depends heavily on only one or two tests. Also, U.S. colleges are more "student-responsible" than those in some other countries. In the United States, students are responsible for asking questions if they do not understand or if they want to question a point. In many other countries, it is considered disrespectful to question or interrupt the instructor, so some ESL students may prefer to leave class confused rather than appear rude. You many want to help ESL students feel comfortable about asking their professors questions. (Usually, this takes more than a one-time invitation.)

One especially troublesome manifestation of ESL students' reluctance to question instructors occurs when assignments or directions are given to a class. ESL students often say that they understand an assignment only to ask another student to explain it to them later. Misunderstandings are easily spread. One way to anticipate this problem is to give students clear, concise written instructions, whether handed out or written on the board with ample time for students to copy them.

DETERMINERS TO USE WITH COUNT AND NONCOUNT NOUNS

176

- With every **singular count noun**, always use one of the determiners listed in Group 1.

  NO   We live in **apartment** in large, white **house.**

  YES   We live in **an apartment** in **that** large, white **house.**

  #### GROUP 1: DETERMINERS FOR SINGULAR COUNT NOUNS

  a, an, the

a house	**an egg**	**the car**

  one, any, some, every, each, either, neither, another, the other

any house	**each egg**	**another car**

  my, our, your, his, her, its, their, nouns with *'s or s'*

your house	**its egg**	**Connie's car**

  this, that

this house	**that egg**	**this car**

  one, no, the first, the second, and so on

one house	**no egg**	**the fifth car**

- With every **plural count noun**, use one of determiners listed in Group 2. Count nouns are sometimes used without determiners, as discussed fully in Chapter 42.

  YES   Be sure that **the tomatoes** you select are ripe.

  YES   **Tomatoes** are tasty in salad.

  #### GROUP 2: DETERMINERS FOR PLURAL COUNT NOUNS

  the

the bicycles	**the rooms**	**the ideas**

  some, any, both, many, more, most, few, fewer, the fewest, a number of, other, several, all, all the, a lot of

some bicycles	**many rooms**	**all ideas**

  my, our, your, his, her, its, their, nouns with *'s or s'*

our bicycles	**her rooms**	**students' ideas**

  these, those

these bicycles	**those rooms**	**these ideas**

  no, two, three, four, and so on, *the first, the second, the third,* and so on

no bicycles	**four rooms**	**the first ideas**

> **DETERMINERS TO USE WITH COUNT AND** 176
> **NONCOUNT NOUNS** *(continued)*
>
> ■ With every **noncount noun** (always singular), use one of the
> determiners listed in Group 3. Noncount nouns can also be used
> without determiners, as discussed fully in Chapter 42.
>
> | | |
> |---|---|
> | YES | I bought **the fish** we ate for supper. |
> | YES | I bought **fish** for supper. |
>
> ### GROUP 2: DETERMINERS FOR NONCOUNT NOUNS
>
> *the*
>
> | | | |
> |---|---|---|
> | **the rice** | **the rain** | **the pride** |
>
> *some, any, much, more, most, other, the other, little, less, the
> least, enough, all, all the, a lot of*
>
> | | | |
> |---|---|---|
> | **enough rice** | **a lot of rain** | **more pride** |
>
> *my, our, your, his, her, its, their,* nouns with *'s or s'*
>
> | | | |
> |---|---|---|
> | **their rice** | **its rain** | **your pride** |
>
> *this, that*
>
> | | | |
> |---|---|---|
> | **this rice** | **that rain** | **this pride** |
>
> *no, the first, the second, the third,* and so on
>
> | | | |
> |---|---|---|
> | **no rice** | **the first rain** | **no pride** |

41c Using singulars and plurals with *one of*
constructions, with nouns as adjectives,
and with *States* in names or titles

One of constructions

One of constructions include *one of the* and *one of* followed by a
pronoun° in the possessive case° (*one of my, one of your, one of his, one
of her, one of its, one of their*). Always use a plural noun as the object
when you begin a phrase with *one of*.

NO	One of the **reason** to live here is the beach.
YES	One of the **reasons** to live here is the beach.
NO	One of her best **friend** has moved away.
YES	One of her best **friends** has moved away.

The verb° in *one of* constructions is always singular. The verb agrees with *one*, not with a plural noun: *One of the most important inventions of the twentieth century* **is** [not *are*] *television.*

Nouns Used as Adjectives

Some words that function as nouns can also function as adjectives°.

> The bird's wingspan is ten **inches**. [*Inches* functions here as a noun.]

> The bird has a ten-**inch** wingspan. [*Inch* functions here as an adjective.]

Adjectives in English do not have plural forms. When you use a noun as an adjective, therefore, do not ad -*s* or -*es* to the adjective even when the noun or pronoun it modifies is plural.

> **NO**   Many **Americans** students are avid basketball fans.

> **YES**   Many **American** students are avid basketball fans.

Names or Titles that Include the Word **States**

The word *states* is always plural. However, names such as the *United States* or the *Organization of American States* refer to singular things—a country and an organization—so they are singular nouns and therefore require singular verbs.

> **NO**   The United **State** has a large television industry.

> **NO**   The United **States have** a large television industry.

> **YES**   The United **States has** a large television industry.

41d   Using nouns with irregular plurals

Some English nouns have irregular spellings. In addition to those discussed in sections 22d-1 and 22d-4, here are others that often cause difficulties.

Plurals of Foreign Nouns and Other Irregular Nouns

Whenever you are unsure whether a noun is plural, look it up in a dictionary. If no plural is given for a singular noun, add an -*s*.

Many nouns from other languages that are used unchanged in English have only one plural. If two plurals are listed in the dictionary, look carefully for differences in meaning. Some words, for example, keep the plural form from the original language for scientific usage and have another English-form plural that is used in non-science contexts. Examples include *antenna, antennae, antennas; formula, formulae, formulas; appendix, appendices, appendixes; index, indices, indexes; medium, media, mediums; cactus, cacti, cactuses;* and *fungus, fungi, funguses.*

Words of Latin origin that end in *-is* in their singular form become plural by substituting *-es: parenthesis, parentheses; thesis, theses; oasis, oases,* for example.

Other Words

Medical terms for diseases involving an inflammation end in *-itis: tonsillitis, appendicitis.* They are always singular.

The word *news,* although it ends in *s,* is always singular: *The news is encouraging.* The words *people, police,* and *clergy* are always plural even though they do not end in *s: The police are tough.*

EXERCISE 41-1

Consulting Chapter 41, select the correct choice from the words in parentheses and write it in the blank.

EXAMPLE   In the United States, the (popularities, popularity) **popularity** of cats as pets (are, is) **is** rapidly outstripping that of dogs.

1. One of the main (reason, reasons)_____may be the recent change in (American, Americans)_____lifestyles.
2. Many people in the (United State, United States)_____are moving from big houses with large yards to small apartments with (ten-feet, ten-foot)_____balconies.
3. Dogs must be walked, even in (rain, rains)_____and (snow, snows)_____.
4. People also are spending (many, much)_____time away from home.
5. As long as they have sufficient (food, foods)_____and (waters, water)_____, cats can safely be left alone for a few days.

ANSWERS & COVERAGE: EXERCISE 41-1

1. reasons [41c, plural obj. with *one of*] **American** [41c, singular for noun used as adj]

2. United States [41c, *States* plural in *United States*] **ten-foot** [41c, singular for noun used as adj]

3. rain, snow [41a, singular for noncount nouns]

4. much [41b, *much* the correct determiner with noncount noun *time*]

5. food, water [41a, noncount nouns always singular]

42 ESL Articles

HOW TO USE CHAPTER 42 ESL EFFECTIVELY

1. Use this chapter together with these handbook sections.
   - 7a articles° and nouns°
   - 41a singulars° and plurals° with count nouns° and noncount nouns°
   - 41b singulars and plurals with expressions of quantity

2. Remember that throughout this handbook, **a degree mark (°)** after a word indicates that you can find the definition of the word in the Glossary of Terms toward the back of the book.

3. Also, use any **cross-references** (usually given in parentheses) to find full explanations of key concepts.

This chapter gives you guidelines for using articles. Section 42a discusses using articles with singular count nouns. Section 42b discusses using articles with plural count nouns and with noncount nouns (which are always singular). Section 42c discusses using articles with proper nouns° and with gerunds° and infinitives°.

42a Using *a, an,* or *the* with singular count nouns

The words *a* and *an* are called **indefinite articles**. The word *the* is called a **definite article**. Indefinite and definite articles comprise one type of determiner. (For other types of determiners, see Chart 176 in 41b.) When you use a singular count noun° (see 41a), always precede it with a determiner.

NO	I bought **book**.
YES	I bought **a book**.
YES	I bought **the book**.
YES	I bought **my book**.
YES	I bought **one book**.

To choose between using an indefinite article (*a* or *an*) and a definite article (*the*) before a singular count noun, you need to determine whether the noun is specific or nonspecific. A noun is considered specific when anyone who reads your writing can understand from the context of your message exactly and specifically to what the noun is referring.

When a singular noun is nonspecific, use *a* (or *an*). When a singular noun is specific, use *the* or a determiner other than an article. Use Chart 177 to help you determine when a noun is specific—and therefore requires the article *the*.

One common exception affects Rule 4 in Chart 177. Even when a noun has been used in an earlier sentence, it may require *a* (or *an*) if one or more descriptive adjectives come between the article and the noun: *I bought **a sweater** today. It was **a** [not *the*] **red sweater***. Other information may make the noun specific so that *the* is correct. For example, *It was **the red sweater that I saw in the store yesterday*** uses *the* because the *that* clause lets a reader know which specific red sweater is meant.

❖ USAGE ALERT: Use *an* before words that begin with a vowel sound. Use *a* before words that begin with a consonant sound. Words that begin with *h* or *u* can have either a vowel or a consonant sound. Make the choice based on the sound of the first word after the article, even if that word is not the noun.

a carpet	**an i**dea	**a g**ood idea
a uniform	**an u**mbrella	**a u**nique umbrella
a hand	**an h**onor	**a h**istory book ❖

WHEN A SINGULAR NONCOUNT NOUN IS SPECIFIC AND REQUIRES *THE*

177

- **Rule 1: Use *the* when the noun names something unique or generally known.**

    The sun has risen above the horizon. [Because *sun* and *horizon* are generally known nouns, they are specific nouns in the context of this sentence.]

- **Rule 2: Use *the* when the noun names something used in a representative or abstract sense.**

    Benjamin Franklin favored **the turkey** as **the national bird** of the United States. [Because *turkey* and *national bird* are representative references rather than references to a particular turkey or bird, they are specific nouns in the context of this sentence.]

- **Rule 3: Use *the* when the noun names something defined by a word, phrase°, or clause° elsewhere in the same sentence.**

    The ship *Savannah* was the first steam vessel to cross the Atlantic Ocean. [The word *Savannah* indicates a specific ship.]

    The carpet in my bedroom is new. [The phrase *in my bedroom* defines exactly which carpet is meant, so *carpet* is a specific noun in this context.]

    The carpet that I bought yesterday is new. [The clause *that I bought yesterday* indicates a specific carpet.]

- **Rule 4: Use *the* when the noun names something defined in an earlier sentence.**

    I have **a computer** at the office. **The computer** is often broken. [In the first sentence, *computer* is not specific, so it uses *a*. The second sentence uses *the* because *computer* has become a specific noun that was defined in the first sentence.]

- **Rule 5: Use *the* when the noun names something that can be inferred from the context.**

    I had to call **the technician** on Monday to fix it. [If this sentence follows the two sentences above about a computer, *technician* is specific in this context.]

42b Using articles with plural count nouns and with noncount nouns

With plural nouns and noncount nouns, you must decide about articles whether to use *the* or to use no article at all. (For guidelines about using determiners° other than articles with nouns, see Chart 176 in section 41b.)

What you learned in section 42a about nonspecific and specific nouns can help you make the choice between using *the* or using no article. Chart 177 in section 42a explains when a singular count noun's meaning is specific and calls for *the*. Plural count nouns and noncount nouns with specific meanings usually use *the* in the same circumstances. However, a plural count noun or a noncount noun with a general or nonspecific meaning usually does not use *the*.

Geraldo grows **flowers** but not **vegetables** his garden. He is thinking about planting **corn** sometime.

Plural Count Nouns

A plural noun's meaning may be specific because it is widely known.

The oceans are being damaged by pollution. [Because the meaning of *oceans* is widely understood, *the* is correct to use. This example is related to Rule 1 in Chart 177.]

A plural noun's meaning may also be made specific by a word, phrase°, or clause° in the same sentence°.

Geraldo sold **the daisies from last year's garden** to the florist. [Because the phrase *from last year's garden* makes *daisies* specific, *the* is correct to use. This example is related to Rule 3 in Chart 177.]

A plural noun's meaning usually becomes specific by being used in an earlier sentence.

Geraldo planted **tulips** this year. **The tulips** will bloom in April. [*Tulips* is used in a general sense in the first sentence, without *the*. Because the first sentence makes *tulips* specific, *the tulips* is correct in the second sentence. This example is related to Rule 4 in Chart 177.]

A plural noun's meaning may be made specific by the context.

Geraldo fertilized **the bulbs** when he planted them last October. [In the context of the sentences about tulips, *bulbs* is specific and calls for *the*. This example is related to Rule 5 in Chart 177.]

Noncount Nouns

Noncount nouns are always singular in form (see 41a). Like plural count nouns, noncount nouns use either *the* or no article. When a noncount noun's meaning is specific use *the* before it. If its meaning is general or nonspecific, do not use *the*.

> Kalinda served **rice** to us. She flavored **the rice** with curry. [*Rice* is a noncount noun. This example is related to Rule 4 in Chart 177: By the second sentence, *rice* has become specific, so *the* is used.]

> Kalinda served us **the rice that she had flavored with curry**. [*Rice* is a noncount noun. This example is related to Rule 3 in Chart 177: *Rice* is made specific by the clause *that she had flavored with curry*, so *the* is used.]

Generalizations with Plural or Noncount Nouns

Rule 2 in Chart 177 tells you to use *the* with singular count nouns used in a general sense. With generalizations using plural or noncount nouns, omit *the*.

NO	**The dogs** require more care than **the cats** do.
YES	**Dogs** require more care than **cats** do.
NO	**The tulips** are **the flowers** that grow from **the bulbs**.
YES	**Tulips** are **flowers** that grow from **bulbs**.

Using *the* with proper nouns and with gerunds and infinitives

Proper Nouns

Proper nouns name specific people, places, or things (see 7a). Most proper nouns do not require articles°: *We visited **Lake Mead** with **Asha** and **Larry***. As shown in Chart 178, however, certain types of proper nouns do require *the*.

Gerunds and Infinitives

Gerunds are present participles (the *-ing* form of verbs°) used as nouns: ***Skating** is challenging*. Gerunds usually are not preceded by *the*.

PROPER NOUNS THAT USE *THE*   178

- **Nouns with the pattern *the* _____ *of* _____**

  the United States **of** America   **the** fourth **of** July
  the President **of** Mexico   **the** University **of** Paris

- **Plural proper nouns**

  the Johnsons   **the** Rocky Mountains
  the Chicago Bulls   **the** Falkland Islands
  the United Arab Emirates   **the** Great Lakes

- **Collective proper nouns (nouns that name a group)**

  the European Economic Community
  the Society of Friends

- **Some (but not all) geographical features**

  the Amazon   **the** Gobi Desert   **the** Indian Ocean

NO	**The constructing** new bridges is necessary to improve traffic flow.
YES	**Constructing** new bridges is necessary to improve traffic flow.

The word *the* does precede a gerund when two conditions are met: (1) the gerund is used in a specific sense (see 42a) and (2) the gerund does not have a direct object°.

NO	**The designing** fabric is a fine art. [*Fabric* is a direct object of *designing*, so *the* should not be used.]
YES	**Designing** fabric is a fine art. [*Designing* is a gerund, so *the* is not used.]
YES	**The designing of fabric** is a fine art. [*The* is used because *fabric* is the object of the preposition° *of* and *designing* is meant in a specific sense.]

Infinitives are the simple form° of verbs, usually preceded by the word *to*. Infinitives used as nouns do not take an article or any other kind of determiner°.

NO	**The to design** fabric takes artistry and technical skill.
YES	**To design** fabric takes artistry and technical skill.

42c
ESL

ANSWERS & COVERAGE: EXERCISE 42-1

1. *a* result [nonspecific use of singular count noun]; *the* first surgeon to cut into [singular count noun made specific by the word *first* and the phrase *to cut into* . . . , Rule 3 in Chart 177]; *the* human heart [representative use of singular count noun, Rule 2]

2. *the* middle of *the* twentieth century [widely understood meaning of singular count nouns, Rule 1]

3. *an* African-American surgeon [first use of noun, *an* before vowel sound]

4. *An* injured young man, *a* Chicago hospital, *a* knife wound [first use of nouns, *an* or *a* depending on vowel or consonant sound]; *the* heart [wide comprehension of noun's meaning and the context make use specific, Rules 1 & 5]

5. *the* heart [wide comprehension, context, Rules 1 & 5]

EXERCISE 42-1

Consulting Chapter 42, select the correct choice from the words in parentheses and write it in the blank.

EXAMPLE   For centuries, (a, an, the) **the** heart was regarded with awe by physicians.

1. As (a, an, the)_____result, (a, an, the)_____first surgeon to cut into (a, an, the)_____human heart had to overcome many fears and superstitions.

2. Asked to guess when this surgery was first tried, most people would say in (a, an, the)_____middle of (a, an, the)_____twentieth century.

3. Heart surgery actually was first performed in 1893 by (a, an, the)_____African-American surgeon named Daniel Hale Williams.

4. (A, An, The)_____injured young man was brought to (a, an, the)_____Chicago hospital with (a, an, the)_____knife wound in (a, an, the)_____heart.

5. Surgeon Williams cast aside age-old taboos and dared to operate—successfully—on (a, an, the)_____heart.

43 ESL Word Order

HOW TO USE CHAPTER 43 ESL EFFECTIVELY

1. Use this chapter together with these handbook sections.
   - 7k-7o sentence° patterns
   - 7e adjectives°
   - 7p sentence types
   - 7f adverbs°
   - 7m modifiers°
   - 11f verbs° in inverted word order
   - 7o clauses°

2. Remember that throughout this handbook, **a degree mark (°)** after a word indicates that you can find the definition of the word in the Glossary of Terms toward the back of the book.

3. Also, use any **cross-references** (usually given in parentheses) to find full explanations of key concepts.

This chapter can help you with several issues of word order in sentences. Section 43a discusses the most common pattern for English sentences and two variations on standard order. Section 43b discusses the placement of adjectives. Section 43c discusses the placement of adverbs.

43a Understanding standard and inverted word order in sentences

The **standard word order** in English sentences is the most common word order. In it, the subject° comes first and the predicate° after. (To better understand these concepts, review sections 7k-7o.)

SUBJECT   PREDICATE
↓   ↓
That book   was heavy.

Inverted word order is common for direct questions° in English. With inverted word order, the main verb° or an auxiliary verb° comes before the subject.

MAIN VERB   SUBJECT
↓   ↓
Was   that book heavy?

AUXILIARY   MAIN
VERB   SUBJECT   VERB
↓   ↓   ↓
Did   you   hear the noise?

When a form of *be* is the main verb or is an auxiliary verb, it comes first in inverted order.

MAIN VERB   SUBJECT
↓   ↓
Was   the noise loud?

AUXILIARY   MAIN
VERB   SUBJECT   VERB
↓   ↓   ↓
Am   I   going to get in trouble?

With main verbs other than *be*, a very common way to form questions is to use inverted order with a form of the verb *do* as an auxiliary verb before the subject and the simple form° of the main verb after the subject.

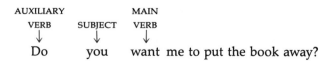

AUXILIARY   MAIN
VERB   SUBJECT   VERB
↓   ↓   ↓
Do   you   want me to put the book away?

Also, use inverted order when a question begins with a question-forming word like *why, when, where,* or *how*.

AUXILIARY VERB	SUBJECT	MAIN VERB
↓	↓	↓
Where does	the book	belong?

When a question has more than one auxiliary verb, put the subject after the first auxiliary verb.

FIRST AUXILIARY	SUBJECT	SECOND AUXILIARY	MAIN VERB
↓	↓	↓	↓
Would	you	have	replaced the book?

You may sometimes see a question formed with the main verb *have* at the beginning.

MAIN VERB	SUBJECT	
↓	↓	
Have	you	another book for me?

It is equally correct and more common to see the question formed with *do* as an auxiliary and *have* as a main verb following the pattern of *auxiliary verb–subject–main verb.*

Do you have another book for me?

♣ USAGE ALERT: Use inverted word order only with direct questions, not with indirect questions° (indirect questions use standard word order: *She asked **how I dropped the book***). ♣

The same rules apply to emphatic exclamations: ***Was** that book heavy!* ***Did** she enjoy that book!*

Also, word order deliberately inverted can be effective, when used sparingly, to create emphasis in a sentence that is neither a question nor an exclamation (see 19f).

43b Understanding the placement of adjectives

Adjectives modify—that is, they describe or limit—nouns°, pronouns°, and word groups that function as nouns (see section 7e). In English, an adjective comes directly before the noun it describes. However, when more than one adjective describes the same noun,

179

WORD ORDER FOR MORE THAN ONE ADJECTIVE

1. **Determiners°, if any:** an article°, a possessive°, a demonstrative pronoun°: *a, an, the, my, your, Jan's, this, that, these, those*, and so on

2. **Expressions of order, including ordinal numbers, if any:** *first, second, third, next, last, final*, and so on

3. **Expressions of quantity, including cardinal (counting) numbers, if any:** *one, two, three, few, each, every, some*, and so on

4. **Adjectives of judgment or opinion, if any:** *pretty, happy, ugly, sad, interesting, boring*, and so on

5. **Adjectives of size and/or shape, if any:** *big, small, short, round, square*, and so on

6. **adjectives of age and/or condition, if any:** *new, young, broken, dirty, shiny*, and so on

7. **Adjectives of color, if any:** *red, green blue*, and so on

8. **Adjectives that can also be used as nouns, if any:** *French, Protestant, metal, cotton*, and so on

9. **The noun**

1	2	3	4	5	6	7	8	9
A		few		tiny		red		ants
The	last	six					Thai	carvings
My			fine		old		oak	table

several sequences may be possible. Chart 179 shows the most common order for positioning several adjectives.

43c **Understanding the placement of adverbs**

Adverbs modify—that is, describe or limit—verbs°, adjectives°, other adverbs, or entire sentences (see section 7f). A one-word adverb or an adverb phrase° can fall in three different places in a clause°: first, middle, or last. Chart 180 summarizes adverb types, what they tell about the words they modify, and where each type can be placed.

TYPES OF ADVERBS AND WHERE TO POSITION THEM

180

- **Adverbs of manner**
  - describe *how* something is done
  - usually come in middle or last position

    > Nick **carefully** groomed the dog
    > Nick groomed the dog **carefully**.

- **Adverbs of time**
  - describe *when* or *how long* about an event
  - usually come in the first or last position

    > **First**, he shampooed the dog.
    > He shampooed the dog **first**.

  - include *just, still,* and *already*, and similar adverbs, which usually come in the middle position

    > He had **already** brushed the dog's coat.

- **Adverbs of place**
  - describe *where* an event takes place
  - usually come in the last position

    > He lifted the dog **into the tub**

- **Adverbs of frequency**
  - describe *how often* an event takes place
  - usually come in the middle position

    > Nick has **never** been bitten while grooming a dog.

  - come in the first position when they are modifying an entire sentence (see Sentence adverbs below)

    > **Occasionally**, he is scratched while shampooing a cat.

- **Adverbs of degree or emphasis**
  - describe *how much* or *to what extent* about other modifiers
  - come directly before the word they modify

    > Nick is **extremely** calm around animals. *extremely* modifies *calm*]

  - include *only*, which is easy to misplace (see 15b-1)

ANSWERS & COVERAGE: EXERCISE 43-1

1. The **beautiful antique glass** vase [Chart, 43b: adjective of judgment precedes adjective of age; adjective of age precedes adjective derived from noun]

2. her **mother's favorite jar** [Chart, 43b: determiner precedes descriptive adjective]

3. that **she almost** cried [43c, adverb of degree is positioned before word it modifies, *cried*]

4. **"Are you** all right?" [43a, inverted word order for questions, form of *be* precedes subject]

5. had **accidentally broken**, was **not extremely angry** [43c, adverbs of degree precede the word they modify]

TYPES OF ADVERBS AND WHERE TO POSITION THEM *(continued)*

■ **Sentence adverbs**
   • **modify the entire sentence rather than just one word or a few words**
   • **include transitional words and expressions** (see 4d-1) **as well as *maybe, probably, possibly, fortunately, unfortunately, incredibly*, and others**

   Incredibly, he was once asked to groom a rat.

❖ PUNCTUATION ALERT: Unless they are very short (fewer than five letters), adverbs in the initial position are usually followed by a comma. ❖

❖ USAGE ALERT: Do not place an adverb in a middle position that separates a verb from its direct object° or indirect object° (see section 15b-3). ❖

EXERCISE 43-1

Consulting Chapter 43, find and correct any errors in word order.

1. The antique glass beautiful vase shattered on the floor.
2. Lu Mi had not meant to break her favorite mother's jar.
3. She was so upset that almost she cried.
4. When Lu Mi's mother heard the sound of shattering glass, she ran into the room asking, "You are all right?"
5. Knowing that Lu Mi had broken accidentally the vase, her mother was not angry extremely.

44 ESL Prepositions

HOW TO USE CHAPTER 44 ESL EFFECTIVELY

1. Use this chapter together with these handbook sections.
   - 7g prepositions°
   - 21a using appropriate language

2. Remember that throughout this handbook, **a degree mark (°)** after a word indicates that you can find the definition of the word in the Glossary of Terms toward the back of the book.

3. Also, use any **cross-references** (usually given in parentheses) to find full explanations of key concepts.

TEACHING TIP

The use of prepositions in any language is idiomatic, so prepositions can be especially difficult for ESL students. In practice, the closer a first language is to English in structure and derivation, the fewer problems a speaker of that language will have with prepositions. Students who speak an Indo-European language (French, German, Spanish, etc.) usually have fewer problems. One important exception is Spanish speakers and the English prepositions *in, on,* and *at.* Spanish uses a single preposition, *en,* for all the meanings covered by *in, on,* and *at.* Consequently, Spanish speakers often need help in distinguishing among the three English prepositions.

Students who speak languages that are not related to English at all (Japanese, Korean, Chinese, Arabic, etc.) have the most difficulty with prepositions. These students need to understand that prepositions are idiomatic and that patience and practice are needed to learn them. (Vietnamese students who have studied French in school may benefit more by referring to a French-English dictionary for meanings and uses of prepositions rather than a Vietnamese-English dictionary.

Prepositions function with other words in prepositional phrases°, which often describe relationships in time or space (see section 7g). The meaning of prepositions in combination with other words is often idiomatic in American English. Therefore, knowing which preposition to use in a specific context takes much experience reading, listening to, and speaking the language. A dictionary like the *Longman Dictionary of Contemporary English* or the *Oxford Advanced Learner's Dictionary* can be especially helpful when you need to find the correct preposition to use.

This chapter can help you with two common uses of prepositions. Section 44a discusses prepositions with some expressions of time and place. Section 44b discusses combinations of prepositions and verbs°.

767

Some of the most obvious errors that ESL students make are with idiom. Idiomatic errors stand out in a sentence and can distract the reader from what is being said. However, many of the more glaring idiomatic errors, such as misuse of articles and prepositions, are actually rather trivial in germs of meaning and grammar. In many cases, "proper" idiom varies from state to state, even from city to city. In addition, most idiomatic errors are not going to disappear in a single semester; students have to work them out over time with more exposure to idiomatic English and more experience with English idiom. How, then, are teachers to judge what idiomatic errors are worth correcting? The following three criteria can be helpful: (1) Is the meaning of the sentence obscured or confused by the error? (2) Does the idiomatic error excessively distract the reader from the meaning of the sentence? (3) Is the idiomatic phrase common enough to cause the student trouble in the future?

ESL students can become frustrated because their problems with English idiom sometimes stubbornly persist despite extensive effort to make them "go away." Some ESL students can become obsessed with sentence-level errors, often to the point of overlooking major issues of logic, organization, and support. Instructors can help such students maintain a proper perspective by reminding them that grammar and idiom are only a small part of the overall writing process and that eliminating idiomatic errors is a matter of practice rather than knowledge.

44a Using prepositions with expressions of time and place

Chart 181 shows how to use the prepositions *in, at,* and *on* to deliver some common kinds of information about time and place. The chart, however, does not cover every situation. For example, it does not explain the subtle difference in meaning delivered by the prepositions *at* and *in* in these two correct sentences: *I have a checking account **at** that bank* and *I have a safe-deposit box **in** that bank.* Also, the

---

USING *IN, AT,* AND *ON* TO SHOW TIME AND PLACE 181

TIME
- *in* **a year or a month** (*during* is also correct but less common)

  in 1995   **in** May
- *in* **a period of time**

  in a few months (seconds, days, years)
- *in* **a period of the day**

  in the morning (afternoon, evening)
  in the daytime (morning, evening) *but* **at** night
- *on* **a specific day**

  on Friday   **on** my birthday
- *at* **a specific time or period of time**

  at noon   **at** 2:00   **at** dawn   **at** nightfall
  at takeoff (the time a plane leaves)
  at breakfast (the time a specific meal takes place)

PLACE
- *in* **a location surrounded by something else**

  in the province of Alberta   **in** Utah
  in downtown Bombay   **in** the kitchen
  in my apartment   **in** the bathtub
- *at* **a specific location**

  at your house   **at** the bank
  at the corner of Third Avenue and Main Street

chart does not include expressions that operate outside the general rules. (Both these sentences are correct: *You ride in the car* and *You ride on the bus*.)

44b Using prepositions in phrasal verbs

Phrasal verbs, also called *two-word verbs* and *three-word verbs*, are verbs° that combine with prepositions to deliver their meaning.

In some phrasal verbs, the verb and the preposition should not be separated by other words: ***Look at*** *the moon* [not ***Look*** *the moon* ***at***]. In **separable phrasal verbs,** other words in the sentence can separate the verb and the preposition without interfering with meaning: *I* ***threw away*** *my homework* is as correct as *I* ***threw*** *my homework* ***away***.

Here is a list of some common phrasal verbs. The ones that cannot be separated are marked with an asterisk (*).

LIST OF SELECTED PHRASAL VERBS

ask out	get along with*	look into
break down	get back	look out for*
bring about	get off*	look over
call back	go over*	make up
drop off	hand in	run across*
figure out	keep up with*	speak to*
fill out	leave out	speak with*
fill up	look after*	throw away
find out	look around	throw out

Usually, you should position a pronoun° object° between the words of a separable phrasal verb: *I threw* ***it*** *away*. Also, you can position an object phrase of several words between the parts of a separable phrasal verb: *I threw* ***my research paper*** *away*. However, when the object is a clause, do not let it separate the parts of the phrasal verb: *I threw away* ***all the papers that I wrote last year***.

Many phrasal verbs are informal and are used more in speaking than in writing. For academic writing, a more formal verb may be more appropriate than a phrasal verb. In a research paper, for example, *propose* or *suggest* might be better choices than *come up with*.

ANSWER: EXERCISE 44-1

Answers will vary.

EXERCISE 44-1

Consulting Chapter 44 and using the list of phrasal verbs in section 44b, write a one- or two-paragraph description of a typical day at work or school in which you use at least five phrasal verbs. After checking a dictionary, revise your writing, substituting for the phrasal verbs any more formal verbs that you think may be more appropriate for academic writing.

45 ESL Gerunds and Infinitives

HOW TO USE CHAPTER 45 ESL EFFECTIVELY

1. Use this chapter together with these handbook sections.
   - 7d verbals°
   - 11a subject-verb agreement°
   - 7k-7l subjects° and objects°
   - 18a-18c parallelism
   - 8b principal parts° of verbs

2. Remember that throughout this handbook, **a degree mark (°)** after a word indicates that you can find the definition of the word in the Glossary of Terms toward the back of the book.

3. Also, use any **cross-references** (usually given in parentheses) to find full explanations of key concepts.

Gerunds and **infinitives** are types of **verbals**. (A verbal is a verb form that functions, not as a verb, but as a noun° or a modifier°, as explained fully in section 7d.)

A gerund uses the present participle (a verb's *-ing* form) as a noun.

Because **running** and **jogging** can strain joints and muscles, **swimming** and **walking** can be safer ways to exercise. [*Running, jogging, swimming,* and *walking* are gerunds.]

An infinitive can function as a noun. (An infinitive consists of the simple form° of a verb, usually preceded by the word *to.*)

45a
ESL

Because I want **to exercise** regularly, I plan **to join** a health club.
[*To exercise* and *to join* are infinitives.]

This chapter can help you choose between gerunds and infinitives. Section 45a discusses gerunds and infinitives used as subjects. Section 45b discusses verbs that are followed by gerunds, not infinitives. Section 45c discusses verbs that are followed by infinitives, not gerunds. Section 45d discusses how meaning changes when certain verbs are followed by a gerund or an infinitive. Section 45e explains that meaning does not change for certain sense verbs no matter whether they are followed by a gerund or an infinitive.

A dictionary like the *Longman Dictionary of Contemporary English* or the *Oxford Advanced Learner's Dictionary* will alert you to words that require a gerund or an infinitive object.

45a Using gerunds and infinitives as subjects

Gerunds are used more commonly than infinitives as subjects.

Choosing the right health club is important.
To choose the right health club is important.

❖ VERB ALERT: When a gerund or an infinitive is used alone as a subject, it is singular° and requires a singular verb. When two or more gerunds or infinitives create a compound subject°, they require a plural verb. (See sections 7k and 11d.) ❖

45b Using a gerund, not an infinitive, as an object following certain verbs

Some verbs° must be followed by gerunds° used as direct objects°. Other verbs must be followed by infinitives°. Still other verbs can be followed by either a gerund or an infinitive. (A few verbs can change meaning depending on whether they are followed by a gerund or an infinitive; see 45d.) Chart 182 lists common verbs that must be followed by gerunds, not infinitives.

Yuri **considered** *calling* [not *to call*] the mayor.
He **was having trouble** *getting* [not *to get*] a work permit.
Yuri's boss **recommended** *taking* [not *to take*] someone who speaks English and Russian to the agency that issues the permits.

182
VERBS AND EXPRESSIONS THAT USE GERUNDS AFTER THEM

acknowledge	detest	mind
admit	discuss	object to
advise	dislike	postpone
anticipate	dream about	practice
appreciate	enjoy	put off
avoid	escape	quit
cannot bear	evade	recall
cannot help	favor	recommend
cannot resist	finish	regret
complain about	give up	resent
consider	have trouble	resist
consist of	imagine	risk
contemplate	include	suggest
defer from	insist on	talk about
delay	keep (on)	tolerate
deny	mention	understand

Gerund After **go**

Go is usually followed by an infinitive: *We can* **go to see** [not *go seeing*] *a movie tonight.* Sometimes, however, *go* is followed by a gerund in phrases such as phrases as *go swimming, go fishing, go shopping,* and *go driving: I will* **go shopping** [not *go to shop*] *after work.*

Gerund After **be** + *Complement* + *Preposition*

Many common expressions use a form of the verb *be* plus a complement° plus a preposition. In such expressions, use a gerund, not an infinitive, after the preposition. Here is a list of some of the most frequently used expressions in this pattern.

LIST OF SELECTED *BE* + **COMPLEMENT** + **PREPOSITION EXPRESSIONS**

be (get) accustomed to	be interested in
be angry about	be prepared for
be bored with	be responsible for
be capable of	be tired of
be committed to	be (get) used to
be excited about	be worried about

We **are excited about** *voting* [not *to vote*] in the next election.

Who will **be responsible for** *locating* [not *to locate*] our polling place?

❖ USAGE ALERT: Always use a gerund, not an infinitive, as the object of a preposition. Be especially careful when the word *to* is functioning as a preposition in a phrasal verb (see 44b): *We are **committed to** changing* [not *to change*] *the rules*. ❖

45c Using an infinitive, not a gerund, as an object following certain verbs

Chart 183 lists selected common verbs° and expressions that must be followed by infinitives°, not gerunds°, as objects°.

She **wanted** *to go* [not *wanted going*] to the lecture.

Only three people **decided** *to question* [not *questioning*] the speaker.

VERBS AND EXPRESSIONS THAT USE INFINITIVES AFTER THEM			183
afford	claim	hope	promise
agree	consent	intend	refuse
aim	decide	know how	seem
appear	decline	learn	struggle
arrange	demand	like	tend
ask	deserve	manage	threaten
attempt	do not care	mean	try
be left	expect	offer	volunteer
beg	fail	plan	wait
cannot afford	give permission	prepare	want
care	hesitate	pretend	would like

Infinitives After be + Complement

Gerunds are common in constructions that use forms of the verb *be*, a complement°, and a preposition° (see 45b). However, use an infinitive, not a gerund, when *be* plus a complement is not followed by a preposition.

> We **are eager** *to go* [not *going*] camping.
>
> I **am ready** *to sleep* [not *sleeping*] in a tent.

Infinitives to Indicate Purpose

Use an infinitive in expressions that indicate purpose: *I read a book **to learn** more about Mayan culture*. This sentence means "I read a book for the purpose of learning more about Mayan culture." *To learn* delivers the idea of purpose more concisely (see Chapter 16) than expressions such as "so that I can" or "in order to."

Infinitives with the first, the last, the one

Use an infinitive after the expressions *the first, the last*, and *the one: Keno is **the first to arrive*** [not *arriving*] *and the last **to leave*** [not *leaving*] *every day.*

Unmarked Infinitives

Infinitives used without the word *to* are called **unmarked infinitives** or **bare infinitives**. An unmarked infinitive may be hard to recognize because it is not preceded by *to*. Some common verbs followed by unmarked infinitives are *feel, have, hear, let, listen to, look at, make* (meaning "compel"), *notice, see*, and *watch*.

> Please let me **take** [not *to take*] you to lunch. [unmarked infinitive]
>
> I want **to take** you to lunch. [marked infinitive]
>
> I can have Kara **drive** [not *to drive*] us. [unmarked infinitive]
>
> I will ask Kara **to drive** us. [marked infinitive]

The verb *help* can be followed by either a marked or an unmarked infinitive. Both are correct: *Help me **put** [or **to put**] this box in the car.*

♣ USAGE ALERT: Be careful to use parallel structure (see Chapter 18) correctly when you use two or more gerunds or infinitives after verbs. If two or more verbal objects° follow one verb, put the verbals into the same form.

NO	We went **sailing** and **to scuba dive**.
YES	We went **sailing** and **scuba diving**.

NO	We heard the wind **blow** and the waves **crashing**.
YES	We heard the wind **blow** and the waves **crash**.
YES	We heard the wind **blowing** and the waves **crashing**.

Conversely, if you are using verbal objects with compound predicates°, be sure to use the kind of verbal that each verb requires.

| NO | We enjoyed **scuba diving** but do not want **sailing** again. [*Enjoyed* requires a gerund object and *want* requires an infinitive object; see Charts 182 and 183.] |
| YES | We enjoyed **scuba diving** but do not want **to sail** again. ❖ |

45d Knowing how meaning changes when certain verbs are followed by a gerund or an infinitive as an object

With stop

The verb *stop* followed by a gerund° means "finish, quit." *Stop* followed by an infinitive means "stop or interrupt one activity to begin another."

We **stopped eating**. [We finished our meal.]
We **stopped to eat**. [We stopped another activity, such as driving, in order to eat.]

With remember *and* forget

The verb *remember* followed by an infinitive means "not to forget to do something": *I must* ***remember to talk*** *with Isa. Remember* followed by a gerund means "recall a memory": *I* ***remember talking*** *in my sleep last night.*

The verb *forget* followed by an infinitive means "to not do something": *If you* ***forget to put*** *a stamp on that letter, it will be returned. Forget* followed by a gerund means "to do something and not recall it": *I* ***forget having put*** *the stamps in the refrigerator.*

45e Understanding that meaning does not change whether a gerund or an infinitive follows certain sense verbs

Sense verbs° include words such as *see, notice, hear, observe, watch, feel, listen to,* and *look at.* The meaning of these verbs is usually not affected whether it is followed by a gerund° or an infinitive° as an

45e
ESL

object°. *I saw the water **rise*** and *I saw the water **rising*** both have the same meaning in American English.

EXERCISE 45-1

Consulting Chapter 45, write the correct form of verbal object (either a gerund or an infinitive) for each verb in parentheses.

EXAMPLE   Everyone would like (find) **to find** easier ways to use computers.

1. Think about (hold)＿＿a computer on your lap and (write)＿＿on its screen with a pen.
2. Several new computers will let you (do)＿＿just that.
3. Engineers have developed these new machines, called ''pen-based'' computers, (replace)＿＿pencil and paper.
4. No bigger than spiral notebooks and called electronic notebooks, pen-based computers have a special stylus for (write) ＿＿directly onto the flat screen.
5. No (train)＿＿or (type)＿＿is required.
6. Manufacturers hope (open)＿＿up whole new markets.
7. Pen-based computers will help (revive)＿＿slow sales of computers.
8. Many people who never considered (buy)＿＿a computer before are starting (look)＿＿seriously at the pen-based computer.
9. People who cannot be tied to a desk by a computer cord can now enjoy the convenience and power of a computer simply by (put)＿＿down their clipboard and (pick)＿＿up an electronic notebook.
10. I remember (wish)＿＿for a notebook computer myself.

1. holding [45b, gerund after preposition]
2. do [45c, unmarked infinitive with *let*]
3. to replace [*replacing* also acceptable]
4. writing [45b, gerund after preposition]
5. training, typing [45a, gerunds as subjects]
6. to open [45c, infinitive following *hope*]
7. revive *or* to revive [45c, unmarked or marked infinitive with *help*]
8. buying [45b, gerund with *consider*]; to look [45c, infinitive with *look at*]
9. putting, picking [45c, *putting* is gerund use after preposition; *picking* is same form for compound objects]
10. wishing [45b, gerund with *wish*]

It may help ESL students to realize that the extensive auxiliary verb system of English is linguistically quite unusual. Most languages alter the single verb form for conjugation instead of adding one or more auxiliary verbs. For this reason auxiliary verbs can present special difficulties, particularly the use of *do* in questions and negative statements. ESL students who try to translate into their first language can become confused by this "extra" word that carries no meaning in a question (*Do* you like pizza?) or a negative statement (I *do* not like pizza). To further complicate matters, forms of *do* can have an emphatic function in declarative sentences (I *do* like pizza; I *do* have time to eat some pizza).

46 ESL Modal Auxiliary Verbs

HOW TO USE CHAPTER 46 ESL EFFECTIVELY

1. Use this chapter together with these handbook sections.
   - 7c recognizing verbs°
   - 8j progressive tenses°
   - 8e auxiliary verbs°
   - tense sequence
   - 8g verb tense°
   - 8l-8m subjunctive mood°

2. Remember that throughout this handbook, **a degree mark (°)** after a word indicates that you can find the definition of the word in the Glossary of Terms toward the back of the book.

3. Also, use any **cross-references** (usually given in parentheses) to find full explanations of key concepts.

Auxiliary verbs are known as *helping verbs* because adding an auxiliary verb to a main verb° helps the main verb convey additional information (see 8e). For example, the auxiliary verb *do* is important in turning sentences into questions. *You have to sleep* becomes a question when *do* is added: *Do you have to sleep?* The most common auxiliary verbs are forms of *be, have,* and *do.*

Modal auxiliary verbs are one type of auxiliary verbs. They include *can, could, may, might, should, had better, must, will, would,* and other forms discussed in this chapter. Modal auxiliary verbs differ from *be, have,* and *do* used as auxiliary verbs in the three ways listed in Chart 184.

DIFFERENCES BETWEEN MODAL AUXILIARY VERBS AND OTHER AUXILIARY VERBS 184

- Modal auxiliary verbs are always followed by the simple form° of a main verb: *I might* **go** *tomorrow*.

- One-word modal auxiliary verbs have no *s* ending in the third-person singular°: *She* **could** *go with me, you* **could** *go with me, and they* **could** *go with me*. Exceptions include the modal auxiliary verb *have to*, which expresses necessity. Auxiliary verbs other than modal auxiliary verbs usually change form for third-person singular: *I* **have** *talked with her, he* **has** *talked with her*.

- Modal auxiliary verbs convey meaning about ability, necessity, advice, possibility, and other conditions: for example, *I can go* means "I am able to go." Modal auxiliary verbs do not indicate actual occurrences.

This chapter can help you use modal auxiliary verbs to convey shades of meaning. Section 46a discusses using modal auxiliary verbs to convey ability, necessity, advisability, and probability. Section 46b discusses using modal auxiliary verbs to convey preferences, plans or obligations, and past habits. Section 46c introduces modal auxiliary verbs in the passive voice°.

46a Conveying ability, necessity, advisability, and possibility with modal auxiliary verbs

Conveying Ability

The modal auxiliary verb *can* conveys ability now (in the present) and *could* conveys ability before (in the past). These words deliver the meaning of "able to." For the future, use *will be able to*.

We **can** work late tonight.
I **could** work late last night, too.
I **will be able to** work late next Monday.

Adding *not* between a modal auxiliary verb and the main verb makes the clause° negative: *We* **can not** (or **cannot**) *work late tonight; I* **could not** *work late last night; I* **will not be able** *to work late next Monday*.

❖ USAGE ALERT: You will often see negative forms of modal auxiliary verbs turned into contractions°: *can't, couldn't, won't, wouldn't,* and others. Because contractions are considered informal usage by some instructors, you will never be wrong if you avoid them in academic writing except for reproducing spoken words. ❖

Conveying Necessity

The modal auxiliary verbs *must, have to,* and *need to* convey the message of a need to do something. *Must* implies future action; *have to* and *need to* are used in the full range of tenses°. (Also, *have to* and *need to* add *-s* for third-person singular°; see 8c.)

You **must** leave before midnight.
She **has to** leave when I leave.
You **will need to** put the lights out after we go.

Conveying Advisability or the Notion of a Good Idea

The modal auxiliary verbs *should* and *ought to* express the idea that doing the action of the main verb is advisable or is a good idea. The past-tense forms are *should have* and *ought to have.*

You **should** go to class tomorrow morning.
I **ought to have** called my sister last week.

The modal auxiliary *had better* delivers the meaning of good advice or warning or threat. It does not change form for tense.

You **had better** see the doctor before your cough gets worse.

Need to is often used to express strong advice, too. Its past-tense form is *needed to.*

You **need to** take better care of yourself.

Conveying Possibility

The modal auxiliary verbs *may, might, could,* and *must* can be used to convey an idea of possibility or likelihood. They deliver a meaning that a guess is being made.

We **may** become hungry before long.
We **could** eat lunch at the diner next door.

The past-tense forms for *may, might, could,* and *must* use these words followed by *have* and the past participle of the main verb.

I **must have neglected** to eat breakfast.

EXERCISE 46-1

Consulting section 46a, fill in the blanks with the past-tense modal auxiliary verb that expresses the meaning given in parentheses.

EXAMPLE   I (advisability) **should have** gone to bed at the regular time last night.

1. I (advisability)_____learned my lesson after what happened in class today.
2. Because I (necessity, no choice)_____finish writing a paper, I stayed up until 3:00 a.m.
3. In class today, I (ability)_____not stay awake.
4. The instructor (making a guess)_____seen my eyes close.
5. I woke up instantly when I heard him say, "You (advice, good idea)_____stayed in bed if you (necessity, no choice)_____sleep, Mr. Lee."

ANSWERS & COVERAGE: EXERCISE 46-1

1. should have *or* ought to have [46a, past-tense form of auxiliary]

2. had to *or* needed to [46a, past-tense form of auxiliary]

3. could [past-tense form of auxiliary]

4. may have, might have, could have, must have [45a, any of the past-tense forms for conveying possibility and making a guess are acceptable here]

5. should have *or* ought to have [46a, either past-tense form is acceptable here]; had to *or* needed to [46a, either past-tense form is acceptable]

46b Conveying preferences, plans, and past habits with modal auxiliary verbs

Conveying Preferences

The modal auxiliary verbs *would rather* and *would rather have* express a preference. *Would rather* (present tense°) is used with the simple form° of the main verb° and *would rather have* (past tense°) is used with the past participle° of the main verb.

> We **would rather see** a comedy than a mystery.
> Carlos **would rather have stayed** home last night.

Conveying Plan or Obligation

A form of *be* followed by *supposed to* and the simple form of a main verb delivers a meaning of something planned or of an obligation.

> I **was supposed to meet** them at the bus stop.

Conveying Past Habit

The modal auxiliary verbs *used to* and *would* express the idea that something happened repeatedly in the past.

ANSWERS & COVERAGE: EXERCISE 46-2

1. should have been [46c, passive modal auxiliary verb with *Devi* receiving the action of the verb]

2. must have landed [46a, correct form for past-tense modal auxiliary verb expressing likelihood]

3. ought not to have [46a, correct form for modal auxiliary verb expressing advisability]

4. should not [46a, correct modal for expressing negative advisability rather than negative ability]

5. might not have [46c, correct form for active modal auxiliary verb expressing likelihood or possibility]

I **used to** hate going to the dentist.
I **would** dread visiting the dentist each time.

♣ USAGE ALERT: Both *used to* and *would* can be used to express repeated actions in the past, but *would* cannot be used for a situation that lasted for a duration of time in the past.

| NO | I **would** live in Arizona. |
| YES | I **used to** live in Arizona. ♣ |

46c Recognizing modal auxiliary verbs in the passive voice

Modal auxiliary verbs use the active voice°, as shown in sections 46a and 46b. In the active voice, the subject does the action expressed in the main verb° (see 8m-8o).

Modal auxiliary verbs can also use the passive voice°. In the passive voice, the doer of the main verb's action is either unexpressed or is expressed as an object° in a prepositional phrase° starting with the word *by*.

PASSIVE	The waterfront **can be seen** from my window.
ACTIVE	I **can see** the waterfront from my window.
PASSIVE	The tax form **must be signed by** the person who fills it out.
ACTIVE	The person who fills out the tax form **must sign** it.

EXERCISE 46-2

Consulting Chapter 46, select the correct choice from the words in parentheses and write it in the blank.

EXAMPLE   I (would, used to) <u>used to</u> collect stamps.

1. Devi (should have, should have been)_____hired by the bookstore manager.

2. The plane (must be landed, must have landed)_____on time.

3. You (ought not to have, ought not have)_____said that.

4. I am going to have some ice cream even though I (cannot, should not)_____.

5. You (might not have been, might not have)_____left your checkbook at home.

Appendix A:
Writing with a Computer

Some people write with a pen, some with a typewriter, and some—an increasing number—with a computer. Unlike other writing tools, computers make relatively painless the activities of planning, shaping, drafting, revising, and editing (see Chapters 2 and 3). If you do not have a computer and word-processing program at your disposal, worry not. The usual methods of writing will continue to serve you well. If you can use a word processor, you will likely agree with most writers who rejoice over a new-found flexibility.

As much as possible, tailor your use of a computer to your personal needs. Some experienced writers prefer to use a computer only for preparing the final copy. Others like to plan and shape (see Chapter 2) by hand and to write all drafts on a computer. Still other writers feel more comfortable writing out drafts by hand and then revising with a computer. Yet others like to use a computer throughout the writing process. See what works best for you in each writing situation.

A1 Basic operations in word processing

You can write with any computer equipped with any word-processing software and printer. You need to type, but you do not have to be an expert typist. You need also to know how to make your particular equipment perform the operations you want. To use a computer to greatest benefit, expect to take the time to learn its various operations. Once you can handle word processing with ease you will not have to interrupt your writing process to figure out how to do something mechanical. Each program is a little different, and many call their functions by different names. Become familiar with your word processor's jargon so that you can learn from a manual or discuss the program's functions with other people.

Here are more or less generic terms you will likely encounter in word processing.

THE LANGUAGE OF WORD PROCESSING

ADD = insert material

BLOCK = mark off a specific section of material on the screen

COPY = reproduce material in an additional location

CURSOR = the highlighted (sometimes pulsing) spot on the screen that signals where material can be typed in or operations begun

DELETE (CUT) = erase

FILE = a document identified by a name you create

INSERT = add material to what is already on screen

MOVE (PASTE) = transfer material from one place to another

PRINT = have the printer produce a "hard" (paper) copy

RETRIEVE (GET) = bring to the screen

SAVE = record on disk

SCROLL = look up and down the material on screen

SEARCH = locate a specific word or group of words on a page or in an entire document

TEXT = the typed material appearing on screen

Do not assume that your work is safe simply because it is on a computer disk. Disks are highly vulnerable, especially to magnetism. Place a disk too close to a magnetic source and, quick as a cursor's flash, your hours of work can be irretrievably garbled. In general, floppy disks do not survive well when they have to coexist with dust, cigarette ashes, food, or high humidity. Do not touch or bend your disks. Save your work frequently. Make a rule for yourself to save your work, say, every two pages or every ten to fifteen minutes. Some writers print out regularly. Having a printout, also called hard copy, means you have a record of your work, even if your disk incurs problems.

Relieved of the sometimes tedious work of copying and recopying material, many writers feel more creative when they use a computer. Their ideas seem to flow more freely when each new thought does not lead to a recopying job. Nevertheless, some writers find that recopying by hand helps them think of new ideas. Be careful, therefore, not to ignore what has always served you well when you wrote by hand. Also, do not let yourself be seduced by the wonders of a computer. It is only a machine.

A2 Using the computer for gathering ideas

At a computer terminal, you can record your thoughts as they occur to you. Try freewriting (2f) or brainstorming (2g). Consider using **invisible writing** by turning off your monitor so that you cannot see what you are writing. This helps you avoid the temptation of editing while you are getting ideas "on paper." After a while, turn your monitor back on to see what you wrote.

As you use idea-gathering techniques, resist the temptation to delete material. Disks hold a great deal. You never know what you might want later. A computer can save everything together for you legibly—without arrows, paper clips, or Scotch tape—then retrieve it when you are ready to decide which material you might use and in what order. If you are writing a research paper (see Chapter 32), be careful to keep full documentation of your sources also on disk.

A3 Using the computer for organization

You can shape, or outline, your essay (see 2n) at a computer. Read what you have written, and put a symbol near what seems most important. Now look over the marked parts, and copy them to the bottom of your text so that you can look at them grouped together. Shuffle them into several different orders. Does it matter which part comes first, second, and so on? Are the parts equally important, or do some seem subordinate to others? Try indenting the subordinate parts to make a rough outline (see 2n). Although what you have written may be so full of typos that only you can decipher it, it will still be more legible than its hand-written equivalent.

A4 Using the computer for drafting and development

Whether you are working with freewriting, invention notes, an outline, or all three, at some point you must create a "real draft." Try to write a whole draft at one session, second-guessing and rewriting as little as possible. If you have questions, or think you may want to elaborate on something but cannot think how at the moment, insert a symbol that will alert you to "talk to yourself" later. When you finish the draft and begin revising, your symbols will help you focus on areas that need reworking.

If your planning techniques result in clusters of ideas or freewriting, try picking any item (probably the one you know the most about) and adding details. Finish that item, whether it takes one or several paragraphs, and then move to another item and do the same thing. If you outlined, flesh out each section as you get to it. The computer automatically will move the remaining sections down to make room for what you add.

Be aware that even a handwritten draft may seem complete—simply because it has a beginning and end, with paragraphs in between. Many writers feel the urge to consider a rough draft the final version, and they type it up. Understandably, this urge is even stronger with computer drafts, which appear finished because they are already typed. Resist the urge to think neatness means completion. Rough drafts are excellent as springboards to revising. You can use them to ask a peer critic (see 3c-5) to react. Keep telling yourself not to confuse a draft with a final version.

A5 Using the computer for revision

Revision—addition to, deletion from, substitution for, and rearrangement of material—is a many-faceted activity (see 3c). You think through your ideas, and you change sentences and words. Because the computer can neither read nor think, you must decide what needs to be done.

As you read through your draft, word by word, use symbols and notes to yourself in brackets to alert you to what you want to revise. Remember, the computer screen does not become illegible from too many notations, as a written or typed draft can. Alternatively, some writers prefer to make changes on hard copy and enter those changes on disk.

If you think of something to add—for instance, something an expert said on your subject—move the cursor to the place in the draft that might be improved by the detail and type the detail in. You can add anything from a word to a many-paragraph segment. If you are unsure about the best place for an addition, type it at the end of the draft, then move the addition into more than one place. See where it helps most, then delete the extras.

Delete with caution. Move material you think you want to drop to the end of your document. Later you may find you want to return the deletion to your draft, so save it where you can find it. This method works for the deletion of a single word or of many pages.

Sometimes you may want to rearrange material. The computer

makes rearranging relatively painless. You may make endless versions of your draft until you are satisfied with the order. Try reordering your body paragraphs, splitting or joining some existing paragraphs, and moving your last paragraph to the first position. You may be surprised. Save the most promising versions. Try printing several versions and asking your peers to react to them.

A6 Using the computer for editing and proofreading

Editing takes place throughout your writing. Proofreading takes place after the last draft has been written. Read your printed copy aloud, or listen to someone else read it. Note items that need to be corrected. Also, you can use the screen to help you proofread and edit. Use the block command to highlight a five- or six-line section, and read each section slowly and carefully. This strategy allows you to work in small segments, and thus you can reduce the tendency to read too quickly and thereby fail to detect errors.

You might try making your own "spell-and-style checker" by keeping a file of the mistakes that you have made in the past. For example, if the difference between *its* and *it's* always escapes you or if you know that you tend to misuse the colon, call up your mistake file, and search your draft for those items. Each time the search stops, check the item against the rules in this handbook.

After you have edited and proofread and you are ready to print out your final version, make sure that your hard copy conforms to manuscript format requirements from your instructor, or use Appendix B.

A7 Using writer's aid programs

A growing number of special programs—some of them built into word processors—are designed specifically to help writers.

Most *prewriting programs* ask you questions to help you generate ideas on a topic. You will quickly learn the questions, but having "someone to talk to" can help get you started. These programs do not give you ideas, but they do help you find ideas within yourself.

Outline programs can help you set up an outline fast, automatically realigning and renumbering to accommodate changes you make.

Spell-checking programs call attention to any of your words that they cannot match to their own dictionaries. The programs are a big help for spotting typos. These programs, however, have limits. Suppose you intended to type "west" but instead typed "rest." Because "rest" appears as a correctly spelled word in the program's dictionary, the program will not call "west" to your attention. You must read your work carefully yourself.

Thesaurus programs are no different from printed thesauruses. You must evaluate each suggested substitution for sense within the context of what you are writing.

Style-checking programs examine your file against grammar, usage, and punctuation rules, alerting you to what they do not find in their programs. Fixing what mistakes they find is still your job. You should use a style-check program with caution. For example, if you are told some of your sentences are in the passive voice, change them to the active voice only when you think the change is needed (see 8m and 8n for a discussion of occasional cases when the passive voice is needed). Bring the same level of critical thinking to other information that the program might provide.

Tutorials like **Blue Pencil,** available with the *Simon & Schuster Handbook,* offer you sets of exercises for you to work at your own pace. It closely resembles the editing process. It scores your answers, and, if you have entered an incorrect answer, the program explains what is wrong and how to fix it. **Blue Pencil** also refers you to the appropriate section in this handbook.

Appendix B:
Following Guidelines for Typing Essays and Research Papers

B1 Following standard practices for typing or handwriting marks of punctuation

After each heading in this section, you will find typewritten and handwritten examples of each mark of punctuation.

PERIOD, QUESTION MARK, EXCLAMATION POINT . ? !

Do not space before these marks. Space twice after each mark when it ends a sentence.

```
I do.  Do you?  You do!  I know you do.
```

In typing initials used in personal names, leave one space after each period.

```
B. A. Jones
W. E. B. Du Bois
```

In other abbreviations, practice varies both for the use of periods and for spacing after periods. An up-to-date dictionary can guide you.

COMMA, SEMICOLON, COLON , ; :

Do not space before these marks. Space once after them in sentences. (See 26c for cases where the colon separates numbers with no space before or after.)

```
Usually, I call first; nevertheless, I did not today.
My reason is this: I saw you walking out of your house.
```

APOSTROPHE '

Do not space before or after an apostrophe within a word.

```
Isn't that Ken's car?
```

Space once after a final apostrophe followed by another word.

```
He must be using the Clarks' garage.
```

When an apostrophe ends the word that ends a sentence, do not leave a space between the apostrophe and the final period, question mark, or exclamation point. Put the apostrophe before the final mark of punctuation.

```
Those cars in the driveway are the Clarks'.
```

QUOTATION MARKS " " ' '

Do not space between quotation marks and whatever they enclose. Do not space between double and single quotation marks.

```
I said, "'Here Comes the Sun' makes me smile whenever I hear
it."
```

Space once after a closing quotation mark unless it ends a sentence. In that case, space twice.

```
He said "plaster."  I heard "blister," but I guess I was
wrong.
```

HYPHEN -

Do not space before or after a hyphen except to use one space after a "suspended" hyphen—that is, a hyphen showing that two prefixes or suffixes refer to one root word.

```
Many athletes trade the agony of defeat for pre- and
post-game shows.
```

When a hyphen occurs at the end of a line, always make it the last mark on the line. Do not carry the hyphen over to start a new line.

DASH --   —

In typed manuscripts, make a dash by striking the hyphen key twice, with no space between. In handwritten manuscripts, make a dash with a single line a little longer than a hyphen. Do not space before or after a dash.

```
All of us--all of us!--think sentimentally about
adolescence.
```

SLASH /   /

Do not space before or after a slash except when you use the slash to separate lines of quoted poetry.

```
and/or   1/16
```

When separating up to three lines of poetry, space once before and once after the slash. If four or more lines, display them (see B2).

```
Consider these lines from Shakespeare's "Sonnet 30":
"When to the sessions of sweet silent thought / I summon up
remembrance of things past."
```

BRACKETS, PARENTHESES [ ] ( )   [ ] ( )

Do not space between brackets or parentheses and whatever they enclose.

```
The letter continued, "Parrish was borne [sic] June 30,
1830. At least that's what Ada Jencks (my great grandmother)
wrote."
```

ELLIPSES . . .   . . .

Use three evenly spaced dots for an ellipsis. Use one space before, between, and after the dots.

```
"Turning away . . . they began to laugh."
```

Use four evenly spaced dots to indicate the omission of one or more sentences. Because the first dot serves as the period at the end of the sentence, leave no space before it. After the first dot, use three evenly spaced dots. (See 29d about using other punctuation with ellipses.)

```
"The shopper felt crowded. . . . Moving away was natural."
```

UNDERLINING (ITALICS)

When you underline more than one word, you may use either style shown here—with or without breaks between words. Whichever style you choose, use it consistently throughout a paper.

```
Zen and the Art of Motorcycle Maintenance
Zen and the Art of Motorcycle Maintenance
```

B2 Following standard practices when preparing the final copy of a paper

The appearance of a paper sends important messages to your instructor. Although no paper will earn an *A* only because it looks exceptionally neat and shows your attention to the conventions of manuscript format, a first-rate appearance suggests to the instructor that you took the assignment seriously and that you value what you have written.

APPEARANCE

Paper: For typed papers, use 8½ × 11-inch white, standard typing paper. Do not use onionskin or erasable paper: onionskin is for copies only, and erasable paper smudges easily and resists handwritten corrections. Double space between lines. Type on only one side of each sheet of paper.

If your instructor accepts handwritten papers, use ruled 8½ × 11-inch standard white, lined paper. Do not use colored paper or paper torn from a spiral-bound notebook. Write on only one side of each sheet of paper. Some of your instructors might require that you write on every other line, to provide space for you to make neat corrections and for them to write comments. If you are unsure of your instructor's requirements, ask. Make your handwriting as clear as you can. If your handwriting is not easily readable, slow down and work to improve it. Be consistent in your presentation; letters and spacing should be uniform.

Ink: Use a black typewriter ribbon, and keep the typewriter keys clean so that the letters will be clear, not blurred.

For handwritten papers, use dark blue or black ink, not red, green, brown, or other colors. Do not use pencil.

Computer printouts: If a printer has both capital and lowercase letters and produces an easy-to-read type, most instructors accept papers prepared on word processors. Ask first, however. When you submit the paper, be sure to tear off the hole-punched edges and separate the pages.

FORMATS

First page: At the end of this appendix is a sample of a first page when a cover page is not used. It shows where to place name, date, course, and other information that your instructor might specify. The format conforms to the recommendations of the Modern Language Association (MLA). A sample cover page, along with a first page when a cover page is used, in MLA style appears at the beginning of Amy Brown's research paper in Chapter 34.

Page from the body of a paper: At the end of this appendix is a sample page from the body of a paper. It shows the measurements for layout and the entry for writer's name and page number. It also illustrates how a displayed quotation is indented.

Works Cited page: At the end of this appendix is a sample first page of a Works Cited list. It shows the measurements for layout and the style of indentation for each entry on the list according to MLA style. A detailed discussion of the features of a Works Cited list appears at the end of Amy Brown's research paper in Chapter 34.

Displaying quotations: When a prose quotation runs more than four typed lines or four handwritten lines, it is displayed. It starts on a new line, and all lines are indented ten spaces. The first line of a paragraph within the displayed quotation is indented an additional three spaces. See examples in 28a and in Amy Brown's research paper in Chapter 34.

When you quote more than three lines of poetry, set the quotation off from your own words. Start a new line and lay the quoted poetry out so that it looks as much as possible like the printed version you are quoting from. If indenting ten spaces from the left causes you to have to break lines, you can indent less than ten spaces or not at all.

```
O Captain! my Captain! our fearful trip is done,
The ship has weather'd every rack, the prize we sought is won,
The port is near, the bells I hear, the people all exulting,
While follow eyes the steady keel, the vessel grim and daring;
```

```
But O heart! heart! heart!
  O the bleeding drops of red,
    Where on the deck my Captain lies,
      Fallen cold and dead.
```

Punctuation leading into a displayed quotation: When the words that lead into a displayed quotation are a complete sentence, end the sentence with a colon (for an example, see 28a-1). When the words are not a complete sentence and flow directly into the wording of the displayed quotation, use no punctuation (for an example, see the sample page from the body of a paper shown at the end of this appendix). ❖ PUNCTUATION ALERT: In MLA documentation style (explained in Chapter 33), the source of a displayed quotation is given in parentheses two spaces after the end punctuation of the quotation. ❖ You will find other examples in Chapter 34 (Amy Brown's research paper, page 2) and in sections 37e-2 and 37e-3. Chapter 33 presents MLA and APA documentation systems and references for other documentation systems. Check with your instructor for which system to use.

B3 Making careful handwritten corrections and insertions in typed papers

If your typewriter lacks any special characters that you need, such as accent marks, you can handwrite them. You can also make a few handwritten corrections in a paper that you intend to hand in. Use the standard correction marks shown below. Note, however, that if you have more than three handwritten corrections on a page, you should retype the page.

Draw one line through words you want to take out.

```
These ~~extra words~~ are deleted.
```

To insert words, make a caret (∧) where the missing words should be, and then write them in above the caret.

```
                    where words
A caret shows should be inserted.
             ∧
```

To transpose letters, use a mark like this:

```
squiggel
```

You can transpose words in a similar way:

Transpose⌊in the⌐words⌋wrong order.

You can indicate the start of a new paragraph like this:

Molly's actions primarily met her needs. ¶Overall, Molly exemplifies the behavior of one type of typical toddler.

You can close up space between letters this way:

Avoid in⌢correct spacing.

You can open space between letters this way:

Leave one space between words in/a sentence.

You can drop a letter and close up the remaining letters this way:

Some spellers have trouble with doub⌢ble letters.

FIRST PAGE WITHOUT COVER PAGE

Amy W. Brown	Name
Professor Wellington	Instructor
English 101, Section A1	Course, Section
10 December 19XX	Date submitted
Personal Space:	} Double space
An Intercultural Perspective	} Double space
	} Double space

When she returned home after a year in South America, Judith Martin, a North American writer, began to have a problem. People kept interpreting her behavior as flirta-tious, but she was not flirting. Fairly soon she figured

---

795

PAGE FROM THE BODY OF A PAPER,
WITH DISPLAYED QUOTE

1″   ½″
Brown 7

personal space.   Clearly, what is considered obnoxious in

one culture might be considered polite in another (Fisher,

Bell, and Baum 167).   As Hall explains, virtually every-

thing people are and do

          is associated with the experience of space. . . .

10 space
indent for Therefore, people from different cultures,
displayed
quotation when interpreting each other's behavior, often

          misinterpret the relationship, the activity, or

          the emotions.   This leads to alienation in

          encounters or distorted communications.

          (Hidden 171)

½″
Brown 10

1″

Indent 5 spaces after
first line of entry   Double space throughout

Works Cited

Davis, Martha, and Janet Skupien, eds.   Body Movement and

     Nonverbal Communication: An Annotated Bibliography

     1971–1981.   Bloomington, IN: Indiana UP, 1982.

Fast, Julius.   Body Language.   New York: Evans, 1970.

Fisher, Jeffrey D., Paul A. Bell, and Andrew Baum.

     Environmental Psychology.   2nd ed.   New York:

     Holt, 1984.

Hall, Edward T.   The Hidden Dimension.   New York:

     Doubleday, 1966.

---.   Interview.   "Learning the Arabs' Silent Language."

     With Kenneth Friedman.   Psychology Today Aug. 1979:

     44–54.

796

Usage Glossary

A **glossary** is a list of words or phrases singled out for special attention. This glossary relates to **usage**, the customary manner of using particular words or phrases.

The term "customary manner" refers to usage by educated people, as demonstrated especially in books, newspapers, and speeches. "Customary manner," however, is not as firm in practice as the term implies. Indeed, little demonstrates as dramatically as does a usage glossary that standards for language use change. Some words slip away from usage: for example, *thee* and *thou* are no longer used in everyday life. Some constructions considered nonstandard a decade ago are accepted as standard today; for example, *shall* used to be required for the first-person future (*I shall finish the work tomorrow*), but today most dictionaries and usage surveys report that *shall* and *will* can be used interchangeably in such constructions.

This Usage Glossary, which contains over 200 entries in alphabetical order, reflects customary practice for academic writing—as of the date this handbook was published. If you think that any information reported here might have changed, consult one of the dictionaries discussed in Chapter 20 with a publication (or revision) date later than this handbook's. The entries in this Usage Glossary cover matters of usage as well as many frequently confused homonyms and commonly confused words. Additional homonyms and commonly confused words appear in section 22b.

You will find this glossary easier to use if you understand two terms used frequently in the discussion: *Informal* indicates that the word or phrase occurs commonly in speech but should be avoided in academic writing. *Nonstandard* indicates that the word or phrase is unacceptable for standard spoken English and for writing.

This glossary can help you in at least two ways: (1) You can browse through it to become familiar with the words and phrases that are subject to usage constraints in academic writing. (2) You can consult it as a reference when you are editing your writing to make sure that you are using the words or phrases correctly.

As in the rest of this book, words marked here with a degree symbol (°) are defined in the Glossary of Grammatical and Selected Composition Terms in this handbook.

a, an Use *a* before words beginning with consonant sounds: *a dog, a grade, a hole*. Also, use *a* before words beginning with vowels that sound like consonants: *a unit, a European*. Use *an* before words beginning with vowel sounds or a silent *h*: *an apple, an onion, an hour*. (7a, 42aESL)

accept, except To *accept* means "to agree to" or "to receive." To *except* (verb°) means "to exclude or leave out"; *except* (preposition°) means "leaving out." (22b)

> **Except** [preposition] for one or two details, the striking workers were ready to **accept** [verb] management's offer. The workers wanted the no-smoking rule **excepted** [verb] from the contract.

advice, advise *Advice* (noun°) means "recommendation"; to *advise* (verb°) means "to give a recommendation." (22b)

> I **advise** you to follow your doctor's **advice**.

affect, effect To *affect* means "to influence" or "to arouse the emotions"; to *effect* means "to bring about"; *effect* (noun°) means "result or conclusion." (22b)

> One **effect** [noun] of the weather is that it **affects** [verb°] some people's moods. We **effected** [verb] some changes in our system for weather forecasting.

aggravate, irritate *Aggravate* is used colloquially to mean *irritate*. Each word has a precise meaning, however: to *aggravate* means "to intensify or make worse"; to *irritate* means "to annoy or make impatient."

> The executive was **irritated** by her assistant's carelessness, for it further **aggravated** the company's financial problems.

ain't is a nonstandard contraction for *am not, is not, are not, has not*, and *have not*.

all ready, already *Already* means "before or by this time"; *all ready* means "completely prepared." (22b)

> The new players were **all ready**; the warmup had **already** begun.

all right is two words, never one (not *alright*). (22b)

all together, altogether *All together* means "in a group, in unison"; *altogether* means "entirely or thoroughly." (22b)

> The sopranos, altos, and tenors were supposed to sing **all together**, but their first attempt was not **altogether** successful.

allude, elude To *allude* means "to refer to indirectly or casually"; to *elude* means "to escape notice of." (22b)

> The researchers **alluded** to budget cuts when they discussed why the identification of the virus had **eluded** them.

allusion, illusion An *allusion* is a reference to something; an *illusion* is a false impression or idea. (22b)

> The candidate wanted to create the **illusion** that he was sympathetic to the poor, so he made a snide **allusion** to his rival's wealth.

a lot (two words, not *alot*) is informal for *a great deal* or *a great many* and should be avoided in academic writing.

a.m., p.m. (or A.M., P.M.) are used only with numbers, not as substitutes for the words *morning, afternoon,* or *evening*. (30h)

Our class, which usually meets early in the **morning** [not *a.m.*], will meet at 7:10 **p.m.** tomorrow.

among, between Use *among* for three or more people or things; use *between* for two people or things.

>The problem was discussed **among** the three students. They had to choose **between** staying in school and getting full-time jobs.

amount, number Use *amount* for concepts or things that are collective rather than separate (wealth, work, happiness); use *number* for anything that can be counted (coins, jobs, joys).

>A large **number** of people had to do a great **amount** of work.

an, and *An* is an article° (see *a, an*) and should not be confused with *and*, which is a conjunction°. (7h)

>They saw **an** eagle **and** its chicks in the nest.

and/or occurs in business or legal writing when either one or both of the items it connects can apply.

>The office needs a modem **and/or** fax machine to transmit data.

In the humanities and most other disciplines, alternatives are usually expressed in words (*The office needs a modem, a fax machine, or both to transmit data*). (29e-3)

anybody, any body *Anybody* is any person not specified; *any body* is a specific person, object, or group. (22b)

>The purity of **any body** of water can be tested by **anybody** with the correct materials.

anyone, any one See *anybody, any body.*

anyplace is informal for *any place* or *anywhere*. Avoid it in academic writing.

anyways, anywheres are nonstandard for *anyway, anywhere.*

apt, likely, liable *Apt* and *likely* are loosely interchangeable. Strictly, however, *apt* is used to indicate a tendency or inclination; *likely* is used to indicate a reasonable expectation that something will happen. *Liable* means "having undesirable consequences."

>Although the roads are **apt** to be icy, you **likely** will arrive on time. However, you are **liable** to have an accident if you speed on icy roads.

as, like, as if

1. Use *like*, not *as*, in a comparison when resemblance but not equivalence is suggested.

>Mexico, **like** [not *as*] Argentina, is a Spanish-speaking country.

2. Use *as*, not *like*, in a comparison when equivalence is suggested.

>John served **as** [not *like*] moderator of the debate. [John = moderator]

3. *As* functions as a subordinating conjunction° or a preposition°, depending on the meaning of the sentence. *Like* functions only as a preposition. To start a clause°, use *as*.

>That hamburger tastes good, **as** [not *like*] a hamburger should. [subordinating conjunction]
>That hamburger tastes **like** chopped leather. [preposition]

4. Use *as if*, not *like*, with the subjunctive mood°. (8m)

> This hamburger tastes **as if** [not *like*] it has been grilled for an hour.

assure, ensure, insure To *assure* means "to promise or convince"; to *ensure* or to *insure* means "to make certain." *Insure* is reserved for financial or legal certainty, especially related to insurance.

> The insurance agent **assured** me that I could **insure** my life, but he explained that no one could **ensure** that I would have a long life.

as to should be avoided as a substitute for *about*.

> The pilot was unsure **about** [not *as to*] the airplane's safety.

awful, awfully *Awful* (adjective°) means "causing fear"; it should not be used as a substitute for intensifiers such as *very* or *extremely*. *Awfully* (adverb°) is informal for *very* or *extremely* and should be avoided in academic writing.

> The cyclone was an **awful** phenomenon to watch. It caused **serious** [not *awful*] damage. It came **very** [not *awfully*] close to our house.

a while, awhile *A while* is an article° and a noun°; it functions as a subject° or object°. *Awhile* is an adverb°; it modifies verbs°. (22b) In a prepositional phrase°, the correct form is *a while: for* **a while,** *in* **a while,** *after* **a while.**

> We waited **awhile** for our friends to arrive, but after **a while** we had to leave.

bad, badly *Bad* is an adjective° (*bad* feelings); it is used after linking verbs° such as *feel* or *felt* (*He felt* **bad**). *Badly* is an adverb° and is nonstandard after linking verbs. For more information, see 12d.

> The farmers felt **bad** [not *badly*]. [*Felt* in this example is a linking verb.]
> The **bad** drought had **badly** damaged the crops.

been, being *Been* is the past participle° of *to be*; *being* is the progressive form° of *to be*.

> Alcohol abuse has **been** [not *being*] on the rise recently. We see lives **being** [not *been*] ruined by drinking.

being as, being that are nonstandard for *because* or *since*.

> **Because** [not *being as* or *being that*] the catcher injured his arm, he had to leave the game.

beside, besides *Beside* (preposition°) means "next to or by the side of"; *besides* (when functioning as a preposition) means "other than or in addition to"; *besides* (when functioning as an adverb°) means "also or moreover."

> With keys in her hand, she stood **beside** the new car. No one **besides** her had a driver's license. **Besides,** she owned the car.

better, had better Used in place of *had better, better* is informal. Avoid it in academic writing.

> We **had better** [not *we better*] be careful.

between, among See *among, between*.

breath, breathe *Breath* is a noun°; *breathe* is a verb°.

> The jogger had to rest and **breathe** rapidly before he could catch his **breath.**

bring, take Use *bring* for movement from a distant place to a near place; use *take* for any other movement.

The coach will **bring** her team to our college, and then she will **take** the team on a tour of the campus.

broke is nonstandard for past participle° *broken.* Avoid it in academic writing, except as the past tense°. (8d)

The jogger's ankle was **broken** [not *broke*]. He **broke** it yesterday.

burst, bust To *burst* means "to break apart suddenly and violently"; its principal parts are *burst, burst, burst* (not *bursted*). To *bust* is slang for to *burst* and should be avoided in academic writing. (8d)

The bubble **burst** [not *busted* or *bursted.*]

but, however, yet Use *but, however,* and *yet* alone, not in combination with each other. (7h)

The economy is strong, **but** [not *but yet* or *but however*] unemployment is still high.

but that, but what are nonstandard for *that.* Avoid them in academic writing.

The supervisor does not doubt **that** [not *but that* or *but what*] the job can be done.

calculate, figure, reckon are informal for *imagine* or *expect.* Avoid such informal uses in academic writing.

The farmers **expect** [not *figure* or *reckon*] that they will have a good crop.

can, may *Can* indicates ability or capacity; *may* requests or grants permission. In the negative, however, *can* is acceptable in place of *may.*

May I leave the room so that I **can** have a cigarette?
Why **can't** I?

can't hardly, can't scarcely are double negatives and are nonstandard; use *hardly* and *scarcely* only. For more information, see 12c.

They can **hardly** [not *can't hardly* or *can't scarcely*] see through the fog.

censor, censure To *censor* means "to judge" or "to delete objectionable material"; to *censure* means "to condemn or officially reprimand."

The town council **censured** the mayor for permitting a citizen's committee to **censor** books in the public library.

chairman, chairperson, chair Usage is changing concerning *chairman,* which has a masculine implication. The gender-free terms *chairperson* and *chair* often are preferred, although *chair* seems to be more widely used at this time. (21b)

choose, chose *Choose* is the simple form of *to choose; chose* is the past tense of *to choose.* (8d)

Today I will **choose** the college I will attend. Yesterday she **chose** the college she will attend.

cloth, clothe *Cloth* (noun°) means "fabric"; to *clothe* (verb°) means "to dress" or "to cover with garments."

The king wanted to **clothe** himself with garments made of fine **cloth.**

complement, compliment To *complement* means "to complete" or "to supplement"; to *compliment* means "to express praise or flattery."

The instructor **complimented** the student for her research project, saying that it **complemented** work done twenty years before.

conscience, conscious *Conscience* (noun°) means "a sense of right or wrong"; *conscious* (adjective°) means "being aware or awake."

The thief was **conscious** that his **conscience** was bothering him.

consensus of opinion is a redundant phrase. Use *consensus* only.

continual, continuous *Continual* is occurring repeatedly; *continuous* is going on without interruption in space or time.

Although all essential systems of the spacecraft were expected to operate **continuously,** the astronauts **continually** checked their instrument panels. The washing machine **continually** breaks down, and then it makes a **continuous** humming sound.

couple, couple of are nonstandard for *a few* or *several.*

You should rest for **a few** [not *a couple* or *a couple of*] minutes before you begin again.

data is the plural of *datum,* a rarely used word. Informal usage now treats *data* as singular, but it should be treated as plural in academic writing.

These [not *this*] **data show** [not *shows*] that the virus is spreading.

different from, different than *From* is the preferred preposition after *different,* although *than* is commonly used in speech.

Football is **different from** [not *different than*] soccer.

disinterested, uninterested *Disinterested* means "impartial"; *uninterested* means "indifferent or not concerned with."

They were **uninterested** in hearing my side of the story, so we agreed to ask a **disinterested** person to settle our dispute.

done is a past participle°; it cannot substitute for the past tense *did.* (8d)

The farmers raised [not *done* raised] a fine crop. They **did** [not *done*] a good job.

don't is a contraction for *do not,* not for *does not (doesn't).*

She **doesn't** [not *don't*] like loud music.

due to Many people object to *due to* as a preposition° meaning "because of." As an adjective°, *due to* following a form of the verb *to be* is acceptable.

He was late **because of** [not *due to* as a preposition] an accident.
His being late was **due to** [an adjective following a form of *to be*] an accident.

effect, affect See *affect, effect.*

emigrate from, immigrate to To *immigrate to* means "to enter a new country to live there." To *emigrate from* means "to leave one country to live in another."

After the ballet star **emigrated from** Russia, he **immigrated to** the United States to start a new life.

ensure, assure, insure See *assure, ensure, insure.*

enthused as an adjective° is nonstandard for *enthusiastic.*

The student was **enthusiastic** [not *enthused*] about going to college.

especially, specially *Especially* and *specially* are not interchangeable. *Especially* means "mainly or particularly"; *specially* is for a special purpose.

> Because the quarterback was **especially** tired, he could not attend the **specially** organized party celebrating his team's victory.

etc. is the abbreviation for the Latin *et cetera,* meaning *and the rest.* Do not use it in academic writing; acceptable substitutes are *and the like, and so on,* or *and so forth.*

> The Greenlawn Resort offers water sports such as snorkeling, scuba diving, windsurfing, **and the like** [not *etc.*].

everyday, every day *Everyday* is an adjective°; it means "daily" and modifies nouns. *Every day* is an adjective-noun combination that functions as a subject° or object°. (22b)

> I missed the bus **every day** last week. Arriving at work late has become an **everyday** occurrence.

everywheres is nonstandard for *everywhere.*

except, accept See *accept, except.*

explicit, implicit *Explicit* means "directly stated or expressed"; *implicit* means "implied or suggested."

> The warning on cigarette packs is **explicit:** Smoking may be dangerous to your health. The warning's **implicit** message is that people should not smoke.

farther, further are used interchangeably, although many writers prefer to use *farther* for geographical distances and *further* for all other cases.

fewer, less Use *fewer* for anything that can be counted (*fewer dollars, fewer* jobs, fewer *joys*); use *less* for concepts or things thought of collectively, not separately (less *money,* less *work,* less *happiness*). (12E-2)

figure, calculate, reckon See *calculate, figure, reckon.*

fine, find *Fine* can be a noun° (*The fine was $100*). *Fine* can be an adjective° (*She bought a fine electric drill*); it is nonstandard for *well* or any other adverb° (not *The new electric drill worked fine*). *Find* is the simple form of the verb *to find* (*We find new evidence each day*).

former, latter When two ideas or things are referred to, *former* refers to the first of the two, and *latter* refers to the second of the two. When more than two ideas or things are referred to, do not use these words.

> Brazil and Ecuador are two Latin American countries. The **former** is Portuguese-speaking, the **latter** Spanish-speaking.

further, farther See *farther, further.*

gender, sex *Gender* is attributed to words, *sex* to people and animals. (21b)

> My instructor uses **gender-free** [not *sex-free*] language, like *police officer* instead of *policeman.*
> What **sex** [not *gender*] is the guard dog?

given, giving *Given* is the past participle° of *to give; giving* is the progressive° form.

A reward was **given** to a citizen for **giving** the police valuable help in preventing a robbery.

goes, says *Goes* is nonstandard for *says.*

> He **says** [not *goes*] we will have a test tomorrow.

gone, went *Gone* is the past participle° of *to go; went* is the past tense° of *to go.* (8d)

> *They* **went** [not *gone*] to the concert after their friends **had gone** [not *had went*] home.

good and is nonstandard for *very.*

> *He was* **very** [not *good and*] sorry.

good, well *Good* is an adjective° (*good idea*); it is nonstandard as an adverb; *well* is an adverb° (*run well*). (12d)

> The **good** writer spoke **well.**

got, have *Got* is the past tense° of *to get (He* **got** *an A)* and is also one of the past participles° of *to get (She has* **got**—or **gotten**—*excellent grades). Got* is nonstandard in place of *have; got to* is nonstandard as a substitute for an intensifier such as *must.* (8d)

> What do we **have** [not *got*] for dinner?
> You **must** [not *got to*] help me.

great is an informal adjective meaning "good," "wonderful," "skillful," or "clever." Reserve it for its precise meaning: "a high degree of," "eminent," "large," "grand."

> **Yes** Einstein was a **great** scientist.
> **Yes** Her work gave her **great** satisfaction.
> **No** She has a **great** personality.

had ought, hadn't ought are nonstandard for *ought* and *ought not.*

> He **ought** [not *had ought*] to call home.

hanged, hung Use *hanged* only to refer to executions (*The prisoner was* **hanged** *this morning*). Use *hung* for all other meanings (*They* **hung** *her portrait in the living room*). (8b)

have, got See *got, have.*

have, of *Have,* not *of,* should be used after such verbs as *could, may, might, must, should.*

> They *could* **have** [not *of*] telephoned. They *may* **have** [not *of*] tried to call.

he, she, he or she Using *he* to refer to both males and females is avoided by people who want to avoid using sexist language°. Many writers use *he or she* or *he/she.* If at all possible they switch to plural nouns and pronouns. (21b, 11q)

> If **they** want [not *he* wants] to avoid accidents, **drivers** [not *a driver*] should drive defensively.

himself, herself See *myself, yourself, himself, herself.*

hisself is nonstandard for *himself.*

hopefully is an adverb° that means "with hope," "in a hopeful manner," or "it is hoped that." It can modify a verb°, an adjective°, or another adverb.

Some people use it as a sentence modifier° meaning "I hope," but this usage is not appropriate in academic writing. Always say in your sentence who is doing the hoping.

No   **Hopefully**, the plane will land safely.
Yes   They waited **hopefully** for the plane to land safely.
Yes   They **hoped** that the plane would land safely.

however, yet, but See *but, however, yet.*

hung, hanged See *hanged, hung.*

if, whether *If* is a subordinating conjunction°. *Whether* occurs in three situations: (1) in an indirect question *(She asked **whether** I had heard from the hikers)*, (2) to express doubt *(She was not sure **whether** they would be safe in the storm)*, and (3) to express alternatives with or without *or not (I did not know **whether** [or whether or not] to search for them).*

illusion, allusion See *allusion, illusion.*

immigrate to, emigrate from See *emigrate from, immigrate to.*

implicit, explicit See *explicit, implicit.*

imply, infer To *imply* means "to hint or suggest without stating outright"; to *infer* means "to draw a conclusion from what has been written or said."

The governor **implied** that she might not seek reelection, and the reporters **inferred** that she had decided to run for president.

incredible, incredulous *Incredible* means "extraordinary" or "not believable"; *incredulous* means "unable or unwilling to believe." A person would be *incredulous* in response to something that is *incredible.*

Their families were **incredulous** as the freed hostages told of the **incredible** cruelty they had suffered while captives.

individual, person, party are not interchangeable in academic writing. Use *individual* to emphasize the uniqueness of a single human being; otherwise use *person.* Use *party* only for a group of people.

The Constitution guarantees every **individual** certain rights.
Each **person** received a written invitation.
The governor and his **party** entered the room together.

infer, imply See *imply, infer.*

inside of, outside of are nonstandard when used with *of (She waited **outside** [not outside of] the dormitory).* Also, *inside of* is nonstandard when referring to time *(She waited **about** [not inside of] five minutes).*

insure, assure, ensure See *assure, ensure, insure.*

into, in to Use *into* as a preposition° (I walked *into* the house). Use *in to* when *to* is part of an infinitive (I walked *in to* greet the guests).

irregardless is nonstandard for *regardless.*

irritate, aggravate See *aggravate, irritate.*

is when, is where In giving definitions, *is* should not be followed by *when* or *where.*

Defensive driving means that [not *is when*] drivers stay on the defense against accidents that might be caused by other drivers.

its, it's *Its* is a personal pronoun in the possessive case *(The dog lost its bone).* *It's* is a contraction of *it is* or *it has* (***It's** a warm day;* ***It's** been a hot day.)* (22b)

-ize is a suffix used to change a noun° or adjective° to a verb° *(hospital + ize = hospitalize, brutal + ize = brutalize).* Be careful not to attach *-ize* indiscriminately to create new words rather than using good words that already exist. When in doubt, check your dictionary to see if a word ending in *-ize* is acceptable.

kind, sort are singular words and should therefore be paired with *this,* not *these. These* can be paired with *kinds* or *sorts.*

kind of (a), sort of (a) *Kind of* and *sort of* are nonstandard if used as adverbs° meaning "in a way" or "somewhat." Also, the *a* with these phrases is nonstandard.

> The hikers were **somewhat** [not *kind of*] tired when they got home.
> That **kind of** [not *kind of an*] exercise is healthy.

later, latter *Later* means "after some time" or "subsequently"; *latter* refers to the second of a pair of ideas or things. (22b)

> That restaurant opens **later** than we had thought. It serves lunch and dinner, the **latter** starting at 7 p.m.

latter, former See *former, latter.*

lay, lie *Lay* (principal parts: *laying, laid*) is always followed by a direct object°. As a substitute for *lie* (principal parts: *lying, lay, lain*), *lay* is nonstandard. (8f)

> **Lay** the blanket on the beach so you can **lie** [not *lay*] down and rest.

learn, teach *Learn* is nonstandard for *teach.* Students *learn;* teachers *teach.*

> The instructor will **teach** us [not *learn* us] chemistry.

leave, let To *leave* means "to depart"; to *let* means "to permit." *Leave* is nonstandard for *let* unless *leave* is followed by *alone.*

> I had to **leave** the classroom early because I was ill. My instructor will **let** [not *leave*] me take a retest tomorrow. She will have to find a proctor, because she cannot **leave** a student alone during an exam.

less, fewer See *fewer, less.*

lie, lay See *lay, lie.*

like, as See *as, like, as if.*

likely, apt, liable See *apt, likely, liable.*

loose, lose, loss *Loose* means "not tight"; to *lose* means "to be unable to find"; *loss* means "that which cannot be found or retrieved."

> Before I **lose** this **loose** belt, I had better tighten it.
> The **loss** from the fire included most of his clothing.

lots, lots of, a lot of are informal for *many, much, a great deal of.*

> **Many** [not *a lot of*] bees were in the hive.

may, can See *can, may.*

may be, maybe *May be* is a verb phrase°; *maybe* is an adverb°. (22b)

> Our team **may be** out of practice, but **maybe** we will win anyway.

media is the plural of *medium* and therefore requires a plural verb.

The **media** *cover* [not *covers*] the elections, but the **medium** that reaches most people is television.

mighty is a nonstandard substitute for *extremely* or *very*.

mind, mine *Mind* is a noun° *(She had a good **mind**)*; *mine* is a personal pronoun° *(That key is **mine**)*.

morale, moral *Morale* (noun°) means "a mental state relating to courage, confidence, or enthusiasm." *Moral* (noun) means "the conclusion of, or lesson from, a story"; *moral* (adjective°) means "right in conduct or character." (22b)

> The president's good **moral** character boosted the country's **morale**
> The **moral** of that story is that people should be kind to animals.

most is nonstandard for *almost* (**Almost** [not *most*] *all of the people agree*). *It is correct as an adjective°* (**most** *people agree*) *and in superlative forms of adjectives and adverbs°* (*the **most** important fact; the **most** lively debate*). (12e)

Ms. is the title free of reference to marital status for women; it is equivalent to the male title *Mr.* Unless a woman specifically requests *Miss* or *Mrs.*, use *Ms.*

myself, yourself, himself, herself are reflexive pronouns° *(I told **myself** to stay home)* and intensive pronouns° *(I **myself** will volunteer)*. They are nonstandard when used as a subject° or an object in a prepositional phrase°.

> The dean and **I** [not *myself*] will explain the facts to the president.
> First, however, the class has to explain them to the dean and **me** [not *myself*].

nothing like, nowhere near are nonstandard for *not nearly*.

> Last month's rain was **not nearly** [not *nowhere near*] enough.

nowheres is nonstandard for *nowhere*.

number, amount See *amount, number*.

of, have See *have, of*.

off of is nonstandard for *off*.

> He fell **off** [not *off of*] the chair.

OK, O.K., okay are acceptable, but avoid them in academic writing in favor of a word more specific to the meaning of the sentence.

> The weather was **satisfactory** [not *okay*] for the race. Course officials gave the **approval** [not *okay*] for the final lap.

on account of is wordy for *because, because of*.

> **Because of** [not *on account of*] the rainy weather, we stayed home.

outside of, inside of See *inside of, outside of*.

party, individual, person See *individual, person, party*.

per The Latin word *per* is acceptable in technical and commercial contexts *(miles **per** hour, **per** capita income)*. For writing in the humanities and some other academic areas, *per* is not preferred.

> A mine shaft collapsed **as reported in** [not *per*] this morning's newspaper.

percent, percentage *Percent* is used with specific numbers *(two percent, 95 percent)*. *Percentage* is used with descriptive words or phrases *(a small percentage)*, but only for amounts that have been expressed as percentages.

Do not use it as a synonym for *part, portion, number, amount,* or other words denoting quantity.

> **Several people** in my class are bilingual [not *A percentage* of my class is bilingual].
>
> A large **percentage** of the voters watch the presidential debates on television.

person, individual, party See *individual, person, party.*

plenty is nonstandard for words such as *quite* and *very (She was **very*** (not *plenty) tired from the workout).* When used as a noun meaning *a large amount, plenty* must be followed by *of (They must have **plenty of** food for the winter).*

plus is acceptable as a preposition° meaning "in addition to." *Plus,* however, should not be used (1) as a substitute for *and* between independent clauses° and (2) as a transitional word° such as *besides, moreover, in addition.*

> **No**   He studied hard **plus** he played hard.
> **No**   **Plus,** he had a long commute between his home and campus.
> **Yes**   She had talent **plus** good work habits.

p.m., a.m. See *a.m., p.m.*

practical, practicable *Practical* means "useful or sensible"; *practicable* means "capable of being put into practice."

> The mayor wanted a **practical** evacuation plan, but none of the proposals was **practicable** for a large city.

precede, proceed To *precede* means "to come before"; to *proceed* means "to continue." (22b)

> The attorney **preceded** her client to court and then **proceeded** to unpack her briefcase.

pretty is informal for words such as *rather, quite, very,* and *somewhat.* Avoid such use in academic writing.

> The flu epidemic was **quite** [not *pretty*] severe.

principal, principle *Principle* means "a basic truth or rule." *Principal* (noun°) means "chief person" or "main or original amount"; *principal* (adjective°) means "most important." (22b)

> The school **principal** paid interest on the **principal** of her bank loan.
>
> One of the **principal** values in the United States is the **principle** of free speech.

proceed, precede See *precede, proceed.*

raise, rise *Raise* (principal parts: *raised, raising*) needs a direct object° *(Please **raise** your hand); rise* (principal parts: *rose, risen, rising*) does not take a direct object *(The sun will **rise**).* Using these verbs interchangeably is nonstandard. (8f)

> The governor will **rise** [not *raise*] to speak after we **raise** [not *rise*] the flag.

rarely ever is an informal expression for *rarely* or *hardly ever;* avoid it in academic writing.

> He **rarely** [not *rarely ever*] came to class, so I **hardly ever** [not *rarely ever*] saw him.

real is nonstandard for intensifiers such as *really* (informal) or *very.*

really is informal for intensifiers such as *very* and *extremely.*

reason is because is redundant; drop *because.* (15d-2)

> One **reason** we moved away **is** [not *is because*] we got new jobs.

reason why is redundant; drop *why.*

> The **reason** [not *reason why*] they left home is a mystery.

reckon, calculate, figure See *calculate, figure, reckon.*

regarding, in regard to, with regard to are used in some legal and technical writing but are too stiff for most academic writing. Useful substitutes are words such as *about* and *concerning.*

> The committee members asked **about** [not *regarding, in regard to,* or *with regard to*] the plan for a new park.

respectful, respectfully; respective, respectively *Respectful* and *respectfully* relate to showing respect; *respective* and *respectively* refer to items that are in the given sequence.

> The staff **respectfully** requested that the dean hear their complaints.
> He suggested that the typist and telephone operators go back to their desk and switchboards, **respectively.** They then returned to their **respective** jobs.

right is nonstandard for intensifiers such as *very* or *extremely.*

> The workers were **very** [not *right*] pleased to hear that the factory will reopen.

rise, raise See *raise, rise.*

says, goes See *goes, says.*

seen is a nonstandard substitute for *saw. Seen* is the past participle° of *to see* and must be used with an auxiliary verb° such as *have, has,* or *had.* (8d)

> *They* **saw** [not *seen*] the film. I **had seen** [not *I seen*] it last week.

set, sit *Set* (principal parts: *set, setting*) is nonstandard as a substitute for *to sit* (principal parts: *sat, sitting*). *Set* means "to place" and is followed by a direct object°. *Sit* means "to be seated." (8f)

> After you carefully **set** [not *sit*] the rare Chinese vase on the table, please **sit** [not *set*] down.

sex, gender See *gender, sex.*

shall, will Use *shall* for questions in the first person (***Shall** I leave?*) or in very formal settings (*The judge **shall** render her verdict after hearing the testimony*). In all other cases, *will* is now accepted for the future tense in first, second, and third persons.

she, he, he or she See *he, she, he or she.*

should, would Use *should* to express obligation (*They **should** practice what they preach*) or condition (*If you **should** need advice, call me*). Use *would* to express a wish (*I wish my family **would** buy a VCR*) or habitual action (*I **would** tape all the comedy specials*).

sit, set See *set, sit.*

so is colloquial as an intensifier like *very* and *extremely.*

some is both nonstandard and vague as a substitute for modifiers such as *somewhat, a little,* and *remarkable.*

> That was **a remarkable** [not *some*] performance.

U GL

somebody, some body See *anybody, any body.*

someone, some one See *anybody, any body.*

sometime, sometimes, some time *Sometime* means "at an unspecified future time"; *sometimes* means "now and then"; *some time* is a span of time. (22c-3)

> **Sometime** next semester we have to take qualifying exams.
> **Sometimes** I worry about the tests. I need **some time** to get used to the pressure.

sort, kind See *kind, sort.*

sort of (a), kind of (a) See *kind of (a), sort of (a).*

specially, especially See *especially, specially.*

stationary, stationery are not interchangeable. *Stationary* means "standing still"; *stationery* refers to paper and related products. (22b)

such is informal and overused as an intensifier such as *very* or *extremely.* Avoid it in academic writing, unless it is part of a comparison including *that.*

> **No** It was **such** a poorly written play.
> **Yes** It was a **very** poorly written play.
> **Yes** It was **such** a poorly written play **that** no one went to see it.

supposed to, used to The final *d* is essential in both expressions. (8b-1)

> The weather is **supposed to** [not *suppose to*] improve. It **used to** [not *use to*] be sunny this time of year.

sure is nonstandard when used as an adverb° meaning *surely* or *certainly.*

> I **surely** [not *sure*] hope to go to college.

sure and, try and See *try and, sure and.*

take, bring See *bring, take.*

teach, learn See *learn, teach.*

than, then *Than* indicates comparison (*One is smaller **than** two*). *Then* relates to time (*He tripped and **then** fell*).

that there, them there, this here, these here are nonstandard for *that, those, this,* and *these,* respectively.

that, which Use *that* with restrictive (essential) clauses°; *which* can be used today for both restrictive and nonrestrictive (nonessential) clauses°; many writers prefer to reserve *which* for nonrestrictive (nonessential) clauses only. (10f)

> We visited the house **that** Jack built. Jack built the house, **which** is on Beanstalk Street, for his large plant collection.

their, there, they're *Their* is possessive; *there* means "in that place" or serves as an expletive°; *they're* is a contraction of *they are.* (22b)

> The students attended **their** classes in the lecture hall, which is over **there**. At this college, **there** are many courses to take, but **they're** all scheduled in the morning.

theirself, theirselves, themself are nonstandard for *themselves.*

them is nonstandard when used for *these* or *those.*

> Let's buy **those** [not *them*] strawberries.

then, than See *than, then*.

thusly is nonstandard for *thus*. Because *thus* is already an adverb°, the *-ly* ending is not needed.

till, until are both acceptable, although most writers prefer *until* in academic writing. Avoid the contraction *'til* in academic writing.

to, too, two *To* is a preposition°; *too* is an adverb°; *two* is the number. (22b)

> They went **to** the game. They ate at a restaurant, **too.** The check was not **too** expensive for the **two** of them.

toward, towards are both acceptable, although some writers prefer *toward*.

try and, sure and are nonstandard for *try to* and *sure to*.

> She wanted to **try to** [not *try and*] get a part-time job. Therefore, she had to be **sure to** [not *sure and*] prepare a résumé.

type is nonstandard for *type of*.

> That *type of* [not *type*] test is hard.

uninterested, disinterested See *disinterested, uninterested*.

unique is an absolute word and therefore cannot be modified by intensifiers such as *very* or *most*.

> Her talent was **unique** [not *very unique* or *most unique*].

until, till See *till, until*.

used to, supposed to See *supposed to, used to*.

wait on is informal when used instead of *wait for*. It is correct when used in the context of waiting on tables.

ways is colloquial for *way*.

> California is a long **way** [not *ways*] from New York.

well, good See *good, well*.

went, gone See *gone, went*.

what is nonstandard when used for *that* or *who*. (10f)

> The house **that** [not *what*] Jack built contains a beanstalk.

where is nonstandard when used for *that*.

> I read in the newspaper **that** [not *where*] tuition will be increased.

where . . . at is redundant; drop *at*.

> **Where** is the house [not *house at*]?

whether, if See *if, whether*.

which, that See *that, which*.

who, which Use *which* to refer to things or ideas; use *who* to refer to people.

who, whom Use *who* for the subjective case° *(The person **who** can type has an easier time in school)*. Use *whom* for the objective case° *(I asked to **whom** my professor was speaking)*. (9e)

who's, whose *Who's* is the contraction of *who is; whose* is possessive.

> **Who's** going to run for mayor?
> **Whose** campaign is well organized?

will, shall See *shall, will.*

-wise The suffix *-wise* means "in a manner, in a direction, or in a position" (*clockwise, otherwise*). Be careful not to attach *-wise* indiscriminately to create new words rather than using good words that already exist. When in doubt, check your dictionary to see if a word ending in *-wise* is acceptable.

> The **weather** [not *Weatherwise, the*] outlook is excellent.

would, should See *should, would.*

Xmas is an abbreviation for *Christmas;* avoid using it in academic writing.

yet, however, but See *but, however, yet.*

your, you're *Your* is possessive; *you're* is the contraction of *you are.* (22b)

> **You're** generous to share **your** food with us.

yourself See *myself, yourself, himself, herself.*

Glossary of Grammatical and Selected Composition Terms

The first time that a term is used in this handbook, it is defined. After that, the term is marked with a degree symbol (°) to signal that it is defined in this glossary. Also, when a definition in this glossary uses terms that are themselves defined here, the terms are marked with a degree symbol. Each definition here concludes with a reference, in parentheses, to the handbook section(s) or chapters where the term is most fully discussed.

absolute phrase A phrase containing a subject° and a participle° and modifying an entire sentence: *Summer being over, we left the seashore.* (7n)

abstract noun A noun° that names things not knowable through the five senses: *idea, guilt.* (7a)

acronym A word made up of the first letters of other words that acts as an abbreviation for those words: *NASA.* (30i)

active voice The form of a verb° in which the subject° performs the action named by the verb. This voice° emphasizes the doer of the action, in contrast to the passive voice°, which emphasizes the action. (8n, 8o)

adjective A word that describes or limits (modifies) a noun° or pronoun° or word group functioning as a noun: *silly, three.* (7e, 12, 43b-ESL)

adjective clause A dependent clause° that usually begins with a relative pronoun° and that modifies nouns° or pronouns°. (7o-2)

adverb A word that describes or limits (modifies) verbs°, adjectives°, other adverbs, or whole sentences: *wearily, very.* (7f, 12, 43c-ESL)

adverb clause A dependent clause° that begins with a subordinating conjunction° and that modifies verbs°, adjectives°, adverbs°, or whole sentences. (7o-2)

agreement The match in expressing number° and person° required between a subject° and its verb° or a pronoun° and its antecedent°. For pronouns and antecedents, expressions of gender° must match as well. (11)

analogy An explanation of the unfamiliar in terms of the familiar, analogy compares objects or ideas from different classes, things not normally associated with each other. Analogy is also a method of developing one or more paragraphs. (4f-8, 21c, 38b)

analysis A thinking process, analysis divides something into its component parts to make clear the relationship between the whole and the parts. Sometimes called *division,* analysis is also a method of developing one or more paragraphs. (4f-6, 5a)

antecedent The noun° or pronoun° to which a pronoun refers. (10, 11m-11r)

antonym A word opposite in meaning to another word. (20a)

APA style See *documentation style.*

appositive A word or group of words that renames a noun° or a noun group preceding it: *my favorite month,* **October.** (7m-3)

argument A written argument seeks to convince a reader to agree with the writer concerning a topic open to debate. (1b, 6)

articles The words *a* and *an* are indefinite articles°. The word *the* is a definite article°. Articles are also called *determiners°, limiting adjectives°, and noun markers.* (7a, 42-ESL)

assertion A statement that gives a position about a debatable topic and that can be supported by evidence, reasons, and examples (including facts, statistics, names, experiences, and experts). (6b)

audience The readers to whom a piece of writing is directed. Knowing the characteristics of the audience can help the writer shape the message so that it will effectively inform or persuade readers. (1c, 6d)

auxiliary verb Also known as a *helping verb,* an auxiliary verb is a form of *be, do, have, can, may, will,* and others that combine with main verbs° to make verb phrases°. Auxiliary verbs help main verbs to express tense°, mood°, and voice°. See also *modal auxiliary verbs.* (7c, 8a, 8e, 43a-ESL, 46-ESL)

balanced sentence A sentence that uses parallelism° to enhance the message of similar or dissimilar ideas. (18f)

base form See *simple form.*

bibliography A list of sources used in a paper. In MLA style°, it is called Works Cited°, and in APA style°, it is called References°. (33a, 33c, 38g)

brainstorming An invention technique° that calls for listing all the ideas that come to mind in connection with a topic and then grouping the ideas according to patterns that emerge. (2g)

bureaucratic language Stuffy, overblown language that is marked by jargon°, euphemism°, and unnecessary complexity. (21e-5)

case The way a noun° or pronoun° changes form to show whether it is functioning as a subject°, an object°, or a possessor: *she, her, hers.* (9)

cause-and-effect analysis Examination of the relationship between outcomes (effects) and the reasons for them (causes). Cause-and-effect analysis can be used to develop one or more paragraphs°. (4f-9, 5f)

chronological order An arrangement of ideas according to a time sequence. Paragraphs°, essays, and larger works may be in chronological order. (2l-2, 4e)

citation Information writers give to identify a source° referred to in a piece of writing. See also *documentation*. (31, 33, 38g)

clarifying sentence See *limiting sentence*.

classical pattern of argument A structure developed by the ancient Greeks and Romans that is used in writing argument. (6c)

classification A method of developing a paragraph° or a larger piece of writing in which separate categories that share some characteristics are grouped together. Classification is often used along with analysis°. (4f-6)

clause A group of words containing a subject° and a predicate°. A clause that delivers full meaning is called an *independent clause*° (or main clause). A clause that needs another sentence structure to deliver full meaning is called a *dependent clause*° (or subordinate clause). (7o)

cliché An overused, worn-out phrase that has lost its capacity to communicate effectively: *smooth as silk, ripe old age*. (21d)

climactic order An arrangement of ideas in a paragraph° or larger piece of writing from least important to most important. Climactic order is sometimes called *emphatic order*. (2l-2, 4e)

climactic sentence See *periodic sentence*.

clustering See *mapping*.

coherence The clear progression from one idea to another in a piece of writing. Transitional expressions°, pronouns°, selective repetition, and parallelism° enhance coherence. A piece of writing is coherent when its parts relate to one another. (4d)

collective noun A noun° that names a group of people or things: *family, team*. (7a, 11h, 11r)

colloquial language Language characteristic of conversation and informal writing. (21a-3)

comma fault See *comma splice*.

comma splice The error that occurs when only a comma connects two independent clauses°. (14)

common noun A noun° that names general groups, places, people, or things: *dog, house*. (7a)

comparative The form of an adjective° or adverb° that reflects a different degree of intensity between two: *blue, **bluer;** easy, **more easily.*** See also *positive* and *superlative*. (12e-1)

comparison and contrast A pattern for developing a paragraph° or whole essay in which the similarities (comparison) and differences (contrast) of subjects are discussed. (4f-7)

complement A word or group of words in the predicate° of a sentence that renames or describes a subject° or object° in that sentence. (7m-1)

complete predicate See *predicate*.

complete subject See *subject*.

complex sentence A sentence containing one independent clause° and one or more dependent clauses°. (7p-3)

compound-complex sentence A sentence containing at least two independent clauses° and one or more dependent clauses°. (7p-4)

compound predicate See *predicate.*

compound sentence A sentence containing two or more independent clauses° joined by a coordinating conjunction. (7p-2)

compound subject See *subject.*

concrete noun A noun° that names things that can be seen, touched, heard, smelled, or tasted: *smoke, sand.* (7a)

conjunction A word that connects words, phrases°, or clauses°, including coordinating conjunctions°, correlative conjunctions°, and subordinating conjunctions°. (7h)

conjunctive adverb A kind of adverb° that creates logical connections between independent clauses°: *therefore, however.* (7f)

connotation The emotional associations suggested by a word that, along with its denotation°, make up its complete meaning. (20b-1)

coordinate adjectives Two or more adjectives that equally modify a noun° or pronoun°. They are separated by a comma: ***heavy, round*** *paperweight.* (24d)

coordinating conjunction A conjunction that joins two or more grammatically equivalent structures. The seven coordinating conjunctions are *and, or, for, nor, but, so,* and *yet.* (7h)

coordination The technique of using grammatically equivalent forms to show a balance or sequence of ideas. (17a-17d)

correlative conjunction A pair of words that joins equivalent grammatical structures, including *both . . . and, not only . . . but also, either . . . or, neither . . . nor,* and *whether . . . or.* (7h)

count noun, noncount noun A count noun is a noun° that names items that can be counted: *radio, street, idea, fingernail.* In contrast, a noncount noun names things thought of as a whole: *electronics, traffic, knowledge, rice.* (41a-41b-ESL, 42a-42b-ESL)

cumulative sentence A sentence that begins with the subject° and verb° and then adds modifiers°—the most common kind of sentence. Also known as a *loose sentence.* (19e-2)

dangling modifier A modifier° that describes something implied but not stated: ***Walking down the street,*** *the Sears Tower came into view.* (15c)

deadwood Empty, unneeded words and phrases that increase the word count but do not add to the meaning. Also called *padding.* (16b)

declarative sentence A sentence that makes a statement: *I walked home.* (opening section ''Structures of the Sentence,'' Chapter 7)

deduction The process of reasoning from general claims to a specific instance. (5g-2)

definite article, indefinite article English has two indefinite articles°: *a* and *an.* In contrast, English has only one definite article: *the.* Articles are one kind of determiner°. (42 ESL)

demonstrative pronoun A pronoun° that points out the antecedent°. The demonstrative pronouns are *this, these, that,* and *those.* (7b)

denotation The dictionary definition of a word. (20b-2)

dependent clause A clause° that cannot stand alone as an independent grammatical unit, usually preceded by a relative pronoun° or subordinating conjunction°. (7o-2)

descriptive adjective An adjective° that describes the condition or properties of the noun° it modifies and has comparative° and superlative° forms: *round, rounder, roundest.* (7e)

descriptive adverb An adverb° that describes the qualities of the verb° and has comparative° and superlative° forms: *happily, more happily, most happily.* (7f)

determiner Words or word groups, traditionally identified as adjectives°, that tell "how much" or "how many" about nouns°. Also called *expressions of quantity, articles°,* limiting adjectives°, and *noun markers.* (7a, 42-ESL)

diction Word choice. (20a, 20b)

dictionary form See *simple form.*

direct address Words of direct address indicate the person or group spoken to and are set off by commas: *The answer,* **Phil,** *may be found at the end of the chapter.* (24f)

direct discourse In writing, words that repeat speech or conversation exactly, requiring the use of quotation marks. (15a-4, 24g, 28a-3)

direct object A noun° or pronoun° or group of words functioning as a noun that receives the action—that is, completes the meaning—of a transitive verb°. (7l, 8f)

direct question A sentence that asks a question and ends with a question mark: *Are you going?* (23c)

direct quotation See *quotation.*

division See *analysis.*

documentation Acknowledging the sources used in any piece of writing, by giving full and accurate information about the source's author and the work's title, date of publication, and related facts. (31-b, 32j, Chapter 33)

documentation style Any of various systems for providing information in your writing about sources that you quote, paraphrase, or summarize. Two of the most widely used styles are those of the Modern Language Association (MLA) and the American Psychological Association (APA). (31b, 32j, Chapter 33)

double negative A nonstandard statement that contains two negative modifiers°, the second of which repeats the message of the first. (12c)

doublespeak Evasive language intentionally used to hide the truth. (21e-4)

drafting A part of the writing process° in which writers compose ideas in sentences and paragraphs. (2a, 3b)

edited American English Also called *standard English,* the language that conforms to established rules of grammar, sentence structure, punctuation, and spelling. (21a-2)

editing A part of the writing process° in which writers check the technical correctness of their grammar, spelling, punctuation, and mechanics°. (2a, 3d)

elliptical clause See *elliptical construction.*

elliptical construction A sentence structure, such as a clause° or phrase°, that deliberately omits words that have already appeared in the sentence and can be inferred from the context. (7o-2, 15e-1)

etymology The study of a word's origins and historical development, including its changes in form and meaning. (opening section Chapter 20; 20a)

euphemism Language that attempts to avoid the harsh reality of some truths by using more pleasant-sounding, overly "tactful" words. (21e-3)

evaluative reading A part of the reading process in which the reader determines the author's tone, differentiates between fact and opinion, and assesses the author's reasoning. (5d-3)

evidence Facts, statistical information, examples, and opinions of others used by a writer to support assertions and conclusions. (5e)

exclamatory sentence A sentence that expresses strong emotion by making an exclamation: *That's ridiculous!* (opening section "Structures of the Sentence" Chapter 7, 19c)

expletive A term that describes the function of *there* and *it* when they combine with a form of the verb *to be* to postpone the subject of the sentence: ***It is*** Mars that we want to reach. (11f, 15-ESL)

expository writing See *informative writing.*

expression of quantity See *determiner.*

extended definition A definition that includes in addition to the denotation° of a word or phrase, its connotations° as well as concrete details to clarify abstract terms. An extended definition may require an entire paragraph° or more. (4f-5, 6e)

faulty predication An error that occurs when a subject° and its predicate° do not make sense together. (15d-2)

finite verb A verb° form that shows tense°, mood°, voice°, person°, and number° while expressing an action, occurrence, or state of being. (8b-2)

first person See *person.*

freewriting Writing nonstop for a specified time in order to generate ideas by free association of thoughts. Freewriting that starts with a set topic or that builds on one sentence taken from an earlier piece of freewriting is called "focused freewriting." (2f)

fused sentence The error of running independent clauses° together without a semicolon or a comma and a coordinate conjunction° between them. Also called a *run-on* or *run-together sentence*. (14)

future perfect progressive tense The form of the future perfect tense° that describes an action or condition ongoing until some specific future time: *they **will have been talking.*** (8g, 8j)

future perfect tense The tense° indicating that an action will have been completed or a condition will have ended by a specified point in the future: *they **will have talked.*** (8g, 8i)

future progressive tense The form of the future tense° showing that a future action will continue for some time: *they **will be talking.*** (8g, 8j)

future tense The form of a verb, made with the simple form° and either *shall* or *will*, expressing an action yet to be taken or a condition not yet experienced: *they **will talk.*** (8e, 8g)

gender Concerning languages, the labeling of nouns° and pronouns° as masculine, feminine, or neutral. This division occurs in English only in third person singular personal pronouns (*he, she, it*) and in a few nouns (*prince, princess*). (34b)

gerund A verbal°, the present participle° functioning as a noun°: ***Walking*** *is good exercise.* (7d, 42c-ESL, 45-ESL)

gerund phrase A gerund, its modifiers, and/or object(s). A gerund phrase can function as a subject: ***Walking briskly to school*** *invigorates me.* It can also function as an object: *I am invigorated by **walking briskly to school.*** (7n)

helping verb See *auxiliary verb.*

homonyms Words spelled differently that sound alike: *to, too, two.* (22b)

idiom A word, phrase°, or other construction that has a meaning different from its usual meaning: *He **lost his head.** She **hit the ceiling.*** (20a-1, 44-ESL)

illogical predication See *faulty predication.*

imperative mood The mood° that expresses commands and direct requests: *Go.* It uses the simple form° of the verb. (8k)

imperative sentence A sentence that gives a command: *Go home now.* (opening section "Structures of the Sentence" Chapter 7)

incubation The time you give your ideas to grow and develop. (2k)

indefinite article See *definite article, indefinite article.*

indefinite pronoun A pronoun° that refers to nonspecific persons or things but that takes on meaning in context: *any, few.* (7b, 11g, 11p)

independent clause A clause° that can stand alone as an independent grammatical unit. (7o-1)

indicative mood The mood° of verbs° used for statements about real things, or highly likely ones, and questions about fact: *I think Grace will be there.* (8l)

indirect discourse The reporting of speech or conversation, which is not enclosed in quotation marks because it does not give the speaker's exact words. (15a-4, 24g, 28a-3)

indirect object A noun° or pronoun° or group of words functioning as a noun that tells *to whom* or *for whom* the action expressed by a transitive verb° was done. (7l)

indirect question A sentence that reports a question and ends with a period: *I wonder whether you are going.* It contrasts with a direct question°. (23c)

indirect quotation See *quotation.*

induction The process of arriving at general principles from particular facts or instances. (5g-1)

inferential meaning A part of the reading process that calls for the reader to read "between the lines" and thereby understand what is implied but unstated. (5d-2)

infinitive A verbal° made of the simple form° of a verb and usually, but not always, *to*. It functions as a noun°, adjective°, or adverb°. (7d, 8b-2, 9h, 42c-ESL, 45-ESL)

infinitive phrase An infinitive°, its modifiers°, and/or object. It functions as a noun°, adjective°, or adverb°. (7n)

informal language Word choice that creates a tone° appropriate for casual writing or speaking. The words may be slang°, colloquial language°, or regional language°. (21a-1)

informative writing Also known as *expository writing,* informative writing gives information and, when necessary, explains it. (1b-1)

intensive pronoun A *-self* form of a pronoun°, which intensifies the antecedent. (7b, 9i)

interjection A word (or words) conveying surprise or another strong emotion. (7i)

interrogative pronoun A pronoun° that asks a question, such as *whose* or *what.* (7b)

interrogative sentence A sentence that asks a question: *Did you see that hat?* (opening section of "Structures of the Sentence" Chapter 7)

intransitive verb A verb that does not take a direct object° and is not a linking verb°. (8f)

invention techniques Ways writers gather ideas. Some techniques are keeping an idea book or journal, freewriting°, brainstorming°, using the journalist's questions, mapping°, reading, and incubating. (2d–2k)

inverted word order In contrast to standard order°, the main verb° or auxiliary verb° comes before the subject° in inverted word order. The occasional use of inverted word order can bring variety and emphasis to writing: *In walked the mayor.* Also, most questions and some exclamations use it: *Was the book heavy?* (19f, 43a-ESL)

irony Suggesting the opposite of the usual sense of the words. (21c)

irregular verb A verb that forms the past tense and past participle° in some way other than by adding *-ed* or *-d: see, saw, seen.* (8d)

jargon Specialized vocabulary of a particular field or group that a general reader might not understand. The unnecessary use of jargon creates pretentious language°. (21e-2)

level of formality The degree of formality as reflected by word choice and sentence structure. A *highly formal level* is used for certain ceremonial and other occasions when stylistic flourishes are appropriate. A *medium level,* which is neither too formal nor too casual, is acceptable for most academic writing. (21a)

levels of generality In grouping information or ideas, moving from the most general to the most specific. (21)

limiting adjective An adjective° that limits the noun° it modifies by pointing out, questioning, enumerating, showing possession, or showing its relation to other words in the sentence. See also *articles, determiner.* (7a, 7e, 41b-ESL)

limiting sentence A sentence that follows the topic sentence in a paragraph and narrows the focus of the paragraph; sometimes called *clarifying sentence.* (4b)

linking verb A main verb° that connects a subject° with a subject complement°. Linking verbs indicate a state of being, relate to the senses, or indicate a condition. (7c, 11i, 12d)

literal meaning A part of the reading process that calls for the reader to read "on the line" and thereby get information about major and minor points that are explicitly stated. (5d-1)

logical appeal The use of logical, sound reasoning in a written argument. Also called *logos.* (6f)

logical fallacies Flaws in reasoning that lead to illogical statements. Common fallacies are hasty generalization, false analogy, circular argument, irrelevant argument, false cause, self-contradiction, red herring, argument to the person, bandwagon, false or irrelevant authority, card stacking, the either-or fallacy, taking something out of context, appeal to ignorance, and ambiguity and equivocation. (5h)

loose sentence See *cumulative sentence.*

main clause See *independent clause.*

main verb A verb that expresses action, occurrence, or state of being. It shows mood°, tense°, voice°, number°, and person°. (7c, 8b, 43a-ESL)

mapping An invention technique° for generating ideas. This process is also called *webbing* and *clustering.* (2i)

mass noun A noun° that names "uncountable" things: *furniture, weather.* (7a)

mechanics Conventions regarding the use of capital letters, italics, abbreviations, and numbers. (30)

medium level of formality A level of language that is neither too scholarly nor too casual. This level, which uses standard vocabulary, conventional sentence structure, and few or no contractions, is acceptable for academic writing. (21a-1)

metaphor A comparison between otherwise dissimilar things. It does not use a word like *like* or *as* to form the comparison, as a simile° does, but directly equates the things being compared. (21c)

misplaced modifier A modifier° that is incorrectly positioned in a sentence, and thus distorts meaning. (15b)

mixed construction A sentence that begins by setting up one grammatical form but switches unintentionally to another, thus garbling the meaning of the sentence. (15d-1)

mixed metaphors Incongruously combined images. (21c)

MLA style See *documentation style.*

modal auxiliary verbs Auxiliary verbs°, most of which have only one form: *can, could, may, might, should, would, must,* and *ought.* They add such information as a sense of needing, wanting, or having to do something, a sense of possibility, likelihood, obligation, permission, or ability. (8e, 46-ESL)

modifier A word or group of words that describes or limits other words, phrases°, or clauses°. The most common modifiers are adjectives° and adverbs°. (7m-2)

mood The ability of verbs° to convey the attitude that the writer or speaker is expressing toward the action. English has three moods: indicative°, imperative°, and subjunctive°. (8l)

noncount noun See *count noun, noncount noun.*

nonessential element See *nonrestrictive element.*

nonfinite verb A participle° or infinitive° functioning as a noun° or modifier°. Also known as a *verbal*°. (8b-2)

nonrestrictive element A limiting or descriptive word, phrase°, or dependent clause° that provides information not essential to understanding the element it modifies. A nonrestrictive element, sometimes called a *nonessential element,* is set off by commas. (24e)

nonsexist language See *sexist language.*

nonstandard Generally taken to mean language not written in edited American English°. (opening section Usage Glossary)

noun The name of a person, place, thing, or idea. Nouns can be classified as proper°, common°, concrete°, abstract°, collective°, or mass°. Nouns function as subjects°, objects°, and complements°. (7a)

noun clause A dependent clause° that functions as a subject°, object°, or complement°. (7o-2)

noun determiner See *determiner.*

noun phrase A noun° and its modifiers° functioning as a subject°, object°, or complement°. (7n)

number Relates to how many subjects act or experience an action, one (singular) or more than one (plural). (8a, 11a)

object A noun° or pronoun° or group of words functioning as a noun or pronoun that receives the action of a verb° (direct object°), tells to whom or for whom something is done (indirect object°), or completes the meaning of a preposition° (object of a preposition°). (7l)

object complement A noun° or adjective° that immediately follows a direct object° and either describes or renames it. (7m-1)

objective case The case° of the pronoun° functioning as direct object°, indirect object°, object of a preposition°, or object of a verbal°. (9)

padding See *deadwood.*

paragraph A group of sentences that work together to develop a unit of thought. Introductory paragraphs prepare the reader for what will follow in a piece of writing. Concluding paragraphs bring a sense of completion to a piece of writing. Transitional paragraphs link major sections within a piece of writing. Most paragraphs are topical paragraphs°, stating a main idea and offering specific, logical support of that idea. (4)

paragraph development Specific, concrete details (RENNS) to support a generalization. Arrangement and organizational patterns include general to specific, specific to general, climactic order°, problem to solution, spatial order°, chronological order°, narration, description, process, example, definition, analysis°, classification°, comparison and contrast°, analogy°, and cause-and-effect analysis°. (4)

parallelism The use of equivalent grammatical forms or matching sentence structures to express equivalent ideas. (18)

paraphrase A restatement of someone else's ideas in language and sentence structure different from those of the source. (31d)

parenthetical documentation Information enabling a reader to identify the source of ideas or of direct quotations°. This information is placed in parentheses immediately after the quotation or information. (33b)

parenthetical reference See *parenthetical documentation.*

participial phrase A phrase containing a present participle° or past participle°, and any modifiers, that functions as an adjective°. (7n)

passive construction See *passive voice.*

passive voice The form of a verb° in which the subject° is acted upon. If the subject is mentioned in the sentence, it usually appears as the object of the preposition° *by.* This voice° emphasizes the action, in contrast to the *active voice°,* which emphasizes the doer of the action. (8n, 8o)

past participle The third principal part° of the verb°. In regular verbs°, it adds *-d* or *-ed* to the simple form° and is identical to the past tense°. In irregular verbs°, it often differs from the simple form and the past tense. To function as a verb, it must have an auxiliary verb°. Used alone, it functions as an adjective°. (7d, 8b-1, 8c)

past perfect progressive tense The past perfect tense° form that describes an ongoing condition in the past that has been ended by something stated in the sentence: *I had been talking.* (8j)

past perfect tense The tense° that describes a condition or action that started in the past, continued for a while, and then ended in the past: *I had talked.* (8i)

past progressive tense The past tense form° that shows the continuing nature of a past action: *I was talking.* (8j)

past tense form The second principal part of the verb°. It shows an action or occurrence or state of being completed in the past. The past tense of regular verbs° add -*ed* or -*d* to the simple form°: *watched.* The past tense of irregular verbs° changes in spelling or uses a different word than the simple form°: *wrote.* (8b-1, 8c)

perfect tenses The three tenses—the present perfect°, the past perfect°, and the future perfect°—that show complex time relationships in the present, past, and future. (8i)

periodic sentence A sentence that begins with modifiers° and ends with the independent clause°, thus saving the main idea—and the emphasis—for the end of the sentence. Also called *climactic sentence.* (19e-2)

person Who or what acts or experiences an action. First person is the one speaking *(I, we);* second person is the one being spoken to *(you, you);* and third person is the person or thing spoken about *(he, she, it; they).* (11a)

personal pronoun A pronoun° that refers to people or things, such as *I, you, them, hers,* and *it.* (7b, 9)

personification A type of figurative language that gives human traits to nonhuman things: *Mother earth.* (21c)

persuasive writing Persuasive writing seeks to convince the reader about a matter of opinion. (1b-2, 6)

phrasal verbs Verbs° that combine with prepositions° as *two-word verbs* or *three-word verbs* to deliver their meaning. In some phrasal verbs, the verb and preposition should not be separated by other words *(Look at the teacher),* but in other phrasal verbs, other words can separate them *(I threw my homework away).* (44b-ESL)

phrase A group of related words that does not contain a subject° and predicate°. It cannot stand alone as an independent grammatical unit. A phrase functions as a noun°, verb°, or modifier°. (7n)

plagiarism Plagiarism occurs when a writer presents another person's words or ideas without giving credit to that person. Writers must use documentation° to give proper credit to their sources. Plagiarism is a serious offense, like stealing. It is a form of intellectual dishonesty that can lead to course failure or expulsion. (31a)

planning An early part of the writing process° in which writers gather ideas, often using invention strategies°. Along with shaping°, planning is sometimes called *prewriting°.* (2a-2d)

plural See *number.*

positive The form of an adjective° or adverb° when it is not being compared. Also see *comparative, superlative.* (12e-1)

possessive case The case° of a noun° or pronoun° that shows ownership or possession. (9)

predicate The part of the sentence that contains the verb° and tells what the subject° is doing or experiencing or what is being done to the subject. A *simple predicate* contains only the main verb° and auxiliary verb°, if any. A *complete predicate* contains the verb and all its modifiers°, objects°, and other related words. A *compound predicate* contains two or more verbs and their objects and modifiers. (7k, 43a-ESL, 44b-ESL)

predicate adjective An adjective° used as a subject complement°. (7m-1)

predicate nominative See *subject complement.*

prefix One or more syllables in front of a root word° that modify its meaning. (20c, 22d)

premise In the syllogism of a deductive argument, the first premise is an assumption and the second premise is either a fact or another assumption based on evidence. These two premises are followed by a conclusion. See also *syllogism.* (5g-2)

preposition A word that shows a relationship between a noun° or pronoun° and other words in the sentence. A preposition is followed by a noun or pronoun object°. (7g, 44-ESL)

prepositional phrase A preposition° and its object° and any modifiers° of its object. A prepositional phrase often shows a relationship in time or space. Prepositional phrases function as adjectives° or adverbs°. (7g, 7n)

present participle Used with one or more auxiliary verbs° in a main verb phrase°, shows action, occurrence, or state of being: *I am **running**.* As a verbal°, the *-ing* form of the verb° functioning as an adjective° (***running** water*) or a noun° (***running** pleases me*). (6d, 8b-1)

present perfect progressive tense The present perfect tense form° that describes something ongoing in the past that is likely to continue into the future. *I **have been talking**.* (8j)

present perfect tense The tense° indicating that an action or its effects continue into the present though begun or perhaps completed in the past: *I **had talked**.* (8i)

present progressive tense The present tense° form of the verb° that indicates something taking place at the time it is written or spoken about: *I **am talking**.* (8j)

present tense The tense that describes what is happening, what is true at the moment, and what is consistently true. It uses the simple form° (*I talk*) and in the third person singular, it uses the *-s* form° (*she **talks**).* (8b-1, 8g, 8h)

pretentious language Showy, overblown writing that calls attention to itself with complex sentences and long words for their own sakes. (21e-1)

prewriting A term for all activities in the writing process before drafting°. See *planning* and *shaping.*

primary evidence First-hand evidence from direct observation by the writer or an authoritative reporter. (5e)

primary source An original work of an author—novels, poems, short stories, autobiographies, diaries—and first-hand reports of observations and of research. (32a)

progressive forms Verb forms made in all tenses° with the present participle° and forms of *to be*. These forms show that an action is ongoing. (8j)

pronoun A word that takes the place of a noun°. Types of pronouns are personal°, relative°, interrogative°, demonstrative°, reflexive°, intensive°, reciprocal°, and indefinite°. Pronouns function in the same ways that nouns° do. (7b)

pronoun-antecedent agreement The match in expressing number°, person°, and gender° required between a pronoun° and its antecedent°. (11m–11r)

pronoun case The way a pronoun changes in form to reflect its use as the agent of action (subject case°), the thing being acted upon (objective case°), or the thing showing ownership (possessive case°). (9)

pronoun reference The relationship between a pronoun° and its antecedent°. (10)

proofreading The final step in the writing process°, proofreading calls for the writer to read the final copy of a piece of writing to find and correct typing errors or handwriting illegibility. (2a, 3e)

proper adjective An adjective° formed from a proper noun°: *Victorian, American.* (7e, 30e)

proper noun A noun° that names a specific person, place, or thing: *St. Louis, Toni Morrison, Corvette.* (7a, 30e, 42c-ESL)

purpose The goal or aim of a piece of writing: to express oneself, to provide information, to persuade, or to create a literary work. (1b)

quotation Repeating or reporting the words another person has spoken or written. Direct quotation repeats the words of the source exactly and encloses them in quotation marks. Indirect quotation reports what the source said, without quotation marks except around any words repeated exactly from the source. Both direct and indirect quotation require documentation° of the source to avoid plagiarism. See also *indirect discourse*. (24g, 28a, 31)

reciprocal pronoun A pronoun° that refers to individual parts of a plural antecedent°: *each other, one another.* (7b)

References In the APA style° of documentation, the list of sources cited in a research paper. (33c-2, 33d)

reflexive pronoun A *-self* form of the pronoun° that reflects the antecedent°. A reflexive pronoun cannot substitute for subjects° or objects°. (9i)

regional language Language specific to a geographic area. (21a-3)

regular verb A verb° that forms its past tense° and past participle° by adding *-ed* or *-d* to the simple form°. Most English verbs are regular. (8d)

relative adverb An adverb° that is used to introduce an adjective clause°: *The lot **where I usually park my car** was full.* (7f, 16-ESL, 17e, 24e-1)

relative clause See *adjective clause.* (7c, 7o-2)

relative pronoun A pronoun° that introduces certain noun clauses° and adjective clauses°, for example, *who, which, that, what,* and *whomever*. A relative pronoun is a subordinating word°. (7b, 7o-2)

restrictive appositive An appositive° renaming a noun° or pronoun° by giving information that is essential to distinguish it from other things in its class: *the college instructor **Pat Murphy.***

restrictive clause A dependent clause° that limits a noun° or pronoun° by giving information necessary to distinguish it from others in its class. In contrast to a nonrestrictive clause°, this kind of dependent clause is never set off with commas. (24e)

restrictive element A word, phrase°, or dependent clause° that provides information essential to the understanding of the element it modifies. In contrast to a nonrestrictive element, a restrictive element is never set off with commas. (24e)

revision A part of the writing process° in which writers evaluate their rough drafts and, based on their decisions, rewrite by adding, cutting, replacing, moving, and often totally recasting material. (2a, 3c, 6h, 32r)

rhetoric The area of discourse that focuses on arrangement of ideas and choice of words as a reflection of the writer's purpose° and sense of audience°. (1)

Rogerian argument An argument form adapted from the principles of communication developed by psychologist Carl Rogers. (6d)

root word The central part of a word to which a prefix° and/or suffix° is added. (20c-2)

run-on (run-together) sentence See *fused sentence.*

second person See *person.*

secondary evidence Evidence° from experts, reliable sources in their fields. Reliable secondary evidence appears in respected publications, is current, and is stated in relatively objective language. (5e, 32g)

secondary source A source that talks about someone else's original work. It explains events, analyzes information, and draws conclusions. (5e, 32a, 37b, 37d)

sentence See *simple sentence, compound sentence, complex sentence, compound-complex sentence.*

sentence fragment A portion of a sentence that is punctuated as though it were a complete sentence. (13)

sexist language Language that unfairly assigns roles or characteristics to people on the basis of sex. Language that avoids stereotyping according to sex is called *nonsexist language.* (21b)

shaping An early part of the writing process° in which writers consider ways to organize their material. Along with planning°, shaping is sometimes called prewriting°. (2l)

simile A comparison, using *like, as* or *as if,* between otherwise dissimilar things. (21c)

simple form The form of the verb° that shows action (or occurrence or state of being) taking place in the present. It is used in the singular° for first and second person° and in the plural° for first, second, and third person°. It is also the first principal part° of a verb. The simple form is also known as the *dictionary form* or *base form.* (8b-1)

simple predicate See *predicate.*

simple sentence A single independent clause° with no dependent clauses°. The subject° or predicate° or both may be compound. (7p-1)

simple subject See *subject.*

simple tenses The present°, past°, and future tenses°, which divide time into present, past, and future. (8g)

singular See *number.*

slang Coined words and new or extended meanings for established words, which quickly pass in and out of use. Inappropriate for any but the most informal communications. (21a-3)

slanted language Biased or emotionally loaded language. (21a-4)

source A book, article, document, other work, or person providing information. (5e-2, 32a, 32g)

spatial order A description of objects according to their physical relationship to one another, often in terms of a central reference point. Spatial order is a pattern that may be used to organize a paragraph°. (2e-2, 4e)

speaker tag Explanatory words that identify the speaker of directly quoted words: *"Stay,"* **said the dog trainer.** (24g)

split infinitive One or more words coming between the two words of an infinitive° (a verb form that starts with *to: to sing, to dance).* (15b-3)

standard English See *edited American English.*

standard word order The most common order for words in English sentences: the subject° comes before the predicate°. (19f, 43-ESL)

subject The word or group of words in a sentence that acts, is acted upon, or is described by the verb°. A *simple subject* includes only the noun° or pronoun°. A *complete subject* includes the noun or pronoun and all its modifiers°. A *compound subject* includes two or more nouns or pronouns and their modifiers. (7k, 43a-ESL)

subject complement Also called a *predicate nominative,* a noun° or adjective° that follows a linking verb° and describes or renames the subject° of the sentence. (7m-1, 8e)

subjective case The case° of the pronoun° functioning as subject°. (9)

subject-verb agreement The match of the subject° and verb° in expressing number° and person° required between a subject° and its verb°. (11b–11l)

subjunctive mood The verb mood° that expresses wishes, recommendations, indirect requests, and speculations: *I wish I **were going.*** (8m)

subordinate clause See *dependent clause.*

subordinating conjunction A conjunction that introduces an adverbial clause°, showing its relationship to the independent clause°. (7h, 7o-2)

subordination The technique of using grammatical structures to reflect the relative importance of ideas. A sentence with subordinated information contains an independent clause° to express important ideas in the sentence, and it contains dependent clauses° or phrases° to express ideas of lesser importance. (17g–17i)

suffix A syllable or syllables added to the end of a root word° that modify its meaning. (20c-2, 22e)

summary A condensed version of the essentials of ideas originally expressed in a longer version. (31e)

superlative The form of the adjective° or adverb° when three or more things are being compared: *green, greener, **greenest;** quickly, more quickly, **most quickly.*** (12e-1)

syllogism The structure of an argument reflecting deduction°. It has two premises°, the first one an assumption and the second a fact or an assumption based on evidence°. The conclusion, which is about a specific instance, follows logically from the premises. (5g-2)

synonym A word that is close in meaning to another word. (20a)

synthesis A component of critical thinking in which one makes connections among ideas. (4a)

tag sentence A sentence that consists of a helping verb, a pronoun, and often the word *not*, generally contracted. A tag sentence is set off by commas: *The soup was too hot, **wasn't it?*** (24f)

tense The time at which the action of the verb° occurs—in the past, present, or future. (8k)

tense sequence The accurate matching of verbs° to reflect the logical time relationships in sentences that have more than one verb. (8k)

thesis statement A statement of the central theme of an essay that makes clear the main idea of the essay, the writer's purpose, and the focus of the topic. It may also suggest the organizational pattern of the essay. (2m, 3c-2, 6b)

third person See *person.*

tone The writer's attitude towards his or her material and reader, especially as reflected in the writer's choice of words. (1d, 5d-3, 21a)

topic The subject of a piece of writing. (2c)

topical paragraph See *paragraph.*

topic sentence The sentence in a paragraph° that contains the main idea of the paragraph. (4a)

transition The logical connection of one idea to another in a piece of writing. Transition is achieved through the use of transitional expressions°, pronouns°, parallelism°, and the repetition of key words and phrases. (4d)

transitional expressions Words and phrases that signal connections among ideas and create coherence. A transitional expression lets the reader know how one idea connects to the next. (4d-1)

transitional words See *transitional expressions.*

transitive verb A verb° that takes a direct object. (8f)

understatement Deliberate restraint for emphasis. (21c)

unity The clear and logical relationship between the main idea of a paragraph° and the supporting evidence for that main idea. (4b)

usage The customary manner of using particular words or phrases. (20a; opening section Usage Glossary)

valid A term applied to an argument based on deduction° when the conclusion logically follows from the premises°. Validity has to do with the structure of the argument, not the truth of the premises. An argument based on untrue premises is valid if the conclusion follows from those premises. (5g-2)

verb The part of the predicate° in a sentence that acts or describes a state of being. Verbs change form to show time (tense°), attitude (mood°), and role of the subject (voice°). Verbs can be main verbs° or auxiliary verbs°, and they appear in verb phrases°. Verbs can be described as transitive° or intransitive° depending on whether they take a direct object°. (7n, 8)

verb phrase A verb° and its modifiers°. A verb phrase functions as a verb in the sentence. (7c)

verbal phrase A group of words that contains a verbal°—an infinitive°, participle°, or gerund°—and its modifiers°. Verbals function as nouns° or modifiers° rather than as verbs°. (7d, 7n)

verbals Verb parts functioning as nouns°, adjectives°, or adverbs°. Verbals include infinitives°, present participles°, past participles°, and gerunds°. (7d, 45-ESL)

voice An attribute of a verb° showing whether the subject° acts (active voice°) or is acted upon (passive voice°). (8n)

webbing See *mapping.*

Works Cited In the MLA style° of documentation, the list of sources cited in a research paper. (33c-1, 33d)

writing process Stages of writing in which a writer gathers and shapes ideas, organizes material, expresses those ideas in a rough draft, evaluates the draft and revises it, edits the writing for technical errors, and proofreads it for typographical mistakes or illegibility. The stages often overlap and do not always proceed in a linear progression: that is, the writing process is recursive. See planning°, shaping°, drafting°, revising°, editing°, and proofreading°. (2, 3)

Index

A degree symbol (°) after an index entry signals that the term is defined in the Glossary of Grammatical and Selected Composition Terms. All entries in boldface italics (*advice, advise,* for example) are discussed in the Usage Glossary and any other place listed. Section numbers are in boldface type and page numbers in regular type. The listing **6a:** 160 thus refers you to page 146, which is in section 6a.

-d, -ed, **8b-1:** 195, **8d:** 197, **22e:** 443–44
dairy, diary, **22b:** 437
Dangling modifiers°, **15c:** 323–24
Dashes, **29a:** 520–22
    with appositives, **29a-1:** 521
    with asides, **29a-2:** 521–22
    with contrasts, **29a-2:** 520–21
    with a definition, **29a-1:** 521
    with an example, **29a-1:** 521
    with other punctuation, **29a-2:** 521–22
    vs. parentheses, **29b:** 522
    quotation marks with, **28e-3:** 518
data, **U GL:** 6
Databases, computerized, **32m:** 598,
    32oh: 600–603
Dates
    abbreviations with, **30h:** 541
    APA citation style, **33c-2:** 623–24
    doubtful, **23d:** 454
    MLA citation style, **33c-1:** 649
    numbers in, **30m:** 547
    parenthetical reference, APA style,
        33b-2: 618
    punctuation of, **24h:** 477, 479
    year of publication, MLA-APA styles
        compared, **33c:** 620
Days of the week, capitalization of, **30e:**
    536
Deadwood°, **16b:** 345–47. *See also*
    Wordiness
Debate, topics open to, **6a:** 146–47
Decimal figures, **30l:** 547
Declarations, emphatic, **23e:** 454–55
Declarative sentences°, **7j:** 178–79
    varying with other types, **19c:** 386–87
Deduction°. *See* Deductive reasoning
Deductive reasoning, **5g-2:** 135–38, **6f:**
    154
    comparison with inductive reasoning,
        5g: 134
    in general-to-specific paragraphs, **4e:**
        89–90
    and position of topic sentence, **4b:**
        74–76
    summary, **5g:** 138
    syllogisms°, **5g:** 135
Definite article°, **42-ESL:** 754–60
Definitions
    circular, **5h:** 140, 143
    in dictionary entries, **6e:** 153, **20a-1:** 403
    emphasizing with dashes, **29a-1:**
        520–21
    extended, **6e:** 153
    as introductory device, **4g:** 106
    as paragraph development pattern, **4f:**
        98
    in the social sciences, **38b:** 717
    in written argument, **6e:** 152–53
Demonstrative adjectives, **7e:** 171
Demonstrative pronouns°, **7b:** 166

antecedents°, **10c-3:** 241
Denotation°, **20b-1:** 408–10
Dependent (subordinate) clauses°, **7o-2:**
    187–90. *See also* Adjective clauses°;
    Adverb clauses°
    in complex sentences°, **7p-3:** 192
    in compound-complex sentences°, **7p-4:**
        192–93
    elliptical, **7o-2:** 190
    introduced by *if* and *unless,* **8m-1:** 216
    introductory, **19e:** 390, **24b:** 461–63
    noun°, **7o-2:** 190
    restrictive° and nonrestrictive°, **7o-2:**
        189, **24e-1:** 471
    revising independent clauses° as, **14d:**
        301–2
    and semicolon misuse with
        independent clause°, **25e-1:** 492
    as sentence fragments°, **13a,b:** 285–86,
        287–88, **14d:** 301–2
    subordination° of, **17:** 362–69
    tense sequences° in, **8k-1:** 211–13
    use of *who, whoever* or *whom, whomever,*
        9e-1: 231–33
descent, dissent, **22b:** 437
Description, **1a:** 3, **4f:** 96–97
Descriptive adjectives°, **7e:** 171
Descriptive adverbs°, **7f:** 172
Descriptors, **32h-4:** 587
dessert, desert, **22b:** 437
Details, developing paragraphs with, **4c:**
    78–80
Determiners°, noun, **7a:** 165, **42-ESL:**
    754–60
Developmental paragraphs, **4a:** 71–73. *See
    also* Topical paragraphs
Development patterns. *See* Paragraph
    development
device, devise, **22b:** 437
Dewey Decimal System, **32n:** 599
Dialect
    and expository writing, **21a-3:** 421
    usage label, **20a-1:** 404
DIALOG Information System, **32o:**
    600–601, 602, 603
Dialogue, broken-off. *See* Direct discourse
Diction°, **20b:** 408–12, **21a:** 418–19. *See
    also* Language; Tone; Words
Dictionaries, **20a:** 401–8
    abridged, **20a-4:** 406–7
    biographical, **32k:** 592
    information in entries, **20a-1:** 401–4
    as a research tool, **32k:** 592
    specialized, **20a-5:** 407–8
    as a spelling aid, **22:** 434
    unabridged, **20a-3:** 405–6
Dictionary form° (of verb). *See* Simple
    form° (of verb)
die, dye, **22b:** 437
different from, different than, **U GL:** 6

Editors
  citing, **33d:** 628
  letters to, MLA and APA citation styles
    for, **33d:** 634
effect, affect, **22b:** 436, **U GL:** 6
Effect, subordinating conjunctions°
    expressing, **7h:** 177
-ei-, -ie-, spelling rules, **22f:** 444
either . . . or. See Correlative conjunctions°
either-or fallacy, **5h:** 142, 143
Elements of writing. *See* Writing
elicit, illicit, **22b:** 437
Elizabethan English, 400
Ellipsis, **29d:** 527–28
  for omissions from quotations, **29d:**
    527–28, **31c-1:** 559
Elliptical clauses°, **7o-2:** 190
Elliptical constructions°, **15e-1:** 328–29
  to reduce clauses°, **16a-3:** 341–42
elude, allude, **22b:** 436
emigrate from, immigrate to, **U GL:** 6
eminent, immanent, imminent, **22b:** 437
Emotional appeal in written argument, **6f:**
    154–55
Emphasis, **19:** 382–93
  achieving, **19a:** 382, 392–93, 412–15
  with added modifiers°, **19e:** 388–90
  conjunctive adverbs° showing, **7f:** 173
  with dashes, **29a:** 520–22
  with inverted word order, **19f:** 391–92
  with italics (underlining), **30g:** 540
  with repetition, **19g:** 392–93
  with sentence fragments°, **13d:** 291–92
  and subject choice, **19c:** 403–4
  understanding, **19a:** 382
  with varied sentence lengths, **19b:**
    399–402
  with varied sentence types, **19c:** 402–3
Emphatic declarations, **23e:** 454
Emphatic order. *See* Climactic order
Empty words and phrases, **16b:** 345–47
Encyclopedias, **32k:** 591. *See also*
    Reference books
Endnotes, **33e:** 639–40, **34b:** 665, 671
  as content notes, **33e:** 640
  first-reference, **33f:** 642–43
  for documenting sources, **33f:** 641–43
  formatting, **33e:** 639–44
  second and subsequent references, **33f:**
    643
End punctuation, **23:** 452–53. *See also*
    Exclamation points; Periods; Question
    marks
ensure, assure, insure, **U GL:** 6
enthused, **U GL:** 6
envelop, envelope, **22b:** 437
Equivalent grammatical form, **18a:** 371.
    See also Parallelism
Equivocation, **5h:** 142–43
-es, -s endings, **8c:** 196, **11b:** 251–52

especially, specially, **U GL:** 7
Essays. *See also* Papers; Writing process
  form of, **2l:** 32–3
  length of, **2a:** 17
  revision checklist, **3c-3:** 56–58
  sequencing ideas in, **2l-2:** 34–35
  thesis statements, **2m:** 35–38, **4g:** 105–6
  titles of, **3c-2:** 54–56, **28b:** 514–15, **28d:**
    516–17
  typing guidelines, **App. B:** 789–96
  unity in, **3b:** 51–52
  unpublished, MLA and APA citation
    styles for, **33d:** 631
Essay tests, **40:** 736–42
  cue words and key words in, **40a:**
    736–39
  strategies for taking, **40c:** 741–42
  writing effective responses in, **40b:**
    739–41
et al., **33b-1:** 613, **33b-2:** 617, **33d:** 627
etc., **30k:** 542; **U GL:** 7
Ethical appeal in written argument, **6f:** 155
Etymologies, **20:** 400
  in dictionary entries, **20a-1:** 402
  specialized dictionaries for, **20a-5:** 407
Euphemisms°, **21e-3:** 428
Evaluation
  of evidence, **5e:** 126–28
  in reading, **5d-3:** 120–24
  of sources, **5e:** 128–30, **32g:** 581–82
Evaluative reading, **5d-3:** 120–24
every
  agreement° of pronoun° with, **11n:** 264
  agreement° of verb° with, **11d:** 255
everyday, every day, **U GL:** 7
everywheres, **U GL:** 7
Evidence°, **5e:** 126–30
  guidelines for using, **5e:** 126–28
  and logical reasoning, **6f:** 154
  primary and secondary, **5e-2:** 128–30
  using to think critically, **5e:** 126–30
  in written argument, **6c:** 150–51
Exact words, **20b:** 408–10
Examples
  as cause of comma splices° or fused
    sentences°, **14a:** 298
  choice of, in research papers, **34b:** 659
  as clue to word meaning, **20c-2:** 417
  in dictionary entries, **20a-1:** 404
  emphasizing with dashes, **29a-1:**
    520–21
  for paragraph development, **4c:** 79–80,
    4f: 98
  in parentheses, **29b-1:** 523
  RENNS, for, **4c:** 78–79
  transitional expressions for, **4d:** 81–83
except, accept, **22b:** 436, **U GL:** 7
Exclamation points
  with commands, **8l:** 215, **19c:** 386, **23e:**
    478–79

Ideas (*cont.*)
    shaping, **2l:** 32–35
Idiom°, **20a-1:** 403–404; **44-ESL:** 767
-ie-, -ei-, spelling rules, **22f:** 444
if, whether, **U GL:** 9
if clauses, in subjunctive mood, **8m-1:** 216
Ignorance, appeal to, **5h:** 142, 143
Ignoring the question, **5h:** 140–41, 143
illicit, elicit, **22b:** 437
Illogical coordination°, **17d-1:** 359–60
Illogical predication°, **15d-2:** 326–27
Illogical subordination°, **17h:** 367
illusion, allusion, **22b:** 436, **U GL:** 9
Imagery, literary analysis of, **37d-4:** 719
immanent, imminent, eminent, **22b:** 437
immigrate to, emigrate from, **U GL:** 9
Imperative mood°, **8l:** 215, **15a-3:** 316
Imperative sentences°, **7j:** 179, **19c:** 386.
    See also Commands
implicit, explicit, **U GL:** 9
Implied subjects, **8l:** 215, **13a:** 284
Implied topic sentence, **4b:** 76
in, in citations, **33d:** 629–30
including, no colon following, **26a:** 497,
    26d: 499
Incomplete sentences, **15e:** 328–30
    elliptical constructions°, **15e-1:** 328–29
    inadvertent omissions, **15e-3:** 330
    incomplete comparisons, **15e-2:** 329–30
    sentence fragments°, **13:** 282–92
incredible, incredulous, **U GL:** 9
Incubating ideas, **2d:** 24, **2k:** 32
Indefinite adjectives°, **7e:** 171
Indefinite articles°, **42-ESL:** 754–60
Indefinite pronouns°, **7b:** 166
    agreement°: with personal pronouns°,
        11p: 265; with verbs°, **11g:** 257–58
    as implied subjects, **8l:** 215
    possessive form, **27a-1:** 502–3
Indentation
    in APA citation style, **33c-2:** 624
    of displayed quotations, **28a-1:** 511
    in formal outlines, **2n:** 41
    in MLA citation style, **33c-1:** 622–23
    for paragraphing, **4a:** 71
Independent (main) clauses°, **7o:** 187
    adverbs° modifying, **7m:** 183
    colons after, **26a:** 497–98
    comma spliced° or fused°, **14:** 296–304
    conjunctive adverbs° joining, **14e:**
        303–4, **25c:** 490–91
    coordinating conjunctions° joining, **14c:**
        299–300, **17:** 357–58, **24a:** 458–60
    modified by adverb clauses°, **7o-2:**
        187–88
    revising as dependent clauses°, **14d:**
        301–2
    semicolons between, **14b:** 299, **14e:**
        303–4, **25a,b,c:** 489–91, **25e:** 492
    and subordinated information, **17:**

362–68
    tense° in, **8k-1:** 211–13
    in various sentence types, **7p:** 191–93
Index cards
    for bibliographic data, **33a:** 610
    for note taking, **32i:** 589, **34a:** 648
    as a research tool, **32f:** 581
Indexes to periodicals, **32m:** 595–97
Indicative mood°, **8l:** 215, **15a-3:** 316–17
Indirect discourse°
    quotation marks not used with, **28a-3:**
        513
Indirect objects°, **7l:** 181, **9:** 226
Indirect questions°, **23a:** 452
Indirect quotations°, **24g:** 475–76, **28a-3:**
        512–14, **31b-31e:** 557–72
Indirect requests, **8m-3:** 217
Indirect sources, parenthetical references
        in MLA style, **33b-1:** 611–15, **34b:**
        655, 657, 661, 663
Indirect titles, **3c-2:** 55–56
individual, person, party, **U GL:** 9
Induction°. *See* Inductive reasoning
Inductive reasoning, **5g-1:** 134–35, **6f:** 154
    compared with deductive reasoning, **5g:**
        134
    in specific-to-general arrangement of
        paragraph, **4e:** 90
    summary, **5g-1:** 135
infer, imply, **U GL:** 9
Inferential meaning°, **5d-2:** 119–20
Infinitive phrases°, **7n:** 185
    introductory, comma with, **24b-2:** 462
Infinitives°, **7d:** 170, **8b-2:** 195–96
    objective case° with, **9g:** 234
    repetition of *to* in parallel forms, **18d-3:**
        374–75
    split, **15b-3:** 320–21
    and tense sequences°, **8k:** 213
    the with, **42c-ESL:** 758–60
    vs. gerunds°, **45-ESL:** 771–77
Informal language level°, **21a-1:** 419
Informal outlines, **2n:** 40-41
    for research paper, **32q:** 606
Information, **6c:** 150
    background, **4g:** 106
    on documentation, recording, **31a:** 555
    sending for, **32h-2:** 585–86
    for which documentation is not
        required, **31a:** 556–57
Information services, MLA and APA
        citation styles for, **33d:** 639
Informative writing°, **1b-1:** 4–5, **2b:** 18
    about literature, **37b:** 696
    thesis statements, **2m:** 36–37
    topical paragraphs°, **4:** 71–72
Initialisms, capitalization of, **30e:** 537
Initials of authors' names, **33d:** 626–27
Inquiry, methods of
    in literature, **37a:** 695

CHARTS IN TINTED BOXES

CHARTS IN TINTED BOXES (*continued*)

CHARTS IN TINTED BOXES (*continued*)

Response Symbols

Here are two lists of symbols your instructor might write on your papers. The first list shows traditional correction symbols; the second list shows complimentary symbols. You can find material related to each item by consulting the handbook sections or chapters given.

Correction Symbols

ab	abbreviation error, **23b, 30h-k**	*pro ref*	pronoun reference error, **10**
ad	error in adjective or adverb, **12**	*pro agr*	pronoun agreement error, **11m-11r**
agr	agreement error, **11**		
ca	error in pronoun case, **9**	*p*	punctuation error, **23-29**
cap	needs capital letter, **30a-e**	*,*	comma error, **24**
cl	avoid cliché, **21d**	*;*	semicolon error, **25**
coh	needs coherence, **4d**	*:*	colon error, **26**
coord	faulty coordination, **17a-d**	*'*	apostrophe error, **27**
cs	comma splice, **14**	*" "*	quotation marks error, **28**
dev	needs development, **4a, 4c, 4f**	*ref*	pronoun reference error, **10**
dm	dangling modifier, **15c**	*rep*	repetitive, **16**
e	needs exact language, **20b**	*shift*	shift, **15a**
emph	needs emphasis, **19**	*sl*	avoid slang, **21a-3**
frag	sentence fragment, **13**	*sp*	spelling error, **22**
fs	fused sentence, **14**	*subord*	faulty subordination, **17e-h**
hyph	error in hyphenation, **22g**	*sxt*	sexist language, **21b**
inc	incomplete sentence, **15e**	*t*	verb tense error, **8g-k**
ital	italics (underlining) error, **30f-g**	*trans*	needs transition, **4b-1, 4b-6**
k	awkward construction, **15, 16, 21e**	*u*	needs unity, **4b, 4d**
lc	needs lower-case letter, **30a-e**	*us*	usage error, **Usage Glossary**
log	faulty reasoning, **5e-h**	*v*	verb form error, **8b-8f**
mixed	mixed construction, **15d**	*v agr*	verb agreement error, **11a-11l**
mm	misplaced modifier, **15b**	*var*	needs sentence variety, **19**
ms	incorrect manuscript form, **Appendix B**	*w*	wordy, **16**
		wc	word choice error, **20, 21**
num	error in number use, **30l-m**	*ww*	wrong word, **20, 21**
¶	start new paragraph, **4**	∧	insert, **Appendix B**
no ¶	do not start new paragraph, **4**	⊔⊓	transpose, **Appendix B**
//	parallelism error, **18**	⌒	close up, **Appendix B**
pl	plural error, **22c**	*?*	meaning unclear

Complimentary Symbols

gd coh	good coherence, **4d**	*gd th*	good thesis statement, **2m, 3c-2, 6b, 32p**
gd coord	good coordination, **17a-c**		
gd dev	good development, **4c, 4f**	*gd trans*	good transitions, **4d-1, 4d-5**
gd log	good logic, **5h**	*gd ts*	good topic sentence, **4a**
gd //	good parallelism, **18**	*gd u*	good unity, **4b, 4c**
gd rea	good reasoning, **5e-5h**	*gd var*	good sentence variety, **19**
gd rev	good revising, **3c**	*gd wc*	good word choice, **20, 21**
gd sub	good subordination, **17d-f**	*gd wp*	good writing process, **1, 2, 3**

How to Use Your Handbook

You can use your *Simon & Schuster Handbook for Writers* as a reference book, just as you do a dictionary or an encyclopedia. To look up information in the *Handbook,* you must rely not only on alphabetical order but also on numerical order. The following steps will guide you.

STEP ONE: DECIDE where in the *Handbook* you need to look.
- Scan the **overview of contents** (on inside front cover).
- **OR** scan the **Table of Contents.**
- **OR** scan the Index at the back of the book (a detailed list of all major and minor contents).

STEP TWO: LOCATE what you are looking for.
- Find the **chapter number** that you need.
- **OR** find the **number-letter combination** that tells the chapter number and subsection letter that you need.
- **OR** find the **page number** that you need.

STEP THREE: CHECK "landmarks" to confirm your location.
- Check the **red tabs** at the top corner of the page for the number-letter combination that you need.
- Check the **shortened title** at the top of each page (left side for chapter title, and right side for subsection titles).

STEP FOUR: READ the material that you have located.
- Note the rule or guiding principle given in the red "headline."
- Note the three e's that follow each headline: **explanation,** sometimes with a chart to summarize or expand the discussion; **examples;** and **exercises** at the end of one or more subsections within a chapter.

STEP FIVE: STUDY the material, using "special features" when available.
- Use the **charts in tinted boxes** that highlight guidelines, checklists, grammar patterns, and summaries.
- Use any **cross-references** (usually given in parentheses) that say where key concepts are explained in more detail.
- Use the **degree mark** (°) after a word to cue you that the word is defined in the "Glossary of Terms" at the back of the book.
- Use the ✤ALERT✤ reminders that help you to recall related issues of punctuation, mechanics, or usage.
- If you are a student for whom English is a second language (ESL), use these three resources: ESL notes, ESL subsections at the end of selected chapters, and Part 9 which consists of six chapters of major ESL topics.